W9-BJJ-621

AN INTRODUCTION TO THE NEW TESTAMENT

THE ANCHOR BIBLE REFERENCE LIBRARY is designed to be a third major component of the Anchor Bible group, which includes the Anchor Bible commentaries on the books of the Old Testament, the New Testament, and the Apocrypha, and the Anchor Bible Dictionary. While the Anchor Bible commentaries and the Anchor Bible Dictionary are structurally defined by their subject matter, the Anchor Bible Reference Library will serve as a supplement on the cutting edge of the most recent scholarship. The series is open-ended; its scope and reach are nothing less than the biblical world in its totality, and its methods and techniques the most up-to-date available or devisable. Separate volumes will deal with one or more of the following topics relating to the Bible: anthropology, archaeology, ecology, economy, geography, history, languages and literatures, philosophy, religion(s), theology.

As with the Anchor Bible commentaries and the Anchor Bible Dictionary, the philosophy underlying the Anchor Bible Reference Library finds expression in the following: the approach is scholarly, the perspective is balanced and fair-minded, the methods are scientific, and the goal is to inform and enlighten. Contributors are chosen on the basis of their scholarly skills and achievements, and they come from a variety of religious backgrounds and communities. The books in the Anchor Bible Reference Library are intended for the broadest possible readership, ranging from world-class scholars, whose qualifications match those of the authors, to general readers, who may not have special training or skill in studying the Bible but are as enthusiastic as any dedicated professional in expanding their knowledge of the Bible and its world.

David Noel Freedman
GENERAL EDITOR

THE ANCHOR BIBLE REFERENCE LIBRARY

AN INTRODUCTION TO THE NEW TESTAMENT

BY

Raymond E. Brown, S.S.

Doubleday

NEW YORK LONDON TORONTO SYDNEY AUCKLAND

THE ANCHOR BIBLE REFERENCE LIBRARY

PUBLISHED BY DOUBLEDAY
a division of Bantam Doubleday Dell Publishing Group, Inc.
1540 Broadway, New York, New York 10036

THE ANCHOR BIBLE REFERENCE LIBRARY, DOUBLEDAY, and the portrayal
of an anchor with the letters ABRL are trademarks of Doubleday,
a division of Bantam Doubleday Dell Publishing Group, Inc.

Library of Congress Cataloging-in-Publication Data
Brown, Raymond Edward.
An introduction to the New Testament / by Raymond E. Brown. —
1st ed.
p. cm — (The Anchor Bible reference library)
Includes bibliographical references and index.
1. Bible. N.T.—Introductions. 2. Bible. N.T.—Theology.
3. Bible. N.T.—Canon. I. Title. II. Series.
BS2330.2.B76 1997
225.6′1—dc21 96-37742
CIP

Nihil obstat
Myles M. Bourke, S.T.D., S.S.L.
Censor deputatus
Imprimatur
✠Patrick J. Sheridan, D.D.
Vicar General, Archdiocese of New York
November 19, 1996
The *nihil obstat* and *imprimatur* are official declarations that a book or pamphlet is free of doctrinal or moral error. No implication is contained therein that those who have granted the *nihil obstat* and *imprimatur* agree with the contents, opinions, or statements expressed.

ISBN 0-385-24767-2

Printed in the United States of America
October 1997

20 19

To
a remarkable group of doctoral candidates
who studied at Union Theological Seminary (NYC)
in the years J. Louis Martyn and I taught New Testament
and who now teach me by their writings

FOREWORD AND ACKNOWLEDGMENTS

The Goal of this Volume

Though the title *An Introduction to the New Testament* would seem to explain the purpose of this volume, a number of clarifications are necessary for readers to know what is intended.

First, the readership that is envisioned has implications. This book is introductory, and therefore not written for fellow scholars.[1] I envision both readers who have become interested in the NT on their own and readers who take NT beginning courses on different levels (e.g., Bible study groups, religious education, college surveys, and initial seminary classes). As part of a Reference Library series, the book must also supply inquirers with general information on the NT. In other words I have attempted a book that the first time one reads intensively parts of the NT can give guidance and later help to answer more specific questions. The envisioned goal and readership has led to the following decisions:

- Readers of the NT who know Greek, the language in which it was written, can make their own informed efforts to grasp what the authors were trying to communicate. Without a knowledge of Greek, plays on words are often lost; moreover some basic concepts of NT theology (e.g., *koinōnia*) defy adequate translation. Nevertheless, the purpose of this *Introduction* is to encourage, not to discourage. The vast majority of the readers envisioned will not know Greek; but they may be assured that with English as the only linguistic tool, it is possible to have a good knowledge of the Scriptures, even if not a professional one.
- Only bibliography in English will be cited because those addressed will probably not be able to consult biblical research in foreign languages. Significant ideas from that important scholarship will enter the discussion but without references to works not translated.

[1]Though I would not expect scholars to learn from the book, I would hope they judge that their beginning students can learn from it. By way of comparison, I judge the *Introduction* by W. G. Kümmel, which is erudite, to be most helpful to scholars, but absolutely deadly for beginning students. I am attempting an introductory volume very different from that.

- Because this *Introduction* is to be used in courses at different levels (in some of which readings or papers will be assigned) the contents of the bibliographies will vary. For example, they will list both elementary and more detailed studies, short and lengthy commentaries.
- The bibliographies will favor books over journal articles because books are more likely to be available to the general reader. They will also favor more recent literature, although classics from an earlier period will be noted.

Second, this book concentrates on the New Testament, not on "Early Christianity." Why? The study of early Christianity moves into church history and so is a much wider field than biblical research. Only in a limited way is Christianity a "religion of the book." Those who followed and proclaimed Christ existed for some twenty years before a single NT book was written (i.e., before AD 50). Even when the NT books were being composed (*ca.* AD 50–150), Christian communities existed in areas where no preserved book was authored; and surely they had ideas and beliefs not recorded in any NT book. (Indeed some who thought of themselves as followers of Christ probably had ideas rejected or condemned by NT writers.) Furthermore, during the last few decades in which NT books were being penned, Christians were producing other preserved writings (e.g., *Didache, I Clement,* Epistles of Ignatius of Antioch, *Gospel of Peter, Protevangelium of James*). While I shall mention those works where appropriate and give brief background for them in Appendix II, my concentration will be on the twenty-seven books accepted as the canonical NT.[2] Such a concentration is legitimate because they have had a uniquely normative place in Christian life, liturgy, creed, and spirituality.[3] Moreover, these books exist, and in that sense are more certain than conjectural, undocumented, or sparsely documented reconstructions of early Christianity.

Let me supply a specific illustration of the approach taken in this *Introduction.* Many readers of the NT want to know what Jesus was like, what he thought of himself, and what he said precisely; but here the issue of the historical Jesus will be treated only in Appendix I. The concern more central to the *Introduction* will be the study of the extant Gospels, i.e., portraits of the activities of Jesus written twenty-five to seventy years after Jesus' death by authors who may never have seen him. We do not have exact reports composed in Jesus' lifetime by those who knew him. Rather what we are

[2]Unanimously by the churches of the West; with variations by the churches of the East (see NJBC 66.85).

[3]Some scholars, challenging the dominant status attributed to the canonical books, would substitute scholarly reconstructions of early Christianity as normative for Christian life, on the plea that the church context of the canon represents thought control. Yet no conflict need exist between scholarship and church, for the latter can allow considerable freedom of interpretation; and indeed, of the two, scholarship may be more authoritarian in its judgments.

given pertinent to the life and ministry of Jesus comes to us in a language other than the one that he regularly spoke and in the form of different distillations from years of proclamation and teaching about him.[4] In one sense that attenuated reminiscence might seem an impoverishment; in another sense, however, the Gospels understood in this way illustrate how Christians, dependent on word of mouth, kept alive and developed the image of Jesus, answering new questions. Did they do so in fidelity to him? The answer to that question is related to the theology of divine inspiration discussed in Chapter 2 below.

Third, this book concentrates on the extant text of the NT books, not on their prehistory. More scholarly attention has been devoted to the NT than to any other literature of comparable length in the world, and this attention has resulted in an uncontrollably large variety of theories about sources (not preserved) that were combined or corrected to produce the books that have come down to us. Such research is often fascinating; a certain percent of it presents plausible results; but none of it is certain. For an introductory book to concentrate on nonextant "originals" is to impose on beginning readers too much theorizing. It is far better to devote most space to what actually exists, supplying only brief guidance to the principal hypotheses about what might have been.

Nevertheless, a minor concession will be made to scholarly theorizing by treating the books in a combined logical and chronological order rather than in the order that has become canonical. Over the centuries in various church listings the NT books have appeared in different sequences, so that the canonical order now familiar in our Bibles was not always followed. Some of it is governed by principles that have little to do with meaning, e.g., the Pauline letters to communities are arranged by size from the longest to the shortest. A glance at the Table of Contents will show that I propose to study the NT books in three groups (Parts II, III, and IV). The first group of eight involves "the Gospels and Related Works," with the Synoptic Gospels studied first in the probable chronological order (Mark, Matthew, Luke); next Acts, which was written to follow Luke as a second volume; and finally John and the Johannine Epistles/Letters (since the latter in some ways comment on issues raised by the Gospel). The second group involves the thirteen Epistles/Letters that bear Paul's name, divided into two batches: the undisputed seven most likely written by Paul himself, arranged in plausible chronological order; then the six deuteroPauline works possibly or probably written by Pauline disciples. The third group involves a somewhat topical

[4]For those who believe in providence, this indirect and not totally consistent witness to Jesus would have been a vehicle chosen by God—something forgotten by those who spend their efforts "improving" on it by harmonizing the Gospels.

arrangement of six works that are hard to date: Hebrews is put first because it has a slight relation to Pauline theology and was often counted as the fourteenth Pauline letter; then four of the Catholic Epistles, beginning with I Peter, which is close to Pauline theology (and sent from the church of Rome, which may have been the church addressed by Hebrews); next James, which, like I Peter, represents the Jerusalem missionary endeavor (but is hostile to a Pauline slogan about faith and works); then Jude (attributed to the brother of James); and II Peter, which draws on Jude. This group ends with Revelation, which deals with the completion of God's plan in Christ.

Fourth, the primary goal is to get people to read the NT books, not simply to read about them. Accordingly only one fifth of this *Introduction* is given over to general or topical discussion (Chapters 1–6,15–17,25). The rest consists of Chapters devoted one by one to the books of the NT, and it is of those Chapters that I now speak. If I were teaching an introductory course, my first assignment in every instance would be for the students to read the respective NT writing. Many *Introductions* assume that the audience is eager or even required to read the NT; I assume that often the audience needs to be shown how engaging the NT books are and how they speak to people's lives and concerns. Accordingly I shall regularly leave the (often disputed) issues of sources, authorship, dating, etc., to the latter part of each Chapter[5] and begin with a *General Analysis of the Message* designed to accompany the reading of the respective NT book. It will point out the flow of thought, elements that are characteristic of the author, and what is significant and interesting. At times this *Analysis* will be almost a minicommentary that should help to make the NT intelligible and enjoyable.

The design of my Chapters on individual NT books varies according to a number of factors: the length of the book, its importance, and its difficulty. An estimation of what will best serve the readers' interests is a governing consideration, for at times the factors play against each other. For instance, the Gospels and Acts are the longest NT books; yet they are narratives and more easily understood than the argumentation in the Epistles or Letters. Among the Pauline writings Romans may be the most important, but its thought is very difficult for the uninitiated. Accordingly, in choosing an Epistle to be featured for special study, I encourage concentration on I Corinthians because most readers will easily see its application to enduring problems in their times and lives. As for the other NT Letters/Epistles, since

[5]Since readers may be curious about such issues because they have heard of disputes, basic information will be boxed in a short summary on the second page of the Chapter, partially with the goal of avoiding a longer discussion at the start.

these are rarely treated in detail in introductory courses, I have tried to offer enough material to encourage readers to study them on their own.

Fifth, religious, spiritual, and ecclesiastical issues raised by the NT will receive ample attention throughout this book. Indeed, in most of my Chapters the last subsection before the Bibliography will be one of "Issues and Problems for Reflection," where readers are invited to think about questions raised by a NT book, related to God, Christ, other NT figures, the church, etc. Although it is certainly possible to study the NT from a secular or noninvolved standpoint or from that of comparative religion, the majority of readers will be interested in it because it is supposed to be important for them religiously.

Probably the greatest number of readers will be Christian in background. I am a Roman Catholic, and at times I shall illustrate how NT passages or issues are related to Catholic teachings and observance. Yet I spent much of my academic life teaching other Christians (Protestant, Episcopal, Orthodox), and so the wider range of Christian practice and belief are very much my concern—and should be in this ecumenical era.[6] Most of the main NT figures and possibly all the writers were Jews, and NT affirmations have had a major role (often devastating) in relations between Jews and Christians. Their ongoing import (more benevolent, I hope) for those relations must not be neglected. Finally, the NT has had an impact on world society and ethics beyond any religious adherence. I cannot hope to do justice to all these factors, but at least I shall try not to forget them.

Sixth, the book aims to be centrist, not idiosyncratic. Readers should know that this choice is made against the background of disputes in the academic world. An introduction has the duty of reporting where scholars stand today. Yet estimating that stance is not easy. New and bold theses tend to attract attention and may well bring those who propose them academic positions and advancement. In reporting such proposals, the media can give the impression that scholars in general now hold them. To be sure, one or another of these new views may win wide acceptance; but all too often what catches media attention has small following and little plausibility.[7] To serve readers

[6]My book has been granted an *imprimatur* declaring that, from the Roman Catholic viewpoint, this *Introduction* is free of doctrinal and moral error. Sometimes that declaration strikes nonCatholics as threatening; but I would think that, were such a declaration a universal custom, the same could be said of my book by Orthodox, Episcopal, and mainline Protestant authorities who are not literalist in their interpretation of the NT. After all, the various churches proclaim themselves to be faithful to the NT, and so a nonproselytizing work describing what is in the NT should be doctrinally unobjectionable. The differences among today's Christians sprang up after NT times and most often have their roots in whether the respective church thinks that postNT developments can be normative.

[7]Its proponents, dismissing the scholarly majority as entrenched and unwilling to change, may promote themselves as the "cutting edge" of contemporary scholarship.

best I shall try to judge what most scholars hold[8]—even when on a particular point I might be inclined toward a minority opinion. Inevitably, however, judgments about the majority stance are not totally free of one's own prejudices.

Acknowledgments

In this, as in past books, David Noel Freedman has been a truly contributive editor; and Prof. John Kselman of Weston School of Theology has been a meticulous reader. That combination of two extremely careful scholars working over every page of my manuscript has saved me many errors. Because I wanted this work to serve a wide range of readers, I have shown sections to professors of various backgrounds to whom I am very indebted: Craig Koester (Luther Northwestern Seminary), John Meier (Catholic University of America), Marion Soards (Louisville Presbyterian Seminary), Phyllis Trible (Union Theological Seminary, NYC), and Ronald Witherup (St. Patrick's Seminary, CA). Dr. Cecil White, librarian at the last mentioned institution, greatly facilitated my research. As always the Doubleday editors have been most helpful and graceful to work with: Thomas Cahill, Eric Major, and most immediately Mark Fretz. Maureen Cullen has been a very observant copy editor, improving the consistency of the book. To one and all sincere thanks.

[8]When a famous scholar's name is particularly associated with the majority thesis, perhaps as its first proponent, I shall include that by way of useful information. However, far more often I shall simply refer to "most scholars" rather than listing the names of five or ten advocates that would have little or no meaning to the readers I envision.

TABLE OF CONTENTS

Foreword and Acknowledgments vii

INTRODUCTORY BACKGROUND MATERIAL xxiii–xlv

Abbreviations xxv
Useful Information about the Bible as a Whole xxxiii
Chronological Table of People and Events Pertinent to the NT xxxviii
Maps of Palestine and the Mediterranean Area xlii

PART I: PRELIMINARIES FOR UNDERSTANDING THE NEW TESTAMENT 1–96

Chapter 1. The Nature and Origin of the New Testament **3–19**
(A) The Nature of the New Testament 3
(B) How the First Christian Books Were Written, Preserved, and Collected 5
Bibliography 15

Chapter 2. How To Read the New Testament **20–47**
(A) Survey of Methods of Interpretation (Hermeneutics) 20
(B) Special Issues Raised by Views on Inspiration and Revelation 29
(C) The Literal Sense 35
(D) Wider Meanings beyond the Literal 41
Bibliography 46

Chapter 3. The Text of the New Testament **48–54**
(A) Manuscript Evidence for the Text 48
(B) Observations about the Use of the Evidence 51
Bibliography 53

Chapter 4. The Political and Social World of New Testament Times **55–73**
(A) The Political World 55
(B) The Social World 63
Bibliography 70

Chapter 5. The Religious and Philosophical World of New Testament Times **74–96**
(A) Jewish Religious World 75
(B) NonJewish Religious World 83
(C) Greco-Roman Philosophies, Philo, and Gnosticism 88
Bibliography 93

PART II: THE GOSPELS AND RELATED WORKS 97–405

Chapter 6. Gospels in General; Synoptic Gospels in Particular **99–125**
Use of the Word "Gospel" 99
Origin of the Gospel Genre 102
The Three Stages of Gospel Formation 107
The Synoptic Problem 111
The Existence of "Q" 116
Bibliography 123

Chapter 7. The Gospel According to Mark **126–170**
General Analysis of the Message 126
Sources 149
How To Interpret Mark 152
Authorship 158
Locale or Community Involved 161
Date of Writing 163
Issues and Problems for Reflection 164
Bibliography 168

Chapter 8. The Gospel According to Matthew **171–224**
General Analysis of the Message 173
Sources and Compositional Features 203
Authorship 208
Locale or Community Involved 212
Date of Writing 216

Issues and Problems for Reflection 217
Bibliography 222

Chapter 9. The Gospel According to Luke **225–278**
General Analysis of the Message 227
Sources and Compositional Features 262
Authorship 267
Locale or Community Involved 269
Purpose 271
Date of Writing 273
Issues and Problems for Reflection 274
Bibliography 276

Chapter 10. The Acts of the Apostles **279–332**
General Analysis of the Message 279
Sources and Compositional Features 316
"Luke" the Historian 319
Authorship 322
Issues and Problems for Reflection 327
Bibliography 331

Chapter 11. The Gospel According to John **333–382**
Stylistic Features 333
General Analysis of the Message 337
Is John a Genuine Gospel? Combined Sources or Development of Tradition? 362
Comparison of John to the Synoptic Gospels 364
Unity and Cohesiveness of John 365
Authorship and the Beloved Disciple 368
Influences on Johannine Thought 371
History of the Johannine Community 373
Issues and Problems for Reflection 376
Bibliography 379

Chapter 12. First Epistle (Letter) of John **383–394**
General Analysis of the Message 383
Composition 389
Issues and Problems for Reflection 392
Bibliography (Johannine Epistles and I John) 393

Chapter 13. Second Letter of John **395–400**
The Background 395
General Analysis of the Message 396
Presbyters 397
Issue for Reflection 399
Bibliography 399

Chapter 14. Third Letter of John **401–405**
General Analysis of the Message 401
Diagnosis of the Situation 403
Issue for Reflection 404
Bibliography 405

PART III: THE PAULINE LETTERS 407–680

Chapter 15. Classifications and Format of New Testament Letters **409–421**
(A) Classifications 410
(B) Format 412
(1) Opening Formula (*Praescriptio*) 413
(2) Thanksgiving 415
(3) Body or Message 415
(4) Concluding Formula 418
(C) How This Volume Will Treat the Individual Letters 419
Bibliography 420

Chapter 16. General Issues in Paul's Life and Thought **422–445**
(A) The Life of Paul 422
(B) The Theology of Paul 437
Bibliography 442

Chapter 17. An Appreciation of Paul **446–455**
(A) Images of Paul 446
(B) Paul's Motivation 448
(C) Paul's Living Heritage 450

Chapter 18. First Letter to the Thessalonians **456–466**
The Background 456
General Analysis of the Message 459
Issues and Problems for Reflection 462
Bibliography 465

Chapter 19. Letter to the Galatians **467–482**
The Background 468
General Analysis of the Message 470
The Aftermath of Galatians in Paul's Career 473
To Where and When? 474
The "Faith [*pistis*] of Christ" (2:16, etc.) 477
Issues and Problems for Reflection 478
Bibliography 481

Chapter 20. Letter to the Philippians **483–501**
The Background 483
General Analysis of the Message 485
Hymns in NT Letters and the Christological Hymn of 2:5–11 489
From Where and When? 493
Unity: One Letter or Two or Three? 496
Issues and Problems for Reflection 498
Bibliography 500

Chapter 21. Letter to Philemon **502–510**
The Background 502
General Analysis of the Message 505
Social Import of Paul's View of Slavery 506
From Where and When? 507
Subsequent Career of Onesimus 508
Issues and Problems for Reflection 509
Bibliography 510

Chapter 22. First Letter to the Corinthians **511–540**
The Background 511
General Analysis of the Message 515
Those Criticized by Paul at Corinth 526
Paul's Critique of Fornicators and Homosexuals (6:9–10) 528
Charisms at Corinth (Chaps. 12 and 14) and Today 531
The "Hymn" to Love (Chap. 13) 533
Paul and the Risen Jesus (Chap. 15) 534
Issues and Problems for Reflection 535
Bibliography 538

Chapter 23. Second Letter to the Corinthians **541–558**
The Background 541
General Analysis of the Message 544
One Letter or a Compilation of Several Letters? 548
Imagery in 4:16–5:10 552
Paul's Collection of Money for Jerusalem (Chaps. 8–9) 553
The Opponents or False Apostles in Chaps. 10–13 554
Issues and Problems for Reflection 556
Bibliography 557

Chapter 24. Letter to the Romans **559–584**
The Background 559
General Analysis of the Message 564
The Unity of Romans and Chap. 16 575
Justification/Uprightness/Righteousness/Justice 576
Paul's View of Jewish Observance of the Law 578
Original Sin and 5:12–21 580
Issues and Problems for Reflection 581
Bibliography 583

Chapter 25. Pseudonymity and DeuteroPauline Writing **585–589**
(A) Pseudonymous Composition in General 585
(B) Problems about Pseudonymity 587
Bibliography 588

Chapter 26. Second Letter to the Thessalonians **590–598**
General Analysis of the Message 590
Did Paul Write II Thessalonians? 592
The Purpose of II Thessalonians 594
Issues and Problems for Reflection 596
Bibliography 598

Chapter 27. Letter to the Colossians **599–619**
The Background 599
General Analysis of the Message 601
The Christological Hymn (1:15–20) 603
The False Teaching (2:8–23) 604
Household Code (3:18–4:1) 608
Did Paul Write Colossians? 610
From Where and When? 615
Issues and Problems for Reflection 617
Bibliography 618

Chapter 28. Epistle (Letter) to the Ephesians **620–637**
General Analysis of the Message 620
Ecclesiology of Ephesians and Early Catholicism 625
To Whom and By Whom? 626
What Genre? 631
Background of the Ideas 633
Issues and Problems for Reflection 635
Bibliography 637

Chapter 29. Pastoral Letter: To Titus **638–652**
The Pastoral Letters in General: Title, Interrelationship 638
The Background (of Titus) 640
General Analysis of the Message 641
Presbyter/bishops in the Pastorals 645
Issues and Problems for Reflection 649
Bibliography on the Pastoral Letters in General and on Titus 650

Chapter 30. Pastoral Letter: The First to Timothy **653–671**
The Background 653
General Analysis of the Message 656
Who Wrote Titus and I Timothy? 662
Implications of Pseudepigraphy for the Pastoral Letters 668
Issues and Problems for Reflection 670

Chapter 31. Pastoral Letter: The Second to Timothy **672–680**
II Timothy and Possibilities about the Pastorals 672
General Analysis of the Message 675
Inspired Scripture (3:15–16) 678
Issues and Problems for Reflection 679
Bibliography 680

PART IV: THE OTHER NEW TESTAMENT WRITINGS 681–813

Chapter 32. Letter (Epistle) to the Hebrews **683–704**
General Analysis of the Message 683
Literary Genre, Structure 689
Thought Milieu 691
By Whom, From Where, and When? 693
To Which Addressees? 697
Issues and Problems for Reflection 701
Bibliography 703

Chapter 33. First Letter of Peter **705–724**
The Background 706
General Analysis of the Message 708
The Suffering Described: Imperial Persecution or Alienation? 713
I Pet 3:19; 4:6 and the Descent of Christ into Hell 714
Relation to the Pauline Tradition 716
From and To Whom, Where, and When? 718
Issues and Problems for Reflection 722
Bibliography 724

Chapter 34. Epistle (Letter) of James **725–747**
The Background 725
General Analysis of the Message 728
Jas 2:24 and Paul on Faith and Works 732
Jas and Matt on the Jesus Tradition 734
Anointing the Sick (5:14–16) 736
Literary Genre 739
By and To Whom, Where, and When? 741
Canonicity of Jas 743
Issues and Problems for Reflection 745
Bibliography 746

Chapter 35. Letter (Epistle) of Jude **748–760**
The Background 748
General Analysis of the Message 750
Jude's Use of Noncanonical Literature 754
Literary Genre 755
By and To Whom, From Where, and When? 756
Canonicity of Jude 759
Bibliography 760

Chapter 36. Second Epistle (Letter) of Peter **761–772**
The Background 761
General Analysis of the Message 762
By and To Whom, Where, and When? 766
Canonicity and Early Catholicism 769
Issues and Problems for Reflection 770
Bibliography 771

Chapter 37. The Book of Revelation (The Apocalypse) **773–813**
The Literary Genre of Apocalyptic 774
General Analysis of the Message 780
Structure of the Book 796
The Role of Liturgy 798
Millenarianism (The Thousand-Year Reign: 20:4–6) 800
Authorship 802
Date and Life-Situation: Persecution under Domitian? 805
Issues and Problems for Reflection 809
Bibliography 811

APPENDIXES 815–840

I. The Historical Jesus **817–830**
Two Hundred Years (1780–1980) of the Modern Quest 817
After 1980: The Jesus Seminar and Related Scholars 819
After 1980: Miscellaneous Views 824
Evaluative Observations 827
Bibliography 829

II. Jewish and Christian Writings Pertinent to the NT **831–840**
Jewish Writings 831
Christian (and Gnostic) Writings 835
Bibliography 840

INDEXES 841–878

Bibliographical Index of Authors 843–866
Index of Subjects 867–878

ILLUSTRATIVE TABLES

1. Chronology of People and Events Pertinent to the New Testament xxxviii
2. Material Usually Allotted to Q 118
3. Luke's Infancy Narrative Structure 230
4. Luke's Use of Mark 263
5. Paul's Activities in the Letters and Acts 424
6. Pauline Chronology 428
7. Comparing Ephesians and Colossians 628
8. The Letters to the Angels of the Churches (Rev 2–3) 784

INTRODUCTORY BACKGROUND MATERIAL

(Data that will be of service throughout this whole volume)

Abbreviations

Useful Information about the Bible as a Whole

Chronological Table of People and Events Pertinent to the New Testament

Maps of Palestine and the Mediterranean Area

ABBREVIATIONS

(For an abbreviated title of a book following the family name of the author, e.g., Culpepper, *Anatomy,* see the *Bibliographical Index of Authors* at the end of this volume. The titles of articles cited in footnotes are usually not given unless required for clarity or particular relevance.)

AAS	*Acta apostolicae sedis*
AB	The Anchor Bible (Commentary Series; Garden City/New York: Doubleday)
ABD	*The Anchor Bible Dictionary* (6 vols.; New York: Doubleday, 1992)
A/F	Augsburg and/or Fortress publishers (Minneapolis)
AH	Irenaeus, *Adversus Haereses*
AJBI	Annual of the Japanese Biblical Institute
AnBib	Analecta Biblica
ANRW	*Aufstieg und Niedergang der römischen Welt*
Ant.	The *Antiquities* of Flavius Josephus
ATR	*Anglican Theological Review*
AugC	Augsburg Commentaries (Minneapolis: Augsburg)
BA	*Biblical Archaeologist*
BAR	*Biblical Archaeology Review*
BBM	R. E. Brown, *The Birth of the Messiah* (2d ed.; New York: Doubleday, 1993)
BBR	*Bibliographies for Biblical Research,* ed. W. E. Mills (Lewiston, NY: Mellen)
BCALB	R. E. Brown, *The Churches the Apostles Left Behind* (New York: Paulist, 1984)
BDM	R. E. Brown, *The Death of the Messiah* (2 vols.; New York: Doubleday, 1994)
BECNT	Baker Exegetical Commentary on the New Testament (Series; Grand Rapids: Baker)
BEJ	R. E. Brown, *The Epistles of John* (AB 30; Garden City, NY: Doubleday, 1982)

BETL	Bibliotheca Ephemeridum Theologicarum Lovaniensium
BGJ	R. E. Brown, *The Gospel According to John* (2 vols.; AB 29, 29A; Garden City, NY: Doubleday, 1966, 1970)
BHST	R. Bultmann, *The History of the Synoptic Tradition* (New York: Harper & Row, 1963)
BINTC	R. E. Brown, *An Introduction to New Testament Christology* (New York: Paulist, 1994)
BJRL	*Bulletin of the John Rylands University Library of Manchester*
BMAR	R. E. Brown and J. P. Meier, *Antioch and Rome* (New York: Paulist, 1983)
BNTC	Black's New Testament Commentaries (London: Black; British printing of HNTC)
BNTE	R. E. Brown, *New Testament Essays* (New York: Paulist, 1983; reprint of 1965 ed.)
BR	*Biblical Research*
BRev	*Bible Review*
BROQ	R. E. Brown, *Responses to 101 Questions on the Bible* (New York: Paulist, 1990)
BSac	*Bibliotheca Sacra*
BTB	*Biblical Theology Bulletin*
BulBR	*Bulletin for Biblical Research*
BZ	*Biblische Zeitschrift*
BZNW	Beihefte zur ZNW
CAC	*Conflict at Colossae: Illustrated by Selected Modern Studies,* eds. F. O. Francis and W. A. Meeks (Sources for Biblical Study 4; Missoula, MT: SBL, 1973)
CBA	The Catholic Biblical Association
CBNTS	Coniectanea Biblica, New Testament Series
CBQ	*Catholic Biblical Quarterly*
CBQMS	Catholic Biblical Quarterly Monograph Series
CC	Corpus Christianorum
CCNEB	Cambridge Commentary on the New English Bible (Series; Cambridge Univ.)
cf.	compare
CGTC	Cambridge Greek Testament Commentary (Series; Cambridge Univ.)
chap.	chapter (in biblical books or books by other authors). Cross-references to other Chapters in this *Introduction* are always written out and capitalized as: Chapter; or marked § in page headings.

CHI	*Christian History and Interpretation,* eds. W. R. Farmer, et al. (J. Knox Festschrift; Cambridge Univ., 1967)
CLPDNW	R. F. Collins, *Letters That Paul Did Not Write* (Wilmington: Glazier, 1988)
CRBS	*Currents in Research: Biblical Studies*
CSEL	Corpus scriptorum ecclesiasticorum latinorum
CTJ	*Calvin Theological Journal*
CurTM	*Currents in Theology and Mission*
DBS	H. Denzinger and C. Bannwart, *Enchiridion Symbolorum,* rev. by A. Schönmetzer (32d ed.; Freiburg: Herder, 1965). Refs. to sections.
DSS	(Qumran) Dead Sea Scrolls
EBNT	*An Exegetical Bibliography of the New Testament,* ed. G. Wagner (4 vols.; Macon: Mercer, 1983–96). Verse by verse.
EC	Epworth Commentaries (London: Epworth)
ed., eds.	edition, editor(s)
EH	Eusebius, *Ecclesiastical History*
EJ	*L'Évangile de Jean,* ed. M. de Jonge (BETL 44; Leuven Univ., 1977)
Eng	English
ETL	*Ephemerides Theologicae Lovanienses*
EvQ	*Evangelical Quarterly*
ExpTim	*Expository Times*
FESBNT	J. A. Fitzmyer, *Essays on the Semitic Background of the New Testament* (London: Chapman, 1971)
FGN	*The Four Gospels 1992,* ed. F. Van Segbroeck (3 vols.; F. Neirynck Festschrift; Leuven: Peeters, 1992)
FTAG	J. A. Fitzmyer, *To Advance the Gospel: New Testament Studies* (New York: Crossroad, 1981)
GBSNT	Guides to Biblical Scholarship, New Testament (Commentary Series; Philadelphia/Minneapolis: Fortress)
GCHP	*God's Christ and His People,* eds. J. Jervell and W. A. Meeks (N. A. Dahl Festschrift; Oslo: Universitet, 1977)
Ger	German
GNS	Good News Studies (Commentary Series; Wilmington: Glazier)
GNTE	Guides to New Testament Exegesis (Series; Grand Rapids: Baker)
GP	*Gospel Perspectives,* eds. R. T. France and D. Wenham (Series; Sheffield: JSOT)

HBC	*Harper's Bible Commentary,* eds. J. L. Mays et al. (San Francisco: Harper & Row, 1988)
HJ	*Heythrop Journal*
HNTC	Harper New Testament Commentary (Series; New York: Harper & Row)
HSNTA	E. Hennecke and W. Schneemelcher, eds., *New Testament Apocrypha* (2 vols; rev. ed.; Louisville: W/K, 1991–92)
HTR	*Harvard Theological Review*
HUCA	Hebrew Union College Annual
HUT	Hermeneutische Untersuchungen zur Theologie
IB	*Interpreter's Bible* (12 vols.); see NInterpB
IBC	Interpretation Biblical Commentary (Series; Atlanta or Louisville: W/K)
IBS	*Irish Biblical Studies*
ICC	International Critical Commentary (Series; Edinburgh: Clark)
IDB	*The Interpreter's Dictionary of the Bible* (4 vols.; Nashville: Abingdon, 1962)
IDBS	Supplement to the above (1976)
ITQ	*Irish Theological Quarterly*
JB	*The Jerusalem Bible* (1966). See NJB
JBap	John the Baptist
JBC	*The Jerome Biblical Commentary,* eds. R. E. Brown et al. (Englewood Cliffs, NJ: Prentice Hall, 1968). References (e.g., 67.25) are to an article (67) and to a section (25) or sections within the article. See NJBC
JBL	*Journal of Biblical Literature*
JETS	*Journal of the Evangelical Theological Society*
JHC	*Journal of Higher Criticism*
JR	*Journal of Religion*
JRS	*Journal of Religious Studies*
JSNT	*Journal for the Study of the New Testament*
JSNTSup	JSNT Supplement Series
JTS	*Journal of Theological Studies*
KENTT	E. Käsemann, *Essays on New Testament Themes* (SBT 41; London: SCM, 1964)
KJV	*King James* or *Authorized Version* of the Bible. For several centuries the standard Protestant Bible in English; unfortunately in the NT this translation frequently rendered an inferior Greek textual tradition

LD Lectio Divina (Series; Collegeville: Liturgical)

LS *Louvain Studies*

LTPM Louvain Theological & Pastoral Monographs

LXX Latin way of writing 70, a rounded number used for the (Septuagint) Greek translation of the OT, traditionally supposed to have been done (independently) by seventy-two translators from Hebrew/Aramaic in Alexandria *ca.* 250 BC. In certain biblical books, like Jeremiah, the chapter divisions of the LXX differ greatly from those of the Hebrew OT; in the psalms the LXX number is frequently one lower than the Hebrew number, e.g., LXX Ps 21 is Ps 22 in Hebrew (and most English translations).

MNT *Mary in the New Testament,* eds. R. E. Brown et al. (New York: Paulist, 1978)

ms., mss. manuscript(s)

n. cross-reference to *footnote(s)*—in the same Chapter unless otherwise indicated

NAB *New American Bible* (1970)

NABR *New American Bible* (rev. NT, 1986)

NCBC New Century Bible Commentary (Series; Grand Rapids: Eerdmans)

NClarBC New Clarendon Bible Commentary (Series; Oxford: Clarendon)

NIBC New International Biblical Commentary (Series; Peabody, MA: Hendrickson)

NICNT New International Commentary on the New Testament (Series; Grand Rapids: Eerdmans)

NIGTC New International Greek Testament Commentary (Series; Grand Rapids: Eerdmans)

NInterpB New Interpreter's Bible (Commentary Series; Nashville: Abingdon)

NIV *New International Version* of the Bible

NIVAC NIV Application Commentary (Series; Grand Rapids: Zondervan)

NJB *New Jerusalem Bible* (1985)

NJBC *The New Jerome Biblical Commentary,* eds. R. E. Brown, J. A. Fitzmyer, R. E. Murphy (Englewood Cliffs, NJ: Prentice-Hall, 1990). References (e.g., 67.25) are to an article (67) and to a section (25) or sections within the article.

NovT *Novum Testamentum*

NovTSup Supplements to *Novum Testamentum*

NRSV *New Revised Standard Version* of the Bible

NS	new series (of a periodical)
NT	New Testament
NTA	*New Testament Abstracts*
NTG	New Testament Guides (Sheffield: JSOT/Academic)
NTIC	The New Testament in Context (Valley Forge, PA: Trinity)
NTIMI	*The New Testament and Its Modern Interpreters,* eds. E. J. Epp and G. W. MacRae (Philadelphia: Fortress, 1989)
NTM	New Testament Message (Commentary Series; Collegeville: Glazier/Liturgical)
NTR	New Testament Readings (London: Routledge)
NTS	*New Testament Studies*
NTSR	New Testament for Spiritual Reading (Commentary Series; New York: Herder & Herder)
NTT	New Testament Theology (Series; Cambridge Univ.)
OT	Old Testament
OTP	*The Old Testament Pseudepigrapha,* ed. J. H. Charlesworth (2 vols.; New York: Doubleday, 1983–85)
P	papyrus ms. (usually of a biblical writing)
PAP	*Paul and Paulinism,* eds. M. D. Hooker and S. G. Wilson (London: SPCK, 1982)
PAQ	*Paul and Qumran,* ed. J. Murphy-O'Connor (London: Chapman, 1968)
PBI	Pontifical Biblical Institute (Press)
PC	Pelican Commentaries (Harmondsworth: Penguin)
PG	J. Migne, Patrologia graeca
PL	J. Migne, Patrologia latina
pl.	plural
PNT	*Peter in the New Testament,* eds. R. E. Brown et al. (New York: Paulist, 1973)
ProcC	Proclamation Commentaries (Philadelphia/Minneapolis: Fortress)
PRS	*Perspectives in Religious Studies*
Q	*Quelle* or source for material shared by Matthew and Luke but absent from Mark
RB	*Revue Biblique*
ResQ	*Restoration Quarterly*
rev.	revised
RevExp	*Review and Expositor*
RNBC	Readings: a New Biblical Commentary (Series; Sheffield: Academic)

RSRev	*Religious Studies Review*
RSV	*Revised Standard Version* of the Bible
SBL	Society of Biblical Literature
SBLDS	SBL Dissertation Series
SBLMS	SBL Monograph Series
SBLRBS	SBL Resources for Biblical Study
SBLSP	SBL Seminar Papers
SBT	Studies in Biblical Theology (London: SCM; Naperville, IL: Allenson)
sg.	singular
SJT	*Scottish Journal of Theology*
SLA	*Studies in Luke-Acts,* eds. L. E. Keck and J. L. Martyn (P. Schubert Festschrift; 2d ed.; Philadelphia: Fortress, 1980)
SNTSMS	Society for New Testament Studies Monograph Series
SP	Sacra Pagina (Commentary Series; Collegeville, MN: Glazier/Liturgical Press)
SSup	*Semeia* Supplement
ST	*Studia Theologica*
StEv	Studia Evangelica (volumes published in Texte und Untersuchungen)
STS	*Searching the Scriptures: Volume Two: A Feminist Commentary,* ed. E. Schüssler Fiorenza (New York: Crossroad, 1994)
TBAFC	*The Book of Acts in Its First Century Setting,* eds. B. W. Winter et al. (6 vols.; Grand Rapids: Eerdmans, 1993–97)
TBC	Torch Bible Commentary (Series; London: SCM)
TBOB	*The Books of the Bible,* ed. B. W. Anderson (2 vols.; New York: Scribner's, 1989)
TBT	*The Bible Today*
TD	*Theology Digest*
TDNT	*Theological Dictionary of the New Testament,* eds. G. Kittel and G. Friedrich
TH	Translator's Handbook (Series; United Bible Societies)
TIM	W. R. Telford, ed., *The Interpretation of Mark* (2d ed.; Edinburgh: Clark, 1995)
TIMT	G. N. Stanton, ed., *The Interpretation of Matthew* (2d ed.; Edinburgh: Clark, 1995)
TNTC	Tyndale New Testament Commentary (Series; Grand Rapids: Eerdmans)
TPINTC	Trinity Press International NT Commentary (Series; London: SCM)

TRD	*The Romans Debate,* ed. K. P. Donfried (rev. ed.; Peabody, MA: Hendrickson, 1991)
TS	*Theological Studies*
TTC	*The Thessalonian Correspondence,* ed. R. F. Collins (BETL 87; Leuven: Peeters, 1990)
TZ	*Theologische Zeitschrift*
v., vv.	verse, verses
VC	*Vigiliae Christianae*
VE	*Vox Evangelica*
WBC	Word Bible Commentary (Series; Waco/Dallas: Word)
WBComp	Westminster Bible Companion (Series; Louisville: W/K)
W/K	Westminster and John Knox publishers (Louisville)
WUNT	Wissenschaftliche Untersuchungen zum Neuen Testament
ZNW	*Zeitschrift für die neutestamentliche Wissenschaft*

Standard abbreviations are used for the biblical books and the Dead Sea Scrolls. (For information about the major scrolls, see Appendix II.) The OT in general and the psalms in particular are cited according to Hebrew chapter and verse numbers (see LXX above). The KJV, RSV, NRSV number of a psalm *verse* is frequently one number lower than the Hebrew, e.g., Hebrew Ps 22:2 is RSV Ps 22:1. In other passages where versification differs, I supply alternative (usually NRSV) verse numbers in parentheses. Readers are sometimes puzzled to find references like Mark 14:9a, 9b, and 9c. That means that a scholar has subdivided Mark 14:9 into three parts: with a as the first part, b as the middle part, and c as the end part. (Since the a, b, c, etc. do not appear in printed Bibles, it is not always clear where the scholar is drawing the subdividing line.) Even greater confidence is shown by a subdivision like 14:a*a* and 14:a*b,* where the first of the three parts is divided still further!

USEFUL INFORMATION ABOUT THE BIBLE AS A WHOLE

The NT does not stand by itself; it joins books that Christians call the OT to form the Bible. Thus the Bible is a collection; indeed, we can speak of a library with the OT representing the selected sacred books of ancient Israel and the NT representing the selected books of the early church. There is unity to the collection; yet one should be cautious of statements claiming "The Bible says . . ." even as one would not state, "The Public Library says . . ." when one means to quote from Jane Austen or Shakespeare. The better phrasing names a specific book or author: "Isaiah says" or "Mark says," thereby recognizing that individuals from different periods of time with different ideas wrote the individual books of the Bible. Although the books take on added meaning because they are part of the whole Bible, their individuality cannot be overlooked.

To speak of the sacred books of ancient "Israel" is a generalization. The span from Abraham to Jesus covers at least 1,700 (and perhaps more than 2,000) years, and different terms designate the principal groups involved in that narrative.[1] Often "Hebrews" describes the ancestors before Moses and Sinai. "Israel" is appropriate for the confederation of tribes that emerged after Sinai and became a kingdom in the land of Canaan/Palestine. (After Solomon's death [*ca.* 920 BC] "Judah" was the southern kingdom centered on Jerusalem, and "Israel" the northern kingdom centered on Samaria.) "Jews" (etymologically related to Judah) is appropriate from the time when the captivity in Babylon came to a close and Persian rule was extended to Judah (6th century BC).[2] More precisely, "Early Judaism" or "Second-Temple Judaism" designates the period from the rebuilding of the Jerusalem Temple after the return from captivity (520–515 BC) until the Roman destruction (AD 70)—a period toward the end of which Jesus lived.

[1]The period before 1000 BC is extremely complicated; for a brief overview see NJBC 75.26–63.

[2]Some react to the labels BC and AD as reflecting Christian bias, especially inappropriate to designate happenings within Israel or Judaism. Often they prefer "BCE" (before the common era) and "CE" (common era) as more professionally neutral, even though, of course, that dating is still calibrated by the putative date of the birth of Christ. Because of their usage in the media, however, BC and AD remain the more recognized and intelligible designation.

Although they incorporate earlier components, oral and written, the *books* that constitute the OT were authored in the period 1000–100 BC. The title "Old Testament" is a Christian designation, reflecting belief in a second collection of sacred books related to Jesus, known as the "New Testament." Actually a contemporary trend among some Christians and Jews avoids the designation "Old Testament" as if it were pejorative ("old" in the sense of out-of-date, passé). The frequently proposed alternative "Hebrew Bible" or "Hebrew Scriptures"[3] is a problem for a number of reasons: (1) The designation "Hebrew" may be understood as pertaining to the Hebrews as a people (see above) rather than to the Hebrew language; (2) Parts of Ezra and Daniel accepted as canonical Scripture by both Jews and Christians were written in Aramaic, not Hebrew; (3) Seven books in the biblical canon used by Roman Catholics and some other Christians are preserved totally or most fully in Greek, not Hebrew; (4) For much of Christian history the Greek Bible was used in the church rather than the Scriptures in Hebrew; (5) The norm for many centuries in the Western church was the Latin Vulgate, not the Scriptures in Hebrew; (6) "Hebrew Scriptures" gives (and is probably meant to give) the books thus designated an autonomy, while OT implies a relationship to NT. Yet there is no Christian Bible without the interrelated two parts. If Christians continue to use "Old Testament" (and in my judgment that is preferable[4]), they must make clear that the term is not pejorative, but descriptive, serving the purpose of distinguishing the books so designated from the NT. In traditional Christian thought the OT is Scripture, just as sacred and enduringly valid as the NT.

Although the Jews of Jesus' time had a sense of fixed sacred writings in the two areas of "the Law" and "the Prophets," there was as of yet no unanimity on which books constituted "the Writings."[5] Some works like Psalms were accepted early as part of that category (see Luke 24:44), but wide general agreement fixing the contents of Sacred Scripture for the majority of Jews came only in the course of the 2d century AD. All the books recognized at that time were ones preserved in Hebrew or Aramaic.

[3]This is not a classic or traditional Jewish designation for the Holy Scriptures. Sometimes the acronym "TANAK" is used, formed from the initials of the Hebrew names for the three major divisions: *Torah* ("Law"), *Nebi'im* ("Prophets"), and *Ketubim* ("Writings"). See n. 5 below. C. R. Seitz, "Old Testament or Hebrew Bible?" *Pro Ecclesia* 5 (1996), 292–303 offers a challenging discussion.

[4]As a terminology that avoids the difficulties of both "Old Testament" and "Hebrew Scriptures," some would argue for "First Testament" and "Second Testament." However, these alternative designations would scarcely be understood by general readers, e.g., if they appeared in a newspaper.

[5]"The Law" refers to the first five OT books (the Pentateuch). "The Prophets" refers to Joshua, Judges, I-II Samuel, and I-II Kings, Isaiah, Jeremiah, Ezekiel, and the Twelve (Minor) Prophets. Eventually "the Writings" came to include Psalms, Proverbs, Job, Song of Songs (or Canticle), Ruth, Lamentations, Ecclesiastes (or Qohelet), Esther, Daniel, Ezra, Nehemiah, and I–II Chronicles.

From earliest attestation, however, because Christians preached about Jesus in the Greek language, they tended to quote the Jewish Scriptures in Greek translation, chiefly the version called the Septuagint (LXX). This tradition, derived from Alexandrian Jews, regarded as sacred not only the books listed in n. 5 but also some books that were first composed in Greek (e.g., the Wisdom of Solomon) or preserved in Greek (even if originally written in Hebrew or Aramaic, e.g., I Maccabees, Tobit, Sirach). Following the guidance of the LXX meant that the Latin, Greek, and Eastern churches[6] took over as canonical a larger OT than the collection of Scriptures that found acceptance among Jews of the rabbinic period. Many centuries later in the Western church some Protestant Reformers opted for considering authoritative only the shorter Jewish canon, but the Roman Catholic Church at the Council of Trent recognized as canonical seven other books that it had used for centuries in church life (Tobit, Judith, I-II Maccabees, Wisdom, Sirach, Baruch, plus parts of Esther and Daniel)—books known as "Apocrypha" in Protestant Bibles, and "Deuterocanonical" in Catholic parlance.[7] All these books were composed before Jesus' time, and probably some of them were known and quoted by NT authors.[8] Accordingly a familiarity with them is desirable whether or not they are canonical Scripture in one's tradition. Possession of a Bible that contains them is highly recommended.

Which is the best English Bible translation to read? By way of a general answer, the most appropriate translation must be judged from one's purpose in reading. Public worship usually has a solemn tone; therefore highly colloquial translations of the Bible may not be appropriate in that context. Private reading, on the other hand, for the purpose of spiritual reflection and refreshment, is sometimes best served by a translation that has an eye-catching, user-friendly style.

For the purpose of careful reading or study, which concerns us here, one must recognize that sometimes the biblical authors did not write clearly, so that the original texts contain certain phrases that are ambiguous or difficult to understand. In some instances translators have to guess at the meaning. They must choose either to render literally and preserve the ambiguity of the

[6]E.g., the Coptic Church in Egypt and the Ethiopian Church. On the OT canon of these churches, see NJBC 66.47.

[7]These books would be considered canonical by some Anglicans and (along with other books) by many Orthodox and Eastern Christians. See S. Meurer, ed., *The Apocrypha in Ecumenical Perspective* (New York: United Bible Societies, Monograph 6, 1992). To be precise, the Protestant list of the Apocrypha sometimes contains books (*First and Second Esdras, Prayer of Manasseh, Third and Fourth Macabees, Ps 151*) not considered Deuterocanonical by Roman Catholics.

[8]E.g., John 6:35 seems to echo Sirach 24:21. Quotation need not mean that these books were placed on the same level as the Law and the Prophets. Also quoted in the NT are books not considered canonical by Jews, Protestants, or Roman Catholics: see Chapter 35 on Jude below.

original,[9] or to render freely and resolve the ambiguity. A free translation, then, represents a choice already made by translators as to what *they* think an obscure passage means—they have built a commentary into the translated text.[10] That product, albeit easier reading, is most difficult for study purposes. Accordingly here I call the attention of readers to a number of relatively literal translations. Unless specified otherwise the complete editions (with Apocrypha/Deuterocanonical books) are discussed, but the value judgments are particularly in reference to the NT.

- *New Revised Standard Version* (NRSV). The *Revised Standard Version* (RSV), supported by the National Council of Churches, was an American revision (1946–52) of the *Authorized (King James) Version* (KJV—for many Protestants still the authoritative Bible). Not a totally new translation, the RSV remained faithful to its antecedent where possible. Despite the occasionally stilted Bible English (including "thou" and "thee"), it was in many ways the best Bible for study purposes. The NRSV, an ecumenical reworking (1990) that has replaced it, has less Bible English and manifests a sensitivity for inclusive language; the price is a certain loss of literalness. A *Catholic Edition* NRSV (1993) has the Deuterocanonical Books inserted within the OT in the usual Catholic order.
- *New American Bible* (NAB). This Roman Catholic translation from the original languages (1952–70), done with Protestant cooperation, had a superior OT but an inferior NT, resulting from uneven editing. A new translation of the NT (1987: called a revision) is much better and makes the NAB a serious candidate for study purposes. Its language is mildly inclusive.
- *New Jerusalem Bible* (NJB). In 1948–54 the French Dominicans of Jerusalem produced *La Sainte Bible,* a learned translation accompanied by copious (but conservative) introductions and notes. The English translation, called the *Jerusalem Bible* (JB, 1966), was less scholarly than the French and uneven in the way it took account of the original languages. The NJB (1985), based on heavy revisions in the French, is overall a significantly improved translation with better introductions.

[9]In a "Study Bible" a literal translation is accompanied by footnotes or a commentary suggesting possible resolution of the obscurities in the translation.

[10]An attractive free translation is "Today's English Version—The Good News Bible" (1966–79), by R. G. Bratcher, sponsored by the American Bible Society. A cautionary word, however, needs to be said about "The Living Bible" (1962–71), by the conservative businessman K. A. Taylor, whose background was in the Inter-Varsity Fellowship. Rather than a real translation, it is professedly a paraphrase: "A restatement of the author's thought, using different words than he did." Taylor's theological bias (which he characterized as "a rigid evangelical position") creates extraordinary christological readings, e.g., the replacement of "the Word" by "Christ" in John 1:1, and the substitution of "Messiah" for "Son of Man." J. P. Lewis, *The English Bible from KJV to NIV* (Grand Rapids: Baker, 1981), 246, echoing words of Thomas More, suggests that the errors of "The Living Bible" are as ubiquitous as "water in the sea."

- *New International Version* (NIV, 1973–78), sponsored by the New York International Bible Society, has been dubbed a conservative alternative to the RSV. Clear and generally literal, but not so literal as the RSV and somewhat uneven, it can be useful for study purposes. As of 1997, it had no edition with Apocrypha/Deuterocanonical Books.
- *Revised English Bible* (REB). The *New English Bible* (NEB, 1961–70) was produced by the Protestant churches of the United Kingdom in vigorous contemporary British English. The OT was too free and idiosyncratic, but the NT had significant value. The REB (1989), a thorough reworking of the NEB done in the 1980s, is a more even work.

Overall, according to one's purpose (study, prayer, public reading), one should choose a translation carefully. No translation is perfect, and readers can learn much from comparing them.

TABLE 1. CHRONOLOGY OF PEOPLE AND EVENTS PERTINENT TO THE NEW TESTAMENT

<table>
<tr><th>Roman Emperors</th><th>Important Jewish High Priests</th><th colspan="3">Jewish and Roman Rulers in Palestine</th><th>Events
Christian events italicized</th></tr>
<tr><td rowspan="4">Augustus
(30 BC–AD 14).</td><td></td><td colspan="3">Herod the Great (37–4 BC).</td><td>—Jesus born ca. 6 BC.
—Revolts at the death of Herod the Great; Augustus divides Herod’s kingdom among Herod’s three sons.</td></tr>
<tr><td rowspan="3">Annas (Ananus I)
(AD 6–15).</td><td>Judea</td><td>Galilee</td><td>E-NE of Galilee</td><td rowspan="2">—Judea made a Roman province when Archelaus is deposed (AD 6); census of Quirinius; revolt of Judas the Galilean.</td></tr>
<tr><td>Archelaus,
ethnarch of Judea
(4 BC–AD 6).</td><td rowspan="4">Herod Antipas,
tetrarch of Galilee
and Transjordan
(4 BC–AD 39).</td><td rowspan="4">(Herod) Philip,
tetrarch of Ituraea
and Trachonitis
(4 BC–AD 34).</td></tr>
<tr><td>Beginning of First Period of Roman Prefecture
Coponius
(AD 6–9).</td><td rowspan="2">—No record of major violent revolts in Judea from AD 7 to 36. Rebuilding of Jerusalem Temple, begun by Herod the Great, continues.</td></tr>
<tr><td rowspan="2">Tiberius
(AD 14–37).</td><td rowspan="2">Caiaphas
(son-in-law
of Annas)
(AD 18–36).</td><td>Valerius Gratus
(AD 15–26).</td></tr>
<tr><td>Pontius Pilate
(AD 26–36).</td><td>—Early incidents under Pilate show him as imprudent but not vicious or dishonest.
—Jesus begins his public ministry and John the Baptist is executed ca. AD 28.
—Jesus is crucified in 30 or 33.
—Pilate’s repression of the Samaritans in 36 causes Vitellius, prefect of Syria, to send him to Rome (36/37).
—Death of Stephen and conversion of Saul (Paul) ca. 36.</td></tr>
</table>

Gaius Caligula (37–41).	Jonathan (son of Annas) (37). Theophilus (son of Annas) (37–41).	Marcellus (36–37). Marullus (37–41?).	Transferal of this region to Herod Agrippa I (39).	Transferal of this region to Herod Agrippa I (37).	—Agrippa I comes from Rome to Palestine, visits Alexandria—antiJewish outburst (38). *—Paul escapes from Damascus and goes to Jerusalem (39); then on to Tarsus.* —Caligula orders his statue to be set up in the Jerusalem Temple. Syrian legate Petronius stalls till Caligula's assassination.
Claudius (41–54).		**End of First Period of Roman Prefecture.** Transferal of Judea to Herod Agrippa I (41).			
		From 41 to 44 Herod Agrippa I rules the area once ruled by Herod the Great.			*—Execution of James, brother of John; Peter arrested under Agrippa I but escapes.* *—Paul in Tarsus (41–44).*
		Second period of direct Roman prefecture or procuratorial rule (44–66)—at first over all Palestine.			
		Galilee and Judea		**E-NE of Galilee**	
		Fadus (44–46). Tiberius Alexander (46–48). Cumanus (48–52).			—Fadus beheads "the prophet" Theudas (45). —Famine under Claudius (45–48). —Tiberius Alexander crucifies two sons of Judas the Galilean. *—Paul comes to Antioch in Syria; "First Missionary Journey" (46–49).* —Under Cumanus uprisings in Jerusalem and Samaria. *—Meeting of James, Peter, and Paul in Jerusalem (49). Paul's "Second Journey" (50–52); he writes I Thess (51).* —Agrippa II intercedes with Claudius and Cumanus is removed.

TABLE 1. *Continued*

Roman Emperors	Important Jewish High Priests	Jewish and Roman Rulers in Palestine		Events *Christian events italicized*
Nero (54–68).	Ananias (47–59). Ananus II (son of Annas) (62).	Felix (52–60). Festus (60–62). Albinus (62–64). Florus (64–66).	In 53 Herod Agrippa II given the realm of Ituraea and Trachonitis.	—*Paul's "Third Missionary Journey" (54–58); he writes principal letters.* —In Palestine under Felix hostile uprisings, including bandits (*lestai*), knife-wielding terrorists (Sicarii), and an Egyptian "prophet." *Imprisonment of Paul in Caesarea (58–60). High priest Ananias prosecutes him. The next procurator Festus brings Paul before Herod Agrippa II; Paul is sent to Rome (60).* —After the death of Festus, a Sanhedrin convoked by the high priest Ananus II condemns *James, the "brother of the Lord," who is stoned to death.* Ananus is removed under the next procurator. Jesus son of Ananias is seized by the Jerusalem Jewish authorities (early 60s) for warning that God would destroy the city and the Temple; he is handed over to the Romans to be put to death; but after maltreating him, Albinus releases him. Albinus and Florus are corrupt and tyrannical governors, setting the stage for revolt. —Rome burns (64); Nero persecutes Christians there; *Peter and Paul put to death.*
Galba, Otho, Vitellius (68–69). *Accession of the Flavian family of Emperors.*		Roman armies led by Vespasian and (after 69) by Titus struggle against revolutionaries in the First Jewish Revolt (66–70).	Herod Agrippa II remains faithful to the Romans during the Revolt.	—In May 66 Florus is forced by street battles to leave Jerusalem; mobs take over the city. Revolution throughout Galilee and Judea. Groups of Zealots (for the Law) kill Jews opposed to revolt. *Supposedly Christians leave Jerusalem for Pella in the Transjordan.* Josephus goes over to the Romans.
Vespasian (69–79).		Destruction of the Jerusalem Temple by the Romans (August 10, 70). **Roman rule.**	Herod Agrippa II keeps his territory till death *ca.* 100.	—Yohanan ben Zakkai, a teacher of the Law who escaped Jerusalem, founds the rabbinical school at Jamnia (Yavneh).

Emperors after AD 70	**Palestine and Judaism after AD 70**	**Christianity after AD 70**
Vespasian reigned till 79. (*Titus' Triumph celebrated in Rome in 71*). Titus (79–81). Domitian (81–96).	Roman rule in Palestine. —Eleazar, grandson of Judas the Galilean, overcome at Masada in 74. In Rome Josephus writes the *War*. —Rabbinical teachers replace the high priests as leaders of Palestinian Judaism. Rabbi Gamaliel II (90–110) is a major figure. —In Rome Josephus writes the *Antiquities*.	—Many NT writings (Gospels, deuteroPaulines, Heb (?), I Pet, Jas, Jude, Rev, I-II-III John); *I Clement* (from Rome, *ca.* 96?). —Supposedly relatives of Jesus dominate Palestinian churches. —Under Domitian grandsons of Jude (Jesus' brother) supposedly interrogated; perhaps other local harassments of Christians.
Nerva (96–98). Trajan (98–117).	—Jewish apocalyptic (*IV Ezra, II Baruch: ca.* 95–120). —Jewish revolts in Egypt, Cyrene, Cyprus, Mesopotamia (115–119).	—*Didache* (after 100); Letters of Ignatius (110); *Letter of Polycarp.* —Ignatius martyred in Rome (110); Polycarp bishop in Smyrna.
Hadrian (117–138).	—Jerusalem rebuilt as Aelia Capitolina (*ca.* 130 on). —Second Jewish Revolt under Simon ben Kosibah (Bar Cochba—approval of Rabbi Akiba: 132–135). —After defeat Jews driven out of Jerusalem; temple to Jupiter built on Temple site.	—II Pet, *Shepherd of Hermas* (130s?), *Secret Gospel of Mark, Gospel of Peter, Protevangelium of James.* —Supposedly *ca.* 130 end of Jewish Christian leadership in Jerusalem, ceding to Gentile bishops. —Polycarp lives on in Smyrna.

MAPS OF PALESTINE AND THE MEDITERRANEAN AREA

The NT writings about Jesus and his disciples relate a story enacted on the stage of history. Real people and real places involve geography, so that eventually readers will need to consult maps. Matthews and Moyer (p. 73 below) survey atlases, but more conveniently many "study Bibles" have an excellent series of maps. The two maps that follow here are simply a basic geographical guide.

The map of Palestine, while it supplies place names useful for all the NT stories situated in that land, shows boundaries roughly as they existed in the late 20s, i.e., the time of Jesus' public ministry. Those boundaries would have changed already within a decade after his death (the early 40s, when all of Palestine, including what had been the Roman province of Judea, was placed under the rule of the Jewish king Herod Agrippa I), and again by the 50s and 60s, and still again after the suppression of the first Jewish Revolt in AD 70. In terms of physical terrain it is helpful to realize that Palestine has three principal geographical features, running parallel to each other. As one moves inward from the Mediterranean, a north-south coastal plain slopes upwards to a north-south chain of mountains that runs like a spine through the center of the land. On the eastern side of those mountains, the land slopes downward to a dramatic rift-valley that (once more, north to south) contains the Sea of Galilee, the Jordan valley, and the Dead Sea. The great NW-SE plain of Esdraelon offers a break through the mountains and direct access from the coast to the valley.

Similarly the map of the Mediterranean Area is meant to be helpful for the NT books where the story moves beyond Palestine, especially Paul's Letters, Acts, and the Revelation. Yet there is no way one map can depict the constantly changing 1st-century Roman provincial boundaries or developing road networks. Our map attempts only a sketch combining the situation in the 50s (when Paul flourished) with place names important at various moments in the NT period (e.g., the seven cities of the Apocalypse, marked as stars).

PALESTINE IN NEW TESTAMENT TIMES

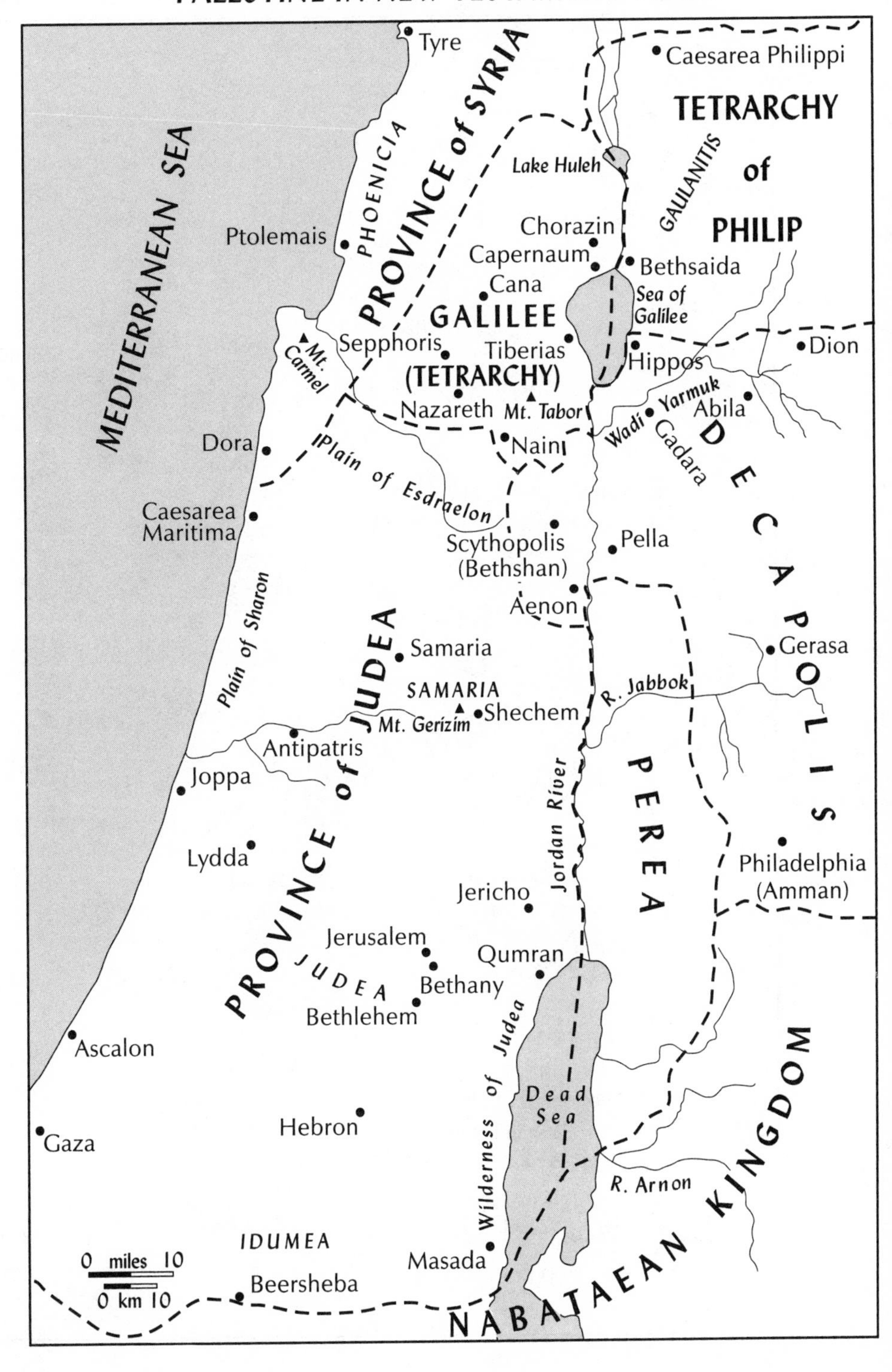

THE MEDITERRANEAN REGION

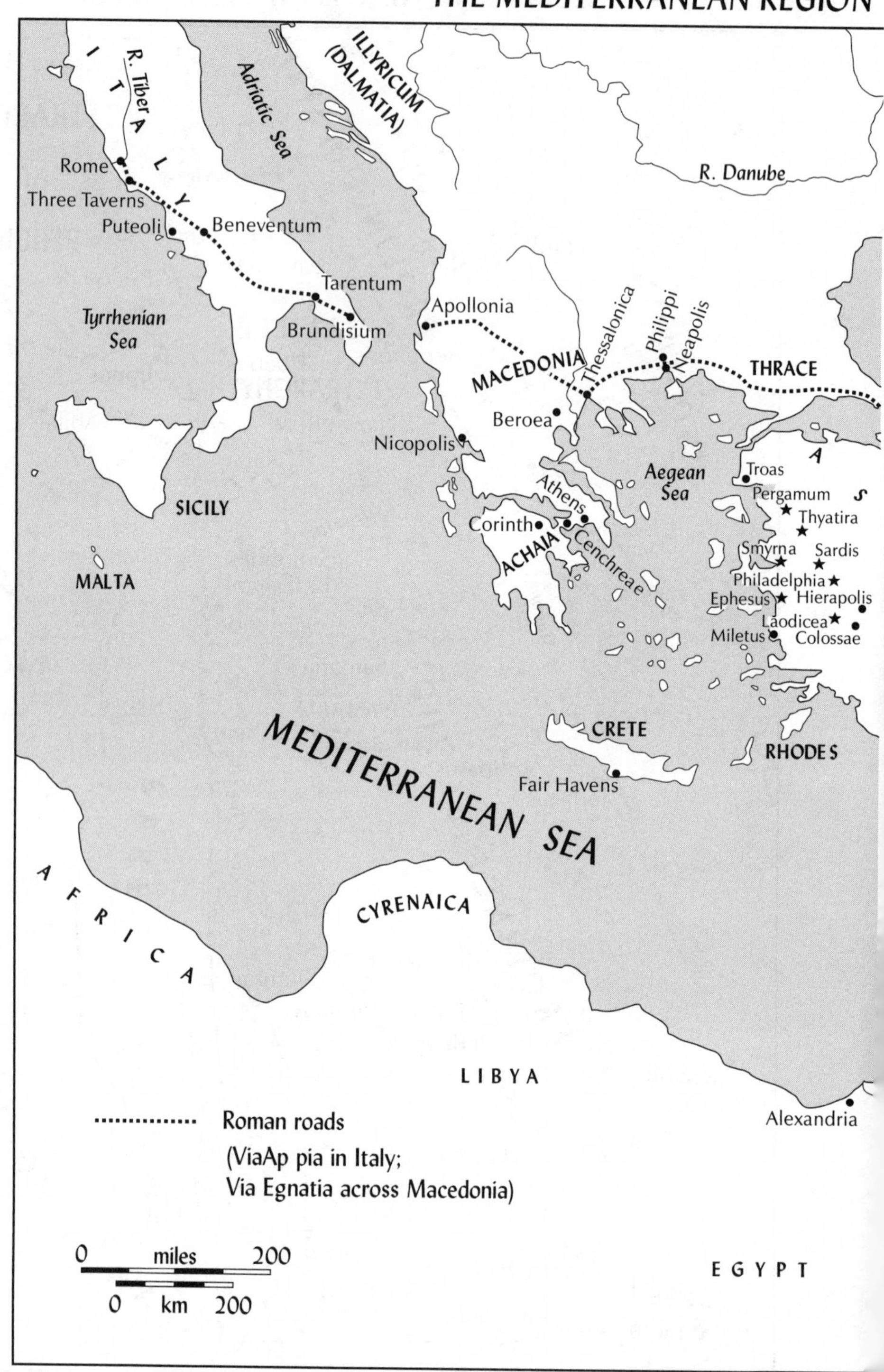

IN NEW TESTAMENT TIMES

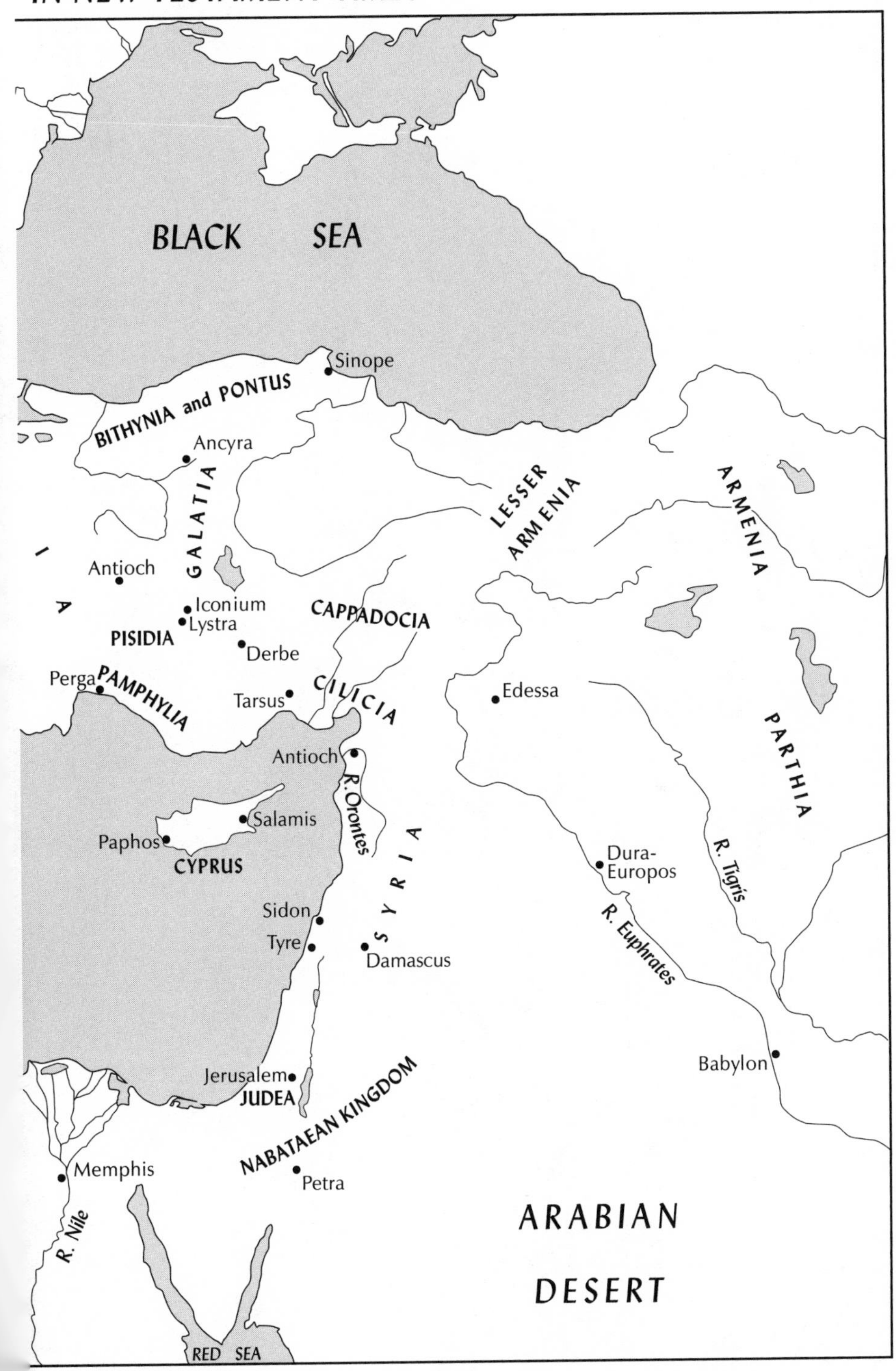

PART I

PRELIMINARIES FOR UNDERSTANDING THE NEW TESTAMENT

The Nature and Origin of the New Testament

How To Read the New Testament

The Text of the New Testament

The Political and Social World of New Testament Times

The Religious and Philosophical World of New Testament Times

CHAPTER 1

THE NATURE AND ORIGIN OF THE NEW TESTAMENT

Although the term "New Testament" evokes for us a body of Christian literature, that understanding is the product of a long development.

(A) The Nature of the New "Testament"

Before the term "testament" was applied to a set of writings, it referred to God's special dealing with human beings. In the story of the Hebrews and of Israel we hear of a "covenant" (agreement or pact[1]) by which God made a commitment to Noah, to Abraham, and to David, promising special help or blessings. In the tradition, however, the most notable covenant was that which God made with Moses and Israel (Exod 19:5; 34:10,27), whereby Israel became God's special people.

Almost 600 years before Jesus' birth, at a moment when the monarchy in Judah and Jerusalem was collapsing before foreign armies, Jeremiah reported an oracle of the Lord: "The days are coming when I will make a new covenant with the house of Israel and the house of Judah. It will not be like the covenant I made with their ancestors the day when I took them by the hand to lead them forth from the land of Egypt. . . . I will place my law within them and write it upon their hearts. I will be their God and they shall be my people" (Jer 31:31–33).[2] "New" here has a connotation of "renewed" even though the renewal is "not like the covenant made with their ancestors"; and it may have had that force when first used by believers in Jesus, as they echoed the language and ideals of Jeremiah (II Cor 3:6; Gal 4:24–26). All the accounts of the eucharistic words at the supper on the night before Jesus died[3] have him relate the term "[new] covenant/testament" to his own blood. Through the death and resurrection of Jesus, therefore, Christians believed

[1]The Hebrew word *bĕrît* was rendered in the Greek Bible by *diathēkē,* which in secular Greek referred to a particular type of covenant or agreement related to death, a testament or will.

[2]The theme of the new covenant reappears in Jer 32:40; Ezek 16:60,62; 37:26; but after those 6th-century BC usages it virtually disappears until it is revived in the DSS and the NT.

[3]Mark 14:24; Matt 26:28; Luke 22:20; I Cor 11:25.

that God had renewed the covenant with a fresh dimension; and they came to understand that this time the covenant reached beyond Israel to include the Gentiles in God's people. Eventually Christian theological reflection and hostile relations between Christians and some Jews who did not accept Jesus led to the thesis that the new testament (in the sense of covenant) had taken the place of the old, Mosaic covenant which had become "obsolete" (Heb 8:6; 9:15; 12:24).[4] Of course, even then the Scriptures of Israel remained the Scriptures for Christians.

Only in the 2d century do we have evidence of Christians using the term "New Testament" for a body of their own writings, ultimately leading to the use of the designation "Old Testament" for the Scriptures of Israel. It would still be several centuries more before Christians in the Latin and Greek churches came to wide agreement[5] about the twenty-seven works to be included in a normative or canonical collection. The next subsection below will treat in general the history of when a NT book was acknowledged as canonical.

The instinct that prospective readers of the NT books need background appeared early. Details about NT books (author, circumstances of composition) were supplied by "Prologues" attached to the Gospels and some of the Epistles (in the late 2d century if not earlier) and by an ancient fragment that bears the name "Muratorian" (which may date from the same period).[6] The first known introductory work to be entitled as such is the short *Introduction to the Divine Scriptures* of Hadrian or Adrian—a treatise on hermeneutics, or the ways of interpreting the Bible.[7] In the next thousand years various works that could be considered introductions gathered and repeated information from past traditions about biblical books. The honor, however, of being the first scientific NT introduction belongs to a series of writings in 1689–95 by the French priest Richard Simon, who studied how the NT books were written and preserved in various texts and versions. His conclusions were regarded as scandalous by more traditional Protestants and Catholics alike.

[4]Many Christians today would hesitate to call obsolete the old testament/covenant in the sense of God's pact with Israel, even though they think that the Mosaic Law is no longer binding on those who have accepted the new covenant.

[5]That agreement still left diversity about the NT canon in the Syrian, Coptic, and Ethiopic Churches; for a sketch of the complexities of the NT canon in the Oriental churches, see NJBC 66.85.

[6]This important witness to the NT canon has been dated to the 4th century by a few scholars, e.g., A. C. Sundberg, Jr., HTR 66 (1973), 1–41, and Hahneman, *Muratorian.* But see the review of the latter in CBQ 56 (1994), 594–95, and E. Ferguson, *Studia Patristica* 17 (1982), 677–83.

[7]Probably he was an early 5th-century monk of Antioch. Before him the *Liber regularum* of the Donatist Tyconius (*ca.* 380) discussed hermeneutics. As we shall see in Chapter 2, hermeneutics is still an issue that demands treatment in a NT *Introduction* today.

By the end of the 18th century and throughout the 19th "Introductions" became the vehicle for conflicting speculations about the history of early Christianity, as scholars attributed various NT books to different schools of 1st- and 2d-century thought. To some extent this tendency has been continued on the contemporary American scene by the NT *Introductions* of Norman Perrin (1st ed.) and Helmut Koester. Yet as the Bibliography at the end of this Chapter indicates, today there is a wide variety of NT *Introductions,* many of them with the simpler goal of reporting information on the books rather than of constructing overall theories of early Christian history.

(B) How the First Christian Books Were Written, Preserved, and Collected

Many people assume that Christians always had Bibles even as we have today, or that Christian writings existed from the beginning. Rather, the formation of the NT, which involved the coming into being and preservation of books composed by followers of Jesus, was a complicated affair.

The Coming Into Being of Books Written by Christians

The introductory section above, "Useful Information about the Bible," reported that by the time of Jesus Jews had become very conscious of sacred writings: the Law, the Prophets, and the other books; and that is what early Christians meant when they spoke of Scripture. Why were the first Christians somewhat slow in writing their own books? A major retarding factor was that, unlike Moses who by tradition authored the Pentateuch, Jesus did not produce a writing that contained his revelation. He is never recorded as setting down even a word in his lifetime or telling any of his disciples to write. Accordingly the proclamation of the kingdom of God made present in Jesus did not depend on writing. Moreover, the first Christian generations were strongly eschatological: For them the "last times" were at hand, and undoubtedly Jesus would return soon—"Maranatha" (= *Marana tha;* I Cor 16:22); "Come Lord Jesus" (Rev 22:20). Such anticipation of the end of the world did not encourage Christians to write for future generations (who would not be around to read books).

Letters. It is no accident, then, that letters were the first Christian literature of which we know: Since they can be designed to answer immediate, pressing problems, they were consistent with an urgent eschatology. That these letters were written by Paul clarifies another factor in the appearance of Christian literature. Paul was a traveling apostle who proclaimed Jesus in one town and then moved on to another. Letters became his means of communication with converts who lived at a distance from him.[8] Thus in the 50s of the 1st century Paul produced the earliest surviving Christian documents: I Thess, Gal, Phil, Phlm, I and II Cor, and Rom. There is a somewhat different tone and emphasis to each, corresponding to what Paul perceived as the needs of the respective community at a particular time. This fact should make us cautious about generalizations in reference to Pauline theology. Paul was not a systematic theologian but an evangelizing preacher, giving strong emphasis at a certain moment to one aspect of faith in Jesus, at another moment to another aspect—indeed to a degree that may seem to us inconsistent. On the grounds that Paul does not mention an idea or practice, very adventurous assumptions are sometimes made about his views. For example, the eucharist is mentioned in only one Pauline writing and there largely because of abuses at the eucharistic meal at Corinth. Except for that situation scholars might be misled to assume that there was no eucharist in the Pauline churches, reasoning that Paul could scarcely have written so much without mentioning such an important aspect of Christian life.

By the mid-60s death had come to the most famous of the earlier generation (i.e., those who had known Jesus or who had seen the risen Jesus: see I Cor 15:3–8), e.g., Peter, Paul, and James, "the brother of the Lord." The passing of the first generation of Christians contributed to the production of works of a more permanent nature. Letters/epistles remained an important means of Christian communication even if they were written now not by Paul himself but in his name to preserve his spirit and authority. Many scholars assign II Thess, Col, Eph, and the Pastoral Letters (I and II Tim and Titus) to this category of "deuteroPauline" writings, composed in the period 70–100 (or even later), after Paul's death. A plausible explanation is that disciples or admirers of Paul were dealing with the problems of the post-70 era by giving advice they thought faithful to Paul's mind. While still dealing with immediate problems such as false teachers or counterfeit letters, the deuteroPauline letters often have a tone that is more universal or permanent. For instance, the idea of the second coming of Jesus was not lost but had become less emphatic, and so II Thess warns against those who overemphasize its immediacy. Col and Eph theologize about "the church" rather than about local churches as in earlier Pauline writings. The structure advocated

[8]If the geographical spread of Christianity contributed to the production of Christian letters, it may be no accident that we do not have any letters of the Twelve Apostles to the Jewish Christian community of Jerusalem. From what is reported in the NT (as distinct from later legends) we might assume that, with the exception of Peter, the Twelve traveled little. Accordingly they could have communicated orally to a Jerusalem audience, and indeed the spoken mode seems to have remained the privileged or expected form of proclamation even after there were written accounts (see Rom 10:14–15). Attestation to this is given by Papias as late as AD 125 (EH 3.39.4).

by the Pastorals, consisting of presbyter/bishops and deacons, is meant to help the church survive for future generations.

In the view of many scholars, to this post-70 period also belong the epistles attributed by name to Peter, James, and Jude, i.e., letters in the name of the great apostles or members of Jesus' family addressing the problems of later Christian generations. Once again these letters often have a universal or permanent tone. Indeed (along with I, II, III John) they eventually became known as "Catholic" (or "General") Epistles, a term that in Eastern Christianity was seen as appropriate to works addressed to the church universal.

Gospels. Literary genres other than letters also appeared of which "Gospel" is the most noteworthy. (In this volume the term "evangelists" will be confined to the writers/authors of the canonical Gospels: "evangelizers" covers the wider category of those who preached about Jesus.) According to the common scholarly view, somewhere in the 60s or just after 70 the Gospel According to Mark was written, offering an account of Jesus' deeds and words remarkably absent from the letters discussed above. Experiences stemming from the decades that separated Jesus from the evangelist colored this presentation. Relevance to Christian problems determined the selection of what was preserved from the Jesus tradition. For instance, the Marcan Jesus' emphasis on the necessity of suffering and the cross may reflect persecution undergone by Christians addressed by Mark. Expansion or explication of the Jesus tradition was demanded because the hearers and readers were no longer the Palestinian Jews of Jesus' lifetime but Gentiles to whom Jewish customs and ideas were strange (see Mark 7:3–4).

The Gospels According to Matthew and to Luke, probably written ten to twenty years after Mark, offer much more of the Jesus tradition, especially by way of sayings (thought to be drawn from a lost collection of sayings known as Q). This wider tradition betrays experiences different from Mark's church background. Still another form of the Jesus tradition found expression in the Fourth Gospel (John), written around 90–100—a form so different that scholars have labored extensively to reconstruct the peculiar community history behind this composition. Despite the local colorings of all four canonical Gospels, their overall import was to preserve for late-1st century readers (and indeed, for those of all time) a memory of Jesus that did not perish when the eyewitnesses died.

None of the Gospels mentions an author's name, and it is quite possible that none was actually written by the one whose name was attached to it at the end of the 2d century (John Mark, companion of Paul and then of Peter; Matthew, one of the Twelve; Luke, companion of Paul; John, one of the

Twelve).[9] Nevertheless, those names constitute a claim that Jesus was being interpreted in a way faithful to the first and second generation of apostolic witnesses and preachers.

Acts; Revelation; Other Literary Genres. Another form of early Christian literature of a more permanent nature than letters is exemplified in the Acts of the Apostles. Intended by the author to constitute the second part of a work that commenced with the Gospel According to Luke (which began and ended in Jerusalem), this book moved the story of Christianity beyond Jerusalem and Judea to Samaria and even to the ends of the earth. The atmosphere in which the work was written is suggested by Acts 1:6–11: Knowledge of the time of the second coming has not been given to the disciples of Jesus, and the spread of Christianity is more important than looking to heaven in expectation of that coming. Acts signals this spread by beginning in Jerusalem with the Twelve and ending in Rome with Paul, whose last words proclaim that the future of Christianity lies with the Gentile world (28:25–28). Such a work envisions an enduring Christianity that needs to know of its continuity with Jesus, Peter, and Paul, and to be certain that its development has not been haphazard but guided by the Spirit received from Jesus.

The Book of Revelation (also called the Apocalypse) represents still another genre in the Christian writing of the post-70 period. With roots in Ezekiel and Zechariah, this book is an example of "apocalyptic" literature, a designation derived from a Greek noun meaning "disclosure" or "revelation." Such apocalyptic literature was well known in Judaism, as exemplified by Daniel and by two books written after the destruction of the Jerusalem Temple in AD 70, namely, *IV Ezra* and *II Baruch.* (The latter two would have been roughly contemporary with Rev.) Persecution of God's people by the great world empires challenged the extent to which history is under God's control. Apocalyptic literature responds to this by visions that encompass what is happening in heaven and on earth at the same time—visions that can be expressed only in luxuriant symbols. The parallelism of heaven and earth gives assurance that what happens below is under the control of God above, and that earthly persecution reflects struggles between God and the major evil spirits. A special aspect of Rev is that the apocalyptic message has been attached to letters to specific churches, so that by expressing the attributes of God in a symbolism that goes beyond rational description, the author is reminding those Christians of the late 1st century that the kingdom of God

[9]The claim that Luke wrote the Third Gospel and Acts is the most plausible of the four attributions, closely followed by the claim that Mark was an evangelist.

is larger than the history they were experiencing. It gives them hope, nay assurance, that despite (or even because of) the setbacks they have suffered, God would make them victorious. Unfortunately, many modern readers have forgotten the 1st-century addressees; and not knowing this type of literature and the plasticity of its images and time symbols (so prevalent in the Jewish apocalypses cited above), they think of Rev as an exact prediction of the future revealing arcane secrets to them. Rather, the grandeur of "the Alpha and Omega, the first and the last" (Rev 22:13) lies beyond chronology and human calculation.

Still other forms of early Christian literature existed, concealed under the designation "letter" or "epistle." Precisely because letters were the dominant literary production of the first Christians, later works that were not letters in the ordinary sense were classified as such. I Pet and Jas are borderline cases: They have elements of a letter format, but the content is closer to a homily (I Pet) or a type of oratorical debate known as a diatribe (Jas). The "Epistle" to the Hebrews has the conclusion of a letter but no epistolary address, so that the destination "to the Hebrews" prefixed to the work by an early scholar derives from an analysis of its contents. The polished style is that of Hellenistic or Alexandrian oratory. Although the work envisions a particular problem (seemingly backsliding from aspects of Christian adherence because of the attractions of Judaism), it elaborates a profound christology of God's Son, who is like us in everything except sin—one who is superior to the angels (who gave the Law) and to Moses, and who replaced by his death the Israelite cult and priesthood. The distance in style and development between this "epistle" and the early Pauline letters is striking. I John, which has no letter format and never mentions John, is extremely difficult to classify. It may be seen as the application of Fourth Gospel themes to a situation in which the Johannine community is no longer racked by expulsion from the synagogue but by internal disagreement and schism.

Thus in various literary genres, Christians after 70 continued to wrestle with problems and threats, but the phrasing of their answers created works that could easily speak to Christian situations of other times and places—to the point that often it is no longer possible to analyze the particular problem or situation the author had in mind. Accordingly, while the earlier Christian literature (the "protoPauline" letters written during Paul's lifetime) can be dated with reasonable accuracy, allowing a variance of only a few years or even a few months, one almost always has to allow a margin of several decades for the suggested dating of the postPauline works. Indeed, in the instance of a few NT writings (Mark, Acts, II Pet) the different dates suggested by well-informed scholars vary by fifty to one hundred years.

THE PRESERVATION AND ACCEPTANCE OF BOOKS WRITTEN BY CHRISTIANS

The Christian compositions we have been discussing, most likely written between the years 50 and 150, were not only preserved but eventually deemed uniquely sacred and authoritative. They were placed on the same level as the Jewish Scriptures (the Law, Prophets, and other Writings) and evaluated as a NT alongside them (so that the Jewish Scriptures became the OT). How did this development come about? Again here I shall consider the issue only in general, leaving details to the discussion of individual books. Indeed we do not know fully the process of preservation;[10] but several factors played a role.

First, apostolic origin, real or putative. I mentioned above how letters not physically written by Paul, Peter, and James could become very important because they were written in the name, spirit, and authority of the apostles. The Gospels were eventually attributed either to apostles (Matthew, John) or to "apostolic men" (Mark, a companion of Peter; Luke, a companion of Paul). The Book of Revelation, containing the visions of a prophet named John (1:1–2; 22:8), won acceptance in the West partly because he was assumed to be John the apostle. When Dionysius of Alexandria perceptively argued around 250 that Rev could not have been written by the author of the Fourth Gospel and of the Johannine Epistles (who was also assumed to have been John the Apostle), the acceptance of the book waned in the East (EH 7.25.6–27). Heb had the opposite fate. Although cited at Rome by late-1st century and early-2d century Christians, Heb was not accepted in the first Western lists of sacred writings. Christians in the East, however, from the end of the 2d century thought that it was written by Paul (EH 6.14.4), an attribution which the Western churches long denied but which played a role in the inclusion of Heb in the canon. Finally in the 4th and 5th centuries the Latin church also came to regard Heb as Pauline and canonical.

Nevertheless, apostolic origin was not an absolute criterion for either preservation or acceptance. Letters written by Paul or in his name to the Corinthians (II Cor 2:4) and to Laodicea (Col 4:16) have not survived. Moreover, some letters purporting to be by Paul were to be discounted according to II Thess 2:2, even if scholars today have no idea how such letters were distinct from the deuteroPauline letters. In the late 2d century the *Gospel of Peter* was rejected by a bishop because of its content, without any debate as to whether or not it came from Peter. Many apocryphal works rejected by later

[10]On a wider level the issues of literacy, publication, circulation, and libraries are discussed by H. Y. Gamble, *Books and Readers in the Early Church* (New Haven: Yale, 1995).

church authorities as spurious or false bore the names of apostles. One must look, then, for other criteria of preservation and acceptance.

Second, importance of the addressed Christian communities. Those for whom the writings were intended had a role in preserving and winning acceptance for them. Apparently no work addressed to the Jerusalem or Palestinian communities has survived, although some of the sources of the Gospels and Acts may have been Palestinian. The disruption of that area by the Jewish Revolt against Rome in 66–70 probably contributed to such a hiatus. Plausibly Antioch in Syria received Matt,[11] a Gospel that became extremely influential. Seemingly the churches of Asia Minor (e.g., Ephesus) and Greece preserved the largest part of the NT, namely, the Pauline and Johannine writings, and perhaps Luke-Acts as well. The church of Rome is thought to have preserved Rom and perhaps Heb and Mark; it is another candidate for the locus of Luke-Acts. When *ca.* 170 Irenaeus rejected the gnostics' claims to apostolic origin for their writings (AH 3.3), the traceable connections of apostles to major churches in Asia Minor, Greece, and, above all, Rome were important arguments for the inclusion of works he considered part of the canonical NT. This factor of the receiving church (catalyzed at times by the influence of some personality mentioned in a NT book who later was prominent in the particular church) may account for the preservation of works like Philemon and Jude, which are not lengthy or significant enough easily to be explained otherwise.

Third, conformity with the rule of faith. The term "canon" or norm may have first referred to the standard beliefs of the Christian communities before it referred to the collection of writings that became standard. The importance of conformity with belief may be illustrated by a story told by Eusebius (EH 6.12.2–6) of Serapion, the bishop of Antioch (*ca.* 190), who found the congregation in nearby Rhossus reading from the *Gospel of Peter,* a work with which he was unfamiliar. At first hearing, he found the work a bit strange but was inclined to tolerate it. When he later learned that this gospel was being used to support docetic teaching (that Jesus was not truly human[12]), Serapion forbade further church use of the work. Some gnostic writings reflected the thesis that Jesus did not truly die on the cross, a view that consequently led to disparagement of Christian martyrdom. By comparison, the four Gospels and the letters of Paul, which highlighted the centrality of the cross and the death of Jesus, along with the Acts of the Apostles with its description of the death of Stephen, would have been preferred by Christian communities in which the blood of the martyrs had proved to be the seed of

[11]Antioch or Syria is also a locus suggested for Mark, John, and Luke-Acts.

[12]Docetists may have appealed to the passage in *GPet* 4.10 that has Jesus silent as if he felt no pain when crucified.

the church. The reason for the uneasiness of Dionysius of Alexandria about Rev and what caused him to examine carefully the authorship of the book was that it described Christ reigning on earth for 1,000 years (Rev 20:4–5): a millenarian or chiliastic doctrine that he denied.

Although contributing to the preservation and importance of certain writings, these three factors scarcely do full justice to what also seems to have involved a church intuition as to what was Spirit-guided.

The Collecting of Early Christian Writings

The various literary genres just discussed had different histories of preliminary collection, and these histories throw light on the attitudes that shaped the final NT compilation.

Paul's Letters. Paul's name appears on thirteen NT letters addressed to separate communities or individuals and written over a period of some fifty years—or even longer if the Pastorals were written after 100. If one posits that Paul himself[13] and the four or five writers of the deuteroPauline letters kept copies, we still do not know how these copies would have been gathered. If copies were not kept by the senders, recipient communities not too distant from each other may have exchanged letters (Col 4:16), thus gradually amassing collections. Some letters, however, seem to have been edited after being sent, and such a literary process would require more than a community interchange. A plausible suggestion is that, after Acts was written and the career of Paul more widely known, his letters were collected systematically. Scholars have attributed such a collection to Onesimus (Phlm 10), to Timothy, or to a Pauline school of writers (perhaps some of the authors of the deuteroPauline letters); but the attempt would have had to continue after the first postPauline generation. While writers *ca.* 100–120 (such as Ignatius of Antioch and the authors of *I Clement* and II Pet) betray knowledge of several Pauline letters, the first clear evidence of a large collection comes several decades later, with Polycarp and Marcion. The latter's acceptance of ten letters did not include the Pastorals.[14] By the end of the 2d century, thirteen were increasingly accepted in the West, with a fourteenth (Heb) soon being added in the East; only by the 4th century was this last book generally acknowledged in the West.

The Gospels. The church eventually accepted four Gospels composed in

[13]D. Trobisch, *Paul's Letter Collection* (Minneapolis: A/F, 1994), maintains that Paul collected and edited some of his letters. H. Y. Gamble, JBL 94 (1975), 403–18, however, presents the case for several different collections of the Pauline letters.

[14]For the absence of the Pastorals and Philemon from P[46], the Chester Beatty Papyrus II of the Pauline letters from *ca.* AD 200, see n. 2 in Chapter 15 below.

the period *ca.* 65–100. Why four? Although Paul is not referring to a written account, his warning in Gal 1:8–9 against a "gospel contrary to what we have preached to you" suggests that the idea of only one gospel may have been axiomatic (see I Cor 15:11). The Gospel According to Mark, which most scholars judge to have been written earliest, calls itself majestically "the gospel [good news] of Jesus Christ (the Son of God)," without suggesting that there was another version of the proclamation. When the author of Matt wrote several decades after Mark, he incorporated other material, especially from the collection of sayings that scholars call Q, into a reshaped Mark, seemingly supposing that now there would be no need for readers to consult either of those two earlier sources. Although the author of Luke (1:1–4) knows of "many" previous narratives, he has set out to produce his "orderly account" with the idea that Theophilus (and other readers) should know the truth more effectively. The fact that there is never a citation from Mark, Matt, or Luke in the Johannine Epistles, even where the Synoptic themes could have served the author well, suggests that for the Johannine community "the message we have heard" (I John 1:5; cf. 3:11) was the Fourth Gospel alone. Bishop Papias (*ca.* 125) knew of several Gospels, but before 150 there is no clear example of more than one Gospel being read as publicly authoritative in a given church.

Indeed the practice of using one Gospel at times had a disturbing exclusivity. Some Jewish Christians used a gospel of their own composition, but many preferred Matt because of the Jewishness of that Gospel and its insistence on every jot and tittle of the Law (Matt 5:18). They did this, presumably, as a polemic against Gentile Christians, who used other writings to support nonobservance of the Law. Gnostic commentaries on John appeared early, for that Gospel could undergird a gnostic rejection of the world.[15] Thus, concentration on one Gospel could sometimes be used to support a theology rejected by the larger number of Christians. By reaction to such exclusivity, the acceptance of more than one Gospel became the practice in "the Great Church."[16] Four Gospels received ever-widening acceptance after 150. Tatian attempted a compromise between the one and the four by composing a single harmonized account out of the four (the *Diatessaron*)—a compromise that was accepted as authoritative for several centuries by the Syriac-speaking churches in the East but not by the Greek- and Latin-

[15]See the Johannine Jesus' statements that he had come from above, that neither he nor his believing followers were of this world (8:23; 17:16), and that he would take them with him to another world (14:2–3).

[16]A term used by the nonbeliever Celsus according to Origen, *Against Celsus* 5.59. The shift in written form from the scroll to the book or codex form, which seemingly took place in the first half of the 2d century, enabled Christians to hold together several Gospels copied one after the other. See G. N. Stanton, NTS 43 (1997), 321–51.

speaking churches. Irenaeus in the West and Origen in the East were influential in establishing the view that God wanted four separate Gospels for the church.

Marcion (*ca.* 100–160)[17] played a peculiar role in catalyzing the formation of the NT canon. Reared a Christian (perhaps even the son of a bishop) and a brilliant theologian, he came from the East to Rome *ca.* 140 proclaiming that the creator attested in the OT was only a demiurge ("the god of this world": II Cor 4:4) who insisted on strict justice. That creator was not the all-high, loving God (a God "alien" and "foreign" to this world) responsible for sending Jesus in human form.[18] Given the increasing separation of Christians from the Law, the cult, and the synagogue as attested in Paul, Heb, and John, the total rejection of the Jewish heritage by Marcion was not surprising. Yet it was decried as heresy by the presbyters of the church of Rome *ca.* 144, causing him to set up a church with its own structures which endured for some three centuries.

Marcion found particular justification for his view in the writings of Paul whom he interpreted as altogether rejecting the Law (and the OT). He selected a canon of Christian writings that could be interpreted as favorable to his thesis, namely, one Gospel (Luke without chaps. 1–2: the *euaggelion*) and ten Pauline letters (without the Pastoral Epistles, the *apostolikon*).[19] Reaction to Marcion's rejection of the OT influenced the larger church's determination to maintain the OT as God's word for the Christian people. So also opposition to Marcion's truncated canon was a factor[20] that pushed the churches toward a larger *euaggelion* (four Gospels rather than Luke alone) and a larger *apostolikon* (at least thirteen Pauline letters rather than ten). An expansion of the latter may also be seen in the inclusion of the Acts of the Apostles, the second half of the Lucan work. With its narrative about the work of Peter, the chief of the Twelve companions of Jesus, prefaced to its account of the work of Paul, Acts could logically stand between the as-

[17]ABD 4.514–20; J. Knox, *Marcion and the New Testament* (Chicago Univ., 1942); E. C. Blackman, *Marcion and His Influence* (London: SPCK, 1948); R. J. Hoffman, *Marcion: On the Restitution of Christianity* (Chico, CA: Scholars, 1984).

[18]Not through real incarnation, however. In his thought Marcion came close to other 2d-century heresies, e.g., docetism. Although the antignostic church writers considered him a gnostic (see p. 92 below), he may simply have shared some viewpoints with the gnostics, e.g., dualism, demiurge.

[19]Marcion also emended the Greek text, removing passages that he disagreed with. Even if myopic, Marcion's emphasis on Paul was an early witness to the power of the great Apostle's writings. A number of scholars would see value in Marcion's exaggerations, as preserving Paul's own radical opposition to the Law over against the early Christian harmonizing of Paul with general church thought and with the other apostles (as in Acts—yet see p. 326 below). Marcion has been looked on as a forerunner of Luther in using Paul to challenge the church.

[20]Other factors, as we have seen, included opposition to Jewish Christians and to gnostics, liturgical usage, loyalty to tradition, and the need for reassurance in the face of martyrdom.

sembled four Gospels dealing with Jesus and the assembled letters of Paul. The same instinct for favoring the Twelve probably explains the inclusion of I Pet and I John. However that may be, in the decades just before and after AD 200, church writers in Greek and in Latin widely accepted a collection of twenty works[21] as a NT alongside the Jewish OT.

Completing the Collection. The remaining seven works (Heb, Rev, Jas, II and III John, Jude, II Pet) were cited from the 2d to the 4th centuries and accepted as Scripture in some churches but not in all. Finally, however, by the late 4th century in the Greek East and the Latin West there was a wide (but not absolute) accord on a canon of twenty-seven works.[22] This standardization involved churches accepting from other churches books about which they had some doubts, and such "ecumenism" reflected an increasing contact and communion between the East and the West. Origen went to Rome and learned the biblical views of the church where Peter and Paul had been martyred and which had struggled against Marcion. On the other hand, later Western thinkers like Ambrose and Augustine became familiar with the works of Origen and through him with the biblical views of the highly literate Alexandrian Christianity. The most learned Latin church father, Jerome, spent much of his life in Palestine and Syria. Thus, in a sense, the larger canon in the 4th century, like the shorter collection in the late 2d century, testified to the experience of what Ignatius had earlier called "the catholic church" (*Smyrnaeans* 8:2).

We shall never know all the details of how the twenty-seven books were written, preserved, selected, and collected; but one fact is indisputable. Joined as the NT, they have been the single most important instrument in bringing untold millions of people from different times and places into contact with Jesus of Nazareth and the first believers who proclaimed him.

Bibliography

For the topics and books of the NT one may profitably begin with the pertinent articles in the following six works. With that understanding, articles from these works will be cited only by exception in the individual Bibliographies that conclude the Chapters in this book:

The Anchor Bible Dictionary (6 vols.; New York: Doubleday, 1992). Abbreviated ABD.

The Books of the Bible, ed. B. W. Anderson (2 vols.; New York: Scribner's, 1989). Vol. 2 has articles on each book of the NT. Abbreviated TBOB.

[21]Four Gospels; thirteen Pauline letters; Acts; I Pet, and I John.

[22]This is the NT count known to us today. The Syriac-speaking communities eventually replaced the Diatessaron with the four Gospels but did not include the minor Catholic Epistles and Rev. The Ethiopian Church used a larger canon often estimated at thirty-five books.

Harper's Bible Commentary, eds. J. L. Mays et al. (San Francisco: Harper & Row, 1988). Abbreviated HBC.

The Interpreter's Dictionary of the Bible (4 vols. 1962; supplementary vol. 1976; Nashville: Abingdon). Abbreviated IDB and IDBS.

New Jerome Biblical Commentary, eds. R. E. Brown et al. (Englewood Cliffs, NJ: Prentice Hall, 1990). Abbreviated NJBC. Refs. to articles and sections, not pages.

The New Testament and Its Modern Interpreters, eds. E. J. Epp and G. W. MacRae (Philadelphia: Fortress, 1989). Reports of the state of research on all aspects of the NT. Abbreviated NTIMI.

General Bibliographies on the NT:

NTA (a periodical begun in 1956, giving brief abstracts in English of all articles and most books on the NT, is the most useful resource).

Elenchus bibliographicus biblicus (an annual, formerly part of the magazine *Biblica,* is the most complete index to all writing on the whole Bible).

Fitzmyer, J. A., *An Introductory Bibliography for the Study of Scripture* (3d ed.; Rome: PBI, 1990). Offers helpful, balanced evaluations.

France, R. T., *A Bibliographic Guide to New Testament Research* (3d ed.; Sheffield: JSOT, 1983).

Harrington, D. J., *The New Testament: A Bibliography* (Wilmington: Glazier, 1985).

Hort, E., *The Bible Book: Resources for Reading the New Testament* (New York: Crossroad, 1983).

Hurd, J. C., *A Bibliography of New Testament Bibliographies* (New York: Seabury, 1966—includes bibliographies of NT scholars).

Krentz, E., "New Testament Library. A Recommended List for Pastors and Teachers," CurTM 20 (1993), 49–53.

Langevin, P.-E., *Bibliographia biblique. Biblical Bibliography . . . 1930–1983* (3d ed.; Quebec: Laval Univ., 1985—covers the whole Bible).

Metzger, B. M., *Index to Periodical Literature on Christ and the Gospels* (Leiden: Brill, 1966). Covers up to 1961 and so is useful for the period before NTA.

Martin, R. P., *New Testament Books for Pastor and Teacher* (Philadelphia: Westminster, 1984).

Porter, S. E., and L. M. McDonald, *New Testament Introduction* (Grand Rapids: Baker, 1995). Annotated bibliography (to be updated every five years).

Introductions to the New Testament

(*Some of the most recent and/or the most important, representing various approaches*):

Beker, J. C., *The New Testament. A Thematic Introduction* (Minneapolis: A/F, 1994).

Brown, S., *The Origins of Christianity: A Historical Introduction to the New Testament* (2d ed.; New York: Oxford, 1993).

Childs, B. S., *The New Testament as Canon: An Introduction* (Philadelphia: Fortress, 1984).

Collins, R. F., *Introduction to the New Testament* (New York: Doubleday, 1983).

Conzelmann, H., and A. Lindemann, *Interpreting the New Testament* (Peabody, MA: Hendrickson, 1988, from the 8th German ed.).

Davies, W. D., *Invitation to the New Testament* (Sheffield: JSOT, 1993 reprint).

Freed, E. D., *The New Testament: A Critical Introduction* (Belmont, CA: Wadsworth, 1986).

Fuller, R. H., *A Critical Introduction to the New Testament* (London: Duckworth, 1974).

Guthrie, D., *New Testament Introduction* (4th ed.; Downers Grove, IL: InterVarsity, 1990). An important, very conservative contribution.

Johnson, L. T., *The Writings of the New Testament* (Philadelphia: Fortress, 1986).

Kee, H. C., *Understanding the New Testament* (5th ed.; Englewood Cliffs, NJ: Prentice Hall, 1993).

Koester, H., *Introduction to the New Testament* (2 vols.; Philadelphia: Fortress, 1982; 2d ed. vol. 1; New York: de Gruyter, 1995).

Kümmel, W. G., *Introduction to the New Testament* (rev. enlarged ed.; Nashville: Abingdon, 1986). A classic.

Mack, B. L., *Who Wrote the New Testament? The Making of the Christian Myth* (San Francisco: Harper, 1995).

Martin, R. P., *New Testament Foundations: A Guide for Christian Students* (rev. ed.; 2 vols.; Grand Rapids: Eerdmans, 1986).

Marxsen, W., *Introduction to the New Testament* (Philadelphia: Fortress, 1968).

Metzger, B. M., *The New Testament: Its Background, Growth, and Content* (2d ed.; Nashville: Abingdon, 1983).

Moffatt, J., *An Introduction to the Literature of the New Testament* (3d ed.; Edinburgh: Clark, 1918). A scholarly classic.

Moule, C.F.D., *The Birth of the New Testament* (3d ed.; London: Black, 1981).

Patzia, A. G., *The Making of the New Testament* (Downers Grove, IL: InterVarsity, 1995).

Perkins, P., *Reading the New Testament* (2d ed.; New York: Paulist, 1988).

Perrin, N., and D. C. Duling, *The New Testament, an Introduction* (3d ed.; Fort Worth: Harcourt Brace, 1994). Major changes from Perrin's 1st ed. (1974).

Price, J. L., *Interpreting the New Testament* (2d ed.; New York: Holt, Rinehart and Winston, 1971).

Puskas, C. B., *An Introduction to the New Testament* (Peabody, MA: Hendrickson, 1989).

Schweizer, E., *A Theological Introduction to the New Testament* (Nashville: Abingdon, 1991).

Spivey, R. A., and D. M. Smith, *Anatomy of the New Testament* (5th ed.; Englewood Cliffs: Prentice Hall, 1995).

Stott, J.R.W., *Men with a Message: An Introduction to the New Testament* (rev. ed.; Grand Rapids: Eerdmans, 1995).

Wikenhauser, A., *New Testament Introduction* (New York: Herder and Herder, 1960). A translation of a Roman Catholic classic of which the most recent German ed. by J. Schmid is the 6th (1973).

Wright, N. T., *The New Testament and the People of God* (Minneapolis: A/F, 1992).

THEOLOGIES OF THE NEW TESTAMENT (some of which are virtually Introductions):

Balz, H., and G. Schneider, eds., *Exegetical Dictionary of the New Testament* (3 vols.; Grand Rapids: Eerdmans, 1990–93). Very useful; supplies transliterations for those who cannot read the Greek alphabet.

Bultmann, R., *Theology of the New Testament* (2 vols.; London: SCM, 1952, 1955). A classic.

Caird, G. B., *New Testament Theology* (Oxford: Clarendon, 1994).

Conzelmann, H., *An Outline of the Theology of the New Testament* (New York: Harper & Row, 1969).

Cullmann, O., *Salvation in History* (New York: Harper & Row, 1967).

Goppelt, L., *Theology of the New Testament* (2 vols.; Grand Rapids: Eerdmans, 1981–82).

Kittel, G., and G. Friedrich, eds., *Theological Dictionary of the New Testament* (Grand Rapids: Eerdmans, 1964–76). German orig. 1932–79. A classic, abbreviated TDNT. Also a one-volume abridgment by G. W. Bromiley (Grand Rapids: Eerdmans, 1985) with transliterations.

Kümmel, W. G., *The Theology of the New Testament According to Its Major Witnesses: Jesus—Paul—John* (Nashville: Abingdon, 1973).

Ladd, G. E., *A Theology of the New Testament*, rev. by D. A. Hagner (Grand Rapids: Eerdmans, 1993).

Léon-Dufour, X., *Dictionary of the New Testament* (San Francisco: Harper & Row, 1980).

Marxsen, W. *New Testament Foundations for Christian Ethics* (Minneapolis: A/F, 1993).

Matera, F. J., *New Testament Ethics* (Louisville: W/K, 1996).

Richard, E., *Jesus: One and Many. The Christological Concept of New Testament Authors* (Wilmington: Glazier, 1988).

Richardson, A., *An Introduction to the Theology of the New Testament* (New York: Harper & Bros., 1959).

———, *A Theological Word Book of the Bible* (New York: Macmillan, 1950).

Schelkle, K.-H., *Theology of the New Testament* (4 vols.; Collegeville: Liturgical, 1971–78).

Spicq, C., *Theological Lexicon of the New Testament* (3 vols.; Peabody, MA: Hendrickson, 1994). French orig. 1978.

Stauffer, E., *New Testament Theology* (London: SCM, 1955).

CANON OF THE NEW TESTAMENT:

Farmer, W. R., and D. M. Farkasfalvy, *The Formation of the New Testament Canon* (New York: Paulist, 1983).

Gamble, H. Y., *The New Testament Canon: Its Making and Meaning* (Philadelphia: Fortress, 1985).

Hahneman, G. M., *The Muratorian Fragment and the Development of the Canon* (Oxford: Clarendon, 1992).

Lienhard, J. T., *The Bible, the Church, and Authority* (Collegeville: Liturgical, 1995).

McDonald, L. M., *The Formation of the Christian Biblical Canon* (Peabody, MA: Hendrickson, 1995).

Metzger, B. M., *The Canon of the New Testament* (Oxford: Clarendon, 1987).

Souter, A., *The Text and Canon of the New Testament* (2d ed.; London: Duckworth, 1954).

Westcott, B. F., *A General Survey of the History of the Canon of the New Testament* (4th ed.; London: Macmillan, 1875). A classic that reprints the basic ancient texts pertinent to canon.

SURVEYS OF NEW TESTAMENT RESEARCH:

Baird, W., *History of New Testament Research* (several vols.; Minneapolis: Fortress, 1992–). Vol. 1 treats 1700–1870.

Bruce, F. F., "The History of New Testament Study," in Marshall, *New* (1977), 21–59.

Fuller, R. H., *The New Testament in Current Study* (New York: Scribner's, 1962).

Hall, D. R., *The Seven Pillories of Wisdom* (Macon, GA: Mercer, 1990). An elegant, conservative critique of the reasoning encountered in NT research.

Harrisville, R. A., and W. Sundberg, *The Bible in Modern Culture . . . from Spinoza to Käsemann* (Grand Rapids: Eerdmans, 1995).

Hunter, A. M., *Interpreting the New Testament 1900–1950* (London: SCM, 1951).

Kümmel, W. G., *The New Testament: The History of the Investigation of Its Problems* (Nashville: Abingdon, 1972).

Morgan, R., "New Testament Theology," in *Biblical Theology: Problems and Perspectives,* eds. S. J. Kraftchick et al. (J. C. Beker Festschrift; Nashville: Abingdon, 1995), 104–30.

Räisänen, H., *Beyond New Testament Theology* (Philadelphia: Trinity, 1990).

Riches, J., *A Century of New Testament Study* (Valley Forge, PA: Trinity, 1993).

CHAPTER 2

HOW TO READ THE NEW TESTAMENT

In the general description of Chapter 1 we saw that different kinds of Christian writings became part of the NT. Now let us look in more detail at how such differences affect the way we read or interpret. The discussion brings us into a very active area in modern scholarship called *hermeneutics,* the study of interpretation, or the quest for meaning.[1] This study employs various approaches to written documents, each called a "criticism," e.g., Textual Criticism, Historical Criticism, and Source Criticism. (This is not "criticism" in the more common sense of unfavorable judgment but in the sense of careful analysis.) Subsection A surveys briefly different types of biblical criticism; Subsection B comments on the impact of theories of inspiration and revelation; Subsection C covers the literal sense of Scripture; Subsection D discusses wider meanings beyond the literal sense.

(A) Survey of Methods of Interpretation (Hermeneutics)

To be blunt, the study of different kinds of interpretation is difficult—indeed at times too difficult for beginners. Nevertheless, so many books on Scripture refer to methods of interpretation that some knowledge of the subject is essential. This subsection offers a wide-ranging, though brief, overview. Fuller treatments of fundamental aspects of interpretation will come later, and so beginners who find themselves a bit lost in the overall picture may wish to return to this subsection. In order to prevent the discussion from becoming too abstract, we shall use the Gospels as concrete examples for surveying how the various types of investigation apply. (But keep in mind that the "criticisms" have a much wider application than the Gospels; both

[1]The Greek word *hermēneia* covered a broad scope of interpretation and clarification—a scope that modern scholars are trying to recapture and expand in their understanding of the hermeneutical task. There is interpretation by speech itself as language brings to expression what is in one's mind, interpretation by translation from one language to another, and interpretation by commentary on and explanation of what someone else has said or written. The latter form of interpretation is often the focus in modern hermeneutics. For more detail, see Thiselton, *New.*

Green, *Hearing* and McKenzie, *To Each,* have essays on each type of criticism, with broader examples.)

1. TEXTUAL CRITICISM. Almost two thousand years ago evangelists wrote four Gospels in Greek. We do not have the original manuscripts (mss.) that came from the evangelists' pens, or for that matter the original of any NT work. What we do have are many handwritten Greek copies made anywhere between 150 and 1,300 years later—for all practical purposes until the invention of printing. Many times, but mostly in minor matters, these copies do not agree among themselves because of copyists' mistakes and changes. The comparison of the diversities in Greek copies (as well as in ancient translations and quotations from the NT) is called Textual Criticism. It is a highly specialized area of research, but Chapter Three will supply general information to help readers understand disputes over the "best reading" of a verse and differences among English Bible translations.

2. HISTORICAL CRITICISM. The four evangelists were trying to convey a message about Jesus to their respective readers. That message is called the literal sense, i.e., what the author literally meant to say; and its detection is *one* aspect of Historical Criticism.[2] Many times the literal sense is relatively easy to discern; at other times it requires a good knowledge of the ancient languages, grammar, idioms, customs, etc. For instance, in Mark 7:11–12 Jesus says, "If people say to their father or mother, 'What support you would have had from me is *Qorban* (that is, dedicated to God),' then you no longer permit them to do anything for father and mother." What custom is involved? What was the logic behind it? Why is the issue meaningful to Mark's intended readers? These and other questions would have to be discussed in order to understand Mark's portrayal of Jesus' attitude. Detection of the literal sense is fundamental to all other forms of interpretation, and so a whole subsection (C below) will be devoted to it.

3. SOURCE CRITICISM. This is the study of the antecedents from which the NT writers drew their information. Gospel sources are a particular concern because in all likelihood the evangelists were not eyewitnesses of Jesus' life. Since people preached about Jesus, at an early stage there was oral tradition; then some of that tradition began to be written down. Can we detect and reconstruct such sources when they have not been preserved? Close parallels among the extant Gospels, especially among the first three (Mark, Matt, and Luke), provide a way of exploring this question. Did one evangelist use as a

[2]This term is understood differently by different interpreters. For a while it served as an umbrella designation for all "scientific" investigation, and so it included what is now more commonly separated off as Source Criticism and Form Criticism. That imprecision should be remembered when one reads exaggerations about the "barrenness" of Historical Criticism. What is being attacked is often not the search for the literal sense but the concentration on sources.

basis another Gospel that had already been written? If so, what was the order of dependence, e.g., Matt on Mark, or Mark on Matt? Such questions should be studied, but not elevated to primary importance. Priority of attention in interpretation must be given to the actual NT works, not to their largely hypothetical sources. The question of Gospel Source Criticism will be discussed in Chapter Six below, as part of a general treatment of all the Gospels, but also in the Chapters dealing with the individual Gospels.

4. FORM CRITICISM. We do not read everything the same way. When we look through a newspaper, we read the front page with the assumption that it consists of reasonably reliable reporting; but when we turn to the advertising pages, we know we have to be much more cautious about the reliability of what is claimed. When one picks up a book in a bookstore, it usually has a jacket or cover identifying it as fiction, history, biography, etc. In technical language the jacket specifies the literary genre or "form"—a helpful step, for once more we read the different genres with different expectations. As we saw in the last Chapter, the NT contains different genres, e.g., Gospels, letters, and apocalypse. Yet there is a need to be more exact. Chapter 6 below will discuss whether the Gospels are a unique literary genre, or are close enough to other ancient forms to be classified as histories or biographies. Similarly Chapter 15 will discuss the classification of NT letters in light of ancient genres. This type of investigation is called Form Criticism.

Pressing beyond the general classification of whole writings, scholars have studied the genres or literary forms of components. Some are rather obvious. Below in the Chapters on the Gospels, for instance, we shall study parables and miracle stories, infancy narratives and passion narratives. The more advanced classification of forms, however, is a highly technical enterprise. For the Gospels they would include: wisdom maxims, prophetic or apocalyptic sayings, rules or laws for community life, "I sayings," metaphors, similes, sayings within a narrative framework, short anecdotes, longer miracle stories, historical narratives, unhistorical legends, etc.[3]

Although discussion of such precise genres lies beyond this *Introduction,* aspects of Form Criticism are important on a general level. Theoretically, each form or genre has its own characteristics. The absence or presence of an expected feature in a particular parable or miracle story, therefore, can be

[3]The main form critics of the 20th century were German (Karl Ludwig Schmidt, Martin Dibelius, Rudolf Bultmann); in developing (different) systems of classification, they assigned German designations, sometimes derived from Greek. Their classic studies are available in English translation: Dibelius, *From Tradition to Gospel* (rev. ed.; New York: Scribner's, 1965); and Bultmann, BHST. See the brief introduction by E. V. McKnight, *What Is Form Criticism?* (GBSNT; Philadelphia: Fortress, 1969); and the more technical K. Koch, *The Growth of the Biblical Tradition. The Form-Critical Method* (New York: Scribner's, 1969). Good examples of commentaries systematically applying form criticism are V. Taylor's on Mark and J. A. Fitzmyer's on Luke.

studied to help determine how that parable or story was passed down in the tradition. For instance, if Mark has a parable that is missing a traditional feature and Matt has the same parable including the feature, that disparity *may* tell us that Matt preserves the original better. Yet the vagaries of human composition are unpredictable. One cannot be sure that the less complete form was not original, because the more complete form may reflect the tendency to supply the expected.

In itself the diagnosis of form tells us nothing about the historicity of the material molded into the form of a saying, parable, or miracle story. Did Jesus utter this saying or parable? Did he work the miracle? Did a supernatural event take place? Form Criticism cannot answer those historical questions.[4] Interpreters sometimes overlook this limitation, as Bultmann's own classification of "legends" exemplifies. Despite the form, for Bultmann these are not miracle stories in the proper sense but religious, edifying accounts that are not historical. That last judgment is not based simply on an identification of form but on a supposition about what can be historical. The stories of the Last Supper are simply cult legends, Bultmann tells us (BHST 244–45), even though others point out that a tradition about a eucharistic supper on the night that Jesus was given over was already established when Paul became a Christian in the mid-30s (I Cor 11:23–26).

5. Redaction Criticism. The inclusion of individual components (miracles stories, parables, etc.) in the final product (the whole Gospel) modifies drastically their significance; and the meaning of the whole Gospel is a primary concern for those who read the NT. In the history of NT scholarship in the 20th century, the development of Redaction Criticism, after an earlier dominance of Form Criticism, dealt with this concern. Form Criticism concentrated on the preexisting units compiled by the evangelists; Redaction Criticism, or at least the branch of it that is better called Author Criticism,[5] recognized that the writers creatively shaped the material they inherited. Attention thus shifted to the evangelists' interests and the work they produced. Where it is possible to know with reasonable assurance the material an author used, one can diagnose theological emphasis by the changes the author

[4]This caution is worth remembering when we discuss the issue of the historical Jesus in Appendix I below.

[5]"Redactor" is another term for "editor," although it may imply a major editor. There was a form of Redaction Criticism that concentrated on the isolation and history of *preGospel* traditions (distinct from the editorial additions by the evangelists) and the historical circumstances in which they were edited. The view that the evangelists were editors is better than the view that they were only compilers but still does not do justice to them as authors giving narrative and theological orientation to what was received. "Composition Criticism" or "Author Criticism" are names emphasizing the latter outlook. An overview is offered by N. Perrin, *What Is Redaction Criticism?* (GBSNT; Philadelphia: Fortress, 1969); and an excellent analysis and bibliography by J. R. Donahue in Malbon/McKnight, *New* 27–55. For applications, see Bornkamm *Tradition* (Matt); Marxsen, *Mark.*

made in what was taken over from the source. For example, if Matt and Luke used Mark, the fact that they greatly esteemed the Twelve is made evident by their omission of Marcan verses stressing the failure of the apostles and by their addition of segments showing the apostles in a good light (Luke 9:18–22 omits from Mark 8:27–33, and Matt 16:13–23 adds to it). Judgments become much more speculative when the reconstruction of the source is uncertain, a problem that has plagued studies of the theology of Mark and John.[6] Even when we do not know the sources, however, the theology of the redactors/authors emerges in the final works they produced. No matter what the components, when a Gospel is read as it has come to us, it speaks theologically. When taken in this direction Redaction Criticism leads into Narrative Criticism (see below).

6. CANONICAL CRITICISM. In some ways this approach[7] may be considered an extension of the interest in the final product evident in Redaction Criticism. Although each NT book has its own integrity, it has become Sacred Scripture only as part of the collected NT; and it has acquired new meaning from its relationship to other books in that canonical collection. (See Chapter 1 above for how the individual works were gathered and grouped.) Whereas other forms of criticism study the meaning of a passage in itself or in the context of the biblical book in which it appears, Canonical Criticism examines the passage in the light of the whole NT or even the whole Bible wherein other books/passages offer insights. Subsection D below develops this criticism.

7. STRUCTURALISM. Though Form Criticism and Redaction Criticism have literary components, these come to the fore in a number of other approaches. Structuralism (or Semiotics) concentrates on the final form of the NT works.[8] Although overall structure as guide to the intention of the author has long been a feature of interpretation, and it is almost de rigueur that biblical introductions supply an outline of every NT book, "structure" in this approach is far more than a general outline. Particularly in the contributions

[6]A good evaluation is given by C. C. Black, JSNT 33 (1988), 19–39.

[7]It was initiated by OT scholars, especially B. S. Childs, *Introduction to the Old Testament as Scripture* (Philadelphia: Fortress, 1979); and J. A. Sanders, *Torah and Canon* (Philadelphia: Fortress, 1972); *Canon and Community* (Philadelphia: Fortress, 1984). NJBC 71.71–74 offers comparison and evaluation; for Childs, see also his *New,* and M. O'Connor, RSRev 21 (#2; 1995), 91–96. Although theoretically Childs accepts Historical Criticism, he can be one-sidedly critical of NT commentaries, no matter how theological, that work on the historical level.

[8]An explanation of structuralism for beginners (in which I include myself) is provided by D. Patte, *What Is Structural Exegesis?* (GBSNT; Philadelphia: Fortress, 1976). More technical are J. Calloud, *Structural Analysis of Narrative* (SSup 4; Philadelphia: Fortress, 1976—treating the very influential method of A. J. Greimas); R. M. Polzin, *Biblical Structuralism* (SSup 5; Philadelphia: Fortress, 1977); and D. C. Greenwood, *Structuralism and the Biblical Text* (Berlin: de Gruyter, 1985). D. O. Via, *Kerygma and Comedy in the New Testament* (Philadelphia: Fortress, 1975), applies structuralism to Mark; Boers, *Justification,* to Gal and Rom.

of Francophone literary theorists, Semiotics has become a highly technical study, akin to mathematics. The structure that is detected is not the outline that meets the eye, for the deepest structures are not apparent on the surface but help to generate the text (whether or not they were consciously understood by the author). These structures must be brought to light in order that the text can be perceived as a coherent whole. Often structuralists propose outlines of frightening complexity, causing nonstructuralists to wonder whether such intricacy is helpful and whether semiotic analysis produces results that could not have been obtained by commonsense exegesis.[9] Readers are invited to do more investigation, for a simple example is not easy to supply. Most of the time Structuralism goes beyond the level of this *Introduction.*[10]

8. NARRATIVE CRITICISM. More obviously and immediately productive is an approach that, when applied to the Gospels, would concentrate on them as stories.[11] At first blush the terminology employed in this exegesis may seem formidable. For example, Narrative Criticism distinguishes the real author (the person who actually wrote) from the implied author (the one who can be inferred from the narrative), and the real audience (those in the 1st century who actually read/heard what was written, or even those who read it today) from the implied audience (those whom the author envisions in writing). Yet these distinctions make sense, and attention paid to the flow of the narrative can cast light on many exegetical problems.

In particular, Narrative Criticism is fruitful for continuous stories like

[9]Not all Francophone biblical scholars are enthusiastic. Writing about the semiotic exegesis of the Gospel infancy narratives by R. Laurentin, L. Monloubou (*Esprit et Vie* 93 [Nov. 24, 1983], 648), asks point-blank whether Semiotics adds anything new to interpretation and gives an answer that I translate:

> "This surging ocean of semiotics whose foaming waves swept over the tranquil beaches of exegesis is now in the process of retreating. It has left certain places on the exegetical beach reshaped; it also leaves various debris. An improper amount of importance given to the formal elements of a text irresistibly recalls the excesses of formal logic so appreciated by a decadent scholasticism."

[10]So also does Deconstructionism, sometimes called PostStructuralism. This recent and highly disputed approach challenges many ideas about meaning developed in the Western intellectual tradition. Not the deepest structures of a text, but the deepest levels of the mind generate meanings that, like language, remain inherently unstable. The most prominent defender of the philosophical validity of this approach is the French scholar, J. Derrida. See S. D. Moore, *Poststructuralism and the New Testament: Derrida and Foucault at the Foot of the Cross* (Minneapolis, A/F, 1994); D. Seeley, *Deconstructing the New Testament* (Leiden: Brill, 1994); A.K.M. Adam, *What Is Postmodern Biblical Criticism?* (GBSNT; Minneapolis: A/F, 1995).

[11]W. A. Beardslee, *Literary Criticism of the New Testament* (Philadelphia: Fortress, 1970); N. R. Petersen, *Literary Criticism for New Testament Critics* (Philadelphia: Fortress, 1978); M. A. Powell, *What Is Narrative Criticism?* (GBSNT; Minneapolis: A/F, 1990); M. Minor, *Literary-Critical Approaches to the Bible: An Annotated Bibliography* (West Cornwall, CT: Locust Hill, 1992). Examples of this approach are offered by Rhoads, *Mark;* Kingsbury, *Matthew as Story;* and Culpepper, *Anatomy* (= John); also R. C. Tannehill on the Gospels in general in NInterpB 8.56–70.

those of Jesus' birth and death. Too often microscopic focus on the text sees problems that exegetes can more easily explain if they appreciate a simplified narrative that takes much for granted. Is it really a problem, for instance, that the Marcan Pilate knows enough to ask Jesus "Are you the King of the Jews?" without explicitly being told about this issue? Does that imply that Pilate was involved in the arrest of Jesus from the start? Or rather are readers to *assume* that the authorities explained the problem to Pilate when they brought Jesus to him, even if we are never told that in the abbreviated, fast-running Marcan account? Again, logically the chief priests cannot have taken Jesus off to Pilate in Matt 27:2 and still have been in the Temple sanctuary when Judas returned the thirty pieces of silver in Matt 27:3–5. Yet is it not the thrust of this narrative to highlight simultaneity? When Gospel passages are read aloud, have not hearers made the kind of interpretative assumptions that the writer intended, at least until scholars noticed a problem? Narrative Criticism counters the excesses of historical investigation and helps to highlight the author's main interest.

Unfortunately some scholars who have embraced Narrative Criticism argue that it is hermeneutically irrelevant whether what is narrated in the Gospels ever happened. In response, two factors must be kept in tension. On the one hand, the effectiveness of the Gospels stems to a major degree from their presentation of Jesus in a long, unified, attention-getting narrative (quite unlike the memories of the great rabbinic sages[12]). On the other hand, by its own self-understanding Christianity is too fundamentally based on what Jesus actually said and did to be cavalier about historicity.

9. RHETORICAL CRITICISM. Related to Narrative Criticism is an approach that analyzes the strategies used by the author to make what was recounted effective,[13] e.g., the discovery of suitable material to be narrated; the organized arrangement of that material; the choice of appropriate words. (The classification of rhetorical argumentation into judicial, deliberative, and demonstrative, will be discussed in Chapter 15 below in relation to letters.)

[12]The Gospels, even in the areas where they recall Jesus' teaching, differ markedly from the Mishna, the collection of rabbinic legal views (*ca.* AD 200—p. 83 below) that, although not Scripture, has become virtually as authoritative for Judaism as the NT is for Christianity. Interestingly the major part of both works was collected at the same time.

[13]A. N. Wilder, *Early Christian Rhetoric: The Language of the Gospel* (London: SCM, 1964); G. A. Kennedy, *New Testament Interpretation Through Rhetorical Criticism* (Chapel Hill: University of North Carolina, 1984); W. Wuellner, "Where Is Rhetorical Criticism Taking Us?" CBQ 49 (1987) 448–63; S. E. Porter and T. H. Olbricht, eds., *Rhetoric and the New Testament* (JSNTSup 90; Sheffield: JSOT, 1993). D. F. Watson and A. J. Hauser, *Rhetorical Criticism of the Bible: A Comprehensive Bibliography with Notes on History and Method* (Leiden: Brill, 1994). A very helpful explanation of both ancient and modern techniques, using Jonah as an example, is supplied by P. Trible, *Rhetorical Criticism* (Minneapolis: A/F, 1994), who calls attention to the significant role of J. Muilenburg. Trible (32–48) distinguishes between two sides of rhetoric: artfully composing the speech/writing, and effectively persuading the audience.

Rhetorical Criticism assumes that the written text discloses the contexts of both the author and the reader, and so is concerned not only with the aims and methods of the writer but also with the interests, values, and emotions of past and present readers.

Both Narrative and Rhetorical Criticism take the Gospels seriously as literature. Previously, by comparison with the great classics of Greco-Roman writing, the Gospels were considered "minor" literary productions (*Kleinliteratur*) of a popular type. Now, however, literary critical studies are doing more justice to an undeniable historical fact: The narrative power of the Gospels centered on the person of Jesus has been of unique efficacy in convincing millions to become Christians.[14] Although I shall point to Jewish lives of the prophets (especially the career of Jeremiah) as partially anticipating the Gospel approach, there are no close equivalents in the preserved Jewish literature of the time to these NT compositions.

10. SOCIAL CRITICISM[15] studies the text as a reflection of and a response to the social and cultural settings in which it was produced. It views the text as a window into a world of competing views and voices. Different groups with different political, economic, and religious stances shaped the text to speak to their particular concerns. This important branch of NT research has contributed to a revival in historical study. Chapter 4 below will discuss the raw material for this criticism, i.e., NT political and social background, and supply applications.

11. ADVOCACY CRITICISM is an umbrella title sometimes given to Liberationist, African American, Feminist, and related studies,[16] because the proponents advocate that the results be used to change today's social, political,

[14]Although the Pauline letters have very persuasive passages about the effectiveness of the death and resurrection of Christ for justification and salvation, they never paint "the face" of the Christ whom Paul proclaims and loves. In terms of the kind of a life he lived, the Gospels showed the world much more of who Jesus was.

[15]H. C. Kee, *Knowing the Truth: A Sociological Approach to New Testament Interpretation* (Minneapolis: A/F, 1989); B. Holmberg, *Sociology and the New Testament* (Minneapolis: A/F, 1990); J. J. Pilch, *Introducing the Cultural Context of the New Testament* (New York: Paulist, 1991); D. M. May, *Social Scientific Criticism of the New Testament: A Bibliography* (Macon, GA: Mercer, 1991); B. J. Malina and R. L. Rohrbaugh, *Social-Scientific Commentary on the Synoptic Gospels* (Minneapolis: A/F, 1992); G. Theissen, *Social Reality and the Early Christians* (Minneapolis: A/F, 1992); J. J. Pilch and B. J. Malina, *Biblical Social Values and Their Meaning: A Handbook* (Peabody, MA: Hendrickson, 1993); J. H. Elliott, *What Is Social-Scientific Criticism?* (GBSNT; Minneapolis: A/F, 1993—excellent bibliography); D. C. Duling, BTB 25 (1995), 179–93 (survey). This criticism is applied to Matt by Balch, *Social History*, and Saldarini, *Matthew's;* to Luke by Neyrey, *Social.*

[16]The pertinent bibliography is enormous. Representative examples are: R. M. Brown, *Unexpected News. Reading the Bible with Third World Eyes* (Philadelphia: Westminster, 1984); C. H. Felder, ed., *Stony the Road We Trod. African American Biblical Interpretation* (Minneapolis: A/F, 1991); E. Schüssler Fiorenza, ed., *Searching the Scriptures: A Feminist Commentary* (New York: Crossroad, 1994); and her major work *In Memory of Her* (2d ed.; New York: Crossroad, 1994). P. Trible, *Christian Century* 99 (1982), 116–18, summarizes three different approaches to women in Scripture.

or religious situation. (A familiar maxim is that liberation of the oppressed is the only optic through which Scripture should be read.) This approach is defended on the grounds that the biblical writers and writings were not without their own advocacy, e.g., written by men or church leaders and thus reflecting a patriarchal or ecclesiastical viewpoint. Accordingly the surface biblical narrative may promote their views, squelching alternatives, so that the slightest clues must be examined to recover what may have been suppressed consciously or unconsciously. Others, however, see in this method the danger of reading into Scripture what one would like to find and of not acknowledging that the NT sociological situation may have been in fact (and not simply through suppression of data) unfavorable to modern causes. Without our settling that dispute, all should acknowledge that, by asking important questions that previous exegetes (largely First World, white, and male) never asked, advocacy researchers have valuably enlightened the NT situation.

12. OVERVIEW. How can readers of the NT cope with so many different "criticisms"? *Different approaches to the text must be combined so that no "criticism" becomes the exclusive manner of interpretation.* Interpreters who employ the various forms of criticism in a complementary way will arrive at a much fuller meaning of the biblical text.[17]

To describe the total range of that meaning, S. Schneiders (*Revelatory*) envisions three "worlds," namely, behind the text, of the text, and before the text. Let us use the Gospels to illustrate this. (a) *The world behind the text* would include both the life of Jesus and the religious reflection on him through faith, preaching, and community religious experience. (b) *The world of the text* as it now stands (no matter how it came to be) contains the written witness of the evangelists, reflecting their own understanding and experience of Jesus and their abilities to express that witness. (More will be said about this in Subsection C below.) Two observations need to be made. On the one hand, although the Gospels are written, the tradition behind them was orally proclaimed and the marks of orality are still strong in the written accounts.[18] In the thesis that Matt and Luke used Mark, we must not assume that their dependence on a written account erased the evangelists' personal memories of what they had heard about Jesus. On the other hand, once written, the Gospel texts had a life of their own, so that there may be meanings conveyed

[17]This was insisted on by the Roman Pontifical Biblical Commission in 1993; see Fitzmyer, *Biblical Commission.*

[18]See J. Dewey, ed., *Orality and Textuality in Early Christian Literature* (*Semeia* 65 [1994]). For appreciation of orality in Mark, see her articles in *Interpretation* 43 (1989), 32–44; CBQ 53 (1991), 221–36; for the passion accounts, see BDM 1.51–53.

that go beyond what the authors envisioned or the original audiences understood. (c) *The world before the text* concerns the interaction of the Gospels with the readers who by interpretation enter into them, appropriate their meaning, and are changed by it. (See the last part of subsection D below: "Subsequent Readings.") At this interpretative level, Gospel explanation/commentary plays an important role. Also many believers would assume that a personal spiritual engagement with the Jesus portrayed in the Gospels is necessary for a full appropriation of the text—an assumption that runs against the sometimes enunciated view that only those who are not committed religiously can be objective interpreters.

In this introductory subsection I have concentrated on the Gospels to illustrate the importance of various hermeneutical approaches. The different "criticisms" (Form, Redaction, Rhetorical, etc.) are applied to the other NT writings as well, e.g., Acts, the letters, Rev, where special issues peculiar to the individual genre arise. However, once the general idea has been illustrated through the Gospels, we may wait until the Chapters treating those writings to make the immediate and practical import of hermeneutical issues more evident.

(B) Special Issues Raised by Views on Inspiration and Revelation

This overview of hermeneutics may well provoke an obvious objection on the part of many readers. After all, these "criticisms" treat the NT books with the assumption that they were written by time-limited human beings according to the literary conventions of the era, so that interpretative approaches suitable for other books can be applied to them as well. Yet through the centuries most Christians have read biblical books not as examples of literature but because God inspired them. Does that belief, if valid, qualify the rules of interpretation? And how does the view that Scripture is a uniquely important element in divine revelation affect interpretation?

Inspiration

Four different (and even contradictory) general positions in reference to inspiration come into play.

(1) Some maintain that the inspiration of the Scriptures is a pious theological belief that has no validity. Much NT criticism that emerged in Germany at the end of the 18th century and during the 19th century was a reaction to

traditional Christian theology.[19] This reactive factor is still to be reckoned with, for some scholars and teachers counteract biblical literalism by debunking any special religious status for the NT writings. For them, NT Christianity should be judged only in terms of its sociological import as a minor religious movement in the early Roman Empire.

(2) Without committing themselves to any view positive or negative about inspiration, many interpreters would regard references to it as totally inappropriate in a scholarly study of the Scriptures. The fact that both Testaments were produced by believers for believers and were preserved by believers to encourage belief is not a factor that should enter into interpretation. When passages that have theological import present difficulties, no appeal can be made to inspiration or any other religious factor (e.g., church tradition) in interpreting them. Whether by intention or not, this attitude has the effect of making a doctrine of inspiration irrelevant.

(3) The literalist end of the spectrum of biblical interpreters would make divine inspiration so dominant a factor that the limitations of the human writers become irrelevant, even as do many of the hermeneutical issues I have raised in the preceding subsection. God knows all things and God communicates through the Scriptures; therefore the Scriptures respond to problems of all times, even those that the human authors never thought of. This stress on inspiration is often correlated with a sweeping theory of inerrancy whereby biblical data relevant to scientific, historical, and religious issues are deemed infallible and unquestionable. Practically, then, all biblical literature is looked on as historical; and apparent contrarieties, such as those between the infancy narratives of Matt and Luke, must be harmonized.

(4) A number of interpreters take an intermediate position.[20] They accept inspiration, deeming it important for the interpretation of Scripture; but they do not think that God's role as an author removed human limitations. In this approach, God who providentially provided for Israel a record of salvific history involving Moses and the prophets also provided for Christians a basic record of the salvific role and message of Jesus. Yet those who wrote down the Christian record were time-conditioned people of the 1st and early 2d century, addressing audiences of their era in the worldview of that period. They did not know the distant future. Although what they wrote is relevant to future Christian existence, their writing does not necessarily provide

[19]The writing of H. S. Reimarus, D. Strauss, and F. C. Baur rejected with skepticism virtually all elements of the supernatural in the careers of Jesus and the apostles. See NJBC 70 for the history of NT criticism.

[20]Sometimes designated "centrist," these may well constitute the majority of teachers and writers in the NT area.

ready-made answers for unforeseeable theological and moral issues that would arise in subsequent centuries. God chose to deal with such subsequent problems not by overriding all the human limitations of the biblical writers but by supplying a Spirit that is a living aid in ongoing interpretation.

Within position (4) there are different attitudes on inerrancy. Some would dispense altogether with inerrancy as a wrong deduction from the valid thesis that God inspired the Scriptures. Others would contend that inspiration did produce an inerrancy affecting religious issues (but not science or history), so that all theological stances in the Scriptures would be inerrant. Still others, recognizing diversity within the Scriptures even on religious issues, would maintain only a limited theological inerrancy. Finally, another solution does not posit a quantitative limitation of inerrancy confining it to certain passages or certain issues,[21] but a qualitative one whereby all Scripture is inerrant to the extent that it serves the purpose for which God intended it. Recognition of this type of limitation is implicit in the statement made at Vatican Council II: "The books of Scripture must be acknowledged as teaching firmly, faithfully, and without error that truth which God wanted put into the sacred writings for the sake of our salvation."[22] Yet even this response runs up against the problem of finding a criterion: How exactly does one know what God wanted put into the Scriptures for the sake of our salvation?

Two proposed criteria for what Scripture teaches authoritatively reflect divisions in Western Christianity since the Reformation. One is that the Spirit guides the individual reader of the Bible to religious or theological truth, i.e., "private interpretation" of the Bible. The other is that the Spirit supplies guidance through church teaching. Each criterion has difficulties. Private interpretation is logically paralyzed when two who claim to have the Spirit disagree. Not every spirit is from God (I John 4:1–3), but how does one know which spirit is? Moreover, at least in the mainline churches that emerged from the Reformation, church tradition of various kinds (e.g., creeds, confessions of faith) has had a role, explicit or implicit, in guiding private interpretation. Roman Catholics who appeal explicitly to Spirit-guided church teaching are often unaware that their church has seldom if ever definitively pronounced on the literal meaning of a passage of Scripture, i.e., what an author meant when he wrote it. Most often the church has commented on the ongoing meaning of Scripture by resisting the claims of those who would reject established practices or beliefs as unbiblical. Moreover,

[21]Any effort to maintain that only certain passages in the NT are inerrant is problematic if inerrancy flows from inspiration that covers all the Scriptures. For a general treatment, see N. Lohfink, *The Inerrancy of Scripture* (Berkeley: Bibal, 1992).

[22]*Dei Verbum* (Nov. 18, 1965) 3.11.

church interpretations of Scripture in Roman Catholicism are affected by qualifications laid out in reference to church teaching in general which have the effect of recognizing historical conditioning.[23]

In an *Introduction* meant to speak to a broad audience of readers, how is one to judge the four positions on inspiration listed above? The religious interest of most would not be met by the skepticism of (1) or even by the silence of (2). As for (3), an outlook on NT inspiration and inerrancy that would vitiate hermeneutical investigations comparable to those employed for other books would not facilitate open inquiry. A form of (4) would have the greatest following among those interested in the religious implications of the NT. Consequently in treating individual NT books I shall call attention to passages that have been the subject of major Christian debate, illustrating how variant theological interpretations have emerged from differing views about the role of the Spirit and/or tradition in interpreting God's inspired word.

Revelation

Part of the reason that people consider the issue of inspiration to be crucial is that they look on Scripture as having a unique position in God's revelation to human beings, a revelation that affects their lives and destinies. Once again, Christians have different outlooks on biblical revelation, and these can be listed in a sequence corresponding to the above list of positions about inspiration. (1) Radical Christians deny the existence of any revelation coming from God other than that already implied in creation. Basing themselves on either metaphysics or their understanding of God, they regard as superstition all claimed communications from above. Accordingly they do not view Scripture as involving divine revelation, even as they dismiss inspiration. (2) Some who may believe in divine revelation allot it no role in interpretation, any more than they allowed inspiration to intrude. Scripture conveys humanly conditioned ideas, and logic rather than faith determines whether they should be accepted. (3) Many, more conservative Christians think of Scripture as the product of revelation, so that every word of it constitutes a divine communication of truth to human beings. This approach, which iden-

[23]*Mysterium Ecclesiae,* issued June 24, 1973 by the Congregation for the Doctrine of the Faith (formerly the Holy Office; AAS 65 [1973], 394–407), states: (1) The meaning of faith pronouncements "depends partly on the power of language used at a certain . . . time"; (2) "Some dogmatic truth is at first expressed incompletely (but not falsely) and later . . . receives a fuller and more perfect expression"; (3) Pronouncements usually have a limited intention "of solving certain questions or removing certain errors"; (4) The truths being taught "may be enunciated in terms that bear the traces" of "the changeable conceptions of a given epoch" and may need to be reformulated by the teaching church to present more clearly their meaning.

tifies Scripture with revelation, runs up against the objection that some passages in Scripture (lists of names, temple measurements, poetic descriptions, etc.) do not seem to involve truth or, at least, truth that affects a way of life or salvation. Such an objection has been met in several ways. Particularly in times past allegorizing interpretations found a hidden spiritual meaning beneath the surface of even the most pedestrian passages, partly on the assumption that knowledge communicated by God must be important whether or not we understand why. Without an appeal to allegory, that assumption is fairly widespread even today.[24]

(4) Other Christians, not finding revelation in every biblical passage, contend that Scripture is not revelation but contains it. Yet within this view, particularly in the West, Christians are divided as to whether Scripture is the only normative attestation of or witness to revelation. If one is allowed a simplification, many Protestants tend to answer affirmatively, while Catholics do not. With the honing of a sharper sense of historical development, however, the situation has become more complicated. No matter how earnestly modern Christians may affirm that they hold nothing except what is found in Scripture, they are so far from the worldview of the OT and NT authors that they cannot look at spiritual realities the way those authors did. Implicitly interpretations that developed from facing later problems have influence. Thus many Protestants acknowledge a reformulation of the biblical revelation through the centuries. Nevertheless, for the most part they do not accept as revealed or normative any affirmations that are not to some degree explicit in Scripture.

The Roman Catholic position has also undergone changes. This Church formally teaches doctrines that cannot be found literally in Scripture, e.g., Mary's Immaculate Conception and Assumption. There have been several popular ways of justifying such teaching. Some Catholics would appeal to a more-than-literal sense of certain biblical passages in which they would find the doctrines hidden. Thus they find the Immaculate Conception in Luke 1:28, "Hail, O one who has been favored [notice the past tense]," and the Assumption in Rev 12:1 with its portrait of the woman in heaven with the sun, moon, and stars. Another approach would posit a second source of revelation different from Scripture, namely, Tradition that was known in the 1st century (but never written down) and passed on orally. Neither of these two views has much knowledgeable following today; indeed Vatican Council II rejected a proposal that would have spoken of two sources of revelation.

One modified (and simplified) Roman Catholic view would be that revela-

[24]For instance, logically one can ask why many Christians are absolutely firm that one must take as literally revealed the biblical account of creation. It is almost as if a knowledge of how the world began (and how it will end) is necessary to salvation.

tion involves both God's *action* for human salvation and the *interpretation* of that action by those whom God has raised up and guided for that purpose. In terms of revelatory action, Scripture describes what God has done in Israel and in Jesus Christ. Scripture also offers interpretation of that action, e.g., the interpretation of the Sinai covenant by the prophets and the interpretation of Jesus' mission by himself and the apostles. Of all interpretation of God's revelatory action the scriptural is the most important and essential; it should guide all subsequent interpretation, so that in ongoing thought there is an enduring responsibility to Scripture. Yet the scriptural interpretation is limited, for it reflects the understanding of God's action only in a period that extends from approximately 1000 BC to AD 125. In Christian faith God's action climaxed in Jesus Christ who is once for all time (Heb 10:10) so that after the gift of the divine Son no further revelation is needed—whence the theological axiom that revelation closed with the death of the last apostle. Yet there is no reason to think that God ceased to guide a developing interpretation of that action. Indeed, the subsequent role of the Spirit in human history, in the history of the church and its pronouncements, in the writings of the Fathers and theologians enters into *a Tradition that embodies the post-scriptural interpretation of the salvific action of God described in Scripture.*[25] The Bible has unique importance because it contains both the narrative of the foundational salvific action of God and the basic interpretation of that action, but there can be subsequent *normative* interpretation of that action which is not found in Scripture. Thus, for example, the raising from death to glory of all the faithful disciples of Christ is an interpretation of salvation revealed in the NT; and although not found in Scripture, the doctrine of the Assumption of Mary can be seen by Roman Catholics as a particular application of that interpretation—an interpretation developing from a late NT tendency visible in Luke and John to see Mary as a privileged disciple.

Besides the theories of revelation broadly described as Protestant and Catholic, others have been advanced, but all have difficulties. Those laid out above are sufficient to enable readers of this *Introduction* to reflect on their own stance. Some teachers of NT courses may be surprised to find these pages, for in their own courses they would not think it proper to raise the issue, lest it detract from an objective or scientific approach to Scripture. Yet it would be surprising if many of their students do not have presuppositions (often very simple) about the relation of revelation to Scripture and questions that spring from those presuppositions. Also, whether consciously or unconsciously, an outlook on revelation inevitably does affect one's approach to

[25]Of course, in a wider sense Scripture itself is tradition, viz., the written tradition of Israel and of the early church.

Scripture, not least the approach of those who would profess themselves agnostic on the subject.

(C) The Literal Sense

Subsection A above offered a survey of many approaches to the NT (types of "criticism")—approaches that should be seen as complementary. Let me now return to one of those approaches that gave rise to modern biblical studies and that remains fundamental even if controverted: Historical Criticism.[26] In part the controversy stems from a lack of agreement on what is implied. For many people Historical Criticism has had almost an aura of pure science in studying the sources from which a biblical book was composed: their historical value; the circumstances of composition; the author; and the objective contents. Yet, since historical investigation was often combined with an antipathy toward theology, the results have appeared barren to readers looking for spiritual meaning applicable to their lives. Indeed this critical approach does not seem to explain the NT as vitally important religious literature. The decline and fall of Historical Criticism has been announced several times; but, as Mark Twain found in reading his own obituary, the funeral was a bit premature. In 1995, for instance, a new periodical *The Journal of Higher Criticism* was founded bearing on its cover a picture of F. C. Baur, the radical exponent of Historical Criticism 150 years ago!

To an important degree, the stubborn survival of Historical Criticism has been due to its concern for something very fundamental to all other forms of interpretation (even though ardent adherents of those other "criticisms" may not agree). When one strips off some of the abuses (e.g., overenthusiasm for detecting sources;[27] arbitrary judgments about historical circumstances), Historical Criticism is concerned with the commonsense observation that readers of any book of Scripture will want to know what the author of that book tried to convey. To highlight this aspect of Historical Criticism (and to avoid some of its unfortunate "baggage") some writers (of whom I am one) choose to speak of the essential necessity of determining "the literal sense" of biblical passages.

The literal sense means what the biblical authors intended and conveyed to their audiences by what they wrote. This sense does not exhaust the meaning of Scripture but has a fundamental relationship to meanings

[26]See E. Krentz, *The Historical Critical Method* (Philadelphia: Fortress, 1975).

[27]Frequently scholars have thought that they could assign every verse in a Gospel to one or another source or to the author's editing; see, for example, the description of thirty-five different source analyses of the Marcan passion narrative offered by M. L. Soards in BDM 2.1492–1524. The one thing certain about any scholar's source analysis is that another scholar will disagree with it.

gained by other forms of "criticism." That the literal sense may not be easy to determine becomes apparent when we reflect one by one on the individual components of that description.

BY WHAT THE BIBLICAL AUTHORS WROTE. The NT books were written some 1,900 years ago in Greek. From the viewpoint of language, even the most competent English translation cannot render all the nuances of the original Greek. From the viewpoint of culture and context, the authors and their audiences had a worldview very different from ours: different background, different knowledge, different suppositions about reality. We cannot hope to open a NT book and read it responsibly with the same ease as we read a book written in our own culture and worldview. Consequently, an intelligent effort to understand the background and outlook of the NT authors can be of great assistance and will be a major concern of this *Introduction.*

Since they wrote in different times and different places, all the authors did not necessarily have the same background or outlook. Let me give some examples of possible differences that affect meaning. It seems likely that most or all the NT authors were of Jewish birth. How well did they know Judaism and with what particular outlook? Was the Greek in which they wrote a language they had grown up with; or was either Aramaic or Hebrew their mother tongue, so that they (or a secretary) were mentally translating into Greek? The authors knew the Jewish Scriptures, but in what language? The Scriptures in Hebrew differ considerably at times from the LXX and from the Targums or Aramaic translations (most of which were made later than the LXX). There is evidence that Matt, John,[28] and Paul may have known Aramaic and/or Hebrew, while Mark and Luke may have known only Greek—but we are far from certain. The Gospels and Acts situate scenes in Jerusalem, Judea, Galilee, Antioch, and other parts of the ancient world; how many of the authors had ever been in the places they mention? Those who had may have written with knowledge; those who had not presumably wrote with imagination or on the basis of what they had heard.

TO AUDIENCES.[29] The writers were addressing particular audiences in the

[28]Throughout this *Introduction* Mark, Matt, Luke, and John are used both for the Gospels and their writers. These traditional designations should be retained, even though, as we shall see, authorship is often more complex. In the abstract we do not know that all the books were written by men, and some modern commentators insist on referring to an unknown NT author as he/she. More concretely, however, nothing in early tradition about the authors suggests that any one of them was a woman; indeed, both the education at that time and customs about public positions among Jews make that possibility highly unlikely. While, except in giving *literal* quotes of Scripture in reference to God, I shall always try to respect modern sensitivities against using masculine pronouns for those who are not male, I do not think that the likelihoods warrant a feminine pronoun in reference to NT authors.

[29]Here we have to take into account both the actual audiences to whom the NT writings were first read, and the intentional audiences, i.e., the readers the authors envisioned as we can tell from

1st and early 2d centuries. How did those audiences understand what was written? We cannot answer with certainty, but certain factors should be considered. First, author's intention and audience's understanding may differ. For instance, after reflecting on the Jewish background of a NT author and the meaning he was trying to convey, we may need to ask how an audience consisting of Christians of Gentile birth who had acquired only a partial familiarity with Judaism understood what he wrote. Paul's description of Jesus as the Son of God most likely had its roots in the promise of Nathan to David that God would treat David's royal offspring as a son (II Sam 7:14). Yet what was the understanding of the title among Paul's hearers/readers[30] who had rendered public honor to male and female gods and their divine children—at least until horrified Jewish Christian missionaries corrected misunderstanding? To what extent must such possibilities be brought into a discussion of the meaning of Scriptures?

Second, although the contents of a NT book enter into the reconstruction of both author and addressees, we have limited knowledge about the identity of the audiences addressed (with the exception of the named communities of some Pauline letters). For example, in Mark 7:3 the evangelist explains that the Pharisees, and indeed all Jews, wash their hands and purify themselves as part of a ritual process antecedent to eating and drinking. From that one may surmise that the author was either a Jew or knew about Jewish customs, whereas the audience knew little about them. That surmise can play a role in judging the meaning of a difficult Marcan passage such as 15:38 involving the rent veil of the Temple sanctuary (parallels in Matt 27:51; Luke 23:45b). There were a number of Temple veils with different functions and decorations (described by the Jewish historian Josephus). Scholars have developed different interpretations of the scene, depending on which veil they think was rent and the significance of that veil. But did the evangelists, one or all, know that there were different sanctuary veils; had anyone of them ever seen the Temple building or the decorated veil? If one had while the others had not, the evangelists may have had different understandings of the rending of the veil. More to the point, is there any chance that Mark's audi-

indications in the writings. (See p. vii above for the intentional audience of this *Introduction,* but at times it may actually be read by others.) See E. V. McKnight, ed., *Reader Perspectives on the New Testament* (*Semeia* 48 [1989]).

[30]We *read* the Pauline letters. Although literacy in the Roman Empire was respectably high, originally the letters were probably read aloud publicly; and that means that most of those reached by the letters *heard* them. The Gospels represent a stage when the traditions about Jesus were put into writing; yet copies of them in the early years would have been kept in church archives and read aloud in community services. Indeed until the combination of printing and the Reformation, most Christians knew the Scriptures through hearing rather than by reading; that situation continued in many Roman Catholic communities till the present century and may still be the dominant situation in Christian missions.

ence would have understood a recondite reference to a specific Jerusalem Temple veil when they did not have an elementary knowledge of Judaism? How about the audiences addressed in Matt and Luke? On the level of literal sense, can one speak properly of a "meaning" of a passage when there is little chance that the original intended audience would have understood such a meaning? Probably one cannot interpret the rending of the veil of the sanctuary to convey more than the words themselves would imply to anyone who had ever been in a temple, namely, that a veil partitioning off the sacred place in the Temple of Jerusalem had been rent from top to bottom, thus depriving that place of what made it God's sanctuary and set it off in holiness from other places in the enclave.

Third, a particular debate centers on the extent to which the audiences of the individual NT writers understood "Scripture," i.e., the sacred Jewish writings of the period before Jesus to which the evangelists frequently appealed.[31] Would the intended audiences have caught subtle allusions? If a passage is cited, would they have been aware of the OT context, so that more of the pericope than the cited line would have sprung to mind? Would vocabulary used by the writer in a cited Scripture passage have evoked in the readers' minds other passages of Scripture containing the same vocabulary, as scholars sometimes assume in their comments? Would the audiences have known living Jewish tradition that had expanded the meaning of a biblical text? The answers may vary from audience to audience.

Fourth, beyond being alert to the intellectual and religious background of the audience addressed, modern hermeneutics has concentrated on sociological analysis of both the author and his audience. Historical studies of churches addressed by Paul or Rev have long been popular; but modern sociology, fortified by a more astute application of archaeological technique, has made us aware of differences centered on citizenship, wealth, education, and social status within the churches addressed (Chapter 4B below). Sometimes, of course, scholars are not at one in their diagnosis of the sociopolitical situation, e.g., of the political unrest in the Palestine of Jesus' public ministry (in my judgment, relatively little unrest, so that Jesus was not a revolutionary) as distinct from the situation fifteen to twenty-five years later (very serious unrest). Diagnosis of the sociopolitical situation of the Gospel audiences generally depends on internal evidence and is a highly speculative quest.

WHAT THE BIBLICAL AUTHORS INTENDED AND CONVEYED. The two verbs are an attempt to do justice to a complex situation. The importance of "convey" is relatively obvious. The NT writers certainly knew more of the Chris-

[31]For a host of problems on the use and understanding of the OT in the NT, see G. K. Beale, ed., *The Right Doctrine from the Wrong Text?* (Grand Rapids: Baker, 1994).

tian tradition than they were able or chose to convey in their writings; John 21:25 is specific about that. Therefore we should maintain a certain distrust of negative arguments from silence, as if the failure to write meant the failure to know. For instance, only Matt and Luke tell us about Jesus' virginal conception. Failure of other NT writers to mention it does not necessarily mean that they did not know of it (or, a fortiori, would deny it[32]); yet neither can we assume that the knowledge was widespread. On the level of the literal sense, exegesis that embraces what the evangelists did not actually convey *in writing* becomes very speculative.

A more delicate issue is the relationship between what the written words convey and what the writers intended. There is a span of possibilities: According to the skill of the writer, a writing may convey what the author wished, or something less, or the opposite, or something other than the author wished or foresaw.[33] In interpreting any work, however, one must start by supposing a *general* correspondence between what the author intended and what the author conveyed. Only by exception, then, do commentators on the Bible have to alert readers to instances where what the words seem to convey may not be what the author intended.

One may well object, "How can a modern interpreter know that ancient authors intended something different from what their words convey?" Sometimes guidance can be found in the context or in other passages. By way of example, one may note Luke does not report a scourging of Jesus by Roman soldiers as do Mark/Matt; accordingly, in Luke 23:26 the antecedent of the "they" who led Jesus away to be crucified is grammatically "the chief priests and the rulers and the people" of 23:13. Many commentators would read this passage as a deliberate Lucan attempt to make the Jews the agents of the crucifixion and to exculpate the Romans. Yet careless use of antecedents is not infrequent in writing.[34] Eventually Luke makes clear that there were (Roman) soldiers involved in the crucifixion (23:36), and elsewhere he indicates that the Gentiles killed Jesus (18:32–33; cf. Acts 4:25–27). From other NT evidence one may suspect that all or most Christians would have heard and known of the Roman role in crucifying Jesus, and so Luke's audience would have understood the "they" of Luke 23:26 in that sense (as have Christian audiences ever since). Most likely, then, the grammatical sense of what Luke wrote was not what he intended to convey.

[32]A "hermeneutics of suspicion" detects conscious or unconscious suppression by scriptural authors—often suppression of what one would like to find there or thinks should have been there. Allowance must be made, however, that the "suppressed" idea never occurred to the ancient writer.

[33]Below I shall speak about the "plus value" or wider meaning of a writing when new generations see possibilities in the text that are harmonious with but also beyond the author's intention.

[34]Indeed, Luke is sometimes a careless editor: He reports Jesus' prophecy about being scourged (18:33) but then, by omitting the Roman scourging, leaves the prophecy unfulfilled.

Nevertheless, one should resort only rarely to such interpretation distinguishing between what was written and what was intended. Often commentators detect contradictions in the sequence of a NT book and assume that one writer could not have been responsible for the text as it now stands or that the writer combined diverse sources without recognizing that they were irreconcilable. Such a solution is not impossible, but not necessarily probable. The account as it now stands made sense to someone in antiquity, and so what seems contradictory to modern interpreters may not be really contradictory. For instance, some commentators would find a contradiction between Mark 14:50 that says of the disciples, "And having left him, they all fled," and Mark 14:51 that still has a certain young man following Jesus, and Mark 14:54 that has Peter following him from a distance. In this type of narrative are these really contradictory, or are they cumulative ways of illustrating the failure of the disciples? All fled or went away denying Jesus, including eventually even those who, by still following, attempted not to flee.

A last note on the issue of the author's intention is that we are speaking of the final or substantial author of a NT book. At times NT authors used sources, most of which are no longer extant. For instance, the majority view is that Matt and Luke (in addition to their use of Mark) drew upon Q, a collection in Greek of the sayings of the Lord detected through what is common between Matt and Luke but absent from Mark. As we shall see in Chapter 6, there is a cottage industry of books about Q, analyzing the exact order and theology of this nonextant source, possible sayings that were not preserved, the nature of the community to which Q was addressed, and how Q might have been closer to Jesus than is any preserved work, etc. Although this research is defensible as scholarly enterprise, the putative meaning of Q should not be presented as an authoritative biblical or NT meaning. Discernment of the complex origins of a biblical book should enter into a diagnosis of the meaning of that book; but *the canonical NT to the authority of which Christians are committed consists of whole books, not reconstructed sources as fascinating as they may be.*

Such insistence partially shelters NT study from a common objection, namely, that every few years scholars change their views about composition and sources and Christianity cannot be dependent on the whims of changing scholarship. Ironically, since the designation "scholars" could refer to the great Christian writers of antiquity, i.e., the "Church Fathers," the churches have in fact been dependent on scholarship. But in terms of this specific objection, the churches or their representatives need not (and even should not) base their preaching or practice on hypothetical, nonextant sources. Although scholars also disagree about the exegesis of texts in the extant books of the NT, that area is far less speculative than the reconstruction of sources.

(D) Wider Meanings beyond the Literal

Although basic, the literal sense is not the only sense of a passage, just as correspondingly Historical Criticism is not the only form of interpretation. In particular, the nature of the Bible makes three issues of wider meaning extremely important.

Wider Meaning from Recognizing God's Role as Author

Above in Subsection B four different attitudes toward the divine inspiration of the Bible were explained, and the fourth was treated as the most plausible approach for those interested in the religious implications of the NT. That view of inspiration customarily speaks of twofold biblical authorship, divine and human—"authorship" not in the sense that God dictated the Bible to human copyists; but that the composition of biblical books by human writers was part of God's providence, so that the OT and the NT might articulate revelation and provide enduring guidance for God's people. As a result of God's active role in producing the Scriptures, it is not illogical to propose that beyond the literal sense intended and conveyed by the human authors could be a fuller sense intended by God. In the history of biblical interpretation from OT times (e.g., at Qumran) through the Reformation this dimension of Scripture was recognized in various ways (see NJBC 71.31–44 for a brief history). Most often the Christian appeal to a more-than-literal sense stemming from divine authorship centered in two areas: the use of the OT in the NT, and the use of the Bible in postbiblical church practice and preaching. It was recognized that the NT authors saw in the OT anticipations of Jesus that went beyond what the original human authors had foreseen, and that church liturgy and imagery in areas such as christology, mariology, and sacramentalism saw anticipations of later beliefs that went beyond the specific NT teaching.

This type of interpretation has been described in various ways: spiritual sense, typology,[35] promise and fulfillment. The main problem faced by such more-than-literal exegesis is the establishment of criteria for reading God's intention in the Scriptures, so that it is kept distinct from simple human ingenuity in reflecting on the Scriptures. Suggested criteria include a wide agreement (including Church Fathers) on the proposed interpretation and some basis in already existing scriptural patterns. For instance, the use of Melchizedek as a type of Christ in Heb 7 is invoked to justify the liturgical

[35]Certain people or things of an earlier period were thought to foreshadow people or things of a later period.

interpretation of Melchizedek's presentation of bread and wine (Gen 14:18) as a type or anticipation of the eucharist.

In the period 1925–70, particularly in Roman Catholic circles, a more technical approach developed in terms of a *sensus plenior* ("fuller sense") of Scripture, understood as the deeper meaning intended by God (but not clearly intended by the human author) seen to exist in the words of Scripture when they are studied in the light of further revelation or of development in the understanding of revelation.[36] As one of the criteria the *sensus plenior* had to be homogeneous with the literal sense. However, since the 1970s, as Catholic exegesis melded into the larger Christian centrist approach to Scripture, at least some of the appreciation for a more-than-literal sense underlying the *sensus plenior* movement has found voice in the two hermeneutical approaches described next.

Wider Meaning Gained from the Placement of a Book within the Canon

If the primary biblical meaning is that of a NT book and not that of its hypothetical preexistent parts or sources, at the other end of the spectrum the book has meaning not only by itself but in relation to the other biblical books. Indeed, a book is truly biblical only because the book became part of an authoritative collection, i.e., the NT or even the whole Bible. No NT writer knew that what he wrote would be included in a collection of twenty-seven books and read as an enduring message centuries or even millennia later. Indeed, given their strong emphases on certain issues, some writers might not have been happy about having works of a different cast set alongside their own with similar authority. In view of what he wrote in Gal 2:11–14 about Cephas (Peter) and "certain men from James," Paul might have deemed it strange to find his letter in the same Testament as two epistles attributed to Peter and one attributed to James.[37] Luke might be annoyed to find his second book (Acts) separated from his first (the Gospel) and placed as if it were of another genre. Nevertheless, being part of the canon is an essential dimension of the meaning of the books we are discussing.

I spoke in subsection A above of "Canonical Criticism," but that designation can have different nuances. If I may use an OT example, the book of Isaiah is thought to consist of three major divisions composed over a long period of time: protoIsaiah (8th century BC), deuteroIsaiah (mid-6th cen-

[36]A treatment of the *sensus plenior* is offered in JBC 71.56–70 and a shorter treatment in NJBC 71.49–51.

[37]Yet Paul's testimony in I Cor 15:5–11 to a teaching and faith shared in common with Cephas and James might mean that his final attitude would have been inclusive.

tury), and tritoIsaiah plus other segments (late 6th century onwards). Scholars write commentaries on each of those parts; but the "canonical meaning," in one sense, would be the meaning that passages from those parts have in the context of the *whole book.* With other nuances it would be the meaning the passage has within the context of the prophetic corpus, then within the OT, then within the *whole Bible,* including the NT—in other words the canonical meaning could include as much as 800 years of interpretation.[38]

The whole canonical dimension is often neglected in two ways. First, some earnest believers are under the false impression that the biblical message is always (and indeed, necessarily) uniform, whereas it is not. One may explain that there is no *contradiction* between Rom 3:28 ("justified by faith, apart from the works of the law") and Jas 2:24 ("justified by works and not by faith alone"); but one can scarcely imagine that Paul's attitude was the same as that of James. When people quote Paul, "Christ is the end of the Law" (Rom 10:4), they may need to add that in Matt 5:17–18 Jesus says, "Do not think that I have come to abolish the Law . . . not the smallest letter nor the smallest part of a letter of the Law will pass away till all these things have come to pass." Then one has a fuller picture of what the NT says about a Christian's relation to the Law. Whether consciously or unconsciously, the church has placed side by side in the same canon works that do not share the same outlook. The response to the canon is not to suppress or undervalue the sharp view of an individual biblical author, but to make up one's mind in face of diverse views existing side by side.

Second, on a more scholarly level where this diversity of view is recognized, there is sometimes a thrust toward defining "the center of the canon" or "the canon within the canon." All must recognize that certain biblical books by their length and profundity are more important than other books; e.g., it would be a bizarre interpreter who would attribute to Jude and Rom the same importance. A preferential religious status has been given within the OT to the Pentateuch or Torah (first five books), and within the NT to the Gospels. The traditional church lectionary for Sundays has assigned importance within the canon by what is chosen to be read. That selection has had its problems: Before the 1970s the Roman Catholic lectionary massively neglected Mark in favor of Matt and Luke—a choice that deprived Christian audiences of hearing the unique sharpness of the Marcan witness. One may excuse the deficiencies of such past practice as indeliberate, stemming from the naive assumption that virtually everything in Mark was contained in the other two Gospels. But selective emphasis in our times is often deliberate.

[38]This appreciation would be another reason why Christians should be aware that they are not simply interpreting books that constitute the "Hebrew Scriptures" (p. xxxiv above) but books that form an OT united to a NT in the same Bible.

Recognizing that there are diverse views in the NT, some scholars decide that certain works are misleading, inferior, or harmful and should receive little emphasis[39] or even be excluded from the NT. Appealing to the Pauline distinction between letter and spirit (II Cor 3:6–8), they contend that Christians cannot make the NT an infallible authority but must distinguish the real spirit within the NT. In particular, there has been a reaction by more radical scholars against works in which aspects of "early Catholicism" are detected, i.e., the initial stages of sacramentalism, hierarchy, ordination, dogma, etc.[40] For instance, some Protestant academics have queried whether II Pet deserves to be in the canon since 3:15–17 warns against the dangers of private interpretation of Paul's letters as perilous—implicitly a step toward church control of Scripture. Yet these are exactly the scriptural passages that other Christians would cite to justify later ecclesiastical developments. In other words, differences among today's Christians are being used as a standard to judge what is important or justifiable in the NT and to push to the fringes works with tendencies to which one objects. This movement has rendered the service of concentrating attention on the acuteness of the problem raised by diversities in the NT, but the direction of the solution is questionable.

Consistently in the course of history, Christians who were arguing to prove they were right and others were wrong have appealed to select NT passages and books, unconsciously ignoring other passages and assuming they were following the whole NT. Is that remedied by consciously ignoring other passages? Might not those who profess to follow the NT profit more by paying serious attention to the passages they find problematic and by asking whether those passages highlight something defective in their own perception of Christianity? Might they not profit more by maintaining the whole canon even if that means that they are challenged by its diversities? Readers could then allow Scripture to serve as both conscience and corrective.

[39]To a certain extent one may trace the modern tendency to Martin Luther's early effort (Sept. 1522) to rearrange the order of the books of the NT, placing Heb, Jas, Jude, and Rev at the end as of lesser quality than the "true and certain main books" of the NT because in former times they were seen in a different light (i.e., not of apostolic origin). Theological problems might be found in the assertion of Heb 10:26 that if one committed serious sin after conversion, there was no possibility of atonement for sin; in Jas' lack of redemptive christology and its emphasis on works (2:24); in the citation of a noncanonical book (*I Enoch*) by Jude 14–15; and in the millennial expectation (thousand-year reign of Christ on earth) in Rev 20:4–6.

[40]In his 1900 work *What Is Christianity?* (English ed.; New York: Harper, 1957) the famous liberal church historian and NT scholar A. Harnack attributed many of these features to 2d-century Christianity that distorted the original import of the NT. In 1951 E. Käsemann (KENTT 95–107) sharpened the issue by pointing to the existence of such features in the NT itself. A debate was opened with the response by H. Küng, *Structures of the Church* (New York: Nelson, 1964), 151–69.

Wider Meanings from Subsequent Reading

We have just been discussing what the NT authors *meant* and also the dimension of meaning that their writings *took on* when placed in the context of the whole canon. Such past tenses, however, do not do justice to the whole issue of meaning. People have continued finding in the NT meaning for their own lives as they face new issues; they have asked what the NT books *mean,* not simply what they meant. That issue can be raised in an ingenuous way by the assumption that the NT writings are addressed directly to the modern world, i.e., by reading a Pauline letter with the assumption that Paul was speaking to the problems of a parish audience in our time. This approach is naive because the NT authors were human beings who composed at a particular time and place and who, even when they looked to the future, conceived of that future in terms of their own experience.

Yet another way of looking at the issue is not at all naive. Once a work is written, it enters into dialogue with its readers, including future readers. In modern contextual approaches to hermeneutics (e.g., in narrative criticism and rhetorical criticism as seen above), the literary work is not simply the written text as once completed; it comes into being when writing and reader interact. The text is not simply an object on which the interpreter works analytically to extract a permanently univocal meaning; it is a structure that is engaged by readers in the process of achieving meaning and is therefore open to more than one valid meaning. Once written, a text is no longer under the author's control and can never be interpreted twice from the same situation.[41] Although the hermeneutical phraseology is recent, there has been an ongoing meaningful engagement with the text through the centuries. The NT has given rise to theological, spiritual, and artistic reflection that, while it goes beyond what the author envisioned, is not mere accommodation to the spirit of a later age. The major problem in judging such reflection lies once more in the criteria for determining an authentic development from a distortion. For example, in terms of impact, when he introduced the creche or Christmas crib, Francis of Assisi became history's most important interpreter of the infancy chaps. of Matt and Luke.[42] One can appreciate that enormous contribution and still be obliged to wonder whether, through fostering maudlin sentimentality, the crib/creche might *in certain circumstances* become false to the main theological purposes of those narratives.

The concern is particularly acute in judging theological developments that

[41]See S. M. Schneiders, NJBC 71.63–64, and a full treatment in her book *Revelatory.*

[42]The creche conflates the Gospels (Matthean magi, Lucan shepherds), the biblical and nonbiblical (the stable and cave), and OT echoes (camels, oxen, sheep). It highlights the dramatic potentialities and the relation to simple family life.

have invoked Scripture. The Reformation brought to the fore radically different theological positions with the claim that they were based on the NT; and so the Western church was split over issues such as whether Christ intended two or seven sacraments. That problem is real; yet modern discussions have to recognize that the NT never speaks of "sacrament," and probably no such umbrella term existed in the 1st century to cover diverse sacred actions such as baptism and the eucharist. In the ongoing ecumenical discussion of the number of sacraments, a modern approach would be to study common elements in the NT understandings of baptism and the eucharist that would lead to the postNT development of "sacrament" as an umbrella term, and the possible existence in the NT period of other sacred actions that in one way or another shared this communality.

From time to time in this *Introduction* I shall ask readers to reflect on issues pertinent to NT books that go beyond the literal sense. Without deciding the disputed issue, recognition of this "plus value" may clarify the subsequent differences and perhaps help to defuse judgments about whose view is truly biblical.

Bibliography on Interpretation

(Bibliography for individual approaches to the NT is found in footnotes attached to the discussions of the respective form of criticism.)

Blount, B. K., *Cultural Interpretation: Reorienting New Testament Criticism* (Minneapolis: A/F, 1995).

Braaten, C. E., and R. W. Jenson, eds., *Reclaiming the Bible for the Church* (Grand Rapids: Eerdmans, 1995).

Fee, G. D., *New Testament Exegesis: A Handbook for Students and Pastors* (rev. ed.; Louisville: W/K, 1993).

Fitzmyer, J. A., *Scripture: the Soul of Theology* (New York: Paulist, 1994). Treats different forms of exegesis.

———, *The Biblical Commission's Document: "The Interpretation of the Bible in the Church"* (Subsidia Biblica 18; Rome: PBI, 1995).

Green, J. B., ed., *Hearing the New Testament: Strategies for Interpretation* (Grand Rapids: Eerdmans, 1995). Essays.

Lührmann, D., *An Itinerary for New Testament Study* (Philadelphia: Trinity, 1989). Various types of criticism, including textual criticism (Chapter 3 below).

McKenzie, S. L., and S. R. Haynes, eds., *To Each Its Own Meaning. An Introduction to Biblical Criticisms and Their Application* (Louisville: W/K, 1993).

McKim, D. K., ed., *A Guide to Contemporary Hermeneutics. Major Trends in Biblical Interpretation* (Grand Rapids: Eerdmans, 1986).

McKnight, E. V., *Meaning in Texts: The Historical Shaping of a Narrative Hermeneutics* (Philadelphia: Fortress, 1978).

Malbon, E. S., and E. V. McKnight, eds., *The New Literary Criticism and the New Testament* (JSNTSup 109; Sheffield: JSOT, 1994). Various types of criticism.

Marshall, I. H., *New Testament Interpretation* (rev. ed.; Exeter: Paternoster, 1985).

Meyer, B. F., *Reality and Illusion in New Testament Scholarship: A Primer in Critical Realist Hermeneutics* (Collegeville: Liturgical, 1994).

Porter, S. E., and D. Tombs, eds., *Approaches to New Testament Study* (JSNTSup 120; Sheffield: JSOT, 1995).

Pregeant, R., *Engaging the New Testament: An Interdisciplinary Introduction* (Minneapolis: A/F, 1995). Wide array of methods.

Ricoeur, P., *Essays on Biblical Interpretation* (Philadelphia: Fortress, 1975).

Ryken, L., ed., *The New Testament in Literary Criticism* (New York: Ungar, 1984).

Schneiders, S. M., *The Revelatory Text: Interpreting the New Testament as Sacred Scripture* (San Francisco: Harper, 1991).

Schottroff, L., *Let the Oppressed Go Free: Feminist Perspectives on the New Testament* (Louisville: W/K, 1993).

Stenger, W., *Introduction to New Testament Exegesis* (Grand Rapids: Eerdmans, 1993).

Thiselton, A. C., *New Horizons in Hermeneutics. The Theory and Practice of Transforming Biblical Reading* (Grand Rapids: Zondervan, 1992).

Tompkins, J. P., ed., *Reader-Response Criticism: From Formalism to Post-Structuralism* (Baltimore: Johns Hopkins, 1980).

Van Voorst, R. E., *Readings in Christianity* (Belmont, CA: Wadsworth, 1997). An interesting text that combines biblical readings with the documents of later theology.

CHAPTER 3

THE TEXT OF THE NEW TESTAMENT

The NT familiar to readers has been translated into a modern language from the ancient Greek in which the NT books were originally composed. The issue of where one finds that Greek text is complicated, and I shall present here only an elementary summary of what may be of use to the nonspecialist.

(A) Manuscript[1] Evidence for the Text

Approximately 3,000 mss. of the Greek NT (part or whole) have been preserved, copied between the 2d and 17th centuries, plus over 2,200 lectionary mss. containing sections (pericopes) of the NT arranged for reading in church liturgy from the 7th century on. These witnesses to the text of the NT do not agree among themselves in myriad ways, but relatively few of the differences are significant.[2] No autograph or original ms. of a NT book has been preserved; the differences came in the course of copying the original. Not all the differences stemmed from mistakes by copyists;[3] some arose from deliberate changes. Copyists, at times, felt impelled to improve the Greek of what they received, to modernize the spelling, to supplement with explanatory phrases, to harmonize Gospels, and even to omit something that seemed dubious. One might think that the oldest preserved copies of the Greek NT (part or whole) would be the best guide to the originals; but that is not necessarily so. For instance, a 6th-century ms. might be the only remaining exemplar of a much earlier, now lost copy that was closer to the autograph than an extant 2d- or 4th-century copy.

[1]The word "manuscript" (ms.) means "handwritten," as distinct from printed works (which began with Gutenberg in 1456). Two types of handwriting were used: *uncial,* which might be compared to our handprinted block capital letters that have no connections between them, and *minuscule,* or cursive (connected) small letters. Sometimes the ancient text is marked with section divisions according to breaks in the sense (at times corresponding to the liturgical readings). The modern chapter division began with Stephen Langton in the 13th century, and the modern verse division began with a printed version of Robert Stephanus (Estienne) in 1551. For more precise subdivision of verses, e.g., Mark 14:9a, see p. xxxii above.

[2]Metzger, *New* 281, states, "No doctrine of the Christian faith depends solely upon a passage that is textually uncertain."

[3]Copyists' mistakes occurred through both the eye (misreading and carelessly copying from a text) and the ear (misunderstanding a person who was dictating the text aloud). One should allow too for a misreading by the person who was dictating to the copyists.

Textual Families. Scholars have bunched together into groups or families mss. that share similar readings and peculiarities,[4] but none of these text groupings has an uncontaminated descent from the originals. The most commonly recognized are the following:

Alexandrian: By the end of the 2d century, Christian scholarship was flourishing in Alexandria, and within the next centuries mss. were copied there with care by scribes who had a sophisticated appreciation of Greek (leaving sometimes the problem whether the plausible readings that mark this group of mss. were original or scholarly improvements). It is marked by shorter readings.

Western: This is a catchall group, named from the Western (North Africa, Italy, Gaul) circulation of some of the Greek mss. that belong to it. Yet alongside them are Greek mss. that can be related to Egypt and to the Syriac-speaking churches of the East. Often the paraphrastic textual readings of this group are longer than the lean and spare Alexandrian readings as if words have been added (interpolations); but in a number of significant instances in Luke, the Western text omits what is found in the Alexandrian (so-called "non-interpolations," e.g., the eucharistic words in Luke 22:19b–20). In Acts the text is almost one-tenth longer than that found in the Alexandrian tradition.

Caesarean: In the 3d and 4th centuries Caesarea on the coast was the most important Christian center in Palestine, glorying in a major library and the scholars who used it. The basic text in this group, dating from the early 3d century, was probably brought there from Egypt; subsequently it spread to Jerusalem and then through Armenian missionaries to Georgia in the Caucasus. In its development the Caesarean text tradition stands between the Alexandrian and the Western.

Byzantine (or Koine):[5] This conflated text that smooths out difficulties and harmonizes differences was used in the liturgy of the Byzantine church (becoming almost normative from the 6th century on), and is generally looked on as a quite late and secondary development. Yet some of its readings are ancient and go back to the church at Antioch *ca.* 300. The *Textus Receptus* (see below) that underlay the KJV NT exemplified this tradition.

Textual Witnesses. A selection of the most important ancient NT textual witnesses gives an idea of the diversity. (Helpful pictures of most of the following may be found in Metzger, *Manuscripts.*) Scholars distinguish three types of Greek mss.:

[4]The name given to a group reflects (sometimes imprecisely) the origin or distribution of many of the mss. that belong to it.

[5]M. A. Robinson and W. G. Pierpont, *The New Testament in the Original Greek According to the Byzantine/Majority Textform* (Atlanta: Original Word, 1991).

(1) *Papyri* (abbreviated P).[6] Egypt has continued to yield very ancient NT fragments and books of the Greek NT on papyrus; since 1890 a hundred have been discovered, dating from the 2d to the 8th centuries. (Dating is based on handwriting style, i.e., paleography.) Among the oldest are:

- P^{52}: (John Rylands Papyrus 457), consisting of a scrap smaller than an index card on which is inscribed part of John 18:31–34. Its date *ca.* 135 makes theories of a very late dating of John impossible.
- P^{46}: (Chester Beatty Papyrus II), consisting of 86 codex (book) pages, *ca.* 200 or earlier, containing the Pauline epistles, including Heb (following Rom—an order based on decreasing length), but not the Pastorals. It belongs to the Caesarean group.
- P^{66}: (Bodmer Papyrus II), *ca.* 200, containing a heavily corrected text of much of John. It belongs to the Alexandrian group, close to the text of Codex Sinaiticus (see below).
- P^{75}: (Bodmer Papyri XIV–XV), *ca.* 225, containing Luke 2:18–18:18 and Luke 22:4–John 15:8. It belongs to the Alexandrian group, close to Codex Vaticanus (see below).

(2) *Great Uncial Codices.* These books, consisting of vellum or parchment pages written in block Greek letters (uncials: n. 1 above), were most prominent from the 3d to the 9th centuries. The emperor Constantine declared tolerance for Christianity in the early 4th century, making possible the public existence of centers of learning and monasteries where many of the codices were copied and preserved. Often they contain the whole Greek Bible and, at times, some early noncanonical Christian works. Of some 300 known uncial codices the most important (designated by capital letters), beginning with the earliest, are:

- B (Codex Vaticanus), mid-4th century, lacking the last part of the NT. It exemplifies the Alexandrian type of text and is thought by most scholars to be the best witness to the original NT text.
- S or א (Codex Sinaiticus), mid-4th century, containing the whole NT plus *Barnabas* and *The Shepherd of Hermas.* It follows the Alexandrian tradition in Gospel and Acts, although elsewhere it has Western readings.
- A (Codex Alexandrinus), early 5th century, once contained the whole NT plus

[6]Ancient writings were on either papyrus or parchment. Papyrus, a type of paper, was made by slicing vertically the stalk of a marsh reed, laying sheets of the sliced strips crosswise on top of each other and pressing them down to form one sheet. It was not overly durable and could survive the centuries only in dry climates (e.g., the Egyptian desert and the area around the Dead Sea). Parchment and the higher quality vellum were prepared animal skins and more durable. Scrolls consisted of sheets of papyrus fastened together side by side and rolled up; codices, like our books, consisted of sheets stacked on top of each other and fastened together at the back. Obviously if one was searching for a page in the middle, a codex was more convenient than a scroll that would have to be unrolled.

1 and 2 Clement and the *Psalms of Solomon;* unfortunately, pages have been lost. In the Gospels the text is Byzantine, but Alexandrian in the rest of the NT.

- D (Codex Bezae), 5th century, contains Matt, John, Luke, Mark, III John, and Acts in Latin and Greek on facing pages. It is the chief representative of the Western text tradition.

(3) *Minuscules.* About the 9th century a cursive (connected letters) writing style began to supersede the uncial, and there are nearly 2,900 NT mss. in this script. Two families of them (named after the scholars K. Lake and W. H. Ferrar) are witnesses of the Caesarean text tradition.

In addition to what we know from these mss., information about the early NT is supplied by versions or translations into other ancient languages, since they bear witness to a Greek text that was the basis of the translation. *Ca.* 200 translations were made into Latin and Syriac, called the Old Latin (OL) and the Old Syriac (OS), to distinguish them respectively from the late–4th century Latin translation (the Vulgate) by St. Jerome that became the standard Bible of the Western church, and from the 4th-5th century Syriac translation (the Peshitta) that became the standard Bible of the Syriac church. The Old Latin and the Old Syriac are generally assigned to the Western text tradition. Comments on the Scriptures by early church writers also supply information about the Greek text or translation that lay before them.

(B) Observations about the Use of the Evidence

When we put all this together, a number of observations emerge:

- Many differences among the textual families visible in the great uncial codices of the 4th and 5th centuries existed already *ca.* 200 as we see from the papyri and early translations. How could so many differences arise within a hundred years after the original books were written? The answer may lie in the attitude of the copyists toward the NT books being copied. These were holy books because of their content and origins, but there was no slavish devotion to their exact wording. They were meant to be commented on and interpreted, and some of that could be included in the text. Later when more fixed ideas of the canon and inspiration shaped the mind-set, attention began to center on keeping the exact wording. The Reformation spirit of "Scripture alone" and an ultraconservative outlook on inspiration as divine dictation intensified that attention.
- At times a choice as to which of competing readings is more plausible cannot be decided on the ms. evidence alone because the weight of the textual witnesses may be about evenly divided. One then has to raise the question of which way copyists are more likely to have thought, and that question can give

us insight into their theology.[7] For example, there are Western mss. that lack Jesus' words in Luke 23:34a, "Father, forgive them, for they do not know what they are doing." Did a pious copyist add it to the original Lucan text that lacked it because he thought that surely Jesus would have thought this way? Or did a copyist delete it from the original because it forgave Jesus' Jewish enemies, and Church Fathers were teaching that one could not forgive those who put the Son of God to death (see BDM 2.971–81)?

- There was a major thrust in the Reformation to get vernacular translations from the original Greek because they would be more accurate and more accessible to people than the Latin Vulgate. The standard English translation (the *Authorized* or *King James Version* of 1611) was made on the basis of Erasmus' edition of the Greek NT (first published in 1516) especially as republished by Robert Stephanus (Estienne) in 1550 and 1551—referred to as the accepted or received Greek NT, the *Textus Receptus.* Unfortunately Erasmus drew heavily on 12th- and 13th-century mss. of the Byzantine tradition; he had available none of the papyri and used none of the great codices listed above. Ironically the Latin Vulgate, translated 1,100 years before, was based on better Greek mss.; and the English translation from the Vulgate (Rheims NT) at times was more accurate, e.g., in omitting the doxology ("For thine is the kingdom . . .") at the end of Matt's form of the Lord's Prayer (6:13).
- Scholarship at the end of the 19th century finally won the battle to replace the inferior *Textus Receptus* by new editions of the Greek NT based on the great uncial codices and other evidence made available since Erasmus' time, and those editions have undergone corrections ever since in the light of further discoveries. The one most familiar to students is the Nestle-Aland edition (constantly updated[8]), which is also used in the United Bible Societies Greek NT edition. Admiration for the scholarship that has gone into that truly critical edition should not make us overlook an important fact: The text printed therein is eclectic, drawing on one tradition for one verse and another tradition for another verse. In other words before the first Nestle edition was printed in 1898, the Nestle-Aland text never existed as a unit in antiquity and was never read in any Christian community. A corollary is that while NT books are canonical, no particular Greek text should be canonized; and the most one can claim for a critically prepared Greek NT is scholarly acceptance.
- The Roman Catholic Church decided canonicity on the basis of long steady use in the liturgy, not on scholars' judgments about who wrote or copied what. Thus the story of the woman caught in adultery in John 7:53–8:11 and the long ending of Mark (16:9–20) were designated by the Council of Trent as

[7]Sometimes a theological outlook can be detected throughout a ms., e.g., Codex Bezae seems to exacerbate the antiJewish tendencies found in the NT.

[8]The 27th ed. appeared in 1993.

belonging to Scripture, even though they are missing from many NT textual witnesses. Catholics remain free to accept the judgment of competent scholars that these passages were not part of the original text of the respective Gospels.

- As I warned at the beginning of the Chapter, textual criticism can be a very difficult pursuit; and most beginners in NT study find it uninteresting or too difficult since it involves a technical knowledge of Greek. Metzger, *Textual Commentary,* is very helpful, going through the Greek NT verse by verse, explaining textual diversities and the rationale of why scholars prefer one reading over another. Recent translations of the NT into English sometimes include at the bottom of the page indications of readings that differ from those chosen in the text. To sample the interesting side of textual criticism, look up the following examples in a translation that has such alternative readings, and reflect on the results of the decision:

John 1:18: "It is God, the only Son" or "It is the only Son"—the former calls the Son "God."

Luke 24:12, describing Peter's running to the tomb of Jesus, is missing in some witnesses. If original, it constitutes a very close relationship between Luke and John, the only other Gospel that has Peter run to the tomb (20:3–10).

Eph 1:1: Some witnesses have no reference to Ephesus. One suggestion is that this was a general missive having a blank space that could be filled in with the place-name of the congregation to which it was being read.

John 7:53–8:11, the story of Jesus forgiving the adulteress, is missing from many mss. and probably was inserted into John long after the original Gospel was completed. Many think, however, that it was an early Jesus story. Why was this story a problem to scribes? Was it because it ran contrary to the early Christian practice of refusing public forgiveness to adulterers?

Mark 16:9–20 and two other, alternative endings (p. 148 below) were apparently added by scribes to alleviate the abruptness of terminating the Gospel with 16:8. What are the implications if Mark originally ended without describing a postresurrectional appearance? Since Mark 16:9–20 is found in most Bibles, what is the impact when 16:1–20 is read sequentially?

Bibliography on New Testament Textual Criticism

Aland, K. and B., *The Text of the New Testament* (2d ed.; Grand Rapids: Eerdmans, 1989).

Aland, B., and J. Delobel, eds., *New Testament Textual Criticism, Exegesis and Church History* (Kampen: Kok, 1995).

Birdsall, J. N., "The Recent History of New Testament Textual Criticism," ANRW (1992) II.26.1.99–197.

Comfort, P. W., *Early Manuscripts and Modern Translations of the New Testament* (Wheaton: Tyndale, 1990).

Ehrman, B. D., *The Orthodox Corruption of Scripture. The Effect of Early Christological Controversies on the Text of the New Testament* (New York: Oxford, 1993).

Ehrman, B. D., and M. W. Holmes, eds., *The Text of the New Testament in Contemporary Research* (B. M. Metzger Festschrift; Grand Rapids: Eerdmans, 1995). Excellent scholarly survey.

Elliott, J. K., and I. Moir, *Manuscripts and the Text of the New Testament* (Edinburgh: Clark, 1995). Introductory.

Epp, E. J., and G. D. Fee, *Studies in the Theory and Method of New Testament Textual Criticism* (Studies and Documents 45; Grand Rapids: Eerdmans, 1993).

Greenlee, J. H., *Introduction to New Testament Textual Criticism* (rev. ed.; Peabody, MA: Hendrickson, 1995). Introductory.

Kilpatrick, G. D., *The Principles and Practice of New Testament Textual Criticism* (BETL 96; Louvain: Peeters, 1990).

Metzger, B. M., *The Early Versions of the New Testament* (Oxford: Clarendon, 1977).

———, *Manuscripts of the Greek Bible: An Introduction to Palaeography* (New York: Oxford, 1981). Excellent illustrations of important mss.

———, *The Text of the New Testament* (3d ed.; New York: Oxford, 1992).

———, *A Textual Commentary on the Greek New Testament* (2d ed.; Stuttgart: United Bible Societies, 1994). An extraordinarily valuable help.

Vaganay, L., and C.-B. Amphoux, *An Introduction to New Testament Textual Criticism* (2d ed.; Cambridge Univ., 1991).

CHAPTER 4

THE POLITICAL AND SOCIAL WORLD OF NEW TESTAMENT TIMES

In Chapter 2 we saw that it is important to know the background and worldview of both the author and the audience. Most of the NT was composed in the 1st century AD. What was the political situation at that time both in Palestine and in the Roman Empire as a whole? What was life like (social world) and how did that affect the proclamation of belief in Jesus? What was the religious situation among Jews? What was the religious context of Gentiles? Those questions are treated in this Chapter and the next. The goal is to offer readers a *general* understanding of the period that frames the NT; an ample *Bibliography* will be offered in each Chapter for in-depth reading.

(A) The Political World of New Testament Times

The discussion, concentrating on the Roman Empire in general and Palestine in particular, will open by describing the situation that preceded the 1st century AD. Then for convenience' sake we shall divide the 1st century into thirds. In relation to the NT the first third of that century was the period in which most of Jesus' life was lived. The second third was the period of Christian oral proclamation and of the composition of the main Pauline letters. The last third was the period of increasing Gentile dominance in the Christian communities and of the composition of most NT works. In order to cover any overlap, the first part of the 2d century, when the very last NT books were composed, will be treated together with the last third of the 1st century.

What Preceded the 1st Century AD

Although trade contacts between Greek lands and Palestine had existed for centuries, in 332 BC a new period began. After conquering Tyre in Phoenicia, Alexander the Great extended his control over Samaria and Judea,[1]

[1]Legends arose about Alexander's visit to Jerusalem and paying homage at the Temple. Factually he may have granted the Jews rights to live in accordance with their ancestral laws. Although seem-

previously under Persian governance. This was more than a military conquest, for now the Jews of the Palestine-Syria area (and quickly those of Egypt) became part of that amalgam of Greek and Eastern civilization that we know as the Hellenistic world.[2]

323–175 BC: Dominance of Palestine by Competing Hellenistic Kings. After Alexander's death, his empire was split up among his generals (referred to as the Diadochoi). Politically the high priests in Judea were caught in between ambitious dynasties in Egypt (the Ptolemies) and in Syria (the Seleucids), both descended from the Greek generals. For the first one hundred years the Ptolemies generally dominated Judea. By successfully dealing with the rulers of Egypt, a major Jewish merchant family, the Tobiads, came to prominence in the Transjordan; and by a policy of political and financial cooperation the Jerusalem high priests avoided Ptolemaic interference in religion for most of the period. In Egypt Jews became an important minority, and by the early 3d century BC the process of translating the Scriptures into Greek (the LXX) was well underway there.[3]

The situation changed when in a series of campaigns (223–200 BC) the Seleucid Syrian ruler Antiochus III humiliated the Ptolemies and gained control of all Palestine. During this period of conflicting allegiances, the Jews felt persecuted by the Ptolemies as attested by the legends in *III Maccabees*. At first Antiochus, as the new Seleucid master, seemed less oppressive in financial demands; he even promised subsidies for the Jerusalem Temple. Yet after defeat by the Romans (190 BC), who imposed a huge war indemnity, the Syrian need for money grew. Under Antiochus' son Seleucus IV (187–175), the Syrian general Heliodorus is remembered as having plundered the treasury of the Jerusalem Temple.

175–63 BC: Antiochus Epiphanes, the Maccabean Revolt, and the Hasmonean High Priests. The predicament brought on by the Seleucids became

---

ingly he picked up Samaritan mercenaries for his army, evidence of a brutal Greek suppression of a Samaritan rebellion is supplied by recent finds in caves in the Wadi ed-Daliyeh near the Jordan valley (including the bones of hundreds of refugees). Samaria was refounded as a Greek military colony. The thesis that Alexander built the Samaritan Temple on Mt. Gerizim may be a simplification of Samaritan relocation and building.

[2]The actuality was more complex. Alexander and his generals were Macedonians, often despised by other Greeks as barbarians; and they were more interested in magnifying power than in extending culture to the East. Nevertheless, their victories brought about a complicated interpenetration of cultures.

[3]The origins of the LXX are complex, since the books were translated at different times by scholars of varying skill, and preserved with varying fidelity. The fictitious *Letter of Aristeas to Philocrates* (2d century BC) supplies the legend of the translation of the Pentateuch by 72 elders under Ptolemy II (285–246 BC). In the 1st and 2d centuries AD there were more literal renderings, revising the LXX (sometimes almost to the point of constituting new translations). Associated with the names of Lucian, Aquila, Symmachus, and Theodotion, they are partially preserved, often mixed in with LXX. At times NT citations of the OT in Greek are literally from or close to the LXX; at other times they are closer to these (or other unknown) revisions.

extremely grave under the unstable Antiochus IV Epiphanes[4] (175–164). Antiochus proceeded systematically to gain unity among his subjects by having them all share the same Greek culture and religion. The venality and ambition of the high priests in Jerusalem, whom he kept changing, served his purposes. He punished attempts at resistance by attacking Jerusalem (169 and 167), slaughtering the population, plundering the Temple, erecting a statue to Zeus on the Temple altar of burnt offering ("the abomination of desolation" of Dan 11:31; 12:11; cf. Mark 13:14), and installing a permanent Syrian garrison in a fortress (the Akra) in the city. This persecution constituted the context of the Book of Daniel, which used descriptions of the Babylonian kings of the 6th century BC to decry the Syrian rulers of the 2d century BC. In 167 there broke out a Jewish revolt led by Mattathias, a priest living in Modein, NW of Jerusalem; it was continued over a period of thirty-five years successively by his sons Judas Maccabeus, Jonathan, and Simon.[5] A number of the very pious (the Hasideans) joined the revolt hoping that victory would put an end to the corruption of the Temple worship by the Seleucid kings. In a seesaw war the Syrians kept manipulating the high priests, playing on their greed and lust for power; and the Maccabees took advantage of internal changes in Syrian politics, playing one kingly claimant against the other and seeking to get Rome involved on their side. Key moments included the Jewish victory in 164 that led to the purification and rededication (whence "Hanukkah") of the altar site; the appointment of Jonathan to the high priesthood in 152; and the capture of the Akra and expulsion of the Syrian garrison in 142.[6]

Final freedom from Syrian attempts to dominate Palestine came only in the first part of the reign of the high priest John Hyrcanus I (135/4–104 BC), the son of Simon, when Rome recognized Jewish independence. Hyrcanus destroyed the Samaritan sanctuary on Mt. Gerizim, magnifying the already existing hatred between Samaritans and Jews. His son Aristobulus (104–103) took the title of king. This combination of high priesthood and kingship would be maintained by his successors for the next forty years, with the political interests of the position often dominating the religious. Wars waged by Alexander Jannaeus (103–76) extended the boundaries of the kingdom. Dissolute and cruel, he stooped to crucifying his Jewish enemies. He was followed by his widow Salome Alexandra (76–69) and subsequently by two

[4]As a mocking substitute for Epiphanes ("Manifestation" as a god), his subjects nicknamed him "Epimanes" ("Madman").

[5]The brothers are often known as the Maccabees; the dynasty that began with Simon's son John Hyrcanus, even though of the same family, is most often called Hasmonean, perhaps after the name (Asamōnaios) of the great-grandfather of Mattathias.

[6]This is often looked on as the beginning of the independence of Judea which lasted until Pompey conquered Jerusalem in 63 BC.

sons, Hyrcanus II and Aristobulus II whose squabbling for power opened the way for Roman intervention in the person of Pompey, who entered Jerusalem and the Temple in 63 BC. For practical purposes the Romans then became the rulers of the land, even if they worked through subservient high priestly rulers and kinglets.

63–4 BC: Roman Dominance, Herod the Great, Augustus. The Romans favored the weak Hyrcanus II (63–41) over Aristobulus as high priest; but through murder and marriage an Idumean adventurer,[7] Antipater II, emerged as a major force in Palestine, first as an advisor to Hyrcanus and then, with Julius Caesar's approval, as a procurator or overseer in his own right. Antipater's son, Herod (the Great), cleverly shifted his allegiances during the Roman civil wars following the assassination of Caesar (44 BC). By 37 BC, through brutality and expeditious marriage into the Hasmonean family, he became undisputed king of Judea, a kingship approved and enlarged by Octavian in 31/30.[8] Regarded with contempt by many Jewish subjects as only half a Jew,[9] Herod's sympathies were clearly with Greco-Roman culture. His reign was marked by extensive building projects including: the reconstructed ancient capital of the Northern Kingdom of Israel, Samaria, now become Sebaste; the new harbor city Caesarea Maritima; and in Jerusalem the Fortress Antonia, a Royal Palace, and a massive extension of the Temple.[10] His distrust of possible rivals led to the construction of inaccessible fortress palaces (including Machaerus in the Transjordan in which JBap would die years later) and the murder of some of his own sons. The brutal cruelty, indeed virtual insanity, of Herod's last years gave rise to Matthew's account of this king's willingness to slaughter all the male children at Bethlehem up to age two as part of his desire to kill Jesus. At the death of Herod (*ca.* 4 BC) Josephus (*War* 2.4.1–3; #55–65) recounts how three adventurers with royal pretensions used force in attempts to succeed him; instead Rome chose Herod's sons, as we shall see.

As for the wider Roman world, the achievements of Octavian, who was the survivor of the wars that followed the death of Julius Caesar on the Ides of March in 44 BC, were recognized by the Senate's grant of the title "Augustus" in 27 BC. Latching on to the mantle of peacemaker, this master of

[7]Idumea at this time was an area south of Judea; the inhabitants were descendants of the Edomites driven west from the area SE of the Dead Sea by the encroaching spread of the Nabatean Arabs.

[8]Herod eventually felt strong enough to dispense with the Hasmonean heritage; he executed Hyrcanus II in 30 BC and his own wife Mariamme I (granddaughter of both Hyrcanus II and Aristobulus II) in 29. By the 20s (BC) a new line of high priests was installed.

[9]*Ant.* 14.15.2; #403: He was from an Idumean family that had converted to Judaism only a half century earlier.

[10]Names like "Sebaste" (Augustus), "Caesarea" (Caesar Augustus), and "Antonia" (Mark Anthony) were meant to flatter Roman patrons of Herod.

propaganda dotted the empire with monuments celebrating his achievements. The Greek cities of Asia Minor adopted his birthday as the first day of the year; indeed an inscription at Halicarnassus called him "savior of the world." The altar of peace at Rome, dedicated to the achievements of Augustus, was part of the creation of his mystique. The Lucan infancy narrative (2:11,14) with angels singing peace on earth and the resounding proclamation: "To you this day there is born in the city of David a Savior who is Messiah and Lord" may well be echoing the publicity of Augustus in the course of whose census the birth of Jesus was placed. When Augustus began his governance, Rome was a republic. He moved gradually to gain more permanent *imperium* ("the supreme administrative power") until he was granted it for life with the right to veto Senate decrees; and effectually, therefore, by his last years Rome was ruled by an emperor.[11] Part of the political expansion of his authority was the creation of new provinces in the territories controlled by Rome, imperial provinces directly responsible to him rather than to the Senate as in former times.

The First Third of the 1st Century AD

Although this may be considered the period of Jesus' lifetime, he was born a bit earlier, before the death of Herod the Great (4 BC).[12] After Herod's death, Augustus split the realm among three of Herod's sons. In the two areas that most touched Jesus' life, Archelaus became ethnarch of Judea, Samaria, and Idumea, while Herod Antipas became tetrarch of Galilee and part of the Transjordan.[13] The rule of Archelaus was autocratic and aroused the hatred of his subjects to the extent that they sent a delegation to Rome to ask for his removal (a situation some think echoed in the parable of Luke 19:14). Augustus responded in AD 6 by making Archelaus's territory the imperial

[11]It is well to note, however, that in the 1st century AD much of the apparatus and exterior facade of the republic remained, with acknowledgment given to the Senate and the Roman people, so that the emperors were not like Egyptian or Syrian kings. The emperor was still at least theoretically responsible to the will of the Roman people.

[12]Dating the birth to the era of Herod the Great is one of the few features that appear in both the Gospel infancy narratives (Matt 2:1; Luke 1:5). On the assumption that the reference is accurate, the anomaly that Jesus was born "before Christ" results from an ancient mistake in calculating the year of his birth. In the 6th century AD Dionysius Exiguus (Denis the Short) proposed to reckon years no longer from the foundation of Rome (A.U.C.) but from the birth of the Lord. Dionysius chose 754 A.U.C. as the birth year, a date too late because by the *most plausible* calculation Herod died in 750 A.U.C.

[13]For the complicated Herodian family tree, see NJBC p. 1245, or ABD 3.175. The third ruling son was Philip, who ruled from 4 BC to AD 34 in the region east and north of the Lake of Galilee (Luke 3:1). Towns like Bethsaida and Caesarea Philippi mentioned in the Gospel accounts were in his territory. "Ethnarch" (governor of an ethnic or minority community) and "tetrarch" (prince of a small area) were lesser titles than "king."

province of Judea. Quirinius, the Roman legate of Syria (an older province) conducted a census for tax purposes as part of the Roman takeover, a census that produced a rebellion by Judas the Galilean. This census is mentioned in Acts 5:37 and is probably in mind also in Luke 2:1–2.[14] Judas' rebellion, which occurred when Jesus was about twelve years old and some twenty-five years before his crucifixion, was the only recorded serious Jewish uprising in Palestine during the period of Jesus' boyhood and maturity. Inevitably during that period, as always with foreign rule, there were disturbances and tense moments; yet two of the prefects of the era, Valerius Gratus and Pontius Pilate, lasted ten years each—an indication that this was not a time of violent revolution.[15] The Roman historian Tacitus (*History* 5.9) reports that in Judea under the Emperor Tiberius (AD 14–37) "Things were quiet."

This then was the Palestine of Jesus' maturity: a crafty and vain Herodian "king" in charge of Jesus' home country of Galilee and a Roman prefect controlling Jerusalem and Judea where Jesus spent his last days and was crucified. Both Philo (*Ad Gaium* 38; #300) and the NT (Luke 13:1; 23:12) tell us that the relations between Herod (or the Herodian princes) and Pilate were not always smooth. Some years after Jesus' death, Pilate's severe use of force to suppress a Samaritan religious movement led to the intervention of the Roman legate in Syria who sent Pilate off to Rome in AD 36.[16] The four-year reign of the Emperor Caligula (37–41) had a frightening aspect for the inhabitants of Jerusalem since he attempted to have a statue divinizing him erected in the Temple.

The Second Third of the 1st Century AD

The first period of direct Roman governance in Judea by prefects ended in AD 39/40. Herod Agrippa I, who had earlier succeeded to the territories of his uncles Philip and Herod Antipas, was a friend of both Caligula and the new Emperor Claudius (41–54). Accordingly he was made king over all Palestine (AD 41–44), restoring the realm of his grandfather Herod the Great. Agrippa won the goodwill of the Jewish religious leaders and made efforts

[14]The wrong temporal sequence in the Acts reference suggests that the Luke-Acts author did not know precisely when this census took place—in fact it occurred after the deposition of Archelaus—and so he may have mingled it with the troubled times after the death of Archelaus's father, Herod the Great, ten years before. Yet see Chapter 10 below, n. 33.

[15]Philo, the Jewish philosopher, presents an extremely hostile picture of Pilate, decrying his "briberies, insults, robberies, outrages, wanton injuries, constantly repeated executions without trial, ceaseless and supremely grievous cruelty" (*Ad Gaium* 38; #302; written *ca.* AD 39–40). Many today would judge that this was a prejudiced view, rhetorically designed to build up the case for replacing Roman prefects with Herod Agrippa I. The Gospels paint a much less hostile portrait of Pilate, but scarcely show him as a model of Roman justice.

[16]Josephus (*Ant.* 18.4.1–2; #85–89).

to appear pious. Acts 12 attributes to him a persecution that killed James the brother of John, son of Zebedee. After Agrippa's death (dramatized in Acts 12:20–23) another period of Roman rule began; but the procurators of the period 44–66 were of low caliber, vicious and dishonest, provoking intense unrest by their injustice. Theirs was a misrule that gave rise to Sicarii (knife-wielding terrorists), Zealots (ruthless adherents of the Law), and a major Jewish revolt against the Romans.[17] Of particular significance for Christians in the last decade of this period was the execution of James, the "brother of the Lord" (AD 62). This was after a hearing by a Sanhedrin called by Ananus (Annas) II, a high priest who was subsequently removed by the procurator Albinus for having acted illegally. Only two years later, after the great fire in Rome in July 64, Emperor Nero (54–68) persecuted Christians in the capital, a persecution in which, according to respectable tradition, both Peter and Paul were martyred. Thus by the mid-60s the most famous Christian personalities of the Gospels and Acts were dead, so that the last third of the 1st century may be called subapostolic or postapostolic.

Major Roman forces and the best generals were involved in suppressing the Jewish Revolt. A somewhat uncertain tradition reports that the Christians in Jerusalem refused to join the Revolt and withdrew across the Jordan to Pella.

The Last Third of the 1st Century AD and the Beginning of the 2d Century

The Flavian family of emperors reigned from AD 69 to 96. Vespasian, the first, had taken command in Judea in 67 and turned around the hitherto unsuccessful Roman effort to quell the Jewish Revolt. But after Nero's suicide in 68 Vespasian's attention was directed toward Rome, and in 69 the legions proclaimed him emperor. This left his son Titus as commander to press the campaign in Judea to its termination; Jerusalem was taken and the Temple destroyed in 70.[18] The arch of Titus in the Roman forum depicts the Jewish sacred paraphernalia and captives brought to the capital in triumph in 71. By way of relations to the Jews, in the 70s Vespasian imposed a special punitive tax whereby they were supposed to pay two drachmas for the support of the temple of Jupiter Capitolinus in Rome in lieu of what they had

[17]For the Sicarii and Zealots, see BDM 1.688–93. The struggle of AD 66–70 is often called the First Jewish Revolt to distinguish it from the later one led by Simon bar Cochba (ben Kosiba) in 132–135. In it there was vicious infighting among various Zealot leaders such as John of Gischala, Menahem (son of Judas the Galilean), and Simon bar-Giora. The last-mentioned was carried off to Rome to be executed in Titus' triumphal parade.

[18]Jewish resistance continued at the fortress of Masada by the Dead Sea until 74.

hitherto contributed to the Jerusalem Temple. *Ca.* 75 Titus lived openly in Rome with his mistress, the Jewish princess Berenice, sister of Herod Agrippa II. Also in Rome under the patronage of these emperors, as reflected in the appended name he took (Flavius), the Jewish writer Josephus wrote his account of the Jewish War and in the early 90s his great history of the Jews, the *Antiquities*—invaluable sources for understanding 1st-century Judaism.

In this dynasty of emperors Domitian, Vespasian's younger son, had the longest reign (81–96). Autocratic and vengeful, in his quest to restore the purity of Roman religion he executed under the charge of atheism some who were attracted to Judaism. There is evidence that he was hostile to Christianity as well (see pp. 805–9 below). Yet, as shown by the letter addressed to the church of Corinth from the church of Rome (*I Clement*), presumably written *ca.* AD 96, the model of Roman imperial order was starting to affect the Christian mindset.

During the reign of the three Flavian emperors, Jerusalem began to be outdistanced in importance for Christians by other centers that had significant Christian communities, e.g., Antioch, Ephesus, and Rome. This would probably also have been the time when the number of Gentile Christians surpassed the number of Jewish Christians. In the synagogues, relations between Jews and believers in Jesus probably varied regionally depending on the makeup of the Christians (e.g., whether there were Samaritans and Gentiles among the Jewish Christians), the way they phrased their theology (e.g., did they use a term like "God" for Jesus that might be understood as denial of monotheism), and their temperament (e.g., did they appear arrogant in debating issues—see John 9:34). In certain Christian communities a strong antipathy arose toward the leaders of the Jewish synagogues as reflected in a series of passages in Matthew (6:2,5; 23:6); the accusation was made that synagogues persecuted Christians (Matt 10:17; 23:34) and expelled them (John 9:22; 12:42; 16:2). A statement such as John 9:28 makes a sharp distinction between the disciples of Jesus and the disciples of Moses; and in some NT passages "the Jews" (and their Law) are treated as alien (Matt 28:15; John 10:34; 15:25).

Shortly after the assassination of Domitian, another dynasty of emperors arose; and the last period with which we shall be concerned in this book was lived under Trajan (98–117) and his successor, Hadrian (117–138). An efficient administrator inclined to intervene in the provinces, Trajan issued regulations that led to a persecution of Christians in Asia Minor as attested in the correspondence between the emperor and Pliny (the Younger), the governor of that region. In his search for Christians Pliny expected to find them among the slave class, especially slave women; he mentions Christians gathering to sing hymns to Christ "as to a god." The need for well-articulated order in the Christian churches if they were to survive is attested by Ignatius the bishop of Antioch who, while he was being taken to Rome as a prisoner to be martyred (*ca.* 110), addressed letters to the churches insisting on the importance of remaining united to the bishop.[19] At the end of Trajan's reign (115–117) and in the early years of Hadrian's there were Jewish riots throughout the eastern part of the Empire. Hadrian's insistence on having in Jerusalem a shrine to Jupiter Capitolinus on the site of the Temple that had been destroyed in 70 and his banning circumcision contributed to the Second Jewish Revolt led by Simon ben Kosiba, known as Bar Cochba or Kochba.[20] The latter designation means "Son of the Star" (see the Davidic star in Num 24:17), and according to later tradition he was acknowledged by the famous Rabbi Akiba (Aqiba) as the Messiah. The Romans ruthlessly suppressed the revolt; Akiba was martyred; and henceforth no Jew was permitted to enter Jerusalem under pain of death. Over the site of the ancient city of Jerusalem a new Gentile city was built, Aelia Capitolina. Although relatives of Jesus are supposed to have been influential in the churches of Palestine during the time of Domitian (EH 3.20), that precedence had come to an end in the time of Trajan (EH 3.32.6); and under Hadrian the leadership of the church in Palestine is said to have passed into Gentile hands (EH 4.6.3–5).

(B) The Social World of New Testament Times

The preceding section gave an overall picture of the political history of the Roman Empire in general and of Palestine in particular during the period of our concern. The NT, however, tells us about the western spread of Christianity outside Palestine, especially to the cities of Asia Minor and Greece. To try to offer a history of that area comparable to the one given of Palestine would be impractical because each region, sometimes each city, had its own particular history. In discussing the Pauline letters this will be illustrated as we study briefly the individual city addressed. What can be done more profitably in this general Chapter is to look at some social features of Mediterranean life during the early Empire that are useful to know when one reads the NT.

The first believers in Jesus were Jews; perhaps all the authors of the NT were Jews. The memories of Jesus and the writings of his followers are filled

[19]If at an earlier period there was in many churches a twofold order consisting of presbyter-bishops (plural) and deacons, by Ignatius' time in some churches in Asia Minor the bishop had emerged as the highest authority with the presbyters and the deacons under him—the famous threefold order that for all practical purposes became universal by 200.

[20]Letters from him and to his followers have been found in the Dead Sea region at Murabba'at (NJBC 67.119).

with references to the Jewish Scriptures, feasts, institutions, and traditions. Therefore there is no doubt about the influence of Judaism on the NT. Yet, as we have seen, since the time of Alexander the Great, the Jews had been living in a Hellenistic world. For a century before Jesus' birth most of them had been living in areas dominated by Roman armies; and by the time of his birth a fair percentage, perhaps even a majority, of the world's Jews spoke Greek. The biblical books composed in Hebrew and Aramaic had been translated into Greek, and some of the Deuterocanonical biblical books like II Macc and Wisdom were composed in Greek—the latter showing at least a popular awareness of Greek philosophical thought.[21] Jews bought goods with coins minted by Roman-Greek overlords and often imprinted with the image of gods. In varying ways and degrees, through commerce, schools, and travel, Jews were influenced by a world quite different from that described in much of the OT. Thus in the social background of the NT much more than Judaism must be taken into account.

Most Christian communities mentioned in the NT were in cities. That is not surprising on several grounds. The Roman system of roads, originally built for military purposes, often facilitated the travels of Jewish Christian preachers, bringing them to the cities on the routes. Jewish merchants had also followed the roads; thus there would be synagogue communities in many cities to which these preachers could make an appeal.[22] Moreover, the cities had denser populations than the countryside, and the evangelizers wanted to reach as large an audience as possible.

The interplay of people of different backgrounds was important in the cities. In Asia Minor and Syria existing city populations had been brought into the Greek sphere by the conquests of Alexander the Great, and now after more than 300 years there would have been a long history of a mixed population. Greece had been a battleground in the Roman civil wars, and the custom of giving soldiers a reward of territory created new Roman settlements in sections of Greece. Which dwellers in a city had the privilege of being citizens depended on particular circumstances. Although there was a special classification assigned to Jews in the Empire, in some cities they were granted citizenship.[23] Inevitably the customs of one group placed limitations on others: Foreigners were barred access to the temple of Hera at Argos in Greece; no nonJews were permitted to enter the Jerusalem Temple;

[21]Lieberman, *Hellenism,* maintains that Greek logic in the form of Alexandrian hermeneutic principles was introduced into Jewish thought at Jerusalem already in the time of Hillel the Elder (late 1st century BC), if we may trust the historicity of traditions about him.

[22]For evidence of Christian activity in synagogues, see Mark 13:9 and par.; Acts 9:20; 13:5,14; 14:1; 17:1–2; 18:4.

[23]Acts 21:39 has Saul/Paul describe himself as "a native of Tarsus in Cilicia, a citizen of no mean city."

only Greeks could be initiated into the Eleusinian mysteries (p. 86 below). In general, Roman administration tried to keep peace among different segments of the population, although a Roman official in Alexandria in AD 38 was sympathetic to the antiJewish rioters.

Perhaps because populations were mixed and because there was considerable population mobility, there seems to have been a felt need "to belong." This is suggested by the number of associations or clubs that existed: associations to maintain gymnasia where body and mind were trained; profession and trade associations that functioned as guilds, unions, and brotherhoods; religious associations for those involved in cults other than public worship; and clubs for young people and the elderly. In particular, those who were not citizens achieved a sense of community in these associations.

Jews were alienated from aspects of common civic life by their religion[24] and dietary laws, although some Jewish officials and wealthy members of society made accommodations, e.g., by contributing patronage or money to a festival. At times, how far to go in participation depended on personal judgment. Philo would not participate in Pagan cults[25] and advocated capital punishment for those Jews who did and thus became idolaters; yet he praised the gymnasium and frequented the theater (where performance could very well include Pagan cultic acts). In Miletus an inscription at the theater honored Jews. Dining with nonJews was particularly sensitive, not only because forbidden foods might be served but because the food might have been dedicated to a Pagan god. Such dining was also a subject of acrimonious debate among Jews who believed in Jesus according to Gal 2:12. Paul condemned participation of Christians at Pagan altar-tables where sacrifices were performed (I Cor 10:21). Yet on the principle that Pagan gods do not exist, he maintained that eating food from sacrifices was not idolatrous. Nevertheless, because some who did not have this perception might sin by eating such food, one had to be sensitive about their consciences (I Cor 8:4–13). Rev 2:14,20 is harsher, condemning altogether the eating of food dedicated to idols.

People who do not share common practices and beliefs are always suspect, and antiJudaism was frequent in sections of the Empire. Nevertheless, the peculiar convictions and commitments of the Jews were protected legally by privileges granted by Julius Caesar and reaffirmed by his successors. Christians probably received similar protection so long as they were thought

[24]The Roman notion of *religio* involved fixed rites on behalf of the whole community (in which Jews did not participate). Foreign cults with strange ceremonies were *superstitio* to the Romans.

[25]Helpful here is a brief article on the participation of Jews and Christians in Pagan cult by P. Borgen in *Explorations* 8 (#1, 1994), 5–6. I shall use "Pagan" (capitalized) in a technical, nonpejorative sense to cover a religious belief that is not Jewish (or Christian).

of as Jews; but once most of the Christians were Gentiles or Jewish Christians rejected by synagogues, they no longer had a legal umbrella. Moreover, Christians were more dangerous to society than Jews. Although Jews gained some converts and sympathizers, predominantly their numbers were constituted through birth. Christians, on the other hand, aggressively converted others, and through much of the 1st century were too new a phenomenon to have many of their members born to a Christian family. Popular opposition to Christians is echoed in Acts 28:22: "As for this sect, we know that everywhere it is spoken against." From evidence pertaining to official persecution clearly the alien behavior of Christians in regard to civic expectations was highly suspect: Surely they were atheists and antisocial, and probably doing unmentionable things in their secretive cult. On the other side of the coin, alienation was taxing on the Christian psyche. Having given up so much of their former community life on every level, Christians needed to be reassured. I Peter is addressed to believers who had become aliens and sojourners (2:11) and were reviled as evildoers (2:12) and insulted (3:9); it gives them assurance that they are a chosen race, a royal priesthood, a holy nation, and God's own people (2:9–10).

How Roman rule was evaluated by the population depended on previous history: Sometimes it was an improvement; sometimes it was not. Under the early Empire, not all cities were treated the same way; Tarsus was a free, allied city exempted from imperial taxation; cities like Corinth and Philippi, because of Roman rebuilding or resettlement, bore the title of a *colonia* in which the agricultural land was not subject to taxation. In the older cities traditional names of officials were preserved (and Acts shows skill in reporting these titles). Nevertheless, former democratic government where offices were open to all citizens was gradually replaced, and the Roman preference for an aristocratic administration meant that other classes, even citizens, were excluded from certain offices. Under the Empire there was a reform of taxation which had become oppressive during the civil wars at the end of the republic. Roman administrators, however, in matters of taxes were judged not only by their own actions but also by the behavior of local officials whom they employed. Tax collection was often farmed out to the highest bidder, so that a tax regarded as oppressive may have been so in itself or because of the collectors' greed and ruthlessness.[26] There is a mixed picture of Gentile authorities in Acts, which is not always specific as to whether the local authorities/magistrates who dealt with Paul were Roman: In

[26]Matt 9:10; 11:19; 21:31 places tax collectors on a level with public sinners and prostitutes; Luke 3:12–13 has JBap warn tax collectors to stop collecting more than what is prescribed, and 19:7–8 has the tax collector Zacchaeus defend himself against the charge of being a sinner by promising that if he had extorted anything, he would repay four times over.

16:22,36–38 and 17:6–9 they are unjust or indifferent; in 13:12 and 19:35–40 they are sympathetic or fair.

Wealth/poverty and the class society found in cities of the Roman Empire created their own problems for early Christians, and both need to be discussed lest they be misunderstood in the light of modern experience. There are many references in the NT to the "poor";[27] and readers might envision their poverty as similar to that of the Third World today where people have no place to live or even scraps to eat and so are in constant danger of perishing. In the Gospels, however, which in part reflect Jesus' own life situation in Galilee, the poor were small farmers with inadequate or barren land, or serfs on large estates; in the cities without the assistance of produce from the land the poor were somewhat worse off. Yet the situation of both groups of NT poor was economically better than that of the desperately poor of the modern world. As for Jesus himself who is remembered as showing an affection for the poor, according to Mark 6:3 he was a *tektōn,* i.e., a "woodworker" who made doors or furniture for the stone or mud-brick houses and plows and yokes for farmers. As a craftsman in a village he might be compared to "a blue collar worker in lower-middle-class America."[28]

As for slaves, NT translations render Greek *doulos* both as "servant" and "slave";[29] but those so described should not be imagined in 19th-century patterns of either British household servants or African slaves in America. Slavery had existed for several centuries by NT times, even if it was beginning to decline. Ancient sources of slaves were pirate raids and the frequent wars that preceded the inauguration of the Roman Empire, since prisoners and sometimes the entire population of a conquered town were sold into slavery. The peace brought about by Augustus partially dried up the supply, and the shortage was aggravated because at the same time many slaves were being set free. Nevertheless, the huge Roman estates needed an abundance of slaves to manage them. The status of slaves varied. Those who rowed in galleys or worked in the quarries had a brutal existence; and at times (especially in Italy before the inauguration of the Empire) slaves became restive socially and politically, as in the revolt of Spartacus (73–71 BC). Yet slaves had legal rights, and under the Empire abusing or killing slaves constituted a punishable crime. Besides working in business, farming, and households, slaves could be administrators, physicians, teachers, scholars, and poets, and

[27]Sometimes it is a spiritual designation for those who do not value wealth; but other times it refers to the economically poor and that is our concern in the text above.

[28]I draw here on the excellent treatment in Meier, *Marginal* 1.280–85, who shows the fragility of other interpretations.

[29]An intriguing issue is whether the feminine form in the Magnificat (Luke 1:48) is meant to describe Mary as the "handmaid" (servant) of the Lord or the "slave," with the latter offering possibilities for identifying her with an element in the Christian audience of Luke.

accumulate wealth. Moreover, noble Pagans denounced slavery, and some Eastern religions accepted slaves without prejudice.

Christian preachers made converts among the city poor and slaves, but they also made considerable inroads among the middle class. Although there were a few wealthy Christians, the least number of converts would have been among that social class and among aristocrats. In I Cor 1:26 Paul is probably more than oratorical when he says, "Not many wise . . . not many powerful, not many of noble birth." A particular occasion of Christian social tension seems to have been the eucharistic meal. For a number of Christians to meet together, a large room would have been necessary. To this room, often on the second floor of a private house of an economically better-off believer, there would have been invited lower-class Christians who otherwise would have no contact with the proprietor. One interpretation of I Cor 11:20–22,33–34 is that some proprietors had found a way around this socially awkward situation by inviting only friends for a meal first, so that they had eaten and drunk before the wider group was welcomed to the eucharist. Paul condemns such procedure as unchristian because it makes those who have nothing feel ashamed. The short Letter to Philemon shows Paul struggling with the issue of a runaway slave who had become a Christian. He asks the owner to take the runaway back as a brother and implicitly not to impose severe penalties on him. Thus for Paul manumission is desirable. Yet the fact that Paul, who thought that the end of the world was coming soon, did not condemn the social structure with its massive number of slaves was tragically misinterpreted for many centuries as Christian justification for the existence of slavery, indeed, of a slavery often harsher than existed in NT times.

Education is also an issue to be considered in reflecting on the NT: the education of Jesus and the preachers, and the education of the audience. There is a major dispute about the nature and extent of Jewish education in this period, for some scholars would draw on the picture of schooling given two hundred years later by the Mishna (p. 83 below) and posit both Jewish elementary schools for reading the Bible in all the towns and advanced schools for studying the Law. Others (Cohen, *From* 120–22) are skeptical, and it is probably wiser to posit that there were not as yet such established institutions. Yet we cannot judge the extent of literacy from that, for Josephus, *Against Apion* 2.25 (#204), interprets Jewish law to order children "to be taught letters concerning the laws and deeds of their forefathers." Whether that was done might depend on the piety of their parents and the nearby presence of a synagogue. Jesus' ability to debate about Scripture suggests that he could read Hebrew (as imaged in Luke 4:16–21). The same is possible for his disciples who had their own trade or profession (fishers, tax collectors), since the derogatory, rhetorical "uneducated, ordinary men" applied to Peter and John in Acts 4:13 need mean no more than not learned in the Law.

The pattern of Greek schooling, well established throughout the Roman Empire,[30] consisted of an elementary school (about seven years) for teaching reading, writing, music, and athletics; then tutoring in grammar, particularly poetry; and finally (for a small number) an upper level education in rhetoric and philosophy. As regards influence on Jesus, there is little evidence that Greek schools were widespread in Palestine in NT times. Although through social science and archaeology our knowledge of 1st-century AD Galilee has grown apace in recent decades,[31] the life setting of Jesus there is not clear. The influence on him of culture from Hellenistic cities like Tiberias on the Lake of Galilee (near where he preached) and Sepphoris (only four miles from Nazareth) should not be exaggerated.[32] On the one hand, village folk are notoriously distrustful of the alien city; on the other hand, there may well have been economic contacts between Sepphoris and Nazareth, for instance, in terms of hired labor and purchased produce. That the young Jesus plied a woodworking trade in Sepphoris is a romantic guess, and material contacts do not necessarily establish the existence of a syncretized cultural ethos that is supposed to have affected him. Although excavations at Sepphoris have not yielded indications of public Pagan cult that would horrify Jewish peasants, the fact that both it and Tiberias served as capitals for Herod Antipas may have made them abominations for Jesus, who spoke with contempt of "that fox" (Luke 13:32). In any case there is no Gospel indication of Jesus' contacts with such cities. Nor do we have concrete evidence that Jesus or his most often mentioned Galilean disciples spoke Greek to any significant extent, or that he phrased any of his teachings in that language, even if it is plausible that he and the disciples would have been familiar with some phrases from contact with Greek-speakers in commerce or practical daily life.

As for Saul/Paul who knew Greek quite well, it is debated whether he grew up in the diaspora or in Jerusalem (see Chapter 16). If in the diaspora, he might well have had basic Greek schooling.[33] Moreover we must remember that at a center like Tarsus there were also public sources of education

[30]In the 1st centuries BC and AD there was a very strong Greek component in Roman culture; particularly under Augustus there was a renewal of Greek influence in architecture and art.

[31]Survey by J. A. Overman, CRBS 1 (1993), 35–57.

[32]Unfortunately R. A. Batey, *Jesus and the Forgotten City* (Grand Rapids: Baker, 1991) overstates Jesus' relationship to Sepphoris. Balance is supplied by S. Freyne, "Jesus and the Urban Culture of Galilee," in *Texts and Contexts,* eds. T. Fornberg and D. Hellholm (Oslo: Scandanavian Univ., 1995), 597–622, who contends that the Hellenistic cities and the Galilean rural hinterland had very different value systems.

[33]In discussing epistle/letter classification below in Chapter 15 we shall see that different types of rhetoric (according to Aristotle's classification) have been identified in Paul's writing.

that could have influenced him, e.g., libraries and theaters where the plays of the Greek poets would be performed. A few Christian preachers may have had a more elaborate Greek education, e.g., Apollos whom Acts 18:24 describes as eloquent, and the author of Heb whom many judge to have written the best Greek in the NT. But in general the NT writings were in the Koine, or everyday spoken Greek of the period.[34] The heavy Semitic influence on the Greek of some NT books, the colloquial character of Mark, and the grammatical mistakes of Rev might well have made these works sound crude to better educated audiences who had the whole course of schooling. Understandably then, by way of implicit self-defense Paul acknowledges that he did not preach "in words taught by human wisdom" (I Cor 2:13).

Bibliography on the Political and Social World

(See also *Bibliographies* for Chapter 5 and Appendix I.)

Bauckham, R. J., *Palestinian Setting,* vol. 4 of TBAFC.

Boccaccini, G., *Middle Judaism. Jewish Thought, 300 B.C.E. to 200 C.E.* (Minneapolis: A/F, 1991).

Bruce, F. F., *New Testament History* (London: Nelson, 1969). Very useful for students.

Cohen, S.J.D., *From the Maccabees to the Mishnah* (Philadelphia: Westminster, 1987).

Conzelmann, H., *Gentiles—Jews—Christians* (Minneapolis: A/F, 1992).

Esler, P. F., *The First Christians in Their Social Worlds* (London: Routledge, 1994).

Feldman, L. H., *Jew and Gentile in the Ancient World: Attitudes and Interactions from Alexander to Justinian* (Princeton Univ., 1973).

Ferguson, E., *Backgrounds of Early Christianity* (2d ed.; Grand Rapids: Eerdmans, 1993). Good textbook.

Freyne, S., *The World of the New Testament* (NTM 2; Wilmington: Glazier, 1980).

———, *Galilee from Alexander the Great to Hadrian 323 B.C.E. to 135 C.E.* (Wilmington: Glazier, 1980).

Gager, J. G., *Kingdom and Community: The Social World of Early Christianity* (Englewood Cliffs, NJ: Prentice Hall, 1975).

Gill, D.W.J., and C. Gempf, *Greco-Roman Setting,* vol. 2 of TBAFC.

Grabbe, L. L., *Judaism from Cyrus to Hadrian* (2 vols.; Minneapolis: A/F, 1991).

Hammond, N.G.L., and H. H. Scullard, eds., *The Oxford Classical Dictionary* (2d ed.; Oxford: Clarendon, 1970). Very helpful for succinct information about classical antiquity.

[34]Koine was a dialect of Attic Greek (i.e., of the Greek of Athens, which, with admixtures of Ionic Greek, had been spread by Alexander the Great throughout the Hellenistic world). There were different levels of Koine, e.g., a more cultivated literary form showing the influence of Attic Greek, and the ordinary vernacular Koine found in inscriptions, private correspondence (preserved in papyri found in Egypt), and the NT (with Heb and Luke showing some touches of literary Koine).

Hengel, M., *Judaism and Hellenism* (2 vols.; Philadelphia: Fortress, 1974; 1-vol. ed., 1981).

———, *Jews, Greeks and Barbarians: Aspects of the Hellenization of Judaism in the pre-Christian Period* (Philadelphia: Fortress, 1980).

Kraft, R. A., and G.W.E. Nickelsburg, eds., *Early Judaism and Its Modern Interpreters* (Atlanta: Scholars, 1986).

Leaney, A.R.C., *The Jewish and Christian World, 200 BC to AD 200* (Cambridge Univ., 1984).

Lieberman, S., *Hellenism in Jewish Palestine* (New York: Jewish Theological Seminary, 1950).

McLaren, J. S., *Power and Politics in Palestine . . . 100 BC–AD 70* (JSNTSup 63; Sheffield: JSOT, 1991).

Malina, B. J., *Windows on the World of Jesus* (Louisville: W/K, 1993).

Mendels, D., *The Rise and Fall of Jewish Nationalism* (New York: Doubleday, 1992).

Momigliano, A., ed., *On Pagans, Jews, and Christians* (Middletown, CT: Wesleyan, 1987).

Moore, G. F., *Judaism in the First Centuries of the Christian Era* (3 vols.; Cambridge, MA: Harvard, 1927–30). A classic.

Neusner, J., ed., *Christianity, Judaism and Other Greco-Roman Cults* (M. Smith Festschrift; 3 vols.; Leiden: Brill, 1975).

Neusner, J., et al., eds., *The Social World of Formative Christianity and Judaism* (Philadelphia: Fortress, 1988).

Nickelsburg, G.W.E., "The Jewish Context of the New Testament," NInterpB 8.27–42.

Reicke, B., *The New Testament Era* (Philadelphia: Fortress, 1968). Still a useful handbook.

Rhoads, D. M., *Israel in Revolution 6–74 C.E.* (Philadelphia: Fortress, 1976).

Riches, J., "The Social World of Jesus," *Interpretation* 50 (1996), 383–92.

Safrai, S., and M. Stern, et al., *The Jewish People in the First Century* (2 vols.; Philadelphia: Fortress, 1974–76).

Sanders, J. T., *Schismatics, Sectarians, Dissidents, Deviants: The Final One Hundred Years of Jewish-Christian Relations* (Valley Forge, PA: Trinity, 1993).

Schürer, E., *The History of the Jewish People in the Age of Jesus Christ* (*175 B.C.–A.D. 135*) (rev. ed. [G. Vermes et al.]; 3 vols. in 4; Edinburgh: Clark, 1973–87). A classic.

Schwartz, D. R., *Studies in the Jewish Background of Christianity* (Tübingen: Mohr-Siebeck, 1992).

Segal, A. F., *Rebecca's Children: Judaism and Christianity in the Roman World* (Cambridge, MA: Harvard, 1986).

Sherwin-White, A. N., *Roman Society and Roman Law in the New Testament* (Oxford: Clarendon, 1963).

Smallwood, E. M., *The Jews under Roman Rule* (Leiden: Brill, 1976).

Stambaugh, J. E., and D. L. Balch, *The New Testament in Its Social Environment* (Philadelphia: Westminster, 1986).

Tcherikover, V., *Hellenistic Civilization and the Jews* (3d ed.; Philadelphia: Jewish Publ. Society, 1966).

White, L. M., and O. L. Yarbrough, eds., *The Social World of the First Christians* (W. A. Meeks Festschrift; Minneapolis: A/F, 1995).
Wilson, S. G., *Related Strangers: Jews and Christians 70–170 C.E.* (Minneapolis: A/F, 1995).
Zeitlin, S., *The Rise and Fall of the Judaean State* (3 vols.; Philadelphia: Jewish Publ. Society, 1962–78).

JOSEPHUS:

Loeb Classical Library: Nine volumes (original plus translation).
Rengstorf, K. H., *A Complete Concordance to Flavius Josephus* (5 vols.; Leiden: Brill, 1973–83).
Cohen, S., *Josephus in Galilee and Rome* (Leiden: Brill, 1979).
Feldman, L. H., *Josephus and Modern Scholarship (1937–1980)* (Berlin: de Gruyter, 1984). A bibliography.
———, *Josephus: A Supplementary Bibliography* (New York: Garland, 1986).
———, "Flavius Josephus Revisited," ANRW II.21.2 (1984), 763–862.
———, "Josephus," ABD 3.981–98.
———, and G. Hata, eds., *Josephus, Judaism, and Christianity* (Detroit: Wayne State Univ., 1987).
Mason, S., *Josephus and the New Testament* (Peabody, MA: Hendrickson, 1992).
Rajak, T., *Josephus: The Historian and His Society* (London: Duckworth, 1983).
Rappaport, U., ed., *Josephus Flavius: Historian of Eretz-Israel in the Hellenistic-Roman Period* (Jerusalem: Yad . . . Ben-Tsivi, 1982).
Schwartz, S., *Josephus and Judaean Politics* (Leiden: Brill, 1990).
Thackeray, H.St.J., *Josephus, the Man and the Historian* (New York: Jewish Institute, 1929). A classic.

ARCHAEOLOGY, CHRONOLOGY, GEOGRAPHY:

Bibliography of the Roman period in Palestine (63 BC–AD 70): Meyers, E. M., et al., CRBS 3 (1995), 129–52. Covers more than archaeology.
Avi-Yonah, M., ed., *Encyclopedia of Archaeological Excavations in the Holy Land* (4 vols.; London: Oxford, 1975–78). See the new ed. by Stern.
Báez-Camargo, G., *Archaeological Commentary on the Bible* (Garden City, NY: Doubleday, 1986). Pertinent information for chap. and verse.
Bickerman, E. J., *Chronology of the Ancient World* (2d ed.; Ithaca: Cornell, 1980).
Doig, K. F., *New Testament Chronology* (San Francisco: Mellen, 1991).
Finegan, J., *The Archaeology of the New Testament,* vol. 1: *The Life of Jesus and the Beginning of the Early Church* (rev. ed.; Princeton Univ., 1992); vol. 2: *The Mediterranean World of the Early Christian Apostles* (Boulder, CO: Westview, 1981).
———, *Handbook of Biblical Chronology* (rev. ed.; Peabody, MA: Hendrickson, 1997).
Frend, W.H.C., *The Archaeology of Early Christianity* (London: Chapman, 1996).
Hoppe, L. J., *The Synagogues and Churches of Ancient Palestine* (Collegeville: Liturgical, 1994).
Jeremias, J., *Jerusalem in the Time of Jesus* (Philadelphia: Fortress, 1969).

Kopp, C., *The Holy Places of the Gospels* (New York: Herder and Herder, 1963).
Matthews, V. H., and J. C. Moyer, "Bible Atlases: Which Ones Are Best?" BA 53 (1990), 220–31. Good survey.
Meyers, E. M., ed., *The Oxford Encyclopedia of Archaeology in the Near East* (5 vols.; New York: Oxford, 1997).
Murphy-O'Connor, J., *The Holy Land: An Archaeological Guide from Earliest Times to 1700* (3d ed.; New York: Oxford, 1992).
Stern, E., *The New Encyclopedia of Archaeological Excavations in the Holy Land* (4 vols.; New York: Simon & Schuster, 1993).
Yamauchi, E., *The Archaeology of New Testament Cities in Western Asia Minor* (Grand Rapids: Baker, 1980).
Wilkinson, J., *Jerusalem as Jesus Knew It: Archaeology as Evidence* (London: Thames and Hudson, 1978).

CHAPTER 5

THE RELIGIOUS AND PHILOSOPHICAL WORLD OF NEW TESTAMENT TIMES

The Jews of this period would have had some knowledge of the nonJewish religions of the peoples with whom they had contact; many of those peoples would have had some knowledge of Jewish religion. Often, on either side, such knowledge would have been partial, inaccurate, and even prejudiced. Therefore, although I shall attempt to present a sympathetic view of the Jewish,[1] Pagan,[2] and syncretistic religious world in which Christianity was born and developed, readers should remember that this presentation may not be what ordinary people perceived. Also, although the subject will be treated under the headings of "Jewish" and "nonJewish," readers should be alert to the dangers of compartmentalizing. In Palestine, even in areas where most of the population was Jewish, there was strong Hellenistic influence, but not necessarily evenly spread. Very Greco-Roman cities in Galilee, for instance, could be surrounded by villages whose inhabitants had little enthusiasm for Gentile thought and practice and other villages whose commerce brought them into closer contact with Hellenism. Similarly, in the cosmopolitan cities of the diaspora, Jews were not of one mind about Hellenistic institutions and culture, with attitudes ranging from enthusiastic participation and acculturation to ghettolike rejection.

[1]In the first decades most believers in Jesus were Jews, but in this comparative Chapter I shall use the term to refer to the beliefs and practices of Jews unaffected by Jesus or claims about him.

[2]As explained in Chapter 4 above, n. 25, capitalized "Pagan" is being used without pejorative implication as a technical reference to a religious belief that is not Jewish or Christian. In NT times it would cover the religions honoring the gods of the Greeks and the Romans, and the various religions of the Near East and Egypt (honoring Baal, Adonis, Osiris, Isis, Mithra, etc.) that Jews and early Christians could or would have known, been influenced by, or struggled with. Jews in Babylon would have had some contact with Zoroastrianism; but Jewish contact with Hinduism and Buddhism that might have played a role in the NT is most uncertain, despite attempts to find influence of those world religions on christology.

(A) Jewish Religious World

As explained on p. xxxiii above, the designation "Judaism" is appropriate for the period of Israelite history that began in 539 BC with the Persian release of the captives from Judah who had been held in Babylon so that they might return to Jerusalem and its environs.[3] In many ways the postexilic religion of Judaism was the heir of the preexilic religion of the Kingdom of Judah. The Temple was rebuilt; sacrifices were offered; hymns or psalms were sung; the main pilgrimage feasts were celebrated.[4] Yet eventually meetings for prayer, devout reading, meditation, and instruction known as synagogues[5] also became an important factor in Jewish life. The figure of the prophet became much less common; and Judaism took on a particular religious coloration from Ezra's proclamation of the Law (Neh 8:1–9:37) *ca.* 400 BC.[6] Certainly from that period obedience to the Law of Moses (the Torah) became more and more a paramount obligation of the Jew as a corollary of accepting the One God. While up to AD 70 attitudes toward the Temple often divided Jews, internal religious divisions centered on different interpretations of the Law existed before and after 70, as we can see from the DSS.

Amidst his depiction of the Maccabean struggle under Jonathan (*ca.* 145 BC), Josephus wrote a famous description: "At that time there were three *haireseis* [parties, sects, schools of thought—from which "heresies" in later usage] of the Jews which held different opinions about human affairs: the first of them was called Pharisees, the second Sadducees, the third Essenes" (*Ant.* 13.5.9; #171).[7] In interpreting this we should be careful. First, for example, we may learn from the tendency to divide Americans into Catholics,

[3]From the time of the return most people known as "Jews" would be descendants of the tribe of Judah with an admixture of Levites and Benjaminites (see I Kgs 12:23), e.g., Saul/Paul was of the tribe of Benjamin (Rom 11:1). The aged Anna in Luke 2:36 is of the (northern) tribe of Asher. The Samaritans claimed to be the descendants of the ten northern tribes of Israel, but in Palestine were not considered "Jews"—see F. Dexinger in E. P. Sanders, *Jewish Christian,* 2.88–114.

[4]Unleavened Bread, Weeks (Pentecost), Tabernacles (Tents, Booths), when Jews were expected to go to Jerusalem. The Passover feast was gradually joined to Unleavened Bread (Mark 14:1), and the lamb to be eaten at the meal by the pilgrims in Jerusalem was sacrificed in the Temple by the priests. New feasts were added, e.g., the Day of Atonement, Hanukkah (Dedication), Purim. Since the Temple, sacrifices, and feasts play a role in the NT, readers would be wise to gain more detailed knowledge of them (NJBC 76.42–56,112–157).

[5]"Synagogue" in its earliest usage may have referred to a community rather than a building. Probably in the time after the Babylonian exile and first in the diaspora (i.e., outside Palestine) buildings used for prayer and teaching came into existence, but they may have been used for other purposes as well. We do not know when the distinctive synagogue building became common. Archaeological ruins of synagogues constructed before AD 70 are very rare. See Hoppe, *Synagogues* 7–14; S. Fine, BRev 12 (#2; 1996), 18–26,41.

[6]The dating of this man (Ezra 7:6: "a scribe skilled in the Law of Moses that the Lord God had given") is uncertain and there are legendary elements in the description of him as a second Moses.

[7]In *Ant.* 18.1.2; #11, in a setting of AD 6 Josephus reports: "From most ancient times there were among the Jews three philosophies pertaining to ancestral tradition, that of the Essenes, that of the

Protestants, and Jews, ignoring the large number who are without firm religious identity. Similarly one may be sure that the differences among Josephus' three groups had no importance for many Jews. Second, the differences were on a wider scale than those we might consider purely religious. Third, our knowledge of how these divisions came about is very limited, and there are many guesses in what scholars have written about their history. Fourth, it is difficult to know the precise coloration of the thought of each group: Josephus simplifies in trying to explain them to Roman readers, and later rabbinic information reflects prejudices. With those cautions I present the most likely picture from the present state of the evidence.

The roots of the *Sadducees* were probably in the Zadokite Temple priesthood and its admirers.[8] They seem to have emerged as a distinct group in Maccabean times by remaining identified with the priesthood of the Jerusalem Temple when others turned away. The complications of that identification should become apparent to readers who review the one hundred years from the Maccabean struggles with the Seleucids beginning in 175 BC to Roman intervention in 63 BC (Chapter 4 above). The Sadducees became increasingly identified with the ruling Hellenized aristocracy, supposedly having little in common with the people. Yet our knowledge of the Sadducees is particularly defective; Josephus tells us little and later rabbinic writings portray them polemically.[9]

Some place the origins of the *Essenes ca.* 200 BC in the atmosphere of Jewish apocalyptic expectations,[10] but most scholars see them as springing from an opposition to developments in the Temple after 152 BC. They would be Hasideans or pious ones who had joined the Maccabean revolt (I Macc 2:42), partly because of the Syrian practice of replacing Zadokite high priests, and who felt betrayed by Jonathan and Simon, the brothers of Judas Maccabeus, who accepted this honor from the Syrian kings.[11] What we know

Sadducees, and the third of the system called the Pharisees." In 18.1.6; #23 he speaks of a fourth philosophy of which Judas the Galilean set himself up as leader; except for an extreme passion for liberty, this group agreed with the Pharisees in all other respects. Judas was a revolutionary, as were some of his children.

[8]The purest priestly descent was claimed to derive from Zadok, a high priest in the time of David and Solomon (I Sam 8:17; I Kings 2:35; I Chron 29:22; Ezek 44:15–16). The piety expressed in Sirach, which shows no awareness of an afterlife and in chap. 50 exalts the high priest Simon II (*ca.* 200 BC) as "the glory of his people," may represent the antecedents of Sadducee thought.

[9]Saldarini, *Pharisees* 299: "The task of reconstructing the Sadducees from the sources is daunting and in many respects impossible."

[10]Thus García Martínez, *People;* he thinks of the DSS community as schismatics, breaking away from the main Essene group later in the 2d century BC under the leadership of the Righteous Teacher—the time assigned by the majority to Essene beginnings.

[11]From the DSS we have knowledge of changes in Temple customs, e.g., of the calendric calculations of feasts, that exacerbated opposition. For the names and contents of these Qumran documents and their contents, see Appendix II below; also NJBC 67.78–117 or ABD 2.85–101.

about the Essenes has been greatly enlarged by the discovery beginning in 1947 of scrolls or fragments of some 800 mss. near Qumran by the Dead Sea (the DSS) because in the majority view these documents stem from a settlement of Essenes at that site from *ca.* 150 BC to AD 70.[12] In *War* 2.8.2–13; #119–161 Josephus provides a long, admiring description of the extraordinary piety and community life of the Essenes who in some ways resembled a monastic group.[13] Numerous features of this description seem to have been verified in the DSS and in the excavations of the Qumran site near the Dead Sea. Josephus (*Ant.* 13.5.9; #172) highlights the Essene theory that all things are determined by fate; this may be a way of explaining in Hellenistic terms the Qumran thesis that all human beings are guided by either the Spirit of Truth or the Spirit of Falsehood. The "Righteous Teacher" honored in the DSS may have been a Zadokite priest who led these Hasideans into the desert where the ancient Israelites were purified in the time of Moses. Disdaining the Temple now presided over by those who in their judgment were wicked priests, the Qumranians formed the community of the new covenant seeking to become perfect by an extraordinarily strict practice of the Law (interpreted for them by the Teacher), and awaiting an imminent messianic coming by which God would destroy all iniquity and punish their enemies.

The *Pharisees* were not a priestly movement and seemingly the Maccabean assumption of the priesthood was not a factor in their thought. Yet their very name, which implies separation, probably results from the fact that they too ultimately became critical of and split from the Hasmonean descendants of the Maccabees who became increasingly secularized rulers. The Pharisees' approach to the written Law of Moses was marked by a theory of a second, oral Law (supposedly also derived from Moses); their interpretations were less severe than those of the Essenes and more innovative than those of the Sadducees who remained conservatively restricted to the written Law.[14] For instance, by way of difference from the Sadducees, the Pharisees professed a belief in the resurrection of the body and angels—beliefs that came to the fore in the postexilic period.

[12]See Beall, *Josephus.* That they were Essenes, not Sadducees as claimed by a minority, is argued persuasively by J. A. Fitzmyer, HJ 36 (1995), 467–76. A crucial text in the discussion is 4QMMT; see BAR 20 (#6; 1994), 48ff.

[13]Comparatively our documentation about the Essenes is abundant, for Philo describes them (*Quod Omnis Probus* 12–13; #75–91; *Hypothetica* 11.1–18), as well as supplying an account of a similar group in Egypt, the Therapeutae (*De Vita Contemplativa*). Also Pliny the Elder, *Natural History* 5.15.73.

[14]Josephus reports this (*Ant.* 18.1.4; #16), but inevitably the Sadducees had their own customs. Probably, however, they did not have a system of interpretation/law that they acknowledged as going beyond the written Law, whereas the Pharisees did acknowledge the more-than-biblical character of some of their interpretations.

Relations among these groups were at times vicious. It is worthwhile documenting some instances of the hostility so that one can place in context the religious enmity one finds in the NT. High priests who were aligned with the *Sadducees*[15] were responsible for many violent deeds. Probably in the late 2d century BC an unnamed high priest sought the death of the Qumran Teacher of Righteousness on the Day of Atonement celebrated on a date peculiar to the Essene calendar (1QpHab 11:2–8); in 128 BC John Hyrcanus destroyed the sanctuary of the Samaritans on Mt. Gerizim where the Hebrew patriarchs had worshiped God (*Ant.* 13.9.1; #255–56); a few decades later Alexander Jannaeus massacred 6,000 Jews at the feast of Tabernacles over a challenge (by Pharisees?) to his legal qualifications to hold the priestly office (*War* 1.4.3; #88–89; *Ant.* 13.13.5; #372–73); later he crucified 800 (seemingly including Pharisees) while their wives and children were butchered before their eyes (*War* 1.4.6; #97; 1.5.3; #113; *Ant.* 13.14.2; #380). In the period 135–67 BC *Pharisees* incited hatred among the masses against the high priests John Hyrcanus (*Ant.* 13.10.5–6; #288, 296) and Alexander Jannaeus (*Ant.* 13.15.5; #402); and, once let loose on their enemies by the Jewish queen Salome Alexandra, they executed and exiled their religious/political adversaries (*Ant.* 13.16.2; #410–11).[16] The Dead Sea Scroll writers, presumably *Essenes,* railed against the Sadducee hierarchy in Jerusalem, condemning them as wicked priests who broke the commandments, and at the same time disparaged the Pharisees. For instance they criticized "the furious young lion [the high priest Alexander Jannaeus] . . . who carries out revenge on the seekers of smooth things [Pharisees] and who hangs people alive" (4QpNah 3-4.1.6–7). In exalting the Righteous Teacher, they spoke of another person (an Essene?) as a scoffer and liar who persecuted the seekers of smooth things (CD-A 1.14–21). All these incidents took place before the time of Herod the Great and the Roman prefecture in Judea (and thus before Jesus' lifetime), perhaps because strong rulers like Herod and the Romans would not tolerate such internecine religious behavior.

Three major questions flowing from the Jewish religious background need to be considered as part of a study of the NT and Jesus. (1) During the time of Jesus' public ministry, which religious group was the most important? Josephus (*War* 2.8.14; #162; *Ant.* 18.1.3; #14) calls the Pharisees the leading sect, extremely influential among the townspeople. That may explain why Jesus is remembered as having been more often in confrontation with them

[15]At least by presumption; very few individuals are identified by name as Sadducees.

[16]E. J. Bickerman, *The Maccabees* (New York: Shocken, 1947), 103: "Early Pharisaism was a belligerent movement that knew how to hate." E. P. Sanders, *Jewish Law* 87–88, lists rabbinic accounts of strong intraPharisee disputes.

than with any other group—a backhanded compliment to their importance.[17] More problematic is the picture of them in Josephus' *Ant.* 18.1.3,4; #15,17 whereby all prayers and sacred rites were performed according to Pharisee interpretation and the Sadducees had to submit to what the Pharisees said. In some incidents where *Ant.* highlights the importance and dominance of the Pharisees, Josephus' earlier writing, the *War*, fails to mention them. This difference raises the serious possibility that Josephus fictionally enhanced the Pharisee image in *Ant.* written in the 90s. The latter was the time of emerging rabbinic influence, and Josephus may have wanted to convince his Roman sponsors that the Pharisee ancestors of the rabbis (see below) were also important.[18] Accordingly, for instance, we may doubt that the high priests' legal proceedings with Jesus were conducted according to the rules of the Pharisees (who are for the most part singularly absent from the Gospel accounts of those proceedings).

(2) Who were Pharisees and what views did they hold? The Gospels often portray the Pharisees as hypocrites[19] and heartless legalists. Few doubt that this picture is hostilely exaggerated, reflecting later polemics between Christians and Jews. Partly as a refutation of that, there has been a tendency to look to the later rabbis as the mirror image of the Pharisees, and to attribute to the Pharisees of Jesus' lifetime rabbinical views attested in the Mishna (codified *ca.* AD 200)—views that are not at all hypocritical or narrowly legalistic. More specifically, famous teachers of the period before the destruction of the Temple in AD 70 are often identified as Pharisees even though there is no supporting ancient confirmation of that.[20] There are certainly lines of development from the early 1st-century AD Pharisees to the 2d-century AD rabbis, and undoubtedly there were Pharisee teachers of sensitive ethics during Jesus' lifetime. Yet the Jewish scholar S.J.D. Cohen wisely warns against a general attribution of prerabbinic traditions to the Pharisees. (Indeed one must be careful about employing in Gospel interpretation other

[17]There are a half-dozen confrontations with Pharisees in Mark, but only one with Sadducees (12:18); Essenes are never mentioned in the NT. Certainly the Gospel pictures are influenced by post-70 AD conflicts between Christians and the emerging rabbinic teachers (closer to the Pharisees than to other groups), but just as surely this is a heightening of a historical conflict in Jesus' lifetime rather than a total creation. One of few people in this period ever identified by name as a Pharisee, Saul/Paul (Phil 3:5), states that he persecuted the early followers of Jesus (Gal 1:13).

[18]The pros and cons of this thesis are discussed in BDM 1.353–57.

[19]In part the overly negative picture may stem from English connotation; the Greek *hypokritēs* means "overscrupulous, casuistic," but not "insincere" (Albright and Mann, *Matthew* cxv–cxxiii). The adjective "pharisaic" can have the same meaning as "pharisaical," i.e., "marked by hypocritical censorious self-righteousness." To avoid any suggestion of that, in this discussion I am using the noun "Pharisee" as an adjective.

[20]In fact, in the NT, Josephus, and the Mishna only a dozen people are identified by name as Pharisees.

material in the Mishna, e.g., the description of how the Passover seder is to be celebrated and the description of what constitutes blasphemy. What took place in AD 70 changed many details in such issues; and the Mishna represents an idealized 2d-century outlook.) A particular complication in the Gospel picture is the relation of the scribes to the Pharisees. Historically the Sadducees and the Essenes surely had scribes attracted to their way of thought; but it may well be factual that the majority of functionaries trained in law and procedure were Pharisees.

(3) How was Jesus related to these groups? Scholars disagree, sometimes with the assumption that surely he belonged to one. There is no serious reason to think of Jesus as a Sadducee; neither a priest nor an aristocrat, he had beliefs that were contrary to those of the Sadducees.[21] His belief in angels and in the resurrection of the body, and the eschatological expectations attributed to him in the Gospels bring him much closer to Essene and Pharisee theology. Even before the discovery of the DSS, adventurous scholars had painted Jesus as an Essene. He seemed to fit Josephus' and Philo's descriptions of their extraordinary piety, disdain of worldly goods, appreciation of celibacy, etc. After the scrolls were discovered, some found a parallel to Jesus in the picture of the Righteous Teacher; others thought that Jesus got some of his ideas from the Essenes.[22] However, no memory in the NT would attach Jesus to such a distinct community; he is remembered as visiting the Jerusalem Temple at the times other Jews came to Jerusalem for feasts (not according to the special calendar of the Qumran Essenes); his somewhat free attitude toward the Law is scarcely in conformity with the ultrastrictness of the Essenes. Most frequently Jesus has been identified as a Pharisee[23] on the assumption (queried above) that we know the views of the Pharisees in Jesus' lifetime and they were like those later enunciated in the Mishna. The failure of the Gospels to relate Jesus to any specific group probably represents a more accurate picture of the historical situation (see Meier, *Marginal* 1.345–49—he was simply a pious Jewish layman).

Beyond the issue of Jesus there has been considerable literature seeking

[21]The Jerusalem high priests are remembered as principal figures in condemning Jesus, in attempting to silence Peter and James (Acts 4:6; 5:17; see "Sadducees" in 4:1; 5:17), and in hostilely pursuing Paul (Acts 24:1). Ananus II, specifically identified as a Sadducee, was responsible for the stoning of James, the "brother" of Jesus (Josephus, *Ant.* 20.9.1; #199–200).

[22]For a judgment on the plausibility of suggested relationships, see R. E. Brown, "The DSS and the NT," in *John and the Dead Sea Scrolls,* ed. J. H. Charlesworth (New York: Crossroad, 1990), 1–8. More plausibly JBap might have been influenced by the Qumran Essenes (without having been one of them). Partial connections-parallels would include the area near the Jordan where both the Qumranians and JBap flourished, his insistence on water baptism, and the description of him as preparing the way of the Lord in the desert.

[23]For instance, H. Falk, *Jesus the Pharisee* (New York: Paulist, 1985), would make Jesus a Pharisee of the Hillel persuasion, bitterly opposed by other Pharisees of the Shammai persuasion.

to relate the early Christians to the Qumran sectarians.[24] Some of it borders on nonsense, e.g., attempts to find symbolic references to Christian figures like Jesus and Paul in the DSS. At times these implausible connections have been accompanied by claims of conspiracies on the part of Christian scholars or even the Vatican to hide the revolutionary implications of the DSS that would disprove Christianity. Unfortunately because of media "hype" such fantasy is often better known than the serious possibilities presented by the DSS.[25] One responsible proposal involves the likelihood that the structures of the early church may have been influenced by structures extant among Jewish groups. Besides asking whether the Christian presbyters/elders were patterned on the elders of the synagogue, one should consider whether the Christian overseers/bishops (*episkopoi*) were patterned on the overseers described in the DSS. Does the designation of the Christian movement as "the Way" and the stress on "commonness/community" (*koinōnia*) reflect the ideology of the Qumran Essenes of having gone into the desert to prepare the *way* of the Lord and their designation of their community directives as "the Rule for the *Oneness*"? Theologically, some would find traces of Qumran influence in the dualism of the Gospel of John phrased in terms of light and darkness, truth and falsehood; in the struggle between the light of the world (Jesus) and the Power of darkness (Luke 22:53); and in the struggle between the Spirit of Truth and the Prince of this world (John 16:11).

The Jewish revolt of AD 66–70 and the destruction of the Jerusalem Temple changed the dynamics of religious grouping. Revolutionaries such as the Sicarii, the Zealots, and the Fourth Philosophy were exterminated; the Qumran Essene settlement was destroyed in 68; the cessation of sacrifices at the Temple weakened the power base of the Sadducees insomuch as their leadership consisted of the priestly families. We do not have clarity on the way in which the Pharisees fed into the rabbinic movement.[26] Nevertheless, in the post-70 period rabbinic teachers, the sages of Israel, gradually won recognition as the guides of the people; and those assembled at Jamnia (Yavneh) on the Palestinian coast were dealt with by the Roman authorities as spokesmen for the Jews. From *ca.* 90–110 Gamaliel II, the son and grandson

[24]For the thesis that fragments of Christian documents have been found among the DSS, see Chapter 7 below, n. 95.

[25]Sober debunking of the folly may be found in Fitzmyer, *Responses;* García Martínez, *People* 24–29, 194–98; and especially O. Betz and R. Riesner, *Jesus, Qumran and the Vatican* (New York: Crossroad, 1994).

[26]Cohen, *From* 226–28, points out that the Mishna, a rabbinic work, does not betray a Pharisee self-consciousness or stress Pharisee ancestry. In part that may be because the Pharisees were remembered as a group over against other groups such as the Sadducees and the Essenes and in that way as having a sectarian mentality. The rabbinic movement was inclusive, not sectarian; there were legal disputes among the rabbis but not internecine violence. See also his "The Significance of Yavneh," HUCA 55 (1984), 27–53.

of famous interpreters of the Law, presided at Jamnia.[27] Christian writings of the post-70 period, when they spoke of Judaism, would increasingly have been thinking of this emerging rabbinic Judaism. In some areas the conflict between those who believed in Jesus and the leaders of the Jewish synagogues was sharp, as attested in strong antiPharisee depiction (Matt 23), in the alienated reference to "their synagogues" as places where Jesus' followers would be scourged (Matt 10:17); and in the portrayal of the expulsion of "a disciple of that fellow" from a synagogue (John 9:28,34). The *Birkat ha-mînîm* or synagogue "blessing" (really a curse) against deviants is often mentioned.[28] The dating of it to AD 85 is dubious, and the idea that it was a universal Jewish decree against Christians is almost certainly wrong. Local synagogues at different times in different places no longer tolerated the presence of Christians.[29] Gradually (early 2d century?) a "blessing" formula denouncing heretics or deviants of various sorts was understood to include Christians and much later to be specifically aimed at them. Everywhere by the late 2d century the lines of demarcation and division between Jews who did not believe in Jesus and Christians were sharply drawn, although that demarcation may have happened over a century earlier in some places.

Readers of the NT also need to know about postbiblical Jewish literature, most of it dating from a period after all the NT documents were written.[30] The **Targums** (Targumim) are Aramaic translations—some of them literal, some of them very free—of the biblical books, made for Jews who no longer spoke Hebrew. Targums of Job from before AD 70 have been discovered at Qumran (as well as the parabiblical *Genesis Apocryphon,* a free Aramaic embellishment of Gen). Later Targums to the Pentateuch and to the Prophets, stemming both from Palestine and Babylon, have been preserved (NJBC 68.106–15); the roots of the earliest of them may date to the 2d century AD. Works designated **Midrash,** written from the 3d century AD on, are free commentaries on the books of the Pentateuch (and eventually on other biblical books).[31]

The **Mishna** is a written codification in Hebrew of Jewish oral law under

[27]Among the younger sages influenced by him would have been Rabbi Akiba (Aqiba), who played a significant role in the Second Jewish Revolt by the support he gave Simon ben Kosibah (Bar Cochba).

[28]See Chapter 11 below, n. 102.

[29]Surely for various reasons: their Gentile component; their free interpretation of the Law; their proclamation of Jesus' divinity; their proselytizing, etc.

[30]Useful manuals for further information are J. Neusner, *Introduction to Rabbinic Literature* (New York: Doubleday, 1994); H. L. Strack and G. Stemberger, *Introduction to the Talmud and Midrash* (2d printing [= rev. ed.]; Minneapolis: A/F, 1996).

[31]The style of imaginative interpretation that is used in these midrashes (or midrashim) is called "midrashic," and one can find instances of that style earlier, e.g., in the recounting of the exodus story in Wis 11:2ff.

the editorship of Rabbi Judah the Prince made *ca.* AD 200; the term means "second," indicating that it was placed alongside the (first) Law preserved in the Pentateuch. Although it attributes its materials to about 150 teachers living between 50 BC and AD 200, in dealing with issues crucial to Jewish living it is a literary response to the influence of Roman occupation on the situation of Jews, especially after AD 70. Many of its rules are idealistic, e.g., provisions for the Temple and its maintenance long after the Temple was destroyed. The **Tosepta** (Tosefta) is another collection of laws and comments, usually dated to the 3d or 4th century AD. In a sense it is a complement to the Mishna, arranged in the same way; yet some of the traditions vary and may be older. There are two lengthy Aramaic commentaries on the Mishna: the **Palestinian Talmud** (completed in the 5th century) and the **Babylonian Talmud** (6th century)—extraordinarily rich compilations of minute legal discussions, traditions, Scripture interpretations, stories, etc.

There is a major problem about the use of this Jewish material in NT work. Since almost all of it was committed to writing after the main NT books, to what extent may it be used to enlighten the accounts of Jesus' life and reflections on the early church? A number of scholars, assuming that the traditions in these and even later works reflect early Jewish thought, practice, and terminology, feel free to cite passages written down anywhere from 100 to 1,000 years after the time of Jesus. Others (among whom I count myself) advocate extreme caution and want confirmation that what is being quoted was known before AD 70.[32]

(B) NonJewish Religious World

There is no doubt that Jesus, the early Christian preachers, and the NT writers were influenced by both the OT and early post-OT Judaism. More debatable is the extent to which they were influenced by the nonJewish religions and philosophies of the Greco-Roman world. In Chapter 4B above under the title "Social World," we saw that in varying degrees and ways Jesus, Paul, and Christians were in contact with this world which offered them possibilities and problems. In this and the next subsection we are asking a more precise question about the extent to which engagement with Greco-Roman culture, education, economy, and religion affected the way they thought about God, worship, morality, etc. If we start with Jesus himself, the answer is that we do not know. In the Synoptic Gospel memory he

[32]J. A. Fitzmyer, *A Wandering Aramean* (SBLMS 25; Missoula, MT: Scholars, 1979), 1–27; also "Problems of the Semitic Background of the New Testament," in *The Yahweh/Baal Confrontation*, eds. J. M. O'Brien and F. L. Horton, Jr. (E. W. Hamrick Festschrift; Lewiston, NY: Mellen, 1995), 80–93.

has little contact with Gentiles or Pagans, forbids his disciples to go near them (Matt 10:5) or imitate their ways (Matt 6:32), betrays Jewish prejudice toward them ("dogs" in Mark 7:27–28; "even the Gentiles" in Matt 5:47). His judgment that they are wordy in their prayers (Matt 6:7) need not imply that he had experienced this personally. Nor do we know the extent to which the early Galilean Christian preachers were influenced by the Pagan religious/philosophical world.

NonJewish influence on Paul is plausible: He came from Tarsus; he wrote and spoke Greek, and he used some Greek oratorical devices in his letters. The speech that Acts attributes to Paul in the Athens Areopagus[33] is addressed to Epicurean and Stoic philosophers (17:17–31) and is phrased in terms that reflect a popular knowledge of Pagan religion and philosophy; but the context indicates that Paul was adaptating himself to the Athenian milieu for the sake of proselytizing, and so the speech does not provide evidence of major influence on his thought. In fact there is sparse evidence of Pagan religious ideas in the letters of this man who calls himself "a Hebrew of the Hebrews." As we shall see in the next subsection, there is greater possibility of philosophical influence.

The attempts to see the evangelists' portrayals of Jesus as influenced by the Pagan "divine man" (*theios anēr*) ideology are highly controverted.[34] The contention that early Christian christology (hailing Jesus as "Lord" and "Son of God") stemmed from Hellenizing the memory of Jesus under the influence of Pagan polytheism was once popular but is now a minority view. John's picture of a world divided into the children of light and the children of darkness, once thought to be phrased in a language derived from the non-Jewish religious sources, is now attested in the DSS. In short, scholars have not demonstrated that in a dominant way Pagan *religion* shaped the theology or christology of the NT.

Why, then, should those who wish to study the NT become familiar with the Pagan religious (and philosophical) world? The mindset of the audience that received the NT message must be taken into account. For instance, listeners with a polytheistic background may have understood preaching about the "son of God" in the light of one Greek god having been begotten by another. Syncretism was much à la mode; and it would be surprising if the Christian gospel were not blended by some of the evangelized into their own

[33]Whether or not the historical Paul is portrayed accurately in this scene, Acts shows how several decades later Paul was remembered or imagined.

[34]That this "divine man" was even a well-defined category has been seriously questioned; see D. L. Tiede, *The Charismatic Figure as a Miracle Worker* (SBLDS 1; Missoula, MT: Scholars, 1972); C. R. Holladay, *THEIOS ANER in Hellenistic Judaism* (SBLDS 40; Missoula, MT: Scholars, 1977); A. Pilgaard in *The New Testament and Hellenistic Judaism,* eds. P. Borgen et al. (Aarhus Univ., 1995), 101–22.

preconceptions, as in the instance of Simon Magus in Acts 8:9–24. Others who heard the Christian preaching may have fitted the message of Jesus or of Paul into one of the philosophies with which they were familiar whether or not that occurred to the preachers. Still others may have regarded the preached message ridiculous when compared with their own more sophisticated philosophical views. Paul surely never thought of himself as a preacher of philosophy (I Cor 1:22–25; 2:1–2), no matter to what extent he was influenced by the rhetorical techniques of the philosophers; but to some who heard him and observed the way he lived, he may have appeared to be a Cynic. To get a sense of all these possibilities, let us survey in this subsection the nonJewish religions and then in the next subsection the Greco-Roman philosophies.

THE GODS AND GODDESSES OF CLASSICAL MYTHOLOGY. Just as Greek culture was a stronger factor in the NT world than Roman culture, so the dominant tone in the pertinent Greco-Roman religion was Greek. Nevertheless, by this era the cult of the Greek and the Roman deities had been amalgamated, and the resultant hybrid blurred the different thrust of the two religions that had existed in antiquity. The Greek Zeus, Hera, Athena, Aphrodite, Hermes, and Artemis were now identified with the Roman Jupiter, Juno, Minerva, Venus, Mercury,[35] and Diana. There were temples, priesthoods, and feasts dedicated to the patron god or goddess of a city or region; statues to the deities dotted the forums of the cities; and popular mythology centered on their intervention.[36] Augustus promoted the traditional ceremonies in honor of the gods. Even though the comic playwrights had lampooned the sexual peccadilloes of these deities, Acts 19:23–40 (where Paul offends the adherents of Artemis/Diana of the Ephesians) shows how dangerous a whipped-up fervor in defense of the official cult could be. Nevertheless, for many this official cult of the ancient gods and goddesses did not translate itself into genuine religious devotion, whence the demythologizing of the deities by the philosophers (e.g., the Stoic identification of Zeus with the *logos* or reason that pervades the universe), the appeal of newer religions

[35]From the combination Hermes-Mercury there further developed the figure of Hermes Trismegistos (the Thrice-Greatest), wherein the messenger of the gods had become an all-wise embodiment of the divine word (*logos*) and a redeemer. A significant literature developed as exemplified by the *Corpus Hermeticum,* consisting of philosophical/theological tractates in Greek (2d–5th centuries AD), with some similarities to ideas and expressions in John and Paul. Some see Hermeticism as originating from the combination of a Pagan gnosticism (p. 92 below) with Greek philosophy. The most significant tractate for comparative purposes is *Poimandres* (translated in Layton, *Gnostic* 452–59), which seems to reflect a worshiping community context. Scholars are divided on the direction of the influence, but most likely the NT and Hermetic writings have been influenced independently by a common milieu.

[36]That mind-set is manifested in Acts 14:11–18 where the crowds at Lystra think Barnabas and Paul are Zeus and Hermes come among them.

from the East and/or mystery religions, and the prevalence of divining, consulting oracles, magic (amulets, charms, formulas), and astrology.[37]

EMPEROR WORSHIP. Even in the official cult there were changes in the 1st century AD. Particularly in the East with its history of deifying rulers, there was a tendency to regard the emperor as divine and place him in the pantheon.[38] Augustus, who was so hailed and yet rejected deification during his lifetime, was deified after his death. Caligula wanted divinizing statues set up in his honor, and Nero regarded himself as divine. Domitian insisted on divine honors, and his styling himself "Lord and God" probably explains the hatred in the Book of Revelation for Roman power as usurping what belongs to God. Pliny the Younger (*ca.* AD 110) made a willingness to offer sacrifice to the emperor's image a test to determine who were Christians and who were not.

THE MYSTERY RELIGIONS[39] involved secret religious dramas and ceremonies by which those initiated could be brought to share in the immortal life of the gods. The initiates who came from all classes were bonded into an enduring fellowship. Some scholars have sought here the source of the Pauline use of *mystērion* in reference to Christ (I Cor 15:51; Rom 11:25; 16:25; Col 1:26–27); but that usage reflects a Semitic background, i.e., the hidden decisions of the heavenly court surrounding God.[40] A more plausible relationship to Christianity would be that those preaching a victory over death through the crucifixion and resurrection of Jesus would have to compete with these cults and myths (varying from country to country) that offered salvation without insistence on social or personal morality.

The most famous of the Greek mystery cults, the *Eleusinian mysteries,* honored Demeter (Ceres), the protectress of agriculture. When her daughter Persephone was carried off to the netherworld by Hades, Demeter in her anger did not permit the earth to produce fruit. As a compromise Persephone stayed in the netherworld for four months a year (the time when seed is in the ground), but the other eight months (when crops grow) she was with

[37]Judaism was influenced by both magic and astrology. In the magical papyri from the Roman era there was a considerable proportion of Jewish material (forms of Hebrew names for God and transcribed Hebrew phrases). Horoscopes based on astrology have been found at Qumran, and in the synagogues from a postNT period there are zodiacal decorations. M. Smith, *Jesus the Magician* (San Francisco: Harper & Row, 1978) would equate Jesus' miracles with magical practice. Without our accepting that equation (see Meier, *Marginal* 2.538–52), surely some who heard about him might have put him in that category (notice the interest in Christianity expressed by Simon Magus in Acts 8:18–19 and the attempt of Jewish exorcists to invoke Jesus' name in 19:13).

[38]A good survey is offered by D. L. Jones, "Christianity and the Roman Imperial Cult," ANRW II.23.2.1023–54; also ABD 5.806–9.

[39]M. W. Meyer, ed., *The Ancient Mysteries: A Sourcebook* (San Francisco: Harper & Row, 1987).

[40]R. E. Brown, *The Semitic Background of the Term "Mystery" in the New Testament* (Facet Biblical Series 21; Philadelphia: Fortress, 1968). See H. Rahner, in J. Campbell, ed., *Pagan and Christian Mysteries* (New York: Harper, 1963), 148–78.

her mother. At Eleusis, just west of Athens, an annual ceremony and secret religious rites were celebrated, insuring life to the initiates.

Another cult was centered on the wine-god *Dionysus* (Bacchus), the son of Zeus and Semele, who in various forms of the legend was saved from destruction. Through ceremonies and drinking, participants (among whom women were prominent) became frenzied and in that ecstatic state had contact with the god who offered them the gift of life. Euripides (5th century BC) presents a vivid account of an orgiastic frenzy in *The Bacchae,* and in 186 BC because of scandal in the Bacchanalia the Roman Senate took corrective measures.

THE EASTERN RELIGIONS. The cult of *Isis* stemming from Egypt was popular in the empire, particularly among women. After her consort Osiris was hacked to pieces, the goddess, persistently searching for the pieces, managed by magical rites to revive Osiris, who became the god of the underworld.[41] The myth is associated with annual flooding of the Nile that brought fertility. There were authoritative actions against the Isis cult in Rome before it received official recognition under Caligula. The 2d-century Latin author Apuleius in his *Metamorphoses* (*Golden Ass*)[42] describes the mystery rite by which an initiate reenacted Osiris' journey to death and thus was insured life after death. In other developments Isis was honored as mistress of the universe and omniscient—a wisdom figure.

A somewhat similar motif in the form of a dying and rising god appears in the story of *Adonis,* the beloved of Aphrodite: He died of a wound from a boar; and the anemone, which flowers in the spring, sprouted from his blood. The grief of the goddess moved the gods of the lower world, who allowed Adonis to spend six months a year with Aphrodite on the earth. This myth, based on the death of nature in winter and revival in spring, was of Phoenician origin and was celebrated in annual festivals. *Attis,* involved with the mother goddess Cybele, was another vegetation god; but his death involved self-castration; and the rites involved in this myth had an orgiastic character. (Romans were not permitted to participate.) Similarly the worship of the *Kabiroi* or Cabiri, originally Phrygian deities, had phallic rites; it was eventually woven together with aspects of the cult of Dionysus and even with that of the emperor.

The cult of *Mithras,* restricted to men, was carried far and wide by Persian and Roman soldiers. With its roots in the Persian Zoroastrian pantheon, Mithraism involved a mediator between human beings and the god of light

[41]In some forms of the cult Osiris was replaced by the syncretized god Serapis.

[42]A good translation of this important work is supplied by P. G. Walsh, *Apuleius, "The Golden Ass"* (Oxford: Clarendon, 1994).

(Ahura Mazda). The setting for the cult was usually a cave sanctuary (Mithraeum), in the center of which was a statue of Mithras slaying a bull. From the bull's wounds came stalks of grain. The overall symbolism is the overcoming of evil and the bringing of life to the initiates who underwent a bath in blood.

(C) Greco-Roman Philosophies, Philo, and Gnosticism

Even though "philosophy" is a word that occurs only once in the NT (Col 2:8), Greco-Roman philosophies and combinations of them with Jewish and Pagan religious motifs also deserve attention. In various ways they considered the origin, place, and destiny of human beings in relation to the cosmos, as well as the role of a universal guiding force. Sometimes they came much closer to monotheism than did any of the Pagan religions; and often they held up a demanding code of behavior, again much more than most of the religions. Although I shall discuss the philosophies individually, interest was often eclectic since people chose attractive elements from different systems.

PLATONISM. The philosophy that Plato (427–347 BC) formulated in dialogues in which Socrates was the chief speaker, had declined as such by NT times; but it influenced other philosophies (and would have enormous influence on the Church Fathers). The most important doctrine was that in this world people see only the insubstantial shadows cast by another world of realities where perfect truth and beauty exist. To fulfill their destiny people must escape the material world and go to their true home in that other world. Some would find Platonic influence (directly or through Hellenistic Judaism) on John's contrast between the world below and the world above, and his description of a Jesus who has come from above to offer true realities (see John 3:31; 1:9; 4:23). By way of Pagan polemic against Christianity, Socrates' composed and cheerful acceptance of a death that was forced upon him was contrasted with the way Jesus faced death. Scorn and mockery were directed to the picture of Jesus prostrate on the ground, his soul sorrowful unto death, begging the Father to take away the cup (Mark 14:33–36).

CYNICS. These stem from another disciple of Socrates but one who disagreed with Plato, namely, the Athenian Antisthenes—a figure overshadowed by his more famous disciple Diogenes of Sinope (*ca.* 412–323 BC). Behavior rather than abstract thought characterized the Cynic outlook, specifically frugality and a return to nature, rejecting (sometimes satirically) artificial conventions. Overall the Cynics showed no interest in talking about god/s. Wandering Cynics took over the Socratic method of asking questions; but instead of addressing them to colleagues or students, they went into the streets to ordinary people and challenged them. In particular, they engaged in the "diatribe," not a raving attack but a pedagogical discourse characterized by conversational style, rhetorical questions, paradoxes, apostrophes, etc. (Some scholars now, however, contend that the full diatribe pattern consisting of thesis, demonstration by antithesis and examples, and the answering of objections, was developed in the classroom rather than in public preaching.) Diatribe patterns appear in Seneca, Epictetus, and Plutarch and have been detected as well in Paul,[43] e.g., the series of questions in Rom 3:1–9,27–31; and the "Do you not know?" sequence with slogans in I Cor 6. By appealing to the Q sayings shared by Matt and Luke some would classify Jesus as a Cynic preacher,[44] a point that will be discussed in Appendix I below. The apocalyptic eschatology associated with both Jesus and Paul, however, would not fit Cynic thought. Some would identify Cynicism as the false teaching attacked in the Pastorals.

EPICUREANS. Another philosophical tradition stems from Epicurus (342–270 BC). In English an epicure is one devoted to sensual pleasure, especially in food and wine; and even in antiquity that may have been a popular evaluation of the Epicurean outlook. Yet Epicurus himself was a virtuous and decent man. He devalued myths and abstractions and appealed to the common people by making sensation the standard of truth—feelings and sense perceptions are trustworthy. His was a philosophy designed to free people from fears and superstitions: There is no need for religion since events are determined by the movement of atoms; gods have nothing to do with human existence; death is final, and there is no resurrection. Conventicles of Epicureans were bound together by friendship and care for each other. This thought was popular among the educated classes, e.g., the Roman poets Lucretius (95–51 BC) and Horace (65–8 BC). It is not surprising then that Acts 17:18,32 includes Epicureans among the audience who mocked when Paul spoke of God's demands and of resurrection from the dead.[45] Epicurean thought could explain why Paul can say that the preaching of Christ crucified is folly to the Greeks (I Cor 1:23).

[43]R. Bultmann's 1910 doctoral dissertation was on the Cynic-Stoic diatribe in Paul. Although this is the majority opinion, an important caution has been issued by K. P. Donfried, "False Presuppositions in the Study of Romans," CBQ 36 (1974), 332–55; reprinted in TRD 102–25. Following some classicists, he wonders whether there is a distinct literary form known as the diatribe since many of the features are found in the general philosophical dialogue. Moreover, he challenges the thesis that if Paul uses the dialogue format, that stereotyped format makes the material in the diatribe useless for determining the historical situation in the community addressed.

[44]Thus Downing, *Cynics;* Mack, *Lost;* see the critique of Mack by P. Perkins, *Christian Century* 110 (1993), 749–51, who rightly points out that this picture implausibly removes Jesus from much of the well-known Jewish context of his times. Also A. Denaux's review of Vaage, *Galilean,* in JBL 115 (1996), 136–38. On perilous reconstructions based on Q, see Chapter 6 below and Tuckett, "A Cynic Q?"

[45]When Paul says, "If the dead are not raised, 'Let us eat and drink, for tomorrow we die'" (I Cor 15:32), he is citing Isa 22:13; but he may also be echoing a prevalent Epicurean motif.

STOICISM. This philosophy stemmed from a contemporary of Epicurus, the Cypriot Zeno (333–264 BC), who lectured in a colonnaded porch (*stoa*) at Athens and who had been trained by a Cynic from whom he derived the tenet that virtue is the only good. Stoicism regarded the universe as a single organism energized by a world-soul, the *logos* or divine reason that guides all things. There is no separate world of ideas as in Plato's philosophy. As part of the universe, if people live according to the guiding reason or natural law, they can remain tranquil in the face of adversity. Affections and passions are looked on as pathological states from which people could be delivered. Thus, this was a system of thought that developed moral values and the conquest of self. Yet the emphasis on divine reason, almost monotheistic in tone, accommodated diverse mythologies as the gods became symbols of the government of nature. A famous hymn by the 3d-century BC Stoic Cleanthes[46] praises Zeus above all gods: He is the one from whom the world began, whose law rules over all things, and who is king over all forever—a hymn parts of which would fit the God of Israel. Stoics had a deterministic outlook on what would happen, with astrology and natural science as the tools for detecting the already fixed plan that would culminate in a great purging conflagration, before a new cycle of ages would begin. There were several chronological stages in the history of stoicism, e.g., the Middle Stoa (2d century BC) in which there was an increased appreciation of the older philosophies of Plato, Philo, and Aristotle. By the Christian period Later Stoicism had become the dominant philosophy, exemplified by Seneca (a contemporary of Paul), Epictetus, and Marcus Aurelius. Acts 17:25,28 has Paul echoing Stoic formulas; and Phil 4:11, "I have learned to be content in whatever state I am," approaches Stoic thought (see also I Cor 4:11–13). Some would argue that Paul's use of diatribe is closer to Stoic usage (Epictetus) than to Cynic usage. Yet in I Cor 6:12 Paul may be attacking a Stoic formula; and in Rom 1:19,23 Paul's argument that idols distort the knowledge of God that was revealed to all is the opposite of the Stoic contention that such artifacts reflect a human yearning for the divine (Malherbe, "Cultural" 19–20).

SOPHISTS. Although there were Sophist philosophers, there was no Sophist philosophy. Sophists were teachers who made a profession of going from city to city teaching for a fee. The most famous early ones were Protagoras (480–411 BC), who taught virtue or efficient conduct of life, and Gorgias (483–376 BC), who taught effective and artistic speech even though he despaired of attaining positive knowledge. Sophists emphasized material success and were able to argue for any viewpoint, true or not (whence the pejo-

[46]Text in Barrett, *NT Background* 67.

rative tone of "sophistic"). At the time of the early Roman Empire a Second Sophistic wave concentrated on the practice of rhetoric, an important element in higher education.[47] Some would see Paul's insistence that he preached God's gospel without cost at Corinth (II Cor 11:7–10) as an implicit contrast with the practice of Sophistic teachers in the city.

Two other items of religious background that should be brought to the attention of readers of the NT represent a combination of Jewish and Gentile motifs, namely, the writings of Philo and gnosticism.

PHILO (*ca.* 20 BC–AD 50) came from a wealthy, Hellenized Jewish family of Alexandria; his schooling gave him an excellent command of Greek language, philosophy, poetry, and drama; and he was a leader in the large Jewish community there. Although he did not have a knowledge of the Scriptures as detailed as that of the rabbis and may not have known Hebrew, he was faithful to Jewish practice, knew the LXX, and was well equipped to translate his religious tradition in a way that a Hellenized world could understand. In numerous writings Philo involved himself in political issues, defended his fellow Jews against calumny, argued that Judaism was a religion with a respectable heritage, and described the life of the Essenes. More important for our purposes, Philo tried to integrate philosophy with biblical principles both directly and through allegorical interpretation of the Bible (especially Gen).[48] He was familiar with Aristotelianism and with Pythagorean numerical speculations; but his dominant approach reflected Platonism (especially in some of its later Middle-Platonic developments) and Stoicism. The descent of the soul into the body was explained in Platonic terms; and although Philo related the Law of Moses to the Stoic idea of rational order in nature, he rejected Stoic determinism in favor of freedom. Whether Philo influenced NT thought is debated. Middle-Platonic ideas detected in the Epistle to the Hebrews resemble those in Philo, but independently both may be reflecting a common Hellenistic Jewish (and even Alexandrian) milieu. Some have found a parallel between John's use of *logos* (the Word) as the one through whom all things were created and Philo's use of *logos* as God's mental activity during the act of creating and also as a radiation from the One God relating that God to human beings.[49] Once again, however, probably both Phi-

[47]G. Anderson, *The Second Sophistic. A Cultural Phenomenon in the Roman Empire* (London: Routledge, 1993) sees more widespread traces of Sophistic influence.

[48]Even though allegorical interpretations are more characteristic of his philosophical bent, Philo also interpreted Scripture literally as well and may have homilized the Jewish audience in the Alexandrian synagogue.

[49]Positing Philo's influence on John is R. G. Hamerton-Kelly, *Pre-existence, Wisdom, and the Son of Man* (SNTSMS 21; Cambridge Univ., 1973); rejecting it, R. M. Wilson, ExpTim 65 (1953–54), 47–49.

lonic and Johannine *logos* are independently related to the personified Wisdom of Jewish OT Wisdom Literature.

GNOSTICISM (from *gnōsis,* "knowledge") is a term, very difficult to define, used to describe a pattern of religious thought, often with Jewish and Christian elements, advocated by groups in the eastern section of the Roman Empire (Syria, Babylonia, Egypt). Our information comes from different sources. The Church Fathers wrote about these groups, explaining the gnostic systems in the course of polemicizing against them.[50] Then in 1945 at Nag Hammadi, 300 miles south of Cairo in Egypt, there was a major discovery of 13 Coptic codices (containing 50 discrete tractates) buried about AD 400 and seemingly stemming from a monastery (Chenoboskion?) infiltrated by gnostics. Many of these are translations of texts composed in Greek in the 2d century AD. Gnostic elements are found also in the literature of the Manicheans (4th–10th century) and the Mandaeans (still existing in Iraq).

The attraction of gnosticism was that it offered answers to important questions: Where did we come from; where should we go; how do we get there? Despite the many differences among gnostics, relatively common theses were that human souls or spiritual principles do not belong in this material world (which is often described as evil and ignorant),[51] and they can be saved only by receiving the revelation that they belong in a heavenly realm of light (the *plēroma* or "fullness"), where there is a hierarchy of emanations from the true God. Ascent to this realm is sometimes through baptism, sometimes through elaborate cultic rituals (often involving anointing), sometimes more through philosophical reflection. Some gnostic groups had their own hierarchy and virtually constituted a counterchurch.[52]

The origins of gnosticism are disputed: a Hellenization of Christianity, or a Hellenization of Judaism and its traditions about Wisdom, or a derivative from Iranian myth, or a combination of Greek philosophy and Near Eastern mythology, or radical novelty derived from experiencing the world as an alien place. Semitic names are used for the divine emanations, but names of Pagan gods like Seth are also involved. Many gnostic authors thought that Jesus brought the revelation enabling a return to the divine world. Yet there are gnostic strains where the imagery seems to be rooted in syncretistic Judaism, so that Christianizing appears as a secondary development. Similari-

[50]Irenaeus, *Adversus haereses* (*ca.* 180) is a prime example.

[51]The usual explanation is that an evil principle entrapped particles of light in this world, or there has been a fall in which a female Wisdom figure generated a defective being who is the OT creator of this world.

[52]Some feminist scholars have contended that the ecclesiastical and theological roles allotted by the gnostics to women were more positive than those allowed in the "Great Church." D. L. Hoffmann, *The Status of Women and Gnosticism in Irenaeus and Tertullian* (Lewiston, NY: Mellen, 1995) argues strongly to the contrary.

ties between John and gnosticism have been detected, e.g., John's motif of not being of this world (17:16) and of eternal life consisting in knowing (17:3). Yet the claim that John was heavily influenced by gnosticism runs against the objection that the available evidence for developed gnosticism dates from a time *after* John was composed. More likely, gnostic thought in relation to John represents an exaggerated interpretation of that Gospel. It may well be that the "antichrists" who left the Johannine community (I John 2:18–19) became gnostic and brought the Gospel into that ambiance.

Bibliography on the Religious and Philosophical World

(See also the *Bibliography* of Chapter 4 since many books treat both political and religious backgrounds.)

DOCUMENTATION AND BACKGROUND IN GENERAL:

Barrett, C. K., *New Testament Background: Select Documents* (rev. ed.; London: SPCK, 1987).

Boring, M. E., et al., *Hellenistic Commentary to the New Testament* (Nashville: Abingdon, 1995). Almost 1,000 Jewish and nonJewish selections arranged according to the pertinent NT passages.

Cartlidge, D. R., and D. L. Dungan, *Documents for the Study of the Gospels* (rev. enlarged ed.; Minneapolis: A/F, 1994).

Crossan, J. D., *Sayings Parallels* (Philadelphia: Fortress, 1986). Arranged according to the sayings of Jesus in the Gospels.

Deissmann, A., *Light from the Ancient East. The New Testament Illustrated by Recently Discovered Texts of the Graeco-Roman World* (4th ed.; Grand Rapids: Baker, 1978; reprint of 1927 ed.). A classic.

Funk, R. W., ed., *New Gospel Parallels* (rev. ed.; Sonoma, CA: Polebridge, 1990).

Murphy, F. J., *The Religious World of Jesus* (Nashville: Abingdon, 1991).

New Documents Illustrating Early Christianity (an annual translating Greek documents).

Winter, B. W., and A. D. Clarke, *Ancient Literary Setting,* vol. 1 of TBAFC.

JEWISH RELIGIOUS WORLD:

Beall, T. S., *Josephus' Description of the Essenes Illustrated by the Dead Sea Scrolls* (SNTSMS 58; Cambridge Univ., 1988).

Holladay, C. R., *Fragments from Hellenistic Jewish Authors* (4 vols.; Chico, CA, and Atlanta: Scholars, 1983–96).

Mason, S., *Flavius Josephus and the Pharisees* (Leiden: Brill, 1991).

Neusner, J., *Judaism in the Beginnings of Christianity* (Philadelphia: Fortress, 1984).

Saldarini, A. J., *Pharisees, Scribes and Sadducees in Palestinian Society* (Wilmington: Glazier, 1988).

Sanders, E. P., *Jewish Law from Jesus to the Mishnah* (London: SCM, 1990).

———, *Judaism: Practice and Belief 63BCE–66CE* (Philadelphia: Trinity, 1992).

———, et al., eds., *Jewish and Christian Self-Definition: Vol. Two: Aspects of Judaism in the Greco-Roman Period* (Philadelphia: Fortress, 1981).

Schüssler Fiorenza, E., ed., *Aspects of Religious Propaganda in Judaism and Early Christianity* (Notre Dame Univ., 1976).
Stemberger, G., *Jewish Contemporaries of Jesus: Pharisees, Sadducees, Essenes* (Minneapolis: A/F, 1995).
Stone, M. E., ed., *Jewish Writings of the Second Temple Period* (Compendium Rerum Iudaicarum ad Novum Testamentum, 2.2; Philadelphia: Fortress, 1984).
Urbach, E. E., *The Sages: Their Concepts and Beliefs* (2 vols.; Cambridge, MA: Harvard Univ., 1979).

DEAD SEA SCROLLS (QUMRAN):

Cross, F. M., Jr., *The Ancient Library of Qumran and Modern Biblical Studies* (rev. ed.; Minneapolis: A/F, 1995).
Fitzmyer, J. A., *The Dead Sea Scrolls: Major Publications and Tools for Study* (SBLRBS 20; Atlanta: Scholars, 1990).
———, *Responses to 101 Questions on the Dead Sea Scrolls* (New York: Paulist, 1992). Very useful in correcting sensationalist nonsense about the Scrolls.
———, "The Dead Sea Scrolls and Early Christianity," TD 42 (1995), 303–19.
García Martínez, F., *The Dead Sea Scrolls Translated* (Leiden: Brill, 1994). Best collection, as of 1996.
García Martínez, F., and J. Trebolle Barrera, *The People of the Dead Sea Scrolls: Their Writings, Beliefs, and Practices* (Leiden: Brill, 1995).
García Martínez, F., and D. W. Parry, *A Bibliography of the Finds in the Desert of Judah, 1970–1995* (Leiden: Brill, 1996).
Jongeling, B., *A Classified Bibliography of the Finds in the Desert of Judah, 1958–1969* (Leiden: Brill, 1971).
VanderKam, J. C., *The Dead Sea Scrolls Today* (Grand Rapids: Eerdmans, 1994).
Vermes, G., *The Dead Sea Scrolls in English* (4th ed.; London: Penguin, 1995). Convenient handbook, but only every fifth line is numbered, leaving it difficult to find references.
———, *The Complete Dead Sea Scrolls in English* (New York: Allen Lane/Penguin, 1997).

GRECO-ROMAN RELIGIOUS AND PHILOSOPHICAL WORLD (beyond Judaism):

Bell, I. H., *Cults and Creeds in Graeco-Roman Egypt* (Liverpool Univ., 1953).
Benko, S., *Pagan Rome and the Early Christians* (Bloomington: Indiana Univ., 1984).
Burkert, W., *Greek Religion* (Cambridge, MA: Harvard, 1985).
Downing, F. G., *Cynics and Christian Origins* (Edinburgh: Clark, 1992).
Finegan, J., *Myth & Mystery: An Introduction to the Pagan Religions of the Biblical World* (Grand Rapids: Baker, 1989).
Grant, F. C., ed., *Hellenistic Religions: The Age of Syncretism* (New York: Liberal Arts, 1953). Translates texts pertinent to religions, cults, philosophers.
———, *Ancient Roman Religion* (New York: Liberal Arts, 1957). Translation of texts.
Koester, H., *Introduction,* vol. 1. Very complete.
Long, A. A., *Hellenistic Philosophy* (London: Duckworth, 1986).

Malherbe, A. J., "The Cultural Context of the New Testament: The Greco-Roman World," NInterpB 8.12–26.
———, *Paul and the Popular Philosophies* (Minneapolis: Augsburg, 1989).
Roetzel, C. J., *The World That Shaped the New Testament* (Atlanta: Knox, 1985).
Rose, H. R., *Religion in Greece and Rome* (New York: Harper & Row, 1959). A classic.

PHILO:

Loeb Classical Library: Ten volumes (original plus translation).
Yonge, C. D., *The Works of Philo* (new ed.; Peabody, MA: Hendrickson, 1993). Convenient one-vol. translation of all the writings.
Barraclough, R., "Philo's Politics," ANRW II.21.1 (1984), 417–553.
Borgen, P., "Philo of Alexandria: A Critical and Synthetical Survey of Research since World War II," ANRW II.21.1 (1984), 98–154.
———, "Philo of Alexandria," ABD 5.333–42.
———, "Philo's Writings," *Philo, John and Paul* (Atlanta; Scholars, 1987), 7–16.
Goodenough, E. R., *An Introduction to Philo Judaeus* (2d ed.; Lanham, MD: University Press of America, 1986; reprint of 1962 ed.).
Mendelson, A., *Philo's Jewish Identity* (Atlanta: Scholars, 1988).
Radice, R., and D. T. Runia, *Philo of Alexandria: An Annotated Bibliography, 1937–1986* (Supplements to VC 8; Leiden: Brill, 1988).
Sandmel, S., *Philo of Alexandria* (Oxford Univ., 1979).
Terian, A., "Had the Works of Philo Been Newly Discovered," BA 57 (1994), 86–97.
Wolfson, H. A., *Philo: Foundations of Religious Philosophy in Judaism* (2 vols.; Cambridge, MA: Harvard, 1947). A classic.

GNOSTICISM:

Foerster, W., *Gnosis* (2 vols.; Oxford: Clarendon, 1972–74). Translation of select patristic evidence and texts.
Layton, B., *The Gnostic Scriptures* (Garden City, NY: Doubleday, 1987). Translation of select patristic evidence, Nag Hammadi, and other texts with helpful background.
Robinson, J. M., *The Nag Hammadi Library* (3d ed.; San Francisco: Harper & Row, 1988). The complete corpus translated.
Evans, C. A., et al., *Nag Hammadi Texts and the Bible: a Synopsis and Index* (Leiden: Brill, 1993).
Franzmann, M., *Jesus in the Nag Hammadi Writings* (Edinburgh: Clark, 1996).
Hedrick, C. W., and R. Hodgson, *Nag Hammadi, Gnosticism, and Early Christianity* (Peabody, MA: Hendrickson, 1986).
Jonas, H., *The Gnostic Religion* (2d ed.; Boston: Beacon, 1963). A classic.
Logan, A.H.B., *Gnostic Truth and Christian Heresy* (Edinburgh: Clark, 1995).
———, and A.J.M. Wedderburn, *The New Testament and Gnosis* (R. M. Wilson Festschrift; Edinburgh: Clark, 1983).
MacRae, G. W., *Studies in the New Testament and Gnosticism* (Wilmington: Glazier, 1987).
Pagels, E. H., *The Gnostic Gospels* (New York: Random House, 1979).

Perkins, P., *The Gnostic Dialogue: The Early Church and the Crisis of Gnosticism* (New York: Paulist, 1980).

———, *Gnosticism and the New Testament* (Minneapolis: A/F, 1993).

Rudolph, K., *Gnosis: The Nature and History of Gnosticism* (San Francisco: Harper & Row, 1983).

———, "Gnosticism," ABD 2.1033–40.

Scholer, D. M., ed., *Nag Hammadi Bibliography, 1970–1994* (Leiden: Brill, 1996).

———, *Studies in Early Christianity. Vol. 5: Gnosticism in the Early Church* (New York: Garland, 1993).

Wilson, R. M., *Gnosis and the New Testament* (Philadelphia: Fortress, 1968).

Yamauchi, E., *Pre-Christian Gnosticism* (2d ed.; Grand Rapids: Eerdmans, 1983).

PART II

THE GOSPELS AND RELATED WORKS

Gospels in General; Synoptic Gospels

Mark

Matthew

Luke

Acts of the Apostles

John

Three Johannine Epistles

CHAPTER 6

GOSPELS IN GENERAL; SYNOPTIC GOSPELS IN PARTICULAR

This Chapter deals with two interrelated problems. There is a serious debate about the extent to which the literary genre of a Gospel is unique to Christianity or is a modification of the pattern of Jewish lives of the prophets or of Pagan biographies.[1] The answer in part depends on the relationship of the Gospels to Jesus: Does the earliest canonical Gospel derive from memories of what Jesus did and said in his lifetime, or is it mostly an imaginative creation retrojecting beliefs about the postresurrectional Jesus into his lifetime? The first three subdivisions of this Chapter will treat general Gospel questions: *Use of the word "gospel"; Origin of the Gospel genre;* and the *Three stages of Gospel formation.*

Beyond the general picture there are questions about the Synoptic Gospels in particular. The very close parallels among these three Gospels suggest borrowing from one another, but in what direction? Was Mark the earliest Gospel, so that Matt and Luke drew upon it? Or was Mark a digest from Matt and Luke? Were Matt and Luke written independently of each other, or did the Lucan writer draw on Matt (as well as on Mark)? Two final subdivisions will treat the *Synoptic problem* and the *Existence of "Q."*

Use of the Word "Gospel"

In NT times *euaggelion* ("good announcement," the word we translate "gospel") did not refer to a book or writing but to a proclamation or message. This is understandable given the background of the term. Words related to it were employed in nonChristian Greek for good news, especially news of victory in battle; and in the imperial cult the emperor's birth and presence constituted good news for the Roman world. LXX words related to *euaggelion* translate words from the Hebrew *bśr,* which has a similar range of proclaiming good news, especially of Israel's victory or God's victory. More

[1]The debate centers on the Synoptic Gospels since the more radical wing of scholarship does not consider John a Gospel in the sense in which the others are (p. 362 below).

widely it can cover the proclamation of God's glorious acts on behalf of Israel.

Scholars debate whether Jesus himself used "gospel" to describe his proclamation of the kingdom. Certainly his followers did, with an emphasis that the good news involved what God had done in Jesus. In Rom 1:3–4 Paul describes his gospel in terms that were probably already known to the Romans; it comprises the twofold identity of Jesus, namely, from the seed of David according to the flesh, and designated Son of God in power according to the Spirit of holiness by resurrection of/from the dead. More commonly for Paul the heart of the gospel is centered in Jesus' suffering/death/resurrection and its power for justification and ultimately salvation (Rom 1:16).

Mark 1:1 opens his account with the words: "The beginning of the gospel of Jesus Christ." The good news of what God has done, once proclaimed to Israel, will now be proclaimed in and through Jesus Christ to all the nations (13:10). It involves the kingdom or rule of God that is made present in Jesus' forgiving sins, healing the sick, feeding the hungry, raising the dead, calming storms—a kingdom/rule proclaimed in his teachings and parables that seek to point out and counteract human obstacles. Jesus is a king whom God makes triumphant even when enemies have crucified him. While neither Matt nor Luke begins in the same way as Mark, their basic gospel outlook is much the same. Matt has Jesus proclaiming the gospel of the kingdom (4:23; 9:35; 24:14), and Luke uses the verbal form *euaggelizein* ("to proclaim the good news") to describe this activity (8:1; 16:16). Since both these writings commence with two chapters of infancy story, their version of the good news also involves the marvelous conception and birth of Jesus (e.g., Luke 2:10). Although John has content about Jesus similar to that of the Synoptics, neither *euaggelion* nor the verbal form appears. However I John (1:5; 3:11) uses the related term *aggelia* ("message") which may have been the Johannine designation for what we know as the Gospel according to John.

The 2d century furnishes attestation of *euaggelion* employed for Christian writings.[2] The plurality of written gospels necessitated the utilization of distinguishing designations, and so by the end of the 2d century titles were prefaced to the canonical Gospels in the pattern "The Gospel according to . . ." (For the debate about the number of authentic Gospels, see p. 13 above.) The existence of gospels beyond the canonical is a question complicated by issues of terminology: (a) Relatively few noncanonical works call

[2]Teachings are said to be found or not found in "the Gospel" by *Didache* 15:3–4; *II Clement* 8:5; *Martyrdom of Polycarp* 4:1. H. Koester, NTS 35 (1989), 361–81, would trace the usage to Marcion who was protesting against oral traditions to which churches attributed apostolic authority.

themselves gospels. For instance, the *Protevangelium* (i.e., Protogospel) *of James,* most of the Nag Hammadi collection, and what we have of the *Gospel of Peter* do not describe themselves as "gospel"; (b) The title "gospel" has been used to refer to noncanonical works independently of their self-designation. Sometimes the usage is neutral and intended simply to designate a work about Jesus, as distinct from epistles, apocalypses, etc. Sometimes the usage is tendentious, wishing to claim for a noncanonical work rank equal to that of a canonical work. In antiquity this might have been a claim of those whom the larger church designated as heretics; today it is sometimes the practice of revisionist scholars trying to dethrone the canon. As an example of the wideness of use, under the title *The Complete Gospels* (Sonoma, CA: Polebridge, 1992) R. J. Miller (ed.) gives the text of seventeen works (plus some loose sayings): the four canonical Gospels; two completely hypothetical reconstructions (a collection of signs from John, and Q from Matt and Luke); four fragments of papyrus that bear no self-designation; two works about Jesus' infancy, neither of which designates itself a gospel; four Nag Hammadi collections of sayings, none of which in its own text designates itself a gospel;[3] and *the Secret Gospel of Mark* that Clement of Alexandria describes as a conflated form of canonical Mark.

Because of these terminological complications it may be useful to keep distinct two categories: "Jesus material" (infancy and passion narratives, sayings collections, miracle collections, discourses attributed to the risen Jesus—without arguing whether or not they were called "gospels" in antiquity or should be called that today); and "gospels," i.e., full narratives such as we encounter in the four canonical writings (covering at least a span of public ministry/passion/resurrection, and combining miracles and sayings).[4] Let me emphasize that this distinction is only a judgment of utility for the sake of the following discussion about the genre of full narrative "gospels," not a prejudicial judgment relative to the value or antiquity of the "Jesus material."

[3]An appended title calls the *Gospel of Thomas* a gospel; it and the *Gospel of Mary* speak of preaching the good news.

[4]Here as elsewhere, except in italicized titles of works, capital "G" will be kept for the canonical gospels. In the apocrypha of the first few centuries we have preserved no full narrative gospels. Some might wish to argue that *Secret Mark,* since it was a conflated form of Mark, was a full narrative gospel; however, we possess only two small passages and therefore are not certain to what extent the whole work was truly distinct from Mark. Of the *Gospel of Peter* (*GPet*) we have preserved only a partial passion/resurrection narrative. Origen knew of a Petrine gospel that contained an infancy narrative (BDM 2.1337)—if that was the same work, *GPet* was probably a full narrative gospel.

Origin of the Gospel Genre

How did the idea of writing the Gospels come about? Did it have its origin in the OT? Was it an imitation of a Greco-Roman genre? Was it a unique creative insight of Mark, with the implication that Matt, Luke, and John then copied Mark's approach? Or was it rather a natural development from early Christian preaching so that the basic idea could be preMarcan and more widespread? Scholars have tended to advocate with exclusiveness one or the other of those approaches.[5] Let me explain elements that contribute to the various solutions, holding open the possibility of combining some of them.

ORIGIN IN THE OT AND JEWISH DEVELOPMENTS DERIVATIVE FROM THE OT. Swartley, *Israel's Scripture,* contends that the structure of the Synoptic Gospels was dictated by the OT story of God's dealing with Israel. In the Book of Jeremiah, one has the prophet's background and dating (1:1–3), a report of his call (including a reference to God's planning before he was born: 1:4–10), an account of his words or speeches and of his prophetic actions (see especially his actions and words in the Temple area in chap. 7), warnings of impending doom for Jerusalem, and a type of passion narrative (chaps. 26, 37–38). Although the proportion of Jeremiah's oracular speeches is much higher than that of Jesus' words in the canonical Gospels, the Book of Jeremiah illustrates the joining in one work of many elements that are joined in the Gospels. By the 1st century AD we find a Jewish work, the *Lives of the Prophets,*[6] which recounts a few or many details about the various prophets: e.g, birth, signs, dramatic deeds, death, and burial place. Probably written in Greek, this work may reflect the influence of the ancient biographies we now describe. (Readers are cautioned not to think of modern biographies.)

ORIGIN IN IMITATION OF SECULAR BIOGRAPHIES. Among the abundant Greco-Roman literature of the centuries immediately before and after Christ were various types of biography, e.g., Plutarch's *Lives* of famous Greeks and Romans, Suetonius' *Lives of the Caesars,* Philostratus' *Life of Apollonius of Tyana,* and Diogenes Laertius' *Lives of the Ancient Philosophers.*[7] Those proposed as counterparts to the Gospels have divergent tonalities.

First, scholars sometimes speak of "aretalogy" as a special genre of biog-

[5]In general I shall reserve to Chapter 11 below a discussion of other hypotheses peculiar to the study of John.

[6]*Lives* (OTP 2.385–99) has a complicated history, including seemingly some Christian additions. See Appendix II below.

[7]One could include also the *Memorabilia* of Socrates by Xenophon and the biographical elements about Socrates in Plato's *Dialogues;* see the study of Votaw, *Gospels* 30–62. (In part the biography parallels were offered as a reaction to the thesis that the Gospels were a type of popular literature distinct from the more classical literature.) Votaw, Talbert, Burridge, and Stanton (for Matt) have been leading exponents of the biography approach to the Gospels.

raphy where a divine man (*theios anēr*) with preternatural gifts works miracles. Despite the appeal to Philostratus, it is not clear that such a definable genre existed; and many of the parallels are postMarcan. Second, Shuler, *Genre,* points to the "laudatory biography" where the primary concern was to show the greatness of the figure. In the case of the philosophers especially, there is emphasis on their teachings and an idealization of the noblest in their life, designed to encourage appreciation and imitation. However, diversities among the proposed laudatory biographies have to be overlooked to isolate such a subgenre, and so its definability is uncertain. Third, Talbert, *What,* considers the portrayal of "immortals" and of "eternals." Humans (sometimes sired by gods) could become immortals at death, whereas eternals were divine beings who descended to earth, lived as humans, and then ascended to heaven again. He contends that Matt, Mark, and Luke present Jesus as an immortal, whereas John portrays him as an eternal—a comparison that needs serious qualification.[8]

In fact, considerable differences exist between Greco-Roman biographies and the Gospels, specifically in the latter's anonymity, their clear theological emphasis and missionary goal,[9] their anticipated ecclesiology, their composition from community tradition, and their being read in community worship. Especially Mark differs from a biography pattern that would highlight the unusual birth and early life of the hero, plus his triumph—or if he was unjustly treated, his fearless and noble acceptance. However, these dissimilarities between the Gospels and Greco-Roman biography are observable from the scholarly point of view and take into account what the evangelists probably intended. It is likely that many 1st-century hearers/readers familiar with Greco-Roman biographies would not have been so precise and would have thought of the Gospels almost as lives of Christ, particularly Matt and Luke which begin with an infancy narrative.

CREATIVITY AND THE GOSPELS. If Mark was the earliest Gospel, was the Gospel a unique Marcan creation? Despite the suggestions in the two preceding paragraphs, there is a uniqueness to the Gospels. Even though the idea of writing a description of Jesus' career might have been catalyzed by the existence of lives of the prophets, famous philosophers, and world figures, what is narrated about Jesus is scarcely governed by a simple desire to

[8]The Synoptic Gospels do not present Jesus simply as a mortal who gains immortality as a reward; rather the resurrection primarily confirms the truth of what he already was before death. John does not present an eternal descending to earth and living as a human, but rather a divine Word that *became* flesh and remained flesh. Aune, "Problem," offers an extended critique of Talbert.

[9]One could argue that the Gospels are christology in narrative form, and Tolbert, *Sowing,* points to the ancient novel. Stanton, "Matthew," however, objects that, while there are some similar literary conventions, novels were meant to supply entertainment and titillation—scarcely the goal of the Gospels.

provide information (although there is an element of that in Luke [1:3–4], the closest of the four Gospels to a Greco-Roman biography) or to encourage emulation. As we saw above in discussing the word *euaggelion,* there is a sense in which what is reported is to receive a response of faith and to bring salvation. To a considerable degree John's statement of purpose in 20:31 fits all the Gospels, "These things are written that you may believe that Jesus is the Messiah, the Son of God, and that believing you may have life in his name." The appearance of the word *euaggelion* in Paul covering a content that would have a similar purpose (Rom 1:1–4; I Cor 15:1–8; cf. I Cor 11:23–26) means that Mark was certainly not the first to put together Jesus material for a salvific purpose, even though his was the earliest preserved full narrative.

How much ingenuity was required to construct a full gospel narrative about Jesus? The answer depends in part on the historicity of the narrative: Largely fiction, or largely fact? (I shall describe historical-Jesus research briefly in Appendix I, which develops many observations made in this paragraph.) On the one hand, a variety of scholars would judge much of what Mark narrates as fiction. For some the passion narrative is fictional, largely created from reflections on the OT. For some Jesus was a wisdom teacher, and the narratives of miracles and resurrection were propagandistic creations in order to make Jesus competitive with other wonder-working figures. For some Jesus was a magician who healed by various means, and the wisdom teaching was a creation in order to make him respectable. Were any of this true, much creativity would have been required to move from what Jesus was in fact to the plausible but very different picture painted in the Gospels. (In Appendix I, however, we shall see how tenuous is the evidence on which many of these claims are made.) On the other hand, an even larger number of scholars would judge much of what Mark narrates as factual. Suppose that Jesus was baptized by JBap and did proclaim the coming of God's kingdom both by sayings/parables that challenged people's entrenched attitudes and by healing the sick and expelling what he regarded as demons; suppose that he aroused the antipathy of Jewish leaders by exercising too sovereign a freedom toward the Law, by claiming to speak for God in a way they regarded as arrogant, and by challenging Temple administration through actions and warnings—then Jesus himself would have supplied the kinds of material that ultimately went into the Gospels, no matter how much that material developed over the decades that separated him from the evangelists.[10]

[10]There is a rough outline of Jesus' activity in the sermons of Acts, e.g., 2:22–24, and especially 10:37–41: It began in Galilee after JBap's baptism when Jesus was anointed with the Holy Spirit

PORTRAITS OF JESUS. Nevertheless, even in the latter understanding the production of Gospels required selection from the Jesus material. Accordingly it is helpful to keep distinct three portraits: the actual Jesus, the historical Jesus, and the Gospel Jesus. A portrait of *the actual Jesus* would involve everything of interest about him:[11] exact dates of birth and death; revealing details about his parents and family; how he got along with them and how he grew up; how and where he worked for a living before he began preaching; what he looked like; what his preferences were in food and drink; whether he got sick from time to time; whether he was humorous, friendly, and liked by villagers of Nazareth, etc. We have nothing like that detail in the Gospels, and the very lack of it is why many scholars resist describing the Gospels as biographies or lives of Christ. Awareness of that deficiency is important for readers who might otherwise approach the Gospels in the same way they would approach the life of a famous modern figure, without any sense of tendentious Gospel selectivity.

A portrait of *the historical Jesus* is a scholarly construct based on reading beneath the Gospel surface and stripping off all interpretations, enlargements, and developments that could possibly have taken place in the thirty to seventy years that separated his public ministry and death from the written Gospels. The validity of the construct depends on the criteria employed by the investigating scholars. The detailed recognition that the Gospel picture reflects developments beyond Jesus' lifetime was first and most ardently promoted in the last two centuries by skeptics who wished to challenge traditional Christian theology; and so the initial quest for the historical Jesus had a debunking tone, as if the Christ of faith had little to do with the Jesus of history. Still today leaders of "the Jesus Seminar" (Appendix I) have publicly stated a goal of liberating Jesus from the church's proclamation of him. In fact, however, as illustrated by Meier, *Marginal,* investigation of the historical Jesus, while it can never be purely objective, needs not be slanted by such prejudices. Indeed, given our modern curiosity this investigation is inevitable and justifiable and even helpful—a point that some who criticize the

---

and power; he went about doing good and healing those oppressed by the devil in the country of the Jews and Jerusalem; they hanged him on a tree, but God raised him up on the third day, and he was seen by God's chosen witnesses who ate and drank with him. C. H. Dodd (ExpTim 43 [1931–32], 396–400) suggested that this was the common preaching outline fleshed out by the Gospels. Far more likely this is an outline distilled from Luke's own Gospel which he inserted into the sermons, and which he got from Mark. Although the preaching contained Jesus material, the ordering from Galilee to Jerusalem probably reflects Mark's simplification. In the majority view John is not dependent on Mark; and while John begins with JBap's baptism and contains words and deeds of Jesus, there is no smooth movement from Galilee to Jerusalem but frequent goings back and forth.

[11] All biographies have to be selective; but here I refer to what gives vitality and color to lives of past figures so that they become understandable and their personality emerges.

excesses of the Jesus Seminar (e.g., L. T. Johnson) do not seem to appreciate sufficiently. Yet cautions are needed in such investigation. The portrait of the historical Jesus is a construct based on limited evidence and designed to produce a minimalist view that can be scientifically agreed on. It can give us at most a tiny fraction of the detail and coloring of the actual Jesus, and it will constantly change as scholarly method is refined or revised. Since the investigation strips off the christological appreciation of Jesus by his followers, the two-dimensional picture that emerges will be singularly lacking in theological and spiritual depth and almost surely will be partially distorted because it will reflect what the investigators wish to highlight. The notion that Christian faith should depend on reconstructions of the historical Jesus is a dangerous misunderstanding.

The Gospel Jesus refers to the portrait painted by an evangelist. It stems from his highly selective arrangement of Jesus material in order to promote and strengthen a faith that would bring people closer to God. The evangelist included only information that served that purpose, and the needs of the envisioned audience affected both contents and presentation. That is why the Gospels written by different evangelists for different audiences in different decades had to differ.

It may be noted that in giving names to the three pictures of Jesus I have refrained from speaking of "the real Jesus," a designation that has connotations both of truth and value. The life of the real Jesus attracted and convinced disciples who proclaimed him throughout the known world. How do the portraits of the actual Jesus, the historical Jesus, and the Gospel Jesus match up to "real" in that sense? Major aspects of the actual Jesus are unreported and thus unknowable; functionally, then, this picture of Jesus can only be partly real to subsequent generations. Because of what it excludes, especially of a religious and theological nature, the depiction of the historical Jesus (or better the "reconstructed Jesus") is the farthest from giving us the real Jesus. As we shall see in Appendix I, it is hard to see how the historical Jesus reconstructed by many scholars would attract the ardent commitment to the point of death that we know Jesus evoked from those who had known him. If one accepts that the portraits in the Gospels retain significant amounts of material from the actual Jesus and their missionary goal was not alien to his, then those portraits are as close to the real Jesus as we are likely to get. As stated in the Foreword, this *Introduction* is meant to acquaint readers with what in fact exists in the NT. Primarily, therefore, it will be concerned with the Jesus of the Gospels. Working with views held by most middle-of-the-road scholars rather than with the highly speculative, the next subsection will expound in simplified form a theory of three stages that contributed to the Gospel presentations of Jesus.[12] In terms of helping those who are not specialists to understand the Gospels, this is the most important part of the Chapter.

The Three Stages of Gospel Formation

(1) THE PUBLIC MINISTRY OR ACTIVITY OF JESUS OF NAZARETH (the first third of the 1st century AD). He did things of note, orally proclaimed his message, and interacted with others (e.g., JBap and Jewish religious figures). Jesus chose companions who traveled with him and saw and heard what he said and did. Their memories of his words and deeds supplied the raw "Jesus material." These memories were already selective since they concentrated on what pertained to Jesus' proclamation of God, not the many trivia of ordinary existence (or elements of the "actual Jesus"). On a practical level it is important for modern readers to keep reminding themselves that these were memories of what was said and done by a Jew who lived in Galilee and Jerusalem in the 20s. Jesus' manner of speaking, the problems he faced, his vocabulary and outlook were those of that specific time and place. Many failures to understand Jesus and misapplications of his thoughts stem from the fact that Gospel readers remove him from space and time and imagine that he was dealing with issues he never encountered.[13] There can even be a sophisticated form of misrepresenting Jesus by imposing on him categories that really do not fit, e.g., peasant[14] or freedom-fighter.

(2) THE (APOSTOLIC) PREACHING ABOUT JESUS (the second third of the 1st century AD). Those who had seen and heard Jesus had their following of him

[12]Critical Protestant scholarship developed the three-stage approach by discussing the effect of the variations in the *Sitz im Leben* (life-context) of a passage, i.e., the context it had in the life of Jesus, the context it had in the life of the church as it was proclaimed, and the context it has in the Gospel in which it has been incorporated. In a church document that has binding authority for Roman Catholics ("Instruction on the Historical Truth of the Gospels," April 21, 1964; NJBC 72.35) the Roman Pontifical Biblical Commission proposed the three-stage development as a way of explaining that, although they contain historical material, the Gospels are not literal history.

[13]Whether liberal or conservative, Christians make that mistake. They may ask whether Jesus would serve as a soldier in a modern war (e.g., in Vietnam) or how many sacraments he planned. The exact answers to such questions is that a Galilean Jew would not have known of the existence of Vietnam or of mechanized war, and that there was not even a word for "sacrament" at this period. What Jesus did and said has implications for these later problems; but in Christian faith the Holy Spirit clarifies that implication by a process of translating from Jesus' time to our time. When church confessional documents speak about the actions of "Jesus Christ," they are not simply talking about the Jesus of the public ministry but about the Jesus portrayed in apostolic preaching and subsequent tradition.

[14]Criticized by Meier, *Marginal* 1.278–82: Jesus lived in an agrarian society but had a trade as a woodworker (Mark 6:3). By way of modern parallel, Meier maintains that Jesus would have been closer "to a blue-collar worker in lower-middle-class America" than to a peasant. See p. 67 above.

confirmed through postresurrectional appearances (I Cor 15:5–7); and they came to full faith in the risen Jesus as the one through whom God had manifested ultimate salvific love to Israel and eventually to the whole world—a faith they vocalized through confessional titles (Messiah/Christ, Lord, Savior, Son of God, etc.). That postresurrectional faith illumined the memories of what they had seen and heard during the preresurrectional period; and so they proclaimed his words and deeds with enriched significance. (Modern readers, accustomed to a media goal of uninvolved, factual reporting, need to recognize the very different atmosphere of early Christian preaching.) We speak of these preachers as "apostolic" because they understood themselves as sent forth (*apostellein*) by the risen Jesus, and their preaching is often described as kerygmatic proclamation (*kērygma*) intended to bring others to faith. Eventually the circle of missionary preachers was enlarged beyond the original companions of Jesus, and the faith experiences of newcomers like Paul enriched what was received and proclaimed.

Another factor operative in this stage of development was the necessary adaptation of the preaching to a new audience. If Jesus was a Galilean Jew of the first third of the 1st century who spoke Aramaic, by midcentury his gospel was being preached in the diaspora to urban Jews and Gentiles in Greek, a language that he did not normally speak (if he spoke it at all). This change of language involved translation in the broadest sense of that term, i.e., a rephrasing in vocabulary and patterns that would make the message intelligible and alive for new audiences. Sometimes the rephrasing (which has left visible traces in the written Gospels) affected incidentals, e.g., a type of tile roof familiar to a Greek audience in Luke 5:19, as contrasted with the Palestinian-style roof through which a hole was opened in Mark 2:4. But other rephrasing had theological repercussions, e.g., the choice of *sōma,* "body" for the eucharistic component in the Synoptics and I Cor 11:24 (as distinct from the more literal translation *sarx,* "flesh" in John 6:51 and Ignatius, *Romans* 7:3). That choice may have facilitated the figurative use of body in the theology of the body of Christ of which Christians are members (I Cor 12:12–27). Thus developments in the Jesus tradition were promoting the growth of Christian theology.

Most often "preaching" serves as the umbrella term for this second stage of Gospel development, although other formative elements contributed to the Gospel end-products. For instance, liturgy or worship became part of Christian life as seen in Gospel baptismal and eucharistic formulas. The shaping of material by catechesis can be detected in Matt. Community controversies supplied coloration, e.g., struggles with Jewish synagogue leaders (in Matt and John) and internally with some who cry "Lord, Lord" in Matt 7:21 (against spiritual enthusiasts?).

(3) THE WRITTEN GOSPELS (the last third of the 1st century, approximately). Although in the middle of the previous period as the Jesus material was being preached some early written collections (now lost) would have appeared, and although preaching based on *oral* preservation and development of the Jesus material continued well into the 2d century,[15] the era 65–100 was probably when all four canonical Gospels were written. As for the evangelists or Gospel writers/authors, according to traditions stemming from the 2d century and reflected in titles prefaced to the Gospels *ca.* 200 or even earlier, two Gospels were attributed to apostles (Matthew and John) and two to apostolic men (i.e., companions of the apostles: Mark [of Peter] and Luke [of Paul]). Yet most modern scholars do not think that the evangelists were eyewitnesses of the ministry of Jesus. This surely represents a change of view;[16] but the denial of the tradition may not be so sharp as it first seems, for the early traditions about authorship may not always have referred to the evangelist who composed the final Gospel. Ancient attribution may have been concerned with the one responsible for the tradition preserved and enshrined in a particular Gospel (i.e., to the *authority* behind the Gospel), or to the one who wrote one of the main sources of the Gospel. See p. 209 below for the problem of what Papias meant when he stated, "Matthew arranged in order the sayings [*logia*] in the Hebrew [= Aramaic?] language, and each one interpreted/translated them as he was able" (EH 3.39.16).

The recognition that the evangelists were not eyewitnesses of Jesus' ministry is important for understanding the differences among the Gospels. In the older approach, wherein the evangelists themselves were thought to have seen what they reported, it was very difficult to explain differences among their Gospels. How could eyewitness John (chap. 2) report the cleansing of the Temple at the beginning of the ministry and eyewitness Matthew (chap. 21) report the cleansing of the Temple at the end of the ministry? In order to reconcile them, interpreters would contend that the Temple-cleansing happened twice and that each evangelist chose to report only one of the two instances.[17] However, if neither evangelist was an eyewitness and each had received an account of the Temple-cleansing from an intermediate source, neither one (or only one) may have known when it occurred during the pub-

[15]*Ca.* AD 115 Papias, bishop of Hierapolis, was seeking out those who had been with the older apostolic generation or their immediate followers, looking for oral tradition independent of the written Gospels that he also knew (EH 3.39.3–4).

[16]At least about Matt and John. Luke 1:2–3 states clearly that the writer was not one of the eyewitnesses although he drew on them.

[17]Many other examples of improbable reconciliations could be offered. Since Matt has a Sermon on the Mount and Luke has a similar Sermon on the Plain (Matt 5:1; Luke 6:17), there must have been a plain on the side of the mountain. Since Matt has the Lord's Prayer taught in that sermon and

lic ministry. Rather than depending on a personal memory of events, each evangelist has arranged the material he received in order to portray Jesus in a way that would meet the spiritual needs of the community to which he was addressing the Gospel. *Thus the Gospels have been arranged in logical order, not necessarily in chronological order.* The evangelists emerge as authors, shaping, developing, pruning the transmitted Jesus material, and as theologians, orienting that material to a particular goal.

Corollaries of this approach to Gospel formation would include the following:

- The Gospels are not literal records of the ministry of Jesus. Decades of developing and adapting the Jesus tradition had intervened. How much development? That has to be determined by painstaking scholarship which most often produces judgments ranging from possibility to probability, but rarely certainty.
- A thesis that does not present the Gospels as literal history is sometimes interpreted to mean that they are not true accounts of Jesus. Truth, however, must be evaluated in terms of the intended purpose. The Gospels might be judged untrue if the goal was strict reporting or exact biography; but if the goal was to bring readers/hearers to a faith in Jesus that opens them to God's rule or kingdom, then adaptations that make the Gospels less than literal (adding the dimension of faith, adjusting to new audiences) were made precisely to facilitate that goal and thus to make the Gospels true.
- To some such an approach to Gospel truth is unsatisfactory since, if there have been developments and adaptations, how do we know that the Gospels offer a message faithful to that of Jesus? Scholars cannot be certain guides since they disagree widely on the amount of alteration, ranging from major to minor. This is a theological issue, and so a theological answer is appropriate. Those who believe in inspiration will maintain that the Holy Spirit guided the process, guaranteeing that the end-product Gospels reflect the truth that God sent Jesus to proclaim.
- Much time has been spent in the history of exegesis harmonizing Gospel differences, not only in minor matters but also on a large scale, e.g., trying to make one, sequential narrative out of the very different Matthean and Lucan infancy narratives, or out of Luke's account of appearances of the risen Jesus in Jerusalem and Matt's account of an appearance on a mountain in Galilee. Besides asking whether this is possible, we need to ask whether such harmonization is not a distortion. In an outlook of faith, divine providence furnished

---

Luke has it later on the road to Jerusalem (Matt 6:9–13; Luke 11:2–4), the disciples must have forgotten it, causing Jesus to repeat it. Mark 10:46 places the healing of the blind man after Jesus left Jericho, while Luke 18:35; 19:1 places it before Jesus entered Jericho. Perhaps Jesus was leaving the site of OT Jericho and entering the site of NT Jericho!

four different Gospels, not a harmonized version; and it is to the individual Gospels, each with its own viewpoint, that we should look. Harmonization, instead of enriching, can impoverish.

- In the last half of the 20th century respect for the individuality of each Gospel had an effect on church liturgy or ritual. Many churches have followed the lead of the Roman Catholic liturgical reformation in introducing a three-year lectionary where in the first year the Sunday Gospel readings are taken from Matt, in the second year from Mark, and in the third year from Luke. In the Roman church this replaced a one-year lectionary where without any discernible theological pattern the reading was taken one Sunday from Matt, another Sunday from Luke, etc. A major factor in making the change was the recognition that Gospel pericopes should be read sequentially within the same Gospel if one is to do justice to the theological orientation given to those passages by the individual evangelist. For instance, a parable that appears in all three Synoptic Gospels can have different meanings depending on the context in which each evangelist has placed it.

The Synoptic Problem

A further stage in Gospel development is required to explain the interrelationship of the first three Gospels, called "Synoptic" because they can be reviewed side by side (syn-optically). These Gospels have so much in common that in the third stage described above there must have been some dependence of one or two on the other or on a common written source. Although much scholarly attention and even passion has been devoted to this problem, most readers of the NT find the issue complex, irrelevant to their interests, and boring—a fact that causes me to be succinct in my treatment. Ample bibliography will be given; but beginners are warned that the subject tends to generate complexity, and they may want to settle for the most common conclusions that I have italicized below (pp. 114, 115, 122).

Statistics and terminology: Mark has 661 verses (vv.); Matt has 1,068, and Luke has 1,149. Eighty percent of Mark's vv. are reproduced in Matt and 65 percent in Luke.[18] The Marcan material found in both the other two is called the "Triple Tradition." The approximate 220–235 vv. (in whole or in part) of nonMarcan material that Matt and Luke have in common is called the "Double Tradition." In both instances so much of the order in which that common material is presented, and so much of the wording in which it is phrased are the same that dependence at the written rather than simply at

[18]Numbers drawn from Neirynck, NJBC 40:5. Very few Marcan pericopes have no parallel in either Matt or Luke.

the oral level has to be posited.[19] Let me simply list some proposals offered to explain these statistics, including for each the main argument(s) pro and con. Finally I shall draw out corollaries from the most commonly accepted solution.

SOLUTIONS THAT POSIT ONE OR MORE PROTOGOSPELS. There have been many proposals (some having no major following today) that would explain the interrelationships of the Synoptic Gospels by positing a gospel that existed before they were written. In the 18th century G. E. Lessing suggested that all three Synoptic Gospels drew on a no-longer-extant Aramaic Gospel, a theory developed by J. Eichhorn, who thought of this source as a full life of Christ. A variant of this thesis has been revived by those who would make apocryphal gospels the source of the canonical Gospels. (The *Gospel of Thomas* will be discussed in relation to the Q hypothesis mentioned below.) *Secret Mark,* a conflated form of Mark known to Clement of Alexandria and thought by many to have been composed in the early 2d century, is claimed by M. Smith to represent more closely than do the canonical Gospels the oldest detectable Christian gospel source, and H. Koester would contend that *Secret Mark* itself was actually written before canonical Mark. The fact that all we know of this gospel is two small fragments and that they can be understood as drawn from the canonical Gospels has discouraged wide acceptance of such claims.[20] In addition to *Secret Mark* J. D. Crossan posits the priority of a shorter form of the *Gospel of Peter* from which all four canonical Gospels drew their passion accounts. Again the majority view is that *GPet* is dependent on the canonical Gospels.[21]

In a more traditional search for a protogospel, some would invoke Papias ("Matthew arranged in order the sayings in the Hebrew [= Aramaic?] language": p. 209 below) and contend that he was speaking not about the Matt

[19]Tuckett, ABD 6.263–64, cites two examples of order and wording as demanding more than oral dependence. Matt (14:3–12) and Mark (6:17–29) both stop the narrative of Jesus' ministry after his return to Nazareth to report the death of JBap; all three Gospels have the same interrupted sentence when Jesus speaks to the paralytic (Matt 9:6; Mark 2:10–11; Luke 5:24). The order of Mark may agree with that of Matt, or that of Luke, or with that of both—however, Matt and Luke never agree against Mark in order. (For seven proposed instances to the contrary, see Fitzmyer, *Luke* 1:68–69: Five are instances of dependence on Q rather than on Mark; two are very dubious.) In itself, that pattern of agreement would not prove that Mark was written first and the other two drew on it, but only that Mark somehow stands between Matt and Luke.

[20]M. Smith, *Clement of Alexandria and a Secret Gospel of Mark* (Cambridge, MA: Harvard, 1973); also HTR 75 (1982), 449–61; H. Koester in *Colloquy on New Testament Studies,* ed. B. Corley (Macon, GA: Mercer, 1983), 35–57; M. W. Meyer, *Semeia* 49 (1990), 129–53. Critique: R. E. Brown, CBQ 36 (1974), 466–85; F. Neirynck, *Evangelica II* (BETL 99; Leuven Univ., 1991), 716–24.

[21]J. D. Crossan, *Four Other Gospels* (Minneapolis: Winston, 1985); *The Cross That Spoke* (San Francisco: Harper & Row, 1988); *Semeia* 49 (1990), 155–68. Critique: R. E. Brown, NTS 33 (1987), 321–43; BDM 2.1317–49; F. Neirynck, *Evangelica II,* 2.732–49; D. F. Wright, *Themelios* 12 (2; Jan. 1987), 56–60; A. Kirk, NTS 40 (1994), 572–95.

we know but about an earlier collection (at times designated M) on which Mark drew and also canonical Matt (whether directly or through Mark). Supposedly this hypothetical collection contained what cannot easily be explained by deriving Mark from canonical Matt or vice versa.[22] Other scholars judge necessary a more complex multidocument theory, e.g., the source was not simply Aramaic M but a Greek translation of M, plus an Aramaic collection of sayings translated into Greek. Oral sources alongside the written are also posited. In a three-volume French Synopsis produced in the 1970s, M.-É. Boismard and A. Lamouille detect four source documents drawn on by the Synoptic evangelists, not directly but on a preGospel level: Document A of Palestinian and Jewish Christian origin *ca.* AD 50; Document B, a reinterpretation of A for Gentile Christians written before AD 58; Document C, an independent Palestinian tradition in Aramaic, very archaic and perhaps the memoirs of Peter—used also in John; Document Q containing material common to Matt and Luke. This type of theory virtually posits a new source to solve every difficulty. It cannot be proved wrong or right, but most will find it too complex to help in the ordinary study of the Gospels. In fact, the scholarly majority in its effort to explain Synoptic differences and similarities, rather than positing no-longer-extant protogospels and very early apocrypha, draws on a relationship among the extant Gospels, i.e., mutual-dependence solutions to which we now turn.

SOLUTIONS IN WHICH MATT WAS THE FIRST GOSPEL, AND LUKE USED MATT. This hypothesis, dating back to Augustine in the 4th century, is the oldest explanation; it was generally accepted by Roman Catholics up to the mid-20th century, and still has respectable advocates (B. C. Butler; J. W. Deardorf; J. Wenham). In this Augustinian approach the canonical order is also the order of dependence: Matt was written first, Mark severely abbreviated Matt, and then came Luke and John, with each drawing on its predecessors. In 1789 J. J. Griesbach proposed a theory of dependence in which the order was Matt, Luke, and Mark.[23] The underpinning of the Matthean priority proposal is that from antiquity Matt has been considered the first Gospel. Explaining Mark is the greatest difficulty in any hypothesis that gives priority to Matt. In the Augustinian hypothesis what was Mark's logic in omitting so much of Matt's account? The Griesbach hypothesis attempts to meet that difficulty by placing Mark last and evaluating it mostly as a digest that re-

[22]Other protogospel theories include *protoMark* (C. Lachmann; H. J. Holtzmann), which Matt and Luke used rather than canonical Mark, and *protoLuke* (B. H. Streeter), consisting of Q and special Lucan material and composed by Luke before he added material influenced by Mark.

[23]He was not clear as to whether Luke depended on Matt, but the modified Griesbach hypothesis advocated today does suppose such dependence. Prominent supporters are W. R. Farmer, B. Orchard, and D. L. Dungan.

ports material where Matt and Luke agree. Yet Mark omits the whole Double Tradition where they do agree!

The main support for the thesis that Luke used Matt lies in passages in the Triple Tradition where Luke and Matt agree, over against Mark, i.e., the "Minor Agreements." For instance, in the Jewish mockery of Jesus both Matt and Luke have Jesus being asked an identically worded question absent from Mark: "Who is it that struck you?"—a quotation that makes better sense of the challenge to prophesy (Matt 26:68; Luke 22:64; Mark 14:65). If Luke and Matt wrote independently of each other, could such an agreement have come about by pure coincidence? Is it not more plausible that Luke copied the question from Matt?[24] Yet there are major arguments against Lucan dependence on Matt (see Fitzmyer, *Luke* 1.73–75). Where Luke and Matt have almost contradictory accounts, why did Luke not make some effort to reconcile the difficulty? For example, Luke's infancy narrative is not only massively different from Matt's, but also in details is virtually irreconcilable with it, e.g., about Joseph and Mary's home (in Bethlehem in Matt 2:11 [house]; in Nazareth in Luke 2:4–7, with no home in Bethlehem) and about their travels after the birth of Jesus (to Egypt in Matt 2:14; to Jerusalem and Nazareth in Luke 2:22,39). Or again, Luke's account of the death of Judas in Acts 1:18–19 is scarcely reconcilable with Matt 27:3–10. As for order, if Luke used Matt, why does Luke's placing of the Q material differ so greatly from Matt's (except for the words of JBap and the temptation story: see Table 2 below)? That argument becomes stronger if Luke used Mark as well (Augustinian thesis), for Luke follows Mark's order closely. Another problem would be Luke's failure to report the Matthean additions to Mark, e.g., Matt 3:14–15; 12:5–7; 16:17–19; 21:14–16; 26:52–54.

SOLUTIONS BASED ON MARCAN PRIORITY. Mark was written first and both Matt and Luke drew on it. There is a form of this approach that goes on to hold that Luke drew on Matt as well, but it faces the difficulties recounted in the last paragraph. *The most common thesis, therefore, posits that Matt and Luke depended on Mark and wrote independently of each other.* What they have in common and did not derive from Mark (the Double Tradition) is explained by positing Q (a source reconstructed entirely from Matt and Luke to be discussed in the next subsection). Thus this is known as the Two-Source Theory.[25]

[24]W. D. Davies and Allison, *Matthew* 109–14, answer carefully objections raised against Q on this basis by Stoldt (*History*); also see n. 26 below. Ironically, the Minor Agreements offer difficulties for the rest of the Griesbach hypothesis, e.g., in the example just cited from the mockery, if Mark used Matt and Luke, why did Mark omit the question that both Gospels have and that improves the sense?

[25]Actually both Matt and Luke are posited to have drawn on special material for many passages that appear in only one of the two Gospels, and thus on a type of third source; but here we are discussing solutions offered for what the Synoptics have in common.

We may compare it to the Griesbach hypothesis thus:

The basic argument for Marcan priority is that it solves more problems than any other theory. It offers the best explanation for why Matt and Luke so often agree with Mark in order and wording, and allows reasonable surmises for why Matt and Luke differ from Mark when they do so independently. For instance, neither evangelist liked Mark's redundancies, awkward Greek expressions, uncomplimentary presentation of the disciples and Mary, and embarrassing statements about Jesus. When using Mark, both expanded the Marcan accounts in the light of postresurrectional faith. The basic argument against Marcan priority rests on the Minor Agreements cited above in reference to the Griesbach hypothesis. Good explanations can be offered for many of them,[26] but some remain very difficult.

A realistic conclusion is that *no solution to the Synoptic Problem solves all difficulties.* Modern authors whose own books require research and who attempt after several decades the almost impossible task of reconstructing precisely how they had put their sources together in writing those books will be sympathetic to our inability to reconstruct precisely the way the evangelists proceeded 1,900 years ago. The process was probably more complex than the most complex modern reconstruction. If one cannot resolve all the enigmas, it is realistic to accept and work with a relatively simple solution to the Synoptic Problem that is largely satisfactory. That is the spirit in which the theory of Marcan priority (as part of the Two-Source Theory) is recommended to Gospel readers. Even though it remains a hypothesis, one should be aware that important consequences flow from accepting it.

These are some *points to be kept in mind when working with Marcan priority:*

- Even when Mark was written, the remembrance of oral tradition about Jesus did not cease. Too often we imagine the composition of the Gospels as totally

[26]See Neirynck, *Minor Agreements* and "The Minor Agreements and Q" in Piper, *Gospel,* 49–72. Also T. A. Friedrichsen in *L'Évangile de Luc,* ed. F. Neirynck (rev. ed.; BETL 32: Leuven: Peeters, 1989), 335–92; R. H. Stein, CBQ 54 (1992), 482–502. Omissions are less difficult since coincidentally both evangelists may have found Mark needlessly troublesome, e.g., both Matt 26:45 and Luke 22:46 omit the virtually untranslatable *apechei* ("it is enough/paid") of Mark 14:41. As for augmentations, in a few of the Minor Agreements a minority of textual witnesses to Mark agree with what Matt and Luke have added (e.g., adding "and perverse" in Mark 9:19, to agree with Matt 17:17; Luke 9:41); but that may result from copyists' harmonizations.

a written endeavor. Yet Papias is a witness to continued interest in oral tradition in the 2d century (n. 15 above). Scholars differ on how much of the oral tradition was memorized (on a rabbinic model) as distinct from repeated word-of-mouth transmission.[27] Many think that some problems not resolved by the Two-Source Theory can be met by bringing into the picture the influence of orally transmitted remembrances. For instance, the identical question, "Who is it that struck you?", shared by Matt and Luke over against Mark (see above), might be explained as independent use of a traditional question in the blindman's-buff treatment of Jesus (BDM 1.579).

- If both Matt and Luke used Mark, their theology can at times be studied by the changes they made in Mark's report—redaction criticism. This has been the linchpin of some ecumenical studies tracing the development of ideas in 1st-century Christianity by moving from Mark through Matt to Luke.[28]
- If one decides that Matt or Luke has added material to what was taken from Mark, that addition, sometimes coming from the special material peculiar to either of those evangelists, need not be dated later than the Marcan material. A sensitive instance would be Matt 16:17–19 added between material borrowed from Mark 8:29 and 8:30. The added material, which has a very strong Semitic cast, may well be early.

The Existence of "Q"[29]

"Q" is a hypothetical source posited by most scholars to explain what was called above the Double Tradition, i.e., agreements (often verbal) between Matt and Luke on material not found in Mark.[30] Behind the hypothesis is the plausible assumption that the Matthean evangelist did not know Luke

[27]For some a written Gospel was an attempt, conscious or unconscious (and perhaps somewhat antagonistic) to control the vagaries of oral tradition—a theory that does not do justice to the role of apostolic authority in fashioning the Jesus tradition (I Cor 15:11). See W. H. Kelber, *The Oral and the Written Gospel* (Philadelphia: Fortress, 1983), who is debated by B. Gerhardsson, *The Gospel Tradition* (Coniectanea Neotestamentica 15; Lund: Gleerup, 1986). Cf. also *Jesus and the Oral Tradition,* ed. H. Wansbrough (Sheffield: Academic, 1991); B. W. Henaut, *Oral Tradition and the Gospels* (JSNTSup 82; Sheffield: JSOT, 1993).

[28]Thus PNT and MNT. The views of Peter and Mary grow more favorable (in a trajectory pattern) as one passes through the Gospels in the order Mark-Matt-Luke. Although some Roman Catholics have praised the Griesbach hypothesis as a more traditional approach, they are left with an unfavorable trajectory since the latest of the Synoptics (Mark) would then be the least appreciative of Peter and Mary (see p. 165 below).

[29]The designation "Q" from the German *Quelle,* "source," is thought to have begun with J. Weiss in 1890. See F. Neirynck, ETL 54 (1978), 119–25.

[30]Or at least not found in Mark in the form found in Matt and Luke. For instance Mark 1:12–13 mentions the tempting of Jesus by Satan but not in the extended form found in Matt 4:1–11 and Luke 4:1–13. Mark 3:22 reports the Beelzebul (Beelzebub) controversy but not attached to casting out a demon from a mute as in Matt 12:22–24 and Luke 11:14–15. Havener, *Q* 153–60, prints out the text of Marcan passages parallel to Q; and Fleddermann, *Mark,* offers a thorough discussion. A few scholars maintain that Mark knew Q; see I. Dunderberg, NTS 41 (1995), 501–11.

and vice versa, and so they must have had a common source. Many cautions are necessary before Q is reconstructed. The contents are usually estimated at about 220–235 verses or parts of verses.[31] Independently, however, both Matt and Luke omit passages found in Mark; therefore it is plausible that independently they have omitted material that existed in Q. Sometimes only Matt or only Luke will preserve material in Mark; it is also possible that material found only in one of the two Gospels might have existed in Q.[32] We are not certain of the sequence of material in Q because Matt and Luke do not present it in the same order; nevertheless most reconstructions follow the Lucan order, since it seems that Matt worked Q material into his large sermons (e.g., the Sermon on the Mount in chaps. 5–7, and the Mission Discourse in chap. 10). The accompanying Table shows generally agreed on contents of Q in the Lucan order; and henceforth, unless otherwise specified, in this Chapter *references to Q material will be through the Lucan versification.* Q is normally reconstructed as a Greek written document because the only guide is two Greek Gospels and because a purely oral body of tradition would not explain the large parts of the Double Tradition that are in the same order. Since Matt and Luke often do not agree in the wording of what they have derived from Q (any more than they agree in what they have derived from Mark), one has to study the tendencies of each Gospel to determine which version more likely represents a change wrought by the individual evangelist. Also it is unlikely that there was only one copy of Q in existence to which Matt and Luke had independent access, and it is possible that *some* of the differences of wording between Matt and Luke are derived from slightly variant copies of Q.[33]

Reconstructed Q consists of sayings and some parables with an absolute minimum of narrative setting;[34] and thus there is a strong sapiential tone. The discovery of the Coptic *Gospel of Thomas,* representing a Greek original

[31]Kloppenborg's very useful *Q Parallels* gives a Greek text and English translation of Q. An English text is printed out in Havener, *Q* 123–46; and in Miller, *Complete Gospels* 253–300. Lists are offered in Neirynck, NJBC 40.14; Davies and Allison, *Matthew* 1.117–18; and at the beginning of Edwards' *Concordance* (with Aland synopsis numbers). Virtually a commentary is offered by Catchpole, *Quest.* There is a vigorous scholarly debate about some verses and words; J. M. Robinson, "International," reports on the discussion of each verse.

[32]Neirynck, NJBC 40.13, mentions proposed passages: Matt 10:5b–6; 10:23; Luke 6:24–26; 9:61–62; 12:32,35–38,49–50(54–56); 15:8–10; 17:28–29. Havener, *Q* 147–51, prints out disputed texts possibly pertaining to Q.

[33]A different approach is to assume that the original of Q was in Aramaic (F. Bussby, ExpTim 65 [1954–55], 272–75—in that case Q might be identified with the supposed collection of the logia of the Lord arranged by Matthew in Hebrew/Aramaic). Matt and Luke would then have drawn on different Greek translations of that Aramaic. Relatively few differences, however, can be plausibly explained through that hypothesis.

[34]There are three narratives of note: the tempting of Jesus; the centurion's sick servant; disciples of JBap come to Jesus.

TABLE 2. MATERIAL USUALLY ALLOTTED TO Q

Matthew	Luke	Contents
3:7b–12	3:7–9,16–17	JBap: warnings, promise of one to come
4:2b–11a	4:2–13	three temptations (testings) of Jesus by the devil (different order)
5:3,6,4,11–12	6:20b–23	beatitudes (different order, wording)
5:44,39b–40,42	6:27–30	love of enemies; turn other cheek; give coat; give to beggars
7:12	6:31	what you wish others to do to you, do to them
5:46–47,45,48	6:32–33,35b–36	love more than those who love you; be merciful as the Father is
7:1–2	6:37a,38c	judge not and be not judged; measure given is measure received
15:14,10:24–25a	6:39–40	can blind lead the blind; disciple not above teacher
7:3–5	6:41–42	speck in brother's eye, log in one's own
7:16–20 (12:33–35)	6:43–45	no good tree bears bad fruit; no figs from thorns
7:21,24–27	6:46–49	calling me Lord and not doing; hearing my words and doing them
8:5a–10,13	7:1–2,6b–10	centurion at Capernaum begs help for sick servant, marvelous faith
11:2–11	7:18–28	disciples of JBap; message to him; praise of JBap as more than a prophet
11:16–19	7:31–35	this generation pleased by neither JBap nor Son of Man
8:19–22	9:57–60	Son of Man has nowhere to lay head; to follow him let dead bury dead
9:37–38; 10:7–16	10:2–12	harvest plentiful, laborers few; mission instructions
11:21–23; 10:40	10:13–16	woe to Chorazin, Bethsaida; whoever hears you, hears me
11:25–27; 13:16–17	10:21–24	thanking the Father for revealing to infants; all things given to the Son who alone knows the Father; blessed eyes that see what you see
6:9–13	11:2–4	the Lord's prayer (variant forms—Matt's longer)
7:7–11	11:9–13	ask and it will be given; if you give good gifts, how much more the Father
12:22–30	11:14–15,17–23	demons cast out by Beelzebul; strong man guards his palace; not with me, against me
12:43–45	11:24–26	unclean spirit gone out of someone returns and brings seven others, making worse
12:38–42	11:29–32	generation seeks sign; sign of Jonah; judgment by people of Nineveh, queen of south
5:15; 6:22–23	11:33–35	not putting lamp under bushel; eye lamp of body, if unsound, darkness
23:25–26,23,6–7a,27	11:39–44	Pharisees cleanse outside of cup; woe for tithing inconsequentials, seeking first place
23:4,29–31	11:46–48	woe to lawyers for binding heavy burdens, building tombs of the prophets
23:34–36,13	11:49–52	I speak/God's wisdom speaks: Will send prophets who will be persecuted; woe to lawyers

TABLE 2. *Continued.*

Matthew	Luke	Contents
10:26–33; 12:32	12:2–10	all covered to be revealed; fear not killers of body; acknowledging me before God
10:19–20	12:11–12	before synagogues, Holy Spirit will help
6:25–33	12:22–31	don't be anxious about the body; consider lilies of field; Father knows what you need
6:19–21	12:33–34	no treasures on earth but in heaven
24:43–44,45–51	12:39–40,42–46	householder and thief; faithful servant preparing for master's coming
10:34–36	12:51–53	not come to bring peace but sword; divisions of family
16:2–3	12:54–56	ability to interpret weather signs should enable to interpret present times
5:25–26	12:58–59	settling before going before the magistrate
13:31–33	13:18–21	kingdom of heaven/God: like growth of mustard seed; like leaven woman puts in meal
7:13–14,22–23; 8:11–12	13:23–29	narrow gate through which few will enter; householder refusing those who knock; people coming from all directions to enter kingdom of heaven/God
23:37–39	13:34–35	Jerusalem, killing the prophets, must bless him who comes in the Lord's name
22:2–10	14:16–24	kingdom of heaven/God: a great banquet, invitees make excuses, others invited
10:37–38	14:26–27	anyone coming must prefer me over family and must bear a cross
5:13	14:34–35	uselessness of salt that has lost its savor
18:12–14	15:4–7	man who leaves 99 sheep to go after lost one
6:24	16:13	cannot serve two masters
11:12–13; 5:18,32	16:16–18	law and prophets till JBap; not a dot of Law will pass; divorcing wife and marrying another is adultery
18:7,15,21–22	17:1,3b–4	woe to tempters; forgive brother after rebuking; Peter: how often to forgive
17:20	17:6	if you had faith like grain of mustard seed, could move mountains
24:26–28	17:23–24,37	signs of the coming of the Son of Man
24:37–39	17:26–27,30	as in the days of Noah, so will be the coming of the Son of Man
10:39	17:33	whoever finds one's life will lose it; whoever loses will find it
24:40–41	17:34–35	on that night, of two, one taken and the other left
25:14–30	19:12–27	parable of the pounds/talents
19:28	22:38,30	followers will sit on thrones judging the twelve tribes of Israel

probably of the 2d century, shows that there were Christian compositions consisting of collections of sayings. (The exact relationship between Q and *Thomas* is highly disputed, since some would date *Thomas* early while others contend that *Thomas* was produced a century after Q and with considerable dependence on the canonical Gospels.[35]) Presumably, as with other Gospel material, these sayings were preserved because they were thought to be of relevance to existing Christians. Looking down the Contents column of the Table helps to highlight the emphases of Q. There is a strongly eschatological thrust in the warnings, woes, and some of the parables. One gets the impression that judgment is imminent; yet Luke 12:39–40 shows that the hour of the master's coming is not known; 17:23–24 warns that there will be deceptive signs; and 19:12–27 suggests that there is a time period for the recipients to make profit with the pounds/talents. Accordingly Jesus' followers are expected to live a highly moral life observing even the Law (16:17) without superficial hypocrisy (11:39–44). There is expectation of persecution and encouragement for those who bear it for the sake of the Son of Man (6:22–23).

Many would attribute to Q a low christology since in it Jesus emerges simply as a Sophist or Cynic wisdom teacher. Yet the Q Jesus is to come and baptize with the Holy Spirit, as proclaimed by JBap (3:16–17; 7:18–23). He is greater than Solomon and greater than Jonah the prophet (11:31–32). He is portrayed as the Son of Man who will come in judgment (Luke 17:23–27,30,37) and as the Son of Man who is rejected and suffers in his lifetime (7:31–35; 9:57–60). He is the Son to whom all has been given; he is known only by the Father, and only he knows the Father (10:22). It is insufficient simply to call Jesus Lord; one must hear his words and do them if one is to survive (6:46–49). Jerusalem must bless him (13:34–35), and one must prefer him over family (14:26–27). He can proclaim with assurance that in the kingdom those who follow him will sit on thrones, judging the twelve tribes of Israel. Such a Jesus is far more than a wisdom teacher.

That issue leads us to a highly debatable aspect of recent Q studies: the attempt to reconstruct a Q community, its history, its theology, where it was written (usually Palestine or Syria), and its leadership (perhaps prophets). Indeed, Q has been analyzed to contain anywhere from two to four redactional layers with a theological outlook assigned to each. True, it is virtually certain that, like the rest of the Gospel material, the Q material has undergone changes (redaction) during the period before its reception into Matt

[35]Contrast S. J. Patterson, *The Gospel of Thomas and Jesus* (Sonoma, CA: Polebridge, 1993) and C. M. Tuckett, ETL 67 (1991), 346–60.

and Luke, and that sometimes by comparing the version of a saying in those two Gospels we can trace a pattern of changes. However, the assumption that we can attribute *with considerable accuracy* different emphases to different stages of growth[36] presupposes an unlikely systematization in Christian life. Much publicity has been attached to this form of reconstruction, and so for the sake of balance readers should be informed that the claims made for it are widely disputed or doubted, and not only by conservative commentators.[37]

Let me briefly report some of the claims. (*Then in parentheses I shall report observations indicating the precarious aspect of the reasoning.*) Some now refer to "the Q Gospel," often with the assumption that it has every right to be considered as important as the canonical Gospels. The classification is thought to be justified by the observation that a collection of sayings bears the name "The *Gospel* of Thomas." (Yet that title is a secondary appendage, perhaps by 2d-century gnostics trying to give *Thomas* status. F. Neirynck[38] prefers to retain the designation "the [Synoptics] Saying *Source* Q" as a reminder that Q remains a hypothetical text to which we have no direct access.) Often a basic presupposition is that Q was produced in a single community whose view it represented. (An individual, having heard sayings and parables attributed to Jesus, could have made a collection. Is there really a coherent theology that marks these juxtaposed sayings that frequently are grouped around different unifying motifs? A look at the sequence in the Contents column of Table 2 gives a rather haphazard impression.) The next presupposition is that Q represents the whole (or enough of the) outlook of those who collected it that it may be used to diagnose their stance as Christians. (The very fact that independently it was preserved by Matt and Luke only in combination with Marcan material may slant the likelihood in the other direction, i.e., that it was never more than an additional collection of teaching for those who accepted the Jesus story.) The argument from silence becomes a major factor in such a presupposition. For example, because there is no reference in the Q material to crucifixion or resurrection, it is claimed that the Q Christians ignored, rejected, or gave little importance to such belief. (In the combination they made, Matt and Luke found no contradiction

[36]Jacobson, *First,* and Kloppenborg, *Formation,* are strong advocates. For example, one approach posits a first stage of Q that was sapiential (and was close to the historical Jesus, who was not an apocalypticist), a second stage where Q was apocalypticized, and a third stage where there was a movement toward narrative and Jesus became an advocate of strict Torah observance (which made Q amenable to Matthew).

[37]See H. W. Attridge, "Reflections on Research into Q," *Semeia* 55 (1992), 222–34.

[38]"Q: From Source to Gospel," ETL 71 (1995), 421–30. Although the Q saying in Luke 7:22 speaks of the poor having the gospel preached to them (*euaggelizein*), that is borrowed from Isa 61:1.

between Q and Mark with its strong emphasis on the passion or between Q and their own emphasis on the resurrection. One cannot assume that independently two evangelists took over a source they wished to correct; rather a justifiable assumption is that Matt and Luke agreed with Q or they would not have used it. Moreover, there are some Q parallels in Mark—could the theology of Mark and Q have been so contradictory? What proof is there that any early-1st-century Christians believed in a Jesus who was not uniquely distinguished by the fact that he had been crucified and raised?[39] A rejection of crucifixion/resurrection is characteristic of a gnosticism not clearly datable before the 2d century.)

In the hypothesis that Matt and Luke used both Q and Mark, it is not unreasonable to assume that Q was as old as Mark and in existence in the 60s. Some, however, make the unprovable claim that Q is older than Mark and is indeed the oldest Christian presentation of Jesus. There is evidence against too early a dating, since certain sayings in Q suggest that an interval has passed since the time of Jesus. One has the impression from Luke 11:49–52 that Christian prophets and apostles have been persecuted. Luke 11:39–44,46–48 shows considerable hostility toward the Pharisees and lawyers; intense conflicts with Pharisees probably developed later in the history of Palestinian Christians rather than earlier.

Extravagant hypotheses based on this hypothetical document have left their mark on modern "Historical Jesus" research (see Appendix I). The portrait of Jesus the wisdom teacher or Cynic philosopher with no apocalyptic message and no messianic proclamation emerges from speculations about stage one of Q theology—a portrait that some would substitute for the Jesus of the Gospels and the Jesus of church faith.[40] A bit abrupt but worthy of reflection is the proposal of J. P. Meier, *Marginal* 2.178, that every morning exegetes should repeat, "Q is a hypothetical document whose exact extension, wording, originating community, strata, and stages of composition cannot be known." Linnemann, "Is There," is even more acerbic. That having been said, in the judgment of most, *the existence of Q (without many of the added hypotheses) remains the best way of explaining the agreements between Matt and Luke in material they did not borrow from Mark.*

[39]Q sayings relate Jesus' rejection and death to the similar fate of the prophets (13:34; 11:49; 6:23); yet there is no evidence that this connection meant that the resurrection of Jesus lacked unique value for the Christians who read/heard Q.

[40]One need not agree with Farmer's defense of the Griesbach hypothesis to realize that he is right (*Gospel*) in arguing that the solution proposed for the Synoptic Problem has pastoral relevance.

Bibliography on the Gospels in General

INTRODUCTION AND GOSPEL GENRE:

Aune, D. E., "The Problem of the Genre of the Gospels," GP 2 (1981), 9–60.
Burridge, R. A., *What Are the Gospels? A Comparison with Graeco-Roman Biography* (SNTSMS 70; Cambridge Univ., 1992).
Goosen, G., and M. Tomlinson, *Studying the Gospels: An Introduction* (Ridgefield, CT: Morehouse, 1994). Interesting popular text.
O'Grady, J. F., *The Four Gospels and the Jesus Tradition* (New York: Paulist, 1989).
Robbins, V. K., "Mark as Genre," SBLSP 1980, 371–99.
Shuler, P. L., *A Genre for the Gospels* (Philadelphia: Fortress, 1982).
Stanton, G. N., "Matthew: *Biblos, Euaggelion,* or *Bios,*" FGN 2.1187–1201.
Swartley, W. M., *Israel's Scripture Traditions and the Synoptic Gospels. Story Shaping Story* (Peabody, MA: Hendrickson, 1994).
Talbert, C. H., *What Is a Gospel? The Genre of the Canonical Gospels* (Philadelphia: Fortress, 1971).
Votaw, C. W., *The Gospels and Contemporary Biographies in the Greco-Roman World* (Facet Biblical Series 27; Philadelphia: Fortress, 1970).

THE SYNOPTIC PROBLEM:

Barr, A., *Diagram of Synoptic Relationships* (new ed.; Edinburgh: Clark, 1995).
Bellinzoni, A. J., et al., eds., *The Two-Source Hypothesis* (Macon GA: Mercer, 1985). Various views.
Butler, B. C., *The Originality of St. Matthew* (Cambridge Univ., 1951). Augustinian hypothesis.
Deardorff, J. W., *The Problems of New Testament Gospel Origins* (San Francisco, CA: Mellen, 1992). Augustinian hypothesis.
Dungan, D. L., ed., *The Interrelations of the Gospels* (BETL 95; Leuven: Peeters, 1990).
Farmer, W. R., *The Synoptic Problem* (2d ed.; Dillsboro: Western North Carolina, 1976). For Griesbach.
———, "Modern Developments of Griesbach's Hypothesis," NTS 23 (1976–77), 275–95.
———, *The Gospel of Jesus: The Pastoral Relevance of the Synoptic Problem* (Louisville: W/K, 1994).
Johnson, S. E., *The Griesbach Hypothesis and Redaction Criticism* (SBLMS 41; Atlanta: Scholars, 1991). Against Griesbach.
Longstaff, T. R. W., and P. A. Thomas, eds., *The Synoptic Problem: A Bibliography, 1916–1988* (Macon, GA: Mercer, 1988).
Neirynck, F., ed., *The Minor Agreements of Matthew and Luke against Mark* (Gembloux: Duculot, 1974).
Neville, D. J., *Arguments from Order in Synoptic Source Criticism* (Macon, GA: Mercer, 1994).
New, D. S., *Old Testament Quotations in the Synoptic Gospels and the Two-Document Hypothesis* (Atlanta: Scholars, 1993). Against Griesbach.

Orchard, B., *Matthew, Luke, and Mark* (Collegeville: Liturgical, 1976). For Griesbach.

Orchard, B., and H. Riley, *The Order of the Synoptics. Why Three Synoptic Gospels?* (Macon, GA: Mercer, 1987). For Griesbach.

Riley, H., *The Making of Mark* (Macon, GA: Mercer, 1989). For Griesbach.

Stanton, G. N., *The Gospels and Jesus* (New York: Oxford, 1989).

———, *Gospel Truth?* (Valley Forge, PA: Trinity, 1995).

Stein, R. H., *The Synoptic Problem* (Grand Rapids: Baker, 1987).

Stoldt, H.-H., *History and Criticism of the Markan Hypothesis* (Macon, GA: Mercer, 1980). Against Marcan priority.

Strecker, G., ed., *Minor Agreements* (Göttingen: Vandenhoeck & Ruprecht, 1993).

Styler, G. M., "The Priority of Mark," in Moule, *Birth* 285–316. Good confirmatory examples.

Taylor, V., *The Formation of the Gospel Tradition* (London: Macmillan, 1953). Still important.

Theissen, G., *The Gospels in Context: Social and Political History in the Synoptic Tradition* (Minneapolis: A/F, 1991).

Tuckett, C. M., *The Revival of the Griesbach Hypothesis* (SNTSMS 44; Cambridge Univ., 1982). Against Griesbach.

Wenham, J., *Redating Matthew, Mark & Luke* (Downers Grove, IL: InterVarsity, 1992). Augustinian hypothesis.

"Q" RESEARCH:

Boring, M. E., *Sayings of the Risen Jesus* (SNTSMS 46; Cambridge Univ., 1982).

———, *The Continuing Voice of Jesus* (Louisville: W/K, 1992). A revision of the above.

Catchpole, D. R., *The Quest for Q* (Edinburgh: Clark, 1993).

Downing, F. G., "A Genre for Q and a Socio-Cultural Context for Q," JSNT 55 (1994), 3–26.

Edwards, R. A., *A Concordance to Q* (Missoula, MT: Scholars, 1975).

———, *A Theology of Q* (Philadelphia: Fortress, 1976).

Farrer, A., "On Dispensing with Q," in *Studies in the Gospels,* ed. D. E. Nineham (R. H. Lightfoot Festschrift; Oxford: Blackwell, 1955).

Fleddermann, H. T., *Mark and Q. A Study of the Overlap Texts* (BETL 122; Leuven: Peeters, 1995).

Havener, I., *Q: The Sayings of Jesus* (Wilmington: Glazier, 1987).

Jacobson, A. D., "The Literary Unity of Q," JBL 101 (1982), 365–89.

———, *The First Gospel: An Introduction to Q* (Sonoma, CA: Polebridge, 1992).

Kloppenborg, J. S., *The Formation of Q* (Philadelphia: Fortress, 1987).

———, "Bibliography on Q," SBLSP 24 (1985), 103–26.

———, *Q Parallels, Synopsis, Critical Notes & Concordance* (Sonoma, CA: Polebridge, 1988).

———, "The Sayings Gospel Q: Recent Opinions on the People behind the Document," CRBS 1 (1993), 9–34. Long bibliography.

———, ed., *The Shape of Q* (Minneapolis: A/F, 1994).

Kloppenborg, J. S., et al., *Q-Thomas Reader* (Sonoma, CA: Polebridge, 1990).

Kloppenborg, J. S., and L. E. Vaage, eds., *Early Christianity, Q and Jesus* (*Semeia* 55: Atlanta: Scholars, 1992).

Linnemann, E., "Is There a Gospel of Q?" BRev 11 (#4; Aug. 1995), 18–23, 42–43.

Lührmann, D., "The Gospel of Mark and the Sayings Collection Q," JBL 108 (1989), 51–71.

Mack, B. L., *The Lost Gospel. The Book of Q and Christian Origins* (San Francisco: Harper, 1993).

Meyer, P. D., "The Gentile Mission in Q," JBL 89 (1970), 405–17.

Neirynck, F., "Recent Developments in the Study of Q," in *Logia—The Sayings of Jesus,* ed. J. Delobel (Leuven: Peeters, 1982), 29–75.

———, *Q-Synopsis: The Double Tradition Passages in Greek* (rev. ed.; Leuven: Peeters, 1995).

Piper, R. A., *Wisdom in the Q-tradition* (SNTSMS 61; Cambridge Univ., 1989).

———, ed., *The Gospel behind the Gospels: Current Studies on Q* (NovTSup 75; Leiden: Brill, 1995).

Robinson, J. M., "LOGOI SOPHON: On the Gattung of Q," in *Trajectories through Early Christianity,* eds. Robinson and H. Koester (Philadelphia: Fortress, 1971), 71–113.

———, "International Q Project," JBL 109 (1990), 499–501 and subsequent years.

———, ed., *Documenta Q* (Leuven: Peeters, 1996–). The first volume deals with reconstructions of the last two centuries. Eventually each of 235 verses of Q will be discussed.

Tuckett, C. M., "A Cynic Q?" *Biblica* 70 (1989), 349–76.

———, "On the Relationship between Matthew and Luke," NTS 30 (1984), 130–42.

———, *Studies on Q* (Edinburgh: Clark, 1995).

———, *Q and the History of Early Christianity* (Peabody, MA: Hendrickson, 1996).

Turner, N., "Q in Recent Thought," ExpTim 80 (1969–70), 324–28.

Vaage, L. E., *Galilean Upstarts: Jesus' First Followers According to Q* (Valley Forge, PA: Trinity, 1994).

Vassiliadis, P., "The Nature and Extent of the Q Document," NovT 20 (1978), 49–73.

Worden, R. D., "Redaction Criticism of Q: A Survey," JBL 97 (1975), 532–46.

CHAPTER 7

THE GOSPEL ACCORDING TO MARK

The first step in considering any book of the NT is to read it through slowly and attentively. Careful reading should precede (and make intelligible) all scholarly speculation about the book. It is particularly important for the Gospels because people are often more familiar with them than with any other section of the NT; and, unless they read carefully, their presuppositions rather than actual texts govern responses. To facilitate observant reading of Mark, the initial *General Analysis* will ignore the prehistory of the material and treat the narrative as it has come to us, attempting to see its features and emphases. In the Gospels (and Acts) the *Analysis* will almost constitute a minicommentary in which inductively the peculiarities of the writer's thought and technique are brought to light through the biblical text. Proportionately the *Analysis* treatment of Mark will be somewhat longer than the *Analyses* of Matt and of Luke because many Gospel features are first encountered here (e.g., parables, miracles). Afterwards subdivisions will be devoted to: *Sources, Interpreting Mark, Authorship, Locale or community involved, Date of writing, Issues and problems for reflection,* and *Bibliography.*

General Analysis of the Message

Many scholars find a major dividing point in Mark 8, approximately halfway through the account of Jesus' ministry. There, after having been consistently rejected and misunderstood despite all he has said and done, Jesus starts to proclaim the necessity of the suffering, death, and resurrection of the Son of Man in God's plan. This development, which serves to reveal the christological identity of Jesus, is meant by Mark to teach a lesson. Readers can learn much about Jesus from the traditions of his parables and mighty deeds; but unless that is intimately combined with the picture of his victory through suffering, they cannot understand him or the vocation of his followers.

Summary of Basic Information

DATE: 60–75, most likely between 68 and 73.

AUTHOR BY TRADITIONAL (2D-CENTURY) ATTRIBUTION: Mark, the follower and "interpreter" of Peter, usually identified as the John Mark of Acts, whose mother had a house in Jerusalem. He accompanied Barnabas and Paul on the "First Missionary Journey" and may have helped Peter and Paul in Rome in the 60s. Some who reject this attribution allow that the author may have been an otherwise unknown Christian named Mark.

AUTHOR DETECTABLE FROM CONTENTS: A Greek-speaker, who was not an eyewitness of Jesus' ministry and made inexact statements about Palestinian geography. He drew on preshaped traditions about Jesus (oral and probably written) and addressed himself to a community that seemingly had undergone persecution and failure.

LOCALE INVOLVED: Traditionally Rome (where Christians were persecuted by Nero). Others suggestions: Syria, the northern Transjordan, the Decapolis, and Galilee.

UNITY: No major reason to think of more than one author; a few would argue for different editions to explain differences in Matt's and Luke's use of Mark.

INTEGRITY: Mark probably ended with 16:8. Mss. have appended other secondary endings recounting the appearance(s) of the risen Jesus. The "longer ending" (16:9–20) is the one most often considered canonical.

DIVISION:*

1:1–8:26: **Part One: Ministry of Healing and Preaching in Galilee**

1. Introduction by JBap; an initial day; controversy at Capernaum (1:1–3:6)
2. Jesus chooses the Twelve and trains them as disciples by parables and mighty deeds; misunderstanding among his Nazareth relatives (3:7–6:6)
3. Sending out the Twelve; feeding 5,000; walking on water; controversy; feeding 4,000; misunderstanding (6:7–8:26)

8:27–16:8: **Part Two: Suffering Predicted; Death in Jerusalem; Resurrection**
+ 16:9–20

1. Three passion predictions; Peter's confession; the transfiguration; Jesus' teaching (8:27–10:52)
2. Ministry in Jerusalem: Entry; Temple actions and encounters; eschatological discourse (11:1–13:37)
3. Anointing, Last Supper, passion, crucifixion, burial, empty tomb (14:1–16:8)
4. An ending describing resurrection appearances appended by a later copyist (16:9–20).

*This way of dividing Mark is designed to enable readers to follow the flow of thought, but no claim is made that the evangelist would have divided the Gospel thus (although the beginning of passion predictions in chap. 8 does seem to be an intentional major divider). In particular the distinction between units (marked numerically above) and their subunits is very hazy, for the latter could easily be elevated to units. Different structures are offered by Achtemeier, *Mark* (ABD) 4.546; Perkins, *Mark* (NInterpB) 521–23; and Humphrey, *Risen* 4 (chiastic pattern). A tripartite division with 8:27–10:45(52) as the centerpiece devoted to discipleship is widely advocated, e.g., E. Best in his writings.

Part One: Ministry of Healing and Preaching in Galilee (1:1–8:26)

Mark, like the other Gospels, prefaces the beginning of Jesus' public activities with JBap's proclamation. Then the first half of the Gospel describes a ministry of preaching and powerful deeds (healings, multiplying loaves, calming storms) and teaching in Galilee and its environs. Although Jesus attracts great interest, he struggles with demons, with misunderstanding (by his family and, more significantly, by the Twelve whom he chose to be with him), and with hostile rejection (by Pharisees and scribes).

1. Introduction by JBap; an Initial Day; Controversies at Capernaum (1:1–3:6). Is this a unit with three or four subunits, or should all the subunits be elevated to separate units? More important, Mark clearly tends to group things either by time (in a day), or by subject matter (controversies), or by form (parables in chap. 4).

Mark's opening (*1:1–15*) presents the beginning of the gospel of Jesus Christ[1] as the fulfillment of Mal 3:1 and Isa 40:3. JBap is the prophesied messenger crying in the wilderness to prepare the way of the Lord. That preparation consists in announcing the one who will baptize with the Holy Spirit, namely, Jesus. A voice from heaven, echoing Ps 2:7 and Isa 42:1, speaks to him as God's beloved Son; and at his baptism the Spirit descends.[2] The affirmations that Jesus was tested by Satan (the opponent of the Spirit) and that JBap was arrested suggest to the reader from the start that Jesus' proclamation of the kingdom will encounter major obstacles. Although some would translate the proclamation to mean that the kingdom or rule of God has come, the best translation of the verb *eggizein* is probably "come near"—the kingdom is making itself felt but has not fully arrived. Jesus begins by *calling four men to be his followers and "fishers" who will catch people* (*1:16–20*), thus presaging that these men will have a role in the proc-

[1]Although Mark 1:1 is often treated as a title, the evangelist may have thought of it as a proclamation. The phrase "Son of God," though supported by major mss., may be a copyist's addition. If genuine it provides an inclusion with the identification of Jesus as "Son of God" by the Roman centurion in 15:39 towards the end—the first believing confession of Jesus under that title in the Gospel.

[2]This has been read in an adoptionist way, as if Mark thought Jesus to be an ordinary human being whom God was now adopting as son and endowing with divine power. There is nothing positive in the text to support that interpretation, but Marcan silence about the "when" of divine sonship may have raised the idea among some. Was it to correct adoptionism that Matt and Luke, who drew on Mark, each prefaced the Marcan material with an infancy narrative that makes clear that Jesus was God's Son from the moment of conception, and that John, who knew the general tradition about Jesus, began with a Prologue that presents Jesus as God's Word even before creation? J. Marcus, NTS 41 (1995), 512–21, thinks that a vision that Jesus had (see Luke 10:18) underlay the baptismal accounts.

lamation. Indeed, the reactions of these disciples will mark major stages in the Gospel.

In describing what appears to be *the initial day of Jesus' ministry* (*1:21–38*), Mark familiarizes the readers with the type of things done in proclaiming the kingdom: teaching in the Capernaum synagogue with authority, exorcising an unclean spirit (the continued opposition of Satan), healing Simon's mother-in-law, healing many more diseased and possessed, and finally seeking a place to pray on the following morning, only to be importuned by his disciples pressing demands on him. Several factors should be noted. Teaching and an exercise of divine power in healing and driving out demons[3] are united in the proclamation of the kingdom, implying that the coming of God's rule is complex. Those who claim to be God's people must recognize that some of their attitudes stand in the way and must change their minds; the presence of evil visible in human affliction, suffering, and sin must be contravened; and the demonic must be defeated. Jesus can teach with authority unlike other people, and even the demons must obey him—all this is related to his being Son of God. Yet Mark never describes Jesus being given such authority and power; he simply has it because of who he is (n. 2 above). Paradoxically the unclean spirit that opposes him recognizes that he is the Holy One of God, while the disciples who follow him do not understand him fully despite his teaching and powerful deeds.

In 1:34 Jesus forbids the demons to speak "because they knew him." This is the first instance of what scholars call Mark's "Messianic Secret," whereby Jesus seems to hide his identity as the Son of God until it is made apparent after his death on the cross. We shall comment later (p. 153 below) on W. Wrede's detection and interpretation of the Secret, but the simplest meaning in the narrative is that demonic knowledge of him, although it invokes a true title, does not catch the mystery of his person (which, as we shall see, involves suffering and death). A struggle in Jesus' vocation between tranquil prayer and activity is glimpsed in 1:35–38.

The expansion of Jesus' activity (*1:39–45*). Jesus' ministry of preaching, driving out demons, and healing moves through the towns of Galilee, a geographical range that will be enlarged in subsequent chaps. of Mark. Notice

[3]Because of his exorcisms and miracles, there is a tendency to dismiss Jesus as a typical exorcist or magician of his time. Yet Achtemeier (*Mark,* ABD 4.555) points out how Jesus differs from the usual exorcist who must find out the name of the demon and delude it into thinking that he (the exorcist) has more supernatural power. An exorcism that does not involve a sickness/disease (as exemplified in Mark 1:21–27) is rare in proposed Hellenistic parallels. For vocabulary differences, see H. C. Kee, NTS 14 (1967–68), 232–46; for the historicity of Jesus' exorcisms, G. E. Sterling, CBQ 55 (1993), 467–93. Meier, *Marginal* 2.537–52, makes a clear distinction between Jesus and magicians.

that the silence (or secrecy) motif is now extended to the healed leper[4] because publicity would make it impossible for Jesus to circulate openly. Implicitly, too, enthusiasm for the wonderful could give the wrong understanding of Jesus.

Controversies at Capernaum (*2:1–3:6*). At this town on the Lake of Galilee, which now has become Jesus' home, Mark centers five incidents where objections are raised by the scribes and the Pharisees and others to his forgiving sins, to his association with sinners, to the failure of his disciples to fast, and to their and his doing what is not lawful on the Sabbath. Clearly Jesus is being presented as one who, on the basis of his own higher authority (2:28: "the Son of Man is lord even of the Sabbath"), does not fit into the religious expectations of his contemporaries—an attitude that gives rise to a plot on the part of the Pharisees and Herodians to destroy him. The proclamation of God's kingdom is opposed not simply by demons but by human beings, and that opposition will be aimed at Jesus the proclaimer.

2. Jesus Chooses the Twelve and Trains Them as Disciples by Parables and Mighty Deeds; Misunderstanding Among His Nazareth Relatives (3:7–6:6). Mark closes the previous section and begins this section with *a summary* (*3:7–12*)[5] showing that Jesus' ministry was attracting people from an ever widening region beyond the Galilee of 1:39. Amid this appeal to many, Jesus goes up to the mountain and *summons the Twelve* (*3:13–19*), whom he wants to be with him and whom he will send forth (*apostellein,* related to "apostle") to preach. The next chaps. show what he does and says when they are with him, presumably to train them for being sent forth (6:7).[6] It may be observed that Luke 6:13–15 and Acts 1:13 present a list of the Twelve that differs from that in Mark (and in Matt 10:2–4) in one of the last four names;[7] and so by the time the evangelists wrote, amidst agreement about Jesus' choice of the Twelve, recollection of the minor members was uncertain (see pp. 208, 725, 748 below and NJBC 81:137–46).

In the sequence 3:20–35 we encounter a narrative arrangement that scholars acknowledge as a feature of Marcan style, an intercalation sometimes

[4]Leprosy in the NT is a type of skin affliction, not Hansen's disease which we know today as leprosy.

[5]On the disputed function of summaries, see C. W. Hedrick, NovT 26 (1984), 289–311. Do they mark off literary structure (Perrin), or do they intentionally expand the ministry beyond the few specific incidents in the surrounding narrative?

[6]If that motif of sending packages this section by way of inclusion, so also does the issue of Jesus' relationship to his family, for in 3:20–21 (plus 3:31–35) they come from where they are to Capernaum to fetch him, whereas in 6:1–6 Jesus goes to Nazareth where they are—in both scenes they are presented as not understanding.

[7]Thaddaeus in Mark and most mss. of Matt; Lebbaeus in some western mss. of Matt; Judas (Jude) in Luke-Acts. All three are Semitic names and scarcely refer to the same person even though later hagiography created the composite Jude Thaddaeus. See B. Lindars, NTS 4 (1957–58), 220–22.

called inelegantly the "Marcan sandwich."[8] In it Mark initiates an action that requires time to be completed, interrupts it by another scene filling in the time (the meat between the surrounding pieces of bread), and then resumes the initial action bringing it to a close. Here the action begins with Jesus' relatives, who do not understand this turn of life where he is not even taking the time to eat (3:20–21) and want to bring him back home. The time it requires to move from Nazareth where they are to Jesus' new "home" at Capernaum is filled in by scribes who come from Jerusalem (3:22–30). The relatives' objection "He is beside himself" is matched by the scribes' "He is possessed by Beelzebul [Beelzebub]," the one expressing radical misunderstanding and the other antagonistic disbelief. At the end of the intercalation (3:31–35), the mother and brothers of Jesus finally arrive; but, now that the proclamation of the kingdom has begun, they have been replaced: "Whoever does the will of God is my brother, and sister, and mother."[9] The intermediary scene with scribes from Jerusalem constitutes one of the Marcan Jesus' clearest statements about Satan, whose kingdom opposes the kingdom of God. With the appearance of Jesus the two kingdoms are locked in struggle. The allegorical parable[10] in 3:27 suggests that Satan is the strong one in possession of his house and goods (this world) and that Jesus is the stronger one who has come to bind him and take his possessions away. The unforgivable blasphemy in Mark 3:28–30 is to attribute Jesus' works to an unclean spirit rather than to the Holy Spirit.[11]

The next subsection (*4:1–34*) is a collection of parables and parabolic sayings pertinent to the kingdom of God, most of them dealing with the growth of seed. Even though Jesus' ministry is centered at Capernaum on the Sea of Galilee, and the setting of these parables is a boat, it seems that the material of Jesus' parables is taken from the villages and farms of the Nazareth

[8]See J. R. Edwards, NovT 31 (1989), 193–216; T. Shepherd, NTS 41 (1995), 522–40.

[9]It is christologically significant that Jesus does not say "father." Since this scene seems to disparage Mary, Roman Catholics often find it difficult; and seemingly so did Matt and Luke. Matt (12:24–50), which preserves the rest of the Marcan material from the scene, omits the prelude where Jesus' "own" think that he is beside himself; and Luke (8:19–21) omits not only that but also any contrast between the natural mother/brothers and the disciples. See also n. 21 below. An appreciation that the mother of Jesus was a special disciple grows in the later Gospels (including John). For further discussion, see the ecumenical book MNT; also S. C. Barton, *Discipleship and Family Ties in Mark and Matthew* (SNTSMS 86; Cambridge Univ., 1994).

[10]Following the German commentator A. Jülicher (1888), interpreters tended to make a sharp distinction between parable (an image making one point) and allegory (individual figures in the symbolism have a meaning). Subsequent attention to OT and rabbinic use of figurative language has challenged such a sharp distinction, and it is now widely recognized that some of the NT parables have allegorical features (NJBC 81.62–63).

[11]The idea of an unforgivable sin appears elsewhere in the NT (Heb 6:4–6; 10:26; I John 5:16–17). R. Scroggs, JBL 84 (1965), 359–73, relates Mark 3:28–29 to I Cor 12:2–3 and the problem of ecstatic Christianity that would accept no limitation on actions in the Spirit. See also M. E. Boring, NovT 18 (1977), 258–79.

hill-country of his youth. There is no real doubt that historically Jesus phrased his teaching in parables.[12] Because they are polyvalent, the particular point of parables takes on coloration from the context in which they are uttered or placed. Scholars have spent much time reconstructing the original context of the parables in Jesus' lifetime and distinguishing it from the subsequent reinterpretations and accretions that took place as the parables were preached in the early Christian decades[13] (both of which preGospel contexts are speculative). The only certain context is the placing of the parables in the extant Gospels—the fact that at times the context differs in Mark, Matt, and Luke exemplifies the creative use of tradition by the evangelists for their own pedagogical purposes.

In the present Marcan narrative sequence three seed-parables (the sower and the seed, the seed that grows by itself, and the mustard seed) serve as a commentary on what has been happening in Jesus' proclamation of the kingdom.[14] In the parable of the sower, the emphasis is on the different kinds of soil. The interpretation supplied in Mark, even if not derived from Jesus himself, may be close to the original idea: Only some have accepted the proclamation of the kingdom, and even among them there are failures. Yet the seed has its own power and will ripen in its own time; it is like the mustard seed with a small beginning and a large growth. Those who heard/read Mark were meant to see these parables as explaining failures and disappointments in their own experience of Christianity and as a sign of hope that ultimately there would be tremendous growth and abundant harvest.

Woven into the seed-parables are comments and parabolic sayings about the "purpose" of the parables. In particular, Mark 4:11–12[15] where Jesus says

[12]The study of Gospel parables has generated an immense literature and sharp debates, to which readers are well introduced in NJBC 81.57–88 and the handbook of H. Hendrickx, *The Parables of Jesus* (San Francisco: Harper & Row, 1986). Books representative of different approaches include: C. H. Dodd, *The Parables of the Kingdom* (rev. ed.; New York: Scribner's, 1961); J. Jeremias, *The Parables of Jesus* (8th ed.; New York: Scribner's, 1972); J. D. Crossan, *In Parables* (New York: Harper & Row, 1973) and *Cliffs of Fall* (New York: Seabury, 1980); N. Perrin, *Jesus and the Language of the Kingdom* (Philadelphia: Fortress, 1976); M. I. Boucher, *The Mysterious Parable* (CBQMS 6; Washington: CBA, 1977); M. A. Tolbert, *Perspectives on the Parables* (Philadelphia: Fortress, 1979); J. Lambrecht, *Once More Astonished* (New York: Crossroad, 1981); J. R. Donahue, *The Gospel in Parable* (Philadelphia: Fortress, 1988); D. Stein, *Parables in Midrash . . . Rabbinic Literature* (Cambridge, MA: Harvard, 1991); C. W. Hedrick, *Parables as Poetic Fictions* (Peabody, MA: Hendrickson, 1994).

[13]For instance, the explanation of the sower and the seed in 4:13–20 is generally perceived as a sermonic interpretation of Jesus' parable, focusing on the obstacles encountered by Christians and using Greek terms exemplified in the epistles.

[14]But also as an introduction to what follows, namely, the unfolding incomprehension of the disciples: N. R. Petersen, "The Composition of Mark 4:1–8:26," HTR 93 (1980), 185–217. See the excellent treatment of these parables by J. Marcus, *The Mystery of the Kingdom of God* (SBLDS 90; Atlanta: Scholars, 1986); also Henaut, *Oral.*

[15]M. A. Beavis, *Mark's Audience. The Literary and Social Setting of Mark 4,11–12* (JSNTSup 33; Sheffield: JSOT, 1989).

that parables are given to those outside in order that they may *not* see, understand, or be converted, is an offensive text if one does not understand the biblical approach to divine foresight where what has in fact resulted is often presented as God's purpose. (Thus, in Exod 7:3 God tells Moses of the divine plan to make Pharaoh obstinate so that he will not listen to Moses—a hindsight description of the fact that Pharaoh resisted.) Mark is really describing what he sees as the negative *result* of Jesus' teaching among his own people, the majority of whom did not understand and were not converted. Like the symbolic visions accorded to Daniel in the OT, the parables constituted a "mystery" the interpretation of which was given by God only to the select (Dan 2:22,27–28). Others do not understand, and the mystery becomes a source of destruction. Isa 6:9–10, which foresaw the prophet's failure to convert Judah, was widely used in the NT to explain the failure of Jesus' followers to convince most Jews (Rom 11:7–8; Acts 28:26–27; John 12:37–40); and Mark employs it here (4:12) in comment on the parables. That Jesus' purpose (in the proper sense) was not to obscure is made clear by the sayings about the lamp and the hidden things in 4:21–23 and also by the summary in 4:33–34 that has Jesus speaking the word to them in parables "as they were able to understand it."

Four miraculous actions follow in 4:35–5:43. These serve to remind today's readers that the 1st-century worldview was very different from our own. Many modern scholars dismiss completely the historicity of the miraculous;[16] others are willing to accept the healings of Jesus because they can be related to the coming of the kingdom as a manifestation of God's mercy but reject the historicity of "nature" miracles such as the calming of the storm in Mark 4:35–41. However, that distinction finds no support in an OT background where God manifests power over all creation. Just as sickness and affliction reflect the kingdom of evil, so also does a dangerous storm; accordingly Jesus rebukes the wind and the sea in 4:39 just as he does a demon in 1:25. (Lest one think this picture impossibly naive, one should

[16]Almost half Mark's account of the public ministry (*ca.* 200 of 450 vv.) deals with miracles. The evangelist describes them as *dynameis* (related to English "dynamite" = "acts of power"), not using a Greek word that would call attention to the wondrous, as does English "miracle" (related to Latin *mirari,* "to wonder at"). The study of Gospel miracles, like that of parables, has produced an extensive discussion to which readers are introduced in NJBC 81.89–117 and in the handbook of H. Hendrickx, *The Miracle Stories of the Synoptic Gospels* (London: Chapman, 1987). Books representative of different approaches include A. Richardson, *The Miracle-Stories of the Gospels* (London: SCM, 1941); R. H. Fuller, *Interpreting the Miracles* (London: SCM, 1963); H. van der Loos, *The Miracles of Jesus* (NovTSup 9; Leiden: Brill, 1965); A. Fridrichsen, *The Problem of Miracle in Primitive Christianity* (Minneapolis: Augsburg, 1972; orig. 1925); H. C. Kee, *Miracle in the Early Christian World* (New Haven: Yale, 1983); C. Brown, *Miracles and the Critical Mind* (Grand Rapids: Eerdmans, 1984); D. Wenham and C. L. Blomberg, eds., *The Miracles of Jesus* (GP 6; Sheffield: JSOT, 1986); Meier, *Marginal,* 2.507–1038.

note that when a storm causes death and destruction today, people wonder why God has allowed this; they do not vent their anger on a high-pressure system.) The victory of Jesus over the storm is seen as the action of the stronger one (3:27) whom even the wind and sea obey.

The struggle of Jesus with the demonic is even more dramatic in the healing of the Gerasene madman (5:1–20), where Jesus drives out "Legion." The pattern of the miracle resembles that of the demoniac story in 1:21–28, including the recognition of Jesus' identity. However, the colorful, imaginative elements are stronger here, e.g., the prolonged description of the man's violence; the need of the demons for a place to stay,[17] leading to the transferral to the pigs; and the detailed portrayal of the healed man. The ending where the healed man is sent off to proclaim to the Decapolis what the Lord has done is significant since it runs contrary to the thrust of the "Messianic Secret." The two miracles in 5:21–43 are another instance of Marcan intercalation (pp. 130–31 above: the "sandwich"): Jesus sets out for Jairus' house in 5:21–24 and arrives to raise Jairus' daughter in 5:35–43, while the time in between is filled in by the healing of the woman with the hemorrhage in 5:25–34. In the story of the woman, notice that power is portrayed as a possession of Jesus that can go out from him without his knowing where it goes. The question "Who has touched my clothes?", the disciples' sarcastic response, and the confession of the woman add to the drama. Yet, perhaps unintentionally, they give the impression that Jesus did not know all things—that may be why the much shorter form of the story in Matt 9:20–22 omits such details. Jesus' declaration "Your faith has saved you" (5:34; 10:52) shows that Mark has no mechanical understanding of the miraculous power of Jesus. In the Jairus story we hear of the threesome Peter, James, and John chosen to accompany Jesus.[18] They were the first called of the Twelve; and evidence in Paul and Acts suggests they were the most widely known. The "mighty deed" of Jesus is to resuscitate the young girl to ordinary life, but Christian readers may have been meant to see the request of the father "that she may be saved and live" (5:23) and the result that the girl "rose" (5:42) as a foreshadowing of Jesus' gift of eternal life.[19] The scene ends with another instance of Marcan secrecy (5:43).

[17]Cf. Matt 12:43–45. There is a major geographical problem in Mark's location of the scene where the pigs can run down the embankment and drown in the sea. Gerasa is a site over thirty miles from the Sea of Galilee, and the alternative reading Gadara is no real help since that is about six miles from the sea.

[18]Also 9:2; 13:3 (with Andrew); 14:33.

[19]See Chapter 11 below, n. 41. Mark's use of the transcribed Aramaic formula *Talitha koum* (5:41), which, as usual, he takes care to translate for his readers, has suggested to some that he is preserving a magical formula (cf. Acts 9:40). However, in describing such a stupendous example of divine power, Mark may choose to use Aramaic to give a sense of authenticity, as most probably in

In 6:1–6 Jesus returns to Nazareth, his native place; and this constitutes an inclusion with his dealings with "his own" from Nazareth at the beginning of the scene (3:21,31–35). His teaching in the synagogue produces skepticism. The local people remember him as a carpenter and know his family,[20] and so both his religious wisdom and his mighty works have no plausible origin. Jesus acknowledges that a prophet is without honor in his own region, among his own relatives, and in his own house.[21] Despite all the parables and the miracles we have seen in the intervening chaps., Jesus' ministry has not produced faith among those who should know him, and his power (which, as we have seen, is related to faith) is ineffective there.

3. Sending out the Twelve; Feeding 5,000; Walking on Water; Controversy; Feeding 4,000; Misunderstanding (6:7–8:26). Again one can debate whether this section constitutes one unit with subunits or a number of distinct units. It begins with sending out of the Twelve and ends with their continued misunderstanding, and has as a major theme Jesus' failed attempt to bring these disciples to satisfactory faith—a failure that will lead to the second part of the Gospel where he proclaims that only by his own suffering and death can that be brought about.

In the subsection dealing with *the mission of the Twelve and Herod* (*6:7–33*) we encounter once more Marcan intercalation; for the sending out (*apostellein*) of the Twelve is narrated in 6:7–13 and their return in 6:30–32, with an account of Herod's activity "sandwiched" between in 6:14–29 to occupy the intervening time. The disciples' mission to preach a change of mind, drive out demons, and cure the sick is an extension of Jesus' own mission; and he gives them the power to accomplish this. The austere conditions (no food, money, luggage) would make it clear any results were not effected by human means; and probably Marcan Christians had come to expect such austerity of missionaries.[22] Between the beginning and the end of the mission we are told that King Herod (Antipas) has killed JBap, and now he is worried that Jesus might be JBap come back from the dead.[23] The fate of

---

Jesus' last words in 15:34. Possibly later generations would attribute magical efficacy to what seemed to them an exotic expression.

[20]The description which mentions the mother, brothers, and sisters suggests that the unmentioned Joseph is dead. As for the debate over whether the brothers and sisters were children of Mary, see Chapter 34 below, n. 2, and BROQ 92–97.

[21]The parallel scene in Matt 13:53–58 omits the indication that a prophet is without honor among his own relatives; and Luke 4:24 omits the lack of honor both "among his own relatives" and "in his own house." See n. 9 above.

[22]Also a welcoming house and staying there. In 6:13 the sick are to be anointed with oil. Jesus does not do that, and again Mark's description may be influenced by early church practice (Jas 5:14–15).

[23]Mark 6:17 is inaccurate (Herodias was the wife not of Philip but of another brother named Herod), and many doubt that a Herodian princess would dance in the manner described. This may

JBap is a warning of what the fate of Jesus is likely to be—and the fate of those sent to carry on his work.

The feeding of the 5,000 and the walking on the water (*6:34–52*) constitute a unit in all four Gospels. Variations of the feeding miracle in John and the presence of what may be another form of it as the feeding of the 4,000 in Mark 8:1–9[24] (also Matt) suggest a very old tradition that has undergone many adaptations in the preaching period. It is an interesting example of multilayered meaning. On the most direct narrative level the multiplication represents Jesus' divine power put to the service of a hungry multitude whose predicament touches his heart. There are also OT echoes however, e.g., Elisha's feeding of 100 with loaves in II Kings 4:42–44, and perhaps the manna miracle in Moses' time ("wilderness place" in 6:32), even as Jesus' walking on the water may echo the dry-shod crossing of the Red Sea. Beginning with Jesus and developing strongly in church preaching, the highlighting of parallels between Jesus' career and OT scenes became a major element in understanding God's total plan. Still another layer of meaning was probably apparent to Mark's readers, for Jesus' action in 6:41 anticipates what he will do at the Last Supper in 14:22–23 in relation to the bread which is his body, an action they would have been familiar with in their own eucharists.[25] Either as part of that symbolism or separately the multiplication may also have been seen as an anticipation of the messianic banquet. Thus, like the parables, the miracles of Jesus could be polyvalent; and indeed a miracle could take on a parabolic role.

In the second miracle, the walking on the water, Mark offers a type of theophany or epiphany; for the divine identity of Jesus is suggested not only by the extraordinary character of the miracle but also by Jesus' answer in 6:50, "I am."[26] It is all the more poignant, then, that the disciples understood neither this miracle nor the multiplication, for their hearts were hardened (6:52). Following the paired miracles there is *a Marcan summary* (*6:53–56*) about the enthusiasm of Galilean villagers for Jesus' many healings, some accomplished simply by the touch of his garments; but the readers are left to suspect that such enthusiasm is not true understanding or faith.

---

well be a popular story—further dramatized in art, music, and drama under the heading of Salome's dance of the veils, whereas the biblical account mentions neither Salome nor veils.

[24]R. M. Fowler, *Loaves and Fishes* (SBLDS 54; Chico, CA: Scholars, 1981) argues that Mark composed 6:30–44 on the basis of the traditional 8:1–9.

[25]A banquet with loaves and fish became a standard representation of the eucharist in early catacomb art. In a different way John's account of the multiplication develops both the Elisha and eucharistic motifs, so that these interpretations may have been common in the early church.

[26]For the use of *egō eimi* as a divine name, see p. 347 below. Mark may represent an incipient form of the usage in the Jesus tradition.

A controversy over ritual purity (*7:1–23*) is the next illustration of misunderstanding. Despite all the miracles, what specifically bothers the Pharisees and scribes who come from Jerusalem is that some of Jesus' disciples do not observe ritual purity, a concept that 7:3–4 has to explain to the readers. The controversy leads Jesus to condemn overly narrow interpretations as human tradition that disregards and even frustrates the real thrust of God's commandment for purity of heart. While the basic attitude toward the Law in 7:8,15 plausibly comes from Jesus, many scholars suggest that the application that has him declare all foods clean (7:19) represents an insight developed within the tradition that Mark espouses. The hard-fought struggles over kosher food attested in Acts and Paul would be difficult to explain if Jesus had settled the issue from the beginning.[27] A sharp contrast to the hostility of the Jewish authorities is supplied by the faith of *the Syrophoenician woman* (*7:24–30*) in the Tyre area. (It is scarcely accidental that Mark places in sequence a controversy over food and the surprising faith of a Gentile who comes spontaneously to Jesus; they were the two major issues that divided early Christians.) Some have been offended by Jesus' response in 7:27 which is not egalitarian since it places the Jews first (the children) and refers to Gentiles as dogs.[28] Such scandal, however, may reflect a failure to accept Jesus as a 1st-century Jew. Paul too put Jews first (Rom 1:16), and I Peter 2:10 echoes the OT thesis that the Gentiles had no status as a people. If the woman's child is healed at a distance, the next miracle, *the deaf man* (*7:31–37*), describes an unusual amount of contact between Jesus and the afflicted, including putting his spittle on the tongue and using the transcribed Aramaic formula *Ephphatha.*[29] Mark indicates that the people's enthusiasm about Jesus' power overrides his command to secrecy.

Even if in origin *the feeding of the 4,000* (*8:1–9*) may have been a duplicate of the earlier feeding, it has a strong cumulative effect in Mark as another manifestation of Jesus' stupendous power. Once again the context is a multitude without anything to eat, and the use of the verb *eucharistein* (8:6) supports eucharistic interpretation.[30] What follows in the scene with *the disciples in the boat* (*8:10–21*) dramatizes climactically the utter unlikelihood that Jesus will be accepted or understood. After all that he has done, the Pharisees who come forward still seek a sign to test him; and the disciples

[27]E.g., Gal 2:11–14; Rom 14:14–21; Acts 10:14–15. See the differing views expressed by N. J. McEleney, CBQ 34 (1972), 431–60 and H. Räisänen, JSNT 16 (1982), 79–100.

[28]The translation of the Greek diminutive for "dogs" as "puppies" is probably not a justified amelioration, for in this period diminutives (more frequent in Mark) are often insignificant variants.

[29]Cf. n. 19 above on 5:41. Only Mark and John (9:6) have spittle miracles. Did other strains of Gospel tradition eliminate that element lest it be interpreted as magic?

[30]See N. A. Beck, CBQ 43 (1981), 49–56.

in the boat are specifically pictured as not having understood the two multiplications. *The healing of the blind man* (*8:22–26*) serves as a parabolic commentary on the situation. The man regains his sight only in stages, for the first action by Jesus gives him only blurry vision. This is also the situation of the disciples stemming from all that Jesus has done for them thus far. Only when Jesus acts a second time does the man see clearly. The next half of the Gospel will describe what Jesus must do to make the disciples see clearly, namely, suffer, be put to death, and rise.

Part Two: Suffering Predicted; Death in Jerusalem; Resurrection (8:27–16:8 + 16:9–20)

Jesus signals a change of tone by predicting clearly his fate three times—the third time as he moves to Jerusalem where all that he predicts will take place. A narrative change of pattern is observable in this second half since relatively few acts of power (miracles) take place, almost as if Jesus recognizes that miracles will not lead his disciples to understand. His activities in Jerusalem are appreciated by the multitude, but hated by the chief priests and the scribes. Finally they hatch a plot to kill him; and with the cooperation of Judas they are able to arrest him after he has eaten a Passover supper with his disciples. He is brought before the chief priest and the Roman governor and condemned to be crucified. After his death a Roman centurion recognizes Jesus' identity as God's Son. On the third day after this, the tomb in which he was buried is found empty; and a young man (angel) there proclaims that Jesus has been raised and will be seen in Galilee.

1. Three Passion Predictions; Peter's Confession; the Transfiguration; Jesus' Teaching (8:27–10:52). Part Two begins with *Peter's confession of Jesus, the first passion prediction, and its aftermath* (*8:27–9:1*). Early in Part One we heard negative judgments about Jesus ("He is beside himself"; "He is possessed by Beelzebul"). Peter's confession (8:27–30) comes amid more positive evaluations of him as JBap, Elijah, and one of the prophets. This spokesman of the disciples who has been with him since 1:16 goes even further by proclaiming Jesus as the Messiah, but Jesus greets this with the same command to silence with which he modified the demons' identification of him as God's Son (3:11–12). The two titles are correct in themselves, but they have been uttered without including the necessary component of suffering. Jesus now commences to underline that component more clearly with a prediction of his own passion (8:31).[31] Peter rejects this por-

[31]The three Marcan predictions of the passion of the Son of Man in chaps. 8, 9, and 10 (drawn on by Matt and Luke, with perhaps an independent form in John 3:14; 8:28; 12:34) have been

trait of the suffering Son of Man; and so Jesus categorizes his lack of understanding as worthy of Satan. Not only will Jesus have to suffer but so too will those who would follow him (8:34–37). In 8:38 Jesus warns that those who are ashamed of him will be judged with shame when the Son of Man comes in the glory of his Father with the holy angels. This remarkable christological claim apparently refers to the parousia (or second coming of Christ), but does the next verse (9:1) also when it speaks of some there not tasting death before they see the kingdom of God come with power? (Matt 16:28 speaks of the coming of the Son of Man.) Or does it refer to the transfiguration which follows immediately (as is implied in the enumeration of the verse as 9:1 instead of 8:39), an interpretation that makes the "not taste death" easier?[32]

The transfiguration (*9:2–13*) produces a reaction that is another example of the inadequate faith of the disciples. At the beginning of Part One the identity of Jesus as God's Son was proclaimed during his baptism by a voice from heaven; but the disciples were not present at that time, and thus far in the public ministry no follower of Jesus has made a believing confession of that identity. Now at the beginning of Part Two, as the hitherto hidden glory of Jesus is made visible to three of his disciples (n. 18 above), the heavenly voice reidentifies Jesus. The scene echoes the greatest OT theophany, for it takes place on a mountain amidst the presence of Moses and Elijah who encountered God on Sinai (Horeb). The "after six days" of 9:2 seems to recall Exod 24:16 where cloud covers Sinai for six days and only on the day after that does God call to Moses. Awkwardly Peter proposes to prolong the experience by building three tabernacles, even as the Tabernacle was built after the Sinai experience (Exod 25–27; 36–38); but in reality he is terrified and does not know what to say (Mark 9:6). The discussion on the way down from the mountain brings up echoes from the passion prediction (namely, that the Son of Man must suffer and will rise from the dead), but now in relation to Elijah. The implicit identification of Elijah as JBap who came before Jesus and was put to death (9:13) may represent the result of early church reflection on how to relate the two great Gospel figures in the light of the OT.

---

the subject of much contention. Is it possible for someone to predict the future? Are the "predictions" totally shaped after the events they describe? For a discussion and bibliography, see BDM 2.1468–91.

[32]See E. Nardoni, CBQ 43 (1981), 365–84. The transfiguration then anticipates a glorious parousia. The idea that it is a resurrection appearance transposed to the ministry is implausible. (Where does one find evidence for the risen Jesus appearing surrounded by OT saints, or a heavenly voice different from his identifying him as the Son?) There has been considerable scholarly debate about the historicity of the transfiguration. Clearly it is related to Jesus' baptism, and in both instances an incident in Jesus' career may have become the subject of heavy christological reflection and dramatization.

The story of a boy with a demon (*9:14–29*),[33] whom Jesus' disciples are not able to cure while he is up on the mountain, is recounted by Mark at unusual length. The symptoms are typical of epilepsy (as Matt 17:15 recognizes), and yet in the Gospel worldview the evil done to the boy by such an illness is described as demonic possession. The question as to why the disciples could not drive out the demon exasperates Jesus: This is a faithless generation (9:19); and there is also a lack of faith implicit in the father's request for help, "If you can" (9:23). The "mute and deaf spirit" obeys Jesus' command to depart; but readers are left with a sense of mystery at the end (9:29) when he tells the disciples, "This kind can come out in no other way except through prayer."

A journey through Galilee begins with Jesus' *second prediction of the passion* (*9:30–32*), which once again the disciples do not understand. (The difficulty in dismissing all these predictions as totally postJesus creations is exemplified in 9:31 where many scholars recognize Semitic features and old tradition.) In Capernaum and eventually as he sets out on a portentous journey to Judea (10:1,17), Jesus gives his disciples *a varied instruction pertinent to the kingdom* (*9:33–10:31*). Mark has gathered here what he envisions as important last communications before Jesus arrives in Jerusalem to die.[34] In 9:33–35 Jesus warns the Twelve not to seek to be greatest in the kingdom but a servant. The inclusiveness of the kingdom is exemplified in 9:36–41[35] by Jesus' command to receive a child (i.e., an insignificant person) in his name and his maxim "Whoever is not against us is for us." The protectiveness against scandal (i.e., causing to sin: 9:42–48) that Jesus extends to the little ones who believe would be heard by Mark's readers as pertaining not only to his lifetime but to theirs. The Twelve are challenged to be like fire and salt (9:49–50), both purifying and seasoning before the period of judgment.

The journey to Judea, instructing the crowds, and a question of the Pharisees are the context for Jesus' teaching on marriage and divorce (10:1–12). The Pharisees on the basis of Deut 24:1–4 would allow a husband to write out a note divorcing his wife because of "an indecency in her," and rabbis debated whether that indecency had to be something very serious or could

[33]See P. J. Achtemeier, CBQ 37 (1975), 471–91 for how a tradition going back to Jesus has been interpreted by Mark.

[34]The connection among some of these teachings seems to be established on chain words or ideas: The notion of not losing a reward for giving a cup of water to those who belong to Christ in 9:41 leads into what happens by way of punishment in Gehenna for those who cause scandal in 9:42; and the fire of Gehenna in 9:48 leads into being salted by fire in 9:49. The fact that in 9:41 the Marcan Jesus speaks of belonging "to Christ" shows the extent to which the Gospel has "modernized" the language from Jesus' time to the time of the church.

[35]Note the high christological import in 9:37: "Whoever receives me, receives not me but the One who sent me."

be trivial. But Jesus, appealing to Gen 1:27; 2:24 for the unity created by marriage, would forbid breaking the marriage bond, so that remarriage after a divorce constitutes adultery. (The same attitude is found among the Jews who produced the Dead Sea Scrolls.[36]) A form of the prohibition is preserved in Matt (twice), Luke, and I Cor 7:10–11; and so it is not unlikely that historically there was a controversy in Jesus' life between him and other Jews who held different views about the issue. The difficulty of his position was recognized by early Christians, and the saying soon gathered comments.[37] For instance, Mark 10:12, which extends the statement to a wife divorcing her husband (not a practice envisioned in OT law), is probably an adaptation to the situation of the Gentile hearers of the Gospel where women could divorce men.

Jesus returns to the issue of those who enter the kingdom (10:13–31). Most think that underlying the children passage in 10:13–16 there is the correction of a wrong attitude that would demand achievement, abilities, behavior, or status on the part of those who are brought to the kingdom, whereas for Jesus the kingdom/rule of God requires only human receptivity of which the child is a good symbol. This interpretation brings Mark quite close to Paul's notion of justification by faith.[38] But how do adults show or express receptivity? That is the issue behind the question of the rich man in 10:17. In response[39] Jesus does not depart from the commandments of God enunciated in the OT; but when the man says he has observed them, Jesus lovingly asks him to sell his possessions and give the proceeds to the poor. Is that part of what is necessary to inherit eternal life, or does it apply only to a special discipleship of walking with Jesus? Certainly not all the early Christians sold their possessions, and 10:24–27 shows that Jesus is demanding what is impossible by human standards but not by God's. Those

[36]Especially 11QTemple[a] 57:17–19 and CD 4:20–21; see the important article of J. A. Fitzmyer, FTAG 79–111.

[37]That continues today. The observation that Jesus issued this demand in a time-conditioned situation is really meaningless, since every statement ever made on the face of the earth was made in a time-conditioned situation. The issue is whether this is to be considered as an enduring demand binding Jesus' followers (Roman Catholic position for marriages considered sacramental) or only as an ideal which for all practical purposes can be dispensed from, either relatively easily (many Protestant churches) or for a grave, specific reason such as adultery (Orthodox position, drawing on Matt 19:9).

[38]E.g., Rom 3:28. In addition, others have thought that an openness to the baptism of infants might be the issue.

[39]"No one is good but God alone" (10:18) is difficult. Many treat it as a pedagogical device: Do not call me good unless you recognize I am God. Others understand it in the opposite direction, I am not God. However, such a distancing of Jesus from God is not a Marcan theme. A third possibility is that, although Jesus would be perceived as divine ("God" in our sense), the term "God" was not yet being used for him in the Marcan sphere because that referred to Jesus' Father in heaven. Ultimately to apply the term "God" to Jesus, Christians had to expand it to include both the Father in heaven and the Son who had an earthly career.

who make great sacrifices for Jesus' sake will be rewarded both in this age and the age to come (10:29–31); but the phrase "with persecutions," whether from Jesus or Mark, is an important realistic touch about their fate.

That realism finds expression also in *the third prediction of the passion* (*10:32–34*)—more detailed than the others as the anticipated events come closer. Caught up in this immediacy, James and John raise the issue of *the first places in the kingdom* (*10:35–45*). The challenge by Jesus to imitate him in drinking the cup and being baptized is symbolically a challenge to suffering. (The flight of the disciples at Gethsemane will show that their confident "We can" response is overly optimistic.) Although there are distinguished places prepared (by God), the disciples must learn that the Gentile pattern where kings lord it over people is not to be followed in the kingdom that Jesus proclaims. There service is what makes one great. "The Son of Man did not come to be served but to serve and to give his life as a ransom for many" (10:45) is a fitting summary of the spirit of this kingdom, a spirit anticipated in Isa 53:10–12.

The journey toward Jerusalem has a final scene in the Jericho area when *Jesus heals the blind Bartimaeus* (*10:46–52*). This man who persists in crying out to Jesus for mercy when others tell him to be silent is symbolic of the many who will come to Christ and hear "Your faith has saved you." Mark gives us this scene of gaining sight as a positive element before the somber scenes he is about to describe in Jerusalem.

2. Ministry in Jerusalem: Entry; Temple Actions and Encounters; Eschatological Discourse (11:1–13:37). The narrative gives the impression that everything described in these chaps. takes place on three days (11:1,12,20). On the first day *Jesus enters Jerusalem* (*11:1–11*). Two disciples are sent from Jesus' base of operations on the Mount of Olives, and all is as he foretold. He sits on the colt that they bring back (perhaps an implicit reference to Zech 9:9 about the coming of Jerusalem's king); and he is acclaimed by a hosanna cry of praise, by a line from Ps 118:26, and by the crowd's exclamation about the coming of the kingdom of "our father David." Thus Jesus is being proclaimed as a king who will restore the earthly Davidic realm—an honor but another misunderstanding. A Marcan intercalation ("sandwich") governs actions on the next day and the beginning of the following day: *cursing the fig tree, cleansing the Temple, and finding the fig tree withered* (*11:12–25*).[40] To curse the tree because it had no fruit seems to many irrational since, as Mark reminds us, this time just before Passover

[40]See W. R. Telford, *The Barren Temple and the Withered Tree* (JSNTSup 1; Sheffield: JSOT, 1980). For the significance of Jesus' action, see BDM 1.454–60; W. W. Watty, ExpTim 93 (1981–82), 235–39; C. A. Evans, CBQ 51 (1989), 237–70. Extreme skepticism about historicity is represented by D. Seeley, CBQ 55 (1993), 263–83.

was not the season for figs. However, the cursing is similar to the prophetic actions of the OT whose very peculiarity attracts attention to the message being symbolically presented (Jer 19:1–2,10–11; Ezek 12:1–7). The barren tree represents those Jewish authorities whose failures are illustrated in the intervening action of cleansing the Temple, which has been made a den of thieves instead of a house of prayer for all peoples (Jer 7:11; Isa 56:7). In particular, the chief priests and the scribes seek to put Jesus to death, and their future punishment is symbolized by the withering of the tree. The miraculous element in the cursing/withering becomes in 11:22–25 the occasion for Jesus to give the disciples a lesson in faith and the power of prayer.[41] (The instruction to the disciples to forgive in order that God may forgive them resembles a motif that Matt 6:12 places in the Lord's Prayer.)

The malevolence of the authorities aroused by the cleansing of the Temple continues in *the challenge to Jesus' authority* (*11:27–33*). This is the first of several "trap" episodes by which Mark shall show Jesus' superior wisdom when confronted by mean-spirited opponents. Notice that in the storyline, even though he is dead, JBap remains a figure to be reckoned with. *The parable of the wicked tenants* (*12:1–12*) who are ultimately deprived of the vineyard[42] has the same motif as the cursing of the fig tree, much to the annoyance of the authorities. More traps are laid for Jesus in the questions of the Pharisees and Herodians about *taxes for Caesar* (*12:13–17*)[43] and of the Sadducees about *the resurrection* (*12:18–27*). These have the effect of showing the wide-ranging hostility to Jesus among the authorities of all groups, but they may also have been instructive for Marcan Christians who faced similar issues: the primacy of God and the hope for resurrection. (It is difficult to know the extent to which the evangelist [or Jesus] was adjudging a contemporary political dispute about taxes.) Although Mark paints Jesus' adversaries with a broad brush, he makes an exception in the portrayal of a sensitive scribe who asks about *the greatest commandment* (*12:28–34*) and wins Jesus' approbation as being not far from the kingdom of God. The opening line of Jesus' response is fascinating; for it cites the Jewish daily

[41]S. E. Dowd, *Prayer, Power, and the Problem of Suffering: Mark 11:22–25* (SBLDS 105; Atlanta: Scholars, 1988).

[42]The vineyard stands for Israel as the background in Isa 5:1–2 shows; the owner is God and the son is Jesus (a rare instance of this self-description in Mark). Many think the servants are the prophets, and the others to whom the vineyard is given are the Gentiles. See n. 10 above on allegorical features in the Gospel parables. There is a form of this parable in *Gospel of Thomas* 65.

[43]For a form of this see *Papyrus Egerton 2*, frag 2 (HSNTA 1.96–99). Like Nicodemus in John 3:2, the opponents begin, "Jesus, Teacher, we know that you have come from God," and continue, "Is it lawful to pay kings what pertains to their rule?" Jesus answers angrily, citing Isaiah as he did earlier (Mark 7:6). Some, like Crossan, would argue that *Egerton* is more primitive than the canonical Gospels, but most think of it as a melange from them. There is also a developed form of the story in *Gospel of Thomas* 100, where the coin is gold and the claim is: "Caesar's agents demand taxes."

prayer, the Shema ("Hear, O Israel . . .") from Deut 6:4.[44] This means that decades after Christian beginnings Gentiles were still being taught to pray a Jewish prayer as part of the fundamental demand placed by God! The two commandments inculcated by Jesus, combining Deut 6:5 and Lev 19:18, share a stress on love that became what Christians would like to think of as the identifying characteristic of their religion—a characteristic, alas, too often lacking.

In response to so many hostile questions, Jesus poses his own difficult *question about David's son* (*12:35–37*). Whether or not the issue arose in Jesus' lifetime, early Christians had to struggle with the perception that acclaiming Jesus as the Messiah meant more than his being the anointed king of the House of David (see FESBNT 113–26). The *denunciation of the public display of the scribes* (*12:38–40*) provides a background for an account of genuine religious behavior, *the widow's mite* (*12:41–44*).

Most of Jesus' activity in Jerusalem thus far has been in the Temple area; and it is after reflecting on the magnificent Temple buildings that, seated on the Mount of Olives, he delivers *the eschatological discourse* (*13:1–37*)—the last speech of his ministry that looks to the end times. The discourse is a collection of dire prophetic warnings (demolition of the Temple buildings; forthcoming persecution of the disciples; need to be watchful) and apocalyptic signs (deceivers; wars; desolating abomination standing where it should not be; phenomena in the sky). Interpretation presents many problems.[45] Assuming that it is sequentially arranged and that Jesus had a detailed knowledge of the future, some have attempted to identify from our point of view what has already happened and what is yet to come. (Literalism particularly distorts the meaning if symbolic elements from OT and intertestamental apocalyptic are taken as exact descriptions of expected events; p. 777 below.) Even those who appreciate the symbolic nature of apocalyptic and do not take a literalist approach think that in part the Marcan account is colored by what the evangelist knows to have already taken place, e.g., persecution in synagogues and before governors and kings.[46] For most readers the "bot-

[44]B. Gerhardsson, *The Shema in the New Testament* (Lund: Novapress, 1996).

[45]L. Hartman, *Prophecy Interpreted* (CBNTS 1; Lund: Gleerup, 1966); W. S. Vorster, TIM 269–88; T. J. Geddert, *Watchwords. Mark 13 in Markan Eschatology* (JSNTSup 26; Sheffield: JSOT, 1989); C. C. Black, in *Persuasive Artistry,* ed. D. F. Watson (JSNTSup 50; Sheffield: JSOT, 1991), 66–92; A. Yarbro Collins, FGN 2.1125–40; J. Verheyden, FGN 2.1141–59; G. R. Beasley-Murray, *Jesus and the Last Days* (Peabody, MA: Hendrickson, 1993 = revision of his books of 1953 and 1963).

[46]That approach is complicated by the hypothesis that Mark took over and edited an earlier apocalypse in which the time indications might be to an earlier period. E.g., is the "abominable desolation" a reference to Caligula's attempt in AD 40 to have a statue of himself set up in the Jerusalem Temple (so N. H. Taylor, JSNT 62 [1996], 13–41), or does it refer to events in Jerusalem toward the end of the Jewish Revolt of AD 68–70?

tom line" from reading through the discourse is that no precise timetable is given: On the one hand Jesus' followers are not to be misled by speculations and claims that the end is at hand; on the other hand they are to remain watchful.

3. Anointing, Last Supper, Arrest, Trials, Crucifixion, Burial, Empty Tomb (14:1–16:8). Another Marcan inclusion is formed by *Judas' treachery and the anointing of Jesus* (*14:1–11*) since the anointing is sandwiched in the time between the plot of the authorities to arrest Jesus and Judas' coming forward to give him over to them. That the anointing is for burial tells the reader that the plot will succeed. For the unidentified woman who does the anointing, see Chapter 9 below, n. 33. *The preparations for Passover* (*14:12–16*) not only supply a ritual context for Jesus' action at the Last Supper but also exemplify Jesus' ability to foretell what will happen. The latter theme will continue when Jesus predicts what Judas, the disciples, and Peter will do. *The Last Supper* (*14:17–25*), narrated very briefly in Mark, provides the context for the first of those predictions; and the idea that Judas will give Jesus over offers a dramatic contrast to Jesus' self-giving in the eucharistic blessing of the bread and wine as his body and blood.

The *Gethsemane section* (*14:26–52*) begins the suffering portion of Mark's passion narrative,[47] as Jesus moves from the supper to the Mount of Olives. In that transition the predictions of the disciples' flight and of Peter's denials set a tragic tone, and in what follows the element of failure and abandonment is stronger in Mark than in any other passion narrative. The isolation of Jesus is dramatized in three steps[48] as he moves away from the body of the disciples, from the chosen three, and then falls to the earth alone to beseech the Father three times to take the cup from him—a cup of suffering that in 10:39 he had challenged his disciples to drink! When the Father is silent and the disciples are found asleep three times, Jesus accepts God's will and proclaims that now the Son of Man is to be given over to sinners—as he had three times predicted. The first step in a long sequence of giving over is when with a kiss (a dramatic touch) Judas gives him over to the crowd that comes from the chief priests and the scribes.[49] Not only do all the dis-

[47]For a bibliography, see BDM 1.97–100. It includes: J. R. Donahue, *Are You the Christ? The Trial Narrative in the Gospel of Mark* (SBLDS 10; Missoula: Scholars, 1973); W. H. Kelber, ed., *The Passion in Mark* (Philadelphia: Fortress, 1976); D. H. Juel, *Messiah and Temple* (SBLDS 31; Missoula, MT: Scholars, 1977); D. P. Senior, *The Passion of Jesus in the Gospel of Mark* (Wilmington: Glazier, 1984).

[48]The frequency of threes, explicit or implicit, emphasizes the highly narrative character of the passion, for a pattern of three is a well-known feature in jokes (Irishman, Scotsman, Englishman) and other oral recounting.

[49]It is noteworthy that in Mark, unlike the other Gospels, Jesus does not respond to Judas; also the unnamed sword-wielder who cuts off the ear of the high priest's servant is not identified as a disciple.

ciples flee, but a young man who was following Jesus runs away naked. Attempts to identify the young men are probably in vain (BDM 1.294–304); he symbolizes failure: Those who had left everything to follow him have now left everything to get away from him.

The Jewish trial: Jesus is condemned by a Sanhedrin and mocked while Peter denies him (*14:53–15:1*). The arresting party gives Jesus over to the chief priests, elders, and scribes who meet as a Sanhedrin[50] to determine his fate. Switching back and forth to depict simultaneity, Mark recounts two contrasting scenes: In one Jesus bravely confesses that he is the Son of God; in the other Peter curses him and denies knowing him. Ironically, at the very moment Jesus is being mocked as a false prophet, the third of his prophecies about his disciples is being fulfilled. Although the authorities do not believe that Jesus can destroy the sanctuary or that he is the Messiah, the Son of the Blessed (God),[51] there will be a verification of both themes at his death. Here Marcan readers were probably hearing anticipations of debates of their own time, for ultimately Christians saw the condemnation of Jesus as what moved God to allow the Romans to destroy Jerusalem, and the identity of Jesus as the Son of God became a principal point of division between Christians and Jews.

The Roman trial: Jesus is handed over to be crucified by Pilate and mocked (*15:2–20a*). The Jewish authorities give Jesus over to Pilate. Mark draws a clear parallel between the two trials in a way that effectively highlights the main point of each. In each a principal representational figure, respectively the chief priest and Pilate, asks a key question reflecting his interests: "Are you the Messiah, the Son of the Blessed?" and "Are you the King of the Jews?"[52] There are false witnesses in the Jewish trial; and Pilate knows that Jesus was handed over out of envy. Yet Jesus is condemned at the end of each trial, spat on and mocked—as a prophet by the Jewish Sanhedrin members, and as the King of the Jews by Roman soldiers. Rejected by all, Jesus is given over by Pilate to the Roman soldiers to be crucified.

The crucifixion, death, and burial (*15:20b–47*). Before the crucifixion, on

[50]Many interpreters of Jesus' passion draw on the later portrayal of the Sanhedrin in the Mishna (*ca.* AD 200). In Jesus' time, however, a Sanhedrin does not seem to have consisted of a fixed number of members or to have met regularly or to have served primarily as a court. From the 1st-century historian Josephus we get the impression that the chief priest called together a Sanhedrin of aristocrats and priests and other important figures when there was an issue on which he needed advice or support, especially issues that involved dealing with the Romans.

[51]It is noteworthy that Mark does not portray the Pharisees as having an active role in the final actions against Jesus or make disputes over the Sabbath or the Law part of the charges against him. The lethal opposition comes from the Temple authorities.

[52]For Mark, Jesus is truly both but not in the hostile, disbelieving way intended by either interrogator. That is why he responds by adding the corrective "Son of Man" saying in 14:62, and by "That is what you say" in 15:2.

the way to the place called Golgotha, Mark highlights the help rendered by Simon of Cyrene, and after Jesus' death on the cross, that rendered by Joseph of Arimathea—ironically the only ones who assist him are those who, so far as we know from Mark, had no previous contact with him. The crucifixion details that Mark mentions are redolent of OT descriptions of the suffering just one, e.g., the two wine drinks, with myrrh at the beginning and vinegary wine at the end (Prov 31:6–7; Ps 69:22); the division of the clothes (Ps 22:19). Three time periods are indicated: the third, sixth, and ninth hours (9:00 a.m.; noon; 3 p.m.), with an increasingly tragic coloring. In the first period, three groups are given a role at Jesus' cross: passersby, chief priests and scribes, and co-crucified criminals. All of them mock him, indeed by reviving the issues from the Jewish trial (destruction of the sanctuary, identity as the Messiah). In the second period darkness comes over the land. In the third period Jesus speaks from the cross for the only time. Mark began Jesus' passion in 14:36 with his prayer in transcribed Aramaic and Greek, "*Abba,* Father . . . take away this cup from me." Mark closes Jesus' passion in 15:34 with another prayer, citing in Aramaic and Greek the desperate words of Ps 22:2, "*Elōi, Elōi, lama sabachthani* . . . My God, my God, why have you forsaken me?"[53] Feeling forsaken and no longer presuming to use the intimate family term "Father," Jesus is reduced to a form of address common to all human beings, "My God." Still, no answer comes before Jesus dies. Yet in a stunning reversal, the moment he expires, God vindicates him in terms of the very issues raised at the Jewish trial: The veil that marked off the Temple sanctuary is torn, depriving that place of its holiness, and a Gentile recognizes a truth that the chief priest could not accept, "Truly this man was God's Son."

Women who had ministered to Jesus in Galilee and followed him to Jerusalem are now introduced as having observed the death of Jesus from a distance. Since they also observe the place where he is buried, they serve as an important link between the death and the discovery of the empty tomb that reveals the resurrection.[54] The burial is done by Joseph of Arimathea, a pious member of the Sanhedrin, who presumably wanted to observe the law that the body of one hanged on a tree should not remain overnight.

The empty tomb and the resurrection (*16:1–8*). Jesus' body was buried hastily; and so early Sunday morning, after the Sabbath rest, the women buy spices to anoint him. The dramatic rhetorical question about moving the

[53]Many commentators stress that this is the opening of a psalm that continues for thirty verses and ends on a positive tone. That does not do justice to the fact that the most pessimistic line in the psalm is quoted, not a victorious one. See V. K. Robbins, FGN 2.1175–81.

[54]With the exception of Luke 8:2, Mary Magdalene is mentioned only in relation to the crucifixion, burial, and empty tomb. See Chapter 9 below, n. 33.

stone underlines the divine intervention in the scene: The tomb is open; a young man who is almost surely to be understood as an angel is there, but not the body of Jesus. The ringing proclamation, "He has been raised . . . he is going before you to Galilee where you will see him," represents the triumph of the Son of Man predicted three times by Jesus (8:31; 9:31; 10:34).[55] The reaction of the women in 16:8 is astounding. They disobey the young man's command to report to the disciples and Peter; they flee, and out of fear say nothing to anyone.[56] Mark's theology is consistent: Even a proclamation of the resurrection does not produce faith without the hearer's personal encounter with suffering and carrying the cross.

4. An Ending Describing Resurrection Appearances Appended by a Later Copyist (16:9–20). What I have just written above is the majority view: The original Gospel ended with Mark 16:8. Yet there are scholars who argue strongly for a lost ending (a final codex page that became detached?), contending that Mark would surely have narrated the appearance in Galilee promised in 16:7 (as does Matt 28:16–20). A proclamation of the good news (a Gospel) that ends with the women saying "nothing to anyone, for they were afraid" (16:8) is troubling.[57] The problem was noted in antiquity, since mss. of Mark witness to three different endings added by copyists, presumably in an attempt to correct the abruptness of 16:8.

The best attested ending, discussed here, is called the Marcan Appendix or the Longer Ending and is printed as part of the text of Mark in many Bibles.[58] It records three appearances of the risen Jesus (to Mary Magdalene, to two disciples in the country, to eleven at table) and an ascension. Despite the later origins of this Appendix, the ordinary reader today reads it in sequence to 16:1–8. The women were afraid to speak in 16:8; now, however, the appearance of Jesus to Mary Magdalene brings her to belief. She shares the news with Jesus' disciples, but they do not believe her. Nevertheless,

[55]The attempt to see Mark 16:7 as referring not to an appearance of the risen Jesus in Galilee but to the parousia is very forced, especially given these three predictions. Resurrection appearances are to a restricted audience, but a parousia confined to the disciples and Peter is unintelligible. Moreover, it would imply that, in describing an appearance in Galilee, Matt misunderstood or disagreed with Mark.

[56]P. L. Danove, *The End of Mark's Story. A Methodological Study* (Leiden: Brill, 1993).

[57]This may be a suspended ending, however, where the readers are expected to complete the story from the hint in the text. Then Mark would be affirming and communicating a postresurrectional reunion without narrating it. See J. L. Magness, *Sense and Absence* (Semeia Studies; Atlanta: Scholars, 1986). Opponents respond that this is an attractive answer, but one that supposes considerable subtlety.

[58]W. R. Farmer, *The Last Twelve Verses of Mark* (SNTSMS 25; Cambridge Univ., 1974). The Council of Trent declared 16:9–20 to be canonical Scripture; but there is no obligation for Roman Catholics to believe that it was written by Mark. The material resembles resurrection accounts found in Matt and Luke-Acts (and perhaps in John [for Mary Magdalene]), but whether the copyist who composed it drew directly from those Gospels or simply from similar traditions is uncertain. The promised "signs" in 16:17–18 resemble some of the miracles recounted in Acts.

when Jesus appears to two of them, they too come to believe. They tell the others who refuse to believe. Finally Jesus appears to the eleven, rebukes them for not having believed, and sends them into the whole world to proclaim the gospel: "Whoever believes and is baptized will be saved." The three examples of those who wrongly refused to believe on the basis of others' words are meant to admonish those who have to believe on the disciples' word. The Appendix ends on the consoling note of the Lord working with missionary disciples and confirming them through miraculous signs.

Sources

No matter what his sources, Mark[59] was a genuine author who created an effective whole. As indicated above, the Gospel has an overall plan, leading up through Part One to the first passion prediction in Part Two. A reference at the conclusion of Part One (8:18–21) brings together the two multiplications of loaves in order to highlight the disciples' misunderstanding. The two trials of Jesus are carefully paralleled. The predictions of Jesus about the disciples are all fulfilled by the middle of the passion account, and the themes brought up at the middle (Jewish trial) are fulfilled at the end as Jesus dies. Some of this organization could have come from sources, but much of it probably came from Mark himself. His authorship, then, is manifested in the way he arranged material, connected stories, chose details to report, and highlighted themes. Did it also consist in total creation of parables, or miracles, or other stories not hitherto present in the Jesus tradition? Scholars debate that issue, but obviously the answer depends on the nature and extent of Marcan sources and our ability to reconstruct them. Here are some of the proposals:

EXTANT SOURCES EXTERNAL TO MARK. The *Secret Gospel of Mark* has been proposed as a source for Mark, and a short form of the *Gospel of Peter* as a source for the Marcan passion. This theory requires a major exercise of imagination and has little following; readers interested in it are invited to read the critiques listed in Chapter 6, n. 20,21 above. A few scholars would contend that Mark knew Q and drew upon it;[60] but since by definition Q consists of material shared by Matt and Luke not found in Mark, this thesis almost passes beyond our control.

BLOCKS OF MATERIAL PRESERVED IN MARK. A large number of scholars

[59]We shall use this name for the evangelist, although as will become clear later, we may not know his identity.

[60]E.g., B. H. Throckmorton, JBL 67 (1948), 319–29; J. P. Brown, JBL 80 (1961), 29–44; J. Lambrecht, NTS 38 (1992), 357–84. See the rejection of this approach by F. Neirynck, ETL 72 (1996), 41–74.

argue that there was a written preMarcan passion narrative (or narratives) that can be detected beneath Mark's passion. Unfortunately the reconstructions differ widely. In BDM 2.1492–1524 M. Soards surveys thirty-five scholars' views of the preMarcan passion, and there is scarcely one verse that all would assign to the same kind of source or tradition. Those who think that John wrote independently of Mark use agreement between those two Gospels as an index of preGospel passion material, but that agreement does not supply the wording of a consecutive account. The likelihood that there was a preMarcan passion account does not remove a real doubt whether we have the methodology to reconstruct it exactly or at length.

Sources for smaller blocks of material have also been proposed. For instance, there is a debate whether the five controversies in 2:1–3:6 were taken over by Mark from a source.[61] Widely proposed is a source (or even an oral and a written source) for the parables in 4:1–34.[62] As for Marcan miracle-stories, there are several theories. For example, P. J. Achtemeier would posit that two cycles have been joined together,[63] each consisting of a miracle worked at sea, three healings, and a multiplication of loaves (respectively within 4:35–6:44 and 6:45–8:26)—into each Mark would have interpolated a block of material (respectively 6:1–33 and 7:1–23). Also there has been considerable debate as to whether a preMarcan apocalypse underlies Mark 13 (n. 46 above).

Why is there so much disagreement in detecting preMarcan written sources? At the roots of the issue are doubts about the applicability of the criteria employed in determining what Mark contributed to the (nonextant) source(s) he employed.[64] For instance, there have been very careful studies of Marcan style, vocabulary, and syntax; and they are most helpful in discussions of the Synoptic problem in order to distinguish Mark's writing from that of Matt and Luke.[65] It is far more difficult to be certain how to use the information gained from them in recognizing Mark's putative sources. Was the style of such a source different from Mark's style? It is not inconceivable

[61]M. J. Cook, *Mark's Treatment of the Jewish Leaders* (Leiden: Brill, 1978), isolates three different written sources from which the author drew his accounts of Jesus' controversies; see also J.D.G. Dunn, NTS 30 (1984), 395–415. However, J. Dewey, JBL 92 (1973), 394–401 (reprinted in TIM 141–51) argues that Mark himself put independent units together in 2:1–3:6, employing a chiastic pattern wherein the first matches the fifth, and the second matches the fourth.

[62]V. Parkin, IBS 8 (1986), 179–82. In JBL 108 (1989), 613–34, P. Sellew distinguishes between didactic scenes taken over from preMarcan tradition and those composed by Mark.

[63]JBL 89 (1970), 265–91. For other analyses of the miracle catenae or sequences see L. E. Keck, JBL 84 (1965), 341–58; T. A. Burkill, JBL 87 (1968), 409–17.

[64]See the careful study of C. C. Black, "The Quest of Mark the Redactor," JSNT 33 (1988), 19–39; and chaps. 7–8 in his *Disciples according to Mark* (Sheffield: JSOT, 1989). In particular one must be careful not to place Mark in a dialectical relationship to his putative sources.

[65]F. Neirynck, *Duality in Mark* (rev. ed.; BETL 31; Leuven Univ., 1988) detects a consistent pattern of duality throughout Mark.

that Mark acquired his religious writing style from that of a source he considered authoritative (and even sacred) enough to use, even as some modern English-speaking evangelists consciously or unconsciously pick up their oratorical phrasing and style from the KJV. If the style of the source was different from Mark's, did Mark copy it slavishly, thus enabling us to distinguish it from his own additions? Or having read what was in the source, did he rephrase its contents in his own style? The latter technique would make it virtually impossible to distinguish between what he took over and what he originated.

The signs of joining (seams) are often appealed to as a guide to what is Marcan and what is preMarcan; yet these are not so satisfactory an indicator as many assume. Looking at Mark (or any Gospels), we can see that a certain sequence is awkward because at a particular spot the transition from one section to another is poor. If the material on either side of this "seam" is somewhat dissonant, we might judge that the awkwardness comes not from poor writing but because someone has joined two bodies of material that originally did not go together. But here the questions begin. Was it Mark who did the joining, or was the awkward union already in the source? Is the joining really awkward, or is the awkwardness in the eye of the beholder who judges from a standpoint that never occurred to the evangelist? (See Meagher, *Clumsy,* for examples.) On that point, one must recognize that the present text, which is deemed awkward, made sense to the final writer/editor whether he copied it or composed it.

Again, the presence in Mark of material in different styles is urged as a criterion for distinguishing Marcan composition from the putative sources. But this criterion too has its perils. Did Mark deliberately vary his style according to what he was describing? If Mark was not always consistent, the presence of different styles is not a certain guide for distinguishing between the preMarcan and the Marcan. Furthermore, in judging style we must take into account the strong influence of orality on Mark. The tradition about Jesus was preached for decades; and even when it was written down, that oral influence continued. Some like W. H. Kelber (Chapter 6, n. 27 above) would see a sharp break between orality and textuality in Mark, the first written Gospel. However, Kelber's models of orality are taken from a preliterate society, whereas Jesus and those who proclaimed him lived in a Judaism where the paradigm for preserving God's word was Scripture, and thus in a religious context where orality and textuality were combined.[66] Best,

[66]L. W. Hurtado, JSNT 40 (1990) 15–32, esp. 16–17, points to models of combined orality and textuality in the Greco-Roman world; see also P. J. Achtemeier, JBL 109 (1990), 3–27; R. Scholes and R. Kellogg, *The Nature of Narrative* (New York: Oxford, 1966), esp. 1–56.

Mark, The Gospel as Story, insists that there is strong continuity between oral tradition and the written form of Mark. Indeed, signs of orality are evident in Mark's writing, as J. Dewey has argued convincingly.[67] This orality is manifested not only in what Mark took over but in the way he presents it. In a context where orality and textuality were mixed, was Mark always consistent in the way he treated his putative source(s), or did he sometimes copy and sometimes rephrase, especially where he was joining material from an oral background to material from a written background? Such a possibility weakens arguments for sources based on different styles in the Marcan Gospel.

These difficulties have not been mentioned to depreciate the intensive study that has gone into the detection of Marcan sources, but they do highlight the uncertainty of the results. The importance of that observation will become apparent in the next subsection.

How To Interpret Mark

Mark has been interpreted in many different ways. Part of the variety stems from the different methods of interpretation employed today. In the *Bibliography* below, these are exemplified by chaps. in the Anderson and Moore book, but more extensively by whole books on Mark devoted to redaction criticism, reader-response criticism, forms of structuralism, narrative criticism, sociorhetorical criticism, and sociopolitical criticism.[68] That in whole or part Mark had its origins in liturgy has been proposed, e.g., composed of lessons to be read in church (Carrington), or shaped by a paschal baptismal liturgy (young man in white robe on Easter Sunday in 16:5), or by Good Friday prayer hours (14:17–15:42: a day broken up by Mark's indications of three-hour intervals). Bilezikian, *Liberated,* sees Mark set up on the classic pattern of a Greek tragedy; and Robbins, *Jesus,* would compare the Gospel to Xenophon's account of Socrates, i.e., the biography of a disciple-gathering teacher. Humphrey sees the OT personification of Wisdom, especially in the Book of Wisdom, as a guiding pattern. Readers may learn from these approaches (or from disagreeing with them), but let me concentrate here on particular problems that scholars have found (or created) in interpreting Mark, often reflected in radically different interpretations.

[67]*Interpretation* 43 (1989), 32–44; CBQ 53 (1991), 221–36. This is maintained also by T. P. Haverly in his doctoral dissertation, "Oral Traditional Narrative and the Composition of Mark's Gospel" (Edinburgh Univ., 1983); also P. Sellew, NTS 36 (1990), 234–67; Bryan, *Preface,* esp. 67–151. On the Marcan story as discourse and effect of rereading, see E. S. Malbon, JBL 112 (1993), 211–30.

[68]See Davidsen, Fowler, Hamerton-Kelly, Heil, Myers, Robbins, Tolbert, and Waetjen in the *Bibliography* below; also Chapter 2 above.

Sometimes a problem is detected in the Gospel as it now stands, especially in enigmatic passages. These include: the seemingly negative purpose for telling parables to outsiders (4:11–12: that they may not understand and turn again and be forgiven); the symbolism of the young man who flees away naked (14:51–52); and the abrupt ending where the women do not transmit the news that Jesus has been raised or tell Peter and the disciples to go to Galilee (16:8). Yet these difficult passages are not insuperable or overly numerous.

Beyond them, one may cite special problems highlighted in different approaches to the Gospel. In 1901 the German scholar W. Wrede[69] proposed his theory that a secret about the Messiah was an important factor in Mark: Although Jesus is the Messiah (or Son of God), he hides this and tells his disciples not to reveal his miraculous healings to others, with the result that only demons recognize his identity. Wrede regarded this picture as historically implausible. The Messianic Secret had been invented (even before Mark, but made central by him) to facilitate bringing early traditions that were nonmessianic into a proclamation of Jesus as the Messiah. Wrede's thesis received very wide acceptance in Germany and became a key factor in showing that Mark was a highly theological composition, rather than a basically historical account. However, there are objections to this thesis. Although Mark is clearly a theological work, it is possible to posit that christology goes back to the earliest levels and even to Jesus himself (see BINTC 73–80). Marcan secrecy (which many would judge that Wrede exaggerated) may have its roots in Jesus' historical rejection of some messianic aspirations of his own time and his having no developed theological language to express his identity. In any case and for various reasons, probably the majority of scholars would no longer think of the Messianic Secret as the key issue in interpreting Mark.

Because of his reputation as a literary critic, F. Kermode's narrative criticism of Mark[70] has received a good deal of attention. Writing disparagingly of much biblical criticism, Kermode stresses Marcan obscurity, so that amid moments of radiance, basically the Gospel remains a mystery like the parables, arbitrarily excluding readers from the kingdom. Leaving aside the critiques of Kermode's book as to whether he has understood exegesis and has not substituted art for science, one may object that he has isolated Mark's

[69]*The Messianic Secret* (London: Clarke, 1971). See J. L. Blevins, *The Messianic Secret in Markan Research 1901–1976* (Washington: Univ. Press of America, 1981); C. M. Tuckett, ed., *The Messianic Secret* (Philadelphia: Fortress, 1983); H. Räisänen, *The "Messianic Secret" in Mark's Gospel* (Edinburgh: Clark, 1990).

[70]*The Genesis of Secrecy* (Cambridge, MA: Harvard, 1979). See the review by J. R. Donahue, CBQ 43 (1981), 472–73, and the important critique by J. Marcus, JBL 103 (1984), 557–74.

writing from its ultimate Christian theology. The motifs of disobedience, failure, misunderstanding, and darkness are prominent in Mark; but the death of Jesus on the cross, which is the darkest moment in the Gospel, is not the end. God's power breaks through, and an outsider like the Roman centurion is not excluded but understands. No matter how puzzled the women at the tomb are, the readers are not left uncertain: Christ is risen and he can be seen.

MORE PROBLEMS OF INTERPRETATION ARE BASED ON PRESUPPOSITIONS ABOUT WHAT PRECEDED MARK. From the start, two cautions are worth underlining (and they will reappear in the remarks below). *First,* while a large majority of scholars thinks that Matt and Luke drew on Mark and on Q, the sources of Mark and John are much more hypothetical. Reconstructing the theology of those nonextant sources (as if a source represented the total outlook of those who wrote/heard it) is doubly hypothetical. Then evaluating Marcan or Johannine theology on the basis of corrective changes made in what was received from the sources is triply hypothetical. *Second,* commentators also use the putative changes to construct the history of the Marcan community and/or Mark's intention to correct other groups of Christians. All four evangelists, whether or not they were in active contact with Jews, condemn hostilely the Jewish failure to acknowledge Jesus as the Messiah. Among the Gospels, however, only John (6:61–66; 12:42) criticizes specifically groups of believers in Jesus whose faith he finds inadequate; and so it is legitimate to read John to have been written at least in part as a corrective of other Christians. There is no such overt criticism in Mark, and to interpret Mark similarly goes considerably beyond the text. Here are some examples:[71]

(a) If Mark knew the *Secret Gospel of Mark,* the *Gospel of Peter,* and/or some of the known gnostic apocrypha, by correcting/rejecting them Mark may be looked on as supporting a more staid and believable christology over against extravagantly imaginative, exotic (and even erotic) views of Christ that were more original. For instance, theoretically Mark would have been omitting the statement that Jesus felt no pain on the cross (*GPet*), or the picture of a gigantic risen Jesus accompanied by a cross that moved and spoke (*GPet*), or the scene where Jesus ate and spent the night with a virtually naked young man whom he had raised from the dead (*Secret Mark*). Or Mark, with his references to the Twelve and his description of the women as failing to speak about the resurrection, may be supporting a male, authoritarian Christianity against a charismatic Christianity, in which women had an

[71]It should be added that some of these interpretations of Mark have the effect of supporting modern social or religious agenda.

equal role and received postresurrectional revelations (gnostic gospels). Although scholars like Crossan and H. Koester suppose Marcan dependence on such apocryphal works, the evidence is so slim that this approach is rejected by most scholars. Without any imputation of intention, one may debate whether such an interpretation does not implicitly depreciate a confessing Christianity that regards Mark as normative for faith.

(b) If Mark drew on a preGospel collection of miracles, he may be rejecting the approach to Jesus as a *theios anēr* ("divine man") in such a source.[72] (In more general comment on the miracles T. J. Weeden[73] thinks that the *theios anēr* christology was prevalent in the community addressed by Mark and associated by them with the disciples of Jesus; Mark writes to discredit those disciples and the miraculous christology-without-suffering associated with them.) Beyond the hypothetical character of such a miracle source and Mark's corrective use of it, there are the problems of whether there was in circulation a *theios anēr* ideology (pp. 84, 103 above), of whether the OT cycles of Elijah and Elisha miracles do not offer a better analogy to the Gospel miracles than do the proposed deeds of Hellenistic wonder-workers, and of whether the miracle-worker-corrective approach is not a reflection of modern skepticism about any picture of Jesus as a miracle worker. If one accepts the possibility of miracles (healings, resuscitations of the dead, multiplication of loaves, etc.), then a source in which Jesus worked them would endow him with supernatural powers. (In the Gospel only disbelievers attribute his power to Beelzebul, and so a Christian source would attribute them to Jesus' great status or to his personal relationship to God.) Mark gives no evidence of skepticism about the factuality of Jesus' *dynameis,* or mighty deeds.[74] Still, the Gospel may be seen as criticizing two views about miracles. Explicitly the Marcan Jesus refuses to work miracles to show off or prove his powers, and implicitly the picture of him as a man who does mighty works is combined with him as an authoritative teacher and one who suffers. Thus if Mark used a source that viewed Jesus only as a triumphant miracle worker or as one who made a vain display of miracu-

[72]See p. 84 above and the dispute in the Keck and Burkill articles in n. 63 above. Also P. J. Achtemeier, JBL 91 (1972), 198–221; *Interpretation* 26 (1972), 174–97; O. Betz, in *Studies in New Testament and Early Christian Literature* (A. Wikgren Festschrift; Leiden: Brill, 1972), 229–40.

[73]ZNW 59 (1968), 145–58 (reprinted in TIM 89–104); see also N. Perrin, "Towards"; (and JR 51 [1971], 173–87; reprinted in TIM 125–40). A number of scholars connect a hostile Marcan picture of the disciples with hostility to the wrong ecclesiology (dynastic, elitist: Trocmé, *Formation*), or to the wrong eschatology (awaiting the parousia in Jerusalem: Kelber, *Mark's Story*), or to the Jerusalem church which had the wrong christology (advocating Jesus as a royal Messiah: J. B. Tyson, JBL 80 [1961], 261–68).

[74]There is no discussion in Mark as to whether Jesus was given miraculous power at a given moment of his existence, and so the thesis that the source presented Jesus as an ordinary human being whom God elevated by suddenly giving him miraculous power is pure speculation.

lous power, it has corrected that source. As for the disciples, E. Best[75] has argued persuasively that Mark's depiction of their failure was meant to function as a pastoral example to the recipients who had also encountered failure, rather than as a polemic against a false position. The readers are to recognize themselves in the disciples.

(c) If Mark drew on a preGospel collection of parables, perhaps in that source Jesus was simply a wandering sophistlike teacher challenging the ordinary mores of the times. Mark would then have been imposing a christology on the source by combining it with material that presented Jesus as the Messiah and Son of God. Such a view is in some ways a derivative from Wrede's theory of the Marcan Secret, but combined with theses about the priority of Q and the view of Christ in the Q community (pp. 120–22 above; 826 below). Again however, nonchristological preMarcan stages of Christianity are purely hypothetical and run against much evidence.

Although many reputable NT scholars construct their analyses of Marcan thought in terms of the corrections of putative sources, the uncertainty of source reconstruction makes their analyses very debatable. Moreover, even when Mark does criticize a certain pattern of thought, e.g., a christology without suffering, that faulty pattern could simply be a general Christian tendency without there being a specific Gospel source or even a specific group of Christians to support it.

READING THE GOSPEL FOR ITS SURFACE IMPRESSION.[76] It may seem naive, but I would recommend that for practical purposes readers being introduced to Mark should ignore the scholarly presuppositions based on controversies detected in sources as well as theories of deliberate obscurity. They will understand Mark better by reading on a surface level. In particular, the likelihood that both Matt and Luke based themselves on Mark may mean that Mark's christology was widely preached.[77] Let me give a thumbnail descrip-

[75] *Following Jesus: Discipleship in the Gospel of Mark* (JSNTSup 4; Sheffield Univ., 1981). For J. R. Donahue, *The Theology and Setting of Discipleship in the Gospel of Mark* (Milwaukee: Marquette Univ., 1983), Mark is presenting the implications of discipleship to the house-churches addressed, stressing service over against a tendency to authoritarian institutionalization. See also W. Shiner, *Follow Me! Disciples in the Markan Rhetoric* (Atlanta: Scholars, 1995) and the discussion raised by E. S. Malbon, *Semeia* 62 (1993), 81–102.

[76] Gundry, *Mark* 1, has a wonderful list of twenty-five noes rejecting presuppositions in interpreting Mark: "No ciphers, no hidden meanings . . . no ecclesiastical enemies . . . no riddle wrapped in a mystery, inside an enigma." Since we do not know whether or not any of these factors existed, it is better to read Mark without them: "Mark's meaning lies on the surface."

[77] C. R. Kazmierski, *Jesus the Son of God* (Würzburg: Echter, 1979), argues that Mark preserved Son of God traditions that he received from earlier preaching; he did not try to correct that christology with the Son of Man positions, nor did he shape his christology by correcting false views in his sources. Cole, *Mark* 12, warns against constructing complex theories of early Christian messianism not supported by Mark. See also Kingsbury, *Christology*.

tion of the basic Marcan story that emerges from a surface reading, allowing the various christological titles for Jesus (Son of Man, Messiah, Son of God) to color each other harmoniously.[78]

Fulfilling Isaiah's prophecies and introduced by JBap, a new divine action to deliver God's people has begun. A heavenly voice, echoing Ps 2, tells readers from the beginning that Jesus is God's unique Son. In order to bring God's kingdom or rule to this world he has the power to teach and do acts that go beyond all anticipation. Yet he is tested and opposed by Satan or the demons who already have control—a foreshadowing of the denouement of the story in the passion. Jesus' healings, calming the storm, feeding the hungry, and forgiving sin are all a manifestation that evil is being overcome; yet the demons resist this invasion of their territory by God's kingdom. Other opposition is exhibited by those who reject Jesus' teaching and challenge his power, a rejection vocalized particularly by the Pharisees and scribes. Finally, opposition is reflected in the fact that those who come to accept and follow Jesus do not understand him. They have their own views about kingship: It should be marked by immediate triumphal success and lordship over others in the manner of the kings of this world. Jesus tries to show his followers that God's values are different: Those who have no power are more open to the rule of God than those who are powerful, and there is nothing more effective than suffering to make one recognize a need for God. Yet, by the middle of the Gospel, it is clear that Jesus is not succeeding, and so he begins to proclaim that he himself will have to suffer and die. (Even though Jesus predicts his resurrection, his words in Mark 13 show that the end will not come immediately and that his disciples will not be spared persecution and failure.) His disciples still do not understand, and they all fail when he is arrested. He is abandoned in his passion as he is condemned unjustly by the chief priest of his people and the Roman governor and is mocked by all. Even God does not seem to hear him; and yet at the very moment that he has plumbed the depths of suffering in death, God vindicates him by showing that what Jesus said was true. He is raised from the dead with the indication that his disciples will see him in Galilee. In the place where they first came to follow him they will follow him again, but now after having begun to learn the lesson of suffering.

By the time Mark wrote, Jesus had been preached as the Christ for several decades. To appreciate what this earliest preserved written portrayal contributed to our Christian heritage, one might reflect on what we would know about Jesus if we had just the letters of Paul. We would have a magnificent

[78]See Achtemeier, *Mark* (ABD) 4.551–53, 556.

theology about what God has done in Christ, but Jesus would be left almost without a face. Mark gets the honor of having painted that "face" and made it part of the enduring gospel.

Authorship

If we work backwards, the title "The Gospel According to Mark" was attached to this writing by the end of the 2d century (or perhaps earlier; see Hengel, *Studies* 64–84). In the mid-2d century Justin (*Trypho* 106.3) refers to "Peter's memoirs" as containing a passage that is found only in Mark 3:16–17. Eusebius (EH 3.39.15–16) records an early-2d-century tradition about Mark and Matt that Papias received from "the elder":[79]

> "Mark, having become the interpreter/translator of Peter, wrote down accurately, however, not in order, all that he recalled of what was either said or done by the Lord. For he had neither heard nor followed the Lord; but later (as I said) he followed Peter, who used to adapt his instructions to the needs [of the moment or of the audience], but not with a view of making an orderly account of the Lord's sayings [*logia*]. Accordingly Mark did no wrong in thus writing down some things as he recalled them, for he made it his aim to omit nothing he had heard and to state nothing therein falsely."
>
> Such things did Papias recount of Mark; but about Matthew he said these things:
>
> "Now Matthew arranged in order the sayings [*logia*] in the Hebrew [= Aramaic?] language, and each one interpreted/translated as he was able."

Leaving aside for the moment the historical value of the Papias tradition, let us ask about the Mark of whom it speaks. The name Mark (Greek *Markos,* from the Latin *Marcus*) was not infrequent (e.g., Mark Antony), and that helps to complicate the NT references to one so named. Acts supplies information about a man whom three times it calls "John whose surname was Mark" but only once (15:39) simply "Mark," and whom it associates with Peter, Paul, and Barnabas.[80] In Phlm 24, an undisputedly authentic let-

[79]Papias' notion of elder (*presbyteros*) will be explained on p. 398 below. The Matt portion of the quoted tradition will be discussed in the next Chapter. For diverse views of this tradition, Kümmel, *Introduction* 95–97; H.E.W. Turner, ExpTim 71 (1959–60), 260–63; Hengel, *Studies* 47–50. More generally, C. C. Black, *Mark: Images of an Apostolic Interpreter* (Columbia: Univ. of S. Carolina, 1994).

[80]In Acts 12:12, on his release from prison *ca.* AD 42–43, Peter went to the Jerusalem house of Mary, the mother of this man. (Presumably, then, John Mark was a Jerusalemite, unless we are to

ter sent between 55 and 63, Paul mentions a Mark as a fellow worker who was with him in the place from which he writes (perhaps from Rome, but more likely from Ephesus during "the Third Missionary Journey"). Col 4:10, which assumes the same situation as Phlm and may be dependent on it, elaborates the picture of this Mark; he is the cousin of Barnabas.[81] I Pet (5:13), written from Rome, identifies Mark as Peter's "son" who is with him there. In II Tim 4:11, when Paul is purportedly dying in prison (in Rome?), he asks that Mark be brought to him, "for his service is useful to me." It is *possible* to combine all this into a composite picture of a John called Mark: He was known to Peter in Jerusalem; he was subsequently a companion of Paul, but quarreled with him in the 46–50 period; after a few years this Mark was reconciled to the apostle and once more became a companion, ultimately coming to Rome in the 60s where he was useful to both Paul and Peter before their martyrdom.

Most likely the Papias tradition was referring to this (John) Mark as the one who wrote down what was said and done by the Lord. How plausible is the tradition? On the one hand, if Papias did get it from the elder, we would be dealing with a tradition shaped within a few decades of the writing. If someone was inventing a tradition about authorship, why attribute the Gospel to such a minor Christian figure? On the other hand, the internal evidence of the Gospel supplies little to support the Papias picture and much to call it into question. That in Mark, Peter is the most important of the Twelve and almost their representative need not mean that Peter was the Gospel's source. One would get a somewhat similar impression of Peter from Paul in Gal and I Cor, and so Peter's importance was simply factual. That the author of this Greek Gospel was John Mark, a (presumably Aramaic-speaking) Jew of Jerusalem who had early become a Christian, is hard to reconcile with the impression that it does not seem to be a translation from Aramaic,[82] that it

think that he and his mother had come to Jerusalem from Cyprus with his cousin Barnabas). When Barnabas and Saul returned from Jerusalem to Antioch sometime in the 40s, they brought with them John Mark (Acts 12:25) and on "the First Missionary Journey" (*ca.* 46?) took him along to Cyprus; but he left them and returned to Jerusalem when they went on to Asia Minor (13:4,13). At the beginning of the "Second Missionary Journey" *ca.* 50 from Antioch, Barnabas wanted to enlist John Mark again; but because of his previous behavior, Paul refused and took Silas instead. Barnabas took Mark with him and sailed to Cyprus (15:36–40).

[81]That information makes it very likely that this Mark of Col is the same as John called Mark, even though no Pauline writing uses the "John" identification. There is a good possibility, however, that Col is pseudepigraphical, written in the 80s, when later Christians began to identify the Mark mentioned in Phlm as the John Mark with whom (according to Acts) Paul refused to travel.

[82]The author supplies translations of some Aramaic words. Was he simply preserving the meaning of terms that had come down to him in the Jesus tradition? (See Cole, *Mark* 59–60.) The proportionately high number of Aramaic words persuades Hengel otherwise: The author "was a Greek-speaking Jewish Christian who also understood Aramaic" (*Studies* 46).

seems to depend on traditions (and perhaps already shaped sources) received in Greek, and that it seems confused about Palestinian geography.[83] (The attempt to claim that Mark used geography theologically and therefore did not bother about accuracy seems strained.) If those observations do not fit the NT John Mark and one wants to give some credibility to the Papias tradition, one might speculate that earlier tradition attributed the Gospel to an otherwise unknown Christian named Mark, who subsequently was amalgamated with John Mark.

Did the relationship of (John) Mark to Peter in Acts and I Peter give rise to the Papias tradition that Mark the evangelist drew on Peter? A few precisions about the Papias statement are important. "Interpreter" need not mean that Peter spoke Aramaic and that Mark translated him into Greek; it could mean that he rephrased Peter's preaching.[84] Papias indicates that Mark was not an eyewitness, that he depended on preaching, and that he had imposed his own order on what he wrote—all that could match the internal evidence of the Gospel about the evangelist. Yet the close, immediate relation posited by Papias between the evangelist and Peter (an eyewitness) is difficult; for some accounts of the words and deeds of Jesus in Mark seem secondary to accounts in Q or the other Gospels. Again if one wants to grant at least limited credibility to Papias, one might regard "Peter" as an archetypal figure identified with the Jerusalem apostolic tradition and with a preaching that combined Jesus' teaching, deeds, and passion.[85] (The observations of form critics detecting different types of sayings, parables, narratives, controversies, etc., in Mark would be no obstacle to such an approach, for these would have been shaped during the preaching.) *Papias could, then, be reporting in a dramatized and simplified way that in his writing about Jesus, Mark reorganized and rephrased a content derived from a standard type of preaching that was considered apostolic.* That could explain two frequently

[83]Mark 5:1,13 betrays confusion about the distance of Gerasa from the Sea of Galilee (n. 17 above). Mark 7:31 describes a journey from Tyre through Sidon to the Sea of Galilee in the midst of the Decapolis. In fact one goes SE from Tyre to the Sea of Galilee; Sidon is N of Tyre, and the description of the Sea of Galilee in the midst of the Decapolis is awkward. That a boat headed for Bethsaida (NE side of the Sea of Galilee) arrives at Gennesaret (NW side: 6:45,53) may also signal confusion. No one has been able to locate the Dalmanutha of 8:10, and it may be a corruption of Magdala. In judgment on confused directions as a criterion of origin, however, one must admit that sometimes even natives of a place are not very clear about geography.

[84]However, Papias' use of the same terminology in reference to Matt may tilt the likelihood toward translation: Peter spoke Aramaic; and Mark, who wrote in Greek, translated him. Matthew composed in Hebrew/Aramaic, and it was up to each individual to translate him into Greek.

[85]Several passages in Paul indicate that historically Peter was known as a preacher and perhaps a font of tradition about Jesus (a combination of I Cor 15:3,5,11; one interpretation of Gal 1:18). Later Acts personifies Peter as *the* preacher of the Jerusalem community. The ecumenical book PNT contends that after his lifetime Peter became an idealized figure for certain functions in the church. II Pet 1:13–19 embodies the picture of Peter as the preserver of the apostolic memory.

held positions about Gospel relationships: first, that the Marcan Gospel was so acceptable within a decade as to be known and approved as a guide by Matthew and Luke writing in different areas; second, that John could be independent of Mark and still have similarities to it in outline and some contents. Many would dismiss entirely the Papias tradition; but the possibilities just raised could do some justice to the fact that ancient traditions often have elements of truth in a garbled form.

Locale or Community Involved[86]

Do we have evidence of where the Gospel was written from or written to (or both, if the author lived among the addressees)? Some proponents of literary criticism contend that the audience implied in the Gospel text may not have been the historical audience who actually received the Gospel. Even without such a thesis (which would make impossible the detection of the actual locale addressed), the internal indications do not tell us whether we are dealing with the outlook of the author or that of the addressees or of both. That difficulty is why I have used the neutral word "involved" in the title of this subsection.

By the end of the 2d century Clement of Alexandria (EH 6.14.6) cites Rome as the place where Mark wrote the Gospel, a thesis supported by a large number of scholars.[87] However, since there was a strong tradition that Peter was martyred at Rome, the ancient claim may have been an imaginative derivation from the connection that Papias made between Mark and Peter. Several internal factors are thought to support Rome as the locale. The presence in Mark of Greek loanwords derived from Latin and of expressions reflecting Latin grammar may suggest a locale where Latin was spoken.[88] Although many of the Latinisms, which are commercial or military words, could be found anywhere in the Roman Empire, Hengel (*Studies* 29) would counter that the description of the woman as a Greek and Syrophoenician in Mark 7:26 represents linguistic usages of the West (and thus possibly of Rome). Also it is claimed that the *kodrantēs* (Latin: *quadrans*) coin of 12:42 was not circulated in the East. Again parallels have been detected between

[86]J. R. Donahue, FGN 2.819–34; CBQ 57 (1995), 1–26; P.J.J. Botha, JSNT 51 (1993), 27–55.

[87]See B. Orchard, FGN 2.779–800; E. E. Ellis, FGN 2.801–16; M. Hengel, *Studies* 28; D. P. Senior, BTB 17 (1987), 10–20; C. C. Black, ExpTim 105 (1993–94), 36–40. Later in antiquity the tradition that Mark became bishop of Alexandria led to a suggestion that the Gospel was written there. *The Secret Gospel of Mark* is supposed to represent additions made at Alexandria to the "Acts of the Lord" that Mark brought from Rome.

[88]E.g., *Legiōn* ("legion") in 5:9,15; *dēnarion* ("denarius") in 6:37; 12:15; 14:5; *kentyriōn* ("centurion") in 15:39; *hodon poiein* in 2:23 representing *iter facere* ("to make one's way"); *to hikanon poiēsai* in 15:15 representing *satisfacere* ("to make enough, satisfy").

Mark and Paul's letter to the Romans. For instance, Mark's "he declared all foods are clean" (7:19) resembles Rom 14:14: "I know and am convinced in the Lord Jesus that nothing is unclean in itself." The strong emphasis on the failure of the disciples to understand and on their flight when Jesus was arrested has suggested that Mark addressed a community that had been persecuted and failed. Perhaps this was a Roman persecution, for 10:42 strongly criticizes those who rule over the Gentiles and lord it over them. Although Christians were harassed in various places, only the capital city's Christian community is known to have undergone major Roman persecution before AD 70, namely, under Nero. During that persecution both *I Clement* 5:2–7 (reference to jealousy) and Tacitus (*Annals* 15.44: "their disclosures") hint at failure and Christian betrayal of other Christians.

Others would localize Mark's addressees closer to Palestine, in Syria or in the northern Transjordan. If Matt and Luke were both written in the Antioch area (dubious speculation!), their knowing Mark independently could be explained if Mark were written nearby. H. Kee (*Community*) finds indications of southern Syria in the references to Tyre and Sidon in 3:8 and especially 7:24,31.[89] Galilee is another suggestion. A thesis associated with the name of E. Lohmeyer and continued by R. H. Lightfoot and W. Marxsen points to a contrast between Galilee and Jerusalem in Mark, so that the future of the believing community lies in Galilee as the promised land of salvation (Mark 16:7) or as a symbol of the Gentile world (although, in fact, Galilee was strongly Jewish and nationalistic). W. Kelber thinks that the prophets of the Jerusalem church expected a parousia that would bring protection against the Romans; but after the destruction of Jerusalem Mark was written as a Galilean Christian polemic against the failed Jerusalem Christian outlook. More simply, however, the fact that Jesus came from Galilee may explain Mark's interest in that area. Even were Galilee a factor in the composition of Mark, it would probably be the place *from* which the Gospel was written rather than the place *to* which. Aramaic terms are translated as if the receiving audience does not know that language (3:17; 7:34; 10:46; 15:22,34), and that would scarcely be true in Galilee. Also the author would not have to explain basic Jewish purification practices (7:3–4) to most Galileans.

The recognition that we cannot know precisely the locale addressed by Mark leaves us free to concentrate on what can be detected about the addressees from a careful reading of Mark, no matter where they lived. *By way*

[89]See also Mack, *Myth* 315–18. The cities of the Decapolis, the Hellenistic area of Palestine, and the Transjordan have also been proposed: J. Marcus, JBL 111 (1992), 441–62; R. I. Rohrbaugh, *Interpretation* 47 (1993), 380–95; BTB 23 (1993), 114–27.

of summary, in whole or in part the Gospel's envisioned audience consisted of Greek-speakers who did not know Aramaic. Either the author or the audience or both lived in an area where Latin was used and had influenced Greek vocabulary. For the most part the recipients were not Jews since the author had to explain Jewish purification customs to them.[90] Yet he could assume that they would know religious terms stemming from Judaism (Satan, Beelzebul, Gehenna, Rabbi, Hosanna, and Amen), so that they were probably Christians who had been converted by evangelizers familiar directly or indirectly with Jewish Christian tradition. Most likely they had heard a good deal about Jesus before Mark's Gospel was read to them.[91] Theologically the recipients had an overheated expectation of an imminent parousia (wherefore Mark 13), probably activated by persecution which they had undergone and during which a considerable number had failed.

Date of Writing

Among those who give credence to the Papias tradition, the usual understanding is that Mark wrote just before or after Peter's death and thus in the mid- or late 60s.[92] Internally that dating is supposed to be supported by the failure of Mark to show any knowledge of the details of the First Jewish Revolt against Rome in AD 66–70 and to mention the fall of Jerusalem. Some who posit a post-70 date for Mark ask whether many people outside Palestine knew details of the Revolt, and whether the fall of Jerusalem warranted symbolic mention in a Gospel before it was seen as God's judgment because of what happened to Jesus. Yet the attention that Josephus and the Jewish apocalypses give to that fall and to the destruction of the Temple leads others to object that Christians with Jewish roots could scarcely have ignored the symbolism of these events after they had occurred.[93]

As for a terminus after which Mark is not likely to have been written,

[90]Other Jewish details in Mark would be known widely to outsiders: that Jews keep the Sabbath, go to synagogues, and do not eat pork (5:1–20).

[91]E.g., Mark 15:1 does not have to identify Pilate for them; 15:21 suggests that Alexander and Rufus, the sons of Simon of Cyrene, were known to them. Presumably they understood who Pharisees and scribes were from traditions about Jesus rather than from personal contact with those figures.

[92]Hengel (*Studies* 21–28) would date the atmosphere of Mark 13 to the period after the suicide of Nero—specifically to AD 69, when three emperors lost their lives.

[93]Matt 22:7 and Luke 21:20 are seen as more precise with respect to the destruction of Jerusalem than is Mark; and during Jesus' passion Matt 27:25 and Luke 23:28 warn the Jerusalem populace of punishment for the "children" (next generation). Yet the references are still only by allusion. The failure of NT works to make specific and detailed mention of the destruction of Jerusalem and the Temple is very hard to explain. J.A.T. Robinson, *Redating the New Testament* (London: SCM, 1976), has used this factor entirely too simply to date most of the NT before AD 70; but we should not pretend that we have a satisfactory answer.

Synoptic relationships constitute an argument. If Mark was used independently by both Matt and Luke and they were written in the 80s or early 90s, as most scholars believe, a date beyond 75 seems unlikely.[94]

The other end of the spectrum is more problematic, for there is no way of knowing with certainty how early Mark was written. This remains true despite the claim of J. O'Callaghan in 1972 to have found a few words of Mark 6:52–53 on a Qumran (DSS) Greek papyrus fragment (7Q5) that paleographically has been dated between 50 BC and AD 50 (give or take twenty-five years). Such identification might imply that the Gospel was in circulation a decade or more before the destruction of the Qumran community in 68. Few scholars have agreed,[95] and most surmise that the developed state of the Greek Jesus tradition in Mark implies that several decades have passed since the time of Jesus. Therefore, *there is wide scholarly agreement that Mark was written in the late 60s or just after 70.*

Issues and Problems for Reflection

(1) As explained in Chapter 6, this *Introduction* works with the thesis that Matt and Luke used Mark. Yet for many centuries the dominant view was Augustine's thesis that Mark was little more than an epitome of Matt; and recently attention has been given to the (modified) Griesbach hypothesis wherein Mark drew on Matt and Luke (p. 113 above). It is instructive to test the theological consequences of positing Marcan dependence on the other Synoptics. For instance, Mark would have omitted the Lord's Prayer and the four beatitudes that Matt and Luke agree upon. As for christology, if Mark was written after Matt and drew on it, at a period when the title

[94]H. Koester ("History" 54–57) appeals to the lack of citations of Mark in early extra-NT church writers to argue unconventionally that final canonical Mark may stem from the late 2d century, although he posits an earlier form of Mark related to *Secret Mark* would have antedated Matt and Luke and from which sections judged unfit were eliminated.

[95]C. P. Thiede has defended it in *The Earliest Gospel Manuscript?* (Exeter: Paternoster, 1992); also (with M. D'Ancona) *Eyewitness to Jesus* (New York: Doubleday, 1996). *First,* however, the exclusively Greek collection of Qumran Cave 7 need not have come from a member of the DSS community. Indeed, relatively few Greek fragments have been found in the other caves, and they were mixed in with a high number of Hebrew and Aramaic mss. Theoretically it is possible that a Christian came to Qumran about the time the settlement was destroyed and used Cave 7 to deposit a ms. *Second,* there are serious problems with the Marcan identification. All other known early papyrus mss. of the Gospels have been from codices; 7Q5 is from a scroll. It has only some ten complete Greek letters on four lines with only one full word (*kai,* "and"). For it to be Mark there has to be missing from 6:52–53 a Greek phrase ("to land") that is found in all other Greek mss. and early versions. Thiede argues that, if one accepts his (highly disputed) reading of partial Greek letters, the combination of these twenty letters on five lines can be shown by computer to exist only in Mark amidst all other known Greek literature. Obviously, however, 7Q5 could be from a hitherto unknown Greek composition. See the response of G. Stanton, *Gospel Truth?* 20–29. *Third,* such an early dating would not prove either that the Gospel was written by John Mark or that it is literal history, as some would claim.

"God" for Jesus was becoming more common, Mark 10:17–18 would have complicated Matt 19:16–17 by gratuitously introducing an objection to giving Jesus a title that belonged to God alone. Mark 6:5 would have introduced the idea that Jesus could not do miracles at Nazareth, changing the statement in Matt 13:58 that he did none. Some claim that Matthean priority and Marcan dependence support traditional Roman Catholic positions, but Mark's presentation of Mary and Peter becomes all the more difficult if the evangelist knew Matt and/or Luke. Mark would have deliberately omitted the infancy narratives of Matt and Luke, even the details in which they both agree, including the conception of Jesus by Mary through the Holy Spirit. Mark would have consciously added two items lacking in Matt and Luke pertinent to Mary, namely, that Jesus' own family thought he was "beside himself" (3:19b–21) and that he received no honor from his own relatives (6:4). As for the Marcan view of Peter and the apostles, Mark would have deliberately omitted both Matt 16:16–19 that makes Peter the rock on which the church was built, and Luke 22:31–34 that has Peter strengthening his brothers after his own failure. (Even though those are not passages shared by both Matt and Luke, Mark can scarcely not have noticed the impact of omitting such positive passages.) Mark would have deliberately omitted the promise of Jesus to the disciples in Matt 19:28 and Luke 22:29–30 whereby they would sit on thrones judging the twelve tribes of Israel. Mark 4:38 would have made the disciples more rude to Jesus than they were in Matt 8:25. Using a book with the Gospels in parallel columns, readers are invited to test other examples of Marcan thought and procedure in the Griesbach hypothesis.

(2) Leaving aside the issue raised under (1) and taking Mark on its own merits, we note that a number of scholars interpret this Gospel as an attack upon the apostles to the point that after their failure in the passion they are never redeemed (also pp. 138, 156 above). When one reads through the Gospel, however, is such a negative interpretation justified? Is their constant misunderstanding not simply human bumbling of which all might be guilty? Does Jesus really abandon them even when he knows they will fail? Do not 14:28 and 16:7 engender confidence that Jesus will bring them back to the role he envisioned when he sent them out in 6:7–13?[96] (Some scholars would argue that these passages represent Mark's additions to an earlier source, but they belong to the Gospel as it comes to us.)

(3) If one had only Mark and not Matt, one would miss the colorful infancy narrative of Herod and the magi, the Sermon on the Mount, the Lord's

[96]True, Mark ends in 16:8 without telling us that the disciples did go to Galilee to see the risen Jesus, but the readers are expected to finish the story (p. 148 above). That the disciples were not rejected, see R. C. Tannehill, JR 57 (1977), 386–405; reprinted in TIM 169–95.

Prayer, the establishment of the church on Peter, and some of the more imaginative elements in the passion (e.g., Judas' suicide). If one had only Mark and not Luke, one would miss the sensitive portrayal of Mary in the infancy narrative, the story of the shepherds, some of the most beautiful parables (the Good Samaritan, the Prodigal Son), and very tender scenes in the passion (healing the servant's ear, the Jerusalem women on the way of the cross, the "Good Thief"). That recognition of impoverishment has sometimes led to a low evaluation of Mark as a poor cousin to the other Synoptic Gospels. By way of corrective, a worthwhile exercise is to read through Mark, excluding all knowledge of Jesus from the other Gospels, and to reflect on how rich a picture of Jesus it offers (see p. 157 above).

(4) In the Marcan passion narrative the chief priests with the scribes and the elders plot against Jesus, come together as a Sanhedrin seeking testimony in order to put him to death, condemn him as deserving to die, spit on and strike and mock him, accuse him before Pilate, stir up the crowd to demand his death, and mock him again while he hangs on the cross. Some scholars would see this as a picture created to promote antiJudaism. That evaluation needs qualification. Clearly the passion narrative has dramatized events; but in terms of underlying reality, it is quite likely that Jewish Temple and Sanhedrin authorities were seriously involved in the death of Jesus and handed him over to the Romans who executed him. This likelihood is supported by the statement of Paul within twenty years of Jesus' death that there was Jewish participation in the death of Jesus (I Thess 2:14–16), by the evidence of the 1st-century Jewish historian Josephus that Pilate condemned Jesus to the cross "upon indictment of the first ranking men among us" (*Ant.* 18.3.3; #64), and by the confirmatory parallel evidence of actions taken against other Jews in Jerusalem in the 60s who were either handed over for execution to the Roman procurator by the Jewish leaders after a beating (Jesus, son of Ananias) or, during the absence of the Roman perfect, directly executed by the high priest who had convened a Sanhedrin (James, brother of Jesus).[97]

In the Christian picture of what was done to Jesus, at first there was nothing antiJewish in depicting the role of the Jewish authorities in his death; for Jesus and his disciples on one side and the Jerusalem Sanhedrin authorities on the other were all Jews. The depiction of those Jews opposed to Jesus as plotting evil was not different from the OT depiction of the wicked plotting against the innocent. For instance, in Wisdom 2:17–21 the wicked contend that if the just one be the son of God, God will defend him; and they resolve

[97]All this is spelled out in BDM 1.364–68, 372–83, 539–41. On the issue of antiJudaism, see BDM 1:383–97.

to revile him and put him to death. The abuse and travail of Jesus took on the hues of the plaintive hymnist of Ps 22 and the Suffering Servant of Isaiah 52–53. Were all the Jewish authorities opposed to Jesus in fact evil? No—no more than six hundred years earlier all who disagreed with Jeremiah's policies for Judah were wicked. Yet the OT account portrayed them thus, simplifying their motives and dramatizing their actions. Indeed some of the most sensitive words in the passion of Jesus are found in Jer 26.[98]

Nevertheless, the account of Jesus' passion was eventually "heard" in an antiJewish way. A major factor was the conversion of Gentiles to the following of Jesus. Sometimes the early Christian communities encountered the hostility of local synagogue leaders, and they saw a parallel between this hostility and the treatment of Jesus by the authorities of his time. Now, however, the issue was no longer on an intraJewish level: That other group, the Jews, were doing these things to us Gentile Christians and were responsible for the death of Jesus. Thus the case of Jesus became different from that of Jeremiah. Both Jews who did not accept Jesus and early followers of Jesus could read the story of Jeremiah as Scripture. Jewish leaders persecuted Jeremiah; yet, even though the language of bloodguilt appears in the account, no one suggested that the blood of Jeremiah needs to be avenged. Rather, for both Jews and Christians Jeremiah was an outstanding example of the innocent made to suffer by the leaders of God's own people; and the prophet's sufferings offered the opportunity for self-examination on what *we* who consider ourselves God's people do to *our* prophets whom God raises up among us. Although much the same story was told of Jesus, the case became emotionally dissimilar because those who thought that Jesus was right ultimately became another religion. Jews and Christians were not able to say in this instance that one of *our* own whom God raised up was made to suffer by *our* leaders. Instead, Christians spoke to Jews of *your* leaders doing this to our savior, while for Jews (in centuries past) it was our leaders doing this to *their* (false) prophet.[99] Fortunately attitudes on both sides are now changing; yet it remains very difficult to overcome the "our," "your," and "their" outlook. It will help readers of the NT if they can remember that it was not thus when the crucifixion was taking place and when the story was first taking shape.

[98]When with God's authority Jeremiah threatened the destruction of the Temple, the priests and *all the people* heard him, and the priests and the prophets demanded his death. Jeremiah warned them that they were bringing *innocent blood* on Jerusalem and its citizens.

[99]Notice that I have spoken in one instance of "your" and in the other of "their." Christian evangelism over the centuries has forced on Jews direct debate about the crucifixion because it was an issue of importance for Christians. Jews have not looked on the issue as of key Jewish importance, and until recent times Jewish writing about the crucifixion has often been for inner consumption by way of (explicit or implicit) comment on Christian accusations.

Bibliography on Mark[100]

COMMENTARIES AND STUDIES IN SERIES: Achtemeier, P. J. (ABD 4.541–57; ProcC, 2d ed., 1986); Anderson, H. (NCBC, 1976); Cole, R. A. (TNTC, 2d ed., 1989); Cranfield, C.E.B. (CGTC, 1959); **Guelich, R. A.** (chaps. 1–8; WBC, 1989); Hare, D.R.A. (WBComp, 1996); **Hooker, M. D.** (BNTC, 1991); Hunter, A. M. (TBC, 1974); Hurtado, L. W. (NIBC, 1989); Johnson, S. E. (BNTC, 2d ed. corrected, 1977); Juel, D. H. (AugC, 1990); Lane, W. L. (NICNT, 1974); Mann, C. S. (AB, 1986); Moule, C.F.D. (CCNEB, 1965); Nineham, D. E. (PC, 2d ed., 1968); Perkins, P. (NInterpB, 1994); Telford, W. R. (NTG, 1996); Williamson, L. (IBC, 1983).

BIBLIOGRAPHIES: Humphrey, H. M., *A Bibliography for the Gospel of Mark, 1954–1980* (New York: Mellen, 1981); TIM 307–26; Wagner, G., EBNT (1983); Neirynck, F. et al., *The Gospel of Mark: 1950–1990* (BETL; Leuven: Peeters, 1992); Mills, W. E., BBR (1994).

SURVEYS OF RESEARCH: Martin, R. P., *Mark, Evangelist and Theologian* (Grand Rapids: Zondervan, 1973); Kealy, S. P., *Mark's Gospel: A History of Its Interpretation* (New York: Paulist, 1982); Matera, F. J., *What Are They Saying about Mark?* (New York: Paulist, 1987); Telford, W. R., TIM 1–61; also FGN 2.693–723 on the preMarcan tradition.

* * *

(See also the *Bibliography* in Chapter 6 on the Synoptic Problem and on Q Research.)

Ambrozic, A. M., *The Hidden Kingdom—A Redaction-critical Study of the References to the Kingdom of God in Mark* (CBQMS 2; Washington: CBA, 1972).

Anderson, J. C., and S. D. Moore, eds., *Mark and Method* (Minneapolis: A/F, 1992).

Best E., *Mark: The Gospel as Story* (Edinburgh: Clark, 1983). A brief treatment of issues.

———, *The Temptation and the Passion: the Markan Soteriology* (SNTSMS 2; 2d ed.; Cambridge Univ., 1990).

Bilezikian, G. C., *The Liberated Gospel: A Comparison of the Gospel of Mark and Greek Tragedy* (Grand Rapids: Baker, 1977).

Broadhead, E. K., *Prophet, Son, Messiah: Narrative Form and Function in Mark 14–16* (JSNTSup 97; Sheffield: Academic, 1994). Christology.

Bryan, C. A., *A Preface to Mark* (Oxford Univ., 1993).

Carrington, P., *According to Mark* (Cambridge Univ., 1960).

Cook, J. G., *The Structure and Persuasive Power of Mark. A Linguistic Approach* (Atlanta: Scholars, 1996).

Davidsen, O., *The Narrative Jesus: A Semiotic Reading of Mark's Gospel* (Aarhus Univ., 1993).

Elliott, J. K., ed., *The Language and Style of Mark* (NovTSup 71; Leiden: Brill, 1993). Development of C. H. Turner's studies in the 1920s.

[100]Boldface indicates a few important, major works, usually commentaries.

Fowler, R. M., *Let the Reader Understand: Reader-Response Criticism and the Gospel of Mark* (Minneapolis: A/F, 1991).

Gundry, R. H., *Mark* (Grand Rapids: Eerdmans, 1993).

Hamerton-Kelly, R. G., *The Gospel and the Sacred: Poetics in the Gospel of Mark* (Minneapolis: A/F, 1994). R. Girard's mimetic theory.

Heil, J. P., *The Gospel of Mark as a Model for Action: A Reader-Response Commentary* (New York: Paulist, 1992). Application to reader in "Action" section.

Hengel, M., *Studies in the Gospel of Mark* (Philadelphia: Fortress, 1985).

Humphrey, H. M., *He is Risen! A New Reading of Mark's Gospel* (New York: Paulist, 1992). Chiastic arrangement; wisdom pattern.

Juel, D. H., *A Master of Surprise: Mark Interpreted* (Minneapolis: A/F, 1994).

Kee, H. C., *Community of the New Age. Studies in Mark's Gospel* (rev. ed.; Macon, GA: Mercer, 1983).

Kelber, W. H., *Mark's Story of Jesus* (Philadelphia: Fortress, 1979).

Kingsbury, J. D., *The Christology of Mark's Gospel* (Philadelphia: Fortress, 1983).

———, *Conflict in Mark* (Minneapolis: A/F, 1989).

Kinukawa, H., *Women and Jesus in Mark* (Maryknoll: Orbis, 1994).

Koester, H., "History and Development of Mark's Gospel," in *Colloquy on New Testament Studies,* ed. B. Corley (Macon, GA: Mercer, 1983), 35–57.

Lightfoot, R. H., *The Gospel Message of St. Mark* (Oxford: Clarendon, 1950).

Mack, B. L., *A Myth of Innocence. Mark and Christian Origins* (Philadelphia: Fortress, 1988). Skeptical historical evaluation.

Malbon, E. S., *Narrative Space and Mythic Meaning in Mark* (San Francisco: Harper & Row, 1986). Structural analysis.

Marcus, J., *The Way of the Lord: Christological Exegesis of the Old Testament in the Gospel of Mark* (Louisville: W/K, 1992). Set in context of DeuteroIsa.

Marxsen, W., *Mark the Evangelist* (Nashville: Abingdon, 1969). Redaction criticism.

Meagher, J. C., *Clumsy Construction in Mark's Gospel* (Toronto: Mellen, 1979).

Morton, A. Q., *The Making of Mark* (Lewiston, NY: Mellen, 1995). Numerical regularity in Marcan structure.

Myers, C., *Binding the Strong Man: A Political Reading of Mark's Story of Jesus* (Maryknoll: Orbis, 1988). Exegesis.

———, *Who Will Roll Away the Stone?* (Maryknoll: Orbis, 1994). Theology.

Perrin, N., "Towards an Interpretation of the Gospel of Mark," in *Christology and a Modern Pilgrimage,* ed. H. D. Betz (Claremont, CA: New Testament Colloquium, 1971), 1–78.

Petersen, N. R., ed., *Perspectives on Mark's Gospel* (*Semeia* 16, 1980).

Quesnell, Q., *The Mind of Mark* (AnBib 38; Rome: PBI, 1969).

Rhoads, D. M., and D. Mitchie, *Mark as Story. An Introduction to the Narrative of a Gospel* (Philadelphia: Fortress, 1982).

Robbins, V. K., *Jesus the Teacher: A Socio-Rhetorical Interpretation of Mark* (Philadelphia: Fortress, 1984).

———, *New Boundaries in Old Territories: Form and Social Rhetoric in Mark* (New York: Lang, 1994).

Robinson, J. M., *The Problem of History in Mark* (SBT 21; London: SCM, 1957). See also *Union Seminary Quarterly Review* 20 (1964–65), 131–47.

Schmid, J., *The Gospel according to Mark* (Staten Island: Alba, 1968).

Schweizer, E., *The Good News according to St. Mark* (Richmond: Knox, 1970).

Stock, A., *The Method and Message of Mark* (Wilmington: Glazier, 1989).

Taylor, V., *The Gospel according to St. Mark* (2d ed.; London: Macmillan, 1966). A classic.

Tolbert, M. A., *Sowing the Gospel: Mark's World in Literary-Historical Perspective* (Minneapolis: A/F, 1989).

Trocmé, E., *The Formation of the Gospel according to Mark* (Philadelphia: Westminster, 1975).

van Iersel, B.M.F., *Reading Mark* (Collegeville: Liturgical, 1988).

Via, D. O., *The Ethics of Mark's Gospel—In the Middle of Time* (Philadelphia: Fortress, 1985).

Waetjen, H. C., *A Reordering of Power: A Sociopolitical Reading of Mark's Gospel* (Minneapolis: A/F, 1989).

Weeden, T. J., *Mark: Traditions in Conflict* (Philadelphia: Fortress, 1971). Thesis summed up in an article in TIM 89–104.

Williams, J. F., *Other Followers of Jesus. Minor Characters as Major Figures in Mark's Gospel* (JSNTSup 102; Sheffield: JSOT, 1994).

Yarbro Collins, A., *The Beginning of the Gospel: Probings of Mark in Context* (Minneapolis: A/F, 1992).

CHAPTER 8

THE GOSPEL ACCORDING TO MATTHEW

Matt (*ca.* 18,300 words in Greek) is more than 50 percent longer than Mark (*ca.* 11,300 words), with much of the greater length explained by the two chaps. of prefaced infancy narrative and the long sermons consisting of sayings material absent from Mark. The healings of the centurion's servant boy and of the blind and mute demoniac (Matt 8:5–13; 12:22–23), taken from Q, are the only entirely nonMarcan miracle-stories in the Matthean Jesus' ministry. Otherwise it is estimated that Matt reproduces about 80 percent of Mark.

Although modern Gospel courses tend to give Mark the most attention among the Synoptics, Matt stood first in the great ancient biblical codices and has been the church's Gospel par excellence. Indeed, Matt has served as the NT foundational document of the church, rooting it in the teaching of Jesus—a church built on rock against which the gates of hell would not prevail. Matt's Sermon on the Mount, the (eight) beatitudes, and the Lord's Prayer are among the most widely known treasures in the Christian heritage. Organizational skill and clarity, plus a penchant for unforgettable images, have given this Gospel priority as the church's teaching instrument.

Once again we shall begin with a *General Analysis* crafted to bring the evangelist's thought and technique to light through the Gospel text. Here, however, there is a special problem: Much of the Matthean storyline is parallel to the Marcan storyline, and an *Introduction* has neither the space nor the leisure to repeat. More attention will have to be given to what was not already discussed in the preceding Chapter. The *Analysis* is not the place for a debate about Matt's sources. Yet all recognize that Matt has sections parallel to Mark, as well as sections parallel to Luke but absent from Mark (the Q material of Table 2 in Chapter 6); and attention to what is the same and what is different in those sections can help to highlight Matt's own outlook. (This is a form of redaction criticism, discussed Chapter 2A above.) Nevertheless, as I caution below (p. 208), we cannot afford to lose sight of Matt's highly effective narrative because of attention to comparative details. By way of procedure, let me suggest that readers go through a whole subsec-

Summary of Basic Information

DATE: 80–90, give or take a decade.

AUTHOR BY TRADITIONAL (2D-CENTURY) ATTRIBUTION: Matthew, a tax-collector among the Twelve, wrote either the Gospel or a collection of the Lord's sayings in Aramaic. Some who reject this picture allow that something written by Matthew may have made its way into the present Gospel.

AUTHOR DETECTABLE FROM CONTENTS: A Greek-speaker, who knew Aramaic or Hebrew or both and was not an eyewitness of Jesus' ministry, drew on Mark and a collection of the sayings of the Lord (Q), as well as on other available traditions, oral or written. Probably a Jewish Christian.

LOCALE INVOLVED: Probably the Antioch region.

UNITY AND INTEGRITY: No major reason to think of more than one author or of any sizable additions to what he wrote.

DIVISION:

1:1–2:23: **Introduction: Origin and Infancy of Jesus the Messiah**
1. The who and how of Jesus' identity (1:1–25)
2. The where and whence of Jesus' birth and destiny (2:1–23)

3:1–7:29: **Part One: Proclamation of the Kingdom**
1. Narrative: Ministry of JBap, baptism of Jesus, the temptations, beginning of the Galilean ministry (3:1–4:25)
2. Discourse: Sermon on the Mount (5:1–7:29)

8:1–10:42 **Part Two: Ministry and Mission in Galilee**
1. Narrative mixed with short dialogue: Nine miracles consisting of healings, calming a storm, exorcism (8:1–9:38)
2. Discourse: Mission Sermon (10:1–42)

11:1–13:52 **Part Three: Questioning of and Opposition to Jesus**
1. Narrative setting for teaching and dialogue: Jesus and JBap, woes on disbelievers, thanksgiving for revelation, Sabbath controversies and Jesus' power, Jesus' family (11:1–12:50)
2. Discourse: Sermon in parables (13:1–52)

13:53–18:35 **Part Four: Christology and Ecclesiology**
1. Narrative mixed with much dialogue: Rejection at Nazareth, feeding the 5,000 and walking on the water, controversies with the Pharisees, healings, feeding the 4,000, Peter's confession, first passion prediction, transfiguration, second passion prediction (13:53–17:27)
2. Discourse: Sermon on the church (18:1–35)

19:1–25:46 **Part Five: Journey to and Ministry in Jerusalem**
1. Narrative mixed with much dialogue: Teaching, judgment parables, third passion prediction, entry to Jerusalem, cleansing the Temple, clashes with authorities (19:1–23:39)
2. Discourse: Eschatological Sermon (24:1–25:46)

26:1–28:20 **Climax: Passion, Death, and Resurrection**
1. Conspiracy against Jesus, Last Supper (26:1–29)
2. Arrest, Jewish and Roman trials, crucifixion, death (26:30–27:56)
3. Burial, guard at the tomb, opening of tomb, bribing of the guard, resurrection appearances (27:57–28:20).

tion of the Gospel text (the parameters of which are indicated in the *Analysis* by boldface), sometimes short, sometimes covering several chaps., in order to appreciate the storyflow–Matt's admirable organization facilitates that. Then my observations about the subsection, calling attention to what is uniquely Matthean, will be more productive for understanding Matthean thought.

After the *Analysis,* subdivisions will treat *Sources and compositional features, Authorship, Locale or community involved, Date of writing, Issues and problems for reflection,* and *Bibliography.*[1]

General Analysis of the Message

Two chaps. of infancy narrative preface Matt's account of the ministry. The climax of the Gospel comes in the account of the passion, death, and resurrection, aspects of which match the infancy narrative as an inclusion. The Matthean account of Jesus' public ministry is placed between the infancy and the passion narratives. Notable in that account is a pattern of five long discourses or sermons, marked off by similar clauses but not identical features.[2] The basic inspiration for these sermons may have come from the two Marcan discourses (parables in Mark 4; eschatology in Mark 13). Thus the most popular outline divides the body of Matt into five parts of alternating narrative and discourse, and I shall follow that in the *Analysis* below as the most helpful for initial understanding. Again the pattern is not perfect, as I have indicated in Division outlined on the Summary Page. (It is unlikely that Matt was trying to match the Pentateuch of Moses, as proposed in the classic presentation of B. W. Bacon.) Though we must be careful to distinguish between a division that corresponds to modern interests and the document's own rhetorical structure, there is a good chance that the schema represents the way the evangelist proceeded, even if he would not necessarily

[1]Those who wish to do further reading and research need only consult the excellent bibliographies in W. D. Davies and Allison, *Matthew.*

[2]The five-discourse pattern was recognized in antiquity. The *Sermon on the Mount* (5:3–7:27) begins with a setting of the disciples on the mountain in 5:1–2 and terminates with 7:28–29: "And it happened when Jesus finished these words . . ." The *Mission Sermon* (10:5–42) begins by introducing the Twelve in 10:1–4; it is followed by a transition in 11:1: "And it happened when Jesus finished instructing the twelve disciples . . ." The *Sermon in parables* (13:3–52) begins in 13:1–2 with Jesus sitting by the sea and the crowds gathering; it is followed by a transition in 13:53: "And it happened when Jesus finished these parables . . ." The *Sermon on the church* (18:1–35) contains at its beginning a dialogue with the disciples; it is followed by a transition in 19:1: "And it happened when Jesus finished these words . . ." The *Eschatological Sermon* (24:4–25:46) has a double introduction in the dialogue of 24:1–2 and the disciples' question of 24:3; it is followed by a transition in 26:1: "And it happened when Jesus finished all these words"—the "all" indicating that this is the last discourse.

have thought in terms of formally dividing his work in so detailed a manner.[3]

Introduction: The Origin and Infancy of Jesus the Messiah (1:1–2:23)[4]

The opening Greek phrase of the Gospel, *biblos geneseōs* (1:1), illustrates the difficulty of being sure of the evangelist's outlook.[5] (a) Most likely it means "*the record of the generations* [= birth record] of Jesus Christ," representing the Hebrew phrase *sēper tôlĕdôt* of Gen 5:1. Although in the OT that phrase is followed by a list of descendants, here it would constitute the title of a genealogy of Jesus' ancestors (Matt 1:2–16, which throughout employs the cognate Greek verb form *egennēsen,* "begot"). (b) That interpretation does not exclude a play on *genesis,* meaning "origin," so that the opening phrase in 1:1, understood to mean "the story of the origin," could cover the whole of chap. 1 and thus include the conception and birth of Jesus Christ. (Others would include chap. 2, and make the phrase cover whatever preceded the opening of the ministry, or even include 3:1–4:16 and everything before Jesus began to preach.) (c) Some commentators would associate the use of *genesis* in Matt 1:1 with the Greek title given to the first book of the Scriptures of Israel. Thus, to replace Mark's "The beginning of the gospel of Jesus Christ, the Son of God," Matt would be using a title for his whole Gospel with a comprehensive echo of Israelite history: "The Book of Genesis as effected by Jesus Christ, son of David, son of Abraham." (d) A polyvalent sense of *genesis* is a possibility: The phrase prefaces the ancestral origin, birth, and beginnings of Jesus; but it also encompasses a view of the whole story of Jesus as a new creation, even greater than the old.

1. The Who and How of Jesus' Identity (1:1–25). This chap. deals with the genealogy and the conception of Jesus. *The Matthean genealogy (1:2–*

[3]Other divisions have been suggested: Davies and Allison, *Matthew* 1.58–72; Senior, *What* 20–27; Boring, *Matthew* 110–18; Meier, *Matthew* (ABD) 4.627–29. A geographic division would be the preGalilean preparation (1:1–4:11), Jesus in Galilee (4:12–18:35); Jesus in Judea and Jerusalem, and return to Galilee (19:1–28:20). Kingsbury (*Matthew: Structure*) has attracted attention with a tripartite division: 1:1–4:16 dealing with the person of Jesus as the Messiah, 4:17–16:20 dealing with the proclamation of Jesus the Messiah, and 16:21–28:20 dealing with suffering, death, and resurrection of Jesus the Messiah. (Also D. R. Bauer, *The Structure of Matthew's Gospel* [JSNTSup 31; Sheffield: Almond, 1988].) Kingsbury believes that the "from that time Jesus began" in 4:17 and 16:21 are Matt's structural markers. However, there are serious objections, e.g., "from that time" occurs also in 26:16; and more plausibly the infancy narrative is a separate unit from what follows in 3:1. See BBM 48–50, 584; Meier, *Vision* 56, 95.

[4]An exhaustive bibliography through 1992 is offered for every aspect of Matt 1–2 in BBM.

[5]Davies and Allison, *Matthew* 1.149–60, favor position (c) with elements of (d). J. Nolland, NTS 42 (1996), 463–71 argues for (a).

17) has sparked an immense literature (discussed in BBM 57–95, 587–600). How the fourteens are counted in 1:17 is not clear, but the overall impression is that God has made mathematically precise preparations for the coming of the Messiah. Given such meticulous care, plausibly there is a common factor among the four OT women mentioned (Tamar, Rahab, Ruth, Uriah's wife [Bathsheba]), perhaps preparing for the community's Christian experience and/or for Mary. The first three women were not Israelites, and the fourth was not married to an Israelite. Does that factor in the antecedents of the Messiah prepare for nonJews accepting the proclamation of the Messiah, and thus for Matt's mixed congregation of Jews and Gentiles? The backgrounds to the marital unions of all four women with the husbands mentioned in the genealogy were irregular, as we see from Gen 38; Josh 2; Ruth 3; and II Sam 11. Yet the women themselves were the instruments of God in continuing the messianic line. Does that prepare for the unusualness of Mary's conceiving and her union with Joseph? More certain is the theological import of the whole genealogy: It brings into the story of Jesus a lengthy span of Israelite history, involving the patriarchs (the first fourteen names), the kings (second fourteen), and even the unknowns (third fourteen). In this way Matt has dramatized Abraham and David motifs found elsewhere in the NT (Gal 3:16; Rom 1:3).

The broken pattern in 1:16 (not "Joseph begot Jesus" but "of Mary was Jesus begotten") prepares the way for the extraordinary manner of *Jesus' conception* (*1:18–25*). As in Luke 1, but more clearly, Mary conceives a child not by male seed but from the Holy Spirit—the virginal conception (for historicity, see *Issue* 4 below). In Matt's book of *genesis* a new creative act brings into being the Messiah in a way that makes him uniquely related to God. Yet he is also the kingly Son of David[6] because Joseph of the House of David acknowledges him as his child by taking Mary his wife home and giving the child a name. Thus Joseph, a Jew most observant of the Law (1:19), becomes the fulfiller of God's plan begun long ago when Abraham begot Isaac. This first chap. of Matt tells readers *who* Jesus is (the Messiah, the one uniquely conceived from the Holy Spirit, Emmanuel or "God with us") and *how* that was brought about.

2. The Where and Whence of Jesus' Birth and Destiny (2:1–23). After the birth of Jesus, *magi come to pay homage to the King of the Jews* (*2:1–12*), and *Herod's plans are foiled as Joseph takes the family to Egypt and then to*

[6]BBM 586; D. R. Bauer, CBQ 57 (1995), 306–23. In the infancy narrative Matt does not explicitly call Jesus "Son of God" although that is implied in 2:15. J. Nolland, JSNT 62 (1996), 3–12, may be too absolute in excluding this christology from 1:18–25.

Nazareth (*2:13–23*). The magi are Gentiles guided by a star (a revelation in nature to those who do not have the Scriptures); the title "the King of the Jews" will reappear as Jesus is crucified, when again Gentiles recognize the truth about him (27:54), while those who have and can read the Scriptures do not believe. Herod, "all Jerusalem," the chief priests, and the scribes of 2:3–4 in their troubled reaction and seeking Jesus' life (2:20: "those" [pl.]) anticipate Pilate, "all the people," the chief priests, and the elders of Matt's passion narrative. In both instances God frustrates the plans of these hostile adversaries (through Jesus' return from Egypt, and through the resurrection). Chap. 2 enlarges the OT background. Chap. 1 highlighted the patriarch Judah, the son of Jacob/Israel, because he was the ancestor of David. Now the patriarch Joseph, another son of Jacob/Israel, comes to the fore, because Joseph, Jesus' legal father, is shaped in his image: Both interpret dreams and save the family by going to Egypt.

The Moses[7] story also comes into the picture when the wicked ruler (pharaoh, Herod) tries to slay all the male children (of the Hebrews, of the Bethlehemites), only to have one (Moses, Jesus) escape and become the savior of his people. The magi contribute to the Moses parallelism, for in Jewish legends of Jesus' time the pharaoh received information from wise men. Also, later when Moses was leading Israel through the Transjordan, the wicked King Balak summoned Balaam (whom Philo calls a *magos*) from the East to curse Israel; but instead he saw the star of the Davidic king arise (Num 22–24).

Finally, to top off his OT coverage, Matt weaves into his account five formula citations from the prophets,[8] showing that God prepared for a virginal conception, for the birth of the Messiah at Bethlehem, for the suffering of other children near Rachel's tomb there, and ultimately for the coming back of God's Son from Egypt and his going to Nazareth. If chap. 1 of Matt dealt with the *who* and *how* of Jesus' identity, the scriptural citations help chap. 2 to bring out the *where* of his birth and the *whence* or place to which his childhood brought him. When readers finish the infancy narrative, they have been given a whole OT background from the Law and the prophets. This is preparatory for the public appearance of Jesus, the kingly Messiah of the House of David and the unique Son of God, who will come from Galilee to be baptized by JBap.

[7]For the many parallels between Jesus and Moses in Matt, see D. C. Allison, *The New Moses* (Minneapolis: A/F, 1993).

[8](1) Matt 1:23 = Isa 7:14; (2) 2:6 = Micah 5:1 + II Sam 5:2; (3) 2:15 = Hos 11:1; (4) 2:18 = Jer 31:15; (5) 2:23 = Isa 4:3?; Judg 16:17? The general Matthean use of formula or fulfillment citations will be discussed below in the subsection on *Sources*.

PART ONE: PROCLAMATION OF THE KINGDOM (3:1–7:29)

1. Narrative: (3:1–4:25): *Ministry of JBap, baptism of Jesus, the temptations, beginning of the Galilean ministry.*[9] Mark's opening pattern is followed. The appearance of Jesus is introduced by *JBap's ministry* (*Matt 3:1–12*), preaching in the wilderness as Isaiah had foretold, and baptizing with water in anticipation of the one who would baptize with the Holy Spirit. In addition, from Q Matt has incorporated JBap's condemnation of the Pharisees and Sadducees and threats of destruction (3:7–12). He thus makes explicable their rejection of JBap to be reported in 21:26. There is a noteworthy Matthean insert in *the account of Jesus' baptism* (*3:13–17*) designed to deal with an implicit christological problem: JBap recognizes that Jesus, who is greater, should be doing the baptizing, but Jesus accepts baptism from JBap as part of God's salvific plan related to the kingdom ("righteousness"; see 6:33). Mark's baptismal heavenly voice was directed to Jesus ("You are my beloved Son"); Matt's voice, "This is my beloved Son," is more widely directed.

Complementing the mention in Mark 1:12–13 that Jesus was tempted (tested) for forty days in the wilderness by Satan, Matt's *narrative of the temptations* (*4:1–11*)[10] fills in from Q their contents, which have been partially shaped from the kinds of testing Jesus underwent during the ministry. The three temptations try to divert the proclamation of God's kingdom so that it will become a kingdom according to the standards of this world. The devil tests Jesus to turn stones into bread for his personal convenience; Jesus will multiply loaves of bread but only for others (14:13–21; 15:32–38). The devil tests Jesus by offering him all the kingdoms of the earth; Jesus will receive all power in heaven and earth (28:18), but not by seeking it and only when it is given by God.[11] Jesus' refusals to have his goals distorted are all phrased in quotations from Deut 6–8, where during the forty-year testing of Israel in the wilderness God spoke through Moses to the people who were tempted to rebel against the divine plan by their complaints and false wor-

[9]Here Matt joins Mark. I shall assume that readers have read the *General Analysis* of Mark, so that there is no need to repeat what was explained there.

[10]B. Gerhardsson, *The Testing of God's Son* (CBNTS 2/1; Lund: Gleerup, 1966); J. B. Gibson, *The Temptations of Jesus in Early Christianity* (JSNTSup 112; Sheffield: Academic, 1995).

[11]Scenes in John show clearly that the three "temptations" or testings (gaining kingly power, working a bread-miracle for the wrong purpose, showing off greatness in Jerusalem), dramatized in Matt and Luke as a direct conflict between Jesus and the devil or Satan, had a counterpart in Jesus' ministry. The crowd in John 6:15 reacts to the multiplication of the loaves by trying to make Jesus an earthly king, and in John 6:26–27 by seeking more such easily obtained bread. In John 7:1–9 the brothers of Jesus want him to leave the "backwoods" of Galilee to go to Judea where he can show himself off to the world.

ship. At the end (Matt 3:10), after Jesus has demonstrated that he is the Son of God who completely serves God's will, Satan is dismissed.

Afterwards *Jesus goes to Galilee to begin his ministry and to call his first four disciples to become fishers of "men"* (*4:12–22*). To this sequence taken from Mark, Matt adds a geographical precision relating Capernaum to Zebulun and Naphtali, which prepares for a formula citation (p. 207 below) from Isa 8:23–9:1 that speaks of "Galilee of the Gentiles." Once more Matt has in view his mixed congregation with many Gentiles. The *summary of the spread of the Gospel* (*4:23–25*), although drawn from Mark, makes a special point that his fame went out "through all Syria," perhaps because the Gospel was written there (see under *Locale* below).

2. Discourse: Sermon on the Mount (5:1–7:29).[12] This is Matt's greatest composition. It weaves together Q material[13] with uniquely Matthean passages into a harmonious masterpiece of ethical and religious teaching. More than any other teacher of morality, the Matthean Jesus teaches with *exousia*, i.e., divine power and authority, and by this empowerment makes possible a new existence. There are parallels between Moses and the Matthean Jesus. The OT conveyer of divine revelation encountered God on a mountain; *the NT revealer speaks to his disciples on a mountain* (*Matt 5:1–2*). For Christians, next to the Ten Commandments as an expression of God's will, *the eight beatitudes* (*5:3–12*)[14] have been revered for expressing succinctly the values on which Jesus placed priority. In the comparable Lucan passage from Q (6:20–23) there are only four beatitudes (phrased more concretely: "you who are poor . . . hungry now . . . weep now . . . when people hate you"); and it is likely that Matt has added spiritualizing phrases ("poor *in spirit* . . .

[12]Of the abundant literature, the following may be noted: W. D. Davies, *The Setting of the Sermon on the Mount* (Cambridge Univ., 1964); W. S. Kissinger, *The Sermon on the Mount: A History of Interpretation and Bibliography* (Metuchen, NJ: Scarecrow, 1975); R. A. Guelich, *The Sermon on the Mount* (Waco: Word, 1982); H. D. Betz, *Essays on the Sermon on the Mount* (Philadelphia: Fortress, 1985); K. Syreeni, *The Making of the Sermon on the Mount* (Helsinki: Suomalainen Tiedeakatemia, 1987—redaction criticism); G. Strecker, *The Sermon on the Mount* (Nashville: Abingdon, 1988); W. Carter, *What Are They Saying about Matthew's Sermon on the Mount?* (New York: Paulist, 1994); H. D. Betz, *The Sermon on the Mount* (Hermeneia; Minneapolis: A/F, 1995); R. Schnackenburg, *"All Things Are Possible to Believers"* (Louisville: W/K, 1995); W. Carter, CRBS 4 (1996), 183–215.

[13]Unconventional is H. D. Betz's view (*Essays*) that Matt thoroughly reoriented a virtually complete Jewish Christian form of the Sermon on the Mount that lacked significant christology and soteriology and presented Jesus as an orthodox teacher of the Law. This would have been an epitome that presented the theology of Jesus in a systematic fashion, resembling the epitomes of the Greco-Roman rhetorical tradition, and would have been directed against the thought of Paul (who is criticized in 5:19)! See the critique in Stanton, *Gospel* 310–18.

[14]Beatitudes (from the Latin *beatus*) are sometimes called macarisms (from the Greek *makarios*). They are not an expression of a blessing conferred, but a recognition of an existing state of happiness or blessing—an approving proclamation, often signifying that eschatological joy has come. There are some twenty-eight different beatitudes in the NT, including four other beatitudes in Matt (11:6; 13:16; 16:17; 24:46). See R. F. Collins, ABD 1.629–31.

hunger and thirst *for righteousness*) and four spiritual beatitudes (meek . . . merciful . . . pure in heart . . . peacemakers). Seemingly Matt's community has people who are not physically poor and hungry; and the evangelist wants them to know that there was an outreach of Jesus for them as well, if they have attitudes attuned to the kingdom. Jesus teaches these beatitudes to the disciples who are to be *the salt of the earth and the light of the world (5:13–16)*.

The ethics of the new lawgiver (*5:17–48*) constitutes a remarkable section, not only for the way it has shaped the Christian understanding of Jesus' values but also for its implicit christology. The Matthean Jesus presents God's demand not by dispensing with the Law[15] but by asking for a deeper observance that gets to the reason why its demands were formulated, i.e., to be "perfect as your heavenly Father is perfect" (5:48). The polemics of Matt's time are illustrated by the evaluation of Jesus' righteousness as exceeding that of the scribes and Pharisees. In the series of six slightly variant "You have heard it said . . . but I say to you" clauses, Jesus dares explicitly to modify or correct what God said through Moses. He makes the demand of the Law more penetrating (e.g., by prohibiting not only killing but anger, not only adultery but lust); he forbids altogether what the Law allows (no divorce,[16] no oath); and he turns from the Law to its opposite (not retaliation [Deut 19:21], but generosity to offenders; not hating enemies [Deut 7:2] but loving them). In other words the Matthean Jesus, speaking more confidently than any 1st-century rabbi, implies that he is more authoritative than Moses, and seems to legislate with all the assurance of the God of Sinai.

In *6:1–18 Jesus reshapes the exercise of piety: almsgiving, prayer, fasting.* His warnings are not against pious practices but against ostentation, a warning that will be reiterated in 23:1–27, where the scribes and Pharisees are repeatedly called hypocrites. (For this term, see Chapter 5 above, n. 19; for an application to our times, see *Issue* 8 below.) The Lord's Prayer, taken from Q,[17] has been shaped by Matt partially along the familiar lines of synagogue

[15]Some have tried to avoid the implication of 5:18 that not even the smallest part of the Law will pass away (an assurance which would seem to demand that the followers of Jesus observe the whole OT Law; see also 23:23) by stressing the last clause "until all is accomplished" and arguing that with Jesus' death it has been accomplished. But the statement is written in a postresurrectional Gospel, and certainly some Christians were hearing this as an ongoing demand—probably Christians similar to "the men from James" who opposed Paul at Antioch (Gal 2:12). When one reads what follows in Matt, however, the manner of observance is subtle indeed. Many scholars judge that Matt's main struggle would not have been with Pauline Christianity, but with interpretations of the law offered by the Pharisees and emerging rabbinic Judaism.

[16]On the divorce issue in general, see p. 141 above in relation to Mark 10:1–12. The Matthean exceptive clause in 5:32, "except on the ground of immorality [*porneia*]," will be discussed below under 19:9.

[17]The shorter Lucan form (11:2–4) may be closer to the original Q wording (e.g., "Father") and form (lacking the petitions about God's will and the deliverance from evil). Some of the original

prayer, e.g., the reverential "Our Father who art in heaven." The organization into six petitions reflects Matt's love of order. The first three, "May your name be hallowed, may your kingdom come, may your will come about on earth as in heaven" are different ways of asking God to bring about the kingdom definitively. (This prayer then, at least in its earlier emphasis, was not far from the tone of *Marana tha*—"Come, Lord Jesus" [I Cor 16:22; Rev 22:20].) The second three deal with the fate of the petitioners as they anticipate that future moment. The coming of the kingdom will involve the heavenly banquet, and so they ask a share of its food (bread); it will involve judgment, and so they ask forgiveness on the criterion of forgiving others that Matt emphasizes (25:45); it will involve a dangerous struggle with Satan, and so they ask to be delivered from the apocalyptic trial and the Evil One. (The KJV addendum "For thine is the kingdom . . ." is discussed in *Issue* 2 below.)

Drawn from Q, *further instructions on behavior for the kingdom* (*6:19–7:27*) touch on total dedication to God, as opposed to worrying about things of this world. Examining oneself carefully rather than examining others is urged; God's generosity in answering prayers is assured; and the golden rule (7:12) is proposed: "Do to others what you would have them do to you." Cautions about the narrowness of the gate (for entering the kingdom) and the danger of false prophets who misuse "my name" (presumably Christians active within Matt's ambiance) lend an apocalyptic tone to the ending of the sermon. The praise of those who hear Jesus' words (7:24–27) as building a well-founded house almost constitutes a judgment against those who reject him. The "When Jesus finished these words" formula (n. 2 above) terminates the sermon, with the accompanying theme of astonishment at the authority of Jesus' teaching.

Part Two: Ministry and Mission in Galilee (8:1–10:42)

1. Narrative Mixed with Short Dialogue (8:1–9:38): *Nine miracles*[18] *consisting of healings, calming a storm, exorcism, interspersed with dia-*

---

eschatological tone has been lessened by Matt's adaptation to ordinary life, also by the disputable translation of Matt's *epiousios* before "bread" as "daily." Fitzmyer, *Luke* 2.901, offers an Aramaic reconstruction. From the abundant literature, note the following: R. E. Brown, TS 22 (1961), 175–208 (reprinted in BNTE 217–53); E. Lohmeyer, *Our Father* (New York: Harper & Row, 1965); J. Jeremias, *The Prayers of Jesus* (SBT NS 6; London: SCM, 1967); P. B. Harner, *Understanding the Lord's Prayer* (Philadelphia: Fortress, 1975); J. J. Petuchowski and M. Brocke, eds., *The Lord's Prayer and Jewish Liturgy* (New York: Seabury, 1978); J. L. Houlden, ABD 4.356–62.

[18]Some count ten by separating the sandwiched healing of the hemorrhaging woman from the raising of Jairus' daughter in 9:18–26. There is a good chance, however, that three patterns of three are meant (see Chapter 7 above, n. 48).

logues, mostly pertaining to discipleship. Thus far Matt has largely presented Jesus as a preacher and teacher of the kingdom—a Messiah of the word. Now, illustrating his love for the arrangement of material with a common import, Matt rejoins the Marcan outline (interspersing a few Q passages) and concentrates on the mighty deeds (miracles) of Jesus effected by his word.[19] First, he performs *a series of three healings* (*8:1–17*), involving: a leper, the centurion's servant boy (from Q), and Peter's mother-in-law, with a summary about many sick. Amid those attracted by his power, a scribe who desires to follow causes Jesus to comment on *the severe requirements of discipleship* (*8:18–22*). That the following of Jesus is a higher demand than burying one's father (in rabbinic thought a duty beyond most others) again reflects extraordinary implicit christology. His maxim is probably to be understood as "Let the spiritually dead (i.e., those who refuse to accept the kingdom) bury the (physical) dead." *Jesus' authority is expressed in another series of three miracles* (*8:23–9:8*) drawn from Mark: He calms the storm and thus gives rise to amazement that wind and sea obey him; he drives out demons who recognize him as Son of God; he heals a paralytic when challenged about his power to forgive sins, something God alone can do. These miracles too have implications for both discipleship and christology. They lead into *dialogues about Jesus' followers and discipleship* (*9:9–17*), caused by the call of Matthew, a tax-collector (Matt's adaptation of the Marcan call of Levi). Jesus justifies his behavior by announcing that he has come to call sinners not the righteous, that his disciples do not have to fast while he (the bridegroom) is with them, and that new wine should not be put into old wineskins—words reflecting the startlingly different character of what he is inaugurating. There follows still another *series of three healings* (*9:18–34*), involving: Jairus' daughter together with the hemorrhaging woman, two blind men, and a mute demoniac.[20] These prepare for the recognition that the *harvest of the crowds needs laborers* (*9:35–38*), and in turn that leads to Jesus' addressing the laborers whom he has chosen and is going to send on a mission.

[19]For miracles in general: Chapter 7 above, n. 16; for Matthean miracles: H. J. Held in Bornkamm, *Tradition* 165–299. B. Gerhardsson, *The Mighty Deeds of Jesus according to Matthew* (Scripta Minora 5; Lund: Gleerup, 1979), emphasizes that the Matthean miracles fulfill prophecies.

[20]Although the interwoven account of the healings of Jairus' daughter and the hemorrhaging woman is drawn from Mark 5:21–43, Matt's account of the curing of the woman is much briefer, ignores the rudeness of the disciples, and shows Jesus in absolute control without any suggestion of limited knowledge. The story of the two blind men (9:27–31) is peculiar to Matt; but it resembles closely the healing of the two blind men in Matt 20:29–34, which is derived from Mark's account (10:46–52) of the blind Bartimaeus. (Matt has a penchant for doubles, perhaps related to the ability of two witnesses to confirm.) Although the healing of the mute demoniac in 9:32–34 is peculiar to Matt, it is almost a doublet of the Q healing of the mute demoniac in Matt 12:22–23; Luke 11:14. Thus there is considerable creative Matthean writing here.

2. Discourse: Mission Sermon (10:1–42). Composed mostly from Mark and Q,[21] this is set in a context of sending out twelve "disciples" with authority over unclean spirits and the power to heal. Jesus is giving them his power to proclaim the kingdom (cf. 10:7 with 4:17). Matt stops to recite the names of the Twelve "Apostles,"[22] thus relating the mission of the disciples in the midst of the ministry to the apostolic sending after the resurrection (28:16–20). Even before he was crucified, Jesus knew that others had a role to play in spreading the good news of the kingdom; and the directives in the sermon have an ongoing force in the Christian mission known to Matt's readers. The sermon begins in 10:5–6 with the warning not to go to the Gentiles and the Samaritans but to "the lost sheep of the house of Israel." As we shall see in the subsection on *Locale* below, this may reflect the history of Matthean Christianity where there was at first almost exclusively a mission to the Jews, and only later a mission to the Gentiles (28:19: "Make disciples of all nations").[23] The demands of Matt 10:9–10 for austerity in the provisions and clothing of the itinerant preachers have curious minor differences from Mark 6:8–9, e.g., no permission to have a staff and sandals. (Are those items not necessary in Matt's situation?) In describing the reception likely to be given to the missionary preachers, Matt 10:12–13,15–16 stresses the hostile judgment on those who refuse. Matt 10:17–22 warns of the fate of the preachers by shifting to here material from the eschatological discourse in Mark 13:9–12. Thus in a sending that takes place during the ministry Matt anticipates the kind of persecution that will greet the postresurrectional apostles. (The mixing of two time periods would be recognizable even if we knew nothing about Mark, since Jesus has forbidden the disciples to go near the Gentiles and yet speaks of their being put on trial by the Gentile as well as Jewish authorities.) Although the Spirit of the heavenly Father will enable those on trial to speak bravely, families will be divided by trials. And the persecuted disciples are to flee from one town to the next: "Amen, I say to you, you will not have finished all the towns of Israel before the Son of Man comes."[24]

[21]For a literary critical analysis, see D. J. Weaver, *Matthew's Missionary Discourse* (JSNTSup 38; Sheffield: Academic, 1990).

[22]This list in 10:2–4 agrees substantially with Mark's list but not with that found in Luke-Acts (Chapter 7 above, n. 7). See n. 82 below for the "Matthew" who appears in all the lists.

[23]Yet scholars are divided about the point of demarcation. Was the time of the mission to Israel just the public ministry of Jesus ending with his death and resurrection, or his whole lifetime to be followed by the church's mission to the Gentiles, or even the period until AD 70 and the destruction of the Jerusalem Temple?

[24]Although 10:23 is peculiar to Matt, some have attributed it to Q and suggested that Luke eliminated it. It was a key verse in A. Schweitzer's thesis that the deluded Jesus expected the final judgment in his lifetime and went to his death hoping to bring it about. If it was spoken by Jesus and is joined to Mark 9:1 and 13:30, it could support the thesis that Jesus had no precise knowledge as to when the final judgment would come and that he made statements expressing implicitly both a hope for it to come soon and an allowance for a long interim (BINTC 52–58). What meaning did Matt

Words of encouragement assuring divine care (10:26–33) follow this prediction of persecution. Then Jesus warns that his coming will bring division and require difficult choices (10:34–39), indeed sacrifices touching on life itself. The Q passage in Matt 10:32–33 has very high christology, making reaction to Jesus the basis of judgment in heaven. Matt's ending of the sermon (10:40–42) extends that correlation to those whom Jesus sends out: Receiving them is receiving him, and receiving him is receiving the God who sent him. Thus the mission of the disciples involves extending God's salvation to all.

PART THREE: QUESTIONING OF AND OPPOSITION TO JESUS (11:1–13:52)

1. Narrative Setting for Teaching and Dialogue (11:1–12:50): *Jesus and JBap, woes on disbelievers, thanksgiving for revelation, Sabbath controversies and Jesus' power, Jesus' family.* Since this section is not one of the five Matthean sermons, it is sometimes listed as narrative. However, the narrative verses are brief and introductory to teaching. Matt sets material combined from Mark and Q in the context of Jesus moving about and entering a synagogue in "their" cities (i.e., of Galilee: 11:1,20; 12:9). Although we have not been told that the disciples returned from their mission, they are with him in 12:2,49. Matt's *treatment of JBap and Jesus* (*11:2–19*) is introduced by an imprisoned JBap who has heard of the deeds of the Messiah, so that 11:4–6 explains that Jesus is the kind of Messiah prophesied by Isaiah (in 29:18–19; 35:5–6; 61:1). Then Jesus reveals who JBap is (Matt 11:7–15). More than a prophet, he is the angelic messenger sent by God to lead Israel to the promised land (Exod 23:20) and the Elijah sent to prepare Israel for God's action (Malachi 3:1,23–24 [4:5–6]). JBap accomplished this by having prepared the way for Jesus, thus becoming the greatest human being ever born before the kingdom of heaven came.[25] (Matt 11:12–15 is not clear as to whether JBap precedes the time of the kingdom [i.e., belongs to the time of the prophets and the Law] or belongs to it [more likely].) Apocalyptic

---

give to the statement? Did the evangelist see a judgmental coming of the Son of Man in the apocalyptic events surrounding Jesus' death (27:51–53; see 26:64), so that literally the mission to Israel was not finished before his death? Or given the failure of Christian preachers to convert great numbers of Jews, was Matt indicating a pessimism that all the Jews would be converted to Christ before the end of the world? This would then constitute another Matthean difference from Paul (Rom 11:25–27).

[25]Whether *preChristian* Jews regarded Elijah as preparing the way for the Messiah is disputed (JBL 100 [1981], 75–86; 103 [1984], 256–58; 104 [1985], 295–96), but early Christians came to interpret Malachi as foretelling such a role. Matt 11:14 clearly identifies JBap with Elijah, as does 17:12–13 (cf. Mark 9:13).

struggle introduces the full coming of the kingdom, and the imprisonment and ultimately the execution of JBap are marks of that. (Of course, in their experience Matt's readers would have seen more marks of violence.) Having spoken about his own identity and that of JBap, in 11:16–19 Jesus criticizes sharply "this generation" for being willing to accept neither. A combination of 11:2 and 19 suggests that Matt is presenting Jesus as both the Messiah and divine Wisdom,[26] but a disbelieving generation cannot recognize his works.

The corrective note on which the JBap section ends leads into the *woes addressed to disbelieving cities on or near the Sea of Galilee* (*11:20–24*). Jesus now switches to a prophetic pattern: For not having paid attention to Jesus' mighty works (miracles), the Galilean cities will have a fate worse than those addressed by Isaiah (23:1) or Ezekiel (26–28), and condemned in Gen 19:24–28. Yet there are people who have responded; and in reference to them Jesus speaks in the style of divine Wisdom by *thanking the Father for revelation* (*11:25–27*) given to those who are childlike, including those who do not count in this world. This jubilant cry, drawn from Q, represents a type of high christology very close to what we find in John's Gospel, where Jesus calls himself the divine Son to whom the Father has given all things (3:35; 5:22,26–27), and where no one knows God except that Son (John 1:18; 14:9), and where he reveals the Father to the chosen (John 17:6).[27] And the "Come to me" *invitation to the heavy-laden* (*11:28–30*), which Matt adds to the Q material, duplicates both Wisdom and Johannine style (Prov 9:3–5; Sirach 24:19; 51:23; John 1:39; 6:44). Like God in Exod 33:14 and Wisdom in Sirach 6:23–31, Jesus promises rest to those who take on themselves the obligations of the kingdom, using some of sweetest words ever attributed to him—words that make intelligible Paul's appreciation for "the meekness and gentleness of Christ" (II Cor 10:1).

Next Matt sets Jesus' teaching in a series of controversies. The first, which involves the disciples' *plucking grain on the Sabbath* (*12:1–8*), has a christological import since Jesus not only claims the right to do what David did but declares that his presence is greater than the Temple and that the Son of Man is lord of the Sabbath. *Healing on the Sabbath* (*12:9–14*) leads to another challenge. We are not sufficiently informed from Jewish sources about the attitude in Jesus' time toward healing on the Sabbath; but Matt attributes to the Pharisees a negative attitude so that they are portrayed as more worried

[26]M. J. Suggs, *Wisdom, Christology and Law in Matthew's Gospel* (Cambridge, MA: Harvard, 1970); M. Johnson, CBQ 36 (1974), 44–64.

[27]Inevitably there has been debate whether this Q passage came from Jesus himself and thus whether he called himself "Son." See Mark 13:32; BINTC 80–89. Intimacy based on mutual knowledge echoes the relationship of God and Moses in Exod 33:12ff. God revealed the divine name to Moses, and so Moses knew God and revealed God to the people of Israel. See in I Cor 13:12 the eloquent words of one to whom God revealed Jesus as Son.

about human precepts than God's intention. In correcting them Jesus is acting in the spirit of the prophets (12:7 = Hosea 6:6). The controversies end on an ominous note with the Pharisees planning to destroy Jesus. Aware of that, Jesus withdraws, followed by a multitude; yet *he heals many as the prophet predicted* (*12:15–21*).[28] The beautiful Isaian passage (42:1–4) reinforces Matt's picture of the tenderness of Jesus, who does not break a bruised reed or quench a smoldering wick.

A *controversy with the Pharisees over Jesus' power* (*12:22–37*) draws heavily from material in Mark 3:22–30. Previously (11:2) JBap associated Jesus' deeds with the Messiah; now the same identification ("Son of David") is suggested to the amazed people when Jesus heals a blind and mute demoniac (a miracle that duplicates 9:32–34; see n. 20 above). In hostile reaction the Pharisees attribute this power over the demon to Jesus' subservience to Beelzebul. Jesus refutes the charge, compares his expulsion of demons to plundering the strong man's house (i.e., the realm of Satan), and warns that blasphemy against the Holy Spirit (i.e., obstinately attributing to the devil the power of God) will not be forgiven. The tone of the condemnation becomes sharper in 12:33–36 (adapted from Q), for Jesus calls the Pharisees a brood of vipers from whom evil emerges and whose works will condemn them on judgment day. When the *scribes and Pharisees request a sign* (*12:38–42*), Jesus offers them only the signs of Jonah (who produced repentance at Nineveh) and of the queen of the South (who appreciated the wisdom of Solomon)—an a fortiori argument: One who is greater is here, and this generation does not appreciate him.[29] He has driven out evil spirits, but *the return of the evil spirits* (*12:43–45*) will make the last state of this evil generation worse than the first. The unexpected arrival of Jesus' mother and brothers raises *the issue of Jesus' family* (*12:46–50*). Now that the kingdom is proclaimed, the disciples who do the will of the heavenly Father are brother, sister, and mother to Jesus.

2. Discourse: Sermon in Parables (13:1–52).[30] Structurally the center of the Gospel, these parables serve as a varied commentary on the rejection

[28]Matt is rejoining Mark here, but he carefully omits Mark 3:19b–21 where Jesus' absorption in his ministry causes his own family members to think that he is beside himself and to set out to seize him. (Thus the arrival of the mother and brothers in Matt 12:46 is unexpected.) Having reported Mary's conception of Jesus from the Holy Spirit, how could the Matthean evangelist have her think this of him?

[29]This seems to duplicate material that appears in Matt 16:1–4. Although found in Q, it probably already had a history of composition there.

[30]For parables in general, see Chapter 7 above, n. 12. For parables in Matt, see J. Lambrecht, *Out of the Treasure* (Louvain: Peeters, 1993); also J. D. Kingsbury, *The Parables of Matthew 13* (Richmond: Knox, 1969), emphasizing redaction criticism. Matt's chap. of eight parables represents collecting genius: One (sower and seed + interpretation) taken from Mark; another (mustard seed) from Mark, but perhaps mixed with Q; one (leaven) is from Q; five peculiar to Matt (weeds +

of Jesus by the Pharisees in the two preceding chaps. In presenting the *parable of the sower and its interpretation* (*13:1–23*) Matt adds two elements: a formula citation (13:14–15) of Isa 6:9–10 that was implicitly quoted in Mark, and a Q blessing enlarging the good fortune of those who have been favored with knowing the secrets of the kingdom (13:16–17). This parable emphasizes the different kinds of obstacles and failures encountered by the proclamation of the kingdom. In Matt 13:13 Jesus speaks in parables "because seeing, they do not see"—a much easier reading than Mark 4:11–12 [p. 133 above] where parables are given to those outside "in order that" they may not see. The next Matthean parable, *the weeds among the wheat and its interpretation* (*13:24–30,36–43*), seems to move to another level of concern. After the proclamation has won adherents to ("sons of") the kingdom, they will be living together in the world with evil people (who are "sons of" the Evil One).[31] Why not eliminate the evil? That could lead to the good being pulled out as well, and so the separation has to be left to a future judgment by the Son of Man.

The paired parables of *the mustard seed and the leaven* (*Matt 13:31–33*)[32] illustrate the present small beginnings of the kingdom and its great future by using examples of extraordinary growth familiar respectively to a man and to a woman. *The purpose of the parables* (*13:34–35*) is glossed by a formula citation from Ps 78:2, so that now part of the purpose is to fulfill the Scriptures. After the interpretation of the parable of the weeds come the paired parables of *the hidden treasure and the pearl of great price* (*13:44–46*). They stress the great value of the kingdom and the necessity of taking the once-for-all opportunity to gain it, even if that requires selling off everything else. The parable of *the dragnet and its interpretation* (*13:47–50*), like that of the weeds, postpones the separation of the good and bad in the kingdom till the close of the age. The sermon ends with a summary parable of *the householder and the new and old treasure* (*13:51–52*). The listeners (13:2)

interpretation, hidden treasure, pearl of great price, net, householder). Neither Matt nor Luke chose to repeat Mark's parable of the seed that grows by itself. Independently did each regard it as puzzling or too fatalistic? Matt's parable of the weeds sowed among the wheat is substituted for it. The parable chap. is divided in different ways by different scholars, e.g., Davies and Allison, *Matthew* 2.370–72, divide it into three parts: 13:1–23 ending with discussion of parables and an interpretation of the sower; 13:24–43 ending with discussion of parables and an interpretation of the weeds; 13:44–52 ending with discussion of understanding these things and being instructed in the kingdom of heaven.

[31]D. R. Catchpole, SJT 31 (1978), 555–70, relates the judgment motif in this parable to the dragnet parable at the end of the chap. Interestingly the world seems to be identified in 10:41 as the kingdom of the Son of Man, and distinguished from the future kingdom of the Father. Many have suggested that at least on the level of Matt's address to his audience the parable would be understood of the presence of good and evil people in the church. For the church as the kingdom of God's Son, see Col 1:13.

[32]R. W. Funk, *Interpretation* 25 (1971), 149–70, and E. Waller, *Union Seminary Quarterly Review* 35 (1979–80), 99–109 offer interesting insights into the parable of the leaven.

who reply that they have understood the parables are like trained scribes who appreciate the new revelation in Jesus and the old revelation in Moses.[33] The evangelist probably considered himself in this light.

Part Four: Christology and Ecclesiology (13:53–18:35)

1. Narrative Mixed with Much Dialogue (13:53–17:27): *Rejection at Nazareth, feeding the 5,000 and walking on the water, controversies with the Pharisees, healings, feeding the 4,000, Peter's confession, first passion prediction, transfiguration, second passion prediction.* In 13:10–11 Jesus said that he spoke in parables because the disciples were to know the mysteries of the kingdom of heaven; accordingly, in what now follows, Jesus turns his main attention to the disciples from whom the church will develop, especially to Peter the rock on whom the church will be built. The *rejection at Nazareth* (*13:53–58*) helps to explain why Jesus must concentrate on his disciples since even his townspeople do not accept him. To show greater reverence for Jesus and his family Matt makes three small changes in the Nazareth story taken from Mark 6:1–6: He does not report that Jesus was a carpenter, or was a prophet without honor "among his own relatives," or "could do no miracle there." (Matt's substitution of "son of a carpenter" for Mark's "carpenter" gave rise to the artistic custom of depicting Joseph as a carpenter.) The lack of faith at Nazareth is followed by an account of *how Herod killed JBap* (*14:1–12*) *and was superstitiously uneasy about Jesus.* In an attempt to get away from Herod Jesus withdraws to a lonely place where he *feeds the 5,000 and subsequently walks on the water* (*14:13–33*).[34] For the main theological emphases in these two miracles (OT, eucharistic, and christological), see p. 136 above. The end of the walking-on-the-water scene is remarkable in Matt; for in 14:33 the disciples, instead of failing to understand as in Mark 6:52, worship Jesus as "Son of God." (Mark would have expected *the readers* to recognize Jesus' identity; but Matt dots the "i" and crosses the "t.") Most significant is the added Matthean scene where Jesus invites Peter to come to him on the water, and as Peter begins to sink, Jesus helps him (14:28–31). This is the first of three instances of special Petrine material in Matt (see PNT 80–83). Peter's impetuousness, the inadequacy of his faith, and Jesus' individual care to lead Peter farther are quite character-

[33]Note the order: "new" before "old" in 13:52; Jesus Christ becomes the lens through which Moses is read. Cf. 9:17 on not putting new wine into old wineskins.

[34]In both 14:1–12 and 14:13–33 Matt abbreviates from the more colorful stories in Mark 6:14–52. In the feeding miracle Matt drops the sarcastic question of the disciples about going to buy bread, and omits the confusing intention to sail to Bethsaida, as well as such touches as the crowd like sheep without a shepherd, and their sitting down in groups of hundreds and fifties.

istic. As a man of little faith who would sink unless the Lord saved him, Peter is representative of the other disciples; their faith and his in the Son of God gains strength from Jesus' powerful, helping hand.

The boat brings Jesus and the disciples to *Gennesaret where Jesus heals all the sick* (*14:34–36*) and then *Pharisees and scribes from Jerusalem debate him over what defiles* (*15:1–20*), a controversy into which both the people and the disciples enter. The attack on the Pharisees is sharp in Matt: They are blind guides who will be rooted out (15:12–14). Whereas in Mark 7:17 the disciples ask him about what defiles, in Matt 15:15 Peter does the asking; and Matt omits the comment that Jesus made all things clean (Mark 7:19b)—a comment that not only offers historical difficulties, as we saw, but also might have offended Matt for whom the Law is not so easily abolished (Matt 5:17).[35] After that, moving on to Tyre and Sidon, *Jesus heals the daughter of the Canaanite woman* (*15:21–28*),[36] a story remarkably like that of the healing of the centurion's servant boy in 8:5–13. As Jesus moves on, passing along the Sea of Galilee, *a summary about the healing of many sick* (*15:29–31*) is used by Matt to replace Mark's story in 7:31–37 of the spittle healing of a deaf mute (omitted because it might be understood as magic?). Then we are told of *the second multiplication of loaves, namely, for the 4,000* (*15:32–39*).

In the Matthean sequence *hostile confrontations with the Pharisees and Sadducees*[37] (*16:1–12*) follow the miracles that Jesus has been doing. Those miracles make intelligible Jesus' response to the disbelieving request for a sign: The Pharisees and Sadducees cannot interpret the already present signs of the times.[38] Criticizing his disciples as people who have little faith for they have not fully understood the bread miracles, Jesus warns them against the leaven or teaching of the Pharisees and Sadducees, whom he equates with an evil and adulterous generation. (Presumably this warning was still appropriate for Matt's readers/hearers in the 80s who might be influenced by rabbinic teaching; but it is not easily reconcilable with 23:2–3, where Jesus

[35]Meier, *Vision* 103, argues, however, that nothing substantial is altered by the omission and Matt accepted the revocation of the food laws—a debated subject at Antioch where Matt may have been written (p. 213 below). On Matt and the Law, see G. Barth in Bornkamm, *Tradition* 58–164; C. E. Carlston, NTS 15 (1968–69), 75–96.

[36]This story has an unusually large number of differences from Mark, including the description of the woman (Syrophoenician to Canaanite—more redolent of the OT?); and some would opt for Matt's drawing on a different version. Probably, however, Matt modified the Marcan story of the healing of a Gentile's daughter in the light of Jesus' previous command to the disciples not to go to the Gentiles (Matt 10:5) and the reiteration in 15:24 from 10:6 that his mission was only to the lost sheep of the house of Israel.

[37]Four times in this section Matt introduces the Sadducees where they were not present in Mark. See p. 211 below for the way scholars have used this fact.

[38]In 16:4 Jesus also says that only the sign of Jonah will be given, a passage echoing 12:38–41.

says that his disciples are to practice and observe whatever the scribes and the Pharisees tell them because they sit on the chair of Moses.)

Yet Jesus' disciples have considerable faith as seen in the climactic *confession of Peter at Caesarea Philippi and the first prediction of the passion* (*16:13–23*). Beyond Mark's account (8:27–30) where, amidst the favorable evaluations of Jesus made by others, Peter confessed him to be the Messiah, in Matt 16:16b–19 there is more Petrine material. Peter now confesses that Jesus is the Son of the living God—a revelation from the Father in heaven, not a matter of human reasoning ("flesh and blood"). The revelation of Jesus' divine sonship to Paul is phrased in almost the same language (Gal 1:16). If that revelation constituted Paul an apostle, this one constitutes Peter[39] the rock on which Jesus will build his church, a church that even the gates of hell (i.e., probably Satanic destructive power) will not prevail against. The OT background of Peter's acknowledgment of Jesus as the Davidic Messiah, the Son of God, is the prophecy of II Sam 7: David's descendant will reign after him and God will treat him as a son. That promise was provoked by David's desire to build a house or temple for God; and so Jesus' promise to build a church on Peter, who acknowledges him as the fulfillment of the promise to David, is not illogical. Isa 22:15–25 describes the establishment of Eliakim as the new prime minister of King Hezekiah of Judah: God places on his shoulder "the *key* of the House of David; he shall *open* . . . and he shall *shut*." The italicized words are echoed in Matt 16:19 as Jesus gives to Peter the keys of the kingdom, so that whatever he binds/looses on earth is bound/loosed in heaven. There are debates about what is meant by this binding/loosing. Is it the power to forgive/not forgive sins (as in John 20:23) or to teach what must be observed, with the result that Peter is the chief rabbi?[40] That this section follows a warning against the teaching of the Pharisees and Sadducees may tilt the odds in favor of the latter, and notice that in 23:13 the scribes and Pharisees are criticized for locking the kingdom of heaven to human beings. (*Issue* 7 at the end of this Chapter will discuss the subsequent application of the Matthean passage to the Roman papacy.) Matt's picture of

[39]That Jesus changed Simon's name to *Petros,* "Peter," or *Kēphas,* "Cephas" (Greek forms respectively translated and transliterated from Aramaic *Kephā'*), is well attested (cf. Mark 3:16; Luke 6:14; John 1:42). On the name see FTAG 112–24. An explanation highlighting the future significance of Peter's name change (cf. Abraham and Jacob in Gen 17:5; 32:29) is offered only by Matt, who plays on the underlying Aramaic: "You are *Kephā'* (= Greek *Petros,* Peter), and upon this *kephā'* (= Greek *petra,* rock) I will build my church." Davies and Allison, *Matthew* 2.627, describe as wasted ingenuity the various attempts (some ancient, some designed to refute Roman Catholics) to avoid the purport that Jesus' church is built on a Peter who has confessed what God revealed to him. These include proposals that *kephā'* means "stone," not "rock," or that the rock is not Peter but Christ or Peter's faith.

[40]PNT 95–101; TIMT 101–14. There is a possibility that the power may have different connotations in 16:19 (teach) and in 18:18 (excommunicate).

the exaltation of Peter because of his professing what God revealed to him does not cause the evangelist to eliminate Jesus' subsequent chastisement of Peter as Satan who thinks on a human level because he does not accept the notion of Jesus' suffering in the prediction of his passion. If anything, Matt sharpens the Marcan reproof, for 16:23 adds, "You are a scandal to me."

This sobering correction leads into directives to the disciples about the *suffering required for discipleship* (*16:24–28*). Encouragingly, however, the suffering of the present is contrasted with future glory; and Jesus, as the Son of Man, is to be the key figure in that glory by bringing with him the kingdom in which his disciples are to have a role. Some of the differences from Mark 8:34–9:1 should be noted. For instance, in Matt 16:27 the Son of Man comes with "his" angels, and in 16:28 instead of seeing the kingdom of God, those standing there are to see "the Son of Man coming in his kingdom." What is Matt's interpretation of the timeline in this promised seeing of the coming? Whatever Mark 9:1 means (p. 139 above), Matt is scarcely referring to the transfiguration that follows immediately since no angels are mentioned there. Does he refer to the crucifixion and resurrection where there is angelic presence? Is that event the coming of the kingdom of the Son of Man as distinct from the coming of the kingdom of God which will take place at the end of time? Or is this another parousia passage vaguely phrased because Jesus had no precise knowledge of when it would occur (n. 24 above)?

The *account of the transfiguration* (*17:1–13*) also shows unique Matthean features.[41] That Jesus' face shone like the sun (17:2) echoes the description of Moses in Exod 34:29–35 and heightens the parallelism to the great theophany on Sinai. Peter's role is highlighted, for he himself will make the three booths. The voice from the cloud in 17:6 repeats more exactly what the voice from heaven said at Jesus' baptism (3:17: "This is my beloved Son with whom I am well pleased"). Accordingly this is another step in the Matthean christological sequence pertaining to divine sonship that runs from the angelic annunciation to Joseph that the child was conceived through the Holy Spirit (1:20), through God's revelation about "my Son" (2:15), to the voice from heaven at the baptism speaking of "my beloved Son" (3:17), to the disciples' recognition after the walking on the water (14:33), culminating in Peter's confession (16:16). Clearly "Son of God" is a major Matthean motif. The question about Elijah, raised by the prophet's presence on the mountain, terminates the transfiguration as Jesus and the disciples descend.[42]

[41]A.D.A. Moses, *Matthew's Transfiguration Story and Jewish-Christian Controversy* (JSNTSup 122; Sheffield: Academic, 1996).

[42]Matt's identification of Elijah with JBap is more specific than Mark's (n. 25 above). Also Matt has smoothed out Marcan ambiguities, e.g., "as it is written of him" (Mark 9:13) in reference to the

In the *story of the epileptic boy* (*17:14–21*) Matt shortens almost by half the vivid Marcan account;[43] and although he does not deny that the boy had a demon (17:18), he greatly suppresses that imagery in favor of a diagnosis of epilepsy (17:15). The explanation of why the disciples could not cure the boy is improved by the introduction of a form of a Q passage on their inadequate faith: Faith as small as a mustard seed could do the impossible, viz., move the mountain (of the transfiguration). Matt continues with the *second prediction of the passion* (*17:22–23*). That Matt does not eliminate this as a doublet, as he often does with Marcan repetitions, may indicate the fixed character of the three-prediction pattern. Then there follows another special Matthean Petrine scene centered on the (*Temple?*) *tax* (*17:24–27*). This story reflects oral tradition, with the finding of the stater coin in the fish's mouth adding almost a folkloric touch. More important is the issue involved. During Jesus' lifetime Jews would have been expected to pay for the support of the Temple.[44] However, Matt never mentions the Temple, and one could be dealing with the denarius tax envisioned in 22:15–22. If we think of the period after AD 70 when Matt wrote, the tax could be the punitive didrachma (= two denarii) tax imposed on Jews for the support of the temple of Jupiter Capitolinus in Rome, or even a collection to support the rabbinical academy at Jamnia. Whatever may be meant, significantly Peter is the intermediary in this story teaching Christians to avoid public offense by paying the tax on a voluntary basis and thus to be peaceable citizens (Rom 13:6–7; I Pet 2:13–16). His role is all the more important if on the Gospel level Matt is dealing with a problem faced by Christians after Peter was dead. (See *Issue* 7 below on the continuation of the Petrine function.)

2. Discourse: Sermon on the Church (18:1–35). This somewhat disparate collection of ethical teaching, much of it once addressed to Jesus' disciples, has been given a perspective that makes it strikingly suited to an established church, the type of church that only Matt has Jesus mention (16:18). Matt connects ecclesiology and christology,[45] for the apostles are to interpret and teach all that Jesus commanded (28:20). Nevertheless, even if a structured church becomes the way in which the tradition and memory of

---

maltreatment of Elijah is dropped—there is no overt Scripture passage to that effect, as seemingly Matt knew. Yet see M. Black, *Scottish Journal of Theology* 39 (1986), 1–17.

[43]As does Luke. That they both omit many of the same lines from Mark (9:14b–16,20–25a,25c–26,28a,29) is a difficulty for the theory of their independent use of Mark.

[44]Exod 30:11–16 describes a half-shekel to be contributed to the Lord. However, we are not totally clear whether the offering for the Temple was a tax or a partially voluntary payment by more observant Jews, e.g., the Pharisees. See R. J. Cassidy, CBQ 41 (1979), 571–80; S. Mandell, HTR 77 (1984), 223–32; D. Daube, in *Appeasement or Resistance and Other Essays on New Testament Judaism* (Berkeley: Univ. of California, 1987), 39–58; D. E. Garland, SBLSP 1987, 190–209.

[45]On this topic see C. E. Carlston, FGN 2.1283–1304.

Jesus are preserved, Matt recognizes the danger that any structure set up in this world tends to take its values from the other structures that surround it. This chap. is meant to insure that those values do not smother the values of Jesus. To readers who struggle with church issues today, this may be the most helpful Matthean discourse.[46]

The sermon is prefaced by the *dispute about greatness in the kingdom of heaven* (*18:1–5*), seemingly taken over with considerable adaptation from Mark. In Jesus' ministry this may have pertained to the ultimate establishment of God's kingdom when the Son of Man comes. Yet we have seen that Matt speaks of a *kingdom* of the Son of Man in this world, so that we are hearing a dispute that would also have meaning for the church, where inevitably there would arise ambition for authoritative positions. In Jesus' set of values the humble are more important than the powerful, for dependence on God is what makes one open to God's rule; and so the little child is held up as an example. The *condemnation of scandals and temptations* (*18:6–9*) that can cause believers to sin would be appropriate for the church Matt addressed, if we can judge from disputes in the Pauline communities (I Cor 8:13; 11:19; Rom 8:13). The Matthean adaptation of the Q *parable of the lost sheep* (*18:10–14*), i.e., the straying sinner, also has institutional application, for by most worldly standards organizations are successful to the extent that they take care of the majority. A political leader who could retain 99 percent of his constituency would have the most favorable poll ratings in history, reflecting the "Caiaphas principle" of John 11:49–50: It is better to let one person perish than to have the whole institution destroyed. However, Jesus who came to save the lost (Matt 10:6; 15:24) has different values, which he phrases in an "impractical" directive that catches his eschatological outlook, i.e., to leave the ninety-nine and go in search of the one who is lost.[47] No large church (or in our times, no large parish) could follow that as a regular practice, for the 99 percent of those who had not strayed would revolt at being neglected. Nevertheless Jesus' values must not be forgotten; for when they are put in practice, however seldom, at that moment and in that place God's kingdom has been made a reality.

Matt now presents a body of material largely special to this Gospel. The instructions on *a procedure for reproving one's "brother* [*and sister*]*," the disciples' access to heaven, and the frequency of forgiveness* (*18:15–22*) are

[46]BCALB 124–45, especially 138–45; W. G. Thompson, *Matthew's Advice to a Divided Community, Mt. 17,22–18,35* (AnBib 44; Rome: PBI, 1970).

[47]The stress is on the joy of finding the one lost sheep, but the fact that the search is done at the cost of caring for the ninety-nine should not be overlooked. Other such directives include: 5:32 (no divorce); 5:39–40 (turning the other cheek; letting someone who takes your coat have your cloak as well); 10:9–10 (taking nothing along in the proclaiming of the gospel); 20:1–15 (paying the one-hour worker as much as the fully employed).

clearly adapted to a church situation; for after the unsuccessful efforts of individuals to win over the reprobate, a report is to be made to the "church" (= local community, unlike the use of "church" in 16:18). The process is designed to prevent too early and too frequent use of authority—a danger in any structured community. The quarantine of the recalcitrant reprobate in 18:17 "as a Gentile and tax-collector" sounds very definitive, reinforced by the power to bind and loose in 18:18.[48] Yet we must remember that Matt's community was a mixed one of Jews and Gentiles, and that Jesus' final instruction was to go out to the Gentiles and teach them (28:19). Moreover, Jesus had shown a particular interest in a tax-collector named Matthew, inviting him to follow (9:9; 10:3). Therefore, the repudiated Christian may still be the subject of outreach and concern. The plausibility of that interpretation is enhanced by 18:21–22 concerning the ongoing forgiveness of the brother (/sister) "who sins" (the same expression used for the person to be corrected in 18:15). Peter is once more (see 17:24–27) a figure of authority getting instruction from Jesus on how he should act. Although he is being a bit "legalistic" in trying to find out how often he should forgive, his offer is quite generous—except for the family circle few people forgive someone seven times. Jesus gives a remarkable answer: Seventy-seven is an infinite number of times (cf. Gen 4:24). Christian forgiveness, then, is to imitate the unlimited range of God's forgiveness, as is confirmed by the eloquent *parable of the unforgiving servant* (*18:23–35*) that invokes divine judgment on those who refuse to forgive. All this has a very real application in church life, for the number of people who turn away from the church where they have not found forgiveness is legion. Overall, to the extent that churches listen to the Jesus who speaks to his disciples in this chap., they will keep his spirit alive instead of memorializing him. Then Matt 18:20 will be fulfilled: "Where two or three are gathered in my name, there am I in the midst of them."

PART FIVE: JOURNEY TO AND MINISTRY IN JERUSALEM (19:1–25:46)

1. Narrative Mixed with Much Dialogue (19:1–23:39): *Teaching, judgment parables, third passion prediction, entry to Jerusalem, cleansing the*

[48]See Lev 19:15–18; Deut 19:15. The procedure in the Dead Sea Scroll community (1QS 5:24–6:1; CD 9:2–8,16–20) is similar to that in Matt. For quarantining or expelling Christians, cf. I Cor 5:1–5; II Thess 3:14; Titus 1:13. Jesus is portrayed as extending the power to bind/loose to his disciples in his lifetime, but it has an ongoing import so that the Matthean community's judgments also are ratified in heaven. Sometimes 18:18 is used to offset 16:19 with the claim that the power given to Peter should not be exaggerated because it was given to all the disciples. To be precise, however, we note that they are not made the rock on which Jesus will build his church nor given the keys of the kingdom of heaven.

Temple, clashes with authorities. Jesus has revealed his intention to found his church and has given instructions about the attitudes that must characterize it. With that done, he now goes up to Jerusalem, where his predictions about the death and resurrection of the Son of Man will be fulfilled.

The narrative of what happened on the road to Jerusalem[49] begins with an example of Jesus' standards for the kingdom. *The question about divorce* (*19:1–12*) is set in the context of the testing of Jesus by the Pharisees. The most notable Matthean feature (see p. 141 above) is the addition of the exceptive phrase in 19:9: "Whoever divorces his wife *except for immorality* [*porneia*] and marries another commits adultery [verb: *moichasthai*]," an exception that also appeared in Matt 5:32, but in none of the other three forms of the divorce prohibition (Luke, Mark, I Cor, though the last two have their own adaptations of Jesus' command). This exception is important mainly for the Christian churches that regard Jesus' prohibition of divorce as normative. What is meant by *porneia*? The Greek word covers a wide range of immorality, but to allow divorce for every kind of unchastity would seem to nullify the force of the prohibition. Some interpret the exception as adultery and so permit divorce and remarriage of the innocent party in a marriage where the other was an adulterer. However, *moicheia* is the proper word for adultery, as attested in the related Matthean verb for "commits adultery." A more likely interpretation would find a reference to marriages within what Jews regarded as forbidden degrees of kindred.[50] Matt would be insisting that Jesus' prohibition of divorce did not apply to such marriages contracted by Gentiles who had come to believe in Christ—indeed those marriages should be dissolved as if they had never occurred (see FTAG 91–97). The consternation of the disciples at Jesus' severity is peculiar to Matt (19:10–12). In reply Jesus raises the possibility about being eunuchs (i.e., totally abstinent) for the sake of the kingdom of God. Like marriage without the possibility of divorce, such celibacy is an eschatological value (see Isa 56:3–5); both impose demands that this world regards as impossible.

The passage about the *rejection of the children by the disciples* (*19:13–15*) in Matt not only lacks the indication in Mark 10:14 that Jesus was indignant at the disciples but also supplies a more ecclesiastical atmosphere for bringing the children: "that he might lay hands on them and pray." The story of the *rich young man and its aftermath* (*19:16–30*) adds to the commandments of the Decalogue the demand to love one's neighbor as oneself (19:19); yet

[49]Matt 19–20 is close to Mark, but there are Q and special Matthean parables.

[50]In Acts 15:20 four items are prohibited to Christian Gentiles; since the other three echo the prohibitions of Lev 17, most think that the fourth, *porneia,* refers to intercourse with close kin as described in Lev 18. The outrageous *porneia* condemned by Paul (I Cor 5:1) is a man living with his stepmother.

even then one is not perfect without sacrificing all possessions to follow Jesus. Once again the severity of the eschatological demand creates consternation among the disciples. In the response of Jesus, Matt 19:28 incorporates an important promise from Q about the exalted future role of the disciples: In the regeneration (*palingenesia*) they will sit on twelve thrones judging the twelve tribes of Israel. Whether the twelve tribes are a reference to the old Israel or to the Christian church is debated, but more widely the judgment may include all who worship the Lord God (see also Rev 21:14). The reward at the end has the same upside-down character as the kingdom: It is not given to the first and most powerful of this world, but to the last who have left behind precious things for the sake of Jesus' name (Matt 19:29–30). The themes of the first and last and of reward also govern the *parable of the workers in the vineyard (20:1–16),* which is peculiar to Matt and regarded by some as an interpretative illustration by the evangelist to highlight God's sovereignty and a graciousness that is not based on what is earned.[51]

Amidst these reflections on ultimate reward the *third prediction of the passion* (*20:17–19*) constitutes a paradoxical consideration of the role of suffering in the victory. That prediction leads into the misunderstanding represented by the *request for the places in the kingdom* (*20:20–28*). To avoid dishonoring the disciples, Matt shifts the request from the sons of Zebedee to their mother.[52] The Twelve have been guaranteed thrones of judgment when the Son of Man sits in glory; evidently that is not the same as sitting at the right and left in the kingdom. The key difference may lie in the warning against lording it over others; for whether it be the Son of Man or the Twelve, the necessary attitude is that of service. The continuing journey to Jerusalem brings Jesus to Jericho[53] and the *healing of two blind men* (*20:29–34*). This clearly is Matt's variant of the Marcan healing of one man, the blind Bartimaeus; it exemplifies Matt's preference for two (perhaps reflecting the demand for two as legal witness).

The entry into Jerusalem (*21:1–9*) is based on Mark with the addition in 21:4–5 of a formula citation of Isa 62:11 and Zech 9:9 that stresses the

[51]Any attempt to justify the parable in terms of social justice or labor relations misunderstands the point. For a study of Matt 19–20 against the background of the social situation in Antioch, see W. Carter, *Households and Discipleship* (JSNTSup 103; Sheffield: Academic, 1994).

[52]Also Matt omits the complicated symbolic reference in Mark 10:38 to a baptism to be baptized with (see Meier, *Vision* 142).

[53]Mark 10:46 reads: "And they came to Jericho and as he was leaving Jericho." Matt, presumably by way of simplification, has chosen to report only the last part: "As they went out from Jericho." These references to Jesus' leaving Jericho constitute a famous conflict with Luke 18:35 that mentions only, "As he drew near to Jericho." There are implausible harmonizations (e.g., leaving OT Jericho, drawing near NT Jericho); but the standard critical explanation is vocalized by Fitzmyer (*Luke* 2.1212): "The account of a cure . . . in the vicinity of Jericho has given rise to different literary traditions about it."

meekness and peacefulness of the messianic king. Famously illogical is the Matthean combination in 21:7 of ass and colt (originally meant as parallel designations of one animal) so that Jesus sat "on them."[54] The sequence of *cleansing the Temple* (*21:10–17*) and the *cursing and withering of the fig tree* (*21:18–22*) reorganizes Mark 11:12–25, where the cleansing is sandwiched between the cursing and the withering. The cleansing of the Temple now takes place on the day on which Jesus entered Jerusalem (rather than on the next day as in Mark) and is set in the context of the whole city being stirred up and recognizing Jesus as *the* prophet (Matt 21:10–11). Also the joining of the cursing and withering has the effect of heightening the miraculous, for now the fig tree withers on the spot when Jesus curses it (rather than being discovered the next day).

To the *challenge to Jesus' authority* (*Matt 21:23–27*) by the priests and the elders, answered in terms of JBap, Matt joins a parable of his own, *the two sons* (*21:28–32*). Comparing the authorities to the son who says he will obey the father but does not, Jesus fashions a highly polemic contrast: Tax-collectors and harlots who believed JBap will enter the kingdom of God before the authorities. The sharpness of the judgment continues in *the parable of the wicked tenants* (*21:33–46*), for in vv. 43,45 the chief priests and the Pharisees understand themselves to be the target of the warning that the kingdom of God will be taken away and given to a nation that will produce fruits. Matt is thinking of the church composed of Jews and Gentiles who believe in Jesus. *The parable of the marriage feast* (*22:1–14*), seemingly adapted from Q, is another instance of the rejection of the leaders. Those invited first by the king are unworthy and do not come; and since they kill the servants sent with the invitation, the king sends his troops and destroys their city. The once independent parable about the man without a wedding garment, which has been added as an ending, deals with a reality that Matt knows well: Into the church have been brought both bad and good, so that those who have accepted the initial call have to face further judgment. Those Christians who are not worthy will suffer the same fate as those who formerly had the kingdom but were not worthy to keep it (cf. 8:11–12). Thus in none of these three parables is it simply a question of the replacement of Israel by the church or of Jews by Gentiles; the issue for Matt is the replacement of the unworthy in Judaism (especially the leaders) by a community

[54]Some would use this as a proof that the author was a Gentile who did not understand Hebrew parallelism (two ways of saying the same thing). Yet in the NT, synonymous parallelism is frequently neglected in favor of literal fulfillment, e.g., in John 19:23–24 "garments" (*himatia*) and "clothing" (*himatismon*) are taken as two different items; and in Acts 4:25–27 "kings" and "rulers" are treated as different people.

of Jews and Gentiles who have come to believe in Jesus and have worthily responded to his demands for the kingdom.

As in Mark there now follows a series of three trap questions: *taxes for Caesar* (*Matt 22:15–22*) proposed by Pharisees and Herodians; *the resurrection* (*22:23–33*) proposed by Sadducees; *the great commandment* (*22:34–40*) proposed by a Pharisee lawyer.[55] These are followed by a question proposed by Jesus to the Pharisees about the Messiah as *David's son* (*22:41–46*). To emphasize the superiority of Jesus, Matt adds observations, e.g., in 22:33 about the crowd's astonishment at Jesus' teaching, and in 22:46 about none daring to ask Jesus any more questions.

Serving as a bridge to the last great discourse, *the denunciation of the scribes and Pharisees* (*23:1–36*) is an extraordinary Matthean construction.[56] The hostility manifested by these authorities in the trap questions of chap. 22 is returned by Jesus' attack on their proud behavior and love for titles,[57] and by his seven "woes" against their casuistry—woes that function almost as the antitheses of the beatitudes in chap. 5. The initial directive (23:2–3) to observe whatever the scribes and Pharisees say for they sit on the chair of Moses is puzzling since elsewhere the Matthean Jesus criticizes their sayings or teaching (e.g., 15:6; 16:11–12; 23:16–22). It is not totally satisfactory to contend that Matt preserves this statement simply as past tradition even though he disagrees with it.[58] The scribe and Pharisee opponents are criticized for talk or pretense not accompanied by action and also for acting from base motives. (Compare the criticism of Jesus' followers in

[55]In Mark (12:28–34) the questioner is a well-disposed scribe who agrees with Jesus' response; all the verses favorable to the questioner are omitted in Matt. Also Matt omits the Jewish prayer, the Shema, with which Mark 12:29 prefaces Jesus' response—an indication perhaps of Matt's break with the synagogue.

[56]It stems from Mark, Q, and Matt's own material. D. E. Garland, *The Intention of Matthew 23* (NovTSup 52; Leiden: Brill, 1979); A. J. Saldarini, CBQ 54 (1992), 659–80; K.G.C. Newport, *The Sources and Sitz im Leben of Matthew 23* (Sheffield: Academic, 1995).

[57]Matt 23:6–10 attacks three titles being used in Jewish (rabbinical) circles when the Gospel was written, "Rabbi," "Father," "Teacher." AntiCatholic literalists have appealed to this passage in criticizing the practice that developed in English-speaking circles of addressing priests as "Father," even though they seem to have no problem of addressing learned people as "Professor" or "Doctor," which are the modern secular equivalents of "Rabbi" and "Teacher." Matt's text criticizes a love for being honored—a love that will find expression in different titles in different times. The real lesson is that, no matter what titles are used, "all are brothers [and sisters]" in Christ, and the greatest must be a servant.

[58]Matt does not hesitate to change Mark when he disagrees with what that Gospel reports about Jesus, so why would he hesitate to change this tradition? Was this principle still condoned in Matt's community for Jewish Christians as part of what could be tolerated in the kingdom of the Son of Man until the harvest at the end of time (13:39)? M. A. Powell, JBL 114 (1995), 419–35, argues that "sit on Moses' chair" does not endorse the authority of the scribes and Pharisees to teach or interpret the Law but acknowledges that they are in control of the copies of the Torah and thus can report what Moses said.

7:21–23 for praising Jesus as Lord but not doing the will of God, and see under the *Issues* section below for modern repercussions in Jewish Christian relations.) Although the seven woes are portrayed as Jesus' critiques of the Jewish leaders of his time, Matt's readers would probably hear them as critiques of synagogue leaders in their time over a half-century later.[59] (And Christians today should hear them as a critique of what generally happens in established religion and thus applicable to behavior in Christianity.) Some of the woes involve disputes about the Law, but the last (23:29–35) associates the scribes and Pharisees with murderers of prophets, wise men, and scribes.[60] For the Christians of Matt's church the crucifixion of Jesus would have sharpened the tone of such polemic, and "Amen, I say to you, all these things will come upon this generation" (23:36) would have been seen as fulfilled in the capture of Jerusalem and destruction of the Temple in AD 70. The chap. ends with an *apostrophe to Jerusalem* (*23:37–39*), drawn from Q. Jesus has failed to persuade the city. Therefore her house (the Temple) is forsaken and desolate, and Jerusalem will not see Jesus again until she says, "Blessed is he who comes in the name of the Lord."

2. Discourse: Eschatological Sermon (24:1–25:46).[61] Thus Matt has prepared the way for a long speech on the last times that fittingly is the last of the five great discourses. *A series of warnings* (*24:1–36*) begins with the disciples' question in 24:3. They pick up the distinction from 23:38–39 by asking about both the destruction of the Temple buildings and the second coming.[62] The sequence in Matt 24 preserves the apocalyptic obscurity of Mark 13, which mixed the Gospel present time with the future. A few adaptations may exemplify the history and times known to Matt, e.g., the doubled reference to false prophets leading people astray (24:11,24) may reflect a struggle with Christian enthusiasm. In Matt 24:15 the prediction of the desolating sacrilege is clearly localized in the Temple (cf. the obscurity in Mark

[59]Of particular interest is 23:15 about the scribes and Pharisees traversing sea and land to make converts—converts to Judaism or to Pharisaism? M. Goodman, *Mission and Conversion* (Oxford: Clarendon, 1994), denies that at this time there was insistent missionary activity by Jews to make Gentile converts. J. C. Paget, JSNT 62 (1996), 65–103, however, challenges the evidence for such a thesis and thinks it likely that there was missionary consciousness among some Jews.

[60]The span from Abel (Genesis) to the blood of Zechariah killed between the sanctuary and altar (II Chron 24:20–22) covers a range from the beginning of the Hebrew Bible (the first book of the Law) to the end (the Writings). However, it also involves a famous inaccuracy because the Zechariah described was the son of Jehoiada, not of Barachiah (BINTC 38).

[61]It contains in 24:1–36 material taken over largely from the eschatological discourse of Mark 13, and in the rest of chap. 24 and in chap. 25 material from Q and Matt's own tradition. The result is a discourse almost twice as long as Mark's. F. W. Burnett, *The Testament of Jesus-Sophia. A Redaction-Critical Study of the Eschatological Discourse in Matthew* (Washington, DC: Univ. of America, 1981).

[62]This clarification is not found in the parallel question of Mark 13:4 and suggests that Matt is writing in the period between the two events.

13:14) and thus is more applicable to the Roman profanation of the Holy Place. The Jewish background of some of Matt's audience is reflected in the prayer that the flight in the last times not be on a Sabbath (24:20), a sensitive issue whether they were still observing that day or would not want to antagonize other Jews who were. Mark had already indicated that there was no precise timetable for the final events, and the *watchfulness material in Matt 24:37–51* underlines that one cannot know when the Son of Man is coming. The warning that the servant who is not waiting when the master comes will be put out with the hypocrites (24:51) shows that unfaithful Christians (and perhaps specifically church leaders) will be judged no less harshly than the scribes and Pharisees. Watchfulness continues in the uniquely Matthean *parable of the ten virgins* (*25:1–13*).[63] The judgment motif grows stronger in the Q *parable of the talents* (*25:14–30*)—a parable that shows how far Matt and Luke (19:12–27) can vary in reporting the same material. The message for Matt's readers[64] is not one of meriting reward but of dedicated and fruitful response by the Christian to God's gift in and through Jesus. The discourse ends with material peculiar to Matt: *the enthroned Son of Man judging the sheep and the goats* (*25:31–46*).[65] Since the Son of Man speaks of God as "my Father," this is the Son of God in the apocalyptic context of the judgment of the whole world. The admirable principle that the verdict is based on the treatment of deprived outcasts is the Matthean Jesus' last warning to his followers and to the church, demanding a very different religious standard both from that of those scribes and Pharisees criticized in chap. 23 and from that of a world that pays more attention to the rich and powerful.

Climax: Passion, Death, and Resurrection (26:1–28:20)

1. Conspiracy Against Jesus, Last Supper (26:1–29).[66] By having Jesus predict at the very beginning that the Son of Man would be given over at this Passover (a type of fourth passion prediction), Matt emphasizes the foreknowledge of Jesus. In *Judas' disloyalty and the anointing of Jesus* (*26:1–16*) the setting of the plot against Jesus is localized in the palace of the high priest Caiaphas in order to prepare for the setting of the Jewish trial later on.

[63]It illustrates well that often a parable makes only one point. If this parable were a general picture of ideal Christian life, the wise virgins should have had the charity to share their oil with the foolish. K. P. Donfried, JBL 93 (1974), 415–28, would find this parable a key to Matthean theology.

[64]There is considerable debate about what the parable may have criticized when uttered during Jesus' ministry; L. C. McGaughy, JBL 94 (1975), 235–45. In the form cited in the *Gospel of the Nazaraeans* 18 (HSNTA 1.161) the man to be punished is not one who hid the talent but one who lived dissolutely and squandered it—a moralizing interpretation.

[65]See J. R. Donahue, TS 47 (1986), 3–31.

[66]With some minor changes, until the end of the Jewish trial, Matt closely parallels Mark 14.

The sum paid (not simply promised) to Judas is specified as *thirty* pieces of silver to echo Zech 11:12. *The preparations for Passover* (*26:17–19*) are briefly recounted, leading directly into *the Last Supper account* (*26:20–29*).[67] Matt makes specific the identification of the one who will give Jesus over (which Mark had left obscure). Judas is not only named but also answers Jesus by calling him "Rabbi," the very title Jesus had forbidden in Matt 23:7–8.

2. Arrest, Jewish and Roman Trials, Crucifixion, Death (26:30–27:56).[68] In the *Gethsemane section* (*26:30–56*) Matt's tendency to avoid duplications causes the omission of Jesus' praying that if it were possible the hour might pass from him—the twin in Mark 14:35 of the direct discourse prayer that the cup might be removed. Additionally this omission serves the purpose of making the Matthean Jesus seem less desperate. Matt also fleshes out the pattern of Jesus' praying three times by supplying in 26:42 a wording for the second prayer (echoing the Lord's Prayer of 6:10). In the arrest (Matt 26:49–50) Judas once more addresses Jesus as "Rabbi," and Jesus responds in a way that manifests his awareness of what Judas has planned. Since Matt makes it clear (contrast Mark) that it was one of Jesus' followers who cut off the ear of the high priest's servant, it is morally important that Jesus comment unfavorably on such force. That the Father would have sent more than twelve legions of angels if Jesus appealed (26:53: some 72,000!) softens the failure of the Father to answer Jesus' prayer to have the cup removed. Typically Matthean is the stress in 26:54 and 56 that what is happening fulfills the Scriptures, in harmony with the many fulfillment citations throughout the Gospel.

The Jewish Trial: Jesus is condemned by the Sanhedrin and mocked while Peter denies him (*26:57–27:1*). Matt includes the name of the high priest Caiaphas, and heightens the iniquity because the authorities are said to have been seeking *false* witness from the start. The indication that two witnesses came forward and the failure to designate their testimony as false (contrast Mark) means that for Matt Jesus did say, "I am able to destroy the sanctuary of God, and within three days I will build (it)." This assertion plus the nonrejection of the title "Messiah, the Son of God" constitute the basis of the

[67]A minor Matthean touch is to add "for the forgiveness of sins" to the words of Jesus identifying the cup of wine as his blood; clearly Jesus' death is presented as an expiatory sacrifice. In Mark 1:4 it is JBap's baptism that is for the forgiveness of sins.

[68]There is abundant literature on the Matthean passion narrative (listed in BDM 1.100–1). In particular, see D. P. Senior, *The Passion Narrative according to Matthew* (BETL 39; Louvain Univ., 1975); *The Passion of Jesus in the Gospel of Matthew* (Wilmington: Glazier, 1985); R. D. Witherup, *The Cross of Jesus: A Literary-Critical Study of Matthew 27* (Ann Arbor: University Microfilms, 1986).

charge of blasphemy. For the question "Who is it that struck you?" mocking Jesus as a prophet-Messiah (26:68), see pp. 114, 116 above. The irony of Peter's denying that he knows Jesus at the very moment when Jesus confesses to being the Messiah, the Son of God, is heightened in Matt, for that is the very title that Peter confessed in 16:16. Matt's sense of order has three different agents (not two as in Mark) provoking Peter's three denials.

The Roman Trial: As Jesus is being handed over to Pilate, Judas seeks to avoid the bloodguilt; Pilate sentences Jesus who is then mocked (*27:2–31a*). In this section of the passion narrative we encounter major episodes unique to Matt. The storyline remains the same as in Mark: questioning by Pilate, Barabbas, the intervention of the chief priests and the crowds, the flogging and handing over to crucifixion, and the mockery by Roman soldiers. Yet the special Matthean material makes the account more vivid and dramatizes responsibility for Jesus' death through the imagery of "innocent blood." (See p. 206 below for this type of Matthean material, almost every line of which echoes the OT and is perhaps taken directly from popular oral tradition.) Matt 27:3–10 interrupts the beginning of the Roman trial with the story of Judas' reaction to the Jewish decision against Jesus. Judas does not want to be responsible for innocent blood (see Matt 23:34–35; Deut 21:9; 27:25). Neither do the chief priests, and so they use the thirty pieces of silver for which Judas had sold Jesus[69] in order to buy a Potter's Field (Zech 11:12–13; Jer 19:1–13; 32:9). Judas' hanging himself echoes the suicide of Ahithophel (David's trusted advisor who went over to David's rebellious son Absalom), the only OT figure who hanged himself (II Sam 17:23).[70] Just as in Matt's infancy narrative there were dream revelations and the Gentiles were responsive when the Jewish authorities were not, so here Pilate's wife receives a dream revelation that Jesus is a just man (27:19). (The title "the King of the Jews" is also shared by this scene and the infancy narrative.) Pilate washes his hands to signify that he is innocent of Jesus' blood; but finally "all the people" say, "His blood on us and our children" (27:24–25). This is not a self-curse by the Jewish people; it is a legal formula taking responsibility for the death of one considered a criminal. Matt knows what the people do not, namely, that Jesus is innocent; and he judges that the responsibility (and punishment) for the death of this just man was visited on all the Jewish

[69]Judas has the same name as Judah, one of the twelve sons of Jacob, who in Gen 37:26–28, rather than shed his brother Joseph's blood, sold him for twenty (or thirty) pieces of silver.

[70]The Ahithophel story in II Sam 15–17 is woven into an earlier section of Jesus' passion also, for in his flight from Absalom David went to the Mount of Olives and wept and prayed. Matt's account of Judas' death differs from two others that, in turn, differ among themselves: Acts 1:16–20 and Papias (BDM 2.1404–10).

people later when the Romans destroyed Jerusalem and the Temple (wherefore the reference to "children").[71]

The crucifixion and death (27:31b–56).[72] Matt (27:36) specifies that the Roman soldiers who crucified Jesus sat and kept watch over him; thus the Roman centurion had (Gentile) companions in confessing that Jesus was truly God's Son (27:54). The challenge of the Jewish authorities to the crucified Jesus (27:41–43) is lengthened to echo the Scriptures (Ps 22:9; Wisdom 2:17–18). The two drinks offered to Jesus become wine mixed with *gall* and vinegary wine (27:34,48) to match the gall and vinegar of Ps 69:22. The major Matthean addition, once more of the vivid, popular type, expands poetically what happened as Jesus died. Not only was the veil of the sanctuary rent from top to bottom; but the earth was shaken, the rocks were rent, the tombs opened, and many bodies of the fallen-asleep holy ones raised, to come out and enter the holy city after Jesus' resurrection (27:51–53). This is a scriptural way of describing the last times. If the birth of Jesus was marked by a sign in the heavens (a star's rising), his death is marked by signs on the earth (a quake) and under the earth (tombs). His death brings judgment on the Temple but also the resurrection of the saints of Israel. Human relationships to God have been changed, and the cosmos has been transformed.

3. Burial, Guard at the Tomb, Opening of the Tomb, Bribing of the Guard, Resurrection Appearances (27:57–28:20). Although in Mark the burial is part of the crucifixion account, Matt has reorganized the sequence to relate the burial more closely to the resurrection. In a pattern resembling that of the infancy narrative Matt has five subsections in an alternating pattern of favorable to Jesus, unfavorable, favorable, etc.; cf. 1:18–2:23 and the alternating Joseph and Herod subsections. *The burial account (27:57–61)* clarifies that Joseph from Arimathea was a rich man and a disciple of Jesus. The placing of *the guard at the tomb (27:62–66)*, unique to Matt, reflects apologetics meant to refute Jewish polemic against the resurrection. The cooperation of Pilate with the chief priests and the Pharisees[73] in using soldiers

[71]That type of judgment, as harsh as it seems to our ears, was not foreign to the time, e.g., the Jewish historian Josephus, *Ant.* 20.8.5; #166, contends that God visited destruction by the Romans on Jerusalem because of Jewish impiety. And the Matthean language echoes the OT, e.g., Jeremiah (26:12,15) warns the princes and "all the people": "If you put me to death, you are bringing innocent blood on yourselves, on this city . . ." Nevertheless, tragically the Matthean passage has been used to support horrendous antiJudaism that must be repudiated (BDM 1.388, 396, 831–39). See *Issue* 8 below on Matt's antiJewish tone.

[72]Matt is still following the Marcan sequence. Minor omissions from Mark include the names of Simon the Cyrenian's sons and that Jesus was crucified at the third hour (9 a.m.). The mother of the sons of Zebedee is substituted for Mark's Salome among the named women who looked on the crucifixion from afar.

[73]In the passion narrative Pharisees are not mentioned at all by Mark and Luke, and only this once by Matt.

to forestall the resurrection/removal of Jesus' body resembles the cooperation of Herod, the chief priests, and the scribes in sending to kill the baby Jesus (2:16–18 [+ 2:4 and the pl. in 2:20]).

The middle subsection of the five in both infancy and burial/resurrection accounts shows a divine intervention to frustrate the hostile plot, for Matt's story of *the empty tomb* (*28:1–10*) is significantly different. There was an earthquake; an angel descended and rolled back the stone, and the guards were struck with fear like dead men. The angel's message to the women about Jesus' victory has a different reaction from the message in Mark; for they run with joy to tell the disciples, and indeed Jesus himself appears to them. The alternating pattern of subsections then turns attention to *the bribing of the guard* (*28:11–15*) by the chief priests and the lie that the disciples stole the body. The finale comes when *Jesus appears to the Eleven* (*28:16–20*) on a mountain in Galilee. As we shall see with resurrection appearances in Luke and John, there are typical details: doubt, reverence for Jesus, and a commission. The mountain is the Matthean symbolic place for Jesus' revelation (5:1), and the exalted Jesus who speaks has been given all power in heaven and earth. (This echoes Dan 7:14; and so Meier, *Vision* 212, speaks of this as the Son of Man coming to his church in a proleptic parousia.) The sending to all nations here at the end revises the restricted sending to the lost sheep of the house of Israel and not to the Gentiles in the middle of the Gospel (10:5–6). The baptismal formula in the name of three divine agents was presumably in use in the Matthean church at this period,[74] having replaced an earlier custom of baptizing in the name of Jesus (Acts 2:38; 8:16; etc.). The instruction to teach all the nations "all that I have commanded you" probably refers to the contents of Matt's five great discourses or even all that Matt has narrated (see 26:13). The final verse "I am with you all days until the end of the age" is an inclusion with God's revelation about Jesus through the prophet Isaiah at the beginning of the Gospel (1:23): "His name shall be called Emmanuel (which means 'God with us')."

Sources and Compositional Features

Those who accept Marcan priority and the existence of Q (Chapter 6 above) work with those two written sources of Matt. We shall discuss them first, and then turn to other commonly agreed-on compositional elements.

(a) MARK. This is Matt's principal source. Although the evangelist might

[74]The roots of the triadic pattern may be in OT apocalyptic, e.g., the Ancient of Days, a son of man, and the interpreting angel in Dan 7. See J. Schaberg, *The Father, the Son, and the Holy Spirit* (SBLDS 61; Chico, CA: Scholars, 1982). Also B. J. Hubbard, *The Matthean Redaction of a Primitive Apostolic Commissioning* (SBLDS 19; Missoula, MT: Scholars, 1974).

have reflected on Mark as it was read in the community liturgy, the detailed work implies that Matt had a written form of Mark before him. The idea that a later evangelist rewrote an earlier Gospel is not foreign to the biblical scene, for the Deuteronomist rewrote earlier Pentateuchal material, and the Chronicler (I-II Chron) rewrote material in Sam and Kings. Mark had been designed to make Jesus intelligible to a Gentile audience; and Matt, in order to serve a community that was becoming more and more Gentile, found Mark a useful framework into which to incorporate Q, a very Jewish collection of Jesus' teaching.[75]

Overall Matt is remarkably faithful to Mark, almost as a scribe copying his source. Nevertheless, in the changes (minor in length) to what is taken over from Mark, one can detect Matthean thought and proclivities. The more characteristic changes made by Matt are listed below with some examples of each:

- Matt writes Greek with more polish than Mark by eliminating difficult phraseology and double expressions and by smoothing out patterns, e.g., Matt 15:39 changes the unrecognizable place-name of Mark 8:10, "Dalmanutha"; 26:34 drops the first time indicator in Mark 14:30, "today, this very night"; 26:45 drops the untranslatable Greek word *apechei* of Mark 14:41; 26:42 supplies words for Jesus' second Gethsemane prayer, contrasted to Mark 14:29.
- Matt omits or changes passages in Mark unfavorable to those whose subsequent career make them worthy of respect, e.g., the *omission* of Mark 3:21 where Jesus' family thinks he is beside himself, of Mark 8:17 where Jesus asks whether the disciples' hearts are hardened, of Mark 8:22–26 which dramatizes the slowness of the disciples to see, and of Mark 9:10,32 where the disciples do not understand the concept of resurrection from the dead; also the *change* of the ambitious questioner from the sons of Zebedee in Mark 10:35 to their mother in Matt 20:20.
- Reflecting christological sensibilities, Matt is more reverential about Jesus and avoids what might limit him or make him appear naive or superstitious, e.g., Matt 8:25–26 changes the chiding question posed by the disciples to Jesus in Mark 4:38 and eliminates Jesus' speaking to the wind and sea in the next Marcan verse; 9:22 eliminates the implication in Mark 5:30–31 that Jesus did not know who touched him and that the disciples thought he had asked a foolish question; 13:55 changes to "carpenter's son" the description in Mark 6:3 of Jesus as a carpenter; 15:30–31 omits Mark's account (7:32–36) of the spittle healing of the deaf mute; 19:16–17 changes Mark 10:17–18 to avoid the implication that Jesus cannot be called good, for God alone is good; 21:12–13 omits Mark 11:16 and the picture of Jesus blockading the Temple.

[75]Indeed it has been suggested that the combination with Mark prevented an overly free further development of Jesus' teaching in a gnostic direction that would divorce it from his earthly career.

- Matt heightens the miraculous element found in Mark, e.g., Matt 14:21 increases Mark's 5,000 in the multiplication of the loaves by adding women and children; 14:24 increases the distance of the boat of the disciples from the shore in the walking-on-the-water scene; 14:35 insists that Jesus healed *all* who were sick; 15:28 has the woman's daughter healed instantly.

(b) Q SOURCE. By including Q material, Matt gives a strong emphasis to Jesus as a teacher. Many would diagnose other Matthean thought and proclivities by the changes the evangelist makes in Q; but since Q is a hypothetical construction derived in part from Matt, we must recognize uncertainties and be careful of circular reasoning. In terms of content Matt appears to be reasonably faithful to Q even as he was to Mark. Yet the way in which Q is used is not consistently the same, and the order of Q is adapted to Matt's sense of order. For example, Matt rearranges the Q material into sermons or discourses. To a group of four beatitudes (Luke 6:20–23) Matt 5:3–11 adds others to enlarge the number to eight. Matt 6:9–13 fleshes out the Lord's Prayer by bringing to it additional petitions lacking in Luke 11:2–4.

(c) SPECIAL MATTHEAN MATERIAL (often called M). When one discusses material in Matt not found in Mark or Q, one enters an area that is not homogeneous and about which scholars seriously disagree. How much represents the Matthean evangelist's own composition/creation and how much did he draw from a source or sources (M) known to him alone among the four evangelists? Certainly the evangelist could create his own compositions modeled on what he found in Mark and Q;[76] yet he does seem to have had other sources that he followed, e.g., a body of special material about Peter (14:28–31; 16:17–19; 17:24–27). Let me illustrate the issue from the infancy and the passion narratives. BBM 52 contended that Matt's infancy narrative drew on several different kinds of raw materials: lists of names of patriarchs and kings; a messianic family tree (1:13–16, to which Matt added Joseph and Jesus); an annunciation of the Messiah's birth patterned on OT annunciations of birth; more importantly, *a birth story with several dreams involving Joseph and the child Jesus, patterned on the patriarch Joseph and the legends surrounding the birth of Moses;* and *a magi-and-star story patterned on the magus*[77] *Balaam who came from the East and saw the Davidic star that would rise from Jacob.* The last two items (which I have italicized) are reconstructed as preMatthean sources in BBM 109, 192 with the warning that this material has been edited so thoroughly that often we can detect only contents, not the original wording. Similarly in the passion narrative I

[76]Stanton, *Gospel* 326–45.

[77]A person with special occult powers: a magician, diviner, soothsayer—in the biblical outlook usually a negative figure, e.g., the magus Simon in Acts 8:9 and the magus Bar-Jesus or Elymas in 13:6,8.

maintain that Matt added source material to what was taken over from Mark (BDM 1.755): Judas hanging himself (27:3–10), Pilate's wife's dream (27:19), Pilate washing his hands of Jesus' blood (27:24–25), a poetic quatrain about the extraordinary events that followed Jesus' death (27:51b–53), and the story of the guard at the tomb (27:62–66; 28:2–4,11–15). Characteristic of this birth and passion material are vivid imagination (dreams, murder of infants, bloodguilt, suicide, plotting, lies), extraordinary heavenly and earthly phenomena (angelic interventions, star moving to the west and coming to rest over Bethlehem, earthquake, dead rising), an unusual amount of scriptural influence (almost as if the stories had been composed on the basis of the OT, rather than simply glossed by OT references), and (alas) sharp hostility toward Jews who did not believe in Jesus, matched by sympathetic presentation of Gentiles (magi, Pilate's wife)—characteristics reflecting the imagination, interests, and prejudices of ordinary people[78] and for the most part missing elsewhere in Matt. Senior and Neirynck, who stress almost exclusively Matt's written dependence on Mark, would regard much or all of this material as a Matthean creation, perhaps on the basis of vague tradition. Is it likely that the Matthean evangelist, who elsewhere has worked closely with Mark and Q, making conservative changes in a scribal manner, suddenly releases a creative urge producing vivid stories different in tone from the changes introduced in those two sources? More plausibly, in my judgment, Matt had a popular, perhaps oral, source consisting of folk traditions about Jesus (which may have had a historical nucleus no longer recoverable).

In addition to these large blocks of material, there are minor Matthean passages and phrases not derived from Mark and Q. Some of these may represent Matthean creativity;[79] some of them may represent a particular type of received tradition. From the oral preaching about Jesus that gave birth to Christianity, the Matthean evangelist surely knew about Jesus before he ever read Mark; and so it is possible, nay even likely, that some minor additions represent his use of oral tradition and phrases to expand what he found in the written sources.[80] In a pericope taken over from Mark, a key to the preMatthean existence of oral tradition could be the independent presence in Matt and Luke of what is lacking in Mark. (Some of the "minor

[78]Some of the passion material is found with developments in the *Gospel of Peter,* which has the characteristics of a gospel reflecting popular Christianity with imaginative elements that go beyond Matt, e.g., a talking cross. Serapion, the bishop of Antioch, found it being read in a small town of Syria, a context in which its fantasy was appreciated. See p. 836 below.

[79]They would be motivated by the same interests we saw under (a). For example, 3:14–15 is added to the baptismal account to insure christological recognition that Jesus is not subservient to JBap.

[80]Meier, *Vision* 12, argues that Mark and Q came to Matt encrusted with oral traditions and that Matt drew on those.

agreements"; see the example on p. 116 above of Matt 26:68; Luke 22:64 where there may have been oral influence on both evangelists.)

(d) FORMULA OR FULFILLMENT CITATIONS. In some ten to fourteen instances where Matt cites the OT (Isaiah in eight of them), the scriptural passage is accompanied by the following formula (with slight variants): "All this took place to fulfill what the Lord had spoken by the prophet who said." This is almost a Matthean peculiarity among the Synoptic Gospels.[81] That Jesus is to be related to the Scriptures is a commonplace in early Christianity, but Matt has uniquely standardized the fulfillment of the prophetic word. In finding this fulfillment, Matt usually makes no attempt to interpret the large contextual meaning of the cited OT passage; rather there is a concentration on the details where there is a resemblance to Jesus or the NT event. Some would contend that there is an apologetic motif in these citations (proofs directed to the synagogue); but then one would expect to find more of them in the account of Jesus' passion, which was the "stumbling block to the Jews" (instead of only 26:56; 27:9–10). More likely the citations have a didactic purpose, informing Christian readers and giving support to their faith. Some are attached to the minutiae of Jesus' career, as if to emphasize that the whole of Jesus' life, down to the last detail, lay within God's foreordained plan. Probably Matt is continuing the invocation of Scripture begun in early Christian preaching, but is doing so now when the primary address is to settled Christian communities who need to be taught.

Did these citations create the narrative they accompany, or are they appended to a narrative that already existed? Instances of each of these processes may exist, but the better arguments favor the latter as a general pattern. For instance, in the infancy narratives in four cases out of five (1:22–23; 2:15b,17–18,23b) the storyline makes perfect sense without the citations and even flows more smoothly. It is hard to imagine how the story in 2:13–23 could have been made up out of the three formula citations contained therein. In an instance over which we have outside control, Mark 1:14 and Luke 4:14 agree that after his baptism Jesus went to Galilee; thus the formula citation in Matt 4:12–16 did not give rise to that story, but colored it with a reference to the Gentiles. Sometimes Matt may have introduced into material taken from Mark a citation already being used more widely (Matt 21:4–5

[81]Luke 22:37 is the only other uncontested Synoptic formula citation although it speaks of accomplishment rather than fulfillment. Less certain are Mark 15:28; Luke 18:31; 24:44. John has nine fulfillment citations but with a less standardized formula (see Chapter 11 below, n. 43). The literature on the subject is considerable: J. A. Fitzmyer, NTS 7 (1960–61), 297–333 (reprinted FESBNT 3–58); R. H. Gundry, *The Use of the Old Testament in Matthew's Gospel* (NovTSup 18; Leiden: Brill 1967); K. Stendahl, *The School of St. Matthew and Its Use of the Old Testament* (2d ed.; Philadelphia: Fortress, 1968); G. M. Soares-Prabhu, *The Formula Quotations in the Infancy Narrative of Matthew* (AnBib 63; Rome: PBI, 1976); also the summary discussion in BBM 96–104.

draws on Zech 9:9, which is also echoed in John 12:15–16). Many times, however, it is hard to imagine that the Matthean citations could have been used independently of their present context. Most likely, therefore, Matt originated the use of many of the citations introduced by a formula.

As to the linguistic background of Matt's formula citations, Gundry, *Use,* maintains that Matt, when copying citations found in Mark (even implicitly), closely adheres to LXX wording. In nonMarcan usage of Scripture, whether in formula citations or not, Matt is freer. Stendahl, *School,* reminds us that there was available in the 1st century a multiplicity of textual traditions of Scripture—not just a standardized Hebrew (MT) and Greek (LXX) tradition, but variant Hebrew wordings, Aramaic targums, and a number of Greek translations, including some closer to the MT than is the LXX. When we add to these the possibility of a free rendering by the evangelist himself, the process of deciding what scriptural wording is Matthean and what preMatthean becomes most uncertain. In the many instances where the Matthean evangelist was the first to see the possibilities of an OT fulfillment, he would presumably choose or even adapt a wording that would best fit his purposes. Matt's choice need not have represented the studies of a school of writers as Stendahl has suggested, but at least we are dealing with a careful and erudite choice worthy of a Christian scribe. Besides using the formula citations to fit the general theology of the unity of God's plan, the Matthean evangelist selected them to serve his particular theological and pastoral interests in addressing a mixed Christian community of Jews and Gentiles.

Let me conclude this subsection with a note of caution. Although the evangelist did draw on previously existing bodies of written and oral material, he did not produce a collection of glued-together sources. Working with a developed christology, ecclesiology, and eschatology, he produced a highly effective narrative about Jesus that smoothly blended together what he received. That narrative won important parts of the ancient world to faith in Christ. It may be academically useful to detect the sources he employed, but to concentrate on the compositional background and miss the impact of the final product is to miss the beauty of the forest while counting the trees.

Authorship

If we work backwards, the title "According to Matthew"[82] was attached to this writing by the latter half of the 2d century (or perhaps earlier; Davies

[82]A "Matthew" appears in all four NT lists of the Twelve (as one of the second group of four names); only in Matt's list (10:3) is there an identification: "the tax-collector." That is related to his only other appearance, i.e., the story of Jesus' call of a tax-collector whom Matt 9:9 calls Matthew but whom Mark 2:14 and Luke 5:27 call Levi. (By birth a man would not have had two Semitic

and Allison, *Matthew* 1.7–8). *Ca.* 125 Papias wrote, "Matthew arranged in order the sayings in the Hebrew [= Aramaic?] language, and each one interpreted/translated as he was able" (EH 3.39.16). On p. 158 above I deliberately printed the Papias reference to Matt in its actual context *following* the reference to Mark, a sequence that would not suggest that Papias thought that Matt wrote before Mark. (The claim that Matt was the first Gospel appears with Clement of Alexandria, Origen, and Eusebius.) There has been considerable debate as to whether in referring to "sayings" (*logia*) Papias meant that Matthew wrote a full Gospel (as later writers understood, thinking of canonical Matt, e.g., EH 5.8.2–3). *Logoi* would have been the usual word for "sayings" in the sense of "words," and so *logia* might mean whatever constituted the "revelations" of Jesus (see Acts 7:38 for the *logia* or revelations delivered by Moses). Moreover, since Papias reported that Mark was a follower of Peter who did not make an orderly account of the Lord's *logia* and it is widely agreed that Papias was referring to the *Gospel* of Mark, plausibly he would have been referring to a gospel when he says that Matthew arranged in order the *logia* in Hebrew/Aramaic.[83] The meaning of *syntassein,* which I have translated "arranged in order," is not certain. It need have no connotation of chronological or even logical order; it could refer to a persuasive or pleasing literary arrangement or even to a fuller account.

The canonical Matthean Gospel exists in Greek—was Papias referring to a Semitic original from which it was translated? Three different observations point in that direction. (1) In antiquity there was a Jewish gospel probably in Aramaic used by Palestinian Christians and associated by the Church Fathers with Nazaraean (or Nazorean) Jewish Christians, especially in the Aleppo area of Syria.[84] References to this gospel relate it closely to Matt; Jerome claimed that he translated it into Greek and at times he treats it al-

---

names; and so if one identifies Levi with Matthew, a member of the Twelve, one would be presuming that Jesus had changed his name.) The usual harmonizing solution is that only the Matthean evangelist, because he was Matthew, knew that this Levi was Matthew; therefore in the story he substituted the name "Matthew" for that of Levi. Less unlikely is that he had a list that identified Matthew one of the Twelve as a tax-collector and that he jumped to the conclusion that this man should be identified with Levi the tax-collector, since in the story Levi became a disciple of Jesus. Possible too is a play on the resemblance of *Maththaios* to *mathētēs,* "disciple."

[83]"Hebrew" among writers in Greek, including the evangelists, often refers to Aramaic. In an oft-quoted 1960 German article, J. Kürzinger maintained that Papias meant that Matthew composed in a Hebrew *manner,* not language. For a critique, see Davies and Allison, *Matthew* 1.14–16. On not making too much of Eusebius' castigation of Papias as a man of little intelligence, see Davies and Allison, 1.13–14.

[84]Later it came to be known as the *Gospel of the Nazaraeans;* but because it was written with Hebrew characters, at times Church Fathers confusingly refer to it as the Hebrew Gospel or the Gospel according to the Hebrews. However, there was another work, the *Gospel According to the Hebrews,* which seems to have been composed in Greek and is not closely related to Matt. There was also a Jewish Christian gospel used by the Ebionites, probably dependent on the Synoptic Gospels.

most as if it were the Semitic original behind Matt. When compared to the canonical Gospel, however, the few Nazaraean passages preserved in patristic quotations seem to be secondary expansions of Matt or interpolations. (2) There are medieval Hebrew forms of Matt that most scholars think of as retroversions from the Greek of canonical Matt, often made to serve in arguments between Christians and Jews. However, some claim that these texts are a guide to the original Hebrew of Matt.[85] (3) Still other scholars think they can reconstruct the original Hebrew or Aramaic underlying the whole or parts of the Greek text of canonical Matt on the assumption that the original was in Semitic.[86]

The vast majority of scholars, however, contend that the Gospel we know as Matt was composed originally in Greek and is not a translation of a Semitic original. As for Papias' attribution of the *logia* to Matthew, if canonical Matt drew on canonical Mark, the idea that Matthew, an eyewitness member of the Twelve, would have used as a major source a noneyewitness, Greek account (Mark) is implausible. (That objection is not really met by the thesis that Matthew wrote an Aramaic gospel that was translated into Greek only after Mark was written and thus under the influence of Mark—not only the Greek wording of Matt but also its organization and material content seem to have been influenced by Mark.) Thus either Papias was wrong/confused in attributing a gospel (sayings) in Hebrew/Aramaic to Matthew, or he was right but the Hebrew/Aramaic composition he described was not the work we know in Greek as canonical Matt.

In the latter hypothesis, did what Matthew wrote in Aramaic/Hebrew play any role in the background of canonical Matt, thus explaining the title given to the latter work? Since Papias speaks of "sayings," was he describing Q, which canonical Matt used? Yet Q as reconstructed from Matt and Luke is a *Greek* work that has gone through stages of editing. Papias could not have been describing that, but was he referring to the Semitic original of the earliest Greek stage of Q, a stage that we can reconstruct only with difficulty and uncertainty? Others posit an Aramaic collection of sayings on which Matt, Mark, and Q all drew. One cannot dismiss these suggestions as impossible, but they explain the unknown through the more unknown.

By way of overall judgment on the "Matthew" issue, it is best to accept the common position that *canonical Matt was originally written in Greek by*

[85]French scholars like J. Carmignac and M. Dubarle have contributed to this thesis; see G. E. Howard, *The Gospel of Matthew According to a Primitive Hebrew Text* (Macon, GA: Mercer, 1987); *Hebrew Gospel of Matthew* (Macon, GA: Mercer, 1994).

[86]Ancient Greek-speakers like Clement of Alexandria and Origen had no problem positing that canonical Matt was translated from Semitic, but that may have been largely because they accepted as received tradition the existence of a (lost) Semitic original.

a noneyewitness whose name is unknown to us and who depended on sources like Mark and Q. Whether somewhere in the history of Matt's sources something written in Semitic by Matthew, one of the Twelve, played a role we cannot know. It is not prudent for scholarship 1,900 years later to dismiss too facilely as complete fiction or ignorance the affirmation of Papias, an ancient spokesman living within four decades of the composition of canonical Matt.

Today a more divisive issue is whether the unknown canonical evangelist was a Jewish Christian or a Gentile Christian. Current scholarship runs about four to one in favor of a Jewish Christian; but significant commentators argue for Gentile authorship.[87] For instance, sometimes they detect mistakes in Matt that they cannot conceive a Jew making, e.g., the evangelist's joining the Pharisees and Sadducees four times in chap. 16 as if they had the same teaching (16:12). Yet that joining may simply be a shorthand way of putting together Jesus' enemies,[88] and 22:34 shows that the evangelist is aware of differences between them. In support of identifying the evangelist as a Jewish Christian, the Papias tradition at least suggests a Jewish background for Matt. The evangelist's use of the OT indicates that he knew Hebrew and perhaps even Aramaic—an unlikely accomplishment for a Gentile. Although not conclusive and possibly reflecting sources rather than the evangelist himself, there are many features of Jewish thought and theology in Matt:[89] the infancy narrative with a genealogy, a Moses parallelism for Jesus, and a knowledge of Jewish legends; the Sermon on the Mount with modifications of the Law; debates with the Pharisees; images of Peter's authority (keys of the kingdom, binding and loosing); a command to obey those who sit in Moses' seat (23:2–3); worry about flight on a Sabbath (24:20); and the special material in the passion narrative that is almost a midrash on OT passages. Overall likelihood, then, favors the Jewish Christian identity of the evangelist.

Yet what type of Jewish Christian? Matt's Greek is probably not translation Greek; the evangelist often corrects Mark's style, and there are Greek wordplays. This linguistic skill could suggest diaspora upbringing (witness

[87]Besides P. Nepper-Christensen (1958) and G. Strecker (1962), who wrote in German, see K. W. Clark, JBL 66 (1947), 165–72; M. J. Cook, HUCA 53 (1984), 135–46; Meier, *Vision* 17–25. An oft-made argument for Gentile authorship is that Matt omits or substitutes Greek for some of Mark's Aramaisms (*Boanērges, talitha koum, korban, Bartimaios, rabbounei, Abba*); much of that, however, may be simply a matter of stylistic preference or communicability.

[88]Matt's antipathy toward the Sadducees may be influenced by the fact that a Sadducee high priest was responsible for the execution of James, Jesus' brother, in the early 60s. Also the joining of Pharisees and Sadducees may reflect the confused period after 70 where the Jewish leaders at Jamnia (Yavneh), though closer to the Pharisees in their intellectual heritage, gained the public influence possessed before 70 by the Sadducee chief priests.

[89]Davies and Allison (*Matthew* 1.26–27) are very helpful here.

Paul). Theologically, the evangelist was neither of the more conservative extreme that opposed the admission of uncircumcised Gentiles to Christian communities (see 28:19), nor of the more liberal extreme that deemed the Law irrelevant (see 5:17–18). Yet the exact Matthean mind-set toward the Law is hard to reconstruct; for as we shall see in the next subsection, the Gospel reflects a complicated community history. Many would find the evangelist's self-description in 13:52: "a scribe trained for the kingdom of heaven . . . a householder who brings out of his treasure new things and old." That reverence for what has gone before is attested in the Matthean addition (9:17) to Mark 2:22, which emphasizes that both old and new are preserved. If we compare the evangelist to Paul, the other great writer on the Law in the NT, even though on practical issues the two might agree and both reverenced the Ten Commandments (Matt 19:18–19; Rom 13:9), each might find the other's slogans too sweeping: "I have not come to abolish the Law" (Matt 5:17); "You are not under the Law" (Rom 6:14–15).

Locale or Community Involved[90]

By the end of the 2d century, church writers were placing the composition of Matt in Palestine.[91] Probably that was a surmise based on the earlier tradition that Matthew wrote in Hebrew/Aramaic, and on the internal evidence of controversies with Jews. However, some of the proposed Palestinian background (e.g., portrayal of how the Pharisees behave in public in 23:5) may reflect Jesus' own time, rather than the situation of the Gospel. *The majority view relates Matt to Syria and specifically to Antioch.* "Syria" is added in Matt 4:24 to Mark's description of the spread of Jesus' activity. The early Jewish *Gospel of the Nazaraeans* related to Matt (n. 84 above) circulated in Syria. The argument drawn from Matt's use of Greek that we should posit a Syrian *city* because Aramaic was spoken in the countryside is uncertain; but urban locale may be suggested by twenty-six uses in the Gospel of "city," compared to four of "village." The dominant influence that Matt would have in subsequent Christianity suggests that it served as the Gospel of a major Christian church in an important city, such as Antioch. If, as noted below in

[90]I remind readers of the cautions enunciated on p. 161 above which make it difficult to know whether the evidence pertains to where the Gospel was written from or written to, or both if the author lived among the addressees, as is normally supposed.

[91]Irenaeus, AH 3.1.1., locates Matt "among the Hebrews in their own language"; the second paragraph of the "AntiMarcionite" Prologue to Luke (Fitzmyer, *Luke* 1.38–39) speaks of Matthew writing in Judea; and Eusebius (EH 3.24.6) places the composition before Matthew's departure from Palestine. For a listing of the scholars who support the various locales, see Davies and Allison, *Matthew* 1.138–39. I shall not attempt here to treat minority proposals, even though proposed by very respectable scholars, e.g., Alexandria, Caesarea Maritima, Galilee, Pella, Edessa, and the seacoast of Syria.

the discussion of dating, Ignatius and the *Didache* supply the earliest evidence of knowledge of Matt, Ignatius (certainly) and *Didache* (probably) are associated with Antioch. However, the most persuasive evidence stems from the correspondence of the internal evidence with what we know of the church at Antioch, as we shall now see.

The interplay of Jewish and Gentile interests in Matt is complex. There are passages that strongly echo the interests of a Law-abiding Jewish Christianity (5:17–20; 10:5–6; 23:1–3); yet other passages revise the Law or Jewish observances (5:17–48; 23:1–36). Despite all the Matthean discussions centered on points of Jewish Law, "the Jews" are referred to as alien in 28:15, as are the synagogues of the Jewish authorities (10:17; 23:34). Matt has taken over Mark, a Gospel addressed to Gentiles, but omitted the explanation of Jewish customs in Mark 7:3–4, as if the Gentile section of the Matthean community would know the issue of cleanliness in eating. *The most plausible interpretation is that Matt was addressed to a once strongly Jewish Christian church that had become increasingly Gentile in composition;* and J. P. Meier (BMAR 45–72) has shown how the history of Christianity at Antioch fits that situation. There were probably more Jews at Antioch than at any other place in Syria, and their ceremonies attracted many Gentiles (Josephus, *War* 7.3.3; #45). It is not surprising then that when Hellenist Jewish Christians were scattered from Jerusalem after the martyrdom of Stephen (*ca.* AD 36; Acts 8:1) and came to Antioch, they spoke of Christ to Gentiles there as well (Acts 11:19–20). The list of "prophets and teachers" in Antioch (13:1: in the early 40s?) includes a childhood companion of Herod Antipas, and so the Christian community there may have had people of prestige and wealth.[92] Paul's mission to the Gentiles, begun with Barnabas, was under the auspices of the Antioch church; and the objections of some ultraconservative Jewish Christians to its success led to the Jerusalem meeting of AD 49. After the agreement there that Gentiles could be received without circumcision, it was at Antioch that Paul, Peter, and men from James (the "brother of the Lord") disagreed sharply over how Jewish food laws affected the table relationships of Jewish and Gentile Christians. Paul lost this battle and departed from Antioch, so that for the period immediately after 50 Christianity in that area would have been dominated by a more conservative outlook on how the Law obliged Gentile converts (as spelled out in the decree from James and Jerusalem in Acts 15:28–29, including the avoidance of *porneia*). Peter played a moderating role keeping the community together (BMAR 40–41).

[92]Elements of wealth have been detected in Matt's community: Only in Matt (10:9) are the disciples warned against carrying gold and silver; the parables in 18:23–35; 25:14–30 deal with huge amounts of money; Joseph from Arimathea is described as a wealthy man (27:57).

In the 60s another major change would have come. Peter was executed in Rome in that decade, and James in Jerusalem. Christians were scattered from Jerusalem as the Jewish Revolt (66–70) began. There and in Antioch the antipathy of Jews for Jewish Christians may have increased since the latter did not stand with their confreres in the Revolt.[93] The Jewish image at Antioch would have been affected in this period by the renegade Jew Antiochus who aroused Gentiles to fury with false tales about Jewish plots to burn the city (Josephus, *War* 7.3.3; #46–53). In the 70s after the crushing of the First Jewish Revolt by the Romans (p. 61 above), at Jamnia on the Palestinian coast an academy of scholars close emerged as an influential force; they were close to Pharisee thought and honored as rabbis. In this same post-70 period at Antioch Gentiles probably became the majority in the Christian group (BMAR 47–52), while the extreme conservative wing of Jewish Christians broke the *koinōnia* ("unity, communion") and separated. They would become the source both of the Syrian Ebionites[94] and of those who were later responsible for the *Pseudo-Clementine Recognitions* that called on the memory of James of Jerusalem as the great hero.

This history of shifting relationships between Jewish and Gentile Christians would fit much of what we find in Matt. Peter and James were prominent at Antioch. Peter appears more prominently in this Gospel (14:28–31; 16:17–19; 17:24–27) than in any other; and to the list of the Twelve taken over from Mark, Matt 10:2 adds "first" before Peter's name. The Q material preserved in Matt is very close to the epistle attributed to James (p. 734 below).[95] As for the variety of views that marked the history of Antiochene Christianity, a sharp rejection of a Gentile mission is enunciated in Matt 10:5–6; 15:24; yet later on a mission to the Gentiles is commanded by Jesus in 28:19. In the opening chapter's story of the magi such an outcome is foreshadowed as God's plan, but historically was it the opposition of the syna-

[93]The way that christology was being vocalized and the presence of Gentiles in the Christian group would have raised doubts in the synagogue about the followers of Jesus: Were they still faithful to Israel's belief in the one God? Some scholars appeal to the *Birkat ha-mînîm,* supposedly dated to AD 85, as evidence of the expulsion of Christians from the synagogue; but see the qualifications on p. 82 above.

[94]The Ebionites are mentioned in patristic literature, especially in the 2d to 4th centuries, as a (heretical) Jewish Christian group who observed parts of the Mosaic Law and had a low christological view of Jesus (not divine in origin, no virginal conception). For the *Pseudo-Clementine* literature, see Chapter 34 below, n. 6 and 44.

[95]Was Q in circulation at Antioch? Luke is said in the tradition to have lived at Antioch (p. 267 below) and could have known Q in a form that circulated there. Mark, even if it was composed in Rome, could also have been known at Antioch, for communication between Rome and the capital of Syria was good. In the post-70 period Rome, where Peter was martyred, may have taken over some of the heritage of the Jerusalem leadership by keeping up relations to churches founded by the Jerusalem missionaries (BMAR 51–53,132).

gogue that drove Christian preachers towards the Gentiles?[96] If there were Christian libertines among the Gentile converts who misunderstood Christian freedom, Matt would serve as a firm corrective for them. Matt 5:18 affirms a reverence for the smallest part of a letter of the Law; Matt 5:21–48 shows a very demanding attitude toward the spirit of the Law; Matt 19:9 introduces into Jesus' rejection of divorce (cf. 5:32) a clause opposed to *porneia.* Yet there are other sections that show sharp hostility toward external Jewish practices and treat the Pharisees as casuistic legalists (the designation *hypokritēs* is used over a dozen times, compared to twice in Mark). The Matthean rejection of the title "Rabbi" (23:7–8) is unique. Davies, *Setting,* has made a strong case that Matt was written as a Christian response to the Judaism that was emerging after AD 70 at Jamnia where the rabbis were revered as interpreters of the Law. Perhaps the Matthean Christians lived in the shadow of a larger Jewish community that resented them. If the two groups shared the same Scriptures and many of the same convictions, their differences may all the more have been the subject of dispute. All this fits the Antioch situation, so that Matt's church could plausibly have been the antecedent of the Antiochene church that two or three decades later would have Ignatius as its bishop (BMAR 73–86).[97]

Had the Christian audience envisioned by Matt left or been ejected from the local Jewish synagogues? Much depends on whether certain statements in the Gospel represent the past (pre-70; see *Dating* subsection below) or the final, present status (80s?). Matt 10:17 predicts that Jesus' disciples will be scourged in synagogues; thus Matt knows of Christians, past or present, who were subject to synagogue authority. Matt 23:2–3 says that the scribes and the Pharisees have succeeded Moses and so one must observe what they say (but not what they do). If that is the present situation, the Matthean Christians would still be under synagogue obedience. However, five times Matt (4:23; 9:35; 10:17; 12:9; 13:54) has Jesus teach in "*their* synagogue(s)"; and in 23:34 Jesus addresses the scribes and Pharisees: "I send to you prophets and wise men and scribes[98] . . . some of them you will scourge in *your* synagogues." In 28:15 we are told: "This story has circulated

[96]D. C. Sim, JSNT 57 (1995), 19–48, argues that there is no proGentile bias in Matt and that the focus remained on the Jews, for this was a group persecuted by the Gentiles. However, Matt's community was a group that understood itself persecuted by both Jews and Gentiles (10:17–18; 23:34).

[97]If Matt struggled with both overly conservative Jewish Christians who adhered to the Pharisees' interpretations of the Law and overly liberal Gentile Christians who needed to be taught ethical behavior implicit in the Law, so also Ignatius seems to have struggled with a Judaizing group on one side and a gnosticizing docetic group on the other.

[98]Although Matt seems to envision a structured church, we have to guess about those who administered it. The passage in 23:34 may reflect a situation similar to that of the Antiochene church with its prophets and teachers (Acts 13:1).

among Jews to the present (day)." Such language of alienation suggests separation from Judaism[99] on the part of the Jewish Christians who together with Gentile Christians formed a self-subsistent church. See also n. 55 above for the possibility that Matt's church no longer recited the basic Jewish prayer, the Shema; it has even been suggested that the Matthean "Our Father" was taught so that the emerging church would have its own prayer to match what was being recited in the synagogues.

Date of Writing

The majority view dates Matt to the period 70–100; but some significant conservative scholars argue for a pre-70 dating. On the upper end of the spectrum, Papias may have flourished as early as 115; if he knew of canonical Matt, a 2d-century date is ruled out.[100] Matt betrays no awareness of the problem of gnosticism; therefore, if Matt was written in the Antioch area, it was probably written before the time of Ignatius (*ca.* 110), for whom gnosticism was a threat. Further confirmation of that is supplied if Ignatius in *Eph.* 19 shows knowledge of Matt 2, and in *Smyrn.* 1.1, of Matt 3:15; and if *Didache* 1.4 shows knowledge of Matt 5:39–41, and *Did.* 8.2, of Matt 6:9–15.[101] *The Gospel of Peter,* plausibly dated about AD 125, drew on Matt.

On the lower end of the spectrum most who think that the apostle Matthew himself wrote the Gospel tend toward a pre-70 dating (although obviously the apostle could have lived till later in the century).[102] There are

[99]This is the view of Meier, Hare, and Stanton vs. Bornkamm, Barth, and Hummel. (Saldarini, *Matthew's,* argues that the Matthean Christians were a Torah-obedient, defiant group within 1st-century Judaism, dislodged from local synagogues in Syria, who legitimized themselves by delegitimizing emerging rabbinic Judaism.) In my judgment the Matthean separation has not left so sharp a sense of alienation as that found in John.

[100]Davies and Allison, *Matthew* 1.127–28, lists the datings proposed by some fifty scholars. Five from the last century but none from this century opt for a date after 100.

[101]Writing in German in 1957, H. Koester would argue that these parallels could simply exhibit knowledge of oral Jesus tradition; but writing in French in 1950, E. Massaux argues for Ignatius' dependence on Matt. Many would regard 3:15 as Matthean redaction; if so, Ignatius knew Matt. For further discussion: J. Smit Sibinga, NovT 8 (1966), 263–83; C. Trevett, JSNT 20 (1984), 59–67; and especially J. P. Meier in Balch, *Social History* 178–86.

[102]Prominent among ancient papyri copies of Matt are $P^{64/67}$, a total of five fragments preserved at Oxford's Magdalen College and Barcelona, hitherto dated to the late 2d century AD (C. Roberts, HTR 64 [1953], 73–80). In Dec. 1994, however, amidst a barrage of newspaper publicity C. P. Thiede made startling (and probably implausible) claims about the early dating of the Magdalen fragments, e.g., Thiede, *Eyewitness* 125: "The fragments at Oxford and Barcelona belong to a particular type of uncial writing that flourished in the mid-first century A.D." (Such dating for a Gospel copy would favor a very early date for the composition of Matt.) Stanton, *Gospel Truth?* 11–19, points to inadequacies in the arguments of Thiede (who employs a Qumran fragment to date Mark very early as well!—Chapter 7 above, n. 95); and during 1995 two specialists in epigraphy, K. Wachtel and S. Pickering, contended against Thiede that the Roberts dating of the Magdalen papyrus is correct; see also T. C. Skeat, NTS 43 (1997), 1–34.

weighty arguments, however, against positing such an early composition. For instance, the omission in Matt 21:13 of the description of the Jerusalem Temple as serving "for all the nations" (Mark 11:17) and the reference in Matt 22:7 to the king burning the city[103] may reflect the destruction at Jerusalem by the Roman armies in AD 70. In terms of theological development, the triadic formula in Matt 28:19 ("the name of the Father and of the Son and of the Holy Spirit") is the most advanced NT step in a trinitarian direction and easier to understand as coming at the end of the NT period—so also the stress on the abiding presence of Jesus in 28:20 rather than on the second coming. The controversies with the Pharisees in Matt and the condemnation of free use of the title "Rabbi" fit well into the atmosphere of the early rabbinic period after 70. Two passages (27:8; 28:15) describe items in the Matthean passion narrative that are remembered "to this day," using an OT phrase to explain place names from long ago (Gen 26:33; II Sam 6:8). Such a description would be very inappropriate if Matt was written only two or three decades after AD 30/33. Probably the best argument for a post-70 date is the dependence of Matt on Mark, a Gospel commonly dated to the 68–73 period.

All this makes AD *80–90 the most plausible dating; but the arguments are not precise, and so at least a decade in either direction must be allowed.*

Issues and Problems for Reflection

(1) The best-attested reading of 1:16 is "Jacob was the father of Joseph, the husband of Mary; of her was begotten Jesus, called the Christ." There are variant readings of Matt 1:16 (BBM 61–64), one designed to avoid calling Joseph "the husband of Mary," another preserving the usual pattern of X begot Y but still calling Mary a virgin. It is most unlikely that the variant readings represent a different understanding of Mary's conception; they are awkward copyists' attempts to straighten out the grammar of the best-attested reading.

(2) The KJV of Matt 6:13 has a doxology or ascription concluding the Lord's Prayer, "For thine is the kingdom, and the power, and the glory, for ever. Amen," drawn from the (inferior) Greek mss. used in the translation history of that version. The clause was lacking in Jerome's Vulgate on which Roman Catholic translations were based; and so there developed an ecumen-

[103]This fits awkwardly into the parable as if it were added by Matt. See also Matt 21:43,45: the kingdom taken away from Jewish authorities (the priests and Pharisees) and given to a people that will bear fruit; 23:38: God's house (Temple) will be abandoned and desolate; 27:25: all the people accept responsibility for the blood of Jesus "on us and on our children," implying reckoning for a generation who lived after Jesus' time.

ical problem: In the English-speaking world there were two different ways to end the Lord's Prayer. Today the great majority of text-critics recognize that the ascription was not written by the Matthean evangelist but was an ancient expansion for liturgical use based on I Chron 29:11. (Some forms of it end with a reference to the Father, the Son, and the Holy Spirit.) The earliest attestation is in *Didache* 8.2, "For yours is the power and glory forever," following the Lord's Prayer but also appearing two other times (9.4; 10.5) and in a eucharistic context. The ecumenical situation has been partially solved today; for in the Roman Catholic Mass, after the Lord's Prayer and a short invocation, the ascription has been incorporated: "For the kingdom, the power, and the glory are yours, now and forever."

(3) The main theological emphases of Matt, especially when compared to Mark, are often listed as christology, ecclesiology, and eschatology. Let me mention a few aspects under each as an invitation to readers to pursue the topics at greater depth. *Christologically:* The divine revelation concerning Jesus as the Messiah, the Son of the living God, comes in the middle of the Gospel (Matt 16:16); the Son of God and Son of Man motifs are prominent throughout; and the Emmanuel motif appears at the beginning and the end. Jesus is implicitly compared with Moses in the infancy narrative and the Sermon on the Mount; and Davidic parallelism is strong in the genealogy and the last days of Jesus' life. The theme of Jesus as divine Wisdom also appears (see 11:19,27). The Son is placed together with the Father and Holy Spirit at the end of the Gospel. *Ecclesially:* Not only are there reflections of Matthean community life throughout, but also the theme of church foundation appears in 16:18–19; and qualities to be emphasized in church life are found in chap. 18. The kingdom of heaven[104] has become quite complex, embracing both a sweep of salvation history and eschatological consummation. The church is not coterminous with the kingdom of heaven but has a role as the place where Jesus is confessed as Lord. In 21:43 the kingdom is transferred from the disbelieving Jewish authorities to a worthy people producing fruit, who constitute the church. The concentration on Peter among the Twelve in scenes peculiar to Matt also has an ecclesial function since he is the rock on which the church is founded. The discourses that set the tone for discipleship (especially chap. 18) also function in church life. *Eschatologically:* The appearance of Jesus as marking a decisive change of times is already anticipated in the infancy narrative, where his birth is signaled by a star in the heavens. Inclusively that motif is picked up by the peculiarly Matthean events that accompany both Jesus' death (earthquake,

[104]See R. K. McIver, JBL 114 (1995), 643–59.

raising the saints, appearance in Jerusalem) and his resurrection (earthquake, angel descending to open the tomb). In Matthean moral teaching some of the most difficult demands reflect eschatological morality (n. 47 above). The eschatological sermon in chaps. 24–25 is much longer than the parallel in Mark and terminates in the great last-judgment parable of the sheep and goats. The appearance of Jesus that ends the Gospel echoes Daniel's vision of the final triumph, and the promised presence of Jesus till the end of time brings us already into the victory of the Son of Man.

(4) Matt 1:16,18–25 clearly describes a virginal conception of Jesus. Although Matt's interest is theological (Jesus is truly *God's* Son), there is no reason to think that the evangelist disbelieved the historicity of this conception. Modern scholars, however, are divided. On the one hand, many do disbelieve, advancing various arguments that I report as follows (with my own queries/comments in parentheses): (a) Such a miracle is impossible. (How does one know that?) (b) This is simply an imaginative account based on the LXX of Isa 7:14: "Behold the virgin will conceive and will give birth to a son," which Matt 1:23 cites. (The Hebrew of Isa 7:14 clearly and the LXX less clearly do *not* predict a virginal conception [see BBM 145–49], and there was no Jewish expectation of the virginal conception of the Messiah.) (c) This is a Christian adaptation of Pagan legends in which a god's seed begets a child of a woman. (Those are not virginal conceptions but divine matings; there is nothing sexual in Matt's or Luke's account; Matt 1–2 almost certainly arose in Jewish Christian circles, which were not likely to have appreciated such alien legends.) (d) The Matthean evangelist writes symbolically, even as did Philo, the Jewish philosopher, who described allegorically the birth of the patriarchs: "Rebekah, who is perseverance, became pregnant from God." (Philo is describing virtues, not the real birth of people.) (e) It is a pious Christian attempt to disguise the fact that Mary was raped and Jesus was illegitimate. (This theory is mostly guesswork with no explicit NT evidence to support it; moreover, such a cover-up would have had to take place extremely early since it is common to Matt and to Luke.)

On the other hand, there are serious scholars who believe in the literal historicity of the virginal conception: (a) Independently it is affirmed by Matt and Luke, which suggests a tradition earlier than either evangelist; (b) In both Gospels the virginal conception is situated in awkward circumstances: Mary becomes pregnant before she goes to live with Joseph, to whom she has been married—an unlikely invention by Christians since it could lead to scandal; (c) As just indicated, the nonhistorical explanations are very weak; (d) There is theological support for a virginal conception: Some Protestants would accept it as true on the basis of inerrancy or biblical authority; Catholics would accept it on the basis of church teaching; and some theologians relate it closely to their understanding of Jesus as divine. For full discussion and bibliography, see BBM 517–33, 697–712.

(5) The Matthean Jesus is often described as an ethical teacher, e.g., in the Sermon on the Mount. Despite the 1st-century context, most Christians would regard as still binding his critique of ostentation in almsgiving, prayer, and fasting (6:1–8,16–18). Yet one should also recognize that if Jesus were speaking to some 20th-century contexts, he might strike out at the opposite vice. Often a highly secular society would be embarrassed by any pious action, including prayer, and would see no sense in fasting as self-denial. Jesus might well say in such a situation: When you pray, pray publicly to challenge those who never pray and see no sense in prayer; when you fast, let others see it so that their presuppositions about comfort may be challenged. Readers may find it fruitful to see if there are other injunctions in Matt that might have to be rephrased to make 20th-century audiences catch the *challenge* of the kingdom of God. Rephrasing, however, is not without peril because it may lead to presenting Jesus as permissive of what some Christians today would want him to permit. The "challenge" of the kingdom that put stern demands on people should not be rephrased away.

(6) As indicated in Appendix II below, some of Jesus' sayings appear in both the canonical Gospels and the *Gospel of Thomas;* and there is a debate whether the *GTh* sayings are derived from or independent of the Gospel sayings (or both). Matt 13, with its mixture of parables derived from Mark, Q, and M, offers a good opportunity for comparative study that readers are invited to make. *GTh* 9 can be compared with Matt 13:3–8,18–23 (sower and the seed and its interpretation, from Mark) and *GTh* 57 with Matt 13:24–30,36–43 (weeds among the wheat and its interpretation, from M). In both instances the *GTh* parable is shorter and lacks the interpretation. Is that because it is more original or because the author of the *GTh* collection rejected the canonical explanation and wanted the parables left open to gnostic applications? The paired parables of the mustard seed and the leaven (Matt 13:31–33, from Q) appear separated in *GTh* 20 and 96, in a shorter form but with a somewhat different thrust: The mustard seed puts forth immense foliage because it falls upon plowed terrain, and the leaven produces huge loaves of bread. Are these gnostic elements (even as in *GTh* 107, the parabolic lost sheep is the largest of the flock)? The paired parables of the treasure in the field and the pearl of great price (Matt 13:44–46, from M) appear separated in *GTh* 109 and 76 in a lengthier form with much more stress on the hidden aspect of the treasure and the pearl. Does that reflect the gnostic idea of the divine hidden in the material world? The canonical pairing may be a secondary organizing of once independent parables, but

can we be sure that *GTh* does not represent a further reorganization, stemming from gnostic usage of Matt?

(7) Matt 16:16c–19 ("You are Peter . . .") is one of the most discussed passages in the NT,[105] largely because Roman Catholics have used it to support the role of the pope. The unusually heavy Semitic background of the phraseology makes it likely that this was not created by Matt but drawn by the evangelist from an earlier source. Many would deny that it was spoken by Jesus himself, e.g., on the grounds that it was missing from the presumably older account of the scene in Mark, and that it contains a reference to "church" (meaning "church" at large) that is unique in the Jesus tradition. However, Bultmann, BHST 258, would argue that Matt preserved an older account of the Caesarea Philippi confession than did Mark. A more widely followed thesis is that Matt has added to the Marcan form of Peter's Caesarea confession of Jesus as the Messiah a Petrine confessional passage that originally had another setting. A postresurrectional setting would be appropriate on several scores: It is when provision for the future church is found in the NT pictures of Jesus, when Paul received a revelation from God about Jesus as "God's Son," which was not dependent on flesh and blood (Gal 1:16), and when the power to forgive or retain sins is given in John 20:23. In any case this Petrine passage can be set alongside Luke 22:31–32 (Jesus promises that Simon [Peter] will not fail despite Satan's attempt to destroy him and will turn and strengthen his brothers) and John 21:15–17 (Jesus three times tells Simon Peter to feed his lambs/sheep) as evidence that in the Gospels written in the last third of the 1st century, after Peter's death, he was remembered as a figure to whom Jesus had assigned a special role in support of other Christians. This NT evidence is a manifestation of what many theologians call the Petrine function in the ongoing church (see PNT 157–68). Obviously it was a major step from that NT picture to the contention appearing later in history that the bishop of Rome is successor to Peter. That development would have been facilitated by various factors: Rome was the capital of the Roman Empire and thus of the Gentile world to which increasingly the Christian mission was directed (Acts 28:25–28); the martyrdom of Peter (and Paul) took place at Rome; and the church there that regarded Peter and Paul as pillars (*I Clement* 5) began in its letters to manifest care for other churches in the Empire (BMAR 164–66). Christians today are divided, mostly along denominational lines, on whether the development of the papacy should be considered as God's plan for the church; but given the NT evidence pertinent

[105]See PNT 83–101; Davies and Allison, *Matthew* 2.602–52 (both with bibliographies). On Peter in general, besides PNT, see Perkins, *Peter.* The fact that in the early Christian view Jesus was a successor to JBap may have facilitated the idea that Jesus' principal disciple would be a successor to him.

to the growth of the image of Peter, it is not easy for those who reject the papacy to portray the concept of a successor to Peter as contradictory to the NT.

(8) Matt's extremely hostile critique of the scribes and Pharisees as casuistic (especially in chap. 23)[106] is not untypical of the harsh criticism of one Jewish group by another Jewish group in the 1st centuries BC and AD[107]—a criticism that at times crossed the borderline into slander. Tragically, as Christianity began to be looked on as another religion over against Judaism, Matt's critique became the vehicle of a claim that Christianity was balanced and honest while Judaism was legalistic and superficial. "Pharisaic" became a synonym for hypocritical self-righteousness. The Matthean passages have remained sensitive in relations between Christians and Jews, for many of the recorded views of the rabbis of the second century AD (often looked on as the heirs of the Pharisees) are not casuistic but sensitive and ethical. R. T. Herford's book, *The Pharisees* (New York: Jewish Theological Seminary, 1924) was a major contribution in alerting Christians against a simplistic, prejudiced view. Yet some would note that in the rabbinical writings we are hearing the intellectual, saintly representatives of Jewish love of the Law who were not necessarily characteristic of thought and behavior on a local level (any more than the Church Fathers were characteristic of Christian thought and behavior on a local level). Be that as it may, more important is the realization that Matt is using the scribes and Pharisees to characterize attitudes that he did not want Christians to imitate and that he would condemn among believers in Jesus as strongly as among their Jewish opponents. The casuistic approach to law criticized by Matt is inevitable in any established religion, including the church. Making some adaptations from the local coloring of the 1st century to that of our century, those studying Matt might profitably go through chap. 23 seeking parallels in Christianity and/or society for the condemned behavior.

Bibliography on Matthew

COMMENTARIES AND STUDIES IN SERIES: Albright, W. F., and C. S. Mann (AB, 1971); Betz, H. D. (Hermeneia, 1995; on Matt 5–7); Boring, M. E. (NInterpB, 1994); Davies, M. (RNBC, 1993); **Davies, W. D., and D. C. Allison** (3 vols.; ICC, 1988, 1991, 1998); France, R. T. (TNTC, 1985); Hagner, D. A. (2 vols.; WBC, 1993, 1995); Hare, D.R.A. (IBC, 1993); Harrington, D. J. (SP, 1991); Hill, D. (NCBC, 1972); Kingsbury, J. D. (ProcC, 1977); Luz, U. (NTT, 1995); Meier, J. P. (ABD 4.622–41); Mounce, R. H., (NIBC, 1991); Overman, J. A. (NTIC, 1996); Riches, J. (NTG, 1996); Smith, R. H. (AugC, 1988).

[106]On "hypocrite," see Chapter 5 above, n. 19.

[107]See L. T. Johnson, JBL 108 (1989), 419–41.

BIBLIOGRAPHIES: Davies and Allison, *Matthew,* have excellent bibliographies for every section of Matt; Wagner, G., EBNT (1983); Mills, W. E., BBR (1993); Neirynck, F. et al., *The Gospel of Matthew (1950–1992)* (BETL 126; Leuven: Peeters, 1996).

SURVEYS OF RESEARCH: Harrington, D. J., *Heythrop Journal* 16 (1975), 375–88; Bauer, D. R. in *Summary of the Proceedings of the American Theological Library Association* 42 (1988), 119–45; Anderson, J. C., CRBS 3 (1995), 169–218; Stanton, G. N., *The Interpretation of Matthew* (2d ed.; Edinburgh: Clark, 1995—abbreviated TIMT), 1–26; Senior, D. P., *What Are They Saying about Matthew?* (2d ed.; New York: Paulist, 1996).

* * *

(See also the *Bibliography* in Chapter 6 above on the Synoptic Problem and on Q Research.)

Anderson, J. C., *Matthew's Narrative Web* (JSNTSup 91; Sheffield: Academic, 1994). Rhetorical, narrative criticism.

Bacon, B. W., *Studies in Matthew* (London: Constable, 1930).

Balch, D. L., ed., *Social History of the Matthean Community* (Minneapolis: A/F, 1991). Collected essays illustrating crossdisciplinary approach.

Bauer, D. R., and M. A. Powell, *Treasures New and Old* (Atlanta: Scholars, 1996). Important essays.

Blomberg, C. L., *Matthew* (Nashville: Broadman, 1992).

Bornkamm, G., et al., *Tradition and Interpretation in Matthew* (Philadelphia: Westminster, 1963). Redaction criticism.

Byrskog, S., *Jesus the Only Teacher* (CBNTS 24; Stockholm: Almqvist & Wiksell, 1994). Teaching authority and transmission in Israel and Matt.

Carter, W., *Matthew: Storyteller, Interpreter, Evangelist* (Peabody, MA: Hendrickson, 1995).

Deutsch, C., *Lady Wisdom: Jesus and the Sages* (Valley Forge, PA: Trinity, 1991).

Ellis, P. F., *Matthew: His Mind and His Message* (Collegeville: Liturgical, 1974). Overuse of chiasm.

Goulder, M. D., *Midrash and Lection in Matthew* (London: SPCK, 1974).

Gundry, R. H., *Matthew* (2d ed.; Grand Rapids: Eerdmans, 1994).

Howell, D. B., *Matthew's Inclusive Story* (JSNTSup 42; Sheffield: Academic, 1990). Narrative rhetoric.

Kilpatrick, G. D., *The Origins of the Gospel according to Matthew* (Oxford: Clarendon, 1946).

Kingsbury, J. D., *Matthew: Structure, Christology, Kingdom* (Philadelphia: Fortress, 1975).

———, *Matthew as Story* (2d ed.; Philadelphia: Fortress, 1988). Narrative criticism.

———, "The Rhetoric of Comprehension in the Gospel of Matthew," NTS 41 (1995), 358–77.

Luz, U., *Matthew 1–7* (Minneapolis: A/F, 1989).

———, *Matthew in History* (Minneapolis: A/F, 1994).

Malina, B. J., and J. H. Neyrey, *Calling Jesus Names: the Social Value of Labels in Matthew* (Sonoma, CA: Polebridge, 1988).

Meier, J. P., *Law and History in Matthew's Gospel* (AnBib 71; Rome: PBI, 1976).
———, *The Vision of Matthew* (New York: Paulist, 1979). Good introduction.
———, *Matthew* (Wilmington: Glazier, 1980).
Menninger, R. E., *Israel and the Church in the Gospel of Matthew* (New York: Lang, 1994).
Overman, J. A., *Matthew's Gospel and Formative Judaism* (Minneapolis: A/F, 1990).
Patte, D., *The Gospel according to Matthew* (Philadelphia: Fortress, 1986). Structuralism.
Powell, J. E., *The Evolution of the Gospel* (New Haven: Yale, 1994). Commentary—idiosyncratic.
Powell, M. A., *God with Us: A Pastoral Theology of Matthew's Gospel* (Minneapolis: A/F, 1995).
Przybylski, B., *Righteousness in Matthew and His World of Thought* (SNTSMS 41; Cambridge Univ., 1980).
Saldarini, A. J., *Matthew's Christian-Jewish Community* (Univ. of Chicago, 1994).
Schweizer, E., *The Good News according to Matthew* (Atlanta: Knox, 1975).
Stanton, G. N., *A Gospel for a New People: Studies in Matthew* (Edinburgh: Clark, 1992). Good introduction.
Stock, A., *The Method and Message of Matthew* (Collegeville: Liturgical, 1994).
Wainwright, E. M., *Toward a Feminist Critical Reading of the Gospel According to Matthew* (BZNW 60; Berlin: de Gruyter, 1991).

CHAPTER 9

THE GOSPEL ACCORDING TO LUKE

This is the longest of the four Gospels. Yet it is only half of the great Lucan writing, for it was originally joined to Acts as part of a two-volume work that in length constitutes over one quarter of the NT—a magnificent narrative that blends together the story of Jesus and that of the early church.[1] Luke departs from Mark more than does Matt and can be said to stand part way between Mark/Matt and John theologically. Indeed, although all the evangelists are theologians, the number of writings on the theology of Luke is astounding. In my treatment of each Gospel I have made the recounting of the narrative in the *General Analysis* the occasion for pointing out the characteristics and thought patterns of the evangelist. Rather than devoting a special subsection to Lucan theology, I shall weave observations pertinent to it into the *Analysis;* for perhaps more than in any other Gospel the story is intrinsic to the theology. Part of the theology is the way the Gospel story of Jesus prepares for what happens in Acts, especially to Peter, Stephen, and Paul. That preparation will be highlighted in the *Analysis.* Afterwards subdivisions will be devoted to these special issues: *Sources and compositional features, Authorship, Locale or community involved, Purpose, Date of writing, Issues for reflection,* and *Bibliography.*[2]

[1]The unity of the two volumes is maintained by the overwhelming number of scholars, based on continuity of style, thought, and plan. Talbert, *Literary Patterns,* shows how the relationships go beyond what meets the eye. However, a challenge is presented by M. C. Parsons and R. I. Pervo, *Rethinking the Unity of Luke and Acts* (Minneapolis: A/F, 1993). Recalling the separation of Luke and Acts already in the 2d century and the early canonical lists, they stress that two different genres (biography, historiography) are involved. However, the use of "us" in the Gospel Prologue to include the author anticipates the similar use of "we" in Acts (n. 84 below)—a similarity that makes one doubt that the author thought he was writing two books in different genres. Already in antiquity the suggestion was made of a lost third Lucan book that treated the subsequent career of Paul after his Roman imprisonment of 61–63. Yet the supporting arguments are weak, e.g., the thesis that Acts 1:1 speaks of the Gospel as "the first book" (of three) rather than more correctly as "the former book" (of two).

[2]Throughout this chapter I shall give preference to books and articles written after 1980; for the preceding period those who wish to do further reading and research need only consult the excellent bibliographies in Fitzmyer, *Luke,* e.g., 1.259–70 on theology.

Summary of Basic Information

DATE: 85, give or take five to ten years.

AUTHOR BY TRADITIONAL (2D-CENTURY) ATTRIBUTION: Luke, a physician, the fellow worker and travelling companion of Paul. Less well attested: a Syrian from Antioch.

AUTHOR DETECTABLE FROM CONTENTS: An educated Greek-speaker and skilled writer who knew the Jewish Scriptures in Greek and who was not an eyewitness of Jesus' ministry. He drew on Mark and a collection of the sayings of the Lord (Q), as well as some other available traditions, oral or written. Probably not raised a Jew, but perhaps a convert to Judaism before he became a Christian. Not a Palestinian.

LOCALE INVOLVED: To churches affected directly or indirectly (through others) by Paul's mission. Serious proposals center on areas in Greece or Syria.

UNITY AND INTEGRITY: Western Greek mss. lack significant passages found in other mss. (Western Non-Interpolation: *Issue* 1 below).

DIVISION:*

1:1–4 **Prologue**

1:5–2:52 **Introduction: Infancy and Boyhood of Jesus**

1. Annunciations of conceptions of JBap and Jesus (1:5–45; 1:56)
2. The Magnificat and the other canticles (1:46–55)
3. Narratives of birth, circumcision, and naming of JBap and Jesus (1:57–2:40)
4. The boy Jesus in the Temple (2:41–52)

3:1–4:13 **Preparation for the Public Ministry**

Preaching of JBap, baptism of Jesus, his genealogy, the temptations

4:14–9:50 **Ministry in Galilee**

1. Rejection at Nazareth; activities at Capernaum and on the Lake (4:14–5:16)
2. Reactions to Jesus: Controversies with the Pharisees; choice of the Twelve and preaching to the multitude on the plain (5:17–6:49)
3. Miracles and parables that illustrate Jesus' power and help to reveal his identity; mission of the Twelve (7:1–9:6)
4. Questions of Jesus' identity: Herod, feeding of the 5,000, Peter's confession, first and second passion prediction, transfiguration (9:7–50)

9:51–19:27 **Journey to Jerusalem**

1. First to second mention of Jerusalem (9:51–13:21)
2. Second to third mention of Jerusalem (13:22–17:10)
3. Last stage of journey till arrival in Jerusalem (17:11–19:27)

19:28–21:38 **Ministry in Jerusalem**

1. Entry into Jerusalem and activities in the Temple area (19:28–21:4)
2. Eschatological discourse (21:5–38)

22:1–23:56 **Last Supper, Passion, Death, and Burial**

1. Conspiracy against Jesus, Last Supper (22:1–38)
2. Prayer and arrest on the Mount of Olives, Jewish and Roman trial (22:39–23:25)
3. Way of the cross, crucifixion, burial (23:26–56)

24:1–53 **Resurrection Appearances in the Jerusalem Area**

1. At the empty tomb (24:1–12)
2. Appearance on the road to Emmaus (24:13–35)
3. Appearance in Jerusalem and ascension to heaven (24:36–53).

*Although one may divide the body of the Lucan Gospel geographically in terms of Galilee and the road to Jerusalem, further subdivision is difficult and inevitably arbitrary, since one episode runs into another. Convenience of treatment has played a large role in the subdivisions given above.

General Analysis of the Message

Among the four evangelists only Luke and John write a few verses explaining reflectively what they think they are about: John at the end (20:30–31), Luke at the beginning.

PROLOGUE (1:1–4)

This is one long sentence in a style more formal than that found elsewhere in the Gospel,[3] written to guide the reader. Commentators have pointed to parallels in the classical prefaces of Greek historians (Herodotus, Thucydides) and of the Hellenistic medical and scientific treatises or manuals.[4] There have been many writers, and now the evangelist too will write. The source for all this writing is a previous generation: "the original eyewitnesses and ministers of the word." Some, especially those who make a historicizing claim that the eyewitnesses included Mary for the infancy narratives, interpret Luke as referring to two groups: eyewitnesses and ministers. Most, however, favor two descriptions for the one group: Those who were eyewitnesses of his ministry and became ministers of the word, viz., the disciples/apostles. Again with a historicizing interest, some would understand "after following everything accurately . . . to write for you in order" in v. 3 to mean that the evangelist was a follower of the apostles who wrote literal history. Probably the author means no more than that he traced things with care and reordered them logically. The theological goal is spelled out to "most excellent Theophilus,"[5] namely, assurance concerning the Christian instruction that had been given him. The "assurance" is about the saving value of what is narrated, not primarily about its historicity or objective reporting—even though that reporting has its roots in traditions stemming from the original eyewitnesses and ministers of the word. Luke-Acts is a narrative (1:1: *diēgēsis*) written by a believer to encourage belief.

Lucan theology is dramatized in history and geography. Drawing on the inspiration of Conzelmann (*Theology*), commentators have traced with many

[3]Verses 1–2 are a subordinate clause, vv. 3–4 are the main clause; and each has three parallel segments. The Prologue is partially comparable to Luke 3:1–2; 9:51; and Acts 1:1–2, which serve as subprefaces.

[4]See the notable discussion of the Prologue by H. J. Cadbury, in Foakes Jackson, *Beginnings* 2.489–510; also V. K. Robbins, PRS 6 (1979), 94–108; R. J. Dillon, CBQ 43 (1981), 205–27; T. Callan, NTS 31 (1985), 576–81; L. Alexander, NovT 28 (1986), 48–74, and *The Preface to Luke's Gospel* (SNTSMS 78; Cambridge Univ., 1993).

[5]Although some have wondered whether the name "friend to God" is purely symbolic for every Christian, the odds favor a real and influential person (of whom we know nothing else) who believed in Jesus or was attracted to what was preached about him. In part Luke may have chosen Theophilus as the addressee because his name could apply also to other desired readers.

variations three stages of Lucan salvation history.[6] One workable proposal offers this analysis: *Israel* (= a story recounted in the Law and the Prophets or OT; see Luke 16:16[7]), *Jesus* (= a story recounted in the Gospel, beginning in Luke 3:1), the *Church* (= a story recounted in Acts, beginning in 2:1, and continuing beyond to the ends of the earth until the Son of Man comes). Jesus is the centerpiece binding together Israel and the Church; and his time may be calculated from the baptism to the ascension (Acts 1:22). Transitional from the OT to Jesus and from Jesus to the Church respectively are two bridges constructed by the evangelist. In Luke 1–2 OT characters representing Israel (Zechariah, Elizabeth, the shepherds, Simeon, Anna) come across the bridge to meet Gospel characters (Mary, Jesus); in Acts 1 the Jesus of the Gospel comes across the bridge to instruct the Twelve and prepare them for the coming Spirit, who will establish the Church through their preaching and miracles. Thus there is continuity from the beginning of God's plan to the end. With that plan in mind, let us turn to the first bridge.

Introduction: Infancy and Boyhood of Jesus (1:5–2:52)

Seven episodes are recognizable: two annunciations of conception (JBap, Jesus), the visitation of Mary to Elizabeth, two birth narratives, presentation of Jesus in the Temple, the boy Jesus in the Temple at age twelve. There are minor differences among scholars about the arrangement and subordination of the episodes,[8] but a careful parallelism in the first six is generally recognized. The accompanying Table 3 is virtually a commentary on the very popular proposal that Luke intended two diptychs. The universal Gospel tradition that JBap appeared on the scene before Jesus has been applied to conception and birth, and they now are presented as relatives. Yet no doubt is left that Jesus is greater.

1. Annunciations of Conceptions of JBap and Jesus (1:5–45,56). We

[6]Particularly disputable is Conzelmann's contention that salvation was offered in the past and will be offered again in the future, but is not offered now in the time of the Church. (Some have refined this by suggesting that there is now individual salvation after death.) Flender, *St. Luke,* argues that to some extent the coming of the Spirit in Acts replaces the parousia because, with the ascension of Jesus, victory is won in heaven. An attractive solution is that Luke thinks of salvation as existentially applicable to those who believe in Jesus and have become part of the church, which, however, still has the task of renewing the world (Powell, *What* 79).

[7]Conzelmann has the period of Israel end in Luke 4:13, and the "Satan-free" period of Jesus end in Luke 22:3. This division totally neglects the infancy narrative, assigns JBap to Israel, and does not do justice to the clear opening of Acts.

[8]See BBM 248–53,623–25; that volume gives an exhaustive bibliography complete through 1992, which I shall not repeat here. Since then especially worthy of note is M. Coleridge, *The Birth of the Lukan Narrative . . . Luke 1–2* (JSNTSup 88; Sheffield: JSOT, 1993)—a literary critical approach.

saw that Matt started his infancy narrative with an echo of the Book of Genesis, Abraham begetting Isaac. Luke draws on the same first biblical book, not by naming Abraham and Sarah but by recalling them in the portrayal of Zechariah and Elizabeth[9]—a technique similar to a photograph that has undergone double exposure so that one set of figures is seen through another. The angel Gabriel who makes the announcement is named in the OT only in the Book of Daniel, which stood toward the end of the canon of Jewish Scriptures (among the Writings—thus in his own way Luke is covering the span of the Scriptures). In Daniel, as in Luke, Gabriel comes at the time of liturgical prayer; and the visionary is struck mute (Dan 9:21; 10:8–12,15). More important, Gabriel interprets the seventy weeks of years, a panoramic description of God's final plan in the last part of which "everlasting justice will be introduced, vision and prophecy will be ratified, and a Holy of Holies will be anointed" (Dan 9:24). This time period is now beginning with the conception of JBap,[10] who will play the role of Elijah (Luke 1:17), the one who according to the last prophetic book (Mal 3:23–24 [or 4:5–6]) will be sent before the coming Day of the Lord.

If the annunciation of JBap's conception is evocative of what has gone before in Israel, the annunciation of Jesus' birth catches to a greater degree the newness that God has begun to bring about. Not to aged parents desperate for a child but to a virgin who is totally surprised by the idea of conception does the angel Gabriel now come. And the conception will not be by human generation but by the creative Spirit of God overshadowing her,[11] the Spirit that brought the world into being (Gen 1:2; Ps 104:30). The child to be born is the subject of a twofold angelic proclamation. First, the expectations of Israel will be fulfilled; for the child will be the Davidic Messiah. Gabriel proclaims this in 1:32–33 by echoing the prophetic promise to David that was the foundation of that expectation (II Sam 7:9,13,14,16). Second, the child will go far beyond those expectations; for he will be the unique Son of God in power through the Holy Spirit. Gabriel proclaims this in 1:35 by anticipating the christological language of the Christian kerygma (Rom 1:3–4). Mary's response, "Be it done unto me according to your word" (Luke 1:38), meets the Gospel criterion for belonging to the family of discipleship

[9]These are the only couples in the Bible who become parents although the men are aged and the wives both aged and barren. Zechariah answers the angel, "How am I to know this?" (see Gen 15:8) and ultimately Elizabeth rejoices (see Gen 21:6–7).

[10]Luke probably understood Dan's "anointed" as a reference to the anointed one, i.e., Christ. JBap belongs in an anticipatory way to the time of Jesus, and what is predicted of JBap by Gabriel echoes what will be said of him during Jesus' public ministry (compare 1:15 to 7:27,28,33).

[11]That Luke intended a virginal conception, see BBM 298–309,517–33,635–39,697–712; also p. 219 above.

TABLE 3. LUKE'S INFANCY NARRATIVE STRUCTURE

Annunciation Diptych
(First Stage of Lucan Composition)

1:5–25	1:26–45,56
Annunciation about John the Baptist	Annunciation about Jesus
Introduction of the dramatis personae: Zechariah and Elizabeth, of priestly family, aged, barren (5–7).	*Introduction:* The angel Gabriel sent to Mary, a virgin betrothed to Joseph of the House of David (26–38).
Annunciation of the conception of John the Baptist delivered by an angel of the Lord (Gabriel) to Zechariah in the Temple (8–23).	*Annunciation* of the conception of Jesus delivered by Gabriel to Mary in Nazareth.
Setting (8–10): The priestly customs: Zechariah's turn to offer incense.	
Core (11–20):	
1. Angel of the Lord appeared to Zechariah.	1. Gabriel came to Mary.
2. Zechariah was startled.	2. Mary was startled.
3. The message:	3. The message:
a. Zechariah	a. Hail . . . Mary
	b. Favored one
c. Do not be afraid	c. Do not be afraid
	d. You will conceive
e. Elizabeth will bear you a son	e. and give birth to a son
f. You will call his name John	f. You will call his name Jesus
g. He will be great before the Lord, etc. (15–17).	g. He will be great, etc. (32–33).
4. How will I know this? The angel's response (19).	4. How can this be? The angel's response (35).
5. The sign: Behold you will be reduced to silence.	5. The sign: Behold your relative has conceived.
Conclusion (21–23): Zechariah emerged from the Temple unable to speak. He went back home.	Mary responded with acceptance and the angel went away.
Epilogue: Elizabeth conceived; she reflected in seclusion in praise of the Lord (24–25).	*Epilogue:* Mary, went to the house of Zechariah and greeted Elizabeth, who was filled with the Holy Spirit and proclaimed the praise of the mother of the Lord. Mary returned home (39–45,56).

TABLE 3. *Continued*

Birth Diptych
(First Stage of Lucan Composition)

1:57–66,80 Birth/Naming/Greatness of John the Baptist	2:1–12,15–27,34–40 Birth/Naming/Greatness of Jesus
Notice of Birth: rejoicing by neighbors (57–58).	*Scene of Birth* (1–20): Setting (1–7): Census involving the two parents; birth at Bethlehem.
Scene of Circumcision/Naming (59–66): Two parents involved in wonders surrounding the naming, indicating the future greatness of the child.	Annunciation (8–12): 1. Angel of the Lord appeared to shepherds nearby. 2. Shepherds are filled with fear. 3. The message: c. Do not be afraid; great joy e. This day there is born in the city of David f. A Savior who is Messiah and Lord 5. The sign: a baby wrapped and lying in a manger.
	Reactions (15–20): Shepherds went to Bethlehem, saw the sign; made known the event;
All astonished; Zechariah spoke praising God; All the neighbors feared; All who heard stored events up in their heart.	Hearers astonished; Mary kept these events in her heart; Shepherds returned, glorifying and praising God.
	Notice of Circumcision/Naming (21).
	Scene of presentation in Temple (22–27,34–38): Setting (22–24): Purification of parents; consecration of firstborn, according to the Law. Greeting by Simeon (25–27,34–35): Moved by the Holy Spirit, Simeon blessed parents, and prophesied the child's future. Greeting by Anna (36–38).
Conclusion (80): Refrain on growth of child. His stay in the desert.	*Conclusion* (39–40): Return to Galilee and Nazareth. Refrain on growth of child.

(8:21). Thus proleptically the angel heralds the gospel of the twofold identity of Jesus, son of David and Son of God, and Mary becomes the first disciple.

Although some would classify the visitation (1:39–45) as a separate scene bringing together the dramatis personae of the two annunciations, it can be seen as an epilogue to the annunciation to Mary; for she is fulfilling with haste the first duty of discipleship by sharing the Gospel with others. JBap within his mother's womb begins his role of alerting people to the coming Messiah (see 3:15–16), and Elizabeth's reaction of blessing Mary as the mother whose womb gives birth to the Messiah and then as one who has believed the Lord's word anticipates Jesus' priorities in 11:27–28.

2. The Magnificat (1:46–55) and Other Canticles. In the table of diptychs I have referred to "the First Stage of Lucan Composition" in order to allow for the common thesis that at a second stage (not necessarily in time) Luke added to his basic outline canticles taken from a collection of early hymns in Greek: the Magnificat, the Benedictus (1:67–78), the Gloria in excelsis (2:13–14), and the Nunc dimittis (2:28–32).[12] All these could easily be removed from their present context and indeed, except for an occasional verse or phrase that may have been inserted (e.g., 1:48,76), are not specific in their references to the action being described in the context. The canticles reflect the style of contemporary Jewish hymnology as seen in I Macc (preserved in Greek) and the Qumran Thanksgiving Psalms (*Hodayot,* in Hebrew), for every line echoes the OT so that the whole is a mosaic of scriptural themes reused for a new expression of praise. Thus the canticles complement the promise/fulfillment motif of the infancy narratives.[13] (Beyond that, the Magnificat is clearly patterned on the hymn of Hannah, the mother of Samuel, in I Sam 2:1–10.) The christology is indirect, proclaiming that God has done something decisive but never spelling this out in reference to Jesus' career[14]—whence the suggestion that these may stem from very early Christians. In a sense, Luke remains faithful to the origin of the canticles by putting them on the lips of the first to hear about Jesus. The Magnificat spoken by Mary, the first disciple, is especially meaningful because having heard that her child would be the son of David and the Son of God, she translates this into good news for the lowly and the hungry and woe for

[12]There is more agreement about the first two than about the last two, which some think of as Lucan compositions. That the canticles were translated from Hebrew or Aramaic is a minority thesis, often advanced by scholars with the historicizing desire to attribute composition to those whom the Gospel pictures as speaking them. See BBM 346–66,643–55.

[13]See S. Farris, *The Hymns of Luke's Infancy Narratives* (JSNTSup 9; Sheffield: JSOT, 1985).

[14]Contrast the more developed, explicitly christological hymns in Phil 2:6–11; Col 1:15–20; John 1:1–18. A few scholars would contend that the Magnificat and Benedictus were Jewish not Christian compositions; but their past (aorist) tenses suggest that they were composed by those who thought that God's decisive action had taken place, whereas Jewish hymns of this period look to God's future intervention.

the powerful and the rich. In Luke her son does the same. The heavenly voice says, "You are my beloved Son" (3:22); and Jesus translates that into beatitudes for those who are poor, hungry, and mournful, and woes to those who are rich, contented, and mirthful (6:20–26). Accordingly the Magnificat has had prominence in liberation theology (BBM 650–52).

3. Narratives of Birth, Circumcision, and Naming of JBap and Jesus (1:57–2:40). In this diptych the similarities between the two sides are not so close as in the annunciation diptych because the greater dignity of Jesus gets such extensive attention. The events surrounding JBap echo the annunciation scene: Elizabeth unexpectedly gives the name John to the child, and Zechariah recovers his speech. The Benedictus extols the fulfillment of all that has been promised to Israel. The description of JBap's growing up and becoming strong in spirit (1:80) echoes the growth of Samson (Judg 13:24–25) and of Samuel (I Sam 2:21).

The setting for the birth of Jesus is supplied by the decree of Caesar Augustus for a census of the whole world, the first enrollment when Quirinius was governor of Syria. Historically this description is fraught with problems: There never was a census of the whole Empire under Augustus (but a number of local censuses), and the census of Judea (not of Galilee) under Quirinius, the governor of Syria, took place in AD 6–7, probably at least ten years too late for the birth of Jesus. The best explanation is that, although Luke likes to set his Christian drama in the context of well-known events from antiquity, sometimes he does so inaccurately.[15] Theologically, by associating Jesus' birth with the decree of Augustus, Luke is introducing a divine plan that will culminate when Paul proclaims the Gospel in Rome (Acts 28). The events Luke will describe actually took place in a small town in Palestine, but by calling Bethlehem the city of David and setting them in a Roman census Luke symbolizes the importance of those events for the royal heritage of Israel and ultimately for the world Empire. The announcement of the angels, "To you this day there is born in the city of David a Savior who is Messiah and Lord" (2:11), is imitative of an imperial proclamation. If Augustus is portrayed in inscriptions as a great savior and benefactor, Luke is portraying Jesus as an even greater one.[16] This is an event on the cosmic stage, as the angelic multitude underlines by affirming glory to God in heaven and peace

[15]On the census see BBM 412–18,547–56,666–68. In 23:45 Luke explains the eschatological darkness at the death of Jesus as an eclipse of the sun; but in the Near East there was an eclipse on Nov. 29, not at Passover of 30 or 33. In Acts 5:36–37 *ca.* AD 36 he has Gamaliel speak about Theudas' revolt which occurred *ca.* 44–46 and thinks that Judas "at the time of the census" came after Theudas, when in fact he was forty years earlier. Those convinced of Bible literalism are hard pressed to explain away all these inexactitudes.

[16]Danker, *Luke* 28–46, develops at length the comparison of Jesus with those exalted as benefactors in the Roman world.

on earth (see *Issue* 2 below).[17] The shepherds with whom the revelation about Jesus is shared and who react by praise are Luke's counterparts to Matt's magi. Eventually both shepherds and magi depart from the scene and never reappear, and so both Luke and Matt avoid contradicting the wider tradition that public christological recognition of Jesus did not exist at the time of his baptism. Mary is the only adult who survives from the infancy narrative into the public ministry of Jesus. Luke 2:19,51 use formulas about pondering, taken from Jewish visionary descriptions (Gen 37:11; Dan 4:28 LXX), to indicate that Mary did not yet fully understand the implications of what had occurred. That preserves her status as a disciple even after all the revelation that has been given; she still has to learn about the identity of her Son as revealed through the suffering of the ministry and the cross. Accordingly, she is told in Luke 2:35, "A sword will pierce through your own soul."

As with the visitation, so also with the presentation of Jesus in the Temple (2:22–40), classification as a separate scene is possible; but there is a parallelism between 1:80 and 2:39–40 and thus a basis for keeping the scene within the diptych pattern (see Table 3). We should note that there are two important matching themes: how Jesus' parents were faithful to the Law,[18] and how Simeon and Anna, representative of devout Jews waiting for the fulfillment of God's promises to Israel, accepted Jesus. This is part of Luke's thesis that neither Jesus nor his proclamation was contradictory to Judaism; e.g., at the beginning of Acts he will show thousands of Jews readily accepting the apostolic preaching. Nevertheless, the light that is to be a revelation for the Gentiles and a glory for Israel is set for the *fall* as well as the rise of many in Israel (2:32,34).

4. The Boy Jesus in the Temple (2:41–52). From the viewpoint of sources, this seems to have come to Luke independently of the other infancy material; in 2:48–50 there is no indication of previous revelation about the identity of Jesus as God's Son or of his extraordinary conception. There was a genre of Jesus' boyhood or "hidden life" stories, best attested in the *Infancy Gospel of Thomas,* which recounts "the mighty childhood deeds of our Lord Jesus Christ" between ages five to twelve. The implicit rationale is a response to a question that must have arisen: If during the public ministry Jesus worked miracles and could speak for God, when did he acquire such

[17]There is debate about whether the two-line Gloria in excelsis (2:13–14) is long enough to be characterized as a hymn; but Luke 19:38 may give us another line of an originally larger composition (perhaps antiphonal, earth responding to heaven) as the disciples sing praise: "Peace in heaven and glory in the highest heavens."

[18]2:22–24,39 (also 2:41). On Luke's view that Jesus supplements the Law which has not been done away with, see Fitzmyer, *Luke Theologian* 176–87.

powers? At his baptism? The boyhood stories are designed to show that he had these powers from an early age (see BINTC 126–29).

No matter what the origin of the story of Jesus at age twelve, by placing it between the infancy and public ministry accounts, Luke has constructed a most persuasive christological sequence. In the annunciation an angel proclaims that Jesus is God's Son (1:35); at age twelve Jesus, when speaking for the first time, makes clear that God is his Father (2:49); at age thirty at the beginning of Jesus' public ministry God's own voice from heaven says, "You are my beloved Son" (3:22–23). Once again, however, since historically such self-revelation at an early age could conflict with later local ignorance at Nazareth about his unique identity (4:16–30), we are assured that Jesus was obedient to his parents when he went back to Nazareth (2:51), presumably by not provoking any more revealing incidents like that in the Temple.

Preparation for the Public Ministry: Preaching of JBap, Baptism of Jesus, His Genealogy, Temptations (3:1–4:13)[19]

We see Luke's feel for history and his theology of world import in the subpreface (3:1–2) that he uses to mark off the beginning of the era of Jesus and the Gospel proper. There is a sixfold synchronism dating it (probably *ca.* AD 29) by imperial, gubernatorial, and high priestly reigns. *JBap's preaching ministry* (*3:1–20*), which inaugurates the Jesus era (Acts 1:22), fulfills Gabriel's prediction to Zechariah in Luke 1:15b–16. Luke combines material from Mark, from Q (3:7b–9),[20] and material of his own (3:10–15). By the expression "the word of God came to John the son of Zechariah" (3:2) Luke assimilates JBap's call to that of an OT prophet (Isa 38:4; Jer 1:2; etc.). The Isaian prophecy that is connected to JBap in all four Gospels is extended (Isa 40:3–5) to include "all flesh shall see the salvation of God" as part of Luke's theological concern for the Gentiles. The vituperation that Matt 3:7 directs to the Pharisees and Sadducees, Luke 3:7 directs to the multitudes—a reflection of the Lucan tendency to remove some of the local Palestinian color and generalize the message. Particularly Lucan is JBap's teaching in 3:10–14 with its emphasis on sharing goods, justice for the poor, and kind sensitivity. All this is similar to what the Lucan Jesus will emphasize, a simi-

[19]In this *Analysis* I give more lengthy treatment to the material peculiar to Luke (such as the infancy narrative); in treating material that Luke shares with Mark (triple tradition) and with Matt (Q material), I shall avoid repetition of information conveyed in the last two Chapters. One might also preview Luke's typical changes of Mark described in the subsection *Sources* below.

[20]The Q problem is acutely demonstrated. Sixty of sixty-four words here are identical with those in Matt 3:7b–10; yet one must explain that without knowing Matt, Luke has placed those words in the same sequence as did Matt amidst the material borrowed from Mark.

larity that explains 3:18, where JBap is said already to be preaching the gospel. Amid the Synoptics only Luke (3:15) raises the issue of whether JBap was the Messiah,[21] a question used to introduce JBap's preaching about the one to come (3:16–18). Then exhibiting his love for order (1:3), Luke in 3:19–20 anticipates the reaction of Herod to JBap from Mark 6:17–18 in order to finish the story of JBap's ministry before beginning the story of Jesus' ministry. Thus Luke avoids any subordination of Jesus to JBap, who is not even mentioned in the following baptismal scene.

The Lucan story of *the baptism of Jesus* (*3:21–22*) indicates that Jesus is praying (a Lucan theme that will also end the ministry: 22:46[22]) and in response the Holy Spirit descends in *bodily* form (Lucan imagery to stress reality; see 24:39–43). This same Holy Spirit who comes on Jesus at the beginning of the Gospel will come on the Twelve at Pentecost at the beginning of Acts (2:1–4). Luke stops here to recount *Jesus' genealogy* (*3:23–38*).[23] While Matt's genealogy descended from Abraham to Jesus, Luke's genealogy mounts to Adam (to prepare the way for all humanity, beyond the physical descent of Israel) and even to God (3:38). The localization of the genealogy before Jesus begins his ministry imitates Exod 6:14–26, where Moses' genealogy is given after his prehistory and before he begins his ministry of leading the Israelites from Egypt. *The testing/temptations of Jesus* (*4:1–13*) are introduced by the indication that Jesus was "full of the Spirit," a Lucan emphasis to prepare for the prominent role of the Spirit in Acts (e.g., 6:5; 7:55). Derived from Q, the Lucan temptations, like the Matthean, correct a false understanding of Jesus' mission.[24] Particularly noteworthy is that, unlike Mark and Matt, Luke has no angels come to minister to Jesus and specifies that the devil left him till an opportune time. At the beginning

[21]That view is reported among the postNT followers of JBap as part of their rejection of Jesus. See John 3:25–26.

[22]See S. F. Plymale, *The Prayer Texts of Luke-Acts* (New York: Lang, 1991); D. M. Crump, *Jesus the Intercessor: Prayer and Christology in Luke-Acts* (WUNT 2/49; Tübingen: Mohr-Siebeck, 1992)—redaction criticism.

[23]There are many differences from Matt's genealogy (especially from David on), and those who think of Luke as having tradition stemming from Mary have tried to argue that his is the true family genealogy of Jesus (or of Mary, despite 3:23!) or even to reconcile the two genealogies. Inspiration does not guarantee historicity or reconcilability; otherwise God should have inspired the two evangelists to give us the same record. While Luke's list may be less classically monarchical than Matt's, there is little likelihood that either is strictly historical. See BBM 84–94,587–89. Both serve a theological purpose, e.g., Luke has a pattern of sevens even as Matt had a pattern of fourteens to show divine planning.

[24]P. 177 above. The most obvious difference between Matt and Luke is the order of the last two temptations, which constitutes a real test for redaction criticism (p. 23 above). Was the Q order the same as Luke's, so that Matt changed it to have the scene end on the mountain, matching the mountain motif of Matt 5:1; 28:16? Or was Q order the same as Matt's, so that Luke changed it to have the scene end at the Jerusalem Temple, where the Gospel ends in 24:52–53? Most judge Matt's order more original.

of the passion, Luke alone among the Synoptics will be specific about the presence of Satan, the power of darkness (22:3,31,53); and on the Mount of Olives when Jesus is tested again, an angel will come to strengthen him (22:43–44).

MINISTRY IN GALILEE (4:14–9:50)

With his sense of theological geography, Luke calls attention to Jesus' return to Galilee (4:14)[25] and to his departure from there toward Jerusalem (9:51). In between Luke places most of the public ministry account that he takes over from Mark, on which he imposes his own order.

1. Rejection at Nazareth; Activities at Capernaum and on the Lake (4:14–5:16). To explain why Jesus of Nazareth spent most of his ministry in Capernaum, Luke begins the story with *the rejection of Jesus at Nazareth (4:14–30)*, which takes place considerably later in Mark 6:1–6 and Matt 13:54–58. Also, the Nazareth scene is much expanded beyond Mark's "on the Sabbath he began to teach in the synagogue," for Luke supplies that teaching as Jesus comments on the scroll of the prophet Isaiah (the sole Gospel evidence that Jesus could read). The passage (Isa 61:1–2), which reflects the Jubilee-year amnesty for the oppressed,[26] is used to portray Jesus as an anointed prophet and is programmatic of what Jesus' ministry will bring about. (Presumably it would have appealed strongly to those of Luke's addressees among the lower classes.) The rejection of Jesus the prophet by those in his own native place echoes Mark; but there is no Lucan suggestion that those rejecting him included his own household or his relatives (cf. Mark 6:4). Jesus' turning to outsiders is justified by prophetic parallels. The fury of the people against Jesus, even to the point of trying to kill him, goes far beyond the Marcan account and serves from the very beginning to prepare readers for his ultimate fate.

Luke recounts *four activities connected with Capernaum (4:31–44)*, which now becomes the operational center of Jesus' Galilean ministry. The first of twenty-one Lucan miracles (deeds of power: Chapter 7 above, n. 16) is an exorcism—even though the devil has departed until a more opportune time, Jesus will struggle with many demons. The healing of Simon's mother-in-law (4:38–39) omits the presence of the four fishermen-disciples from

[25]Most scholars start the Galilean ministry here; but others, influenced by Mark's outline, begin it in 4:31. Summaries are characteristic of Lucan style (especially in Acts); and Luke 4:14–15 serves as a preliminary summary of the type of activity Jesus engages in during his Galilean ministry.

[26]R. B. Sloan, Jr., *The Favorable Year of the Lord: A Study of Jubilary Theology in the Gospel of Luke* (Austin: Schola, 1977); S. H. Ringe, *Jesus, Liberation, and the Biblical Jubilee* (Philadelphia: Fortress, 1985).

Mark's account because in Luke, Jesus has not yet called them. In a summary of Jesus' deeds at Capernaum (4:40–41) Luke avoids the exaggeration in Mark 1:33 that the whole city gathered around the door—perhaps an illustration of Luke's sense of better order. What happens when Jesus goes to a deserted place (Luke 4:42–44) exhibits typical Lucan universalizing, since the people rather than Simon and his companions come to seek out Jesus. Compared to Mark 1:39, which has Jesus going through the synagogues of all Galilee, Luke 4:44 localizes the synagogues in Judea. That may illustrate the vagueness of Luke's ideas of Palestinian geography, since in the next verse (5:1) Jesus is still in Galilee, at the Lake. Or does Luke's Judea simply mean "the country of the Jews"?

The *miraculous catch of fish and the call of the disciples* (*Luke 5:1–11*) illustrates ingenious Lucan (re)ordering. The call of the first disciples that Mark had placed before the four Capernaum episodes has been moved after them and indeed after a fishing miracle that only Luke among the Synoptics records. That Jesus has healed Simon's mother-in-law and effected a tremendous catch of fish[27] makes more intelligible why Simon and the others followed Jesus so readily as disciples. The call of a Simon who confesses himself an unworthy sinner is a dramatic presentation of vocation and prepares the way for a calling of Paul who was also unworthy because he had persecuted Christians (Acts 9:1–2; Gal 1:13–15). The theme of leaving "everything" to follow Jesus (Luke 5:11) illustrates Luke's stress on detachment from possessions. Next, Luke narrates *the healing of a leper* (*5:12–16*).

2. Reactions to Jesus: Controversies with the Pharisees; Choice of the Twelve and Preaching to the Multitude on the Plain (5:17–6:49). Drawing on Mark 2:1–3:6, Luke presents a series of *five controversies* (*5:17–6:11*) in all of which Pharisees[28] play a role. The controversies involve a paralytic, the call of Levi, fasting, picking grain and healing on the Sabbath. In them Pharisees criticize many aspects of Jesus' behavior: his claim to be able to forgive sins, his associates, his failure to have his disciples fast, their picking grain and his own healing on the Sabbath. Notice the Lucan emphasis on Jesus' prayer (5:16). The healing of the paralytic becomes more solemn as Luke broadens the audience to Pharisees and teachers of the Law from every village of Galilee, Judea, and Jerusalem, and we are told the power of the Lord was with him to heal (5:17). To make the setting more intelligible to

[27]Here we encounter Luke's occasional similarity to John, for the fishing miracle occurs in a postresurrectional setting in John 21:3–11. Brown, *John* 2.1089–92 and Fitzmyer, *Luke* 1.560–62 favor the postresurrectional setting as more original. Arguing from the conservative view that if one event were described by the two evangelists there would not be differences, Bock, *Luke* 1.448–49 opts for two different miracles!

[28]D. B. Gowler, *Host, Guest, Enemy, and Friend. Portraits of the Pharisees in Luke and Acts* (New York: Lang, 1991)—a combination of social and narrative criticism.

his Hellenistic audience (in Greece?), Luke 5:19 describes a roof of tiles rather than the matted reed and dried mud roof of Palestine through which one would have to dig (Mark 2:4). In the call of Levi, out of Lucan respect for Jesus, the ire of the Pharisees and their scribes is now directed against the behavior of his disciples (Luke 5:30) rather than against Jesus (as in Mark 2:16). In the question about fasting and the response about the new and the old, Luke 5:39 is unique in stressing the superiority of the old. Is this Luke's gesture of respect for those of Jewish descent among his addressees who have had a difficult time leaving behind their former adherence? These controversies lead Jesus' enemies to plot against him (Luke 6:11). The Herodians of Mark 3:6, however, drop out of the picture as meaningless to Luke's audience (also cf. Luke 20:20 to Mark 12:13).

Luke turns to the favorable side of the reaction to Jesus by recounting *the choice of the Twelve, and the healing and preaching to the multitude on the plain (6:12–49)*—a parallel to Matt's Sermon on the Mount which was directed to the Twelve (Matt 5:1–2).[29] In his sense of order Luke has transposed the two scenes of Mark 3:7–12 and 3:13–19, the healing of the multitude and the calling of the Twelve,[30] so that the Twelve are with Jesus when he heals "all" among a great multitude on a plain (Luke 6:17–19). That means that the Lucan Sermon on a Plain which begins in 6:20 is directed to all disciples, not only to the Twelve. Four Lucan beatitudes open the sermon, echoing the program for the ministry read aloud in the Nazareth synagogue. These beatitudes address those who are actually poor, hungry, mournful, and hated "now." The accompanying "woes," perhaps of Lucan creation and resembling the contrasts in the Magnificat, hint at the antagonisms engendered among the addressees by the affluent. The comparable condemnation in Jas 2:5–7; 5:1–6 might suggest that the reason for the violent dislike was the practice of injustice by the rich. Yet, as we shall in later chaps., at times but not consistently, Luke seems to regard the very possession of wealth (unless distributed to the poor) as corrupting one's relationship to God. Luke's ideal is the Jerusalem community of those believers who give their possessions to the common fund as he describes in Acts 2:44–45; 4:32–37.

Without the "You have heard it said . . . but I say to you" that characterizes Matt 5:17–48, Luke 6:27–36 enunciates Jesus' values. Although sometimes these are called "the ethics of the kingdom," that designation is far more appropriate for Matt, where "kingdom" occurs eight times in the course of

[29]Luke's composition from his own material (L), Mark, and Q is only about 30 percent as long as Matt's. It inaugurates Luke's "Little Interpolation" into Mark, as will be explained under *Sources* below. For the extent of the Q material in this sermon, see Table 2 in Chapter 6 above.

[30]The Lucan list of the Twelve Apostles (see also the Eleven in Acts 1:13) seems to stem from a different tradition from that of Mark 3:16–19 and Matt 10:2–4 (see Chapter 7 above, n. 7).

the Sermon on the Mount, than for Luke, who mentions "kingdom" only once in the whole sermon (6:20). Thus there is less eschatological tone to the startling demands of the Lucan Jesus for his disciples to love those who hate and abuse them. The passage on not judging (6:37–42, expanded over Matt 7:1–5) is an extension of love. We are reminded that the demands are addressed to all who would hear (6:27,47), and that the demands are not met by those who do not bear good fruit and simply say "Lord, Lord" (6:43–49).

3. Miracles and Parables that Illustrate Jesus' Power and Help to Reveal His Identity; Mission of the Twelve (7:1–9:6). The Lucan form of *the healing of the centurion's servant in 7:1–10* (a Q miracle), where two deputations are sent to Jesus rather than having the official come himself, and where a servant (*doulos*) is cured rather than a boy/son (cf. Matt 8:5–13; John 4:46–54), may be secondary. The story contrasts a Gentile's faith-response to Jesus with the Jewish authorities' rejection of him. This is a Gentile who has loved the Jewish nation and built the synagogue and thus foreshadows Cornelius, the first Gentile to be converted in Acts (10:1–2). The next miracle, *the raising of the son of the widow of Nain* (*7:11–17*), is uniquely Lucan. This awesome manifestation of power gains Jesus christological recognition (7:16 echoes the prophet and divine visitation motif of 1:76–78), but also shows his compassionate care for a mother deprived of her only son. (For resuscitations, see Chapter 11 below, n. 41.)

Returning to Q material (= Matt 11:2–19), Luke gives us *a scene dealing with JBap* (*7:18–35*) that clarifies his relationship to Jesus.[31] The response of the Lucan Jesus to JBap's disciples in terms of Isaiah is consistent with his having read from Isaiah proleptically at Nazareth. Luke alone (7:29–30) mentions that Jesus' praise of JBap suited all the people and the tax-collectors, who were baptized by JBap and recognized his role in the plan of God (3:10–13), but not the Pharisees and the lawyers, who were unbaptized and rejected that plan. That reaction helps to explain the Q comparison to petulant children who cannot be pleased (7:31–34). The Lucan form of the final verse (7:35) has wisdom justified by "all her children," i.e., JBap and Jesus and those who are their disciples. Perhaps as a continuation of the objection to the Son of Man who has come eating and drinking (7:34), Luke adeptly narrates, in the context of eating at the table of Simon the Pharisee, a beautiful story involving *a penitent sinful woman who weeps over and*

[31]It is interesting to see the effect of the different arrangements: Jesus mentions to JBap's disciples that he has raised the dead: in Matt that refers to the daughter of Jairus (Matt 9:18–26: a scene that has preceded); in Luke it has to refer to the son of the widow.

anoints Jesus' feet (*7:36–50*).[32] It may be composite since it involves a parable comparing two debtors. Is the Lucan story the same as that of the anointing of Jesus' head by a woman at the house of Simon the leper in Mark 14:3–9 and Matt 26:6–13, and that of the anointing of Jesus' feet by Mary, the sister of Martha and Lazarus, in John 12:1–8?[33] There is also a debate as to whether Luke's sinful woman was forgiven because she loved much or whether she loved much because she had already been forgiven. Either meaning or both would fit Luke's stress on God's forgiveness in Christ and a loving response. After the story of this woman, the last part of Luke's "Little Interpolation" into the Marcan outline describes the *Galilean women followers of Jesus* (*8:1–3*), who had been cured of evil spirits and diseases. Three of them are named: Mary Magdalene, Joanna, wife of Chuza, Herod's steward, and Susanna; the first two will reappear at the empty tomb (24:10). Interestingly the other Gospels name Galilean women exclusively in relation to the crucifixion and resurrection, so that only Luke tells us of their past and that they served (*diakonein*) the needs of Jesus and the Twelve out of their means—a picture of devoted women disciples.[34] In part this support anticipates the picture of women in Acts, e.g., Lydia at Philippi (16:15).

Rejoining the Marcan outline at its parable chapter (4:1–20), Luke next recounts *the parable of the sower and the seed and its explanation, interrupted by the purpose of the parables* (*8:4–15*). Particularly interesting is the simplification of the seed that fell into good soil. Only a hundredfold yield is mentioned (not thirty or sixty), and this seed is interpreted as those who hear the word, hold it fast in an honest and good heart, and bring forth fruit with patience (8:15). The brief array of *parabolic sayings centered on the lamp* (*8:16–18*) also ends on the theme of hearing and heeding and leads into the *arrival of Jesus' mother and brothers* (*8:19–21*). Although drawn from Mark 3:31–35, the import is entirely changed. There is no longer an

[32]D. A. Neale, *None but the Sinners: Religious Categories in the Gospel of Luke* (JSNTSup 58; Sheffield: Academic, 1991) discusses the idea of "sinner" in various scenes in Luke, including this one.

[33]Many think that two stories, one of a penitent sinner who wept at Jesus' feet during the ministry and the other of a woman who anointed Jesus' head with costly perfume, have become confused in the tradition that came down to Luke and John. Others argue for one basic story (see Fitzmyer, *Luke* 1.684–86). Hagiographic tradition and legend glued these three stories together and further confused the situation by identifying Mary, sister of Martha, with Mary Magdalene, whence all the art depicting Mary Magdalene as a penitent prostitute with her hair loosed. See M. R. Thompson, *Mary of Magdala: Apostle and Leader* (New York: Paulist, 1995).

[34]Rosalie Ryan, BTB 15 (1985), 56–59, points out that some women scholars (E. Tetlow, E. Schüssler Fiorenza) accuse Luke of a patriarchal attitude reducing women to household tasks. Ryan argues that these women and the Twelve are described similarly in proclaiming the good news of the kingdom. Also J. Kopas, *Theology Today* 42 (1986), 192–202; R. J. Karris, CBQ 56 (1994), 1–20. Overall see B. E. Reid, *Women in the Gospel of Luke* (Collegeville: Liturgical, 1996).

unfavorable contrast between the natural family and a family of disciples; rather there is only praise of the mother and brothers as hearing the word of God and doing it—they exemplify the good seed and fit the criterion of discipleship.

Luke now gives *a sequence of four miracle-stories* (*8:22–56*): calming the storm at sea, healing the Gerasene demoniac,[35] resuscitating Jairus' daughter, and healing the woman with a hemorrhage. The miracles in this chapter are elaborate, as can be seen by comparing the exorcism in Luke 8:26–39 to that in 4:33–37; and the grandeur of Jesus is fully displayed as he exercises power over the sea, demons, long-lasting illness, and death itself. Next[36] Luke continues with *the sending out of the Twelve* (*Luke 9:1–6*). Having manifested his power, Jesus now shares it with the Twelve by giving them authority over demons[37] and sending them to preach the kingdom/gospel and to heal (9:2,6).

4. Questions of Jesus' Identity: Herod, Feeding of the 5000, Peter's Confession, First and Second Passion Prediction, Transfiguration (9:7–50). While the Twelve are away, we are told of *Herod's having beheaded JBap* (*Luke 9:7–9*). Luke omits the whole Marcan account of Herod's banquet and the dance of Herodias' daughter, reflecting perhaps a distaste for the sensational. The important point for Luke is the "tetrarch's" (3:1) curiosity about Jesus (preparing for 13:31 and 23:8). The theme of Jesus' identity is followed out in the subsequent scenes. They begin with *the return of the Twelve Apostles and the feeding of the 5,000* (*9:10–17*), an adapted form of Mark 6:30–44. Luke then skips over Mark 6:45–8:26 (the "Big Omission"), leaving out everything from after the feeding of the 5,000 to after the feeding of the 4,000.[38] Presumably the Lucan evangelist saw these as doublets and decided to report only one; but the differences from the Marcan account of the 5,000 and the presence of another variant in John 6:1–15 may mean that he combined two accounts in the one multiplication of the loaves he reports. (On the eucharistic possibilities, see pp. 136, 345.)

[35]The description of the area in 8:26 as "opposite Galilee" is often diagnosed (along with Luke's later omission of the story of the Syrophoenician woman; n. 38 below) as reflective of Luke's theological geography, keeping the whole of this first part of the ministry in the confines of Galilee.

[36]Luke follows the general sequence from Mark 4:35–6:13, but skips Mark 6:1–6a (Jesus at Nazareth) which was employed earlier in Luke 4:16–30.

[37]This authority takes on special significance in Luke-Acts because of Peter's struggle with Simon Magus (Acts 8:9–25) and Paul's encounter with Bar Jesus and the seven sons of Sceva (13:4–12; 19:13–20). See S. R. Garrett, *The Demise of the Devil: Magic and the Demonic in Luke's Writings* (Minneapolis: A/F, 1989).

[38]The Big Omission includes: the walking on the water, the discussion about what defiles a person and Jesus' declaring all foods clean, the plea of the Syrophoenician woman for her daughter, the healing of the deaf man, the feeding of the 4,000, and healing of the blind man in stages. See *Sources* and Table 4 below.

Rejoining Mark's outline at 8:27 in that Gospel, Luke has next *the threefold proposal about who Jesus is and Peter's confession (9:18–20)*, introduced by the typical Lucan note that Jesus was praying. In the sequence Peter's "the Christ of God" is Luke's way of answering Herod's "Who is this?" ten verses earlier.[39] This confession is greeted by Jesus' *first passion prediction (9:21–22)*, but there is in Luke (unlike Mark/Matt) no misunderstanding by Peter and no chastisement of him. Rather Jesus continues by *teaching about the cross and judgment (9:23–27)*. If the Son of Man must suffer, so also must his followers if they hope to share in his glory. Interesting Lucan features in this series of loosely attached sayings about discipleship include the demand that the cross must be taken up "daily" and the specification that the Son of Man has his own glory alongside that of the Father (9:26). *The transfiguration (9:28–36)*, set in the context of Jesus praying, describes that glory as present already in Jesus' earthly career (9:32).[40] Yet it also affirms the suffering aspect of the Son of Man, for Jesus talks to Moses and Elijah about his "exodus," i.e., his departure to God through death in Jerusalem. Both glory and suffering are affirmed by God's voice that identifies him as Son and Chosen One (Suffering Servant). *The story of the boy with a demon (9:37–43a)* is not so explicit about epilepsy as is Matt 17:15 and abridges the graphic Marcan account even more than does Matt. In particular, Luke suppresses most of the Marcan emphasis on the incapacity of the disciples to heal this child, being more interested in the miracle as manifesting "the majesty of God." Similarly in *the second prediction of the passion and the dispute about greatness (9:43b–50)* Luke again softens the Marcan picture by explaining that the disciples did not understand because Jesus' saying was concealed from them and by moderating the confrontation over which of them was the greatest. Not only is the least among them the greatest, but even an outsider who uses Jesus' name has a place.

Journey to Jerusalem (9:51–19:27)

At this point Luke writes another subpreface (somewhat comparable to 3:1–2) to mark off major change. The time is coming for Jesus to be taken

[39]Kingsbury and others would see this as a central confessional title for Jesus in Luke's Gospel. A comparison with Peter's confession in the other Gospels is presented under *Issue* 3 below.

[40]There are many variations from Mark, as well as parallels with Matt; and the question has been raised whether Luke drew upon a nonMarcan account. See B. E. Reid, *The Transfiguration* (Paris: Gabalda, 1993). Luke omits the account in Mark 9:9–13 of the dialogue about Elijah as Jesus descends from the mountain, perhaps because the angel Gabriel has already identified JBap as Elijah in Luke 1:17.

up (to heaven), and so he sets his face for Jerusalem where he is to die. Luke is portraying a Jesus who knows his destiny and accepts it from God. The long journey[41] is (an artificial) framework for the "Big Interpolation" (9: 51–18:14), as Luke leaves the Marcan outline for almost all this second half of the Gospel and inserts large blocks from Q and from his own sources (L). This section of the Gospel is most characteristically Lucan. The material may be divided into three subsections according to the points in 13:22 and 17:11 where Luke reminds us of the framework of the journey.[42]

1. First to Second Mention of Jerusalem (9:51–13:21). We have seen some parallels between the Gospels of Luke and John, but now we perceive that they are also far apart. Among the Gospels only Luke has *the hostile encounter with a Samaritan village (9:51–56)*, which is diametrically the opposite of the warm reception given Jesus by the Samaritans in John 4:39–42. Very Lucan is Jesus' refusal of the vengeance upon the Samaritans proposed by James and John. The dialogue with *three would-be followers (9:57–62)* highlights the absolute demand imposed by the kingdom. We saw a sending of the Twelve in Mark 6:7–13, Matt 10:5–42 (woven into the Mission Discourse), and Luke 9:1–10. Only Luke has a second mission, *the sending of the seventy-two (10:1–12)*. Actually he seems to have created it out of the same Q material used for the sending of the Twelve. The doubling may be designed to prepare for Acts where the Twelve function prominently at the beginning of the mission, but then the initiative passes to others, like Paul, Barnabas, and Silas. The need for a second sending in the Gospel (10:2) is explained by the size of the harvest. Does the designated "seventy-two" echo for Luke the LXX numbering of the nations in Gen 10:2–31 and thus prognosticate the ultimate extent of the harvest?[43] The proclamation that "the kingdom of God has come near" has an element of judgment in it, for it is followed by *woes to the disbelieving cities (10:13–16)*.

Joy at the subjection of the demons marks the Lucan *return of the seventy-two (10:17–20)*—compare the unemotional return of the Twelve in 9:10.

[41]The Jesus who preaches during this journey anticipates Paul's preaching journeys. H. L. Egelkraut, *Jesus' Mission to Jerusalem: A Redaction Critical Study of the Travel Narrative* (Frankfurt: Lang, 1976), sees a conflict motif running throughout, so that the material in the journey explains God's judgment on Jerusalem, while at the same time Jesus teaches disciples who will go on to constitute a believing community. D. P. Moessner, *The Lord of the Banquet: The Literary and Theological Significance of the Lukan Travel Narrative* (Minneapolis: A/F, 1989), finds an antecedent in Moses' journey in Deuteronomy. More immediately it was inspired by a verse in the Lucan "Big Omission" from Mark (namely, 10:1) where Jesus leaves Galilee and goes to Judea and beyond the Jordan. The summary in Acts 10:37–39 distinguishes from the Galilee ministry "all that he did in the country of the Jews."

[42]C. L. Blomberg, GP 3.217–61, offers chiastic arrangements.

[43]Mss. are divided on whether to read seventy-two or seventy. The former (6×12) is an unusual number, and has probably been simplified by scribes to the more usual seventy, perhaps under the influence of Exod 24:1 where Moses had seventy assistants.

Jesus sums up their mission (and perhaps the mission of the church as Luke has known it) in terms of the fall of Satan. The authority over serpents and scorpions given to them in 10:19 is similar to that in the postresurrectional mission in the Marcan Appendix (16:17–18). Why the disciples should rejoice because their names are written in heaven (Luke 10:20) is explained by what follows. *Jesus thanks the Father for revelation* (*10:21–22*), a passage that has Johannine parallels (p. 184 above). That the disciples have been chosen by the Son to receive the revelation is shown in *the blessing of the disciples* (*10:23–24*), a macarism that acknowledges what they have seen. Luke's next episode involves *the lawyer's question about eternal life and Jesus' response about the love of God and neighbor* (*10:25–28*).[44] Although the lawyer is posing a test, Jesus likes his answer; and that leads into further probing by the lawyer and the *Lucan parable*[45] *of the good Samaritan* (*10:29–37*). Since the commandment to love leads to (eternal) life, the lawyer seeks casuistically to know to whom the commandment applies; but he is told that one can define only the subject of love, not the object. The Samaritan is chosen to illustrate a subject whose range is unlimited, perhaps preparing for Acts 8 with its positive picture of the reaction of Samaritans to the gospel.

The story of *Martha and Mary* (*10:38–42*) is another instance where material peculiar to Luke has Johannine parallels (John 11:1–44; 12:1–8). Yet there are also major differences: The brother Lazarus is absent from Luke, and the family home at Bethany in John is two miles from Jerusalem, not a village on the way from Galilee and Samaria to Jerusalem. The import of the Lucan story is that heeding the word of Jesus is the only important thing—a lesson harmonious with the earlier answer about the love of God and neighbor as the basic observance necessary for eternal life. It demonstrates that what is required is not complicated. Similarly uncomplicated is the instruction given to the inquiring disciple about the *Lord's Prayer* (*11:1–4*)—a shorter and in some ways older wording than that preserved in Matt, but also less eschatological.[46] The encouragement to pray is continued by the

[44]This is similar to the question and response in Mark 12:28–31 involving the scribe and the issue of the preeminent commandment.

[45]The exclusively Lucan parables, as well as being in harmony with the theology of the Gospel and using some adept storytelling techniques (e.g., the rule of three in the number of characters), are very rich in human characterization and detail and fascinating insights into Palestinian attitudes. The good Samaritan and the prodigal son are the most popular; Fitzmyer offers two full pages of bibliography on each. See K. E. Bailey, *Poet and Peasant and through Peasant Eyes. A Literary-Cultural Approach to the Parables in Luke* (combined 2 vols.; Grand Rapids: Eerdmans, 1983), with the caution that at times he is overoptimistic about the applicability of examples from the present Near East to ancient Palestine.

[46]"Each day" instead of "today"; "as we forgive" instead of "as we have forgiven"; and the lack of Matt's added petition about deliverance from the Evil One. See Chapter 8 above, n. 17.

uniquely Lucan *parable of the insistent friend* (*11:5–8*), a story redolent of Palestinian local color, for it envisions the whole family crowded into a single-room house. Q material on *insistence in asking* (*11:9–13*) is added to make the point. The most important variant from Matt 7:7–11 is the promise in Luke 11:13 to those who ask: Matt has good things given by the heavenly Father; Luke has the Holy Spirit given, as verified in Acts.

Abruptly in this friendly sequence where Jesus has been teaching his disciples, Luke shapes *a controversy passage and sayings about the evil spirit* (*11:14–26*). The reference to the struggle between the strong man (Beelzebul) and the stronger one (Jesus) prepares readers for the struggle to take place at Jerusalem in the passion. Peculiarly Lucan is *the beatitude from the woman in the crowd* (*11:27–28*). The pattern of two blessings with priority being given to obedience to God's word has already been anticipated in 1:42–45. In *the warning signs for this generation, parabolic sayings about light, and woes to the Pharisees* (*11:29–12:1*), there are noteworthy Lucan features. Unlike Matt 12:40 that interprets the sign of Jonah in terms of the three days in the whale's belly (preparatory for Jesus' burial and resurrection), Luke 11:32, like Matt 12:41, interprets it as the preaching to the people of Nineveh. Very typical is Luke 11:41 in its stress on the importance of almsgiving, indeed giving from what really matters. While in Matt 23:34 Jesus utters a saying in his own name (simply "I"), Luke 11:49 attributes the same saying to "the Wisdom of God," raising the issue of whether here he identifies Jesus as divine Wisdom. Whereas Matt 23:13 accuses the scribes and Pharisees of locking up the kingdom of heaven, Luke 11:52 has the lawyers taking away the key of knowledge. Finally Luke ends the passage with a warning to the crowds to beware of "the leaven of the Pharisees which is hypocrisy." This is the closest Luke comes to the frequent Matthean designation of the Pharisees as hypocrites (see Chapter 5 above, n. 19).

The *exhortation to confess fearlessly* (*12:2–12*) promises reward for anyone who proclaims the truth and warns of judgment for one who does not. Even a Gospel so emphatic on forgiveness as Luke preserves the tradition of the unforgivable blasphemy against the Holy Spirit (12:10). The assurance that "the Holy Spirit will teach you what you ought to say" when facing hostile synagogue and secular authorities (Luke 12:11–12) takes on added significance in stories that illustrate the trials of Christians in Acts. The pericope on *greed and the parable of the rich barn-builder* (*12:13–21*) is distinctively Lucan. The hopes to divide an inheritance equally or to enlarge a growing business, understandable in themselves, run against the contention that a strong interest in material possessions is not reconcilable with interest in God. Ideally Christians are asked to live by the maxim "One's life does not depend on what one possesses" (12:15; see Acts 2:44; 4:34). The fate of the barn-builder reflects the expectation of an individual judgment taking place before the general judgment at the end of the world. A passage *decrying cares about earthly things* (*12:22–34*) illustrates how well off one can be without such cares. The instruction, "Sell your possessions and give alms" (12:33) is very Lucan in its outlook.

Luke now changes the topic with a section on the *necessity of faithful watchfulness* (*12:35–48*). In the midst of Q material (that Matt 24:43–51 has incorporated into the Eschatological Sermon) Luke 12:41 is an insert: a question by Peter as to whether this teaching is "for us or for all," which is never specifically answered. However, since the next saying involves a *steward* who takes good care of the household, one may judge that there is a greater obligation on the apostles and on Christian leaders. The Q material, which ends in 12:46 with a threat of punishment for the servant who does not watch, is qualified by the Lucan addendum in 12:47–48 distinguishing between the punishment of those who had knowledge and those who did not. (In narrating the hostile treatment of Jesus in the passion, Luke will be the most attentive of all the Gospels to distinguish between the people and their leaders.) That distinction leads into a frightening description of *the diverse results of Jesus' ministry* (*12:49–53*). In eschatological language Jesus speaks of the fire he is to bring on the earth and the baptism of being tested that is part of his destiny. Division, not peace, will be the result; the prediction in Luke 2:34 that Jesus was set for the fall and rise of many in Israel is now made more precise in terms of how families will be split. Since other statements esteem peace (2:14; 19:38) and unified families (role of JBap in 1:17), the results of Jesus' ministry are ambivalent, with a thrust in both directions. Evidently much of this will happen soon, for Jesus expresses ire at *people's inability to read the signs of the present time* (*12:54–56*). To Q material related to *settling before being judged* (*12:57–59*), Luke adds his own *examples of destruction to inculcate repentance* (*13:1–5*). We have no other knowledge of Galileans who were killed by Pilate while offering sacrifice (at Jerusalem), or of the fall of a tower in Siloam (the fountain of Jerusalem), although some have thought that the former incident explains the enmity between Herod (the tetrarch of Galilee) and Pilate that Luke reports in 23:12. *The parable of the fig tree* (*13:6–9*) offers one more chance for the tree's bearing fruit before being cut down. Many have wondered if it is not a benevolent Lucan form of the cursing of the fig tree in Mark 11:12–14,20–23 and Matt 21:18–21, and thus a miracle that has become a parable. Luke next portrays Jesus teaching in a synagogue on a Sabbath and compassionately *healing a crippled woman* (*13:10–17*), a deed that makes the ruler of the synagogue indignant. Although the healing causes rejoicing among the people, it shames the authorities and in the present sequence may illustrate that some will not repent and listen. Nevertheless, *the twin parables of the mustard seed and the leaven* (*13:18–21*) give assurance that the kingdom will ultimately spread and be great despite its small beginnings.

2. Second to Third Mention of Jerusalem (13:22–17:10). Stopping to remind us that Jesus is on the way to Jerusalem, Luke provides an opening question as to how many will be saved. This introduces material on *exclusion from and acceptance into the kingdom* (*13:22–30*). Many who may claim to know Jesus will be shut out, while outsiders from all over the world will get in. The Pharisees' report of *Herod's homicidal hostility* (*13:31–33*) offers the explanation for Jesus' going on to Jerusalem. The reader is probably meant both to think that the Pharisees are telling the truth and to distrust their motives; for they may have been trying to get Jesus off the scene by urging him to save his life through departure from Galilee. Paradoxically, Jesus knows that going to Jerusalem will lead to his death. (Herod will reappear during the Roman trial when Pilate turns Jesus over to him for judgment.) Jesus' thoughts about his destiny leads into the plaintive *apostrophe to Jerusalem* (*13:34–35*): As a prophet Jesus will die there, but the city will be punished for what it does to prophets.[47]

The next three episodes are set in the home of a prominent Pharisee: *the Sabbath cure of a man with dropsy, two instructions about conduct at dinner, and the parable of the great banquet* (*14:1–24*). The cure of the man almost forms a pair with the Sabbath healing of a woman in 13:10–17 and has much the same message. (Actually at Qumran there was a prohibition of pulling a newborn animal out of a pit on the Sabbath: CD 11:13–14.) The first instruction, i.e., not taking the privileged place at dinner, comes close to prudential good manners, especially if the goal is judged as enjoying greater honor at table (Luke 14:10). Yet it does warn against self-honor. The second instruction, i.e., inviting the disadvantaged rather than one's peers, is at home in the upside-down values of the kingdom where the poor are more important than the rich. The eschatological outlook is explicit in the final line (14:14) where the recompense of this behavior is promised at the resurrection of the just. The parable of the great banquet[48] passes a judgment of rejection on those who were first invited because they had priorities that they put before the invitation to the kingdom.

[47]See C. H. Giblin, *The Destruction of Jerusalem according to Luke's Gospel* (AnBib 107; Rome: PBI, 1985).

[48]W. Braun, *Feasting and Social Rhetoric in Luke 14* (JSNTSup 85; Cambridge Univ., 1995). Luke 14:15–24 resembles (but with many differences) the parable of the marriage feast given by the king for his son in Matt 22:1–10. The antiquity of still another form in the *Gospel of Thomas* 64 is favored even by some who are not enthusiastic about the priority of apocryphal gospels. In *GTh* a man prepared a dinner and sent his servant to four guests, all of whom refuse: One has to stay at home because merchants are coming; one has just bought a house and people need him there; one

Then, without mentioning Jesus' departure from the Pharisee's home, Luke has Jesus talking to the great multitudes who accompanied him about *the cost of discipleship* (*14:25–35*). Peculiarly Lucan are the prudential parables about the need to calculate the cost before starting a house or beginning a war (14:28–32)—parables worthy of an OT wisdom teacher. This message is very different from the more prophetic stance of not worrying about the needs of this life, inculcated earlier in 12:22–34.

The whole next chapter consists of *three parables: lost sheep, lost coin, lost* (*prodigal*) *son* (*15:1–32*). Matt 18:12–14 works the lost sheep parable into the Sermon on the Church addressed to the disciples;[49] Luke addresses it (and his own other two parables) to the Pharisees and scribes who object to Jesus' keeping company with sinners. The references to joy in heaven show that the parables give a lesson in God's loving mercy and dramatize the value of those whom others despise as lost. In the first two Luke has a man and woman respectively as dramatis personae (shepherd, housekeeper) similar to the man-woman combination in the mustard seed and yeast parables of 13:18–21. The lost or prodigal son stresses that the elder brother should not be jealous of the father's benevolent treatment of the sinful younger brother, and that fits the context of correcting the Pharisees' attitude toward sinners. Beyond that, the point made in the middle of the parable at 15:20 is important for understanding the concept of Christian love. The portrayal of the father running to the younger son and kissing him before he can give the prepared speech of repentance could serve as an illustration of Rom 5:8: "God's love for us is shown in that, while we were yet sinners, Christ died for us," and I John 4:10: "In this is love, not that we loved God but that God loved us" (p. 533 below).

Many have found difficulty with the uniquely Lucan *parable of the unjust steward* (*16:1–15*) because it seems to commend to the disciples shady business practice; but what is praised is the prudent energetic initiative of the steward, not his dishonesty.[50] Diverse sayings dealing with wealth have been

---

has to arrange a dinner for a friend who is getting married; one has just bought a village and has to go collect the rent. When the servant reports back, the master tells him to go out into the streets and bring in those whom he finds. "Buyers and sellers shall not come into the places of my Father." This point differs from the points made by Matt and Luke.

[49]For the forms of the parable in *Gospel of Thomas* 107 (the largest sheep that Jesus loved most) and *Gospel of Truth* 31:35–32:9 (playing on the symbolism of 99), and arguments that neither is more primitive than the canonical forms, see Fitzmyer, *Luke* 2.1074.

[50]One group of interpreters contends that in the contemporary practice the agent could legitimately lend his master's property at a commission and that this man was doing nothing dishonest in canceling the commission. If that was Luke's idea, he has written with extraordinary obscurity; and the point of the prudent endeavor of the steward is not strengthened. Moreover, the use of *adikia* ("lack of justice") in v. 8 to describe the steward seems to imply dishonesty beyond the squandering mentioned in v. 1.

attached to the parable, but it is debated at which verse they begin: 8b, 9, or 10. Overall they serve Luke's theological tenet that abundant money corrupts and that the right way to use it is to give it away to the poor and thus make friends who, when they go to heaven, can help. At the end of the pericope Luke 16:14–15 shifts to challenging the Pharisees who are "lovers of money" and justify/exalt themselves before others. Perhaps Pharisee devotion to the Law supplies the mental connective to the following Q *sayings about the Law and divorce* (*16:16–18*). The better interpretation of v. 16 is that the coming of JBap marks both the end of the Law and the prophets and the beginning of preaching the gospel of the kingdom (3:1–2,18). There is no discontinuity between the two eras, for in Jesus' teaching not even the smallest part of a letter of the Law drops out (v. 17). What is the relation of the saying on divorce (v. 18) to the preceding principle about the Law? Clearly Jesus' prohibition of divorce does not agree with the permission given the man to divorce in Deut 24:1–4. Although Luke does not mention Gen 1:27; 2:24 as do Mark 10:6–12 and Matt 19:4–9, had that reference (which is part of the Law) become an inherent part of the Christian interpretation so that forbidding divorce was seen to agree with the Law? It was part of the Qumran adherence to the Law (p. 141 above). The theme of the damning effects of wealth returns in the uniquely Lucan *parable of the rich man and Lazarus* (*16:19–31*).[51] The different fates after death are not based on the rich man having lived a life of vice, and Lazarus having been very virtuous; they are based on the rich man having had a comfortable and well-fed life, while Lazarus was hungry and miserable (16:25). This attack on the Pharisees' love for money (which would also serve as a warning for Christians, e.g., Acts 5:1–11) is made sharper by a second point, made at the end of the parable. If they do not listen to Moses and the prophets, they will not listen to someone come back from the dead. To Luke's readers/hearers this would appear prophetic, for Acts will show that people did not listen even after Jesus came back from the dead.

The topic changes as Jesus addresses to his disciples four unrelated *warnings on behavior* (*17:1–10*). Cautioning against scandalizing others, they stress forgiving fellow disciples, the power of faith, and the distinction between great achievement and duty. The last warning, which is peculiarly Lucan, is an interesting challenge: The disciples who have followed Jesus might get the idea that they had done something great, but they are to tell themselves that they are unprofitable servants who have only done their duty.

[51]This is another similarity between Luke and John: Only they mention a Lazarus, and the theme of resurrection from the dead is connected with him in both Gospels.

3. Last Stage of Journey till Arrival in Jerusalem (17:11–19:27). This begins with the uniquely Lucan *cleansing of the ten lepers, including the thankful Samaritan* (*17:11–19*). Jesus has been traveling toward Jerusalem since 9:51, and in 9:52 his messengers entered a Samaritan village. That at this point in the story he is still passing between Samaria and Galilee tells us that the journey is an artificial framework (and also that Luke may not have had a precise idea of Palestinian geography). Yet the framework explains why there is a Samaritan among the lepers, indeed, the sole leper to show gratitude and thus to receive salvation. His reaction anticipates the glad reception of the good news about Jesus by Samaritans in Acts 8:1–25. Since Jesus' journey will soon come to an end with his departure from this world, it is appropriate that Jesus now gives to the Pharisees and then to his disciples *eschatological teaching* (*17:20–37*), drawn together from Q, L, and Luke's own composition, as an anticipation and almost a doublet of the eschatological discourse to be presented in chap. 21. The teaching warns against being deceived, on the one hand, by bogus claims that the kingdom or the days of the Son of Man have visibly arrived and, on the other hand, by thoughtless living as if there will never be a judgment. The more interesting Lucan features include: that the kingdom of God cannot be observed and is among us (see *Issue* 4 below), and that the judgment is unpredictably discriminatory, choosing one person and leaving another (17:31).

In face of this judgment, the uniquely Lucan *parable of the unjust judge* (*18:1–8*) is designed to encourage the disciples by an a fortiori principle. If continued petitioning persuades a totally amoral judge, how much more will their persistent, confident prayer be heard by God who vindicates the chosen ones. The theme of prayer leads into the Lucan *parable of the Pharisee and the publican* (*or tax-collector: 18:9–14*). Beyond exhibiting God's mercy to sinners, the story raises the issue of the rejection of the Pharisee, who is not justified. The Pharisee is not a hypocrite; for, although a bit boastful, he has lived faithful to God's commandments as he understood them. Is the problem that although he thanks God, he has not shown any need of God or of grace or forgiveness? Or does the Lucan Jesus come close to Pauline thought that observing commanded works does not justify by itself? The example of God's graciousness to the outcast tax-collector leads Luke to recount Jesus' *kindness to little children* (*18:15–17*),[52] who serve as a model of dependence on God for entering the kingdom.

[52]Finally here Luke ends his "Big Interpolation" begun after 9:50 (= Mark 9:39–40) to rejoin Mark (at 10:13–16). Just as the Pharisee would regard the tax-collector as unworthy of God's mercy, the disciples regard the little children as unworthy of Jesus' notice. The sinfulness of the tax-collector is related to the corrective in 3:12–13 about collecting no more than what has been assigned.

In turn this leads to the ruler's question of *what is necessary for eternal life and the obstacle offered by riches* (*18:18–30*). Although Luke is following Mark carefully now (with the noteworthy exception that Luke does not say that Jesus "looked with love" on this rich man), the theme is harmonious with Luke's insistence on selling *all* and distributing to the poor. Even those who observe the commandments must be challenged to go farther, not simply in order to be perfect as in the more tolerant Matt 19:21, but in order to enter the kingdom. Luke 18:29 adds "wife" to the list of what will be left behind (cf. Mark 10:29) for the sake of the kingdom—is he thinking of his hero Paul in Acts who was unmarried? Luke 18:30 promises that those who make the sacrifices will receive "manifold" in this life—a more prudent assurance than the hundredfold, houses, brothers, sisters, etc. in Mark 10:30. What Jesus himself will sacrifice is articulated in *the third prediction of the passion* (*18:31–34*). It hews close to Mark 10:32–34 even to the point of predicting that the Gentiles will spit upon and scourge the Son of Man—something that never happens in the Lucan passion narrative![53]

The *healing of the blind man as Jesus comes near Jericho* (*18:35–43*) is a variant of the healing of Bartimaeus as Jesus leaves Jericho (Mark 10:46) and the healing of two blind men as Jesus leaves Jericho (Matt 20:29). Probably Luke has moved the scene geographically to Jesus' entering the city because next he wishes to introduce a colorful scene of his own involving *Zacchaeus* (*19:1–10*) within Jericho. Beyond Jesus' kindness to a tax-collector deemed a sinner, the story illustrates Luke's attitude toward wealth: Zacchaeus is a rich man, but salvation can come to his house because he gives half his goods to the poor.[54] The theme of correct use of wealth continues in the *parable of the pounds* (*19:11–27*). The story of the nobleman going away and giving each of ten servants a pound that one of the servants turns into ten pounds, another into five pounds, and a third simply preserves,[55] resembles the Matthean story (25:14–30) of a man who gives to three servants talents, respectively five, two, and one, that are turned into another five, another two, and simply preserved. In each case the last servant is chastised. The thrust of the parable is to challenge the disciples to make profit-

[53]Curiously Luke omits the element in Mark 10:33 that the Son of Man will be delivered to the chief priests and the scribes (even though similar information was included in the first Lucan passion prediction and the deed actually happens in the Lucan passion narrative) and that they will condemn him to death (even though Luke 24:20 attributes to the chief priests and "our" rulers the condemnation to death).

[54]In 18:22–23 Jesus will ask a very wealthy would-be follower to give away *all* that he has to the poor. Is the spirit of sacrifice rather than the percentage the important issue?

[55]We never hear of the other seven servants. Is Matt more original in having only three servants, or has he honed the account, excising the unecessary?

able use of all that Jesus has revealed to them about the kingdom. Beyond some differences from Matt that may represent editing of a common Q story, Luke seems to have interwoven another story about a nobleman who goes to a far country to receive a kingship: His citizens hated him and sent an embassy to try to prevent his being appointed king, only to have him come back as king and slay them.[56] This prepares for the rejection of Jesus in Jerusalem, his crucifixion as King of the Jews, his return in resurrection, and the ultimate destruction of Jerusalem.

MINISTRY IN JERUSALEM (19:28–21:38)

At the end of his long journey that began in 9:51 Jesus arrives at Jerusalem where his "exodus," or departure to God, will take place.[57] He will stay overnight at Bethphage and Bethany in the near environs of Jerusalem, but most of his activity there will be centered in the Temple area, and at the end he will deliver an eschatological discourse.

1. Entry into Jerusalem and Activities in the Temple Area (19:28–21:4). *The royal entry into Jerusalem* (*19:28–38*) stays close to the Marcan account (11:1–10) but changes the theme from the bystanders' enthusiasm for the arrival of the kingdom to the disciples' praise of Jesus as king (see John 12:13). In Luke 7:18–19 the disciples of JBap posed to Jesus their master's question, "Are you the one to come?" Now the disciples of Jesus confirm that he is. Luke includes a refrain about peace and glory that resembles the Gloria in excelsis (2:14). When the Pharisees want the disciples rebuked, *Jesus reluctantly predicts the destruction of Jerusalem* (*19:39–44*). This is a continuation of the Lucan warnings in 11:49–52 and 13:34–35, but now the possibility of reform seems to be a thing of the past. (Scholars debate whether the description in 19:43 is so precise that Luke must have written [or at least rephrased] it after the historical destruction by the Romans.) That Jesus wept when he uttered this prophecy is indicative to Luke's readers that Christians should not rejoice over that destruction. Unlike Mark 11:11–19 that places the cleansing of the Temple area on the day after Jesus entered Jerusalem, but like Matt 21:10–13, Luke places his (less violent) picture of *the cleansing of the Temple* (*19:45–46*) on the same day on which Jesus

[56]The background of Luke 19:12,14,15a,27 may have been suggested by the history of Archelaus, the son of Herod the Great. After his father's death he went to Rome, seeking to be confirmed king by Emperor Augustus. While he was gone from Palestine, riots broke out against his rule; and later, after having returned as ethnarch, he was brutal toward his subjects.

[57]B. R. Kinman, *Jesus' Entry into Jerusalem in the Context of Lukan Theology and the Politics of His Day* (Leiden: Brill, 1995).

entered Jerusalem.[58] Otherwise Luke begins a section where most of his material is taken from Mark with minor changes.

Jesus now starts daily *teaching in the Temple area, provoking the question of authority* (*19:47–20:8*). In a typical summary Luke describes how the chief priests and the scribes seek to destroy Jesus for this teaching; and then tells how, frustrated by his popularity among "all the people," the most they can do is to challenge his authority—a challenge offset by his own counter-challenge about JBap. (Luke does not need to tell the readers that Jesus' authority comes from God; see 4:43.) The *parable of the wicked attendants* (*20:9–19*) serves as a critique of these authorities (as they recognize in v. 19), because they have not given back fruit from the vineyard. Indeed, the uniquely Lucan v. 18 makes it a threat, for the stone they rejected not only becomes the cornerstone of a new building but also fractures and crushes people. The authorities react by spying on Jesus and seeking to trap him with *a question concerning the tribute to Caesar* (*20:20–26*), which he deftly avoids. Another attempt to lessen Jesus' teaching authority is made by the Sadducees with their *question about the resurrection* (*20:27–40*), but the quality of his answer draws approbation even from scribes (vv. 39–40). Skipping over the scribe's question in Mark 12:28–34 about the most important commandment, Luke continues with Jesus' own *question about David's son* (*20:41–44*). These confrontations end with Jesus' withering *condemnation of the scribes* (*20:45–47*). The charge that they "devour widows' houses" leads into the story of *the widow's offering* (*21:1–4*), which, although taken and shortened from Mark, has a special resonance in Luke, since it favors the poor over the ostentatious rich and illustrates giving away all that one has.[59]

2. Eschatological Discourse (21:5–38). As in Mark/Matt, admiration of the Temple buildings elicits from Jesus a *prediction of the destruction of the Temple* (*21:5–6*); and that leads into a discourse on the last things—a discourse complicated by the fact that Jesus has already exhorted to eschatological vigilance in 12:35–48 and given eschatological teaching in 17:20–37. Unlike Mark/Matt, Luke situates the discourse in the Temple as a continuation of his daily teaching there (19:47; 20:1; 21:38); and there is more interest in what happens to Jerusalem, which is separated from what will happen to the whole world. In the *body of the discourse* (*21:7–36*) some would main-

[58]The historicity of the event, particularly in its more elaborate Marcan form, is debated. If one posits that a simpler prophetic action has been dramatized, there is still the debate whether this took place early in the ministry (as in John 2:13–17) or shortly before Jesus died. In both accounts Jesus is in Jerusalem as Passover comes or is at hand.

[59]A variety of interpretations, many of them quite foreign to the text (e.g., giving according to one's means), are discussed by A. G. Wright, CBQ 44 (1982), 256–65.

tain that 21:8–24 refers to the fate of Jerusalem and 21:25–36 refers to the fate of the world when the Son of Man comes.[60] These points are peculiarly Lucan: 21:12 speaks of persecution for the sake of Jesus' "name" (see Acts 3:6,16; 4:10; etc.); 21:13–15 promises a wisdom that cannot be contradicted to be given when it is time to bear testimony (see 7:35; 11:49; Acts 6:3,10; 7:10); 21:18 supplies extra confidence to Jesus' followers, for not a hair of their head will perish (see 12:7); in place of Mark's abomination of desolation, 21:20 speaks of Jerusalem surrounded by armies (from a knowledge of what happened in AD 70?); between the destruction of Jerusalem and the final times, 21:24 seems to allow a long period: Jerusalem will be trampled "until the times of the Gentiles are fulfilled"; 21:28 speaks of future redemption; 21:33ff. omits Mark's indication (13:32) that no one, not even the Son, knows the day or the hour (a motif that Luke reserves until Acts 1:7, without the limitation on the Son's knowledge); 21:34–36 is an exhortation that serves to end the discourse as Jesus warns about judgment to come on the entire earth. After this ending Luke 21:37–38 supplies a summary describing Jesus' daily activity to serve as a transition to the passion narrative.

Last Supper, Passion, Death, and Burial (22:1–23:56a)

We have seen that when Luke follows Mark, he does so with substantial fidelity; but the passion narrative is an exception. Although many scholars posit dependence on a preLucan passion narrative separate from Mark, a more plausible case can be made for Luke's dependence on Mark combined with some special traditions. Here Luke may simply have done more reordering than elsewhere, perhaps in a desire to make this most important narrative more effective. In particular, both in the passion and resurrection accounts Luke draws on traditions that have left a trace in John as well.

1. Conspiracy Against Jesus, Last Supper (22:1–38). The first Lucan reordering is exemplified by the *conspiracy against Jesus* (*22:1–6*), which Mark interrupts to intercalate the story of Jesus' anointing[61] but which Luke holds together as a unit. Luke explains that Satan entered into Judas (also John 13:2,27). After the temptations in the desert the devil had left Jesus till a more opportune time (Luke 4:13); now he has resumed the direct attack on Jesus. Also arrayed against Jesus, alongside the chief priests, are the captains or officers (of the Temple: 22:4,52; Acts 4:1; 5:24,26).

Peter and John are specified as the disciples who went ahead to prepare

[60]However, decision about structure depends on whether one judges that Luke has dissociated the parousia from the events of contemporary history. See V. Fusco, in O'Collins, *Luke* 72–92.

[61]See above for the issue of whether Luke 7:36–50 is a variant of the anointing in Mark 14:3–9.

for the *Last Supper* (*22:7–38*), the Lucan account of which is twice as long as the Marcan or the Matthean. Jesus' earnest desire to eat this Passover meal with his apostles catches the warmth of the relationship, especially now that this hour has come (22:14–15; cf. John 13:1). The clauses about Jesus not eating or drinking again "until it is fulfilled in the kingdom of God" or "until the kingdom of God comes" (Luke 22:16,18) enhance the eschatological symbolism of the Supper but are obscure in their precise reference. (In Luke 24:30–31 after the resurrection Jesus will break bread with his disciples, which may be considered a form of the coming of the kingdom.) An even greater problem is presented by Luke's having Jesus speak of the cup twice (22:17–18 and 20), before and after he speaks of the bread.[62] Probably the first cup belongs to Luke's description of the ordinary Passover meal (22:15–18), while the second cup that is preceded by the bread belongs to Luke's description of the eucharist (22:19–20). The latter is parallel to the eucharistic description in Mark 14:22–24; Matt 26:26–28, but with the differences italicized in what follows: "my body *which is given for you; do this in remembrance of me*" (resembling I Cor 11:24: "my body which is for you; do this in remembrance of me"), and not "blood of the covenant" but "This *cup is the new covenant in my blood which is poured out for you*" (the first part resembling I Cor 11:25). Thus there may have been two traditions of Jesus' Last Supper, one preserved in Mark/Matt, the other in Paul and Luke. The feast of Passover had a remembrance (*anamnēsis*) motif: "remember the day of your departure from the land of Egypt all the days of your life" (Deut 16:3), but for Christians this is shifted to a remembrance of Jesus. The Lucan clauses that have the body and blood given or poured out "for you"[63] stress the soteriological thrust of Jesus' death and of the eucharist.

Mark and Matt have three predictions of the fate of the disciples: one (involving Judas) made at the Last Supper, two (involving the body of the disciples and Peter) made on the way to the Mount of Olives. Luke's more "orderly" account places all three at the Last Supper (as does John). The prediction of the giving over of Jesus by Judas (22:21–23) is substantially a reworking of Mark 14:18–21, except that in Mark it precedes the eucharistic words.[64] The prediction about the body of the disciples/apostles (Luke 22:24–30), composed and adapted from Mark and Q, is very Lucan in its

[62]This is complicated by a textual problem because in some Western textual witnesses (Codex D, Old Latin) 22:19b–20, containing the second cup passage, is missing; see *Issue* 1 below. The best solution is to recognize that the shortening represents a scribal emendation to get rid of what appeared as repetition.

[63]Cf. John 6:51: "The bread that I shall give is my flesh for the life of the world."

[64]By having the prediction of Judas' betrayal (see the "traitor" designation in 6:16) come after he had participated in the eucharist, is Luke pedagogically cautioning his readers that participation in the eucharist is no automatic guarantee of right behavior?

benevolence. In reaction to a dispute about which of them is the greatest, Jesus praises them for their fidelity to him in his trials and promises them places at table in his kingdom and thrones from which to judge the twelve tribes. This is virtually the opposite of the prediction in Mark 14:27 that they will all be scandalized and scattered; and indeed, unlike Mark, Luke will never describe the flight of the disciples when Jesus is arrested. Similarly Luke 22:31–34 is a unique introduction that modifies the prediction of Peter's threefold denial; for amidst Satan's effort to sift all the apostles like wheat, Jesus promises to pray for Simon (Peter) that his faith will not fail. When he has turned back, he is to strengthen his "brothers" (the other apostles, all believers, or both?). Proper to Luke, too, is dialogue that leads to the assertion that the apostles have two swords (22:35–38). The situation of a mission without provisions (as in 10:4—the seventy-two) is now changed; everyone needs to be prepared, having purse, or bag, or sword, for Jesus will be reckoned with outlaws. The apostles misunderstand the figurative language, and Jesus responds "Enough of that" to their report that they have two swords.[65]

2. Prayer and Arrest on the Mount of Olives, Jewish and Roman Trials (22:39–23:25). Luke has no dialogue on the way from the Supper when Jesus is going to a "customary" place (cf. John 18:2) on the mountain opposite Jerusalem where *Jesus prays and is arrested* (*22:39–53*). Luke simplifies Mark's dramatic description of the alienation of Jesus from the disciples. There is no separation of Jesus in stages from the body of the disciples, and then from Peter, James, and John, to go off by himself; nor is there a description of Jesus' emotions and his falling to the ground. With composure the Lucan Jesus kneels to pray (a position familiar to Christians: Acts 7:60; 9:40; 20:36; 21:5); he prays only once (not three times) and finds the disciples sleeping only once (and then "out of sorrow"). If 22:43–44 (the appearance of an angel to Jesus) was written by the evangelist rather than added by a later copyist (see BDM 1.179–86), Luke differs from Mark/Matt by having Jesus' prayer answered, a touch illustrative of the Lucan Jesus' closeness to his Father. In Mark/Matt, after Jesus was tested by the devil for forty days in the desert, angels ministered to him. Luke omitted that; but now an angel strengthens Jesus, making him ready to enter the second and greater testing or trial.

Jesus' words during the arrest show that he knows the evil intention behind Judas' kissing him (Luke 22:48). Picking up on the discussion about

[65]Why they have two swords here and one of them has a sword when Jesus is arrested is not clear (BDM 1.268–71), but this scarcely turns them into revolutionaries! For a detailed study of Luke 22:24–30, see P. K. Nelson, *Leadership and Discipleship* (SBLDS 138; Atlanta: Scholars, 1994).

the swords at the Supper, the disciples demonstrate their continuing misunderstanding by asking about striking with the sword. This question causes Jesus to tell them to desist, advice that Luke would pass on to Christians facing arrest or persecution in their time. Alone among the Gospels, Luke has the chief priests themselves come to the Mount of Olives; and Jesus reminds them of his daily teaching in the Temple area as a challenge to the armed force being used to arrest him (cf. the interrogation of Jesus by Annas in John 18:20). Luke's theology of the scene finds expression in 22:53: This hour belongs to the power of darkness. Yet even in this desperate moment the mercy of Jesus is demonstrated as (in Luke alone) he stops to heal the right ear of the servant of the high priest who came to arrest him.

In Mark/Matt and in John the denials of Jesus by Peter are interwoven (in different ways) with the night scene where Jesus stands before Jewish authorities; Luke's orderliness causes him to put the *denials by Peter* (*22:54–62*) first, before the Jewish trial, with the result that Jesus is present in the courtyard while Peter is denying him. The poignant moment when the Lord turns and looks at Peter recalls the promise at the Last Supper that Jesus would pray for Simon Peter so that his faith would not fail. Luke also places in the night courtyard setting the *Jewish mockery of Jesus* (*22:63–65*) and has it done by those who were holding him captive, whereas Mark/Matt have it at the conclusion of the Jewish trial and done by the Sanhedrin members. This rearrangement causes Luke to simplify the presentation of the *Jewish trial* (*22:66–71*)[66] and to set it all in the morning. The chief priests ask Jesus about being the Messiah, the Son of God; but this question is divided into two segments and a direct answer to the first is avoided because they would not believe—features found in John 10:24–25,33,36.

The Lucan account of the *Roman trial* (*23:1–25*) departs significantly from Mark. A set of charges is presented to Pilate: Jesus is misleading the nation, as exemplified in forbidding taxes to Caesar and claiming to be Messiah king. Luke knows the pattern of Roman trials (cf. the charges presented in the trial of Paul in Acts 24:5–9), and he is fitting the tradition about Jesus into that pattern. Luke 23:4,14,22 dramatizes Jesus' innocence, for three times Pilate says that he finds no guilt in him—cf. the three times in John 18:38; 19:4,6 where Pilate finds no case against Jesus. Only Luke (23:6–12) reports that Pilate sent Jesus to Herod who questioned and mocked him—a

[66]The question has been raised whether one should speak of a trial in Luke because his account has no witnesses, no reference to the high priest as an interrogator, no charge of blasphemy, and no death sentence. Yet in the total Lucan picture "trial" is not inappropriate. At the end of the procedure (22:71) the Sanhedrin members say, "What further need of testimony (witness) do we have?" Luke 24:20 says that the chief priests gave him over to a death sentence (*krima*). Acts 13:27–28 speaks of the Jerusalem rulers having judged (*krinein*) him.

continuation of the special Herod material (9:7–9; p. 267 below), but also an anticipatory parallel to the trial in Acts 25–26, where the perplexed Roman governor Festus turns Paul over to the Herodian king Agrippa II to be interrogated. In both cases (Luke 23:15; Acts 26:32) the accused is returned to the governor without being found guilty. Especially Lucan is the observation that Jesus' presence before Pilate and Herod healed the enmity that had existed between them. The Jesus who healed so many during the public ministry continues to heal throughout the passion. After Jesus comes back, Pilate tries twice again to release him, even offering the lesser penalty of whipping; but finally he gives Jesus over "to their will" (Luke 23:25). That is done without Luke's recording the scourging and mockery of Jesus by the Roman soldiers found in the other three Gospels.[67] Was the omission prompted by a dislike of repetition because Jesus had already been mocked before Herod?

3. Way of the Cross, Crucifixion, Burial (23:26–56). Elevating *the way of the cross* (*23:26–32*) beyond the transitional sentence found in the other Gospels, Luke constructs an episode that has a key place in the structuring of Jesus' death. Here immediately before Jesus is crucified, Luke groups Simon the Cyrenian, a large multitude of people, and the "daughters of Jerusalem"; in 23:47–49 immediately after Jesus dies on the cross he groups the Roman centurion, the crowds, and the women from Galilee—a triptych with the crucifixion in the center and a group of three parties favorable to Jesus on either side. Luke reported that when Jesus was born there were many Jews who received him favorably; he insists that this is true also when Jesus died, only now a Gentile has also entered the picture. Echoing the OT, the warnings of Jesus to the weeping daughters of Jerusalem (23:28–32) represent a continuation of the theme whereby Jesus reluctantly proclaimed the fate of the city to be sealed (19:41–44)—despite the presence of some who are sympathetic. The specification "yourselves and your children" recognizes that the burden of the coming catastrophe will fall on another generation.

Luke also reshapes the *incidents culminating in death on the cross* (*23:33–46*). Only in Luke does Jesus speak at the moment of crucifixion. Some manuscripts of Luke lack Jesus' words in 23:34a, "Father, forgive them, for they do not know what they do" (BDM 2.971–81); but the extension of forgiveness would fit the Lucan outlook admirably. Mark describes three groups of mockers at the cross before Jesus died: the passersby, the

[67]This omission means that Luke does not mention soldiers until 23:36, halfway through the crucifixion account; and that has led to the (wrong) charge that Luke portrays the Jewish participants as physically crucifying Jesus. See p. 39 above and BDM 1.856–59.

chief priests, and the two co-crucified. After separating out the people as simply observing, Luke has his mocking threesome consist of the rulers, the soldiers, and one of the co-crucified. The unique scene with the other co-crucified in 23:40–43 is a masterpiece of Lucan theology. The generosity of Jesus goes far beyond what the criminal[68] asks for, and he becomes the first one to be taken to Paradise! The trusting and confident final word of Jesus on the cross, "Father, into your hands I place my spirit" (23:46) is quite different from the Marcan Jesus' plaintive cry of being abandoned. All the negative signs that accompanied the crucifixion, including the rending of the sanctuary veil, are placed before Jesus dies, so that the positive, salvific results of the death can stand out clearly.

To exemplify those results Luke recounts the *reaction of the three parties to the death of Jesus, followed by the burial (23:47–56)*. The Roman centurion joins his testimony to that of Herod, Pilate, and the one co-crucified wrongdoer that Jesus was a just man and did nothing wrong. The crowds express sorrow. The women followers stand at a distance looking on; and they will be the connective to the future, for they will also look on at the burial[69] and come to the tomb. The final touch is to tell us that the women observed the Sabbath law. Luke was very insistent to report that at the birth of Jesus everything was done according to the Law; from one end of his life to the other Jesus has lived within the confines of Judaism.

Resurrection Appearances in the Jerusalem Area (24:1–53)[70]

Luke deviates from the Marcan indication that the risen Jesus would appear in Galilee, and concentrates his three appearance-scenes around Jerusalem. This makes the sequence with the passion tighter. More important, Luke can thus finish the Gospel in the place where it began, the city that symbolizes Judaism.

1. At the Empty Tomb (24:1–12). Although Luke follows Mark 16:1–8, he greatly modifies it, adding clarifications (v. 3: when the women went in, they did not find the body), a dramatic question (v. 5: "Why do you seek the living among the dead?"), and adaptations (v. 6: not an appearance in Galilee but a remembrance of what Jesus said there; and v. 9: The women did not

[68]He is often called the "penitent thief"; but Luke calls him a "wrongdoer" without specifying his crime, and although the man recognizes that he is being justly punished, he never expresses penitence. (See Luke 15:20 above.) Is it accidental that this wrongdoer is the only one in this or any Gospel to call Jesus simply, "Jesus," without an additional modifier?

[69]There Luke develops the portrayal of Joseph from Arimathea to explain that although he was a member of the Sanhedrin, he had not consented to the decision against Jesus.

[70]R. J. Dillon, *From Eyewitnesses to Ministers of the Word: . . . Luke 24* (AnBib 82; Rome: PBI, 1978).

stay silent but told all this to all the rest). Luke has his own tradition about the presence of Joanna (the wife of Chuza: 8:3). Truly novel is the textually dubious v. 12 which reports that, although the women were not believed, Peter ran to the tomb, saw only the burial wrappings, and went home wondering. It is extremely close to what is reported in John 20:3–10 (without the disciple whom Jesus loved, however). Luke's later plural reference to this in 24:24, after the visit of the women to the tomb, is puzzling: "*Some* of our number went to the tomb."

2. Appearance on the Road to Emmaus (24:13–35). This dramatic and very long appearance account is entirely proper to Luke, although it is echoed in the Marcan Appendix (16:12–13). There are some good storytelling techniques, e.g., the disappointed hope of the disciples that Jesus might have been the deliverer; Jesus pretending to want to go on farther. Yet there are also curious elements, e.g., an Emmaus sixty stadia (seven miles) from Jerusalem is not easily located; we know nothing of this Cleopas or, a fortiori, of his unnamed companion; it is hard to calculate how the time allotments at the end of the day (vv. 29,33) are possible; finally Luke (v. 34) does not tell us the circumstances of the appearance to Simon (Peter) that took place before evening on this day.[71] It is typically Lucan that the first account of an appearance should occur on a journey; and just as on the long journey to Jerusalem, so also in 24:27 Jesus gives important revelation to disciples: He appeals to the whole of Scripture in order to explain what he has done as Messiah. In the Book of Acts the apostolic preachers will do this, and Luke wants to root their use of Scripture in revelation given by Jesus. Yet even though the disciples' hearts glowed when Jesus opened to them the meaning of the Scriptures, they recognized him only when he broke bread. This prepares for the (eucharistic) breaking of the bread in the Christian community described in Acts[72] and (together with the other postresurrectional meals) may well have been at the root of Christian belief in the presence of the risen Lord in the eucharistic banquet.

3. Appearance in Jerusalem and Ascension to Heaven (24:36–53). As in John (and seemingly in the Marcan Appendix 16:14–18), the *first appearance to the assembled disciples in Luke* (*24:36–49*) is set in Jerusalem on the evening of the resurrection day. In both Luke and John (20:19–29) these features are found: Jesus stands in their midst and says, "Peace be to you"; there is reference to Jesus' wounds (hands and feet in Luke, hands and side

[71]There is support for this in I Cor 15:5 which lists Jesus' appearance to Cephas first.

[72]The combination of reading the Scriptures and breaking the bread would eventually become the basic component of Christian worship and thus the nourishment of Christian life. On Luke-Acts see A. A. Just, Jr., *The Ongoing Feast: Table Fellowship and Eschatology at Emmaus* (Collegeville: Liturgical, 1993).

in John); and the mission given by Jesus involves forgiveness of sins and the role of the Spirit (explicit in John, symbolically designated as "what my Father has promised" in Luke). Luke is particularly insistent on the reality of Jesus' appearance, for Jesus eats food and affirms that he has flesh and bones. (In his references to a risen body, Paul speaks of one that is spiritual and not flesh and blood [I Cor 15:44,50].) Jesus explains the Scriptures to these disciples too—a sign that this is fundamental to any understanding of what God has done in him. Here the revelation consists of a mission (cf. Matt 28:18–20;[73] John 20:22–23): a mission to all the nations beginning from Jerusalem of which a more detailed program will be given in Acts 1:8. Jesus commissions his disciples to be witnesses of these things that have happened to him in fulfillment of Scripture. Luke had promised at the beginning of the Gospel that his systematic account would be based on what the original eyewitnesses and ministers of the word passed on; clearly, then, he thinks that the disciples fulfilled their mission.

The appearance ends with an *ascension scene* (*24:50–53*)[74] when Jesus goes out to Bethany, blesses his disciples, and is carried up into heaven. Then the disciples return with joy to Jerusalem and the Temple, praising God. This ascension scene, which takes place on Easter Sunday night, terminates the Gospel story of Jesus. The Gospel began in the Temple when an angel came down from heaven to Zechariah; by inclusion it ends in the Temple as Jesus has gone to heaven.

Sources and Compositional Features

The evangelist acknowledges sources: "The original eyewitnesses and ministers of the word" passed on reports of what had come to pass, and many had already undertaken to compile accounts (1:1–2). The Gospel frequently looks forward to Acts; and that orientation affects the way Luke treats his sources. For instance, while the Matthean evangelist incorporated into his account of Jesus' ministry advanced christological insights, e.g., through the disciples' and Peter's confessions of Jesus as the Son of God, the Lucan writer can postpone such confessions until the apostolic preaching of Acts. The stress on Pauline journeys in Acts influences Luke 9:51 and 19:28–29 in using the indications of Jesus' journey to Jerusalem in Mark 10:1,32; 11:1

[73]In Matt the mission will succeed because there the risen Jesus to whom all power in heaven and on earth is given will be with the Eleven all days until the end of the age; in Luke it will succeed because the promised Spirit will invest the Eleven with power.

[74]The Western text (see *Issue* 1 below) omits "he was taken up into heaven"—in my judgment the omission is either a copyist's mistake (as his eye skipped Greek words) or an excision to avoid having two ascensions in Luke-Acts, pace Ehrman, *Orthodox* 227–32.

TABLE 4. LUKE'S USE OF MARK

Material from Mark in Luke		*Major Lucan Interpolations*
Mark 1:1–15	= Luke 3:1–4:15	
		4:16–30 (at Nazareth)
Mark 1:21–3:19	= Luke 4:31–44; 5:12–6:19	5:1–11 (catch of fish)
		6:20–8:3 (Little Interpolation)
Mark 4:1–6:44	= Luke 8:4–9:17	
Mark 8:27–9:40	= Luke 9:18–50	
		9:51–18:14 (Big Interpolation)
Mark 10:13–13:32	= Luke 18:15–43; 19:29–21:33	19:1–28 (Zacchaeus, parable)
Mark 14:1–16:8	= Luke 22:1–24:12	

to frame ten chapters (Luke 9:51–19:27), so that this journey becomes the setting for most of Jesus' teaching. At times too, anticipation of Acts affects the ordering of material, as when the Roman governor Pilate refers Jesus to Herod for a decision, even as in Acts 25 the Roman governor Festus will hand Paul over to (Herod) Agrippa for a decision. As with Matt, we shall treat first two written sources, Mark and Q, of which one can speak with more assurance, and then other compositional material.

(a) MARK.[75] The material taken from Mark constitutes about 35 percent of Luke. In the majority scholarly view the Lucan evangelist had a written form of Mark before him, although some have questioned whether in all details it was identical with the form of Mark used by Matt. The Lucan procedure is to follow the Marcan order and take over Marcan material in large blocks. Notice that Luke omits two sequential Marcan sections: the "Big Omission" of Mark 6:45–8:26 (from after the first multiplication of the loaves to after the second multiplication) and the "Little Omission" of Mark 9:41–10:12 (temptations to sin, teaching on divorce). The reason for these omissions is not totally clear; but probable factors, in addition to Luke's theological preferences,[76] were a desire to avoid repetition and to work material into the planned geographical flow of the story.

Although in general Luke is quite faithful to Mark, he made changes that enable us to detect Lucan thought and proclivities. In what follows the more characteristic changes made by the Lucan evangelist are listed with some examples of each.

- Luke improves on Mark's Greek, bettering the grammar, syntax, and vocabulary, e.g., in 4:1,31,38 and passim by omitting Mark's overused "immedi-

[75]Comparable to the 80 percent of Mark reproduced in Matt, only about 65 percent is reproduced in Luke, which is slightly longer than Matt.

[76]M. Pettem, NTS 42 (1996), 35–54, contends that Luke disagreed with the thesis in Mark 7:18–19 ("Big Omission") that Jesus himself contradicted the Law on food; cf. Acts 10.

ately"; in 20:22 by changing a Latinism like *kēnsos* (= *census*) from Mark 12:14; in 20:23 by substituting the more exact "craftiness, treachery" for the "hypocrisy" of Mark 12:15.

- Luke states at the beginning his intention to write carefully and in an orderly manner (1:3); accordingly he rearranges Marcan sequence to accomplish that goal, e.g., Jesus' rejection at Nazareth is put at the opening of the Galilean ministry rather than after some time had elapsed (Luke 4:16–30 vs. Mark 6:1–6) in order to explain why his Galilean ministry was centered at Capernaum; the healing of Simon's mother-in-law is placed before the call of Simon and companions (4:38–5:11 vs. Mark 1:16–31) in order to make more logical Simon's willingness to follow Jesus; Peter's denials of Jesus are put before the Sanhedrin trial in preference to Mark's complicated interweaving of the two. At times Luke's orderliness is reflected in avoiding Marcan doublets (Luke does not report the second multiplication of loaves) whereas Matt likes to double features and persons. Yet Luke has a double sending out of the apostles/disciples (9:1–2; 10:1).
- Because of changes made in material received from Mark, Luke occasionally creates inconsistencies, e.g., although in Luke 5:30 the partners in the conversation are "the Pharisees and their scribes," 5:33 speaks of "the disciples of the Pharisees," as if the Pharisees were not present; although in 18:32–33 Luke takes over from Mark the prediction that Jesus will be mocked, scourged, and spit on by the Gentiles, Luke (unlike Mark 15:16–20) never fulfills that prediction; Luke has changed the Marcan order of the denials of Peter and the Jewish mockery of Jesus but forgotten to insert the proper name of Jesus in the new sequence, so that at first blush Luke 22:63, in having "him" mocked and beaten, seems to refer to Peter, not Jesus. See also n. 67 above.
- Luke, even more than Matt, eliminates or changes passages in Mark unfavorable to those whose subsequent career makes them worthy of respect, e.g., Luke omits Mark 3:21,33,34 and (in 4:24) changes Mark 6:4 in order to avoid references detrimental to Jesus' family; Luke omits Mark 8:22–26 which dramatizes the slowness of the disciples to see, and Mark 8:33 where Jesus calls Peter "Satan"; in the passion Luke omits the predicted failure of the disciples, Jesus' finding them asleep *three* times, and their flight as reported in Mark 14:27,40–41,51–52.
- Reflecting christological sensibilities, Luke is more reverential about Jesus and avoids passages that might make him seem emotional, harsh, or weak, e.g., Luke eliminates: Mark 1:41,43 where Jesus is moved with pity or is stern; Mark 4:39 where Jesus speaks directly to the sea; Mark 10:14a where Jesus is indignant; Mark 11:15b where Jesus overturns the tables of the money changers; Mark 11:20–25 where Jesus curses a fig tree; Mark 13:32 where Jesus says that the Son does not know the day or the hour; Mark 14:33–34 where Jesus is troubled and his soul is sorrowful unto death; Mark 15:34 where Jesus speaks of God forsaking him.

- Luke stresses detachment from possessions,[77] not only in his special material (L), as we shall see below, but also in changes he makes in Mark, e.g., followers of the Lucan Jesus leave *everything* (5:11,28), and the Twelve are forbidden to take even a staff (9:3).
- Luke eliminates Mark's transcribed Aramaic names and words (even some that Matt includes) presumably because they were not meaningful to the intended audience, e.g., omission of Boanerges, Gethsemane, Golgotha, *Elōi, Elōi, lama sabachthani.*[78]
- Luke may make Marcan information more precise, presumably for better storyflow, greater effect, or clarity, e.g., Luke 6:6 specifies that the next scene (Mark 3:1: "again") took place "on another Sabbath"; Luke 6:6 specifies "the *right* hand" and 22:50 "the right ear"; Luke 21:20 clarifies or substitutes for Mark's "abomination of desolation."

(b) Q SOURCE. The material taken from Q constitutes just over 20 percent of Luke; it adds a strong ethical tone to the portrayal of Jesus. Unlike the Matthean evangelist who moves around Q material to form five major sermons or discourses, the Lucan writer is thought for the most part to have preserved the original order of the Q document (Table 2 above). Occasionally Luke inserts Q material within a block borrowed from Mark, e.g., the teaching of JBap (3:7–9,16c–18) within the first block that describes JBap. Most Q material, however, he inserts in two places where he opens up the Marcan sequence (Table 4 above), namely: a smaller body of Q material in 6:20–8:3 as part of the Little Interpolation, and a larger body of Q material in 9:51–18:14, the Big Interpolation (depicted as part of Jesus' journey to Jerusalem). In both instances he mixes it with other material of nonMarcan origin. As we saw in the *General Analysis,* in order to reflect his own theological views Luke adapts the Q material in many ways. Yet because we do not possess Q, it is often difficult to know whether it is Matt or Luke that has effected a change. The parables of the great supper and the talents/pounds, where the two accounts differ so greatly (Matt 22:2–10; 25:14–30 vs. Luke 14:16–24; 19:12–27), illustrate the difficulty of knowing exactly what Luke has added.

(c) SPECIAL LUCAN MATERIAL (often designated L). Between one third and 40 percent of Luke is not drawn from Mark or Q. Given the evangelist's acknowledgment of the original eyewitnesses/ministers of the word and of

[77]W. E. Pilgrim, *Good News to the Poor: Wealth and Poverty in Luke-Acts* (Minneapolis: Augsburg, 1981); L. T. Johnson, *Sharing Possessions* (Philadelphia: Fortress, 1981); D. P. Seccombe, *Possessions and the Poor in Luke-Acts* (Linz: Plöchl, 1982).

[78]Related to this would be Luke's omission or modification of Mark's local color, e.g., people at a Passover meal dipping in the same dish (Mark 14:20), and Luke's correction of dubious Marcan claims, e.g., that at the feast Pilate used to release any prisoner whom the Jewish crowds requested (Mark 15:6).

many writers who had already undertaken to compile orderly accounts (Luke 1:1), it is not surprising that scholars have posited traditions and sources peculiar to Luke—even more numerous than those peculiar to Matt. Yet there are two major difficulties when we consider the percentage of the Gospel that is not found in Mark or Q. First, since Luke is a very capable rewriter, it is extremely difficult to decide how much material the evangelist freely composed himself, and how much he took over from already shaped traditions or sources. Second, where the author has taken over material, it is not easy to distinguish preLucan traditions from possible preLucan sources. (In this *Introduction* L is understood as covering both.) Pages 232 and 255 above illustrated the issue in reference to the infancy and passion narratives. If I may insert my personal views, although I think Luke knew certain traditions about the origins and death of Jesus and about JBap, I doubt that there were composed Marian (family) and JBap sources available to Luke or a complete passion narrative other than Mark. There are certain agreements between Luke and Matt over against Mark, but I see no convincing evidence that Luke knew the Matthean Gospel.[79] There are clear Lucan parallels to John, but I doubt that Luke knew the Johannine Gospel; rather certain similar traditions came down to both.[80]

However, scholars have plausibly posited some sources for the Gospel (for Acts' sources, see p. 316 below), e.g.: (1) a collection of early hymns or canticles (Magnificat, Benedictus, Gloria in excelsis, Nunc dimittis); (2) a story of Jesus at age twelve—an example of a wider genre of Jesus' boyhood stories; (3) a Davidic genealogy of popular provenance in circulation among Greek-speaking Jews; (4) a group of special parables, which may have included these:[81] good Samaritan, persistent friend, rich barn-builder, barren fig tree, lost coin, prodigal son, Lazarus and the rich man, dishonest judge, and the Pharisee and the publican; (5) a group of miracle-stories, which may have included these: the catch of fish, resuscitating the widow's son, and the cures of the crippled woman on the Sabbath, of the man with dropsy, and of ten lepers. In addition, and distinct from larger sources, the author seems to have had particular items of tradition or information about JBap (family origins), Mary the mother of Jesus, Herod Antipas, and the Galilean women disciples. Some of this probably came through people whom the author

[79]BBM 618–19; Fitzmyer, *Luke* 1.73–75. Major efforts to establish Lucan dependence on Matt are Drury, *Tradition;* Goulder, *Luke;* and Franklin, *Luke.*

[80]BGJ 1.xlvi–xlvii; BDM 1.86–92; Fitzmyer, *Luke* 1.87–88. Those who posit dependence usually work in the other direction: John drew on Luke (p. 365 below).

[81]Parables and miracles unique to Luke are the key to the parable and miracle sources discussed above. Granted that Luke drew on those sources, he may well have composed some parables and/or miracle-stories in imitation of those in the sources.

mentions, e.g., knowledge about Herod (9:7–9; 13:31–32; 23:6–12) coming through Manaen of the church of Antioch (Acts 13:1).

As we end this discussion of Lucan sources, we should remind ourselves, just as we did for Matt (p. 208 above), that the evangelist has done far more than collect and organize disparate material. At the very beginning of Luke's work he speaks of orderly narrative, and all that he received or created has been woven into an epic sweep that begins in the Jerusalem Temple and ends at the imperial court in Rome. This epic can be read for itself without any knowledge of sources,[82] and probably that is the way it was heard or read by the first audiences. Luke is a gifted storyteller, e.g., manifesting a truly artistic sense (the beautifully balanced infancy narrative), and presenting scenes of exquisite tenderness (the "penitent thief"). His choice or creation of L material includes some of the most memorable passages in all the Gospels, e.g., the parables of the good Samaritan and the prodigal son. Accurately Dante described him as "the scribe of the gentleness of Christ"—more than any other evangelist Luke has given the world a Jesus to love. If we combine this with the theological motifs noted in the *General Analysis* above and remember that the same writer also produced the Book of Acts, we must acknowledge the third evangelist as a most significant shaper of Christianity.

Authorship

By the latter half of the 2d century (title of P^{75}, Irenaeus, Muratorian Fragment) this book was being attributed to Luke the companion of Paul. Three references in the NT (Phlm 24; Col 4:14; II Tim 4:11) speak of him as a fellow worker and beloved physician who was faithful to Paul in a final imprisonment. The way that Col 4:11 is phrased, i.e., all the men listed before that verse are of the circumcision, suggests that Luke who is listed after that verse is not a Jew.[83] The NT information is greatly increased by the assumption that Luke was part of the "we," i.e., a form of self-reference in certain passages of Acts where Paul is not traveling alone (intervals in the period AD 50–63).[84] Outside the NT a Prologue from the end of the 2d century adds that Luke was a Syrian from Antioch who died in Boeotia in Greece (see Fitzmyer, *Luke* 1.38–39). Scholars are about evenly divided on whether this

[82]Tannehill, *Narrative,* is helpful on this point.

[83]The name *Loukas,* which is a shortened Greek form of a Latin name (Lucius?), does not tell us whether he was Gentile or Jew.

[84]The "we" passages are 16:10–17 ("Second Missionary Journey," from Troas to Philippi); 20:5–15; 21:1–18 (end of the "Third Missionary Journey," from Philippi to Jerusalem); 27:1–28:16 (Paul sent as a prisoner to Rome).

attribution to Luke should be accepted as historical, so that he would be the author of Luke-Acts.[85]

The main objection against authorship by a companion of Paul comes from Acts in terms of historical and theological differences/discrepancies from the Pauline letters; but we shall leave that problem until we discuss authorship in the next Chapter. It does not make a great deal of difference whether or not the author *of the Gospel* was a companion of Paul, for in either case there would be no reason to think of him as a companion of Jesus.[86] Therefore as a second- or third-generation Christian he would have had to depend on traditions supplied by others—as posited under *Sources* above.

What can be deduced from the Gospel about the evangelist? The last observation in the preceding paragraph seems to be confirmed in 1:1–3, where he includes himself among those who received knowledge of the events passed along from the original eyewitnesses and ministers of the word. Of the four evangelists he had the best control of Greek and facilely uses several styles.[87] In Acts he exhibits a knowledge of the rhetorical conventions of Greek historians and some knowledge of Greek literature and thought. It is not clear that he knew either Hebrew or Aramaic; but he certainly knew the LXX, as seen not only in his citations of Scripture but also in his heavy use of Septuagintal style in appropriate parts of his work. This ability in Greek has caused many to posit that the evangelist was a Gentile convert to Christianity. The knowledge of the OT, however, is so detailed that others have contended that he must have come to Christ with a Jewish background. Yet the mistake about purification in Luke 2:22 ("their" wrongly implies the purification of the father) is implausible on the part of one who grew up in a Jewish family. A solution that does justice to both sides of the issues is to posit that the evangelist was a Gentile who had become a proselyte or a God-fearer, i.e., was converted or attracted to Judaism some years before he was evangelized.[88]

[85]Fitzmyer, *Luke Theologian* 1–22, and Franklin, *Luke* argue strongly in favor. A minority view is that Luke the companion of Paul, after Acts, also wrote the Pastoral Epistles, so that their geographical and biographical information makes up for the abrupt ending of Acts. See J. D. Quinn in Talbert, *Perspectives* 62–75; S. G. Wilson, *Luke and the Pastoral Epistles* (London: SPCK, 1979), and n. 1 above on the theory of three volumes.

[86]In the late 4th century Epiphanius (*Panarion* 51.11.6) claimed that Luke was one of the seventy-two disciples (Luke 10:1). Yet almost two centuries earlier Tertullian (*Adv. Marcion* 4.2.1–2) kept Luke, as an "apostolic man," clearly distinct from the apostle eyewitnesses.

[87]E.g., imitative introductory formulation in his Prologue, Septuagintal style in the infancy narrative, classical polish in Paul's Areopagus declamation in Athens (Acts 17:16–31), and a pattern in Stephen's preaching different from that of Peter and Paul. It has been claimed that Lucan style becomes less biblical and more Hellenistic as the narrative moves from the Gospel (centered in Palestine) to Acts (on the way to Rome).

[88]If the first "we" passage (Acts 16:10–17) is extended to 16:20, the "we" companion would be described as a Jew.

The Gospel is inaccurate on Palestinian geography (see 4:44; 17:11 above); that seems to rule out an evangelist from Palestine (but also seems to question whether he could have been the "we" companion who seemingly spent the years 58–60 there). The knowledge of the church at Antioch exhibited in Acts 11:19–15:41 (ending about AD 50) has been advanced as support for the extra-NT tradition that he was an Antiochene[89] (or did it give rise to that tradition?). Many think that the eucharistic formula in I Cor 11:23–25, which Paul says he received from tradition, came from the practice of the church at Antioch from which Paul had been sent forth on his missionary journeys. Luke's form of the formula in 22:19–20 is not derived from Mark and is close to that of Paul, and thus could show contact with the Antioch church. There have been several attempts to establish that the evangelist was a physician, as Luke was, by pointing to technical medical language and perceptions introduced into material taken over from Mark.[90] However, in a series of writings H. J. Cadbury won over most scholars to the viewpoint that the Lucan expressions are no more technical than those used by other educated Greek writers who were not physicians.[91] More will be added to the picture of the author when we discuss Acts in Chapter 10.

Locale or Community Involved

External tradition that Luke (identified as the evangelist) was from Antioch does not tell us from or to where the Gospel was written. The tradition that Luke was a companion of Paul raises a likelihood that Luke-Acts was addressed to churches descended from the Pauline mission. More specifically a late-2d century Prologue reports that the Gospel was written in Greece (Achaia) and that Luke died there (Fitzmyer, *Luke* 1.38–39).

From the internal evidence of the two-volume Lucan work, the concentration in the last half of Acts on Paul's career (independently of the "we" identification) makes it likely that the addressees were somehow connected with that apostle's proclamation of the gospel message. The Lucan Gospel differs in many ways from Matt. If Matt was written for the church at Antioch, it is quite unlikely that Luke was addressed to the same church (e.g., two such

[89]There is a "we" passage of dubious value that appears in Codex Bezae of Acts 11:28, a scene set in the church of Antioch about AD 44. Fitzmyer, *Luke* 1.43–47, would add the possibility that Luke was a native Syrian inhabitant of Antioch (i.e., a Gentile Semite).

[90]For instance, Luke 4:38 adds "high" to the fever in Mark 1:30; Luke 8:43 softens the harsh criticism of physicians in Mark 5:26. W. K. Hobart, *The Medical Language of St. Luke* (Dublin: Hodges, Figgis, 1882) was the great proponent. He was not very adept at biblical criticism (e.g., 80 percent of his list of four hundred words is found in the LXX); yet the thesis won support from well-known scholars: W. M. Ramsay, *Luke the Physician and Other Studies* (New York: Doran, 1908), and Harnack, *Luke*.

[91]See Cadbury, *Style* 50–51; JBL 45 (1926), 190–206; 52 (1933), 55–65.

very diverse infancy narratives would not have been shaped in the same area for the same people). Occasionally an address to Rome has been suggested because Acts ends there, but Rome in the finale of Acts is primarily symbolic as the center of the Gentile world. Also, if the Gospel was written after AD 70 to the capital, one would have expected some echo of Nero's persecution in the mid-60s. (If Mark was written to Rome, would another Gospel have been needed there?) By way of narrowing the field, the last lines of Acts (28:25–28), attributed to Paul, indicate that the future of the Gospel lies with the Gentiles,[92] not with the Jews. That would be strange if the Luke was addressing a largely Jewish Christian audience.[93] Luke's references to the synagogue have a different tone from Matt's. As Meier, *Vision* 17, plausibly observes, for Matt's church the synagogue has become a foreign institution, while for Luke's addressees the synagogue always was a foreign institution.[94] We have seen that Luke drops Marcan Aramaic expressions and place-names as well as references of local color (packed-mud roofs, Herodians) as if they would not be understood, and he substitutes what would be more intelligible to people of Greek background. (Thus, if there were Jewish Christians among the addressees, seemingly they were not Aramaic speakers.) Features in the presentation of Jesus reflecting the Gentile world have been detected in the Gospel, e.g., the prefacing of a narrative dealing with Jesus' infancy and youth gives the Gospel somewhat the aspect of a Hellenistic biography. Jesus' lectures at a banquet have been compared to those of a sage at a symposium (14:1–24). The resistance to portraying Jesus as suffering during the passion befits a Hellenistic resistance to portraying emotions.[95] All this would make sense if Luke-Acts was addressed to a largely Gentile area evangelized directly or indirectly (through disciples) by the Pauline mission.[96] Of course, that description could fit many places. Specifically, the early tradition that it was written in and to an area of Greece would match

[92]Tyson, *Images,* thinks that the envisioned readers were Gentiles attracted to Judaism (God-fearers) and that the purpose of the Lucan writing was to get them to accept Christianity rather than Judaism. I would judge that such Gentiles might have been an important element among the addressees but not the total constituency. The tone of Luke-Acts that favors this direction could result in part from the address to Theophilus (Luke 1:3; Acts 1:1) who may well have been a Gentile sympathetic to Judaism. The name is attested for both Jews and Gentiles.

[93]Jervell, *Luke,* and Tiede, *Prophecy,* argue for an audience of Jewish Christians. According to Tiede they would have been puzzled by the destruction of the Temple, so that Luke would have had to explain that this resulted from Israel's failure to heed the prophets and Jesus. However, Gentile Christian converts, who had been taught the validity of the OT covenant, could have been equally puzzled by what happened to Jerusalem.

[94]An extremely interesting comparison of the different communities addressed by Matt and Luke is offered by E. A. LaVerdiere and W. G. Thompson, TS 37 (1976), 567–97.

[95]J. H. Neyrey, *Biblica* 61 (1980), 153–71.

[96]The Gospel's emphasis on the poor and critique of the rich, and the idealization in Acts of voluntarily sharing goods may mean that the community had a greater proportion of the lower classes

this internal evidence and might find some confirmation in Acts 16:9–10, which portrays Paul's movement from Asia Minor to Macedonia as dictated by divine revelation. Notice that I have spoken of an area; for rather than thinking of Luke's intended audience as a single house-church or even as living in one city, perhaps we should think of Christians of the same background spread over a large region.

Purpose

Closely related to the issue of addressees is the highly disputed issue of the purpose of Luke-Acts.[97] Much depends on the relations to the Romans and the Jews pictured therein. Since the Lucan Pilate three times declares Jesus not guilty, was Luke trying to persuade Greco-Roman readers that the Jews were totally responsible for the crucifixion? Yet Acts 4:25–28 clearly blames Pilate. Because Acts ends with Paul having been taken to Rome as part of an appeal to the emperor, it has been suggested that the author envisioned a defense brief for Paul. However, then would he not have reported the results of Paul's trial in Rome? Another proposal is that through some of his descriptions of perceptive Roman officials (e.g., of Gallio in Acts 18:14–15) the author was trying to persuade Roman officials to deal fairly with Christians. Yet he also depicts weak Roman officials who are browbeaten by hostile Jewish leaders (Pilate, the magistrates at Philippi, and Felix). Moreover, the proposal that Pagan authorities were likely to read such a work as Luke-Acts is very speculative. A similar objection can be raised to the thesis of O'Neill, *Theology,* that Acts sought to persuade educated Romans to become Christians, a thesis complicated by his idiosyncratic dating of Acts to 115–130 designed to establish a comparison between Acts and the apologetic writing of Justin Martyr.[98]

A more plausible suggestion is that the Lucan writing could help the Christian readers/hearers in their own *self-understanding,* especially when calumnies were circulated among nonbelievers, whether Jews or Gentiles. Christians needed to know that there was nothing subversive in their origins, nothing that should cause them to be in conflict with Roman governance, and that it was false to assimilate Jesus and his immediate followers to the

---

of society. See H. Moxnes, *The Economy of the Kingdom: Social Conflict and Economic Relations in Luke's Gospel* (Philadelphia: Fortress, 1988); also L. T. Johnson, *The Literary Function of Possessions in Luke-Acts.* (SBLDS 39; Missoula, MT: Scholars, 1977).

[97]Bock, *Luke* 1.14, lists eleven suggestions of which I shall treat only the most prominent. C. H. Talbert, *Luke and the Gnostics: An Examination of the Lucan Purpose* (Nashville: Abingdon, 1966), has not had much following in his thesis that, by emphasizing Jesus' humanity and suffering and by stressing a legitimate line of authority, Luke wrote against gnostics; see Fitzmyer, *Luke* 1.11.

[98]H.F.D. Sparks, JTS NS 14 (1963) 457–66, offers a critique of the 1st edition of O'Neill's book.

Jewish revolutionaries[99] who had embroiled the Roman armies in war in the late 60s. As for the relation of Luke's audience to Jews who did not believe in Jesus, some would detect an overwhelmingly hostile picture, so that Luke would be writing to describe the rejection of the Jews.[100] Yet Luke's portrayal of the role of the (Jewish) people in the passion is more nuanced and more favorable than that of the other Gospels, and in Acts he portrays many Jews as coming to believe in Jesus. There is no doubt that Acts describes Jewish leaders both in Jerusalem and in the diaspora synagogues as resisting the proclamation of Christ (and indeed that may be historical), but this description seems to spring from a desire to explain why Christian preachers and especially Paul turned to the Gentiles.

Indeed, the whole flow of Luke-Acts suggests an endeavor to explain the status quo. In the three stages of salvation history, the Gospel comes after the Law and the Prophets because Jesus is loyal to Israel—in him God has not changed the divine plan but fulfilled it. Acts follows as the third stage because the Spirit that comes after Jesus' departure makes the apostles' ministry the legitimate continuation of Jesus' proclamation of the kingdom. The revelation to Peter about Cornelius, Jesus' call of Paul, and the agreement of Paul, Peter, and James at Jerusalem all legitimize Paul's ministry to the Gentiles as part of this continuation. By divine providence a Gospel that had its beginning in Jerusalem, the capital of Judaism, ultimately came to Rome, the capital of the Gentile world. The Gentiles addressed by Luke-Acts could thus be assured that their acceptance of Jesus was no accident or aberration but part of God's plan reaching back to creation, a plan that ultimately includes the conversion of the whole Roman world. Also although they were evangelized by those who had not seen Jesus, the gospel they received went back to "eyewitness and ministers of the world." Thus, not apologetics against adversaries but assurance to fellow Christians was the goal[101] as the author himself indicated at the start: "So that you may realize what certainty you have of the instruction you have received" (Luke 1:4). If the author was

[99]Cassidy, *Jesus,* would find potentiality for revolution in the reversal of values in the Magnificat and the beatitudes; others prefer to speak of a nonviolent revolution or even pacifism; J. M. Ford, *My Enemy Is My Guest: Jesus and Violence in Luke* (Maryknoll: Orbis, 1984).

[100]There is considerable writing on the subject: R. L. Brawley, *Luke-Acts and the Jews: Conflict, Apology, and Conciliation* (SBLMS 33; Atlanta: Scholars, 1987); J. T. Sanders, *The Jews in Luke-Acts* (Philadelphia: Fortress, 1987); F. J. Matera, JSNT 39 (1990), 77–93 (helpful nuance); J. B. Tyson, ed., *Luke-Acts and the Jewish People: Eight Critical Perspectives* (Minneapolis: Augsburg, 1988); J. B. Tyson, *Images of Judaism in Luke-Acts* (Columbia, SC: Univ. of South Carolina, 1992—very good bibliography); and J. A. Weatherly, *Jewish Responsibility for the Death of Jesus in Luke-Acts* (JSNTSup 106; Sheffield: Acadmic, 1994).

[101]Squires, *Plan,* shows how readers in the Hellenistic world could find parallels in Greco-Roman literature stressing providence.

a Gentile Christian addressing fellow Gentile Christians, he wrote with the assurance that "they will listen" (Acts 28:28).

Date of Writing

The same ancient Prologue that locates the Lucan addressees in Greece tells us that Luke's age at death was eighty-four and that he wrote after Matthew and Mark. That Luke used Mark is most plausible from internal evidence; and if Mark is to be dated in the period 68–73, *a date earlier than 80 for Luke is unlikely.* (Since Matt and Luke seem to be totally independent of each other, there is no way from internal evidence to decide which is older.) The constant Lucan pessimism about the fate of Jewish leaders and Jerusalem makes it likely that Jerusalem has already been destroyed by the Romans in 70.[102]

Objection to a post-80 date stems largely from the fact that Acts ends *ca.* 63 with Paul's two-year imprisonment in Rome, and the contention that if Luke had written much later than that, he would have reported Paul's subsequent career and death. As we shall see in the next Chapter, however, that objection probably misunderstands the purpose of Acts which was not to tell the life of Paul but to dramatize the spread of Christianity, culminating with the symbolism of the great missionary coming to Rome, the capital of the Gentile empire. Indeed, the relation espoused by the Paul of Acts 28:25–28 between the mission to the Gentiles and the failure of the mission to the Jews is so different from what Paul himself wrote in Rom 9–11 *ca.* 57/58 that it is hard to imagine a date in the early 60s for Acts.

How long after 80 was Luke-Acts written? *A date no later than 100 is indicated.*[103] The Gospel's symbolic interest in Jerusalem as a Christian center does not match the outlook of 2d-century Christian literature. For Asia Minor and specifically for Ephesus the writer of Acts seems to know only a church structure of presbyters (Acts 14:23; 20:17). There is no sign of the

[102]Luke 11:49–51; 13:34–35; 19:41–44; 21:20–24; 23:28–31. There is a debate whether 19:43–44 is so exact that it had to be written after the destruction of the city; 19:46 omits from the parallel Marcan description that the Temple would be a house of prayer "for all the nations," presumably because the Temple has been destroyed when Luke is writing; 21:20 substitutes a picture of Jerusalem surrounded by armies for Mark's symbolic "abomination of desolation"; 21:23 omits the Marcan reference to flight in winter (because Luke knew that Jerusalem was destroyed in August/September?). Nevertheless, we admit that the absence of an indisputable, clear, specific Gospel (or, indeed, NT) reference to the destruction of the Temple as having taken place remains a problem, since it should have had an enormous impact on Christians (Chapter 7 above, n. 93).

[103]A minority view dates Luke-Acts to the 2d century (sometimes as late as AD 150), written to correct heterodox movements of that period, e.g., O'Neill, *Theology;* J. T. Townsend, in Talbert, *Luke-Acts* 47–62.

developed pattern of having one bishop in each church so clearly attested by Ignatius for that area in the decade before 110. Nor does the writer of Acts show any knowledge of the letters of Paul, which were gathered by the early 2d century. Within the range between 80 and 100, in order to preserve the possibility that there is truth in the tradition that the author was a companion of Paul, the best date would seem to be *85, give or take five to ten years.*

Issues and Problems for Reflection

(1) A particular textual problem, awkwardly called Western Non-Interpolations,[104] affects the interpretation of Luke 22:19b–20; 24:3b,6a, 12,36b,40,51b,52a and perhaps other verses. The Western family of textual witnesses often has readings longer than those in other ms. traditions, but in these verses it has shorter readings. Following the lead of the famous 19th-century textual critics Westcott and Hort, many scholars and translators have followed the Western brevity and omitted from Luke the better attested longer readings. Some of them are important, e.g., 22:19b–20 describes the eucharistic cup of wine; 24:12 describes Peter going to the empty tomb. The recent trend, however, is to accept them as genuine, in part because P^{75}, the earliest ms. of Luke known to us, published in 1961, contains them.

(2) "Glory in the highest heavens to God, and on earth peace to people of good will" (2:14). In the second clause there are four items, the first three of them undisputed ("on earth," "peace [nominative]," "to people [literally, men: dative]"). For the fourth and final item the oldest and best Greek mss., followed by the Latin Vulgate, read a genitive of *eudokia,* "good will, favor," leading to the classical Roman Catholic translation, "and on earth peace to *men of good will.*" Inferior Greek mss. known to the KJV translators read a nominative, and Luther favored that because it avoided any suggestion that God granted peace in proportion to human merit, whence the classical Protestant translation, "and on earth peace, *good will toward men.*" Modern scholars, rejecting the nominative, have sought to solve the theological problem by appealing to Hebrew and Aramaic phrases in the DSS: "a man/children of His good will," so that Luke's genitive of *eudokia* could mean not "of [human] good will" but "of [God's] favor," extending peace to people favored by God. For the ongoing debate see BBM 403–5,677–79.

(3) The confession of Peter appears in all four Gospels and illustrates theories of interGospel relationships:

[104]See K. Snodgrass, JBL 91 (1972), 369–79; G. E. Rice, in Talbert, *Luke-Acts* 1–16; A. W. Zwiep, NTS 42 (1996), 219–44.

Mark 8:29: "You are the Messiah";
Matt 16:16: "You are the Messiah, the Son of the living God" (followed by the giving of the name "Peter");
Luke 9:20: "The Messiah of God";[105]
John 6:69: "You are the Holy One of God."

In the Two-Source Theory Matt and Luke have expanded Mark in different ways. In the Griesbach hypothesis Mark, using Matt and Luke, chose the one element common to both. Those who maintain that Luke knew Matt think he shortened the Matthean formula, perhaps under the influence of Mark's shorter form. The likelihood that there is a special relationship between Luke and John might account for the genitival modifier ("of God") in both. Yet the relationship to John is complicated, for there are Johannine parallels to Matt as well. In John 1:40–42 Andrew calls his brother Simon (Peter) and tells him, "We have found the Messiah," on which occasion Jesus gives the name Peter; and in John 11:27 Martha confesses, "You are the Messiah, the Son of God." Is all this because John knew the Synoptics or because common traditions fed into the Synoptic and Johannine strains of Gospel formation?

(4) Luke has texts that illustrate the complexity of the notion of the kingdom of God.[106] There is ambivalence about whether the concept involves kingship or kingdom, whether and to what extent it has come and/or is still coming, and whether it is visible or invisible. Palpable images like gate and table and expulsion from the kingdom are employed in 13:24,28,29; and in 9:27 there are those standing here who will not taste death until they have seen the kingdom of God. Yet in 17:20–21 Jesus contends that the coming of the kingdom is not a matter of observation so that one can say, "Here or there it is." In 11:2 the disciples are taught to pray for the kingdom to come. In 10:9 disciples are told to proclaim to the towns they visit: "The kingdom of God has come near"; in 11:20 Jesus says that if it is by the finger of God that he drives out demons, "The kingdom of God has reached you"; and in 11:21 he says, "The kingdom of God is in/among you." In 21:31–32 (the eschatological discourse) upon seeing the signs of the last times, one can say, "The kingdom of God is near"; and all this will happen before this generation passes away. This varied outlook is a reflection of the problem of futuristic and realized eschatology that occurs elsewhere in the NT (see *Issue* 2 in Chapter 10 and p. 342 below).

[105]The Messiah theme reappears strongly in Acts; see M. L. Strauss, *The Davidic Messiah in Luke-Acts* (JSNTSup 110; Sheffield: Academic, 1995).

[106]Very helpful here is Fitzmyer, *Luke,* with its exact translation of verbs in the kingdom passages and many treatments of the kingdom topic (e.g., 1.154–57; 2.1159).

Bibliography on Luke

(See also the *Bibliography* in Chapter 6 on the Synoptic Problem and on Q Research. Books marked below with an asterisk treat Acts also.)

COMMENTARIES AND STUDIES IN SERIES: **Bock, D. L.** (2 vols.; BECNT, 1994, 1996); Browning, W.R.F. (TBC, 3d ed., 1972); Caird, G. B. (PC, 1963); Craddock, F. B. (IBC, 1990); Culpepper, R. A. (NInterpB, 1995); Danker, F. W. (ProcC, 2d ed., 1987); Ellis, E. E. (NCBC, 2d ed., 1974); Evans, C. A. (NIBC, 1990); Evans, C. F. (TPINTC, 1990); **Fitzmyer, J. A.** (2 vols.; AB, 1981, 1985); Geldenhuys, N. (NICNT, 1951); Green, J. B. (NTT, 1995); Johnson, L. T. (ABD 4.403–20; SP, 1991); Leaney, A. R. C. (BNTC, 2d ed., 1966); Marshall, I. H. (NIGTC, 1978); Morris, L. (TNTC, 1974); Nolland, J. (3 vols.; WBC, 1989, 1993); Plummer, A. (ICC, 5th ed., 1922); Reiling, J., and J. L. Swellengrebel (TH, 1971); Stöger, A. (2 vols.; NTSR, 1969); Thompson, G.H.P. (NClarBC, 1972); Tiede, D. L. (AugC, 1988); Tinsley, E. J. (CCNEB, 1965); Tuckett, C. M. (NTG, 1996).

BIBLIOGRAPHIES: Fitzmyer, *Luke,* has excellent bibliographies for every section of Luke, and accordingly this Bibliography gives more attention to works after 1980; Wagner, G., EBNT* (1985); Van Segbroeck, F., *The Gospel of Luke: A Cumulative Bibliography 1973–1988* (BETL 88; Leuven: Peeters, 1989); Green, J. B., and M. C. McKeever, *Luke-Acts and New Testament Historiography** (Grand Rapids: Baker, 1994—annotated); Mills, W. E., BBR (1995).

SURVEYS OF RESEARCH: Barrett, C. K., *Luke the Historian in Recent Study** (London: Epworth, 1961); van Unnik, W. C., in Keck, *Studies* (1966) 15–32; Talbert, C. H., *Interpretation* 30 (1976), 381–95; Karris, R. J., *What Are They Saying about Luke and Acts?** (New York: Paulist, 1979); Fitzmyer, *Luke* 13–34; Bovon, F., *Luke the Theologian: Thirty-Three Years of Research (1950–1983)** (Allison Park, PA: Pickwick, 1987); Powell, M. A., *What Are They Saying about Luke?* (New York: Paulist, 1989).

* * *

Brown, S., *Apostasy and Perseverance in the Theology of Luke* (AnBib 36; Rome: PBI, 1969).

*Cadbury, H. J., *The Style and Literary Method of Luke* (2 vols.; Cambridge, MA: Harvard Univ., 1920).

*———, *The Making of Luke-Acts* (2d ed.; London: SPCK, 1958). A classic.

*Carroll, J. T., *Response to the End of History: Eschatology and Situation in Luke-Acts* (SBLDS 92; Atlanta: Scholars, 1988).

Cassidy, R. J., *Jesus, Politics and Society: A Study of Luke's Gospel* (Maryknoll: Orbis, 1978).

*———, and P. J. Scharper, *Political Issues in Luke-Acts* (Maryknoll: Orbis, 1983).

Conzelmann, H., *The Theology of St. Luke* (New York: Harper, 1960).

Creed, J. M., *The Gospel according to St. Luke* (London: Macmillan, 1930).

Danker, F. W., *Jesus and the New Age: A Commentary on St. Luke's Gospel* (rev. ed.; Philadelphia: Fortress, 1988).

*Darr, J. A., *On Character Building: The Reader and Rhetoric of Characterization in Luke-Acts* (Louisville: W/K, 1992).

Dawsey, J. M., *The Lukan Voice: Confusion and Irony in the Gospel of Luke* (Macon: Mercer, 1986).
Drury, J., *Tradition and Design in Luke's Gospel* (London: DLT, 1976). Midrashic approach.
Edwards, O. C., Jr., *Luke's Story of Jesus* (Philadelphia: Fortress, 1981).
*Ellis, E. E., *Eschatology in Luke* (Facet Biblical Series 30; Philadelphia: Fortress, 1972).
*Esler, P. F., *Community and Gospel in Luke-Acts: The Social and Political Motivations of Lucan Theology* (SNTSMS 57; Cambridge Univ., 1987).
*Evans, C. A., and J. A. Sanders, *Luke and Scripture: The Function of Sacred Tradition in Luke-Acts* (Minneapolis: A/F, 1993).
*Fitzmyer, J. A., *Luke the Theologian* (New York: Paulist, 1989).
*Flender, H., *St. Luke: Theologian of Redemptive History* (Philadelphia: Fortress, 1967).
*Franklin, E., *Christ the Lord: A Study in the Purpose and Theology of Luke-Acts* (Philadelphia: Westminster, 1975).
*———, *Luke: Interpreter of Paul, Critic of Matthew* (JSNTSup 92; Sheffield: JSOT, 1994).
Goulder, M. D., *Luke: A New Paradigm* (2 vols.; JSNTSup 20; Sheffield: JSOT, 1989).
*Harnack, A. (von), *Luke the Physician: The Author of the Third Gospel and the Acts of the Apostles* (New York: Putnam's, 1907).
*Hastings, A., *Prophet and Witness in Jerusalem: A Study of the Teaching of Saint Luke* (Baltimore: Helicon, 1958).
Interpretation 48 (Oct. 1994): issue dedicated to Luke.
*Jervell, J., *Luke and the People of God: A New Look at Luke-Acts* (Minneapolis: Augsburg, 1972).
*———, *The Unknown Paul: Essays on Luke-Acts and Early Christian History* (Minneapolis: Augsburg, 1984).
*Juel, D. H., *Luke-Acts: The Promise of History* (Atlanta: Knox, 1983).
Karris, R. J., *Invitation to Luke* (Garden City, NY: Doubleday, 1977).
———, *Luke: Artist and Theologian* (New York: Paulist, 1985).
*Keck, L. E., and J. L. Martyn, *Studies in Luke-Acts* (P. Schubert Festschrift; Nashville: Abingdon, 1966). Abbreviated SLA.
Kilgallen, J. J., *A Brief Commentary on the Gospel of Luke* (New York: Paulist, 1988).
Kingsbury, J. D., *Conflict in Luke: Jesus, Authorities, Disciples* (Minneapolis: A/F, 1991).
Kodell, J., "The Theology of Luke in Recent Study," BTB 1 (1971), 115–44.
*Kurz, W. S., *Reading Luke-Acts* (Louisville: W/K, 1993).
*Maddox, R., *The Purpose of Luke-Acts* (Edinburgh: Clark, 1982).
*Marshall, I. H., *Luke: Historian and Theologian* (Grand Rapids: Zondervan, 1971).
*Mattill, A. J., Jr., *Luke and the Last Things* (Dillsboro, NC: Western North Carolina, 1979).
*Morton, A. Q., and G.H.C. Macgregor, *The Structure of Luke and Acts* (London: Hodder & Stoughton, 1964).
Navone, J., *Themes of St. Luke* (Rome: Gregorian Univ., 1970).

*Neyrey, J. H., *The Social-World of Luke-Acts* (Peabody, MA: Hendrickson, 1991).
*O'Collins, G., and G. Marconi, *Luke and Acts* (New York: Paulist, 1991). Essays.
*O'Fearghail, F., *Introduction to Luke-Acts: A Study of the Role of Lk 1,1–4,44 in the Composition of Luke's Two-Volume Work* (AnBib 26; Rome: PBI, 1991).
*O'Toole, R. F., *The Unity of Luke's Theology: An Analysis of Luke-Acts* (GNS 9; Wilmington: Glazier, 1984).
*Ravens, D.A.S., *Luke and the Restoration of Israel* (JSNTSup 119; Sheffield: Academic, 1996).
Reicke, B., *The Gospel of Luke* (Richmond: Knox, 1964).
*Richard, E., ed., *New Views on Luke and Acts* (Collegeville: Liturgical, 1990). Essays.
*Richardson, N., *The Panorama of Luke: An Introduction to the Gospel of Luke and the Acts of the Apostles* (London: Epworth, 1982).
Robinson, W. C., Jr., *The Way of the Lord: A Study of History and Eschatology in the Gospel of Luke* (Basel: dissertation, 1962).
Schweizer, E., *The Good News According to Luke* (Atlanta: Knox, 1984).
*Sheeley, S. M., *Narrative Asides in Luke-Acts* (JSNTSup 72; Sheffield: JSOT, 1992).
*Shepherd, W. H., Jr., *The Narrative Function of the Holy Spirit as a Character in Luke-Acts* (SBLDS 147; Atlanta: Scholars, 1994).
*Squires, J. T., *The Plan of God in Luke-Acts* (SNTSMS 76; Cambridge Univ., 1993).
*Talbert, C. H., *Literary Patterns, Theological Themes and the Genre of Luke-Acts* (SBLMS 20; Missoula, MT: Scholars, 1974).
*———, ed., *Perspectives on Luke-Acts* (Edinburgh: Clark, 1978). Important articles.
*———, ed., *Luke-Acts: New Perspectives from the Society of Biblical Literature Seminar* (New York: Crossroad, 1984). Articles.
———, *Reading Luke. A Literary and Theological Commentary on the Third Gospel* (New York: Crossroad, 1986).
*Tannehill, R. C., *The Narrative Unity of Luke-Acts: A Literary Interpretation* (2 vols.; Philadelphia/Minneapolis: A/F, 1986, 1990).
*Tiede, D. L., *Prophecy and History in Luke-Acts* (Philadelphia: Fortress, 1980).
*Tuckett, C. M., ed., *Luke's Literary Achievement* (JSNTSup 116; Sheffield: Academic, 1995).
*Walasky, P. W., *"And So We Came to Rome": The Political Perspective of St. Luke* (SNTSMS 49; Cambridge Univ., 1983). An apology addressed to the Roman Empire.
*Wilson, S. G., *The Gentiles and the Gentile Mission in Luke-Acts* (SNTSMS 23; Cambridge Univ., 1973).
*———, *Luke and the Law* (SNTSMS 50; Cambridge Univ., 1983).
*———, "Lukan Eschatology," NTS 16 (1969–70), 330–47.

CHAPTER 10

THE ACTS OF THE APOSTLES

Since Luke-Acts constitutes one book in two volumes, the subsections on *Purpose* and *Date of writing* in the previous chapter apply to Acts as well. After the *General Analysis,* subdivisions will be devoted to these special issues: *Sources and compositional features, "Luke" the historian, Authorship, Issues for reflection,* and *Bibliography.*

General Analysis of the Message

The author gave no title to this book any more than he gave a title to the Gospel; but later church writers dubbed it "Acts" (in the sense of deeds), thus implicitly comparing it to Hellenistic writings of the same name describing the career and accomplishments of famous men. The modifier "of the Apostles"[1] is not precise, for there are only two major figures: Peter (who is one of the Twelve Apostles, and appears at first with John) is prominent in nine or ten chaps., and Paul (who is only twice called an apostle, and appears at first with Barnabas) is prominent in seventeen chaps. Occasionally, therefore, scholars prefer the designation: Acts of Peter and Paul. In what follows proportionately more discussion will be devoted to the pre-Pauline beginnings, because nowhere else in the NT are they reported in any detail. In this material attention will be given to the continuity of Acts with the portrayal of Jesus in Luke. As for the Pauline section of Acts, in addition to the treatment here, Chapter 16 below surveys Paul's life,[2] and Chapter 17 offers an appreciation of Paul.

Introduction: Preparing Jesus' Followers for the Spirit (1:1–26)

1. Jesus Instructs His Disciples and Ascends to Heaven (1:1–11). At the beginning in *1:1–2, a type of subprologue* (cf. Luke 1:1–4), the author

[1]In twenty-eight chapters there are occasional references to apostles (e.g., 1:2; 4:36–37; 5:12; 8:1), who consistently are the Twelve (cf. 6:2,6), with the exception of Paul and Barnabas in 14:4,14. The only figure who gets lengthy treatment in Acts besides Peter and Paul (and Barnabas as Paul's companion) is Stephen, who is not designated an apostle.

[2]Table 5 in that Chapter compares data from Acts with data from the Pauline letters; Table 6 sketches Pauline chronology.

Summary of Basic Information

DATE, AUTHOR, LOCALE: Same as for Luke (p. 226 above).

INTEGRITY: Western Greek mss. have a significant number of passages (many of them with additional information) missing from other mss.

DIVISION:

1:1–2 **Introduction: Preparing Jesus' Followers for the Spirit**
1. Jesus instructs his disciples and ascends to heaven (1:1–11)
2. Awaiting the Spirit; replacement of Judas (1:12–26)

2:1–8:1a **Mission in Jerusalem**
1. The Pentecost scene; Peter's sermon (2:1–36)
2. Reception of the message; Jerusalem communal life (2:37–45)
3. Activity, preaching, and trials of the apostles (3:1–5:42)
4. The Hellenists; toleration; Stephen's trial and martyrdom (6:1–8:1a)

8:1b–12:25 **Missions in Samaria and Judea**
1. Dispersal from Jerusalem; Philip and Peter in Samaria (8:1b–25)
2. Philip and the Ethiopian eunuch en route to Gaza (8:26–40)
3. Saul en route to Damascus; return to Jerusalem and Tarsus (9:1–31)
4. Peter at Lydda, Joppa, Caesarea, and back to Jerusalem (9:32–11:18)
5. Antioch; Jerusalem; Herod's persecution; Peter's departure (11:19–12:25)

13:1–15:35 **Mission of Barnabas and Saul Converting Gentiles; Approval at Jerusalem**
1. Antioch church sends Barnabas and Saul: Mission to Cyprus and SE Asia Minor (13:1–14:28)
2. Jerusalem conference and approval; return to Antioch (15:1–35)

15:36–28:31 **Mission of Paul to the Ends of the Earth**
1. From Antioch through Asia Minor to Greece and return (15:36–18:22)
2. From Antioch to Ephesus and Greece, and return to Caesarea (18:23–21:14)
3. Arrest in Jerusalem; imprisonment and trials in Caesarea (21:15–26:32)
4. Journey to Rome as a prisoner (27:1–28:14a)
5. Paul at Rome (28:14b–31).

takes pains to relate his second volume to his first. Not only does he mention once more Theophilus to whom the Gospel was dedicated (Luke 1:3); but he sums up the import of the Gospel: "In the first book I have narrated all that Jesus began to do and teach *until the day he was taken up,* after he had given instruction through the Holy Spirit to the apostles whom he had chosen." In this new book what Jesus began is continued through the same Spirit working in the apostles. The italicized clause prepares us for a seeming duplication: Luke 24:50–51 recounted the ascension or taking up of Jesus to heaven on Easter Sunday night from Bethany (on the Mount of Olives), but Acts 1:9–12 will recount an ascension of Jesus to heaven at least forty days later from the Mount of Olives.[3] In his storyline the author is using the single resurrection-ascension complex as a hinge. From God's viewpoint the ascension of the risen Jesus after death is timeless, but there is a sequence from the viewpoint of those whose lives it touched. For the Gospel the ascension visibly terminates the activity of Jesus on earth; for Acts it will prepare the apostles to be witnesses to him to the ends of the earth.

The risen Jesus appears to his disciples for forty days after his passion (*1:3–7*) as a preparation for the coming of the Spirit. Early tradition speaks of plural appearances of Jesus,[4] but architectonically Acts has fitted them into forty days to match the forty days in Luke 4:1–2,14 that Jesus spent in the desert before he went in the power of the Spirit to begin his ministry in Galilee. In both instances the author is evoking the forty years in the desert during which God prepared Israel for entry into the Promised Land. (For the correlation of forty days and forty years, see Num 14:34; Ezek 4:6.) Here the preparatory period allows Jesus to give proofs of the resurrection (Acts 1:3; cf. the apologetic tone in Luke 24:36–43) and to present clearly his notion of the kingdom. The apostles are to wait in Jerusalem for baptism with the Holy Spirit as promised by JBap (Luke 3:16). Most important, in relation to the full coming of the kingdom Jesus tells them, "It is not for you to know the times or seasons."[5] Countering many speculations about the endtime, this firm answer was essential for the composition of Acts in the 80s: If the end were coming immediately, it would not be sensible to write a book for future readers or to envision a mission that would reach the whole world.

The outline of this second volume is supplied in Acts 1:8 through a directive of Jesus to the apostles: "You will be my witnesses in Jerusalem, all Judea and Samaria, and to the end of the earth."[6] The Acts story that begins in Jerusalem will end in Rome (chap. 28), the center of an empire extending to the known ends of earth. Having thus prepared his disciples for the future, *Jesus is taken up to heaven* (*1:9–11*). Two men in white suddenly are stand-

[3]M. C. Parsons, *The Departure of Jesus in Luke-Acts: The Ascension Narratives in Context* (JSNTSup 21; Sheffield: JSOT, 1987).

[4]E.g., I Cor 15:5–8, but presumably over a much longer time since Paul is included.

[5]Acts 1:7 is a Lucan variation of Mark 13:32: "Of that day or hour no one knows, not even the angels in heaven, nor the Son, but only the Father." Acts omits the lack of knowledge of the Son, since it is now the risen Lord who speaks.

[6]Acts presents these as the risen Jesus' words; but that must be understood correctly, for the book goes on to show that the disciples had no awareness of having been informed of such a plan. Writing some fifty years after the early evangelizing, the author looks back on the geographical expansion that had taken place and understands it as what Christ willed for his church, whence the attribution to the risen Jesus, who had prophesied it.

ing there to interpret the event for Jesus' followers, even as two (angelic) men in dazzling apparel were standing by the empty tomb as interpreters for the women (Luke 24:4–7). Since the ascension takes place from the Mount of Olives, where God will come in the final judgment and manifest kingship over all the earth (Zech 14:4–21), the two can predict that Jesus will come back in the same way as he has been seen going.

2. Awaiting the Spirit; Replacement of Judas (1:12–26). *Those who await the promised coming of the Spirit are listed and numbered in 1:12–15.* Praying together in Jerusalem in the upper room are the Eleven (apostles minus Judas), the women, Mary the mother of Jesus (chronologically the last NT reference to her), and his brothers. This listing too represents continuity with the Gospel. The apostles could bear witness to the public ministry and the risen Jesus; the women, to the burial and empty tomb (Luke 23:55–24:10); Mary, to events of Jesus' birth and youth (Luke 1–2). An estimate in 1:15 puts the number of believers at about 120 and reflects the author's penchant for numbers and symbolism. He next recounts how the apostolic number left vacant by Judas was filled out to complete the Twelve (120 = 10 believers for each of the 12?).

Peter takes the initiative in this completion by telling *how Judas lost his share in the apostolic ministry* (*Acts 1:16–20*). The account of Judas' suicide in Matt 27:3–10 is quite different (p. 201 above; BDM 2.1404–10). From what the two stories have in common we may suspect that Judas died quickly and violently and that the early Christians called upon the death of wicked OT figures to explain God's punishment of the man who had handed Jesus over.[7]

The place of Judas is filled by *the selection of Matthias* (*Acts 1:21–26*). That italicized description does not do justice to the key element. Matthias has no personal import and will never again be mentioned; what is essential is that the number of the Twelve be complete. Israel of old had twelve patriarchs representing the twelve tribes; in the course of time Levi lost a regular share in the Promised Land (even though it had cities), and the sons of Joseph (Ephraim and Manasseh) were counted so that the pattern of twelve might be preserved. The story of the Israel renewed in Jesus can start with no fewer than Twelve. They are not to be an ongoing institution in the church of subsequent centuries, but are a once-for-all symbol for the whole of the renewed Israel, never to be replaced when they die (see Acts 12:2 below). Judas deserted and did not go to one of the twelve heavenly thrones for judging Israel to which the others will go, as promised by Jesus (Luke 22:30;

[7]As we saw, Matt shows parallelism with the death of Ahithophel, echoing II Sam, Deut, Jer, Zech. Acts shows parallelism with the death of the antiGod figure Antiochus IV Epiphanes (II Macc 9:7–12), echoing Wisdom 4:19; Ps 69:26; 109:8.

Matt 19:28).[8] Just as the Twelve were originally chosen by Jesus (John 15:16), by means of lots, the choice of Judas' replacement is left to God's will. The community is now prepared for the coming of the Spirit.

Mission in Jerusalem (2:1–8:1a)

1. The Pentecost Scene; Peter's Sermon (2:1–36). The Feast of Weeks or Pentecost (so called because it was celebrated seven weeks or fifty days after Passover) was a pilgrimage feast when pious Jews came from their homes to the Temple or central shrine in Jerusalem. The plausible historical nucleus of *the coming of the Spirit described in Acts 2:1–13* is that on the next pilgrimage feast after Jesus' death and resurrection his Galilean disciples and his family came to Jerusalem and that, while they were there, the presence of the Spirit[9] was charismatically manifested as they began to speak in tongues. This was seen as a sign that they should proclaim publicly what God had done in Jesus.

Acts has re-presented that nucleus with theological insight, highlighting its central place in the Christian history of salvation. In the re-presentation the meaning of Pentecost plays a key role. An agricultural feast of thanksgiving celebrated in May or June, like the other Jewish feasts it had acquired additional meaning by recalling what God had done for the chosen people in "salvation-history." The deliverance from Egypt in the middle of the first month (Exod 12) was commemorated at Passover. In the third month (19:1), and thus about a month and a half later, the Israelites arrived at Sinai; and so Pentecost, occurring at roughly the same interval after Passover, became the commemoration of God's giving the covenant to Israel at Sinai—the moment when Israel was called to be God's own people.[10]

In depicting God's appearance at Sinai, Exod 19 includes thunder and smoke; and the Jewish writer Philo (contemporary with the NT) describes angels taking what God said to Moses on the mountaintop and carrying it out on tongues to the people on the plain below. Acts, with its description of

[8]We may think of these men as "wearing two hats": They were the Twelve and they were also apostles (see the distinction in I Cor 15:5–7). *The Twelve* were irreplaceable eschatological figures, not part of church administrative structure. *The apostles* (a wider group inclusive of the Twelve) founded and nurtured communities, and "bishops" (figures in church structure) succeeded the apostles in the care of those churches.

[9]The Spirit plays an enormous role in Acts; see J.H.E. Hull, *The Holy Spirit in the Acts of the Apostles* (London: Lutterworth, 1967); J.D.G. Dunn, *Jesus and the Spirit: A Study of the Religious and Charismatic Experience . . . in the New Testament* (Philadelphia: Westminster, 1975); R. P. Menzies, *The Development of Early Christian Pneumatology, with Special Reference to Luke-Acts* (JSNTSup 54; Sheffield: JSOT, 1991).

[10]In the OT no salvation-history meaning is supplied for Weeks (Pentecost), but in later rabbinical writings the meaning given above is attested. Thanks to *Jubilees* and the DSS, we now have evidence that this meaning was known in Jesus' time.

the sound of a mighty wind and tongues as of fire, echoes that imagery, and thus presents the Pentecost in Jerusalem as the renewal of God's covenant, once more calling a people to be God's own. According to Exodus, in the Sinai covenant the people who heard the invitation to be God's own and accepted it were Israelites. After Sinai in biblical language the other nations remained "no people."[11] Acts 2:9–11, with its broad sweep from the eastern extremities of the Roman Empire (Parthians, Medes, and Elamites) to Rome itself, describes the nationalities who at Pentecost observed and heard what was effected by the Spirit at the Jerusalem renewal of the covenant. Thus Acts anticipates the broad reach of the evangelizing, now begun, that will ultimately make even the Gentiles God's own people (Acts 28:28).[12] Implicitly this Pentecost is more momentous and wider-reaching than the first Pentecost at Sinai.

Reaction to the Spirit-filled disciples speaking in tongues—ecstatic behavior that looked to observers like drunkenness—causes Peter to deliver *the first sermon (2:14–36),* a sermon that Acts conceives of as the fundamental presentation of the gospel.[13] Peter interprets the action of the Spirit at Pentecost as the fulfillment of the signs of the last days foretold by the prophet Joel—an interpretation that matches the strong stress placed by Acts on prophecy.

Worth noting is the fact that Peter begins this proclamation in what we would call OT terms, by quoting a prophecy. This opening affirms the basic consistency of what God has done in Jesus Christ with what the God of Israel did for and promised to the people of the covenant. Then Peter turns to tell what God has done in Jesus: a brief summary of his mighty works, crucifixion and resurrection, culminating in scriptural evidence that he was the Lord and Messiah (2:36). In a certain sense this concentration on christology represents a change from Jesus' own style as narrated in Luke's

[11]By implication in Deut 32:21; "no people" is a category to which a disobedient Israel is symbolically reduced in Hos 1:9; see I Pet 2:10.

[12]A possibility is that the list in 2:9–11 describes the areas evangelized by missionaries from the Jerusalem church (e.g., the East and Rome), as distinct from areas evangelized from other centers like Antioch (e.g., through the journeys of Paul). In Acts 2:5 Luke describes the people from these areas as devout Jews, an identification that fits the pilgrimage feast context. Yet we may be meant to see here an anticipation that all from these nations (2:17: "all flesh") would be evangelized. For traditions underlying 2:1–13 see A.J.M. Wedderburn, JSNT 55 (1994), 27–54.

[13]In the subsections below on *Sources* and *"Luke" the historian* the question of historicity will be raised. Did Peter actually deliver a sermon on Pentecost itself? What did he say? The sermon in Acts is composed by the author of the book, but did he have a tradition about the nucleus of the apostolic preaching? The speaking in tongues should make us cautious in judging. At an early level of recounting, the speaking was ecstatic, whence the appearance of drunken babbling. It has been reinterpreted in Acts as speaking in other tongues or languages that are understandable—a reinterpretation that has not wiped out the earlier tradition.

Gospel. There, although both an angel and God testified to Jesus as Messiah and divine Son, and the disciples called him Lord, Jesus did not talk directly about himself. He spoke about God's kingdom and its challenge to accepted values. Yet Acts confirms the evidence of Paul that early preachers shifted the primary focus of their proclamation to Jesus himself, almost as if they could not announce the kingdom without first telling of him through whom the kingdom was made present. The fundamental gospel became centered on the christological identity of the risen Jesus as Messiah and Son of God (see Rom 1:3–4).

2. Reception of the Message; Jerusalem Communal Life (2:37–45). Having presented this model of preaching, *Acts 2:37–41 now dramatizes in question and answer form the fundamentals of accepting the gospel.* What must be done once people believe the christological proclamation (2:36–37)? Peter makes specific demands and then gives a promise. The *first* demand is to "repent."[14] Acts is showing continuity between the beginning of the public ministry of Jesus (where JBap preached "a baptism of repentance": Luke 3:3: *metanoia*) and the beginning of the church, between the first demand of the proclamation of the kingdom and the first demand of apostolic preaching.

Second, Peter demands that people be baptized for the forgiveness of their sins (Acts 2:38b). Although JBap insisted that people receive the baptism of repentance, Jesus did not; in the first three Gospels he is never shown as baptizing anyone.[15] Forgiveness of sins was through the power of his word. For Acts Jesus' power over sin remains, but now it is exercised through baptism; and so in his second demand Peter is going beyond the pattern of Jesus' lifetime. Baptism as a public action[16] is important for our reflection here: Peter is portrayed as asking people to make a visible and verifiable profession of their acceptance of Jesus. This is tantamount to asking people to "join up." The basic Israelite concept is that God chose to save *a people,* and the renewal of the covenant on Pentecost has not changed that. There is a

[14]Literally the Greek verb *metanoein* (*meta* = "across, over"; *noein* = "to think") means "to change one's mind, way of thinking, outlook"; for sinners changing one's mind involves repentance. The demand placed on religious people to change their minds cannot fully be met by a once-for-all-time response; they must be willing to change when a new presentation of God's will confronts them. See R. D. Witherup, *Conversion in the New Testament* (Zacchaeus Studies; Collegeville: Liturgical Press, 1994).

[15]Once in John (3:22) he is said to baptize, but that is corrected and denied in 4:2. In a postresurrectional appearance the Matthean Jesus tells the Eleven (the Twelve minus Judas) to make disciples of all nations, baptizing them (Matt 28:19). There is no reason to think that the readers of Acts would have known this command found only in Matt, especially since it embodies the retrospective experience of the Matthean community toward the end of the 1st century.

[16]Baptism is looked at in different ways in the different books of the NT, and the later theology of baptism represents an amalgamation from those different views.

collective aspect to salvation, and one is saved as part of God's people. The time of the church is beginning, and the importance of the church for God's plan is a direct derivative from the importance of Israel.

Third, Peter specifies that baptism must be "in the name of Jesus Christ." The fact that JBap baptized and that Jesus himself was baptized by John was surely an important factor in moving the followers of Jesus to insist on baptism; yet Acts 18:24–19:7 contends that there was a clear distinction between the baptism of John and baptism "in the name of the Lord Jesus" (19:5). We are not certain about procedures in the earliest baptismal practice; but most likely "in the name of" means that the one being baptized confessed who Jesus was (and in that sense spoke his name),[17] e.g., "Jesus is Lord"; "Jesus is the Messiah (Christ)"; "Jesus is the Son of God"; "Jesus is the Son of Man."[18] Such baptismal confessions would explain why titles were so commonly applied to Jesus in the NT.

Fourth, after spelling out the demands on those who believe in Jesus, Peter makes a pledge (2:38–39): "You shall receive the gift of the Holy Spirit, for the promise is . . . to as many as the Lord God calls." (Although there is a challenge to the hearers to change their lives, the priority in conversion belongs to God.) Peter and his companions have received the Holy Spirit, and now they promise that the same Holy Spirit will be given to all believers. In terms of the fundamentals of Christian life there will be no second-class citizens, and the same equality in receiving the gift of the Spirit will prove true when the first Gentiles are baptized (Acts 10:44–48). This principle will need to be recalled when inevitably bickering arises over special roles (I Cor 12).

Acts 2:41 reports that about three thousand of those who heard Peter's sermons met his demands and were baptized; it then proceeds to describe how they lived. The memories are highly selective, so that we have as much a theology of the early church as a history. *A summary in 2:42–47 lists four features in the communal life of the early believers.*[19] The first years in Jerusalem (until about AD 36) are idealized as the time when Christians[20] were

[17]The use of the triadic formula in Matt 28:19 ("name of the Father and of the Son and of the Holy Spirit") would have been a later development, giving a fuller picture of God's plan of salvation.

[18]John 9:35–38 may be echoing that church's baptismal ceremony involving a question from the baptizer, "Do you believe in the Son of Man?" with the response, "Lord, I believe"; and then an act of worship.

[19]On the role of summaries in Acts, see under *Sources* below. The selection of these four features is made from the later vantage point of what the author of Acts judges most important and enduring—the primitive community embodying what a Christian community should be.

[20]Throughout these early chapters of Acts, set in immediately postresurrectional Jerusalem, to speak of Christians or Christianity is an anachronism; no designation is as yet given for those who believed in Jesus. If the author of Acts (11:26) is historically correct, it was at Antioch (seemingly

of one mind (1:14; 2:46; 4:24; 5:12). The four features will be treated in this order: *koinōnia,* prayers, breaking of the bread, and apostles' teaching.

First, koinōnia ("fellowship, communion, community"). We have seen that the introduction of baptism showed a remarkable drive toward "joining up," so that those who believe quickly constitute a group. The wide distribution in the NT of the term *koinōnia* (related to *koinos,* "common" as in Koinē Greek) shows that the believers felt strongly that they had much in common. Sometimes translated as "fellowship," more literally it is "communion," i.e., the spirit that binds people together, or "community," i.e., the grouping produced by that spirit. Indeed, *koinōnia* may reflect in Greek an early Semitic name for the Jewish group of believers in Jesus, comparable to the self-designation of the Jewish group responsible for the Dead Sea Scrolls as the *Yaḥad,* "the oneness, unity."[21] An important aspect described in Acts 2:44–45; 4:34–5:11 is voluntarily sharing goods among the members of the community. While the idealism of Acts exaggerates ("all goods"), the fact that there were common goods in the Dead Sea Scrolls community shows that a picture of sharing is plausible for a Jewish group convinced that the last times had begun and that this world's wealth had lost its meaning.[22] Did such "Christian socialism" impoverish the Jerusalem community? Paul refers to the poor (Christians) in Jerusalem for whom he was collecting money (Rom 15:26; Gal 2:10; I Cor 16:1–3). The willingness of Gentiles in distant churches to share some of their wealth with the Jewish Christians in Jerusalem was for Paul a tangible proof of the *koinōnia* that bound Christians together—an external manifestation of the common faith and common salvation that was at the heart of "community." The importance of keeping this communion is exemplified in Gal 2:9 where Paul deems the outcome of the Jerusalem discussion about the Gentiles *ca.* AD 49 to have been a great success because at the end the leaders of the Jerusalem church gave to him and Barnabas the right hand of *koinōnia.* For Paul it would have been against the

---

in the late 30s) that the believers were first called Christians. Yet having noted that, for the sake of simplicity I shall anticipate the terminology.

[21]Another early name may have been "the Way," e.g., Acts 24:14: "According to the Way . . . I worship the God of our Fathers" (also Acts 9:2; 19:9,23; 22:4; 24:22). This was also a DSS self-designation: "When these people join the community [*Yaḥad*), they . . . go into the wilderness to prepare the way of the Lord." It reflects the idealism of the return of Israel from exile (Isa 40:3), when Israel came along "the way" prepared by God to the Promised Land. The designation that became the most popular, i.e., *ekklēsia,* "church," plausibly reflects the first exodus in which Israel came into being, for in Deut 23:2 the Greek OT rendered *qāhāl,* "assembly," by *ekklēsia* to describe Israel in the desert as "the church of the Lord."

[22]More than other Gospels Luke is insistent that wealth is an obstacle to the acceptance of Jesus' standards and that the rich are endangered (1:53; 6:24; 12:20–21; 16:22–23). Although Christians do not know the times or seasons for the final intervention of God's rule/kingdom (Acts 1:7), they esteem values consonant with a theology that this world is not a lasting entity.

very notion of the one Lord and the one Spirit if the *koinōnia* between the Jewish and the Gentile churches had been broken.[23]

Second, prayers. Praying for each other was another aspect of *koinōnia,* and the Pauline letters bear eloquent testimony to his constant prayer for the communities he founded. What kind of prayer forms were used by the first Jews who came to believe in Jesus? Since they did not cease to be Jewish in their worship, they continued to say prayers that they had known previously, and new prayers would have been formulated according to Jewish models. Among the latter Acts 2:42 would probably have included the hymns or canticles of the Lucan infancy narrative, which most likely were Christian compositions that Luke adapted and placed on the lips of the first characters of his Gospel (p. 232 above). Like the Jewish hymns of this time (as exemplified in the Books of the Maccabees and the DSS) they are a pastiche of OT echoes. In addition the early Christians would have adopted Jesus' own prayer style, visible in the Lord's Prayer preserved in Luke 11:2–4, some petitions of which echo petitions of synagogue prayers (p. 179 above). Gradually Christian prayer did center on recalling and praising what Jesus had done, reflecting increasing Christian distinctiveness.

Third, breaking bread. Acts portrays early Christians like Peter and John going frequently, or even daily, to the Temple to pray at the regular hours (2:46; 3:1; 5:12,21,42). This implies that the first Jews who believed in Jesus saw no rupture in their ordinary worship pattern. The "breaking of bread" (presumably the eucharist) would, then, have been in addition to and not in place of the sacrifices and worship of Israel. Notice the sequence in 2:46: "Day by day attending the Temple together and breaking bread in their homes." How did the first Christians interpret the eucharist? Paul, writing in the mid-50s (I Cor 11:23–26), mentions a eucharistic pattern that was handed on to him (presumably, therefore, from the 30s) and says, "As often as you eat this bread and drink this cup, you proclaim the Lord's death until he comes." The recalling of the Lord's death *may* echo the Jewish pattern of Passover re-presentation (Hebrew: *zikkārôn;* Greek: *anamnēsis*), making present again the great salvific act, now shifted from the exodus to the crucifixion/resurrection. The "until he comes" reflects an eschatological outlook visible in the Lord's Prayer and *Marana tha* (*Māráná' 'āthā':* "Our Lord, come"), but now attached to a sacred meal. This expectation may have had a special Jewish background, for the DSS community envisioned the presence of the Messiah at the meal of the last times. That the risen Jesus showed

[23]Only toward the end of the NT period do we get clear evidence that the Christian *koinōnia* has been broken. The author of I John, for whom having *koinōnia* "with us" is necessary in order to have *koinōnia* with the Father and the Holy Spirit, condemns "those who went out from us" as antichrists (1:3; 2:18–19).

himself present at meals (Luke 24:30,41–43; John 21:9–13; Mark 16:14), so that his disciples recognized him in the breaking of the bread (Luke 24:35), may be related to belief in his coming at the celebration of the eucharist.[24] A sacral meal eaten only by those who believed in Jesus was a major manifestation of *koinōnia* and eventually helped to make Christians feel distinct from other Jews.

Fourth, teaching of the apostles. The Scriptures were authoritative for all Jews, in particular the Law and the Prophets; this would have been true for the first followers of Jesus as well. Thus, early Christian teaching would for the most part have been Jewish teaching.[25] Points where Jesus modified the Law or differed from other established interpretations of the Law were remembered and became the nucleus of a special teaching. As they passed this on, the Christian preachers would have made their own application to situations that Jesus had not encountered; [26] and this expanded form of what stemmed from Jesus was probably what Acts means by the teaching of the apostles. Such teaching, while secondary to the teaching of the Jewish Scriptures, was authoritative in regard to the specific points it touched. When it was committed to writing, the resultant compositions were on the way to becoming a second set of Scriptures.

The four features characteristic of Jerusalem communal life selected by Acts show both continuity with Judaism and distinctiveness that marked off Jews who believed in Jesus from other Jews. These aspects were in tension, pulling in opposite directions: The first held the Christians close to their fellow Jews whom they met in the synagogal meetings; the second gave to the Christian *koinōnia* identity and the potentiality of self-sufficiency. External factors of rejection and reaction, however, would have to take place before Christians would constitute a distinguishably separate religious group, and that development will be the subject of later chaps. of Acts. Meanwhile chaps. 3–5 use the actions of Peter and John to focus narratives of the earliest interchanges with fellow Jews (before AD 36).

3. Activity, Preaching, and Trials of the Apostles (3:1–5:42). The summary statements in 2:43 (wonders done by the apostles) and 2:46 (daily Temple attendance) prepare the way for *the dramatic account of the healing*

[24]In these different details we can find the background of a later theology of the eucharist, e.g., the celebration of the eucharist as a sacrifice can be related to recalling the death of the Lord, and the concept of the real presence of Christ in the eucharist can be related to believing that the risen Lord appeared at meals and would return again at the sacred meal.

[25]This fact is sometimes overlooked by those who search out NT theology or ethics. The points of unique importance mentioned in the NT are like the tip of the iceberg, the bulk of which is the unmentioned, presupposed teaching of Israel.

[26]See the example of two instructions on marriage and divorce, one from the Lord and one from Paul, in I Cor 7:10,12.

that takes place when Peter and John go up to the Temple (3:1–10). Jesus began his ministry by manifesting the healing power of God's rule (kingdom) to the amazement of all (Luke 4:31–37); now we see that Peter and the apostles carry on the same work with the same power. The healing is "in the name of Jesus Christ of Nazareth" (Acts 3:6), i.e., worked through the power of the heavenly Christ, not through any self-sufficiency of the apostles. "By faith in his name, his name has made this [lame] man strong" (3:16).[27]

The Lucan account of Jesus' ministry combined healings and words; here in a similar pattern *Peter's healing is followed by a sermon (3:11–26)*. This sermon is meant to illustrate the presentation of Jesus to Jews. As with Peter's sermon on Pentecost,[28] it amalgamates OT echoes and what God has done in Jesus. If the Pentecost sermon began its challenge with the prophecy of Joel that was seen to be fulfilled in what was happening, this sermon will terminate (3:22–26) with a challenge based on the promise of Moses in Deut 18:15 that God would raise up a prophet like him who must be heeded. In 3:19 the demand to "repent" or "change one's mind" (*metanoein*) appears once more, but now with greater specification. The Jews of Jerusalem delivered up and denied Jesus the servant of God in the presence of Pilate who had decided to release him (3:13 = Luke 23:16); they denied the Holy and Just One and asked for a murderer (3:14 = Luke 23:18–19,25: Barabbas). Yet they acted in ignorance (3:17 = Luke 23:34a)[29] as did their rulers, and accordingly they are being offered this chance to change. In the face of the apostolic preaching, however, ignorance ceases to be an excuse, and change of mind/heart is necessary if they are to receive Jesus as the Messiah when he is sent back from heaven (Acts 3:19–21). The story that follows in Acts will insist that many of the people did change, but most of the Jewish leaders did not.

The apostolic preaching and its success (4:4: five thousand) stirs up wrath and leads to *the arrest Peter and John (4:1–22)*. Jesus' own attitude toward resurrection had aroused the opposition of the Sadducees, "who say there is no resurrection" (Luke 20:27–38); and now the priests and the Sadducees are disturbed that Peter and John have been proclaiming in Jesus the resurrection from the dead (Acts 4:2). A meeting of the Sanhedrin consisting of rulers, elders, scribes, and chief priests is convened against them (4:5–6), just as a Sanhedrin of the elders of the people, and chief priests and scribes

[27]Jewish respect for the personal name of God (YHWH or Yahweh) and its awesome power is reflected in Christian respect for the name (most often, "Lord") given to Jesus at which "every knee should bow in heaven, on earth, and under the earth" (Phil 2:9–11).

[28]R. F. Zehnle, *Peter's Pentecost Discourse . . . Acts 2 and 3* (SBLMS 15; Nashville: Abingdon, 1971) thinks some of the material in Acts 3 is older than that in Acts 2.

[29]Also Acts 13:27; Rom 10:3; not all the people wanted Jesus to die (Luke 23:27,48).

was convened against Jesus (Luke 22:66). (In neither case are the Pharisees mentioned as having been directly involved, and that may be historical.) The interrogators focus on the miracle, demanding, "By what name did you do this?"—a question that prepares for the response of Peter: "By the name of Jesus Christ of Nazareth whom you crucified, whom God raised from the dead . . . There is no other name under heaven given to the human race by which we must be saved" (Acts 4:10,12).

Annoyed at the boldness of the religious proclamation of the apostles who were not formally educated in religious matters or the Law of Moses,[30] the Sanhedrin authorities blusteringly cut short debate and arbitrarily order Peter and John not to speak in the name of Jesus (4:18). Less than two months before, Peter in the high priest's house had denied Jesus three times; now before a battery of chief priests he cannot be silent about Christ (4:19–20). Among the Gospels Luke alone (22:31–32) had Jesus pray that, although Satan desired to sift Peter and the others like wheat, Peter's faith would not fail and he would turn and strengthen his brethren. Here we see the prayer fulfilled as Peter and John emerge unyielding from the Sandhedrin to report to their fellow believers what has happened—a report that consists of *a triumphal prayer of praise to God* (*Acts 4:23–31*) comparing the forces that had been aligned in Jerusalem against Jesus (Herod and Pilate, the Gentiles, and the "peoples" of Israel) to the forces now uttering threats against his followers. All the believers are filled with the Holy Spirit and, thus strengthened, proceed to speak the word of God with boldness (4:31).[31]

To demonstrate that Jesus' followers were of one heart and soul, *a summary* (*4:32–35*) emphasizes some of the same features as the earlier summary in 2:42–47, especially holding things in common (*koinos*). Two examples follow. The first involves *Barnabas* (*4:36–37*), who sold a field and brought the money to the apostles to contribute to the common fund. Besides exemplifying positively the spirit of *koinōnia,* this reference prepares for future narrative. Barnabas is a Levite, and Acts 6:7 will tell us that many priests (who would have been from the tribe of Levi) came to believe. Moreover, Barnabas is from Cyprus; and when later at Antioch he becomes a missionary with Paul, they will first go to Cyprus (13:1–4).

The other example, involving *Ananias and Sapphira* (*5:1–11*), is negative and illustrates divine punishment of those violating the purity of the early community. No story captures better the Israelite mentality of the early be-

[30]That is the probable meaning of *agrammatoi,* "unlettered," in Acts 4:13. An exaggerated interpretation would portray the apostles as illiterate.

[31]Matt 27:51; 28:2 had the earth quake as a manifestation of supportive divine power when Jesus died and rose; Acts has it quake as the Holy Spirit manifests God's supporting presence in the community of believers.

lievers. The Twelve were meant to sit on thrones judging Israel (Luke 22:30); here through Peter judgment is exercised on the renewed Israel. In the OT (Josh 7) Israel's attempt to enter victoriously beyond Jericho into the heart of the Promised Land was frustrated because Achan had secretly hidden for himself goods that were to be dedicated to God. His deception caused God to judge that Israel had sinned and needed purification. Only when Achan was put to death and his goods burned could Israel proceed as a people who had to be perfect as God is perfect. So also the renewed Israel has been profaned by the deceptive holding back of goods which were claimed to have been contributed to the common fund. Satan entered into Judas, one of the Twelve, to give Jesus over (Luke 22:3–4); and now he has entered into the heart of Ananias, a believer in Jesus, to lie to the Holy Spirit (Acts 5:3). The impurity is eradicated by the judgment of Peter that brings about the fatal action of God. It is in describing the fear produced by this intervention that Acts uses the term "church" for the first time (5:11).[32]

The *second confrontation of the apostles with the Sanhedrin* (*5:12–42*), having many parallels to the first, illustrates the author's affection for symmetrically paired passages as a way of intensifying an issue. This time not one healing but many signs and wonders are involved. People even from the surrounding villages begin to bring their sick to be cured by the apostles, especially by Peter. Once again the high priests and the Sadducees have the apostles arrested but are frustrated when an angel of the Lord releases them so that they return to the Temple—a release all the more ironical because the Sadducees do not believe in angels. Thus the Sanhedrin session called to discuss the apostles has to have them arrested again; and as with the arrest of Jesus (Luke 22:6), care has to be taken not to arouse the people (Acts 5:26). Peter expresses his defiance of the high priest with a memorable line: "We must obey God rather than human beings," and then gives a christological sermon as though he hoped to convert the Sanhedrin (5:30–32).

The engendered fury reaches the point of wanting to kill the apostles (5:33), but is interrupted by the intervention of the famous Pharisee Gamaliel I (who would have been living in Jerusalem at this time). Scholars have debated endlessly whether this part of the scene is historical.[33] Far more important is the place of the scene in the Lucan storyline. Acts has not mentioned Pharisees as opposed to the followers of Jesus; and now it has Gama-

[32]Obviously the author does not think that such an act of judgment is alien to the nature of the church. We are very close here to an early understanding of the power to bind and to loose!

[33]There are anachronisms in Gamaliel's speech, e.g., he mentions Theudas' revolt and "after him Judas the Galilean." If this Sanhedrin session took place around AD 36, Theudas' revolt had not yet taken place, and Judas' revolt had taken place thirty years before.

liel the Pharisee advocating tolerance for them.[34] Offering examples of other movements that failed, he summarizes the situation, "If this work is from human beings, it will fail; if it is from God, you will not be able to overthrow it."[35] Gamaliel's advice carries the day. Although the apostles are beaten, they are released; and tacitly the Sanhedrin adopts the policy of leaving them alone as they continue every day to preach Christ publicly and privately (5:42).

4. The Hellenists: Toleration; Stephen's Trial and Martyrdom (6:1–8:1a).[36] After the Sanhedrin session at which Gamaliel spoke, Acts begins (*ca.* AD 36?) an era in which, except for the brief rule of the Jewish king Herod Agrippa I over Palestine (AD 41–44; Acts 12:1–23), the branch of the Jerusalem church closely associated with the Twelve was not persecuted.[37] (That period would come to an end in AD 62 when James, the brother of the Lord and leader of the Jerusalem church, was put to death.) This is not implausible, for within those years (36–40, 45–62) Paul could go to Jerusalem at least three times and see the church leaders without any indication of secrecy.

However, the removal of the external threat did not mean that all was well. Suddenly, after the picture of the church as being of one mind, *Acts 6:1–6 tells us about a hostile division among Jerusalem Christians,* a division that will bring persecution on a segment of them and lead eventually to a great missionary enterprise. Probably here Acts draws on an old tradition, and the account is sketchy. Common goods are no longer a sign of *koinōnia,* for two groups of Jewish believers within the Jerusalem community are fighting over them. Why? The designation of one group as Hellenists (Greeklike) whose leaders have Greek names (6:5) suggests that they were Jews who spoke (only?) Greek and who were raised acculturated to Greco-Roman civilization. Deductively by contrast, then, the other group called the Hebrews would have spoken Aramaic or Hebrew (sometimes Greek as well) and would have been more culturally Jewish in outlook.[38] Beyond the cultural

[34]Acts (22:3) will present Paul as having studied with this great teacher of the Law who is depicted here as a fair-minded man. Later 23:6–9 will have the Pharisees supporting tolerance for Paul over against the Sadducees.

[35]It may not be true that every religious movement that is of human origin fails; nevertheless, the church would have been wiser many times in its history if it had used Gamaliel's principle to judge new developments in Christianity rather than reacting in a hostile manner too quickly.

[36]E. Richard, *Acts 6:1–8:4: The Author's Method of Composition* (SBLDS 41; Missoula: Scholars, 1978).

[37]To forestall an objection, let me point out that the Hellenist branch of the Jerusalem church (e.g., Stephen) was persecuted; but in that persecution and expulsion the "apostles" were not bothered (Acts 8:1b).

[38]Paul, a strict Law-observant Jew, who probably knew Hebrew or Aramaic as well as Greek, considered himself a Hebrew (II Cor 11:22; Phil 3:5), whether or not that designation meant the same to him as it did to the author of Acts.

difference apparently there was also a theological difference. The apostles, who were clearly Hebrew Christians, have not let their faith in Jesus stop them from worshiping in the Temple (2:46; 3:1; 5:12,21). However, Stephen, who will become the Hellenist leader, speaks as if the Temple has no more meaning (7:48–50). In fact, we know that Jews of this period were sharply divided over whether the Jerusalem Temple was the sole place on earth at which sacrifice could be offered to God; and so it is not improbable that Jews of opposite persuasions on that issue may have become believers in Jesus. In any case the disagreement among these Jerusalem Christians has been translated into finances (as have many inner-church fights ever since) because the Hebrews (surely the larger group) are attempting to force the Hellenists to conformity by shutting off common funds from the Hellenist widows, who presumably were totally dependent on this support.

In order to deal with this situation the Twelve summon "the multitude" of the disciples (perhaps a technical name for those who could vote) to settle the issue. In this session the Twelve avoid the obvious, simple solutions. Although Hebrews themselves, they do not demand that the Hellenists either conform or leave. Moreover, they refuse to take over the administration of the common goods; specifically they do not wish to involve themselves in waiting on or serving[39] tables in order to ensure a fair distribution of food. Rather they wished to allow the Hellenists to have their own leaders and administrators of common goods.

This brief scene offers important subjects for reflection. *First,* nowhere do we see more clearly the unique role of the Twelve maintaining the wholeness of God's renewed people. They preserve the *koinōnia* by their solution, for the Hellenists are to remain as fully recognized brothers and sisters in Christ.

Second, the acceptance of the suggestion made by the Twelve was a decision in the early church for pluralism and for what we have come to call today "the hierarchy of doctrine." The cultural and theological disagreements that existed in Jerusalem between the Hebrews and the Hellenists were implicitly being judged as less important than their common belief in Jesus. Most believers in Jesus decided very early that it was better to tolerate certain differences of practice and thought rather than to destroy a *koinōnia* based on christology (but see n. 23 above).

Third, in terms of church structure, no blueprint had come from Jesus showing how the community of those who believed in him was to be admin-

[39]Because the verb "to wait on, serve" in Acts 6:2 is *diakonein,* this scene has come to be interpreted as the establishment of the first deacons. The position of the Hellenist leaders who are selected in this scene is not similar to that of the deacons described in the Pastoral Letters. See Chapter 30 below, n. 11.

istered. By the time described in Acts 6 (*ca.* AD 36?) believers are increasing in numbers and are arguing with one another—two sociological factors that always produce a need for defining leadership more clearly. Accordingly we hear of the seven who become the administrators for the Hellenist believers. Probably administrators also emerge for the Hebrew Christian community at the same time, for henceforth James (the brother of the Lord) and the elders (presbyters) appear as authorities in Jerusalem, alongside the apostles (Acts 11:30; 12:17; 15:2; 21:18). The choice of administrators in 6:6 is done in the context of praying and the laying on of hands. Although development of church structure reflects sociological necessity, in the Christian self-understanding the Holy Spirit given by the risen Christ guides the church in a way that allows basic structural development to be seen as embodying Jesus Christ's will for his church.

Fourth, as depicted in Acts, the Twelve made a good proposal, approved by "the multitude" of the Jerusalem community. Nevertheless, none of those present at this meeting could have foreseen how far their decision would lead.[40] In keeping the Hellenists within the Christian *koinōnia* the Jerusalem community now becomes responsible for the actions and preaching of the Hellenist leaders. The chief priests and the Sanhedrin had implicitly decided to extend grudging tolerance to those who believed in the risen Christ; but that did not mean they would tolerate attacks on the Temple from believers in Jesus any more than they tolerated it from other Jews.

A *summary* (*6:7*) about the spread of the word of God and the conversion of priests sets the stage for *a conflict centered on Stephen* (*6:8–8:1a*). The first-ranking among the Hellenists, Stephen, stirs up opposition at a Jerusalem synagogue attended largely by foreign Jews. They drag him before a Sanhedrin and level a (false) charge about the message he is preaching—in general his words against Moses and the Law, and specifically that Jesus would destroy the Temple sanctuary. In his long speech (Acts 7:2–53) in response to the Temple charge Stephen will phrase those radical implications in the climactic statement: "The Most High does not dwell in houses made with hands" (7:48).

Although Acts gives us speeches of Peter and Paul, none is so elaborate as the speech of Stephen.[41] His survey of the salvation-history from the patri-

[40]The results of major church decisions can go beyond what was foreseen, with no way to stop at a point judged prudent; see below (pp. 305–6) on the Jerusalem conference of Acts 15.

[41]Is the greater attention because the Christianity that exists in the author's lifetime has now followed the path of Stephen in terms of rejection of the Temple rather than the path of Peter and Paul, both of whom are described as worshiping in the Temple? For overall views: M. H. Scharlemann, *Stephen: A Singular Saint* (AnBib 34; Rome: PBI, 1968); J. J. Kilgallen, *The Stephen Speech* (AnBib 67; Rome: PBI, 1976); *Biblica* 70 (1989), 173–93; D. Wiens, *Stephen's Sermon and the Structure of Luke-Acts* (N. Richland Hills, TX: Bibal, 1995).

arch Abraham to Israel's entrance into the Promised Land under Moses and Joshua has fascinated scholars since elements in it do not seem to reflect standard OT understanding. Some have even proposed that we have here reflections of a Samaritan background[42] harmonious with the mission in Samaria that will soon be undertaken by the Hellenists. The last verses are astoundingly polemic from a prisoner in the dock, for Stephen accuses his hearers of giving over and murdering the just Jesus even as their fathers persecuted the prophets. Not surprisingly this accusation brings rage against Stephen to the boiling point, and he is cast out of the city and stoned to death (7:54–60). The scene is truly significant, not only because Stephen is the first Christian martyr, but also because the death of Stephen in Acts matches so closely the death of Jesus in Luke. Both accounts speak of the Son of Man at the right hand of God (Luke 22:69; Acts 7:56); both have a prayer for the forgiveness of those who are effecting this execution (Luke 23:34a; Acts 7:60); both have the dying figure commend his spirit heavenward (Luke 23:46; Acts 7:59). In the figure of Peter Acts has shown continuity with Jesus' ministry of healing and preaching; in the figure of Stephen Acts has shown continuity with Jesus' death. And just as Jesus' death was not the end because the apostles would receive his Spirit to carry on the work, the death of Stephen is not the end, for observing is a young man named Saul (7:58). He consents to the death (8:1a), but in God's providence he will continue the work of Stephen.

Missions in Samaria and Judea (8:1b–12:25)

1. Dispersal from Jerusalem; Philip and Peter in Samaria (8:1b–25). Acts 1:8 laid out the divine plan of evangelizing: "You shall be my witnesses in Jerusalem and in all Judea and Samaria, and to the ends of the earth." We have heard witness (*martyria*) borne in Jerusalem culminating with the martyrdom of Stephen; now we are to hear preaching in the next two regions as the Hellenists are scattered throughout Judea and Samaria (8:1b; 9:31).[43] The major step of moving outside Jerusalem to preach to a wider audience is not the result of planning but of persecution. Those who are expelled and become the missionaries to other areas are the Hellenists, the more radical Christians in terms of their relation to Jewish Temple worship. Missionary

[42]See the debate between C.H.H. Scobie, NTS 19 (1973), 390–414 and R. Pummer, NTS 22 (1976), 441–43. Also Munck, *Acts,* Appendix V, 285–300.

[43]In the complicated description of 8:1b, Acts tells us that the apostles (and seemingly the Hebrew Christians) were not expelled, presumably because they did not propagandize against the Temple as the Hellenists did. In this persecution a ferocious agent is Saul, whose conversion will be dramatically recounted in Acts 9.

activity in itself might have been neutral in the attitude it inculcated toward Judaism, but with the Hellenists as spokesmen it was bound to be a centrifugal force. Their converts to Jesus would have no deep attachment to prominent features of Jewish worship.

According to Acts 8:5 the Hellenists go to the Samaritans and thus begin preaching Jesus to nonJews. (Later [11:19–20] in Phoenicia, Cyprus, and Antioch some preach to Gentiles.) The Hellenists were ideally suited to evangelize Samaria since Samaritans did not accept the Jerusalem Temple as the only place of worship.[44] Their successful proclamation attracts Simon Magus.[45] Yet the one to confront him is Peter, not Philip, the Hellenist successor of Stephen; for the Jerusalem church, having heard of the Hellenist success, has sent Peter and John that the Samaritans might receive the Holy Spirit.[46] Simon wants the apostles' power and offers money for it, thus forever dubiously immortalizing his name in "simony." Peter challenges him to repent; yet unlike Stephen's prayer for his adversaries, this promotion of repentance is qualified as to whether Simon can really change his heart (8:22–23). On their way back to Jerusalem Peter and John too preach to Samaritans (8:25).

2. Philip and the Ethiopian Eunuch En Route to Gaza (8:26–40). More Hellenist evangelizing takes place in the southern part of Judea, manifesting geographical spread. The Ethiopian eunuch, minister of Candace,[47] is from an exotic region in Africa (probably not modern Ethiopia, but Sudan or Nubia to the south of Egypt—one of "the ends of the earth"). He is reading Isaiah, and the Hellenist Philip's ability to interpret the prophet in order to explain Christ is a continuation of the risen Jesus' interpreting the Scriptures for his disciples (Luke 24:27,44–45). Although Deut 23:2(1) would rule out the admission of the castrated into the community of Israel, Philip has no hesitation about meeting the eunuch's request to be baptized into the community of the renewed Israel. (Was Philip acting out the eschatological

[44]Many think that there is a Hellenist strain in John, the only Gospel where Jesus goes into Samaria and gains Samaritan followers. If so, in John 4:21 we may be hearing the type of preaching done in Samaria by the Hellenists: "You will worship the Father neither on this mountain [Gerizim, the Samaritan holy place] nor in Jerusalem."

[45]This curious figure later became a subject of speculation, figuring in legend as the great adversary of Christianity. Does the designation of Simon as "the Power of God called Great" mean that he related himself to a gnostic emanation that stands between the distant, hidden God and human beings? Is categorizing him as a *magus* Acts' contemptuous classification of a gnostic teacher? Does the author of Acts include the story of Simon's defeat because already gnostics were making Simon a hero?

[46]Acts gives the impression that granting the Spirit required the collaboration of the Twelve. Here one suspects that the basic purpose of the apostolic visitation was to verify whether the conversion of such outsiders as the Samaritans was reconcilable with Jesus' proclamation.

[47]Acts presents Candace as the personal name of the Ethiopian queen; it seems, however, to have been a title.

benevolence of Isa 56:3–5 toward eunuchs?) That openness prepares us for the admission of Gentiles, and by way of transition Acts stops here to tell us about Saul/Paul who would be the great emissary to the Gentiles.

3. Saul En Route to Damascus; Return to Jerusalem and Tarsus (Acts 9:1–30). After narrating here the account of the conversion of Saul/Paul, the author will report it twice more from Paul's lips in his speeches of self-defense (22:3–21; 26:2–23).[48] In those later versions the vocation to evangelize the Gentiles will be blended into the conversion account. Here the author is content to move in stages: Ananias, who cures and baptizes him, is told of the future mission, but not Saul himself. Yet clearly, because of all that is to be accomplished through this "vessel of election" (9:15), Acts is very interested in recounting his dramatic conversion effected by Jesus himself.[49] The dramatic touches of the story are superb, e.g., the personalizing of the Saul's hostility in 9:4, "Saul, Saul, why do you persecute *me*?" The reluctance of Ananias to have anything to do with Saul despite the Lord's instruction highlights the metamorphosis of Saul from a truly fearsome persecutor. Acts is very careful to report that Saul received the Holy Spirit (9:17), for Paul's proclamation will eventually be as potent as was that of Peter and the others who received the Spirit at Pentecost. In significant harmony with Acts' previous stress on christological belief, the new convert preaches that "Jesus is the Son of God" (9:20). Acts also lays the basis for the future activity of Barnabas with Paul by telling us that it was Barnabas who supported Saul against those in Jerusalem who could not believe that the persecutor had now changed.[50] Probably under the constraint of actual chronology, Acts postpones the most famous activities of Saul/Paul by telling us that he went back to Tarsus (9:30); his great mission will be described later after the author tells us more about Peter. By way of narrative procedure the overlapping of the two figures helps to show that the same gospel is preached by both.

[48]For Luke's pattern of recurrent narration see M.-E. Rosenblatt in Richard, *New* 94–105; R. D. Witherup, JSNT 48 (1992), 67–86.

[49]The risen Jesus appeared on earth to the Twelve and then departed to heaven whence he now speaks to Saul. Does that mean that the author of Acts posits a qualitative difference of status between the Twelve and Paul in terms of their experience of Christ? I Cor 15:5–8, from Paul himself, would give the impression that there was no difference in the appearances of the risen Jesus to Peter or the Twelve (or James) and the appearance to Paul (except that they are listed first, he is last).

[50]Acts 9:19b–30 recounts Paul's preaching in Damascus, his facing a Jewish conspiracy after many days, and his being lowered in a basket over the wall to escape to Jerusalem where, after Barnabas brings him to the apostles, he preaches and debates insistently before being sent off to Tarsus. There is a famous discrepancy between this and Paul's own account in Gal 1:15–22: After the revelation he did not go up to Jerusalem to see the apostles but went immediately to Arabia; then he returned to Damascus, before going after three years to Jerusalem for fifteen days, where he saw and conversed only with Cephas (Peter) and James, and finally went on to Syria and Cilicia (still not known by face to the churches of Christ in Judea). Possibly Paul's brief summary of what happened nearly twenty years before is imprecise; probably the author of Acts had heard only a simplified version. See Chapter 16 below, subsection A.

4. Peter at Lydda, Joppa, Caesarea, and Back to Jerusalem (9:31–11:18). The first of the Twelve was the spokesman of apostolic missionary activity in Jerusalem (Acts 2–5); but when the church began spreading to Judea and Samaria, the Hellenists and Saul took center stage (with Peter invoked chiefly to face Simon Magus). Now, however, with the church at peace (*9:31—a transitional summary*), Peter returns to the fore. Previously we have seen that in the name of Jesus Peter could heal and preach. *Peter's cure of Aeneas at Lydda* (*9:32–35*) with the command to rise echoes closely Jesus' cure of the paralyzed man (Luke 5:24–26). Even more closely *Peter's revivification of Tabitha at Joppa* (*9:36–43*) resembles Jesus' action in raising the daughter of Jairus (Luke 8:49–56).[51] No power has been withheld from the church, not even the power over death itself. Now, however, we are about to move beyond the parallels to Jesus' ministry to a new area. The Lucan Gospel account of Jesus began and ended in the Jerusalem Temple. What Peter does next will start a chain of actions that will eventually take Christianity outside Judaism to Gentiles[52] and to Rome, the representative of the ends of the earth.

In 10:1–48 the author as a third-person reporter recounts how Peter is led by the Spirit to baptize Cornelius (and his household), a Gentile who participates in synagogue prayers and accepts the moral demands of Judaism.[53] *In 11:1–18 Peter repeats what happened with a first-person report* as he defends his behavior before the Jerusalem Christians. (As with Paul's repetitions of the story of his conversion, the duplication signals that this is an account of pivotal importance.) There are six subdivisions in the Acts narrative: (a) 10:1–8: The pious Roman centurion Cornelius receives a vision of an angel of God at Caesarea telling him to send to Joppa for Simon called Peter; (b) 10:9–16: At Joppa Peter receives a vision telling him three times that foods traditionally considered ritually unclean are in fact not unclean; (c) 10:17–23a: Pondering the vision, Peter receives the men sent by Cornelius who ask him to come to Cornelius's house; (d) 10:23b–33: Cornelius

[51]The Marcan parallel (5:41) to the latter has "*Talitha koum*(*i*)," which is remarkably like the order "Tabitha, rise" in Acts 9:40. For resuscitations, see Chapter 11 below, n. 41.

[52]The author portrays a gradual enlargement: Peter dealing with a sympathetic Gentile (chap. 10); the Hellenists preaching to the Greek-speaking Gentiles (11:19–20); then Barnabas and Saul sent out from Antioch, at first preaching to the Jews in the synagogues but gradually turning their attention to Gentiles (13:4ff.), who become the chief concern.

[53]Luke refers to such Gentile sympathizers to Judaism who did not become converts as God-fearers (or God-worshipers: 10:2,22; 13:43; 17:4,17). There has been a debate about the accuracy of such a designation: A. T. Kraabel, *Numen* 28 (1981), 113–26; and (with R. S. MacLennan) BAR 12 (#5, 1986), 46–53,64. However, M. C. de Boer in Tuckett, *Luke's Literary* 50–71, shows that Luke scarcely invented this terminology for such people who certainly existed. Tyson, *Images* 35–39, contends that these are the readers to whom the author has directed Luke-Acts, represented in the text by Cornelius, the Ethiopian eunuch, and Theophilus (see Chapter 9 above, n. 92). For an analysis of the Cornelius story, see R. D. Witherup, JSNT 49 (1993), 45–66.

receives Peter and they compare visions; (e) 10:34–49: Peter preaches a sermon, and the Holy Spirit comes upon the uncircumcised present, so that Peter commands them to be baptized; (f) 11:1–18: Returning to Jerusalem, Peter has to account for his boldness in baptizing Gentiles.

Because there are heavenly revelations to both Cornelius and Peter, readers are meant to recognize that what occurs here is uniquely God's will. Such an emphasis was probably necessary because of the controversial nature of the two issues involved. First, were Christians bound by the Jewish rules for kosher foods? The thesis that in God's eyes all foods are ritually clean (10:15) constitutes a major break from Jewish practice, a break now to be supported not only by Hellenist radicals but also by the first of the Twelve. Gradually the extent to which new wine cannot be put into old wineskins (Luke 5:37) is becoming apparent. Often modern Jewish and Christian scholars, studying the history of this early period and regretting the great rift that opened between Christianity and Judaism, suggest that if in the 1st century there had been more tolerance and understanding on both sides, the split could have been avoided. Some indications in the NT, however, suggest that the *radical implications* of Jesus were really irreconcilable with major tenets and practices of Judaism.[54]

Second, did *Gentiles* have to be circumcised to receive baptism and the grace of Christ?[55] Implicitly or explicitly those who insisted that Gentiles needed to be circumcised (i.e., become Jews) were maintaining that being a Jew had primacy over faith in Christ in terms of God's grace. Peter is pictured as rejecting that by word and deed in 10:34–49. Scholars debate whether the author of Acts is historical in presenting Peter as the first to accept uncircumcised Gentiles into the Christian *koinōnia.* One may argue from 11:19–20 that the Hellenists were the first to do this, and clearly later Paul was the greatest spokesman for the practice. Yet since Paul portrays Peter (or Cephas) as present at Antioch dealing with Gentiles (Gal 2:11–12) and perhaps at Corinth (I Cor 1:12; 9:5), what may underlie Acts is the memory that among the Jerusalem leaders Peter was foremost in displaying such openness, whence the ability of Peter or his image to appeal to both sides of the Christian community.[56] In any case Acts 10:44–48 describes the accep-

[54]Related to this issue, see J. Neusner, *A Rabbi Talks with Jesus* (New York: Doubleday, 1993).

[55]The NT (including Paul) does not debate whether *Jewish Christian* parents should have their sons circumcised. Those who did so to insure the extra privileges of being Jews (see Rom 9:4–5) could have constituted a problem theologically only if they thought that circumcision was *necessary* (along with baptism) for someone to become a child of God and part of God's people newly chosen in Jesus Christ.

[56]Paul (Gal 2:7) speaks of Peter's having been entrusted with the gospel to the circumcised; yet a letter attributed to him, I Peter, is clearly written to Gentile Christians (2:10: "You were once no people").

tance of Cornelius as a major step, accompanied by an outpouring of the Spirit manifested through speaking in tongues, comparable to Pentecost—the beginning of the church of the Gentiles comparable to the beginning of the church of the renewed Israel.[57]

The radical character of what Peter has done and proclaimed is challenged in 11:2–3 by confreres in the church of Jerusalem: "Why did you go to the uncircumcised and eat with them?" It is not clear whether at heart this Christian "circumcision party" was altogether opposed to converting Gentiles to belief in Christ or was simply insisting that Gentiles could be converted only after they had become Jews. Peter answers the circumcision party by telling about his visions and the coming of the Spirit upon Cornelius' household. This existential argument silences the circumcision party (for the moment) and leads to the acceptance of Gentiles into existing Jewish Christian groups (11:18). But the issue has not been fully resolved, as Acts 15 will show us after it has depicted an active mission to Gentiles.

5. Antioch; Jerusalem; Herod's Persecution; Peter's Departure (11:19–12:25). Attention now switches from the church in Jerusalem to *the church in Antioch* (*11:19–26*), where the followers of Jesus were first called Christians, the name by which they would be known for the rest of time. As part of his technique of simultaneity, the author now picks up the Hellenists' story broken off in chap. 8 when they were scattered from Jerusalem to Samaria. Belatedly we are told that they went also to Phoenicia, Cyprus, and Antioch (in Syria), preaching at first only to Jews but then gradually to Gentiles as well. Although a Hebrew Christian like Peter did accept a Gentile household into the community, seemingly the aggressive effort to convert Gentiles began with the Hellenists. When Jerusalem heard this, Barnabas was sent to Antioch to check on the development; and he approved it (11:22–23). This becomes the occasion of bringing to Antioch Saul, who was last heard of in 9:30. Thus, while the Jerusalem church in the person of Peter is taking the first steps toward admitting a few Gentiles, Antioch develops as a second great Christian center, more vibrantly involved in mission.[58]

[57]Some today contend that "baptism in the Spirit" is distinct from and superior to baptism in water, basing their position on the sequence in Acts. That is not an issue in Acts, however. According to his purpose and interests the author shows: (a) the Twelve and those together with them receiving the Spirit without (ever) being baptized in water; (b) people being baptized (in water) and then receiving the gift of the Spirit (2:38; 19:5–6); (c) people receiving the Spirit before being baptized in water (here); (d) people having been baptized in water (with the baptism of John) who never even knew that there was a Holy Spirit (18:24–19:7).

[58]There were different missions conducted by the first Jews who believed in Jesus, reflecting different theologies; see my article in CBQ 45 (1983), 74–79. However, M. D. Goulder, *A Tale of Two Missions* (London: SCM, 1994), carries this too far by rejecting the idea of a unified church. From our evidence, despite differences, the first Christians would have thought of themselves as unified in the *koinōnia* of the renewed Israel.

The development of the Antioch base is a grace because just at this time Jerusalem and Judea are hit particularly hard by *a famine foretold by Agabus* (*11:27–30*) and by a changed political situation where direct Roman rule had been replaced in AD 41–44 by a Jewish kingdom leading to *persecution of Christians under Herod Agrippa I* (*12:1–23*). The famine offers the Antiochene Christians a chance to display *koinōnia* by sharing goods with the poorer believers in Judea; the persecution offers the Jerusalem Christians an opportunity to bear witness by martyrdom, for James, son of Zebedee, brother of John, and one of the Twelve, is put to death.[59] Whereas hitherto in Luke-Acts there was a tendency to distinguish between the Jewish people (more favorable to Jesus) and their rulers, 12:3,11 associates the Jewish people with the antiChristian hostility of Herod. Readers are being prepared for a situation in which Judaism and Christianity are not only distinct but hostile.

Great danger threatens when Peter is arrested; but God intervenes through an angel to release him, even as God intervened by an angel to release him when he was arrested by the Sanhedrin (5:19). Later an earthquake will free Paul when he is in prison in Philippi (16:26). These divine interventions show God's care for the great spokesmen of the gospel.[60] That Peter, after his escape from Herod, goes to another place (12:17) has given rise to the imaginative, but probably wrong, tradition that at this juncture Peter went to Rome and founded the church there. That Peter, as he leaves Jerusalem, sends word to James (the "brother" of Jesus but not one of the Twelve) has been interpreted, also wrongly, as his passing the control of the church (and even the primacy) to James. However, one should distinguish between the roles of the two men: Peter, the first of the Twelve to see the risen Jesus, is always named first among them and would have a unique role in the church at large because of that; there is no evidence that Peter was ever local administrator of the Jerusalem church—a role of administration rejected for the Twelve in 6:2. Probably as soon as there was an administrative role created for the Hebrew element of the Jerusalem church, James held it, not illogically because he was related to Jesus by family ties.[61] In any case Peter's

[59]This is James the Greater who in legend went to Spain (venerated at Compostela) and evidently came back again to Judea soon enough to die about AD 41! He must be kept distinct from other NT Jameses, especially James the "brother" of Jesus (Chapter 34 below). As explained above in relation to 1:21–26, members of the Twelve are not replaced when they die.

[60]In the light of such tradition, one can imagine later Christian puzzlement when neither Peter nor Paul escaped Nero's arrest at Rome where they were executed. Would some have judged that the emperor was more powerful than Christ? Perhaps that is why a book like Revelation had to stress so firmly that the Lamb could and would conquer the beast representing imperial power.

[61]This relationship would have been very significant to those who emphasized Jesus as a royal Messiah of the House of David. The dominant Gospel evidence is that the "brothers" of Jesus were not disciples during his lifetime (Mark 3:31–35; 6:3–4; John 7:5); but the risen Jesus appeared to James (I Cor 15:7), and James was an apostle in Jerusalem at the time of Paul's conversion (Gal 1:19; *ca.* AD 36). Cf. W. Schmithals, *Paul and James* (SBT 46; London: SCM, 1965).

departure from Jerusalem was not a permanent one; he had returned by the time of the meeting in that city described in Acts 15 (*ca.* AD 49). Acts finishes the colorful story of the frustrated persecution by describing (12:23) the horrible death of being eaten by worms visited by God on King Herod Agrippa in AD 44. It is quite similar to the death of the great enemy of Israel, King Antiochus Epiphanes, in II Macc 9:9. Both accounts are theological interpretations of sudden death: Those who dare to raise their hand against God's people face divine punishment.

The stories of *famine and persecution at Jerusalem end on a triumphal note* (*12:24–25*): The persecutor has fallen; God's word grows and multiplies; and Barnabas and Saul bring back to Antioch John Mark (the evangelist?—pp. 158–60 above).

Missions of Barnabas and Saul Converting Gentiles; Approval at Jerusalem (13:1–15:35)[62]

1. Antioch Church Sends Barnabas and Saul; Mission to Cyprus and SE Asia Minor (13:1–14:28). This section begins with a *short description of the church of Antioch* (*13:1–3*). If Jerusalem has the apostles (i.e., the Twelve), Antioch has prophets and teachers, among whom Acts places Barnabas and Saul.[63] Barnabas is listed first and Saul, last; only during the mission will the name Paul begin to be used consistently in place of Saul and the order reversed to Paul and Barnabas (e.g., 13:13,43). In other words in the mission the great proclaimer of the gospel will find his identity and status.

We are told that the Antiochene prophets and teachers were "performing a liturgical service [*leitourgein*] to the Lord and fasting." As promised in Luke 5:34–35, the days have now come when the bridegroom has been taken away and fasting has become a part of early church life. What did the liturgical service consist of? Was it a eucharist?[64] In this context of prayer and fasting, hands are laid on Barnabas and Saul. We should not anachronistically speak of this as an ordination; it is a commissioning by the church of Antioch for a mission that is often counted as the first Pauline journey and dated to AD 46–49.

[62]One could start the mission "to the end of the earth" (1:8) here rather than in 15:36 (see below). These chaps. 13:1–15:35 are more initiatory and exploratory than the chaps. that follow.

[63]Cf. I Cor 12:28: "God has appointed in the church first apostles, second prophets, third teachers . . ." Paul thought of himself as an apostle, but not in the Lucan sense of the Twelve.

[64]In Luke 22:14,19 "Do this in commemoration of me" is addressed to the apostles. But in a eucharist at Antioch where the Twelve were not present, who would have presided? About the turn of the 1st century *Didache* 10:7 depicts a situation where prophets celebrated the eucharist, and that may have been the custom earlier as well.

Along with John Mark, *Barnabas and Saul go to Cyprus* (*13:4–12*), Barnabas' home territory; and they speak in the Jewish synagogues. Since in his own writings Paul speaks of converting Gentiles, scholars have wondered whether Acts is accurate here. But the Pauline letters are to churches evangelized in later missionary journeys at a time when Paul had turned to converting Gentiles—a development that may have stemmed from experiment if he found (as Acts indicates) more success with them.[65] Saul's encountering in Cyprus and besting the false prophet and magus, Bar-Jesus, sets up a parallelism with Peter's encountering Simon Magus in Samaria. The enemies of the gospel are not simply earthly forces (as Paul will state clearly in his own letters).

The move from Cyprus *to Antioch of Pisidia in Asia Minor* (*13:13–50*) may have been a more adventurous extension of the mission than Acts indicates, and perhaps that is what caused John Mark to depart and go to Jerusalem (13:13). A later reference (15:37–39) shows that this departure left a bad memory with Paul. The author makes what happened in Asia Minor at Pisidian Antioch almost an exemplar of the Pauline mission. There Paul (henceforth so named) gives a synagogue sermon (13:16–41) that in its appeal to the OT and summary of what God did in Jesus is not unlike the sermons earlier preached by Peter.[66] Thus we get a picture of a consistent message preached by the two great figures who dominate the story of the early church, Peter and Paul.[67] Acts 13:42–43 reports a generally favorable reaction among Jews and their sympathizers to the sermon, but 13:44–49 shows that on the following Sabbath there was hostility from "the Jews" so that Paul and Barnabas shifted their appeal to the Gentiles.

The Jewish hostility at Antioch continues so that Paul and Barnabas are driven from Pisidia and have to *move on to Iconium* (*13:51–14:5*)—a rebuff that evidently does not discourage them, for they are "filled with joy and the Holy Spirit" (13:52). In Iconium, where they spend a considerable period,

[65]That in fact Paul was involved with synagogues is strongly suggested by his statement in II Cor 11:24: "Five times I received from Jews thirty-nine lashes"—a synagogue punishment. Even at the end, Acts will continue to show Paul, when he arrives at Rome *ca.* 61, speaking first to Jews. However, although in Rom 1:16 Paul indicates that Jews came first in the general proclamation of the gospel, in 11:13 he characterizes his own apostolate as "to the Gentiles."

[66]Undoubtedly the author of Acts composed the speech attributed to Paul; yet the composition is not alien to the christological thought attested in Paul's letters. For instance, Acts 13:23 relates Jesus to David's posterity and 13:33 makes God's raising Jesus the moment of saying, "You are my Son; today I have begotten you." In Rom 1:3–4 Paul speaks of the one who was "descended from David according to the flesh and designated Son of God in power according to the Spirit of holiness by resurrection from the dead." In Acts 13:39 there is justification language similar to that of the Pauline letters.

[67]There were disagreements between the two men (Gal 2:11,14); but when it came to the essential message about Jesus, Paul associates himself with Cephas (Peter) and the Twelve (and James!) in a common preaching and a common demand for belief (I Cor 15:3–11).

both procedure and reaction are much the same; and once again they have to *move on—this time to the Lycaonian cities of Lystra and Derbe* (*14:6–21a*). In Lystra Paul is depicted as healing a man crippled from birth just as Peter had healed a cripple from birth in 3:1–10—the healing power of Jesus that was passed on to Peter in dealing with the Jews of Jerusalem has been passed on to Paul in dealing with Gentiles. The vivid Gentile reaction, hailing Barnabas and Paul as the gods Zeus and Hermes,[68] catches the ethos of a different world where the message of the one God (14:15–18) has not really taken root, making it all the more difficult to preach Christ. The hostility aroused by the Jews from the previous city pursues Paul; he is stoned and left for dead. (In his own writing Paul will speak eloquently about his suffering for Christ, including being stoned, e.g., II Cor 11:23–27.) But Paul recovers and then goes on with Barnabas to Derbe. *The two disciples retrace their steps through the Asia Minor cities and then sail back to Syrian Antioch* (*14:21b–28*). In a passing phrase Acts 14:23 has them appointing presbyters (or elders) in every church. Many doubt that this form of structure existed so early.[69] At least we may deduce that by the last third of the 1st century when Acts was written, presbyters existed in these churches and their status was seen as part of the Pauline heritage. The journey ends with a report to the church of Antioch that had sent Paul and Barnabas forth: "God opened a door of faith to the Gentiles" (14:26–27).

2. Jerusalem Conference and Approval; Return to Antioch (15:1–35). What Paul has done does not please the *circumcision party at Jerusalem who now send people to Antioch* (*15:1*) to challenge the acceptance of Gentiles without circumcision. One might have thought that this issue was settled at Jerusalem earlier (Acts 11) when Peter justified his acceptance of the Gentile Cornelius without circumcision. It was, however, one thing to incorporate into a largely Jewish Christian community a few Gentiles; it is another to be faced with whole churches of Gentiles such as Paul had founded—churches that would have little relation to Judaism other than holding in veneration the Jewish Scriptures. We can see in Rom 11:13–26 Paul's understanding of what he thought would happen from his Gentile mission: The Gentiles are a wild olive branch grafted on the tree of Israel; and eventually, through envy, all Israel will come to faith in Christ and be saved. The circumcision party may have been far more realistic in their fears that Paul had

[68]On this slender evidence is based much speculation about the appearance of Paul as short and slight.

[69]Presbyters are never mentioned in the undisputed Pauline letters; the appointment of them is a major issue only in the postPauline Pastoral Epistles. Yet *episkopoi* and *diakonoi* are mentioned in Phil 1:1, and arguments drawn from silence about church structure(s) in Paul's lifetime are very uncertain.

begun a process whereby Christianity would become almost entirely a Gentile religion, which, of course, is what happened. (Ultraconservatives, as distorted as their theology may be, are often more perceptive about the inevitable direction of changes than are the moderates who propose them.) Far from being grafted on the tree of Israel, the Gentile Christians will become the tree. To stop that foreseeable catastrophe Paul's opponents attack the principle that Gentiles may be admitted without becoming Jews (i.e., being circumcised). They cause so much trouble that *Paul and Barnabas have to go to Jerusalem* (*15:2–3*) to debate the issue. There follows a report of what may be judged the most important meeting[70] ever held in the history of Christianity, for implicitly *the Jerusalem conference* (*15:4–29*) decided that the following of Jesus would soon move beyond Judaism and become a separate religion reaching to the ends of the earth.

We are fortunate in having two accounts, one in Acts 15, the other in Gal 2; and this double perspective teaches us much about the great personalities of early Christianity. Scholars tend to prefer Paul's own eyewitness account and to dismiss the Acts account as later bowdlerizing. There is no question that Acts presents a simplified and less acrimonious report; but as regards Gal, we should recognize that a personal account written in self-defense has its own optic, removing it from the realm of the purely objective. For instance, in Gal 2:1 Paul says, "I went up to Jerusalem with Barnabas, taking Titus too along"; Acts 15:2 says that "Paul and Barnabas and some others were appointed to go up to Jerusalem." That they went up commissioned by the church of Antioch may very well be the more accurate picture, even though (as part of his self-defense in Gal) Paul highlights his initiative in cooperating.

Acts indicates that those in Jerusalem had the power of decision on the issue. Paul speaks disparagingly of the "so-called pillars" whose reputation meant nothing to him; but that very title implies that their reputation did mean something to others, and in the long run Paul could not stand alone. Although he received his gospel (of grace freely given to the Gentiles) through a revelation from Jesus Christ and would not change it even if an angel told him to do so (Gal 1:8,11–12), he mentions the possibility that he had run in vain (2:2). If that is more than an oratorical touch, he may have been admitting the power of the "pillars": Should they deny his Gentile churches *koinōnia* with the mother church in Jerusalem, there would be a division that negated the very nature of the church. Thus, despite Paul's certi-

[70]Although often called the "Council" of Jerusalem, this should not be confused with the later ecumenical councils of the church (Nicaea, etc.).

tude about the rightness of his evangelizing, the outcome of the Jerusalem meeting for the communities he had evangelized involved uncertainty.

To have brought along Titus, an uncircumcised Gentile (Gal 2:3), is a shrewd maneuver. Probably some of the Christian Pharisee advocates of circumcision[71] had never seen any of the uncircumcised Gentiles whom they denied to be true Christians; and it is always more difficult to confront others who patently believe in Christ and tell them face to face, "You are not Christians because you do not agree with me." Another prudent step by Paul (Gal 2:2) is first to lay out his argument privately before those at Jerusalem who were of repute. Initial reactions of authorities are often defensive; when uttered in private, they can be modified later without loss of face. Public "eyeball-to-eyeball" confrontations with authorities usually prove little more than nearsightedness.

The public disputation at Jerusalem is the core of the story. Four participants are involved, two predictable (on opposite sides: the circumcision advocates and Paul), one less predictable (Peter), and one unpredictable (James). Understandably, given the goal of Gal, Paul's account is centered on his own role, not yielding submission even for a moment and convincing the reputed pillars of the truth of his gospel. Yet Acts gives the least space to Barnabas and Paul (15:12), sandwiching their report between Peter's words (15:7–11) and those of James (15:13–21)—an arrangement creating the impression that it was the last who carried the day. One needs to read between the lines of both accounts. The issue under discussion was what Paul and Barnabas had done in their missionary activity, and in that sense the conference was centered on Paul. Yet the real suspense may have been centered on what James would say, since he would carry the Jerusalem church with him. Gal 2:9 implies that by listing James first among the so-called pillars of the church, ahead of Cephas (Peter) and John.

What reasoning was advanced by the participants? Paul recounts deeds done among the Gentiles (Acts) and the gospel he preaches to them (Gal), which surely means an account of how such people had come to faith without circumcision. Peter's argument is also experiential (Acts): God had sent the Holy Spirit on the uncircumcised Cornelius. James' argument is reasoned (Acts) and, as might be expected from a conservative Hebrew Christian, draws on the Scriptures. The prophets foretold that the Gentiles would come, and the Law of Moses allowed uncircumcised Gentiles to live among the people of God provided that they abstained from certain listed pollutions.

[71]In place of this more neutral terminology of Acts 15:5, Paul speaks polemically of "false brethren" spying out the freedom of his treatment of the Gentiles.

Unfortunately we do not hear the arguments advanced by the circumcision party, other than the simple statement in Acts 15:5 that the Law of Moses required circumcision.

More significant is a deafening silence about Jesus. No one who favors admitting the Gentiles without circumcision mentions the example of Jesus, saying, "Jesus told us to do so." And, of course, the reason is that he never did tell them to do so. Indeed, one may suspect that the only ones likely to have mentioned Jesus would have been those of the circumcision party, arguing precisely that there was no authorization from him for such a radical departure from the Law. Even Paul remembers Jesus as "born under the Law" (Gal 4:4). This may have been the first of many times when those who have resisted change in the church did so by arguing that Jesus never did this, whereas those who promoted change did so on the import of Christ for a situation that the historical Jesus did not encounter.[72] In any case, both Acts and Gal agree that Peter (and John) and James kept the *koinōnia* with Paul and his Gentile churches. The road was now open for free and effective evangelizing to the ends of the earth. In fact that road would also lead away from Judaism. Even though the Savior for Gentiles was a Jew born under the Law, Christianity would soon be looked on as a Gentile religion quite alien to Judaism, especially to a Judaism for which the Law would become ever more important once the Temple was destroyed.

Now *Paul and Barnabas go back to Antioch* (*15:30–35*), carrying a letter of clarification that circumcision was not to be required of Gentile converts. However, the Gentiles are required to abstain from four things proscribed by Lev 17–18 for aliens living among Israel: meat offered to idols; the eating of blood; the eating of strangled animals (i.e., animals that were not ritually slaughtered); and incestuous unions (*porneia,* "impurity," but here with kin). This is the position that James advocated when he spoke at the Jerusalem conference (15:20). When we compare the picture to Paul's account in Gal 2:11ff., we realize that the history was surely more complicated.

A plausible combination of the two sources of information might yield the following. Paul and Barnabas go back to Antioch with the good news that freedom from circumcision had been recognized. Struggles develop, however, as to whether Gentile Christians are bound by food laws obeyed by the Jewish Christians who constitute the church alongside them. Paul argues that they are not bound, and Peter participates in this free practice until men

[72]The Synoptic Gospels give attention to Jesus' reaching out to tax-collectors and prostitutes. Was part of the reason for preserving that memory an implicit rebuttal of the circumcision position? One could construct the rebuttal thus: Jesus did reach out to those outside the Law, and now in our time the Gentiles are the ones outside the Law. One must recognize, however, that such arguments offer their own difficulties, for they can be used to justify almost any practice.

from James come demanding specific practices of the food laws.[73] Peter accedes to James, much to Paul's anger. Paul's loss of such important support may have influenced his departure on his next mission. Paul's letters show that in the churches he evangelizes (where Gentile Christians would have been the majority) his converts are not bound by Jewish food laws. In the area where James of Jerusalem has influence (Acts 15:23: Antioch, Syria, and Cilicia, where presumably Jewish Christians are the majority), the Gentiles are bound. The Jerusalem conference preserved *koinōnia* about the essential for conversion: Gentiles do not have to become Jews. However, that did not guarantee uniformity of lifestyle. Paul judges freedom from the food laws so important that he calls it an issue of gospel truth (Gal 2:14); apparently others do not think it that important.

Mission of Paul to the Ends of the Earth (15:36–28:31)

The second half of Acts now becomes almost exclusively the story of Paul. The dispute over food laws is not discussed. Rather we hear of a wide range of travel that will twice bring Paul as far as Corinth in Greece and cover the years AD 50–58. More than likely during that period Paul wrote most of his preserved undisputed correspondence. The combination of the Jerusalem decision that enabled churches freely to accept Gentiles and the Antioch dispute that threw Paul more on his own seems to have catalyzed the most creative time of Paul's life.

1. From Antioch through Asia Minor to Greece and Return (15:36–18:22). In the Antioch dispute, Barnabas and John Mark may well have accepted the position demanded by the men from James; for Acts, which is silent about the struggle between Paul and Peter, reports *Paul's quarrel with Barnabas and Mark* (*15:36–39*), so that they could no longer travel together. Consequently *Paul takes Silas as he sets out on another mission* (*15:40–41*),[74] the first part of which brings him through Syria and his native Cilicia. Next *Paul revisits Lystra and Derbe* (*16:1–5*). That visit is the occasion of the circumcision of Timothy, the historicity of which is questioned by schol-

[73]Gal 2:12. Scholars are divided on whether the men from James included Judas and Silas bringing the letter mentioned in Acts. Although Acts 15:25,30 would seem to have Paul and Barnabas carry the letter to Antioch, some ten years later Acts 21:25 has James tell Paul about the letter as if it were news to him.

[74]It is customary to detect in Acts three Pauline missionary journeys, with one journey (AD 46–49) before the Jerusalem conference and two after it (AD 50–52, 54–58—traditional dating; Table 6 below); and when it serves, we shall use that rubric. It is unlikely, however, that Paul understood his missionary life to be so neatly divided; and indeed it is uncertain that the author of Acts made such a division, for it is easy to look on everything from 15:40 to 21:17 as one long journey. What is certain is that, after the Jerusalem decision, Acts describes Paul's major missionary activity as ranging much farther than his first missionary effort.

ars who think it inconceivable that Paul would have changed his stance on circumcision even to win converts. However, if Timothy was looked on as a Jew, there is no clear evidence that Paul would have wanted Jewish Christians to give up circumcision (n. 55 above).

Paul's moves on through Phrygia and Galatia to Troas (*16:6–10*). In the latter site he receives a vision of the man of Macedonia pleading for help that causes him to cross over to Greece. This is seen by the author of Acts as a divinely inspired moment. (The "we" form of narrative begins at Troas and continues through the crossover to Philippi; thus the author's personal participation may have increased his appreciation of the moment—see *Authorship* below.) The spread of Christian faith to Macedonia (and thus to Europe, although Acts does not highlight the continent) is presented almost as manifest destiny; and in retrospect the tremendous contributions of two thousand years of European Christianity could justify that judgment. Far more than the author of Acts dreamed, the appeal of the man of Macedonia ultimately brought Christianity to ends of the earth that in the 1st century were not even known to exist.[75]

The evangelizing at Philippi (*16:11–40*) shows us some of the best and the worst of a mission among Gentiles. The generous openness and support of Lydia,[76] a Gentile devotee of Jewish worship, is a model for the Christian household. On the other hand, the legal and financial problems presented by the girl who had a spirit of divination remind us that Paul was dealing with an alien, superstitious world. As the account continues, the miraculous opening of the prison echoes scenes of Peter's miraculous release from prison and shows that God is with his emissary to the Gentiles. The complexity of Paul's trial because he is a Roman citizen illustrates how the early Christians, in order to survive, had to use every available means, including Roman law. The "we" form of narrative ceases as Paul leaves Philippi, and so it is possible that the anonymous companion stayed there seven years till Paul came back to Philippi (20:6; AD 51–58).

At Thessalonica (*17:1–9*) Paul runs into the same kind of Jewish opposition that marred his mission in Asia Minor before the Jerusalem conference. The list of charges against Paul and his supporters in 17:6–7 resembles the list of charges against Jesus before Pilate in Luke 23:2—a list found only in Luke. We shall see other resemblances between the treatment of Jesus and

[75]Some on other continents who were evangelized from Europe complain that they were indoctrinated with an alien culture. Yet Europeanization would probably have happened in any case; and the fact that the cross of Christ was planted alongside the banner of the respective king was potentially a helpful corrective—both to abuses that existed before Europeans came (that are sometimes forgotten) and to the abuses they brought.

[76]Compare the support of the Galilean women for Jesus in Luke 8:3. See D. L. Matson, *Household Conversion Narratives in Acts* (JSNTSup 123; Sheffield: Academic, 1996).

the treatment of Paul, a parallelism that fitted the theology of Luke-Acts. Forced by Jewish opposition *Paul goes on to Beroea* (*17:10–14*), where in an interesting gesture of evenhandedness the author tells us that the Jews were nobler and less contentious.

Yet the Jews from Thessalonica follow, and so *Paul pushes on to Athens* (*17:15–34*). Just as the author of Acts exhibited a sense of destiny when Paul crossed to Europe, he shows an appreciation of what Athens meant to Greek culture in recounting Paul's stay there. He supplies a dramatic context of Epicurean and Stoic philosophers (17:18)[77] who try to fit this new teaching into their categories. The author knows about the agora or public square (17:17) and the hill of the Areopagus (17:19); he phrases the sermon delivered there in quality Greek and has it show an awareness of the many temples and statues of the city. The play on the altar to an unknown god and the philosophical and poetic quotations offer a cultured approach to the message about Christ, quite unlike the gambits of the other sermons in Acts. The master-touch in the scene may be the reaction to this eloquence from the cosmopolitan audience: Some mock; others put Paul off; some believe.[78] Paul will go from here directly to Corinth, and in I Cor 2:1–2 he describes what may have been a lesson learned: "When I came to you proclaiming the mystery of God, I did not come with lofty words or wisdom. For I decided to know nothing among you except Jesus Christ and him crucified."

Paul's stay at Corinth (*18:1–18*) has an added interest: From there Paul writes I Thess, our oldest preserved Christian writing; and he would direct much later correspondence to Corinth, causing us to know more about that Pauline church than any other. Aquila and Priscilla (Prisca), whom he meets there, will feature later in Paul's correspondence and career. (Acts consistently uses the name Priscilla; Paul consistently uses Prisca.) They had come from Rome (probably already as Christians) and will eventually go back and be part of Paul's contacts ("co-workers in Christ Jesus") with Rome before he ever arrives there (Rom 16:3). We can see Paul forming a circle of colleagues and friends who would be in contact with him all his life (Chapter

[77]B. Gärtner, *The Areopagus Speech and Natural Revelation* (Uppsala Univ., 1955).

[78]A moment's reflection on three major cities is worthwhile. Athens was the center of culture, philosophy, and art; Paul's message had only limited success there, and we are told of no other early mission to that city. Alexandria was the center of learning with its magnificent library tradition; the eloquent preacher Apollos came from there (Acts 18:24), but otherwise (and despite later legends) we know of no pre-70 Christian missionary activity there. Rome was the seat of imperial power and ruled the world. There was a successful Christian mission in the capital by the 40s; Paul could address plural house churches there before 60; various NT writings are thought to have been addressed to or sent by the church of Rome; and ultimately Peter and Paul would die there. Why greater attention to Rome? Evidently early Christians were realists: Neither Athens the museum nor Alexandria the library could sway the world, and so the powerful city that did was a more fruitful target.

17 C below). The reference to tentmaking at the beginning of Paul's stay at Corinth reminds us of the indication in his letters that he normally supported himself and did not ask his hearers for personal financial help (also Acts 20:33–35). Once again we see Jewish hostility, so that Paul is brought before the tribunal of the Roman proconsul Gallio—a figure whose presence at Corinth supplies a most important key for dating Paul's mission there to AD 51–52 (p. 433 below). The unwillingness of the Roman official to get involved in Jewish religious questions is part of the general picture of the pre-Nero period when Rome was not yet hostile to Christians as such. The *return from Corinth to Antioch* (*18:19–22*) is compacted into a brief (and somewhat confusing) account, as Paul passes through Ephesus, Caesarea, and Jerusalem (the "church" of 18:22?) en route.

2. From Antioch to Ephesus and Greece, and Return to Caesarea (18:23–21:14). After a while *Paul sets out from Antioch through Galatia and Phrygia* (*18:23*). While Paul is en route, we are told of *the presence at Ephesus of Apollos from Alexandria* (*18:24–28*) and then at the beginning of *Paul's stay at Ephesus* (*19:1–40*[*41*]) of others, who believed in Jesus but had received only the baptism of John and knew nothing of the Holy Spirit. Little enlightenment is given about how such a situation could exist—were these evangelized by some who knew Jesus during the ministry but left Palestine before the crucifixion and resurrection?

Paul remains at Ephesus about three years.[79] Acts 19:11–19 piques our interest with portraits of Paul the miracle worker and of Jewish exorcists attempting to drive out evil spirits using the name of Jesus (cf. Luke 9:49–50). A struggle among those who appealed to Jesus plays large in much of the Pauline correspondence written from Ephesus (Gal? Phil? Phlm? I Cor). The refrain that "the word of the Lord grew" (Acts 19:20; cf. 6:7; 12:24) signals that, alongside Jerusalem and Antioch, Christianity now has another major center, Ephesus, and that Paul's ministry has been blessed even as was the ministry of the Twelve. Acts 19:21 is the first indication of Paul's ultimate plan to go to Rome via Greece and Jerusalem, an important anticipation for how the book will end. There is a colorful account of the silversmiths' riot centered on Artemis or Diana of the Ephesians (19:23–40[41]) that terminates Paul's stay.

Briefly recounted are *Paul's travels through Macedonia to Greece* (*20:1–3a*), i.e., Corinth, where he stays three months. (In this period, AD 57–58, he writes II Cor before he gets to Corinth, and Rom from Corinth.) Then *he*

[79]Three months in 19:8, plus two years in 19:10; plus added time in 19:21ff. = "three years" of 20:31? From here he seems to have written Gal, Phil, Phlm, and I Cor. Some would detect a deliberate change of missionary style—radiating out from a steady base of operations rather than frenetically moving on after a few weeks in each place.

goes back through Macedonia and Philippi (*20:3b–6*). The "we" form of narrative resumes as Paul crosses from Philippi *to Troas where he raises the dead to life* (*20:7–12*), even as Peter raised Tabitha in Joppa (9:36–42). It would be of interest to know if Paul's breaking bread in 20:11 means that he presided at the eucharist. Hastening on to be at Jerusalem for Pentecost (AD 58), *Paul sails along the Asia Minor coast to Miletus bypassing Ephesus* (*20:13–16*).

At Miletus he gives *an eloquent farewell sermon to the presbyters of the church of Ephesus* (*20:17–38*). It has great value as a guide to how the author of Acts sees the presbyters (cf. 14:23 above) who inherit the care of the church from Paul. In the Pastoral Epistles there is information suggesting that (presumably after going to Rome and being released from prison) Paul came back to Asia Minor in the mid 60s. Acts betrays no knowledge of this, so that the sermon constitutes Paul's final directives to those whom he will never see again (20:25,38).[80] It begins with an *apologia pro vita sua* (20:18–21) as Paul reflects on how he has served the Lord; this yields to foreboding about the imprisonment and afflictions he must now undergo. This man who first encountered the profession of Christ in Jerusalem some twenty years before at the trial and stoning of Stephen is being led by the Spirit to return to that city where he will be put on trial amidst cries for his death (see 22:22). In this portentous context Paul admonishes the presbyters he is leaving behind to be shepherds of the flock in which the Holy Spirit has made them overseers.[81] As we can see from I Peter 5:1–4, the comparison of the presbyters to shepherds of the flock was well established in the late 1st century. Although that image reflects authority, the real emphasis is on the obligation to take care of the flock and not let it be ravaged—in short, what we mean by "*pastoral* care," a terminology derived from shepherding. The most pressing danger to be faced, as also in the Pastoral Epistles, is false teaching: "those who speak perverse things so as to draw away disciples" (Acts 20:30). Paul stresses that he supported himself, coveting no one's silver and gold (20:33–35), and indeed elsewhere the NT advice to presbyters warns against a corrupting love of money (I Peter 5:2; Titus 1:7; I Timothy 3:3), an enduring temptation since the presbyters managed the common funds.

After this farewell at Miletus, the return journey to Palestine continues, bringing *Paul to Tyre* (*Acts 21:1–6*) and another dramatic farewell, and then

[80]This portion of Acts resembles the context of the Pastoral Epistles where the time of Paul's departure has come (II Timothy 4:6–8). In fact both Acts and the Pastorals (in that order) were most likely written after Paul's death. Many scholars think that, of the existing correspondence, Rom was the last letter actually written by Paul and contains his final preserved thoughts.

[81]20:28: pl. of *episkopos,* literally "one who oversees," which is the Greek word for bishop. Once more we are close to the atmosphere of the Pastorals where there are groups of presbyter-bishops in the postPauline churches, i.e., presbyters who oversee the community's life and teaching.

on to Caesarea (*21:7–14*). There at the home of Philip the Hellenist and his four daughter-prophets, the prophet Agabus comes and by symbolism forewarns Paul of imprisonment. Thus Paul's road to Jerusalem and impending suffering echoes Jesus' journey to Jerusalem where he would be seized and put to death (Luke 9:51; 13:33).

3. Arrest in Jerusalem; Imprisonment and Trials in Caesarea (Acts 21:15–26:32). Clearly a climax is reached when *Paul goes up to Jerusalem* (*21:15–17*), where the "we" form of description comes to an end (21:18), not to be resumed until six chapters and two years later. *Paul is received by James and the elders* (*21:18–25*) and reports to them his success among the Gentiles. They match his claims with reports of their own successes among the Jews. Acts cannot disguise the negative feelings raised among the Jerusalem Christian authorities by (false) rumors about what Paul has been teaching.[82] The well-intentioned plan to have Paul show his loyalty to Judaism by purifying himself and going to the Temple (21:24) fails when *fanatics start a riot, claiming that he has defiled the holy place* (*21:26–30*) by bringing Gentiles into it. Paul is saved from the crowd only by *the intervention of a Roman tribune with soldiers* (*21:31–40*); but after being arrested, Paul protests in Greek that he is a Roman citizen. He is allowed to speak in Aramaic to the crowd.

Paul's speech of defense (*22:1–21*) recounts his conversion and its aftermath with some variants from the original account in 9:1–30, e.g., cf. 9:7 and 22:9. *The speech produces conflict* (*22:22–29*): The crowd reacts violently, but Paul's Roman citizenship wins him the tribune's protection. The next day *Paul is brought before a Sanhedrin* (*22:30–23:11*). He arouses dissent between the Sadducees and Pharisees over the resurrection. (There are echoes here of Jesus' appearance before the Sanhedrin as well as his dealing with the Sadducees over the resurrection [Luke 20:27].) Even though the tribune rescues him from the violent melee, a vision of the Lord warns Paul that he will have to testify in Rome. Paul's nephew frustrates the *Jewish plot to kill Paul* (*Acts 23:12–22*), and *Paul is sent to Caesarea and the Roman prefect Felix* (*23:23–35*). The *trial of Paul before Felix* (*24:1–27*), who was procurator in Palestine between 52 and 60, has parallelism to the trial of Jesus before Pilate. The high priest and the Jewish elders present Felix with a list of charges (24:5–6) resembling those presented by the Sanhedrin of the chief priests and elders against Jesus (Luke 23:1–2). The self-understanding of Paul in Acts 24:14 is noteworthy: "I admit to you that according to the Way, which they call a sect, I worship the God of our fathers;

[82]We have no evidence that he taught "all the Jews who live among the Gentiles to forsake Moses" (21:21).

I believe everything conformable to the Law and written down in the prophets."[83] Interestingly we are told that Felix knew about the Way (24:22). Paul says that he brought alms to Jerusalem (24:17), indirectly confirming the many references in his letters to a collection for Jerusalem (especially Rom 15:25–28). Felix hopes for a bribe—Josephus confirms his venality—and Paul is left in prison[84] at Caesarea for two years (AD 58–60) until the end of Felix's procuracy.

Paul is interrogated by Festus (*25:1–12*), the next procurator who ruled in AD 60–62; but the prisoner refuses an offer to be tried in Jerusalem and appeals to Caesar. The author's sense of drama is caught in the lapidary Roman response (25:12): "You have appealed to Caesar; to Caesar you shall go." The parallelism to the Lucan trial of Jesus is heightened, because *Festus passes Paul to the Herodian king Agrippa II* (*25:13–26:32*) to be heard,[85] even as Pilate sent Jesus to Herod (Luke 23:7). Again the Herodian king finds the prisoner not guilty. For a third time Paul's conversion on the road to Damascus is recounted (Acts 26:9–20).

4. Journey to Rome as a Prisoner (27:1–28:14a). Once more employing the "we" format, Acts now recounts a long sea journey up the Syrian coast, over past Cyprus, along the southern coast of Asia Minor, across to the southern coast of Crete, and then amidst a great storm, to Malta, Sicily, and up the west coast of Italy, to a landing at Puteoli, near Naples. This journey probably began in the late summer of 60 and ended in 61. Survival from storm and snakebite illustrates God's care for Paul whose concern for companions on the ship and healings effected at Malta show that his missionary sense has not left him. Vivid details about the navigation and the various ships lend verisimilitude, although some scholars skeptically reject the whole as unhistorical.

5. Paul at Rome (28:14b–31). Paul's arrival after his long and treacherous sea journey is described in a portentous understatement, "And so we came to Rome" (28:14b). This is the ultimate step foreseen by the risen Jesus in 1:8: "You will be my witnesses in Jerusalem, all Judea and Samaria, and *to the end of the earth.*" By this time in the early 60s, Christian communities had been at Rome for about twenty years. But in the flow of the story that has centered on Peter and Paul, a climax comes with the arrival in the capital of the great missionary. Ironically Roman authorities have sent him there because of his appeal to the emperor and thus become responsible for the

[83]For the Way, see n. 21 above. Josephus lists three sects of the Jews (Pharisees, Sadducees, Essenes), and by the time Acts was written Christians may have been categorized as a sect.

[84]B. Rapske in TBAFC 3 (1994) gives an exhaustive treatment of how Paul would have been treated in Roman custody.

[85]R. F. O'Toole, *Acts 26* (AnBib 78; Rome: PBI, 1978).

evangelizing of their own Empire. To the very end Acts shows Paul appealing to the local Jews with the insistence that he has done nothing "against the customs of our fathers." Acts 28:21 is important: The author portrays the Jewish community in Jerusalem as being in close contact with the Jewish community in Rome (which may well be factual).[86] Paul's preaching about Jesus has no success; and the last words attributed to him in the book, despairing of a hearing from the Jews, firmly turn to the Gentiles who will listen.[87] The summary that ends Acts speaks of Paul's preaching for two years in Rome with success.

Sources and Compositional Features

Under this heading we shall consider the various elements that make up Acts: (a) Traditions and/or Sources; (b) Speeches; (c) Summaries.

(a) TRADITIONS AND/OR SOURCES. In Chapter 9 under *Sources* we saw that the Lucan evangelist not only acknowledged the fonts from whom tradition about Jesus came ("the original eyewitnesses and ministers of the word") but also used with reasonable fidelity written sources (Mark, Q). Some would contend that the author did not have similar controls in Acts and was much more creative and therefore fictional. Part of their argumentation is that, while stories about Jesus might be preserved, Christians would not be interested enough in the apostles or churches to preserve *early* stories about them that had a chance of being genuinely historical. (They allow that the author may have used the later traditions of the church of his own time filled with legendary accretions; see Haenchen, *Acts* 81–89.) Actually there is reasonable evidence in the uncontested Pauline writings to the contrary.[88] Moreover since the author indicates a consistency by dedicating both volumes of Luke-Acts to Theophilus, there is no reason to think that the tracing of everything carefully from the beginning promised by Luke 1:3 stopped with the Gospel. Accordingly the following questions are worth pursuing: What fonts did the evangelist have for traditions he included and developed in Acts? Did he have written or, at least, already shaped sources for Acts?

[86]That the Jews in Rome have heard nothing hostile about Paul is odd, since in writing to the Romans Paul seems to expect that when he comes he will find hostility from Christians who are particularly attached to Judaism. See BMAR 111–22.

[87]A number of scholars think that the author expected an ongoing mission to the Jews. True, there is no reason to think that preaching to Jews would be discontinued, but the climactic final judgment attributed to Paul does not prognosticate success.

[88]As J. Jervell and others have pointed out, what happened in one church was reported to other churches (I Thess 1:8–9; II Cor 3:2–3; Rom 1:8). Also there are references to the apostles and known church figures (I Cor 9:5; 15:5–7), to the church in Jerusalem and Judea (I Thess 2:14; Gal 2), and to the customs of all the churches (I Cor 14:33–34). Such references presume that audiences already know something about these figures and communities.

In discussing the Gospel of Luke, we saw that the fonts for some peculiar Lucan material (L) may have been people who appear in Acts, e.g., the Herod Antipas tradition from Manaen in Acts 13:1. On the assumption that the author was the companion of Paul in the "we" passages of Acts (see *Authorship* below), the report that in 21:8–10 "we entered the house of Philip the evangelist" and that Agabus came there has suggested that from one or both of these individuals came the stories about Philip and the Hellenists and Agabus in Acts 6:5; 8:5–40; 11:27–28. If the tradition is accurate that the author was Luke from Antioch, did he have contact there with Barnabas, who told him about Paul's "First Missionary Journey" made with Barnabas and Mark (Barnabas's cousin: Col 4:10)?[89]

Besides personal fonts of information, fixed sources have been proposed. Two factors have contributed to the various suggestions. (1) The diverse contents of Acts cover in chronological sequence (but with some overlapping) the activities of three different agents in three geographical areas, namely, the *apostles* in Jerusalem; the *Hellenists* who were eventually driven out of Jerusalem and had a role in developing the church in Antioch; and finally *Paul* whose missions beginning from Antioch go west to "the end of the earth." (2) Doublets (e.g., chaps. 4 and 5) have been detected in the first half of Acts and explained as the product of the interweaving of two sources. Accordingly a typical proposal[90] detects the following sources (with the first two interwoven):

Jerusalem (Caesarea, Palestine) Source: 1:6–2:40; 3:1–4:31; 4:36–5:11; 5:17–42; 8:5–40; 9:32–11:18; 12:1–23.
Antioch (Hellenist) Source: 6:1–6; 6:8–8:4; 11:19–30; 15:3–33.
Pauline Source: 9:1–30; 13:3–14:28; 15:35–28:31, including "we" passages (n. 98 below).

There is little evidence that the author of Acts was present for much of what he narrates (except the "we" passages), and little likelihood that he invented all of it; and so he must have had at his disposal information or traditions. But had such traditions already been shaped into sequential sources? The argument from style enters the discussion but scarcely resolves the problem. Some detect a strongly Semitic style in the first half of Acts and use this

[89]See R. Glover, NTS 11 (1964–65), 97–106. The author was at Troas when the "we" passages begin (Acts 16:11), but it is not impossible that he had come there from Antioch.

[90]My description draws on Fitzmyer, JBC 45.6. For a thorough survey see Dupont, *Sources.* Probably the most widely proposed is an Antioch source. In the complicated textual theory of the French scholars Boismard and Lamouille (n. 110 below) the now-lost original edition of Acts drew on a highly historical source, composed in Palestine *ca.* 50, in which *Peter* was the main figure. Then from earlier material the author of that edition (a Jewish Christian) composed the travels of *Paul.*

as a proof for a Jerusalem source.[91] Yet stylistic arguments are not overly convincing, for this author is capable of archaizing when he is describing a story that has a decidedly Jewish setting[92]—in this instance Palestine as contrasted with the Gentile areas to the west that will frame the narrative to follow. Moreover, other scholars find marks of Lucan style and vocabulary in the various sections of Acts, so that whether the author used loose traditions or fixed sources, he would have rewritten the material he took over. By way of summary this observation may be made: *Nothing like the wide agreement on the Gospel's use of the sources Mark and Q exists for Acts' use of sources.* Whether Acts drew on traditions or sources, a fundamental issue remains: What is the historical value of the final account? That will be discussed below under *"Luke" the Historian.*

(b) SPEECHES. Roughly one third of Acts consists of speeches, made principally by Peter, Stephen, Paul, and James.[93] Instead of describing in the third person the significance of something that is happening, Acts prefers to offer a speech where one of the main characters explains that significance. Why does Acts adopt this technique? Some regard it simply as a Hellenistic literary device to make the narrative more interesting and vivid. More precisely it has been regarded as a device of ancient historiographers who composed speeches that could serve as appropriate commentaries and put them on the lips of famous men. Thucydides, *History* 1.22.1, says that, although he kept as close as possible to the general sense of the words that were said, he had the speakers say what was in his view called for by the situation.[94] Does that point to a possible combination of a memory of what was said and of the historian's own interpretative imagination? In the case of Acts, once more we must recognize that (if we can judge from the limits of the "we" passages) the author of Acts himself was not present when many of these speeches were supposed to have been made.

More conservative interpreters have suggested that important speeches would have been memorized by the speaker's disciples who *were* present, so

[91]Drawing on syntactical evidence, R. A. Martin, NTS 11 (1964–65), 38–59, argues for Aramaic sources in Acts 1–15.

[92]See, for example, the Semitized style of the infancy narratives because the figures there are the first Jews to encounter Jesus.

[93]The number of speeches is counted between twenty-four and twenty-eight. They have been studied in the past by such distinguished scholars as Cadbury, *Making* 184–93 and Dibelius, *Studies* 138–85; and an excellent summary and reexamination are presented by M. L. Soards, *The Speeches in Acts* (Louisville: W/K, 1994).

[94]Lucian of Samosata, *How To Write History* 58: "If some one has to be brought in to give a speech, above all let his language suit his person and his subject . . . It is then, however, that you can exercise your rhetoric and show your eloquence." Most moderns would regard this process as not truly historical, but evidently Lucian thought it was reconcilable with what he wrote earlier (*How* 39): "The sole task of the historian is to tell it just as it happened."

that we could have substantially what was said. Others think that there was no real memory so that the speeches are virtually pure Lucan creation. Still others opt for different approaches to different speeches in Acts. For instance, Paul's speeches that are custom-designed for an occasion[95] might have been free compositions by the author of Acts interpreting the mind of the great missionary. On the other hand, the somewhat stereotyped kerygmatic speeches of Peter (2:14–36; 3:12–26; 4:8–12; 5:29–32; 10:34–43), and of Paul (13:16–41), who speaks in the same way that Peter does, may have been shaped in Acts from memories of an early apostolic preaching style. As we saw, Stephen's speech is almost unique in outlook and emphases, and some have used this as proof that Acts must have drawn on tradition even in the nonkerygmatic discourses. Whatever the derivation of the material in the speeches, no appeal to purely literary and historiographic conventions does sufficient justice to how the speeches serve to develop the theological thrust of Acts. The progress of Christian insight into God's plan of history finds expression in them, and on that I concentrated in the *General Analysis* above.

(c) SUMMARIES. In the Gospel Luke used and developed some of Mark's summaries as well as adding his own. The account of activities at Jerusalem in Acts uses summaries (2:42–47; 4:32–35; 5:11–16; 6:7) in order to portray the growth and sanctity of the community in its golden age, and mark off steps in the development of the action. Later in the book the latter function is served by one-sentence summaries (9:31; 12:24; 16:5; 19:20; 28:30–31). This effort for transitions enhances the readability of Acts as a smooth-flowing narrative. Some of the summaries involve the author's knowledge of the early Jerusalem Christians. Let us now consider how accurate such knowledge was.

"Luke" the Historian

Our brief analysis of compositional features has pointed to the abilities of the author as theologian and narrator, but left open the very disputed question of his role as historian. Since he starts his two-volume work by talking about an orderly account based on a word passed down from original eyewitnesses, and about tracing everything from the beginning and writing systematically (Luke 1:1–3), by any standard the question of history is appropriate. Yet, no matter what he learned from others about Jesus, how much did the

[95]Acts 17:22–31: on the Areopagus; 20:18–35: at Miletus; 22:3–21: at Jerusalem; 24:10–21: before Felix; 26:1–23: before King Agrippa; and 28:17–20,25–29: to the Jews of Rome.

author know about the early Jerusalem church, about the spread of Christianity, and about Paul? Estimates of his knowledge are reflected in evaluations of Acts ranging from almost purely fictive to remarkably accurate.[96]

Before entering the details of the discussion, all should recognize and admit that Acts' reports are highly selective chronologically and geographically. A reasonable estimate is that a three-year span is covered between chaps. 1 and 8, and almost twenty-five years between chaps. 9 and 28. The incidents narrated in that span of time are few indeed. In concentrating on the Jerusalem Christians and the transition to Antioch, Acts does not tell us when and how the followers of Jesus spread to Damascus (9:2). The author has information about Paul's travels to the west; but he reports nothing about the spread of Christian missionaries to eastern Syria or North Africa, or the initial evangelizing of Rome itself (yet see n. 12 above). Thus even if everything he reports should emerge as accurate historically, it would be a sketchy account.

How much did the author of Acts know about the early Jerusalem and Antioch churches? Since there is no other detailed source for this period, there is much that we can never verify, e.g., about the harassment of Peter and John by the priestly authorities, the existence and martyrdom of Stephen, and the killing of James, son of Zebedee, by Herod Agrippa. (It would, however, take a dedicated skeptic to assume that all such events are fictional.) Two elements that can contribute to an intelligent evaluation of historicity are the determination of *plausibility* through what we know from elsewhere of the Jewish and Christian scenes, and the detection of *provable errors* in what is affirmed. As for judging plausibility we must make allowance for the author's desire to confirm the faith of Theophilus. There is no doubt, for instance, that he romanticizes the early Christian picture at Jerusalem in terms of the rapidity and numbers of conversions, the saintliness of the life, the generosity in giving up possessions, and the single-mindedness. Implicitly he admits this simplification when by way of exception he tells us the stories of the deceptive Ananias and Sapphira, and of the division between the Hebrews and the Hellenists. If one allows for such romanticization and simplification, however, the picture of the values, actions, and organization of an early apocalyptically minded Jewish Christian community is quite plausible when tested by comparable elements in the Dead Sea Scrolls com-

[96]Gasque, *History,* is a good survey. Opposite poles in the earlier critical approach to Acts were represented by F. C. Baur (who saw Acts as a 2d-century compromise between the Gentile followers of Paul and the Judaizing followers of Peter) and W. M. Ramsay (who presented his geographical and archaeological studies of Asia Minor as confirming the historicity of Acts). In the early 1900s strong arguments for historicity were advanced by the liberal church historian, A. (von) Harnack (*Luke*), and by the German classical historian, E. Meyer.

munity. In terms of NT parallels, the importance given to Peter and John among the Twelve receives confirmation from Gal 2:9, even as Peter as the chief missionary evangelist among the Twelve is confirmed by Gal 2:7; I Cor 9:5. As we saw, many scholars analyze the dispute between the Hebrews and the Hellenists in Acts 6 in terms of adherence to the Temple. If so, the Acts picture that it was not the Twelve who evangelized Samaria, but those who had no loyalty to the Jerusalem Temple, may find some confirmation in John 4:23,37–38.

As for provable errors, the most obvious ones are in Palestinian history rather than in Christian history. Whether or not, perhaps for antiSadducee reasons, Gamaliel the elder advocated some tolerance toward the early followers of Jesus (Acts 5:34–39) we cannot know, but his speech is probably for the most part a Lucan creation. Luke 2:2, combined with 1:5, is inaccurate about the date of the census of Quirinius; and there is a similar inaccuracy in Acts 5:37 about the revolt of Judas the Galilean directed against that census (n. 33 above). By the time Acts was written, the Roman cohort Italica was in Syria and could be used when needed in Caesarea; it is not impossible that 10:1 is anachronistic in positing its presence there *ca.* 39. But such minor inaccuracies do not mean that we can dismiss the general historicity of Acts' portrayal of early Christianity, any more than inaccuracies in Josephus and the discrepancies between his *Ant.* and *War* entitle us to dismiss his general historicity.

How much did the author of Acts know about Paul's missionary travels? A large part of this discussion will take place under the subheading *Authorship* below in terms of whether the author could have been a companion of Paul for a limited period of time covered by the "we" passages. (There the author's portrait of Paul's relationship to Jerusalem and his knowledge of Pauline theology will be compared to Paul's self-expression in the letters.) Here we are interested in the facts of Paul's journeys. Long ago the British scholars J. B. Lightfoot and W. M. Ramsay pointed to the extraordinary accuracy of Acts' knowledge of the widely differing titles of municipal and imperial officials in the various towns visited (e.g., 13:12; 17:6; 18:12; 19:31,35)—an accuracy often proved by datable inscriptions discovered in the respective sites. Overall the book is also accurate about the boundaries and alignments of districts and provinces in the 50s. These observations are a major factor in challenging the thesis that Acts was fiction written in the mid-2d century, for by that late date even a meticulous researcher would have been hard put to be accurate about such details. Also much of what Acts tells us correlates very well with what we can determine from Paul's own letters (Table 5 in Chapter 16 below).

Given that he was not an eyewitness of what he narrates and that he is highly selective, the author of Acts does not get bad grades for historical accuracy in the various sections of his book. Though he wrote more in a biblical style than in a classical history style, it is not ridiculous to think that the author might have been a fitting candidate for membership in the brotherhood of Hellenistic historians, even if he would never be made president of the society. Yet in evaluating Luke the historian it is worth remembering that this author who never called his Gospel a gospel never calls his Acts a history. He thought of both as *diēgēsis,* "narrative."[97] In Acts the narrative he recounts is primarily intended to give believers assurance (Luke 1:4) and strengthen them with theological insight. Therefore, whatever history Acts preserves is put to the service of theology and pastoral preaching.

Authorship

In the subsection on *Authorship* in Chapter 9 above we saw the reasonable possibility that the Lucan evangelist was a Gentile (a Syrian from Antioch?) who was converted or attracted to Judaism some years before he was evangelized by Christian preachers. From Acts the detail that he was a companion of Paul has been added both by early church tradition and internal analysis. This is all related to several interconnected assumptions: The "we" passages[98] are historical; only two people were covered by that "we" (Paul and an unnamed companion); and the author of Acts was the "we" companion. Let us look at these assumptions.

There is no major reason to doubt that the "we" passages are historical in the general sense that Paul made the journeys involved. But was there a specific companion who accompanied him (and therefore knew details), or is "we" simply a literary convention in shipboard journeys? In an oft-cited article V. K. Robbins[99] offered examples of "we" used in such sea travels in contemporary Greco-Roman literature. However, Fitzmyer has examined the examples and found them wanting;[100] and it is far from clear that they explain satisfactorily the usage of Acts. If "we" is purely conventional, why does

[97]Fitzmyer, *Luke* 1.17. Pervo, *Profit,* stressing that Acts presents an edifying message in entertaining garb, would argue that the proper classification of Acts among ancient writings would be the popular novel. That is a good classification for some of the apocryphal *Acts,* but does it do justice to the solid historical content of canonical Acts? In the classification of modern literature some "historical novels" contain highly reliable facts woven together on a simplified storyline.

[98]They are 16:10–17 ("Second Missionary Journey," from Troas to Philippi); 20:5–15; 21:1–18 (end of the "Third Missionary Journey," from Philippi to Jerusalem); 27:1–28:16 (Paul sent as a prisoner from Caesarea to Rome).

[99]BR 20 (1975), 5–18; reprinted in Talbert, *Perspectives* 215–42.

[100]*Luke Theologian* 16–22. For instance, some are in the first person singular, not plural, and therefore simply autobiographical; in many parts of the narrative, not simply in journeys, some use a "we" that is only slightly different from an editorial "we."

this pronominal usage not appear throughout all the sea-journeying in Acts instead of in only a few sections separated by years in the narrative? Moreover, in the first "we" passage (Acts 16:10–17), Paul is on land at Philippi in all but two verses. (See also 20:7–12; 21:15–18 within the second and third "we" passages.) Finally, one could argue that "we" in Acts should be related to the "us" of Luke 1:1–2, which has nothing to do with a sea voyage.

A simpler explanation regards the "we" as autobiographical, so that the "we" passages constitute a type of diary describing moments when the writer was with Paul. Normally, then, it would follow that the writer of the diary was the author of the whole Book of Acts, especially since the general style and interests of the "we" passages are those found elsewhere in the book. Nevertheless, scholars who cannot reconcile the picture of Paul in Acts with the "real" Paul revealed by his own letters have proposed that the author got the diary of a true companion of Paul and included sections of it at appropriate moments in the narrative he built around them. Before resorting to such a cumbersome solution we need to examine how irreconcilable Acts and the Pauline letters really are.

Acts gives information about *Paul's early life.* He was from Tarsus and his name was Saul. He was reared and studied in Jerusalem and seemingly did not come there alone, for in 23:16 we find the son of Paul's sister at Jerusalem. Acts recounts that after Paul's conversion he went back to Tarsus (9:30) only to come later to Antioch (11:25–26), but tells us nothing of Paul's life or activities there. Most of this goes beyond information in Paul's letters without contradicting it, although Paul's upbringing in Jerusalem rather than in Tarsus is disputed (Chapter 16 below).

The real challenge to the author's being identified as the "we" companion relates to his knowledge of *Paul's theology and career as a missionary for Christ.* In the preceding subsection on *"Luke" the historian,* we saw that Acts fared reasonably well in the context of ancient historiography. Nevertheless, on the grounds that a true companion would have been very accurate, discrepancies that can be detected between Acts and the Pauline letters are emphasized by those who would challenge the author's identity. In such challenges sometimes a discrepancy is unwarrantedly magnified into a contradiction. For instance, Conzelmann (*Acts* xlv) misstates the evidence: "Luke denies the apostolic title even to Paul." Acts 14:14 speaks of "the apostles Barnabas and Paul." That reference (also 14:4) is often dismissed on the (unprovable) grounds that here Acts means apostles of the church of Antioch, somehow a lesser title. (Would the readers be led by the narrative of Acts to suspect that?) But even were that so, Conzelmann's "denies" is inappropriate, for the evidence shows only that in the usage of Luke-Acts "apostles" normally means the Twelve (which was probably the common usage in the last part of the 1st century, e.g., Matt 10:2; Rev 21:14). There is no sign that this is a conscious rejection of Paul's own usage—it is scarcely a denigration of Paul, who is the exalted hero of the whole second half of Acts.

Nevertheless, when we leave aside exaggerations, there are still significant discrepancies. Major examples involve Acts' account of Paul's return to Jerusalem after his conversion *ca.* AD 36, and Paul's acceptance of the food purity rules after the Jerusalem meeting of 49 (see pp. 298, 308–9 above). Also the author of Acts betrays no knowledge of the Pauline letters[101] and is silent about many of the principal theological themes stressed in those letters. In a famous article, P. Vielhauer[102] argued that Luke-Acts' natural theology, view of obedience to the Mosaic Law, christology (no preexistent or cosmic Christ), and eschatology (not imminent) are different from Paul's. However, others disagree and find no contradictions.[103] At least one should not overlook similarities. The eucharistic formula in Luke 22:19–20 is very close to that in I Cor 11:23–25. That the first appearance of the risen Lord was to Simon Peter is suggested by Luke 24:34 and I Cor 15:5. The picture of Paul in Acts as one who performs miracles is confirmed by II Cor 12:12; Rom 15:18–19. As for differences, even if in general Acts does not emphasize the theme of justification and prefers forgiveness of sins, 13:38–39 speaks of both and maintains that justification comes by belief in Christ rather than by observance of the Law (see also 5:18–19). The basic christology of Jesus as God's Son as phrased in Acts 13:33 is not far from Rom 1:3–4. The natural theology of being able to recognize God from creation is shared by Acts 17:24–30 and Rom 1:19–21; 2:15. Acts certainly puts emphasis on Christ's continuity with the salvation-history of Israel that is hard to reconcile with Paul's radical, apocalyptic understanding of the newness of Christ as expressed in Gal,[104] but not irreconcilable with the picture in Rom 9–11.

Fitzmyer, who thinks Acts was probably written by Luke, points out that

[101]Although this is widely held, see Walker "Acts"; also M. D. Goulder, PRS 13 (1986), 97–112, who argues that Luke knew I Cor and I Thess.

[102]"On the Paulinism of Acts," SLA 33–50 (German orig. 1950–51). Much of his argument uses as a standard of judgment the theology of Gal, Rom, and I-II Cor. K. P. Donfried, TTC 3–26, maintains that the theology of Acts' Paul is quite close to that reflected in I Thess—a Paul still influenced by what he learned at Antioch in Syria and before his stance on justification was sharpened by the later polemic (Gal) against Jewish Christian missionaries who insisted on circumcision and justification through observance of the works of the Mosaic Law.

[103]Gärtner, *Areopagus;* P. Borgen, CBQ 31 (1969), 169–82. Mattill, *Luke,* denies that the author believed that the end was imminent. A large group of scholars would contend that the emphasis in Acts 1:7 points to a theologian who maintained that one does not know when the end will come—an outlook that is reconcilable with alternating between hoping that it will come soon and thinking that it may be delayed. Also see *Issue* 4 in Chapter 9 above.

[104]Fitzmyer, *Luke* 1.21, may be too optimistic: "By casting the primitive Christian message in terms of salvation-history rather than as apocalyptic Luke has again merely played the message in a different key."

the "we" companion was with Paul only at certain times.[105] The "we" references begin at Troas on the "Second Missionary Journey" *ca.* 50; therefore the "we" companion might have had only imprecise knowledge of earlier events. The first "we" passage breaks off after the companion and Paul have gone from Troas to Philippi, and the next picks up when Paul sails from Philippi (20:5) on his way back to Palestine in 58. We are left to surmise that the "we" companion stayed in Philippi for the whole of the intervening period of some seven years (while Paul travelled to Corinth, back to Palestine and Antioch, came to Ephesus and stayed there for a long time, and went to Corinth again). If he did, he was not with Paul during the sending of I Thess, Gal, Phil, Phlm, I-II Cor, and Rom (as dated by the more plausible reckoning—Table 6 in Chapter 16 below). That could explain why if the companion wrote Acts, he shows no knowledge of the letters or of the theology in them shaped by the situations Paul encountered.

There is much to be said for that argument; but as Fitzmyer recognizes, there remain problems. The *first problem* is with Paul's letter to the Philippians written when he was in prison—should not the "we" companion have known of that letter? There are three proposals for dating the writing: from *Ephesus* in 54–56, from *Caesarea* in Palestine in 58–60, and from *Rome* in 61–63. The "we" companion was with Paul in Palestine in 58–60 (but was he at Caesarea or did he stay in Jerusalem?); he went with Paul to Rome in 60–61 (but since the "we" passage ends in Acts 28:16, did he stay with Paul there for the two years described in 28:30?). Actually the best option may be that Phil was written from Ephesus in 54–56 (Chapter 20 below); but then, if the "we" companion was at Philippi from 50 to 58, he would have been there when the letter arrived. If he is Luke, why is he not mentioned in the letter?[106] On the other hand, of all the Pauline communities, the Philippians are the most caring for Paul's welfare, never forgetting to send him help in his activities (Phil 4:14–18) and imprisonment. Was that because one who had come there as a companion of Paul remained at Philippi, guiding that community and making certain that it did not forget the apostle who evangelized it? Could he be the "true yokemate/companion" of Phil 4:3?

The *second problem* revolves around the proposal that because the "we" companion was not with Paul between 50 and 58, he might not have known or at least been affected by the theology of the great debates reflected in the letters of that period. Yet the "we" companion traveled with Paul on long

[105] In this he contradicts what he regards as an exaggeration in Irenaeus, AH 3.14.1: "Luke was inseparable from Paul."

[106] Yet among the Philippian contacts only Epaphroditus, who had brought gifts to Paul, the two bickering women, Euodia and Syntyche, and Clement are mentioned by name in Phil, so that we are not dealing with a letter that gives an exhaustive list.

journeys after 58 and surely should have learned from him about the controversies and the theology developed in response. That objection loses some of its force, however, if Acts was written several decades after Paul's death when his struggles with Judaizers would have been a distant memory and no longer very relevant to the current scene. When Acts is evaluated, some differences from Paul's letters may stem, not from the author's ignorance of Paul's mind, but from his stressing what he deems more appropriate for another generation. Could he, for instance, have known about Paul's difficulties with the Corinthian Christians (reflected in four or more letters and a reprimanding visit) but have chosen to remain silent so as not to scandalize his readers? Or again, if he was familiar with Paul's confidence that all Israel would be saved by coming to Christ (expressed in Rom 11:25–26 in AD 57/58), now twenty-five years later he may have felt that such optimism was no longer justified (Acts 28:25–28). Was it dishonest for Acts to adapt Paul to the later situation by putting a different outlook on his lips? That question assumes that Paul had only one view on the issue—an assumption rendered suspect by the variety of positions attested in the undisputed letters. Was Paul always optimistic about the future of evangelism among the Jews, or rather was not Rom fine-tuned to a community that had loyalty to Judaism? May not the author of Acts have been stressing a more pessimistic vein of Pauline thought (perhaps a minor one) with which he agreed? One may surmise that ancient writers would often have been astounded by what modern analysts see as contradictions.

In summary, it is *not impossible* that a minor figure who had traveled with Paul for small parts of his ministry wrote Acts decades after the apostle was dead, if one makes the allowance that there were details about Paul's early life he did not know, that he simplified and reordered information (even as he did in the Gospel what he took over material from Mark), and that as a true theologian he rethought some of Paul's emphases that were no longer apropos. We have no way of being certain that he was Luke, as affirmed by 2d-century tradition; but there is no serious reason to propose a different candidate. Luke is mentioned only once in the nondisputed letters of Paul (Phlm 24) and twice in the deuteroPaulines (Col 4:14; II Tim 4:11), and so he was scarcely the most obvious Pauline character upon whom to fasten as a fictional author.[107] There is nothing to contradict's Luke's having been with Paul in the places and times indicated by the "we" passages, and he fits the profile of a minor figure. This proposal for authorship has more to recom-

[107]Since some of the best known Pauline companions, like Timothy and Titus, were elsewhere during one or the other of the time periods involved, they can be eliminated. Occasionally it has been suggested that Luke was fastened on because Acts ends in Rome, and according to II Tim 4:11, written from Rome, Luke would have been the only companion with Paul there.

mend it than other theories, but "not impossible" is all that should be claimed.

Issues and Problems for Reflection

(1) Acts has a textual problem more acute than that of any other NT book. We saw in treating Luke (Chapter 9, *Issue 1*) that the Western family of textual witnesses has a shorter reading in eight or more verses. In Acts, however, Western textual witnesses have a Greek Text of the book one-tenth *longer* than the Egyptian or Alexandrian textual tradition![108] (Detachment of Acts from Luke may have led to a different textual history.) The extra material includes phrases, clauses, and whole verses; see 13:27; 15:29; 18:27; 19:1; and 28:31 (Fitzmyer, JBC 45.7). From the ms. and patristic evidence alone, one cannot decide which is the older. The majority view treats the Eastern text as more original, and the Western text as paraphrastic, reflecting copyists' additions of religiously enriching glosses (as in 6:8; 7:55), clarifications (as in 15:34; 16:35–40), and intensified views.[109] Yet there are reasons for dissent: Extra data included in the Western text match the style of the rest of the text, are often neutral, and at times seem to indicate additional accurate knowledge (see 12:10; 19:9; 20:15; and 28:16). To meet the problem most have resorted to a theory of two different editions of Acts (rather than simply tinkering by copyists). Variations of the two-edition theory are (a) Luke did them both, with either the Eastern text as a second, more polished effort, or the Western as a second, expanded effort; (b) A second scribe produced the Western text by glossing the first with notes that Luke left behind; (c) The Western was the original edition, while a shortened edition was produced in the 2d century for wider circulation, or to offer a work of greater polish; (d) An original edition of Acts is no longer preserved; it can be reconstructed from the Western text whose author used it as his principal source; another author produced the Eastern text by revising the Western text in light of the original text to which he had independent access.[110] What-

[108]The latter is most purely represented by Codex Vaticanus, while the most prominent Western witnesses are the Greco-Latin Codex Bezae, a North African Latin version, and a Syriac version (Harclean). Barrett, *Acts* 1.2–29 gives a detailed and balanced discussion of the textual evidence. Most Western readings can be found in the notes to the translation offered in Foakes Jackson, *Beginnings,* vol. 4. It is debated whether there was a single Western text or only Western readings, and whether Irenaeus knew the Western textual tradition *ca.* 180.

[109]E. J. Epp, *The Theological Tendency of Codex Bezae Cantabrigiensis in Acts* (SNTSMS 3; Cambridge Univ., 1966), finds an increased antiJewish tendency in the Western text.

[110]This is the thesis of M.-É. Boismard and A. Lamouille, who beginning in 1984 produced a spectacularly detailed multivolumed French study, summarized by J. Taylor "Making." The author of the Western text is proposed as the one who divided Luke-Acts into two volumes, supplying a preface to each.

ever the solution, most commentaries are based on the shorter, Eastern text.

(2) In terms of God's final establishment of the kingdom (and of the second coming of Jesus), Acts 1:7, "It is not for you to know the times or seasons that the Father has set by his own authority," has become the answer of the large church: belief that these things will come, but ignorance as to when or how. Often in sharp conflict with this position, apocalypticists put great effort into endtime calculations and predictions. Thus far they have always been wrong about the assigned dates, and so Christians of the larger church tend to look with distaste on futuristic predictions as fanatical. However, strongly apocalyptic Christianity renders a service. If those who profess that they do not know the times and seasons begin to neglect the creedal proposition that Jesus will come again to judge the living and the dead, they may start thinking that they can build the kingdom of God. Apocalypticists are very certain that the endtime depends on *God* establishing the kingdom, for human beings on their own usually build only the Tower of Babel. Perhaps Christians need to profess with equal fervor both that they cannot know the times and seasons and that one day, in a way that will probably be a total surprise to all, God will establish the kingdom.

(3) Many sermons or speeches in Acts begin by recounting the OT story before telling the story of Jesus. That pattern may need to be stressed in preaching today.[111] Long centuries after God first called the Hebrew slaves and made them the people of Israel, their self-understanding would be tested as to whether anything had really changed because of that calling, especially when they lost the Promised Land and were carried off into exile. In other words, they lived through beforehand what has often been the Christian experience in the centuries after Jesus. Both Jews and Christians have needed faith in order to see God's realities in and through a long history where at times God seems to be absent. The NT alone covers too short a period of time and is too filled with success to give Christians such lessons. By way of particular example, for centuries the OT (except for verses from the Psalms) was never read in Roman Catholic churches on Sundays, a neglect that left people unfamiliar with what was taught so well there. In the aftermath of Vatican II that defect has been corrected, and yet it is disappointing how seldom the OT readings are the subject of the homily. Preachers turn too easily and quickly to the Gospel readings for their topic, even when the very thing that might most challenge their audience is in the OT passage!

(4) For someone who would eventually be compared, rightly or wrongly,

[111]See "The Preaching Described in Acts and Early Christian Doctrinal Priorities," in my *Biblical Exegesis and Church Doctrine* (New York: Paulist, 1985), 135–46.

to other founders of religions, Jesus was remarkably "unorganizational." True, he is reported as calling a few people (particularly the Twelve) to leave their work and follow him, but otherwise he seems to have been content to leave without follow-up those who encountered him and were visibly moved by what he did and said. The Gospels tell us with vague generalization that they went back to their towns and villages and reported enthusiastically what they had seen and heard, but there is no evidence of their forming "Jesus groups" in his lifetime. After the resurrection, however, his followers show an instinct to gather and hold together those whom they convince about Jesus; and their demanding an identifying sign like baptism is the first step in that process of gathering. Indeed, we have little evidence in early Christian missionary endeavor of people being free to say, "I now believe in Jesus," and then walking off on their own. Rather they are made part of a community. They are justified and can be saved, but not simply as individuals. Today, as all know, there are doctrinal divisions among Christian churches. Yet there may be a more fundamental division, namely, between those who think "church" is important, and those for whom Christianity is really a matter of "Jesus and me," without any concept of being saved as part of a people or church.

(5) In its first description of new believers in Jesus being baptized (2:38–41), Acts speaks of baptism "in the name of Jesus." From the very beginning the identity of Jesus' followers was established by what they believed and professed about Jesus. (Later creeds are an enlarged expression of the faith expressed at baptism.) This was a startling difference from Judaism; for although one could call Jews "disciples of Moses" (John 9:28), no one would ever think of defining them by what they believed about the personal identity of Moses. The need to give expression to the centrality of Jesus in the new covenant made Christianity a creedal religion in a manner dissimilar to Judaism. It would be a fascinating exercise some Sunday to ask everyone in church to write on a slip of paper one sentence explaining what a Christian is. Certainly many responses would consist of behavioral descriptions, e.g., a Christian is one who practices love of neighbor. Indeed, one cannot be much of a Christian without behaving as Jesus taught, but behavior is not sufficiently defining: Christians are not the only ones who exhibit love toward each other. How many responses would reflect the most ancient and basic definition that a Christian is one who believes that Jesus is the Christ?

(6) As with other aspects of Acts' portrayal of the early church, the notion of *koinōnia* ("communion," introduced in 2:42) needs emphasis in our time. It is scandalous that Christian churches have broken *koinōnia* with each other; and the purpose of ecumenism is to see if they can regain communion. After the 16th-century Reformation the Protestant churches seemed to splin-

ter over and over again; and although there has been some reunification within denominations, new divisions arise over sensitive issues. Roman Catholics prided themselves on being united; yet now after the 20th-century self-reformation at Vatican II, Catholics are splintering. Ultraconservatives are convinced that the church has moved too far away from "the good old days"; liberals are convinced that the church is not moving fast enough; and both are extremely critical of the pope for not siding with them. All Christians need to be reminded that breaking the *koinōnia* is scarcely reduplicating the values of the early church.

(7) The *General Analysis* above points out many Jewish features in the life and practice of the first Christians described at the beginning of Acts. A Jewish pattern may also have affected the Christian choice of a time for eating the eucharistic meal. The discovery of the empty tomb early Sunday morning helped to fix Christian attention on what by the end of the 1st century would be known as "the Lord's Day." Yet the choice of Sunday may have also been facilitated by the pattern of the Jewish Sabbath, which ended at sundown on Saturday. Before sundown Jews who believed in Jesus were restricted in movement (a Sabbath day's journey); but when the Sabbath was over (Saturday evening), they would have been free to come from a distance to assemble in the house of another believer to break the eucharistic bread. This may explain the ancient Christian memory of a celebration on the night between Saturday and Sunday.

(8) The discussion of Acts 6:1–6 above enables us to see the development of church structure as the product not only of sociological necessity but also of the guidance of the Spirit. For that reason, certain basic aspects of structure are believed by many Christians to be unchangeable. In other words, on the analogy of the incarnation, there can be both the human and the divine in the church and its structure. A recognition of that will allow certain adaptations in church structure to meet the needs of the day without giving the sense that each generation is free to reinvent the church. The difficult task is to decide which issues are changeable, and the Spirit working in the church and among Christians has to play a role in that decision.

(9) A major issue in Acts 10, 11, and 15 is the admission of Gentiles to Christian *koinōnia* without circumcision. This was not detectably an issue solved by Jesus in his lifetime since he showed little interest in Gentiles.[112] There are those today on both extremes of the ecclesiastical spectrum who think they can appeal to the words or deeds of Jesus to solve any question

[112]The stories of the Syrophoenician woman who asked to have her daughter healed and of the Roman centurion whose faith Jesus praised are of exceptional character and do not really settle the problem.

in the church (parochial, regional, or universal). If Jesus did not solve the most fundamental question of the Christian mission, we may well doubt that his recorded words solve most subsequent debated problems in the church. How was the circumcision issue solved according to Acts? Peter does not act by his own initiative or wisdom; rather God shows him that he should not consider anyone unclean (Acts 10:28). Since Cornelius has received a vision from God, God shows no partiality (10:34). The uncircumcised Cornelius can be baptized because the Holy Spirit has come upon him (10:47). In other words we have the example of Christians facing an unforeseen problem and solving it, not by appeal to a previous blueprint by Jesus for the church,[113] but by insight (gained from the Holy Spirit) as to what Christ wanted for the church.

Bibliography on Acts of the Apostles

(For all categories below, see also the *Bibliography* in Chapter 9 on Luke, especially the works marked there with an asterisk. For material on the presentation of Paul in Acts, see the *Bibliography* in Chapter 16 on Paul's life.)

COMMENTARIES AND STUDIES IN SERIES: **Barrett, C. K.** (2 vols.; ICC, 1994, 1998); **Bruce, F. F.** (NICNT, 2d ed., 1988); Conzelmann, H. (Hermeneia, 1987); Hanson, R.P.C. (NClarBC, 1967); Johnson, L. T. (SP, 1992); Krodel, G. A. (AugC, 1986); Liefeld, W. L. (GNTE, 1995); Marshall, I. H. (TNTC, 1980; NTG, 1992); Munck, J. (AB, 1967); Neil, W. (NCBC, 1973); Ringe, S. H. (WBComp, 1995); Williams, D. J. (NIBC, 1990); Williams, R. R. (TBC, 1965); Willimon, W. H. (IBC, 1988).

BIBLIOGRAPHIES: Mattill, A. J., Jr., and M. B., *A Classified Bibliography of Literature on the Acts of the Apostles* (Leiden: Brill, 1966); Wagner, G., EBNT (1985); Mills, W. E., *A Bibliography of the Periodical Literature on the Acts of the Apostles: 1962–1984* (Leiden: Brill, 1986); BBR (1996).

SURVEYS OF RESEARCH: Dupont, J., *The Sources of the Acts: The Present Position* (New York: Herder and Herder, 1964); Gasque, W., *A History of the Criticism of the Acts of the Apostles* (Tübingen: Mohr-Siebeck, 1975).

* * *

The Book of Acts in Its First Century Setting, eds. B. W. Winter et al. (6 vols.; Grand Rapids: Eerdmans, 1993–1997). Essays covering virtually every aspect of Acts. Abbreviated TBAFC.

Brown, R. E., *A Once and Coming Spirit at Pentecost* (Collegeville: Liturgical, 1993). A brief commentary.

[113] Actually the most conservative group who maintained that circumcision of Gentiles was necessary may have appealed to Abraham and Moses as proof from the Scriptures requiring circumcision and argued that there was no evidence that Jesus had ever changed the requirement.

Bruce, F. F., *Commentary on the Book of Acts* (Grand Rapids: Eerdmans, 1980).
Cadbury, H. J., *The Book of Acts in History* (New York: Harper, 1955).
Cassidy, R. J., *Society and Politics in the Acts of the Apostles* (Maryknoll: Orbis, 1987).
Dibelius, M., *Studies in the Acts of the Apostles* (London: SCM, 1956). Very important essays.
Dupont, J., *The Salvation of the Gentiles: Studies in the Acts of the Apostles* (New York: Paulist, 1979).
Easton, B. S., *Early Christianity: The Purpose of Acts and Other Papers* (Greenwich, CT: Seabury, 1954).
Foakes Jackson, F. J., and K. Lake, eds., *The Beginnings of Christianity: The Acts of the Apostles* (5 vols.; London: Macmillan, 1920–1933). A mine of useful information; vol. 4 is a translation and commentary.
Gaventa, B. R., "Towards a Theology of Acts," *Interpretation* 42 (1988), 146–57.
Goulder, M. D., *Type and History in Acts* (London: SPCK, 1964).
Haenchen, E., *The Acts of the Apostles* (Philadelphia: Westminster, 1971).
Harnack, A. (von), *New Testament Studies III: The Acts of the Apostles* (London: Williams and Newgate, 1909). Classic studies.
Hemer, C. J., *The Book of Acts in the Setting of Hellenistic History* (WUNT 49; Tübingen: Mohr-Siebeck, 1989).
Hengel, M., *Acts and the History of Earliest Christianity* (Philadelphia: Fortress, 1979).
Karris, R. J., *Invitation to Acts* (Garden City, NY: Doubleday, 1978).
Knox, W., *The Acts of the Apostles* (Cambridge Univ., 1948).
Lentz, J. C., Jr., *Luke's Portrait of Paul* (SMTSMS 77; Cambridge Univ., 1993).
Levinsohn, S. H., *Textual Connections in Acts* (SBLMS 31; Atlanta: Scholars, 1987).
Lüdemann, G., *Early Christianity According to the Traditions in Acts: A Commentary* (Philadelphia: Fortress, 1989).
Mattill, A. J., Jr., "The Date and Purpose of Acts: Rackham Reconsidered," CBQ 40 (1978), 335–50.
O'Neill, J. C., *The Theology of Acts in Its Historical Setting* (2d ed.; London: SPCK, 1970).
Pervo, R. I., *Profit with Delight: The Literary Genre of the Acts of the Apostles* (Philadelphia: Fortress, 1987).
———, *Luke's Story of Paul* (Minneapolis: A/F, 1990).
Reimer, J. R., *Women in the Acts of the Apostles* (Minneapolis: A/F, 1993).
Rosenblatt, M.-E., *Paul the Accused: His Portrait in the Acts of the Apotles* (Collegeville: Liturgical, 1995).
Taylor, J., "The Making of Acts: A New Account," RB 97 (1990), 504–24.
van Unnik, W. C., "Luke's Second Book and the Rules of Hellenistic Historiography," in *Les Actes des Apôtres,* ed. J. Kremer (Gembloux: Duculot, 1979).
Walker, W. O., "Acts and the Pauline Corpus Reconsidered," JSNT 24 (1985), 3–23.
Wilcox, M., *The Semitisms of Acts* (Oxford: Clarendon, 1965).

CHAPTER 11

THE GOSPEL ACCORDING TO JOHN

John has some significant stylistic features that should be brought to the readers' attention from the start. Then, as with the preceding chapters, in the *General Analysis* we shall read through the Fourth Gospel in its present form, tracing its thought patterns before theorizing about the origins of this Gospel. That theorizing will come in subdivisions devoted to such topics as: *John as a genuine Gospel, Comparison to the Synoptic Gospels, Unity and cohesiveness, Authorship role of the Beloved Disciple, Influences on Johannine thought, History of the Johannine community, Issues for reflection,* and *Bibliography.*

Stylistic Features[1]

John is a Gospel where style and theology are intimately wedded, as we shall see in features discussed below.

#1. *Poetic format.* In a few sections of John many scholars recognize a formal poetic style, even marked by strophes, e.g., the Prologue and perhaps John 17. But the issue raised here is much wider: a uniquely solemn pattern in the Johannine discourses that some would call semipoetic. The characteristic feature of this poetry would not be parallelism of lines (as in the OT) or rhyme, but rhythm, i.e., lines of approximately the same length, each constituting a clause. Whether or not one agrees that the discourses should be printed in poetic format,[2] the fact that Jesus speaks more solemnly in John than in the Synoptics is obvious. One explanation draws on the OT: There divine speech (God through the prophets or personified divine Wisdom) is poetic, signaling a difference from more prosaic human communication. The Johannine Jesus comes from God, and therefore it is appropriate that his words be more solemn and sacral.

#2. *Misunderstanding.*[3] Although he comes from above and speaks of

[1]Pertinent studies are Wead, *Literary,* Staley, *Print's,* and M. Davies, *Rhetoric;* then for a chapter-by-chapter study, Culpepper, *Anatomy.*

[2]For examples, see BGJ, NAB (earlier NT version), JB, and NJB. C. F. Burney, *The Poetry of Our Lord* (Oxford: Clarendon, 1925), and Bultmann in his theory of a Revelatory Discourse Source (p. 363 below) would trace the poetry to an Aramaic original.

[3]D. A. Carson, *Tyndale Bulletin* 33 (1982), 59–91.

Summary of Basic Information

DATE: 80–110. Those who think that the Gospel was redacted (edited) by another hand after the main writer composed it may place the body of the Gospel in the 90s and the additions of the redactor *ca.* 100–110, about the same time as III John.

TRADITIONAL (2D-CENTURY) ATTRIBUTION: To John, son of Zebedee, one of the Twelve.

AUTHOR DETECTABLE FROM THE CONTENTS: One who regards himself in the tradition of the disciple whom Jesus loved. If one posits a redactor, he too may have been in the same tradition. Plausibly there was a school of Johannine writing disciples.

PLACE OF WRITING: Traditionally and plausibly the Ephesus area, but some opt for Syria.

UNITY: Some think sources (collection of "signs"; collection of discourses; passion narrative) were combined; others think of a process of several editions. In either case, plausibly the body of the Gospel was completed by one writer, and a redactor later made additions (chap. 21; perhaps 1:1–18); but no text of the Gospel has been preserved without these "additions."

INTEGRITY: The story of the woman caught in adultery (7:53–8:11) is an insertion missing from many mss.; see *Issue* 1 below.

DIVISION:

1:1–18: **Prologue:** An introduction to and summary of the career of the incarnate Word.

1:19–12:50: **Part One: The Book of Signs:** The Word reveals himself to the world and to his own, but they do not accept him.

1. Initial days of the revelation of Jesus to his disciples under different titles (1:19–2:11).
2. First to second Cana miracle; themes of replacement and of reactions to Jesus (chaps. 2–4): changing water to wine, cleansing the Temple, Nicodemus, the Samaritan woman at the well, healing the royal official's son.
3. Old Testament feasts and their replacement; themes of life and light (chaps. 5–10):
   SABBATH—Jesus, the new Moses, replaces the Sabbath ordinance to rest (5:1–47);
   PASSOVER—the Bread of Life (revelatory wisdom and the eucharist) replaces the manna (6:1–71);
   TABERNACLES—the Source of living water and the Light of the world, replaces the water and light ceremonies (7:1–10:21);
   DEDICATION—Jesus is consecrated in place of the Temple altar (10:22–42).
4. The raising of Lazarus and its aftermath (chaps. 11–12): Lazarus raised to life, Jesus condemned to death by the Sanhedrin, Lazarus's sister Mary anoints Jesus for burial, entry to Jerusalem, the end of the public ministry and the coming of the hour signaled by the arrival of Gentiles.

13:1–20:31: **Part Two: The Book of Glory:** To those who accept him, the Word shows his glory by returning to the Father in death, resurrection, and ascension. Fully glorified, he communicates the Spirit of life.

1. The Last Supper and Jesus' Last Discourse (chaps. 13–17):

(a) The Last Supper (chap. 13): the meal, washing of the feet, Judas' betrayal, introduction to discourse (love commandment, Peter's denials foretold);

(b) Jesus' Last Discourse (chaps. 14–17):
Division One (chap. 14): Jesus' departure, divine indwelling, the Paraclete;
Division Two (chaps. 15–16): vine and branches, the world's hatred, witness by the Paraclete, repeated themes of Division One;
Division Three (chap. 17): the "Priestly" Prayer.

2. Jesus' passion and death (chaps. 18–19): arrest, inquiry before Annas with Peter's denials, trial before Pilate, crucifixion, death, and burial.
3. The resurrection (20:1–29): four scenes in Jerusalem (two at the tomb, two inside a room).
Gospel Conclusion (20:30–31): Statement of purpose in writing.

21:1–25: **Epilogue:** Galilean resurrection appearances; second conclusion.

what is "true" or "real" (i.e., heavenly reality), Jesus, the Word become flesh, must use language from below to convey his message. To deal with this anomaly, he frequently employs figurative language or metaphors to describe himself or to present his message.[4] In an ensuing dialogue the questioner will misunderstand the figure or metaphor, and take only a material meaning. This allows Jesus to explain his thought more thoroughly and thereby to unfold his doctrine. Stemming from the Johannine theology of the incarnation, such misunderstanding has become a studied literary technique. (See John 2:19–21; 3:3–4; 4:10–11; 6:26–27; 8:33–35; 11:11–13.)

#3. *Twofold meanings.*[5] Sometimes playing into misunderstanding, sometimes simply showing the multifaceted aspect of revelation, a double meaning often can be found in what Jesus says. (a) There are plays on various meanings of a given word that Jesus uses, meanings based on either Hebrew or Greek; sometimes the dialogue partner may take one meaning, while Jesus intends the other. (Various terms in 3:3,8 [n. 20 below]); "lifted up" in 3:14; 8:28; 12:34 (crucifixion and return to God); "living water" in 4:10 (flowing water and life-giving water); "die for" in 11:50–52 (instead or on behalf of). (b) In the Fourth Gospel the author frequently intends the reader

[4]For a thorough treatment, see C. R. Koester, *Symbolism in the Fourth Gospel* (Minneapolis: A/F, 1995); also D. A. Lee, *The Symbolic Narratives of the Fourth Gospel* (JSNTSup 95; Sheffield: JSOT, 1994). In a sense the Johannine figures or metaphors (16:29) are equivalent to the Synoptic parables, for in John the reality represented by the Synoptic kingdom of heaven stands in our midst in the person of Jesus. In the Synoptics the parables are frequently misunderstood just as the metaphors are in John.

[5]R. Shedd in *Current Issues in Biblical and Patristic Interpretation,* ed. G. D. Hawthorne (M. C. Tenney Festschrift; Grand Rapids: Eerdmans, 1975), 247–58; E. Richard, NTS 30 (1985), 96–112.

to see several layers of meaning in the same narrative or in the same metaphor. This is understandable if we think back to the circumstances in which the Gospel was composed, involving several time levels.[6] There is a meaning appropriate to the historical context in the public ministry of Jesus; yet there may be a second meaning reflecting the situation of the believing Christian community. For example, the prediction of Jesus that the Temple sanctuary would be destroyed and replaced in 2:19–22 is reinterpreted to refer to the crucifixion and resurrection of Jesus' body. The Bread of Life discourse seems to refer to divine revelation and wisdom in 6:35–51a and to the eucharist in 6:51b–58. As many as three different meanings may have been intended in the imagery of the Lamb of God (1:29,36: apocalyptic lamb, paschal lamb, and suffering servant who went to slaughter like a lamb). (c) Duplicate speeches. Occasionally a speech of Jesus seems to say essentially the same thing as a speech already reported, sometimes to the point of verse-to-verse correspondence. P. 367 below suggests a possible solution: A redactor (editor who worked over the Gospel after the evangelist had finished the basic work) found in the tradition other versions of discourse material duplicating in part the versions that the evangelist had included and added them at an appropriate place lest they be lost. (Compare *3:31–36* to 3:7–18; *5:26–30* to 5:19–25; *10:9* to 10:7–8; *10:14* to 10:11; *16:4b–33* to chap. 14.) At times there is a different tone in the duplicate material.

#4. *Irony.*[7] A particular combination of twofold meaning and misunderstanding is found when the opponents of Jesus make statements about him that are derogatory, sarcastic, incredulous, or, at least, inadequate in the sense that they intend. However, by way of irony these statements are often true or more meaningful in a sense that the speakers do not realize. (3:2; 4:12; 6:42; 7:35; 9:40–41; 11:50.)

#5. *Inclusions and transitions.* The careful structure of the Gospel is indicated by certain techniques. By inclusion we mean that John mentions a detail (or makes an allusion) at the end of a section that matches a similar detail at the beginning of the section. This is a way of packaging sections by tying together the beginning and the end. Large inclusions are 1:1 with 20:28; 1:28 with 10:40; smaller inclusions are 1:19 with 1:28; 2:11 with 4:54; 9:2–3 with 9:41; 11:4 with 11:40. By way of transition from one subdivision of the Gospel to the next, the evangelist likes to use a "swing"

[6]There are other interpretations of these levels. Reinhartz, *Word,* who holds that the Gospel is fiction, posits a level concerned with Jesus, a level concerned with the Johannine Christians in the 1st-century diaspora, and a cosmological level involving the encounter of the Word of God with the world.

[7]P. D. Duke, *Irony in the Fourth Gospel* (Atlanta: Knox, 1985), treats other Johannine features under this broad title. See also G. R. O'Day, *Revelation in the Fourth Gospel. Narrative Mode and Theological Claim* (Philadelphia: Fortress, 1986).

("hinge") motif or section—one that concludes what has gone before and introduces what follows. E.g., the Cana miracle terminates the call of the disciples in chap. 1, fulfilling the promise in 1:50, but also opens the next subdivision of 2:1–4:54 that runs from the first Cana miracle to the second. The second Cana miracle concludes that subdivision, but by stressing Jesus' power to give life (4:50) prepares for the next subdivision (5:1–10:42) where Jesus' authority over life will be challenged.

#6. *Parentheses or footnotes.*[8] Frequently John supplies parenthetical notes, explaining the meaning of Semitic terms or names (e.g., "Messiah," "Cephas," "Siloam," "Thomas" in 1:41,42; 9:7; 11:16), offering background for developments in the narrative and for geographical features (e.g., 2:9; 3:24; 4:8; 6:71; 9:14,22–23; 11:5,13), and even supplying theological perspectives (e.g., clarifying references from a later standpoint in 2:21–22; 7:39; 11:51–52; 12:16,33; or protecting Jesus' divinity in 6:6,64). Some of these may reflect a situation where a tradition transmitted at first in one context (Palestinian or Jewish) is now being proclaimed in another context (diaspora or Gentile).

General Analysis of the Message

Close attention to the detailed outline at the beginning of the Chapter will be helpful; for, as #5 above indicates, the Gospel has been carefully arranged to illustrate themes chosen by the evangelist.[9]

PROLOGUE (1:1–18)

Serving as a preface to the Gospel, the Prologue[10] is a hymn that encapsulates John's view of Christ. A divine being (God's Word [1:1,14], who is also the light [1:5,9] and God's only Son [1:14,18]) comes into the world and becomes flesh. Although rejected by his own, he empowers all who do accept him to become God's children, so that they share in God's fullness—a

[8]M. C. Tenney, BSac 117 (1960), 350–64.

[9]E.g., two different themes may be found in the same set of chapters (e.g., chaps. 2–4). The outline I have given is the most popular and well supported by the text. (The terminology "Book of Signs" and "Book of Glory" is taken from C. H. Dodd.) The massive chiastic arrangement detected by P. F. Ellis (*The Genius of John* [Collegeville: Liturgical, 1984]), which has had little following, supposes an excessively complicated scheme (twenty-one sequences: the 1st matched by the 21st, the 2d by the 20th, etc.). See the critique in CBQ 48 (1986), 334–35: "a Procrustean bed of chiastic parallelism." C. H. Giblin's tripartite division (*Biblica* 71 [1990], 449–68) neglects what to many seems obvious, namely, the Gospel indicates the beginning of a major new section in 13:1.

[10]There is an abundant literature on the Prologue, e.g., beyond the commentaries: C. K. Barrett, *The Prologue of St. John's Gospel* (London: Athlone, 1971); C. H. Giblin, JBL 104 (1985), 87–103; J. L. Staley, CBQ 48 (1986), 241–64; C. A. Evans, *Word and Glory* (JSNTSup 89; Sheffield: JSOT, 1993); E. Harris, *Prologue and Gospel* (JSNTSup 107; Sheffield: Academic, 1994).

gift reflecting God's enduring love[11] that outdoes the loving gift of the Law through Moses. The background of this poetic description of the descent of the Word into the world and the eventual return of the Son to the Father's side (1:18) lies in the OT picture of personified Wisdom (especially Sirach 24 and Wisdom 9) who was in the beginning with God at the creation of the world and came to dwell with human beings when the Law was revealed to Moses. In agreement with the tradition that JBap's ministry was related to the beginning of Jesus', the Prologue is interrupted twice, viz., to mention JBap before the light comes into the world (1:6–8) and to record JBap's testimony to Jesus after the Word becomes flesh (1:15). This testimony will be picked up in Part One to follow.

Part One: The Book of Signs (1:19–12:50)

This part of the Gospel will show Jesus bringing different types of people to believe in him while at the same time provoking many among "the Jews" to hostility. At the end (12:39–40) the Gospel quotes Isa 6:10 to the effect that God has blinded their eyes and hardened their hearts that they might not see. Thus this "Book" illustrates the theme from the Prologue (John 1:11): "To his own he came; yet his own did not accept him."

1. Initial Days of the Revelation of Jesus to His Disciples under Different Titles (1:19–2:11). In a pattern of separate days (1:29,35,43; 2:1)[12] John shows a gradual recognition of who Jesus is. *On the first day (1:19–28) JBap explains his own role,* rejecting laudatory identifications and predicting the coming of one of whom he is unworthy. *On the next day (1:29–34) JBap explains Jesus' role.* As befits "one sent by God" (1:6), JBap perceptively recognizes Jesus as the Lamb of God, as one who existed beforehand, and as God's chosen one (or Son—disputed reading of 1:34). *On the next day (1:35–42) Jesus is followed by Andrew and another disciple of JBap* (the one who by the second part of the Gospel will have become the disciple whom Jesus loved?). Andrew hails Jesus as teacher and Messiah, and Simon (Andrew's brother) is brought to Jesus, who names him "Cephas" (i.e., rock = Peter; cf. Mark 3:16; Matt 16:18). *On the next day (John 1:43–51) he (An-*

[11]The "grace" and "truth" of 1:14 probably reproduce the famous OT pairing of *ḥesed* and *'ĕmet,* i.e., God's *kindness* (mercy) in choosing Israel independently of any merit on Israel's part and God's enduring *fidelity* to the covenant with Israel that expresses this kindness.

[12]Some would see an implied day in 1:40 after the reference to 4 p.m. in 1:39 and contend that John counts seven days (calculated in BGJ 1.106) in order to signify a week of the new creation (following the Prologue reference to the original creation [John 1:1 to Gen 1:1]). However, although in chap. 1 John specifies four separate days, he jumps to "the third day" in 2:1 (presumably from the last mentioned day)—a strange way to signify seven. Even more dubious is the proposal to find an inclusion in a final week of Jesus' life: 12:1: "Six days before Passover"; 12:12: "the next day"; 13:1: "It was just before Passover."

drew, Peter, or Jesus?) finds Philip, who in turn finds Nathanael, and Jesus is identified successively as the one described in the Mosaic Law and the prophets, as the Son of God, and the King of Israel. Yet Jesus promises that they will see far greater things and speaks of himself as the Son of Man upon whom the angels ascend and descend. The "far greater things" seem to begin in Cana on the third day (2:1–11) when Jesus changes water to wine and his disciples come to believe in him.

Certain Johannine theological emphases appear in this first subsection. A legal atmosphere colors the narrative, e.g., JBap is interrogated by "the Jews,"[13] and he testifies and does not deny—an indication that some of the Johannine tradition was shaped in a forensic context, possibly in a synagogue where Christians were interrogated about their belief in Jesus. As for christology, it can scarcely be accidental that John places in these initial days confessions of Jesus under many of the traditional titles that we find scattered in the other Gospels, most often later in the ministry (see Matt 16:16). It is almost as if the evangelist wants to portray as elementary the christological tradition known to the other Gospels and to begin his Gospel at a stage where the others end. For the other Gospels the sight of the Son of Man accompanied by the angels will come only at the end of time; for John that occurs during the ministry because the Son of Man has already come down from heaven.[14] Also this subsection portrays discipleship. Jesus poses an initial question in 1:38, "What are you looking for?" and follows in 1:39 by "Come and see." Yet it is only when they remain with him that the first followers become believers. Then in a consistent pattern the initial disciples go out to proclaim Jesus to others with a christological perception deepened through that very action, as illustrated in the "higher" titles given to Jesus day after day.

2. First to Second Cana Miracle (chaps. 2–4). The Cana scene is "the first of his signs"[15] (2:11); and thus like a swinging door (*Stylistic Feature*

[13]The evangelist may well be a Jew by birth; yet most often he uses this expression with a hostile tone for those of Jewish birth who distrust or reject Jesus and/or his followers. "The Jews" include Jewish authorities but cannot be confined to them; and the generalizing term may be an attempt to portray the Jewish opponents in the synagogues of John's time—opponents who are persecuting John's community (16:2) even as Jewish opponents in Jesus' time were remembered as persecuting him. Consequently, most often "the Jews" seem to be a disliked group separate from the followers of Jesus; and Jesus at times speaks as a nonJew (or, at least, not as one of those "Jews"): "written in your Law" (10:34); "in their Law" (15:25); "as I said to the Jews" (13:33). See p. 167 above.

[14]Scribes recognized this for they combined John 1:51 with Matt 26:64. No other Gospel affirms that Jesus had come down from heaven, so that the terminology "second coming" really supposes Johannine insight. F. J. Moloney, *The Johannine Son of Man* (2d ed.; Rome: Salesianum, 1978); D. Burkett, *The Son of Man in the Gospel of John* (JSNTSup 56; Sheffield: JSOT, 1991).

[15]John does not use *dynamis,* "act of power" (helping to establish the kingdom of God), which is the Synoptic designation for miracle, but *ergon,* "work," or *semeion,* "sign." The OT description of the exodus from Egypt speaks of the "works" of God (Exod 34:10; Deut 3:24; 11:3) and the

#5 above), it both closes the initial revelation and opens the next major subdivision that terminates in 4:54, where we are told that the healing of royal official's son announced at Cana "was the second sign that Jesus performed on returning again from Judea to Galilee." The theme of replacement runs through Jesus' actions and words in the three chapters thus marked off.

In the initial Cana miracle (*2:1–11*), which John calls a sign, Jesus replaces the water prescribed for Jewish purifications (in stone jars containing more than 120 gallons) by wine so good that headwaiter wonders why the best has been kept until last. This represents the revelation and wisdom that he brings from God (Prov 9:4–5; Sirach 24:20[21]), fulfilling the OT promises of abundance of wine in the messianic days (Amos 9:13–14; Gen 49:10–11). An intertwined motif involves the mother of Jesus, whose family-style request on behalf of the newly married ("They have no wine") is rebuffed by Jesus on the grounds that his hour had not yet come.[16] Yet the mother's persistence that honors Jesus' terms ("Do whatever he tells you") leads him to grant her original request—similarly in the second Cana sign where the royal official's persistence wins his request after a rebuff (John 4:47–50; cf. Mark 7:26–29). The mother of Jesus will reappear at the foot of the cross (John 19:25–27), where her incorporation into discipleship will be completed as she becomes the mother of the Beloved Disciple. Meanwhile, in *a transitional verse* (*2:12*) we find that she and Jesus' "brothers" followed him to Capernaum, but no farther when he began his public ministry by going to Jerusalem.

Situated in Jerusalem near Passover,[17] *the next subsection* (*2:13–22*), *treats Jesus' attitude toward the Temple.* It has parallels in two Synoptic scenes: the cleansing of the Temple (Mark 11:15–19,27–28 and par.) which takes place not long before Jesus is put to death, and the witnesses at the Sanhedrin trial on the night before the crucifixion, who falsely testify that Jesus said he would destroy the Temple sanctuary (Mark 14:58; Matt 26:61; cf. Acts 6:14). In John the scenes are combined and placed early in the ministry; the sanctuary statement is on Jesus' lips (phrased, however, as "*You*

"signs" God did through Moses (Exod 10:1; Num 14:22; Deut 7:19). In their most characteristic Johannine usage, works and signs are miraculous deeds (or statements about the future: John 12:33; 21:19) that manifest who Jesus is, his purpose, his glory, and/or his relation to the Father. "Work" expresses the divine perspective on what is accomplished and so is a fitting description for Jesus himself to apply to his miracles. "Sign" indicates the human viewpoint wherein attention is directed not so much to the miraculous in itself (which may not lead to true faith: 2:23–24; 4:48; 12:37) but to what is revealed by the miracle to those who can see beyond.

[16]Thus this is a scene similar to Luke 2:48–49 and Mark 3:31–35, where Jesus gives relationship to God precedence over relationship to family.

[17]This and the two other Passovers mentioned in John, and the feast of Tabernacles (6:4; 7:2; 11:55) are characterized as "of the Jews"; it would seem then that John's readers/hearers do not consider these feasts their own.

destroy," not as "I will destroy"); and the replacement is not another sanctuary but the same one which will be raised up. Leaving aside the insoluble issue of which tradition is more historical, we note two peculiar Johannine theological emphases. By showing the antagonism of "the Jews" from the very beginning, John illustrates the utter incompatibility between Jesus and his own who do not receive him (see John 1:11). Also in John's interpretation the sanctuary is Jesus' body, "destroyed" by "the Jews" but raised up by Jesus.[18] Thus the Jerusalem Temple, which has been turned into a marketplace, has been replaced by the body of Jesus as the true holy place. *According to 2:23–25 many in Jerusalem believed in Jesus because of signs he was doing,* but he did not trust their faith because it stopped at the miraculous aspect of the sign and did not perceive what was signified. This transitional observation introduces one of these would-be believers to Jesus who appears in the next subsection.

The Nicodemus scene (*3:1–21*) is the first of the important Johannine dialogues. This Pharisee, a member of the Sanhedrin, comes to Jesus "at night" (i.e., because he does not yet belong to the light) and acknowledges him as a "teacher who has come from God." By that designation Nicodemus means only "raised up by God," whereas Jesus has actually come from God. Thus Nicodemus is a representative spokesman of an inadequate faith,[19] as becomes evident when Jesus explains that only begetting from above enables one to enter the kingdom of God, i.e., begetting of water and Spirit.[20] The Johannine Jesus speaks of the very life of God acquired only when one is begotten by God ("from above"), which takes place when one is baptized in water and receives God's Spirit. Nicodemus is thinking of natural birth from a Jewish mother that makes one a member of the chosen people, a people that the OT considers God's child (Exod 4:22; Deut 32:6; Hos 11:1). Such a pedigree is rejected in John 3:6, for the only thing that flesh can beget or give birth to is flesh. The Johannine Jesus, then, is radically replacing what constitutes the children of God, challenging any privileged status stemming from natural parenthood. Typical Johannine irony surfaces in 3:9–11: To the Nicodemus who came saying "We know" but cannot understand, Jesus, speaking on behalf of those who do believe, counterpoises: "We are talking

[18]Whereas in the earlier formulations Jesus is raised up (by God) or God raises Jesus, in John (2:19; 10:17–18) Jesus raises himself. This reflects the thesis in John 10:30: "The Father and I are one."

[19]Subsequent characters representative of different faith-encounters will include the Samaritan woman (chap. 4) and the man born blind (chap. 9). Helpful is Rensberger, *Johannine Faith.*

[20]There are many plays on Greek words in this dialogue, making it very difficult to translate. The same verb can mean "begotten by" (a male principle; see I John 3:9: "God's seed") and born of (a female principle); the same adverb means "from above" and "again"; the same word means wind and Spirit, whence 3:8.

about what we know and we are testifying to what we have seen." Jesus' surety about the need for begetting from above stems from his own having come from above. The dialogue now becomes a monologue as Nicodemus fades into the darkness whence he came (until he reappears still hesitantly as a hidden follower in 7:50–52, and finally publicly in 19:39–42). In 3:15–21 Jesus proclaims for the first time the basic Johannine theology of salvific incarnation: He is God's Son come into the world bringing God's own life, so that everyone who believes in him has eternal life and thus is already judged.[21]

JBap's final witness to Jesus (*3:22–30*), resuming 1:15,19–34, is in the context of Jesus' own baptizing[22] (which helps to reinforce the baptismal reference in the "water and Spirit" of 3:5). Opposition to Jesus on the part of JBap's disciples enables JBap once more to clarify just who he is not and the greatness of the one for whom he has prepared. The image is that of the bridegroom's best friend protectively keeping watch over the house of the bride (Israel), waiting to hear the approach of the bridegroom (Jesus) as he comes to take her to his home.

The style of *the puzzling speech in 3:31–36* is that of the Johannine Jesus; and it seems to duplicate things said in 3:7,11–13,15–18, thus supporting the thesis of those who claim that the redactor supplemented the work of the evangelist by adding other forms of material already found there. However, the context suggests that JBap is the speaker. Like Jesus he has been sent by God, and so does he speak like Jesus? Following this, *4:1–3 supplies a geographical transition* from Judea toward Galilee.

On this journey Jesus stops in Samaria at the well of Shechem/Sychar. The *dialogue with the Samaritan woman and its aftermath* (*4:4–42*) is the first full example of Johannine dramatic ability. In it a character who is more than an individual has been developed in order to serve as a spokesperson for a particular type of faith-encounter with Jesus.[23] The portrayal centers on how one first comes to faith and the many obstacles that stand in the way.

[21]Such "realized eschatology" is dominant in John (see also 5:24); yet there are passages of "final eschatology" as well (5:28–29). Bultmann would attribute the latter to the Ecclesiastical Redactor (p. 367 below) as a corrective to the former, but that is too mechanical. There is no evidence that anyone in the Johannine tradition held one form of eschatology exclusively, and I John, which recalls what was "from the beginning," is emphatic on final eschatology (pp. 386, 389 below).

[22]This is the only reference in the NT to Jesus himself baptizing during his ministry, and it may well be historical despite the denial in 4:2. That denial and the complete silence about Jesus' baptizing in the Synoptic tradition are intelligible if, once JBap had been arrested, Jesus gave up a baptizing ministry and so was not remembered by his followers as a baptizer. The rivalry between adherents of JBap and Jesus, who eventually was more successful than JBap (3:26), may reflect the situation when the Gospel was written; for Acts 18:24–19:7 gives evidence of the continued existence of adherents of JBap, and 2d- and 3d-century writings point to some who argued that JBap, not Jesus, was the Messiah.

[23]See Lee, *Symbolic,* for this motif.

Smarting from the injustice of Jewish treatment of Samaritan women, she rebuffs Jesus' request for a drink. Jesus does not answer her objection but responds in terms of what he can give her, i.e., living water which she misunderstands as flowing water, contemptuously asking him if he thinks he is greater than Jacob. By Johannine irony, Jesus is greater; but once again Jesus refuses to be sidetracked and explains that he is speaking of the water that springs up to eternal life, a water that will permanently end thirst. With masterly touch John shows her attracted on a level of the convenience of not having to come to the well. Then in typical Johannine style Jesus shifts the focus to her husband in order to make progress in another way. Her reply is a half-truth and the all-knowing Jesus shows that he is very aware of her five husbands and her living with a man who is not her husband.[24] The very fact that the story continues shows that Jesus' effort to bring her to faith will not be blocked by the obstacle of a far-from-perfect life, even though that is something she must acknowledge. Confronted with such surprising knowledge of her situation, the woman finally shifts to a religious level, seeking to avoid further probing by bringing up a theological dispute between Jews and Samaritans as to whether God should be worshiped in the Jerusalem Temple or on Mount Gerizim in this very area. Again Jesus refuses to be sidetracked; for although salvation is from the Jews, a time is coming and is now here when such an issue is irrelevant, for cult at both sacred sites will be replaced by worship in Spirit and truth. Nimbly the woman once more seeks to avoid the personal issue by changing the perspective to the distant future when the Messiah comes;[25] but Jesus will not let her escape. His "I am (he)" confronts her with a current demand for faith.

John now (4:27–39) adopts the double-stage technique, reporting the reaction of the disciples as they return to center stage at the well, while the woman goes off backstage to the village. Although the disciples have been with Jesus, their misunderstanding of Jesus' food is just as crass as the woman's misunderstanding of the water. The woman's hesitant "Could this be the Messiah?" means that she is seeking reinforcement, which is supplied by the Samaritans from the village who come to believe when they encounter Jesus (4:40–42). Their words to her, "No longer is our faith dependent on your story, for we have heard for ourselves," reflect Johannine theology that all must come into personal contact with Jesus. Plausibly this story reflects

[24]Many scholars have sought to find a special symbolism in the five husbands, e.g., as reflecting the 8th-century BC transplant to Samaria of colonists from five Pagan cities who brought their gods with them (II Kings 17:24ff. and Josephus, *Ant.* 9.14.3; #288). However, that is unnecessary for the flow of the story.

[25]Much in the story shows a knowledge of Samaria; yet the Samaritans did not expect a Messiah in the sense of an anointed king of the House of David. If the evangelist knew that, he may be translating their expectation into language more familiar to his readers.

Johannine history in which Samaritans came into the community alongside Jews, but that is beneath the surface. More obvious is the continued theme of replacement (here of worship at the Temple) and the contrast between the more open faith of the Samaritans and the less adequate belief of those at Jerusalem (2:23–25) and Nicodemus.

The second sign at Cana (4:43–54) terminates this subdivision. It resembles the first Cana story in that the petitioner is rebuffed but persists, and so has the petition granted. The story of the royal official's son (*huios*) is probably a third variant of the story of the centurion's servant (*pais*), which has two slightly different forms in Matt 8:5–13 and Luke 7:1–10. The variants are of a sort that could arise in oral tradition, e.g., English "boy" (one translation of *pais*) can mean both son and servant. In the sequence of Johannine themes the transitional 4:43–45 speaks of an inadequate faith that gives no honor to a prophet in his own country (cf. Mark 6:4; Luke 4:24).[26] This sets up a contrast to the faith illustrated by the royal official who believes that what Jesus has said will happen and returns home on the strength of it, ultimately leading his whole household to faith (cf. Acts 10:2; 11:14; 16:15,34). To Nicodemus Jesus had spoken of a (life-giving) begetting/birth from above; to the Samaritan woman he had spoken of water springing up to eternal life; now he gives life to the royal official's son. This prepares for a key saying in the next subdivision that the Son grants life to whomever he wishes (5:21).

3. OT Feasts and Their Replacement (chaps. 5–10). That theme of life which will be developed in chaps. 5–7 will yield to the theme of light in chaps. 8–10—both of them motifs anticipated in the Prologue. A more dominant motif, however, is the sequence of Jewish feasts that move through this subdivision (Sabbath, Passover, Tabernacles, Dedication), and on each something Jesus does or says plays on and to some extent replaces a significant aspect of the feast.

On the Sabbath Jesus heals and thus gives life, leading to a hostile dialogue (5:1–47). The combination of a miracle and a discourse/dialogue that brings out the miracle's sign-value is a Johannine technique (see also chap. 6). Here, on the occasion of an unnamed "feast of the Jews" that is also a Sabbath (5:9), Jesus cures a lame man who has been waiting to be healed at the pool of Bethesda.[27] His instruction to take up the mat violates the Sab-

[26]Scholars are divided as to whether "his own country" is Judea (which would mean skipping back over the Samaria scene to 2:23–25) or Galilee as indicated by the immediate context and the other Gospels. The latter interpretation finds support in the (implicit) superficiality of the welcome by the Galileans in 4:45 based on their seeing what Jesus had done in Jerusalem.

[27]By the Sheep Pool or Gate of Jerusalem, this may be what is called in the DSS Copper Scroll (xi 12–13) "Bet 'Ešdatayin," a form indicating a place named Bet 'Ešda where there were two basins. Most likely this site is the trapezoidal pool area (divided by a central partition into two pools) in the

bath law (as verified later in the codified directives of the Mishna). The explanation that Jesus offers to "the Jews" does not appeal to humanitarian grounds, as in Luke 13:15–16; 14:5, but to his supreme authority, as in Mark 2:28 and par. The logic seems to be that, although people should not work on the Sabbath, God continues to work on that day.[28] God is Jesus' Father, and the Father has given to the Son power over life and death. "The Jews" recognize what is being claimed; "They sought all the more to kill him because not only was he breaking the Sabbath but, worse still, he was speaking of God as his own Father, thus making himself God's equal" (5:18). Thus, more than in other Gospels, in John a lethal antipathy toward Jesus appears early and consistently, and a claim to divinity comes through clearly. Understandably many scholars think that we have here double exposure: memories of hostility to Jesus during his ministry on which have been superimposed the later experiences of his followers who were accused of ditheism by Jewish authorities, i.e., of making a God of Jesus and thus violating the fundamental tenet of Israel: The Lord our God is one. The answer in 5:19–30 is subtle: the Son does nothing of himself, but the Father has given all things to him. In 5:31–47 five arguments are advanced as testimony as if they were advanced in synagogue debates: God (Another) has testified on Jesus' behalf; so also JBap, and the works that Jesus is doing, and Scripture, and finally Moses who wrote about Jesus.

At Passover time Jesus multiplies the loaves and fish and gives a discourse on the Bread of Life (6:1–71). There are two Synoptic accounts of the multiplication (followed in the first instance by the walking on the sea); and charts in BGJ 1.239–44 show how in some details John's account seems closer to the first Synoptic account and in other details closer to the second Synoptic account.[29] The introduction of Philip and Andrew as characters who prepare for Jesus' response is typically Johannine (1:40,43–44; 12:22); and John has peculiar features that could heighten the eucharistic symbolism in the multiplication.[30] The combination of marvelously supplied food and walking on water echoes Moses' miracles in the Exodus after the first Passover (manna, Red Sea), even as the murmuring of 6:41 matches the similar action of Israel

NE section of walled Jerusalem, just outside St. Anne's church. The springs there were thought in antiquity to have healing power. John 5:3b–4, concerning the angel stirring the water, is missing from the best mss. and reflects popular tradition.

[28]The fact that people are born and die on the Sabbath shows that God is at work, giving life, rewarding good, and punishing evil.

[29]The two accounts are found respectively in Mark 6:30–53; Matt 14:13–34; Luke 9:10–17; and Mark 8:1–10; Matt 15:32–39. It is very difficult to understand how the fourth evangelist could have made his account from them, and this scene is a strong argument for Johannine independence. As for respective age, in some details John's account seems older; in some details, more recent.

[30]E.g., the verb *eucharistein* in v. 11; *klasma* for fragment (v. 12; used in the eucharistic description in *Didache* 9:4); *synagein* (v. 12: "gather," whence synaxis).

in the desert wanderings (Exod 16:2,8). Accordingly a comparison of Jesus and Moses follows: Moses did not give the true bread from heaven because those who ate the manna died (John 6:32,58). Whereas the Synoptic accounts do not tell us the reaction of those for whom the bread and fish were multiplied, John has the crowd find and put demands on Jesus the next day as evidence that they did not really see beyond the miraculous to what was signified. Jesus did not come simply to satisfy earthly hunger but to give a bread that would nourish people for eternal life, and the discourse that follows[31] seems to give two interpretations of how this would be done.

First, in John 6:35–51a Jesus is the Bread of Life in the sense that his revelation constitutes teaching by God (6:45), so that one must believe in the Son to have eternal life. The language, "No one who comes to me shall ever be hungry, and no one who believes in me shall ever again be thirsty" (6:35), echoes the promise of divine Wisdom[32] in Sirach 24:21(20). Second, in John 6:51b–58 Jesus is nourishment in another sense, for one must feed on his flesh and blood to have eternal life. The themes of 6:35–51a are duplicated but now in language evocative of the eucharist. Indeed 6:51b, "The bread that I shall give is my own flesh for the life of the world," might well be the Johannine eucharist formula comparable to "This is my body which is (given) for you" of Luke 22:19; I Cor 11:24. Taken as a whole the two parts of the discourse in John 6 would reveal that Jesus feeds his followers both through his revelation and his eucharistic flesh and blood. In response some of Jesus' disciples murmur about this teaching (6:60–61) even as did "the Jews" (6:41–43,52). On the level of Jesus' ministry this unfavorable reaction is to his claims about the heavenly origins of the Son of Man; on the level of community life it may reflect a rejection by other Christians of a high view of the eucharist.[33] Simon Peter and the Twelve are among those who do not go away, for they recognize that Jesus has the words of eternal

[31]Echoing Exod 16:4,15; Ps 78:24, the debate over "He gave them bread from heaven to eat" ("He" = Moses or God; "gave" or "gives"; "bread from heaven" = manna or Jesus) leads into a homily, possibly in response to a synagogue argument against the Johannine Christians. Typical of the homily style of the time was the introduction of a prophetic text (6:45 from Isa 54:13) to support the interpretation. See the important contribution by P. Borgen, *Bread from Heaven* (NovTSup 10; Leiden: Brill, 1965; 2d ed., 1981); *Logos Was the True Light* (Univ. of Trondheim, 1983), 32–46. Less likely is the view that there was already a set three-year synagogue lectionary in which the Exodus text was a Passover reading, as was Isa 54—the thesis of A. Guilding, *The Fourth Gospel and Jewish Worship* (Oxford: Clarendon, 1960), critiqued by L. Morris, *The New Testament and the Jewish Lectionaries* (London: Tyndale, 1964).

[32]Wisdom is a very important motif in Johannine christology: M. Scott, *Sophia and the Johannine Jesus* (JSNTSup 71; Sheffield: JSOT, 1992); M. E. Willett, *Wisdom Christology and the Fourth Gospel* (San Francisco: Mellen, 1992). For general OT background, R. C. Hill, *Wisdom's Many Faces* (Collegeville: Liturgical, 1996).

[33]The claim that many of his disciples would not follow him any more (6:66) is found only in John among the Gospels and may reflect a period toward the end of the century when the *koinōnia* was being broken.

life. (Thus despite its failure to speak of "apostles" or give a list of the Twelve, John's Gospel inculcates respect for them.) The Synoptic confessional scene refers to Peter as "Satan" (Mark 8:33; Matt 16:23), but for John 6:70–71 Judas is the devil who, Jesus already knows, will give him over.

The next Jewish feast, Tabernacles (*Tents, Booths*), *seems to cover 7:1 to 10:21,* before the mention of the feast of Dedication in 10:22. This eight-day-long pilgrimage-feast on which Jews went up to Jerusalem, besides celebrating the Sept./Oct. grape harvest, was marked by prayers for rain. A daily procession from the pool of Siloam brought water as a libation to the Temple where the court of the women was lighted by immense torches—thus themes of water and light. Refusing a request of his "brothers" that smacks of disbelief, Jesus goes up to Jerusalem at his own initiative and secretly (7:1–10). Thoughts about him produce a division (7:11–15), reflecting John's theme that Jesus causes people to judge themselves. Jesus' dialogue with "the Jews" in 7:16–36 recalls previous hostility over violating the Mosaic Law and culminates with a warning that he will not remain much longer and is going away to the One who sent him.[34] The replacement for the water theme of the feast comes to the fore on the last day of Tabernacles in 7:37–39 as Jesus announces that from within himself (the more likely reading) shall flow rivers of living water, i.e., the Spirit that would be received when he was glorified (see 19:34). The division over Jesus, leading to a failed attempt to arrest him (7:40–49), brings Nicodemus back on the scene, defending Jesus but still not professing that he is a believer (7:50–52).

The continuation[35] in 8:12–59 introduces the replacement for the light theme of the feast as Jesus proclaims himself to be "the light of the world." The legal atmosphere of defensive testimony against Jewish charges returns,[36] and the situation becomes very hostile, e.g., suggestions of illegitimacy, charges that the devil is the opponents' father. It ends with one of the most awesome statements attributed to Jesus in the NT, "Before Abraham even came into existence, I AM" (8:58), which brings about an attempt to stone Jesus (implicitly for blasphemy).

Chap. 9, describing how the man born blind came to sight, is the master-

[34]Is "Surely he is not going off to the diaspora among the Greeks to teach the Greeks?" in 7:35 an ironic indication of the future of Johannine Christians after expulsion from the synagogue? How ironic is the objection in 7:42 that the Messiah has to come from Bethlehem? Does the evangelist know the tradition that Jesus was born in Bethlehem (found elsewhere only in Matt 2 and Luke 2); or does he judge that earthly birthplace is irrelevant since Jesus is from above; or does he intend both meanings?

[35]For the passage in 7:53–8:11 dealing with the adulterous woman, see *Issue* 1 below.

[36]Particularly puzzling is that hostile objections come from "Jews who believed him" (8:30–31). Does this reflect the Johannine community's struggle with other Christians of a lower christology who could not accept Jesus as the divine "I AM"? This title has been the subject of extensive study, e.g., D. M. Ball, *"I AM" in John's Gospel* (JSNTSup 124; Sheffield: Academic, 1996).

piece of Johannine dramatic narrative, so carefully crafted that not a single word is wasted. "The light of the world" motif (9:5) and the reference to the pool of Siloam (9:7,11) provide a loose relationship with the Tabernacles feast that evidently has kept Jesus in Jerusalem. The man born blind is more than an individual;[37] he has been developed as a spokesperson for a particular type of faith-encounter with Jesus. The Samaritan woman exemplified the obstacles encountered in coming to believe in Jesus on the first encounter. The blind man, having washed in the waters of Siloam (the name is interpreted as "the one sent," a Johannine designation for Jesus), exemplifies one who is enlightened on the first encounter, but comes to see who Jesus really is only later—after undergoing trials and being cast out of the synagogue.[38] This could be seen as a message to Johannine Christians who have had a similar experience, encouraging them that through their trials they have been given an opportunity to come to a much more profound faith than when they first encountered Christ. The intensifying series of questions to which the man born blind is subjected, the increasing hostility and blindness of the interrogators who eject him from the synagogue, the blind man's growing perceptiveness about Jesus under the interrogations,[39] and the parents' apprehensive attempt to avoid taking a stand for or against Jesus—all these are developed masterfully into a drama that could easily be enacted on a stage to illustrate how, with the coming of Jesus, those who claim to see have become blind and those who were blind have come to sight (9:39).

In the narrative sequence the metaphorical discourse on the good shepherd (10:1–21), although it has a certain autonomy, is directed to the Pharisees whom Jesus accused of being blind in 9:40–41. This and the description of the vine in 15:1–17 are the closest that John comes to the parables so common in the Synoptics.[40] In John there is a mixture of metaphors offering different ways of looking at the same reality: Jesus is the gate by which the shepherd goes to the sheep, and by which the sheep come into the fold and go out to pasture; and Jesus is the model shepherd who both knows his sheep by name and is willing to lay down his life for them. On the level of Jesus' ministry this would be aimed at the Pharisees who are the pictured audience; on the level of Johannine church life this may be a critique of other Chris-

[37]Augustine (*In Johannem* 44.1; CC 36.381): "This blind man stands for the human race."

[38]"Enlightenment" was an early Christian term for baptismal conversion, e.g., Heb 6:4; 10:32; Justin, *Apology* 1.61.13. The questions and answers in 9:35–38 may reflect a Johannine baptismal interrogation leading the believer to confess the name of Jesus as Son of Man who has come down from heaven. In early catacomb art the healing of the blind man was a symbol of baptism.

[39]V. 11: "the man they call Jesus"; v. 17: "He is a prophet"; v. 33: a man from God.

[40]Shepherding symbolism is featured there also (Mark 14:27; Matt 18:12; 25:32; see Acts 20:28–29; I Pet 5:2–4; Heb 13:20), reflecting a long history of OT usage (Num 27:16–17; I Kings 22:17; Jer 23:1–4; Ezek 34). J. Beutler and R. T. Fortna, eds., *The Shepherd Discourse of John 10 and Its Context* (SNTSMS 67; Cambridge Univ., 1991).

tians who have introduced human shepherds (pastors) who might seem to rival the claims of Christ. The famous passage in 10:16 where Jesus, referring to other sheep not of this fold, expresses his goal of one sheep herd, one shepherd suggests that, when the Gospel was written, division among Jesus' followers was a problem.

The next Jewish feast is Dedication (*Hanukkah: 10:22–42*) that celebrates the dedication of the altar and the reconstruction of the Jerusalem Temple by the Maccabees (164 BC) after several years of desecration under Syrian rulers. This festal theme is replaced when in the Temple portico Jesus claims to be the one whom the Father consecrated and sent into the world (10:36). The issues raised against Jesus about being the Messiah and blaspheming because he said he was God's Son resemble the substance of the Sanhedrin inquiry recounted by the Synoptic Gospels just before Jesus died (cf. John 10:24–25,36 and Luke 22:66–71). Faced with attempts to stone and to arrest him, Jesus defiantly proclaims, "The Father is in me, and I am in the Father." By way of inclusion the evangelist now has Jesus go back across the Jordan to where the story began in 1:28, and there the witness of JBap still echoes (10:40–42).

4. The Raising of Lazarus and Its Aftermath (chaps. 11–12). This subdivision serves as a bridge between the Book of Signs and the Book of Glory. *Jesus gives life to Lazarus* (*11:1–44*), even as he gave light to the blind man (see 11:37) and thus performs the greatest of his signs; yet paradoxically the gift of life leads to the decision of the Sanhedrin that Jesus must die (11:45–53), a decision that will bring about his glorious return to the Father. In the account of the man born blind a dialogue explaining the sign-value followed the healing; but in the raising of Lazarus the dialogue that explains this sign precedes—to have conversation after Lazarus emerges from the tomb would be an anticlimax. In the dialogue Martha already believes that Jesus is the Messiah, the Son of God (comparable to Peter's confession in Matt 16:16), and that her brother will rise on the last day; but Jesus leads her to an even deeper faith. Jesus is not only the resurrection but also the life, so that whoever believes in him will never die. Lazarus's miraculous return to life fulfills Martha's aspiration but is still only a sign, for Lazarus will die again[41]—that is why he emerges from the tomb still bound with the burial clothes. Jesus comes to give an eternal life impervious to death, as he will symbolize by emerging from the tomb leaving his burial clothes behind (20:6–7).

[41]Jesus' raisings from the dead (Lazarus, the son of the widow of Nain [Luke 7:11–17], the daughter of Jairus [Mark 5:35–43]) are recounted by the evangelists as miraculous resuscitations, similar to those done by the OT prophets Elijah and Elisha (I Kings 17:17–24; II Kings 4:32–37). Jesus' own resurrection is of a higher order, eschatologically anticipating God's raising of the dead in the last days. Resuscitation restores ordinary life; resurrection involves eternal life.

A Sanhedrin session (*11:45–53*) is provoked by the size of the following gained by Jesus and the fear that the Romans might intervene to the detriment of the nation and the Temple ("holy place"). Caiaphas, high priest in that fateful year, is enabled to utter a prophecy, though he does not recognize it. He means that Jesus should die in place of the nation, but John sees this to mean that Jesus will die on behalf of the nation and indeed "to gather together even the dispersed children of God and make them one." Jesus' fate is sealed by the Sanhedrin who plan to kill him, and *the intermediary verses* (*11:54–57*) *prepare for the arrest at Passover.*

The two scenes that follow have parallels in the Synoptics but in reverse order. *At Bethany six days before Passover Mary, the sister of Lazarus, anoints Jesus' feet* (*John 12:1–11*). This action is closely paralleled in Mark 14:3–9; Matt 26:6–13, where at Bethany two days before Passover an unnamed woman pours ointment on Jesus' head.[42] Both forms of the story have the motif of preparing Jesus for burial. The scene on the next day when *Jesus triumphantly enters Jerusalem* (*John 12:12–19*) has a close parallel in the entrance into Jerusalem in Mark 11:1–10; Matt 21:1–9; Luke 19:28–40, which took place considerably earlier. Only John mentions palm branches, and Jesus' choice of an ass seems almost by way of corrective reaction pointing to the king promised in Zechariah who is to bring peace and salvation (Zech 9:9–10).

The end of the public ministry is signaled by the arrival of Gentiles (*12:20–50*), which causes Jesus to exclaim "The hour has come" and to speak of a grain of wheat that dies in order to bear much fruit. The atmosphere resembles that of Jesus' prayer in Gethsemane on the night before he dies in Mark 14:34–36 and par. In both scenes Jesus' soul is troubled/sorrowful. In Mark he prays to the Father that the hour might pass from him; in John he refuses to pray to the Father that he might be saved from the hour since this was why he had come—different reactions mirroring what would later be called the humanity and divinity of Jesus. In Mark he prays that God's will should be done; in John he prays that God's name be glorified—variants of petitions in the "Our Father" and thus reflections of Jesus' prayer style. The responding voice from heaven in John 12:28–29 is mistaken for an angel; this resembles the appearance of an angel as a response in Luke 22:43 and Jesus' claim that if he wanted the Father would have sent more than twelve legions of angels in Matt 26:53—interesting examples of variation within different preservations of the Jesus tradition. The failure of the crowds to accept the proclamation of the Son of Man becomes in John

[42]Luke 7:36–50, another parallel, is a penitential scene set in Galilee where a sinful woman weeps over and anoints Jesus' feet. As with Mark/Matt, it is set in the house of Simon. In no Gospel account is Mary Magdalene the agent, despite subsequent artistic imagination.

12:37–41 a fulfillment of Isaiah's prediction that they will never believe.[43] True, some in the Sanhedrin believe in Jesus; but fearing the Pharisees and not willing to confess, they do not proclaim the glory of God (12:42–43). Once more we suspect that the evangelist also has in mind those in the synagogues of his own time who do not have the courage to confess Christ. The last word of Jesus in the ministry summarizing the Johannine message (12:44–50) resembles the opening summary addressed to Nicodemus in 3:16–21: The light has come into the world constituting the occasion of self-judgment between those who believe in him and are delivered from darkness and those who reject him and are condemned.

Part Two: The Book of Glory (13:1–20:31)

The theme of chaps. 13–20 is enunciated in 13:1 with the announcement that Jesus was aware that the hour had come for him to pass from this world to the Father, showing to the very end his love for his own who were in this world. In the five chapters that describe the Last Supper only "his own" are present to hear Jesus speak of his plans for them, and then in the three chapters that describe the passion and death and resurrection Jesus is glorified and ascends to his Father who now becomes their Father (20:17). Thus this "Book" illustrates the theme of the Prologue (1:12–13): "But all those who did accept him he empowered to become God's children," i.e., a new "his own" consisting of "those who believe in his name," not those who were his own people by birth.

1. The Last Supper and Jesus' Last Discourse (chaps. 13–17). In all the Gospels Jesus speaks at this meal on the night before he dies, but in John the discourse lasts much longer.

(a) In initial sections of the Last Supper (chap. 13), John's narrative has parallels to Synoptic material where at table Jesus talks about Judas[44] and (there or afterwards) warns that Simon Peter will deny him three times. Yet in place of Jesus' words over the bread and wine, John has the washing of the disciples' feet, a loving act of abasement that serves as an example for his disciples.[45] Also unique to John is the presence of "the disciple whom

[43]We saw (p. 207 above) that Matt has ten to fourteen instances of fulfillment citations of the OT; John has nine fulfillment citations of a less standardized pattern. E. D. Freed, *Old Testament Quotations in the Gospel of John* (NovTSup 11; Leiden: Brill, 1965); B. G. Schuchard, *Scripture Within Scripture* (Atlanta: Scholars, 1992).

[44]For John and Luke, Judas is the instrument of the devil/Satan.

[45]I shall discuss Johannine sacramentalism under *Issue* 3 below. Often on a secondary level of symbolism, references to baptism and the eucharist seem to be present; e.g., "If I do not wash you, you will have no heritage with me" (13:8) has caused the footwashing to be seen as a symbol of baptism.

Jesus loved." Acting as an intermediary for Simon Peter, who is placed at a distance from Jesus, this Beloved Disciple leans back against Jesus' chest to ask the identity of the one who will give Jesus over. Mentioned only in the Book of Glory, characteristically the Beloved Disciple is close to Jesus and contrasted with Peter (see p. 369 below).

After Judas has gone out into the night (symbolic of Satanic darkness), John supplies a short introduction (13:31–38) to the Last Discourse as Jesus speaks once more of his coming glorification and issues his new commandment: "As I have loved you, so you too must love one another." This is "new" not because the OT was lacking in love but because there are now two peculiarly Christian modifications: The love is to be empowered and modeled on the way Jesus manifested love for his disciples by dying and rising for them (see also Rom 5:8), and it is a love to be extended to one's fellow Christian disciples.

(b) In the body of JESUS' LAST DISCOURSE (CHAPS. 14–17) he speaks to "his own" as he contemplates his departure. This Discourse is a unique composition, comparable to Matt's Sermon on the Mount or to Luke's collection of Jesus' words spoken on the way from Galilee to Jerusalem. John's Discourse presents as one final message diverse material found in the Synoptics not only at the Last Supper but also scattered through the public ministry. Poised between heaven and earth and already in the ascent to glory, the Johannine Jesus speaks both as still in the world and as no longer in it (16:5; 17:11). This atemporal, nonspatial character gives the Discourse an abiding value as a message from Jesus to those of all time who would believe (17:20). In terms of form and content it resembles a "testament" or farewell speech[46] where a speaker (sometimes a father to his children) announces the imminence of his departure (see John 13:33; 14:2–3; 16:16), often producing sorrow (14:1,27; 16:6,22); he recalls his past life, words, and deeds (13:33; 14:10; 15:3,20; 17:4–8), urging the addressees to emulate and even surpass these (14:12), to keep the commandments (14:15,21,23; 15:10,14), and to keep unity among themselves (17:11,21–23). He may wish the addressees peace and joy (14:27; 16:22,33), pray for them (17:9), predict that they will be persecuted (15:18,20; 16:2–3), and pick a successor (Paraclete passages).

Division One of the Last Discourse (*chap. 14*). Stressing the theme of

[46]See that of Jacob to his twelve children (Gen 49), of Moses to Israel (Deut 33), of Joshua to Israel (Josh 23–24), and of David (II Sam 23:1–7; I Chron 28–29). This literary genre became very popular in the last centuries BC as we can see from the apocryphal literature, e.g., in *Jubilees* the farewells of Noah (10), of Abraham (20–21), and of Rebekah and Isaac (35–36), and the whole of the *Testaments of the Twelve Patriarchs*. In the NT testaments are supplied for Paul in Acts 20:17–38 and II Tim 3:1–4:8, and one for Peter in II Pet. Parallels in this literature to John's Last Discourse are listed in BGJ 2.598–601. More generally see D. F. Tolmie, *Jesus' Farewell to the Disciples* (Leiden: Brill, 1995).

departure, Jesus consoles his disciples by a promise to return to take them to himself so that they may be with him. Throughout, the flow of the Discourse is furthered by those present who pose questions reflecting their misunderstanding, and so Thomas' question (14:5) leads to one of the most famous proclamations in the Gospel: "I am the way and the truth and the life," and Philip's question (14:8) leads to Jesus' "Whoever has seen me has seen the Father . . . I am in the Father and the Father is in me." This mutual divine indwelling leads, in turn, into the theme of how the Spirit (14:15–17), Jesus (14:18–22), and the Father (14:23–24) will all dwell in the Christian.[47]

Of particular interest is the designation of the Spirit as the Paraclete.[48] Unlike the neuter word (*pneuma*) for Spirit, *paraklētos,* literally "the One called alongside," is a personal designation picturing a Spirit called in after Jesus' departure as "advocate"[49] to defend Christians and "consoler" to comfort them. Just as Jesus received everything from the Father and while on earth is the way to know the Father in heaven, so when Jesus goes to heaven, the Paraclete who receives everything from Jesus is the way to know Jesus.[50] Jesus, however, is the divine Word incarnate in one human being whose stay in this world with his followers is temporary; the Paraclete does not become incarnate but dwells in all who love Jesus and keep his commandments and is with them forever (14:15–16). Two features are characteristic: He is in a hostile relationship to the world which cannot see or recognize him (14:17) and he serves as a teacher explaining the implications of what Jesus said.

The latter motif appears in the second Paraclete passage of chap. 14 (v. 26), and then Jesus gives his gift of peace, accompanied by a warning that the Prince of this world is coming (14:27–31b). Jesus' final words in the chapter (14:31c), "Get up! Let us leave here and be on our way," seem to signal the end of the Last Discourse and would lead perfectly into 18:1, "After this discourse Jesus went out with his disciples across the Kidron valley."

[47]The various statements about how all three of these figures will come to believers and remain with them are complicated; see BGJ 2.602–603.

[48]For Johannine Paraclete-Spirit literature see: C. K. Barrett, JTS NS 1 (1950), 1–15; R. E. Brown, NTS 13 (1966–67), 113–32; also BGJ 2.1135–44; H. Windisch, *The Spirit-Paraclete in the Fourth Gospel* (Facet Biblical Series 20; Philadelphia: Fortress, 1968; German orig. 1927, 1933); D. E. Holwerda, *The Holy Spirit and Eschatology in the Gospel of John* (Kampen: Kok, 1959); G. Johnston, *The Spirit-Paraclete in the Gospel of John* (SNTSMS 12; Cambridge Univ., 1970); G. M. Burge, *The Anointed Community. The Holy Spirit in the Johannine Tradition* (Grand Rapids: Eerdmans, 1987).

[49]From Latin for "called alongside," this is a designation for a lawyer. *Paraklētos* in Greek is a forensic or legal term designating a defense attorney, but the Johannine Paraclete is more a prosecutor.

[50]The Johannine Jesus is the truth (14:6); the Paraclete is the Spirit of Truth (14:17; 16:13), a designation not found in the OT but in the DSS (in dualistic opposition to the Spirit of falsehood), and used for the Holy Spirit only by John. See also I John 5:6: "The Spirit is truth."

Division Two of the Last Discourse (*chaps. 15–16*). That three chapters of Discourse follow 14:31c is very surprising and has led many to posit an insertion added later to the original work of the evangelist by a redactor (p. 367 below). That 16:4b–33 seems to treat many themes of Division One and yet to suppose that the audience knows nothing of those themes has suggested that this insertion consisted of an alternative Last Discourse which the redactor did not want to have perish. Be all that as it may, let us look at the individual subsections.

15:1–17: The vine and the branches.[51] Alongside the shepherd comparison of chap. 10, this is the other significant Johannine instance of parabolic/allegorical language. In the OT Israel is frequently pictured as God's choice vine or vineyard, nurtured with consummate care only to yield bitter fruit. We have seen Jesus replacing Jewish institutions and feasts; now he portrays himself as the vine of the New Israel. As branches united to him, Christians will bear fruit pleasing to God, the vinedresser. Although the vine will not wither and fail, branches will fall and have to be removed and burned. Some would compare this image of the Christian community to Paul's image of the body of Christ (I Cor 12:12–31); but while Paul's imagery is invoked to regulate the relation of Christians to each other, John's imagery is concerned only with their indwelling in Jesus. As part of his comments on the image, Jesus proclaims again his commandment, "Love one another as I have loved you" (15:7–17, esp. 12; cf. 13:34–35). That love includes a willingness to lay down one's life for others.

15:18–16:4a: The world's hatred; witness by the Paraclete. Jesus' stress on the necessity of love among his followers is related to his perception of how the world hates him and those whom he has chosen out of the world. If at the beginning of the Gospel we were told that God loved the world (3:16), "the world" is now coterminous with those who have rejected the Son whom God sent to save it. The fact that Jesus has come and spoken makes this rejection sinful (15:22). The Paraclete will come and continue the witness on behalf of Jesus, and those who have been with Jesus from the beginning must bear witness (15:26–27). They should recognize, however, that they will be expelled from the synagogue and even put to death for such witness. This section of the Johannine Last Discourse resembles part of the final speech of Jesus before the Supper in Mark 13:9–13 (see also Matt 10:17–22).

16:4b–33: Themes resembling those of Division One (chap. 14). In 16:4b–7 Jesus reiterates what he said at the beginning of the Discourse

[51]See F. Segovia, JBL 101 (1982), 115–28.

(14:1–5) as he announces his departure, discusses where he is going,[52] and recognizes that his disciples' hearts are troubled. Once more there are two Paraclete passages: The first in 16:7–11 matching that in 14:15–17 in the theme of his conflict with the world (and the Prince of this world: cf. 14:30);[53] the second in 16:13–15 matching that in 14:25–26 in the theme of his teaching anew what Jesus taught. Whereas in 14:16,26 the Father is said to give or send the Paraclete, in 16:7 Jesus is said to send him—an illustration of Jesus' claim that the Father and he are one (10:30).

Although earlier in the Supper (13:33; see 7:33; 12:35) Jesus spoke of being with his disciples only a little while, the development of that theme in 16:16–22 has no close parallel elsewhere in the Last Discourse.[54] Jesus' painful death and his subsequent return are compared to labor pangs and subsequent birth (see the similar imagery for the birth of the Messiah in Rev 12:2,5). In 16:23–24, however, with the issue of asking and receiving, we have once more a theme found in Division One of the Discourse (14:13–14). The section 16:25–33 also has some themes that we have heard before ("The Father loves you because you have loved me" in 16:27 and 14:21,23; "I am going to the Father" in 16:28 and 14:12; the promise of peace in 16:33 and 14:27); but the contrast between figures of speech and speaking plainly and the prediction of the scattering of the disciples are new.[55] Although in terminating Division One of the Discourse Jesus spoke of the Prince of this world having no hold on him (14:30), the simpler "I have conquered the world" is a more resounding termination for this Division.[56]

Division Three of the Last Discourse (*chap. 17*). This sublime conclusion to the Last Discourse is often evaluated as the "Priestly" Prayer of Jesus, the one who consecrated himself for those whom he would send into the world (17:18–19). In the first section (17:1–8) Jesus prays for glorification (i.e., the glory that he had before creation) on the grounds that he has completed all

[52]Evidence that different forms of the Last Discourse may have been placed side by side is supplied by comparing 16:5 ("Not one of you asks me, 'Where are you going?'") with the words of Thomas in 14:5 ("Lord, we don't know where you are going").

[53]The verb in the poetic treatment of the three issues (sin, justice, judgment) in which the Paraclete will be active can mean "expose," "prove wrong about," or "convict." (For similar triadic patterns, see I John 2:12–14,16; 5:7.) Here the Paraclete, acting as an attorney prosecuting the world to establish the justice of Jesus' cause, resembles the heavenly witness in Job (16:19) who after Job's death takes his stand on earth and serves as a vindicator ("redeemer": 19:25–27).

[54]Yet just as 14:15–17, 14:18–22, and 14:23–24 treated sequentially the Spirit, Jesus, and the Father, so also 16:13–15, 16:16–22, and 16:23–27.

[55]In Mark, immediately after the Supper, Jesus predicts that in the passion the disciples will be scandalized and cites Zech 13:7 about the sheep being scattered. In John 16:1 Jesus speaks of the future suffering of the disciples in order to prevent them from being scandalized, and in 16:32 he warns that they will be scattered.

[56]We see how the Christian is conformed to Jesus when we look at I John 5:5 "Who is it that conquers the world but the one who believes that Jesus is the Son of God?"

that the Father has given him to do and revealed God's name. This is not a selfish prayer, since the goal of the glorification is that the Son may glorify the Father properly. In the second section (17:9–19) Jesus prays for those whom the Father has given him that they may be kept safe with the name given to Jesus.[57] He refuses to pray for the world (which by rejecting Jesus has become the realm of evil), for his disciples do not belong to the world. Quite unlike a gnostic savior, Jesus does not ask that his disciples be taken out of the world, but only that they be kept safe from the Evil One (who is the Prince of this world). Praying that they will be consecrated as he consecrates himself, Jesus sends them into the world to bear witness to truth. In the third section (17:20–26) Jesus prays for those who believe in him through the word of the disciples—a prayer that they may be one just as the Father and Jesus are one. (As in 10:16 we get the impression that already in John's time Christians are not one.) A unity brought to completion among believers will be convincing to the world. Magnificent statements about these believers are addressed to the Father: "I have given to them the glory which you have given to me"; "You loved them even as you loved me"; "They are your gift to me"; and finally (17:26) "To them I made your name known, and I will continue to make it known so that the love you had for me may be in them and I may be in them." With that assurance the Johannine Jesus goes on to be lifted up on the cross in his return to the Father.

2. Jesus' Passion and Death (chaps. 18–19). Here John is closer to the overall Synoptic (Marcan) outline than elsewhere. Even though major individual details differ, the same pattern of four "acts" may be detected in both accounts: arrest, interrogation by Jewish high priest, trial before Pilate, crucifixion/burial.

Arrest in the garden across the Kidron (18:1–12). The Synoptic designation for the locale to which Jesus and his disciples went after the Last Supper is Gethsemane and/or the Mount of Olives. John speaks of Jesus crossing the winter-flowing Kidron[58] to a garden. The prayer to the Father about being delivered from the hour, which is found in this context in Mark 14:35, has occurred earlier in John (12:27–28), so that the whole Johannine scene centers on the arrest, with Jesus eager to drink the cup the Father has given him (cf. Mark 14:36).[59] There are peculiar Johannine features: Jesus, knowing

[57]The name of God has power. In Phil 2:9–11 the name ("Lord") is given by God to Jesus after his crucifixion and exaltation; in John Jesus already has the divine name ("I AM"?) before his death.

[58]Both this designation and Ascent of Olives appear in the Greek of the account of David's flight from the attempt of Absalom on his life (II Sam 15:23,30).

[59]Only in John is the one who cuts off the ear of the servant of the high priest identified as Simon Peter. Is that historical information, or does it illustrate a tendency to supply names for the unnamed based on verisimilitude (i.e., this is the type of bold thing Peter was likely to have done)? The fact that John also names the servant (Malchus) complicates the problem.

that Judas is coming, goes out to meet him; and when he identifies himself with the words "I am," the arresting party, consisting of Jewish police and a cohort of Roman soldiers, fall back to the ground before him. This corresponds to the depiction of Jesus in control that governs the passion in John: "No one takes my life away from me; I lay it down of my own accord. I have power to lay it down, and I have power to take it up again" (10:18).

Interrogation by Annas; Peter's denials (*18:13–27*). All the Gospels have the arresting party deliver Jesus to the Jewish high priest's court/palace to be interrogated by that authority—an interrogation that is accompanied by accounts of an abuse/mockery of Jesus and of Peter's three denials. In John alone there is no session of the Sanhedrin to decide on Jesus' death (that took place earlier: 11:45–53); and although Caiaphas is mentioned, Annas conducts the inquiry.[60] Peter's denials are introduced by the presence of another disciple who is known to the high priest—probably the Beloved Disciple who appears only in John.

Trial before Pilate (*18:28–19:16*). All the Gospels have Jesus led from/by the high priest to be tried by the Roman governor, but in John this trial is a much more developed drama than in the Synoptics. Careful stage setting is supplied, with "the Jews" outside the praetorium and Jesus inside. Seven episodes describe how Pilate shuttled back and forth trying to reconcile the two adamant antagonists (diagram in BGJ 2.859). Only John explains clearly why Jesus was brought to Pilate (18:31: the Jews were not permitted to put anyone to death)[61] and why Pilate rendered a death sentence even though he knew that Jesus did not deserve such a punishment (19:12: he would be denounced to the Emperor for not being diligent in punishing a so-called king). Jesus, who scarcely speaks to Pilate in the other Gospels, explains that his kingship is not political; moreover "the Jews" admit that the real issue is not the charge of being "the King of the Jews" but that Jesus claimed to be God's Son (19:7). Pilate is challenged by Jesus as to whether he belongs to the truth (18:37), and thus the scene becomes the trial of Pontius Pilate before Jesus, over whom Pilate has no real power (19:11). The scourging by the Roman soldiers (at the end after condemnation in Mark/Matt) is moved to the center of the trial so that Pilate can present the abused and mocked Jesus to "the Jews" in the famous *Ecce homo* scene, with the

[60]Luke does not name the high priest here but knows of the high priests Annas and Caiaphas (Luke 3:2; Acts 4:6). While in Mark/Matt the authorities abuse/mock Jesus, in Luke and John the Jewish police are the agents.

[61]Historically this has been challenged; but overall it seems likely that John is accurate, namely, except for certain agreed-on crimes, only the Roman governor of Judea could order execution. Of course, that norm would not always have been effectively operative; e.g., when he was away or at a distance and so might not be able to enforce the Roman policy, Jewish authorities/groups could take it into their own hands to punish people for infractions that required death under Jewish law.

vain hope that they will give up their request for the death penalty. Although Pilate yields, "the Jews" are compelled to give up their messianic expectations by saying, "We have no king other than the Emperor" (19:15). In Pilate John has dramatized his thesis that those who would avoid the judgment provoked by Jesus do not themselves belong to truth (9:18–23; 12:42–43).

Crucifixion, death, and burial (19:17–42). Here too John is more dramatic than the Synoptics, making major theological episodes out of details in the tradition. In slightly different wording all four Gospels mention the charge "King of the Jews," but in John this becomes the occasion for Pilate's finally acknowledging the truth about Jesus, proclaiming it in the style of an imperial inscription in three languages. All four Gospels mention the division of Jesus' clothing; but in John the way in which the Roman soldiers thus fulfilled the Scripture to the "nth" degree is spelled out as an illustration of how Jesus remained in charge. After the death of Jesus the other Gospels mention Galilean women standing at a distance; John has them near the cross while he is still alive. There are two other figures whose presence John alone notes and whose names he never gives us: the mother of Jesus[62] and the disciple whom he loved. Jesus brings them into a mother-son relationship and thus constitutes a community of disciples who are mother and brother to him—the community that preserved this Gospel. With this the Johannine Jesus is able to make his final word from the cross, "It is completed," and to hand over his Spirit to the believing community he is leaving behind (19:30). The scene of the piercing of the dead Jesus' side is peculiarly Johannine, fulfilling both 7:37–39 that from within Jesus would flow living water symbolic of the Spirit, and (since the bones of the paschal lamb were not to be broken) 1:29 that he was the Lamb of God. Peculiar to John is Nicodemus (3:1–2; 7:50–52), who had not openly admitted that he believes in Jesus. Now he reappears and (together with the traditional Joseph from Arimathea) publicly gives an honorable burial to Jesus, fulfilling Jesus' promise to draw all to him once he had been lifted up (12:32).

3. Four Scenes in Jerusalem and Faith in the Risen Jesus (20:1–29). Like Luke and Mark 16:9–20 and unlike Matt and Mark 16:1–8, chap. 20 in John places all the appearances of the risen Lord in Jerusalem, with no indication of appearances to take place in Galilee. In John four different types of faith-response to the risen Jesus are dramatized, two in scenes that take place at the empty tomb, two in a room where the disciples are gathered. The second and fourth concentrate on individual reactions: Mary Magdalene and Thomas.[63] Some of the material has parallels in the Synop-

[62]See J. A. Grassi, CBQ 49 (1986), 67–80 (without necessarily adopting his chiastic pattern).
[63]See D. A. Lee, JSNT 58 (1995), 37–49.

tic Gospels,[64] but the arrangement of that and new material reflects John's love for personal encounter with Jesus.

At the tomb (20:1–18). An introduction (20:1–2) consisting of Mary Magdalene's coming to the tomb, finding it empty, and reporting this to Simon Peter and the Beloved Disciple prepares for the two scenes at the tomb. The *first scene* (20:3–10) involves Simon Peter and the Beloved Disciple who run to the tomb. Both enter and see the burial wrappings and head cloth; yet only the Beloved Disciple comes to faith.[65] The fourth evangelist does not challenge the tradition that Peter was the first of the Twelve to see the risen Lord (Luke 24:34; I Cor 15:5); but in his consistent desire to exalt the Beloved Disciple, John has that disciple come to faith even before the risen Lord appears or prophetical Scripture is recalled. Thus the Disciple becomes the first full believer. The *second scene* (20:11–18) has Mary Magdalene return to the tomb where now two angels are present. Neither their speaking to her nor the sudden appearance of Jesus, whom she mistakenly identifies as a gardener, brings her to faith. That is accomplished when Jesus calls her by name—an illustration of the theme enunciated by the Good Shepherd in 10:3–4: He calls his own by name, and they know his voice. Mary is sent to proclaim all this to the disciples,[66] who are now called Jesus' brothers because as a result of the resurrection/ascension Jesus' Father becomes their Father. In the language of the Prologue (1:12), Jesus has empowered those who believe in him to become God's children. In typical Johannine outlook, these two scenes at the tomb relate resurrection faith to intimacy with Jesus; now the Gospel turns to scenes of a more traditional character, where faith and doubt greet the appearance itself.

Inside a room (20:19–29).[67] The *first scene* (20:19–25) takes place on Easter Sunday night in a place where the doors are locked for fear of "the Jews." It involves members of the Twelve (v. 24) and resembles a culminating scene in the other Gospels (Matt 28:16–20; Luke 24:33–49; Mark 16:14–20) where Jesus appears to the Eleven (Twelve minus Judas) and sends them forth on a mission. After extending peace in echo of 14:27 and 16:33, the Johannine Jesus gives to the disciples a mission that continues his own. In a symbolic action evocative of God's creative breath that gave life to the first human being

[64]Mary Magdalene and women ("we" in 20:2) find the tomb empty; angels speak to Mary; Peter goes to the tomb (Luke 24:12—missing in some mss.); appearance to Mary (Matt 28:9–10); appearance to the Twelve and mission for them.

[65]As is the Johannine custom, details are left obscure, e.g., the symbolism (if there is any) of the Disciple's outrunning Peter, and why the sight of the garments told him that Jesus had risen. Scholars' proposed explanations are myriad.

[66]This mission earned her in the later church the designation *apostola apostolorum*, "Apostle to the apostles."

[67]This is sometimes called "the upper room," but that requires harmonization with the scene after the ascension in Acts 1:13 (also Mark 14:15).

(Gen 2:7) and of the demand to be begotten of water and Spirit (John 3:5–8), Jesus breathes on them and gives them a Holy Spirit with power over sin, continuing his own power over sin. The other Gospel appearance scenes always include an element of disbelief on the part of the Eleven, but John more dramatically embodies it in Thomas who vocalizes a determined incredulity (in vv. 24–25, which serve as a transition to the next episode).

The *second scene* (20:26–29) is localized in the same place a week later with Thomas present. Although the proof offered Thomas, viz., examining Jesus' hands with his fingers and putting his hand in Jesus' side,[68] presents a tangibly corporeal image of the risen Jesus, one should note that Thomas is not said to have touched Jesus. To have done so would probably have signified that Thomas' disbelief remained. Rather, his willingness to believe without touching Jesus is genuine faith, with the ironical result that the one who embodied disbelief now utters the highest christological confession in the Gospels, "My Lord and My God"—an inclusion with the Prologue's "The Word was God." In response, Jesus blesses all future generations who will believe in him without having seen (20:29), thus showing an awareness of the Gospel audience for whom John had been writing throughout.

Gospel Conclusion (20:30–31): *Statement of purpose in writing.* Luke explains his purpose at the beginning of his Gospel (1:1–4), but John saves his statement of intention till the end. In selecting material to be included in the Gospel,[69] his goal has been to have people come to faith or increase in faith (disputed reading) in Jesus as the Messiah, the Son of God, and through this faith to possess eternal life in his name. This statement is true to the constant emphases of the Gospel, but also warns against a literalist interpretation of John as if the main purpose were to report eyewitness testimony.

Epilogue (21:1–25)

Although the Gospel concludes at the end of chap. 20, there follows another chapter of resurrection appearances (this time in Galilee)[70] with another con-

[68]John 19:34 told us that Jesus' side was pierced; but only by combining the resurrectional appearances of John 20:25,27 and Luke 24:39 do we get the image that Jesus' hands and feet were nailed to the cross. Riley, *Resurrection,* points out that John has a more fleshly conception of the resurrection than has the partially gnostic *Gospel of Thomas.*

[69]It is not clear what the clause "Jesus performed many other signs" in John 20:30 implies. (See n. 15 above.) The last miracle done by Jesus was the raising of Lazarus in chap. 11, whence the designation of 1:19–12:50 as "The Book of Signs." Does the evangelist mean other unrecorded signs during Jesus' public ministry? (But then one might have expected the clause to be appended to the end of chap. 12.) Or does he evaluate something in chaps. 12–20 as a sign (whence "other" signs in 20:30) even though in these chapters he does not use the term and Jesus performs no miracle? Some would argue that the resurrection is a sign, but that seems more like glorious reality.

[70]The attempt to connect chap. 21 to 20 in 21:14 seems to be an afterthought. Many scholars attribute chap. 21 to a redactor (p. 367 below) who added it to an already completed Gospel. For a

clusion. This chapter contains two scenes, one involving fishing (21:1–14), the other preserving sayings of the risen Jesus to Simon Peter and the Beloved Disciple (21:15–23). The connection between the two scenes and their internal harmony are questionable, but theologically the themes are related.

The *first scene* (*21:1–14*), in which the risen Jesus is not recognized by the disciples (who are supposed to have seen him twice in chap. 20), involves a miraculous catch of fish similar to that during the ministry in Luke 5:4–11. Since Simon Peter hauls the 153 fish ashore and the net is not torn, the catch becomes symbolic of missionary success in bringing people into the one community of Christ. Typically Johannine is the greater perceptiveness of the Beloved Disciple who in 21:7 is the first of the disciples to recognize the risen Lord. The unity of the scene is imperiled by the fact that Jesus suddenly has fish on shore in v. 9 before the catch is brought ashore. The meal he provides of bread and fish (vv. 12–13) may be the Johannine form of the tradition that the risen Lord appeared at meals, often with eucharistic overtones (see chap. 6).

The *second scene* (*21:15–23*) shifts symbolism abruptly as, leaving aside Peter's catch of fish, Jesus talks to him about sheep. Probably this represents a second stage in Peter's image: Known as a missionary apostle (fisherman), Peter has now become a model for pastoral care (shepherd: see I Pet 5:1–4; Acts 20:28). This development may have involved a late Johannine concession to church structure, for chap. 10 portrayed Jesus as the sole shepherd. But the qualifications remain faithful to Johannine idealism: Peter's shepherding flows from his love for Jesus; the flock still belongs to Jesus ("my sheep"); and Peter must be willing to lay down his life for the sheep. The unity of the scene is somewhat challenged by the sudden appearance of the Beloved Disciple, but the contrast between him and Peter is typically Johannine. The tradition that Peter is the symbol for apostolic authority is not challenged, but without that authority the Beloved Disciple still has a position that Peter does not have—the Disciple may last until Jesus returns.[71] The concern for the exact implication of this statement (21:23: "did not say he was not to die"), which has circulated as Johannine tradition, suggests that the Disciple is now dead.

The conclusion in 21:24–25 identifies the Beloved Disciple as the witness who stands behind the Gospel narrative and certifies the truth of his testimony. It also reminds us that the whole Jesus cannot be captured in the pages of any book, even a book such as the Fourth Gospel!

---

defense of unified authorship of chaps. 1–21, see S. S. Smalley, NTS 20 (1973–74), 275–88; P. S. Minear, JBL 102 (1983), 85–98.

[71]This may be the Johannine equivalent of Matt 24:34 that all these things would come to pass before this generation would pass away.

Is John a Genuine Gospel? Combined Sources or Development of Tradition?

Is John a Gospel in the same sense in which Mark, Matt, and Luke are Gospels? According to the majority view, the Synoptic Gospels had their roots in memories of what Jesus actually did and said, even though the material stemming from those memories has undergone selection, theological reflection, narrative embellishment, and simplification in the course of a preaching (and initial writing?) that separated the actual occurrences in the late 20s and the final written composition thirty to seventy years later. Is that description true also of John?

From the 2d to the 18th century that question was answered in the affirmative, with the assumption that John, one of the Twelve Apostles of Jesus, not only supplied the memory of what had happened but also wrote it down. Thus John's Gospel was a surer guide than Mark or Luke, neither of which had been written down by an eyewitness. The differences between John and the Synoptics were explained by supposition that in his old age the apostle read the other Gospels and decided to supplement them with his own, more meditative memories.[72]

In the last two centuries, however, a more critical mind-set recognized that there is in John not the slightest sign that its author intended a supplement, nor has he supplied any key as to how his material could be fitted together with the Synoptic material to which he makes no reference. Accordingly the majority of scholars shifted toward the position that John was not authored by an eyewitness. Initially that perception had the effect of moving the pendulum to the other extreme in relation to historicity: The material in John was now judged to have no historical value (unlike the material in the Synoptic Gospels). Within this approach it was first assumed that for information about Jesus the author of John was entirely dependent on the Synoptics from which he imaginatively reshuffled material into fictional narratives.[73] A number of studies from different perspectives, however, began to gain dominance for the view that John was written independently of the

[72]The classic older lives of Christ reflect this view. Since John (the putative eyewitness) mentions three Passovers (2:13; 6:4; 12:1—the last being the Passover of Jesus' death), it was assumed that Jesus' ministry lasted two or three years (depending on how much time was allotted before the first Passover). Then the Synoptic material was divided and assigned to the years determined from John. Modern scholars deny that the Synoptic material is in chronological order, and would query whether John mentioned all the Passovers of Jesus' ministry and/or whether those he mentioned were cited as historical memories or simply for the purpose of symbolism.

[73]E.g., supposedly having read the story of Martha and Mary (Luke 10:38–42) and the parable of Lazarus (Luke 16:19–31) whom the rich man wanted sent back from the dead, John created the account of Lazarus, the brother of Martha and Mary, who did come back from the dead.

Synoptics.[74] The theory then emerged that the fourth evangelist drew, not on the Synoptics, but on nonhistorical sources. Bultmann's theory of three sources attracted much attention: (a) a Signs (*Semeia*) Source consisting of miracles selected from a larger collection[75]—according to Bultmann miracles do not happen, and so these were fictional stories designed to make projected image of Jesus more competitive in a world that believed in miracle workers; (b) a Revelatory Discourse Source, originally in Aramaic poetic format, containing the speeches of a revealer come down from heaven;[76] these were translated into Greek, adapted to serve as speeches of the Johannine Jesus, and then combined with the Signs material; (c) a Passion and Resurrection Account, drawing on Synoptic material.

By the middle of the 20th century the pendulum began to swing back. Studies in German by E. Schweizer and E. Ruckstuhl[77] found the same stylistic peculiarities in all three sources proposed by Bultmann, an observation leading to the ironic suggestion that the author of the Fourth Gospel would have had to write all three sources himself. Dodd, *Historical,* had a leading role in arguing that at times in the words and deeds of Jesus in John there is tradition that has every right to be considered as old as traditions in the Synoptics. *The theory gained followers that John was a Gospel not unlike the others, undergoing three stages of development even as they did*—a theory that I espouse. (1) At its beginning there were memories of what Jesus did and said, but not the same memories preserved in the Synoptics (specifically in Mark); perhaps the difference stemmed from the fact that unlike the pre-Synoptic tradition, John's memories were not of standardized apostolic origin (see below under *Authorship*). (2) Then these memories were influenced by the life-experience of the Johannine community that preserved them and of the Johannine preachers who expounded them. (3) Finally an evangelist, who plausibly was one of the preachers with his own dramatic and creative abilities, shaped the tradition from the second stage into a written Gospel. Both the Synoptics and John, then, would constitute independent witnesses

[74]P. Gardner-Smith, *St. John and the Synoptic Gospels* (Cambridge Univ., 1938), was influential; similarly R. Bultmann and C. H. Dodd.

[75]The key proofs are the enumeration of signs in John 2:11; 4:54, and the mention of other signs in 12:37; 20:30. For the Greek text of Bultmann's reconstructed Signs Source, see Smith, *Composition* 38–44.

[76]All the parallels offered by Bultmann date from a period later than the writing of John, e.g., the Syriac *Odes of Solomon* and the Mandaean writings. More recently some have claimed to find antecedents in the gnostic documents discovered at Nag Hammadi (4th-century Coptic from 2d-century AD Greek), particularly in the "I" speeches in "The Thunder, Perfect Mind" (VI,2). The reconstructed Greek text of Bultmann's Revelatory Discourse Source is found in Smith, *Composition* 23–34, and an English text in B. S. Easton, JBL 65 (1946), 143–56.

[77]An English article by Ruckstuhl appears in EJ 125–47.

to Jesus, witnesses in which early tradition has been preserved[78] and also undergone theological reflection as the message about Jesus was adapted to ongoing generations of believers. Although John has sometimes been deemed the most theological of the Gospels, the theological difference becomes one of intensity and of the extent to which theological insight is woven creatively and imaginatively into the memories of Jesus.

Although the approach just described has a respectable following, in the last decades of the 20th century one cannot speak of a unanimous approach to John. There are those who think they can detect with great precision the Gospel's sources (or at least the Signs Source, usually seven signs), even if the Bultmannian judgment about nonhistoricity is no longer necessarily part of the picture. Frequently the source is presumed to have originated within the same community that gave rise to the Gospel, so that the difference between a source and an earlier edition becomes somewhat nebulous.[79] As for relationship to the Synoptics, although the majority probably still holds Johannine independence of the Synoptics, an articulate group (whose arguments are urged with determination by F. Neirynck[80]) contends that John drew on Mark and even the other Synoptics. Observations pertinent to these differences will be made in subsections to follow.

Comparison of John to the Synoptic Gospels[81]

A comparison of the Fourth Gospel to the first three Gospels shows obvious differences. Peculiarities of John include: a Jesus conscious of having preexisted with God before he came into the world (John 17:5); a public ministry largely set in Jerusalem rather than in Galilee; the significant absence of the kingdom of God motif (only in 3:3,5); long discourses and dia-

[78]Dodd, *Historical,* is the classic exponent of this; see also Robinson, *Priority* (who has good observations independent of his tendency to date the NT writings too early). One should still recognize that from the first days tradition about Jesus was preserved for theological reasons.

[79]D. A. Carson, JBL 97 (1978), 411–29 surveys Johannine source analysis. Kysar, *Fourth Evangelist* 26–27, describes five different reconstructions of the Signs Source; also see the work of Fortna, Nicol, van Belle, and von Wahlde. Ruckstuhl, who in 1951 isolated some 50 Johannine characteristics, by 1987 had enlarged the count to 153 and developed further his argument that the widespread presence of the same stylistic features throughout the Gospel rendered impossible the isolation of sources; but Fortna, in particular, has argued that a more sophisticated set of criteria enables him to distinguish an earlier account (a gospel, not merely a Signs Source) underlying the present Fourth Gospel. For more on Johannine stylistic features, see N. G. Timmins, JSNT 53 (1994), 47–64. A thorough German study of signs in John by W. Bittner (1987) rejects a Signs Source.

[80]See EJ 73–106; and in *John and the Synoptics,* ed. A. Denaux (BETL 101; Leuven Univ., 1992), 1–62.

[81]Amidst the abundant literature, see B. Lindars, NTS 27 (1981), 287–84; P. Borgen in *The Interrelations of the Gospels,* ed. D. L. Dungan (BETL 95: Leuven Univ., 1990), 408–37; D. M. Smith, *John among the Gospels: The Relationship in Twentieth-Century Research* (Minneapolis: A/F, 1992).

logues rather than parables; no diabolic possessions; a very restricted number of miracles (seven?), including some that are unique (changing of water to wine at Cana, healing a man *born* blind, and the raising of Lazarus). According to statistics supplied by B. de Solages in a French study (1979) there are parallels to Mark in 15.5 percent of John's passion narrative; the parallels to Mark in the Matthean and Lucan passion narratives would be four times higher.

Yet there are also important similarities to the Synoptics, especially in the beginning narrative of the ministry featuring JBap and in the concluding narratives of the passion and empty tomb. In particular, the closest similarities are with Mark, e.g., in the sequence of events shared by John 6 and Mark 6:30–54; 8:11–33; and in such verbal details as "genuine nard of great value" (John 12:3), 300 denarii (12:5), and 200 denarii (6:7). There are parallels with Luke,[82] but more of motif than of wording, e.g., figures like Martha and Mary, Lazarus (parabolic in Luke), and Annas; lack of a night trial before Caiaphas; the three "not guilty" statements in the Pilate trial; postresurrectional appearances of Jesus *in Jerusalem* to his male disciples; the miraculous draught of fishes (John 21). There are fewer similarities with Matthew; yet compare John 13:16 with Matt 10:24; and John 15:18–27 with Matt 10:18–25.

A variety of solutions has been suggested. At one end of the spectrum, some would posit John's knowledge of Mark or even of all three Synoptics. (Such proposals may disagree as to whether John *also* had an independent tradition.) At the other end of the spectrum, the fourth evangelist is thought not to have known any Synoptic Gospel and occasional similarities between John and the others are explained in terms of the Synoptic and Johannine traditions independently reproducing with variations the same deeds or sayings. In between the extremes a median position (that I espouse myself) maintains that Mark and John shared common preGospel traditions, oral or written; and that although the fourth evangelist had not seen the final form of Luke, he was familiar with traditions incorporated later into Luke. Some who make a distinction in John between an evangelist and a final redactor would posit that only the latter knew one or more of the Synoptic Gospels.

Unity and Cohesiveness of John

If we lay aside the issue of sources employed in John, the question remains whether the Gospel is a cohesive whole. There are abrupt transitions (called

[82]J. A. Bailey, *The Traditions Common to the Gospels of Luke and John* (NovTSup 7; Leiden: Brill, 1963); F. L. Cribbs, SBLSP 1978, 1.215–61.

aporias) between parts of John, e.g., with only minimum transitions chap. 4 ends in Galilee; chap. 5 describes Jesus in Jerusalem; chap. 6 has Jesus back in Galilee. Some scholars would rearrange these chapters to the order 4, 6, and 5 on the supposition that the original order was confused. Indeed commentaries have been written on a reconstructed order.[83] The rearrangement proposal faces serious difficulties. First, there is no manuscript evidence to support any such rearrangements, and any theory that the pages of John were confused by chance has to depend totally on imagination. Second, the order that emerges from rearrangements still presents problems unless one makes changes in the wording, e.g., while the order 4, 6, 5, makes better geographic sequence, the transition from the end of chap. 5 to the beginning of chap. 7 is awkward. Third, such rearrangements are based on assumptions about what should have interested the evangelist. Yet John gives us a very schematic account of Jesus' ministry, and does not worry about transitions unless they have theological purpose (e.g., the careful sequence of days in chaps. 1–2). In the series of feasts in chaps. 2, 5, 6, 7 and 10 that serves as the framework for Jesus' ministry, little attention is paid to the long intervals that separate the feasts. Someone was responsible for the Gospel in its final form; and unless one is willing to suppose incompetence, he could scarcely have missed the obviously imperfect sequence, if he regarded that as important.

Yet one cannot deny the presence of certain transition difficulties for which another solution may be proposed. The most awkward is the relatively clear ending of the Gospel in 20:30–31 where the writer acknowledges that there was other material that he could have included but did not choose to do so. The presence of still another chapter (21) and another ending (21:24–25) raises the possibility that, after an earlier form of the Gospel was completed (but before any preserved form of the Gospel circulated), someone made additions. Presumably this someone was *not* the person who composed the earlier form and now had afterthoughts, for that person should have felt free to insert the material of chap. 21 before the ending he had earlier composed in 20:30–31.[84] Accordingly the present Gospel is thought to involve the work of two hands, an evangelist who composed the body of the Gospel and a redactor who later made additions.

In that theory what would have been the goal of this redactor and how did

[83]Schnackenburg shifts these chapters; Bernard calculates the length of a sheet of papyrus and liberally moves papyrus-length passages around; Bultmann makes a large number of rearrangements, some of them of the length of only a few words. This last proposal does not explain how such small fragments got displaced. Was the Gospel written on tiny scraps of papyrus?

[84]Presumably the evangelist himself was no longer available (dead? elsewhere?) to make the additions.

he work? Bultmann, who attributed major sections of the Gospel to redaction, created the image of an Ecclesiastical Redactor. In this approach, the writing left by the evangelist was too radical in its theology; and in order to make it acceptable to the wider church (hence "Ecclesiastical"), a type of censor added sections. For example, to a nonsacramental gospel the Ecclesiastical Redactor added the references to baptism in 3:5 and the eucharist in 6:51b–58 and to both sacraments in 19:34b–35; to a gospel that understood the last things (coming from heaven, judgment, eternal life) to have been already realized in Jesus' ministry, the Ecclesiastical Redactor added the motif of final judgment (5:28–29; 12:48). Positing such censorship smacks too much of a modern mind-set governed by a thesis-antithesis pattern and is unnecessary in the redactor theory.

A much more likely supposition is that one who took the trouble to add to the evangelist's work agreed with it substantially and was of the same community of thought. Indeed the style of the proposed additions shows respect for what was already written and a desire not to tamper with the established pattern, e.g., adding a chapter of resurrection appearances (chap. 21) after the existing ending in 20:30–31 rather than breaking up the careful arrangement of appearances in chap. 20. There are several possible types of material that the redactor would have been adding. (1) Omitted material. There are several indications (20:31; 21:25) of a wider body of tradition that was not included. Some of it may not have been known to the evangelist or have suited his purpose, e.g., the appearances in Galilee. (2) Duplicate material. In the final form of John there appear to be slightly variant collections of substantially the same words of Jesus. E.g., 3:31–36 (which awkwardly lacks a clear indication of the speaker) seems to duplicate things said in 3:7,11–13,15–18. Also parts of 16:4b–33 (spoken at the Last Supper, considerably after the indication in 14:31 that Jesus was leaving) duplicate closely themes already enunciated in chap. 14; and 6:51b–58 duplicates sayings in 6:35–51a.

Why would the redactor have added such material to the evangelist's work? We must speculate from the nature of the proposed additions. At times the added material is not significantly distinctive in tone or emphasis and so may have been included simply because it was in the tradition and the redactor did not want to lose it. At other times the putative additions reflect a different theological emphasis, best explained if community thought varied over time. For instance, 6:51b–58 brings out the eucharistic aspect of the Bread of Life, supplementing the emphasis on the bread as divine revelation or teaching in 6:35–51a. This need not be hardened into a corrective imposed by ecclesiastical censorship, for there were already symbolic references to the eucharist in the account of the multiplication of the loaves

(6:1–15) that served as the basis for the Bread of Life discourse. Plausibly the dialogue in 21:15–17 that gives Simon Peter shepherding responsibility was included because it offered justification for the development of human pastoral authority in a community that hitherto had looked on Jesus as the sole shepherd—a development, some would theorize, necessitated by the type of schismatic division visible in I John. In such an instance, however, one should not jump to the conclusion that, if the motive for the redactor's addition was prompted by circumstances in ongoing community history, the added material itself was necessarily late. Sayings about the manner of Peter's martyrdom (21:18) and the possibility that the Beloved Disciple would not die (21:23) are so vague that they surely preceded the respective deaths. In some instances the redactor would have been reviving and incorporating old tradition.

Plausible as that may be, at most the theory of a redactor solves some of the features observable in the Gospel as it has come to us.

Authorship and the Beloved Disciple[85]

The Gospel calls attention to an eyewitness at the cross (19:35) who seemingly is "the disciple whom Jesus loved" (19:26). John 21:20,24 claims that this anonymous Beloved Disciple both bears witness and "has written these things." Irenaeus (*ca.* AD 180) identified the Disciple as John (one of the Twelve) who lived at Ephesus[86] till Trajan's time (*ca.* 98). (As a boy Irenaeus had known Polycarp, bishop of Smyrna, who is supposed to have known John.) This identification of the Beloved Disciple and evangelist as John (son of Zebedee), with the minor variation that he had assistants, subsequently received church acceptance. Nevertheless, as pointed out above (p. 109), it is now recognized that such late-2d-century surmises about figures who had lived a century before were often simplified; and that authorship tradition was sometimes more concerned with the *authority* behind a biblical writing than with the physical writer. As with the other Gospels it is doubted by

[85]Amidst the literature on the Disciple see: P. S. Minear, NovT 19 (1977), 105–23; M. Pamment, ExpTim 94 (1982–83), 363–67; B. Byrne, JSNT 23 (1985), 83–97; J. A. Grassi, *The Secret Identity of the Beloved Disciple* (New York: Paulist, 1992); J. H. Charlesworth, *The Beloved Disciple* (Valley Forge, PA: Trinity, 1995).

[86]This localization may be the most enduring aspect of Irenaeus's information (AH 3.1.1), for probably the scholarly majority still thinks the Gospel was written in the Ephesus area. See S. van Tilborg, *Reading John in Ephesus* (Leiden: Brill, 1996). A significant minority suggests Syria as the place of composition, with an occasional voice raised for Alexandria. As for traditions about John, see R. A. Culpepper, *John, the Son of Zebedee. The Life of a Legend* (Columbia, SC: Univ. of South Carolina, 1994). M.-É. Boismard, writing in French in 1996, amasses evidence to show that John died with his brother James in Jerusalem in the early 40s, but was subsequently confused with John the Presbyter/Elder of Ephesus (p. 398 below). Yet John met with Paul in a Jerusalem conference (Gal 2:9) that most would date to 49 (Table 6 in Chapter 16).

most scholars that this Gospel was written by an eyewitness of the public ministry of Jesus.[87]

Who was the Beloved Disciple? There are three approaches. *First,* some propose a known NT figure. In addition to the traditional candidate (John, son of Zebedee), other proposals have included Lazarus, John Mark, and Thomas (Charlesworth). Although there may be a passage to support each identification, if the long tradition behind John is rejected, one is reduced to guessing. *Second,* some scholars have evaluated the Beloved Disciple as a pure symbol, created to model the perfect disciple. That he is never given a name and that he appears alongside Peter in scenes known to us from the Synoptic Gospels where no such figure is mentioned[88] have been invoked as a proof of nonhistoricity. However, another unnamed Johannine figure who has a symbolic role and appears where she is absent in the Synoptics, namely, the mother of Jesus (2:3–12; 19:25–27), was certainly a historical figure. The Beloved Disciple's presence at the foot of the cross when all the Twelve had fled need indicate only that he was neither one of the Twelve[89] nor an apostle—a term never used in John. *Third,* still other scholars (with whom I agree) theorize that the Beloved Disciple was a minor figure during the ministry of Jesus, too unimportant to be remembered in the more official tradition of the Synoptics. But since this figure became important in Johannine community history (perhaps the founder of the community), he became the ideal in its Gospel picture, capable of being contrasted with Peter as closer to Jesus in love.

Was the Beloved Disciple the evangelist? That would be the impression given by John 21:20,24: "has written these things." Could this, however, be a simplification by the redactor who added chap. 21, hardening the more accurate 19:35: "This testimony has been given by an eyewitness, and his testimony is true; he is telling what he knows to be true that you too may have faith"? The passage in 19 could mean that the Beloved Disciple was not the evangelist but a witness to Jesus and thus the *source* of tradition that has gone into the Fourth Gospel. The evangelist who wrote that passage could have been a follower or disciple of the Beloved Disciple (whom he describes in the third person) and not himself an eyewitness of the ministry. Indeed, if one posits both a different writer for the Epistles (p. 389 below) and a redactor for the Gospel, one could agree with those who posit a "Jo-

[87]An important exception is Hengel, *Question,* who would identify the author as John the Elder (not John the apostle), who was head of a school in Asia Minor where he had moved from Palestine. As a young man he had known Jesus, and then he modeled himself after the Beloved Disciple.

[88]Compare Mark 14:18–21; 14:54; 16:1–4 with John 13:23–26; 18:15–18; 20:1–10 respectively. There is no Synoptic parallel to John 21:20–23.

[89]For a tradition that there were disciples of Jesus beyond the Twelve involved in the passion, see BDM 2.1017–18,1171–73.

hannine School,"[90] i.e., various disciples employing both a style and material that were traditional in this community—traditional because in whole or in part they were shaped by the Beloved Disciple.

The thesis would explain how some factors in John[91] plausibly reflect origin in the ministry of Jesus, while other factors seem distant from that ministry:

(a) Familiarity with Palestine. John knows the location of Bethany (11:18), the garden across the winter-flowing Kidron (18:1), Solomon's porch in the Temple (10:23), the pools of Bethesda (5:2) and of Siloam (9:7), and the Lithostrotos (19:13). These sites are not mentioned in the other Gospels, and sometimes external evidence supports Johannine accuracy. Other Johannine geographical references (Bethany beyond the Jordan in 1:28; Aenon near Salim in 3:23) have not yet been identified, but we should be cautious about resorting to purely symbolic interpretations of the names.

(b) Familiarity with Judaica. Jewish feasts are mentioned in 5:9b; 6:4; 7:2; and 10:22; and the ensuing dialogue shows a knowledge of festal ceremonies and theology. Jewish customs are mentioned both explicitly (purity regulations in 2:6; 18:28; paschal lamb in 19:36) and implicitly (perhaps the makeup of the high priest's tunic in 19:23).

If the tradition behind John is firmly rooted in Judaism and Palestine,[92] the presentation of that tradition has moved considerably beyond Jesus' ministry. Indeed the evangelist acknowledges this (2:22) and defends such development as guided by the Spirit-Paraclete (16:12–14). Those who confess Jesus have been expelled from the synagogue (9:22; 12:43); indeed, Christians have been killed by pious devotees of the synagogue (16:2). We have seen in n. 13 above that the Johannine use of "the Jews" reflects attitudes developed in the history of the Johannine community. Unlike the Jesus of the Synoptic Gospels, the Johannine Jesus speaks explicitly of his divinity and his preexistence (8:58; 10:30–38; 14:9; 17:5). He is hailed as God (20:28); and the basic argument with "the Jews" is not merely about his violation of the Sabbath rules but about his making himself equal to God (5:16–18; 19:7). Traditional deeds of Jesus, like healing the crippled, multiplying loaves, and opening the eyes of the blind, have become the subject of long homilies involving theological reflection and debate along the lines of the Jewish interpretation of Scripture (5:30–47; 6:30–51a; 9:26–34). Contrary

[90]See Culpepper, *School* 258–59, for the possible meaning of that designation.

[91]We shall continue to call both Gospel and evangelist "John," no matter who the Beloved Disciple and the evangelist were.

[92]Bultmann contended that one of the sources behind John (Revelatory Discourses) was composed in Aramaic, and other scholars have explained passages in John as a translation from Aramaic. See C. F. Burney, *The Aramaic Origin of the Fourth Gospel* (Oxford Univ., 1922); and the discussion in S. Brown, CBQ 26 (1964), 323–39.

to the Synoptic tradition, a significant group of Samaritans believes in Jesus independently of Jesus' first followers (4:28–42).

Such development may be explained best if tradition about Jesus stemming from the Beloved Disciple has been reflected upon over many years and expanded in the light of Johannine community experiences. Beginning with the acceptance of Jesus as the final prophet and the Messiah of Jewish expectations (1:40–49), the tradition has gone on to "greater things" (1:50). Jesus is not only the Son of Man who will come down from heaven at the end of time to judge the world; the hour is already here and he has already come down from heaven. That is the secret of his ministry: What he does and says is what he saw and heard when he was with God before the Word became flesh (5:19; 8:28; 12:49). The teachers of Israel believed in a Moses who climbed up Sinai, had contact with God there, and came down to repeat what he had heard; but Jesus is greater than Moses. He did not have to go up to God but came from heaven above where he saw God, so that whoever believes in him is never judged (3:10–21).[93] The Beloved Disciple may have lived through the historical development of the community (and perhaps through expulsion from the synagogue), and so there may have been a certain symbiosis between him and the Gospel that committed to writing a tradition that not only had its roots in his experience of Jesus but also embodied decades of his ongoing reflection on that experience. The evangelist, who wove the theologically reflected tradition into a work of unique literary skill, would presumably have been a disciple of the Beloved Disciple, about whom he writes in the third person. And the redactor, if there was one, may have been another disciple.

Influences on Johannine Thought

John is often characterized as a Hellenistic Gospel. Its usage of abstract ideas like light and truth; its dualistic division of humanity into light and darkness, truth and falsehood; its concept of the Word—all these were once widely held to be the product of Greek philosophical thought, or of combinations of philosophy and religion (e.g., the Hermetic literature), or of the Pagan mystery religions. An intermediary proposal was that the works of the

[93]Samaritans rejected the work of David; for them Moses was the salvific figure par excellence. It is tempting to speculate that the Samaritans who came to believe in Jesus (John 4:39–42) catalyzed this view of Jesus as the descending Son of Man, a figure like but greater than Moses. Significantly, the Jewish opponents of the Johannine Jesus considered him a Samaritan (8:48). On the issue of Samaritans and John, see: G. W. Buchanan in *Religions in Antiquity,* ed. J. Neusner (Festschrift E. R. Goodenough; Leiden: Brill, 1968), 149–75; E. D. Freed, CBQ 30 (1968), 580–87; C.H.H. Scobie, NTS 19 (1973), 390–414; J. D. Purvis, NovT 17 (1975), 161–98. M. Pamment, ZNW 73 (1982), 221–30.

Jewish philosopher Philo (before AD 50) served as a channel of such thought, particularly in relation to "the Word."[94] Another group of scholars has stressed the relationship of John to (incipient) gnosticism. The Johannine picture of a savior who came from an alien world above,[95] who said that neither he nor those who accepted him were of this world (17:14), and who promised to return to take them to the heavenly dwelling (14:2–3) could be fitted into the gnostic world picture (even if God's love for the world in 3:16 could not). Hitherto, very few actual gnostic works were known, and our knowledge of 2d-century gnosticism came from the reports of the Church Fathers. From them we knew that the first commentator on John (Heracleon, disciple of Valentinus, mid-2d century) was gnostic.[96] Now, however, with the discovery at Chenoboskion (Nag Hammadi) in Egypt in the late 1940s, we have gnostic works in Coptic (some translated from original Greek of the 2d century AD). Although there are occasional stylistic parallels to John (n. 76 above), overall these new documents are very different from a narrative Gospel like John; and most doubt that John borrowed from such gnosticism.[97] Still another proposal would see parallels between John and the later Mandaean writings (p. 92 above), with their syncretistic mixture of Jewish lore and gnostic myth. In substance all these theories agree that the Johannine idiom of language and thought did not stem from the Palestinian world of Jesus of Nazareth.

A very different approach would see the basic origins of Johannine Christianity within that Palestinian world with all its Jewish diversity—a world that had been influenced by Hellenism but where reflection on the heritage of Israel was the primary catalyst. That heritage would be judged not simply from the books of the Law and the Prophets, but also from the protocanonical and deuterocanonical Wisdom Literature (see p. xxxv above), and from apocryphal and intertestamental literature. In particular, the enrichment supplied by the DSS comes into the picture. We find in these documents ideas and vocabulary that the critics once thought were not authentically Palestin-

[94]Dodd, *Interpretation* 10–73, gives a convenient overview of these approaches. See also G. W. MacRae, CBQ 32 (1970), 13–24; R. Kysar, *Fourth Evangelist* 102–46. Borgen, *Bread,* draws heavily but with circumspection on Philo; see also D. A. Hagner, JETS 14 (1971), 20–36.

[95]This picture was painted by W. A. Meeks, "The Man from Heaven in Johannine Sectarianism," JBL 91 (1972), 44–72; see also the collection of M. de Jonge's essays, *Jesus: Stranger from Heaven and the Son of God* (Missoula, MT: Scholars, 1977). For a strong rejection of gnostic influence, see C. A. Evans, *Word.*

[96]Gaius, a learned ecclesiastic of Rome in the late 2d century, is said to have attributed the authorship of John to Cerinthus who had gnostic leanings.

[97]Bultmann and Haenchen posit gnostic influence on John or on his sources. Others think that John wrestled with many of the problems that appear in the later gnostic writings, but did not get his answers (which are quite different) from them; see J. M. Lieu, ExpTim 90 (1978–79), 233–37. On John and the *Gospel of Thomas,* R. E. Brown, NTS 9 (1962–63), 155–77; G. J. Riley, *Resurrection Reconsidered: Thomas and John in Controversy* (Minneapolis: A/F, 1994).

ian, viz., a world divided into light and darkness (John 3:19–21); people under the power of an evil angelic principle (I John 5:19); people walking in light or in darkness (8:12; I John 1:5–7); walking in truth (II John 4; III John 4); testing the spirits (I John 4:1); the spirits of truth and perversity (I John 4:6). The resemblance in vocabulary and thought between the DSS and John should banish the idea that the Johannine tradition could not have developed on Palestinian soil.

There is no evidence for a direct familiarity of John with the DSS; rather there is the possibility of indirect acquaintance with a type of thought and expression current at Qumran, and perhaps in a wider area. There are interesting parallels between what we know of JBap and the beliefs attested in the Scrolls (even though we need not think that JBap was a member of the Qumran community), and in the NT John shows the greatest interest in JBap's disciples. In portraying the first disciples of Jesus as disciples of JBap and Jesus as conducting at least a brief baptizing ministry, John may be historical. This leaves open the possibility that the disciples of JBap were a channel whereby Qumran vocabulary and ideas came into the Johannine tradition.[98] That much of the Qumranlike vocabulary appears in the speeches of Jesus in John (to a much greater extent than in the Synoptics) need not lead us to conclude hastily that the raw materials in those speeches were the artificial compositions of the evangelist. If Qumran exemplifies a wider range of thought, Jesus could well have been familiar with its vocabulary and ideas; for the Word-made-flesh spoke the language of his time. The Johannine tradition, with a special affection for this style of thought, may have been more attentive in preserving it,[99] as well as remembering and emphasizing other ideas that did not seem important to the Synoptic writers. The possibility of Palestinian and Jewish origins for the Johannine presentation of Jesus leads us to the issue of Johannine community development.

History of the Johannine Community

As noted in discussing the Synoptic Gospels, because the Jesus material was shaped by each evangelist for an intended audience, indirectly the Gospels may give us theological and sociological information about the Christians who preserved, shaped, and/or received the memories of him. John's Gospel presentation of Jesus is strongly characterized by debates and adversarial situations, and we have three Epistles of John clearly echoing Jo-

[98]Except for the possible identification of the Beloved Disciple as the unnamed figure alongside Andrew in John 1:35–40, we are not sure that he was a disciple of JBap.

[99]Some characteristically Johannine expressions have a faint echo in the Synoptics (e.g., the "hour" in Mark 14:35; a solemn "I am" in Mark 6:50; 14:62).

hannine thought but more openly addressed to an audience and its problems. Consequently it may be that one can reconstruct more of the background of John than that of any other Gospel. Yet one should not confuse such reconstructive research with exegesis, which has to do with what the Gospel meant to convey to its readers. The evangelist tells us his purpose in 20:31, and it was not to recount background.

I shall now present a reconstruction of the community history,[100] warning that while it explains many factors in the Gospel, it remains a hypothesis and "perhaps" needs to be added to every sentence. The reconstruction covers not only the Gospel and its redaction but also the Johannine Epistles (to be treated in more detail in Chapters 12–14). Four phases are involved. (1) A phase preceding the written Gospel but shaping its thought (up to the 70s or 80s). In or near Palestine, Jews of relatively standard expectations, including followers of JBap, accepted Jesus as the Davidic Messiah, the fulfiller of the prophecies, and one confirmed by miracles (see the titles in John 1). Among them, insignificantly at first, was a man who had known Jesus and become his disciple during the public ministry and who would become the Beloved Disciple. To these first followers were added Jews of an anti-Temple bias who made converts in Samaria (John 4). They understood Jesus primarily against a Mosaic background (as distinct from a Davidic one): Jesus had been with God, whom he had seen and whose word he brought down to this world. The acceptance of this second group catalyzed the development of a high, preexistence christology (seen against the background of divine Wisdom[101]) that led to debates with Jews who thought that Johannine Christians were abandoning Jewish monotheism by making a second God out of Jesus (5:18). Ultimately the leaders of these Jews had Johannine Christians expelled from synagogues (9:22; 16:2).[102] The latter, alienated from their own, turned very hostile to "the Jews," whom they regarded as children of the devil (8:44). They stressed a realization of the eschatological

[100]Explained in detail in R. E. Brown, *Community,* with a chart on pp. 166–67. My views are very similar to those of J. L. Martyn, whose very important work is outlined there in 171–74. The differing views of G. Richter, O. Cullmann, M.-É. Boismard, and W. Langbrandtner are covered in 174–82. See also Mattill, "Johannine"; Neyrey, *Ideology;* Painter, *Quest.*

[101]Parallels between the Johannine Jesus and personified divine Wisdom are given in BGJ 1.521–23; also Scott, *Sophia.*

[102]This thesis is *not* based on the existence, interpretation, or dating (often to AD 85) of the *Birkat ha-mînîm,* inserted as the twelfth of the *Eighteen Benedictions* (*Shemoneh Esreh*), i.e., a Jewish curse on those who were considered deviants. Despite the association of the insertion with Rabbi Samuel the Younger/Small who flourished *ca.* AD 100, we do not know how quickly and widely this curse was adopted. The inclusion of Christians among the deviants may have come considerably later than the composition of John. See the doubts raised by R. Kimelman in *Jewish and Christian Self-Definition,* ed. E. P. Sanders (Philadelphia: Fortress, 1981), 2.226–44; also W. Horbury, JTS NS 33 (1982), 19–61; L. H. Schiffman, *Who Was a Jew?* (Hoboken: Ktav, 1985); V. Martin, *A House Divided* (New York: Paulist, 1995).

promises in Jesus to compensate for what they had lost in Judaism (whence the strong theme of replacement in the Gospel). At the same time the Johannine Christians despised believers in Jesus who did not make the same public break from the synagogue (exemplified by the parents of the blind man in 9:21–23; also 12:42–43). The disciple mentioned above made this transition and helped others to make it, thus becoming the Beloved Disciple.

(2) The phase during which the basic Gospel was written by the evangelist.[103] Since "the Jews" were considered blind and unbelieving (12:37–40), the coming of the Greeks was seen as God's plan of fulfillment (12:20–23). The community or part of it may have moved from Palestine to the diaspora to teach the Greeks (7:35), perhaps to the Ephesus area[104]—a move that would cast light on the Hellenistic atmosphere of the Gospel and on the need to explain Semitic names and titles (e.g., rabbi, Messiah). This context brought out universalist possibilities in Johannine thought, in an attempt to speak to a wider audience. Rejection and persecution, however, convinced Johannine Christians that the world (like "the Jews") was opposed to Jesus. They looked on themselves as not of this world which was under the power of Satan, the Prince of this world (17:15–16; 14:30; 16:33). In their relation to other Christians, they rejected some as having so inadequate a christology that they were really unbelievers (6:60–66). Others symbolized by Simon Peter truly believed in Jesus (6:67–69) but were not deemed so perceptive as the Johannine Christians symbolized by the Beloved Disciple (20:6–9). The hope was that the divisions between them and the Johannine community might be healed and they might be one (10:16; 17:11). However, the Gospel's one-sided emphasis on the divinity of Jesus (shaped by struggles with the synagogue leaders) and on the need for love of one another as the sole commandment (13:34; 15:12,17) opened the way for some in the next generation whose whole knowledge of Jesus came from that Gospel to develop exaggerated views.[105]

(3) The phase during which the Johannine Epistles, I and II John, were written (*ca.* AD 100). The community split in two: (a) Some adhered to the

[103]Plausibly he was a disciple of the Beloved Disciple—not a witness of Jesus' ministry, but perhaps, as the paragraph above suggests, one who was more Hellenized than the Beloved Disciple and/or lived in the diaspora.

[104]See n. 86 above. Given the interest of this Gospel in the disciples of JBap, it is noteworthy that the only place outside Palestine where they are mentioned in the NT is at Ephesus (Acts 19:1–7). Cassidy, *John's Gospel,* would find echoes of Roman persecution in John, but that seems dubious.

[105] Although the Gospel was *not* addressed to "the Jews" (or even to Gentiles who refused evangelization and together with "the Jews" constituted "the world" antagonistic to Jesus), its appeal to believers (20:31) designed to strengthen their faith has been shaped by the hostility encountered in the community's history. One should distinguish between the evangelist's own thought and how the Gospel might have been read by others who had their own presuppositions. Diverse interpretations of how the Gospel presents Jesus' humanity are offered by Schnelle, *Anti-Docetic,* and M. M. Thompson, *Humanity.*

view represented by the author of I and II John (another Johannine writer distinct from the evangelist). He complemented the Gospel by stressing the humanity of Jesus (come in the flesh) and ethical behavior (keeping the commandments); (b) Many seceded (at least, in the view of the author of I John 2:18–19) and were antichrists and children of the devil because they had so exaggerated Jesus' divinity that they did not see any importance in his human career or in their own behavior (beyond simply believing in Jesus—see pp. 390–91 below). Yet in the Johannine community there was no structure sufficiently authoritative to enable the author to discipline the secessionists who were actively seeking more adherents; he could only urge those who were puzzled about truth to test the Spirits (I John 4:1–6).

(4) The phase during which III John was written and the redactor added chap. 21 (AD 100–110?). The disintegration of the Johannine community led to a development of pastoral structure and brought those sympathetic to the christology described under 3a closer to the larger "church catholic." In III John, even though the writer did not like him because he had become authoritative, Diotrephes probably represented this new trend which was alien to the preceding Johannine reliance on the Spirit alone as teacher. Similarly in John 21:15–17 Jesus gives Simon Peter the task of feeding the sheep and thus recognizes human pastors alongside Jesus, the model shepherd. This development would ultimately bring some Johannine Christians into the larger church and preserve the Johannine heritage for that church. On the other hand those sympathetic to the christology described under 3b above (perhaps the larger group) fed their interpretation into docetism (where Jesus was deemed not truly human) and gnosticism (where this world was considered so distorted that it was not God's creation[106]) and ultimately Montanism (where Montanus became the embodiment of the Paraclete to guide the church).

Issues and Problems for Reflection

(1) The passage in 7:53–8:11 dealing with Jesus' judgment on the woman caught in adultery is missing from the best Greek mss. While for many (including Roman Catholics) the story is canonical, inspired Scripture, almost certainly it is out of context here in John, despite possible relationship to 8:15,46a. Some mss. place the story after Luke 21:38 as a continuation of the cunning questions presented to Jesus before his arrest (Luke 20:20–40). We may have here an old story about Jesus' mercy toward sinners (see Papias

[106]As mentioned, the first commentator on John in the 2d century was a Valentinian gnostic; the secessionists may have been the route by which this valuable theological tool was placed at the disposition of that school of gnostic thinkers.

in EH 3.39.17) that traveled independently of the four Gospels and could not be included until there was a change in the church's reluctance to forgive adultery (*Shepherd of Hermas, Mandate* 4.1). The passage supplies an occasion for reflecting on the relationship between the Jesus tradition and church teaching.

(2) In Matt's Sermon on the Mount (5:44), Jesus says, "Love your enemies, and pray for those who persecute you." In the "Love one another" of 13:34; 15:12,17 John's Jesus thinks of love for one's fellow believers who are God's children; but nothing is mentioned of enemies. (And indeed the Johannine Jesus does not pray for the world [John 17:9; see I John 5:16c].) Thus the Johannine "new commandment" of love may seem narrow to some and even sectarian. Yet from another point of view, love of those one has to live with can be the most difficult exercise of love. Christian prayers for those outside the Christian faith and concern for them can be compromised by a lack of love for other believers in Christ. Ironically, churches have fought each other bitterly in missionary areas where they were all proclaiming their love for those who did not yet believe in Christ![107]

(3) There is sharp division on the question of Johannine sacramentalism. One group of scholars sees few or no references to sacraments (especially baptism and eucharist); and indeed some would characterize John as antisacramental. Their case is based on the absence of overt references to baptism (cf. Matt 28:19; Mark 16:16) and to the eucharist (cf. Mark 14:22–24 and par.). From this springs Bultmann's thesis of an Ecclesiastical Redactor who introduced sacramental references to make the Gospel acceptable to the church. Others contend that John is the most sacramental of the Gospels; indeed, they detect some twenty allusive or symbolic references to baptism and the eucharist in John's use of water, bread, wine, gaining sight, etc.[108] To prevent too imaginative a search for these, exterior controls have been suggested, e.g., insisting that the proposed Johannine sacramental symbols be verified in sacramental contexts in other NT or early church writings and/or catacomb art. An in-between position maintains that the Johannine Jesus' words and actions are prophetic anticipations of the sacraments rather than

[107]Roman Catholics might reflect that before Vatican Council II in their prayers they rarely mentioned nonChristians (or even nonCatholics) who suffered from disasters or political persecution; after the Council laudably they have done so with great earnestness. Yet at the same time before that Council they rarely if ever attacked fellow Roman Catholics publicly; afterwards they have done so both vociferously and publicly, as they have fought over liberal and conservative issues. Can they be persuasive in their concern for outsiders if they virtually hate one another?

[108]For various views: O. Cullmann, *Early Christian Worship* (SBT 10; London: SCM, 1953); B. Vawter, TS 17 (1956), 151–66; R. E. Brown, TS 23 (1962), 183–206; also BNTE, chap. IV; B. Lindars, SJT 29 (1976), 49–63; K. Matsunaga, NTS 27 (1980–81) 516–24; R. W. Paschal, *Tyndale Bulletin* 32 (1981), 151–76; C. K. Barrett *Essays,* 80–97; F. J. Moloney, *Australian Biblical Review* 30 (1982), 10–33.

direct references. Beyond the baptismal/eucharistic interpretations, John has been seen as the most sacramental NT writing in the broader sense that *the Johannine Jesus used the language of this world to refer to the realities of the world from which he came*—the earthly used to symbolize the heavenly. In my view the broader sacramental understanding of Johannine symbolism, which is certainly verifiable, tilts the odds in favor of seeing specific symbolic references to baptism and eucharist.

(4) Above (p. 346) a twofold interpretation of the Bread of Life was suggested: Jesus' revelation and Jesus' flesh and blood. In Luke 24:27–35 there are two ways in which the presence of the risen Jesus is recognized: the interpretation of the Scriptures and the breaking of the bread. One may have here incipiently the format of the liturgical service in which through the centuries Christians have sought nourishment: the service of the word (reading and preaching the Scriptures) and the service of the sacrament (eucharist). Churches have at times been divided as to which deserves the most emphasis, but often the ideal has been to include both in the Sunday service. Readers may wish to reflect on their own experience of church life, especially if there have been changes in these last decades, to see how the balance works out.[109]

(5) I insisted above that the investigation of the history of the Johannine community and the discussion of John's sources and composition did not constitute exegesis in the sense of determining what the author intended to convey to his audience. Perhaps proportionately too much attention has been devoted to the background issues and too little to the Gospel's helping readers to believe that Jesus is the Messiah, the Son of God, and thus to possess life in his name (20:31). Clement of Alexandria called John "the spiritual Gospel." Many Johannine emphases facilitate that insight, e.g.: the pedagogically simple picture that through begetting/birth in water and Spirit believers receive God's own life and that through Jesus' flesh and blood that life is fed and nourished; the dramatic stress on one-to-one contacts with Jesus; the everyman and everywoman role of Johannine figures like the blind man and Samaritan woman, personifying different faith reactions; the language of love binding believers to Jesus just as love binds the Son with the Father; the indwelling Paraclete through whom Jesus remains attainable; the importance of discipleship which is a role that all can share. For John there are no second-class citizens among true believers; all of them are God's own children in Christ.

[109]See B. D. Chilton, *A Feast of Meanings. Eucharistic Theologies from Jesus through Johannine Circles* (NovTSup 72; Leiden: Brill, 1994); F. J. Moloney, *A Body Broken for a Broken People: Eucharist in the NT* (Peabody, MA: Hendrickson, 1996).

Bibliography on John

COMMENTARIES AND STUDIES IN SERIES: Beasley-Murray, G. R. (WBC, 1987); Bernard, J. H. (2 vols.; ICC, 1928); Brown, R. E. (2 vols.; AB, 1966, 1970; = BGJ); Burge, G. M. (GNTE, 1992); Haenchen, E. (2 vols.; Hermeneia, 1984); Johnson, T. F. (NIBC, 1993); Kysar, R. (AugC, 1986; ABD 3.912–31); Lindars, B. (NCBC, 1972; NTG, 1990); Macgregor, G.H.C. (Moffatt, 1919); Marsh, J. (PC, 1968); Michaels, J. R. (NIBC, 1989); Morris, L. (NICNT, 1971); Newman, B. M., and E. A. Nida (TH, 1980); O'Day, G. R. (NInterpB, 1995); Richardson, A. (TBC, 1959); Sanders, J. N. and B. A. Mastin (HNTC, 1969); Sloyan, G. S. (IBC, 1988); Smith, D. M. (ProcC, 2d ed., 1986; NTT, 1995); Stibbe, M.W.G. (RNBC, 1993; NTR, 1994).

BIBLIOGRAPHIES: Malatesta, E., *St. John's Gospel 1920–1965* (AnBib 32; Rome: PBI, 1967); Wagner, G., EBNT (1987); Van Belle, G., *Johannine Bibliography 1966–1985* (BETL 82; Leuven Univ., 1988); Haenchen *John* 2.254–346; Mills, W. E., BBR (1995).

SURVEYS OF RESEARCH: Howard, W. F., *The Fourth Gospel in Recent Criticism and Interpretation* (4th ed.; London: Epworth, 1955); Kysar, R., *The Fourth Evangelist and His Gospel* (Minneapolis: Augsburg, 1975)—covering 1955–75; "The Fourth Gospel: A Report on Recent Research," ANRW 2.25.3 (1985), 2391–2480—covering to 1977; "The Gospel of John in Current Research," RSRev 9 (1983), 314–23—covering to 1983; Sloyan, G. S., *What Are They Saying about John?* (New York: Paulist, 1991)—covering 1970–1990; Carson, D. A., *Themelios* 9 (1983), 8–18; Smalley, S. S., ExpTim 97 (1985–86), 102–08; du Rand, J. A., *Johannine Perspectives* (South Africa: Orion, vol. 1, 1991)—covering Epistles and Rev too; Menken, M.J.J. (1993, Johannine christology) in de Boer, *From Jesus* 292–320.

* * *

Abbott, E. A., *Johannine Vocabulary* (London: Black, 1905).

Anderson, P. N., *The Christology of the Fourth Gospel* (WUNT 2.78; Tübingen: Mohr-Siebeck, 1996).

Ashton, J., *Understanding the Fourth Gospel* (Oxford: Clarendon, 1991).

———, ed., *The Interpretation of John* (Philadelphia: Fortress, 1986). Important articles.

Bacon, B. W., *The Gospel of the Hellenists* (New York: Holt, 1933).

Barrett, C. K., *The Gospel According to St. John* (2d ed.; London: SPCK, 1978).

———, *Essays on John* (London: SPCK, 1982).

Beasley-Murray, G. R., *Gospel of Life: Theology in the Fourth Gospel* (Peabody, MA: Hendrickson, 1991).

Brown, R. E., *The Community of the Beloved Disciple* (New York: Paulist, 1979).

Bultmann, R., *The Gospel of John* (Philadelphia: Westminster, 1971; German orig., 1941/1966).

———, *Theology* 2.1–92. Analysis of Johannine theology.

Carson, D. A., *The Gospel According to John* (Grand Rapids: Eerdmans, 1991).

Cassidy, R. J., *John's Gospel in New Perspective* (Maryknoll: Orbis, 1992).

Cullmann, O., *The Johannine Circle* (Philadelphia: Westminster, 1976).
Culpepper, R. A., *Anatomy of the Fourth Gospel: A Study in Literary Design* (Philadelphia: Fortress, 1983).
———, *The Johannine School* (SBLDS 26: Missoula, MT: Scholars, 1975).
———, and C. C. Black, eds., *Exploring the Gospel of John* (D. M. Smith Festschrift; Louisville: W/K, 1996). Important collection of articles.
Davies, M., *Rhetoric and Reference in the Fourth Gospel* (JSNTSup 69; Sheffield: JSOT, 1992).
de Boer, M. C., *Johannine Perspectives on the Death of Jesus* (Kampen: Pharos, 1996).
———, ed., *From Jesus to John. Essays on Jesus and New Testament Christology* (M. de Jonge Festschrift; JSNTSup 84; Sheffield: JSOT, 1993).
Dodd, C. H., *The Interpretation of the Fourth Gospel* (Cambridge Univ., 1953). Background and theology.
———, *Historical Tradition in the Fourth Gospel* (Cambridge Univ., 1963). Comparison to the Synoptics.
Ellis, E. E., *The World of St. John. The Gospel and Epistles* (New York: Abingdon, 1965).
Forestell, J. T., *The Word of the Cross. Salvation as Revelation in the Fourth Gospel* (AnBib 57; Rome: PBI, 1974).
Fortna, R. T., *The Gospel of Signs* (SNTSMS 11; Cambridge Univ., 1970).
———, *The Fourth Gospel and its Predecessor* (Philadelphia: Fortress, 1988). Modifies the reconstruction in the earlier work.
Glasson, T. F., *Moses in the Fourth Gospel* (SBT 40; London: SCM, 1963).
Harner, P. B., *Relation Analysis of the Fourth Gospel: A Study in Reader-Response Criticism* (Lewiston: Mellen, 1993).
Hawkin, D. J., *The Johannine World* (Albany: SUNY, 1996).
Hengel, M., *The Johannine Question* (Philadelphia: Trinity, 1989).
Hoskyns, E., *The Fourth Gospel,* ed. F. N. Davey (2d ed.; London: Faber, 1947).
Interpretation 49 (#4; Oct. 1995): issue is devoted to John.
Käsemann, E., *The Testament of Jesus According to John 17* (Philadelphia: Fortress, 1968).
Kysar, R., *John, The Maverick Gospel* (rev. ed.; Louisville: W/K, 1993).
———, *John's Story of Jesus* (Philadelphia: Fortress, 1984).
Lee, E. K., *The Religious Thought of St. John* (London: SPCK, 1950).
Lightfoot, R. H., *St. John's Gospel,* ed. C. F. Evans (Oxford: Clarendon, 1956).
Lindars, B., *Behind the Fourth Gospel* (London: SPCK, 1971).
Loader, W., *The Christology of the Fourth Gospel* (2d ed.; Frankfurt: Lang, 1992).
Louw, J. P., "On Johannine Style," *Neotestamentica* 19 (1985), 160–76.
Marrow, S. B., *The Gospel of John: A Reading* (New York: Paulist, 1995).
Martyn, J. L., *The Gospel of John in Christian History* (New York: Paulist, 1978).
———, *History and Theology in the Fourth Gospel* (2d ed.; Nashville: Abingdon, 1979).
Mattill, A. J., Jr., "Johannine Communities Behind the Fourth Gospel: Georg Richter's Analysis," TS 38 (1977), 294–315.
Meeks, W. A., *The Prophet-King: Moses Traditions and the Johannine Christology* (NovTSup 14; Leiden: Brill, 1967).

Neyrey, J. H., *An Ideology of Revolt. John's Christology in Social Science Perspective* (Philadelphia: Fortress, 1988).
Nicholson, G. C., *Death as Departure: The Johannine Descent-Ascent Schema* (SBLDS 63; Chico, CA: Scholars, 1983).
Nicol, W., *The Sēmeia in the Fourth Gospel* (NovTSup 32; Leiden: Brill, 1972).
Olsson, B., *Structure and Meaning of the Fourth Gospel* (Lund: Gleerup, 1974).
Pagels, E. H., *The Johannine Gospel in Gnostic Exegesis* (SBLMS 17; Nashville: Abingdon, 1973).
Painter, J., *Reading John's Gospel Today* (Atlanta: Knox, 1980—minor updating of his *John, Witness and Theologian*).
———, *The Quest for the Messiah: The History, Literature and Theology of the Johannine Community* (2d ed.; Nashville: Abingdon, 1993).
Pancaro, S., *The Law in the Fourth Gospel* (NovTSup 42; Leiden: Brill, 1975).
Perkins, P., *The Gospel according to St. John. A Theological Commentary* (Chicago: Franciscan Herald, 1978).
Pollard, T. E., *Johannine Christology and the Early Church* (SNTSMS 13; Cambridge Univ., 1970).
Porter, S. E., and C. A. Evans, eds., *The Johannine Writings* (Sheffield: Academic, 1995). Important articles from JSNT.
Pryor, J. W., *John: Evangelist of the Common People. The Narrative and Themes of the Fourth Gospel* (London: DLT, 1992).
Reim, G., "Jesus as God in the Fourth Gospel: the Old Testament Background," NTS 30 (1984), 158–60.
Reinhartz, A., *The Word in the World: The Cosmological Tale in the Fourth Gospel* (SBLMS 45; Atlanta: Scholars, 1992).
Rensberger, D., *Johannine Faith and Liberating Community* (Philadelphia: Westminster, 1988).
Robinson, J.A.T., *The Priority of John* (London: SCM, 1985).
Schnackenburg, R., *The Gospel according to St John* (3 vols.; New York: Herder & Herder/Crossroad, 1968, 1980, 1982).
Schnelle, U., *Anti-Docetic Christology in the Gospel of John* (Minneapolis: A/F, 1992).
Scroggs, R., *Christology in John and Paul* (Philadelphia: Fortress, 1988).
Segovia, F., *Love Relationships in the Johannine Tradition* (SBLDS 58; Chico, CA: Scholars, 1982).
———, *Farewell of the Word. The Johannine Call to Abide* (Minneapolis: A/F, 1991).
Senior, D. P., *The Passion of Jesus in the Gospel of John* (Wilmington: Glazier, 1991).
Smalley, S. S., *John: Evangelist and Interpreter* (Exeter: Paternoster, 1978).
Smith, D. M., *The Composition and Order of the Fourth Gospel* (Yale Univ., 1953).
———, *Johannine Christianity: Essays on Its Setting, Sources, and Theology* (Univ. of South Carolina, 1984).
Staley, J. L., *The Print's First Kiss. A Rhetorical Investigation of the Implied Reader in the Fourth Gospel* (SBLDS 82; Atlanta: Scholars, 1988).
———, *Reading with a Passion* (New York: Continuum, 1995). An unusual personal application of rhetorical criticism.

Stibbe, M.W.G., *John as Storyteller: Narrative Criticism and the Fourth Gospel* (SNTSMS 73; Cambridge Univ., 1992).
———, ed., *The Gospel of John as Literature* (Leiden: Brill, 1993).
Talbert, C. H., *Reading John* (New York: Crossroad, 1994).
Teeple, H., *The Literary Origin of the Gospel of John* (Evanston, IL: Religion and Ethics Institute, 1974).
Thompson, M. M., *The Humanity of Jesus in the Fourth Gospel* (Philadelphia: Fortress, 1988).
Van Belle, G., *The Signs Source in the Fourth Gospel* (BETL 116; Leuven Univ., 1994).
Vellanickal, M., *The Divine Sonship of Christians in the Johannine Writings* (AnBib 72; Rome: PBI, 1977).
von Wahlde, U. C., "Literary Structure and Theological Argument in Three Discourses with the Jews in the Fourth Gospel," JBL 103 (1984), 575–84.
———, *The Earliest Version of John's Gospel* (Wilmington: Glazier, 1989).
Wead, D. W., *The Literary Devices in John's Gospel* (Basel: Reinhardt, 1970).
Westcott, B. F., *The Gospel According to St. John* (reissue London: Clarke, 1958; orig. 1880). A classic.
Whitacre, R. A., *Johannine Polemic: The Role of Tradition and Theology* (SBLDS 67; Chico, CA: Scholars, 1982).
Wiles, M. E., *The Spiritual Gospel: The Interpretation of the Fourth Gospel in the Early Church* (Cambridge Univ., 1960).
Wind, A., "Destination and Purpose of the Gospel of John," NovT 14 (1972), 26–69.
Witherington, B., III, *John's Wisdom: A Commentary* (Louisville: W/K, 1995).
Woll, D. B., *Johannine Christianity in Conflict* (SBLDS 60; Chico, CA: Scholars, 1981).

CHAPTER 12

FIRST EPISTLE (LETTER) OF JOHN

In style and vocabulary there are so many similarities between I John and John that no one can doubt that they are at least from the same tradition. Indeed, I John makes most sense if understood as written in a period following the appearance of the Gospel,[1] when the struggle with the synagogue and "the Jews" was no longer a major issue. Rather a division among Johannine Christians had now occurred, sparked by different views of Jesus. Both groups accepted the Gospel's profession that the Word was God; but they disagreed about the importance of what the Word had done in the flesh—the way he had "walked." One group felt that his actions set a moral standard to be followed; the other held that simply believing in the Word was all that mattered, and what Christians did had no more importance than what Jesus did. In the *General Analysis* we shall see how that discernment of the situation is verified; then subdivisions will be devoted to *Composition* (author, dating, structure), *Issues for Reflection,* and *Bibliography.*[2]

General Analysis of the Message

As will be explained toward the end of the Chapter, the structure of I John is related to the structure of John.

Prologue (1:1–4)

This resembles a primitive sketch of the Prologue to the Fourth Gospel. We say "primitive," for we certainly do not find here the clarity found in the Gospel. Dominant is the importance of the "we," namely, the tradition-

[1]Perhaps before the final redaction of John, especially the addition of John 21, but dating is discussed under *Composition* below. The closeness of John and I John has caused me to treat the Johannine Epistles here, after the Gospel, rather than in their canonical order among the Catholic Epistles (p. 705 below), following Jas and I-II Pet. That order reflects the view that the Epistles were written by the apostle John, son of Zebedee (see Gal 2:9). Even without our accepting that view, the canon lends valuable support to the recognition the Johannine theology is consonant with the theology attributed to the other prominent early Christian leaders.

[2]In Chapters 12–14 I shall give preference to books and articles written after 1980; for the preceding period those who wish to do further reading and research may consult the very complete bibliographies in BEJ.

Summary of Basic Information

DATE: Most likely after the Gospel according to John; thus *ca.* AD 100.

TO: Christians of the Johannine community who had undergone a schism.

AUTHENTICITY: Certainly by a writer in the Johannine tradition, probably not by the one responsible for most of the Gospel.

UNITY: Great majority of scholars think of unified composition; Bultmann's thesis of combined sources has little following.

INTEGRITY: The "Johannine Comma" or additional Trinitarian material in 5:6–8 (n. 14 below) is a 3d–4th-century Latin theological gloss; otherwise no additions.

FORMAL DIVISION:

1:1–4: Prologue

1:5–3:10: Part One: God is light and we must walk in light

3:11–5:12: Part Two: Walk as the children of the God who has loved us in Christ

5:13–21: Conclusion.

bearers and interpreters of the Johannine School (p. 369 above) who preserve and develop the (eye)witness of the Beloved Disciple. The "beginning" in 1:1 (unlike "the beginning" in John 1:1) refers to the start of Jesus' ministry, where such witness played a role. The object of the eyewitnessing is "the word of life," but with more emphasis on "life" than on "word"—a *life* that was made known. "Word" in the I John Prologue is less personalized than in John's Prologue; for although "the word of life" here means more than simply the news or message about the divine life, it is less than the incarnate Word that possesses and gives life in the Fourth Gospel. The "word," meaning the proclamation of divine life (v. 2) made visible in and through Jesus, constitutes the *aggelia* or "message" of I John 1:5; 3:11 which enables the readers to participate in this life, and thus to have fellowship[3] with the living God. This fellowship (vv. 3–4) is the root of Christian joy and an essential constituent of the Johannine community ("with us").

PART ONE: GOD IS LIGHT AND WE MUST WALK IN LIGHT (1:5–3:10)

The message of I John opens (1:5–7) by reiterating the Johannine view of a world divided into light and darkness (see John 3:19–21), with God as the

[3]*Koinōnia* or "fellowship," i.e., associating and sharing goods and life (p. 287 above), does not occur in the Fourth Gospel.

light of the just.[4] Walking in light and acting in truth guarantee fellowship with one another and "with him," for the blood of Jesus cleanses from sin. *I John 1:8–2:2 turns to the false propagandists who refuse to acknowledge their wrongdoing as sin.* True Christians acknowledge or publicly confess their sins,[5] for which Jesus is expiation. (Notice the emphasis on the salvific value of the death of Jesus, a theme found in only a few passages in John.) To claim sinlessness is to make a liar out of God; lying is characteristic of Satan (John 8:44). I John does not wish to encourage sin, but reminds us that, if we do sin, we have a paraclete with the Father, "Jesus Christ the just one."[6] *Keeping the commandments and thus perfecting the love of God is the theme of I John 2:3–11.* (It is uncertain whether the writer means God's love for us, or our love for God, or both.) Specifically the commandment of love for one's fellow Christian ("brother") is highlighted as in John 13:34; 15:12,17. Although this is an old commandment known to Johannine Christians "from the beginning" when they first were converted to Christ, it is new in the sense that it has yet to be put fully into effect in a world liberated by Jesus from the power of darkness. (The "true light is already shining" in 2:8 echoes John 1:9.)

An oratorically powerful but enigmatic passage, *I John 2:12–14 twice uses three titles for the addressees.*[7] "Children" may be meant as general form of address for all the Johannine Christians, including "fathers" (who have been Christians longer and thus know the One who is from the beginning) and "young people" (more recent Christians who have struggled with and conquered the Evil One). The clause following each address begins with *hoti,* a connective that can mean either "that," informing the respective group, or "because," offering reasons for what the group should already know. The thought of the struggle against the Evil One leads to *an impassioned denunciation of the world (2:15–17)* and its attractions: sensuous lust, enticement for the eyes, and a pretentious lifestyle.[8] The transitory nature of the world introduces the theme of struggle with the agent of the Evil One, the antichrist (or antiGod figure; cf. II Thess 2:3ff.). In a realized apocalyptic outlook *I John 2:18–23 sees this struggle already going on* in the opposition

[4]This picture of the world is reminiscent of DSS phraseology, as are the expressions "walk in light" and "do the truth."

[5]The Council of Trent (DBS 1679) cited I John 1:9 in relation to sacramental confession.

[6]The writer is thinking of him as advocate; the Johannine Epistles do not use *paraklētos* for the Spirit as does John (p. 353 above).

[7]In the semipoetic style of this passage, 2:14 may be repeating 2:12–13 in slightly different wording.

[8]The Evil One appears as "The Prince of this world" in John 12:31; 14:30; 16:11. The attractions have become well known as concupiscence, envy, and pride, related to that larger evil triad: the world, the flesh, and the devil. However, the writer does not give so sweeping a picture; he is simply characterizing the sensual, materialistic society that Christianity had to overcome.

to the author and the true Johannine Christians offered by the false teachers (who are the antichrists) and their followers who have gone out from the community. Satan is the liar par excellence, and his mark is on anyone who denies that Jesus is the Christ (come in the flesh—see I John 4:3). Yet the epistolary writer does not really need to tell his children this, for they have the anointing from the Holy One (i.e., from the Father, the Son, or both?). *This anointing which came at the beginning (2:24–27)*—probably the reception of the Spirit when they became Christians—makes it unnecessary to be taught by such teachers, for true believers have both eternal life and the truth in which they remain.

I John 2:28–3:3 deals with the theme of the appearance of Christ, both ending the section on the last hour begun in 2:18 and turning to the idea of union with God and Jesus. While there was relatively little emphasis in John on the parousia, or return of Jesus at the end of time (see 5:26–29; 14:1–3), that motif is prominent in I John. The connection between the realized eschatology of John and the final eschatology of I John is that although Jesus, who was righteous, is already present to all believers who do what is right, the fullness of union is possible only with his final return. Present union with Jesus enables one to face with confidence his return in judgment (either in death or at the end of the world). Impassioned assurance is proffered in 3:1: "See what love the Father has given us that we may be called the children of God." Paul speaks of *adoptive* childhood or sonship (Gal 4:15; Rom 8:15); an even bolder concept is advanced in *I John 3:4–10: We are children of God because God's seed begot us* (cf. John 1:12–13). The children of God and the children of the devil are plainly distinct because the former act in righteousness and love their brothers and sisters.[9]

Part Two: Walk as the Children of the God of Love (3:11–5:12)

At the beginning of Part One (1:5), the writer proclaimed the *aggelia* or message in terms of light; now *3:11–18 proclaims the message as love.* Using the example of Cain, 3:15 argues that hatred is a form of murder.[10] By contrast Christ laid down his life for us, and so we ought to be willing to lay

[9]One suspects that the author's opponents, even though they might not emphasize the importance of good deeds, would claim to love their brothers and sisters but that would not include a love for the author and his followers. The author's harsh description of his opponents makes it difficult to see that he loves them; but notice that in calling them children of the devil, he does not say they were begotten by the devil. To become a child of God one needs to be begotten by God; it is never explained how one becomes a child of the devil, but probably the author would regard that as a deliberate and hence blameworthy choice.

[10]The devil was a murderer from the beginning (John 8:44).

down our lives for our brothers and sisters (3:16). In particular, the specific demand that those who have means must help a "brother in need" suggests that the secessionists were the wealthier members of the community and so to be equated with the world. Echoing John 14:15,21; 15:12,17, *the necessity of keeping the commandments, specifically of loving, is inculcated in I John 3:19–24.* "We should believe in the name of God's Son, Jesus Christ, and love one another as he commanded us"—the very points of faith and practice in which the false propagandists were deficient.

I John 4:1–6 invokes a test of "by their fruits you shall know them" to discern false prophets with their claim of being led by the Spirit. There is a Spirit of God and a spirit of the antichrist, and every Spirit-led person who acknowledges Jesus Christ come in the flesh belongs to God.[11] More practically the principle "Anyone who knows God listens to us" becomes a way of distinguishing the spirit of truth from the spirit of deceit.[12] Of course, one may guess that the secessionists are directing the same polemic against the author and his followers; for them *he* has the spirit of deceit.

Abruptly *4:7–21 returns to the theme of love for one another* with the ringing proclamation, "God is love" (similar to "God is light" in Part One: 1:5). We know this not because of our initiative of loving God, but because God took the initiative of sending the only Son into the world so that we might have life and that sins might be expiated—a divine love for sinners (cf. John 3:16; Rom 5:8). The clarity and beauty of this thought come to a head in I John 4:12: "No one has ever seen God;[13] yet, if we love one another, God remains in us and God's love is brought to perfection in us." To be practical, the writer gives a test: Any who claim to love God while hating their (Christian) brothers or sisters are liars.

The close interconnection of Johannine motifs is illustrated by the *treatment of faith, love, and commandments in 5:1–5.* Previously we heard that sinlessness and righteousness were marks of those begotten by God (3:9–10); now we are told that everyone who believes that Jesus is the Christ is begotten by God and will conquer the world—a victory won by faith. (Notice that "faith" here seems to involve a christological confessional statement.) Although oratorically powerful, *the three who testify in 5:6–8,* i.e., the Spirit, the water, and the blood, are obscure and seem to echo John 19:34 where the blood flowing from the side of the pierced Christ is intermingled

[11] M. C. de Boer, NovT 33 (1991), 326–46: Coming in the flesh is related to Christ's *death* as a concrete and exemplary act of love.

[12] This section has particularly close affinities with the DSS: in 1QS 3:18–19 people are dominated either by a spirit of truth or a spirit of deceit, and we hear of "testing the spirits" in 1QS 5:20–21 in reference to new members of the community.

[13] Do the secessionists claim special visions of God that give them knowledge?

with water, a sign of the Spirit (John 7:38–39).[14] This emphasis on the salvific witness borne by Jesus' shedding blood is probably corrective of the secessionists who placed all the emphasis in understanding Jesus' salvific action on the moment of his being baptized as the Spirit descended.[15] Later sacramental use of the passage in a liturgical context discovers references to baptism and the eucharist as testifying to faith in Christ. *Part Two of I John culminates in 5:9–12* by stressing that acceptance of such divine testimony leads to belief in God's Son and the possession of (eternal) life.

Conclusion: 5:13–21

Even as the Johannine evangelist chose to clarify his purpose in writing (John 20:31: "That you may believe that Jesus is the Christ, the Son of God, and that believing you may possess life in his name"), so also the epistolary writer: "That you may know that you possess this eternal life—you who believe in the name of the Son of God" (I John 5:13). Connected to that motif is the urging of prayers that sinners may receive life because such prayers will be heard. However, there is an important exception: The writer does not urge prayer for those who commit "deadly sin,"[16] seemingly the sin of joining the secession, which was a form of apostasy.

Three solemn "We know" proclamations are made in 5:18–20 as the writer returns to his dualistic view where God and those begotten by God are opposed to the Evil One and the world that lies in his grasp. The guarantee of knowing God and the truth is the recognition that the Son of God has come. Most likely "He is the true God and eternal life" at the end of 5:20 refers to Jesus, so that I John ends as did John (20:28) with a clear affirmation of the divinity of Christ. The impassioned concluding cry of I John, "Little children, guard yourselves against idols" (5:21), has the secessionists in mind, for their false christology is a form of idolatry.

[14]A meditative addition to I John 5:6–8 (italicized below), with variants, appears among Latin writers in North Africa and Spain in the 3d and 4th centuries: "Because there are three who testify *in heaven: Father, Word, and Holy Spirit, and these three are one; and there are three who testify on earth:* the Spirit and the water and the blood; and the three are of one accord." Missing from the Greek and Oriental textual witnesses before AD 1400, this additional material known as the "Johannine Comma" (a "comma" is part of a sentence) represents dogmatic trinitarian reflection on the shorter original text. See BEJ 775–87 (with bibliography).

[15]See M. C. de Boer, JBL 107 (1988), 87–106. Also B. Witherington, III, NTS 35 (1989), 155–60, on relationship to John 3:5.

[16]He is not making the later theological distinction between mortal and venial sin. See P. Trudinger, *Biblica* 52 (1971), 541–42; D. M. Scholer in *Current Issues in Biblical Interpretation,* ed. G. F. Hawthorne (M. C. Tenney Festschrift; Grand Rapids: Eerdmans, 1975), 230–46.

Composition

AUTHOR. Traditionally it was assumed that the same writer composed John and the three Epistles (or Letters) of John. The similarities shared by I John and John are numerous, as indicated in the *General Analysis.*[17] Indeed, many statements in I John could be placed on the lips of the Johannine Jesus, and there would be no way to distinguish between them and the words actually assigned to him in John. Yet there are also some surprising differences:

- The Prologue of I John does not emphasize the incarnation of the personified Word, as does the Prologue of John; rather it testifies to the *word* (*message*) *of life* which was seen, heard, and felt—the human career of Jesus.
- I John assigns to God features that the Gospel assigns to Jesus, e.g., in I John 1:5 God is light (cf. John 8:12; 9:5); in I John 4:21 and II John God gives the commandment to love one another (cf. John 13:34).
- There is less epistolary emphasis on the Spirit as a person, and the Gospel term "Paraclete" is never used of the Spirit. (Christ is the paraclete or advocate in I John 2:1.) There is a warning that every spirit is not the Spirit of Truth or the Spirit of God, and so spirits must be tested (4:1,6).
- Final eschatology is stronger in I John than in John, where realized eschatology dominates. There is more emphasis on the parousia as the moment of accountability for Christian life (I John 2:28–3:3).
- Especially as to vocabulary, the Dead Sea Scroll parallels are even closer in I John than in John.[18]

Some of these differences give the Epistles the air of being more primitive than the Gospel, but they may reflect the author's claim to be presenting the gospel as it was "from the beginning" (I John 1:1; 3:11). Overall they suggest that the same person may not have written the Epistles and the Gospel. Some would distinguish, then, at least *four figures in the Johannine School* of writers: the Beloved Disciple (who was the source of the tradition), the evangelist who wrote the body of the Gospel, the presbyter who wrote the Epistles, and the redactor of the Gospel.

DATING AND OCCASION FOR WRITING. I John was known by Polycarp and Justin and thus certainly existed before AD 150. How much earlier and how is it related to John and to II-III John? Most scholars think the Johannine

[17]I am concerned here primarily with I John, but I shall occasionally refer to II and III John because in all likelihood the three works come from the same hand (although III John deals with a different issue). BEJ 755–59 lists all the similarities between the Johannine Epistles and John. For the issue of the same or different authors, see C. H. Dodd, BJRL 21 (1937), 129–56; W. F. Howard, JTS 48 (1947), 12–25; A. P. Salom, JBL 74 (1955), 96–102 (grammatical study); W. G. Wilson, JTS 49 (1948), 147–56 (linguistic evidence).

[18]See M.-É. Boismard in Charlesworth, *John DSS,* 156–65.

Epistles were written after the Gospel.[19] More precisely, I would place I and II John in the decade after the body of the Gospel was written by the evangelist (*ca.* 90) but before the redaction of the Gospel (which may have been contemporaneous with III John, just after 100). What particularly differentiates I and II John from the Gospel is the change of focus. "The Jews" who are the chief adversaries in the Gospel are absent; and all attention is on deceivers who have seceded from the community,[20] and by so doing have shown a lack of love for their former brothers and sisters. Such "antichrists" would seduce the writer's adherents on several issues:

(a) *Faith.* The secessionists deny the full import of Jesus as the Christ, the Son of God (2:22–23). Since they were Johannine Christians who believed in Jesus as the divine Son, presumably the denial means that they negated the importance of the human career of Jesus by not confessing him as the Christ come in the flesh (4:3).[21] Probably they thought that salvation came solely from the entrance of the Son of God into the world, so that the historical activity of Jesus had no salvific or exemplary importance. In particular, they seem to have neglected the bloody death of Jesus as an act of love and expiation, a motif that the author emphasizes (1:7; 2:2; 4:10; 5:6).

(b) *Morals.* They (presumably the same group) boast of being in communion with God and knowing God while walking in darkness and not keeping the commandments (1:6; 2:4); indeed, they will not recognize that they have sinned (1:8,10; 3:4–6). This moral stance may be related to their christology if, having denied the importance of what God's Son did in the flesh after the incarnation, they denied the importance of what they themselves did in the flesh after becoming children of God through belief. The author insists that the true child of God avoids sin (3:9–10; 5:18) by acting righteously and keeping the commandments, especially the commandment to love one's fellow Christian (3:11,23; II John 5). The children of God must walk in purity and love just as did Jesus, God's Son (I John 2:6; 3:3,7; 4:10–11).

(c) *Spirit.* Seemingly the secessionist leaders claim to be teachers and even prophets, led by the Spirit. The author disclaims the need for teachers (2:27) and warns against false prophets, "Do not believe every spirit, but test

[19]More complicated theses are possible, e.g., Strecker thinks II and III John were written at Ephesus around AD 100 and that John and I John were written later and independently by other members of the Johannine School.

[20]Secession or going out from us is the picture given by the epistolary writer (I John 2:19; II John 7); but those being attacked probably thought of themselves as preserving true Johannine insights, corrupted by the presbyter and his adherents. (Roman Catholics tend to think of Protestants as having left the [true] church; Protestants think of themselves as restoring the [true] church which had been distorted by Rome.) BEJ 762–63 lists all the statements in I and II John pertinent to the "secessionist" views.

[21]There is no reason to think that they were docetists who denied the reality of Jesus' humanity; rather the religious import of that humanity is at issue.

the spirits to see whether they are of God" (4:1). There is a Spirit of Deceit that leads the antichrists, and a Spirit of Truth that leads the author and his adherents (4:5–6).

There have been attempts to identify the secessionist adversaries of I and II John with known "heretics," e.g., the *docetists* attacked by Ignatius of Antioch (*ca.* 110) who denied that Christ was truly human; or *Cerinthus* (described by Irenaeus as an opponent of John) who held that the Christ, a spiritual being, descended upon Jesus, a normal man, after baptism and withdrew from him before crucifixion;[22] or 2d-century *gnostics,* who regarded the world and flesh as a deception. Such known "heresies," however, may be later descendants of the error encountered in I and II John. *That error (illustrated under three headings above) is plausibly an exaggeration by Johannine Christians of certain features in the Fourth Gospel.* For instance, the Gospel portrays the incarnation of the preexistent Son of God who saves people by his very entrance into the world as the light—anyone who comes to the light is free from being judged and from the guilt of sin (John 3:16–21; 9:39–41). Since people seemed to be saved by faith during the ministry of Jesus, it is not emphasized in John that the death of Jesus is salvific. The Gospel gives little ethical teaching except the commandment to love one another. According to John 14:16–17,26; 16:13, the Paraclete (advocate) or Spirit of Truth comes to dwell in every believer, guiding that person to all truth.

Despite the possibility of developing such Gospel themes to produce the views held by the secessionists, the author of I and II John claims that his views and not those of the secessionists represent the true "gospel" held from the beginning.[23] (The word translated "message" in I John 1:5 and 3:11 is *aggelia,* possibly the Johannine equivalent for "gospel" or *euaggelion.*) He writes as a member of the Johannine School that bears witness to the tradition that comes down from the Beloved Disciple—a "we" who personally or by association have heard, seen, looked upon, and felt Jesus, the embodiment of the life of God (1:1); a "we" who know the importance of how Jesus lived (walked) in the flesh and died for sins. The differences of thought from the Gospel described above make sense as a reaction to the misinterpretation of the Gospel by the secessionists.

GENRE AND STRUCTURE. Scholars disagree about both issues. As for

[22]For what is known about Cerinthus, see BEJ 766–71.

[23]See R. E. Brown in *Text and Interpretation,* eds. E. Best and R. M. Wilson (M. Black Festschrift; Cambridge Univ., 1979), 57–68; U. C. von Wahlde, *The Johannine Commandments: 1 John and the Struggle for the Johannine Tradition* (New York: Paulist, 1990). J. Painter, NTS 32 (1986), 48–71, suggests that the opponents were Gentile converts who were interpreting Johannine tradition in the light of their own background.

genre, I John has *none* of the features of the letter format.[24] Plausibly it is a written exhortation interpreting the main themes of the Fourth Gospel in light of secessionist propaganda that had a certain plausibility and continued to attract followers. Presumably it was circulated in the main center of Johannine Christianity (Ephesus?) where the Gospel was written and the author lived.

As for structure,[25] the author offers no clear indication of plan. He is repetitious, and uses hinge verses that belong both to what precedes and what follows. Bultmann's theory that the author had an early source (written in poetic couplets) that he employed in writing I John[26] has had little following; and most think of I John as a unified work. A tripartite division is popular (three Parts, preceded by a Prologue and followed by an Epilogue).[27] However, those who believe that I John is an interpretation of the Fourth Gospel favor a bipartite division that corresponds to the Gospel division. A Prologue (1:1–4) comments on the hymn that is the Gospel Prologue (John 1:1–18), and a Conclusion (5:13–21) draws on the theme of the preredactional Gospel Conclusion (John 20:30–31). The two main Parts of the Epistle are marked off by the statement "This is the gospel" (*aggelia,* "message") in 1:5 and 3:11. Part One (1:5–3:10) defines the gospel as "God is light" and stresses the obligation of walking in light. Part Two (3:11–5:12) defines the gospel as: "We should love one another" and holds up Jesus as the example of love for one's Christian brother and sister.

Issues and Problems for Reflection

(1) Just as with John (p. 333 above), so also with I John, there is a debate about whether the text should be printed in semipoetic format. BEJ does so because one can divide the Johannine writer's Greek into sense lines of relatively similar length that match each other in rough rhythm.

(2) Sometimes I John's description of the world in 2:15–17 has been criti-

[24]As we shall in Chapter 15, some use "epistle" as a designation for a work that is in letter format but is not truly a letter; but I John really does not fit that designation either. Of course, in speaking of the work in a biblical setting there is no way to avoid the traditional title "Letters/Epistles of John"; but my title for this Chapter puts "Epistle" before "Letter" to signal that I John is not similar to II or III John, which are truly "Letters."

[25]Some scholars find no pattern or structure; some count syllables or three-line strophe patterns; some propose numerical patterns (three, seven, twelve); some detect an epistolary pattern of doctrinal section followed by a paraenetic or hortatory section. See A. Feuillet, BTB 3 (1973), 194–216; F. O. Francis, ZNW 61 (1970), 110–26; P. R. Jones, RevExp 67 (1970), 433–44; E. Malatesta, *The Epistles of St. John: Greek Text and English Translation Schematically Arranged* (Rome: Gregorian Univ., 1973); J. C. O'Neill, *Puzzle.*

[26]See BEJ 38–41 (plus 760–61).

[27]BEJ 764 charts some thirty-five proposed divisions into three Parts; most frequently the first is brought to an end at 2:17, or 27, or 28; the second at 3:24 or 4:6.

cized as too negative, as if the author were forgetting that God created the world and saw that it was good. Be that as it may, I John is describing the world of God's creation after it has been marred by sin. Moreover, an "anything goes" generation may need to be reminded that the condemnation of sensual lust and concupiscence cannot be dismissed simply as "Victorian," but has deep roots in the Judeo-Christian tradition.

(3) Some find almost a contradiction in I John's insistence on love ("God is love") and the refusal to pray for those who commit a deadly sin (5:16c). (Compare the Johannine Jesus' refusal to pray for the world in John 17:9.) It is not arrogance to recognize evil and those who do it; but Christians should be careful about deciding that such people are radically evil in themselves and cannot be prayed for.

Bibliography on the Johannine Epistles in General and on I John

(Some of the *Bibliography* of Chapter 11, e.g., on Johannine theology and community history, treats the Johannine Epistles alongside the Gospel.

Commentaries and Studies in Series (The following all treat I-II-III John): Alexander, N. (TBC, 1962); Brooke, A. E. (ICC, 1912); Brown, R. E. (AB, 1982; = BEJ); Bultmann, R. (Hermeneia, 1973); Culpepper, R. A. (ProcC, rev. ed., 1995); Dodd, C. H. (Moffatt, 1966); Edwards, R. B. (NTG, 1996); Grayston, K. (NCBC, 1984); Haas, C. et al. (TH, 1972); Houlden, J. L. (HNTC, 1973); Johnson, T. F. (NIBC, 1993); Kysar, R. (AugC, 1987); Lieu, J. M. (NTT, 1991); Loader, W. (EC, 1992); Marshall, I. H. (NICNT, 1978); Moody, D. (WBC, 1970); Perkins, P. (NTM, 1979); Ross, A. (NICNT, 1958); Sloyan, G. S. (NTIC, 1995); Smalley, S. S. (WBC, 1984); Smith, D. M. (IBC, 1991); Stott, J.R.W. (2d ed.; TNTC, 1988); Strecker, G. (Hermeneia, 1996); Thüsing, W. (NTSR, 1971); Williams, R. R. (CBC, 1965).

Bibliography and Surveys of Research: Bruce, F. F., "Johannine Studies since Westcott's Day," in Westcott, *Epistles* (1966 ed., below), lix–lxxvi; Briggs, R. C., RevExp 67 (1970), 411–22; Segovia, F., RSRev 13 (1987), 132–39; Wagner, G., EBNT (1987).

* * *

Black, C. C., "The Johannine Epistles and the Question of Early Catholicism," NovT 28 (1986), 131–38.

Bogart, J., *Orthodox and Heretical Perfectionism in the Johannine Community as Evident in the First Epistle of John* (SBLDS 33; Missoula, MT: Scholars, 1977).

Bruce, F. F., *The Epistles of John* (Old Tappan, NJ: Revell, 1970).

Coetzee, J. C., "The Holy Spirit in 1 John," *Neotestamentica* 13 (1981), 43–67.

Cooper, E. J., "The Consciousness of Sin in I John," *Laval Théologique et Philosophique* 28 (1972), 237–48.

Filson, F. V., "First John: Purpose and Message," *Interpretation* 23 (1969), 259–76.

Hobbs, H. H., *The Epistles of John* (Nashville: Nelson, 1983).

Law, R., *The Tests of Life. A Study of the First Epistle of St. John* (Edinburgh: Clark, 1909).

Malatesta, E., *Interiority and Covenant: A Study of* einai en *and* menein en *in the First Letter of St. John* (AnBib 69; Rome: PBI, 1978).

Neufeld, D., *Reconceiving Texts as Speech-Acts. An Analysis of I John* (Leiden: Brill, 1994).

O'Neill, J. C., *The Puzzle of I John: A New Examination of Origins* (London: SPCK, 1966).

Piper, O. A., "I John and the Didache of the Primitive Church," 66 (1947), 437–51.

Richards, W. L., *The Classification of the Greek Manuscripts of the Johannine Epistles* (SBLDS 35; Missoula, MT: Scholars, 1977).

Schnackenburg, R., *The Johannine Epistles* (New York: Crossroad, 1992). German orig. 1975.

Songer, H. S., "The Life Situation of the Johannine Epistles," RevExp 67 (1970), 399–409.

Stagg, F., "Orthodoxy and Orthopraxy in the Johannine Epistles," RevExp 67 (1970), 423–32.

Streeter, B. H., "The Epistles of St. John," in *The Primitive Church* (New York: Macmillan, 1929), 86–101.

Vorster, W. S., "Heterodoxy in 1 John," *Neotestamentica* 9 (1975), 87–97.

Westcott, B. F., *The Epistles of St. John* (Grand Rapids: Eerdmans, 1966; original ed., 1883). A classic.

CHAPTER 13

SECOND LETTER OF JOHN

We saw that a decision about the genre and structure of I John was not easy. There is no similar problem with II and III John; they are almost parade examples of brief ancient letters, close to each other in length, which was probably determined by the measurement of a sheet of papyrus. After the *Background* and *General Analysis,* subdivisions will be devoted to *Presbyters,* an *Issue for reflection,* and *Bibliography.*

The Background

II and III John are alike in their letter format, especially in the Opening and Closing. Both describe the writer as "the presbyter." II John has similarities of content to I John (which has no letter format), especially in vv. 5–7 that emphasize the commandment to love one another (= I John 2:7–8) and condemn the deceivers who have gone forth into the world as the antichrist denying Jesus Christ come in the flesh (= I John 2:18–19; 4:1–2).[1] Thus, though the writer of I John does not identify himself, most scholars think that the presbyter composed all three works—one who on the basis of I John was a disciple of the Beloved Disciple.

II John is sent to a Johannine community at a distance from the center. The secession has not yet reached there, but secessionist missionaries are on the way (II John 10–11). The presbyter instructs that community (the Elect Lady and her children) not to let such false teachers into "the house" (house-church where the community met). The arrival of emissaries, some from the presbyter, some from the secessionists, must have been confusing for such distant Johannine communities. How were they to know who carried the truth until they allowed the emissaries to speak? And by then the damage was done!

[1]I John's "having come in the flesh" clearly refers to the incarnation; probably so does the "coming in the flesh" of II John 7, although some would apply that to the parousia. For a full list of the similarities between II John and I John, see BEJ 755–56.

Summary of Basic Information

DATE: About the same time as I John, thus *ca.* AD 100.

TO: Christians of a Johannine community threatened by the advent of schismatic missionaries.

AUTHENTICITY: By a writer in the Johannine tradition, who wrote III John as well and probably I John.

UNITY AND INTEGRITY: Not seriously disputed.

FORMAL DIVISION:
A. Opening Formula: 1–3
B. Body: 4–12
  4: Transitional expression of joy
  5–12: Message
C. Concluding Formula:13.

General Analysis of the Message

Opening Formula (vv. 1–3). The Sender and Addressee sections of the *Praescriptio*[2] are succinctly phrased: "The presbyter to an Elect Lady and her children," i.e., figuratively, an unnamed local church and its members[3] within the presbyter's sphere of influence. The fact that presbyter will give that church instructions and send along greetings from the children of "your elect sister" (v. 13) suggests he is an authoritative figure in another Johannine church (perhaps the mother church from which the addressed church was founded). The Greeting "grace, mercy, peace" (v. 3), customary for a Christian letter ("grace, mercy" in thirteen letters; "peace" added in I-II Tim), is followed by the Johannine addition of truth and love.

Transitional expression of joy (v. 4). In epistolary format a statement of joy is often transitional to the Body of the letter (and thus a "Body-Opening"), and here the mention of a commandment by the Father in v. 4 is related to the exposition of the commandment in v. 5. Probably the presbyter's rejoicing to find "some of your children walking in truth" in v. 4, which is intended to be gracious (*captatio benevolentiae*), employs "some" generally ("those encountered"), rather than correctively ("some but not all").

[2]See Chapter 15 below for this technical "letter-format" terminology.

[3]Besides this interpretation of "the Elect [or Chosen] Lady," (Greek: *eklektē kyria*), other suggestions are (a) *The lady (named) Electa,* advocated in the Latin translation of Clement of Alexandria (*ca.* 200); this has led to a modern suggestion that II John was a love letter (v. 5). (b) *The noble Kyria,* as proposed by Athanasius; there is better evidence for Kyria as a name than for "Electa." (c) *Dear Lady,* an unnamed woman; yet like the two previous suggestions, this identification of the addressee as an individual is difficult to reconcile with the letter's wider tone, i.e., that all who know the truth love her and her children (v. 1), that some of her children are walking in the truth (v. 4), and that the children of her "elect sister" sent greetings. (d) *The church at large;* this recognizes that no individual person is meant, but then who is "the elect sister" of v. 13?

Message (vv. 5–12). The insistence in 5–6 on the commandment of love and the necessity of walking in the commandment echoes the main ethical thrusts of I John. (On the commandment not being new but from the beginning, see I John 2:7–8; on it being from the Father, see I John 4:21; 5:2–3; on walking, see I John 1:6,7; 2:6,11; on love involving fidelity to the commandments, see I John 5:3.) Similarly the christological thrust of I John is echoed by the insistence in II John 7 on acknowledging Jesus coming in the flesh as the differentiating mark between those whom the presbyter acknowledges as beloved children and the antichrist deceivers who have gone out into the world (see. p. 390 above). That the dangerous teaching of the latter, already clearly present in I John, is only about to make its appearance among the addressees of II John, is suggested by the warnings that they should look to themselves (v. 8) and not receive into their "house (church)" those who bring another doctrine (vv. 10–11). Otherwise they might lose what they have worked for and share in evil. The adversaries (actual or potential) are described in v. 9 as "progressive" (literally as "going ahead and not remaining in the teaching of Christ"). This corresponds to the contention in I and II John that the writer's christology and ethics represent what was from the beginning.[4] That the difference is seen as crucial is affirmed in v. 9: Whoever has the wrong teaching does not have God!

In closing the Body or message of the letter in v. 12, the presbyter has a familiar touch: an apology for the brevity of what has been written (also III John 13–14). The hope to visit soon has to be taken in the same conventional vein, and not as threatened supervisory discipline, even though the presbyter's pastoral heart will rejoice if all goes well. "That our joy may be fulfilled" echoes I John 1:4 where it is clear that such joy stems from the *koinōnia* of Johannine Christians with one another and with God and Jesus Christ.

Concluding Formula (v. 13). The fact that the presbyter sends not his own greetings but those of a sister Christian church illustrates that this letter is sent, not as a personal directive, but as part of the policy of the Johannine "we" whom we heard speaking in I John 1:1–4.

Presbyters

Other NT letters supply the personal name of the author or writer, sometimes with an identifying title like "apostle" or "servant." II and III John are our only Christian examples from the period AD 50–150 of the sender of a

[4]Chapter 12 above suggested that the secessionists probably understood themselves as remaining faithful to directions indicated in the Gospel of John, directions that the epistolary writer regarded as one-sided and dangerous misinterpretations.

letter giving a title or designation and no personal name. One may suppose that in a close-knit body of Christians the recipients would have known the personal name of the sender; yet the designation "the presbyter" must have been customary and/or preferred by him, by them, or by both. (One may wonder whether titles of reverence were not a Johannine trait, for in John such symbolically important figures as the Beloved Disciple and the mother of Jesus are never identified by personal name.) What does the writer of II John mean by the self-designation *ho presbyteros* ("presbyter/elder")? We saw that he speaks authoritatively to other Johannine Christians about the tradition and assumes that when he comes to visit them they will want to hear more from him. In III John he sends out missionaries whom Gaius is asked to receive even though a regional authority, Diotrephes, is ill-disposed. From all this one gets the impression that "the presbyter" has prestige but not judicial authority. If he wrote I John, as seems likely, he is part of a Johannine "we" who speak about tradition held from the beginning. How does this picture drawn from the Johannine Epistles fit into what we know about "presbyters" from elsewhere? At least five different examples of early Christian usage of "presbyter/elder" have been offered as parallels.[5]

(a) An elderly man of dignity and importance, an interpretation favored by those who think of the author as the Beloved Disciple, who has been traditionally pictured as dying at an advanced age (John 21:22–23). Yet the Johannine "we" who speak in John 21:24 are clearly distinct from that figure, and "the presbyter" belongs to the Johannine "we" if he wrote I John. (b) Church officials (many of them also carrying the designation *episkopos*) who in groups were responsible for the administration of local churches in the late 1st century, as attested in Acts 20:17; Jas 5:14; I Pet 5:1; I Tim 5:17; Titus 1:5; *I Clement* 44:5.[6] Yet the Johannine writings do not give any evidence of the church structure with *presbyteroi* attested by those writings. (c) One of the Twelve Apostles, as attested when Peter describes himself in I Pet 5:1 as "*sympresbyteros*" or "fellow presbyter." Papias (EH 3.39.4) speaks of Philip, Thomas, James, John, and Matthew as *presbyteroi.* Yet in both these instances personal names, not the titles, tell us that apostles are involved; furthermore there is no reference to "apostles" having authority in the Johannine tradition. (d) A companion of Jesus who was not one of the Twelve, also a usage attested by Papias who, after he mentions members of the Twelve, speaks of Aristion and the *presbyteros* John, disciples of the Lord, who spoke authoritatively. (e) A disciple of the disciples of Jesus and

[5]On "presbyters," see B. W. Bacon, JTS 23 (1922), 134–60; G. Bornkamm, TDNT 6.670–72; J. Munck, HTR 52 (1959), 223–43; W. C. van Unnik, GCHP 248–60. Also pp. 645–48 below.

[6]Also in most of the letters of Ignatius of Antioch, where *one* of the presbyters served as *episkopos* over the others.

thus a second-generation figure who served as a transmitter of the tradition that came down from the first generation. Irenaeus (AH 4.27.1) claims: "I heard it from a certain presbyter who had heard it from those who had seen the apostles and from those who had taught."

In the theory of composition offered on p. 371, 374–76 above, whereby there was a Johannine School of writers carrying on the vision of the Beloved Disciple, the Beloved Disciple himself might have fitted into category (d), whether or not he was known as "the presbyter," while the evangelist, the epistle writer, and the redactor of the Gospel might have fitted into category (e). It is the last category, then, that would best fit the use of "the presbyter" in II and III John.

Issue for Reflection

Notice the treatment proposed in II John 10–11 for those whom the writer regards as false teachers: They are not to be received into the house or greeted. More than likely, door-to-door evangelists visiting private homes are not envisaged, but those who want to come into a house-church (Rom 16:5; I Cor 16:19; Phlm 2; Col 4:15) in order to preach or teach. An outlook whereby people should be disciplined rather than given the chance to spread falsehood or misbehavior is attested also by Matt 18:17; I Cor 5:3–5; Titus 3:10–11; and Rev 2:2.[7] To some extent the attitude was traceable to an ideal established by Jesus, "Whoever receives the one whom I shall send receives me, and whoever receives me receives the One who sent me" (John 13:20). We see where a strict interpretation of that could lead when with Latin logic Tertullian maintained that heretics have no right to appeal to the Scriptures,[8] and later Christians concluded that the safest way to be certain that heretical ideas were not disseminated was to execute the heretics. True, when positive harm is being done to others, even charity has limits; yet fierce exclusiveness in the name of truth usually backfires on its practitioners. C. H. Dodd once asked, "Does truth prevail the more if we are not on speaking terms with those whose view of truth differs from ours—however disastrous their error may be?"

Bibliography on II John

(See the *Bibliography* in Chapter 12 on I John, which treats the Johannine Epistles in general.)

[7]Irenaeus (AH 3.3.4) reports that John the disciple of the Lord fled from any contact with Cerinthus, the "enemy of truth," and that Polycarp, bishop of Smyrna, shunned Marcion as "the firstborn of Satan."

[8]*De praescriptione haereticorum* 37.1–7; CC 1.217–18.

Bartlet, V., "The Historical Setting of the Second and Third Epistles of St John," JTS 6 (1905), 204–16.
Chapman, J., "The Historical Setting of the Second and Third Epistles of St John," JTS 5 (1904), 357–68, 517–34.
Donfried, K. P., "Ecclesiastical Authority in 2–3 John," in *L'Evangile de Jean,* ed. M. de Jonge (BETL 44; Gembloux: Duculot, 1977), 325–33.
Funk, R. W., "The Form and Structure of II and III John," JBL 86 (1967), 424–30.
Lieu, J., *The Second and Third Epistles of John* (Edinburgh: Clark, 1986).
Polhill, J. B., "An Analysis of II and III John," RevExp 67 (1970), 461–71.
von Wahlde, U. C., "The Theological Foundation of the Presbyter's Argument in 2 Jn (vv. 4–6)," ZNW 76 (1985), 209–24.
Watson, D. F., "A Rhetorical Analysis of 2 John according to the Greco-Roman Convention," NTS 35 (1989), 104–30.

CHAPTER 14

THIRD LETTER OF JOHN

The shortest book in the NT and very similar to II John in format, style, authorship, and length, III John is, nevertheless, quite unlike I and II John in subject matter. There is no critique of moral indifference or christological error, only of complicated church relationships that involve rival authority—a situation very difficult to diagnose. After the *General Analysis* describes what is said in the letter, subdivisions will be devoted to a detailed *Diagnosis of the situation,* an *Issue for reflection,* and *Bibliography.* For the moment the following surface information is sufficient: In one community a certain Diotrephes, who has emerged as a leader, has decided to keep out traveling missionaries, including those from the presbyter. His refusal of hospitality causes the presbyter to write III John to Gaius, seemingly a wealthy person in a neighboring community. Gaius has been providing hospitality on a temporary basis, but the presbyter wants him to take over larger responsibility for helping the missionaries, including the well-known Demetrius, who will soon arrive.

General Analysis of the Message

Opening Formula (vv. 1–2). The Sender and Addressee section (v. 1) is the briefest in the NT, but very close to the secular letters of the time. A health wish (v. 2) is also a feature in the Opening of secular letters, but the presbyter extends his concerns to Gaius' spiritual welfare—a connection of soul and body (cf. Matt 10:28). Clearly the presbyter regards Gaius as very sympathetic.

Transitional expression of joy (vv. 3–4). As with II John 4, this is transitional to the Body of the letter (a "Body-Opening"). The joy that Gaius is walking in the truth is more than conventional, because the presbyter is implicitly holding Gaius up by contrast with Diotrephes, whom he will mention in v. 9. Testimony has been borne to Gaius by "brothers" who have come to the presbyter. Combined with vv. 5–6, this shows that the presbyter has contacts with a group of travelers who are partly missionaries and partly his eyes and ears about church situations.

Message (vv. 5–14). The "brothers" of vv. 5–6, among whom Gaius has

Summary of Basic Information

DATE: Perhaps after I and II John, reflecting attempts to deal with the situation described in those writings; III John may be related to the pastoral development in John 21 and thus written shortly after AD 100.

TO: Gaius, a Johannine Christian friendly to the presbyter, because Diotrephes, who has taken over leadership (in a neighboring community), is not friendly.

AUTHENTICITY: By a writer in the Johannine tradition, who wrote II John as well and probably I John.

UNITY AND INTEGRITY: Not seriously disputed.

FORMAL DIVISION:
A. Opening Formula: 1–2
B. Body: 3–14
  3–4: Transitional expression of joy
  5–14: Message
C. Concluding Formula: 15.

a reputation of being hospitable, are coming from the presbyter's community to that in which Gaius lives; and Gaius is asked to help them farther on their way. We get a picture here of early preachers of Christ who have set out for the sake of "the Name," careful to reject aid from the Pagans (v. 7), and who therefore depend on the assistance of generous local Christians (vv. 5,8). In the presbyter's beautiful expression (v. 8) those who help such persons become "co-workers in the truth." If the letter had ended with v. 8, we would have assumed simply that Gaius was either the wealthiest Christian in a community (but then why not a letter addressed to the community [as was II John] mentioning Gaius with praise?) or the Christian formally or informally leading the community. In vv. 9–10, however, a much more complicated situation is suddenly revealed; for a certain Diotrephes "who likes to be first" in the church[1] does not pay attention to the presbyter[2] and has ignored the presbyter's letter. Beyond that, Diotrephes is spreading evil nonsense about the presbyter, refusing to receive "brothers" (i.e., missionaries apparently sent by the presbyter), hindering those who wish to do so, and expelling them from the church! A more thorough rejection of the presbyter's authority

[1]Most likely a nearby church, not the one in which Gaius lives; for in v. 14 we hear that the presbyter hopes to visit Gaius on a friendly basis, and the visit to the church led by Diotrephes promises to be hostile (v. 10). V. 9 contains the first reference to *ekklēsia* in the whole Johannine corpus (also at the end of III John 10).

[2]More precisely "to us." The plural is interesting given the singular "I wrote" in the same verse. Seemingly the presbyter regards himself as part of a community of tradition-bearers (I John 1:1–5)—see also III John 12: "We give our testimonial as well, and you know our testimony is true."

one can scarcely imagine.[3] One would expect the presbyter simply to order Diotrephes removed or ostracized, but the relatively mild urging not to imitate evil (v. 11) suggests that the presbyter had neither the authority nor the practical power to act against Diotrephes. Rather he writes to Gaius endorsing a figure named Demetrius (v. 12), apparently a missionary for whom this serves as a letter of recommendation.[4]

As in II John 12, the presbyter closes the Body or message of the letter in vv. 13–14 with an apology for brevity and the hope to see Gaius soon.

Concluding Formula (v. 15). II John had the children of an Elect sister church send greetings; III John has "the beloved here" (i.e., in the presbyter's church) send greetings to Gaius and to the beloved there, "each by name."

Diagnosis of the Situation

Ironically the only work in the Johannine corpus to give the personal names of Johannine Christians (Gaius, Diotrephes, Demetrius[5]) is imprecise as to how these are related to one another and the presbyter. (a) Gaius. Does he offer hospitality to those who have recently been rejected by Diotrephes, or does Diotrephes refuse hospitality to those whom Gaius was helping? Most opt for the former, but why then does the presbyter have to tell Gaius about Diotrephes? For oratorical emphasis? Gaius was probably not a member of Diotrephes' house-church (n. 1 above); and Gaius, whom the presbyter likes, was probably not the head of another house-church—a position condemned by the presbyter in v. 9. In other words the presbyter may be dealing with two churches that have different organization. (b) Diotrephes. The things for which he is blamed are: liking to make himself first in a church, paying no attention to the presbyter, refusing to welcome "brothers" (apparently missionaries sent out by the presbyter), and hindering and expelling those who extend that hospitality. Many have suggested that he was, by title or in fact, an example of the emerging presbyter-bishop described with enthusiasm by Ignatius of Antioch (p. 398 above). His emergence would be

[3]Yet the presbyter does not describe Diotrephes as an antichrist, a secessionist, a false prophet, or one who denies that Jesus Christ has come in the flesh (cf. I John 2:18–23; 4:1–2; II John 7), whence my contention that he does not regard Diotrephes as a christological "heretic."

[4]For letters of recommendation identifying Christians to be received, supported, and listened to, see Acts 18:27; Rom 16:1–2; I Cor 16:3; II Cor 3:1; Phil 2:25–30; and Col 4:7–9. This may have been the beginning of the practice in Johannine circles, a practice made necessary by the recent circulation of secessionist missionaries.

[5]All three are Greco-Roman names, not derivative from Hebrew. There are two or three other figures named Gaius in NT circles (I Cor 1:14; Acts 19:29; 20:4), a Demetrius (Acts 19:24) and a Demas (short for Demetrius? Phlm 24; Col 4:14); but there is no convincing reason to identify this Gaius and Demetrius with any of them. Diotrephes is not a particularly common name.

very troubling on the Johannine scene where so little emphasis had been placed on church structure. By contrast, the presbyter-writer would represent the older Johannine situation wherein there might be a "School" of tradition-bearers but these were not authoritative community administrators.[6] (c) Demetrius. A prominent missionary (receiving "a good report from all") was coming to Gaius, either carrying III John or shortly after it would have been received. The seriousness of the testimonial to him reflects the presbyter's view that hospitality must be extended so that the gospel can be proclaimed.

We cannot be sure of all the reasons for the antagonism between the presbyter and Diotrephes; but in my judgment the letter makes the most sense if both figures were opposed to secessionist missionaries. If we assume that the presbyter wrote I John as well, he thought that there was no need for human teachers: Those who have the anointing with the Spirit are automatically taught what is true, and so one must test the spirits to detect false prophets (I John 2:27; 4:1–6). Diotrephes may have judged all this too vague, since the secessionists claimed that they had the true spirit, making it impossible for people to know who was speaking the truth. As had been discovered in other churches (e.g., Titus 1:5–16; I Tim 4), Diotrephes would have decided that authoritative human teachers were needed, namely, those who had the background to know what was erroneous and the administrative authority to keep false teachers away. He took on that role for his local church, keeping all missionaries out, including those of the presbyter. In the presbyter's outlook Diotrephes was arrogant in departing from the principle that Jesus was the model shepherd and all other (human) shepherds were thieves and bandits (John 10). In Diotrephes' outlook the presbyter was naive and impractical. That Diotrephes ultimately won in his view of what would save Johannine Christianity may be indicated by John 21 (the latest element in John, written after I-II John?) where Jesus gives Peter pastoral authority over the sheep, effectively modifying the thrust of John 10.

Issue for Reflection

If the diagnosis of III John offered above has value, we have in the Gospel and Epistles traces of developments within a particular Christian community over several decades: (a) struggles with local Jewish synagogues that rejected as irreconcilable with monotheism the Johannine Christian confession

[6]Attempts to make the presbyter-writer a "heretical" representative of Johannine theology that was too adventurous for the larger church (the Great Church represented by Diotrephes) are refuted by the fact that the views expressed in I and II John would be more traditional by other NT standards than those found in John, as indicated by the epistolary writer's appeal to what was from the beginning.

of Jesus as God; (b) a bitter withdrawal or expulsion of Johannine Christians from the synagogues, accompanied by the Christian counterclaim that Jesus had replaced all the essentials of Judaism (Temple worship, feasts, natural birth from Jewish parents); (c) simultaneously an intensification of the high christological criterion, making the Johannine Christians suspicious of some other Christians as not properly confessing Jesus; (d) an internal division when this high christology was carried by some Johannine Christians to the point of questioning the importance of the humanity of Jesus; (e) an attempt to preserve a christological balance between the human and the divine by appealing to what was traditional in Johannine teaching, and by rejecting as antichrists those who deviated from that balance; (f) a struggle about effective means to combat false teachers; (g) and the gradual acceptance of the kind of authoritarian structure found in the other churches, thus bringing at least part of the Johannine heritage into line with the rapidly emerging Great Church. If one thinks of struggles and divisions in subsequent Christianity, one can realize how often the pattern has repeated itself, in whole or in part.

Bibliography on III John

(See the *Bibliography* in Chapter 12 on I John, which treats the Johannine Epistles in general.)

Hall, D. R., "Fellow-Workers with the Gospel," ExpTim 85 (1973–74), 119–20.

Horvath, T., "3 Jn 11[b]: An Early Ecumenical Creed?" ExpTim 85 (1973–74), 339–40.

Malherbe, A. J., "The Inhospitality of Diotrephes," GCHP 222–32.

Watson, D. F., "A Rhetorical Analysis of 3 John. A Study in Epistolary Rhetoric," CBQ 51 (1989), 479–501.

PART III

THE PAULINE LETTERS

Classifications and Format of New Testament Letters
General Issues in Paul's Life and Thought
An Appreciation of Paul

ProtoPauline (Undisputed) Letters	*DeuteroPauline (possibly Pseudonymous) Letters*
I Thessalonians	II Thessalonians
Galatians	Colossians
Philippians	Ephesians
Philemon	Titus
I Corinthians	I Timothy
II Corinthians	II Timothy
Romans	

CHAPTER 15

CLASSIFICATIONS AND FORMAT OF NEW TESTAMENT LETTERS

Of the twenty-seven books of the NT, half have Paul's name attached, all of them in letter form. Chapters 18–31 below will treat those writings individually, but before that three Chapters will be devoted to an overall picture. Chapter 15 will analyze the letter format that shaped Paul's communication and explain how the individual letters will be approached. Chapter 16 will report what we know of Paul's life and some important aspects of his thought. These two somewhat technical chapters reflect issues raised by the available information. Then on a more humane level Chapter 17 will attempt briefly to offer an appreciation of Paul and to catch his spirit.

As we saw in Chapter 1, the seven undisputed Pauline (or protoPauline) letters were probably the first NT books to be composed. That is explicable, in part, because the early Christians thought that Christ would return soon, and so only "immediate literature" that dealt with existing problems was of import. Yet letters continued to be written even when more permanent literature (Gospels, Acts) had begun to be produced. Indeed, the Table of Contents of printed Bibles lists twenty-one of the twenty-seven NT books as "Letters" or "Epistles"—a surprising statistic when we realize that none of the forty-six OT books[1] carries that designation.

In the canonical order accepted in modern Bibles, all the NT letters, which by name or history are associated with apostles, come after the Acts of the Apostles. The thirteen letters/epistles that bear Paul's name come first. They are divided into two smaller collections: nine addressed to communities at geographical places (Rom, I-II Cor, Gal, Eph, Phil, Col, I-II Thess) and four

[1]The thirty-nine (proto)canonical and seven deuterocanonical books refer to or contain letters. (In some listings of the Apocrypha the Letter of Jeremiah is counted as a separate book rather than as the sixth chap. of Baruch.) For references to letters in the Hebrew sections of the OT, see II Sam 11:14–15; I Kings 21:8–10; Jer 29:1–23; etc. (Remnants of almost fifty extrabiblical letters in Hebrew written during the biblical period have been found, almost all on ostraca, i.e., potsherds). In the Aramaic sections of the OT whole letters are reproduced, e.g., Ezra 4:7–22; 7:11–26. (Some seventy early extrabiblical letters in Aramaic have been preserved on papyrus or skin, plus forty-six on ostraca.) Letters are reproduced also in the Greek sections of the OT, e.g., I Macc 10:18–20,25–45; II Macc 1:1–2:18; 5:10–13; 8:21–32; Baruch 6. See Acts 23:26–30 for a letter within a NT book (by a Roman centurion to the procurator Felix); also Rev 2–3.

addressed to individuals (I-II Tim, Titus, Phlm). Each collection is arranged in descending order of length.[2] Hebrews, long associated with Paul, follows; and then come the so-called Catholic Epistles associated with James, Peter, John, and Jude. The first three are in the order of their names in Gal 2:9, followed by Judas (Jude) who is not mentioned by Paul.

(A) Classifications

We may begin with the terminology "letter" and "epistle." For many these are interchangeable; but A. Deissmann, whose *Light from the Ancient East* (2d ed.; London: 1927) was a major contribution toward highlighting the importance of Greek papyri letters for NT background, made a distinction. "Epistle" for him was an artistic literary exercise, generally presenting a moral lesson to a general audience, and intended for publication, e.g., Seneca's *Epistulae Morales.* "Letter" was a nonliterary means of communicating information between a writer and a real correspondent separated by distance from one another.[3] By that criterion, of twenty-one NT compositions all or most of the thirteen compositions associated with Paul, along with II-III John, might be classified as "Letters," whereas Hebrews and perhaps I-II Pet, James, I John, and Jude would be "Epistles."

Today, however, almost all scholars would nuance Deissmann's distinction (and many would reject it). The ancient rhetorical handbooks show a wide range of Greco-Roman letter types, e.g., letters conveying praise, correction, argumentation, information, etc., so that even a homily meant to persuade can be cast in a letter format. Several of Paul's letters (I Cor and Rom) are so long that they might be classified as letter-essays. As for audience, it is not clear that any of the Pauline writings or even those dubbed "Catholic" (or "General," or "Universal") were addressed to Christians everywhere (even though some of them could easily serve all Christians). True, only some NT letters are addressed to communities in a specific city or cities; but the others may have in mind Christians with a particular heritage, e.g., Johannine Christians (I–III John), Pauline Christians (Eph), or Christians with a strong attachment to Judaism (Jas, Jude). Works in my judgment that are clearly

[2]The one exception is that Gal comes before Eph, even though by most counts Eph is about 200 words longer than Gal. In the Chester Beatty Papyrus II (P^{46}), from *ca.* AD 200, Eph comes before Gal. As an argument against the antiquity of the Pastoral Letters, it is often noted that they are lacking in that ancient papyrus codex, but so is Phlm; and therefore the contents of P^{46} may indicate no more than that the papyrus preserved the first part of the Pauline collection and not the second (addressed to individuals). See J. D. Quinn, CBQ 36 (1974), 379–85.

[3]As with letters today, some could be more formal than others. For Deissmann, epistles were produced in cultured and educated circles, whereas letters were exchanged among people of lower social status and less education. That is a very dubious aspect of his theory. See J. D. Quinn, ABD 6.564.

"Letters," I shall entitle that way. In the instance of I John, Eph, Heb, Jas, Jude, and II Pet, I shall put both "Letter" and "Epistle" in the title of the respective Chapter, placing first the designation that does more justice to the work—provided that one wants to apply (with modification) Deissmann's standards.

Letters could be written in different ways, sometimes by the sender's own hand and sometimes dictated. In the latter case each syllable might be copied by a recording secretary,[4] with an editor introduced to correct infelicities; or after the sender had indicated only the broad lines of the message, more authority to formulate might be given to a scribe, who was almost a co-author, to create the final form. As for Paul, he may have written a short letter like Phlm entirely with his own hand (v. 19). References to lines written by Paul's own hand in a longer letter (I Cor 16:21; Gal 6:11; II Thess 3:17; Col 4:18), however, suggest that the rest of the letter was penned by another writer; and explicitly Rom 16:22 has greetings from "Tertius who wrote the letter." (See also I Pet 5:12 for Peter writing "through Silvanus.") In all this, however, we do not know how literally Paul would have supplied wording to scribes (and thus whether he was working with secretaries or co-authors). He may have dictated some letters exactly and allowed freedom in others, e.g., in Col, which has a style very different from the protoPauline letters.[5]

The NT letters, particularly the Pauline letters, were meant to be read aloud in order to persuade. Consequently, like speeches, they can be judged as rhetoric, in terms of the authority of writer, the quality of the writing, and the desired effect on the audience. In particular, rhetorical criticism (p. 26 above) would pay attention to the way the material has been chosen and structured in a letter and to the way in which it has been expressed (both as to vocabulary and organization) so that it would be easily understood and remembered.

Aristotle (*Ars rhetorica* 1.3; §1358b) distinguished three modes of argumentation in rhetoric, and recently scholars have sought to apply these to NT letters.[6] (1) Judicial or forensic argumentation, such as would be found

[4]Latin shorthand was already in use by this time, and most likely Greek as well. A professional secretary would record dictation with a stylus in shorthand on a wax-coated tablet and then transcribe in longhand on papyrus sheets about nine inches wide. For the latter normally a reed pen was used and black ink (with a chimney-soot base). If a significant letter was being sent, the secretary would make and keep a copy. Murphy-O'Connor, *Paul the Letter-Writer,* is very helpful for the technical information.

[5]Many scholars, however, consider Col deuteroPauline (i.e., written by a disciple of Paul) because not only the style but also the content differ from the protoPauline letters.

[6]Although letters have rhetorical aspects, they were not originally part of the theoretical systems of rhetoric. Only gradually did they make their way into rhetorical handbooks, e.g., the treatment by Julius Victor in the 4th century AD. Indeed, Pseudo-Libanius (4th–6th centuries AD) lists 41 types of letters. Malherbe, *Ancient* 2–14, is very helpful on this background.

in the law courts. At times, for instance, Paul is conscious of charges made against him by those opposed to his policy on circumcision and the Mosaic Law and is defending his ministry and what he has done in the past. (2) Deliberative or hortatory (paraenetic) argumentation, such as would be found in public or political assemblies that are debating what is expedient for the future. It tries to persuade people to make practical decisions and do things. In writing to Corinth Paul insists that if his letter is not received, he will come and argue in person (II Cor 13:1–5). (3) Demonstrative or epideictic argumentation, as in speeches given at a public celebration. It is designed to please or inspire people, affirming common beliefs and values and gaining support in present endeavors. Paul often writes to encourage his converts, praising their faith and observance. By way of application Puskas, *Letters* 37–38, 59–61, 76–77 classifies Gal, I Cor, and Rom respectively as judicial, deliberative, and demonstrative rhetoric, and offers Greco-Roman parallels for each.

Yet caution is indicated about attempts to detect sophisticated rhetorical patterns. There is no way to be sure that Paul would have been aware of the classic analyses of rhetoric and/or would have been consciously following them.[7] The different forms of argumentation may have been simply unconscious responses to what needed to be done. Or, indeed, certain features may reflect OT patterns, e.g., the argumentative and hortatory atmosphere (resembling forensic and deliberative rhetoric) in some passages of Paul's writing may be affected by the *rîb* or *rîv* (covenant lawsuit where God takes the chosen people to court: Isa 3:13–15; Micah 6:1ff.), and not (only) by Greco-Roman rhetoric. The recognition of emotive overstatements, of eloquent exaggeration, of marshaled arguments, etc., is significant for determining what is really being said; but that recognition may come without knowledge of the formal rules of ancient rhetoric. Thus the extent to which disputes about precise rhetorical classification are important for interpretation is not always clear.

(B) Format

The Hellenistic world has left us many Greek and Latin letters of literary quality, as well as papyrus fragments of thousands of letters from Egypt dealing with the concerns of ordinary life (business, legal matters, friendship, and family). Letters tend to follow a set format, and one who lacks

[7]E. A. Judge, *Australian Biblical Review* 16 (1968), 37–50, offers a careful discussion of how much can be diagnosed about Paul's rhetorical knowledge from his upbringing (either at Tarsus or Jerusalem) and his letters.

knowledge of that format can seriously misinterpret a letter. (For example, in a modern English letter one might draw the wrong inference about the relationship between the writer and the addressee if one attributed to "Dear" in the opening its normal value and did not realize that it is stereotyped in a letter.) Accordingly, the influence of standardized letter format on NT letters is an important factor in interpretation.

In what follows I concentrate on a more-or-less standard format detectable in most NT letters (or epistles). Generally four parts of the letter are distinguished: (1) Opening Formula; (2) Thanksgiving; (3) Body or Message; (4) Concluding Formula. Of course, the habitual distinction of parts does not mean that the writers necessarily so divided their thoughts. But having been shaped by the conventions of their times, they would normally follow this progression.

(1) Opening Formula (*Praescriptio*)[8]

The Opening Formula of the Greco-Roman letter consisted of three basic elements (sender, addressee, greeting), although sometimes another element extends the greeting, e.g., one remembering (*mnēmoneuein*) the addressee, or wishing good health to the addressee and reporting on the writer's own (good) health. Let us now examine in detail each of these three or four component elements as they appear in early Christian letters.

Sender (*Superscriptio*). This involves the personal name of the author,[9] sometimes further identified with a title to establish the author's authority. Although in I-II Thess we find simply "Paul," nine times he identifies himself as "an apostle of/through Christ Jesus," twice as "a servant of Christ Jesus," and in Titus also as "a servant of God."[10] II and III John are anomalous in using a title ("the presbyter") for the sender without an attached personal name. Eight of the thirteen Pauline letters name co-senders in various combinations: Timothy (in six), Silvanus (two), Sosthenes (one). Special relationships to the communities addressed do not adequately explain the inclusion of these names; in one way or another the co-senders have contributed to the composition of these writings (Murphy-O'Connor, *Paul the Letter-Writer* 16–34).

[8]Occasionally one finds the term "Address" used for this part of the letter; but it is wiser to keep that designation for what was written on the *outside* of the folded papyrus (on the inside of which a letter was written), namely, the equivalent of our envelope address.

[9]Because of the custom of using scribes already mentioned, the sender or author may not have been the physical writer. In the text above, however, I use the terms interchangeably.

[10]Among the Catholic Letters/Epistles, "apostle" appears in I and II Pet, while "servant" appears in II Pet, Jas, and Jude—the last mentioned also speaks as "brother of James." In the letters of Ignatius of Antioch we find: "Ignatius who is also called Theophorus [God-bearer]."

Addressee (*Adscriptio*). The simplest form is a personal name; but in the few NT and subapostolic letters written to individuals, further identification is supplied (e.g., "to Polycarp who is bishop") and/or an expression of affection (e.g., III John's "to the beloved Gaius"). The addressees in most NT and subapostolic letters are communities in stated regions. In five Pauline letters (I-II Thess, I-II Cor, Gal) the addressees are identified as "church"; in four (Phil, Rom, Col, Eph), as "saints"—note that the communities in Colossae and Rome were not founded by Paul. The addressee of II John, "an elect Lady," is probably a symbolic designation for a church, but the letter is atypical in not stating where the church is.

Greeting (*Salutatio*). Occasionally this was omitted. Jewish letters of the period tend to replace "greetings" (Greek *chairein* = Latin *ave,* "hail") with "peace" (Greek *eirēnē,* reflecting Hebrew *shālôm*) and to be more expansive in its description of the persons involved, e.g., "Baruch, the son of Neriah, to the brothers carried into captivity, mercy and peace" (*II Baruch* 78:2). Some NT examples have the regular *chairein,* e.g., Jas 1:1: "To the twelve tribes in the diaspora, greetings."[11] Yet neither the Jewish "peace" nor the Greek "greetings" used alone is typical of NT letters; for they employ a combination of two or three nouns like "grace, peace, mercy, love," characterized as coming from God the Father (and Jesus Christ)—thus almost all the Pauline letters.[12] II John has "grace, mercy, and peace" but, quite unusually, as a statement of existing Christian fact rather than as a wish. III John has none of these and really lacks a greeting.

Remembrance or Health Wish. In the Greco-Roman personal letter, still within the Opening Formula, the greeting was often expanded by a remembrance or a health wish as the sender prayed for the health of the addressee and gave assurance of the sender's own health. An example of an Opening Formula with this fourth element is: "Serapion, to his brothers Ptolemaeus and Apollonius, greetings. If you are well, it would be excellent; I myself am well."[13] In I Thess the remembrance is part of the Thanksgiving rather than part of the Opening Formula; for after "we give thanks" in 1:2, the letter continues in 1:3, "*remembering* before our God and father your work of faith." III John gives the best and only clear example of an opening health wish in a NT letter: "Beloved, I hope you are in good health." While lacking remembrances and health wishes, most NT letters expand one or the other

[11]Also Acts 15:23, and a secular example in 23:26.

[12]Paul's favorite greeting, "grace" (*charis*) and "peace" (*eirēnē,* probably implying salvation), is often thought to combine a noun resembling the Greco-Roman *chairein* with the Jewish "peace."

[13]Papyrus Paris 43, from 154 BC, cited in Doty, *Letters* 13. When the letter was to be interpreted by a carrier, another feature of the greeting might be a statement establishing the credibility and credentials of the carrier by clarifying his relationship to the sender.

element in the Opening Formula by attaching the high status and privileges of Christians. Rom, Titus, and II Tim expand the designation of the sender in that way, e.g., Paul "set apart for the gospel of God . . ." I Cor and I-II Pet expand the description of the addressee, e.g., "To the exiles of the diaspora . . . chosen according to the foreknowledge of God the Father by sanctification of the Spirit . . ." Gal expands the greeting: "Grace and peace from the Lord Jesus Christ who gave himself for our sins . . ."

(2) Thanksgiving

In Hellenistic letters the Opening Formula is often followed by a statement wherein the sender gives thanks (*eucharistein*) to the gods for specified reasons, e.g., deliverance from a calamity. II Macc 1:11 supplies a good Jewish example: "Having been saved by God from grave dangers, we thank God greatly for taking our side against the king." Sometimes there is prayer that such care will be continued. A different pattern appears in the Pauline Thanksgiving (which is lacking in Gal and Titus).[14] The introductory wording is usually: "I/we give thanks to [my] God because . . ." The specified reason for the thanks is not deliverance from disaster but the faithfulness of the congregation addressed, and the supplication is for the continuance of such fidelity. Often some of the main themes of the Body of the letter are briefly anticipated in the Thanksgiving. Thus admonitions can appear in this section, or a specific paraenetic (urging) tone.[15] In II and III John there is no expression of thanks after the Opening Formula, although the Johannine expressions of joy serve much the same function as a Thanksgiving, i.e., that of a compliment putting readers in a benevolent mood to receive a message (in the Body of the letter) that may contain a demand or even a warning.

(3) Body or Message

The Body of a letter is sometimes defined as what comes between the Opening Formula (+ Thanksgiving) and the Concluding Formula. This de-

[14]One must speak in generalities, for the Pauline Thanksgiving is not so neatly regular as the Opening Formula. It may run a few lines or over 50 percent of the letter (I Thess). In the Thanksgiving of II Cor (1:3–11) an extended blessing (1:3–10) precedes the expression of thanks (1:11); similarly in the Thanksgiving of Eph 1:3–23 a doxology (1:3–14) precedes the thanks (1:15–23). Some would contend that the Thanksgiving of Gal has been replaced by the expression of amazement in 1:6ff., an epistolary feature in letters of ironic rebuke.

[15]It has been suggested that Paul began his oral preaching with a thanksgiving to God and that this practice left its mark on his use of the Thanksgiving in letters. Paul's practice may also reflect a background in Jewish liturgical life with its blessings of God. As to the extent to which Paul's Thanksgivings truly fit epistolary style, see the debate between P. Arzt, NovT 36 (1994), 29–46, and J. T. Reed, JSNT 61 (1996), 87–99.

scription reflects two factors: First, the Body until recently has been the least studied epistolary element from the viewpoint of form; second, the Body has been thought to have little set form.[16] Increasingly, however, thanks to scholars like Funk, Mullins, and White, discrete sections with definite formal characteristics are being recognized in the Body, especially in the transitional sentences at the beginning (Body-Opening) and the end (Body-Closing). In between there is the Body-Middle (for want of a better term), which is more difficult to analyze from a formal viewpoint. Greco-Roman letters offer only limited help for studying the formal characteristics of the Body of most NT letters, because the NT letter Bodies, especially those of Paul and I-II Pet, are considerably longer than the Bodies of ordinary letters. Rather, II-III John, with their brevity determined by the length of a papyrus sheet, would have been closer to the ordinary conventions.

Body-Opening. Since this element introduces the occasion for writing the letter, tactically it tends to proceed from a hint about what is common in the relationship between the writer and the addressee. And so there is a rather narrow range of opening sentences in the Body of secular letters: "I want you to know . . ."; "Do not think that . . ."; "Please do [not] . . ."; "I regretted [or was astonished, or rejoiced] when I heard that you . . ."; "I/you wrote previously about . . ."; "I appeal to you . . ."

Equivalent formulas are found in the Body-Opening of the Pauline letters. Generally they involve an opening expression of joy, chiefly over news of the addressees' welfare. In Phil 1:4 there is joy in praying for the addressees; in II Tim 1:4 the sender longs to see the addressee so that he may be filled with joy; in Phlm 7 joy has already been derived by the sender from the love of the addressee. In Jas 1:2–3 the author tells the addressees to count meeting trials as a joy, since testing produces steadfastness. In II John 4 and III John 3–4 the presbyter expresses joy over the blessed state of the addressees (walking in truth)—the subject that appears in the Thanksgiving of the Pauline letters.[17]

Another feature of the Body-Opening, transitional to the main message, is a petition or request. Mullins points out that this feature characteristically comes near the beginning of the Body of the letter and has set properties: (a) A background for the petition is usually given first as a prelude, often in

[16]Many speak of two parts of the Body of the Pauline letter: first, a doctrinal exposé (the Pauline indicative), and then an ethical, paraenetic exhortation (the Pauline imperative). As valid as that analysis may be, it is based on content rather than form and ignores the stereotyped features at the opening and closing of the Body.

[17]See also Polycarp, *Philippians* 1:1–2. Perhaps one should speak of a step in Christian letter format wherein the blessed state of the addressees was acknowledged by using either *eucharistein,* "to give thanks," or *chairein,* "to rejoice."

terms of joy over the state of the addressee. (b) The petition itself is expressed in terms of one of four verbs of asking. (c) The addressee is written to directly in the vocative. (d) There is an expression of courtesy. (e) The desired action is described.

Body-Closing. The other segment of the Body of a Greco-Roman letter that has predictable characteristics is the Closing. Here the writer solidifies or recapitulates what has been written in the Body, creating a bridge to further correspondence or communication. In both the papyri and the Pauline letters features of this segment include: (a) a statement as to why the letter was written—the motivation; (b) an indication of how the addressees should respond to it—either a reminder of responsibility (often in the papyri) or an expression of confidence (often in Paul); (c) a proposal of further contact by a visit, by an emissary, or by continuing correspondence. The last feature serves an eschatological function for Paul, since through it judging or consoling apostolic authority will be made present to the addressees. (One can use the language of eschatology because in Paul's view that apostolic authority reflects the judgmental authority of God or Christ.) Aspects of the "apostolic parousia," as Funk has dubbed it, involve the hope of being able to visit (granted the possibility of being delayed by a hindrance) and a reference to the mutual benefits and joy that will result therefrom.

A few Pauline formulas illustrate clearly such features: "I myself am satisfied about you, my brothers . . . But I wrote to you boldly on some points as a reminder . . . that by the will of God I may come to you in joy and be refreshed in your company" (Rom 15:14,15,32). "Confident of your compliance I wrote to you, knowing that you will do more than I say. At the same time prepare for me a guest room, for I hope that through your prayers I shall be given back to you" (Phlm 21–22). While scholars treat the promised visit as part of the Body-Closing, normally in Paul it is not the very last feature of the Body (before the Concluding Formula) but occurs earlier. In letters where there is a dispute in the community addressed, the promise of an apostolic visit may be followed by some paraenesis and exhortation. For example, "I shall visit you after I pass through Macedonia . . . Be watchful, stand firm in the faith, and be courageous" (I Cor 16:5,13); and "I am writing this while I am away from you, so that when I come, I may not have to be severe . . . Mend your ways; heed my appeal" (II Cor 13:10–11). Body-Closings are found in II John 12 and III John 13–14, where the presbyter promises a personal visit. In II John the goal of the visit is "so that our joy may be fulfilled"; in III John there are two references to a visit: In v. 10 the presbyter will accuse Diotrephes; in v. 14 he longs to talk to Gaius face to face.

(4) Concluding Formula

Two conventional expressions mark the end of a Greco-Roman letter, namely, a wish for good health[18] and a word of farewell (*errōso*). An example of how brief this can be comes from the last two lines of Papyrus Oxyrhynchus 746: "For the rest take care of yourself that you may remain in good health. Farewell" (Doty, *Letters* 10–11). In the Roman period an expression of greetings (*aspazesthai*) became customary as a third feature. In this area of letter format the Pauline letters do not follow the normal conventions, for Paul never concludes with either the health wish or *errōso*. He does have greetings (*aspazesthai*) coming from the co-workers who are with him and directed to people whom he knows at the community addressed. For example, "Give greetings to every saint in Christ Jesus; the brothers who are with me send greetings; all the saints send you greetings, especially those who are of the household of Caesar" (Phil 4:21–22); and "All those with me send you greetings; greet those who love us in the faith" (Titus 3:15). Both II and III John have greetings sent to the addressee from the community where the letter originated, and III John wants the beloved who are being addressed to be greeted "each by name." (This resembles the Pauline custom of listing by name those to be greeted.)

Besides greetings, Paul's Concluding Formula sometimes contains a doxology of God (Rom 16:25–27; Phil 4:20) and a benediction of the recipients. In eight of the Pauline letters the benediction is a slight variant of this general form: "The grace of our Lord Jesus Christ [be] with you";[19] but five letters have a shorter form: "Grace [be] with you." These features are found in the Concluding Formulas of other NT letters as well; for Heb and I Pet have both greetings and a benediction, while a doxology is found in Heb, I-II Pet, and Jude.[20] III John and I Pet have "peace" instead of "grace"; and the combinations "peace" and "grace" in Eph 6:23–24, and "peace" and "mercy" in Gal 6:16 confirm that "peace" was an alternative benediction in Concluding Formulas of Christian letters.

In four of the Pauline letters (I Thess, I-II Cor, Rom) and in I Pet the greeting is to be done with "a holy kiss."[21] Although kisses were not unusual among family members, there was a reticence about public kisses in Greco-Roman society. Mostly they are described in scenes of reconciliation or of relatives meeting after separation. Throughout his ministry Jesus and his dis-

[18]This sometimes duplicated an acknowledgment of good health earlier in the letter (Thanksgiving).

[19]Expanded by "the love of God and the fellowship of the Holy Spirit" in II Cor 13:13(14).

[20]Greetings (*aspazesthai*) are normal in the Ignatian letters; a benediction appears in *I Clement* and in Ignatius, *To Polycarp;* a doxology appears in *I-II Clement.*

[21]W. Klassen, "The Sacred Kiss in the New Testament," NTS 39 (1993), 122–35.

ciples are not shown exchanging a kiss; but Judas' use of it in Gethsemane in a context where he did not wish to alert Jesus may mean that it was a normal greeting in the group, and certainly the kiss as a greeting is attested in the Bible (Gen 33:4; II Sam 20:9; and Luke 15:20). Evidently the Christian community had adopted the kiss as a sign of fellowship; it was holy because it was exchanged among the saints.

As noted above, at times Paul takes care to include a line stating that he is writing with his own hand. At least for the four longer letters in which he does so (I Cor, Gal, II Thess, Col), besides suggesting that the rest of the letter was physically penned by another, such lines may imply that Paul has checked the whole so that it could justifiably be sent in his own name.

(C) How This Volume Will Treat the Individual Letters

The seven letters called "Catholic" (or "General," or "Universal") will be divided in my treatment. The three Johannine letters were treated in Chapters 12–14, following Chapter 11 on the Gospel according to John. The other four letters are treated in Chapters 33–36 in the order I Pet, Jas, Jude, II Pet. The thirteen letters/epistles that bear Paul's name will be treated in a combined topical and chronological order, so far as the latter can be determined. Chapters 18–24 cover the protoPauline group (i.e., surely written by Paul) in the order I Thess, Gal, Phil, Phlm, I-II Cor, and Rom.[22] After Chapter 25 on Pseudonymity and deuteroPauline writing, Chapters 26–31 cover the deuteroPauline group (perhaps or probably not written by Paul himself) in the order II Thess, Col, Eph, Titus, I Tim, and II Tim. Following them, Hebrews, which is not by Paul but has often been regarded as Pauline, is discussed in Chapter 32.

An important general rule is that all biblical references in a Chapter will refer to the letter being discussed in that Chapter unless otherwise noted. Generally the treatment will begin with a *Background* subsection that recounts the previous history of Paul's dealing with the community addressed (or what we know of Peter, James, and Jude in the instance of the Catholic letters). Then the *General Analysis of the Message* will summarize the main points of the letter. Since the letters vary greatly in both content and tone, the *Analysis* subsection will vary in approach.[23] The number and topics of

[22]We do not know when Phil and Phlm were written (sometime between 54 and 62), but they are conveniently treated together since Paul composed them in prison. We do not know when Gal was written—perhaps as early as 54; but with a different tone it treats some of the issues dealt with more systematically later in Rom (*ca.* 58).

[23]The *General Analysis* of the Gospels and Acts in Chapters 7–11 above consisted of a minicommentary that sought to highlight the features and theology of the respective work through a rapid

the subsequent subsections (authorship, dating, unity, special topics, etc.) will be dictated by the character of each letter. Most often these letters were addressed to the needs and problems of individual Christian communities in the 1st century. Consequently the subsection *Issues and problems for reflection* is especially important for the NT letters, since it is there that the relevancy to life today will be discussed. Often I shall present different views on an issue so that readers can make up their own minds, and the *Bibliography* may be helpful in that enterprise.

Bibliography

Doty, W. G., *Letters in Primitive Christianity* (Philadelphia: Fortress, 1973).

Fitzmyer, J. A., "Aramaic Epistolography," in *Studies in Ancient Letter Writing,* ed. J. L. White (*Semeia* 22; Chico, CA: Scholars, 1982), 22–57.

Funk, R. W., "The Apostolic Parousia: Form and Significance," in *Christian History and Interpretation: Studies Presented to John Knox,* eds. W. R. Farmer et al. (Cambridge Univ., 1967), 249–68.

Kim, Chan-Hie, *Form and Structure of the Familiar Greek Letter of Recommendation* (SBLDS 4; Missoula, MT: Scholars, 1972).

Malherbe, A. J., *Ancient Epistolary Theorists* (SBLRBS 19; Atlanta: Scholars, 1988).

———, *Moral Exhortation: A Greco-Roman Source Book* (Philadelphia: Westminster, 1986).

Mullins, T. Y., "Disclosure: A Literary Form in the New Testament," NovT 7 (1964), 44–50.

———, "Formulas in New Testament Epistles," JBL 91 (1972), 380–90.

———, "Greeting as New Testament Form," JBL 87 (1968), 418–26.

———, "Petition as a Literary Form," NovT 5 (1962), 46–54.

———, "Visit Talk in New Testament Letters," CBQ 35 (1973), 350–58.

Murphy-O'Connor, J., *Paul the Letter-Writer* (GNS 41; Collegeville: Liturgical, 1995). Very informative.

O'Brien, P. T., *Introductory Thanksgiving in the Letters of Paul* (NovTSup 49; Leiden: Brill, 1977).

Puskas, C. B., Jr., *The Letters of Paul: An Introduction* (Collegeville: Liturgical, 1993).

Richards, E. R., *The Secretary in the Letters of Paul* (WUNT 2/42; Tübingen: Mohr-Siebeck, 1991).

Sanders, J. T., "The Transition from Opening Epistolary Thanksgiving to a Body in the Letters of the Pauline Corpus," JBL 81 (1962), 348–52.

Schubert, P., *Form and Function of the Pauline Thanksgivings* (BZNW 20; Berlin: Töpelmann, 1939).

reading of the text. But those NT works were continuous narratives; the letters are not and different approaches are required.

Stirewalt, M. L., Jr., "The Form and Function of the Greek Letter Essay," in TRD 147–71.

Thomson, I. H., *Chiasmus in the Pauline Letters* (JSNTSup 111; Sheffield: Academic, 1995).

Weima, J.A.D., *Neglected Endings. The Significance of the Pauline Letter Closings* (JSNTSup 101; Sheffield: JSOT, 1994).

———, "Rhetorical Criticism of the Pauline Epistles since 1975," CRBS 3 (1995), 219–48.

White, J. L., *The Body of the Greek Letter* (SBLDS 2; Missoula, MT: Scholars, 1972).

———, *Light from Ancient Letters* (Philadelphia: Fortress, 1986). Comparative letter texts for studying NT letters.

———, "New Testament Epistolary Literature in the Framework of Ancient Epistolography," ANRW II/25.2, 1730–56.

CHAPTER 16

GENERAL ISSUES IN PAUL'S LIFE AND THOUGHT

Next to Jesus Paul has been the most influential figure in the history of Christianity. Although all the NT writers are working out the implications of Jesus for particular communities of believers, Paul in his numerous letters does this on the widest scale of all. That range, plus the depth of his thought and the passion of his involvement, have meant that since his letters became part of the NT, no Christian has been unaffected by what he has written. Whether or not they know Paul's works well, through what they have been taught about doctrine and piety, all Christians have become Paul's children in the faith. A general Chapter devoted to what we know about Paul's life and some main points in his thought, therefore, is an essential part of a NT Introduction.

(A) The Life of Paul

There are two sources for his life: biographical details in his own letters and accounts of his career in Acts (beginning with 7:58). There are three views of how to relate these sources. (a) Virtually complete trust in Acts. The traditional lives of Paul are guided strongly by Acts, fitting and adapting information from the letters into the Acts framework. (b) Great distrust of Acts. By way of reaction and as part of a skepticism about the historical value of Acts, what that book reports about Paul has been questioned. Indeed, some scholars have constructed Paul's career entirely or largely leaving out the Acts information, or drastically correcting it by heightening the differences between Acts and the letters into contradictions (e.g., Becker, Knox, Jewett, Lüdemann). (c) A mediate stance uses Paul's letters as a primary source and cautiously supplements from Acts,[1] not hastening to declare apparent differences contradictory. The possibilities of this third stance

[1]A principle formulated by Knox, *Chapters* 32, has won wide acceptance: "We may, with proper caution, use Acts to supplement the autobiographical data of the letters, but never to correct them"—a valid principle provided we allow that autobiography is sometimes slanted (even unconsciously) by the optic of the writer.

will be presented here, and readers should review the discussion of Acts in Chapter 10 above, especially as to whether a companion of Paul could have been the author (pp. 322-27).

There is no doubt that Acts has offered a theological interpretation of Paul, adapting his role to fit an overall view of the spread of Christianity "to the end of the earth" (Acts 1:8). Moreover, the author may have had only a sketchy view of parts of Paul's career, so that he telescoped and compacted complex events. Nevertheless, there is simply too much correspondence between Acts and autobiographical remarks in Paul's epistles for one to dismiss the Acts information: The author knew a great number of facts about Paul. To appreciate that, see Table 5 on the next page.[2] Let us review what can be reconstructed of Paul's life from a critical use of the two sources.

Birth and Upbringing

Paul was probably born *ca.* AD 5–10, during the reign of the Emperor Augustus. He is described in Acts 7:58 as a young man at the stoning of Stephen, and in Phlm 9 (written after AD 55) as an "old man."[3] Jews at this period, especially in the diaspora (i.e., outside Palestine), often had two names, one Greek or Roman, the other Semitic. "Paul" (Paulus) was a well-known Roman family name. Since the apostle describes himself as of the tribe of Benjamin (Rom 11:1; Phil 3:5), there is no reason to doubt Acts that his Jewish name was "Saul"[4] (called after the first king of Israel, a Benjaminite).

Paul never tells us where he was born; but the information in Acts that he was a citizen of Tarsus, the prosperous capital of Cilicia (22:3; 21:39: "no mean city"), is perfectly plausible. Tarsus had a considerable Jewish colony; and by his own testimony, in his early years as a Christian Paul hastened to go to Cilicia (Gal 1:21). Acts 16:37–38 and 22:25–29 identify Paul as a Roman citizen by birth.[5] Some have suggested that Tarsus' inhabitants received that privilege, but citizenship may have come to Paul through his family rather than through the status of Jews in Tarsus.

Probably the majority of scholars maintains that Paul was reared and edu-

[2]This was composed by J. A. Fitzmyer and is printed with his gracious permission and that of the publisher, Prentice-Hall, from NJBC, p. 1331. He drew on T. H. Campbell, "Paul's 'Missionary Journeys' as Reflected in His Letters," JBL 74 (1955), 80–87.

[3]Age bracket usually age 50 to 60; this is a disputed reading.

[4]A Jew having similar sounding Jewish/Gentile names, like Saul/Paul, was not uncommon at this time, e.g., Silas/Silvanus.

[5]Also 25:6–12 since only Roman citizens were supposed to appeal to the emperor. P. van Minnen, JSNT 56 (1994), 43–52, argues strongly for historicity, building a case that Paul was the descendant of one or more freed slaves from whom he inherited citizenship.

TABLE 5. PAUL'S ACTIVITIES IN THE LETTERS AND ACTS

Pauline Letters	Acts
Conversion near Damascus (implied in Gal 1:17c)	Damascus (9:1–22)
To Arabia (Gal 1:17b)	
Return to Damascus (1:17c): 3 yrs.	
Flight from Damascus (II Cor 11:32–33)	Flight from Damascus (9:23–25)
To Jerusalem (Gal 1:18–20)	To Jerusalem (9:26–29)
"The regions of Syria and Cilicia" (Gal 1:21–22)	Caesarea and Tarsus (9:30)
	Antioch (11:26a)
	(Jerusalem [11:29–30; 12:25])
	Mission I: Antioch (13:1–4a)
	Seleucia, Salamis, Cyprus (13:4b–12)
Churches evangelized before Macedonian Philippi (Phil 4:15)	South Galatia (13:13–14:25)
	Antioch (14:26–28)
"Once again during 14 years I went up to Jerusalem" (for "Council," Gal 2:1)	Jerusalem (15:1–12)
Antioch Incident (Gal 2:11–14)	Antioch (15:35); **Mission II**
	Syria and Cilicia (15:41)
	South Galatia (16:1–5)
Galatia (I Cor 16:1) evangelized for the first time (Gal 4:13)	Phrygia and North Galatia (16:6)
	Mysia and Troas (16:7–10)
Philippi (I Thess 2:2 [= Macedonia, II Cor 11:9])	Philippi (16:11–40)
Thessalonica (I Thess 2:2; cf. 3:6; Phil 4:15–16)	Amphipolis, Apollonia, Thessalonica (17:1–9)
	Beroea (17:10–14)
Athens (I Thess 3:1; cf. 2:17–18)	Athens (17:15–34)
Corinth evangelized (cf. I Cor 1:19; 11:7–9)	Corinth for 18 months (18:1–18a)
Timothy arrives in Corinth (I Thess 3:6), probably accompanied by Silvanus (I Thess 1:1)	Silas and Timothy come from Macedonia (18:5)
	Paul leaves from Cenchreae (18:18b)
	Leaves Priscilla and Aquila at Ephesus (18:19–21)
Apollos (in Ephesus) urged by Paul to go to Corinth (I Cor 16:12)	Apollos dispatched to Achaia by Priscilla and Aquila (18:17)
	Paul to Caesarea Maritima (18:22a)
	Paul to Jerusalem (18:22b)
	In Antioch for a certain amount of time (18:22c)
Northern Galatia, second visit (Gal 4:13)	**Mission III**: North Galatia and Phrygia (18:23)
Ephesus (I Cor 16:1–8)	Ephesus for 3 yrs. or 2 yrs., 3 mos. (19:1–20:1; cf. 20:31)
Visit of Chloe, Stephanas, *et al.* to Paul in Ephesus (I Cor 1:11; 16:17), bringing letter (7:1)	
Paul imprisoned (? cf. I Cor 15:32; II Cor 1:8)	
Timothy sent to Corinth (I Cor 4:17; 16:10)	
Paul's 2nd "painful" visit to Corinth (II Cor 13:2); return to Ephesus	
Titus sent to Corinth with letter "written in tears" (II Cor 2:13)	
(Paul's plans to visit Macedonia, Corinth, and Jerusalem/Judea, I Cor 16:3–8; cf. II Cor 1:15–16)	(Paul's plans to visit Macedonia, Achaia, Jerusalem, Rome, 19:21)
Ministry in Troas (II Cor 2:12)	
To Macedonia (II Cor 2:13; 7:5; 9:2b–4); arrival of Titus (II Cor 7:6)	Macedonia (20:1b)
Titus sent on ahead to Corinth (II Cor 7:16–17), with part of II Cor	
Illyricum (Rom 15:19)?	
Achaia (Rom 15:26; 16:1); Paul's third visit to Corinth (II Cor 13:1)	3 mos. in Greece (Achaia) (20:2–3)
	Paul starts to return to Syria (20:3), but goes via Macedonia and Philippi (20:3b–6a)
	Troas (20:6b–12)
	Miletus (20:15c–38)
	Tyre, Ptolemais, Caesarea (21:7–14)
(Plans to visit Jerusalem, Rome, Spain [Rom 15:22–27])	Jerusalem (21:15–23:30)
	Caesarea (23:31–26:32)
	Journey to Rome (27:1–28:14)
	Rome (28:15–31)

cated at Tarsus. He wrote good Greek, had basic Hellenistic rhetorical skills, quoted from the Scriptures in Greek, and knew Deuterocanonical Books composed or preserved in Greek. Tarsus had a reputation for culture and excellent schools; and although those structures would have been Gentile, an essential training in writing, rhetoric, and dialectic may have been made available to Jewish boys in order to allow them to function competitively. Perhaps it was also there that Paul learned a trade that Acts 18:3 defines as tentmaker.[6] Supporting himself by working, even if a burden undertaken for the sake of the gospel, was a point of pride for Paul in his later missionary travels since it meant that he did not have to beg money from those whom he was evangelizing (I Thess 2:9; I Cor 9:14–15; II Cor 11:9).[7] As a tradesman he would have been among the lower social classes, but a step higher than one who had become a citizen by being freed from slavery.

To what extent did upbringing in the diaspora (pockets of Jewish life outside Palestine) influence Paul, besides obvious language and rhetorical abilities? Acculturation by Jews in language and education led to varied degrees of accommodation and even assimilation, so that no universal judgments can be made.[8] He would have known something about the religion of the Gentiles among whom he lived, e.g., have had some awareness, probably prejudiced and unsympathetic, of Pagan myths and Greco-Roman civic religious festivals. As we shall see in discussing the letters, the idea that he borrowed many ideas from the mystery religions (p. 86 above) is overdone; but even non-initiates would often have had a general idea of their ideals and themes. There is a good chance that Paul's education would have included a summary acquaintanceship with the moral or ethical stances of the Stoics, the Cynics, and the Epicureans. On a simpler level Paul would have known how ordinary Gentiles lived and worked, so that later in life he would not have come among them as a stranger to their worries, aspirations, family problems, etc. As we can see from his letters, Paul understood very well the major role of the household in the Greco-Roman culture in which his addressees lived.

There was another side to Paul's upbringing, however, for his thorough knowledge of Judaism and the Jewish Scriptures needs to be explained. The claim in Acts 22:3 that Paul was brought up in Jerusalem and educated by Gamaliel I the Elder, who flourished in Jerusalem *ca.* AD 20–50, probably

[6]This title does not adequately convey to us the wide range of such an artisan. Although the traditional view is that Paul worked with goat hair fabric from his native Cilicia, others have noted that a skilled craft with skins involved leatherworking, making tents and awnings, etc. (see Pliny, *Natural History,* 19:23–24). Murphy-O'Connor, *St. Paul's Corinth,* argues for the last as Paul's special metier. See R. F. Hock, *The Social Context of Paul's Ministry: Tentmaking and Apostleship* (Philadelphia: Fortress, 1980).

[7]Some philosophers did support themselves from the households of the rich who patronized them, much to the disgust of the Cynics (p. 88 above). Rabbis too learned manual trades.

[8]J.M.G. Barclay, JSNT 60 (1995), 89–120.

needs qualification. The letters do not suggest that Paul had seen Jesus during the public ministry or at the crucifixion,[9] and so implicitly cast doubt on Paul's continuous presence in Jerusalem in the years AD 26–30/33. Yet he does describe himself as a Hebrew and a Pharisee (Phil 3:5; II Cor 11:22). This is harmonious with Acts 23:6, which describes Paul as a son of Pharisees, and 26:4–5, which suggests that Paul was a Pharisee from his youth. Paul says he was zealous for the traditions of the ancestors and advanced in Judaism beyond many of his own age (Gal 1:14). Pharisee teachers outside Palestine could not have been overly frequent. Also very likely Paul knew Hebrew (or Aramaic or both—Acts 21:40; 22:2; 26:14). Combining all this information raises the possibility that in the early 30s (before Stephen died) Paul, who was then in his 20s and had already received solid Jewish upbringing in Tarsus, came to Jerusalem to study the Law[10]—something that Acts 22:3 may be simplifying, romanticizing, and exaggerating. In any case it was a man very familiar with two worlds who at a life-determining moment became "a servant/slave of Christ Jesus."

Belief in Jesus and Immediate Aftermath

Paul says that he persecuted the church of God violently and tried to destroy it (Gal 1:13; I Cor 15:9; Phil 3:6). This can be understood to refer to participation in the persecution of Christians of Jerusalem and environs, as affirmed by Acts 8:3; 9:1–2; 22:3–5,19; 26:9–11—see I Thess 2:14, which indicates that the churches of God in Judea had been persecuted. (The statement in Gal 1:22 that three years after his adherence to Jesus the churches in Judea still did not know his face need not contradict his role in such a persecution—his hostile behavior may have been heard about by many followers of Jesus who had never seen him [as in Acts 9:13].) Why did Paul persecute the followers of Jesus? E. P. Sanders (*Paul* [1991], 8–9) argues that the persecution was due to Paul's zeal, not to his being a very observant Pharisee. By making a connection between the clauses of Phil 3:5–6, "according to the Law a Pharisee, according to zeal a persecutor of the church, according to righteousness based on the Law blameless," others suspect that

[9]II Cor 5:16, "even if we once knew Christ according to the flesh," means only that at one time Paul had judged Jesus according to worldly standards.

[10]Acts 23:16 indicates that Paul had relatives in Jerusalem, one of whom at least was loyal to him. Had parts of the family moved here from Cilicia, and were there sections of the family resident in both places? Were they believers in Christ? The suggestion that Paul studied in Jerusalem does not necessarily make Paul a rabbi or support the thesis (J. Jeremias) that he was a great, master teacher of the Law at Jerusalem, or the contention that he was a follower of the school of Hillel (more usual) or Shammai (R. A. Martin, *Studies*). On Paul and Pharisaism, see D. Lührmann, JSNT 36 (1989), 75–94. Van Unnik (*Tarsus*) has argued strongly for Paul's upbringing in Jerusalem, but that remains the minority view.

Paul saw the followers of Jesus proclaiming a message contrary to the Pharisee interpretation of the Law. More precisely, was Paul's hostility toward these people related to their confessing as the God-approved Messiah one who had been condemned by the Jewish authorities as a blasphemer? Acts 26:9 reports that, before conversion, Paul had done many things by way of opposing "the name of Jesus of Nazareth." Did Paul perceive the followers of Jesus as blaspheming against Moses by changing customs that the Law decreed and by advocating the destruction of the Temple sanctuary (i.e., the charges against Stephen: Acts 6:11–14; 8:1)?

After a period of persecuting, according to both Gal 1:13–17 and Acts 9:1–9, Paul received a divine revelation in which he encountered Jesus and after which he stayed at Damascus. That report leaves many issues unresolved. In I Cor 9:1 Paul says he *saw* Jesus (also 15:8); but in none of the three accounts of the experience in Acts does that happen[11] (yet cf. 9:27), even though he does see light. Did Luke rank this appearance from heaven on a lower level than the risen Lord's appearances on earth to the Twelve? For Paul, the appearance of the risen Lord was a major factor in his being an apostle; but some have doubted that he was an apostle in Luke's estimation (pp. 298, 323 above).

Theologically the encounter with the risen Lord revealed to Paul that the scandal of the cross was not the end of the story of Jesus. Acts 26:17 has Jesus say that he is sending Paul to the Gentiles, and in Gal 1:16 Paul says that God was pleased "to reveal His Son to/in me that I might preach him among the Gentiles." Does this mean that from the first moment of his conversion Paul knew of his mission to the Gentiles?[12] Or in later reflection, after he found Gentiles very receptive of his gospel (which did not insist on their deserving the Christian invitation by being circumcised and doing the works of the Law), did Paul relate his appeal to them to his own undeserved call by Christ when he was persecuting the church? The latter better fits the evidence of Acts (13:46–47; 17:4; 18:6).

[11] 9:3–7; 22:6–9; 26:13–18. It is a notorious problem that these three accounts of Paul's "conversion" do not agree in details—an indication that either Luke did not have detailed, fixed, handed-down tradition, or he felt free in his dramatization of the tradition. Although I shall use the conventional term "conversion," I do not wish to imply that Paul's coming to believe in Jesus meant that he started now to lead a good life (Phil 3:6b: He was previously "blameless" in the practice of the Law) or that he was converted away from Judaism to a new religion. In fact, he never speaks of a conversion, but of a calling or commission. Yet Paul did have a change or reversal of values as he reconsidered the import of the Mosaic Law in the light of what God had done in Jesus. See P. F. Craffert, *Scriptura* 29 (1989), 36–47.

[12] Murphy-O'Connor, "Pauline Missions," argues that the knowledge was very early, for he interprets Gal 2:7 (the assignment of Paul to the uncircumcised and Peter to the circumcised) to stem from the meeting between Peter and Paul when Paul came to Jerusalem between 37 and 39 (Gal 1:18); but there is no indication that this assignment was the product of a meeting and not simply a distillation of what the two men had been doing before 49.

TABLE 6. PAULINE CHRONOLOGY

TRADITIONAL	EVENT	*REVISIONIST*
AD 36	**Conversion to Christ**	AD *30/34*
39	**Visit to Jerusalem after Damascus**	*33/37*
40–44 **44–45**	**In Cilicia** **At Antioch**	*after 37*
46–49 see below	**(First) Missionary Journey, beginning in Antioch, to Cyprus and southern Asia Minor, returning to Antioch** *(Second) Missionary Journey, beginning in Antioch, through southern Asia Minor to N. Galatia, Macedonia, Corinth* (I Thess), return to Jerusalem and Antioch	*after 37* *39–41/43* (41–43)
49	**Jerusalem conference**	*47/51*
50–52 (51–52)	**(Second) Missionary Journey, beginning in Antioch, through southern Asia Minor to N. Galatia, Macedonia, Corinth** (I Thess), **return to Jerusalem and Antioch**	see above
54–58 (54–57) (summer 57) (57/58)	**(Third) Missionary Journey, beginning from Antioch through N. Galatia to Ephesus; three-year stay there—imprisoned?** (Gal, Phil, Phlm, I Cor) **Paul goes through Macedonia toward Corinth** (II Cor, Gal?), **winters at Corinth** (Rom), **returns to Jerusalem**	*indistinct from second* (48/55) (after 54)
58–60 **60–61**	**Arrested in Jerusalem; imprisoned two years in Caesarea** (Phil?) **Sent to Rome; long sea journey**	*52–55 or 56–58*
61–63	**Prisoner in Rome for two years** (Phil? Phlm?)	
after summer 64	**Death in Rome under Nero**	

TABLE 6. Continued

OBSERVATIONS:

Cities where Paul made lengthy stays are printed in small caps. Pauline letter titles are abbreviated, printed in Roman, and placed within parentheses; a question mark follows the title to indicate an alternative dating that is possible but less plausible. **The traditional chronology with its principal dates is printed in boldface;** *the revisionist chronology with its principal dates is printed in italics.* The latter is more difficult to portray in a table because it is based on widely differing views of those who advocate it in whole or in part. Those differences can be illustrated from comparing the chronologies of Knox, Buck/Taylor, Lüdemann,* Jewett, Murphy-O'Connor, and Donfried, abbreviated K, B, L, J, M, and D respectively:

- Crucifixion: L = 27 (30); J = 33 (or less likely 30); D = 30
- Conversion to Christ: B = 32; K = 34 or 37; L = 30 (33); J = Oct. 34; M = *ca.* 33; D = 33
- To Jerusalem after Damascus: B = 35; K = 37 or 40; L = 33 (36); J = 37; M = 37–39; D = 36
- Paul's first arrival at Corinth before Jerusalem conference (also usually I Thess): K = *ca.* 41; B** = 41; L = 41; J = 50; M = 49; D = *ca.* 43
- Jerusalem conference: K = 51; B = 46–47; L = 47 (50); J = Oct. 51; M = 51–52; D = *ca.* 50
- L places the confrontation of Paul and Peter at Antioch before the Jerusalem conference; J places it after the Jerusalem conference
- D associates the Gallio confrontation with Paul's later visit to Corinth
- Lengthy (3-year) stay at Ephesus: B = 49–52; L = 48–50 (51–53); J = *ca.* 53–55; M = ending in 54; D = 52–55
- Writing of Romans: K = 53/54; B = 47; L = 51/52 (53/54); J = *ca.* 56; M = 55/56; D = *ca.* 56
- Arrest in Jerusalem: K = 53/54; B = 53; L = 52 (55); J = 57; D = 56/57.***

*Lüdemann (*Paul,* 262–63) gives two sets of dates dependent on whether Jesus was crucified in AD 27 or 30, with the second in parentheses.

**Buck/Taylor place the composition of II Thess before I Thess and separate the arrival at Corinth in 41 from the composition of I Thess in 46.

***Lührmann, *Galatians* 3,135, offers a combination chronology: traditional through the Corinthian stay of 51–52; but then, without an intervening journey to Jerusalem and Antioch, the long Ephesus stay (and return through Macedonia to Corinth) in 52–56. Collection brought to Jerusalem in 56 (then Caesarea); Paul in Rome 58–60 and death about that time.

I shall now have to begin supplying dates for Paul's career as a believer in Jesus. Competing chronologies have been offered by scholars, and in the accompanying Table 6 I present two types. One may be called "Traditional" and is still followed by the majority; the other that I call "Revisionist" has a smaller but articulate group of adherents. As indicated at the end of the Table, differences about the date of Jesus' crucifixion and the reliability of the data in Acts are responsible for many of the assigned datings. (Only rarely does a chronological difference have theological import in reading Paul's letters.) In the discussion to follow I shall follow the Traditional Chronology both because it is the one readers will most often encounter and because it seems more reasonable to me.

When did Paul's conversion take place? Acts 7:58; 8:1; 9:1 associates Paul's persecuting activity with the aftermath of the martyrdom of Stephen. Gal 1:17–18 seems to indicate a three-year interlude between Paul's conversion and his going to Jerusalem (i.e., the interval when he was in Arabia[13] and Damascus); II Cor 11:32–33 reports an escape by Paul from Damascus when King Aretas tried to seize him.[14] The Nabatean King Aretas was given control of Damascus by the Emperor Caligula (37–41); and so many would date Paul's conversion *ca.* 36, and his escape from Damascus and going to Jerusalem *ca.* 39.

According to Gal 1:18–19, at Jerusalem Paul visited and conversed with Peter and saw James the brother of the Lord (but none of the other apostles[15]). At times in his letters Paul will mention what he received *from the tradition* about Jesus (I Cor 11:23; 15:3), and it has been suggested that it was in this period that he learned some or all of that tradition. The stay in Jerusalem was brief (Gal 1:18; Acts 22:18), and then Paul went off to Tarsus in Cilicia (Acts 9:30).[16] How long Paul remained there is not clear, but it may have been several years.

Eventually Antioch in Syria (the third largest city in the Roman Empire, after Rome and Alexandria) became important in Paul's life. Acts 11:25–26 has Barnabas go to Tarsus and bring Paul to Antioch because of the possibilities opened by the spread of Christianity to the Gentiles. Paul is supposed to have spent a year there before being sent to Jerusalem with famine relief (11:26–30). There was a famine in this eastern Mediterranean area during the reign of Emperor Claudius, probably *ca.* 45; but this visit to Jerusalem is very hard to reconcile with Paul's declaration that in his Christian career (up to AD 50) the second time he went to Jerusalem was fourteen years later (Gal 2:1: after his first visit or, more likely, after his conversion?). In any case it was Antioch, not Jerusalem, that was to be the base for Paul's outgoing missionary activity. The Orontes River provided Antioch with access to a port on the Mediterranean, and it was across that sea that Paul would set out to proclaim Jesus more widely.

[13]Not Saudi Arabia but the Nabatean kingdom running south, through the Transjordan to the Sinai, and centered on Petra. J. Murphy-O'Connor, CBQ 55 (1993), 732–37; BRev 10 (#5; 1994), 46–47.

[14]This is not irreconcilable with the report in Acts 9:23–25 about Paul's escape from a Jewish plot to kill him in Damascus.

[15]In the Acts account of the Jerusalem stay, Barnabas brought him to the apostles (9:27).

[16]In Gal 1:21 Paul speaks of Syria and Cilicia. That might mean Antioch on the way to Tarsus, but it could also be a summary description of what Luke narrates as going to Tarsus, coming to Antioch, the whole "First Missionary Journey" (from Antioch to Cyprus, to SE Asia Minor, and back to Antioch)—in short everything between Paul's leaving Jerusalem *ca.* 39 and the meeting there in 49.

First Missionary Journey; the Jerusalem Meeting; the Antioch Aftermath

One of the main objections to using Acts as a guide to Paul's life is that in his letters Paul shows no awareness of numbered (three) missionary journeys. It is argued pungently that if you had asked Paul of the letters, "Which missionary journey are you on now?", he would not have known what you were talking about. But to a certain extent one might say the same about the Paul of Acts, which never explicitly spells out three missionary journeys.[17] Indeed, Acts indicates that during a year and a half Paul was at Corinth and during three years he was at Ephesus, and thus not journeying in the ordinary sense of the word. *The three journeys are only a convenient classification developed by students of Acts, and I shall use them in that sense.* According to Acts 13:3–14:28 a missionary journey from Antioch in Syria took Barnabas, Paul, and John Mark by sea to Cyprus, then on to the Asia Minor cities of Perga (and, after John Mark departed), Pisidian Antioch, Iconium, Lystra, and Derbe, before Paul and Barnabas returned to Antioch in Syria (*ca.* AD 49). Having met opposition in synagogues, Paul addressed himself to Gentiles among whom the gospel was well received.[18] In his undisputed letters Paul gives us no information about such a journey. Yet in Gal 2:1–3 he recalls preaching to the Gentiles before the Jerusalem meeting of AD 49 (to be discussed in the next paragraph), and in II Cor 11:25 he mentions being stoned (as he was at Lystra in Acts 14:19—see also n. 16 above and the place-names in II Tim 3:11).

According to Acts 10:44–48; 11:20–21, there were others before Paul who made converts among the Gentiles (seemingly without any insistence on circumcision), but perhaps in situations where such Gentiles could be absorbed into communities of Jewish Christians. Apparently Paul's innovation was to have formed entire communities of Gentile Christians with little or no attachment to Judaism. What did this portend for the future of Christianity? After Paul (and Barnabas) returned to Antioch, a meeting was held in Jerusalem *ca.* 49 to answer that question (Acts 15:1–29 and Gal 2:1–10). Although there are differences between the two accounts, they agree that Paul, James (brother of the Lord), and Peter (Cephas) were involved, and that there was a group opposed to Paul who insisted that the Gentiles should

[17]Indeed, Acts 18:22–23 does not offer a very clear delineation between the Second and the Third. (On the cities that played a role in Paul's missions and letters, see S. E. Johnson, *Paul*.)

[18]He speaks of the gospel bringing salvation through faith "to the Jews first and also to the Greeks" (Rom 1:16). See Chapter 10 above, n. 65, for Paul's preaching in synagogues. There he would have encountered Gentiles sympathetic to Judaism who might have provided him with his initial converts.

be circumcised. By the medium of speeches, Acts highlights the reasons offered by Peter and James for agreeing with Paul that circumcision could not be demanded.[19] Gal 2:9 reports that these others recognized the grace and apostolate bestowed on Paul and extended to him the right hand of fellowship.

The decision to accept the Gentiles without circumcision did not settle all problems. Were the Gentiles bound by other parts of the Law of Moses, especially the purity laws concerning food? What was the relationship of Jewish Christians who observed these laws to Gentile Christians who did not? Both Acts 15:30 and Gal 2:11,13 agree that after the Jerusalem meeting Paul and Barnabas went back to Antioch. There according to Gal 2:12–14 a major dispute occurred: Peter who had been eating with the Gentiles backed down when men came from James with an objection. To Paul this attempt to compel the Gentiles to live like Jews violated the truth of the gospel! Acts tells us nothing about such a dispute but in a confused way does have a letter sent (as James wished: 15:20) from Jerusalem to Antioch, ordering that in Syria and Cilicia Gentiles keep the Jewish purity laws, especially concerning food.[20] Gal 2:13 reports that at Antioch Barnabas too sided with the men from James, and Acts 15:36–40 indicates that Paul and Barnabas came to an unhappy parting of the ways so that Paul left Antioch with Silas immediately afterward. Apparently, then, Paul lost the battle about food laws at Antioch, and that may explain why Antioch no longer features prominently as the home base of Paul's missionary activity.[21] In his journeys he is now much more on his own.

Second and Third Missionary Journeys

Although, as explained above, this division of journeys is common among scholars, the missionary activity described in Acts 15:40–21:15 can be taken together as Luke's illustration of Paul's wider-ranging enterprise after the Jerusalem decision opened the Gentile world to belief in Jesus without circumcision (AD 50–58).

In the first part of the activity (AD 50–52; the "Second Journey":

[19]See pp. 305–9 above. Acts 15:20 complicates the scene by including the issue of the foods that must not be eaten.

[20]Acts has Paul agreeing with this letter from Jerusalem. That is scarcely accurate, as we can determine not only from Gal, but also from I Cor 8 which emphasizes *freedom* about food dedicated to idols—a food that was prohibited in this letter inspired by James. See L. Gaston, "Paul and Jerusalem," in *From Jesus to Paul*, ed. P. Richardson and J. C. Hurd (F. W. Beare Festschrift; Waterloo, Canada: W. Laurier Univ., 1984), 61–72.

[21]Henceforth Paul would come back from his travels to Jerusalem first or exclusively (Acts 18:22; 19:21; 21:15); in his letters he collects money for Jerusalem but never mentions Antioch again after Gal 2:11.

15:40–18:22) Acts reports that Paul returned to sites in SE Asia Minor evangelized in the First Journey. Then going north (for the first time) to Galatia and Phrygia, he crossed over to Macedonia (Europe) from Troas, clearly under divine guidance.[22] There his travels brought him to Philippi, Thessalonica, Beroea, Athens, and Corinth. To three of those five cities NT letters bearing Paul's name would eventually be sent. Indeed the first preserved Pauline letter, **I Thessalonians,** was written from Corinth as Paul expressed concern for a church he had recently evangelized (AD 50–51). Paul's eighteen-month stay at Corinth was the longest thus far at any church he was founding;[23] ironically he was to leave behind there a community that would be troubled over more issues than any other to which he would write. Aquila and Priscilla (Prisca), whom he met at Corinth[24] and who would sail with him to Ephesus, became lifelong friends and co-workers both at Ephesus and Rome. The fact that at Corinth Paul was haled before Gallio the proconsul of Achaia (Acts 18:12) has been used as a linchpin of Pauline chronology, for an inscription (NJBC 79.9) places Gallio as proconsul at Corinth in the twelfth year of Claudius (41–54), which began on Jan. 25, 52. Gallio seems to have left Corinth by the end of 52.[25] These perimeters suggest dating Paul's stay at Corinth to 50/51–52. Acts 18:18b–22 has Paul depart from Cenchreae, the port of Corinth, touch down at Ephesus and Caesarea (on the Palestinian coast), and then go up to greet the church (at Jerusalem).

In the second part of Paul's wide-ranging missionary activity (AD 53/54–58; the "Third Journey"; Acts 18:23–21:15), after spending "some time" at Syrian Antioch, he went once more through Galatia and Phrygia to Ephesus,[26] the most important city of the Roman province of Asia, where he

[22]It is at this moment that Acts (16:9–10) uses "we" for the first time in reference to the traveling missionaries. Traditionally that has been interpreted as a sign that the writer (Luke?) began to accompany Paul (pp. 325–26 above).

[23]D. P. Cole, BRev 4 (#6; 1988), 20–30, points to a change in Paul's previous pattern of rapidly moving from city to city, a change continued in the subsequent three-year sojourn at Ephesus (AD 54–57). Seemingly Paul now preferred to stay in one place with broad commercial ties where he would encounter many who came and went and from which he could extend his activities.

[24]They were Jewish Christians who had "recently" come to Corinth from Italy "because Claudius had ordered all the Jews to leave Rome" (Acts 18:2). If the information is historical, it probably does not refer to the action of Claudius in AD 41 ordering the overly numerous Roman Jews not to hold meetings but *not* driving them out (Cassius Dio, *Roman History* 60.6.6). Rather it may refer to what Suetonius (*Claudius* 25.4) reports: "He expelled Jews from Rome because of their constant disturbances impelled by Chrestus." *If* these disturbances were over belief in Christ and *if* the 5th-century Christian Orosius was right in dating this expulsion to AD 49, Priscilla and Aquila would have arrived in Corinth about a year before Paul. J. Murphy-O'Connor, BRev 8 (#6; 1992), 40–51,62, however, would have them arrive nine years before Paul. See p. 311 above.

[25]Thus Fitzmyer, NJBC 79:9. J. Murphy-O'Connor, "Paul and Gallio," JBL 112 (1993), 315–17, rejecting the revisionist thesis of D. Slingerland (JBL 110 [1991], 439–49), dates Gallio's presence at Corinth between June and October 51 and Paul's stay from early spring 50 to the autumn of 51.

[26]This itinerary has been called into doubt by some scholars, e.g., Jürgen Becker, *Paul* 27–28, who denies any return to Palestine or Syria but allows a possible visit to Galatia and Phrygia (re-

stayed three years (54 till the spring of 57: Acts 20:31; cf. 19:8,10; I Cor 16:8). Among the events that Acts 19:1–20:1 recounts are Paul's struggle with the seven sons of a Jewish high priest who were exorcists, and the riot led against Paul by the silversmiths devoted to "Artemis/Diana of the Ephesians,"[27] which led to his departure. In his letters Paul never speaks explicitly of these events at Ephesus; yet he may refer to the latter implicitly in the list of hardships in II Cor 11:23–26, in "the affliction that came to us in Asia" (II Cor 1:8), or in "I fought at Ephesus with beasts" (I Cor 15:32; also 16:8–9: "There are many opponents"). In particular, those allusions to Paul's ordeals allow the possibility that the apostle may have been imprisoned at Ephesus, even though Acts describes no such imprisonment. That issue is important because many suggest that Paul wrote from Ephesus the letters to the **Philippians** and to **Philemon,** both of which were written while Paul was a prisoner. More generally agreed is that while at Ephesus he wrote to the **Galatians,** expressing anguished concern over what had happened there in the four or five years since his evangelizing efforts in N. Galatia *ca.* 50. Toward the end of Paul's stay at Ephesus, troubles in the church of Corinth were brought to his attention; and some of the Corinthian correspondence was written at that time (**I Corinthians** [16:8]; and a tearful letter [II Cor 2:3–4: lost?]), interspersed with a painful visit (II Cor 2:1). Acts is completely silent about Paul's difficult dealings with Corinth.

Sometime after Pentecost (late springtime) in 57 Paul left Ephesus for Troas, farther north on the Asiatic shore of the Aegean; but not finding there Titus, whom he had sent to straighten out things in Corinth, he crossed to Europe and Macedonia (Philippi? II Cor 2:12–13) where he met Titus who was bearing the good news that a reconciliation had been effected. Paul then wrote (perhaps in two stages) what is now **II Corinthians.** Finally he went to Achaia and Corinth where he spent three winter months (57/58). There Paul gathered receipts from a collection for the Jerusalem Christians, taken up in various churches he had evangelized; he would bring these funds to Jerusalem on his planned journey. At Corinth Paul also composed **Romans,**

---

flecting the second visit hinted at in Gal 4:13). According to Acts 18:24–26, before Paul arrived at Ephesus, the Alexandrian preacher Apollos had come, speaking eloquently about Jesus' career but inadequately about the Spirit, so that Priscilla and Aquila had to instruct him more fully. Again doubt has been raised about the Apollos episode at Ephesus as Lucan theologizing; but if it was Luke's goal to subordinate the role of Apollos, why did he not have Paul instruct him? Apollos then went on to Corinth (18:27–19:1) and, seemingly unwittingly, gave rise to the Apollos faction there (I Cor 3:4–6). He came back to Ephesus before Paul left in spring 57, and was reluctant to go back to Corinth (I Cor 16:12), perhaps because he feared to create more division. Titus 3:13 portrays Paul years later still concerned about the missionary career of Apollos.

[27]The famous statue of Artemis of Ephesus with many bulbous protusions (breasts? eggs?) is decorated with other signs of fertility, suggesting that she has been amalgamated with the great Mother Goddess of Asia Minor. The bottom part of the statue is a tree trunk; see p. 783 below for the huge Ephesus temple of Artemis built on top of an ancient tree shrine.

alerting the house-churches in the capital of the Empire that he planned to visit there on his way to Spain, once he had taken the collection to Jerusalem (15:24–26). In that letter there is an effort to ingratiate himself as if the Romans had heard exaggerated reports about him.

According to Acts 20:2–17 (spring 58) Paul set out from Corinth to Jerusalem by way of Macedonia, spending Passover at Philippi. Then sailing to Troas, Paul worked his way down the Asian coast to Miletus where he gave a farewell speech to the presbyters of Ephesus who had come to see him (20:17–38).[28] At Miletus and again at Tyre and Caesarea as he reached the Palestinian coast, Paul exhibited a foreboding of imprisonment and death at the end of the journey. There is some confirmation of that in Rom 15:30–31 where Paul asks prayers for his forthcoming visit to Jerusalem that he "may be delivered from the disobedient in Judea."

Paul Arrested in Jerusalem; Imprisoned in Caesarea; Taken to Rome; Death

Most of the last half-dozen years of Paul's life (*ca.* 58–64) is recounted in Acts 21:15–28:31; they were marked by suffering, four of them by imprisonment. (Those who do not attribute **Philippians** and **Philemon** to the putative imprisonment at Ephesus attribute them to the imprisonment at Caesarea or at Rome, thus dating them later. Otherwise this period of Paul's life cannot be confirmed by the Pauline letters.) Only in passing does Acts (24:17) confirm that Paul brought donation money to Jerusalem. A meeting, rather tense beneath surface politeness, took place between Paul and James (the brother of the Lord and head of the Jerusalem Christians) in which Paul was told to behave as a pious, practicing Jew while at Jerusalem (21:17–25). Yet his presence in the Temple court caused a riot so that a Roman tribune had to intervene to save him, and he had to give a long speech of self-defense in Hebrew (Aramaic? 21:26–22:30). Eventually Paul was brought before a Sanhedrin session and managed to create a dispute between his Sadducee and Pharisee judges, causing the tribune to take him away to Caesarea to be judged by the Roman governor Felix, before whom he again defended himself (23:1–24:21). Felix, however, looking for a bribe, put off judgment and left Paul in prison for two years (24:22–27). Only with the advent of Festus, the next procurator, and the continued charges by the Jewish leaders, was Paul's case taken up again (25:1–26:32). In a trial before Festus, Paul argued that he had committed no crime against Jewish Law or against Caesar. The

[28]It is clear from this speech (20:25,38: prophecies that they would never see Paul's face again) that Luke knew of no further activity by Paul in Asia Minor such as posited by the Pastoral Letters.

procurator invited King Herod Agrippa II to hear the case; and although neither ruler found Paul guilty, he was sent to Rome as a prisoner because he had appealed to Caesar.

Paul's hazardous sea journey (end of AD 60, beginning of 61) is described with great verve in Acts 27:1–28:14.[29] Storms, shipwreck, and a winter spent at Malta culminate in "And thus we came to Rome" (important to Acts theologically: p. 315 above). Paul is said to have stayed there two years under a type of house arrest that enabled him to preach to those who came to him. The sentiment of Paul with which Acts 28:26–28 closes the story (*ca.* 63), i.e., the Jews will never hear whereas the Gentiles will, is scarcely that expressed by Paul in Rom 11:25–26 (perhaps the last of Paul's undisputed letters), namely that when the Gentiles have come in, all Israel will be saved. Neither the letters nor Acts tells us of his death; but there is good tradition that he was martyred under Nero (EH 2.25.4–8), either about the same time as Peter (AD 64) or somewhat later (67). Tradition would have Paul buried on the Via Ostiensis, a spot commemorated by the basilica of St. Paul outside the Walls.

Remaining Issues. If Acts is accurate about the terms of Paul's house arrest in Rome (two years), were there further travels between 63 and the time of his death (64 to 67)? Did he follow his intention to go to Spain? Did Luke show some recollection of that when in Acts 1:8 he had Jesus extend the witness to "the end of the earth"?[30] Within thirty years of Paul's death *I Clement* 5:7 reports that Paul "traveled to the extreme west," before he bore witness to the ruling authorities and died. In discussing Acts the *Muratorian Fragment* (*ca.* 180?) makes reference to an account of the departure of Paul from Rome for Spain.

Even more pressing, what are we to think of the geographical information in the Pastoral Letters that would have Paul before his death again visiting Ephesus, Macedonia (from which he writes I Tim [1:5] to Ephesus), and Greece (with plans to winter at Nicopolis [Titus 3:12])? II Tim 3:13 suggests an unprepared departure from Troas (because he was arrested?), and 1:8,16–17 has Paul a prisoner in Rome. If the Pastorals were written by Paul, this information about a "second career" after that described in Acts would have to be treated as historical. If they were written by a Pauline disciple, it might still be historical (drawing on a genuine Pauline itinerary) or it might constitute an imaginative setting for the Letters (but one written in ignorance

[29]Since there is no confirmation in the undisputed (or even the pseudonymous) Pauline letters of the appeal to Caesar and the journey to Rome, some who challenge the historicity of Acts dismiss the account as novelistic fiction.

[30]E. E. Ellis, *Bulletin for Biblical Research* 1 (1991), 123–32.

of Acts; see n. 28 above). Ways of evaluating that will be discussed at the beginning of Chapter 31 below.

(B) The Theology of Paul

Pauline theology is a very large subject to which many books have been devoted, as may be seen from the Bibliography at the end of the chapter. Even a sketch is beyond the scope of this *Introduction.* Possible and fruitful, however, is a listing that supplies orientation on some major issues or problems in the study of Pauline thought so that readers may reflect on them as they study the individual letters.[31]

(1) *Was Paul Consistent?* Whether we are dealing with whole letters (deuteroPauline) or parts of letters (e.g., Rom 9–11), judging what is or is not Pauline is to some extent based on conformity with the rest of Pauline thought. Just how consistent was Paul?[32] Caution is required. If one isolates the agreed-on genuine letters of Paul (I Thess, I-II Cor, Gal, Rom, Phil, Phlm), they certainly do not give us the totality of Paul's theology. Therefore, when one encounters a new idea, e.g., that of the detailed church structure advocated in the Pastorals, it is not so easy to affirm prima facie that this could not come from Paul. One would need to show that this new idea is not reconcilable with Pauline thought. But that criterion presumes that Paul could not or would not change his mind (on theological grounds, not merely as a matter of personal stubbornness). He does say in Gal 1:8: "Even if we or an angel from heaven should proclaim (to you) a gospel other than the one we have preached to you, let that one be anathema." Yet that constancy concerns Paul's basic principle about God's gracious gift of salvation in Christ, independent of the works of the Law. How applicable is such immutability to working out ramifications for Christian life? One might be encouraged to recognize changeableness by I Cor 9:19–23 where Paul stresses he is all things to all: "To the Jews I became like a Jew to win over Jews; . . . to those outside the Law I became like one outside the Law to win over those outside the Law." (That statement, however, may not imply lineal but dialectic development.)

Here are some instances of the problem. May one acknowledge a difference going beyond oratory between Gal 5:2, "If you receive circumcision, Christ will be of no advantage to you," and Rom 3:1–2, "What benefit is

[31]The thought will be judged from the letters, not from Acts.

[32]Räisänen, *Paul,* is one of the most articulate advocates of inconsistency: Paul's statements about the Law are not harmonious and reflect what he decided as he faced different situations.

there in being circumcised? Much in every way"?[33] Could Paul be rethinking with more subtlety the role of circumcision, without, of course, changing his gospel that salvation is possible without it? Such a change might stem from bad reactions at Jerusalem to Paul's caustic criticism of the men who were the pillars of the Jerusalem church (Gal 2:6–9) communicated by those opposed to Paul in Galatia. In Rom 15:30–31 Paul asks Christians at the capital to join in striving for his acceptance at Jerusalem; and could that approach stem from the recognition that in the polemic atmosphere of Gal he had overstated the issue? On another issue, is Paul in I Cor 10:28–33 (not eating food dedicated to idols lest one scandalize weaker Christians) showing tolerance for what Peter may have been doing at Antioch when he stopped eating meals with Gentiles because it scandalized the men from James—an action that Paul challenged for the sake of the gospel (Gal 2:11–14)? A recognition that from one letter to another Paul's statements are not rigidly consistent does not mean that his thought is incoherent or compliant. Rather this recognition that Paul was far from an ideologue underlines the importance of understanding the circumstances that Paul is addressing in each letter and what he is arguing for or against. Paul's coherence amidst diversity stems in part from his pastoral perception of what he thought people needed to hear, whether they liked it or not. There is a great difference between being all things to all in order to please all, and being all things to all in order to save as many as possible (I Cor 9:22).

(2) *What Was Paul's Attitude toward Judaism?* With the exception of Romans, Paul's undisputed letters were addressed to audiences he had evangelized himself; and since he regarded himself as having been entrusted with the gospel to the uncircumcised, he was writing primarily to Gentiles. Many commentators assume that what Paul told them had universal applicability and would have been said to Jews as well. That seems plausible in relation to his basic gospel of salvation through Christ, but are we sure how he would apply that gospel to Jews? In the preceding paragraph I cited Gal 5:2, where Paul states that it is useless for Gentiles to be circumcised. Yet suppose Paul had married a Jewish woman who came to believe in Christ and they had a son: Would he have refused to have the child circumcised? Certainly he would not have thought that circumcision was necessary for salvation since the child would grow up to believe in Christ. But would Paul not have wanted the child to have the privileges of being an "Israelite" described eloquently in Rom 9:4–5? The Paul of Acts 24:14 states that "according to the Way, which they call a sect, I worship the God of our fathers [i.e., ancestors] be-

[33]The latter passage is speaking about the benefit of circumcision to Jews, but the Gentiles who read Rom would gain a better appreciation of the religious value of circumcision than would the Gentiles addressed in Gal.

lieving all things according to Law and what is written in the Prophets." Could or would the historical Paul have said that?[34]

(3) *How Unique Was Paul?* Related to the preceding issue is the question of how new or unique or even idiosyncratic Pauline thought was, not only in relation to Judaism but also in relation to his fellow Christians. It is clear that the revelation of God's Son changed Paul's outlook dramatically; but in his Christian approach to questions, how different was he from other prominent or leading Christians? Several factors have prompted a maximalist answer. Paul's stress on differences from Cephas (Peter) and the men from James in Gal 2:11–14 and his criticism of the superlative apostles in II Cor 11:5 have shaped the picture of Paul as a loner. Throughout Christian history the study of Paul has prompted important theologians to issue radical challenges to the prevailing or popular thought (Marcion, Augustine [against Pelagius], M. Luther, K. Barth), and that has been retroverted into the picture of Paul. Yet there are anachronistic dangers in such retroversion; e.g., as K. Stendahl has pointed out, Luther's struggle with guilt and sin cannot be used to interpret Paul's outlook on his preChristian past.[35] Gal 2:9 has James, Cephas (Peter), and John give the right hand of fellowship to Paul, and I Cor 15:3–11 has Paul join himself to Cephas, the Twelve, James, and all the apostles in a common preaching and a common belief. We may ask, then, whether in seeing a certain harmony between Peter and Paul (Acts, *I Clement* 5.2–5) and expressing in a benevolent way Peter's problems with Paul (II Pet 3:15–16), later works were simply domesticating Paul or validly preserving an insight that he was not hostilely isolated.[36]

(4) *Was Paul the Creator of High Christology?* In certain strands of liberal thought Jesus was simply a Jewish peasant of a reformist bent, criticizing hypocrisy and some of the entrenched religious attitudes and institutions of his time. Paul, it is claimed, hellenized the memory, making Jesus the Son of God; and in that sense Paul was really the founder of the Christian religion. Few would express the contrast so crudely today, but some of the tendency to make Paul the architect of high christology continues. That is challenged in essentials by the realization that Paul scarcely created for Jesus titles like Son of God or the Lord (in an absolute sense) since they had their

[34]A further aspect of this will be discussed below in Chapter 24 (Romans) in a subsection on *Paul's view of Jewish observance of the Law.*

[35]"The Apostle Paul and the Introspective Conscience of the West," HTR 56 (1963), 199–215; reprinted in his *Paul Among Jews,* 78–96. Paul's preChristian state should not be interpreted as if the "I" of Rom 7:13–25 was autobiographical, but according to Phil 3:6: "As to righteousness based on the Law, blameless."

[36]Another way of discussing this point is to discuss the churchly images of Paul in the postapostolic period; see under (8) below; BCALB; M. C. de Boer, CBQ 42 (1980), 359–80; and V. P. Furnish, JBL 113 (1994), 3–17, esp. 4–7.

roots in Palestinian (and even Semitic-speaking) Christianity.[37] Indeed, there is a trend in centrist critical scholarship to see considerable continuity between the christology of Jesus' lifetime and the christology of Paul (see BINTC).

(5) *What Is the Theological Center of Paul's Theology?* Although they widely agree that one should not impose on Paul the organizational principles of later theology, scholars are far from agreement on the key issue in Paul's thought. The Reformation emphasis on justification by faith still has followers, e.g., Käsemann, with modifications. F. C. Baur stressed the antithesis between human flesh and the divine Spirit. Bultmann gives the main thrust to anthropology because the Pauline affirmations concerning God relate the deity to human beings; thus he would divide Paul's thought under the headings: "The human being prior to the revelation of faith" and "The human being under faith." A concept of salvation-history is seen as central to many who do not drive a sharp wedge between Paul and Judaism.[38] Beker stresses a Jewish apocalyptic context: the Christ-event as the consummation and end of history. Fitzmyer prefers the language of "eschatological" over "apocalyptic" and speaks of christocentric soteriology: Christ crucified and raised for our sanctification. All these have their element of truth, provided we realize that they are analytical judgments and that probably Paul never thought out "the center of his theology." He did express himself, however, about his "gospel," and christocentrism is closest to that (see Rom 1:3–4; 4:24–25).

(6) *Is There a Central Pauline Narrative?* In place of a central theological theme some scholars have thought of a narrative. Just as Judaism had a basic story of how God chose and called Israel through Moses (a story shared by Pharisees, Sadducees, Essenes, and nationalist extremists), so also, some would logically suppose, Christians had a basic story that retold God's choice of Israel by recalling how God had renewed the call through the ministry, crucifixion, and resurrection of Jesus. Surely Paul had preached the story about Jesus when he first came to a site.[39] Accordingly we cannot judge Paul's gospel from his letters because those presume the "story" about Jesus he had recounted when he first came to the community addressed, a story

[37]See D. Wenham, *Follower of Jesus or Founder of Christianity* (Grand Rapids: Eerdmans, 1995). J. A. Fitzmyer, an expert in Aramaic, makes a strong case that the prePauline Philippians hymn (2:6–11) with its very high christology dates back to the 30s (Chapter 20 below, n. 23).

[38]W. D. Davies, *Paul.* In another way the debate over salvation-history is related to the similarity or dissimilarity between the thought of Paul and that exhibited in Luke-Acts (p. 324 above). Did Paul see the work of Christ as a harmonious prolongation of what God had done in Judaism (a continuous history of salvation), or was there an apocalyptic change so that what had once been of value was now dross?

[39]See with variations N. T. Wright, *NT People;* S. E. Fowl, *The Story of Christ in the Ethics of Paul* (JSNTSup 36; Sheffield: JSOT, 1990); Hays, *Faith;* Witherington, *Paul's Narrative.*

difficult to reconstruct from what underlies the letters. In many ways this "commonsense" approach to Paul is more convincing than any presentation wherein he was abstractly systematic in his thought.

(7) *What Does Paul Mean by "Righteousness" and "Justification"?* Since Reformation times, righteousness (*dikaiosynē*) has been a major issue in Pauline studies. As mentioned in (5), some would make it the center of Pauline theology, even though the theme is notoriously absent from an early letter like I Thess.[40] (Perhaps "justification" was not Paul's first formulation of what happened through Christ; it may represent language honed in the battles with Jewish Christian missionaries in Galatia.) In numerous passages Paul speaks of "the righteousness of God." With the help of Qumran evidence it is now widely recognized that this phraseology echoes a Jewish apocalyptic description of God's covenant graciousness in the context of judgment. For Paul, it describes God's powerful salvific act through faith in Jesus Christ. The other side of the coin is the effect of the Christ-event: justification (*dikaiōsis;* verb: *dikaioun,* "to justify"), i.e., the relationship of human beings to God effected by God's gracious, unmerited action in Christ: They now stand before God acquitted or innocent. The Reformation debate about whether God simply declares people upright (usually identified as the Protestant position) or actually makes them upright by transforming them (the Catholic position) may be asking for a precision that lies beyond Paul's explicit thinking.[41]

(8) *How Do the DeuteroPauline Writings Fit into the Pauline Picture?* Six letters are involved: II Thess, Col, Eph, I-II Tim, Titus.[42] If in fact they were not written by Paul, were they all written by Pauline disciples so that they represent a genuine continuity? Can change of circumstances explain differences of emphasis from Paul's undisputed letters? Overenthusiasm about the endtimes can explain a corrective emphasis in II Thess, while Col and even Eph can be seen as a development of Paul's own view of the body of Christ in the light of a larger view of the church toward the end of the century. Some would find the emphasis on church structure in the Pastorals so foreign to Paul's own interests that those letters would have to be regarded as an alien implant. However, the structure of settled communities that would en-

[40]This absence contributed to F. C. Baur's rejection of I Thess as a genuine Pauline letter; and P. Vielhauer does not even refer to the letter in his article comparing Paul and Acts (Chapter 10 above, n. 102). The adverb *dikaiōs* is found in I Thess 2:10.

[41]For further discussion and bibliography, see the subsection on *Justification/Uprightness* in Chapter 24 (Romans) below.

[42]Arranged in ascending order of probability of nonPauline authorship. At one end of the spectrum the case for II Thess is about 50/50; at the other end about 80 to 90 percent of critical scholarship rejects Pauline authorship of the Pastorals.

able them to survive was surely a more important question after Paul's lifetime than during it, and so how decisive is the historical Paul's failure to be interested in it? Prima facie, the author of the Pastorals thought his ideas so close to those of Paul that he used the name of the apostle. Do we have sufficient evidence to contradict his judgment? Further discussions of this will be offered in Chapters 25 and 30 below.

Bibliography on Paul's Life, Theology, and Chronology

PAUL (IN GENERAL) AND HIS THEOLOGY:

Study Tools (arranged topically): Metzger, B. M., *Index to Periodical Literature on the Apostle Paul* (Grand Rapids: Eerdmans, 1960); Mills, W. E., *An Index to Periodical Literature on the Apostle Paul* (Leiden: Brill, 1993); Francis, F. O., and J. P. Sampley, *Pauline Parallels* (Philadelphia: Fortress, 1975—parallels among the letters); Ellis, E. E., *Paul and His Recent Interpreters* (Grand Rapids: Eerdmans, 1961); Wedderburn, A.J.M., "... Recent Pauline Christologies," ExpTim 92 (1980–81), 103–8; Sabourin, L., "Paul and His Thought in Recent Research," *Religious Studies Bulletin* 2 (1982), 63–73,117–31; 3 (1983), 90–100.

Aageson, J. W., *Written Also for Our Sake: Paul and the Art of Biblical Interpretation* (Louisville: W/K, 1993).
Banks, R., *Paul's Ideas of Community: The Early House Churches* (2d ed.; Peabody, MA: Hendrickson, 1994).
Barrett, C. K., *Paul: An Introduction to His Thought* (Louisville: W/K, 1994).
Becker, J., *Paul: Apostle to the Gentiles* (Louisville: W/K, 1993).
Beker, J. C., *Paul's Apocalyptic Gospel* (Philadelphia: Fortress, 1982).
———, *Paul the Apostle* (2d ed.; Philadelphia: Fortress, 1984).
Bornkamm, G., *Paul* (New York: Harper & Row, 1971).
Bruce, F. F., *Paul: Apostle of the Heart Set Free* (Exeter: Paternoster, 1984).
Cerfaux, L., *Christ in the Theology of St. Paul* (New York: Herder & Herder, 1959).
———, *The Church in the Theology of St. Paul* (New York: Herder & Herder, 1959).
———, *The Christian in the Theology of St. Paul* (New York: Herder & Herder, 1967).
Chicago Studies 24 (#3, 1985): an issue dedicated to Paul.
Collins, R. F., *Proclaiming the Epistles* (New York: Paulist, 1996). Preaching Paul from the church lectionary.
Cunningham, P. A., *Jewish Apostle to the Gentiles* (Mystic, CT: Twenty-Third, 1986).
Dahl, N. A., *Studies in Paul* (Minneapolis: Augsburg, 1977).
Davies, W. D., *Paul and Rabbinic Judaism* (4th ed.; London: SPCK, 1980).
Dibelius, M., *Paul* (London: Longmans, 1953).
Dodd, C. H., *The Meaning of Paul for Today* (London: Collins, 1958).
Donfried, K. P., and I. H. Marshall, *The Theology of the Shorter Pauline Letters* (Cambridge Univ., 1993).

Drane, J. W., *Paul: Libertine or Legalist?* (London: SPCK, 1975).
Dungan, D. L., *The Sayings of Jesus in the Churches of Paul* (Philadelphia: Fortress, 1971).
Dunn, J.D.G., "Prolegomena to a Theology of Paul," NTS 40 (1994), 407–32.
Ellis, E. E., *Paul's Use of the Old Testament* (Grand Rapids: Baker, 1957).
———, *Pauline Theology: Ministry and Society* (Grand Rapids: Eerdmans, 1989).
Engberg-Pedersen, T., ed., *Paul in His Hellenistic Context* (London: Routledge, 1994).
Evans, C. A., and J. A. Sanders, eds., *Paul and the Scriptures of Israel* (JSNTSup 83; Sheffield: JSOT, 1993).
Fee, G. D., *God's Empowering Presence: The Holy Spirit in the Letters of Paul* (Peabody, MA: Hendrickson, 1994).
Fitzmyer, J. A., *Paul and His Theology* (2d ed.; Englewood Cliffs, NJ: Prentice Hall, 1989)—an enlarged version of NJBC arts. 79 and 82.
———, *According to Paul* (New York: Paulist, 1993).
Freed, E. D., *The Apostle Paul, Christian Jew: Faithfulness and Law* (Lanham, MD: Univ. Press of America, 1994).
Furnish, V. P., *Theology and Ethics in Paul* (Nashville: Abingdon, 1968).
———, "Pauline Studies," in NTIMI 321–50 (excellent bibliography).
———, "On Putting Paul in His Place," JBL 113 (1994), 3–17.
Hanson, A. T., *Studies in Paul's Technique and Theology* (London: SPCK, 1974).
Harrington, D. J., *Paul on the Mystery of Israel* (Collegeville: Liturgical, 1992).
Hawthorne, G. F., et al., *Dictionary of Paul and His Letters* (Downers Grove, IL: Intervarsity, 1993).
Hays, R. B., *Echoes of Scripture in the Letters of Paul* (New Haven: Yale, 1989).
Hengel, M., *The Pre-Christian Paul* (London: SCM, 1991).
Jewett, R., *Paul the Apostle to America: Cultural Trends and Pauline Scholarship* (Louisville: W/K, 1994).
Johnson, S. E., *Paul the Apostle and His Cities* (GNS 21; Wilmington: Glazier, 1987).
Käsemann, E., *Perspectives on Paul* (Philadelphia: Fortress, 1971).
Keck, L. E., *Paul and His Letters* (2d ed.; Minneapolis: A/F, 1988).
Lambrecht, J., *Pauline Studies* (BETL 115; Leuven: Peeters, 1994).
Lincoln, A. T., and A.J.M. Wedderburn, *The Theology of the Later Pauline Letters* (Cambridge Univ., 1993).
Lüdemann (Luedemann), G., *Opposition to Paul in Jewish Christianity* (Minneapolis: A/F, 1989).
Lyons, G., *Pauline Autobiography: Toward a New Understanding* (SBLDS 73; Atlanta: Scholars, 1985).
Marrow, S. B., *Paul: His Letters and His Theology* (New York: Paulist, 1986).
Martin, B. L., *Christ and the Law in Paul* (NovTSup 62; Leiden: Brill, 1989).
Martin, R. A., *Studies in the Life and Ministry of the Early Paul and Related Issues* (Lewiston, NY: Mellen, 1993).
Matlock, R. B., *Unveiling the Apocalyptic Paul* (JSNTSup 127; Sheffield: Academic, 1996).
Meeks, W. A., *The Writings of St. Paul* (New York: Norton, 1972).

———, *The First Urban Christians. The Social World of the Apostle Paul* (New Haven: Yale, 1983).

Meinardus, O.F.A., *St. Paul in Ephesus and the Cities of Galatia and Cyprus* (New Rochelle, NY: Caratzas, 1979).

———, *St. Paul in Greece* (New Rochelle, NY: Caratzas, 1979).

———, *St. Paul's Last Journey* (New Rochelle, NY: Caratzas, 1979). These three books are attractive, short guides.

Munck, J., *Paul and the Salvation of Mankind* (Richmond: Knox, 1959).

Murphy-O'Connor, J., *Becoming Human Together: The Pastoral Anthropology of St. Paul* (2d ed.; Wilmington: Glazier, 1982).

———, *Paul: A Critical Life* (New York: Oxford, 1996).

Neyrey, J. H., *Paul, In Other Words: A Cultural Reading of His Letters* (Louisville: W/K, 1990). An anthropological reading.

O'Brien, P. T., *Gospel and Mission in the Writings of Paul* (Grand Rapids: Baker, 1995).

Patte, D., *Paul's Faith and the Power of the Gospel* (Philadelphia: Fortress, 1983).

Pauline Theology (4 vols. planned; Minneapolis: A/F):

Vol. 1, ed. J. M. Bassler, *Thess, Phil, Gal, Phlm* (1991);

Vol. 2, ed. D. M. Hay, *1 and 2 Corinthians* (1993);

Vol. 3, eds. E. E. Johnson and D. M. Hay, *Romans* (1995).

Penna, R., *Paul the Apostle* (2 vols.; Collegeville: Liturgical, 1996). Exegetical and theological.

Porter, S. E., and C. A. Evans, eds., *The Pauline Writings* (Sheffield: Academic, 1995). Important articles from JSNT.

Räisänen, H., *Paul and the Law* (Philadelphia: Fortress, 1983).

Ramsay, W. M., *St. Paul the Traveller and Roman Citizen* (New York: Putnam, 1904). A classic.

Ridderbos, H. N., *Paul: An Outline of His Theology* (Grand Rapids: Eerdmans, 1975).

Roetzel, C. J., *The Letters of Paul* (2d ed.; Atlanta: Knox, 1985).

Sanders, E. P., *Paul and Palestinian Judaism* (Philadelphia: Fortress, 1977).

———, *Paul, the Law, and the Jewish People* (Philadelphia: Fortress, 1983).

———, *Paul* (Past Masters; New York: Oxford, 1991). Attractive; simpler than the others.

Sandmel, S., *The Genius of Paul* (new ed.; Philadelphia: Fortress, 1979). A Jewish view.

Schmithals, W., *Paul and the Gnostics* (Nashville: Abingdon, 1972).

Schoeps, H. J., *Paul: the Theology of the Apostle in the Light of Jewish Religious History* (Philadelphia: Westminster, 1961).

Schreiner, T. R., *Interpreting the Pauline Epistles* (GNTE; Grand Rapids: Baker, 1990).

———, *The Law and Its Fulfillment. A Pauline Theology of Law* (Grand Rapids: Baker, 1993).

Schütz, J., *Paul and the Anatomy of Apostolic Authority* (SNTSMS 26; Cambridge Univ., 1975).

Schweitzer, A., *Paul and His Interpreters* (New York: Schocken, 1964; German orig. 1911).

Segal, A. F., *Paul the Convert. The Apostolate and Apostasy of Saul the Pharisee* (New Haven: Yale, 1990).

Soards, M. L., *The Apostle Paul: An Introduction to His Writings and Teaching* (New York: Paulist, 1987).

Stendahl, K., *Paul among Jews and Gentiles and Other Essays* (Philadelphia: Fortress, 1976).

Tambasco, A., *In the Days of Paul: The Social World and Teaching of the Apostle* (New York: Paulist, 1991).

Taylor, M. J., *A Companion to Paul: Readings in Pauline Theology* (Staten Island, NY: Alba, 1975).

Taylor, N. H., *Paul, Antioch and Jerusalem* (JSNTSup 66; Sheffield: JSOT, 1992).

Theissen, G., *Psychological Aspects of Pauline Theology* (Philadelphia: Fortress, 1987).

Thompson, W. G., *Paul and His Message for Life's Journey* (New York: Paulist, 1986).

Trilling, W., *A Conversation with Paul* (New York: Crossroad, 1987).

van Unnik, W. C., *Tarsus or Jerusalem: The City of Paul's Youth* (London: Epworth, 1962).

Watson, F., *Paul, Judaism, and the Gentiles* (SNTSMS 56; Cambridge Univ., 1986).

Whitely, D.E.H., *The Theology of St. Paul* (2d ed.; Philadelphia: Fortress, 1974).

Witherington, B., III, *Paul's Narrative Thought World* (Louisville: W/K, 1994).

Ziesler, J. A., *Pauline Christianity* (rev. ed.; New York: Oxford, 1990).

PAULINE CHRONOLOGY:

Buck, C. H., Jr., and G. Taylor, *Saint Paul: A Study in Development of His Thought* (New York: Scribner's, 1969).

Donfried, K. P., "Chronology: New Testament," ABD 1.1011–1022, esp. 1016–1022.

Hurd, J. C., "Pauline Chronology and Pauline Theology," in *Christian History and Interpretation,* eds. W. R. Farmer et al. (J. Knox Festschrift; Cambridge Univ., 1967), 225–48.

Jewett, R., *A Chronology of Paul's Life* (Philadelphia: Fortress, 1979).

Knox, J., *Chapters in a Life of Paul* (Nashville: Abingdon, 1950; rev. ed. Macon: Mercer, 1987).

Lüdemann (Luedemann), G., *Paul: Apostle to the Gentiles: Studies in Chronology* (Philadelphia: Fortress, 1984). Excellent bibliography.

Murphy-O'Connor, J., "Pauline Missions before the Jerusalem Conference," RB 89 (1982), 71–91.

Ogg, G., *The Chronology of the Life of Paul* (London: Epworth, 1968).

Suggs, M. J., "Concerning the Date of Paul's Macedonian Journey," NovT 4 (1960–61), 60–68.

CHAPTER 17

AN APPRECIATION OF PAUL

The preceding two Chapters offer general information that will enable readers to appreciate the Pauline letters when we discuss them individually. Yet in writing those Chapters I have been somewhat embarrassed because they survey the very material that made me restive in the first courses about Paul that I attended. We students had to memorize letter outlines and make maps of the journeys of Paul; the professors spent hours discussing Pauline chronology and whether he went to South Galatia or North Galatia. In my own teaching I have come to recognize that much of that is important; but I have not forgotten that such an emphasis engendered no love for Paul and, at least in some of my classmates, proved a permanent block to savoring the heritage he left. The Gospels engendered spontaneous attraction, but Paul's letters necessitated laborious plodding. Accordingly I want to add a different kind of introductory Chapter, i.e., one centered on appreciating this man who did more than anyone else in his time to lead people to see what Jesus Christ meant for the world.

(A) Images of Paul

What image does Paul evoke? Most of the well-known paintings or statues of Paul are imaginative recreations of dramatic moments in Acts, showing Paul being struck from his horse on the road to Damascus, or Paul debating with the philosophers in the halls of a school in Athens, or Paul being shipwrecked on his sea journey to Rome. Occasionally there is a chiaroscuro of a bald-headed Paul writing a letter in the flickering light of a candle. The common symbolism of Paul with a sword echoes the tradition that Paul was martyred by beheading in Rome.

Paul's own words do not seem to have fed the artistic fancy. Yet his writing is the most autobiographical in the NT; indeed in the whole Bible only Jeremiah matches Paul in self-revelation. In particular, one passage creates indelible images:

> Often near death; five times I have received thirty-nine lashes from Jews; three times I have been beaten with rods; once I was stoned; three times I

> have been shipwrecked; a night and a day I passed on the watery deep; on frequent journeys; in dangers from rivers; in dangers from bandits; in dangers from (my own) kind; in dangers from Gentiles; in dangers in the city; in dangers in the wilderness; in dangers on the sea; in dangers from false brethren; in toil and hardship; many times without sleep; in hunger and thirst; many times not eating; cold and not clothed; and besides other things there is on me the daily pressure constituted by anxiety for the churches. Who is weak and I am not weak? Who is made to stumble into sin, and I am not indignant? (II Cor 11:23–29)

To appreciate the awesome reality of that description modern readers may need some background. For instance, "frequent journeys" gives a vivid mental picture if one understands the difficulties they entailed.[1] It is often affirmed that the famous Roman road network facilitated the spread of Christianity, and films about Roman times picture chariots dashing along the roads paved with hard rock. Undoubtedly Paul took advantage of such roads when he could, but in many regions he would not have had such a luxury. Moreover, Paul was an itinerant artisan who would have had to struggle to get money for food; a wheeled vehicle would have been beyond his means. Horseback travel was difficult; for horses were not used for long distances, and skill was required in riding (given the absence of the saddles and stirrups that we know). Probably Paul would not even have been able or willing to spend money for a donkey to carry his baggage, for soldiers were prone to requisition these animals from travelers who could not offer resistance. And so we have to picture Paul trudging along the roads, carrying his limited possessions in a sack, at the maximum covering twenty miles a day.

At times when he could earn some money with his leatherworking skills and his travel pattern brought him to an inn, he may have been able to rent an overnight spot there—a place on the ground in the courtyard near the fire, or, more expensively, a bed (probably infested with bugs) in a room off the yard. Often, however, he had to sleep somewhere near the road, amidst the cold, rain, and snow. As a poor man he would have been easily victimized by brigands, especially in country areas that were less efficiently controlled by police. Sea journeys were not much safer. Coming east the winds helped, but going west was dangerous; and in either direction there were many shipwrecks. Being a passenger on the open deck of a cargo boat, eating the limited provisions one had brought aboard, was really not much more comfortable than travel on land.

The difficulties were not over when Paul arrived at his intended destina-

[1] I draw freely here on the very helpful article of J. Murphy-O'Connor, "On the Road and on the Sea with St. Paul," BRev 1 (#2, 1985), 38–47.

tion. Today those who walk through the magnificent ruins of a city like Ephesus cannot help but recognize the grandeur and power of Greco-Roman culture embodied in majestic buildings, shrines, temples, and statues. Yet here was a Jew with a knapsack on his back who hoped to challenge all that in the name of a crucified criminal before whom, he proclaimed, every knee in heaven, on earth, and under the earth had to bend. The contempt and mockery of the sophisticated Gentiles for this babbling ragpicker of ideas reported in Acts 17:18 ring true. Further, the Acts accounts of his being hauled before magistrates and imprisoned throw light on Paul's report of "dangers from the Gentiles." Those dangers might have been bearable if his own "kind" (*genos,* "race, stock"; II Cor 11:26) had given him a warm reception when he proclaimed a Messiah descended from David. But both Acts and Paul's letters portray struggle and hostility. Paul did not have the status to command a place in a public building for his message; Acts 16:13 has him preaching at a place of prayer by a riverside. Frequently he must have preached where he lived and worked, namely, in the tenement houses-with-shops of the larger cities. According to Acts he found his way into synagogue house-meetings where often enough he was unwelcome (because he was addressing the Gentiles and stirring up trouble?); that is confirmed by the five times he received the punishment of thirty-nine lashes "from Jews," a punishment associated with synagogue discipline. Paul himself testifies to the fact that his struggles were not over when he brought people to believe in Christ. He devotes much of Gal to countering other Christians whom he considered "false brethren" because they undermined his work by attempting to preach another gospel. The Corinthian correspondence also shows vividly his anxiety for the churches.

(B) Paul's Motivation

Why did Paul subject himself to all this "grief"? Before a dramatic moment in the mid-30s of the 1st century AD Paul had been at peace with his upbringing, with himself, and with his God. The Greek style of his letters shows that he was adequately educated in the dominant Greco-Roman culture. In terms of the Jewish tradition he claims to be advanced beyond many of his contemporaries (Gal 1:14). Seemingly he was well connected with the religious authorities in Palestine.[2] As for religious observance, he was blameless (Phil 3:5–6). What brought about a drastic change whereby all this became so much "dross"? Acts 9:3–8 and Gal 1:12,16 offer a partial

[2]Acts 9:1–2 would have the high priest giving Paul letters to the synagogues in Damascus. Even without this, we might deduce that his persecution of the church (Phil 3:6; Gal 1:13) can scarcely have been a solo enterprise.

explanation: God was pleased to reveal "His Son" Jesus Christ to Paul. "I count everything as loss because of the surpassing worth of knowing Christ Jesus my Lord" (Phil 3:8). Revelation and knowledge, however, do not adequately explain the driven missionary we have seen above, the "new creature" (to use Paul's own language: II Cor 5:17). Nor does scholarly speculation as to whether that revelation brought immediate insight into what Christ meant for the Gentiles who could be justified without performing the works of the Law. Something far more significant had happened on a personal level.

In the revelation Paul, who already knew the love shown by the God of his Israelite ancestors, discovered a love that went beyond his previous imagination. He felt "taken over" by Christ Jesus (Phil 3:12). With awe Paul exclaims: "The Son of God loved me and gave himself for me" (Gal 2:20). What he avows in Rom 8:35–37 must have been uttered many times in the travails described above: "Who will separate us from the love of Christ? Will anguish or persecution or famine or nakedness or peril or the sword? . . . In all these things we are conquerors because of him who loved us." This love became the driving factor of Paul's life when he came to understand how encompassing it was: "The love of Christ impels us once we come to the conviction that one died for all" (II Cor 5:14).

And how can people know the love of Christ unless they hear about it? "And how are they to hear without a preacher? And how can there be preachers unless they are sent?" (Rom 10:14–15). Thus the mission to the Gentiles who would otherwise not hear is not for Paul an abstract conclusion, but an inevitable translation into action of the overflowing love that he had experienced. Although Paul offers arguments for his position that Gentiles were not bound to accept the observance of the Law of circumcision, his most basic argument would have been existential: They had to become aware of the love manifested by God in Christ, and nothing must be allowed to stand in the way. Paul's attitude toward the Law for the sake of the Gentiles was part of his being all things to all that they might be saved (I Cor 9:21–22).

The hardships encountered in the mission became for Paul more than means to be endured toward an end. If the love of God was manifested in the self-giving of Christ, how could the love of Christ be shown to others except in the same way? "We were ready to share with you not only the gospel of God but also our own selves" (I Thess 2:8). By Paul's carrying about in his body the death of Jesus, the life of Jesus was revealed (II Cor 4:10). "If we are afflicted, it is for your encouragement" (II Cor 1:6). To bring an end to divisions at Corinth, Paul offered an extraordinarily moving description of love. His own experience was what caused him to affirm that of all the gifts or charisms given by God in Christ, "the greatest is love"

(I Cor 13:13). In the language of I Cor 13, in order to preach a Christ who embodied the love of God, Paul had to be patient in his love and endure all things. Amid discouragements Paul had drawn on the love of Christ in order to hope for all things; and he had to be sure that the love that burned in him remained Christ's, not seeking its own interests or brooding over injury. In response to God's love whereby "Christ died for us while we were still sinners" (Rom 5:8), it behooved Paul to rejoice when Christ was proclaimed even by those who were seeking to harm Paul (Phil 1:17–18).

In the Chapters to follow we shall discuss whether, where, and when Paul wrote each letter; whether some of them were glued together from several letters; and whether he went to North Galatia or only South Galatia. We shall try to unravel what precisely Paul meant by justification and the righteousness of God; and whether "the faith of Christ" means Christian faith in Christ or Christ's own faith. But our reflections on all such issues must be qualified by the underlying awareness that Paul would grind his teeth if anyone thought any of that was other than dross when compared with experiencing the all-encompassing love of Christ, the goal to which he had devoted every waking hour. As for his own importance, although he is remembered even today as the most zealous proponent of Christ in the NT, he would remind his admirers: "I am the least of the apostles, indeed unfit to be called an apostle . . . Yet it is by the grace of God I am what I am, and God's grace toward me has not been in vain" (I Cor 15:9–10). Because of that grace he could not be defeated: "The transcendent power comes from God, not from us. We are afflicted in every way possible, but we are not crushed; we have our doubts, but we never despair; we are persecuted, but we are never forsaken; we are struck down, but we are never annihilated" (II Cor 4:7–8).

(C) Paul's Living Heritage

A major component in appreciating Paul is the heritage he left: those whom he brought to Christ; his letters; his disciples and their writings.

THOSE WHOM PAUL BROUGHT TO CHRIST. As explained in Chapter 15, Thanksgivings are part of the letter format of this period, but Paul's have their own peculiarities. Surely he was following his heart as well as form when he gave thanks for those who had been chosen to experience God's love in Christ even as he had, and so were not lacking in any spiritual gift (I Cor 1:7). They were his hope, his joy, his crown, the stars in his universe (I Thess 2:19–20; Phil 2:15). He was comforted by their faith; indeed he can say, "We now live if you stand firm in the Lord" (I Thess 3:8). "For as God is my witness, how I long for all of you with the affection of Christ Jesus" (Phil 1:8). Paul was their father in Christ Jesus (I Cor 4:15; I Thess 2:11);

he was in labor like a mother until Christ was formed in them (Gal 4:19), and as gentle with them as a nursing mother (I Thess 2:7). They were his brothers and sisters. Indeed he could call the Philippians (1:7) his partners in the gospel. They completed his joy by being of the same mind about Christ, united in heart with the same love (Phil 2:2,5).

At times Paul could be harsh: He chastised the Galatians bitterly and called them fools (3:1); he warned the Corinthians that when he came again, he would not be lenient (II Cor 13:2). Yet he insisted, "I wrote to you with many tears, not that you might be pained but that you might know the abundant love I have for you" (II Cor 2:4). And he could issue a challenge that few others in Christian history have ever dared to make: "Be imitators of me, as I am of Christ" (I Cor 11:1; also 4:16); and many of those addressed did find Christ in Paul: "You became imitators of us and of the Lord" (I Thess 1:6). That this claim was not self-serving arrogance may be seen from Paul's indignant reaction when some at Corinth confused adherence to him with adherence to Christ: "Was Paul crucified for you?" (I Cor 1:13). Though Paul had failures, the enduring love of his converts and their gratitude for what he revealed of Christ were a major tribute to his apostleship.

PAUL'S LETTERS. No other follower of Jesus in NT times left behind a written testimony comparable to that of Paul. True, Luke-Acts (*ca.* 37,800 words) is longer than the thirteen letters attributed to Paul (32,350 words); but we scarcely know the Lucan author, whereas Paul's personality stands out in his letters. He claims not to be oratorical: "My speech and my message were not in plausible words of wisdom" (I Cor 2:4; II Cor 11:6); yet ironically it is the current vogue in scholarship to expend considerable effort detecting the mode of Greek oratory that he employed. For ordinary readers, however, such classification contributes little to the appreciation of Paul, because whether he is judged by his own self-deprecation (not adept in oratory) or by Aristotelian standards (using oratorical techniques), the way he communicates his love of Christ is often unforgettable. In the whole library of Christianity it is hard to match his impassioned eloquence. To what has already been cited, we may add the following samples. "I died to the Law that I might live for God. I have been crucified with Christ; it is no longer I who live, but Christ who lives in me" (Gal 2:19–20). "For me to live is Christ, and to die is gain" (Phil 1:21). "I decided not to know anything among you except Jesus Christ and him crucified" (I Cor 2:2). "Be it far from me to boast except in the cross of our Lord Jesus Christ through which the world is crucified to me and I to the world" (Gal 6:14). "For in Christ Jesus neither circumcision nor uncircumcision counts for anything, but only faith working through love" (Gal 5:6). "I am convinced that neither death, nor life, nor angels, nor principalities, nor present things, nor future things, nor powers, nor height, nor depth, nor anything else in creation will be able to separate us from the love of God in Christ Jesus our Lord" (Rom 8:38–39). That eloquence has been a key factor in the ongoing appreciation of Paul by audiences in places and times that he would have never envisioned.

PAUL'S DISCIPLES AND THEIR WRITINGS. Paul was a man of great intensity and a wide range of emotions. He must also have been a man capable of engendering deep friendship, for Paul's letters give evidence of extraordinary loyalty on the part of a wide cast of characters.[3] Timothy, Titus, and Silvanus are seen over a number of years carrying Paul's letters and messages, and sometimes acting as ambassadors in very difficult circumstances; apparently their devotion was never in question. Aquila and Prisca (Priscilla) were willing to pick up stakes and move with Paul from Corinth to Ephesus, and then to go ahead to Rome in anticipation of his arrival. The slave Onesimus attached himself to Paul even at the price of offending his master (Phlm), and both Onesimus and the woman deacon Phoebe (whom Paul thinks of as a "sister": Rom 16:1–2) are warmly recommended by the apostle.

Beyond those and other named disciples and companions, a lasting appreciation of Paul stems from the pens of those who themselves remained anonymous while writing about him or in his name. *The author of Acts* (Luke?) has often been criticized for not fully understanding Paul's theology, for highlighting themes that were not Pauline (salvation-history), for simplifying Paul's career, and for avoiding many of the controversies in Paul's life. We should not overlook, however, the extraordinary tribute he paid by devoting to Paul half the book's lengthy description of the spread of Christianity. Whether or not Paul was that important in the estimation of nonPauline Christians, Acts has forever placed Paul alongside Peter in the Christian "pantheon" as the two most important figures in the following of Jesus. In his own writing Paul speaks of God's revelation of the divine Son "in order that I might preach him among the Gentiles" (Gal 1:16). But would subsequent Christianity have understood the full ramifications of that plan without Acts' dramatization that began Paul's story in Jerusalem, the Jewish capital, and led him to Rome, the Gentile capital where he spoke definitively about the future direction of Christianity toward the Gentiles? Again Acts has fleshed out in an unforgettable way the travels, imprisonments, and afflic-

[3]For a complete listing, see E. E. Ellis in Hawthorne, *Dictionary* 183–89. A point worth noting: We know a wide range of named characters surrounding Jesus and surrounding Paul, but in the whole body of the DSS we do not seem to have a single name of a community member, not even that of its founder. In both the strict and the broad sense of the word, the gospel was "incarnate" in individuals.

tions the apostle describes. Paul says, "To the Jews I became like a Jew in order to win over Jews; . . . to those outside the Law I became like one outside the Law . . . in order to win over those outside the Law" (I Cor 9:20–21). Acts graphically embodies that adaptability in the different sermons attributed to Paul: When he addresses a synagogue (Acts 13:15–41), most of what he says is derived from the OT; when he stands in the middle of the Athenian Areopagus (17:22–31), he not only uses more literary Greek but also quotes philosophers. Paul's last discourse, addressed to the elders of Ephesus (Acts 20:17–38), sums up beautifully his career and captures the tender love of his converts for him. Paul's own writings may be remarkably autobiographical, but the biography in Acts contributed enormously to his image.

A greater tribute to Paul came from those disciples who in his name wrote the pseudonymous deuteroPauline literature (see Chapter 25 below).[4] Apparently a half-dozen authors found the apostle, even after his death, an enduring authority to speak to the churches in the last third of the 1st century. For instance, *II Thessalonians* shows Paul facing the great evil of the end-time and reassuring his Christian converts. Paul's life among them continues to be a model they should imitate: "Be firm and hold on to the traditions you were taught by our word or letter" (2:15).

Even more impressive is the contribution of the author of *Colossians.* Master of a graceful liturgical style, he developed with new depth Pauline themes of christology, ecclesiology, and eschatology. Scholars debate the authentic Pauline tonality of some of the magnificent affirmations of Col; perhaps a more meaningful question is whether Paul would not have been pleased to have them incorporated in his heritage. In his lifetime Paul thought largely of local churches; but, along with Col, would he not have seen the necessity to apply his ideas to the larger vision of church now developing? In any case, Paul's ongoing influence is beautifully illustrated by the appeal to his sufferings in Col 1:24—an appeal all the more impressive if Paul was already dead ("absent in the flesh but with you in spirit" [2:5] in a more profound sense). Paul's use of "mystery" and "body" has inspired in Col a luxuriant development of these motifs; and Paul's speaking to the domestic problems of husband, wife, and slave has been systematized and reshaped in a household code (Col 3:18–4:1). The hymn in Col 1:15–20 is a worthy companion to that offered by Paul himself in Phil 2:5–11.

[4]One could extend Paul's influence further. The reference to "our brother Timothy" in Heb 13:23 brought that writing into the Pauline camp, and in much of the church it was attributed to Paul. In many theological stances I Pet is close to Pauline thought; and, as we shall see, some critics (wrongly in my judgment) would put that writing in the Pauline rather than the Petrine school. II Pet 3:15–16 testifies to the influence of the writings of "our beloved brother Paul." Jas 2:24 shows alarm at the circulation of a misunderstood Pauline formula. Some would attribute the letter format of Rev 2–3 to Pauline patterning.

Probably *Ephesians,* although close to Col, was the contribution of another admirer, the most talented of the Pauline writing disciples. We noted above Paul's own impassioned eloquence about Christ. Matching that are the words attributed to Paul in Eph 3:8: "To me, even though I am the very least of all the saints, was given the grace to preach to the Gentiles the unsearchable riches of Christ"; and in 3:17–19: "That Christ may dwell through faith in your hearts, that rooted and grounded in love, . . . you may know the love of Christ that surpasses knowledge, that you may be filled with all the fullness of God." If Paul professed that at the name given to the exalted Jesus every knee should bow in heaven, on earth, and under the earth (Phil 2:9–10), equally majestic is the description in Eph 1:20–21 of what God "worked in Christ by raising him from the dead and seating him at His right hand in the heavens, far above every . . . name that is named not only in this age but also in the one to come." While Paul stresses the theme of "one" (body, bread, spirit, mind: I Cor 10:17; Phil 1:27; Rom 12:5), he never reached the grandeur of the description he motivated in Eph 4:4–6: one body, one Spirit, one hope, one Lord, one faith, one baptism, one God and Father of all. To imitate the master is one form of appreciation; to be inspired by him to go farther is an even greater contribution to his heritage.

The *Pastoral Letters* (Titus, I-II Tim) have sometimes been dismissed as unworthy of the Pauline corpus because of their pedestrian concern with church structure, diatribes against heretical dangers, and downgrading of women. Certainly the writer (or writers) did not have the elegance of some of the deuteroPaulinists just discussed. Yet the very concern that caused these letters to be called "Pastoral" is faithful to Paul, and he might have become more systematic if faced with dangerous church disintegration at the end of the century. Moreover, a general disparagement does not do justice to some admirable passages, e.g., the hymnic language of Titus 3:4–7; I Tim 3:16; 6:15–16, and the moving "sure (faithful) saying" of I Tim 1:15: "Christ Jesus came into the world to save sinners, of which I am the foremost." There is a really remarkable capturing of the Pauline spirit in II Tim (the last written work in the corpus?). Who could hope for an epitaph more poignant than: "I have fought the good fight; I have finished the race; I have kept the faith. For the rest there is laid up for me the crown of righteousness which the Lord, the righteous judge, will grant to me on that day" (II Tim 4:7)? And the heritage goes on, for Paul has prepared a new generation who can be just as effective as he was: "Stir into flame the gift of God that is within you . . . God did not give us a spirit of timidity but of power and love" (1:6–7).

Beyond that tribute the author of II Tim realizes that the bequest of the great preacher, apostle, and teacher (1:11) is not dependent on a generation or two of disciples. In 2:8–9 Paul is heard to say that he is suffering in chains for the sake of the gospel; then he cries out defiantly, "But the word of God is not chained." The ultimate gift of Paul is to have preached a gospel that had enormous power in itself and therefore could not be chained or silenced even when its proponents were. Readers who keep in mind *the apostle whose preaching unchained the gospel* will not allow the Pauline message to be buried beneath details as we now consider the thirteen NT writings that bear Paul's name.

CHAPTER 18

FIRST LETTER TO THE THESSALONIANS

As the oldest preserved Christian writing, this document has a special significance even outside the Pauline corpus. Within the corpus I Thess has at times been neglected because it does not treat the great Pauline theme of justification by faith apart from the works of the Law. Yet that very attitude raises issues of Pauline theology to which readers were alerted in Chapter 16. Can our evaluation of the importance of a Pauline letter be independent of the relation of the letter to the life-situation for and in which it was composed? Is not the expression of Pauline thought shaped by the needs of the particular community (perhaps in this case one not affected by the dispute over the works of the Law)? Or if there was growth in Paul's thought, might we be hearing here a younger Paul—still very close to his experiences in the church of Antioch, but not yet honed by the Galatian crisis that brought the issue of justification to the fore in his thought (Chapter 10 above, n. 102)? The questions just asked imply that an introductory treatment of the *Background* of Paul's dealing with the addressees is important for understanding Thess (or, indeed, any Pauline letter). Then the *General Analysis* will supply guidance as readers go through the text of the letter, and subsections will cover *Issues for reflection* and *Bibliography.*

The Background

Paul, with Silas and Timothy,[1] had crossed over from the province of Asia (Asia Minor or present-day Turkey) to Macedonia (Europe, present-day northern Greece) *ca.* AD 50. Within a relatively short time he would move through Macedonia to Achaia (southern Greece) stopping at Philippi, Thessalonica, Beroea, Athens, and Corinth. Perhaps missions from Jerusalem had brought the name of Christ to Europe earlier;[2] but this was a major step in

[1]And the "we companion" of Acts 16:10ff. who seemingly was neither of them; see pp. 325–27 above.

[2]See Chapter 24 below for the date of the Christian foundation at Rome. A sharp distinction between Asia and Europe is not attested in the literature of this period; yet Acts 16:9–10 dramatizes the significance of going over to Macedonia rather than staying in Asia.

Summary of Basic Information

DATE: The oldest preserved Christian document: 50 or 51 in the Traditional Chronology, during Paul's (Second Missionary) journey, undertaken after the meeting in Jerusalem (or 41–43 in the Revisionist Chronology,* before the Jerusalem meeting).

FROM: Corinth within a few months of Paul's preaching at Thessalonica.

TO: The Christians at Thessalonica, probably of mixed Gentile and Jewish origin.

AUTHENTICITY: Not seriously doubted today.

UNITY: That two letters have been combined to make up I Thess has been suggested by a small number of respected scholars (e.g., W. Schmithals), but unity is overwhelmingly asserted.

INTEGRITY: The Pauline authorship of 2:13–16 is strongly affirmed by the majority; see *Issue* 2 below. A few look on 5:1–11 as an addition to the letter.

FORMAL DIVISION:

A. Opening Formula: 1:1
B. Thanksgiving: 1:2–5 or 1:2–10; or a longer Thanksgiving 1:2–3:13, subdivided into first (1:2–2:12) and second (2:13–3:13)
C. Body: 2:1–3:13 (or 1:6–3:13): Pauline indicative (relationship to Thessalonians)
   4:1–5:22: Pauline imperative (instructions, exhortations)
D. Concluding Formula: 5:23–28.

DIVISION ACCORDING TO CONTENTS:

1:1–10: Address/greeting and Thanksgiving
2:1–12: Paul's behavior at Thessalonica
2:13–16: Further Thanksgiving about the reception of the gospel
2:17–3:13: Timothy's mission and Paul's present relationship to the Thessalonian church
4:1–12: Ethical admonitions and exhortations
4:13–5:11: Instructions about the parousia
5:12–22: Instructions about church life
5:23–28: Concluding blessing, greeting (with a kiss, see pp. 418–19 above).

* For the two Chronologies see Table 6 in Chapter 16 above.

Paul's proclaiming the gospel, and his concerns in later years would often be directed toward the churches established in the evangelization of Greece.

His first preaching was at Philippi where he "suffered and was shamefully treated" (I Thess 2:2).[3] Then proceeding some 100 miles west along the Via Egnatia, the great Roman road across northern Greece, Paul and his companions came to Thessalonica,[4] where he proclaimed the gospel "not only in word, but also in power and in the Holy Spirit and with full conviction"

[3]See the *Background* of Chapter 20 below for the account of Paul's activities in Philippi, which involved being stripped, beaten, and imprisoned.

[4]Founded in 316 BC by Cassiander (a general of Alexander the Great) and named after his wife, Thessalonike, this important commercial city had been under Roman control since 168 BC. The local population was deported, and in 146 BC Thessalonica became the capital of the Roman province of Macedonia.

(I Thess 1:5). How long he stayed there is uncertain. In a compressed and highly stylized picture, Acts 17:2 mentions three consecutive Sabbaths at the synagogue,[5] and afterwards indicates a ministry centered around the house of Jason (17:5–9), followed by a hasty departure. Besides preaching, Paul (I Thess 2:9) recalls that he had labored and toiled, slaving night and day, so that he would not be a financial burden; and in Phil 4:16 he remembers that the Philippians sent money to him at Thessalonica several times—a description that suggests more than a few weeks' stay.

Thessalonica was a city with a Jewish community but marked by a multiplicity of cults, reflecting the mixture of the population. Archaeology and historical records indicate places for worshiping the Roman pantheon and the emperor,[6] as well as a host of Oriental deities, e.g., Cabirus (Kabiroi), Isis, Serapis, and Osiris. The letter that Paul writes back to his converts at Thessalonica who "broke with the worship of false gods" (1:9) implies that they were Gentiles, and (4:1) that they were largely of the working class. Acts 17:4 may not be too askew, then, in reporting that at Thessalonica, although Paul preached first in the synagogue, converting some who heard him there, eventually he attracted many God-fearers and Gentiles.[7] Also Paul's tentmaking, leatherworking trade would have brought him into contact with Gentiles who made their livelihood in a similar way. (Acts is probably mentioning only the more prominent people.) In I Thess 2:2 Paul speaks of "great opposition" at Thessalonica. This might be related to Acts 17:5–10, where Paul's success with the Gentiles angered a group of Jews who in turn aroused the marketplace crowds against him, causing him to flee the city with Silas. Such an enforced hasty departure leaving things unfinished could explain Paul's writing back after he had been gone only a short time (I Thess 2:17) and his intense desire to revisit, so that, being thwarted (2:18), he sent Timothy back from Athens to Thessalonica[8] to prevent the Christians there

[5]Acts 17:2 does *not* state that Paul's whole stay at Thessalonica was of three weeks' duration, although some would increase the friction between Paul's letters and Acts by reading it that way. The fact that the author of Acts knew that the local Thessalonian magistrates were politarchs (17:6,8), a designation confirmed by inscriptions discovered there, should make one cautious about blanket dismissals of the Acts account of Paul's stay at Thessalonica as grossly inaccurate.

[6]See H. L. Hendrix, *Thessalonicans Honor Romans* (ThD dissertation; Cambridge, MA: Harvard, 1984). The goddess Roma and Roman political benefactors were interrelated in worship. A temple of Caesar was built, and already *ca.* 27 BC Thessalonian coins portrayed Julius as a god.

[7]Many reject the Acts information that some converts were Jews. Yet it is difficult to conceive that at least some would not have been, and so it is overly precise to argue from I Thess that *all* the Christians had to be Gentiles. One is caught between the Acts tendency to establish a set pattern of Pauline ministry in the synagogue, and the skeptical overuse of the argument from silence stemming from Paul's failure to mention Jews. For the application of I Thess 1:9–10 to the local situation at Thessalonica, see J. Munck, NTS 9 (1962–63), 95–110.

[8]This itinerary for Timothy (Athens to Thessalonica) differs from the compressed picture in Acts 17:14–15, where Silas and Timothy remained in Beroea while Paul went to Athens. Eventually according to Acts 18:1,5 Paul went on from Athens to Corinth, and Silas and Timothy rejoined him

from being unsettled by hardships (3:2–5) and by what they were suffering from their "compatriots" (2:14–15). What were these hardships and sufferings? It is not unlikely that the opposition that Paul faced from both Gentiles and Jews continued after he left and afflicted his converts.[9] Presumably the "compatriots" he mentions were Gentiles, and yet Paul also compares the sufferings of the Thessalonian Christians to what the churches of God in Judea suffered from the Jews who killed the Lord Jesus and the prophets. In the gospel picture the Jewish authorities effected the death of Jesus through the cooperation of the Roman magistrate, even as Acts 17:5–6,13 would have some Jews at Thessalonica stirring up street rabble and magistrates (presumably Gentile) against Paul. With that background of relationship between Paul and the Thessalonian Christians, what does he say in the letter written shortly after he preached among them?

General Analysis of the Message

Because Paul's thought shifts back and forth in the letter, I shall not attempt a purely sequential *Analysis.*[10] Rather let me suggest that readers go through I Thess quickly to get a surface impression of the contents, and then they may find useful this *Analysis* that highlights the main issues.

Clearly Paul cared for the Thessalonians. He addresses them as his "brothers" (= brothers and sisters) some fourteen times—proportionate to the letter's length this is an intense usage. One way of translating 2:8 is "Having been separated from you, we were ready to share with you not only the gospel of God but also our very own selves." Sometimes Paul benevolently flatters his addressees, but one gets a sense that he was genuinely relieved when Timothy returned to him (at Corinth) with the good news that the Thessalonian Christians had not been unsettled by affliction (3:3) and were holding firm in the Lord (3:6–8). "How can we thank God enough for you, for all the joy that we feel before our God on your account?" (3:9). Indeed, they seem to have taken up the challenge to spread faith in Christ by making the word of the Lord ring out elsewhere in Macedonia and Greece (Achaia;

---

there. According to I Thess 1:1 Silvanus and Timothy were with Paul (at Corinth) when he wrote that letter.

[9]According to Acts 17:5–9 Jason, who gave Paul hospitality, was dragged before the city authorities and made to pay money as security or bail. Seemingly he was a wealthy Jew—the name is borne by a Jewish high priest in II Macc 4:7. If he is the figure mentioned in Rom 16:21, he eventually went to Corinth (from which Rom was written), perhaps under continuing harassment after Paul's departure. See F. Morgan-Gillman, "Jason of Thessalonica," TTC 39–49.

[10]On the Summary Page above, I offer two divisions. The first is a formal division according to the standard letter format explained in Chapter 15, but under *Issue* 1 below I show how hard it is to apply that format to I Thess. The second is a division according to contents, and that shows complications in Paul's flow of thought.

1:7–8; see 4:10). Thus Paul, who cannot come to them soon and perhaps now feels less need to do so, is able to write this gentle letter in which there is encouragement to do more (4:10) but little expressed reproof[11] or major new instructions. Indeed, throughout most of it, using oratorical style, Paul is able to appeal to what the Thessalonians already know.[12] A major exception is 4:13–5:11 where he teaches something new. Presumably his reminders and/or his new teaching respond to issues reported by Timothy and questions proposed by the Thessalonians. Precisely to what extent, however, is Paul motivated by specific dangers or trends present in Thessalonica and by the religious, political, and cultural shaping of those who had come to believe in Jesus in that city?[13] Let us examine that issue in more detail under the rubric of two questions.

FIRST, why in much of the letter does Paul remind the Thessalonians of things they already know? On the simplest level, any community that consisted largely of Gentiles converted after a relatively brief missionary visit by Paul had made an enormous change in accepting belief in the one God of Israel who was also the Father of Jesus Christ; and so reinforcement by recalling what had been preached would be appropriate indeed. More specifically Donfried, "Cults" 338–42, thinks that frenzied Pagan religious observances (Dionysus, Cabiri) at Thessalonica were background for Paul's warnings in 4:3–8: "Stay away from impurity"; "not in lustful passion like the Gentiles who do not know God"; "God has not called us to uncleanness but to holiness."[14] That is an interesting suggestion; yet others argue that much of the archaeological evidence pertinent to the Pagan religions comes from a later time, and so its applicability to the Thessalonica that Paul knew is disputed (see H. Koester in TTC 442–44).

Again Donfried, "Cults" 347–52, points out comparative situational possibilities in I Thess 1:6; 2:2,14; 3:3 where Paul writes of affliction and opposition. Was part of the problem the strange exclusivity of this Christian group whose converts abandoned the public religion? In particular, did Paul's proc-

[11]The admonitions in 5:12–15,19–22 seem to be genuinely corrective of existing attitudes at Thessalonica; those in 4:3–5,11–12 about chastity, marriage, and work could be general directives for all times, but see Donfried's position in the next paragraph of the text above.

[12]The idea of remembering is found in 1:3; 2:9; the phrase "You know" is found nine times (1:5; 2:1,2,5,11; 3:3,4; 4:2; 5:2).

[13]One can argue intelligently that certain features in the letter would be common to any general exhortation. For instance, calling himself a father (2:11) would fit the general stance of inculcating morals (as a parent does to children). A challenge to imitate (1:6) was also typical in moral education.

[14]Does I Thess 4:4, which speaks of acquiring or controlling one's *skeuos* ("vessel") in holiness, refer to the male sexual organ or one's wife? Donfried opts for the former because of the prominence of the phallus in frenzied cults.

lamation of the gospel of the one God of Israel and the Lord Jesus Christ cause affliction and persecution in a city where Roman civic cult was so strong? (Acts 17:7 makes the charge specific: Paul's preaching of Jesus as a king contradicts the decrees of Caesar.) Does Paul need to remind the Thessalonians that he himself underwent suffering when he preached there (2:2) because he is being accused of cowardice in having fled the city and left others to face the results of his preaching (Acts 17:9–10)? In the brief time after Paul's departure from Thessalonica were believers put to death, whence the issue of the fate of the dead in Christ (I Thess 4:16)? Or is Malherbe (*Paul* 46–48) correct in suggesting that the affliction and the suffering of which Paul speaks are not external persecution but internal distress and isolation? That certainly may have been part of the picture; yet in looking back on his activity a few years later (II Cor 11:23–27) Paul speaks of physical beatings, attempts on his life, and external dangers both from Jews and Gentiles; and in Rom 8:35–36, in reference to "the sword" (if he is not being purely rhetorical), he raises the issue of Christians being killed. Physical harassment and persecution had occurred in the earlier years of Paul's mission. There is still another possibility for what Paul refers to by affliction. He reminds his readers of his behavior as a preacher at Thessalonica in I Thess 2:1–13. They had seen that he did not evangelize with impure motives or deception, or with flattery or greed, or seeking praise but gently as a nursing mother (2:7) and as a loving father (2:11), blamelessly preaching not a human word but the word of God. Was this reminder provoked by charges made against him by those afflicting the church there? Was he being compared to the stereotype of the crude and avaricious wandering Cynic philosopher peddling his message?[15] This charge would have been particularly galling to Paul, who argued that he was an apostle of Christ who preached the gospel or word of God (2:2,8,13). Indeed, he echoed Jesus: "You have been taught by God in the love of one another" (4:9; see also "word of the Lord" in 4:15).

SECOND, why in 4:13–5:11, instead of reminding the Thessalonians of what they already know, does Paul indicate that they need further precision? Paul had a strongly apocalyptic or eschatological understanding of what God had done in Christ: The death and resurrection of Jesus marked the change of times, so that all were now living in the endtime. This was a message of

[15]See p. 88 above for Cynics; also A. J. Malherbe, NovT 12 (1970), 203–17; and *Paul* 18–28. The fact that most Thessalonian Christians did *not* have this attitude toward Paul is clear from Timothy's report in 3:6 that Paul was remembered kindly and would be welcomed if he came back. Some parts of Paul's message could resemble respectable Epicurean teaching, e.g., "Live quietly, mind your own business, and work with your hands, as we charged you" (4:11).

hope for all who believed;[16] and Paul had taught the Thessalonians about the ultimate fulfillment of that hope, namely, Christ's second coming[17] from heaven to be seen by all (1:10; 4:16–17). As they underwent affliction and suffering, this expectation supplied strength. Yet, probably because he thought this would take place soon, Paul did not broach the issue of believers who would be dead before that coming. He may not have anticipated how quickly some would be put to death for Christ. Now, perhaps because the Thessalonians asked for instructions, Paul wishes to be specific, drawing on the implication of what he had taught about the salvific value of the death and resurrection of Jesus. Christians may grieve for their dead but not like "others who have no hope" (4:13). Once the parousia has begun, "those who have fallen asleep in Christ" will be raised and together with the living they shall be taken up to meet the Lord in the air (4:14–17). No time or date can be attached to all this; indeed it will come suddenly, so that they should be careful to stay wide awake and sober (5:1–11). Yet overall, the thought of the parousia of the Lord Jesus Christ is encouraging: "Whether we are awake or asleep [in death] we shall still live united to him" (5:10). Notice that the Paul of I Thess is not interested in the details of the parousia as such; his pastoral concern is to calm any disturbance in the community he had evangelized.

Issues and Problems for Reflection

(1) In this *Introduction* we shall not be able to spend much time on exact details of the structure of Pauline letters (beyond the overview in Chapter 15 above), but the unusual pattern of I Thess is worth noting. Paul mentions co-senders Silvanus and Timothy[18] in the Opening Formula but does not identify himself (or them) as an apostle or servant of Christ, as he will do frequently in future letters (yet see 2:6). The Thanksgiving begins in 1:2. Does the expression of thanks in I Thess 2:13 belong to the Body of the letter, constituting a second Thanksgiving after 1:2? Or does the Thanksgiving of

[16]I Thess 2:12 contains one of the few Pauline references to the kingdom of God, and it is optimistic: "God who calls you into His own kingdom and glory."

[17]The term "parousia" occurs four times in I Thess and three in II Thess—half the total Pauline usage. There is no evidence that it was derived from preChristian Jewish apocalyptic. It was used in secular Greek for the solemn arrival of a king or emperor at a place; Paul imagines the solemn coming of the sovereign Jesus from heaven to meet the Christian community. Other Pauline terms for this event include "revelation" (*apokalypsis:* I Cor 1:7; II Thess 1:7), "manifestation" (*epiphaneia:* II Thess 2:8; Pastorals), and "Day of the Lord" (I Thess 5:2; II Thess 2:2; passim).

[18]They are with Paul and are known to the Thessalonians but do not have any role in the letter. As for their previous history with Paul in Thessalonica, Acts 17:1 (see 16:29) mentions Paul and Silas (= Silvanus) coming to Thessalonica; and 16:1–4 suggests that Timothy came with them.

the letter extend to the end of chap. 3?[19] In part, this issue is related to the next question below.

(2) Is 2:13–16 an original part of I Thess written by Paul or was it added by a later editor?[20] It refers to "the Jews who killed the Lord Jesus" and generalizes about them in hostile terms. If written by Paul, who certainly had been in Jerusalem in the 30s, it constitutes a very early, major refutation of the revisionist theory that the Romans were almost exclusively responsible for Jesus' death. *Arguments against Pauline authorship of I Thess 2:13–16 include:* (a) It constitutes a second Thanksgiving in the letter; (b) The statement that the Jews[21] "are the enemies of the whole human race" resembles general Pagan polemic, scarcely characteristic of Paul; (c) The statement that the Jews "are filling up their sins" and divine "wrath has finally overtaken them" contradicts Rom 11:25–26 that "all Israel will be saved." *Arguments for Pauline authorship of I Thess 2:13–16:* (a) All mss. contain it; (b) Paul speaks hostilely of "Jews" as persecutors in II Cor 11:24, and he is not incapable of polemic hyperbole; (c) In Rom (2:5; 3:5–6; 4:15; 11:25) Paul speaks of the wrath of God against Jews, so that the hope of their ultimate salvation does not prevent portrayal of divine disfavor. In Paul's thought the jealous Jews at Thessalonica who harassed both him and those who came to believe in Jesus would represent what Rom 11:25 calls the part of Israel upon whom "hardening" (= the "wrath" of I Thess) had come. If before Paul arrived, Jews who observed the Law had attracted some God-fearing Gentiles and prominent women (Acts 17:4), understandably they might have been infuriated when their converts went over to Paul's proclamation of the Messiah in which Law observance was not required.

(3) The description of the parousia given in I Thess 4:16–17 involves the voice of the archangel, the signal of the heavenly trumpet, and being caught up in the clouds to meet the Lord in the air. In 5:1–2 there is a vagueness about the times and the seasons. Some of this echoes both the language of Jewish apocalyptic (see p. 776 below) and the language attributed to Jesus in the apocalyptic discourses of the Gospels (see p. 144 above on Mark 13). Did Paul mean any or all of this as a literal description? Whether he did or not, should modern readers (including those who believe in the inspiration of Scripture) expect this to be fulfilled literally? If not, to what extent is the

[19]See references supplied in J. Lambrecht, "Thanksgivings in 1 Thessalonians 1–3," TTC, 183–205, as well as the *Bibliography* at the end of Chapter 15 above.

[20]See BDM 1.378–81 for writings for and against. Subsequently C. J. Schlueter, *Filling Up the Measure* (JSNTSup 98: Sheffield: JSOT, 1994), and R. A. Wortham, BTB 25 (1995), 37–44, have joined the majority position favoring Pauline authorship.

[21]To be precise, the Jews "who killed the Lord Jesus . . . and persecuted us," i.e., a restricted group. See F. Gilliard, NTS 35 (1989), 481–502.

parousia a symbolic way of saying that, in order to bring about the kingdom, God has yet something to do that cannot be done by human beings but only through Jesus Christ? How important to Christians is the expectation of the parousia after two thousand years of waiting for Jesus to return?[22] That Jesus Christ will come again (in glory) to judge the living and the dead is part both of the Apostles' Creed and the Nicene Creed. See *Issue* 2 in Chapter 10 above.

(4) If 4:13 means that some Thessalonian Christians have been grieving over those who are asleep as if there were no hope, is that because they are making the expected encounter with Jesus in the parousia the moment of receiving God's gift of life? In 4:14 Paul speaks of Jesus who "died and rose again"; thus the death and resurrection of Christ is the life-giving moment for all who are "in him" (including the dead: 4:17). What does being caught up in the clouds to meet the Lord add? Some modern Christians think of this as the "rapture" and deem it extremely important; others have scarcely heard of it. See G. Wainwright in *The Westminster Dictionary of Christian Theology* (Philadelphia: Westminster, 1983), 485; R. Jewett, *Jesus Against the Rapture* (Philadelphia: Westminster, 1979).

(5) At most Paul was at Thessalonica only a couple of months before he had to depart. Yet shortly afterward when he writes I Thess, he urges the Thessalonians to be considerate to those who are over them in the Lord with the task of admonishing them (5:12). What are the possible ways in which such figures could have gained this authoritative position/function? Did Paul appoint leaders before he left a community he had founded, as Acts 14:23 indicates (even if Acts be judged anachronistic in identifying those leaders with the later presbyters)? How are the figures at Thessalonica to be related to the roughly simultaneous overseers/bishops and deacons in place in Philippi (Phil 1:1) and to those whom God would appoint at Corinth as prophets, teachers, and administrators (I Cor 12:28–30)?[23]

(6) I Thess is the earliest Christian writing to have been preserved; surely Paul was not conscious that he was composing a work that would have that distinction. Nevertheless, the status of I Thess offers interesting reflections. Were this the only Christian work that had survived from the 1st century, what would it tell us of the way Paul worked, of his self-understanding, of his christology, of his conception of the church or Christian community? Given that most Christians claim to adhere to the apostolic faith, it is inter-

[22]Questions about the ultimate victory of Christ were already raised in the 1st and 2nd centuries, as can be seen from Acts 1:6–7 and II Pet 3:3–10.

[23]Even though Phil and I Cor were written later than I Thess, Paul established the Christian communities at Philippi, Thessalonica, and Corinth within a half year in AD 50–51; and the letters to those communities have reminiscences of a church situation dating back to that time.

esting to imagine being transported back to the year 51 and entering the meeting room at Thessalonica where this letter of the apostle Paul was being read for the first time. Within the opening ten verses one would hear references to God the Father, the Lord Jesus Christ, and the Holy Spirit, and to faith, love, and hope. That is a remarkable testimony to how quickly ideas that became standard in Christianity were already in place.

Bibliography on I Thessalonians

COMMENTARIES AND STUDIES IN SERIES (* = also on II Thess): **Best, E.** (HNTC, 1972*); Bruce, F. F. (WBC, 1982*); Donfried, K. P. (NTT, 1993*); Frame, J. (ICC, 1912*); Juel, D. H. (AugC, 1985); Marshall, I. H. (NCBC, 1983*); Morris, L. (NICNT, rev. ed., 1991*); Reese, J. M. (NTM, 1979*); Richard, E. (SP, 1995*); Wanamaker, C. A. (NIGTC, 1990*); Williams, D. J. (NIBC, 1992*).

BIBLIOGRAPHIES AND SURVEYS OF RESEARCH: Richard, E., BTB 20 (1990), 107–15*; see Collins, *Studies* 3–75; Weima, J.A.D., *An Annotated Bibliography of the Thessalonian Letters** (Leiden: Brill, 1997/98).

Barclay, J.M.G.,* "Conflict in Thessalonica," CBQ 56 (1993), 512–30.

Boers, H., "The Form-Critical Study of Paul's Letters: 1 Thessalonians as a Case Study," NTS 22 (1975–76), 140–58.

Bruce, F. F.,* "St. Paul in Macedonia: 2. The Thessalonian Correspondence," BJRL 62 (1980), 328–45.

Collins, R. F., "A propos the Integrity of 1 Thes," ETL 55 (1979), 67–106.

———, *Studies on the First Letter to the Thessalonians* (BETL 66; Leuven: Peeters, 1984).

———, *The Birth of the New Testament* (New York: Crossroad, 1993). Almost the whole book is devoted to I Thess.

———, ed., TTC 1–369 (important articles, many in English).

Donfried, K. P.,* "The Cults of Thessalonica and the Thessalonian Correspondence," NTS 31 (1985), 336–56.

Gillman, J., "Signals of Transformation in 1 Thessalonians 4:13–18," CBQ 47 (1985), 263–81. A comparison with I Cor 15.

Jewett, R.,* *The Thessalonian Correspondence: Pauline Rhetoric and Millenarian Piety* (Foundations and Facets; Philadelphia: Fortress, 1986). Very complete listing of possible outlines; excellent bibliography.

———, "Enthusiastic Radicalism and the Thessalonian Correspondence," *SBL 1972 Proceedings,* 1.181–232.

Johanson, B. C., *To All the Brethren. A Text-Linguistic and Rhetorical Approach to I Thessalonians* (CBNTS 16; Uppsala/Stockholm: Almqvist, 1987).

Kaye, B. N.,* "Eschatology and Ethics in First and Second Thessalonians," NovT 17 (1975), 47–57.

Koester, H., "I Thessalonians—Experiment in Christian Writing," in *Continuity and Discontinuity in Church History,* eds. F. F. Church and T. George (G. H. Williams Festschrift; Leiden: Brill, 1979), 33–44.

Lightfoot, J. B., *Notes on the Epistles of St. Paul* (London: Macmillan, 1895), 1–92. A classic.

Longenecker, R. N., "The Nature of Paul's Early Eschatology," NTS 31 (1985), 85–95.

Lührmann, D., "The Beginnings of the Church at Thessalonica," in *Greeks, Romans, and Christians,* eds. D. L. Balch et al. (A. J. Malherbe Festschrift; Minneapolis: A/F, 1990), 237–49.

Malherbe, A. J., "Exhortation in First Thessalonians," NovT 25 (1983), 238–55.

———, *Paul and the Thessalonians* (Philadelphia: Fortress, 1987). Interesting social analysis of Paul's activities at Thessalonica.

Mearns, C. L.,* "Early Eschatological Development in Paul: The Evidence of I and II Thessalonians," NTS 20 (1980–81), 136–57.

Olbricht, T. H., "An Aristotelian Rhetorical Analysis of 1 Thessalonians," in *Greeks* (see Lührmann above), 216–36.

Pinnock, C. H., "The Structure of Pauline Eschatology," *Evangelical Quarterly* 37 (1965), 9–20.

Plevnik, J., "The Taking Up of the Faithful and the Resurrection of the Dead in I Thessalonians 4:13–18," CBQ 46 (1984), 274–83. A comparison with I Cor 15.

———, "1 Thess 5,1–11: Its Authenticity, Intention and Message," *Biblica* 60 (1979), 71–90.

Schmithals, W.,* "The Historical Situation of the Thessalonian Epistles," *Paul and the Gnostics* (Nashville: Abingdon, 1972), 123–218.

Smith, A., *Comfort One Another: Reconstructing the Rhetoric and Audience of 1 Thessalonians* (Louisville: W/K, 1995).

Stanley, D. M., " 'Become Imitators of Me': The Pauline Conception of Apostolic Tradition," *Biblica* 40 (1959), 859–77.

Wanamaker, C. A.,* "Apocalypticism at Thessalonica," *Neotestamentica* 21 (1987), 1–10.

CHAPTER 19

LETTER TO THE GALATIANS

In some ways this has been considered the most Pauline of the Pauline writings, the one in which anger has caused Paul to say what he really thinks. Only parts of II Cor match it in passion; for with the prophetic fervor of an Amos, Paul discards diplomacy in challenging the Galatians. Not surprisingly, Christian innovators or reformers anxious to get the larger church to do a 180-degree turn have appealed to Gal's vigorous language and imagery. Marcion translated Paul's antinomy between faith and the works of the Law[1] into an antinomy between the creator God and the redeemer God.[2] Luther called it his "pet epistle," for he found in Paul's rejection of justification by the works of the Law support for his rejection of salvation by good works. Indeed Luther's confrontations with the papal emissaries were seen as a reenactment of Paul's publicly condemning Cephas (Peter) on behalf of the truth of the gospel. A sermon on Gal brought great peace of heart to John Wesley. In the 19th century the opposition between Peter and Paul described in Gal was a key factor in F. C. Baur's reconstruction of early Christianity. Others, however, have been embarrassed by the crudeness of the polemic and the lack of nuance about the Jewish heritage. In antiquity Gal may well have contributed to a situation that II Pet 3:15–16 chose to describe diplomatically, "Our beloved brother Paul wrote to you according to the wisdom given him . . . in all his letters; there are some things in them hard to understand that the ignorant and unstable twist to their destruction." One thing is certain: No one can fault the Paul of Gal for making theology dull.

After the *Background* and *General Analysis,* subsections will be devoted to the *Aftermath of Gal in Paul's career, To where and when, "the Faith of Christ," Issues for reflection,* and *Bibliography.*

[1]Here for all practical purposes Paul is speaking of the Mosaic Law, but see pp. 470, 578–80 below.

[2]J. L. Martyn, "Galatians," TBOB 2.283, adds that Marcion hardened the apocalyptic antinomy into an ontological one. See his "Apocalyptic Antinomies in Paul's Letter to the Galatians," NTS 31 (1985), 410–24.

Summary of Basic Information

DATE: 54–55 from Ephesus is more likely than 57 from Macedonia (Traditional Chronology; see Table 6 in Chapter 16 above for Revisionist Chronology).

TO: Churches around Ancyra in ethnic Galatian territory, i.e., north-central section of the province of Galatia in Asia Minor (evangelized in 50 and 54), or, less likely, to churches at Antioch, Lystra, and Derbe in the south of the province (evangelized in 47–48 and 50).

AUTHENTICITY, UNITY, AND INTEGRITY: Not seriously disputed.

FORMAL DIVISION:

A. Opening Formula: 1:1–5
B. Thanksgiving: None
C. Body: 1:6–6:10
D. Concluding Formula: 6:11–18.

DIVISION ACCORDING TO CONTENTS (and Rhetorical Analysis):

1:1–10: Introduction:
- 1:1–5: Opening Formula (already defensive in describing apostleship and what Christ has done)
- 1:6–10: Exordium or introduction (astonishment in place of Thanksgiving), describing the issue, the adversaries and the seriousness of the case (by anathemas)

1:11–2:14: Paul narrates his preaching career to defend his thesis about his gospel stated in 1:11–12

2:15–21: Debate with opponents, contrasting his gospel with theirs: justified by faith in Christ, not by observing the Law; Christians live by faith

3:1–4:31: Proofs for justification by faith not by Law: six arguments drawn from the past experiences of the Galatians and from Scripture, particularly centered on Abraham

5:1–6:10: Ethical exhortation (paraenesis) for them to preserve their freedom, and walk according to the Spirit

6:11–18: Conclusion: authenticating postscript in Paul's own hand (as distinct from scribe who took dictation); recapitulation of attitude toward circumcision; benediction.

The Background

In the years before AD 55 Paul had proclaimed the gospel (perhaps twice[3]) to Gentiles who now constituted the churches of Galatia. (Their precise identity we shall leave to later.) Although his stay among them was brought about or affected by a "weakness of the flesh" (4:13),[4] the Galatians were more than kind during Paul's affliction and treated him as an angel of God. Seemingly they saw him work miracles among them (3:5). This memory sharpens his outrage that the Galatians now (4:16) evaluate him as an enemy who

[3]In 4:13 he describes how he preached the gospel there "originally" or "at first."

[4]The assurance that the Galatians would have plucked out their eyes and given them to him (4:15) and the reference to writing with "large letters" (6:11) have given rise to the suggestion of an eye affliction that incapacitated him.

somehow cheated them in his preaching about Christ. How had this come about?

After Paul left Galatia, Christians of Jewish origin (6:13) had come, probably from Jerusalem,[5] preaching another gospel (1:7), i.e., an understanding of what God had done in Christ different from Paul's. (Had they come to Galatia because Paul had been there, or was this simply a stop on their evangelizing route that accidentally brought them into contact with his past work? Were they as pointedly hostile to him as he was to them?) Their "gospel" has to be reconstructed mirror-wise[6] from Paul's hostile refutation of it—a process marked by uncertainties and not geared to engender a sympathetic understanding of a preaching that most Galatians quickly came to judge more persuasive than what they had heard from Paul.

In subsequent Christian history a sense of the sacredness of NT Scripture and respect for Paul as the great apostle have naturally led Christians to a conviction that his gospel was true to Christ and that of his adversaries was not. Nevertheless, since there is no convincing reason for thinking that "the preachers," as they may be called, were fools or dishonest, I shall seek to show why their gospel, so far as it can be reconstructed, sounded plausible. Paul and the preachers were at one in proclaiming that what God had accomplished through Jesus the Messiah in terms of justification and the gift of the Spirit was for both Jews and Gentiles. But how were Gentiles to receive God's gift in Jesus? According to Paul's preaching, God offered justification through the "faith of/in Christ" (subsection below). According to the preachers faith in Christ had a role, but justification was not complete without observing the works of the Law—a preaching that preserved for the Gentiles the great heritage of Judaism with all its ethical guidance.[7] A key factor in that preaching of works was an insistence on circumcision and observing the calendrical feasts (4:10). As the preachers explained, the one true God had blessed all the nations of the world in Abraham who believed (Gen 15:6) and then, as part of the covenant, gave Abraham the commandment of cir-

[5]See *Issue* 1 below. Their challenging of Paul's gospel by insistence on circumcision is similar to the outlook of the group who had challenged his gospel at Jerusalem *ca.* 49 (Gal 2:1–5; Acts 15:1). Notice that later "certain men from James [of Jerusalem]," whom Paul calls "adherents of circumcision" (2:12), were not deterred by his success at the Jerusalem meeting but came after him to Antioch and created trouble. Although the preachers attacked in Gal may have claimed that they had the support of the Jerusalem authorities (since "men from James" and Peter had shown themselves sensitive to Jewish food laws [Gal 2:11–14]), their insistence on circumcision certainly went beyond the view of James, Peter, and John as expressed in Acts 15:1–29 and Gal 2:1–10.

[6]For criteria see J.M.G. Barclay, JSNT 31 (1987), 73–93; also Martyn, *Galatians* (AB).

[7]If this seems strange, remember that the Jesus of Matt 5:17–18 is recalled as saying that he had not come to abolish the Law but to fulfill it and that not even the smallest part of a letter of the Law would pass away. Strains in the Jesus tradition similar to what we find in Matt probably fed the preachers' christology and vocabulary. Indeed, Betz would see in Matt 5:19 a condemnation of Paul as one who teaches others to relax the commandments.

cumcision (Gen 17:10) and the heavenly calendar. Jews are descendants of Abraham through Sarah (the free wife) and have observed the covenant of circumcision (Gen 17:14) and the Law given by angels to Moses (Gal 3:19); Gentiles are descendants of Abraham through Hagar (the slave wife). Through the preachers the work of Jesus the Messiah was now being extended to the Gentiles, who can be fully included in the covenant if they are circumcised in imitation of Abraham and do the works of the Law. (Borgen maintains that without circumcision the Gentile believers in Christ were proselytes, and circumcision was required if they were to remain in the covenanted people of God.).

Yet had not Paul already brought the gospel to the Gentile believers in Galatia? No! In order to make quick converts Paul had preached a truncated gospel that did not tell them that sharing in the Abraham covenant depended on circumcision. Paul had left them without the guidance of the Law, prey to the "Evil Inclination"[8] and the desires of the flesh; and that is why sin was still rampant among them. This was a persuasive message, especially if the preachers pointed out that Paul, who was a latecomer to the gospel, had not known Jesus as the real apostles had. After all, Jesus, who was circumcised himself, had never exempted anyone from circumcision; and the real apostles at Jerusalem kept the feasts and the food laws. How could Paul answer the preachers and win back the Galatians to recognize that he had preached the truth? As we turn to analyze the letter he wrote, we should keep in mind that controversy with the preachers shapes his expression and phrasing. Too often Paul's "theology" of justification, faith, and freedom is abstracted from Gal without recognizing the apologetic shaping.[9]

General Analysis of the Message

In the OPENING FORMULA (1:1–5), unlike I Thess, Paul designates himself as an apostle, a status stemming not from human beings but from Jesus Christ (1:1—and from God: 1:15).[10] Of the seven undisputed Pauline letters,

[8]See J. Marcus, IBS 8 (1986), 8–21.

[9]Hong, *Law,* is helpful in reminding us to pay attention to Paul's phrasing in the individual letters before generalizing. The dispute between Dunn and Räisänen is also pertinent: Dunn contends that Paul did not attack the Law as such but only from a certain perspective; Räisänen posits a more radical break between Paul and Judaism. Although Paul and the Jewish Christian preachers are thinking about the Mosaic Law, it is interesting to ask what the Galatian Gentiles understood from their own experience when they heard "law" being discussed. See M. Winger, *"By What Law?"* (SBLDS 128; Atlanta: Scholars, 1992).

[10]That may be partially self-defensive, given the hostile preachers mentioned in the letter. Nevertheless his primary goal is not to defend his apostleship but the authenticity of the gospel he proclaimed to the Galatians. (Cf. B. C. Lategan, NTS 34 [1988], 411–30.) The Jerusalem "pillars" acknowledged his apostolate (2:8), and that authority is employed in his interpretation of Scripture in chaps. 3–4 defending his gospel.

if we leave aside Rom which was sent to a community that Paul had not evangelized, Gal is the only one of the remaining six in which Paul does not name a co-sender.[11] He addresses himself "to the churches of Galatia," i.e., a group of communities in the Galatian region or in the larger province of Galatia (see subsection below). Paul is the target of the attack in Galatia, and he makes a personal response—one marked by anger that does not allow for a Thanksgiving.

The BODY opens with a type of *exordium or introduction* (*1:6–10*) that, with a biting tone of disappointed astonishment,[12] quickly lays out the issue, the adversaries, and the seriousness of the case: There is no other gospel than the one proclaimed by Paul when he called the Galatians in the grace of Christ; cursed are those who preach something different.[13] Then, using the rhetorical pattern of court defenses, Paul writes in letter form *an apologia* (*1:11–2:21*), polemical in tone but employing a sequence of rhetorical devices.[14] In an implied courtroom setting, the preachers who have come to Galatia are to be imagined as the accusers, Paul as the defendant, and the Galatians as the judge. To appreciate the points made by Paul, one should keep in mind the claims of the preachers as reconstructed in the *Background* above. Paul's main thesis is that the gospel he proclaims came through divine revelation and not from human beings (1:11–12). As a paradigm[15] of that, Paul relates the story of his conversion and preaching, touching down on key points, e.g.: the initial divine revelation and commission; no dependence on the Jerusalem apostles; the challenge to him from the party insisting on

[11]He does mention "all the brothers who are with me" (1:2); if he wrote from Ephesus, probably Timothy was with him.

[12]In unpublished seminar lectures on Gal, N. A. Dahl points out that in ancient ironic letters an expression of astonishment such as found in Gal 1:6 could take the place of the expression of thanks.

[13]See also the curse in 3:10 and K. A. Morland, *The Rhetoric of Curse in Galatians* (Atlanta: Scholars, 1995).

[14]Judicial or forensic rhetoric is explained by Betz, *Galatians* 14–25, with parallels in Plato, Demosthenes, and Cicero. Betz's rhetorical outline underlies those offered by Fitzmyer, Puskas, and others; see also J. D. Hester, JBL 103 (1984), 223–33; T. W. Martin, JBL 114 (1995), 437–61. Another type of rhetoric, deliberative or epideictic (p. 412 above), has been detected in Gal by R. G. Hall, JBL 106 (1987), 277–87; J. Smit, NTS 35 (1989), 1–26, and Matera, *Galatians* 11–13—an attempt to persuade the Galatians not to accept the preachers' gospel of circumcision. Boers, *Justification,* offers a semiotic approach to Gal; and L. L. Belleville, JSNT 26 (1986), 53–78, a structural analysis of Gal 3:21–4:11. It is questionable whether some of the proposed rhetorical and structural refinements greatly increase our understanding of Paul's message. R. G. Hall, NTS 42 (1996), 434–53, contends that the rhetoric of Jewish apocalyptic is more pertinent to Gal than is Greco-Roman rhetoric.

[15]B. R. Gaventa, NovT 28 (1986), 309–26. Was Paul's recitation of his divinely inspired "conversion" motivated in part by the preachers' attack on his inconsistency: once a strong advocate of strict Pharisaism (obviously including circumcision); now dispensing with it (see 5:11)? An account of Paul's past life comparing Gal and Acts is supplied on pp. 298, 306–9, 323 above. A major difference in reporting the Jerusalem meeting is that Acts 15 weaves in the issue of ritually unclean food that did not come until slightly later according to Gal 2:11–14. See P. J. Achtemeier, CBQ 48 (1986), 1–26.

circumcision for the Gentiles; the agreement reached between him and the Jerusalem authorities rejecting that challenge; and the acknowledgment that he was entrusted with the gospel and apostolate to the uncircumcised (1:13–2:10).

In describing those of the circumcision party who afterwards came to Antioch from Jerusalem claiming to represent James, Paul is suggesting that they were the progenitors of those who have come to Galatia (from Jerusalem?); for he blends his defense of the gospel at Antioch against the earlier adversaries into a type of dialogue with the Jewish Christian preachers in Galatia (2:11–14 with 2:15–21). To paraphrase, "By birth we are both Jewish and so we know the Law; yet we also know that one cannot be justified by the works of the Law; indeed in seeking Christ we Jews found ourselves to be sinners. And so I died to the Law and was justified by the faith of/in Christ who gave himself for me and now lives in me."[16]

Then Paul piles up *six arguments from experience and Scripture to convince the foolish Galatians who have allowed themselves to be bewitched*[17] *(3:1–4:31)*—arguments that I now simplify. *First* (*3:1–5*): When he proclaimed Christ crucified, the Galatians received the Spirit without observing the works of the Law, so how can those works be made necessary? *Second* (*3:6–14*): Against the preachers' insistence on the circumcision of Abraham (Gen 17:10,14) he can cite God's promise that in Abraham all the nations would be blessed (Gen 12:3)—a promise independent of circumcision—so that in giving the Spirit to the uncircumcised Gentiles through faith, God is fulfilling the promise to Abraham, a man whose faith was reckoned as righteousness (Gen 15:6).[18] *Third* (*3:15–25*): A will that has been ratified cannot be annulled by a later addition. The Law came 430 years after the promises to Abraham; how can inheritance from those promises depend on observing the Law? The Law was only a temporary custodian until Christ came. *Fourth* (*3:26–4:11*): The Galatians, who were slaves to the elemental spirits of the universe, have experienced through redemption by God's Son and divine adoption the freedom of the "sons" (= children) of God; why do they want again to become slaves, this time to the demands of the Law? *Fifth* (*4:12–20*): The Galatians treated Paul extremely well, like an angel; how can he have become their enemy, as the preachers would make him? *Sixth* (*4:21–31*): The preachers appealed to Abraham, Hagar, and Sarah but drew

[16]On the rhetorical question about Christ being an agent of sin in 2:17, see M. L. Soards in Marcus, *Apocalyptic* 237–54.

[17]J. H. Neyrey, CBQ 50 (1988), 72–100, studies the formal charge of witchcraft in this passage.

[18]J.D.G. Dunn, NTS 31 (1985), 523–42, diagnoses the "works of the Law" in 3:10 as circumcision and food laws, which summarize the function of the Law as a boundary marker distinguishing the Jewish people.

the wrong lesson.[19] Hagar, the slave woman, does not represent the descendance of the Gentiles but the present, earthly Jerusalem and the enslaving covenant of the Law given on Mt. Sinai; Sarah, the free woman, represents the heavenly Jerusalem and the covenant of God's promise to Abraham—she is the mother of all who have been made free in Christ.

After the arguments Paul finishes the Body of Gal with *a passionate exhortation* (*5:1–6:10*) against the preachers and a warning that the Law will not help the Galatians against the works of the flesh (which are contrasted with the works of the Spirit in 5:19–26).[20] A magnificent affirmation in 5:6, "In Christ Jesus neither circumcision nor uncircumcision has any force, but faith working through love," makes it clear that Paul does not consider circumcision something evil but rather something that has no power to bring justification to the Gentiles. It also suggests that Paul thought of faith accepting the efficacy of what Christ had done as something that had to find expression in love manifested in the life of the believer. (He would see God at work in both the faith and the love, with neither being simply human reactions.) The preachers may speak of "the law of Christ"; that, however, is not the Law of Sinai but the obligation to bear one another's burdens (6:2).

Then, Paul stops the scribe and writes the *Conclusion* (*6:11–18*) against circumcision with his own hand in big letters, so that the Galatians cannot miss the point. If the preachers praised the superiority of Israel, Paul proclaims "the Israel of God" in which it makes no difference whether or not one is circumcised. As for the preachers' attacks on him, "From now on let no one make more trouble for me, for I bear the marks of Jesus on my body." What Paul has suffered as an apostle is more important than the marks of his circumcision!

The Aftermath of Galatians in Paul's Career

We can only guess what happened when this letter was read in the churches of Galatia. Some would have been offended by the intemperate language that called them fools (3:1). Was it proper for a Christian apostle

[19]Martyn, "Galatians," TBOB 277–78, utilizing two tables, gives a fascinating contrast between the two exegeses of the Abraham story. See also "The Covenants of Hagar and Sarah," in *Faith and History,* eds. J. T. Carroll et al. (Festschrift P. W. Meyer; Atlanta: Scholars, 1990), 160–90. Martyn reminds us that Paul's polemical interpretation is directed against an imposition of the Law on Gentiles, and that it is dangerously misunderstood when read as a denigration of Judaism, as if it were a religion that made slaves of people while Christianity makes people free. That the exegesis is allegorical and directed toward the experience of the Galatians, see S. E. Fowl, JSNT 55 (1994), 77–95; Hays, *Echoes.*

[20]Highly unusual is the thesis of J. C. O'Neill, ETL 71 (1995), 107–20, that "spirit," like "flesh," is part of the human being, not the Holy Spirit, and that 5:13–6:10 was originally a Jewish collection of moral aphorisms later incorporated into Paul's letter.

to indulge in gutter crudity by wishing that in the circumcision advocated by the preachers the knife might slip and lop off the male organ (5:12)? What entitled Paul to deprecate as "so-called pillars of the church" members of the Twelve who had walked with Jesus and the one honored as "the brother of the Lord" (2:9)? Was that polemic not a sign of the weakness of his position? Others who had turned away from Paul, remembering the one who had brought Christ to them and realizing that beneath the polemic surface of the missive there was tender concern (4:19), might have been led to reexamine whether they had done right in listening to the preachers. In the end did Paul's letter win the day with the majority? It was preserved after all; and I Cor 16:1 (written later?) tells us that he planned a collection of money from the Galatian churches, presumably with hope of success.

Be that as it may, surely certain elements in the letter did damage to Paul. He had expressed himself intemperately. (Was the scribe bold enough to ask him did he really want to phrase 5:12 the way he did?) The preachers who honestly believed that they were serving Christ by advising the Gentiles of the necessity of circumcision would surely not have forgotten Paul's personal attacks, including one on their integrity and motives (6:12–13).[21] If Phil (3:2ff.) was written shortly after Gal, we may be seeing the preachers' continued pursuit of a mission to correct Paul's deficient evangelizing. His remarks about the so-called pillars of the Jerusalem church, his polemic against Peter who was not on the right path about the truth of the gospel (Gal 2:14), and even his unnuanced contention that the Sinai covenant brought about enslavement (4:24–25) most probably got back to the Jerusalem Christian authorities sympathetic to the Jewish heritage. No wonder that Paul's later plans to return to Jerusalem with the collection made him apprehensive about acceptance (Rom 15:22–32; also pp. 554, 564 below). In the 2d century the vigorous antiLaw phrasing of Gal would serve Marcion's thesis that the OT should be rejected as the work of an inferior god (demiurge)—a thesis Paul would surely have rejected.

To Where and When?

These two questions are related. In this letter addressed "to the churches of Galatia" (1:2) and the "Galatians" (3:1), Paul mentions that his first preaching of the gospel in that area was because of a bodily ailment (which seemingly interrupted his journey unexpectedly) and that he was well re-

[21]Paul accuses them of promoting circumcision in order to avoid persecution, presumably by nonChristian Jews who because of this would not treat them as renegades. Or it might be by Gentile authorities who would regard the circumcised converts they made as Jews and thus protected by imperial policy, rather than as belonging to an illicit superstition.

ceived and treated (4:13–15). Where did the addressees of Gal live? If the meeting in Jerusalem described in Gal 2:1–10 is the same as the meeting in Jerusalem after Paul's "First Missionary Journey" described in Acts 15, as most scholars think, the letter was written after 50 (Traditional Chronology). While writing this angry letter, Paul expresses the wish (obviously unfulfilled) to be present with the Galatians (4:20). Is that merely a rhetorical expression of concern? Or does it mean he is somehow unable to come? Because he is too far away? Because he is in prison? Or because he is too involved in another church situation, e.g., the negotiations with Corinth? Do any of these suggestions help to specify when Paul wrote? Let us look in greater detail at the intertwined issues.

Galatai were Indo-Aryans, related to the Celts and Gauls, who invaded Asia Minor about 279 BC. Within fifty years, after defeat by the kingdom of Pergamum, their territory was restricted to a mountainous central section around Ancyra (modern Ankara). Rome used them as allies in various wars; and when the last Galatian king died in 25 BC, their ethnic homeland was incorporated into the large Roman "Province of Galatia" that extended south toward the Mediterranean, including Pisidian Antioch, Iconium, Lystra, and Derbe.[22] Were Christians in those cities in the southern part of the province of Galatia addressed in Gal (the South Galatian theory)? Or were the ethnic Galatians in the north central region the ones addressed (the North Galatian theory)? The issue, strongly disputed among scholars for the last 250 years, *is not really important for the meaning of Gal;* and so the discussion will be kept brief. Although much of the deliberation centers on a comparison between Gal and Acts, readers should remember that the Acts information may be jumbled and surely is incomplete, not listing all of Paul's travels.

SOUTH GALATIAN THEORY (proposed in the last two centuries and defended by such scholars as W. M. Ramsay and F. F. Bruce). There is clear evidence in Acts that Paul had evangelized the southern part of the province of Galatia, specifically Antioch, Iconium, Lystra, and Derbe (during the "First Missionary Journey" in 46–49 and then again briefly on the "Second Journey" in 50). That evidence, however, leaves little room for Paul's sickness being the occasion of his first visit there. Moreover, Acts never clearly refers to the southern region as Galatia. Indeed, Acts places the southern cities in their districts, not the province: Antioch in Pisidia (13:14), Lystra and Derbe in Lycaonia (14:6). Acts specifies that Paul's mission in the southern cities reached Jews as well as Gentiles, but there is no indication in Gal that any of the addressees are converted Jews. Arguments for the Southern

[22]For what is known of Roman Galatia between 25 BC and AD 114, see articles of R. K. Sherk and S. Mitchell, ANRW VII/2, 954–1081.

theory include Paul's habit of usually (but not always) employing the names of Roman provinces (e.g., Macedonia and Achaia), and the reference to Barnabas in Gal 2:1 as if he were known to the addressees—he was with Paul on the "First Missionary Journey" but not afterward. Yet was Barnabas' name known only to those Christians whom he had personally evangelized? Would not his presence at the famous Jerusalem meeting have been more widely known?

NORTH GALATIAN THEORY (the ancient approach and still the majority theory). While the term "Galatia" might be ambiguous, the address "Galatians" in 3:1 is much less so. It is more appropriate for people who were ethnically of that descent than for the hellenized city populace to the south. When would Paul have come to the ethnic Galatian region? On the "Second Missionary Journey," after Paul revisited the south of the province (*ca.* 50), Acts 16:6–7 reports, "They [Paul, Silas, Timothy] went through Phrygia and the Galatian region, having been hindered by the Holy Spirit from speaking the word in [the province of] Asia. Having come opposite [toward] Mysia, they tried to go into Bithynia, but the Spirit of Jesus did not permit them." Does Acts mean that they moved westward through the Phrygian region of the province of Galatia (thus still not into North Galatia), or does it mean they moved northward through Phrygia into the (North) Galatian territory proper? The former might seem more logical geographically; but if one accepts the latter interpretation, the mysterious comment about being "hindered by the Holy Spirit" might be related to Paul's being ill in Galatia (Gal 4:13) and thus hampered in his missionary enterprise. Whatever Acts meant by "Phrygia and the Galatian region," Paul made converts there, for according to 18:23, early on the "Third Missionary Journey" (AD 54), Paul traveled from place to place through the Galatian region and Phrygia "strengthening all the disciples there," i.e., by implication, disciples made on the earlier journey.[23] (The reversal of the order of the two geographical names shows how hard it is to get precision from Acts, whose author may not have known exactly where Paul went.) While it is not easy to judge, overall the arguments supporting this Northern theory seem more persuasive.

DATING. In the South Galatian theory, Paul could have written Gal anytime after revisiting the southern cities in 50 ("Second Missionary Journey").[24] What dating is suggested by the more accepted North Galatian

[23]Theoretically Paul could have written Gal to those disciples before he returned on the "Third Missionary Journey," but Acts shows no awareness that hostility developed toward Paul between the two visits to Galatia. Concerning the route of this journey, see Chapter 27 below, n. 3.

[24]Some would even have Gal written from Antioch *ca.* 48 after the "First Missionary Journey" on the grounds that Gal 2:1 is not describing the visit to Jerusalem reported in Acts 15 but the earlier

theory? There are two proposals: (1) After passing through the (ethnic) Galatian and Phrygian region a second time, Paul went to Ephesus (Acts 19:1) where he stayed three years (54–56). Word could have reached him that teachers had come and "quickly" (Gal 1:6) won over the Galatians to "another gospel"—news that prompted the angry writing of Gal in 54 or 55.[25] If the letter was successful (or, at least, if Paul hoped it was successful) an attempt at healing could be signaled by Paul's plan in I Cor 16:1, when he was about to leave Ephesus in 57, to have the Galatian churches contribute to his collection for Jerusalem. (2) Some scholars who think there could have been no healing after such a letter as Gal argue that the plan in I Cor 16:1 was formulated before Paul found out what had happened to his converts in Galatia. He was informed of that as he left Ephesus or just afterward; and abandoning the plan for a collection in Galatia,[26] he wrote Gal from Macedonia in late 57 (between II Cor and Rom) as a harsh reproof. The closeness of Gal to Rom (written from Corinth in 58) is also advanced as an argument for this later dating. The dating in the mid-50s has more following, and I judge it more probable; but the evidence leaves the question open.

The "Faith [pistis] of Christ" (2:16, etc.)

A major discussion has centered on what Paul means when he speaks of being justified or of justification (see the subsection in Chapter 24 below), not from the works of the Law but from/through the *faith of* (Jesus) *Christ* (2:16; 3:22; also Rom 3:22,26; Phil 3:9). The construction "from/through faith of Christ" (*ek/dia pisteōs Christou*) can be understood as an objective genitive, i.e., the Christian's faith in Christ, or as a subjective genitive, i.e., the faith possessed or manifested by Christ.[27] The debate also affects the

---

famine visit of Acts 11:30; 12:25. However Acts gives little detail about the famine visit, and it may be a confused memory. It is very unlikely Paul was in Galatia before the Jerusalem meeting of Gal 2:1 or he would have mentioned Galatia in 1:21 along with Syria and Cilicia. Moreover Gal 2:11–14 suggests that Gal was written after Paul broke with the Antiochene community.

[25]Gal may have been the first Pauline letter written from Ephesus. "Quickly," if not purely oratorical, fits poorly with a date three or four years later when Paul was in Macedonia or Corinth. Ephesus was about 350 miles from Ancyra, and thus closer than Macedonia or Corinth to the ethnic Galatian territory.

[26]It is pointed out that in Rom 15:26, written at the end of his collection drive, Paul mentions money raised only in Achaia and Macedonia. However, in writing to the Romans, Paul may have had a different reason for not mentioning the Galatians, viz., reports about what he wrote in Gal had caused hostility in Jerusalem and he feared that the information had been transmitted to the Roman Christians.

[27]The Greek has no article between the preposition and *pisteōs* in reference to Christ. In English one can phrase the objective genitive without an article between the initial preposition and the noun ("from faith in Christ"), but the subjective genitive requires an article ("from *the* faith of Christ").

simpler and more common expression "from faith" (*ek pisteōs*).[28] Both interpretations require comment.

Faith *in* Christ is probably the more common interpretation and may be supported by Gal 3:26 which uses the preposition "in." In that interpretation, however, although faith in what God has done in Christ, especially through the crucifixion and resurrection, can be seen as a response that brings about justification, one needs to emphasize that God also generates the response—a divine grace given to believe, responding to the divine grace manifested in Christ. The faith *of* Christ is sometimes understood as his fidelity to God's plan, a fidelity that brought about justification. Others find that interpretation weak and prefer to think of the faith manifested by Jesus in going to crucifixion without visible divine support, a portrayal that may be justified by the passion narratives of Mark and Matt and by Heb 5:8. Martyn contends that Gal 2:20–21 shows that Christ's faith is Christ's faithful death. Still others combine the two approaches and suggest that Christ's faith manifested in his death is given to his followers through faith in Christ.[29] To survey the discussion among scholars[30] and to ask what all this means for understanding Paul is a basic exercise in the study of Pauline theology.

Issues and Problems for Reflection

(1) There is a considerable literature on the opponents of Paul in Galatia,[31] involving different proposals for identifying them. Since the early 20th century a few scholars have argued that simultaneously Paul was struggling against two groups: Judaizing Christians from Jerusalem who insisted the Gentiles should be circumcised and (either Jewish or Gentile) libertine proponents of the Spirit who claimed that believers could gratify the desires of the flesh.[32] It would have been to the second group that Paul directed 5:16–26. Another proposal is that the preachers did not come from the outside but from inside the Galatian community, e.g., Jewish Christians challenging uncircumcised Gentile members of the community. Still another proposal (Schmithals, *Paul* 13–64) is that the preachers were gnostics who advocated circumcision as a mystical rite that would bring the Galatians to a higher

[28]Gal 3:7,8,9,11,12,24; 5:5; also "through [*dia*] faith" (3:14); "from the hearing of [with] faith" (3:2,5); or simply "faith" (1:23; 3:23,25; 5:6,22; 6:10).

[29]See also A. J. Hultgren, NovT 22 (1980), 248–63; B. Dodd, JBL 114 (1995), 470–73.

[30]For "faith of": Hays, *Faith;* M. D. Hooker, NTS 35 (1989), 321–42; S. K. Williams, CBQ 49 (1987), 431–47; D. A. Campbell, JBL 113 (1994), 265–85. For "faith in": Fitzmyer, *Romans* 345–46 (with bibliography); R. A. Harrisville, NovT 36 (1994), 233–41.

[31]See Brinsmead, Howard, Jewett, Martyn ("Law-Observant"), Munck, Russell (useful summary), and Wilson in the bibliography below.

[32]See J. H. Ropes, *The Singular Problem of the Epistle to the Galatians* (Cambridge, MA: Harvard, 1929).

state of perfection, with or without the Law (6:13). In the majority judgment these proposals introduce unnecessary complications and bypass the dominant evidence that *one group of Jewish Christian preachers came to Galatia, demanding circumcision of Gentiles who became followers of Christ.*

(2) We saw on pp. 469, 472 above that Paul and the preachers disagreed about the interpretation of the Abraham/Sarah/Hagar story, depending on how they combined the motifs of Gen 12, 15, and 17 (God's promise that in Abraham the Gentiles would be blessed; the faith of Abraham that was credited as righteousness; and the covenant of circumcision). Now both Paul and the preachers employed a style of OT interpretation quite different from much of modern exegesis, often because their exegesis, although quite at home in the Judaism of the time, was very free and more-than-literal by our standards (see Chapter 2 above, subsection D). Granted the difference between ancient and modern exegesis, it is worth exploring this question: Which would be the more convincing to modern readers drawing on the literal meaning of the OT, Paul's or the preachers' application of the Abraham story to the issue of whether Gentile believers in Christ should be circumcised if they wished fully to be justified as children of Abraham?

(3) Occasionally, again according to modern standards, there is a problem with Paul's use of the OT because of the textual reading that underlies his interpretation. A famous example is worth considering, namely the reference to faith in Hab 2:3–4, an obscure passage that appears with remarkable diversity in the Hebrew OT, the Greek OT, the DSS, the Letter to the Hebrews, and in Paul's citations in Gal and Rom. (a) According to the Masoretic Hebrew text, the prophet, complaining about injustice against the background of the Neo-Babylonian (Chaldean) conquests *ca.* 600 BC, is told to await a vision that will surely come even if it delays. In contrast to the inflated arrogant person who is not upright, "the just because of *his* faith/fidelity shall live," i.e., presumably because of his fidelity to or trust in the God of the covenant. (b) The LXX translation of Hab, although it speaks of a vision, says even if *he* delays, wait for him, for he will surely come; thus it understands the vision to be of one who comes, perhaps the king of the Chaldeans as God's instrument. God will be displeased if the one in the vision draws back, but "the just/righteous from *my* fidelity shall live," i.e., God's fidelity to promises made. (c) In the DSS commentary on Hab (1QpHab 7:5–8:3) the vision is explained by the Righteous Teacher, and it applies to the community of those who keep the Law. They will be freed from persecution "because of their deeds and because of *their* fidelity to the Righteous Teacher," i.e., because of their observing his interpretation of the Law. (d) The author of Heb 10:37–39 follows the LXX with some changes, seemingly interpreting the coming one in the vision to be Jesus in his second

coming. "My just one from faith shall live," i.e., by being faithful until Jesus comes. (e) In Gal 3:11 (Rom 1:17) Paul writes, "The just/righteous from [= through] faith will live," interpreting Hab 2:3–4 to mean that the just live by faith in or fidelity to Jesus Christ.

(4) The preceding paragraph suggests that some of Paul's arguments for his position on faith and Law might not in themselves be very convincing. Although he offers them, we would be mistaken to think that he derived his position from those arguments. His position is an expression of the gospel that did not come to him from human teachers but through a revelation (*apokalypsis,* unveiling) of Jesus Christ (1:12).[33] That revelation gave Paul a new perspective whereby he could see how God transformed the world through the crucifixion of Christ, and in 3:23,25 he gives an example of how his view changed. Thus, although he has shaped some of the vocabulary and reasoning of Gal in light of the propaganda of the preachers, much of what he affirms about Christ, faith, and freedom could have been said even if the preachers had never arrived. Drawing together the *positive* message of Gal, independent of his polemics, is very helpful in understanding Paul. Note in particular the famous christological affirmation of 4:4–7.

(5) Gal contrasts the Law (32 times) and freedom (11 times with cognates). One of the attractions of the preachers' message may have been the clear ethical directives contained in the Law. Freedom is attractive but needs definition, as we see when we list freedom from sin, freedom from the Law, freedom from obligation and control, freedom for doing what one wishes, freedom for love and service. Freedom can leave the door open to license, as seemingly it had done in Galatia. Paul counterattacks by criticizing a misunderstanding of freedom (5:13) and by warning those who walk by the Spirit not to be involved in "works of the flesh" that he lists (5:17–21). Ironically his very words have become a type of law guiding Christians on these points. In pastoral practice what is the interplay between responsible freedom and clear directives that border on law?

(6) In an apocalyptic mind-set such as Paul's, there is little time for changing this world's social structures. Consequently the famous denial of difference between Jew and Greek, slave and free, male and female (Gal 3:28) is not primarily a statement of social or political equality. It is a statement of equality through Christ in God's plan of salvation: "You are all one in Christ Jesus." The same Paul who phrased it was capable of sanctioning inequalities among Christians: The Gentiles are but a wild olive branch grafted onto the cultivated tree of Israel; those who were slaves when called to Christ

[33]M. Winger, JSNT 53 (1994), 65–86, shows that the gospel itself is not a matter of tradition received by Paul as are descriptions of it, which can vary (Rom 1:3–4). When Paul proclaimed the gospel to the Galatians, their apprehension of it was by divine power.

should stay in that state; women should not be permitted to speak in the churches and should be subordinate (Rom 11:24; I Cor 7:20–21; 14:34). Nevertheless, many Christians recognize a gospel dynamism in Paul's statement that may or even should go beyond his vision. How is that effected theologically without unjustifiably making 3:28 an anticipation of the French Revolution ideal of *égalité*?

(7) Marcion's NT canon was heavily Pauline: Luke and ten Pauline letters (beginning with Gal!). His rejection of the Old Testament and the whole heritage from Judaism is generally looked on as an extreme derivative from Paulinism. Martyn, TBOB 2.283, quotes a memorable sentence from F. Overbeck, "Paul had only one student who understood him, Marcion—and this student misunderstood him." On the other hand, the Jewish Christians of the 2d century came to hate Paul as one who had distorted the Jewish heritage and hindered the success of the gospel among Jews. Going through Gal to find statements about the Law that might feed Marcion's absolutism and later Jewish Christian antagonism allows one to see how Scripture can be read in a way never dreamed of by the author.

Bibliography on Galatians

COMMENTARIES AND STUDIES IN SERIES: Betz, H. D. (Hermeneia, 1979); Bruce, F. F. (NIGTC, 1982); Burton, E. D. (ICC, 1921); Cole, R. A. (TNTC, 1989); Cousar, C. B. (IBC, 1982); Dunn, J.D.G. (BNTC, 1993; NTT, 1993); Fung, R.Y.K. (NICNT, 1988); Guthrie, D. (NCBC, 1974); Krentz, E. (AugC, 1985); Longenecker, R. N. (WBC, 1990); **Martyn, J. L.** (AB, 1997); Matera, F. J. (SP, 1992); Osiek, C. (NTM, 1980); Schneider, G. (NTSR, 1969); Ziesler, J. A. (EC, 1992).

BIBLIOGRAPHIES: Vaughan, W. J., RevExp 69 (#4; 1972), 431–36; Wagner, G., EBNT (1996).

Baasland, E., "Persecution: A Neglected Feature in the Letter to the Galatians," ST 38 (1984), 135–50.

Barclay, J.M.G., *Obeying the Truth: A Study of Paul's Ethics in Galatians* (Edinburgh: Clark, 1988).

Barrett, C. K., *Freedom and Obligation: A Study of the Epistle to the Galatians* (Philadelphia: Westminster, 1985).

Betz, H. D., "The Literary Composition and Function of Paul's Letter to the Galatians," NTS 21 (1974–75), 353–73.

Bligh, J., *Galatians* (London: St. Paul, 1969). Useful if one can leave aside his attempt to fit the letter into chiastic structure.

Boers, H., *The Justification of the Gentiles: Letters to the Galatians and the Romans* (Peabody, MA: Hendrickson, 1994). Semiotic exegesis.

Borgen, P., *Paul Preaches Circumcision and Pleases Men* (Trondheim: Tapir, 1983).

Brinsmead, B. H., *Galatians—Dialogical Response to Opponents* (SBLDS 65; Chico, CA: Scholars, 1982).

Buckel, J., *Free to Love. Paul's Defense of Christian Liberty in Galatians* (LTPM 15; Leuven: Peeters, 1993).
Cosgrove, C. H., *The Cross and the Spirit: A Study in the Argument and Theology of Galatians* (Macon, GA: Mercer, 1988).
Dunn, J.D.G., *Jesus, Paul and the Law: Studies in Mark and Galatians* (Louisville: W/K, 1990).
Ebeling, G., *The Truth of the Gospel: An Exposition of Galatians* (Philadelphia: Fortress, 1985).
Gaston, L., *Paul and the Torah* (Vancouver: Univ. of British Columbia, 1987).
Gordon, T. D., "The Problem at Galatia," *Interpretation* 41 (1987), 32–43.
Hansen, G. W., *Abraham in Galatians: Epistolary and Rhetorical Contexts* (JSNTSup 29; Sheffield: JSOT, 1989).
Hays, R. B., "Christology and Ethics in Galatians," CBQ 49 (1987), 268–90.
———, *The Faith of Jesus Christ: An Investigation of the Narrative Substructure of Galatians 3:1–4:11* (SBLDS 56; Chico, CA: Scholars, 1983).
Hong, I.-G., *The Law in Galatians* (JSNTSup 81; Sheffield: JSOT, 1993).
Howard, G. E., *Paul: Crisis in Galatia* (SNTSMS 35; 2d ed.; Cambridge Univ., 1990).
Jewett, R., "The Agitators and the Galatian Congregation," NTS 17 (1970–71), 198–212.
Lightfoot, J. B., *St. Paul's Epistle to the Galatians* (London: Macmillan, 1865).
Lührmann, D., *Galatians* (Minneapolis: A/F, 1992).
Lull, D. J., *The Spirit in Galatia* (SBLDS 49; Chico, CA: Scholars, 1980).
MacDonald, D. R., *There Is No Male and Female: The Fate of a Dominical Saying in Paul and Gnosticism* (Philadelphia: Fortress, 1986).
Martyn, J. L., "A Law-Observant Mission to the Gentiles," SJT 38 (1985), 307–24.
———, "Galatians" in TBOB 2. 271–84. Anticipates his AB commentary.
Munck, J., "The Judaizing Gentile Christians," in *Paul and the Salvation of Mankind* (Richmond: Knox, 1959), 87–134.
Räisänen, H., "Galatians 2.16 and Paul's Break with Judaism," NTS 31 (1985), 543–53.
Ramsay, W. M., *A Historical Commentary on St. Paul's Epistle to the Galatians* (New York: Putnam's, 1900). A major proponent of the South Galatian theory.
Ridderbos, H. N., *The Epistle of Paul to the Churches of Galatia* (NICNT; 8th ed.; Grand Rapids: Eerdmans, 1953).
Russell, W., "Who Were Paul's Opponents in Galatia?" BSac 147 (1990), 329–50.
Thielman, F., *From Plight to Solution: A Jewish Framework for Understanding Paul's View of the Law in Galatians and Romans* (NovTSup 61: Leiden: Brill, 1989).
Tyson, J. B., " 'Works of Law' in Galatians," JBL 92 (1973), 423–31.
Williams, S. K., "*Promise* in Galatians: A Reading of Paul's Reading of Scripture," JBL 107 (1988), 709–20.
———, "Justification and the Spirit in Galatians," JSNT 29 (1987), 91–100.
Wilson, R. M., "Gnostics—in Galatia?" *Studia Evangelica* 4 (1968), 358–67.
Yates, R., "Saint Paul and the Law in Galatians," ITQ 51 (1985), 105–24.

CHAPTER 20

LETTER TO THE PHILIPPIANS

In some ways this is the most attractive Pauline letter, reflecting more patently than any other the warm affection of the apostle for his brothers and sisters in Christ. Indeed, Phil has been classified an example of the rhetoric of friendship. It contains one of the best-known and loved NT descriptions of the graciousness of Christ: one who emptied himself and took on the form of a servant, even unto death on a cross. Nevertheless, Phil is plagued by much-debated difficulties. We cannot be certain where Paul was when he wrote it and hence the date of its composition. Moreover, we are uncertain of its unity, for some would divide the present document into two or three originally distinct letters. But let us discuss the letter as it now stands before turning to such debates. After the *Background* and the *General Analysis* of Phil, subsections will be devoted to: *Hymns and the Christological hymn of 2:5–11, From where and when, Unity, Issues for reflection,* and *Bibliography.*

The Background

As we recalled on p. 456 above, Paul had crossed over by sea with Silas and Timothy from the Province of Asia (Asia Minor or present-day Turkey) to Macedonia (Europe, present-day northern Greece) in AD 50–51. Passing the mountainous island of Samothrace, they landed at the port of Neapolis, where the great Roman highway across Macedonia, the Via Egnatia, had an access coming down to the sea. It is dubious that such a long highway was always well maintained in these early imperial times, so that Philippi, astride the Egnatia some ten miles inland, depended heavily on commerce coming up the short access road from the Mediterranean. This site, to which the missionaries immediately went, was a major Roman city, where a century before (42 BC) Mark Antony and Octavian (Augustus) had defeated Brutus and Cassius, the assassins of Julius Caesar, and had settled the veterans from the victorious armies.[1] Here Paul proclaimed the gospel and founded his

[1]The earlier history of this city (brought under Macedonian dominion in 356 BC by Philip II, father of Alexander the Great, and named after him; then brought under Roman control in 168 BC) is not relevant for our purposes. Acts 16:12 correctly describes it as a *kolōnia* (a settlement of retired Roman troops). Latin was the official language, but commercial contacts with neighboring cities

Summary of Basic Information

DATE: *Ca.* 56 if from Ephesus. (Or 61–63 from Rome, or 58–60 from Caesarea.)

TO: The Christians at Philippi, a Roman colony (Acts 17:12) where army veterans were allotted property after battles in the civil wars (42 BC), and like Thessalonica (farther west) an important commercial city on the Via Egnatia. Evangelized by Paul *ca.* AD 50 on his "Second Missionary Journey" (see Table 6 in Chapter 16 above for Revisionist Chronology).

AUTHENTICITY: Not seriously disputed.

UNITY: Scholarship about evenly divided: That two or three letters have been combined to make up Philippians is widely suggested, but a respectable case can be made for unity.

INTEGRITY: Today no major theory of interpolations. In the past, proposed interpolations for theological reasons: "bishops and deacons" (1:1), or the christological hymn (2:6–11).

FORMAL DIVISION (of existing, unified letter):

A. Opening Formula: 1:1–2
B. Thanksgiving: 1:3–11
C. Body: 1:12–4:20: Mixture of Paul's prison situation; exhortations, warning against false teachers, gratitude to the Philippians
D. Concluding Formula: 4:21–23.

DIVISION ACCORDING TO CONTENTS:

1:1–11: Address/greeting and Thanksgiving
1:12–26: Paul's situation in prison and attitude toward death
1:27–2:16: Exhortation based on example of Christ (christological hymn)
2:17–3:1a: Paul's interest in the Philippians and planned missions to them
3:1b–4:1: Warning against false teachers; Paul's own behavior (a separate letter?)
4:2–9: Exhortation to Euodia and Syntyche: unity, joy, higher things
4:10–20: Paul's situation and the Philippians' generous gifts
4:21–23: Concluding greeting, blessing.

first church in Europe (Acts 16:11–15; Phil 4:15). A tribute to his planting is paid almost a century later by Polycarp, who (*Philippians* 1:2) speaks of the firmly rooted faith of the Philippians, famous in years past and still flourishing.

Reading Acts 16 one gets the impression of a relatively brief stay and some success among Jews and Gentiles, despite civic harassment. At the beginning (16:13–15) by a stream outside the city gate, Lydia, a merchant woman from Thyatira who sold purple goods and who was attracted to Juda-

meant that Greek was also spoken. Philippi was administered under *ius italicum,* or Roman law applicable within Italy. That may explain why in Acts 16:38–39, when the magistrates find out that they have been maltreating Roman citizens (Paul and Silas), they apologize. Acts 16:12 also describes Philippi as a "first/leading city of the district of Macedonia," but it was not the capital city of either this district of Macedonia or the province (respectively, Amphipolis and Thessalonica, mentioned in Acts 17:1).

ism ("a worshiper of God"), was baptized with her household and offered her house for Paul to stay.[2] This story seems to reflect accurately social realities in Philippi, and especially the prominent position played by women. Some confirmation may be supplied in Phil 4:2 by Paul's mentioning two women, Euodia and Syntyche, who are now bickering but who had been his evangelistic co-workers there. Their names and those of Epaphroditus and Clement in 2:25; 4:3 suggest that there was a high percentage of Gentiles among the Philippian Christians.

More conversions at Philippi are recorded in Acts 16:16–40. The fact that Paul had driven out the spirit from a fortune-telling slave girl caused the owners to haul him and Silas before the local magistrates as troublesome Jews. No wonder that Paul described his time at Philippi as one "when we suffered and were shamefully treated" (I Thess 2:2). Yet, although they had been stripped, beaten, and imprisoned, when an earthquake jarred open the prison doors, Paul and Silas refused to escape—a gesture that led to the conversion of the jailer and his household. Eventually the magistrates apologized for mishandling Roman citizens but asked them to depart, and so they set out west along the Via Egnatia for Thessalonica.[3] With that background, let us look at this letter to "all the saints in Christ Jesus who are at Philippi, with bishops and deacons" (1:1).

General Analysis of the Message

Although my treatment of most of the Pauline letters moves sequentially, following the traditional letter format,[4] here as with I Thess, because Paul's thought shifts back and forth, I suggest that readers go through the letter quickly to get a surface impression of the contents, and then turn to this *Analysis* that highlights the main issues.

Those converted at Philippi by Paul entered into a unique partnership with

[2]Archaeological evidence (V. Abrahamsen, BA 51 [1988], 46–56) of native Thracian and Eastern cults *outside* the Roman city has led to the speculation that Jews also worshiped there, whence the presence outside the gate of both Lydia and Paul. Thyatira was in Lydia, and slaves were sometimes named after their homeland. Since wealthy people (especially women of a household) bought purple, Lydia would have had good contacts for Paul in Philippi.

[3]Acts 17:1. Had Paul been in Philippi again between this first visit and the time he wrote Phil? If he wrote it from Ephesus, we have no evidence that he was at Philippi again *before* he came to Ephesus to spend three years there (54–56); but he may have visited Macedonia and Philippi during that stay (Chapter 23 below, n. 3). If Paul wrote Phil from Caesarea or Rome (58–60 or 61–63), he did go to Macedonia *after* his Ephesus stay on the way to Corinth (*ca.* 57: Acts 19:21; 20:1; I Cor 16:5; II Cor 2:13; 7:5) and then again (specifically to Philippi) after he was in Corinth, on his way to Caesarea and Jerusalem (*ca.* 58: Acts 20:3,6; Rom 15:25–26?).

[4]In addition to the divisions of Phil suggested on the Summary Page, a chiastic arrangement is proposed by A. B. Luter and M. V. Lee, NTS 41 (1995), 89–101, where the prologue in 1:3–11 is matched by the epilogue in 4:10–20; 1:12–26 by 4:6–9, etc.

him (1:5) that lasted from the moment he left for Thessalonica (to which they sent gifts several times: Phil 4:15–16; see also II Cor 11:9) until this very moment when he was writing from prison.[5] Their sending Epaphroditus to Paul has been a new attestation of this fidelity; and now, because of concern over that valuable co-worker's health, Paul has sent him back (4:18; 2:25–26). A strong bond of friendship colors this letter that expresses Paul's gratitude and keeps the Philippians informed; indeed the human attraction of Paul the man is revealed in their loyalty. One cannot dismiss simply as letter-form his emotional words to the Philippians, written in a context that had brought him face to face with the possibility of his own death: "I hold you in my heart" (1:7); "With God as my witness, I yearn for all of you with the affection of Christ Jesus" (1:8); "My beloved and longed-for brothers [and sisters], my joy and my crown" (4:1). Besides the strong attestation of gratitude and friendship, which may be considered the main motivation for the letter, there are important indications about Paul's outlook from prison and the situation at Philippi that need to be considered.

PAUL'S OUTLOOK FROM PRISON: The letter reflects thoughts forced on Paul by his imprisonment for preaching the gospel. *First,* he is not despondent despite what he is suffering. His imprisonment, although made difficult by the legal charge and the guards, advances the gospel since clearly he is suffering for Christ (1:12–13; 3:8); and others have been emboldened by his example to preach without fear (1:14). Unfortunately some are doing that in a spirit of rivalry in order to outdo Paul (1:15),[6] and he shows contempt for such competitiveness both in Phil 1:18 and in the roughly contemporaneous I Cor 1:13; 3:5–9. The preachers do not matter; the only thing that matters is that Christ be preached.

Second, reflection on death is brought on by Paul's current situation, as witnessed both in Phil and the Corinthian correspondence. (It contributes to discussions on pp. 437–38 above by making us wonder to what extent Paul's theology on basic issues developed in the course of time.) Earlier, in I Thess 4:17, Paul used the language of: "We who are alive" at the coming of Christ. If that is not just an editorial "we," Paul expected to survive till the parousia. But in Phil 1:20–26 he wrestles with the possibility of dying

[5]Phil 1:7,13,17; 4:10. Throughout I shall accept the hypothesis that Paul wrote Phil at Ephesus *ca.* 56; in the other hypotheses (Caesarea [58–60], Rome [61–63]) the support of the Philippians for Paul had lasted even longer—as much as ten years! Paul supported himself rather than beg money of members of a community while he was working among them; but seemingly, once he had moved on, he would accept money sent him by way of support for continuing his ministry elsewhere.

[6]Rivalry among preachers or at least among their adherents seems to have been common in these early communities. According to I Cor 1:11–12 groups at Corinth were formed around Paul, Apollos, and Cephas (Peter). Acts 18:24–28 reports that just before Paul came to Ephesus for his three-year stay (54–56), Apollos had been there (and then had gone on to Corinth: 19:1).

(also II Cor 5:1–10), trying to decide whether the immediate access to Christ provided by death is better than the continued ministry of proclaiming Christ. In Phil 3:10–11 Paul speaks of sharing Christ's suffering "that somehow I may attain the resurrection from the dead"—is he contemplating martyrdom?[7]

THE SITUATION AT PHILIPPI: Paul wants the Philippian Christians to be blameless, shining as lights amid a crooked and perverse generation and holding fast to the word of life, so that he will know that he has not run in vain (Phil 2:14–16). Paul wishes to hear that they stand firm in one spirit, striving with one mind for the faith of the gospel—a *koinōnia* of the Spirit (1:27; 2:1). Yet there are some who are troubling the Philippian church. How many groups does Paul have in mind?[8] At least three distinct attitudes are reprimanded in the text.

First, there is internal dissension at Philippi even among those, like Euodia and Syntyche, who had labored side by side with Paul (4:2–3).[9] The cause of the dissension is not clear, but given human nature it probably reflected conceit and a lack of humility which Paul condemns (see 2:2–4). Indeed, it is against conceit and pushing one's own interest that Paul holds up Christ as an example of self-giving service in the christological hymn of 2:5–11 (subsection below).

Second, apart from the squabbling adherents who had worked with Paul, there is an external opposition to the Philippian Christians that causes them to suffer (1:28–29). Seemingly this continues the type of harassment to which Paul himself was subjected when he first came there and which he has also encountered at Ephesus (1:30; Acts 19:23–20:1), namely, people complaining about the strange teaching of the Christians because it does not acknowledge the gods, and appealing to the local authorities to arrest or expel them. Nothing can be done about such injustice, but God will overcome.

Third, there are the workers of evil (3:2–3) whom Paul calls dogs,[10] and whom the Philippians should look out for. They mutilate the flesh, seemingly

[7]R. E. Otto, CBQ 57 (1995), 324–40.

[8]As many as eighteen different analyses of the adversaries have been proposed (see Gunther, *St. Paul's* 2). Some of the multiplication is unnecessary. Those who preach Christ out of envy of Paul (1:15–18) may be at the place of his imprisonment, not at Philippi.

[9]Paul asks someone ("My true *syzyge*") to intervene in the dispute; it is not clear whether that means "my true yokefellow" or "my true Syzygos." Is this the "we companion" of Acts 16:10–16 who came with Paul to Philippi in 50–51 and seemingly stayed there until 58 (20:6)? See p. 325 above.

[10]Paul's use could simply reflect an epithet familiar to Jews (Isa 56:10–11; Matt 7:6; Mark 7:27). Some, however, see here a reference to Cynic preachers since the name "Cynic" (*Kynikos*) was pejoratively derived from *kyōn, kynos,* "dog," supposedly reflecting the disgusting public behavior (urinating and masturbating) associated polemically with them. Yet the Philippian context does not point to such behavior.

by circumcision; and believers in Jesus who worship in the spirit should put no faith in such emphasis on the flesh. Paul can refute these adversaries by describing his own impeccable Jewish credentials—even though he counts all that as loss when compared to the supreme gain of knowing Christ Jesus the Lord (3:4–11). We are not far here from Paul's attack in the roughly contemporaneous Gal on those who insisted on circumcision, namely, Christian Jews. Some think that the Phil passage is a general warning in case such people show up; for, if they were already at work in Philippi, Paul would have devoted more of the letter to them. Or else they may be just beginning to appear in small numbers at Philippi, whereas in Galatia they were having great success.[11]

What complicates the further diagnosis of this third group of adversaries is the tendency of scholars to interpret other parts of chap. 3 as referring to them. Before we enter into details, readers need to be cautioned about such a use of chap. 3 to reconstruct a historical situation,[12] since it shows a certain thematic parallelism to the christological message of chap. 2. (That parallelism also creates doubt that chap. 3 was originally a separate letter, as many scholars maintain; see below.) Just as Paul asked the Philippians to have the mind of Christ (2:5), he can say to them, "Join in imitating me" (3:17). Similar to Christ who was in the image of God and yet emptied himself and took on the form of a servant, Paul, who once had confidence in his fleshly origins as a circumcised Israelite and blameless Pharisee, counted all that as rubbish for the sake of Christ (3:4–9). And just as Christ was elevated, so also Paul, who emphasizes that he is not already perfect, presses upward to God in Christ Jesus (3:12–14). If one accepts such parallelism, how much can be diagnosed from chap. 3 about adversaries?

Is Paul's acknowledgment of imperfection sufficient warrant for theorizing that the adversaries had gnostic leanings, claiming to be perfect and professing a radically realized eschatology in which Christ had already come?[13] In 3:18–19 Paul reiterates a warning given in times past about those who live as enemies of the cross of Christ, making the belly their god, glorying in their shame, and setting their mind on earthly things (implicitly unlike

[11]Somewhat combining what I have designated as the second and third adversaries, M. Tellbe, JSNT 55 (1994), 97–121, argues that the Judaizers were trying to persuade the Philippian Christians that if they were circumcised, they would be tolerated by the Romans as Jews.

[12]D. J. Doughty, NTS 41 (1995), 102–22, argues that 3:2–21 is not addressing a particular community situation involving real opponents; rather it is a deuteroPauline characterization of persons outside the community.

[13]This thesis is related to the detection of gnostic background in the christological hymn of 2:5–11, to the use of *gnōsis* in 3:8, and to the designation "enemies of the cross" in 3:18 (in the sense of denying that Jesus died on the cross and therefore rejecting the resurrection).

Christ, who has been exalted to heavenly things: 2:9–11). Are those people the same as the Judaizing workers of evil of 3:2–3, now described as stressing Mosaic food laws and glorying in the circumcised male organ?[14] (Yet the warning in 3:2–3 seems to be against a new, not a past danger.) Or is this a more general condemnation of libertines based on the inevitabilities of unfettered human desires—a common and not necessarily specific charge? Or even a condemnation of libertines in Ephesus from where he is writing and where he struggled with "wild beasts" (I Cor 15:32). Our inability to answer those questions about 3:12 and 3:18–19 cautions against complicating the clearer condemnation in 3:2–3 of adversaries who would try to put emphasis on circumcision and confuse the Philippians. However, since most of what Paul says about himself and his outlook in chap. 3 would have its value no matter who and how distinct the adversaries were, and the description of those adversaries affects relatively few verses, a decision about them is not essential to reading Phil intelligently.

Hymns in NT Letters and the Christological Hymn of 2:5–11

HYMNS IN NT LETTERS. Although there are references to Christians singing "psalms and hymns and spiritual songs,"[15] the NT does not contain a collected book of hymns similar to the OT Book of Psalms, the DSS *Hodayot* (1QH), or the (Pharisees') *Psalms of Solomon.* Rather 1st-century Christian canticles and hymns are incorporated into larger writings of another genre, e.g., a gospel, letter, apocalyptic vision. (Compare I Macc 4:30–33; II Macc 1:24–29.) Sometimes the NT hymn or song is clearly designated, as in the heavenly singing of Rev 4:8,10–11; 5:9. The canticles of the Lucan infancy narratives, while not designated as songs, are set off from the surrounding text as oracles or praise (p. 232 above). The Johannine Prologue by its very situation at the beginning of the Gospel stands apart.

A greater problem is presented by the proposal that there are hymns woven into the heart of letters and detectable only by scholarly investigation. Most often nothing in the context states that a hymn is being introduced and quoted, although occasionally the transition to the incorporated hymn

[14]H. Koester, NTS 8 (1961–62), 317–32, responds affirmatively: Christian missionaries of Jewish origin preaching perfection based on the Law and Jewish practices—a perfection they had achieved.

[15]Col 3:16; Eph 5:19; also Acts 16:25; Heb 2:12; I Cor 14:15,26; Jas 5:13. "Psalm" is a Christian composition, evidently thought comparable to OT psalms. The letter of Pliny to Trajan (10.96–97), *ca.* 110, says that Christians met before dawn on a stated day and sang in alternation (antiphonally?) "a hymn to Christ as a God." The earliest preserved Christian hymn collection may be the *Odes of Solomon,* a Jewish Christian collection in Syriac of the 2d century. The earliest preserved musically annotated Christian hymn seems to be Oxyrhynchus Papyrus 1786 of the early 3d century.

is awkward. Among the criteria for detecting a hymn the following have been suggested:[16]

(a) Worship milieu, e.g., a proposed baptismal setting for Eph 5:14; and the hymns of I Peter.

(b) Introductory formulae, e.g., "It is said" in Eph 5:14; "We confess" in I Tim 3:16; or in the case of christological hymns, a clause introduced by a relative pronoun, "The one who . . ." (Phil 2:6; Col 1:15; I Tim 4:16), extended by causal connectives.

(c) Rhythmic style, parallel patterns, lines or strophes of equal length, e.g., the series of six aorist passive verbs in I Tim 3:16; the parallel descriptions of God's Son in Col 1:15–16 and 1:18b–19. This is not rhyming poetry; indeed some would argue for prose hymns.

(d) Vocabulary different from that customarily used by the epistolary author—only applicable if the author did not compose the hymn. Similarly a distinctive syntax is often found, e.g., avoiding conjunctions (thus, parataxis).

(e) Not a criterion but often characteristic of the hymns is a high christology, e.g., the description of the Word as God in John 1:1; or of the Son as the one in, for, and through whom all things were created (Col 1:16); or of Christ Jesus as one given the name above every other name (Phil 2:9). Among the themes prominent in the christology are creation, the struggle against evil leading to restoration, and Jesus' death leading to resurrection (exaltation, enthronement). Ps 110:1, "The Lord said to my Lord, 'Sit at my right hand,'" is a motif in a number of hymns (Rom 8:34; Eph 1:20–22; I Pet 3:22), probably on the principle that OT psalms could be seen as addressed to Christ (Heb 1:5,8,13). Some of the hymns addressed to Christ are similar to hymns to God.[17] Col 3:16 relates psalms and hymns to teaching the word of Christ, and so they became early vehicles of a christological gospel. Hengel ("Hymns" 192) claims, "The hymn to Christ . . . is as old as the community itself."

(f) Another characteristic is the free redactional addition of explanatory clauses or phrases to traditional hymns to apply them more directly to the author's theme (see n. 20 and 21 below; also n. 9 in Chapter 27).

The criteria are not easy to apply, and as a result the detection of hymns is an inexact "science." That will be illustrated in debates to be reported

[16]The borderline between hymns and confessional formulae is imprecise. For detecting hymns a pioneering work in German was E. Norden, *Agnostos Theos* (Leipzig: Teubner, 1913). Amid a large bibliography, see J. T. Sanders, *The New Testament Christological Hymns* (SNTSMS 15; Cambridge Univ., 1971); E. Stauffer, *NT Theology*, 338–39; M. Hengel, "Hymns and Christology," *Studia Biblica 1978* (JSNTSup 3; Sheffield: Academic, 1980), 173–97; E. Krentz, BR 40 (1995), 50–97.

[17]Compare Eph 5:19 ("to the Lord") to Col 3:16 ("to God"); Rev 4:8–11 (to "the Lord God Almighty") to 5:9 (a new song to the Lamb).

about the individual hymns—debates as to where they end or how they are to be divided or which lines are original. Moreover, the line of demarcation between hymns and confessional formulae (e.g., I Cor 15:3–8) or doxologies (e.g., I Tim 6:15–16) is not clear. The following is a list of hymns often detected by scholars in NT letters (scholarly estimates run from five to thirty); it does not claim to be complete, and those marked with an asterisk would be the most agreed on:

Phil 2:6–11*	Col 1:15–20*	Heb 1:3
I Cor 13	Eph 1:3–14*	I Pet 1:3–5
Rom 3:24–26	Eph 1:20–23	I Pet 1:18–21
Rom 6:1–11	Eph 2:14–18(22)	I Pet 2:21–25
Rom 8:31–39	Eph 5:14*	I Pet 3:18–22
Rom 11:33–36	Titus 3:4–7	
	I Tim 3:16*	
	II Tim 2:11–13*	

Various backgrounds have been suggested for the formation of such hymns. Among the suggested Pagan parallels are the Orphic Hymns (5th–4th centuries BC), the Isis Hymn of Cyme (2d century BC),[18] and the Mithras Liturgy (pp. 87–88 above). Jewish background is supplied by the personified Wisdom poems of the OT (e.g., Prov 1:20–33; 8–9; Sirach 24; Wisdom 7:22ff.; Baruch 3:9ff.) where before the creation of the world Wisdom is created by or proceeds from God, then comes down to dwell among human beings, and offers them the food and drink of the knowledge of God. This portrait of Wisdom was a major element in shaping NT christology (BINTC 205–10).

THE CHRISTOLOGICAL HYMN OF 2:5–11. This description of Christ as a servant to be imitated is the most famous passage in Phil (and indeed among the most memorable lines ever penned by the apostle). There is an enormous literature devoted to it,[19] and a detailed consideration lies beyond the possibilities of this introductory book. Yet these points are worth mentioning by way of acquainting readers with the issues:

- Most think that Paul wrote but did not create these lines; they are probably a prePauline hymn that the Philippians knew and that Paul may have taught them at the time of his first visit.
- The structure of the hymn is debated, e.g., six strophes of three lines each (E.

[18]R. MacMullen and E. N. Lane, *Paganism and Christianity 100–425 C.E.* (Minneapolis: A/F, 1992), includes a number of ancient hymns.

[19]For bibliography see R. P. Martin, *Carmen Christi: Philippians 2:5–11 in Recent Interpretation* (2d ed.; Grand Rapids: Eerdmans, 1983); also N. T. Wright, JTS NS 37 (1986), 321–52.

Lohmeyer),[20] or three strophes of four lines each (J. Jeremias).[21] In its theological flow, the hymn is bipartite, with the theme of lowliness/abasement in 2:6–8 and that of exaltation in 2:9–11.

- Proposals about the background of the hymn (exclusive or in combination) include: gnostic reflections on the Primal Man; the Poimandres tractate in the Hermetic literature (p. 85 above); the Genesis story of Adam and speculations about a second Adam; the Suffering Servant imagery in deuteroIsaiah;[22] the personified figure of divine Wisdom in postexilic Judaism. A relation to the OT is clear; other proposed references are not.
- Also debated is whether the hymn was originally composed in Greek, probably with its origin in the mission that evangelized Greek-speaking Jews, or in Aramaic with its origin in the Palestinian missionary enterprise. A plausible case can be made for the latter and for the possibility that Paul learned the hymn in the late 30s in the first years after his conversion.[23]
- Dispute about the precise focus of the christology is centered on 2:6–7: Christ Jesus "who being in the form [*morphē*] of God, did not think being equal to God a *harpagmon* [something to be clung to or grasped at], but emptied himself having taken the form of a servant, having become [or been born] in a human form." Is "being in the form of God" the same as being equal to God and thus being uncreated (as in the Johannine Prologue: "The Word was God"), or does it mean being in the image/likeness of God (as in Gen 1:27: "God created Adam in His image") and thus lower than being equal to God? Correspondingly, was Christ Jesus already equal to God but did not *cling* to that, or was he offered the possibility to become equal to God and did not *grasp* at it (as did Adam when tempted by the serpent in Gen 3:5: "You will be like gods")? Is the movement in the hymn from Christ's being first in the form of God (i.e., equal to God) to subsequently becoming human and thus taking on the form of a servant? Or does the hymn start with Christ's simultaneously being both in the form (image) of God (which is not the same as equal to God) and human in the form of a servant, and does the movement consist in accepting the form of a servant rather than grasping at becoming equal to God? In other words does the hymn posit an incarnation of a divine figure as does the Johannine Prologue, or is there a play on two Adam-figures (i.e., human archetypal models): the Adam of Gen who was in the image of God but, by ambitiously trying to go higher, went lower through his sin; and Christ

[20]Strophes matching verses thus: A = v. 6; B = 7a–c; C = 7d–8b; D = 9; E = 10; F = 11. "Even death on a cross" in v. 8c is judged to be Paul's addition to the original hymn. (For the subdivision of verses indicated by letters of the alphabet [7a,b,c,d], see p. xxxii above.)

[21]Thus: A = 6–7b; B = 7c–8b; C = 9–11. Besides "even death on a cross" (8c), "of those in heaven and on earth and under the earth" in 10c and "to the glory of God the Father" in 11c are judged to be Paul's additions.

[22]Listing six proposals, D. Seeley, JHC 1 (1994), 49–72, argues that the hymn contrasts the Isaian servant and the Greco-Roman ruler worshiped as divine and all-powerful.

[23]See J. A. Fitzmyer, CBQ 50 (1988), 470–83; also his summary in NJBC 82.48–54.

who was in the image of God but, by humbly choosing to go lower, ultimately was exalted by being given the divine name (2:9–11)?[24] If the hymn is incarnational and was phrased in Aramaic in the 30s, the highest type of NT christology was articulated early indeed.

- Although in itself the hymn is christological, the paraenetic context is soteriological,[25] i.e., it exhorts the addressees for their own salvation to follow the exalted Christ. Rather than looking out for their own interests and seeking to better themselves (2:3–4), the Philippians are to have the mind of a Christ who showed that the way to God is not by grasping at a higher place on the ladder ("upward mobility") but by becoming humbly obedient to God, even unto death on a cross.

From Where and When?

We glean from Phil itself the following items indicative of Paul's situation when he wrote the letter:[26]

(a*) He was in prison (1:7,13,17).
(b) Where he was imprisoned there were members of the praetorian guard (1:13), as well as Christians among "Caesar's household" (4:22).[27]
(c) Paul mentions the possibility that he might die (1:19–21; 2:17): Imminently as condemnation culminating his imprisonment? Or as a missionary's always-possible fate?
(d*) Yet he also hopes to be delivered (1:24–25; 2:25).
(e*) Timothy was with Paul (1:1; 2:19–23).
(f) Christians with different motives in this area, some envious of Paul, have been emboldened to speak the word of God (1:14–18).
(g) There have been frequent contacts between Paul and Philippi through messengers back and forth:
    1. News reached the Philippians of Paul's imprisonment;

[24]See BINTC 133–35. Incarnational interpretations in L. D. Hurst, NTS 32 (1986), 449–57; C. A. Wanamaker, NTS 33 (1987), 179–93; nonincarnational in J. Murphy-O'Connor, RB 83 (1976), 25–50; G. E. Howard, CBQ 40 (1978), 368–87; see also J.D.G. Dunn, *Christology in the Making* (2d ed.; London: SCM, 1989).

[25]Unfortunately this hymn is often studied in itself without reference to its place in the letter's flow of thought. For that context see Kurz, "Kenotic"; and M. D. Hooker in *Jesus und Paulus,* eds. E. E. Ellis and E. Grässer (Göttingen: Vandenhoeck & Ruprecht, 1975), 151–64.

[26]Asterisks indicate features in Phil that are also true in whole or part of Paul's situation when he wrote Phlm (Chapter 21 below). As for Philippians, if it consists of what were originally two or three letters (see next subsection), one could have been written from one place, and another from another place. (For example, chap. 3 does not mention imprisonment.) But that is too uncontrollable a possibility for our purposes here.

[27]I.e., officials, servants, and slaves in the emperor's administration and/or service, both in Rome and throughout the Empire.

2. They sent Epaphroditus with a gift (4:15);[28] but staying with Paul, he became ill, even to the point of death (2:26,30);
3. News reached the Philippians of Epaphroditus' illness;
4. Epaphroditus heard that this news distressed the Philippians;
5. Paul had sent or is now sending Epaphroditus back to Philippi (2:25–30);
6. Paul hopes to send Timothy soon (2:19–23), and indeed to come himself (2:24).

What sites in Paul's known career would fit these details?

CAESAREA (58–60)—first proposed in 1799. After Paul was arrested in Jerusalem, Acts 23:33–26:32 describes how Paul was taken to Caesarea to be tried before Felix, then imprisoned, and left there for two years until the new procurator, Festus, examined him and sent him to Rome. Details *a, b, c, d* above could fit this situation, particularly *ca.* 60, when Felix arrived and gave Paul hope for release. As for *e,* Timothy set out for Jerusalem with Paul and went as far as Troas (20:4–5), but we never hear of him again in Acts. Are we to think that he went on to Jerusalem and Caesarea and remained with Paul for the two years? And, in terms of *f,* did Paul's imprisonment spark rival evangelistic activity among the Christians of Caesarea of whom we heard earlier in Acts 21:8–14, even though all of them seemed favorable to Paul? The greatest difficulty concerns *g.* Philippi is some 900–1,000 miles from Caesarea by the sea route (which would not always be feasible) and well over 1,000 miles by the very difficult land route. Are all those journeys back and forth from Caesarea to Philippi plausible?[29]

ROME (61–63).[30] Acts 28:16,30 reports that Paul, having been brought to Rome, remained under a type of house arrest (by himself, with a soldier to guard him) for two years at his own expense, and was allowed to preach unhindered.[31] As with Caesarea, details *a, b, c, d* could fit Rome; indeed *b*

[28]One could place Paul's imprisonment after the arrival of Epaphroditus, in which case the Philippians would have been sending the gift simply to help Paul's missionary activity (like the gifts sent to him at Thessalonica [Phil 4:16]).

[29]Paul's original plan was to go from Jerusalem to Rome and Spain (Rom 15:24–28); and if he had been released from Caesarea, Philippi would have been on that route provided he wanted to visit churches he had evangelized on the coast of Asia Minor and in Greece. Yet we should remember that the author of Acts, who is our only source for the Caesarea imprisonment, portrays Paul as having no hope he would ever get back to much of that Asia Minor area (Acts 20:25,38).

[30]This was already suggested in the Marcionite Prologue (*ca.* 200?) and remained traditional into modern times, in part because Phil was associated with Col, Eph, and Phlm as four captivity or prison epistles (and Timothy was a co-sender of both Phil and Col). In that hypothesis Col and Eph best fitted the last part of Paul's career (the 60s). If deemed slightly earlier than the others, Phil was dated at the beginning of the Roman detention.

[31]C. S. Wansink, *Imprisonment for the Gospel: The Apostle Paul and Roman Prisons* (JSNTSup 130; Sheffield: Academic, 1996). Perhaps Paul's imprisonment in Rome is attested by *I Clement* 5:7, written from the church of Rome *ca.* AD 96: "Having come to the limits of the West [see Acts 1:8],

could fit Rome better. As for *e,* there is no evidence in Acts that Timothy was with Paul in Rome in 61–63, and the time distance from the last mention of him (at Troas) is greater; but *f* is more easily fulfilled in Rome, since in Acts Paul's own preaching is mentioned and we know from Rom 14 and 16:17–18 that Christians there were of different views.[32] Again the greatest difficulty concerns *g.* From Rome to Philippi the land route southeast along the Via Appia to Brundisium, across the Adriatic Sea by ship to Macedonia, and along the Via Egnatia to Philippi would be somewhat more than 700 miles; and a sea voyage along the west coast of Italy, across the Adriatic, with disembarkation and reembarkation at the Corinthian isthmus, and up the east coast of Greece (a route that might have been followed if the emissaries wanted to visit the Pauline church at Corinth) would be over 900 miles. Although the distances are shorter than those in the Caesarea hypothesis, they are still a formidable obstacle to the frequency of the journeys necessary to explain the evidence of the letter.

EPHESUS (54–56)—proposed at the beginning of the 20th century. Here *a* is a problem, for we have no specific evidence that Paul was in prison at Ephesus. Yet during his three-year stay there, Acts 19:23–41 mentions an uproar in which Paul's companions were hauled before the magistrates, and Paul himself speaks of having fought "wild beasts"[33] at Ephesus in a context that threatened his life (I Cor 15:32) and of having almost received a sentence of death while in Asia (II Cor 1:8–10). Also in II Cor 6:5; 11:23 (written before he was imprisoned at Caesarea and in Rome) Paul speaks of having already undergone many imprisonments.[34] Thus imprisonment at Ephesus is a distinct possibility, and then *b, c, d,* and *f* would offer no difficulty.[35] As for *e,* Timothy was definitely with Paul at Ephesus (I Cor 4:17; 16:10; Acts 19:22); also the details in *g* fit Ephesus better than either Caesarea or Rome. From Ephesus to Philippi a direct sea journey, or one by land to Troas and then by sea, would be only about 400 miles and take seven to

---

and *having testified before rulers,* he thus departed this world and was taken up to the holy place [i.e., heaven]."

[32]Phil 1:15 speaks of some preaching out of *phthonos* ("envy, zeal"); *I Clement* 5:2 reports that because of *phthonos* the greatest pillars (of the church: Peter and Paul) were persecuted to death (at Rome).

[33]A. J. Malherbe, JBL 87 (1968), 71–80, sees "beasts" as Paul's use of traditional polemic language for opponents. Since, however, Ignatius, *Romans* 5:1, uses this language to describe his own being taken under the custody of guards from Syria to Rome, could Paul be going beyond fierce opponents and referring more specifically to those who imprisoned him at Ephesus?

[34]*I Clement* 5:6 has the tradition that Paul was seven times in bonds. Later, as he journeyed to Jerusalem in 58, was part of the reason for avoiding Ephesus (Acts 20:16–17) that he had been in prison there and might be arrested again?

[35]As for *b,* Ephesus was the most important city of the Roman province of Asia and the site of the proconsular headquarters, so that there would have been a major Roman presence there including a *praitōrion.* "Caesar's household" (n. 27 above) could refer to the staff of the imperial bank in Asia.

nine days. Moreover, the references to Timothy just cited show that Paul did send emissaries into Macedonia when he was at Ephesus. An objection to the Ephesus theory is that I Cor, sent from there, mentions a collection to be taken up for the Jerusalem church throughout the whole Pauline missionary territory, and Phil does not.[36] But neither does Gal[37] (or Phlm), plausibly written at Ephesus, even though the collection would be taken in the Galatian area (I Cor 16:1). Paul's stay at Ephesus and subsequent travel to Corinth (whence he would go to Jerusalem) covered a time span of four years. Gathering and bringing a collection to Jerusalem would not have been a matter of urgency throughout the entire period, especially if during that time he was in prison at Ephesus and might die (obviously without getting to Jerusalem). It would have become more urgent toward the end of the Ephesus period when Paul was released from prison and could plan his travels, and then again, when he had left Ephesus and was journeying through Macedonia to Corinth (see II Cor 8–9; Rom 15:26–28—at which time the Macedonian Christians did contribute). Indeed, the collection argument actually works in favor of Ephesus and a dating *ca.* 55: If Phil were written at Caesarea or Rome, that successful collection would have been past history; why, then, in reciting the history of the Philippians' generosity in Phil 4:10–20, does Paul not mention their contribution to it? Moreover, in 4:14–16 Paul reminisces about what seems to have been his first and only visit to Philippi. If he were writing from Caesarea or Rome, he would have been to Philippi at least three times (n. 3 above).

There is no way to decide this issue; but the best arguments seem to be on the side of Ephesus, and the weakest on the side of Caesarea.

Unity: One Letter or Two or Three?

Although the unity of many of the Pauline letters has been questioned in the endless ingenuity of scholarship, only two have remained subjects of major debate: II Cor and Phil. What external and internal evidence causes uncertainty about the unity of Phil (which began to be doubted at the end of the 19th century)? Externally, in the mid-2d century Polycarp (*Philippians* 3:2) mentions Paul's "letters" to the Philippians.[38] If precise, this could refer to the canonical letter and lost ones, or to the canonical letter and II Thess

[36]On the other hand, as indicated throughout this Chapter, there are close parallels between Phil and I Cor.

[37]Gal 2:10 shows that Paul agreed in the Jerusalem meeting (*ca.* AD 49) to remember the poor, but nothing is said in Gal about a planned collection of money in the various Pauline churches to be carried to Jerusalem such as spelled out in the letters of AD 56–58.

[38]Yet *Philippians* 11:3 (preserved only in Latin) seems to speak of the beginning of Paul's "epistle" (singular).

(Chapter 26, n. 9 below), or to the original form of the canonical correspondence before an editor combined several letters into one. Internally, Phil 3:1b ("To write the same things to you is no trouble to me") suggests that Paul might have written previously to the Philippians. If so, was he referring to a lost letter or to an originally independent section of what now has been collected as Phil? At the end of chap. 2 (vv. 23–30) Paul alludes to his travel plans, which he usually does toward the conclusion of his letters; and the "Finally" in the following verse (3:1a) sounds as if he is about to close the letter; yet two chaps. follow. Is it logical to have the sending back of Epaphroditus mentioned (2:25–30) before his arrival bringing gifts to Paul (4:18)? Some think that (if 3:1b–4:3 were an insert from another letter) 3:1a and 4:4 would fit together uniquely well; also then the different adversaries detected in Phil could be assigned to different letters.

As for the letters thought to be combined in Phil, the common denominator in the several theories is that chap. 3[39] constitutes in whole or in part a separate letter:

- *Two original letters* (G. Bornkamm; J. Gnilka; E. J. Goodspeed; L. E. Keck), e.g.,
  I. 3:1b–4:20: A letter when Paul received the gift brought by Epaphroditus;
  II. 1:1–3:1a + 4:21–23: A letter after Epaphroditus recovered from sickness.[40]
- *Three original letters* (more popular: F. W. Beare, J. A. Fitzmyer, R. H. Fuller, H. Koester; E. Lohse, W. Marxsen, W. Schmithals), e.g.,
  I. 4:10–20: A letter acknowledging the gift received by Paul from the Philippians;
  II. 1:1–3:1a + 4:4–7,21–23: A letter urging a worthy life, rejoicing in the Lord;
  III. 3:1b–4:3 + 4:8–9: A corrective and polemical letter.

There is no doubt that the Body of Philippians (1:12–4:20; see Summary Page) has a mixture of material, wherein Paul switches back and forth between autobiographical description (his position in prison and relations with the Philippians through Epaphroditus and Timothy), exhortations, and warnings against false teachers. The division into two or three letters is really an attempt of scholars to rearrange that material more logically and consistently. Yet one cannot find in Phil two or three distinct Opening and Concluding Formulas, so that if originally there were several letters, the compiler

[39]Described variously as beginning in 3:1b or 3:2 and as terminating in 3:21 or 4:1. Those who split 3:1 into two parts often see the first part of the verse (3:1a) looking back to chap. 2, and the second part (3:1b) looking ahead to the warnings about to be given.

[40]A suggested variation detects I: 1:1–3:1a + 4:2–7,10–23 (a pastoral letter written after both the events above) and II: 3:1b–4:1 + 4:8–9 (a polemical letter written after Paul was released from prison and false teachers had arrived).

abbreviated them. Moreover, his logic in moving segments around (e.g., 4:8–9) and combining these letters into the present irregular sequence is far from clear. Favoring unity is the fact that there are rare Pauline words and a community of ideas shared by the proposed two or three letters. Approximately, therefore, an equal number of scholars still maintains that the present form of Phil is the original form. One can postulate that in prison Paul wrote in a "stream of consciousness" style, communicating his grateful acknowledgments of past relationships and present kindnesses, his exhortations and corrections as they came to mind, without recasting them in a totally logical sequence. In any case this debate[41] need not be of great concern to ordinary readers who, given the very divided state of scholarship, are wiser to read the letter in its present sequence, recognizing that it reflects relationships over a period of time and that more than one danger may be envisioned.

Issues and Problems for Reflection

(1) In discussing the unity of Phil, I suggested that the debate over whether the preserved letter represents a compilation from two or three original letters is not of great importance to most readers. That affirmation may be tested by studying one of the theories of compilation and seeing if there are ways in which it affects the basic meaning of Phil.

(2) It is a worthwhile exercise to review the way in which the Christological Hymn is printed in several modern NT translations. What effect, if any, does a decision about the number of strophes and the lines assigned to each (n. 19 and 20 above) have on meaning?

(3) Paul seems remarkably self-revelatory in Phil. Based on its contents, what would have been Paul's strengths as a pastor in relation to the community at Philippi? He is clearly polemic toward the workers of evil in 3:2ff. How effective is what he says in refuting them? Granted that he is not likely to change their minds, how likely is his approach to protect or correct the Philippians whom both he and they are addressing?

(4) Because of his imprisonment Paul reflects several times in this letter on his relationship to Christ and in that way reveals his own "spirituality." For instance, Paul invites his readers to imitate him (3:17) and to imitate Christ (2:5). Indeed, at the beginning of the letter Paul calls himself a servant of Christ to prepare for speaking of Christ as one who took on or accepted

[41]B. D. Rahtjen, NTS 6 (1959–60), 167–73, argues for three letters; and B. S. Mackay, NTS 7 (1960–61), 161–70, rebuts him. Collange, *Philippians,* argues for three letters; and W. J. Dalton, *Biblica* 60 (1979), 97–102, rebuts him. T. E. Pollard, NTS 13 (1966–67), 57–66, traces thematic connections throughout Phil; and J. T. Reed, JBL 115 (1996), 63–90, thinks that 3:1 does not mark a different letter but is a hesitation formula simply indicating a change in theme.

"the form of a servant" in 2:7. Notice that the imitation is not simply a human undertaking (2:13). How practical is such imitation after nearly two thousand years?

(5) In the Opening Formula Paul addresses himself to the saints at Philippi "with the *episkopoi* [overseers/bishops] and *diakonoi* [ministers/deacons]." Discussion of those two groups of functionaries[42] has been colored by modern Christian attitudes toward bishops, favorable and unfavorable. To avoid such an early presence of bishops (of which there is no evidence in the other protoPauline letters) some scholars have dismissed this as a later interpolation or sought to detect Pauline disdain for such dignitaries (implicitly contrasted with the self-designation of Paul and Timothy who claim only to be "servants" of Christ). Many more scholars today caution that the Philippian *episkopoi* were not the same as the functionaries of that name described at a later era in the deuteroPauline Pastorals. (For instance, since secular *episkopoi* were financial officers of groups, could Paul have been addressing those at Philippi who helped raise the money to support him?) Nothing further, however, is said in Phil; and so scholars' statements about these figures involve considerable guessing. A more helpful exercise, employing the evidence of contemporaneous Pauline writings, is to compare the "overseers" at Philippi to "those over you [*proïstamenoi*] in the Lord" in I Thess 5:12, to the "administrators" (*kybernēseis*) in I Cor 12:28, and to "the one who exhorts" (*parakalōn*) in Rom 12:8. To that may be added what Acts 12:17; 15:2,4,6,22,23; 21:18 reports about James and the elders/presbyters at Jerusalem. Seemingly the churches of the 50s were structured, but not in the same way or with universally used titles.

(6) After reflecting on the different views reported in the subsection above about the christology of the hymn in 2:5–11, one may compare themes in that passage to other Pauline and deuteroPauline passages such as I Cor 8:6; II Cor 5:18–19; 8:9; Rom 5:12–19; Col 1:15–20.

(7) Paul identifies himself as having been a Pharisee (3:5; see Acts 23:6); and therefore, even before believing in Jesus, he would have anticipated the resurrection of the dead. We have seen one modification of his belief in I Thess 4:15–17 where he asserts that the dead in Christ will rise to meet him at the parousia. Yet, even before the parousia, Paul thinks that if he departs this life he will be with Christ (Phil 1:23). In 3:11, perhaps rhetorically, he says, "If possible, I may attain the resurrection from the dead."[43] How does one reconcile these expectations? With what modality are such expectations part of Christian hope today?

[42]Collange and Soards take the words in apposition, so that "overseers" and "ministers" refer to only one group of people. Ministry in Paul is a complicated issue, e.g., see Ellis, *Pauline Theology*.

[43]See R. E. Otto, n. 7 above.

(8) The social situation at Philippi when Paul first came may belong more appropriately to the study of Acts 16:12–40, but Lydia was prominent there even as Euodia and Syntyche were important in the community that Paul wrote to five to ten years later (Phil 4:2). Thomas and Portefaix offer material that invites fascinating reflection on what the gospel of Christ may have meant to women in this Roman city that was the first place in Europe evangelized by Paul.

Bibliography on Philippians

COMMENTARIES AND STUDIES IN SERIES (* = plus Philemon; *** = plus Col, Eph, Phlm): **Beare, F. W.** (BNTC, 3d ed., 1973); Bruce, F. F. (NIBC, 1989); Caird, G. B. (NClarBC, 1976***); Craddock, F. B. (IBC, 1985); Fee, G. D. (NICNT, 1995); Getty, M. A. (NTM, 1980*); Gnilka, J. (NTSR, 1971); **Hawthorne, G. F.** (WBC, 1983); Houlden, J. L. (PC, 1970***); Koenig, J. (AugC, 1985*); Marshall, I. H. (EC, 1992; NTT, 1993*); Martin, R. P. (NCBC, 1980: good bibliographies; and TNTC, 2d ed., 1987); Müller, J. J. (NICNT, 1961*); O'Brien, P. T. (NIGTC, 1991); Silva, M. (BECNT, 1992); Thielman, F. (NIVAC, 1995); Vincent, M. R. (ICC, 1955 reprint [orig. 1897]*: still worth consulting); Witherington, B., III (NTIC, 1994).

Barth, K., *The Epistle to the Philippians* (Richmond: Knox, 1962). A distinguished theologian's approach to the work.

Bloomquist, L. G., *The Function of Suffering in Philippians* (JSNTSup 78; Sheffield: JSOT, 1993).

Collange, J.-F., *The Epistle of St. Paul to the Philippians* (London: Epworth, 1979).

Duncan, G. S., "Were St. Paul's Imprisonment Epistles Written from Ephesus?" ExpTim 67 (1955–56), 163–66.

Furnish, V. P., "The Place and Purpose of Phil. III," NTS 10 (1963–64), 80–88.

Garland, D. E., "The Composition and Unity of Philippians," NovT 27 (1985), 141–73. Good bibliography.

Gunther, J. J., *St. Paul's Opponents and Their Background* (NovTSup 35; Leiden: Brill, 1973).

Holladay, C. R., "Paul's Opponents in Philippians 3," *Restoration Quarterly* 12 (1969), 77–90.

Jewett, R., "Conflicting Movements in the Early Church as Reflected in Philippians," NovT 12 (1970), 362–90.

———, "The Epistolary Thanksgiving and the Integrity of Philippians," NovT 12 (1970), 40–53.

Klijn, A.F.J., "Paul's Opponents in Philippians iii," NovT 7 (1965), 278–84.

Kurz, W. S., "Kenotic Imitation of Paul and Christ in Phil 2 and 3," in *Discipleship in the New Testament,* ed. F. Segovia (Philadelphia: Fortress, 1985), 103–26.

Lightfoot, J. B., *St. Paul's Epistle to the Philippians* (4th ed.; London: Macmillan, 1885). A classic.

Marshall, I. H., "Which Is the Best Commentary? 12. Philippians," ExpTim 103 (1991–92), 39–42.

Peterlin, D., *Paul's Letter to the Philippians in the Light of Disunity in the Church* (NovTSup 79; Leiden: Brill, 1995).

Portefaix, L., *Sisters Rejoice. Paul's Letter to the Philippians and Luke-Acts as Received by First-Century Philippian Women* (CBNTS 20; Uppsala/Stockholm: Almqvist, 1988).

Reumann, J., "Philippians 3:20–21—A Hymnic Fragment?" NTS 30 (1984), 593–609.

Schmithals, W., "The False Teachers of the Epistle to the Philippians," *Paul and the Gnostics* (Nashville: Abingdon, 1972), 65–122.

Thomas, W. D., "The Place of Women in Philippi," ExpTim 83 (1971–72), 117–20.

CHAPTER 21

LETTER TO PHILEMON

That Paul wrote this letter is not seriously disputed even by those who contend that he did not write Col, a letter that has the same setting and many of the same dramatis personae as Phlm. Frequently their assumption is that from the genuine Phlm a pseudonymous writer drew the context for Col. Inevitably the question arises as to why both letters might not be pseudepigraphic; but the counterquestion is why would someone bother to create Phlm, a note with such a narrow goal, and attribute it to Paul. Such speculation leaves much to be desired; but in this *Introduction,* one goal of which is to familiarize readers with what seems reasonable to a centrist scholarly majority, Phlm will be accepted as genuinely from Paul, independently of the position taken on Col. After the *Background* and the *General Analysis,* subsections will be devoted to the *Social import of Paul's view of slavery, From where and when,* the *Subsequent career of Onesimus, Issues for reflection,* and *Bibliography.*

The Background

This is the shortest of the Pauline letters (335 words), and in format closest to the pattern of ordinary Hellenistic letters, especially to those making intercession.[1] One should be careful, however, not to evaluate it simply as a letter from one individual to another asking for a favor. As one who has lived a long life[2] and suffered much in the service of Christ, Paul is writing to the head of a Christian house-church, or even to a church in the person of its host (since Paul anticipates communal pressure on Philemon). He writes as a prisoner, i.e., one who has sacrificed his freedom for Christ, to ask for another's freedom; and in every line just beneath the surface is the basic challenge to the societal rank of master and slave offered by the changed

[1]It is comparable to the shorter letter of Pliny the Younger appealing to Sabinianus for a young freedman who sought refuge in Pliny's home; Pliny offers reasons for Sabinianus to be clement (9.21; in English and Latin in Lohse, *Colossians* 196–97). As for length, there are 245 words in II John, 219 in III John; their shorter length is generally thought to have been dictated by the size of a sheet of papyrus.

[2]In v. 9 the reading *presbytēs,* "old man," is found in all mss., although some prefer to read or substitute *presbeutēs,* "ambassador."

Summary of Basic Information

DATE: *ca.* 55 if from Ephesus; 58–60 if from Caesarea (unlikely); 61–63 if from Rome.

TO: Philemon, with Apphia (his wife?), Archippus, and the church at Philemon's house.

AUTHENTICITY, UNITY, AND INTEGRITY: Not seriously disputed.

FORMAL DIVISION:

A. Opening Formula: 1–3
B. Thanksgiving: 4–7
C. Body: 8–22 (21–22 can be considered a Body-Closing or part of the Conclusion)
D. Concluding Formula: 23–25.

DIVISION ACCORDING TO CONTENTS (and Rhetorical Structure):

1–3: Address, greeting
4–7: Thanksgiving serving as an *exordium* to gain Philemon's good will by praise
8–16: Appeal offering motives to Philemon on behalf of Onesimus (*confirmation*)
17–22: Reiteration and expansion of appeal (*peroration*)
23–25: Concluding greetings, blessing.

relationship introduced by the gospel. Literary criticism and sociology have enriched the study of the letter (Petersen), but Soards is correct in insisting on the primacy of the theological dimension.

Since this letter deals with a slave, a few general remarks about slavery in Paul's time may be appropriate before we look at the specific situation. Society in the provinces of the Roman Empire where Paul conducted missionary activity was highly stratified. At the upper level would have been the Romans appointed by the Senate or the emperor to administer the province politically, fiscally, and militarily; next would come the local privileged class (through heredity or money); then the small landowners, shop owners, and craftspeople. These would have been followed in social rank by the freedmen and freedwomen who had been released from slavery through the action of their masters or by their own purchase of freedom; and then at the bottom would have been the immense number of slaves with whose existence the economic welfare of the Empire was intimately involved. (The dire results of the revolt of the slaves in Italy led by Spartacus in 73–71 BC show that any proposal of the abolition of slavery would have had Empire-shaking potentialities.) People became slaves in various ways: Many were prisoners taken in war; others were kidnapped by slave hunters; still others were enslaved through debt; and, of course, there were the children born to slaves. The slavery many English-speaking readers of the Bible are most familiar with is that of the blacks in America, but the Roman situation was more complicated. Within the general category the most burdensome form of slave life was endured by those who did heavy manual labor, e.g., in the mines, building construction, and the rowing banks on ships. By contrast many who worked in households for understanding masters would not have been much worse off than servants in wealthy British homes at the end of the last century known to TV watchers through "Upstairs, Downstairs." On a particularly high level were the very well-educated slaves who administered their master's estates or businesses, instructed the children, and even earned their own money. These would have been the group from which many emerged by gaining or being given freedom.

The specific slavery situation dealt with in Phlm is well known to Paul, Philemon, and Onesimus. Unfortunately presuppositions are not spelled out, and the sequence of events has to be reconstructed from hints. (To judge the situation we must pay attention not only to the personal names used to identify the dramatis personae but the titles given them that indicate their roles as Christians.) A plausible reconstruction is that Philemon was a well-to-do Christian, Apphia was his wife, and Archippus was close to him;[3] Philemon's home served as the meeting place of a house-church. It is not clear that Paul has ever personally encountered Philemon;[4] at least, however, the evangelizing of the area in which Philemon lived was probably the fruit of Paul's mission, perhaps through Pauline fellow-workers (vv. 23–24: Epaphras?). Onesimus was Philemon's slave who seemingly had run away.[5] The language of begetting in v. 10 suggests that Paul had (recently) converted him. In another city was he thrown into prison (but not as a runaway or he would have been sent back), and was it there that he met Paul who evangelized him? Or was the encounter more deliberate: Without being imprisoned, had

[3]Archippus is variously identified by scholars, e.g., as Philemon's son, or the head of the church that met in Philemon's house (Stöger), or even the owner of Onesimus. (The last identification is maintained by J. Knox; also L. Cope, *Biblical Research* 30 [1985], 45–50—then Paul would have written in order to have Philemon, the church leader, present when the request about Onesimus was made to Archippus.) The last two proposals depend on dubious interpretations of the instruction in Col 4:17 to Archippus to fulfill his ministry, e.g., by administering the church or by freeing Onesimus. (In the latter case, why such bluntness in the Col passage after all the delicacy in Phlm?) The variety of proposals illustrates how little is spelled out in Phlm.

[4]Pointing to *no encounter:* v. 5 "I hear"; pointing to an *encounter:* v. 1 "co-worker" (a term used by Paul mostly to refer to people who had been with him personally) and v. 19 "You owe me your very life." Those who favor an encounter generally suggest that the meeting had not taken place where Philemon now lives (because Paul himself had not evangelized Colossae) but perhaps at Ephesus. Would Apphia and Archippus have been with Philemon, or are we to posit different relationships between Paul and the three people addressed?

[5]We have ancient examples of "wanted posters" offering money for the apprehension of runaway slaves, but it is not clear that Onesimus was being legally pursued—perhaps already an indication of a Christian sensibility on the part of the master. Or Onesimus might not simply have been seeking freedom, e.g.: Perhaps while in service Onesimus had done something that caused Philemon to lose money ("Formerly he was useless to you" in v. 11, plus 18–19); and rather than face his master, he had gone elsewhere to look for someone who would intercede for him.

he, as a fugitive, sought help from a Christian group (and from Paul, of whom he had heard his master speak) in a strange city where he was now in trouble? In any case the fact that Paul has been responsible for the new life shared by both Philemon and Onesimus underlies this message designed to work out the effects of that theological reality on the social plane.

General Analysis of the Message

The letter, designed to persuade, is astute, with almost every verse hinting at something more than is stated. Indeed some (see Church, "Rhetorical") have detected well-known rhetorical canons and techniques. In vv. 4–7, which constitute a *captatio benevolentiae,* Paul flatters (not necessarily insincerely) by reporting what he has heard about Philemon's Christian love and faith—heard from Epaphras and/or from Onesimus, or because everybody in the Pauline circle knows about such an outstanding figure? Then in v. 8 Philemon is given an oblique reminder of Paul's apostolic authority to command; yet by Paul's preference this letter is an appeal about the fate of Onesimus (10). Although as Paul's child in Christ, he is extremely useful[6] to his Christian father in prison and Paul would have liked to keep him as a coworker, Paul will do nothing without Philemon's consent (and probably the approval of the house-church). Consequently he is sending Onesimus back with the wish that Philemon will accept him no longer as slave but as beloved brother. Notice how much is being asked: not simply that Onesimus escape the punishment that could legally be imposed, not simply that Onesimus be freed (which we might have expected as a more noble gesture), but that Onesimus be moved to the plane of the Christian relationship: "Receive him as you would receive me" (v. 17). The request is a dramatic example of Paul's way of thinking in fidelity to the change of values brought about by Christ: His antinomy is not simply slave and free, but slave and new creation in Christ. In vv. 18–19 Paul guarantees with his own hand a promise to pay back anything owed;[7] but by emphasizing that he is one to whom Philemon owes (directly or indirectly) his Christian life, Paul makes any demand for repayment virtually impossible. There is a double rhetorical touch in v. 21, where Paul both reminds Philemon that he owes obedience (to Paul as an apostle or to God and the gospel?) and expresses his confidence that Philemon will do more than asked. The "more" is interpreted by some as a hint

[6]The name Onesimus, common for slaves, means "useful" in Greek; Paul plays on that in v. 11 in the contrast between "formerly worthless to you . . . now of good worth to you and to me."

[7]Many have thought that Onesimus stole something when he fled, but this may be simply a reflection of Roman law that a person who harbors a runaway slave is held accountable to the owner for the loss of work involved.

that Philemon should release from slavery Onesimus who is his Christian brother. Paul will visit after being released (an occasion that Philemon has been praying for: v. 22). Is this a subtle indication that Paul wants to see for himself how Onesimus has been treated? That Philemon reacted generously is almost certain, or the letter would not have been preserved.

Social Import of Paul's View of Slavery

Jesus himself had a strong apocalyptic view: The kingdom/rule of God was present in his ministry; decision was imperative in face of a divine invitation that would not be repeated. In the tradition Jesus avoided spelling out a horarium of the endtimes; but even if the precise moment could not be known, the dominant impression is one of the end coming soon. Paul too had an apocalyptic approach in which the death and resurrection of Christ marked the changing of the times. Strong apocalypticism does not encourage long-range social planning. Structures in society that prevent the proclamation of the gospel must be neutralized. Yet precisely because Christ is coming back soon, other structures that do not represent gospel values can be allowed to stand provided that they can be bypassed to enable Christ to be preached. It will not be for long. The implications of the gospel for slavery are clear to Paul: In Christ Jesus "there is neither slave nor free" (Gal 3:28); all are of equal value. All were baptized into the one body (I Cor 12:13) and should treat one another with love. The only true slavery that remains after the change of the aeons is slavery to Christ (I Cor 7:22). Yet to overturn the massive Roman societal institution of slavery is not a feasible accomplishment in the very limited time before Christ comes. Obviously on the worldly level slaves will seek to gain freedom; but if one is a slave at the time of being called and physical freedom is unobtainable, that situation is not of essential importance. "In whatever state each was called, there let that person remain with God" (I Cor 7:21–22).

To some interpreters Phlm reflects a welcome, stronger Pauline position on slavery, one that would eventually move sensitive Christians as a whole to reject it. Here we see that when Paul can hope for cooperation, he challenges a Christian slave owner to defy the conventions: To forgive and receive back into the household a runaway slave; to refuse financial reparation when it is offered, mindful of what one owes to Christ as proclaimed by Paul; to go farther in generosity by freeing the servant; and most important of all from a theological viewpoint to recognize in Onesimus a beloved brother and thus acknowledge his Christian transformation. (Many today in evaluating Phlm might not appreciate the last-mentioned dimension, but for Paul that was the key demand.) Taking such a gracious stance might have deleterious social implications in the eyes of outsiders and even of less daring Christians. It might make one who acts thus look like a troubler of the social order and a revolutionary; but that is a price worth paying out of loyalty to the gospel.

To other interpreters, Phlm represents a lack of nerve. On the bottom line, despite his implicit encouragement to release Onesimus, Paul does not tell Philemon explicitly that keeping another human being as a slave factually denies that Christ has changed values. Tolerating a social evil while gently protesting in the name of Christianity is tantamount to condoning it and ensuring its survival. And indeed through the centuries Paul's failure to condemn slavery was used by some Bible readers as proof that the institution was not evil in itself. The question was not asked whether Paul's partial toleration was not so fundamentally determined by his apocalyptic outlook that it could not serve as a guide once the expectation of the second coming was moved to the indefinite future. As we shall see below under *Issues,* the social-morality questions that surround this issue can be extended to other issues as well.[8]

From Where and When?

Paul writes this letter from prison, and so we must survey the same three candidates for imprisonment examined for Phil in Chapter 20: Ephesus, Caesarea, Rome.[9] Yet now the situation is more complicated. In itself this letter gives fewer hints than did Phil: Although Paul wants a guest room prepared for his visit (v. 22), we are never told where the addressees live. (Yet one must admit that a request to prepare a guest room if Paul would have to make a long sea journey from either Rome or Caesarea even to draw near the site addressed seems odd.) Several of the key factors (asterisked) on p. 493 above that contributed to determining the place of origin of Phil are verified here; and so, if Ephesus was the more probable candidate there, it might be considered that here as well.

However, one must also take into account the clear relationship of Phlm to Col. The beginning of both letters lists Timothy "our brother" as a co-sender with Paul; and the ending of both is supplied in Paul's own hand (Phlm 19; Col 4:18). Eight of the ten people mentioned in Phlm are men-

[8]Indeed, Burtchaell, *Philemon's Problem,* uses this letter as entrée into issues that constitute the daily dilemma of the Christian.

[9]It is impossible to determine whether this was a confining detention or a type of house arrest where Paul was easily approached. Strangely the 2d-century Monarchian Prologues assign Phlm and Phil to Rome, but Col to Ephesus. In my judgment there is little to recommend Caesarea as the place from which Phlm was sent.

tioned in Col as well.[10] (Nevertheless, it is uncertain that Paul wrote Col, and so details therein may not be factual biography.) Because Onesimus and Archippus are referred to in Col (4:9,17), the vast majority of interpreters assume that Philemon lived in the Colossae region; and that workable assumption[11] favors Ephesus as the candidate of Paul's whereabouts. In terms of a slave's flight that city was only 100–120 miles away, as contrasted with immense distances between Colossae and Rome or Caesarea.[12] There are difficulties, however. The christology of Col is advanced, and if Col is genuinely Pauline, that might favor the Roman captivity (61–63) and the end of Paul's career for the composition of both Col and Phlm. More specifically, of those who were with Paul when he sent Phlm (vv. 1,24), while *Timothy*'s presence favors Ephesus (p. 495 above), *Aristarchus* both was with Paul at Ephesus in 54–57 and set out with him from Caesarea for Rome in 60 (Acts 19:29; 27:2); *Mark* (which one?), *Luke,* and *Demas* are not mentioned in the Ephesus stay, but are later associated with Rome (respectively I Pet 5:13 [Babylon = Rome]; II Tim 4:11 [also Acts 28:16 if Luke is part of "we"]; II Tim 4:10). All this is very uncertain, however; and overall the arguments for Ephesus and composition *ca.* 56 are as good as and even better than those for Rome. Nothing essential by way of interpretation depends on the decision.

Subsequent Career of Onesimus

Presumably Paul wrote a large number of personal letters to individual Christians. Why was this one preserved? The usual and more likely answer is that this letter is more ecclesial than personal, having important pastoral/theological implications (even if, as we have seen, Paul does not determine the future of slavery). But in order to explain preservation, a more romantic proposal, associated with the names of Goodspeed and Knox, has been made. Onesimus was released by Philemon and returned to work with Paul

[10]Timothy, Archippus, Onesimus, Epaphras, Mark, Aristarchus, Demas, and Luke are shared by the two works; Philemon and Apphia are absent from Col. Yet the role assigned to Onesimus in Col 4:9 scarcely corresponds to the role he has in Phlm.

[11]Why workable? *If Col was written by Paul,* one can trust the geographical and historical references therein and theorize that Tychicus and Onesimus carried with them to Colossae the letter to Philemon (Col 4:7–9). Yet Col, which contains many greetings to people at Colossae (and Laodicea), makes no mention of Philemon. Was the house-church that met at his home not in Colossae but in a nearby town in the area? (The precision that Laodicea was the town is related to Knox's adventurous thesis that, after being read by Philemon in Laodicea, Phlm was brought to Archippus in Colossae and so was the letter *from* Laodicea in Col 4:16.) *If Col was not written by Paul,* the mention of Onesimus and Archippus therein was most likely inspired by the genuine letter to Philemon, and the direction of the pseudonymous letter may stem from a reliable tradition that connected these people with Colossae.

[12]With difficulty one could argue for a flight by a slave to Rome to become untraceable in the capital of the empire over 1,000 miles away; but there is less plausibility in a flight to Caesarea.

in Ephesus, remaining there as a principal Christian figure once Paul had left. He was still there more than a half-century later when Ignatius of Antioch, using more developed church-structure language, addressed the Ephesian church "in the person of Onesimus, a man of love beyond recounting and your bishop" (*Eph.* 1:3). In that capacity, and out of an esteemed memory of the man who was his father in Christ, Onesimus was well placed to collect the scattered letters of Paul, now long dead. With understandable pride he included among the great writings that the apostle had addressed to churches a small missive treasured all these years since it involved Onesimus himself and made his whole subsequent career possible. Alas, there is virtually no proof for this truly attractive theory. The Onesimus at Ephesus in AD 110 may have taken that name to honor the slave who was converted there by the imprisoned Paul long before. There is no way to decide; but to adapt an Italian saying, *Se non è vero, è ben trovato:* Even if it is not true, it was still worth being proposed.

Issues and Problems for Reflection

(1) It is a worthwhile exercise to list the main characters with the descriptive titles given them in Phlm. To what extent is Paul using titles to make those involved conscious of what they and he are, through the gift of God in Christ? How does this new theological dimension affect their existing relationship?

(2) Often authority is quickly invoked in settling a church issue. Paul is very clear that he has authority, but he prefers to persuade (vv. 8–9; see also II Cor 8:8), even though shrewdly he includes rhetorical and psychological pressure in the persuasion. (A preference for persuasion is also evinced in Matt 18:15–18.) To what extent is such a preference inherent in *metanoia* or "conversion" when that is understood literally as changing one's way of thinking? The NT does use the language of God's commandment(s) in speaking of the coming of the kingdom. What relationship does that have to the gospel's placing responsibility on the individual?

(3) Paul's partial tolerance of slavery may be related to his apocalyptic view in which this world is passing away. The charge is often made that even today Christians with strongly apocalyptic views are less insistent on social justice. Are there examples in Christian history where strong apocalypticism and a strong demand for changing social structures coexist? How might they coexist today?

(4) Related to (3) is the issue of "interim ethics," i.e., ethical attitudes phrased in a context where the present time is seen as quickly passing because Christ will return soon. On the one hand, belief in the imminent return

of Christ allowed toleration of unjust social institutions for the expected short while (provided one could still proclaim the gospel); on the other hand, heroic demands seem to have been made on Christians precisely because things to which they might become attached were not going to last. If in I Cor 7:20–24 a slave can be told to stay a slave on the principle that one might as well remain in the state in which one was called, the same applies to a single person or to a married person whose lives may also be troubled. "The appointed time has grown short; from now on, let those with wives live as though they had none" (7:29). How does one determine what is permanently demanded by the gospel even if that demand was placed with the presupposition of a short interim?

Bibliography on Philemon

COMMENTARIES AND STUDIES IN SERIES: Stöger, A. (NTSR, 1971). See also the writings asterisked in the Phil *Bibliography* of Chapter 20 above and the Col *Bibliography* of Chapter 27 below.

Burtchaell, J. T., *Philemon's Problem* (Chicago: ACTA Foundation, 1973).

Church, F. F., "Rhetorical Structure and Design in Paul's Letter to Philemon," HTR 71 (1978), 17–33.

Daube, D., "Onesimos," HTR 79 (1986), 40–43.

Derrett, J.D.M., "The Functions of the Epistle to Philemon," ZNW 79 (1988), 63–91.

Elliott, J. H., "Philemon and House Churches," TBT 22 (1984), 145–50.

———, "Patronage and Clientism in Early Christian Society," *Forum* 3 (#4; 1987), 39–48.

Getty, M. A., "The Theology of Philemon," SBLSP (1987), 503–8.

Goodenough, E. R., "Paul and Onesimus," HTR 22 (1929), 181–83.

Harrison, P. N., "Onesimus and Philemon," ATR 32 (1950), 268–94.

Knox, J., *Philemon among the Letters of Paul* (rev. ed.; Nashville: Abingdon, 1959).

Lewis, L. A., "An African American Appraisal of the Philemon-Paul-Onesimus Triangle," *Stony the Road We Trod* (Minneapolis: A/F, 1991), 232–46.

Mullins, T. Y., "The Thanksgivings of Philemon and Colossians," NTS 30 (1984), 288–93.

Petersen, N. R., *Rediscovering Paul: Philemon and the Sociology of Paul's Narrative World* (Philadelphia: Fortress, 1985).

Preiss, T., "Life in Christ and Social Ethics in the Epistle to Philemon," *Life in Christ* (SBT 13; London: SCM, 1954), 32–42.

Riesenfeld, H., "Faith and Love Promoting Hope [Phlm 6]," in *Paul and Paulinism,* eds. M. D. Hooker and S. G. Wilson (London: SPCK, 1982), 251–57.

Soards, M. L., "Some Neglected Theological Dimensions of Paul's Letter to Philemon," PRS 17 (1990), 209–19.

White, J. L., "The Structural Analysis of Philemon," SBLSP (1971), 1–47.

Winter, S.B.C., "Paul's Letter to Philemon," NTS 33 (1987), 1–15.

CHAPTER 22

FIRST LETTER TO THE CORINTHIANS

Paul's known contacts with Corinth lasted nearly a decade, and there is more Pauline correspondence to that city than to any other place. Indeed traces of as many as seven letters have been detected (pp. 548–49 below). The disturbed state of the Christians at Corinth explains the need for so much attention. Paradoxically, the range of their problems (rival "theologians," factions, problematic sexual practices, marital obligations, liturgy, church roles) makes the correspondence exceptionally instructive for troubled Christians and churches of our times. Attempts to live according to the gospel in the multiethnic and crosscultural society at Corinth raised issues still encountered in multiethnic, multiracial, and crosscultural societies today. Paul's style of questions and debate with quoted statements makes his presentation of those issues vivacious and attractive, and has led scholars to discuss the precise rhetoric employed. For those studying Paul seriously for the first time, if limitations mean that only one of the thirteen letters can be examined in depth, I Cor may well be the most rewarding. Accordingly, after the *Background,* the *General Analysis* will delineate the message at greater length than usual; then subsections will be devoted to: *Those criticized by Paul at Corinth,* his *Condemnation of fornicators and homosexuals, Charisms at Corinth* (I Cor 12 and 14), the *Hymn to love* (I Cor 13), *Paul and the risen Jesus* (I Cor 15), *Issues for reflection,* and *Bibliography.*

The Background

The mainland of Greece (Achaia) is connected to the large Peloponnesus peninsula to the south by a narrow, four-mile-wide isthmus, with the Aegean Sea to the east and the Ionian or Adriatic Sea to the west. On a plateau controlling this isthmus, astride the very important north–south land route to the peninsula and situated in between ports on the two seas, was the city of Corinth[1] (towered over on the south by a 1,850-foot-high acropolis hill,

[1]Strabo, *Geography* 8.6.20, speaks of the "master of two harbors." Because of the way the isthmus is twisted, *Cenchreae,* the port that gave access to the eastern sea via the Saronic gulf, lay six

Summary of Basic Information

DATE: Late 56 or very early 57 from Ephesus (or 54/55 in the Revisionist Chronology).

TO: Mixed church of Jews and Gentiles at Corinth converted by Paul in 50/51–52 (or 42–43).

AUTHENTICITY: Not seriously disputed.

UNITY: Some see two or more separate letters interwoven, but unity is favored by an increasing majority, even if the one letter was composed in disjunctive stages as information and a letter came to Paul from Corinth.

INTEGRITY: No widely agreed-on major interpolations, although there is some debate about 14:34–35 and chap. 13; a lost letter preceded (I Cor 5:9).

FORMAL DIVISION:

A. Opening Formula: 1:1–3
B. Thanksgiving: 1:4–9
C. Body: 1:10–16:18
D. Concluding Formula: 16:19–24.

DIVISION ACCORDING TO CONTENTS:

1:1–9:	Address/greetings and Thanksgiving, reminding Corinthians of their spiritual gifts
1:10–4:21:	Part I: The factions
5:1–11:34:	Part II: Problems of behavior (incest, lawsuits, sexual behavior, marriage, food, eucharist, liturgy); what Paul has heard and questions put to him
12:1–14:40:	Part III: Problems of charisms and the response of love
15:1–58:	Part IV: The resurrection of Christ and of the Christian
16:1–18:	The collection, Paul's travel plans, commendations of people
16:19–24:	Greetings; Paul's own hand; "Our Lord, come."

Acrocorinth). Called "the light of all Greece" by Cicero, this spot had already been settled for more than four thousand years when the Greek city effectively came to an end through defeat by the Romans in 146 BC. The replacement city to which Paul came in AD 50/51–52 had been founded a century before (44 BC) as a Roman colony by Julius Caesar. In one sense, then, Corinth was like Philippi; but its strategic placement attracted a more cosmopolitan population, for poor immigrants came from Italy to dwell there, including freed slaves of Greek, Syrian, Jewish, and Egyptian origin. The 1st-century BC Greek poet Crinagoras described these people as scoundrels, but many of them soon became wealthy. Their skills made the site

to seven miles east of Corinth; Lechaion or *Lechaeum,* the port that gave access to the western sea via the gulf of Corinth, lay about two miles north of Corinth. In antiquity a paved road, the *diolkos,* across the isthmus facilitated trade between the two seas; and, in addition to transshipment of merchandise, grooves cut into it allowed light ships to be hauled from one sea to the other, thus saving a dangerous journey of about two hundred miles around the treacherous end of the peninsula. Although Nero began to cut a canal, it was only in 1893 that the two seas were connected by the Corinth Canal.

thrive as a manufacturing (bronze and terra cotta items) and commercial center. Indeed, under Augustus it became the capital city of the province of Achaia, whence the presence of the proconsul Gallio (brother of the famous Seneca) who dealt with Paul (Acts 18:12).

Archaeology enables accurate reconstruction of the Roman city[2] and attests to the multicultural ambiance. Although Latin may have been the first language of the Roman colony, inscriptions show the wide use of Greek, the language of commerce. The standard Greek deities were honored by temples, and the Egyptian cult of Isis and Serapis is attested. Homage to the emperors was augmented by imperial patronage extended to the Panhellenic Isthmian games held every other year in the spring (including AD 51); they were outranked in importance only by the Olympic games. Although archaeological evidence is lacking, except for a synagogue lintel (see Acts 18:4), there was a large 1st-century AD Jewish colony with its own officials and internal management, perhaps augmented by Claudius's expulsion of Jews from Rome in AD 49 (Chapter 16 above, n. 24).

Greek Corinth acquired an overblown reputation (partly through slander) for sexual license, so that Greek words for whoremongers, prostitution, and fornication were coined employing the city's name. Despite references to this "city of love" with a thousand priestesses of Aphrodite (Venus) who were sacred prostitutes, only two small temples to that goddess have been found. Whatever may have been true of Greek Corinth, we should think of Roman Corinth simply as having all the problems of a rough, relatively new boomtown adjacent to two seaports. Yet it also had advantages from Paul's point of view. The travelers passing through Corinth, including those visiting the famous healing shrine of Aesculapius or attending the Isthmian games, would need tents for temporary housing, so that a tentmaker or leatherworker like Paul (and Aquila and Priscilla; Acts 18:2–3) could find work and self-support there.[3] Because of the many who came and went, he would not be rejected as an outsider or even a resident alien; and the seed of the gospel that he sowed in Corinth might well be carried far and disseminated by those whom he evangelized. Furnish ("Corinth") has many interesting suggestions about how what Paul writes was affected by the building projects, festivals, artifacts, and agriculture of the site.

Paul's contacts with Corinth were complicated. It may help to be quite arithmetical in recounting those that led up to I Cor (the continuation leading up to II Cor may be found on p. 541 below). In addition to numerals used to designate the moments of contact, I shall use capital letters of the alphabet

[2]See maps and city plans in Murphy-O'Connor, *St. Paul's Corinth,* 6, 20, 24–25; also Furnish, "Corinth."

[3]See Hock, *Social.*

to designate Paul's letters to Corinth, some of which correspondence has been lost. I shall keep referring to these numerals (#) and letters throughout this Chapter and the next.

(#1) AD 50/51–52. According to Acts 18:1–3 Aquila and Priscilla (almost certainly Jewish Christians) were at Corinth when Paul arrived there. Some challenge that sequence because in I Cor 3:6,10; 4:15 Paul claims that at Corinth he planted and laid the foundation and fathered the Christian community. We may wonder, however, whether that language excludes the possibility that a few Christians were on the scene before he came. Paul's experiences in Philippi and Thessalonica had been marked by hostility and/or rejection, so that he came to Corinth in fear and trembling (I Cor 2:3); yet he stayed there a year and a half. Even if we make allowance for rhetorical overstatement, Paul's claim that he did not speak with the eloquence of human wisdom (2:4–5; also II Cor 11:6) probably means that he would not have appealed to the academically sophisticated—a change of tactics from his approach just before this in Athens, if we can depend on Acts 17:16–34. The picture in Acts 18:2–4 is that Paul began his evangelizing with the Jews, lodging in the house of his fellow tentmakers Aquila and Priscilla and preaching in the synagogue. Then (Acts 18:5–7; I Thess 3:1,2,6) after the arrival of Silas and Timothy from Macedonia with news about the Thessalonian Christians, he shifted to the Gentiles, moving to the house of Jason, a God-fearer (i.e., a Gentile sympathetic to Judaism). From the names mentioned in I Cor 16:15–18 and Rom 16:21–23, we detect the presence of both Jewish and Gentile converts at Corinth, with the latter somewhat in the majority. Predominantly those converted by Paul would have been from the lower to middle strata of society, with artisans and ex-slaves far outnumbering the rich.[4] We shall see that some difficulties about the eucharistic meal may have been caused by the interaction of rich and poor at Corinth. Paul's initial preaching at Corinth must have been strongly eschatological or even apocalyptic, since symbolically he refused to accept money, lived a celibate life (an indication that this was not a lasting world), worked signs and wonders (II Cor 12:12), and spoke in tongues (I Cor 14:18; see p. 284

[4]Altogether we know some 17 names of Christians at Corinth. Becker (*Paul* 147) guesses that Paul left behind 50 to 100 Christians when he departed in AD 52. Theissen, *Social,* has studied the Corinthian Christians sociologically; see also Meeks, *First.* The name "Fortunatus" (I Cor 16:17) may betray slave origin. Apparently Aquila and Priscilla were of a higher social status; at different times they had a home/house at Corinth (Acts 18:3—owned or rented), at Ephesus (I Cor 16:19), and at Rome (Rom 16:3–5). At Corinth Crispus was ruler of the synagogue (Acts 18:8; I Cor 1:14); Gaius had a house (as seemingly did Phoebe at nearby Cenchreae; Rom 16:1), and Erastus was city treasurer or aedile (Rom 16:23)—an inscription thanking the latter for his public generosity has been found (Murphy-O'Connor, *St. Paul's Corinth* 37).

above). Before Paul's stay at Corinth was over, the Jews dragged him before the proconsul Gallio (Acts 18:12–17). That backfired, however: Gallio released Paul, while Sosthenes, the ruler of the synagogue, was beaten.

(#2) AD 52–56? After Paul left Corinth in 52 with Priscilla and Aquila (Acts 18:18), other missionaries came; and the vivacious preaching of a man like Apollos[5] may have catalyzed spirited elements within the Corinthian community, producing some of the enthusiasm that Paul would have to criticize in I Cor. **(#3)** I Cor 5:9 refers to a letter Paul had written (**Letter A,** lost[6]), warning the Corinthians not to have dealings with immoral people.

(#4) (*ca.* AD 56). While staying at Ephesus (54–57), Paul got reports about Corinth, e.g., from "those of Chloe" (I Cor 1:11; also 11:18). We know nothing of Chloe: whether she lived at Corinth (with contacts at Ephesus?) or at Ephesus; whether she was a Christian; whether "those of Chloe" were her family or her household or her business establishment; whether she had sent them or they were traveling from Corinth to Ephesus. **(#5)** About the same time or shortly afterward at Ephesus, Paul received a letter from the Corinthians (I Cor 7:1), perhaps in reply to his Letter A and seemingly brought by Stephanas, Fortunatus, and Achaicus (16:17–18) who probably added their own reports. **(#6)** Paul wrote I Cor from Ephesus **(Letter B).**[7] Although there have been attempts to see I Cor as an amalgamation of once totally distinct letters, it is best evaluated as a single missive sent to the Corinthian Christians, even if composed in two stages responding to #4 and #5 respectively. With that background, let us look through I Cor.

General Analysis of the Message

The OPENING FORMULA (1:1–3) joins to Paul as co-sender Sosthenes (p. 413 above). Seemingly this is the same man, now a Christian, who earlier was the ruler of the Corinthian synagogue and was beaten before the *bēma* when Gallio refused to judge Paul (#1; Acts 18:17). Did Paul dictate the

[5]I Cor 3:6; Acts 18:24–28; 19:1. Although there were Christians at Corinth who identified themselves as followers of Cephas (Peter; I Cor 1:12) and Paul cites the right of Cephas (and the brothers of the Lord) to travel with a believing wife (I Cor 9:5), there is no clear evidence that Peter was at Corinth. When Paul mentions missionary activity at Corinth, he cites only Apollos and himself (3:4–6; 4:6; see 16:12). Also Acts, which speaks about Apollos at Corinth, is silent about any role of Peter there, as is early tradition (I Peter 1:1 has no address to Achaia).

[6]Unless, as some would contend, it is preserved in part in II Cor 6:14–7:1.

[7]Sometime before Pentecost of AD 57 (I Cor 16:8—Traditional Chronology; for Revisionist Chronology, see Table 6 in Chapter 16 above). A number of events took place between the sending of I Cor and Paul's termination of his stay at Ephesus by leaving to pass through Troas to Macedonia and Achaia (summer of 57; #10, p. 543 below). Accordingly, a date of composition in late 56 or very early 57 seems most likely. The sending of the letter is somehow related to the mission of Timothy to Corinth (see n. 13 below, and #7 in Chapter 23 below).

letter to him (16:21)?[8] In the first nine verses, which include the THANKSGIVING (1:4–9), Paul mentions (Jesus) Christ nine times, an emphasis befitting Paul's coming correction of Corinthian factionalism by insisting that they were baptized in the name of Christ and of no other. He also gives thanks that the Corinthians have been given grace (*charis*) enriching them in speech and knowledge and that they were not lacking in any charism—an ironic touch since he will have to castigate them in the letter about their pretended wisdom and their fights over charisms. Another way in which the Thanksgiving anticipates the letter's contents, is that, as it comes to an end, it refers to the day of the Lord, the theme of I Cor 15:50–58, as the letter draws to a close.

PART I OF THE BODY OF THE LETTER (1:10–4:21). Almost four chapters are addressed to the problem of divisions or factions that exist at Corinth, about which Paul has been informed by members of Chloe's household (#4).[9] As a result of the activity described under #2 above, but probably without any incentive from the missionaries themselves,[10] there were now conflicting loyalties among the Corinthian Christians who had declared preferences: " 'I belong to Paul,' or 'I belong to Apollos,' or 'I belong to Cephas [Peter],' or 'I belong to Christ' " (I Cor 1:12).[11] Christians today have become accustomed to being divided; and so, except for the speed with which they occurred, we are not surprised by such divisions. What more likely surprises us is Paul's response, for we are accustomed to people defending their own choice among ecclesiastical divisions and attacking rival positions. Paul does not defend the faction that "belongs" to him or stress his own superiority, since all the preachers are only servants (3:5). "Is Christ divided? Was it Paul who was crucified for you or was it in Paul's name that you were baptized?" (1:13). "Whether Paul, or Apollos, or Cephas . . . you belong to Christ, and Christ belongs to God" (3:22–23).

[8]For co-authorship in the Corinthian correspondence, see J. Murphy-O'Connor, RB 100 (1993), 562–79.

[9]In dealing with these divisions, Paul defends his own apostolate. D. Litfin, *St. Paul's Theology of Proclamation: 1 Corinthians 1–4 and Greco-Roman Rhetoric* (SNTSMS 79; Cambridge Univ., 1994), contends that, when measured against Greco-Roman standards, Paul's eloquence seemed deficient, and that caused him difficulties. Puskas, *Letters* 59–63, speaks of judicial or forensic rhetoric here (p. 411 above).

[10]I Cor 3:6 speaks favorably of Apollos watering what Paul planted, and 16:12 has Paul urging Apollos to visit Corinth. Overall see N. A. Dahl, "Paul and the Church at Corinth according to 1 Cor 1:10–4:21," *Studies in Paul* (Minneapolis: Augsburg, 1977), 40–61.

[11]It is not clear whether "I belong to Christ" was the slogan of a fourth group (who in reaction to the others rejected human leadership) or Paul's own statement correcting the previous slogans. The parallelism favors the former interpretation (most scholars); the latter interpretation gets support from 3:22–23, which mentions only three groups (also *I Clement* 47:3). Snyder, *First Corinthians* 21–22, thinks of the Christ group as a house-church of a gnostic bent who regarded themselves as spiritually perfect and above the law and who were at the root of many of the abuses Paul had to correct in chaps. 5–15.

The existence of these divisions reflected different personal loyalties among the Corinthian Christians. Also, however, in choosing a particular preacher, like Apollos, some Corinthians may have been opting for what sounded like greater wisdom, whereas Paul without eloquence had preached a foolishness really wiser than human wisdom, namely, Christ and him crucified (1:18–2:5).[12] This was the mysterious wisdom of God hidden from the rulers of the present age who crucified the Lord of glory; it was proclaimed by Paul in words taught by the Spirit—thus spiritual truths in spiritual words (2:6–16). Paul laid down a solid foundation, indeed, the only possible foundation, Jesus Christ; and on the day of judgment everything else that is insubstantial will be shown up and burned off (3:10–15). The Corinthians ought to realize that they are God's temple in which the Spirit lives, and despise the wisdom of this world as foolishness in God's sight (3:16–23). In a highly rhetorical manner Paul contrasts "us apostles" (4:9) to the Corinthians, who in their religious stance are proud even though they have nothing that they did not receive (4:7). "Here we are, fools for Christ, while you are so wise in Christ . . ." (4:10–13). This letter is a warning from a father to his children, and Timothy is being sent to Corinth[13] to remind them of Paul's life and teaching before Paul himself comes to test the arrogant. "Shall I come to you with a stick, or with love in a spirit of gentleness?" (4:17–21).

PART II OF THE BODY OF THE LETTER (5:1–11:34). Next Paul turns to various problems of Christian behavior among the Corinthians.[14] Apparently *chaps. 5–6* involve things he has heard about Corinthian Christian practice,[15] and issues of sex and marriage come up in over half his instructions. Today correctives about sex are often dismissed as Victorian, but that gives her Britannic majesty credit for something that goes back to the 1st century in Christianity. Responsible sexual behavior in and out of marriage is a major issue in life; and inevitably what belief in Christ meant for such behavior

[12]Did those who admired Apollos stress eloquence (see Acts 18:24)? Paul uses figurative language to illustrate the shortcomings of the Corinthians and his role among them. They are fleshly, not spiritual, babes not ready for solid food (3:1–4; also I Thess 2:7; Eph 4:13–14). He was not only paternal (4:15) but maternal (3:2; also I Thess 2:7; Gal 4:19); see B. Gaventa, *Princeton Seminary Bulletin* 17 (1996), 29–44.

[13]The verb in 4:17 is aorist ("I sent"); yet in 16:10 Paul says: "Whenever Timothy comes," as if the letter is expected to get there before Timothy arrives. Presumably, then, Timothy has been sent on the indirect route through Macedonia (see Acts 19:21–22). See #7 in Chapter 23 below.

[14]Puskas, *Letters* 59–60, sees this as deliberative hortatory rhetoric (p. 412 above) concerned with decision-making, especially with a practical or expedient tone, and offers Greek parallels. B. S. Rosner, *Paul, Scripture and Ethics. A Study of 1 Corinthians 5–7* (Leiden: Brill, 1994), argues that Paul's ethics here were formed by his Jewish scriptural inheritance rather than by a Greco-Roman background.

[15]Some would argue that this is an oral report other than that received from Chloe's household (1:11), which had been answered in chaps. 1–4. It is not unlikely that those who brought the letter of 7:1 from Corinth (#5) may have supplied Paul with some oral information about Christians there. Hurd and Snyder would argue that, like 1–4, chaps. 5–6 were written after 7–15.

became a problem, especially since the Jews and Gentiles who came to faith did not always share the same presuppositions. The first instance addressed by Paul (5:1–5) involves a man and his stepmother. Seemingly the man's father had died and he wishes to marry the widowed second wife who might be about his own age. From Paul's own teaching that Christians were a new creation, did the man or even the community ("And you are proud") think that previous relationships no longer mattered? Paul's outrage about this behavior betrays his Jewish roots; for marriage within such a degree of kindred was forbidden by the Mosaic Law (Lev 18:8; 20:11). He bases his argumentation, however, on the claim that such behavior was not tolerated even among the Gentiles.[16] That causes many scholars to think that Gentile converts to Christianity at Corinth had mistakenly taken Paul's proclamations of freedom to mean that there were no old rules of behavior (see also I Cor 6:12). Paul's authority to issue an excommunication even from a distance is invoked in 5:4–5; and what follows in reference to the letter he had already sent them (*Letter A;* #3)[17] shows that his main concern is not about the immorality of the world outside the community but sinfulness within the community that might leaven it harmfully (5:6–13; Jewish imagery, from Passover practice).

Paul's Jewish distrust of the standards of the Pagan world is reflected in his insistence that disputes are to be settled by having fellow Christians act as judges rather than going before Gentile courts (6:1–8) and in his list of vices of which the Corinthian Christians were formerly guilty (6:9–11). In 6:12 we hear a slogan in circulation at Corinth that presumably is at the root of much of what Paul condemns: "For me everything is permissible."[18] Paul qualifies it by insisting that not everything brings about good and by insisting that none of our choices must produce mastery over us. Real freedom does not have to be expressed to remain freedom. People do not live in a neutral environment: To indulge in loose behavior is not freedom but bondage to compulsions that enslave. Sexual permissiveness affects the Christian's body, which should be evaluated as a member of Christ's body (6:15) and the temple of the Holy Spirit (6:19). One's body is a means of self-

[16]Euripides' *Hippolytus,* Cicero, and the *Institutes* of Gaius are cited to support Paul's contention that it was not tolerated even among Gentiles; but the marriage of brother to sister in the Egyptian royal family indicates differing Gentile attitudes toward kindred marriage. The very strong Jewish background of Paul's stances in I Cor is emphasized by D. Daube in *Jesus and Man's Hope II,* eds. D. G. Miller and D. Y. Hadidian (Pittsburgh Theol. Seminary, 1971), 223–45; but Daube's appeal to later rabbinic material would be queried by some today.

[17]What he advised them in that letter (5:9) has either been misunderstood or misapplied (5:11). This is related to the issue of the slogans that are quoted in I Cor: Are they Paul's statements that were misunderstood? (See p. 527 below.)

[18]Put together with the list of vices in 6:9–10, does this slogan suggest that behavior among Corinthian Christians was worse than among Pauline converts elsewhere?

communication, and so intercourse produces a union between the partners. Union of one who is a member of Christ with an unworthy partner, such as a prostitute, disgraces Christ, just as marital union glorifies God (6:20).[19]

Turning from what he has heard about the Corinthians, in *chap. 7* Paul begins to answer questions that have been posed to him.[20] The first involves the statement (his own or one coined at Corinth?): "It is good for a man not to touch a woman."[21] (This lively pattern of citing statements or slogans and then discussing them has often been looked on as Paul's imitation of the Cynic diatribe pattern; see p. 89 above.) Although abstention from sex is laudable in itself, Paul does not encourage it within marriage because it could create temptations and effect injustice. He encourages marriage for those who cannot exercise control, even though "I would like everyone to be as I am myself"—Paul seemingly means without a wife (widower or never married?) and, of course, practicing abstinence (7:2–9).

To those already married (perhaps thinking of a specific couple) Paul repeats the Lord's ruling (p. 141 above) against divorce and remarriage (7:10–11), but then adds a ruling of his own that permits separation when one of the partners is not a Christian and will not live in peace with the believer (7:12–16).[22] In 7:17–40 Paul shows the extent to which his thinking is apocalyptic: He would have all people (circumcised Jew, uncircumcised Gentile, slave,[23] celibate, married, widow) stay in the state in which they were when called to Christ because the time has become limited.[24] See pp. 509–10 above for the problem of evaluating "interim ethics," and of determining in

[19]B. Byrne, CBQ 45 (1983), 608–16. In this and in much of what follows Paul deals with what a male does sexually, for the social mores of the time permitted greater sexual freedom on the part of otherwise respectable males than on the part of respectable females. R. B. Ward, BRev 4 (#4; 1988), 26–31, points out that in 18 BC Augustus proclaimed the *Lex Iulia* to encourage marriage and children because many men were avoiding marriage and pursuing all their sexual pleasure with prostitutes and slaves.

[20]There are seven uses of "Now concerning" (7:1,25; 8:1,4: 12:1; 16:1,12) to indicate questions. As for chap. 7, in 7:1–16 Paul treats issues of continence for the married, and in 7:25–40 for the single; in between he discourages changes of life-status. On chap. 7, see J. Murphy-O'Connor, JBL 100 (1981), 601–6; V. L. Wimbush, *Paul, the Worldly Ascetic* (Macon, GA: Mercer, 1987).

[21]See W. E. Phipps, NTS 28 (1982), 125–31; also G. F. Snyder, NTS 23 (1976–77), 117–20 on "It is good" statements.

[22]The separation would seemingly involve divorce and possibly remarriage, although Paul does not address the latter issue. A nonChristian who will live in peace with the believing spouse is sanctified by that union, just as, in the opposite direction, a believer is contaminated by a sexual union with a prostitute (6:16). Surprising, however, is the indication in 7:14 that children are sanctified by their relationship to the believing parent (or parents?). Later it was thought a defect for a Christian to have children who were not believers (Titus 1:6).

[23]S. S. Bartchy, *Mallon Chrēsai: First Century Slavery and the Interpretation of 1 Corinthians 7:21* (SBLDS 11; Missoula, MT: Scholars, 1973); J. A. Harrill, BR 39 (1994), 5–28.

[24]7:29. To what does 7:36–38 refer: a father and his unmarried daughter (keeping her single or marrying her off), or a man and his fiancee, or even a husband in regard to his wife when the two have pledged abstinence (spiritual marriage)? For background see L. B. Elder, BA 57 (1994), 200–34; J. L. White, BR 39 (1994), 62–79; W. Deming, *Paul on Marriage and Celibacy* (SNTSMS

such an outlook of Christ-coming-back-soon what constitutes enduring moral guidance for Christians two thousand years later. Certainly that outlook remains a factor for advocating celibacy: As a Christian virtue it makes no sense unless accompanied by other signs (voluntary poverty, self-giving) projecting faith that this is not a lasting world.

In chap. 8 Paul answers questions about food that had been sacrificed to the gods and then offered to whoever would buy it.[25] Since there are no gods other than the one God, the Father and source from whom are all things,[26] it is quite irrelevant that food has been offered to gods. Thus Christians have freedom: "We are no worse off if we do not eat, nor better off if we do" (8:8). Yet pastorally Paul is concerned about weak converts whose understanding is imperfect and who might think that sitting and eating in the temple of a false god involves worship of that god and thus might commit idolatry by eating. Therefore, one must be careful not to scandalize those weak believers.[27] Paul's stance is governed by the statement with which he opens this discussion (8:2): Knowledge, even correct knowledge, can puff up the self, but love builds up others and thus puts constraints on self-serving behavior. (The notion of pastoral limitations on one's rights can be an important challenge to a generation that constantly speaks of rights but not of responsibilities.) If eating would cause them to fall, it is better not to eat (8:13). Somewhat disjointedly he comes back to this same issue in 10:23–33: "Never be a cause of scandal to Jews or to Greeks or to the church of God" (10:32).

In chap. 9 Paul gives an impassioned defense of his rights as an apostle. Others may deny that he is an apostle; but he has seen the risen Lord, and the work he has done in conversion is proof of his apostleship. It is not insecurity about his status that has caused Paul to pass over his rights as an apostle, e.g., his right to be fed and supported, or to be accompanied by a

---

83; Cambridge Univ., 1995). The latter posits Stoic and Cynic background in chap. 7 (but cf. n. 14 above).

[25]W. L. Willis, *Idol Meat in Corinth. The Pauline Argument in 1 Corinthians 8 and 10* (SBLDS 68; Chico, CA: Scholars, 1985); P. D. Gooch, *Dangerous Food: 1 Corinthians 8–10 in Its Context* (Waterloo, Ont: Laurier Univ., 1993); P. D. Gardner, *The Gifts of God and the Authentication of a Christian* (I Cor 8:1–11:1; Lanham, MD: Univ. Press of America, 1994). Gooch stresses that Paul's "liberalism" extends no farther than the food laws and circumcision; he does not abandon Judaism's conception of the demands implied by the relation of the chosen people to God.

[26]To whom Paul joins the one Lord Jesus Christ, the agent through whom are all things (8:6). Most interpreters think that here Jesus is being presented as the one who brought the cosmos into being, but J. Murphy-O'Connor, RB 85 (1978), 253–67, contends that Paul is echoing baptismal language describing him as the savior of all. For the work of the Spirit, not mentioned here, see 12:4–6 where there is a triadic pattern of the same Spirit, the same Lord, and the same God.

[27]See G. R. Dawes, CBQ 58 (1996), 82–98. In 8:7 Paul speaks of the principle of respecting *syneidēsis*, "conscience"; and as Snyder, *First Corinthians* 125, points out, that is the first known use of the term in Christian history.

Christian wife who would also have to be supported.[28] Rather he supported himself and preached the gospel free of charge lest a request for support put an obstacle to belief (i.e., people would think he was preaching for money). Two wonderfully rhetorical passages (9:15–18,19–23) exhibit Paul at his best. He is clearly proud of what he has accomplished through his sacrifices; and yet in another sense he was under divine compulsion: "Woe to me if I do not proclaim the gospel!" And in this proclamation he became all things to all that he might win over more people: To those under the Law he became as one under the Law; to those outside the Law, as one outside the Law; to the weak, as one who was weak. (This passage should be a warning to all those who would find rigorous ideology in Paul's thought: Foremost he was a missionary—see the discussion of Pauline consistency on p. 437 above.) In 9:24–27 he ends this issue of how he has struggled in his ministry with a fascinating use of imagery from athletic competitions that would be very familiar to the Corinthians, for whom the Isthmian games loomed large.[29] He has subjected himself to punishing disciplinary training lest, after proclaiming the gospel to others, he himself should be disqualified.

Chaps. 10–11 deal with more problems at Corinth, predominantly those affecting community worship. In 10:1–13, citing the exodus where many Israelites who had passed through the sea and received divinely supplied nourishment nevertheless displeased God, Paul warns the Corinthians against sexual immorality, discouragement by trials, and worship of false gods—all examples from the testing of Israel in the desert that "were written as a lesson to us on whom the culmination of the ages has come."[30] In 10:2 and 14–22 Paul writes of baptism and of the eucharistic cup of blessing that is a sharing (*koinōnia*) in the blood of Christ and bread-breaking that is a sharing in the body of Christ (10:16). Here Paul supplies some important insights for subsequent sacramental theology because he makes it clear that through baptism and the eucharist God delivers and sustains Christians, and yet also shows that such exalted help does not immunize those who receive the sacraments from sin or exempt them from divine judgment. Since the many partakers are one body,[31] participation in the eucharist is irreconcilable with participation in Pagan sacrifices that are in fact being offered to demons

[28]From 9:4–6 we learn that other apostles (for Paul this need not mean the Twelve), the brothers of the Lord (including James?), and Cephas (Peter) were accompanied by Christian wives, and seemingly expected support from their converts rather than working for their livelihood while preaching. Barnabas, like Paul, did not behave thus. This favorable reference to Barnabas (*ca.* AD 55) is interesting given the hostile reference in Gal 2:13 to his behavior at Antioch (*ca.* 49–50).

[29]O. Broneer, BA 25 (1962), 1–31; HTR 64 (1971), 169–87.

[30]W. A. Meeks, JSNT 16 (1982), 64–78.

[31]It is not clear whether 10:17 means that the Christian partakers form one collective body (somewhat along the lines of Col and Eph where the church is the body of Christ) or are made participants in the one risen body of Christ; see 12:12ff. and pp. 612–13 below.

and make people partners with demons.[32] One cannot participate both in the table of the Lord and the table of demons. Interrupting the issue of the eucharist, 11:1–16 supplies directions for community "liturgical behavior": A man must pray or prophesy with head bared, while a woman must have her head covered. The theological basis offered for this demand (a man is the glorious reflection of God, while the woman reflects the man; because of angels the woman ought to have a sign of authority on her head[33]) may not have been deemed fully probative even by Paul himself, for at the end (11:16) he resorts to the authority of his own custom and those of the churches.

Then in 11:17–34 Paul returns to the eucharist and the meal in which it was set,[34] bluntly expressing his displeasure with Corinthian behavior. Divisions (those of chaps. 1–4?) are being carried over to "the Lord's Supper," where the Corinthians meet together *as a church* (11:18) to reenact a remembrance of what Jesus did and said on the night he was given over until he comes (11:20,23–26). Seemingly some have a meal that precedes the special bread-breaking and cup of blessing, while others ("those who have nothing") are excluded and go hungry. *Perhaps* this echoes a social situation where the need for a large space means that eucharistic meetings are in the home of a wealthy person; all Christians including the poor and slaves have to be accepted into the hospitality area of the house for the eucharist, but the owner is inviting to his table only well-off friends of status for the preparatory meal.[35] That is not Paul's notion of the church of God (11:22); either all

[32]In 8:1–6 and 10:23–32 Paul is clear that, since the Pagan gods are no-gods, food offered to them is like any other food. But active participation in the sacrifices to them is not a matter of indifference.

[33]Did having her head uncovered give a married woman the appearance of publicly denying marital status? On the appearance of headcoverings: D. W. J. Gill, *Tyndale Bulletin* 41 (1990), 245–60; C. L. Thompson, BA 51 (1988), 99–115. On the social position of Corinthian women: G. Clark, *Theology* 85 (1982), 256–62. On Paul's theology: M. D. Hooker, NTS 10 (1963–64), 410–16; G. Trompf, CBQ 42 (1980), 196–215; O. Walker, JBL 94 (1975), 94–110. The attempt of W. O. Walker, JBL 94 (1975), 94–110, to explain away I Cor 11:2–16 as a nonPauline interpolation is rejected by J. Murphy-O'Connor, JBL 95 (1976), 615–21, who, nevertheless, would lessen the authority of Paul's views therein on the grounds that they are not formally taught. Yet J. P. Meier, CBQ 40 (1978), 212–26, points out that Paul presents his view on having women's heads covered as apostolic tradition.

[34]This is often referred to as the *agapē* or love-meal (Jude 12); the local custom may have varied as to whether it preceded or followed the special bread-cup action that we call the eucharist.

[35]Archaeological remains of wealthy houses at Corinth show a public space (dining room and courtyard) that, allowing for furniture, would hold no more than fifty people. (See Murphy-O'Connor, *St. Paul's Corinth* 153–61.) Perhaps the socially acceptable ate in the dining room (triclinium), while others were in the courtyard. All Christian meeting places, however, were not the same. Murphy-O'Connor, BRev 8 (#6; 1992), 48–50, pictures a rented two-level shop where only ten or twenty believers could come together. Sometimes judgments are made with absolute certitude as to who presided at the eucharist: the head of the house (one side of the modern theological spectrum) or those approved by the Twelve (the other side). We have little evidence about this, and both of the above are guesses. Of help in avoiding naive modernization is R. Banks, *Going to Church in the First Century* (3d ed.; Auburn, ME: Christian Books, 1990).

should come together to eat the meal, or they should eat first in their own homes (11:33–34). The whole purpose of the sacred breaking of the bread is *koinōnia* (10:16), not division of the community. One also sins against the body and blood of the Lord if one eats the bread and drinks the cup unworthily (11:27), seemingly by failing to discern that it is the body and blood of the Lord (11:29).[36] Indeed, Paul contends that judgment is already falling on the Corinthians for some have died and many are sick (11:30). Despite the Book of Job, a correlation between sin and sickness/death has remained strong in Jewish thought!

PART III OF THE BODY OF THE LETTER (12:1–14:40). *Chaps. 12 and 14* deal with the spiritual gifts or charisms given in abundance to the Corinthian Christians, while *chap. 13,* sometimes called a hymn to love, appears as an interruption corrective of any acquisitiveness about charisms.[37] These chaps. have received so much attention that it seems best to discuss them separately and more fully (see subsections below). Here I might comment on only one aspect of what is implied by the picture Paul has painted. Because 12:28 lists apostles, prophets, and teachers as the first charisms, most often the Corinthian community is thought to have been administered by charismatics, i.e., those who were recognized to have been given one of those charisms by the Spirit. Yet the picture is complicated because a special charism of "administration" is also listed in 12:28. Moreover, we know relatively little of how functions were divided among apostles, prophets, and teachers, and to what extent apostles other than Paul were involved. Even if Eph 4:11 was written years later, its order of apostles, prophets, evangelists, pastors, and teachers warns us that the assignment of function may not have been exact or uniform. The description of the speaking of prophets in I Cor 14:29–33 shows how hard it is to be sure what prophets did.[38] In 14:34–35, immediately after a description of prophecy, women are excluded from speaking in

[36]The unworthiness refers to the manner of participation, so that here Paul is not directly thinking of two groups of people, one group worthy, the other unworthy. In the unworthy manner of receiving, the failure to discern means not recognizing the presence of Christ but also not recognizing the communality brought about by participation in the eucharist (10:16–17). Paul's words have relevance to the divisions discussed under *Issue* 8 below.

[37]J. T. Sanders, *Interpretation* 20 (1966), 159–87, surveys research on chap. 13, which is so interruptive that some (Barrett, Conzelmann) consider it a later addendum by Paul. Yet a connection to what precedes is found in 13:1–3 since three previously mentioned charisms (tongues, prophecy, and faith) are cited. Moreover, Paul's thought in this letter seems to come in fits and starts, so that interruption scarcely proves later addition, e.g.: After an interruption, the advice in 7:8–11 to the unmarried and married to stay that way is resumed in 7:17ff.; the issue of freedom and food sacrificed to idols in chap. 8 is resumed in 10:23–33; the treatment of the eucharist in 10:14–21 is resumed in 11:17–34.

[38]T. W. Gillespie, *The First Theologians: A Study in Early Christian Prophecy* (Grand Rapids: Eerdmans, 1995), pays special attention to I Cor.

churches; yet 11:5 allows women to pray or prophesy with their head covered.[39] The idea that in the 50s all the Pauline churches were administered charismatically in the same way as Corinth (and that twenty or thirty years later this changed to a more institutionalized bishop-deacon structure pictured in the Pastorals) is risky because of both the lack of information in most of the other letters written at this time, and the reference to bishops and deacons at Philippi (Phil 1:1).[40]

PART IV OF THE BODY OF THE LETTER (15:1–58). Here Paul describes the gospel in terms of the resurrection of Jesus and then draws implications from that for the resurrection of Christians.[41] I shall devote a subsection below to many subsidiary issues about Paul's notion of the resurrection stemming from this chap., while here I concentrate on the function of the resurrection in Paul's message to Corinth. Some Corinthian Christians have been saying that there is no resurrection of the dead (15:12). It is not clear what these people think happened to Jesus; but the argument makes good sense if they thought that Jesus had risen bodily from the dead,[42] and in 15:1–11 Paul is reminding them of that common tradition. Jesus rose from the dead and appeared to such known figures as Cephas, the Twelve, James (the brother of the Lord), and Paul himself (15:3–8; also 9:1)—a tradition totally conformed to the Scriptures and solidly attested: "Whether, then, it was I or they, thus we preach and thus you believed" (15:11). As for the fate of others, those whom Paul would correct may have thought that the equivalent of resurrection had been accomplished already by the coming of the Spirit so that nothing else was to be expected. Rather, basing himself on what happened to Christ, Paul contends that all the dead are to be raised (15:12–19), that the resurrection is future (15:20–34), and bodily (15:35–50). In this argument he teaches that those fallen asleep in Christ are not lost (also II Cor 4:14). Indeed, Christ is the firstfruits of those fallen asleep: As in Adam all died, so in Christ all

[39]Also Acts 2:17–18 seems to presuppose women prophesying, and 21:9 describes four women prophets. Some have tried to solve the contrariety by maintaining that "speaking" (*lalein*) to people in church involved a role different from prophesying, where the word comes from God. Others have posited that I Cor 14:34–35 is a later interpolation in the style of I Tim 2:11–14, citing the fact that some ancient copyists transposed 34–35 to after v. 40. On 14:33b–36 see R. W. Allison, JSNT 32 (1988), 32–34; C. Vander Stichele, LS 20 (1995), 241–53; L. A. Jervis, JSNT 58 (1995), 51–74; also A. C. Wire, *The Corinthian Women Prophets* (Minneapolis: A/F, 1990); N. Baumert, *Woman and Man in Paul* (Collegeville: Liturgical, 1996); and n. 20 in Chapter 30 below.

[40]See Chapter 20 above, *Issue* 5. It is possible that in places where Paul had a relatively brief stay, he recognized the need to leave behind a more formal structure, whereas in places where he had a longer time to form the community (Corinth), Paul was inclined to leave the assignment of roles to the Spirit through charisms.

[41]I. Saw, *Paul's Rhetoric in 1 Corinthians 15* (Lewiston, NY: Mellen, 1995).

[42]Ruef (*I Corinthians* xxiv), however, thinks they held that, like Elijah, Jesus was elevated into heaven (from the cross) without having died.

shall be made alive (I Cor 15:20–22).[43] There is an eschatological order: first, Christ; then at his return, those who belong to Christ; then at the end, when he has destroyed every dominion, authority and power, and subjected all enemies (with death as the last enemy[44]), Christ hands over to the Father the kingdom; finally, the Son himself will be subjected to God, who put all things under him so that God may be all in all (15:23–28).

Resurrection is not an abstract issue for Paul; rather, the hope of being raised explains his willingness to suffer as he has in Ephesus, from which he writes this letter (15:30–34). In 15:35–58 Paul concentrates on another objection raised at Corinth to the resurrection of the dead: With what kind of body? (This has remained an objection over the centuries as the earthly remains of millions of people have disintegrated and disappeared.) Paul gives a subtle answer: Resurrection will involve a transformed body, as different as the grown plant is from the seed—a body imperishable, not perishable; powerful, not weak; spiritual (*pneumatikos*), not physical (*psychikos*); in the image of heavenly origin, not from the dust of the earth. After all, "Flesh and blood cannot inherit the kingdom of God" (15:50). At the end, whether alive or dead, we shall all be changed and be clothed with the imperishable and immortal (15:51–54). The "bottom line" in response to the Corinthians who deny the resurrection is that death has lost its sting because God has given us victory through our Lord Jesus Christ (15:55–58).

BODY CLOSING (16:1–18) and CONCLUDING FORMULA (16:19–24). The Closing of I Cor gives instructions for the Corinthians to take up the collection for Jerusalem[45] and outlines Paul's plan. Paul wants to stay at Ephesus at least till Pentecost (May/June AD 57?) because, despite opposition, an opportunity for evangelizing work has opened for him. Yet he plans to come to Corinth via Macedonia and perhaps to spend the winter (AD 57–58?) there. Whenever Timothy comes (n. 13 above), he is to be treated well (16:10–11). As for Apollos, although Paul had urged him to return to Corinth, he is unwilling to do so at this time, presumably lest he exacerbate the factionalism there (16:12).

Although the concluding greetings (including those from Aquila and

[43]Paul returns to this motif in 15:29–34 with the added puzzling argument that if the dead are not raised, why are people baptized for them? This text (15:29) has been used in ancient and modern times (respectively by Marcionites and Mormons) to justify vicarious baptism of Christians for the dead. See J. Murphy-O'Connor, RB 88 (1981), 532–43; R. E. De Maris, JBL 114 (1995), 661–82.

[44]M. C. de Boer, *The Defeat of Death* (JSNTSup 22; Sheffield: JSOT, 1988): Jewish apocalyptic speaks of two mutually exclusive "ages," one ruled by a superhuman evil power and the other by God. I Cor 15:26 does not mean that Christ has defeated all powers except death. Rather, death and sin have been defeated by God through Christ; but they both remain the mark of "this age" which in Christ's death and resurrection God has victoriously invaded.

[45]V. D. Verbrugge, *Paul's Style of Church Leadership Illustrated by His Instructions to the Corinthians on the Collection* (San Francisco: Mellen, 1992).

Prisca/Priscilla) are warm, when Paul takes up a pen to add a touch with his own hand, he acts as a judge, cursing anyone at Corinth who does not love the Lord (16:22). Still his last words are positive, not only extending love to all, but also uttering a prayer that evidently even the Corinthians know in the mother tongue of Jesus (Aramaic *Māránā' thā':* "Our Lord, come").

Those Criticized by Paul at Corinth

In chaps. 1–4 Paul corrects factionalism among the Corinthians, not by addressing each group separately but by criticizing the whole community of Christians for allowing themselves to be split up into the three or four groups of adherents (n. 11 above). He does not tell us whether there were theological differences among the groups beyond their loyalties to different individuals; but scholars have felt free to assign distinct individual stances to each.[46] For example, often a conservative adherence to the Law is attributed to the Cephas (Peter) faction, despite the fact that I Cor 15:5,11 indicates that Cephas and Paul preached a common message. There is no evidence that the missionaries whose names designate the factions (Paul, Apollos, Cephas) were blamed by Paul for encouraging such factionalism. Was the formation of the groups spontaneous, or did some of those whose slogans are criticized in subsequent chapters of I Cor have a role in generating the factionalism? In the next paragraphs I shall discuss the ideas criticized by Paul, but there is little evidence that these came from abroad to Corinth. Perhaps the groups gave voice to tendencies already present, e.g., inadequate Gentile understandings of Christian ideas derived from Judaism. Were the three or four factions organized into separate house-churches? Answers to that question are largely guesses since there is little information in I-II Cor on house-churches, beyond their existence (I Cor 16:19; Rom 16:23). Indeed, I Cor 14:23 envisions the possibility of the whole church coming together.

The words *sophia* ("wisdom") and *sophos* ("wise") occur over twenty-five times in chaps. 1–3, as the wisdom of God (which others consider foolishness) is contrasted with human wisdom. The criticism of Jews and Greeks, both of whom reject the Christ who was the wisdom of God, shows that Paul is not criticizing any one view of human wisdom, even if forms of Greek philosophy were included under the wisdom looked for by Greeks (1:22). Although in chaps. 1–4 *gnōsis* occurs only in 1:5, a considerable

[46]D. B. Martin, *The Corinthian Body* (New Haven: Yale, 1995) contends that the disputes at Corinth reflect different ideological constructions of the body. P. Vielhauer, JHC 1 (1994—German original 1975), 129–42, argues that 3:11 is polemically directed against primacy claims made on behalf of Peter. Pogoloff, *Logos,* however, thinks the allegiances were to the preachers not to ideologies, and that throughout the Corinthian Christians were striving for the status of a social elite.

number of scholars has contended that Paul was criticizing a gnostic movement at Corinth.[47] For evidence they sometimes turn to the later chapters of I Cor, e.g., "We all possess knowledge" (8:1) and the discussion of knowledge in 8:7–11; see also 13:2,8; 14:6. Certainly there were Christians at Corinth who were more knowledgeable than other Christians and thought themselves superior. But is the term "gnostics" appropriate for them as if they shared a great deal in common with the 2d-century systems that claimed a special revealed knowledge about how recipients possessed a spark of the divine and could escape from the material world?[48] Paul, the founder of the Christian community at Corinth, departed *ca.* AD 52; had major gnostic teachers come and influenced the Christians by 56? (Peter was no gnostic, and Paul shows no apprehension about Apollos' views in 16:12.) Did the denial of the resurrection of the dead by some at Corinth (15:12,29) stem from a gnostic denial that Jesus was physically a human being who died and/or the contention that true believers were already spiritually raised? Were Christians at Corinth saying "*Jesus* be cursed" (12:3); and if so, were they thereby rejecting the idea that Christ (distinct from Jesus) had a genuine earthly existence?

This leads us into the problem of evaluating a number of slogans in I Cor. Besides those cited above, the following could be included: "All things are permissible for me" (6:12; 10:23); "Food is meant for the stomach, and the stomach for food" (6:13); "Avoid immorality; every other sin that a person may commit is outside the body" (6:18); "It is good for a man not to touch a woman" (7:1). Paul correctively modifies these slogans, and so they are being used by those whom he would admonish at Corinth. That modification, however, leaves open two major possibilities: These statements were originally coined either by Paul in evangelizing the Corinthians (but are now being misused) or by Paul's adversaries.[49] In either case, one could posit their use in a system of thought whereby superior knowledge leads a group

[47]In 2:13–16 Paul speaks of the *pneumatikoi,* or spiritual people, whom he contrasts with the unspiritual; R. A. Horsley (HTR 69 [1976], 269–88) argues for a group of such people at Corinth. See B. A. Pearson, *The Pneumatikos-Psychikos Terminology in 1 Corinthians* (SBLDS 12; Missoula, MT: Scholars, 1973).

[48]Schmithals, *Gnosticism,* is a major study of this issue. R. A. Horsley, NTS 27 (1980–81), 32–51, finding parallels in Hellenistic Jewish theology represented by Philo and the Wisdom of Solomon, argues that the gnosis at Corinth was vocalized by missionaries of that background. (Murphy-O'Connor thinks of Apollos as a conduit of Philo's Alexandrian thought that Paul was ridiculing.) Yet R. M. Wilson, NTS 19 (1973–74), 65–74, doubts that there was a developed gnosticism.

[49]See J. Murphy-O'Connor, "Corinthian Slogans in 1 Cor 6:12–20," CBQ 40 (1980), 91–96; R. A. Ramsaran, *Liberating Words: Paul's Use of Rhetorical Maxims in 1 Corinthians 1–10* (Valley Forge, PA: Trinity, 1996). Hurd, *Origin,* thinks that many of the errors at Corinth stem from Paul's own teaching there: His uncautious advocacy of freedom and overly enthusiastic outlook on the parousia were exaggerated over the years by those who had heard him. See also Conzelmann, *1 Corinthians* 15–16.

(the "Christ" party?) toward libertinism on the principle that the body is unimportant, both as to what one does in the body and to what happens after death.

Finally there are other points in Paul's critique that may have nothing to do with a profound theological stance. The tendencies to go to secular courts with lawsuits (6:1–7) and for women to pray with their heads uncovered (11:5) may reflect nothing more than Corinthian social mores.

There is considerable surmise in this discussion of those whom Paul was correcting, and some have sought clarity by appealing to the portrayal of the opponents in II Cor as if there was a continuity between the two groups. Although that will be discussed on pp. 554–56 below, it explains the obscure through the equally obscure, since the physiognomy of the II Cor opponents is not overly clear.

Paul's Critique of Fornicators and Homosexuals (6:9–10)

Paul warns that those who practice a number of vices will not inherit the kingdom of heaven. Today almost all Christians would still join his condemnation of idolaters, thieves, the greedy, drunkards, slanderers, and robbers, whether or not they would assign to them all the same severe fate. But major problems have developed about three designations: *pornoi, malakoi,* and *arsenokoitai.* (The first and the third, which will be our main concern here, are joined in I Tim 1:10.)

Pornoi is understood to refer to the (sexually) immoral by RSV, NIV, NJB, and AB, and to fornicators by NABR and NRSV. Today, greater tolerance in First World society toward the living together of unmarried men and women and/or sexual intercourse between them has catalyzed a debate as to whether Paul was issuing a blanket condemnation of "fornication."[50] Since in 6:15–18 Paul goes on to forbid a Christian man's joining his body with that of a prostitute (*pornē*) and to condemn *porneia,* and since there was a Corinthian history of sacred prostitutes in the service of Aphrodite, some would argue that by *pornoi* in 6:9 Paul meant only those who indulged in sex for money, i.e., those involved with prostitutes. However, in 5:1, as an example of *porneia* among the Corinthians Paul holds up the man who was living with his stepmother—scarcely sex for profit.[51] Because there is not adequate evidence for narrowing Paul's reference to *pornoi,* "Those who indulge in fornication" is a more accurate translation than "Those who use women prostitutes."

[50]Paul also mentions adultery in this list.

[51]Nor is it reasonable to confine to sex-for-pay the verb *porneuein* in 10:8, used in a context based on what the Israelites did in Exod 32:6.

The next two terms, *malakoi* and *arsenokoitai,* lead us to the issue of homosexuality; and E. P. Sanders (*Paul* [1991] 110–13) is wise in insisting that a necessary preliminary is understanding Greco-Roman attitudes where there was no overall condemnation of sexual relations with a person of the same sex. Indeed in Greek circles the homosexual activity of a grown man with an attractive youth could be considered part of cultured education since the beauty of the male body was highly esteemed. But in general it was shameful for a grown male to be the passive partner or play the woman's role—that was for slaves. (There is less information about female homosexuality, but there may have been a corresponding disdain for the woman who played the male or active role.) As for Jews, as Sanders points out, they condemned homosexuality "lock, stock, and barrel," i.e., both passive and active.[52] Although some scholars disagree, in all likelihood Paul with his two nouns is also condemning passive and active homosexuality.

Malakoi (literally, "soft") could refer to the effeminate, and some would argue for the translation "dissolute." Yet in the Greco-Roman world it was a designation for catamites, men or boys (particularly the latter) who were kept for sexual use, playing the receptive, feminine role. "Boy prostitutes" and "male prostitutes" are translations offered by the NABR and NRSV. (Since there is no serious tendency in today's society to be tolerant toward pederasty or male prostitution, this is not the word that causes the major problem.) The debate has centered on *arsenokoitai* (literally, "those who go to bed with males"), translated as "sodomites" (NRSV) or "homosexuals" (NIV).[53] Movements for justice for gays have led to challenges about such a rendering, and some would contend that Paul is condemning only male prostitution because it brutalizes the active participant as well as victimizing the passive participant. This is highly dubious on several grounds. As indicated above, an attempt to create a parallelism with *pornoi,* understood as those having sex with female prostitutes, is unlikely. Moreover, the linguistic composition of *arsenokoitai* lends little support to confining the term to using male prostitutes.[54] The components *arsēn* and *koimasthai* are found in

[52]*Letter of Aristeas* 152–53; *Sibylline Oracle* 2.73; Philo, *Special Laws* 3.37–42.

[53]The NABR renders the term "practicing homosexuals," a translation designed to correlate with Roman Catholic theology that homosexual orientation is not sinful but homosexual practice is. While Paul was talking about practice, such a distinction was surely not in his mind. RSV's "sexual *perverts*" introduces a note that is not explicit in this passage; see n. 56 below.

[54]R. Scroggs, *The New Testament and Homosexuality* (Philadelphia: Fortress, 1983) would argue that throughout the NT writers were opposing pederasty, which was the only *model* of homosexuality in their contemporary culture; yet see P. Coleman, *Christian Attitudes to Homosexuality* (London: SPCK, 1980), esp. 120ff. The argument that *arsenokoitai* means male prostitutes was developed particularly by J. Boswell, *Christianity, Social Tolerance, and Homosexuality* (Univ. of Chicago, 1980), 335–53. It has been devastatingly challenged by D. F. Wright, VC 38 (1984), 125–53; R. B. Hays, *Journal of Religious Ethics* 14 (1986), 184–215; also M. L. Soards, *Scripture and Homosexuality* (Louisville: W/K, 1995).

Lev 18:22; 20:13, which forbid lying with a male as with a woman, i.e., having coitus with a male. Surely Paul, whose basic Bible was the LXX, had these passages in mind when he used the compound word to condemn homosexuality.[55] The fact that I Cor 6:9–10 places the reference to *arsenokoitai* in the context of many other condemned practices hinders efforts to evaluate how seriously he regarded it. His thought is spelled out more clearly in Rom 1:26–27, where he bases himself on God's creation of man and woman for each other, to cleave together as one. Accordingly he denounces as a graphic distortion of God's created order women who have exchanged natural intercourse for that against nature and men who have abandoned natural relations with women and burned with lust for one another.[56] Overall, then, the evidence strongly favors the thesis that Paul was condemning not only sexual activity by pederasts but also by homosexuals—indeed any sexual activity outside of marriage between a man and a woman.

All statements by human beings, including those in the Bible, are limited by the worldview of those who uttered them. Our attention has been focused on what Paul was condemning in the 1st century. A different but essential question is how binding the Pauline condemnation is for Christians of today. This goes beyond the issue of "interim ethics" (p. 509 above). We know a lot more about the physiology and psychology of sexual activity than did Paul. Nevertheless, the fact that in I Cor 6:16 Paul cites Gen 2:24, "The two will become one flesh," suggests that his condemnation of fornicators and homosexuals in I Cor 6:9 is rooted in God's having created male and female in the divine image (Gen 1:27) and ordained that they might be united in marriage—the same background cited against divorce by Jesus in Mark 10:7–8. An outlook based on the revelation of God's will in creation itself would not be easily changed. Scholarly discussion of the issue will continue, challenging Paul's outlook on the "unnatural." Nevertheless, in insisting on the sexual limits imposed by the divinely commanded state of marriage between a man and a woman, Paul and indeed, Jesus himself, walking among us in our times, would not be frightened by being considered sexually and politically "incorrect," any more than they minded being considered overly demanding in the Greco-Roman and Jewish world of their times.[57]

[55]It may be true that the authors of the Hebrew Bible did not know the whole range of homosexual practice among the Gentiles; it is much less likely that the Alexandrian translators of the Bible into Greek or Paul with his Hellenistic upbringing did not know that range.

[56]Exemplifying different views, Fitzmyer, *Romans* 287–88: "Paul regards such homosexual activity as a perversion [*planē* in 1:27b]"; M. Davies, *Biblical Interpretation* 3 (1995), 315–31, contends that Paul has a blind spot about this OT worldview; J. E. Miller, NovT 37 (1995), 1–11, argues that Rom 1:26–27 rejects "unnatural" (noncoital) *hetero*sexual intercourse.

[57]In forming a position on how permanently binding scriptural positions are, Christians of different backgrounds appeal to different factors: inspiration, inerrancy, biblical authority, and church

Charisms at Corinth (I Cor 12 and 14) and Today

In 12:28 we find a list of charisms, divided first into a numbered group of three consisting of apostles, prophets, and teachers; and then into an unnumbered group consisting of acts of power [miracles], the gifts of healings, forms of help or assistance; administrative capabilities [or leadership], and various kinds of tongues.[58] This is not a total list, for 12:8–10 also mentions utterance of wisdom, utterance of knowledge, faith, and discernment of spirits, plus a distinction made between tongues and the interpretation of tongues;[59] still others appear in Rom 12:6–8. Some who have one charism want another, and in I Cor 12:12ff. Paul uses the image of the human body and its many members, probably borrowed from popular Stoicism (p. 90 above), to stress that diversity is necessary. Even the less presentable parts have an indispensable role. From 14:1–33 we discern that the gift of speaking in tongues,[60] perhaps because it was most visible, was the chief source of strife. Paul critiques the situation in several ways. One needs to interpret the tongues, and consequently an additional gift of interpretation is required (14:13). Compared to tongues, there are more excellent gifts, e.g., prophecy that builds up the church (14:5). Most radically Paul urges seeking after love (*agapē*), which is more important than any charism (13:1–13), whether speaking angelic tongues or prophecy, or miracles. When he has advanced all his arguments, Paul contends that every true prophet and spiritual person will recognize that what he has written is a command of the Lord; and the person who does not recognize that is not to be recognized in the community (14:37–38)! If Paul has to resort to that authoritarian "bottom line," we know we are dealing with a difficult subject.

Although there have always been small churches and even sects of Christians who exulted in charismatic phenomena, in recent years "charismatics" have received more attention and are now found among members of most of the large churches. There is a variety of charisms in these modern experiences, but frequently attention centers on speaking in tongues, "being slain

---

teaching (pp. 29–32 above). For a perceptive and sensitive treatment of this issue, see C. R. Koester, *Lutheran Quarterly* 7 (1993), 375–90.

[58]The Greek is a strange mixture of persons, abilities, and actions, so that one has to supply English words like "forms of" or "qualities of." Clearly "charisms" are varied in their most basic description. On Paul's thought about charisms, see Marrow, *Paul* 149–59; E. Nardoni, CBQ 55 (1993), 68–80.

[59]On the range of the charisms, it is startling to read in I Cor 12:9: "to another faith is given," since all Christians must have faith. Perhaps Paul means a special intensity of faith (13:2: faith so as to move mountains), or a faith especially effective in sustaining others.

[60]See F. A. Sullivan, in *The Spirit of God in Christian Life,* ed. E. Malatesta (New York: Paulist, 1977), 23–74, where endnotes contain ample bibliography.

in the spirit," and detecting demons.[61] It is generally recognized that charismatic experiences have the power to intensify the religious or spiritual life of people. Yet are charismatics today experiencing what is described in I Cor 12?

Some remarks are in order: (a) No person reared in the 20th century has the worldview of a person reared in the 1st century, and therefore it is impossible today to know or duplicate exactly what Paul describes, no matter how genuine the self-assurance of the charismatic. On the basic point of the Spirit, for instance, Christians are now shaped by a trinitarian theology worked out in the 4th century; there is no evidence that Paul had such clarity about the personhood of the Spirit. (b) As for speaking in tongues, Paul claims to speak in tongues to a greater degree than those he is addressing at Corinth (14:18). Yet it is not easy to be certain what he means by "tongues." He makes references to speech that requires interpretation; to speech directed to God but not to others, for nobody understands the speakers; to sounds that in themselves are unintelligible; to a gift that builds up the individual rather than the church (14:1–19); and to the tongues of angels (13:1). Writing a few decades later, the author of Acts seems to offer two interpretations of speaking in tongues (2:4): one in which it is unintelligible babbling as if the speakers were drunk (2:13–15), and another in which it is the speaking of foreign languages that one has not learned (2:6–7). Are different understandings of "tongues" what is meant by "various kinds of tongues"? (c) The charisms described by Paul are gifts given freely by God; they do not all seem to involve emotional experience or dramatic behavior. As already indicated, one gift is *kybernēseis* (administrations, leaderships). Today we may recognize that a person is a gifted administrator and attribute that to God, but normally we do not place such people in the same charismatic category as speakers in tongues. Paul does. (d) Modern appreciation of charisms sometimes neglects the fact that they were very divisive at Corinth. Inevitably, whether a charism or an office is involved, when one Christian claims to have a role others do not have, issues of superiority and envy are introduced. There are NT reflections on the Spirit that almost work against the idea of different charisms. According to John 14:15–16 everyone who loves Jesus and keeps the commandments receives the Paraclete Spirit, and there is no suggestion of different gifts or roles. In John's view all are disciples, and that is what is important. (e) Finally, in evaluating modern charismatics, with loyalty to the NT evidence one may rejoice that the church today

[61]NT attempts to explain the difference between the baptism administered by JBap and that to be introduced by Jesus have sometimes promoted an attempt to distinguish between baptism of water (administered to all Christians) and a baptism of the Spirit surrounded by the outpouring of charisms. According to John 3:5, however, *all* true believers are begotten of water *and* Spirit.

like the church in Corinth is not lacking in any spiritual gift (1:7). Yet one may challenge those who maintain that someone is not a Christian if that person does not receive a special charism, or maintain that when a charism is received, the possessor is a better Christian than others not thus gifted.

The "Hymn" to Love (I Cor 13)

This chapter contains some of the most beautiful lines ever penned by Paul, whence the designation "Hymn." After the contrast between love and charisms (13:1–3), 13:4–8a personifies love and makes it the subject of sixteen verbs (some of which are translated by predicate adjectives in English). This leads into a contrast between a present marked by charisms in which there is but a poor reflection in a mirror, and a future where we shall see face to face. There faith, hope, and love will remain, "but the greatest of these is love" (13:8b–13).

What is meant by Christian love (*agapē*)? Every NT author does not necessarily have the same understanding of the term, but what follows applies to some of the principal passages. An entree is offered by A. Nygren's famous *Agape and Eros* (2 vols.; London: SPCK, 1932–37). To spotlight the uniqueness of Christian *agapē*, Nygren contrasted it with both the highest expression of love (*eros*) among the Pagan philosophers and love described in the OT. The contrast is exaggerated and needs serious qualification; nevertheless, it can be helpful in clarifying what is meant in this chap. of I Cor. Nygren described *eros* as love attracted by the goodness of the object: people reaching out or up for the good they want to possess in order to be more complete.[62] In Platonic philosophy this *eros* would be a motivating factor reaching out for the perfect truth and beauty that exists outside this world. In Aristotelian philosophy *eros* would involve the material or limited reaching out to be less limited and thus moving up the scale of being. God, in whom there is all perfection, would be the supreme object of *eros*. *Agapē*, on the other hand, is unmotivated; it confers goodness on the object loved. Thus *agapē* starts with God who needs nothing from creatures but by love brings them into being and ennobles them. In particular, Paul's notion of love is based on the self-giving of Christ, who loved us not because we were good but while we were still sinners (Rom 5:8). As I John 4:8,10 proclaims: "God is love . . . In this is love, not that we loved God but that God loved us and sent His Son to be the atoning sacrifice for our sins." The eloquent personification of love in I Cor 13:5–8 almost makes love and Christ inter-

[62]Nygren did not discuss sexual love (which is a God-given form of love among human beings). At times in the NT (especially in John) words related to *philia*, "friendship," are almost interchangeable with words related to *agapē*.

changeable. Given worth (justified, sanctified) by Christ's *agapē,* we become the channel of passing that love on to others whom we love, not evaluating their goodness and without motivation: "Love each other as I have loved you" (John 15:12).[63]

Paul and the Risen Jesus (I Cor 15)

The tradition preserved in 15:3ff. shows that there was in place an early sequence of Jesus' death, burial, resurrection, and appearances—the building blocks of a passion narrative (especially when combined with 11:23 that places the Last Supper on the night before Jesus was given over). It offers an argument for recognizing that a tradition about Jesus' earthly career was developing side by side with Paul's preaching that reports few details about that career. Although this chapter was included in I Cor as an argument for the reality of the resurrection of those who have died in Christ, it has become a centerpiece in the argument about the reality of the resurrection of Jesus. In the present form there are two groups of three by whom Jesus "was seen": Cephas (Peter), the Twelve, and more than 500; then James, all the apostles, and "last of all me."[64] The concluding reference to himself is extremely important since Paul is the only NT writer who claims personally to have witnessed an appearance of the risen Jesus.[65] We may list a number of issues:

(a) Paul places the appearance to himself, even if it was last, on the same level as the appearance to all the other listed witnesses. Acts gives a different picture, for after appearances on earth Jesus ascends into heaven (1:9); consequently, a light and voice comes to Paul from heaven (Acts 9:3–5; 22:6–8; 26:13–15). Few would give the Lucan picture priority over the Pauline.

(b) Paul employs the verbal sequence died/buried/raised/appeared in I Cor 15:3–5 and reuses "appeared" (the passive of "to see") three more times in 15:6–8. Nevertheless, some have contended that Paul is not referring to

[63]Nygren wrote almost as if *eros* was to be eradicated in favor of *agapē* when, as a matter of fact, both forms of love should coexist. In Christian love for another, there should be an aspect of the unmotivated, not dependent on how good that person is; but the Christian can scarcely not love the goodness of that other person as well. Again, Nygren, who held that loving God because of the divine goodness would be *eros,* was too purist in arguing that Christians cannot love God since there is nothing that can be bestowed on God. For instance, he had to contend that Jesus' command to love the Lord your God with whole heart, soul, and mind (Mark 12:30, from the LXX of Deut 6:5, both using *agapan*) was an imperfect conception of love. Also Nygren contended wrongfully that there was no *agapē* in the OT. The *ḥesed* or covenant love of God for Israel is a manifestation of *agapē.*

[64]Scholars are divided as to where the received tradition stops and where Paul's addenda begin. See also 9:1, "Have I not seen Jesus our Lord?"

[65]The author of II Pet (1:16–18), speaking as Peter, claims to have seen the transfiguration; the prophetic author of Rev has visions of the heavenly Jesus.

seeing Jesus in a bodily form. Since in Paul's understanding Jesus appeared to more than 500 people at the same time, a purely internal vision seems to be ruled out. Moreover, presumably Paul's experience of the risen Jesus has something to do with his expectations about the raising of the dead in the rest of the chap. There he very clearly talks about a resurrection of the *body* (even if transformed) and uses the analogy of sowing in the ground and what emerges from it (15:35–37).[66]

(c) Much has been made of Paul's silence about Jesus' empty tomb as if that silence were contradictory to the Gospel accounts. Yet there is no a priori reason why he had to mention the tomb, and the burial/resurrection sequence virtually presumes that the risen body is no longer where it was buried.

(d) Luke's description of a risen Jesus who speaks of himself as having flesh and bones and who eats (Luke 24:39,42–43) seems contrary to a Pauline understanding of the risen body as spiritual and not flesh and blood (I Cor 15:44,50). Luke (who does not claim to have seen the risen Jesus) may well have had a more concrete, tangible understanding of the risen body (of Jesus) than Paul had (of the risen bodies of Christians). Once again few would give the Lucan picture priority over the Pauline.

Issues and Problems for Reflection

(1) The common view, adopted here, is that I Cor is a unified letter sent at one time. (Hurd, "Good News," discusses the issue thoroughly.) Motifs in the Thanksgiving (1:5–7, e.g., possessing knowledge, not lacking charisms, awaiting the revealing of Jesus Christ) anticipate themes in 8:1; 12:1; 15:23. Yet there is no visible connection between the factions mentioned in chaps. 1–4 and the corrections issued after 5:1. For example, we get no indication whether members of the Cephas (Peter) or Apollos factions are those who deny that Paul is an apostle (9:2). The two occasions of information mentioned under #4 and #5 above best explain the disjointed nature of the letter, but leave open different theories of composition. Snyder argues that a letter consisting of chaps. 7–16 was composed by Paul in response to the missive from Corinth mentioned in 7:1 (#5). Before he could send his letter, he got news via Chloe of a more serious situation created by the factions at Corinth; and so he prefixed chaps 1–6. De Boer favors the opposite order: Paul's letter consisting of chaps. 1–4 was not sent before the newly arrived missive from Corinth (with accompanying reports) required the addition of 5–16.

[66]M. E. Dahl, *The Resurrection of the Body. A Study of 1 Corinthians 15* (SBT; London: SCM, 1962).

(2) Paul's description of excommunication in 5:4–5 is not very clear except for his insistence that the sinful man had to be expelled from the community. We find in Acts 5:1–11 the extirpation of those whose sinful presence would corrupt the community. How a Christian community might deal with someone who had to be corrected is illustrated in Matt 18:15–17. Yet notice that in neither Matt (see 18:21–22) nor I Cor (5:5b) was the expulsion of the sinner the last word; there was still hope for forgiveness or salvation.

(3) We see examples of Paul's understanding of his apostolic authority in 5:3–5 (to excommunicate), 7:10–16 (to issue a ruling that modifies a ruling of the Lord), and 15:9–11 (to be a spokesman along with others of an authoritative interpretation of the gospel). An old axiom is that revelation ceased with the death of the last apostle. Not to be taken in a mechanical sense, this was meant to signify that the Christian revelation included not only what Jesus said in his ministry but also the interpretation of Jesus by the apostles, particularly as enshrined in the NT. (See also Gal 1:8; Matt 16:19; 18:18; John 20:23.) Yet in modern discussions of disputed issues (particularly of morality), one sometimes gets the impression that if Jesus himself did not affirm something and one must resort to Paul's word, that is less authoritative. Moreover, although the major Christian churches have resisted the notion of postapostolic new revelation, others who believe in Christ, from Montanus in the 2d century to Joseph Smith in the 19th, have held that new revelation could come through a prophet.

(4) In Acts 16:15,33 we find instances of Paul baptizing immediately those whom he had convinced about Christ; but according to I Cor 1:14 in a year and a half at Corinth he personally baptized only Crispus (confirming Acts 18:8) and Gaius. Nevertheless Paul considered himself the one father of the Corinthians in Christ through the gospel. How did baptism fit into Paul's missionary enterprise? If he did not baptize most of the Corinthians, who did? Paul speaks of his planting the seed and Apollos watering it (3:6). Without any pun, did Apollos do the baptizing in water? This would be interesting in the light of Acts 18:24–28 where he had not known that there was a baptism beyond JBap's. What theology of baptism would explain separating the evangelizer from the baptizer? In I Cor 6:11 Paul gives the sequence "washed, sanctified, justified" (a rare reference in I Cor to justification; see 1:30 and 4:4), showing that baptism had a centrality. Chap. 10 compares baptism to Moses' delivering Israel from Egypt in the exodus, and places it in a context that speaks of the eucharist. See also the treatment in Rom 6:1–11.

(5) Paul's attitude in I Cor 7:1–9 is that he would like all to be like himself, unmarried and abstaining from sex, but the affirmation it is better "to marry

rather than to burn,"[67] has been the source of much discussion. See also 7:28: If you do get married it is not a sin, but married people will have hardships; and 7:32–33: The unmarried man can pay attention to the Lord's affairs while the married man pays attention to the affairs of the world and how to please his wife. Granted that these statements are colored by the thought of Christ coming soon, they do not offer an enthusiastic picture of the sanctifying possibilities of married life. In subsequent Christianity the monastic movement for men and women led to the thesis that celibacy for the kingdom of God is better than marriage. On the other hand in Reformation times celibacy was attacked as a distortion of the gospel; and where Protestantism was victorious, priests and nuns were often forced to marry. Today many Catholics and Protestants want to avoid the category of "better" and to recognize that both celibacy and marriage lived in the love of God are noble callings/choices. Reflection on this issue is profitably augmented by study of Matt 19:10–12 and Eph 5:21–33.

(6) Given Paul's pastoral attitude on eating food sacrificed to idols (chap. 8; p. 520 above), what is so wrong about Cephas' (Peter's) behavior at Antioch described in Gal 2:11ff.? A Jewish Christian, he knew that he was free to eat with Gentile Christians; but when men of James came and objected, he ceased to do so. Paul objected to this behavior as timorous and insincere (even though Barnabas sided with Peter); but in Peter's mind might it not have been pastoral behavior to avoid scandalizing the less enlightened Jewish Christians? If there were those at Corinth who insisted on exercising freedom and eating what they wanted, might they not have accused Paul of betraying the gospel of freedom by his cautious attitude, even as he accused Peter of this at Antioch?

(7) In 10:1–4 Paul speaks of the ancestral Israelites having been baptized into Moses in the cloud and the sea, and having all eaten the supernatural food and drunk the supernatural drink. The rock in that scene of desert wandering was Christ. Given the references to the eucharist in 10:14–22, Paul is reflecting on both baptism and the eucharist against an OT background. This is one of our first indications of the close joining of what were to be designated by later Christians as the primary sacraments. How close were they actually associated in early Christian "liturgical" services? The eucharistic passage (also 11:27) implies great care about who could participate. Yet 14:22 suggests an assembly where the word was spoken and unbelievers might enter. Were there separate Christian meetings for the eucharistic meal and for proclaiming the word? (Thus, Becker, *Paul* 252.)

[67]M. Barré, CBQ 6 (1974), 193–202, argues that Paul does not mean "to burn with passion" but "to be burned in the fires of judgment."

(8) Exacerbated by Reformation disputes, differing church theologies of the eucharist have constituted a very divisive factor in Western Christianity. I Cor 10:14–22 and 11:17–34 are extraordinarily important as the only references to the eucharist in the Pauline letters and also the oldest preserved written eucharistic testimony.[68] Comparison of 11:23–25 and Luke 22:19–20 on the one hand with Mark 14:22–24 and Matt 26:26–28 on the other hand suggests at least two different preserved forms of the eucharistic words of Jesus—perhaps three if John 6:51 is brought in. (Paul and Luke may be giving us the form in use at the church of Antioch.) It is sobering to reflect that if there had not been abuses at Corinth, Paul would never have mentioned the eucharist; and certainly many scholars would be arguing that there was no eucharist in the Pauline churches on the grounds that he could not have written so much and been accidentally silent about it. Also, since the second passage mentions divisions over eucharistic practice and understanding at Corinth five years after conversion, we are reminded how quickly the eucharist became a source of contention! A divisive issue among Christian churches today is whether there is a sacrificial aspect in the eucharistic offering. Another divisive issue concerns real presence: Is the communicant truly eating the body and drinking the blood of the Lord? Granted that the Roman Catholic-Protestant debates certainly go beyond Paul's thought, reflection on I Cor 10:14–22 and 11:27–29 contributes to the discussion, along with John 6:51–64. Those passages contain verses that have a sacrificial context and verses that point to realism but also the need for faith.

Bibliography on I Corinthians

COMMENTARIES AND STUDIES IN SERIES (* = plus II Cor): Barrett, C. K. (HNTC, 1968); Bruce, F. F. (NCBC, 1971*); Conzelmann, H. (Hermeneia, 1975); Dunn, J.D.G. (NTG, 1995); Ellingworth, P., and H. Hatton (2d ed.; TH, 1994); **Fee, G. D.** (NICNT, 1987); Fisher, F. L. (WBC, 1975*); Grosheide, F. W. (NICNT, 1953); Harrisville, R. A. (AugC, 1987); Morris, L. (2d ed.; TNTC, 1985); Murphy-O'Connor, J. (NTM, 1979); Orr, W. F. and J. A. Walther (AB, 1976); Robertson, A., and A. Plummer (2d ed.; ICC, 1914); Ruef, J. (PC, 1977); Thrall, M. E. (CCNEB, 1965*); Watson, N. (EC, 1992).

BIBLIOGRAPHIES: Whitely, D.E.H.,* *Theology* 65 (1962), 188–91; Mills, W. E., BBR (1996).

Barrett, C. K., "Christianity at Corinth," BJRL 46 (1964), 269–97.
Belleville, L. L., "Continuity or Discontinuity: A Fresh Look at 1 Corinthians in the

[68]On the eucharist and Lord's Supper in I Cor, see R. A. Campbell, NovT 33 (1991), 61–70; F. Chenderlin, *"Do this as my memorial"* (AnBib 99; Rome: PBI, 1982); Marrow, *Paul* 140–49; J. Murphy-O'Connor, *Worship* 51 (1977), 56–69; J. P. Meier, TD 42 (1995), 335–51.

Light of First-Century Epistolary Forms and Conventions," EvQ 59 (1987), 15–37.

Bieringer, R., ed.,* *The Corinthian Correspondence* (BETL 125; Leuven: Peeters, 1996).

Blenkinsopp, J., *The Corinthian Mirror* (London: Sheed and Ward, 1964).

Broneer, O., "Corinth: Center of St. Paul's Missionary Work in Greece," BA 14 (1951), 78–96.

Brown, A. R., *The Cross and Human Transfiguration: Paul's Apocalyptic Word in 1 Corinthians* (Minneapolis: A/F, 1995).

Carson, D. A., *Showing the Spirit: A Theological Exposition of 1 Corinthians 12–14* (Grand Rapids: Baker, 1987).

Chow, J. K., *Patronage and Power: A Study of Social Networks in Corinth* (JSNTSup 75; Sheffield: JSOT, 1992).

Clarke, A. D., *Secular and Christian Leadership in Corinth . . . 1 Corinthians 1–6* (Leiden: Brill, 1993).

de Boer, M. C., "The Composition of 1 Corinthians," NTS 40 (1994), 229–45.

Ellis, E. E., "Traditions in 1 Corinthians," NTS 32 (1986), 481–502.

Furnish, V. P., "Corinth in Paul's Time," BAR 15 (#3; 1988), 14–27.

Hay, D. M.,* *1 and 2 Corinthians* (*Pauline Theology* 2; Minneapolis: A/F, 1993).

Héring, J., *The First Epistle of Saint Paul to the Corinthians* (London: Epworth, 1962).

Hurd, J. C., *The Origin of 1 Corinthians* (2d ed.; Macon, GA: Mercer, 1983).

———, "Good News and the Integrity of 1 Corinthians," in *Gospel in Paul,* eds. L. A. Jervis and P. Richardson (R. N. Longenecker Festschrift; JSNTSup 108; Sheffield: Academic, 1994).

Kilgallen, J. J., *First Corinthians: An Introduction and Study Guide* (New York: Paulist, 1987).

Lampe, G.W.H.,* "Church Discipline and the Interpretation of the Epistles to the Corinthians," in CHI 337–61.

Marshall, P.,* *Enmity in Corinth* (2d ed.; WUNT 2.23; Tübingen: Mohr-Siebeck, 1991).

Martin, R. P., *The Spirit and the Congregation: Studies in 1 Corinthians 12–15* (Grand Rapids: Eerdmans, 1984).

Mitchell, M. M., *Paul and the Rhetoric of Reconciliation* (Tübingen: Mohr-Siebeck, 1991).

Moffatt, J., *The First Epistle of Paul to the Corinthians* (New York: Harper, 1938).

Morton, A. Q.,* *A Critical Concordance to I and II Corinthians* (Wooster, OH: Biblical Research, 1979).

Murphy-O'Connor, J., *St. Paul's Corinth: Texts and Archaeology* (GNS 6, 1983).

———, "The Corinth that Saint Paul Saw," BA 47 (1984), 147–59.

Pogoloff, S. M., *Logos and Sophia: The Rhetorical Situation of 1 Corinthians* (SBLDS 134; Atlanta: Scholars, 1992).

Quast, K.,* *Reading the Corinthian Correspondence* (New York: Paulist, 1994).

Schmithals, W., *Gnosticism in Corinth* (Nashville: Abingdon, 1971).

Schüssler Fiorenza, E., "Rhetorical Situation and Historical Reconstruction in 1 Corinthians," NTS 33 (1987), 386–403.

Snyder, G. F., *First Corinthians* (Macon, GA: Mercer, 1992).
Talbert, C. H.,* *Reading Corinthians* (New York: Crossroad, 1989).
Theissen, G., *The Social Setting of Pauline Christianity: Essays on Corinth* (Philadelphia: Fortress, 1982).
Walter, E., *The First Epistle to the Corinthians* (London: Sheed & Ward, 1971).
Welborn, L. L., "On the Discord in Corinth," JBL 106 (1987), 83–111.
Witherington, B. III, *Conflict and Community in Corinth* (Grand Rapids: Eerdmans, 1995).

CHAPTER 23

SECOND LETTER TO THE CORINTHIANS

Although there is no doubt that Paul wrote II Cor, transitions from one part of the letter to the other have been judged so abrupt that many scholars would chop it up into once-independent pieces. Nevertheless, it may well be the most oratorically persuasive of all Paul's writings, for in the various hypothetically independent pieces he has left unforgettable passages. Perhaps no other letter of Paul evokes so vividly the image of a suffering and rejected apostle, misunderstood by his fellow Christians. In order not to miss the forest for the trees, after the *Background,* the *General Analysis* will highlight the oratorical power of II Cor. Then subsections will treat: *One letter or a compilation, Imagery in II Cor 4:16–5:10, Paul's collection of money for Jerusalem* (*II Cor 8–9*), *Opponents in II Cor 10–13, Issues for reflection,* and *Bibliography.*

The Background

Beginning on p. 514 above there was a numerical list of contacts (#1–6) between Paul and Corinth up to and including the writing of **Letters A** (lost) and **B** (= I Cor) that were part of Paul's correspondence to the Corinthians. Let us now continue that numerical and alphabetic list as an explanation of the genesis of II Cor.

(#7) After Paul wrote I Cor in late 56 or very early AD 57, Timothy, who had been traveling through Macedonia, came to Corinth (Acts 19:21–22; I Cor 4:17–19; 16:10–11; p. 517 above). This would have taken place in early 57 (after the arrival of I Cor?). Timothy found the situation bad; and many assume that this was the result of the arrival of the false apostles described in II Cor 11:12–15, who were hostile to Paul. Timothy went to Ephesus to report the situation to Paul. **(#8)** This emergency caused Paul to set out from Ephesus and cross directly by sea[1] to pay what turned out to be a "painful

[1]The direct sea route was about 250 miles in length (but could not always be used safely); the Ephesus-Troas-Macedonia-Achaia-Corinth (mostly) land route followed by Timothy and also by Paul on his third visit to Corinth (see #10, #12) involved a journey of about 900 miles.

Summary of Basic Information

DATE: Late summer/early autumn 57 from Macedonia (55/56 in the Revisionist Chronology).

TO: The church already addressed in I Cor.

AUTHENTICITY: Not seriously disputed.

UNITY: Most scholars think that several (two to five) letters have been combined.

INTEGRITY: 6:14–7:1 is thought by some to be a nonPauline interpolation.

FORMAL DIVISION (of existing letter):

A. Opening Formula: 1:1–2
B. Thanksgiving: 1:3–11
C. Body: 1:12–13:10
D. Concluding Formula: 13:11–13.*

DIVISION ACCORDING TO CONTENTS:

1:1–11:	Address/greeting and Thanksgiving, stressing Paul's sufferings	
1:12–7:16:	Part I:	Paul's relations to the Corinthian Christians
		(a) 1:12–2:13: His deferred visit and the "tearful" letter
		(b) 2:14–7:16: His ministry (interruption: 6:14–7:1)
8:1–9:15:	Part II:	Collection for the church in Jerusalem
10:1–13:10:	Part III:	Paul's response to challenges to his apostolic authority
13:11–13:	Concluding greetings, blessings.	

*The RSV divides Greek 13:12 into two verses, so that the final verse (13:13) becomes 13:14.

visit" to Corinth (II Cor 2:1). This second of Paul's three visits to Corinth[2] was a failure. He had threatened to come "with a whip" in I Cor 4:21; yet according to II Cor 10:1,10b he was perceived as timid and ineffective when face to face with the Corinthians. Apparently someone affronted him publicly and undermined his authority with the community (II Cor 2:5–11; 7:12). Paul decided he needed a cooling-off period, and so he left Corinth planning to return quickly, without stopping on the way back to visit the Macedonian churches first (as he had once planned in I Cor 16:5).

(#9) Either before or after Paul's return to Ephesus,[3] he changed his mind about going back to Corinth directly, realizing it would only be another painful visit (II Cor 2:1); and instead he wrote a letter "with many tears" (2:3–4;

[2]II Cor 12:14; 13:1–2. The first visit (#1) saw the foundation of the church; the third will be recounted in #12 below.

[3]Did Paul go by land from Corinth up into Macedonia (Thessalonica, Philippi?); and from there, deciding that it was unwise to return to Corinth so soon, cross over to Ephesus? Or did he go by sea from Corinth to Ephesus; and there, partially because of trouble he encountered, change his plans? (In II Cor 1:8–9 he speaks of suffering beyond endurance in the province of Asia [= Ephesus] and even of a death sentence.) The pertinent II Cor 1:15–16 is very complicated.

7:8–9: **Letter C,** lost[4]). There may have been some severity in the letter, an instance of Paul's being bold once he was away from Corinth (10:1,10). Yet it was meant not to grieve the Corinthians but to let them know his love. Encouraged by Paul's hope that the Corinthians would respond favorably (7:14), Titus carried this letter.[5] **(#10)** Finally Paul departed from Ephesus, probably in the summer of 57, going north to the port of Troas and there crossing over by sea from the province of Asia to Macedonia (I Cor 16:5,8; II Cor 2:12–13; Acts 20:1). Meanwhile, Titus had been well treated at Corinth (II Cor 7:15); indeed, he was even able to begin collecting money for Paul to bring to Jerusalem (8:6); and in the late summer or early autumn of 57 he brought that joyful news to Paul in Macedonia (7:5–7,13b). Although Paul's "tearful" letter had caused sorrow, the Corinthians had repented and expressed concern for the grief they had caused Paul. Indeed, with alarm and some indignation they were anxious to prove themselves innocent (7:7–13). **(#11)** In immediate response (thus from Macedonia [Philippi?] in late summer or early autumn of 57 with Timothy at his side) PAUL WROTE II COR **(Letter D).**[6] It was to be carried by Titus (and two other brothers) as part of a continued mission to raise money at Corinth for Paul to take back to Jerusalem (8:6,16–24). **(#12)** Paul himself went on to Corinth (his third visit there; 12:14; 13:1–2), where he spent the winter of 57–58[7] before taking the collection to Jerusalem through Macedonia, Philippi, and Troas (Acts 20:2–5). **(#13)** There is no clear evidence that he ever returned to Corinth. If the Pastoral Letters contain reliable historical information, II Tim 4:20 may mean that the ship that took Paul from Ephesus to Rome as a prisoner stopped at Corinth. After Paul's death there was an echo of his contacts with Corinth, dating from the end of the 1st century. The letter from the church

[4]Actually many scholars do not think that the "tearful" letter was lost. Some have proposed that the reference is to I Cor which has its corrective sections. (Yet then why was Paul's painful visit [#8; II Cor 2:1], which took place before the "tearful" letter, not mentioned in I Cor?) A much larger number argue that it has been preserved in the strongly corrective II Cor 10–13. The latter is unlikely for several reasons. The "tearful" letter (#9) was written at a time when Paul had made up his mind not to pay another painful visit (II Cor 2:1,4), but in II Cor 10–13 (12:14; 13:1–2) Paul speaks of coming again. Moreover 12:18 indicates that Titus (who carried the "tearful" letter) had been to Corinth and reported back to Paul. Thus II Cor 10–13 was written after the "tearful" letter.

[5]See 7:7: "his coming." Paul and Timothy had failed in previous missions to pacify Corinth, so now another Pauline figure is given a try. It is difficult to know how literally we are to take Paul's almost ecstatic praises in II Cor 7:13–16.

[6]A subsection below will discuss whether II Cor is a unified letter or a collection of once independent letters (two to five), but we shall begin (*General Analysis*) by treating the letter as it now stands.

[7]Murphy-O'Connor would add a year to the sequence: After Paul had sent I Cor from Ephesus before spring, he spent the winter of that year in Macedonia and wrote II Cor 1–9 in the spring of the following year. Later in the summer of that next year, because there was new deterioration at Corinth, he wrote II Cor 10–13 from western Greece or Illyricum (Rom 15:19); only then did he go on to winter in Corinth.

of God at Rome to the church of God at Corinth that we know as *I Clement* was concerned once more with the problem of factionalism at Corinth (1:1); and in chap. 47 it compared the new factionalism with that addressed in the letter written by Paul to Corinth at the beginning of his preaching.

General Analysis of the Message

OPENING FORMULA (1:1–2) and THANKSGIVING (1:3–11). We do not know why here Paul changes the address from that of I Cor 1:2 (to the church of God in Corinth and Christians [saints] everywhere) to include specifically the Christians "in the whole of Achaia." Is it to prepare for the collection that will be taken up throughout Achaia (II Cor 9:2)? In 1:3–11 Paul speaks of the trials he suffered at Ephesus—an experience that highlighted his own weakness and Christ's comfort and also served as background for his recent dealings with Corinth.

PART I OF THE BODY OF THE LETTER (1:12–7:16) discusses those dealings with the Corinthians, both narrating them and looking at them theologically. In *subdivision* (*a*) *1:12–2:13* he concentrates on his change of plans after the painful visit he had paid from Ephesus (#8). The change was not simply an issue of human preference, but part of his "Yes" to what God wants for the Corinthians and for Paul himself. Instead of exposing them to another harrowing confrontation that might make him seem too domineering (1:23–24), he wrote a letter "with many tears" (#9) to change their minds, so that when he did come it might be a joyful experience. From 2:5–11 we learn that the problem during the painful visit had centered around an obstreperous individual.[8] In response to Paul's "tearful" letter the Corinthians have disciplined this person, but now Paul urges mercy and forgiveness.[9] (This is an interesting example both of the use of discipline and of restraints placed on it, all for the sake of the church.) Paul tells the Corinthians that his interest in healing his relations with them was such that (after leaving Ephesus) he interrupted his preaching ministry at Troas in order to cross over to Macedonia to hear from Titus the effect of the tearful letter (2:12–13).

In *subdivision* (*b*) *2:14–7:16* Paul relates his ministry on a larger scale to the Corinthian crisis.[10] That crisis wrings out of Paul passages of remarkable

[8]Some hypothesize that this was the incestuous man reprimanded in I Cor 5:1–2 about whom the community was so proud.

[9]To the theory that II Cor 10–13 constitutes the letter "with many tears," one may object that there is no such concentration on an individual in those chapters.

[10]On II Cor 2:14–3:3, see S. J. Hafemann, *Suffering and Ministry in the Spirit* (Grand Rapids: Eerdmans, 1990). On 3:1–18, L. L. Belleville, *Reflections of Glory* (JSNTSup 52; Sheffield: Academic, 1991); J. A. Fitzmyer, TS 42 (1981), 630–44; W. C. van Unnik, NovT 6 (1964), 153–69; S. J. Hafemann, *Paul, Moses and the History of Israel* (WUNT 81; Tübingen: Mohr-Siebeck, 1995). On 4:8–9; 6:3–10, J. T. Fitzgerald, *Cracks in an Earthen Vessel* (SBLDS 99; Atlanta: Scholars, 1988).

oratorical power, e.g., 5:16–21 describing what God has done in Christ. Many will find Paul's reference to God "appealing through us" (5:20) still true, for the appeal continues to be effective today. If the thought-flow seems to ramble, in part that is because the argument takes its orientation from the activity of would-be apostles at Corinth and their attacks on Paul (of which he will report more in chaps. 10–12). Stressing that he is no peddler of God's word (2:17), Paul insists that he, unlike the others, should need no letter of recommendation to the Corinthians[11]—they themselves, as the result of his ministry, are his letter (3:1–3). Paul then launches into the superiority of a ministry involving the Spirit over a ministry engraved on stone that brought death (3:4–11). Moses put a veil over his face in dealing with Israel, and it remains when Israelites read the old covenant. However, when one turns to Christ, the veil is taken away because the Lord who spoke to Moses is now present in the Spirit (3:12–18). Paul's gospel is not veiled except to those who are perishing because the god of this world has blinded their minds (4:3–4). Paul's power is from God, even though this treasure is carried in an "earthen vessel" (4:7). In a masterpiece of irony (4:8–12),[12] Paul differentiates between his physical suffering and his status in Christ, for "we always carry in our body the death of Jesus so that the life of Jesus may also be revealed in our body."

In 4:16–5:10 in a series of contrasts (outer/inner/; seen/not seen; naked/clothed) Paul explains why he does not lose heart. His troubles are momentary compared to eternal glory; and when the earthly tent is destroyed, there is an eternal, heavenly dwelling from God. In the subsection *Imagery* below we shall examine this passage more closely; but it tells us the extent to which Paul's life draws nourishment from the unseen, as he lives in the tension of the "already" and the "not yet." Although Paul stresses that he is not commending himself to the Corinthians, he is clearly trying to get them to appreciate his ministry for them (5:11–15), which others would denigrate.[13] Whether he means Christ's love for him or his love for Christ or both, Paul's "The love of Christ compels us" (5:14) is a magnificent summary of his devotion. God "gave us the ministry of reconciliation . . . so we are ambassadors of Christ" (5:18–20) describes movingly the vocation that Paul would

[11]On such letters, see W. R. Baird, JBL 80 (1961), 166–72.

[12]There are various examples of irony in II Cor. See C. Forbes, NTS 32 (1986), 1–30, for Paul's use of this literary technique, as well as G. A. Kennedy, *NT Interpretation.*

[13]See J. L. Martyn in CHI 269–87; J. P. Lewis, ed., *Interpreting 2 Corinthians 5.14–21* (New York: Mellen, 1989). In 5:13 Paul speaks of being beside himself for God; is that a reference to his speaking in tongues, which is speaking to God (I Cor 14:2,18)? In 5:16–17 Paul writes about once having known Christ according to the flesh, but now no longer. This does not mean that he had known Jesus during the public ministry, but that he once looked at Christ without the eyes of faith. Now that the old aeon/age has passed away, in the new aeon, which is a new creation, Paul sees him differently.

share with them. Appealing to the Corinthians not to receive God's grace in vain (6:1), Paul assures them that he would put no stumbling block in anyone's path (6:3). In a moving catalogue describing what his life has been like (6:4–10), Paul bares his soul to the Corinthians with a challenge for them to open their hearts to him (6:11–13).

Shifting to dualistic contradictions (6:14–7:1: righteousness/wickedness, etc.), Paul urges them not to become tied to unbelievers. (In the present sequence the passage serves as an indicator that all has not been healed at Corinth and prepares for the corrective chaps. 10–13. Below in a subsection on unity we shall discuss relevant problems of sequence, thought, and derivation.) Then in 7:2 he returns (see 2:13) to explaining his behavior to the Corinthians, telling them how delighted he was when Titus brought to him in Macedonia the good news that his "tearful" letter had produced a good effect (#9, 10 above). He is glad that now he can have complete confidence in them (7:16).

PART II OF THE BODY OF THE LETTER (8:1–9:15) treats Paul's collection for the church in Jerusalem (8:1–9:15). That confidence leads him into daring to request[14] money from them for his collection, a project they had already begun last year (8:10; 9:2, see n. 7 above). He holds up to them the example of the Macedonian Christians, who are being generous despite their poverty (8:1–5), as well as that of Jesus Christ himself "who, though he was rich, for your sake became poor, that you might become rich by his poverty" (8:9). Influenced perhaps by the Jewish custom of sending distinguished men to Jerusalem with the collection for the Temple, and desiring to make his own probity clear, Paul is sending Titus, who recently was favorably received at Corinth, to arrange the collection (and probably to carry II Cor). With him (again to insure probity: 8:16–23) will go a brother famous among all the churches (someone from Achaia [specifically, from Corinth as a diplomatic gesture], working in Macedonia?), and another zealous brother who has helped Paul—two figures we cannot name despite many proposals. The collection for Jerusalem is also the subject of chap. 9, which seems to speak specifically to Achaia (and which some scholars regard as a separate treatment, but see 1:1 and the joining of Corinth and Achaia). Just as Paul is boasting about the generosity of the Macedonians to the Corinthians, he has been boasting about the Corinthians (Achaia) to the Macedonians; and he does not want to be embarrassed if any Macedonians come with him to

[14]8:8; notice that, as in Phlm 8–9, Paul does not choose to command. Earlier the Macedonians, especially the Philippians, had shown their generosity (Phil 4:10–19; II Cor 11:9), but now the situation at Macedonia seems to have been particularly troubled (7:5). The Thessalonian Christians may have been particularly poor because of the confusion involving those who had ceased to work (I Thess 4:11–12; II Thess 3:6–13).

gather the collection. Paul's pronouncement, "God loves a cheerful giver" (9:7) has understandably been an ageless favorite with money raisers.

PART III OF THE BODY OF THE LETTER (10:1–13:10) contains Paul's more detailed response to challenges to his apostolic authority. Whereas chaps. 8–9 were optimistic and enthusiastic about the Corinthian response, abruptly the next four chaps. turn more pessimistic as Paul indicates uncertainty about his reception when he comes a third time. Indeed, he has to threaten to be as severe when he comes as he has been in his writing, presumably including his "tearful" letter of #9 (10:2,6,11; 13:2). Nevertheless, Paul wants to stress that the authority given him by the Lord is for building up, not for pulling down (10:8; 13:10; cf. Jer 1:10). There have been "apostles" (would-be "super-apostles": 11:5; 12:11) undermining Paul at Corinth; but as far as Paul is concerned, they are masqueraders and false apostles (11:13–15) who in the end will be punished. (An extensive literature has been devoted to these opponents, and they shall be treated in a subsection below.) Their enduring contribution is to have drawn forth from Paul the longest and most impassioned description of his own apostolic service.[15] In this crisis-ridden moment of his life, from his soul there rings out a cry of confidence in the power of Christ: "When I am weak, then I am strong" (12:10). Although 12:12 lists signs, wonders, and miracles as "signs of an apostle" that Paul had wrought among the Corinthians, clearly the times he was imprisoned, flogged, lashed, stoned, shipwrecked, imperiled, hungry, thirsty, and stripped naked are more important to him as an expression of his apostolic concern for all the churches (11:23–29).[16] Paul is willing to take the risk of boasting so that he may show the sincerity of his challenge to the Corinthians: "I will most gladly spend and be spent for your souls. If I love you more, will you love me less?" (12:15). Evidently this was the best way he could conceive of getting the Corinthians to respond generously and rid themselves of divisions and corruptions before he came, so that he might not need to be harsh (12:20–13:10).

The CONCLUDING FORMULA (13:11–13) serves as Paul's final exhortation to the Corinthians in the missive as it now stands: "Mend your ways, heed my appeal, think alike, live in peace." Was he successful? Was his third visit peaceful or a struggle? Acts 20:2–3 devotes only one sentence to the three

[15]M. M. DiCicco, *Paul's Use of Ethos, Pathos, and Logos in 2 Corinthians 10–13* (Lewiston, NY: Mellen, 1995), argues that Paul knew and employed the different methods of Aristotelian rhetoric.

[16]A mysterious "thorn" has been given to Paul in the flesh, a messenger of Satan to harass him (12:7). Was it demonic force, psychological stress, physical ailment, or constant human opposition? Gal 4:13 speaks of a weakness of the flesh related to his first preaching to the Galatians. See Furnish, *2 Corinthians* 548–50; T. Y. Mullins, JBL 76 (1957), 299–303; H. R. Minn, *The Thorn That Remained* (Auckland: Moore, 1972); P. H. Menoud, in his *Jesus Christ and Faith* (Pittsburgh: Pickwick, 1978), 19–30.

months that he stayed in Achaia (of which Corinth was the capital) after he had come from Macedonia; it gives no indication of internal Christian conflict. Neither do passages in Rom 16:1,21–23 mentioning Paul's Christian friends at Corinth (from which address he was writing that letter). No matter how the Corinthians reacted, Paul's triadic blessing on them in 13:13 including God and Jesus and the Holy Spirit (the fullest benediction that Paul composed) has served Christians in liturgy even to this day as a model invocation.

One Letter or a Compilation of Several Letters?

Among the letters in the Pauline corpus, the unity of II Cor has been the most challenged (with the unity of Phil, a distant second), and anywhere from two to five once-independent components have been diagnosed. To follow the discussion below, where the alphabetic designation starts with *Letter D,* readers will remember from #3 and #6 on p. 515 above that there was a *Letter A* before I Cor was written, so that I Cor was *Letter B.* Then a "tearful" *Letter C* was written before II Cor (#9, pp. 542–43 above).

Many who evaluate II Cor as a unity think of it as *Letter D,* so that the total fourfold Corinthian correspondence would have consisted of two lost letters and two preserved letters. Supporting unity in II Cor is the fact that there is only one Opening Formula (1:1–2) and one Concluding Formula (13:11–13). If once-independent letters are contained in II Cor, they have been truncated, and one cannot posit a simple gluing together of documents.[17]

On the other hand, the shift of tone in II Cor from the generally optimistic chaps. 1–9 to the more pessimistic 10–13 is sharp; and a majority of scholars would argue for independent origins of at least those two components—thus Bruce, Barrett, Furnish, and Murphy-O'Connor—which would become *Letters D* and *E* in our alphabetic sequence. Beyond that, II Cor 6:14–7:1 has the air of a self-contained unit, and chaps. 8 and 9 seem to involve a certain duplication in referring to the collection. Accordingly G. Bornkamm would find five letters in II Cor. In our alphabetic system these would consist of: *Letter C* = 10:1–13:10 = the "tearful" letter mentioned in 2:3–4; *Letter D* = 2:14–7:14 (minus 6:14–7:1), i.e., the main section of II Cor; *Letter E* = 1:1–2:13 + 6:14–7:1, a letter of reconciliation; *Letter F* = 8:1–24, written

[17]For unity, see W. H. Bates, NTS 12 (1965–66), 56–69; Stephenson, A.M.G., in *The Authorship and Integrity of the New Testament* (London: SPCK, 1965); and Young and Ford, *Meaning.* A. Stewart-Sykes, JSNT 61 (1996), 53–64, criticizes the argumentation in the more complex theories of partitioning I-II Cor into many letters.

to Corinth concerning the collection for Jerusalem; *Letter G* = 9:1–15, a circular missive to Achaia about the collection.[18] In this hypothesis every discrete subject in II Cor has been interpreted as a separate letter.

The problem of sequence may be added to the problem of once-independent units. For instance, Soards (*Apostle* 88), following Bornkamm and D. Georgi, would argue that II Cor 8 was written first and sent with Titus, who brought back news of troubles at Corinth. Then Paul wrote II Cor 2:14–7:4, a letter that failed. Next Paul visited Corinth (#8 above); and when that failed, he wrote the "tearful letter" (#9) consisting of II Cor 10–13. Titus brought back news that this time Paul had succeeded; and so he wrote II Cor 1:1–2:13 and 7:5–16. Finally he wrote II Cor 9. To the obvious question of why any editor reorganized this material in the existing order, some would resort to positing stupidity. Fallon (*2 Corinthians* 7), following Bornkamm, thinks that II Cor was organized after Paul's death as his last testament, with chaps. 10–13 intended as a prediction of false apostles in the future, and 13:11–13 as his farewell and final prayer. Hurd ("Good News") has the simplest explanation: Three letters "to the Corinthians" had been gathered together under that heading in order of descending length, i.e., what we know as I Cor, II Cor 1–9, II Cor 10–13; but the person who split it up into the canonical order did not notice that he had joined two separate letters as II Cor.

What is at the root of these and a dozen other theories? An important factor in judging unity is whether the breaks from one section of II Cor to another are so sharp that they cannot be interpreted as a shift of focus within the same missive. Yet at times other issues enter in. In this *Introduction* we cannot hope to discuss all the problematic sections of II Cor just mentioned, but both chaps. 10–13 and 6:14–7:1 deserve attention. (For fuller detail, see Furnish, *2 Corinthians* 35–48; 371–83.)

(a) II Cor 10–13. One gets the impression from the report brought back by Titus in 7:5–16 that the difficulties between Paul and Corinth have been settled: "I rejoice because I have complete confidence in you." Yet in chaps. 10–13 the atmosphere is different. Paul fears that when he comes he will have to be severe; there are false apostles who are demeaning Paul, and the Corinthians are listening to them. Three explanations have been proposed. The FIRST EXPLANATION is that chaps. 10–13 came from a once-independent letter written at another time. Some who think that letter was composed before chaps. 1–9 would identify 10–13 with *Letter C*, the "tearful" letter men-

[18]For a slightly different analysis of five letters in II Cor, see N. H. Taylor, "Composition"; others would posit more letters than six. Betz, *2 Corinthians* 3–36, gives a history of theories subdividing II Cor. Betz is so convinced that F and G are separate letters that he has written a whole Hermeneia commentary on them.

tioned in II Cor 2:3–4, but there are serious objections to that thesis (n. 4, 9 above). A more plausible suggestion is that after II Cor 1–9 was sent as *Letter D,* a new crisis was created at Corinth by the arrival of would-be super-apostles, forcing Paul to write this new letter of which 10–13 is a truncated remnant (*Letter E*).[19] The SECOND EXPLANATION is that chaps. 10–13 are part of the same letter (*D*) as chaps. 1–9, but were an addendum prompted by new, disturbing information that came to Paul before he sent off chaps. 1–9. Actually, the line between an unexpected addendum to the original letter and a new letter is blurry. The fact that there is no Opening Formula in chap. 10[20] may be easier to explain if we are dealing with an addendum, but then the absence of any indication that disturbing news has reached Paul becomes more puzzling than if we were dealing with a *truncated* new letter. The THIRD EXPLANATION is that chaps. 10–13 are part of the same letter (*D*) as chaps. 1–9, and were intended by Paul from the moment he began writing II Cor. One then has to posit that Paul was reacting to the Corinthian situation in stages. The optimistic relief so tangible in chap. 7 was because Titus brought news that the major crisis had been settled: The obstreperous individual who had publicly embarrassed Paul face to face with the community's cooperation had now been corrected and was about to be disciplined. The community had not decisively rejected Paul. Nevertheless, there was still the danger from those who presented themselves as apostles and made slighting remarks about Paul. Even though Paul had increased confidence about the goodwill of the Corinthians because they had rejected the obstreperous individual, he would have to be corrective if they did not see through the would-be apostles. We saw in discussing I Cor that Paul's sense of sequence is not always smooth, and so this theory cannot be rejected out of hand. The main argument in its favor is that some of the remarks in chaps. 1–9 seem to envision the same opponents as those described in chaps. 10–13 (see subsection below on the false apostles). Nevertheless, can the onslaught in 10–13 really have been planned to follow an appeal for money in chaps. 8–9?

(b) II Cor 6:14–7:1. Here too there is a sequence problem, since the theme of open hearts from 6:13 is picked up again in 7:2, so that clearly 6:14–7:1

[19]The thesis that 10–13 was originally part of an independent letter goes back to J. S. Semler in 1776. F. Watson, JTS NS 35 (1984), 324–46, would identify it with *Letter C;* J. Murphy-O'Connor, *Australian Biblical Review* 39 (1991), 31–43, thinks of 10–13 as Paul's last letter to Corinth, written from Illyricum just before #12.

[20]J. Knox in JBL 55 (1936), 145–53, suggested that an editor joined three separate letters (I Cor; II Cor 1–9; and II Cor 10–13) as a collection "To the Corinthians" by stripping off the original Opening Formulas of the second and third letters. Later another editor split this collection into two, namely, I Cor and II Cor, and copied from the Opening Formula of I Cor to supply an opening for II Cor.

is an interruption. But there are also questions of vocabulary and thought. The passage contains a number of words and usages not attested elsewhere in the undisputed Pauline letters, e.g., Beliar, and its Scripture citations. If the "unbelievers" who are the main target are Gentiles, overly familiar contact with Gentiles has not been an issue in II Cor.[21] Would Paul urge the Corinthians not to be joined together with Gentiles when at Antioch he had argued with Peter (Gal 2:11–13) that eating with Gentiles represented gospel freedom?[22] Or are we to think that Gentile "unbelievers" represented a special moral threat in the licentious atmosphere of the "wide-open" port city of Corinth? The three items in the dualism (righteousness/wickedness, light/darkness, Christ/Beliar) contain some terms familiar in the dualism of the Dead Sea Scrolls, and a number of scholars have suggested that either Paul or an editor of the II Cor took over this passage from that source.[23] Nevertheless, some very prominent commentators would argue that Paul himself composed 6:14–7:1 for its present placement.[24] Can "unbelievers" be seen as polemic terminology for the opponents who will come into clearer focus in chaps. 10–13? Whatever view one accepts, there is still a problem of why this passage was placed here and how it was deemed to fit the thought of the rest of the letter.

These two examples should establish a range from possibility to plausibility for the thesis that II Cor is composite. Surety is not obtainable. The debate about the unity of II Cor has import for a detailed historical knowledge of Paul's dealings with Corinth; but from the earliest times II Cor has been presented in its present format and sequence.[25] Consequently hearers and readers have had the task and opportunity of making sense of the present format. As I have cautioned several times in this *Introduction,* commentaries based on reconstructions are of debatable value. To understand what Paul wants to communicate, it will suffice for most readers to recognize that II Cor contains different topics expressed with different rhetorical emphases.

[21]Some would appeal to I Cor 5:9–11, where Paul says he wrote a letter (*Letter A;* #3) telling the Corinthians not to associate with immoral men. Is II Cor 6:14–7:1 that letter? Would Paul globally identify the unbelieving Gentiles as immoral?

[22]H. D. Betz, JBL 92 (1973), 88–108, has argued that II Cor 6:14–7:1 is an *anti*Pauline fragment, supporting ideas that Paul condemned.

[23]E.g., J. A. Fitzmyer, CBQ 23 (1961), 271–80; FESBNT 205–17, arguing for a nonPauline interpolation. J. Murphy-O'Connor (RB 95 [1988], 55–69) contends there are better parallels in Philo than in the Scrolls; see Chapter 22 above, n. 48.

[24]Lambrecht, Murphy-O'Connor. See also M. E. Thrall, NTS 24 (1977), 132–48; W. J. Webb, *Returning Home: New Covenant and Second Exodus as the Context for 2 Corinthians 6.14–7.1* (JSNTSup 85; Sheffield: Academic, 1993).

[25]W. S. Kurz, JSNT 62 (1996), 43–63, points out that even if II Cor is composite, the original life-situation of the component pieces would have been of little relevance for the audience of the combined form. That insight relativizes the importance of reconstructing original fragments.

Imagery in 4:16–5:10

Paul expresses his thought about mortal existence and eschatological existence in allusive language that is not easy to decipher. His contrast is between the outer human being (*anthrōpos*) and the inner human being. This is not body vs. soul, but human existence in this world as one lives by the life that one got from one's parents, vs. living by the life that one receives through faith from the risen Jesus Christ. The former is mortal, constantly being given over to death; the latter is being renewed and made more glorious day after day as one is changed into the likeness of Christ (4:11; 3:18). In his mortal life Paul has been brought close to death many times; and yet paradoxically each time the life of Jesus has become more manifest in Paul's flesh. As Furnish (*2 Corinthians* 290) points out, whereas in Stoic philosophy one's soul is rendered more perfect by discipline, in Paul's faith the growing perfection comes from the Lord who is the Spirit (3:18).

Yet some of Paul's imagery also gives an insight into what he expects in the other world, and what happens if the earthly tentlike house[26] should be destroyed (5:1)—a tent in which he sighs under a burden (5:4), the body in which he is at home while he is away from the Lord (5:6). Destruction for Paul does not mean that he will be unclothed and found naked (5:3–4); rather he will be more splendidly clothed. To replace the tentlike house there is a building from God, a house not made with hands, eternal in the heavens (5:1). Paul would actually prefer being away from home in the body and being at home with the Lord (5:8; see Phil 1:20–26). If that much seems clear,[27] many other things are not. Is this house not made with hands already in existence or is it made by God when the earthly tent is destroyed? Is it a new spiritual body to replace the mortal body? And if so, when does a believer stand before the judicial bench of Christ (5:10) and become clothed with this body—at the moment of death or at the resurrection from the dead (as in I Cor 15:36–44)? Or is the reference more ecclesiological, involving incorporation into the body of Christ? Or is the reference more apocalyptic, involving a type of heavenly sanctuary? Or without being specific, is the imagery meant simply to contrast transitory present existence with enduring future existence? In any case, would Paul have had special revealed knowledge of what awaited Christian believers beyond death? Or in the imagery was he simply expressing confidence about victory and being with Christ?

[26]II Cor 5:1,4 represent the only uses of tent (*skēnos/ē*) language in the writings of Paul the tentmaker (Acts 18:3).

[27]Yet J. Murphy-O'Connor, RB 93 (1986), 214–21, would argue that "Being at home in the body while we are in exile from the Lord" (5:6b) represents not Paul's thought but a slogan used by Paul's opponents and expressing their misunderstanding.

Paul's Collection of Money for Jerusalem (chaps. 8–9)

In what chronologically should be some time in the 40s, Acts 11:29–30 reports that Paul and Barnabas delivered to the Jerusalem elders a donation from Antioch for "service to the brethren living in Judea"—a gesture hard to fit into Paul's own recollections about his relations to the Jerusalem Christians before the Jerusalem Meeting of AD 49. There Paul acceded to the request of the Jerusalem authorities to remember the poor, something he was eager to do (Gal 2:10).[28] We do not know whether Paul immediately instituted a collection to meet that demand and whether he ceased after "those from James" came and created a problem at Antioch. In any case *ca.* 56–57, a half-dozen years later, the collection for Jerusalem, "the service for the saints," has become a major concern in his missionary career.[29] The Galatian churches and the Corinthians were told to set aside a certain amount of money on the first day of every week (I Cor 16:1–4: presumably the day when Christians came together), and in II Cor 8–9 and Rom 15:26 we have Paul canvassing Macedonia and Achaia.[30] Why was Paul so concerned about the success of this effort?

Generosity to the poor is attested in the OT (Ps 112:9) and was inculcated by Jesus. Those who have plenty should share with the needy—someday the tables may be turned (II Cor 8:14). But why the poor *at Jerusalem*? Surely a factor is Paul's desire to unify his Gentile communities with Jerusalem (*koinōnia;* see Gal 2:9): The Gentiles have shared in the Jews' spiritual blessings, and so they owe it to the Jews to share material blessings with them (Rom 15:27). Thus it will be clear that Gentiles and Jews (especially those in the mother church) are one in Christ. Both psychologically and practically there are few things in life that bind together people and institutions more effectively than sharing their bank accounts.

Was there also a personal issue? If those who are denigrating Paul at Corinth are from Jerusalem and are vilifying Paul as disloyal to the mother Christian community, would a collection for the Jerusalem Christians work toward disproving that? Did Paul's opponents at Galatia pass on his sarcastic comments about the so-called Jerusalem pillars of the church who were of

[28]It has been debated whether a particularly acute poverty at Jerusalem was created by the sharing of goods in common (according to the idealistic description in Acts 2:44–45; 4:32,37); yet see the optimism about shared goods in 4:34–35.

[29]C. H. Buck, Jr., HTR 43 (1950), 1–29; L. E. Keck, ZNW 56 (1965), 100–29; J. Munck, *Paul* 282–308; K. F. Nickle, *The Collection: A Study in Paul's Strategy* (SBT 48; London: SCM, 1966); D. Georgi, *Remembering the Poor. The History of Paul's Collection for Jerusalem* (Nashville: Abingdon, 1992; German orig., 1965).

[30]Seemingly the arrival of the collection in Jerusalem is described in Acts 24:17: "After many years I came to bring alms to my nation."

no importance to him (Gal 2:6,9) and his description of the present Jerusalem as in slavery (to the Law) with her children (4:25); and if so, is Paul hoping that the collection will heal any hard feelings between him and the Jerusalem authorities? Certainly in Rom 15:30–31 Paul seems apprehensive about whether his service in Jerusalem will be acceptable to the Christians there. Between the lines of Acts 21:17–25 one can detect tension between Paul and James when Paul does get to Jerusalem. Thus the collection may have played a spiritual, ecclesiological, and diplomatic function in Paul's ministry—a sampling of the complicated roles that raising money has played in churches ever since.

The Opponents or False Apostles in II Cor 10–13

Although some respectable scholars (Barrett, Käsemann) would argue that the "super-apostles" of 11:5 and 12:11 are different from the "false apostles" (11:13), that is a minority view involving an unnecessary complication.[31] Granted the thesis that only one set of "apostles" is described throughout 10–13, what are their characteristics? Reading through the chapters with that question in mind, one may create a portrait not only from what Paul says in direct critique but also from his self-defense. They seem to have "come" recently to Corinth. They are of Jewish stock but have (presumably Hellenistic) rhetorical skills; they preach Jesus and what passes for a gospel. They boast of extraordinary powers and experiences,[32] and the fact that they ask for support makes the Corinthians feel important. Interestingly, Paul concentrates his attacks on their flashy pretensions and attitudes more than on their doctrine, and he does so largely in a style of one-upmanship. If they are Hebrews and Israelites and servants of Christ, so is he (11:21–23). If the super-apostles talk about their powers, Paul too worked signs, wonders, and miracles when he was at Corinth (12:11–12). If they talk about their experiences, fourteen years ago he was taken up to third heaven and heard things he cannot utter (12:1–5). They have to build on his foundation, boasting about what really are other's labors; but he builds on no one else's (10:15; I Cor 3:10). But more than any other point of comparison, can they match

[31]Most often in this thesis the false apostles are preachers at Corinth whereas the super-apostles are the authorities in Jerusalem, probably the so-called pillars of the church of Gal 2:9. But surely one has to interpret 11:5 ("super-apostles") in the light of 11:4, which describes someone who *comes* and preaches another Jesus. See Furnish, *2 Corinthians* 502–5. More generally: D. Kee, *Restoration Quarterly* 23 (1980), 65–76; M. E. Thrall, JSNT 6 (1980), 42–57.

[32]Georgi, *Opponents,* has argued strongly that the opponents are eloquent Hellenistic Jewish ecstatics, filled with the Holy Spirit, who manifested miracle-working power, related to the image of the "divine man" (*theios anēr*) in the Hellenistic world. Murphy-O'Connor, with modifications, has taken up this theme of "Spirit-people."

his record of suffering and being persecuted for Christ (II Cor 11:23–29)? As for money, Paul's failure to seek support was a sign of strength, not of weakness—precisely to avoid burdening the Corinthians and out of his love for them (11:7–15). He robbed other churches for support in order to serve them. Now, despite the innuendos of the false apostles, when Paul is gathering for the collection, he has taken care to act with careful probity, sending Titus and a brother disciple for the money (12:16–18).

The picture of the false apostles can be enlarged and confirmed by recognizing that Paul had them in mind at times earlier in II Cor (3:1–6:13). They evidently arrived at Corinth with letters of recommendation from other Christians; Paul needs none, for the Corinthians whom he converted to Christ are his letter (3:1–3). Confirmation is found here that they charged for their gospel (2:17) and that they boasted about what they had seen (5:12). Is Paul's defense of his sufferings and life-threatening predicaments (4:7–5:10; 6:4–10) an indication that the false apostles were invoking these as a sign of his failure? Is Paul's insistence that the treasure received from God is held in earthen vessels an indication that the false apostles thought that power now belonged to them rather than to God (4:7)?

As for the doctrine proclaimed by these people, was it intrinsically wrong from Paul's point of view; or was the difficulty simply their pretensions? One cannot tell much from the highly oratorical reference to the possibility of someone coming and preaching another Jesus or a different gospel (11:4).[33] One does not find in II Cor anything comparable to the attack in Gal on those who would require Gentile Christians to be circumcised. Yet Paul does insist on his Hebrew and Israelite background; and in 3:6–18 he praises a new ministry and covenant of the Spirit over what was engraved in letters on stone, and extols the superiority of reflecting the Lord's glory with unveiled face over reflecting it with veiled face as Moses did. This emphasis might suggest that the opponents placed great value on their Jewish heritage.[34] Overall, however, beyond the theological implications of the false apostles' claims about themselves, no clear doctrinal fallacy emerges from II Cor 3–7; 10–13.

What happens if we join I Cor to II Cor? Were those attacked by Paul in I Cor (p. 526 above) the opponents designated as false apostles in II Cor? According to I Cor the Corinthians were divided as to whether to follow Paul, Apollos, Cephas (Peter), or Christ; and at least Peter would have been

[33]In Gal 2:14 he accused Peter of not being straightforward about the truth of the gospel, but in I Cor 15:5,11 he insisted that Peter and he were preaching the same basic message that must be believed. In II Cor 6:14–7:1 Paul warned against unbelievers; could that be oratorical excess for the misguided followers of Christ he is describing in chaps. 10–13?

[34]Gunther, *Paul's Opponents* 299–303, is a strong proponent of the Jewish background.

considered an apostle,[35] even if it remains very uncertain that he was at Corinth. I Cor 9:1–27 defends Paul's rights as an apostle and 15:8–10 defends his status as the recipient of an appearance of the risen Jesus that was given to all the apostles. Nevertheless, precisely because he had not seen Jesus during the public ministry, many times in Paul's lifetime a defense of his apostleship may have been imposed on him by different critics who made no claim to be apostles themselves. Against the identification of the opponents of I Cor with those of II Cor is the impression given by II Cor 3:1; 11:4 that the false apostles had arrived recently; indeed, they may have emerged as the most important force to be counteracted only after Titus' visit with the "tearful" letter (#9). However, since it seems impossible that I Cor vanquished all Paul's opponents mentioned therein, what is more likely than that some of his older enemies joined forces with the newly arrived, so that a type of hybrid had now emerged to create trouble for Paul at Corinth?

Scholars have theorized at length that the false apostles had Jerusalem roots as adherents of the Twelve or of James, or were Hellenistic Jewish preachers who emphasized Jesus as a wonder-worker, or were gnostics. Despite occasional passages that may lend support to one or the other of those theories, there is not enough explicit evidence in the Corinthian correspondence to establish any one of them convincingly. In Gal 2:12 Paul was very specific that "men from James" (or Jerusalem) came to harass him at Antioch; if emissaries from James of Jerusalem were vexing his cause at Corinth, why would he be less specific? We may have to be content that those designated "apostles" were vainglorious about their own marvelous gifts of the Spirit and preached a victorious Christ with little emphasis on his sufferings or Christian imitation of those sufferings.

Issues and Problems for Reflection

(1) "The one who knew no sin—for our sake God made sin" (II Cor 5:21). There is a common NT teaching that Jesus was without sin (John 8:46; 14:30; Heb 4:15; I Pet 2:22; I John 3:5). Does Paul here go against that tradition by claiming that God made Jesus personally a sinner who, then, would be an object of God's disfavor? (Some would support that by claiming that Jesus was trying to avoid drinking the cup of divine *wrath* in Mark 14:36.) If not, there are several possibilities: (a) God allowed Jesus to be *considered* a sinner (blasphemer) and to die a sinner's death. A parallel is Gal 3:13: "Christ became a curse for us, for it is written, 'Cursed is everyone

[35]See C. K. Barrett, "Cephas and Corinth," in *Essays on Paul,* 28–34. F. C. Baur made one of the oldest treatments of Paul's adversaries at Corinth (1831) the cornerstone of his theory that the early church was shaped by a struggle between legalistic Petrine and libertarian Pauline Christianity.

who is hung on a tree' " (the punishment for blasphemy: Lev 24:16 and Deut 21:22–23 are combined by Josephus). (b) God allowed Jesus to stand in for sinful humanity. The rest of the sentence in II Cor 5:21 may favor that interpretation: "so that we might become the righteousness of God in him." (c) God made Jesus an offering for sin. In the Greek of Lev 4:25,29 "sin" is used for sin offering. Yet there is no preparation in the II Cor context for such an idea.

(2) The historicity of Acts with its hero-worshiping portrayal of Peter and Paul, their careers filled with marvels, has often been challenged (even as the miracles attributed to Jesus have often been dismissed as later propaganda). II Cor 12:12 is worth considering in light of those judgments. Paul himself claims the working of "signs, wonders, and miracles" among the Corinthians (also Rom 15:19), even if he does not put the probative value on them that others do. A comparison of Paul's account in II Cor 11:23–33 of what he underwent with the picture in Acts shows that, if anything, Acts might lead us to underestimate the apostle's extraordinary career. Even some of the most challenged aspects of the Acts picture, like Paul's initial preaching in the synagogues and the opposition from the diaspora Jews, find confirmation (11:24,26). There are minor differences, e.g., that Paul's departure from Damascus involved the hostility of King Aretas and not only that of the Jews (cf. 11:32–33 and Acts 9:22–25). Yet the similarities between Acts and Paul's own writings should not be undervalued (Table 5 in Chapter 16 above).

Bibliography on II Corinthians

COMMENTARIES AND STUDIES IN SERIES: Barrett, C. K. (HNTC, 1973); Best, E. (IBC, 1987); Betz, H. D. (Hermeneia, 1985: only chaps. 8–9); Danker, F. W. (AugC, 1989); Fallon, F. T. (NTM, 1980); **Furnish, V. P.** (AB, 1984); Hughes, P. E. (NICNT, 1962); Kreitzer, L. J. (NTG, 1996); Kruse, C. (TNTC, 1987); Martin, R. P. (WBC, 1986); Murphy-O'Connor, J. (NTT, 1991); Omanson, R. L., and J. Ellington (TH, 1993); Tasker, R.V.G., (TNTC, 1958); **Thrall, M. E.** (2 vols.; ICC, 1994, 1998); Watson, N. (EC, 1993). See also asterisked works in the *Bibliography* of Chapter 22 above.

BIBLIOGRAPHIES: Dutile, G., *Southwest Journal of Theology* 32 (#1; 1989), 41–43 (annotated); Bieringer, *Studies* 3–66.

Barrett, C. K., "Paul's Opponents in II Corinthians," NTS 17 (1970–71), 233–54.

Beasley-Murray, G. R., *2 Corinthians* (Nashville: Broadman, 1971).

Bieringer, R., and J. Lambrecht, *Studies on 2 Corinthians* (BETL 112; Louvain: Peeters, 1994).

Bornkamm, G., "The History of the Origin of the So-called Second Letter to the Corinthians," NTS 8 (1961–62), 258–64.

Bultmann, R., *The Second Letter to the Corinthians* (Minneapolis: Augsburg, 1985).

Carson, D. A., *From Triumphalism to Maturity: An Exposition of 2 Corinthians 10–13* (Grand Rapids: Baker, 1984).

Crafton, J. A., *The Agency of the Apostle: A Dramatic Analysis of Paul's Responses to Conflict in 2 Corinthians* (JSNTSup 51; Sheffield: Academic, 1991).

Georgi, D., *The Opponents of Paul in Second Corinthians* (Philadelphia: Fortress, 1986; German orig. 1964).

Hanson, R.P.C., *II Corinthians* (London: SCM, 1954).

Harris, M. J., *2 Corinthians* (Grand Rapids: Zondervan, 1976).

Héring, J., *The Second Epistle of Saint Paul to the Corinthians* (London: Epworth, 1967).

Kent, H.A.A., *A Heart Opened Wide: Studies in II Corinthians* (Grand Rapids: Baker, 1982).

Madros, P., *The Pride and Humility of Saint Paul in His Second Letter to the Corinthians* (Jerusalem: Franciscan, 1981).

Menzies, A., *The Second Epistle of Paul to the Corinthians* (London: Macmillan, 1912).

Oostendorp, D. W., *Another Jesus: A Gospel of Jewish-Christian Superiority in II Corinthians* (Kampen: Kok, 1976).

Savage, T. B., *Power through Weakness. Paul's Understanding of the Christian Ministry in 2 Corinthians* (SNTSMS 86; Cambridge Univ., 1996).

Strachan, R. H., *The Second Epistle of Paul to the Corinthians* (New York: Harper, 1935).

Sumney, J. L., *Identifying Paul's Opponents: The Question of Method in 2 Corinthians* (JSNTSup 40; Sheffield: Academic, 1990).

Taylor, N. H., "The Composition and Chronology of Second Corinthians," JSNT 44 (1991), 67–87.

Thrall, M. E., "A Second Thanksgiving Period in II Corinthians," JSNT 16 (1982), 101–24.

Young, F. M., and D. F. Ford, *Meaning and Truth in 2 Corinthians* (Grand Rapids: Eerdmans, 1987).

CHAPTER 24

LETTER TO THE ROMANS

Longer than any other NT letter, more reflective in its outlook than any other undisputed Pauline letter, more calmly reasoned than Gal in treating the key question of justification and the Law, Rom has been the most studied of the apostle's writings—indisputably Paul's theological chef d'oeuvre. From Augustine through Abelard, Luther and Calvin, to Barth this letter has played a major role in the development of theology. With only slight exaggeration one could claim that debates over the main ideas in Rom split Western Christianity.[1] Indeed, shelves could be filled simply with discussions of its key theme of justification—discussions that are often very difficult for beginners. Much of the analysis is colored by Reformation conflicts about faith and works, and these debated themes of Rom seem remote from ordinary Christian life today. For those who may have time to study in greater depth only one Pauline letter, Rom would not be my recommendation, even though it is the most important. In this *Introduction,* therefore, I give somewhat less space to Rom than to I Cor, where the discussions and the themes were easier to follow and more immediately applicable.[2] After the *Background* and *General Analysis,* subdivisions will be devoted to: the *Unity of Rom and chap. 16, Justification/righteousness, Paul's view of Jewish observance of the Law, Original sin and Rom 5:12–21, Issues for reflection,* and *Bibliography.*

The Background

There are two important introductory issues: the situation in Paul's life that served as the context of the letter, and the history of the Roman community that received it. The first is relatively easy to discern. Paul is writing from near Cenchreae (the port of Corinth) since he commends to the recipients Phoebe, a deacon from that city (16:1–2). He sends along the greetings of Gaius, who is host to the whole church from which Paul writes; and there

[1]Melanchthon's *Loci communes* (1521), the first textbook of Protestant systematic theology, arranged its doctrinal topics according to the general structure of Rom. For the history of interpretation, see J. D. Godsey, and R. Jewett in *Interpretation* 34 (1980), 3–16, 17–31 respectively.

[2]Nor shall I attempt to supply bibliography for all the chapters and topics; Fitzmyer's bibliography in his *Romans* is exhaustive.

Summary of Basic Information

DATE: In the winter of 57/58 from Corinth (55/56 in the Revisionist Chronology).

TO: God's beloved in Rome, where Paul had never been but had friends.

AUTHENTICITY: Not seriously disputed.

UNITY: A very small minority posits the joining of two separate letters; a larger minority maintains that chap. 16 was added later.

INTEGRITY: Besides chap. 16 (or the doxology in 16:25–27), a few have rejected chaps. 9–11 as not truly Pauline.

FORMAL DIVISION:

A. Opening Formula: 1:1–7
B. Thanksgiving: 1:8–10
C. Body: 1:11–15:13
D. Concluding Formulas (15:14–16:23) plus Doxology (16:25–27).

DIVISION ACCORDING TO CONTENTS:

1:1–15: Address/greeting, Thanksgiving, and Proem about Paul's wish to come to Rome

1:16–11:36: Doctrinal Section:
- Part I: 1:16–4:25: Uprightness of God revealed through the gospel
  - 1:18–3:20: God's wrath and sins of Gentiles and Jews
  - 3:21–4:25: Justification by faith apart from the Law
- Part II: 5:1–8:39: God's salvation for those justified by faith
- Part III: 9:1–11:36: God's promises to Israel

12:1–15:13: Hortatory Section:
- Part I: 12:1–13:14: Authoritative advice for Christian living
- Part II: 14:1–15:13: The strong owe love to the weak

15:14–33: Paul's travel plans and a blessing

16:1–23: Recommendation for Phoebe and greetings to people at Rome

16:25–27: Concluding doxology.

was a prominent Gaius at Corinth (16:23; I Cor 1:14). Paul, as he writes, is planning to take a collection to Jerusalem (Rom 15:26–33). The apostle spent the winter of 57/58 (Traditional Chronology) in Corinth, and afterward (Acts 20:2–21:15) went back through Macedonia, Asia, and Caesarea to Jerusalem, where he was arrested. Thus there is virtual scholarly unanimity that Paul wrote to Rome from Corinth (in 57/58, or earlier in the Revisionist Chronology).

The second issue involves the recipients of the letter. One approach considers the history of Christianity at Rome to be irrelevant background. Paul was not the founder of the Roman Christian community,[3] and advocates of this approach suppose that he knew little about it. In his letter he was writing

[3]To the Corinthians Paul was father (I Cor 4:15), and he could correct them with firmness. He has to approach the Romans far more gingerly, almost apologizing for having written boldly (Rom 15:15).

a magisterial compendium of his theology or general reflections based on his past experiences rather than knowledgeably addressing issues of immediate concern to Roman Christians. Often that outlook is tied in with the theory that chap. 16, which contains greetings from Paul to twenty-six people, does not belong to the letter and therefore was not addressed to Christians whom Paul knew at Rome. However, if chap. 16 does belong to Rom (the dominant view now in English-speaking circles) and Paul knew so many people in Rome, presumably he knew something about the Roman church.

Accordingly, a more popular approach is that Christian origins at Rome, the capital of the Empire, and the nature of the Roman church are important background. There were probably 40,000–50,000 Jews in Rome in the 1st century AD;[4] and from the available evidence, beginning in the 2d century BC, many had come as merchants, immigrants, or captives from the Palestine/Syria area. Close political bonds continued for two centuries as Rome carefully supervised client kingdoms in Palestine, and Herodian princes were sent to Rome to be reared. After the fall of Jerusalem in AD 70, the Jewish historian Josephus lived out his life in Rome as a client of the Flavian emperors; and in the 70s the soon-to-be Emperor Titus brought to Rome the Jewish king Agrippa II, whose sister Berenice became Titus' mistress.

Given that history of Jewish presence, it would not have been long before Jews who believed in Jesus and who were making converts in other cities of the Empire, like Damascus and Antioch, made their way to such a promising missionary field. When did the first word about Christ reach Rome? Let us work backwards to answer that question. Tacitus' account of Nero's persecutions after the fire of AD 64 (*Annals* 15.44) implies that it was possible to distinguish between Christians (*Chrestianoi*) and Jews at Rome. The Christians were numerous; and this "pernicious [Christian] superstition" had originated in Judea—an indirect suggestion that Christianity had come to Rome from Judea. Paul's letter in 57/58 implies the Christian community had been in existence for a considerable period of time, since he had been wishing "for many years" to visit (15:23). Indeed, the faith of the Romans "is being reported over the whole world" (1:8), a flattery that would make little sense if Paul was writing to a minuscule group recently founded. Thus it seems that the Roman Christian community must have existed by the early 50s. Acts 18:1–3 reports that when Paul came to Corinth (*ca.* AD 50) he found

[4]Population estimates are uncertain. In the whole Roman Empire, according to Edmundson, *Church* 7, there were about 4,500,000 Jews amid a total population of 54 to 60 million, or one out of every thirteen people. Others estimate the number of Jews at 6 to 7 million. On the Jewish background material for Rom, see R. E. Brown, BMAR and "Further"; W. Wiefel, TRD 85–101; H. J. Leon, *The Jews of Ancient Rome* (Philadelphia: Jewish Publication Society, 1960); J. C. Walters, *Ethnic Issues in Paul's Letter to the Romans* (Philadelphia: Trinity, 1993); M. D. Nanos, *The Mystery of Romans* (Minneapolis: A/F, 1996).

lodging with Aquila and Priscilla (= Prisca), a Jewish couple who had recently come from Italy "because Claudius had ordered all the Jews to leave Rome." Since it is never mentioned that Paul converted them, they came from Rome as Jews who already believed in Jesus. Suetonius (*Claudius* 25.4) states that Claudius "expelled Jews from Rome because of their constant disturbances impelled by Chrestus [*impulsore Chresto*]." As we saw in Chapter 16 above, n. 24, this expulsion may have meant that by AD 49 the Christian mission had been in Rome long enough to cause serious friction in the synagogues. We have no substantial evidence before that,[5] but very likely Christianity had reached Rome by the early 40s.

Whence did the Christian preachers come? *Ca.* 375 Ambrosiaster, living in Rome and writing a commentary on Rom,[6] reports the Romans "received the faith although with a Jewish bent [*ritu licet Judaico*]." Paul had never been to Rome; nothing in Acts' accounts of Antioch suggests that there was a mission from that city to Rome. In fact, there are no arguments for a source other than Jerusalem; and Acts 28:21 relates that Jews in Rome had channels of theological information coming from Jerusalem, a connection supported by Jewish documents describing figures of the late 1st century.

Why is all this important for understanding Rom? It could be of twofold importance if we accept chap. 16 as part of the letter. First, knowing a surprisingly large number of Christians at Rome, Paul would have shaped his letter to speak pastorally to the community there. Acts and Gal indicate that Christianity coming from Jerusalem was likely to have been more conservative about the Jewish heritage and the Law[7] than were the Gentiles converted by Paul. Rom is noticeably more cautious about the value of the Jewish heritage than was Gal, not only because of the presence of chaps. 9–11, but also when individual passages are compared to Gal.[8] (That makes sense if echoes of Gal had reached Jerusalem and were threatening Paul's hope for a benevolent reception there [p. 554 above].) For example, while in Gal 5:2 Paul wrote, "If you receive circumcision, Christ will be of no advantage to you," Rom 3:1–2 asks, "What benefit is there in being circumcised? Much in every way." Paul is not being inconsistent, for unlike the situation envisaged in Gal (and Phil 3) there are no adversaries in Rome proclaiming an

[5]For uncertain suggestions, see BMAR 102–3. Acts 2:10 mentions Jews from Rome among those who heard about Jesus on the first Pentecost.

[6]PL 17:46A; CSEL 81, p. 6, #4(3).

[7]Many scholars contend that, since Jewish Christians had been expelled by the Emperor Claudius earlier, the Roman community known to Paul may have had a large percentage of Gentiles. The Gentiles, however, would mirror the Christianity of the Jews who converted them. Moreover, some Jewish Christians would have returned after the death of Claudius in 54.

[8]J. L. Martyn has called Rom the first commentary on Gal; Metzger, *New* 229, says that if Gal is the Magna Carta of universal Christianity, Rom is its constitution.

antigospel of the necessity of circumcising the Gentiles.[9] Rom is also the most "liturgical" of the undisputed Pauline letters in the sense of employing the language of Jewish worship, e.g., Christ is described as an expiatory sacrifice (3:25); people are urged to present their bodies as a living sacrifice (12:1); and Paul's own ministry is in the priestly service of the gospel (15:16). Could this phraseology have been employed with an eye to recipients who respected the Jerusalem Temple liturgy? Second, Paul was planning to go to Jerusalem; and if Roman Christianity stemmed from Jerusalem, a persuasive letter to Rome from Paul might both help him to anticipate what he might say at Jerusalem and at the same time persuade the Roman Christians to intervene with the Jerusalem authorities on his behalf.

Sometimes Rom is described as Paul's last testament. This may mean no more than that it was the last written of the undisputed letters of Paul—"last" by accident. Something more intentional would be meant if Rom was foreseen by Paul as possibly his final message. I have suggested in the preceding paragraph that Paul may have been apprehensive about bringing the collection of (Gentile Christian) money to Jerusalem. If it were refused, would the *koinōnia* between Paul's communities and Jerusalem be broken? That might mean that Paul would become persona non grata in many places including Rome; and so he might have written this letter in order that the Christians of this very influential church would know the truth about the gospel for which he was willing to die—a literary last testament so that his insights would not be lost. This is too imaginative an hypothesis to base on the slender foundation of Rom 15:22–32. Yet, even without such dire foreboding, Paul surely thought of his forthcoming journey to Jerusalem to bring the collection as a major moment in his missionary career; and he may have decided to send to the Roman house-churches a thought-out statement of his gospel. He would have hoped that his gospel, which had implications for Jew and Gentile, could heal animosities in the mixed congregation at Rome.

The most satisfactory interpretation of Rom combines elements from different proposals.[10] Rom was in a way a summary of Paul's thought, phrased with an air of finality as he pulled together his ideas before going to Jerusalem where he would have to defend them.[11] But why was this summary sent

[9]Rom 16:17–20 does have Paul warn against dissensions in opposition to the teaching that the Romans have learned; but from that passage it is not clear that those who promote such dissension through false teaching are already on the scene. This might represent generalized polemic against those who are likely to appear.

[10]See a dozen different views in TRD 3–171; also Wedderburn, *Romans*.

[11]Many would cite the judgment of Philip Melancthon, Luther's companion in the German Reformation: "a compendium of the Christian religion." Yet in Rom there is an almost disproportionate emphasis on the motifs that appeared in Gal.

to Rome? For several reasons. At this moment in his life Paul had finished his mission in the eastern Mediterranean, and he was hoping to begin a major mission in Spain in the far west. Rome would make an admirable base for that mission (even as Antioch and Philippi had served as bases from which he made his initial moves westward in his earlier excursions).[12] Accordingly Paul thought it important that the Romans get a correct perception of his apostolic ministry, so that, while Rom served as a letter of recommendation for Paul himself (L. T. Johnson), it served even more as a recommendation for his gospel (H. Koester). More pastorally, a careful explanation of Paul's ideas might help to improve relations between Christians of different persuasion at Rome (the "strong" and the "weak" of 14:1–15:1), fulfilling Paul's responsibility to be an apostle to the Gentile areas. In addition, the Roman Christians, if they were convinced that Paul was not prejudiced against Judaism, might be intermediaries with their Jerusalem forebears, paving the way for a favorable acceptance of Paul by the Jewish Christian authorities there. On several fronts, then, Rom was meant to be persuasive; and that may explain the heavy use of the diatribe format (p. 89 above)—a genre employed by Greco-Roman philosophers to demonstrate theses and answer objections.[13] Let us now treat Rom consecutively and see whether these observations are validated.

General Analysis of the Message

The OPENING FORMULA (1:1–7), the THANKSGIVING (1:8–10), and a PROEM (1:11–15) that serves as Body-Opening may be treated together for they have interlocking features of interest. The failure of Paul to use the expression "the church of God that is in Rome" or "the churches of Rome" (cf. I Cor 1:2; II Cor 1:1; Gal 1:2; I Thess 1:1) has been interpreted pejoratively. Although Paul is willing to greet a house-church at Rome (16:5), it is speculated that he did not consider the Roman community a true church because he did not found it or because of its theology. That is almost surely wrong: Paul would not be derogatory in a letter designed to win Roman favor; he could scarcely call a group that he would not consider a church

[12]In 16:1–2 Paul asks for help for Phoebe, who seems to be carrying the letter. She may be meant to work with Prisca and Aquila in setting up such a base; all three had worked with Paul in missionary activity in the eastern Mediterranean.

[13]If one considers Rom to be a didactic letter, parallels exist between Rom and the letters of Epicurus and elements in Plutarch's *Moralia;* see M. L. Stirewalt, Jr., TRD 147–71. Dunn, *Romans* lix, is perfectly correct, however, in maintaining that the distinctiveness of the letter far outweighs its conformity with Greco-Roman literary or rhetorical patterns, and that debates as to whether it is epideictic (demonstrative), or deliberative, or protreptic (persuasive) do not advance very far our understanding of the contents of Rom and Paul's purpose.

"the beloved of God in Rome called to be holy" (Rom 1:7); and the failure to use "church" at the beginning of Phil, addressed to a community that Paul founded and loved, shows how unreliable silence is.

In v. 8 Paul testifies to the faith of the Roman Christians proclaimed in all the world—high praise since it becomes apparent from vv. 11–15 that Paul has never seen them, although he has long desired to visit them. In that context the salutation, the most formal in the Pauline writings, is striking for the way in which Paul introduces himself to the Roman Christians.[14] He uses only his own name—no co-sender—and shows that he is "an apostle set apart for the gospel of God" (1:1) by spelling out: "The gospel concerning God's Son who was born/begotten of the seed of David according to the flesh, designated Son of God in power according to the Spirit of holiness as of resurrection from the dead" (1:3–4). Critical scholarship recognizes that here Paul is not using language of his own coinage but offering a Jewish Christian formulation of the gospel[15]—presumably because such a formulation would be known to the Roman Christians and acceptable to them. If Paul's gospel has been misrepresented or slandered, he is protecting himself from the start by showing that what he preaches agrees with the preaching of those who evangelized the Romans. Thus, he and the Romans can be encouraged by each other's faith (1:12). The transition to the Body of the letter (1:10–15) relates Paul's future plan to come to Rome to preach the gospel of which this missive is an anticipatory statement.

DOCTRINAL SECTION OF THE BODY: PART I (1:16–4:25): *The uprightness/righteousness [dikaiosynē] of God revealed through the gospel.* Paul continues into the main section of his letter by stressing that this gospel is the power of God for the salvation[16] of every believer, first for the Jew, then for the Greek. (Notice the theological sequence, which would be effective against any who claimed that Paul devalued Jewish believers.) A central theme of Rom is that "the righteousness of God" is now revealed (1:17; subsection below), namely, that quality whereby in judgment God acquits people of their sins through their faith in Jesus Christ. (On the use of Hab

[14]Morgan, *Romans* 17, points out that in the opening verses Paul assumes that his hearers will understand a host of theological terms: Messiah (Christ), apostle, gospel, Son of God, Scripture, Spirit of holiness—Christians had developed a shared terminology very early.

[15]E.g., the expression "Spirit of holiness," reflects a Semitic genitival structure in place of Paul's normal and better Greek expression "Holy Spirit." Notice that in the beginning Paul makes no reference to Jesus' crucifixion or death (cf. Rom 4:25). Ambrosiaster, continuing what was quoted on p. 562, says that prior to Paul the mystery of the cross had not yet been laid out for the Romans.

[16]In the genuine Pauline letters salvation is an eschatological, future aspect of God's work in which the intercessory Christ in heaven has a role; Jews would understand it against the OT background of God as saving or delivering Israel, and Gentiles might hear an echo of a king or emperor as "savior" in the sense of protecting a nation or town from evil. Normally Paul keeps salvation distinct from justification, which is a present reality; but, as we shall see, Eph seems to run salvation together with justification.

2:4, "The just through faith will live," see Chapter 19 above, *Issue* 3.) What was the relation of people to God before the coming of the gospel of Christ? Turning first to the Gentiles in this letter to the Christians of the capital city of the whole Roman world, Paul (1:18–23) wishes to explain that a gracious God was knowable from the time of creation.[17] It was only by human fault and stupidity that the divine image was obscured in the Pagan world, whence the wrath of God. A graphic description of Pagan idolatry, and the lust and depraved conduct to which it has led (1:24–32) reflects Paul's Jewish standard of values.[18] In much of the portrayal of Gentiles that opens Rom Paul may be drawing on a standard Hellenistic synagogue depiction with which he was reared. But then in 2:1, in a style known to us from the Stoic diatribe, Paul speaks to an imagined Jewish listener, who might be passing judgment on what Paul has condemned and yet, despite this superior stance, be doing the same things. God does not show favoritism: Eternal life or punishment will be assigned according to what people do, first Jews, judged according to the Law; then Gentiles, judged according to nature (*physis*) and what is written in their hearts and consciences (2:5–16).

In a remarkable section (2:17–24) Paul taunts the proud claims of Jewish superiority. He does not deny that circumcision has value,[19] but only if one observes the Law. Indeed, an uncircumcised person who lives up to the Law's requirements will condemn the circumcised Law-breaker (2:25–29). All human beings are guilty before God. Well then, what is the advantage for circumcised Jews if they too are under God's wrath (3:1–9) and no one is righteous?[20] In 3:21–26 Paul answers: To the Jews were given God's own words of promise, and God is faithful. The apostle describes what was promised or prefigured in the Law and Prophets, namely, the righteousness of God through faith of/in Jesus Christ, justifying without distinction Jew and Greek. God's integrity is vindicated: God is not unfair, for the sins of all

[17]This passage has led to a discussion of whether Paul espouses a natural theology: a discussion complicated by patristic theories of natural revelation and modern scholars' insistence on the purity of Pauline eschatological theology (to which they see a contrariety in an emphasis on the powers of human reasoning). In a nuanced discussion Fitzmyer (*Romans* 271–74) shows that Paul is echoing the kind of Hellenistic Jewish thought about Gentiles found in Wis 13:8–9: "They are not pardonable, for if they were capable of knowing so much that they could investigate the world, how did they not sooner find the Lord of these things?" Paul is not speaking of a natural revelation (*apokalyptein*) comparable to the revelation in Christ; he is speaking of what God has made evident about the divine, eternal power in material creation and what Pagans have culpably ignored.

[18]Wis 14:17–31. For Paul's condemnation of homosexual practices, see p. 529 above. Spivey and Smith (*Anatomy* 342) argue that Paul cites homosexual behavior not because it is the worst sin but because it exemplifies how sin reverses the order that God created (see Jude 7).

[19]Elsewhere Paul is clearly adverse to having Gentile converts circumcised, but here he is talking about Jews. It is scarcely accidental that in Rom Paul discusses his attitude toward Judaism—Roman Christians would be interested in that.

[20]To establish the latter point, in 3:10–20 Paul lists Scripture passages that scholars describe as *testimonia,* i.e., collected texts on a theme, perhaps put together in a liturgical context.

have been expiated by Christ's blood.[21] No one has the right to boast, since God has graciously justified the circumcised and the uncircumcised in the same way, by faith[22] apart from deeds/works of (= prescribed by) the Law (3:27–31).

Paul has cited the Law and the Prophets; and in chap. 4 he reaches back to the first book of the Law and cites Abraham to show that God has worked consistently, for Abraham's righteousness came by faith, not by the Law.[23] We saw on pp. 469–72 above that Paul's appeal to Abraham was probably catalyzed by the use of Abraham among those in Galatia who insisted that circumcision was necessary for salvation. Now the example of Abraham has become a formative part of his understanding of God's plan. The Jews of Paul's time would have looked on Abraham as their forebear, but for Paul he is "father of us all" who share his faith (4:16).[24] The section comes to a close with a concise statement of Paul's thesis: The story of the righteousness attributed to Abraham was written for us who believe in the Lord Jesus, "who was given over for our transgressions and raised for our justification" (4:25). While this salvific action affects individuals, Paul envisions individual believers related to one another in a collectivity—a religious community or church, even as Israel was a covenanted people.

DOCTRINAL SECTION OF THE BODY: PART II (5:1–8:39): *Reconciliation to God in Christ and Its Benefits.* If people are justified through Christ, they are now reconciled to God. This brings many benefits: peace with God, hope of sharing God's glory, and an outpouring of God's love (5:1–5). The description of how Christ's death accomplished justification, salvation, and reconciliation (5:6–11) contains one of the great NT explanations of what is involved in divine love: a willingness to die for sinners who do not deserve such graciousness (see p. 533 above). After having used Abraham as an example of justification by faith in Israel's history, Paul now compares what has been accomplished through Christ with the state of all human beings stemming from Adam: grace and life compared to sin and death. (For Paul, death is not simply the cessation of life but, because it came through sin, the

[21]The model in Paul's mind is the Temple animal sacrifices and the sprinkling of their blood. Fitzmyer, *Romans* 342, argues from vocabulary, much of it ritual, that in 3:24–26 a prePauline formula has been reused—perhaps another instance of Paul casting his gospel in language familiar to Roman Christians. Overall see D. A. Campbell, *The Rhetoric of Righteousness in Romans 3:21–26* (JSNTSup 65; Sheffield: JSOT, 1992).

[22]In 3:28 Luther introduced an adverb not found in the Greek ("*only* through faith," or "through faith *alone*"); the vocabulary of *sola fides* had existed in Latin church writers before Luther, but his addition in Rom heightened the theological contrast with James 2:24: "A person is justified by deeds/works, not by faith alone."

[23]On Abraham in Rom 4, see R. B. Hays, NovT 27 (1985), 76–97.

[24]In the course of his treatment Paul makes one of his severest statements: "The Law produces wrath; where there is no Law, there is no transgression" (4:15). The complaint that this picture is not fair to the Jews of Paul's time will be treated in a subsection below (p. 578).

negation of life.) As the trespass of Adam led to condemnation for all, so the obedient act of righteousness of Christ led to justification and life for all. This passage (5:12–21) gave rise to the theology of original sin; see the subsection below.

In 6:1–11 Paul explains that this effect is brought about through baptism—the longest treatment of the topic in his letters, although even here he never spells out the exact relationship of baptism and faith in this divine work. Our old self was crucified with Christ; we were baptized into his death and buried with him, so that as he was raised from the dead, we too might walk in newness of life.[25] But Sin (personified by Paul) remains an active force, even though we are now under grace rather than under the Law, and 6:12–23 warns against being enslaved by Sin. Some have thought that the apostle is reusing one of his baptismal sermons here, perhaps in order to protect himself against any charge that his gospel of justification apart from the Law fostered licentiousness.

In chap. 7, Paul returns to the issue of the Mosaic Law. The basic principle is that Christ's death has annulled the binding power of that Law. The Law cannot be equated with Sin, but sinful passions are aroused by the Law: "I would not have known sin, if it were not for the Law" (7:5,7). The "I" monologue that runs through 7:7–25 is among the most dramatic of Paul's rhetorical passages in Rom: "I do not understand what I do. I do not do what I wish, but I do the very thing I hate . . . I delight in the Law of God, but I see in my members another law at war with the law of my mind." This impassioned speech has given rise to many interpretations.[26] Fitzmyer, *Romans* 465–66, offers a fascinating parallel from the DSS, where the writer describes an "I" who wrestles with the issue of salvation, beginning with words: "I belong to wicked humanity." Both that writer and Paul are *describing sinful humanity* from a Jewish viewpoint; but for the DSS author deliverance comes from a gracious God through the Law or Torah, while for Paul it comes from a gracious God through faith in Jesus Christ.

[25]On 6:1–4, P. L. Stepp, *The Believer's Participation in the Death of Christ* (Lewiston, NY: Mellen, 1996). Although some would interpret this theology of baptism against the background of mystery-religion initiations (p. 86 above), it should be related to the way Jesus compared his own death to a baptism with which he was baptized (Mark 10:38–39). Gal 2:19–20 speaks of dying and living in Christ without reference to baptism.

[26]Besides the bibliography in Fitzmyer, *Romans* 469–72, see J. Lambrecht, *The Wretched "I" and Its Liberation: Paul in Romans 7 and 8* (Louvain: Peeters, 1992). Prominent among the interpretations is seeing the "I" as autobiographical, i.e., Paul reflecting on his preChristian struggles observing the Law. This fed into Luther's identification of his own struggles with Paul's struggles (his famous description "at the same time righteous and sinner" is related to 7:15–20). An essential corrective is K. Stendahl, "The Apostle Paul and the Introspective Conscience of the West," HTR 56 (1963), 199–215; reprinted in his *Paul among Jews,* 78–96. Important, even if needing correction, is R. Bultmann, "Romans 7 and the Anthropology of Paul," *Existence and Faith* (New York: Meridian, 1960), 147–57; also his *Theology,* 1.288–306.

If Christ delivers from death and sin and brings life, how is that life to be lived, especially since we are still flesh and the flesh is not submissive to God's law? In chap. 8 Paul's answer is that we are to live, not according to the flesh but according to the Spirit of God who raised Christ from the dead. "If you live according to the flesh, you are going to die; but if by the Spirit you put to death the deeds of the body, you will live" (8:13).[27] Thus we become children of God (able to cry out "*Abba,* Father," even as Jesus had), heirs of God and co-heirs of Christ, with the promise that if now we suffer with him, we shall also be glorified with him (8:14–17). The people of Israel had understood that they were God's firstborn or God's sons/children (Exod 4:22; Isa 1:2), but now the relationship had been deepened through the Spirit of him who was uniquely God's Son. (Paul uses for "us" the language of divine "sonship," *huiothesia,* language that John confines to Jesus alone.) In the OT story of creation, the earth was cursed because of Adam's sin (Gen 3:17–19; 5:29); and so in OT apocalyptic there are dreams of a new heaven and a new earth (Isa 65:17; 66:22). Logically, then, as part of his contrast between Adam and Christ, Paul (Rom 8:18–23) speaks also of Christ's healing effect on all material creation (including the human body). It will be freed from the bondage of decay and brought to freedom. We do not yet see all this; we hope and wait with endurance; and to aid our weakness the Spirit intercedes for us with sighs that cannot be spoken (8:24–27). None of this future is left to chance: Both justification and glorification are part of the plan of salvation that God has predestined from the beginning (8:28–30). The God "who did not spare His own Son but gave him over for all of us" is on our side, and that is a source of enormous confidence. In 8:31–39 Paul ends this second Part of the Doctrinal Section of Rom with one of the most eloquent statements in all Christian spiritual writing: "If God is for us, who is against us? . . . I am convinced that neither death nor life, nor angels nor principalities, nor present things nor future, nor any powers . . . will be able to separate us from the love of God in Christ Jesus our Lord."

DOCTRINAL SECTION OF THE BODY: PART III (9:1–11:36): *How is justification through Christ reconcilable with God's promises to Israel?*[28] If there was a divine plan from the beginning leading to Christ, how is it that the Israelites (Jews), who received the promises through the Law and the Prophets, rejected Christ? The logical need to answer that question elicits from

[27]This is not a trinitarian view, for the Spirit in Paul's description does not yet clearly function as a person; but the assignment of such activity to God's Spirit will move Christian thought in that direction. "Flesh" is not evil for Paul, but through it the evil impulse can get a hold on people.

[28]J. Munck, *Christ and Israel: An Interpretation of Romans 9–11* (Philadelphia: Fortress, 1967); C. K. Barrett, "Romans 9:30–10:21: Call and Responsibility of Israel," *Essays on Paul* (Philadelphia: Westminster, 1982), 132–53; A. J. Guerra, RB 97 (1990), 219–37.

Paul chapters so surprising that some scholars (beginning already in the 2d century with Marcion) have deemed them to be foreign to the letter and contradictory. The missionary who had spent so many years proclaiming the gospel to the Gentiles would be willing to be cut off from Christ and be damned for the sake of his Jewish kinsmen! Giving the lie to all who say that he denigrates Judaism, he lists with pride the marvelous Israelite privileges (9:4–5).

In his explanation that the word of God has not failed, Paul cites Scripture to show that not all the offspring of Abraham were reckoned as his children: God chose Isaac not Ishmael, Jacob not Esau (9:6–13). God is not unjust in this but acts like the potter who chooses to make a quality vase and a common vase from the same clay (9:14–23). And so God cannot be asked to account for the choices made. Making use of another list of *testimonia* (9:24–29), Paul seeks to show that God foresaw both Israel's infidelity and the call of the Gentiles. Israel failed because it sought righteousness by deeds, not by faith; and to compound the error, despite its zeal, it has not recognized that God has manifested righteousness to those who believe in Christ and that, in fact, Christ is the end of the Law (9:30–10:4).[29] Paul continues by emphasizing the futility of seeking to be righteous before God on the basis of works, whereas "if you profess with your lips that 'Jesus is Lord' and believe in your heart that God has raised him from the dead, you will be saved" (10:9). In this "you" there is no distinction between Jew and Greek (10:12); and all this fulfills Joel 3:5 (2:32): "For everyone who calls upon the name of the Lord shall be saved."

In 10:14–21 Paul offers Israel little excuse: The gospel was preached already by the prophets, but Israelites did not believe. They cannot even have the alibi of not understanding; for they are a disobedient and defiant people, while the foolish nation of the Gentiles has responded. "Has God then rejected His people?" (11:1). In an indignant negative response to the question he has rhetorically posed, Paul speaks as an Israelite, a descendant of Abraham from the tribe of Benjamin, who has been chosen by grace. He cites examples from Israel's history where the majority failed, but God preserved a remnant (11:2–10). In fact, Paul foresees that everything will work out well (11:11–32). Israel's stumbling and partial hardening of heart have been providential in allowing salvation to come to the Gentiles. Then by reverse

[29]On the validity of this judgment about Israel's view of works-righteousness, see p. 579 below. By "end of the (Mosaic) Law" it is not clear whether Paul means goal of the Law or termination of the Law (Gal 4:4–5), or a combination: the goal of the Law that brings it to an end. See R. Badenas, *Christ the End of the Law* (JSNTSup 10; Sheffield: JSOT, 1985); S. R. Bechtler, CBQ 56 (1994), 288–308; G. E. Howard, JBL 88 (1969), 331–37.

psychology Israel will become jealous, and all Israel will be saved.[30] Gentile believers should not boast; they are but a branch from a wild olive tree that has been grafted onto a cultivated tree in place of some of the branches that have been lopped off. The regrafting of the natural (Israelite) branches will go easier. (It is a bit shocking that the apostle to the Gentiles seems to have seen the conversion of the Gentiles, not as an end in itself, but as a halfway step toward the conversion of Israel.) The Gentiles earlier and Israel now have been disobedient, and God is showing mercy to all. Paul ends this portrayal with a hymn praising the depths of the riches and the wisdom of God: "To him be glory forever. Amen" (11:33–36).

HORTATORY SECTION OF THE BODY: PART I: (12:1–13:14): *Authoritative advice for Christian Living.* Paul now makes suggestions to the Roman Christians about how they should live in response to the mercy of God. On the one hand this is not surprising because from the beginning (1:5) Paul made it clear that the grace of his apostleship was directed to bringing about the obedience of faith. On the other hand this is a brave enterprise since Paul had no personal acquaintance with most Roman Christians. Beginning in 12:3, then, Paul echoes ideas that he also expressed in I Cor written probably less than a year before: one body, many members, different gifts/charisms, among which are prophecy and teaching,[31] and an emphasis on love. Like an OT wisdom writer, in 12:9–21 he offers a series of counsels with a special emphasis on harmony, forbearance, and forgiveness—all as part of not being conformed to this age/world (12:2) and being renewed in a new age or aeon inaugurated by Christ.[32]

The directive to be subject to governing authorities (13:1–7) is particularly appropriate in a letter to the capital. (I Pet 2:13–15, written from the capital, will have a similar tone.) By this time Claudius, who had driven the Jews out of Rome, was dead, and the new emperor (Nero) had not yet shown hostility to Christians; consequently Paul can speak of the (Roman) ruler as God's servant. The instructions to pay taxes and to respect and honor author-

[30]11:26—indeed some by Paul's ministry to the Gentiles (11:13–14). For Stendahl, Paul means God will bring about the salvation of Israel apart from Christ. In my judgment Fitzmyer, *Romans* 619–20, is correct in rejecting that, for such a solution militates against Paul's overall thesis of justification and salvation by grace for all those who believe in the gospel of Christ Jesus.

[31]Exhortation and being generous in contributions are two charisms absent from I Cor 12:8–10,28 but mentioned in Rom 12:8. Is the charism of "administrative capabilities" (*kybernēseis*) in I Cor 12:28 the same as "presiding over others diligently" (*proïstamenoi*) in Rom 12:8?

[32]Apocalyptic: see pp. 461–63, 509, 525 above. It is debated among scholars whether the list of counsels is Paul's own composition, or is drawn from an earlier Greek or Semitic composition. See C. H. Talbert, NTS 16 (1969–70), 83–94; W. T. Wilson, *Love Without Pretense; Romans 12:9–21 and Hellenistic-Jewish Wisdom Literature* (WUNT 2.46; Tübingen: Mohr-Siebeck, 1991).

ity would make model citizens of the Christians. Did Paul's obedient attitude stem from his personal good experience with Roman authority (e.g., with Gallio at Corinth in Acts 18:12–17)? Or were his instructions a defensive strategy against the charge that his theology of freedom and otherworldliness fostered dangerous civil irresponsibility? Or was he pastorally concerned that two relatively recent expulsions of Jews (AD 19 and 49) by annoyed Roman emperors not be repeated in the instance of Christians? (Were Christians, since they were converting Gentiles, potentially more annoying than Jews? See Chapter 8 above, n. 59.) When we discuss Rev, we shall see that by the end of the century a different Christian attitude toward the Roman emperor had developed, shaped by imperial persecution and harassment of Christians. Thus it is unwarranted to absolutize the Pauline instruction as if his were *the* NT view applicable to governing authorities of all times. In 13:8–10, where "Love one another, for whoever loves the neighbor has fulfilled the Law" is accompanied by the contention that the commandments are summed up in "You shall love your neighbor as yourself," Paul comes close to the Jesus tradition in Matt 22:38–40. Rom 13:11–14 concludes Part I of the hortatory section by stressing how critical is the eschatological moment, this *kairos* inaugurated by Christ. (V. 12, with its imagery of night and day, the works of darkness and the armor of light, may reflect a baptismal hymn known to the Romans.) The urgency leads to Paul's advice that they should arm themselves against the desires of the flesh: "Put on the Lord Jesus Christ" (13:14).

HORTATORY SECTION OF THE BODY: PART II: (14:1–15:13): *The strong owe love to the weak.* We are not certain whether the language of "strong" and "weak" that appears here was of Pauline coinage or was already in use among the Roman audience. These designations seem to cover ways of looking at Christian requirements rather than divided factions, such as those who adhered to different Christian figures at Corinth. The "strong" are convinced they can eat anything and need not treat any days as special; the "weak" are cautious about eating, trusting only vegetables, and observe certain holy days. Despite the efforts of some scholars to associate such preferences with Hellenistic gnostic or mystery-religion practices, the issue probably reflects observances stemming from the purity and cultic demands of the Mosaic Law. The "strong" regard those demands as irrelevant, the "weak" (who seem to be equated with "weak in faith" in 14:1) think they are obligatory. Many scholars would identify the "strong" as the Gentile Christian majority at Rome, and the "weak" as Jewish Christians; but this goes beyond (or even against) the evidence. The Gentile Christians may very well have been in the majority, whence the warnings that the Gentiles should not boast because the Jews rejected Christ (11:17–18); but that does not tell us whether or not the Gentile Christians observed the Mosaic Law.[33] If the original evangelizers of Rome had been missionaries from Jerusalem (a possibility suggested above), there may have been many Gentile converts who were observant. The "weak," then, would have been a combination of such Gentiles and some Jewish Christians who returned to Rome after Claudius' death. On the other hand, other Jewish Christians who were friends of Paul and whom he mentions in Rom 16 would have been among the "strong."

Paul is concerned that the two groups should not judge or despise each other (14:3–4,10,13). Whether they eat or abstain, each group should be doing it for the Lord: "Whether we live or we die, we belong to the Lord" (14:6–8). If the Roman Christians, "strong" or "weak," have heard that Paul does not oblige his Gentile Christian converts to observe the Mosaic Law, they are learning, as had the Corinthians before them (I Cor 8:7–13; 10:23–33), that he would never countenance that this freedom be used to divide a community. In particular, he warns the "strong" that it is better not to eat meat or drink wine if it causes the brother or sister to trip or stumble (14:21). Identifying himself with them, Paul proclaims, "We who are strong ought to bear with failings of those who are weak rather than please ourselves" (15:1). Christ did not please himself (15:3) but became a servant of the circumcision to show God's fidelity, confirming the promises made to the patriarchs, so that the Gentiles may glorify God's mercy (15:8–9a). Paul ends this section with another list of testimonia (15:9b–12): This time they are passages from the Prophets, the Law, and the Writings (the three divisions of the OT) that concern God's plan for the Gentiles.

FIRST CONCLUDING SECTION (15:14–33): *Paul's future plans.* The apostle brings his letter to a close with two interrelated sections. The first explains his dealings with the Romans. He knows they are good, but he wrote to them because he has been given grace by God to be a minister to the Gentiles. Just as a Jewish priest was dedicated to the service of God in the Temple, Paul's preaching the gospel is a liturgical service so that the Gentiles might become an acceptable sacrifice dedicated to God (15:16).[34] In executing that service Paul has gone from Jerusalem to Illyricum (western Greece).[35] Now

[33]For instance, the Galatian community converted by Paul may have been entirely Gentile; but after the antiPauline preachers convinced them, many Galatian Gentile Christians accepted circumcision and the obligations of the Law. For scholarly debates about the "strong" and the "weak," see Minear, *Obedience;* R. J. Karris, TRD 65–84; and J. Marcus, NTS 35 (1989), 67–81.

[34]As Fitzmyer, *Romans* 712, points out, however, one cannot deduce from this that Paul was aware of himself as a Christian "priest." The name for the cultic priest of Israel was in Greek *hiereus;* in the NT that term is used for Christ in Heb 5:6 etc., but never for any Christian believer. It will be the end of the 2d century before Christian ministers (bishops) are spoken of as priests.

[35]A region contiguous to Macedonia and containing the Dalmatian coast. When did Paul go there? Perhaps a few months before he wrote this letter as he made his way from Ephesus and Troas through Macedonia on his way to Corinth.

he hopes to push farther west, through Rome whose Christians he has desired for many years to visit, to preach the gospel where Christ has not been named, namely, Spain (15:14–24). But first he must bring to the Jerusalem poor the money he has been collecting in Macedonia and Achaia, and that journey worries him. Will he escape the hostility of the unbelievers in Judea (who seemingly look on him as a traitor who has gone over to the church he once persecuted), and will his collection be accepted by the Christians at Jerusalem (who, we may guess, have been offended by some of the derogatory comments Paul made against the Jerusalem church "pillars"—Gal 2:6,9)? Paul wants the Romans to help him on this journey by praying for him (15:25–33). Does he also hope that they will send a good word for him to their friends in Jerusalem?

SECOND CONCLUDING SECTION (16:1–27): *Greetings to Roman friends.* But since Paul wishes to spend some time at Rome on his way back from Jerusalem to Spain, he also needs a good word put in for him at Rome. First, Phoebe, a woman deacon[36] of the church at Cenchreae a few miles from where Paul is writing and a great help to him, is going to Rome (and perhaps carrying this letter); she should be received well. If there are Roman Christians who are suspicious of Paul, she as an intermediary can help, as can various people already in Rome who know him, twenty-six of whom he now proceeds to greet in 16:3–16. (I am assuming that this chapter was authentically written by Paul as part of Romans; see first subsection below.) We are acquainted with only a few of them from Acts and other Pauline letters—although we know more about Paul than about any other NT Christian, we still know relatively little. References to a house-church in 16:5, and to households in 16:10 and 11, and to associated groups in 16:14 and 15 suggest that the Roman community consisted of a good number of small house-churches; and indeed that pattern is attested in Rome throughout the 2d century. It has caught modern attention that Andronicus and Junia (preferable to "Junias") are "outstanding among the apostles" (16:7). Junia/Junias is most likely a woman's name, and she may have been the wife of Andronicus. This identity would mean that Paul could apply the term "apostle" to a woman.[37] The verse is a problem chiefly for those who, contrary to the NT evidence, confine apostolate to the Twelve. (Since only anachronistically can every apostle be thought of as an ordained priest, the verse is not decisive in the

[36]We do not know whether deacons in the Pauline churches of the 50s (see Phil 1:1) were as structured a group as the deacons of I Tim 3:8–13, a letter written several decades later. However, whatever a male deacon did, presumably a woman deacon did also. (The term "deaconess" is not helpful, for that institution is a much later office, not having the rank of male deacons.)

[37]"Apostle" had many meanings, and for Paul a common meaning is one who saw the risen Jesus and became a preacher of the gospel. Since more than 500 saw the risen Lord at one time (I Cor 15:6), it would be rather surprising if there were not women apostles in this sense.

modern debate as to whether women can or should be ordained eucharistic priests.)

The letter ends (16:21–23) with Paul including greetings from other Christians at Corinth. The scribe Tertius introduces himself (the only time a Pauline secretary does that), presumably because he was a collaborating disciple in the letter. (Some copyists moved the blessing in 16:20b to follow 16:23 and thus constituted a spurious verse 16:24.) The doxology (praise of God) in 16:25–27 is missing from many mss. and may well be an early copyist's or editor's liturgical addition for public reading in church.

The Unity of Romans and Chap. 16

Beatty Papyrus II (P^{46}; *ca.* AD 200) offers evidence for a 15-chapter form of Rom.[38] In the 19th century a theory began to gain favor, particularly in Germany, that chap. 16 was a once-separate Pauline letter of recommendation addressed to Ephesus on behalf of Phoebe, who was going there from Cenchreae (Rom 16:1–3).[39] A very careful study by Gamble, however, has exposed the weakness of any theory that would dissociate chap. 16 from Rom.[40] The textual evidence for chap. 16 as part of Rom is overwhelmingly strong. To have the letter terminate with the last verse of 15, "The God of peace be with you all," would be to posit an ending unlike that of any genuine Pauline letter, whereas 16:21–23 is typically Pauline. The number of people whom Paul greets at Rome in chap. 16 need not be a problem. Paradoxically Paul, who did not greet many named people when writing to a place where he had spent a long time (e.g., in his letters to Corinth), needed friends to recommend him to others at Rome where he had never been. Many names that Paul mentions in chap. 16 would fit the Roman scene,[41] e.g., "Aristobulus" (a grandson of Herod the Great with that name seems to have lived out

[38]There is 6th-century Latin textual evidence for a 14-chapter form (a form already known to Tertullian and Origen and thus in existence *ca.* AD 200). However, since chap. 15 is clearly Pauline and is closely related to 14, the more substantial issue is whether the original Rom consisted of 15 or 16 chapters.

[39]It is argued that Prisca and Aquila who are greeted in 16:3 had been in Ephesus for several years before Rom was written (Acts 18:24–26), indeed as late as 56 (I Cor 16:19), and that Epaenetus who is greeted in 16:5 was the first convert in *Asia.* Yet these people could have moved to Rome after Paul left Ephesus in the summer of 57. Surely some of those greeted at Rome were Jewish Christian fugitives driven out by the Emperor Claudius in 49, whom Paul had met at Corinth and other places; they may have returned to the capital after that emperor died in 54.

[40]In addition to Gamble, *Textual,* see J.I.H. MacDonald, NTS 16 (1969–70), 369–72; K. P. Donfried, JBL 89 (1970), 441–49; N. R. Petersen in *The Future of Early Christianity,* ed. B. Pearson (H. Koester Festschrift; Minneapolis: A/F, 1991), 337–47.

[41]Lightfoot, *Philippians* 174–77, shows that the names of Rom 16 are attested and hence quite plausible in the Rome of the early Christian centuries. Six of the names of those greeted are Latin; eighteen are Greek. Many are typical for slaves and freedmen and may represent Jews and non-Romans employed in the great Roman houses. Clearly those whom Paul calls "kin" (Andronicus,

his life at Rome) and "Narcissus" (the name of a powerful Roman freedman under Claudius). The Muratorian Fragment from the late 2d century sees Rom as one of the Pauline epistles that envisage the whole church. In that same direction the 14-chapter and 15-chapter forms of Rom were probably early abbreviations in order to make the letter less particularly directed to one church, so that it could be read easily in the churches of other places and other times.[42]

Justification/Uprightness/Righteousness/Justice

This key idea in Pauline thought and in Rom is expressed in a number of terms: the verb *dikaioun;* the nouns *dikaiosynē, dikaiōsis;* and the adjective *dikaios.* An enormous literature has been devoted to it, involving remarkably difficult and subtle discussions. I shall use the terms "righteousness" and "justification," but even the translation has been disputed (with some fearing that "righteousness" will be misunderstood as self-righteousness, and "justice" as punitiveness). Here I shall describe briefly and in an elementary way some of the basic issues in order to help readers to pursue the subject further on their own.[43]

Paul speaks of the *dikaiosynē theou,* "the righteousness of God," but how is the genitive to be understood? In times past it has been understood as a possessive genitive, constituting a stative description of an attribute of God's being, a divine virtue, almost equivalent to "the just or righteous God." However, Paul's notion implies activity; and in order to do justice to that, two other understandings have major support today. The phrase can be understood as a possessive genitive, describing an active attribute of God, like the wrath of God or the power of God, equivalent to the justifying activity of God, e.g., Rom 3:25–26, which speaks of God's forbearance[44] "as a proof

---

Junia, Herodion) are Jews. For the problem presented by 16:17–20 with its reference to those who create dissensions, see n. 9 above.

[42]The same goal explains the (poorly attested) textual omission of the address to Rome in 1:7. See N. A. Dahl in *Neotestamentica et Patristica,* ed. W. C. van Unnik (O. Cullmann Festschrift; NovTSup 6; Leiden: Brill, 1962), 261–71.

[43]Very helpful in this survey has been J. A. Fitzmyer, NJBC 82:39,68–69; full bibliography in Fitzmyer, *Romans* 151–54. Books include: J. Reumann, *"Righteousness" in the New Testament* (Philadelphia: Fortress, 1982); M. A. Seifrid, *Justification by Faith* (NovTSup 68; Leiden: Brill, 1992); B. F. Westcott, *St. Paul and Justification* (London: Macmillan, 1913); J. A. Ziesler, *The Meaning of Righteousness in Paul* (SNTSMS 20; Cambridge Univ., 1972). Ecumenically, see *Justification by Faith,* eds. H. G. Anderson et al. (Lutherans and Catholics in Dialogue VII; Minneapolis: Augsburg, 1985). Important is E. Käsemann, "The Righteousness of God in Paul," *New Testament Questions of Today* (Philadelphia: Fortress, 1969), 168–82.

[44]The forbearance or mercy element in the divine exercise of justice is extremely important for understanding Paul. The young Luther was tormented by the *dikaiosynē theou,* understood as the justice by which God punishes sinners. The great discovery in his life was when he began to understand a justice by which God mercifully gives life through faith.

of God's righteousness at the present time: that He Himself is righteous and justifies the person who has faith in Jesus." Or the phrase can be understood as a genitive of source or origin, describing the state of uprightness communicated to human beings as a gift from or by God, e.g., Phil 3:9: "not having my own righteousness which is from the Law but that which is through the faith of/in Christ, the righteousness from [*ek*] God that depends on faith." One may ask, of course, whether Paul would have made such a precise distinction in the implication of his genitives, since both ideas can be found in his thought. What should be retained is a legal background in the root of the word, as if people were being brought before God for judgment and God is acquitting them and thus manifesting divine graciousness. In this just and merciful divine judgment there is also a sense of God asserting authority and power, triumphing over the forces that would mislead people, setting things right, and saving the world. Although such a notion of the righteousness of God, often in other terminology, was a reality for OT Israel, for Paul there was in Jesus a greater, eschatological manifestation of God's *dikaiosynē,* extended to all.

"Justification" is also used by Paul to describe an effect worked in those who believe what God has done in Christ. Since God acquitted people in judgment, they were now justified. This acquitting took place not because people were innocent but because, although they were sinners, the truly innocent Jesus was himself made sin for the sake of others (II Cor 5:21). By an act of love Christ died for sinners (Rom 5:8); "he was given over for our transgressions and raised for our justification" (4:25). For Paul this justification or righteousness took the place of the righteousness under the Law (Phil 3:6). Although Paul did not create the Christian use of this vocabulary of being justified, he developed it as a major motif in several of his letters, and emphasized that it was a grace or gift and received through faith (Rom 3:24–25). Whether Paul understood this theology from the time of God's first revelation of Christ to him or he came to understand it gradually, particularly from his experience with the Galatians, is disputed (p. 427 above). The latter would explain why justification theology and language appear chiefly in Gal, Phil, and Rom. Another major scholarly debate is centered on whether for Paul God simply declares people upright by a type of judicial sentence (forensic or declarative justification) or actually changes people and makes them upright (causative or factitive justification). Yet, is a sharp distinction possible since God's justifying declaration has an element of power that is also causative? Can people be *reconciled* to God without being transformed?

Paul's View of Jewish Observance of the Law

Again we shall have to be content with introductory observations, for an enormous amount of scholarly labor has been expended on this very difficult topic.[45] In the aftermath of the Reformation the dominant interpretation was that Judaism in Paul's time was legalistic, insisting that people were justified only if they did the deeds mandated in the Mosaic Law. Paul's condemnation of such a Judaism was used to refute a legalistic Roman Catholicism that maintained that people could be saved by the good works they performed or had performed on their behalf. Very quickly Catholics protested that, although the function of indulgences may well have been distorted in popular practice and preaching in the 16th century, in careful Catholic theology justification was a free gift of God that could not be earned by good works. Both sides, however, assumed that the Jews of Paul's time thought justification could be merited by good works; and so a challenge among Christians to the accuracy of that picture came more slowly. Modern sensibility about the issue developed from several sides: (a) a growing awareness that Reformation issues were often being retrojected into an understanding of Paul; (b) a realization that many times Paul was polemicizing, not against Jewish thought but against Jewish Christian thought, e.g., of those who maintained that Gentile converts to Judaism could not be justified through Christ unless they accepted circumcision; (c) a demand for greater precision about what Paul actually says about works and the Law; (d) and a protest from Jewish scholars and Christian experts in Judaism that Jews had no simple theology of meriting salvation through works. The last two points need discussion.

As for (c) Rom illustrates the complexity of Paul's attitude toward the Law. He upholds the Law (3:31), sees it as holy (7:20) and fulfilled (8:4), and insists on the commandments (13:8–10; I Cor 7:19; also Gal 5:14). Yet no human being will be justified in God's sight by the works of the Law (Rom 3:20); the Law brings wrath (4:15); it increased sin (5:20; Gal 3:19). Some scholars would distinguish between two different understandings of Law, or two different parts of the Law, with the ethical commandments (against idolatry and sexual behavior) binding on all, Gentile Christians included, but not the cultic demands (circumcision, calendar feasts). E. P. Sanders, in his 1991 book *Paul* (p. 91), is more flexible: Paul rejected aspects of the Law that were against his own mission, those that separated Jew from Gentile in the people of God called in Christ. That evaluation recog-

[45]Fitzmyer (*Romans* 161–64) devotes over two pages of bibliography to it; also F. Thielman, *Paul & the Law* (Downers Grove, IL: InterVarsity, 1994); and the important review article by C. R. Roetzel, CRBS 3 (1995), 249–75.

nizes that Paul's reaction to the Law stemmed from his experience of the graciousness of God in Christ rather than from systematic theorizing.

When we turn to (d), how relevant are Paul's remarks to what we know about the Jewish attitude toward justification/righteousness through works of the Law? Sanders (*Paul and Palestinian Judaism*) has offered a sympathetic explanation of the Jewish attitude that merits attention. God had freely chosen Israel which made a covenant to live as God's people, and that grace could not be earned. Rather, observance of the Law provided a God-given way of living within the covenant, so that properly one should not speak of works-righteousness but covenant-keeping-righteousness (also known by the rarefied designation "covenantal nomism"). Sanders argues that such a position may be justified from Jewish writings, even if it was not universal.[46] Others object that if this were the view that was commonly held in Judaism, Paul should have seen no sharp conflict between it and his own concept that God had graciously extended righteousness through faith in Christ. Yet in a passage like Phil 3:6–7 he clearly contrasts his blameless state in Law-righteousness and what he has found in Christ. Is it sufficient to contend with Sanders that what Paul found wrong in Judaism was that it was not Christianity?

If Paul's objections to Law-righteousness were more substantial, could it be that Paul misunderstood or, in his new-found enthusiasm for Christ, even polemically exaggerated the role of works in his portrayal of the Jewish concept of righteousness? Räisänen (*Paul*), for instance, finds inconsistency in Paul's views and claims that he distorted the Jewish picture. However, should 20th-century reconstructions of 1st-century Jewish thought based on reading ancient documents be preferred to the witness of a perceptive observer like Paul, who lived as an observant Jew in that century? After all, in discussing the 1st century and Paul, one needs to ask whether the subtleties of the relation of Law to covenant-keeping-righteousness were understood on a popular level (anymore than a subtle Catholic theology about indulgences has always been understood on a popular level). There are early rabbinic statements virtually identifying covenant and Law (or more properly, Torah); and such features as circumcision, food laws, and Sabbath observance had be-

[46] J. Neusner (in *Approaches to Ancient Judaism II,* ed. W. S. Green [Chico, CA: Scholars, 1980], 43–63) criticizes Sanders for depending on later rabbinic material not applicable to Paul's time. Barrett, *Paul* 77ff., offers a penetrating challenge to Sanders' analysis; also C. L. Quarles, NTS 42 (1996), 185–95. I. H. Marshall, NTS 42 (1996), 339–58, points out that while some of Paul's opposition to the works of the Law can be explained as flowing from his mission to the Gentiles (i.e., insistence on these symbols of Judaism would have made it too difficult to convert Gentiles), there is a deeper issue: He was opposed to works as something people can depend on for salvation, rather than purely on divine grace.

come visible lines of distinction between Jews and Pagans. Thus observance of works of the Law could easily have been the subject of pride and popularly understood as what made a Jew "right" with God. (See Dunn in TRD 305–6.) When he was writing about the thought of Jews (as distinct from that of his Jewish Christian opponents), Paul could have been protesting against such a legalistic *understanding* of God's covenant with Israel, not because he misunderstood but because he correctly regarded it as the view held by many Jews.

Original Sin and Rom 5:12–21

Paul maintains that sin entered the world through one man, and through sin death, and so death spread to all human beings (5:12). He never uses the wording "original sin," and he does not refer to a fall from previous grace. But it was in reflection on this verse that in the 4th century Augustine developed the theology of original sin (*peccatum originale*), partially in debate with Pelagius. Augustine maintained that by his sin Adam fell from his original supernatural status, and that through human propagation, which involved concupiscence, the lack of grace was passed on to every human being descended from Adam. That discussion belongs to the realm of systematic theology, but some observations about Paul's thought may serve as a clarification:

(1) For parts of the story in Gen 2:4b–3:24 Adam is not an individual male but a figure representative of humanity. For Paul, however, Adam is an individual figure like Jesus; and so the apostle is comparing the first man[47] and the man of the eschaton. (2) Paul's interpretation of Gen may have been shaped in part by interpretations of his time,[48] but what dominates his picture of Adam is his theology of Jesus. In other words, he did not read Gen and come to understand Jesus; he understood Jesus and read Gen in that light. This retrospective approach means that Paul really has nothing novel to teach us about the historical origins of the human race. (3) Paul's view of the universality of sin and death stems from observing the existing world, and he uses the Gen story to explain that. Actually the author of Gen, even if he drew on earlier legends, wrote his story in a similar way, working back from the world he knew to picture its origins. (4) To some the idea of a

[47]Since Paul is thinking backward from Jesus, "man" is a more appropriate translation than "human being."

[48]Jewish sources depict the primordial sin in various ways, e.g., Adam's sin (*IV Ezra* 3:21; 7:116–18; *II Baruch* 54:15–16), or Eve's disobedience (Sirach 25:24[23]), or the devil's envy (Wisdom 2:24), or the sin of sons of God with the daughters of men (Gen 6:1–5), or even the pride of the Prince of Tyre (Ezek 28). See F. R. Tennant, *The Sources of the Doctrine of the Fall and Original Sin* (New York: Schocken, 1968; orig. 1903); J. J. Scullion et al., *Original Sin* (Victoria, Australia: Dove, 1975).

human sinfulness that goes beyond one's personal evil deeds is strange. The total human experience forces many others, however, to recognize a mystery of evil that has collective overtones. Paul has sought to give voice to that by appealing to the imagery of human origins. (5) Paul's primary interest is not in the sin of Adam but in the superabundant grace of Christ. He contends that Christ's act of righteousness led to justification and life for all—something much harder to observe than universal sinfulness. Indeed, some would argue from this passage for universal salvation!

Issues and Problems for Reflection

(1) In subdividing the Doctrinal Section (1:16–11:36) of Rom into three Parts (1:16–4:25; 5:1–8:39; 9:1–11:36) I am following a subdivision pattern that with minor variations is suggested by Achtemeier, Cranfield, Fitzmyer, and others. Puskas, *Letters* 76–78, sees Rom as epideictic rhetoric (p. 412 above), and finds four Parts (1:16/18–3:20 [negative argument]; 3:21–5:21 [positive argument]; 6:1–8:39; 9:1–11:36). Becker, *Paul* 355, contends that Rom 5 has a hinge function, closing 1:18–5:21 and opening 6:1–8:39. Because scholars are convinced that Rom was carefully planned, a diagnosis of its structure is sometimes equivalent to a diagnosis of its theology. See TRD 245–96.

(2) Rom 9:5 has two clauses joined: "Of them [i.e., the Israelites] is the Christ according to the flesh *the one who is over all God blessed forever.* Amen." To whom do the italicized words refer? (a) A period may be placed after "flesh," so that the following words become a separate sentence blessing God. (b) A comma may be placed after flesh, and a period after "forever." This punctuation would mean that Paul calls Christ, "God blessed forever." Grammar favors it, even if the verse then becomes the only example in the undisputed Pauline letters of calling Jesus "God," and the earliest example of that usage in the NT (see BINTC 182–83).

(3) I have opted above for a plausible interpretation of Paul's theological terms, but some of them have been the subject of endless debate. For instance, many take for granted that in Rom "Law" means the Mosaic Law with relative consistency. Yet, for passages in chap. 7 for instance, other suggestions are Roman law, law in general, all God's precepts, or natural law (see Fitzmyer, *Romans* 131–35). The "I" of chap. 7 is plausibly unregenerate humanity as looked at by a Christian Jew, but others have thought it refers to Paul personally, or to a Jewish boy speaking psychologically, or to the Christian struggling after having been converted, or even to Adam. Commentaries should be consulted on the arguments pro and con.

(4) A subsection was devoted to the issue of original sin in 5:12–21, but

there have been debates about how Paul should be understood independently of that issue. The majority would understand the death that came through sin as spiritual death, not simply physical death (even if that goes beyond the Adam story). A Greek prepositional combination in 5:12 has been particularly difficult: "Death thus spread to all human beings, *eph hō* all sinned." Is there a reference to Adam "in whom" or "through whom" or "because of whom" all sinned? Or, without an Adam connection, does Paul mean "to the extent that all sinned," or "inasmuch as all sinned," or "with the result that all sinned." For detailed discussion, see J. A. Fitzmyer, NTS 39 (1993), 321–39.

(5) In the OT the Spirit is a way of describing God's agency in creating (Gen 1:2; Ps 104:30), vivifying (Ezek 37:5), and making people representatives of the divine plan (Isa 11:2; Joel 3:1 [2:28])—an agency that comes from without but also works within people. In the dualism of the DSS there is a great Spirit of Truth—a type of angelic force ruling over people from above but also dwelling within them and guiding their lives. (Fitzmyer, *Romans* 517, supplies examples of the role allotted to the Spirit in the life of those who belong to the DSS group.) Some of these same ideas appear in Paul's picture of the Spirit, a term he employs nineteen times in chap. 8. Other examples of frequent usage in Pauline chaps. are supplied by I Cor 2; 12; 14; II Cor 3; and Gal 5. It is a worthwhile exercise to seek out a total Pauline picture and compare it to other NT concepts of the Spirit. Fee, *God's Presence,* is the most comprehensive treatment of *all* the Pauline Spirit passages; see 472–634 for those in Rom.

(6) In Rom 8:29–30 Paul says that those whom God foreknew, he also "predestined" (from *proorizein,* "to decide before") and those whom God predestined, God also called.[49] In the course of theological history this passage fed into important debates about God's predestining those who would be saved. Without entering those discussions, we should be aware that, despite the wording, the passage is not necessarily meant to cover God's dealings with all human beings of all times. First, it is prompted by a specific problem, namely, that most of the Jews who had been confronted with the revelation in Christ had rejected him. Second, the goal of the predestining is salvific. Paul thinks that the ultimate purpose of the hardening of Israel is "that the full number of the Gentiles may come in and thus all Israel may be saved" (11:25–26). Also, "God has delivered all to disobedience in order that He might have mercy on all" (11:32). This is very far from predestining some people to damnation. Third, a recognition of how Jews thought about divine causality is important. In the DSS we hear that God establishes the entire plan before things exist; yet other texts make it perfectly clear that

[49]Also 9:18: "God has mercy on whomever He wills and hardens whomever He wills."

people act freely. A Western logic whereby, if God has decided beforehand, that must mean that human beings are predetermined, is not easily to be imposed on Paul.

(7) In 11:25–26 Paul speaks of the fate of Israel as a mystery: a hardening until the full number of the Gentiles has come in; and thus all Israel will be saved. Does Paul imply that he has had a revelation of the future fate of Israel, or is he expressing a hope? More likely he thinks of a revelation, for he speaks of a mystery in God's mind. But then one might debate whether God is committed to Paul's interpretation of the revelation. Jeremiah's complaint in 17:15; 20:7–18 implies that God did not support Jeremiah's interpretation of God's word that he had authentically received. Moreover, Paul phrases himself in the language of an apocalyptic sequence, which always has a figurative element that should not be confused with linear history.

(8) It is noteworthy that Rom, which speaks so eloquently about sin and justification, is relatively silent about repentance. In Luke 24:47 there is to be a proclamation that people should *repent* and be forgiven in Jesus' name. Many interpreters would explain that for Paul divine forgiveness is not a response to human repentance but is purely gracious, for God acts without previous human initiative. Is the contrast between Paul and Luke that sharp? Are NT writers who insist on repentance proposing a purely human initiative; or is repentance itself a grace from God? The Lucan proclamation could involve double grace: Be open to the God-given impetus to repent, and receive God-given forgiveness. Would Paul disagree with that approach?

Bibliography on Romans

COMMENTARIES AND STUDIES IN SERIES: Achtemeier, P. J. (IBC, 1985); Barrett, C. K. (BNTC, 2d ed. 1991); Bartlett, D. L. (WBComp, 1995); Best, E. (CCNEB, 1967); Black, M. (NCBC, 2d ed. 1989); Byrne, B. (SP, 1996); **Cranfield, C.E.B.** (new ICC, 2 vols.; 1975, 1979); **Dunn, J.D.G.** (WBC, 2 vols.; 1988); Edwards, J. R. (NIBC, 1992); **Fitzmyer, J. A.** (AB, 1993); Harrisville, R. A. (AugC, 1980); Kertelge, K. (NTSR, 1972); Moo, D. J. (NICNT, 1996); Morgan, R. (NTG, 1995); Sanday, W., and A. C. Headlam (ICC, 5th ed. 1902).

BIBLIOGRAPHIES: Sweet, J.P.M., *Theology* 67 (1964), 382–87; Mills, W. E., BBR (1996); Wagner, G., EBNT (1996).

Barth, K., *The Epistle to the Romans* (Oxford Univ., 1933, from the 6th German ed.).

———, *A Shorter Commentary on Romans* (Richmond: Knox, 1959).

———, *Christ and Adam* (New York: Collier, 1962).

BMAR 92–127.

Brown, R. E., "Further Reflections on the Origins of the Church of Rome," in *The Conversation Continues,* eds. R. T. Fortna and B. R. Gaventa (J. L. Martyn Festschrift; Nashville: Abingdon, 1990), 98–115.

Byrne, B., *Reckoning with Romans* (Wilmington: Glazier, 1986).
Cranfield, C.E.B., *Romans: A Shorter Commentary* (Grand Rapids: Eerdmans, 1985).
Dodd, C. H., *The Epistle of Paul to the Romans* (New York: Harper & Row, 1932).
Donfried, K. P., ed., TRD (a collection of very important essays).
Elliott, N., *The Rhetoric of Romans* (JSNTSup 45; Sheffield: JSOT, 1990).
Fitzmyer, J. A., *Spiritual Exercises Based on Paul's Epistle to the Romans* (New York: Paulist, 1995).
Gamble, H. Y., *The Textual History of the Letter to the Romans* (Grand Rapids: Eerdmans, 1977).
Guerra, A. J., *Romans and the Apologetic Tradition* (SNTSMS 81; Cambridge Univ., 1995).
Heil, J. P., *Paul's Letter to the Romans: A Reader-Response Commentary* (New York: Paulist, 1987).
Hendriksen, W., *Exposition of Paul's Epistle to the Romans* (2 vols.; Grand Rapids: Baker, 1980–81).
Hultgren, A. J., *Paul's Gospel and Mission, The Outlook from His Letter to the Romans* (Philadelphia: Fortress, 1985).
Jervis, L. A., *The Purpose of Romans: A Comparative Letter Structure Investigation* (JSNTSup 55; Sheffield: Academic, 1991).
Käsemann, E., *Commentary on Romans* (Grand Rapids: Eerdmans, 1980).
Kaylor, R. D., *Paul's Covenant Community: Jew and Gentile in Romans* (Atlanta: Knox, 1988).
Leenhardt, F. J., *The Epistle to the Romans* (London: Lutterworth, 1961).
Minear, P. S., *The Obedience of Faith* (SBT NS 19; London: SCM, 1971).
Moxnes, H., *Theology in Conflict: Studies of Paul's Understanding of God in Romans* (NovTSup 53; Leiden: Brill, 1980).
Nygren, A., *Commentary on Romans* (Philadelphia: Muhlenberg, 1949).
Robinson, J.A.T., *Wrestling with Romans* (Philadelphia: Westminster, 1979).
Schlatter, A., *Romans: The Righteousness of God* (Peabody, MA: Hendrickson, 1995; German orig. 1935).
Stendahl, K., *Final Account: Paul's Letter to the Romans* (Minneapolis: A/F, 1995).
Stott, J.R.W., *Romans. God's Good News for the World* (Downers Grove, IL: InterVarsity, 1994).
Stowers, S. K., *The Diatribe and Paul's Letter to the Romans* (Chico, CA: Scholars, 1981).
———, *A Rereading of Romans* (New Haven: Yale Univ., 1994). Read against the background of Gentile culture.
Stuhlmacher, P., *Paul's Letter to the Romans* (Louisville: W/K, 1994; German orig. 1989).
Vorster, J. N., "The Context of the Letter to the Romans: a Critique on the Present State of Research," *Neotestamentica* 28 (1994), 127–45.
Wedderburn, A.J.M., *The Reasons for Romans* (Edinburgh: Clark, 1991).
———, " 'Like an Ever-rolling Stream': Some Recent Commentaries on Romans," SJT 44 (1991), 367–80.
Ziesler, J. A., *Paul's Letter to the Romans* (Philadelphia: Trinity, 1989).

CHAPTER 25

PSEUDONYMITY AND THE DEUTEROPAULINE WRITINGS

Before we enter the problematic terrain of deuteroPauline letters, i.e., those that bear Paul's name but possibly were not written by him, let us discuss the difficult concept of pseudepigraphy (literally, but often misleadingly, "false writing") or pseudonymity ("false name")[1]—terminology employed in biblical discussions with special nuance.

(A) Pseudonymous Composition in General

It may be clearer here to speak of "writer" rather than "author." Normally, for us, "author" means not simply the one responsible for the ideas contained in a work but the one who actually drafted its wording. Ancients were often not that precise and by "author" may have meant only the authority behind a work. We are not totally unfamiliar with such a distinction, for we encounter the phenomenon of "ghost-writers," particularly in the instance of entertainers who wish to write an autobiography but need the help of a skilled writer to cast their story in a correct or attractive way. Now more frequently, however, even a ghost-writer has to be acknowledged in the form of "The Autobiography of John/Jane Doe with the cooperation (or assistance) of John Smith." That phenomenon is close to one ancient use of scribes (p. 411 above) and may be encountered in a genuine Pauline letter if Paul dictated the ideas and someone like Silvanus phrased them in writing. It is *not* what scholars mean by pseudonymity in reference to the NT works.

[1]Unfortunately some confuse pseudonymous compositions (works that claim to be written by someone who did not write them) with anonymous compositions (works that do not identify by name their writer), especially in the instance where the writer has been externally identified. The Gospels, for instance, are anonymous; they do not identify their authors (see, however, John 21:24); the attributions to Matthew, Mark, Luke, and John that appear in titles stem from the (late?) 2d century and are not part of the original works. Anonymous too are Acts, Heb, and I John (II-III John claim to be written by "the presbyter"). The pseudonymous works of the NT, i.e., those whose very wording identifies an author who *may* not have composed them, are II Thess, Col, Eph, I-II Tim, Titus, Jas, I-II Pet, and Jude. (The self-identification of the author is not reasonably disputed in the seven Pauline letters already discussed and in Rev [the prophet John].) In this Chapter I am leaving aside books not accepted into the biblical canon (Appendix II below).

Modern readers also encounter writing under an alias or pen name, a method adopted for various reasons. In the 19th century Mary Anne Evans wrote under the male name George Eliot because it was difficult for women to get serious writing accepted. In the 20th century more than one author of mysteries has written under several names, sometimes with a particular fictional detective featured respectively by each "name," e.g., John Dickson Carr and Carter Dickson are names for the one male author; Ruth Rendell and Barbara Vine are names for the one female author. Writing under an alias is objectionable when deception is intended (e.g., composing a new Sherlock Holmes story and selling it as a recently discovered, unpublished original by Arthur Conan Doyle) but not when one is publicly continuing to write in the style of the now defunct original author (e.g., Sherlock Holmes scripts used in movies featuring him active during World War II).

In NT research some who first proposed that letters attributed to Paul were really pseudonymous hinted that the purpose might be fraudulent, but that connotation has largely disappeared from the discussion.[2] Most often what is being suggested is that one of the Pauline "school" of disciples took it upon himself to write a letter in Paul's name because he wanted it to be received authoritatively as what Paul would say to the situation addressed. Such a situation makes sense if one supposes that Paul was dead and the disciple considered himself an authoritative interpreter of the apostle whose thought he endorsed. Attribution of the letter to Paul in those circumstances would not be using a false name or making a false claim that Paul wrote the letter. It would be treating Paul as the author in the sense of the authority behind a letter that was intended as an extension of his thought—an assumption of the great apostle's mantle to continue his work. Indeed, such attribution could serve to continue the apostle's presence, since letters were considered a substitute for personal face-to-face conversation (J. D. Quinn, ABD 6.564). *Mutatis mutandis* the same may be said of other proposed instances of NT pseudonymity: Those who considered themselves in the school of James (of Jerusalem), or of Peter may have written letters in their authority's name.[3]

Justification for positing this type of pseudepigraphy is found in the OT.[4]

[2]Guthrie, "Development," gives a history of the development of the thesis that NT works could be pseudonymous. The pseudonymous thesis was introduced in the late 1700s, but F. C. Baur was the first to suggest it on a large scale.

[3]The Letter/Epistle of Jude may have been written by a follower of James since the putative author is identified as "brother of James."

[4]Some would appeal to the example of Greco-Roman historians attributing speeches to famous figures; see Chapter 10 above, n. 94. Although occasionally cited, Tertullian, *Adv. Marcion* 4.5.4 (CC 1.551), "It is permissible for words published by disciples to be regarded as belonging to their masters," refers to Luke's writing a Gospel inspired by Paul, and thus not to pseudonymity (D. Guthrie, ExpTim 67 [1955–56], 341–42).

Books of law written 700 or 800 years after Moses' time were written in his name since he was the great lawgiver. Psalms (even those with titles attributing them to others) were collected in a Davidic psalter since David was famed as a composer of psalms or songs. A book like Wisdom written in Greek *ca.* 100 BC was attributed to Solomon, who had lived 800 years before, since he was the wise man par excellence. Prophets in the school of Isaiah continued writing 200 years after the prophet's death and had their compositions included in the Book of Isaiah. Apocalypses, both canonical and noncanonical, tended to invoke the name of famous figures from the past (Daniel, Baruch, Enoch, Ezra) as seers of the visions now being narrated, long after their lifetime.[5] In the centuries just before and after Jesus' time pseudepigraphy seems to have been particularly frequent even in Jewish works of a nonapocalyptic nature: the *Prayer of Nabonidus, Odes of Solomon, Psalms of Solomon.*

(B) Problems about Pseudonymity

True as all that may be, when we posit the pseudonymous character of NT works (as I shall), difficulties remain that should not be overlooked; and readers are asked to keep them in mind in the next Chapters. I have cited OT examples of pseudonymity where centuries separated the person from the writings; consequently they are not really parallel to works written within a few years of Paul's life. We speak of disciples of Paul or adherents to the Pauline school of thought as pseudonymous writers, but we do not know their precise identity. (Silvanus, Timothy, Titus, and even Luke have been suggested for the various works). How close did one have to be to the historical Paul to write in his name? At times was it simply a matter of knowing Paul's writings and using an earlier letter as a basis for further composition? (That suggestion has been made to explain the writing of II Thess in dependence on I Thess, and of Eph in dependence on Col.) Some scholars would date the Pastorals to AD 125 or later when Paul would have been dead a half century or three quarters. How long after the master's death could one still claim authority to write in his name, especially when other Christian writers of the postapostolic generation were writing in their own names? How are canonical pseudonymous works different from apocrypha written in the name of NT figures but rejected by the church as noncanonical?[6]

[5]Since Jesus and the early Christians shared a highly apocalyptic outlook, can one invoke that observation to explain the frequency of pseudonymity in the NT? Yet in the NT apocalypse par excellence, Revelation, there is little reason to doubt the seer's self-designation as John (1:1,4,9; 22:8).

[6]K. Aland, "Problem," raises this issue. In between the two are the subapostolic works (neither canonical nor apocrypha) that are pseudonymous (*Didache,* which describes itself as "The Lord's

Is the audience (church) addressed to be taken as historical? For instance, if pseudonymous, was II Thess written to the church at Thessalonica as I Thess was, or did the writer simply copy that address since he was using I Thess as a guide for his motif? How in the 1st century would a wider audience have received a letter seemingly addressed to the problems of the church at Thessalonica? Did the audience who first received a pseudonymous letter know that it was actually written by another in Paul's name? Would the letter's authority have been diminished if that were known? Did the writer think that such knowledge made any difference? (II Pet makes the author's apostolic identity of key importance, e.g., 1:16.) Would the later church have accepted these letters into the canon had it known they were pseudonymous?[7] The percentage of scholarly opinion holding that the writer was not the claimant varies for each work, and so there remains the obligation to ask and answer the question: What difference does a decision on the question of pseudepigraphy make in how this letter/epistle is understood?

What are the criteria for determining genuineness and pseudonymity? They include internal data, format, style, vocabulary, and thought/theology.[8] Already on pp. 411, 498, 551 above we saw some problems with these criteria; but since scholarship is almost evenly divided on whether Paul wrote II Thess, we can test them more practically in the next Chapter.

Bibliography on New Testament Pseudonymity

Aland, K., "The Problem of Anonymity and Pseudonymity in Christian Literature of the First Two Centuries," JTS NS 12 (1961), 39–49.

Beker, J. C., *Heirs of Paul* (Minneapolis: A/F, 1991).

---

teaching to the Gentiles through the Twelve Apostles") and anonymous (*I* and *II Clement; Epistle of Barnabas,* where the designations do not come from the works themselves but from external attribution). Highly speculative is Aland's own thesis that the attribution of pseudonymous works to the apostles was the logical conclusion of the presupposition that the Spirit was the author and that, when the movement of the Spirit lost its impetus, such attribution ceased. An explanation closer to the circumstances of each work needs to be invoked.

[7]Guthrie, "Development," and Ellis, "Pseudonymity," represent a position sympathetic to characterizing pseudonymous works as forgeries—a designation deemed to be irreconcilable with their being canonical. Meade, *Pseudonymity,* argues that pseudonymous origin or anonymous redaction in no way prejudices either the inspiration or canonicity of the work.

[8]Statistics and computer efficiency in counting words and features have been brought into the discussion. A. Q. Morton and J. McLeman, *Paul, the Man and the Myth* (New York: Harper & Row, 1966), judging literary and theological analysis unsatisfactory, determine by statistics that there are only five genuine Pauline letters: Rom, I-II Cor, Gal, and Phlm. However, A. Kenny, *A Stylometric Study of the New Testament* (Oxford: Clarendon, 1986), employs sophisticated statistical theory to argue that twelve Pauline letters are genuine (possible exception: Titus). K. J. Neumann, *The Authenticity of the Pauline Epistles in the Light of Stylostatistical Analysis* (SBLDS 120; Atlanta: Scholars, 1990), finds that the best set of variables assigns II Thess, Col, and Eph to Paul but not the Pastorals. Using multivaried statistic methods, D. L. Mealand, JSNT 59 (1995), 61–92, would see Col-Eph and the Pastorals separating in different directions from the other Paulines.

Collins, R. F., *Letters That Paul Did Not Write* (GNS 28; Wilmington: Glazier, 1988). Abbreviated CLPDNW.

Ellis, E. E., "Pseudonymity and Canonicity of New Testament Documents," in *Worship, Theology and Ministry in the Early Church,* eds. M. J. Wilkins and T. Paige (R. P. Martin Festschrift; JSNTSup 87; Sheffield: Academic, 1992), 212–24.

Goodspeed, E. J., "Pseudonymity and Pseudepigraphy in Early Christian Literature," *New Chapters in New Testament Study* (New York: Macmillan, 1937), 169–88.

Guthrie, D., "The Development of the Idea of Canonical Pseudepigrapha in New Testament Criticism," *Vox Evangelica* 1 (1962), 43–59.

Lea, T. D., "The Early Christian View of Pseudepigraphic Writings," JETS 27 (1984), 65–75.

Meade, D. O., *Pseudonymity and Canon* (WUNT 39; Tübingen: Mohr-Siebeck, 1986).

Metzger, B. M., "Literary Forgeries and Canonical Pseudepigrapha," JBL 91 (1972), 3–24.

Patzia, A. G., "The Deutero-Pauline Hypothesis: An Attempt at Clarification," EQ 52 (1980), 27–42.

CHAPTER 26

SECOND LETTER TO THE THESSALONIANS

There is considerable dispute as to whether II Thess was written by Paul or by a Pauline disciple. After the *General Analysis,* subsections will be devoted to: *Did Paul write II Thess,* the *Purpose, Issues for reflection,* and *Bibliography.*

General Analysis of the Message

Just as in I Thess, the OPENING FORMULA (1:1–2) lists "Paul, Silvanus, and Timothy," even if Paul is the one who communicates. The only possible reference to a previous missive is in 2:15 where the Thessalonians are told, "Hold to the traditions that you were taught, whether by word or by *our letter.*" The THANKSGIVING (1:3–10) praises the faith and love of the Thessalonians, as well as their steadfastness in the suffering imposed on them. When Jesus appears from heaven, he will inflict vengeance and eternal punishment on their persecutors, while they will be given rest from affliction and glorified. Transitional is a *Prayer (1:11–12)* that God will make them worthy of their call.

As he begins the INDICATIVE SECTION OF THE BODY (2:1–17), Paul does not want the Thessalonians overly excited by "spirit or word,"[1] or any letter alleged to be from him about the immediacy of "the day of the Lord" (2:1–2). Rather, they can relax because the apocalyptic signs that must precede the coming of that day have not yet occurred, namely, the apostasy, the appearance of the lawless one or son of perdition who is antiGod, and the activity of Satan with pretended signs and wonders (2:3–12).[2] Yet the mystery of

[1]Does this expression refer to ecstatic prophets arising among the Thessalonian Christians, or are they coming from the outside? This reflects the issue of whether opponents to Paul were now on the Thessalonian scene.

[2]This is not really a timetable although many interpreters use that term. That the author is taking for granted traditional expectations can be seen from the Marcan "Apocalypse." It speaks of a desolating sacrilege and of false christs and prophets who will lead astray with signs and wonders (Mark 13:14–22), and yet only the heavenly Father knows the day or the hour when heaven and earth will pass away (13:32).

Summary of Basic Information

DATE: If by Paul, probably *ca.* AD 51/52, shortly after I Thess. If pseudonymous, probably late 1st century, when increased apocalyptic fervor was manifest.

FROM: If by Paul, probably from Corinth, like I Thess. If pseudonymous, there is no way to know.

TO: If by Paul, to Thessalonica. If pseudonymous, perhaps the same; yet the address to the Thessalonians may simply have been borrowed from I Thess.

AUTHENTICITY: Scholars are almost evenly divided on whether Paul wrote it, although the view that he did not seems to be gaining ground even among moderates.

UNITY: Queried by very few (see Best, *Commentary* 17–19, 30–35).

INTEGRITY: No major advocacy of interpolations.

FORMAL DIVISION:

A. Opening Formula: 1:1–2
B. Thanksgiving: 1:3–10, plus Prayer (1:11–12)
C. Body: 2:1–17: Pauline indicative (instructions)
3:1–16: Pauline imperative (paraenesis and exhortations)
D. Concluding Formula: 3:17–18.

DIVISION ACCORDING TO CONTENTS:

1:1–2: Greeting
1:3–12: Thanksgiving for Thessalonians' faith and love that will save them at the parousia when their persecutors will be punished; continued prayer for them
2:1–12: Instruction on signs that precede the parousia
2:13–17: Thanksgiving and instructions on God's choosing them for salvation
3:1–5: Paul requests prayer and prays for them
3:6–15: Ethical admonitions and exhortations (against idleness and disobedience)
3:16–18: Concluding blessing, greeting.

lawlessness is already at work, and something/someone is currently restraining the lawless one until he is revealed in the proper time (2:6–7).

Paul then thanks God who chose the Thessalonian believers from the beginning. They are to hold firm to the traditions they were taught "by us," and he prays that they may be comforted (2:13–17).

In 3:1–2, transitional to the IMPERATIVE SECTION OF THE BODY (3:1–16), Paul requests a corresponding prayer "for us . . . that we may be delivered" from evil men.[3] The Lord will strengthen the Thessalonians and protect them from the evil one, and Paul is confident that they will do the things "we command" (3:3–5). Then Paul enunciates a specific command (3:6–13) because of the overheated expectations of the day of the Lord. Some have not been working (probably because they thought that there was only a very short time left and work seemed useless). This is not imitating Paul, who during his stay among them, precisely in order to set an example, worked

[3]Are these evil men actually on the scene, or are they figures expected to arrive in the last times?

night and day. Consequently, "If anyone does not want to work, let that person not eat" (3:10).[4] To impress the seriousness of this command, a further directive is given: "Mark anyone who does not obey our word in this letter and have nothing to do with that person" (3:14). Yet, and here we see a touch of pastoral gentleness, "That person is not to be regarded as an enemy but warned as a brother" (3:15). Just as the first part of the Body closed with a prayerful wish for the Thessalonians in 2:16–17, so also the second part in 3:16, this time a prayer for peace.

In the CONCLUDING FORMULA (3:17–18) Paul switches from the "we" to an "I," as he sends a greeting with his own hand.

Did Paul Write II Thessalonians?

Already in the late 1700s the traditional view that Paul wrote this letter was called into doubt. In 20th-century German scholarship, running from W. Wrede in 1904 to W. Trilling in 1972, arguments presented against Pauline writing gradually made this minority view more and more accepted. English-speaking scholarship (e.g., Aus, Best, Bruce, Jewett, L. T. Johnson, Marshall, and Morris) has tended to defend writing by Paul, but more recently Bailey, Collins, Giblin, Holland, and Hughes have been among the increasing numbers opting for pseudonymity.

Judging the arguments is not easy. II Thess is a bit more than one half the length of I Thess; and close resemblances between I and II Thess have been estimated to affect about one third of II Thess. The *similarity of format* between the two letters is striking—indeed greater than between any other two genuine letters: the same Opening Formulas;[5] a double Thanksgiving (which in a Pauline letter is peculiar) in I Thess 1:2; 2:13 and II Thess 1:3; 2:13;[6] a benediction in I Thess 3:11–13 and II Thess 2:16–17 asking God the Father and the Lord Jesus Christ to strengthen the hearts of the Thessalonians; also the same last verse. (Even beyond format, II Thess 3:8 repeats almost verbatim I Thess 2:9 about Paul's labor and toil night and day.) Why would Paul copy himself in this almost mechanical way? Is not this much more likely

[4]It is worth noting that these forceful words made their way into the constitution of the U.S.S.R.! (Soards, *Apostle* 131.) It has been claimed that the practical solution of imitating the work ethic of Paul because the end is not yet at hand makes virtually irrelevant an eschatological outlook. Yet it keeps the necessary Christian tension between the now and the not-yet.

[5]The suggestion made in Chapter 23, n. 20, above, about the Corinthian correspondence and its Opening Formulas could also be applied to the Thessalonian correspondence and explain this similarity.

[6]There is a third reference to thanksgiving in I Thess 3:9, unmatched in II Thess. Some would use this imperfection in parallelism as a proof of the genuineness of II Thess.

the mark of another writer who in II Thess is assuming the mantle of the Paul who wrote I Thess?

Style and vocabulary arguments[7] are invoked. Remarkable vocabulary similarities between the two letters exist, as well as notable differences peculiar to II Thess. In II Thess 1:3–12 the sentences are longer and more complex than in I Thess, so that in this feature II Thess is close to the statistics of Eph and Col while I Thess is close to the those of the undisputed Pauline letters. II Thess is more formal than I Thess in tone. References to Paul's life in II Thess are less personal; yet that fact might be explicable if II Thess was written very soon after I Thess and thus there was no need to reiterate what Paul had done when he first came to Thessalonica. Moreover, "This greeting is with my own hand, *Paul;* this is my mark in every letter" (II Thess 3:17) is very personal. Certainly the first clause in that sentence favors genuineness. (If II Thess is pseudonymous and if the notion of forgery is to be avoided, the writer is symbolically insisting on the genuineness of the message, not of the penmanship.) On the other hand, the second clause may favor pseudonymity because "every letter" would be more intelligible after there was a tradition of Paul having written many letters rather than only I Thess (which is the sole letter known to have preceded II Thess if the latter was written early by Paul).

Internal indications of the time of composition enter the discussion because Paul died in the mid-60s. It is argued that the reference to the temple of God in II Thess 2:4 shows that the Jerusalem Temple was still standing, and therefore the work was written before AD 70 and close to the time of I Thess. On the other hand, the divine temple could be interpreted symbolically (see Rev 21:22). The oblique suggestion of forged Pauline letters (II Thess 2:2; 3:17) favors a later rather than an earlier period, not only because it is unlikely that Paul would have been such a copied authority near the beginning of his missionary career[8] but also because we have no instance of a Jewish pseudonymous work being attributed to a man who was still alive. If the "man of lawlessness" in II Thess 2:3 symbolizes *Nero redivivus*

[7]Both Krentz and Schmidt agree that II Thess is pseudonymous, but Krentz is more skeptical than Schmidt about the probative value of this type of evidence. (The latter employs a sophisticated grammatical concordance computer analysis.) Best (*Thessalonians* 52–53) thinks that stylistic and linguistic similarities between I and II Thess are a most serious challenge to pseudonymity. Listing some expressions in II Thess that do not occur elsewhere in Paul is not a very impressive argument; writers of more than one work often use a few different expressions in each.

[8]In the 50s Paul's opponents denied his apostolic authority; forgery assumes an established acceptance of that authority. Yet Barclay, "Conflict" 525–30, who thinks that Paul wrote II Thess perhaps a few weeks after I Thess, suspects that the first letter gave rise to an imbalance about apocalyptic among the Thessalonians. Paul was puzzled by this and wondered if someone had falsified a letter to them.

(embodying the expectation that Nero would come back from the dead), that emperor committed suicide in 68; and so II Thess would have had to be written after that date and after Paul's lifetime.

The closeness of II Thess to postPauline works is invoked as an argument for pseudonymity. For instance, the atmosphere of deceptive false teachers (2:2–3,10–11) and of the need to retain traditions previously taught (2:15) resembles the atmosphere of the Pastorals (I Tim 1:6–7; 4:1–2; Titus 1:9). The similarity between the apocalyptic of II Thess and that of Rev would suggest a date near the end of the 1st century.

The purpose of II Thess is cited as a major argument on both sides, but that issue deserves treatment in its own subsection.

The Purpose of II Thessalonians

If Paul wrote this letter, we might assume that, while clarifying that those who had died would still share in the parousia, I Thess had focused too much attention on that event and intensified an expectation of its immediacy. Such expectation could have been sharpened by increased persecution and affliction (1:4). Indeed, some were claiming that Paul had said that the day of the Lord had already come (II Thess 2:2) and had stopped doing any work (3:10–11). Paul now writes a second letter to reassure the Thessalonians that there have to be some apocalyptic signs before the day of the Lord. In considering the thesis that Paul wrote this a few months after his relatively short stay in Thessalonica in the early 50s, we are left wondering by the description of the signs. What is the person or thing restraining the mystery of lawlessness which is already at work? Moreover, can the insistence that noticeable signs must come before the day of the Lord (II Thess 2:3–5) be reconciled with I Thess 5:2, "The day of the Lord will come like a thief in the night," as constituting Paul's consistent thought expressed at the same period of time?[9]

[9]Some who do not wish to regard II Thess as postPauline have struggled with the relationship to I Thess. To explain stylistic differences, a change of Paul's secretaries has been suggested, e.g., Silvanus for one letter, and Timothy for the other. Alternatively, it has been proposed that II Thess, which was sent soon after I Thess, was addressed to a different group within the Thessalonian community (despite I Thess 5:26: "Greet all the brethren"), or else addressed to Thessalonica to be sent on to a neighboring community (Philippi, which Paul visited before Thessalonica—see pp. 496–97 above on several letters to Philippi—or to Beroea, which he visited afterwards). Already in 1641 H. Grotius suggested switching the order of the two letters: Timothy was sent from Athens carrying II Thess (before which there was no other letter: 2:2); it settled the problem, and so from Corinth there was sent the more pacific I Thess which assumes that the Thessalonians had been receptive to Paul's earlier instruction and need only some new pointers (4:9,13; 5:1). This thesis has relatively little following today (Kümmel, *Introduction* 263–64); yet see Manson, "St. Paul," and P. Trudinger, *Downside Review* 113 (1995), 31–35.

Genuine Pauline authorship need not demand a very early date for II Thess, although that calculation is more common. For instance, after writing I Thess Paul most likely visited Thessalonica several times in his journeys to Macedonia (see I Cor 16:5 at the end of his stay at Ephesus *ca.* summer 57; and II Cor 7:5 and Acts 20:1–6 before his final visit to Jerusalem *ca.* 58). These further encounters might explain issues in II Thess if it was written after that period.

If Paul did not write II Thess, in some ways interpretation becomes more complex. It could not have been written too late, for it was already known to Marcion and Polycarp before the mid-2d century. Some would see the letter addressed to a different situation (gnostic dangers[10]) not clearly related to the Thessalonian church described in the earlier letter. Others more plausibly see a continuity with some of the themes in I Thess. Donfried, "Cults" 352–53, thinks it may have been written shortly after I Thess by either Timothy or Silvanus (co-authors of both letters) in Paul's name while he was away.

Perhaps the majority of scholars who opt for pseudonymity would see the letter addressed to the Thessalonian church towards the end of the 1st century, where the dangers corrected would find a better context[11] than in the 50s. (Thus there would have been a continuity of church audience, even if separated by decades.) By the 90s at least in some areas Christians were meeting severe trials (II Thess 1:4,6);[12] and so they began to see evil on a global scale working against believers in Christ. They turned to Jewish apocalyptic written in similar circumstances and reused its symbols, e.g., Daniel's description of hostile world empires as savage animals. The Book of Revelation symbolically identified an evil of Satanic origin at work through the medium of the Roman Empire and emperor worship. Specifically the Emperor Domitian (see pp. 805–9 below), whose distrust of religious deviations seems to have led to local harassment of Christians and who signed himself as Lord and God, may have epitomized the offense. It is possible to see II Thess in the same light since it mentions persecution and evil deceit and associates the activity of Satan with the coming of the lawless one who exalts himself above every god and seeks worship by sitting in the temple of God (2:3,4,9). In this approach a writer who knew I Thess

[10]See H. Koester, *Introd. (NT)* 2.242–46. Attempts to find incipient gnostic opponents in I Thess (e.g., in the sexual libertinism decried there; see Puskas, *Letters* 103) are less plausible than Donfried's suggestions (p. 460 above).

[11]Readers might profitably look to Chapter 37 below on the Book of Revelation for a similar context, and perhaps to Chapter 12 above on I John which in 2:18–19 proclaims that the antichrists have come.

[12]Sufferings are mentioned in I Thess 2:14, but those recounted in II Thess seem to be on a larger scale causing the author to invoke eternal destruction on the persecutors (1:9) and some Thessalonians to think the end was at hand. Nevertheless we must be cautious about the extent to which these descriptions are a literary convention rather than a portrayal of fact.

5:1–2 containing Paul's caution about the times and seasons and the coming of the day of the Lord like a thief in the night decided to write a letter patterned on it. Paul, dead now a quarter of a century, would speak again in the midst of heated apocalyptic expectations, giving a message that is authoritative and to be held fast (II Thess 2:15; 3:4,6). He warns people not to be deceived by the enthusiasm of false teachers (2:3)[13] and reminds the audience of the standard signs associated with the parousia that are still not verified.[14] True, the mystery of lawlessness is at work. Yet something or somebody is restraining the lawless one; and when that figure comes, the Lord Jesus will slay him (2:7–8).

Looking at the arguments for and against Paul's writing II Thess, personally I cannot decide with certitude, even if surety is claimed by some adherents of postPauline writing. Although the current tide of scholarship has turned against writing by Paul himself,[15] biblical studies are not helped by being certain about the uncertain. Moreover keeping open both possibilities challenges readers to think more perceptively about the issues involved.

Issues and Problems for Reflection

(1) It is challenging to list differences of teaching and emphasis between I and II Thess and to make an effort to explain them. Beyond the obvious differences in the respective eschatological teaching, there are more subtle divergences. For instance in I Thess there is a tone of beseeching and exhorting, whereas in II Thess there is a greater appeal to authoritative teaching and the tradition (*paradosis:* a word absent from the earlier letter). In I Thess (1:5; 2:1–9; 3:4) Paul appeals to himself as an example; the Paul of II Thess (2:15; 3:6,14) speaks more as an apostolic authority. Do these features offer an argument for dating II Thess to a postPauline period when he was being revered as a founder of the churches (Eph 2:20)?

(2) What is the christology of II Thess and how may it be compared to that of I Thess? For instance, notice the use of "God" in I Thess 1:4; 5:23,24 and the use of "the Lord [Jesus]" in almost identical phrases in II Thess 2:13; 3:16; 3:3. If II Thess was written at a later period, is the exaltation of Jesus

[13]Some think the appearance of these false teachers was prompted by the delay of the parousia (II Pet 2:1–2; 3:3–4). Hughes, *Early,* argues that the false teachers were *followers of Paul* who taught a fulfilled eschatology (the day of the Lord had come).

[14]To what extent is the description of the man of lawlessness seated in the temple of God dependent on early Christian expectations and even on Jesus' apocalyptic descriptions in the Gospels, e.g., the desolating abomination in Mark 13:14? The latter connection is rejected by R. H. Shaw, *Anglican Theological Review* 47 (1965), 96–102.

[15]This *Introduction* attempts to present the majority view of scholars, and for that reason I have treated II Thess in the deuteroPauline section of the Epistles.

now more advanced?[16] Notice, however, that primarily the lordship of Jesus seems to be connected not with the resurrection but with the parousia. Is this a reappearance of an earlier christology (see BINTC 110–12)?

(3) There is a major dispute about the identity of the man of lawlessness, the son of perdition and agent of Satan, who takes his seat in the temple of God and proclaims himself to be God (whose coming is associated with the apostasy; 2:3–5,9–10), and the identity of the thing or person now restraining him (*to katechon; ho katechōn,* from the verb "to hold back"). We can only touch on the subject here; readers must consult commentaries for arguments pro and con about the suggested identifications. According to the date assigned to II Thess, the man of lawlessness has often been identified with a Roman emperor pretending to be divine (Caligula, Nero, Domitian),[17] and the restrainer identified with Roman law or an agent thereof that/who has prevented the enforcement of emperor worship. Other suggestions for the restrainer are God who in Jewish thought had bound the evil angels till the last days and delayed the time of judgment,[18] or the divine plan that the gospel be proclaimed in the whole world. A few scholars (e.g., Giblin) interpret the *katechon/katechōn* as a "seizing" force/person hostile to God, i.e., a falsely inspired prophet who had misled the Thessalonians about the day of the Lord. Much of the discussion assumes that the author was clear in his own mind as to the identity of both the lawless man and the restrainer. It is not impossible, however, that the author received the imagery from tradition and that, without being able to identify them,[19] in the current situation he believed only that the lawless one had not come and therefore the restrainer must be at work. (That the audience had been told about them and so knew them [2:5–6] need not mean that their precise identity had been revealed.)

Today readers should reflect on a more crucial issue. Are believers still to expect an apostasy, a man of lawlessness, and a restrainer? Throughout Christian history people have thought so, identifying various figures as the antichrist.[20] Already in NT times, however, we find an attempt to deal with

[16]Probably one should not appeal to II Thess 1:12. Although some would read it as "the grace of our God-and-Lord Jesus Christ," the reading "the grace of our God and of the Lord Jesus Christ" is to be preferred. See BINTC 180.

[17]Much apocalyptic imagery was influenced by the Book of Daniel, and there the principal enemy was the Syrian king Antiochus IV who promoted false worship.

[18]See J. M. Bassler, CBQ 46 (1984), 496–510.

[19]He speaks of the "mystery" of lawlessness in 2:7, and the apocalyptic seer often does not fully understand the mystery.

[20]Although 2:4 describes the man of lawlessness as an antiGod figure, the description of his appearing (*apokalypsis*) as an object of worship clearly makes him an antichrist—his is a false parousia counterpoised to the true one. In the NT the term *antichristos* occurs only in I John 2:18,22; 4:3; II John 7 where it is applied to dangerous erroneous teachers. The early Christian idea of a specific embodiment of evil standing against God is treated by L. J. Lietaert Peerbolte, *The Antecedents of AntiChrist* (Brill: Leiden, 1996).

such expectations on a more pedestrian level: The author of I John 2:18–19 sees those who have apostatized from his community as the expected antichrists. May the symbolism of II Thess be accepted simply as meaning that there is always opposition to the kingdom of God, and that before the final coming of that kingdom in and through Christ there will be supreme opposition? Some have claimed that II Thess makes eschatology irrelevant. More simply does it make irrelevant the seeking of precision about exactly what will happen, as if that were a major religious issue?

Bibliography on II Thessalonians

COMMENTARIES AND STUDIES IN SERIES: Aus, R. (AugC, 1984); Krodel, G. A. (ProcC, 1993); Menken, M.J.J. (NTR, 1994). See also the *Bibliography* of Chapter 18 for asterisked books, treating both I and II Thess.

Bailey, J. A., "Who Wrote II Thessalonians?" NTS 25 (1978–79), 131–45.

Collins, R. F., CLPDNW 209–41; also ed. TTC 371–515 (many English articles).

Giblin, C. H., *The Threat to Faith. An Exegetical and Theological Re-Examination of 2 Thessalonians 2* (AnBib 31; Rome: PBI, 1967).

———, "2 Thessalonians 2 Re-read as Pseudepigraphical," TTC 459–69.

Holland, G. S., *The Tradition that You Received from Us: 2 Thessalonians in the Pauline Tradition* (HUT 24; Tübingen: Mohr-Siebeck, 1988).

Hughes, F. W., *Early Christian Rhetoric and 2 Thessalonians* (JSNTSup 30; Sheffield: JSOT, 1989).

Koester, H., "From Paul's Eschatology to the Apocalyptic Schemata of 2 Thessalonians," TTC 441–58.

Krentz, E., " 'Through a Prism': The Theology of 2 Thessalonians as a Deutero-Pauline Letter," SBLSP 1986, 1–7.

Lightfoot, J. B., *Notes on the Epistles of St. Paul* (London: Macmillan, 1895), 93–136. A classic.

Manson, T. W., "St. Paul in Greece: The Letters to the Thessalonians," BJRL 35 (1952–53), 428–47; also in his *Studies in the Gospels and Epistles* (Philadelphia: Westminster, 1962), 259–78.

Menken, M.J.J., "The Structure of 2 Thessalonians," TTC 373–82.

Russell, R., "The Idle in 2 Thess 3:6–12: an Eschatological or Social Problem?" NTS 34 (1988), 105–19.

Schmidt, D., "The Authenticity of 2 Thessalonians: Linguistic Arguments," SBLSP 1983, 289–96.

———, "The Syntactical Style of 2 Thessalonians: How Pauline Is It?" TTC 383–93.

Sumney, J. L., "The Bearing of Pauline Rhetorical Pattern on the Integrity of 2 Thessalonians," ZNW 81 (1990), 192–204.

CHAPTER 27

LETTER TO THE COLOSSIANS

In its vision of Christ, of his body the church, and of the mystery of God hidden for ages, Col is truly majestic, and certainly a worthy representative of the Pauline heritage. That evaluation should not be forgotten amidst the major scholarly debate about whether or not the letter was written by Paul himself, a problem that has cast a long shadow on discussions about Col. After the *Background,* the *General Analysis* will reflect on what is actually communicated in Col since all theories about the writer must do justice to that. Subsections will treat the *Christological hymn* (*1:15–20*), the *False teaching* (*2:8–23*), the *Household code* (*3:18–4:1*), *Did Paul write Col, From where and when, Issues for reflection,* and *Bibliography.*

The Background

An important commercial route passing through the Phrygian Mountains connected Ephesus on the western coast of Asia Minor to Iconium and Tarsus in the SE. About 110 miles from Ephesus along that route, in a volcanic section of the Phrygian region of the province of Asia subject to earthquakes, lies the Lycus River valley. On the riverbank stood *Laodicea,* a sizable commercial and textile center. From there one could take a branch road northward for about six miles and come to *Hierapolis,* famous for its medicinal hot springs, a temple to Apollo, and purple dye. Or one could continue the main route for another eleven miles to the SE and arrive at *Colossae,* also a textile center noted for purple wool products. In Roman times Laodicea had become the most important and Colossae the least important[1] of these three cities, which were arranged roughly like a triangle. Their population would have been largely Phrygian and Greek, but Jewish families from Babylon had been resettled there just after 200 BC. By Paul's time the Jewish population in the Laodicea area seems to have been more than 10,000 and (from a later Talmudic reference) quite hellenized.

Evidently the churches in the three cities had close relations. Paul men-

[1]Indeed it would have been the least important city to which any of the Pauline letters was directed (Lightfoot).

Summary of Basic Information

DATE: If by Paul (or by Timothy while Paul was still alive or had just died), 61–63 (or slightly later) from Rome, or 54–56 from Ephesus. If pseudonymous (about 60 percent of critical scholarship), in the 80s from Ephesus.

TO: The Christians at Colossae, in the Lycus River valley in Phrygia in the province of Asia, not evangelized by Paul but by Epaphras, who has informed Paul about the church and its problems.

AUTHENTICITY: A modest probability favors composition by a disciple of Paul close to certain aspects of his thought (perhaps part of a "school" at Ephesus) who drew on Phlm.

UNITY AND INTEGRITY: Not seriously debated. Probably in 1:15–20 an extant hymn has been adapted.

FORMAL DIVISION:
- A. Opening Formula: 1:1–2
- B. Thanksgiving: 1:3–8
- C. Body: 1:9–2:23: Pauline indicative (instructions)
  3:1–4:6: Pauline imperative (paraenesis and exhortations)
- D. Greetings and Concluding Formula: 4:7–18.

DIVISION ACCORDING TO CONTENTS:

1:1–2:	Opening Formula
1:3–23:	Proem consisting of Thanksgiving (1:3–8), Prayer (1:9–11), Praise of Christ's Lordship including a hymn (1:12–23)
1:24–2:5:	Apostolic office and preaching the mystery revealed by God
2:6–23:	Christ's Lordship vs. human ordinances
3:1–4:6:	Practice: Vices, virtues, household code
4:7–17:	Greetings and messages
4:18:	Paul's own hand; blessing.

tions Epaphras who has worked hard in all three (Col 4:12–13); he asks that the letter to the Colossians be read in the church of the Laodiceans, and that the Colossians read "the one from Laodicea"[2] (4:16; see also 2:1). The personal references in 4:7–17 are understandable if the Christian community at Colossae was a small, close-knit group, largely known by name to each other (Rogers, *Colossians* xiii). This area had not been evangelized by Paul

[2]The NT tells us nothing more about this letter. In the 2d century Marcion thought it was the writing we know as Eph; and in the 20th century J. Knox (followed by E. Schweizer) contended that it was Phlm (Chapter 21 above, n. 11). *A Letter to the Laodiceans,* forged by the Marcionites, is mentioned in the Muratorian Fragment (late 2d century?). By the 4th century in the Eastern Church an apocryphal letter to the Laodiceans was being challenged, but no such letter in Greek has been preserved. In the West from the 6th to the 15th centuries a Latin apocryphon *To the Laodiceans* circulated, along with vernacular translations (including the rev. ed. of Wycliffe); it was rejected by Erasmus, the Council of Trent, and the Protestant Reformers. Shorter than Phlm, this work, which is a patchwork of lines from the genuine Pauline letters beginning with Gal 1:1 (HSNTA 2.42–46), was probably composed between the 2d and 4th centuries in either Latin or Greek, perhaps by Marcionites.

and had never seen his face (Col 2:1).[3] Yet, since Paul feels free to instruct the Colossians (passim) and addresses them (and the Laodiceans) with a sense of pastoral responsibility (1:9,24; 2:1–2), and since they are interested in what is happening to him (4:7,9), it is likely that a Pauline mission had proclaimed Christ in the Lycus valley, perhaps sent out when Paul was in Ephesus in AD 54–57. Acts 19:10 reports that during Paul's years there, "All the residents of [the province of] Asia heard the word of the Lord." Such an intermediate connection of Paul with their being evangelized is supported by the fact that Epaphras, a Gentile and one of their own who had taught them the truth, was now with Paul (Col 1:6–7; 4:12–13).

Paul is imprisoned (4:3,10), and so communicates with Colossae by this letter to be carried by Tychicus, accompanied by Onesimus (4:7–9). Thus, though absent in the flesh, he can be with them in spirit (2:5).

General Analysis of the Message

The OPENING FORMULA (1:1–2) lists Timothy as a co-sender, as in Phil and Phlm (contributing to the tendency to join Col to them as "Captivity" or "Prison Letters"). In the THANKSGIVING (1:3–8) Paul shows knowledge of the situation at Colossae gained through Epaphras and is pleased by it,[4] writing words of encouragement. One gets the impression that the addressees, in Paul's judgment, have received the gospel well and it is bearing fruit among them.

Paul moves smoothly into the INDICATIVE SECTION OF THE BODY (1:9–2:23) by explaining that he wants to deepen their sense of its completeness by appealing to what they know of Christ in whom all the fullness of God was pleased to dwell. He does this through a famous christological hymn (1:15–20) to which a special subsection will be devoted. Paul wants the Colossians to fully understand Christ as the mystery of God in whom are hidden all the treasures of wisdom and knowledge (2:2–3).

The reason for this emphasis is the danger presented by false teaching (2:8–23) that threatens the Lycus valley Christians who, by implication, were Gentiles.[5] The second subsection below will be devoted to a diagnosis

[3]This is odd since according to Acts 18:23; 19:1 on his "Third Missionary Journey" (*ca.* 54) Paul passed through the region of Galatia and Phrygia and through the interior (of the province of Asia) on his way to Ephesus—a journey that might well have brought him on the road through the Lycus valley. The failure to have followed that route may support the theory that Acts refers to *northern* Galatia (p. 476 above).

[4]Mullins, "Thanksgivings," argues that this section in Col is not simply drawn from the parallel Thanksgiving in Phlm. The messages in 4:7–17 also presume a friendly relationship.

[5]They were formerly estranged (1:21); God has chosen to make his riches known among the Gentiles (1:27).

of that teaching; but readers should be warned in advance that what can be discerned about it from Paul's critique is sketchy and uncertain.[6] Far more important is what Col emphasizes positively. Implicitly countering the teaching is the gospel, "the word of truth" (1:5). The Colossians already have acquired profound knowledge through being introduced to God's plan for all in Christ (2:3). No elements of the universe have any power over the Colossians because Christians have been delivered from the power of darkness and transferred to the kingdom of God's beloved Son (1:13). Indeed, all the principalities and powers were created through God's Son, and all things whether on earth or in heaven were reconciled through him; he is preeminent over all (1:16,18,20). Believers in him do not need to worry about food or drink (2:16), for Christ through his death will present them holy and without blemish before God (1:22). Feasts, new moon, and Sabbath were only shadows of things to come; the substance belongs to Christ (2:17).

In the IMPERATIVE SECTION OF THE BODY (3:1–4:6) Paul's message turns from christology to how Christians should live. It is not clear that his commands are directly influenced by reaction to the false teachers. Indirectly, the writer may be saying to the Colossians that this is what they should be paying attention to rather than listening to the specious arguments of the teachers. Having been raised with Christ, they should be thinking about what is above; for when Christ appears, they will appear with him in glory (3:1–4). Col first gives two lists of five vices each to be avoided and then a list of five virtues to be exhibited by those who have put on a new self in Christ (3:5–17). Finally, in a household instruction, which will receive special attention in a subsection below, the author speaks more specifically to various members of the Christian household (wives, husbands, children, slaves, masters), showing how the mystery of God revealed in Christ affects every aspect of day-to-day life (3:18–4:2). Chapter 19 above, *Issue* 6, pointed out that the list in Gal 3:28 of those among whom no difference should be posited ("Neither Jew nor Greek . . .") did not necessarily imply social equality. That becomes apparent here where a similar list in Col 3:11[7] is followed by this instruction embodying the social inequalities of a patriarchal structure.

The GREETINGS AND CONCLUDING FORMULA (4:7–18) mention eight of the ten people alluded to in Phlm. That parallelism is very important for discussing the authorship and setting of Col in subsections below.

[6]For example, 2:8 refers to *anyone who might* captivate the Colossians "by philosophy and empty deceit according to human tradition, according to the elements [or elemental spirits] of the world/universe." Given the directness of Paul's critique of dangers in Gal and I Cor, the vagueness of the description in Col has been used as an argument against writing by Paul himself.

[7]Notice the reversal "Greek and Jew" and the lack of the male/female pair.

The Christological Hymn (1:15–20)

A key element in Colossians' presentation of Christ is a poetic passage describing his role in creation and reconciliation, a passage commonly regarded as a hymn. (For hymns in the Pauline corpus, see the subsection in Chapter 20 above.) This hymn has been the subject of an extensive bibliography, much of it in German;[8] and a detailed consideration lies beyond the possibilities of this introductory book. Yet these points are worth mentioning by way of acquainting readers with the issues:

- Most think that the writer of the letter was using an already existing Christian hymn familiar to the Colossians and perhaps to the whole area evangelized from Ephesus. Finding ideas in the hymn useful for correcting the false teaching, the writer of Col made them sharper by minor additions.[9]
- The structure of the hymn is debated. If one leaves aside suggestions that rearrange lines into a perfect balance, proposed divisions of the existing lines include: (1) three strophes (vv. 15–16: creation; 17–18a: preservation; 18b–20: redemption); (2) two strophes of unequal length (15–18a: creation; 18b–20; reconciliation);[10] or (3) two strophes of approximately the same length (15–16 and 18b–20), separated by a refrain (17–18a, which is sometimes thought to match the preface to the hymn in 13–14). Although the divisions differ in how to deal with 17–18a, they are alike in recognizing that within this hymn to God's beloved Son the most visible parallelism is between the descriptions in 15–16a, "who is the image of the invisible God, the firstborn of all creation, for in him all things were created," and 18b–19, "who is the beginning, the firstborn from the dead . . . for in him all the fullness has been pleased to dwell."
- How exalted is the christology centered on the parallelism of the firstborn? If Jesus was raised from the dead first before all others, was he the first to be created? Answering no, many see a reference to the uniqueness of the Son, a firstborn who existed before all creation (as in John's Prologue hymn). Yet the closest and most commonly accepted background for the description in 1:15–16a is the OT picture of personified female Wisdom, the image of God's goodness (Wisdom 7:26) who worked with God in establishing all other things

[8]For treatments in English see J. M. Robinson, JBL 76 (1957), 270–87; R. P. Martin, VE 2 (1963), 6–32; E. Käsemann, KENTT 149–68; E. Lohse, *Colossians* 41–61; B. Vawter, CBQ 33 (1971), 62–81; W. McGown, EQ 51 (1979), 156–62; P. Beasley-Murray in *Pauline Studies,* eds. D. A. Hagner and M. J. Harris (Grand Rapids: Eerdmans, 1980), 169–83; T. E. Pollard, NTS 27 (1980–81), 572–75; F. F. Bruce, BSac 141 (1984), 99–111; J. F. Balchin, VE 15 (1985), 65–93; J. Fossum, NTS 35 (1989), 183–201; N. T. Wright, NTS 36 (1990), 444–68; J. Murphy-O'Connor, RB 102 (1995), 231–41.

[9]Two frequently proposed are (the italicized) phrases in 1:18a: "He is the head of the body, *the church*"; and 1:20b: "Making peace *through the blood of his cross.*"

[10]This thesis, probably the most popular, is well defended by Lohse, *Colossians* 44–45.

(Prov 3:19)—that Wisdom was created by God at the beginning (Prov 8:22; Sirach 24:9).

- Besides personified Wisdom other backgrounds for the hymn have been suggested. E. Käsemann sees a preChristian text dealing with the gnostic redeemer myth: a primal man who breaks into the sphere of death to lead out those who belong to him. (Yet "the beginning of God's creation" and "firstborn of the dead" are *Christian* terminology in Rev 3:14 and 1:5.) E. Lohmeyer, drawing on the theme of "reconciliation" in Col 1:20a, understands the hymn against the backdrop of the Jewish Day of Atonement when the Creator is reconciled to the people of God. (Is there proof that Jews of this period stressed the creation motif in observing Yom Kippur?) In the same direction S. Lyonnet finds in 1:20 echoes of the Jewish New Year (Rosh Hashanah). What can be said is that while some of the language of the hymn echoes Hellenistic Jewish descriptions of Wisdom, it also has parallels in Platonic, Hermetic, and Philonic terminology (Chapter 5 above). Consequently, its christology, which as we shall see below is very different from that of the syncretistic false teachers attacked in Col, is nonetheless phrased in a language not too distant from theirs.
- The hymn's emphasis on *all* things being created in God's Son (1:16) underlines the superiority of Christ over the principalities and the powers. Special attention has also been paid to all the *plērōma* ("fullness") in 1:19: "For in him all the fullness was pleased to well." In 2d-century Valentinian gnosticism the *plērōma* was the fullness of the emanations that came forth from God, but not God who was above all those. The Hermetic corpus (p. 85 above) could speak of God as the *plērōma* of good, and the world as a *plērōma* of evil. But neither of those is what is meant in Col where 2:9 ("all the *plērōma* of deity" in Christ bodily) interprets 1:19. By divine election God in all fullness dwells in Christ. That is why through him all things can be reconciled to God (1:20a).[11]

The False Teaching (2:8–23)

The teaching that presents a danger at Colossae has to be reconstructed mirror-wise from the letter's hostile polemic against it, and that makes the tone and content of the teaching hard to evaluate. By way of TONE, clearly the situation at Colossae is not like that recounted in Gal where the foolish Galatians were being won over in large numbers to another gospel.[12] Nor

[11]Compare II Cor 5:19: "God was in Christ reconciling the world to Himself."

[12]As pointed out in Chapter 19 above, n. 14, Paul employed judicial or forensic rhetoric to defend himself in Gal. The rhetoric here is more epideictic, or demonstrative, censuring unacceptable thought and practices, but not pointing out wrongs done to Paul or his companions (Puskas, *Letters* 124). Pokorný (*Colossians* 21–31) offers a structural analysis. A. E. Drake, NTS 41 (1995), 123–44, finds deliberately cryptic structural features.

does it resemble that at Philippi which, even though the community was sound, called forth harsh polemics from Paul (Phil 3:2: "Look out for the dogs; look out for the evildoers; look out for the mutilation [i.e., circumcision]"). Indeed, we cannot be certain that the Christians at Colossae were even aware of their peril; and some of the description might be purely potential (e.g., Col 2:8: "Look out lest anyone captivate you"). More than likely, however, already on the scene as a minority were those who would prey on the Colossians. Whether or not they were members of the house-church(es) at Colossae, we cannot know.

By way of CONTENT, we may begin by noting that the cities of the Lycus River valley constituted an area where religious observances reflected a mixture of native Phrygian cults, Eastern imports (Isis, Mithras), Greco-Roman deities, and Judaism with its insistence on one God. In the description of the teaching that threatened the Christians at Colossae, elements that seem related to Judaizing are described; for Col 2:11 emphasizes a circumcision not made by hand, a circumcision of Christ implicitly opposed to the necessity of physical circumcision. Furthermore (2:16) some would judge the Colossian Christians on questions of food and drink (dedicated to idols?) and of observing a feast, a new moon, or Sabbaths (Jewish calendric observances?).[13] Nevertheless, on the assumption that Col envisions one false teaching rather than a plague of totally separate ones, the text seems to require something more complex than an attempt to get the Colossian Christian Gentiles to observe the Mosaic Law for salvation. No arguments from the OT are offered by Paul in refutation, nor does he explicitly connect any of the observances with Judaism.

In 2:8 Paul would have the recipients beware of being seduced by an empty deceitful "philosophy" that is according to human tradition. He could be referring to the thoughts of one of the Greek philosophers,[14] or to the mystery religions (p. 86), which were also called philosophies. Yet that designation need not exclude a Jewish element, since Josephus (*War* 2.8.2; #119; *Ant.* 18.1.2; #11) describes the positions of the Pharisees, Sadducees, and Essenes as philosophies, and Mark 7:8 has Jesus condemn the Pharisees for rejecting the commandment of God in favor of their human tradition.

Col 2:8 goes on to describe the error as putting emphasis on the "elements" (*stoicheia*) of the world/universe. In Greek philosophy these could

[13]Festivals and new moon can, but need not, be Jewish observances; yet in combination with the Sabbath, they probably were. The three terms are combined in Hos 2:13; Ezek 45:17; etc.

[14]Scholars have detected in Col similarities to Pythagorean, or Cynic, or popular Stoic thought, or to Middle Platonism (pp. 88–90 above). For discussions of Paul's adversaries, see especially Arnold, Bornkamm, De Maris, Dunn, Evans, Hartman, Hooker, Lyonnet, T. W. Martin, and E. W. Sanders in the *Bibliography* below.

be the elements that constitute everything (earth, fire, water, air); but in Hellenistic times the term also referred to the cosmic rulers or spirits that dominated the world, including the heavenly bodies that astrologically controlled human affairs. Col's hostile references to "principalities" and "powers" (2:15) and to abasement and the "worship of angels" (2:18) point in that direction.[15] Might the issue of feast, new moon, and Sabbath be involved in this worship? (In his argument against the Judaizing preachers who would impose circumcision and the works of the Law on the Galatians, Paul protested against being made slaves to the elements/spirits of the universe and observing days and months and seasons and years: Gal 4:3,9–10.[16]) Col 2:23 disparages bodily severity. Might extremes of asceticism be in mind in reference to "food and drink" (2:16) rather than food dedicated to idols—an asceticism that manifested obedience to the elemental spirits, the principalities, and the powers?

Combining these elements, many would describe the false teachers at Colossae as Jewish Christian syncretists in whose "philosophy" were combined (hellenized) Jewish, Christian, and Pagan elements: a "self-devised religion [*ethelothrēskia*]" in R. P. Martin's rendering of 2:23. In it angels were associated with the stars and worshiped on feasts, at the new moon, and on the Sabbath almost as deities who rule the universe and human life—elements in a cosmic pattern that people must follow in life. (As "sons of God" in the heavenly court, angels could be understood as similar to the deities of the Greco-Roman pantheon.) This syncretism could incorporate believers in Christ under the proviso that they rated him as subordinate to the angelic principalities and powers. After all, Christ was flesh while the principalities are spirits.

Two other factors are sometimes detected in the teaching. *First,* some would describe the teaching rejected by Col as gnosticism (pp. 92–93 above) because of references to visions,[17] to being inflated by the bodily mind, to the gratification of the flesh (2:18,21–23), and to the elemental spirits if they

[15]F. O. Francis, CAC 163–95; R. Yates, ExpTim 7 (1985–86), 12–15. In Qumran (DSS) thought God had placed all human beings under the control of two spirits who are also angels: the evil spirit of deceit and the good spirit of truth, or Belial and Michael (see E. W. Saunders, "Colossian"; for differences: E. Yamauchi, "Qumran and Colossae," BSac 121 [1964], 141–52). "Worship of angels" probably means worship paid to the angels, but some understand it as worship by angels.

[16]However, T. W. Martin, NTS 42 (1996), 105–19, claims that they are Jewish calendric observances taken over by Paul's community, and he is *not* attacking them. They are not the same observances as those in Gal 4:10.

[17]The Christian gnostic systems are often revealed in an appearance of the risen Jesus. Already Lightfoot identified the Colossian heresy as gnostic, pointing to the thought of Cerinthus. M. D. Goulder, NTS 41 (1995), 601–19, who thinks Col was written by an aging Paul to attack a developing Jewish Christian gnosticism, points to parallels in the thought of the *Apocryphon of John.*

are understood as emanations of God. Yet there is no direct reference to "knowledge" in the critique of the teachers. True, in Col's positive presentation of Christ there is frequent reference to "knowledge," "insight," "wisdom" (1:9–10,28; 2:2–3; 3:10,16; 4:5), and "fullness" (the *plērōma* discussed above); and this could be seen as an implicit critique of the use of the same language by the false teachers. Unfortunately our information about incipient gnosticism in the 1st century is very limited (as contrasted with more detailed knowledge of the developed gnostic systems of the 2d century), so that identifying the teaching as gnostic because of the vague features just mentioned amounts to elucidating the unknown by the less known, and it does not noticeably augment our picture of the situation at Colossae.

Second, in its positive sections Col speaks of the divine mystery (*mystērion*) hidden from past ages but now revealed in Christ—the knowledge of which has been shared with the Colossians (1:26–27; 2:2–3; 4:3). Some would find in that an implicit critique of the false teachers as adherents of a mystery religion. One could point to nearby Hierapolis as a cult center of Cybele, the great Anatolian Mother Goddess (p. 87 above), and the possible use of the obscure word *embateuein* ("to enter into") with "visions" in 2:18 to refer to initiation into the enacted rites of a mystery religion.[18] That the false teachers had some mystery religion connections or used mystery religion language is possible. However, Paul's own use of *mystērion* stems from apocalyptic Judaism[19] and is certainly not dependent on *his* having been exposed to mystery religions.

If these observations leave a picture filled with uncertainties, that is an honest estimate of the state of our knowledge of the teaching. Hartman, "Humble" 28–29, is wise in dividing material in Col pertinent to the false teaching into certain, probable, and possible. Those who write with great certainty about it are, to a considerable extent, guessing. Of course, there is nothing wrong with guessing, provided that all are aware of how much guesswork is involved. At this distance in time and place we may not be able to decipher all the elements that went into the syncretism attacked in Col or identify the end-product with precision. Ordinary readers can rest content with a diagnosis that settles for what is truly probable: The opponents had combined belief in Christ with Jewish and Pagan ideas to shape a hierarchi-

[18]On *embateuein,* see F. O. Francis, CAC 197–207. He relates it to the Apollo sanctuary of Claros near Ephesus with its oracle. M. Dibelius, CAC 61–121, studies Isis initiation and other initiatory rites.

[19]See R. E. Brown, CBQ 20 (1958), 417–43; and *Biblica* 39 (1958), 426–48; 40 (1959), 70–87; and Chapter 5 above, n. 40; also J. Coppens, PAQ 132–58. In apocalyptic thought God revealed the divine plan in the *secret* heavenly council of the angels, and prophets and seers gained knowledge of that *mysterious plan* by being given a vision of the heavenly council.

cal system of heavenly beings in which Christ was subordinated to angelic powers to whom worship was due.

Household Code (3:18–4:1)

This is the first of five NT lists of rules for members of the Christian household that we shall encounter, and perhaps the oldest.[20] Both in OT Wisdom Literature and the ethical discussions of the Greek philosophers the behavior of household members toward each other was discussed. More specifically the popular philosophers developed detailed catalogues of ethical responsibilities toward governing authorities, parents, brothers and sisters, husbands, wives, children, other relatives, and business customers. In the maturing Christian communities believers needed guidance, so that outsiders could see the effect of faith in Christ on their lives and recognize them as beneficial members of society. This need may have been more pressing when and where the majority of Christians were Gentiles who had not been raised with a knowledge of the Jewish Law.

There can be little doubt, then, that both in format and content the NT household codes were influenced by contemporary ethical lists. Yet now there was a new motivation: "In the Lord" (Col 3:18,20; also "Lord" 3:22,24; "Master in heaven" 4:1), a Christ who is over every principality and power. These are rules for households under the Lordship of Christ—"Serve the Lord Christ" is said to the slaves in 3:24 but could be said to all. That principle determines which ethical admonitions will be emphasized and sets the tone—and removes any contradiction with 2:20–22, which warns the Colossians against regulations that are according to human precepts and doctrines. This is illustrated by the fact that the first party in each of the three pairs (3:18–19: *wives*/husbands; 3:20–21: *children*/fathers; 3:22–4:1: *slaves*/masters) is told to be subject or obedient, as subjection to the Lordship of Christ works its way down in terms of specified subjections within the community.[21] The second party in each pair, the one to whom subjection is due, must exemplify characteristics of the Lord who is over all: love, not acting

[20]See Eph 5:21–6:9; Titus 2:1–10; I Tim (2:1–2); 2:8–15 + 5:1–2; 6:1–2; I Pet 2:13–3:7 (also in *Didache* 4:9–11; *I Clement* 1:3; 21:6–8; Polycarp, *Philippians* 4:1–6:2). Treatments of the household codes (sometimes called by the German name *Haustafeln,* "lists of household obligations," derived from the Luther Bible) are found in commentaries on the respective passages; but a particularly helpful comparative table is offered in Selwyn, *1 Peter* 422–39, esp. 423. See also J. E. Crouch, *The Origin and Intention of the Colossian Haustafel* (Göttingen: Vandenhoeck & Ruprecht, 1972); D. C. Verner, *Household* (-codes in the Pastorals); C. J. Martin, "The *Haustafeln* (Household Codes) in African American Biblical Interpretation," in *Stony the Road We Trod,* ed. C. Felder (Minneapolis: A/F, 1991), 206–31.

[21]In Chapter 18 above, *Issue* 5, it was noted that in the oldest preserved Pauline work Christians were told to respect those who were *over* them in the Lord (I Thess 5:12).

in anger, justice. That slaves receive four verses of instruction and masters only one may reflect the Christian social status: many slaves, few wealthy masters. (The relation of Col to Phlm, a letter concerned with the slave/master relationship, also enters the picture.)

How are Christian readers of later times to evaluate these ethical instructions phrased as guidance to 1st-century families? (1) One approach is to debate the issue on the internal biblical level. There are texts in the undisputed Pauline letters acknowledging for all Christians a baptismal equality of salvific benefits (Gal 3:27–29; I Cor 12:13—cf. also Col 3:10–11). Citing those, some will suggest that the household codes of later NT writings are a corruption reflecting an increasingly authoritarian patriarchal church order. Besides pointing to passages in the earlier Pauline letters that make women subordinate to men (e.g., I Cor 14:34–36), others respond that the later writings are just as canonical and authoritative as the undisputed Pauline writings. Acknowledging that, still others point out that not all NT writings work out with the same profundity the gospel implications of equal salvific benefits, and that one must explore carefully the tensions among texts without dismissing any of them.

(2) The second approach, not exclusive of the first, is to debate the issue on the hermeneutical level of translating culturally conditioned texts of the NT into the lives of people today. (a) One view with respect to the present topic treats the codes as virtually Christian law to be obeyed as God's eternal will. This view allows a spectrum in which some laws are regarded as more important than others; but a basic query remains: Does this outlook not canonize a particular 1st-century social arrangement, even if the NT presents it as "in the Lord"? (b) The other basic view gives priority to our contemporary social experience in evaluating the codes. Again there is a spectrum of ways in which interpreters search out the *value* being inculcated in a 1st-century context and seek to translate it into modern societal relations. Some would reinterpret the codes to mean that wives owe deserving husbands respect, not subjection. More radically others would contend that the values of the gospel can require that the directives be rephrased to the point of saying the opposite. Modern slaves (to an economic or political system) should be told not to obey or be subject, but to revolt and throw down their oppressive masters. Because of centuries-long inequities imposed on women, wives should be told to express themselves and at times struggle against their husbands. There is a basic query to be faced in this view as well: Does it not reduce the biblical text to interesting antiquarian information? In seeking a way between this Scylla and Charybdis readers are reminded of the discussion of biblical authority in Chapter 2 B above, for an answer will explicitly or implicitly reflect the stance taken toward inspiration, revelation, and

church teaching—and Christian self-giving love. That few would change the directive given to children serves warning that one attitude toward the household directives may not be appropriate for all the pairings mentioned.

Did Paul Write Colossians?[22]

Thus far I have referred to the one addressing the Colossians as "Paul" because that is the way the letter presents him. Moreover, there is a great deal of vocabulary, style, and theology in Col that is distinctively Pauline; and were the name "Paul" missing from 1:1,23; 4:18,[23] surely the letter would still be placed in the Pauline ambiance. Only in 1805 (E. Evanson) and then beginning systematically in the late 1830s (E. Mayerhoff) were challenges raised to the Pauline writing of Col. As with II Thess, Col offers a good chance to evaluate the kind of reasoning offered. *At the present moment about 60 percent of critical scholarship holds that Paul did not write the letter.*[24] Readers less interested in technicalities can settle for that judgment and skip the following summary of arguments and counterarguments for treating Col as deuteroPauline.

From the start one should note that the discussion is complicated by two very different ideas of pseudonymity in relation to Col. Some scholars are thinking of it as written by someone close to Paul during his lifetime or shortly after his death, perhaps with an idea of what Paul himself wanted to write. Others are thinking of a situation several decades later, where someone in the Pauline heritage takes on himself the mantle of the apostle and speaks to a situation that has only now developed. Thus besides asking whether it is likely that someone other than Paul wrote the letter, one has also to decide which of the two pseudonymous scenarios is more plausible.

(1) VOCABULARY. Col uses 87 words that do not appear in the undisputed Pauline letters (including 34 that appear nowhere else in the NT).[25] Yet Phil,

[22]Although the issue is most often presented as one of Pauline authorship, as I have explained previously, the term "author" offers difficulty. If the letter were written twenty years after Paul's death by a Pauline disciple seeking to present the thought of his master, in the ancient estimation Paul might very well be called the "author," i.e., the authority behind the work. I use "writer" to refer to the person who composed the letter, whether or not that person used a scribe to pen the work.

[23]The repetition of the name has the effect of reminding readers that "*the* apostle" is addressing them. The reference to Paul as "a minister [*diakonos*] of the gospel" and "a minister of the church" and to Paul's vicarious suffering (1:23–25) have been thought to represent a postPauline hagiography wherein he was being highly revered.

[24]CLPDNW 171 surveys the various scholars and the nuances of their views. Two major studies in German about the Pauline writing of Col came to opposite conclusions: E. Percy (1946: yes); W. Bujard (1973: no). Cannon's detailed study favors Paul as the writer.

[25]A detailed presentation underlying points (1) and (2) is found in Lohse, *Colossians* 84–91. Of the 87 words, some 35 are found in Eph. Much of the argument against Paul's writing Col draws on its differences from the undisputed letters and its closeness to Eph. E. P. Sanders, "Literary," how-

genuinely written by Paul and of comparable length, uses 79 words that do not appear in the other undisputed Pauline letters (including 36 that appear nowhere else in the NT). Thus the percentages of unusual words prove nothing; and even if they were much higher in Col, that would not be decisive because the writer might be drawing on the false teaching present at Col for some of his distinctive terminology. Another vocabulary objection to Pauline writing is the absence in Col of favorite Pauline terms: "righteousness/justification," "believe," "law," "freedom," "promise," "salvation." Again this statistic becomes less impressive when we realize that "to justify" is not found in I Thess, Phil, and II Cor; nor is "law" found in I Thess and II Cor; nor "save/salvation" in Gal. Moreover, once more the vocabulary of Col may have been shaped by the problem at hand.

(2) STYLE. There are extraordinarily long sentences in Col hooked together by participles and relative pronouns (sometimes not apparent in translations that break the sentences up), e.g., 1:3–8, 2:8–15. True, there are long sentences in the undisputed Pauline letters (e.g., Rom 1:1–7), but the Col style is marked by pleonastic synonyms, piling up words that convey the same idea.[26] Lohse speaks of its "liturgical hymnic style" influenced by extant tradition and points out similar features in the hymns of the Dead Sea Scrolls. Are such differences reconcilable with Paul's having written Col? Granted that Paul did not personally evangelize Colossae, did he take care to send a message in a style influenced by hymns and liturgical confessions known there, so that his correction of the teaching would not seem alien? Did he employ a scribe who knew Colossae (Epaphras or one influenced by him?) and depend on his cooperation in apposite phrasing? That could explain in part why so many of the minor particles, adverbs, and connective words common to genuine Pauline style are missing in Col. Yet since the differences of style extend to the phrasing of key arguments, many scholars would say that no scribal explanation can account for Col.

(3) THEOLOGY. The developed christology, ecclesiology, and eschatology of Col has become the principal argument against Paul as the writer. (a) *Christologically,* the characteristic Pauline evaluation of the death/resurrection of Christ as the source of justification is missing in Col, although in him we have the redemptive forgiveness of sins (1:14) and, through the blood of his cross, peace and reconciliation (1:20). The shift of emphasis to creation through Christ and his preeminence is undoubtedly shaped by a desire to respond to the false teaching, but is it reconcilable with the historical Paul's

---

ever, contends that Paul did not write Col because passages in it are almost verbatim the same as passages in I Thess, I Cor, and Phil.

[26] 1:11: "endurance and patience"; 1:22: "holy, blameless, irreproachable"; 1:26: "ages and generations"; 2:11: "circumcised with a circumcision," etc.

thought? Those who maintain that it is point to I Cor 8:6: "Yet for us there is . . . one Lord Jesus Christ through whom are all things and through whom we are." At the other end of the christological spectrum Col 1:24 would have Paul say, "I rejoice in (my) sufferings for your sake, and in my flesh I am filling up what is lacking in the afflictions of Christ for the sake of his body, i.e., the church." Although in none of the undisputed letters is Paul so specific about the vicarious value of his sufferings, would that not be explicable if Col was written toward the end of his life after even more opportunity to carry the cross? (b) *Ecclesiologically,*[27] in the undisputed Pauline letters "church" most often refers to the local Christian community as "the churches of Galatia" and "the church of God which is in Corinth," with only a few instances of a more universal use as "the church" (Gal 1:13; I Cor 12:28; 15:9). The local use still appears in the greetings of Col (4:15–16), but in 1:18,24 the Lord exercises his rule over the entire world as the head of his body, the church. Thus the church affects even the heavenly powers. In I Cor 12:12–14,27 (see also 6:13–15; 10:16–17; Rom 12:4–5) Paul spoke of the risen body of Christ of which each Christian is a member, just as different physical parts, including the head, are members of the physical body. Yet he never used the imagery of the church as the body of Christ or Christ as the head—a major theme in Col (and Eph).[28] One gets the impression from Col that the church is part of the supreme accomplishment of Christ, and the goal of Paul's own work (1:24). Can so developed an ecclesiology be attributed to Paul's lifetime? (c) *Eschatologically,* the present status of the Christian is greatly exalted—in other words, realized eschatology seems to dominate future eschatology. Christians are already in the kingdom of God's beloved Son (1:13). In baptism they are raised with Christ (2:12; 3:1), something that is never said in the undisputed writings of Paul and that, according to some scholars, he never would have said. However, such objections may be taking

[27]Lohse, *Colossians* 177–83, develops well the theological arguments against Pauline writing of Col, but on 179 he advances an argument on the basis of silence in Col about church structure. Unless there were an overwhelming reason in Col to appeal to church structure, this argument from silence is not significant.

[28]Col 1:18; 2:17,19; 3:15 (Eph 1:22–23; 2:16; 4:4,12,15–16; 5:23,29–30). The variations of the theology of the body of Christ in the Pauline corpus have been the subject of much discussion: L. Cerfaux, *Church* 262–86; J.A.T. Robinson, *The Body* (SBT 5; London: SCM, 1952); E. Best, *One Body in Christ* (London: SPCK, 1955); P. Benoit, *Jesus and the Gospel* (New York: Seabury, 1974; French orig. 1956), 2.51–92; E. Schweizer, NTS 8 (1961–62), 1–11; B. A. Ahern, CBQ 23 (1961), 199–209; J. T. Culliton, CBQ 29 (1967), 41–59; A.J.M. Wedderburn, SJT 24 (1971), 74–96; D. J. Harrington, HJ 12 (1971), 246–57; 367–78; R. H. Gundry, *Sōma in Biblical Theology* (SNTSMS 29; Cambridge Univ., 1976); W. A. Meeks, GCHP 209–21; B. Daines, EvQ 54 (1982), 71–78; G. S. Worgul, BTB 12 (1982), 24–28; A. Perriman, EvQ 62 (1990), 123–42; G.L.O.R. Yorke, *The Church as the Body of Christ in the Pauline Corpus* (Lanham, MD: Univ. Press of America, 1991); J.D.G. Dunn, in *To Tell the Mystery,* eds. T. E. Schmidt and M. Silva (R. Gundry Festschrift; JSNTSup 100; Sheffield: JSOT, 1994), 163–81.

too literally the symbolism of Col. True, the historical Paul who wrote Phil 3:11–12,20–21 would not say that Christians are so totally glorified that they need not be taken up in a future bodily resurrection to meet the risen Christ; but Col 3:4, which refers to the final coming of Christ and the future glorification of Christians, shows that the writer of Col does not advocate such a totally realized eschatology. Once that misunderstanding is put aside, is being "raised with Christ" so far from the genuine Pauline thought that all died in Christ but now the risen Christ lives in Christians?[29]

The point being made at the end of the last paragraph is important in evaluating the theological arguments against Paul's writing Col. Many scholars work almost with a dialectic of thesis and antithesis. They are confident of the clarity of Paul's thought, which stemmed from the revelation he received, and they can judge with certainty what would be contradictory to it. (We saw an extreme form of that view in the opinion that would reject Rom 9–11 as unauthentic because Paul could not have thought thus about Israel.) Others evaluate the revelation to Paul of God's graciousness in Christ as offering a general theological orientation that was shaped and found articulation in the situations he encountered. Comparing Gal and Rom they can see a remarkable modification and maturing of expression influenced by the pastoral goal of Rom. The contention that Paul could not possibly have held the christological, ecclesiological, and eschatological views advanced in Col is overstated. Yet in itself the theological argument does strengthen the case against Paul's writing Col.

(4) False Teaching. F. C. Baur disallowed Paul as the writer of Col because the heresy described therein belonged to the 2d century. That is clearly exaggerated; but some scholars would contend that, although a struggle against Judaizers makes sense in Paul's lifetime, the struggle against the teaching described in Col (whether gnostic, or syncretistic, or mystery religion) makes better sense later. There is so much guesswork in diagnosing this teaching, however, that any argument for dating based on it is speculative in the extreme.

(5) Characters and Situation. An unusually solemn picture of Paul emerges from his self-designation in Col as apostle by the will of God (1:1), the minister (*diakonos*) of the gospel and of the church according to the economy of God (1:23–25). Epaphras is a fellow minister of Christ *on Paul's behalf* (1:7). The vicarious suffering of Paul for the Colossians is stressed (1:24). Some interpreters would see the writer of Col idealizing Paul, a fig-

[29]See II Cor 5:14–15; Gal 2:20; Phil 1:21. Although Rom 6:4–5 keeps Christian bodily resurrection in the future, it associates the Christian's new way of life with Christ's resurrection.

ure of the past, as a saint; he was "one of the first Christian writers to have a vision of Paul, 'the apostle and martyr'" (CLPDNW 206).

As for other characters, although the pseudonymity of II Thess was favored by the almost complete absence of references to dramatis personae and local situation, Col gives us those references in abundance and with remarkable similarity to Phlm. Besides Paul himself, ten people are named in Phlm: seven where Paul is imprisoned, and three at the place of destination.[30] Even if not in the same order, eight of these people are mentioned in Col: the same seven where Paul is imprisoned (plus two unmentioned in Phlm: Tychicus and Jesus Justus[31]), and one of the same people at the place of destination, Archippus (plus a woman or man named Nympha[s] unmentioned in Phlm). The only two from Phlm not mentioned in Col are Philemon and (his wife?) Apphia—an understandable absence since Phlm was sent to them to deal with a problem in their household that is not in focus in Col. How does one explain this similarity of the dramatis personae and the situation? There are two feasible solutions:[32]

(a) Both letters were written at about the same time by Paul himself (or at his directives by a scribe) and were being carried to the Colossae area in the same journey by Tychicus accompanied by Onesimus. This is by far the easiest solution. As we shall see in the next Chapter, some would add that Eph, a more general letter composed by Paul and addressed to different churches in the same area, was also included in the mail pouch. An objection to the simultaneity posited in this solution is that Onesimus has to be pleaded for in Phlm, whereas in Col 4:9 he seems to be an authoritative envoy.

(b) Paul wrote Phlm and another writer borrowed from it the dramatis personae and situation in order to compose Col.[33] In that hypothesis there are two time possibilities. If both letters were read in Colossae, Col might have been written by Timothy at about the same time that Paul wrote Phlm, perhaps because the rules of Paul's imprisonment had changed in a way that made further communication by his own hand or dictation impossible. Timo-

[30]Timothy (co-sender), Onesimus, Epaphras, Mark, Aristarchus, Demas, Luke, along with Philemon, Apphia, and Archippus. See G. E. Ladd, "Paul's Friends in Colossians 4:7–16," RevExp 70 (1973), 507–14.

[31]Phlm 23 speaks of "Epaphras, my fellow prisoner in Christ Jesus"; but a few would put punctuation between "Christ" and "Jesus," separating the latter name as referring to another of Paul's companions, namely this Jesus Justus mentioned in Col.

[32]The thesis that both letters are pseudonymous with fictional dramatis personae and situation does not have much following, since it is difficult to understand why such relatively unimportant background would have been created.

[33]Influence in the other direction is unlikely because one would scarcely take the trouble to formulate a fictional setting for so short a letter as Phlm. Another theoretical possibility, instead of the dependence of the writer of Col on a genuine Phlm, is dependence on genuine Pauline fragments (e.g., on 4:7–18) that have been incorporated into Col and edited under the influence of Eph.

thy is designated a co-sender, and he could speak authoritatively for Paul who had "no one like him" (Phil 2:20). Yet if Timothy had learned earlier what Paul intended to write to Colossae and was phrasing it on his own, he would really be serving as a type of scribe; and that would remove Col from being classified as pseudonymous in the strict sense. The more difficult possibility that Col was written by someone else years after Paul wrote Phlm is treated in the next subsection.

From Where and When?

The characters involved in Phlm and Col could not have stayed in the same place very long, and so in any solution the composition of Col has to be kept close to that of Phlm, whether in fact or in fiction. In some of the following suggestions one may hear an echo of E. Käsemann's principle: If Col is authentically from Paul's lifetime, date it as late as possible; if it is postPauline, date it as early as possible.

If Col was truly written by Paul when he was in prison,[34] the same three places of origin offered as possibilities for Phil can be invoked here (Rome, Ephesus, Caesarea). Although B. Reicke (along with Kümmel, Lohmeyer, and J.A.T. Robinson) has argued for Caesarea, most scholars reject that site for Col as a most unlikely base for an active missionary enterprise directed to inland Asia Minor. Consequently the choice has usually been between Rome and Ephesus, the two candidates discussed for Phlm in Chapter 21 above. For Phlm *taken alone,* on the assumption that Philemon lived in the Colossae region, geographical closeness made Ephesus more logical than Rome as the place from which the letter was sent; and nothing in the contents prevented a dating of Phlm *ca.* 55. Yet because the theology of Col seems developed and because parallels have been detected between Col and Rom (see Lohse, *Colossians* 182), Rome and a later dating *ca.* 61–63 are favored by most proponents of authenticity.[35] (Obviously then Phlm would also have to be attributed to that place and date.)

If Col was not written by Paul and the characters and situation were copied

[34]The imprisonment referred to in Col (and Phlm and Eph) seems much less oppressive and threatening than that referred to in Phil (1:20–23,29–30; 2:17). If written by Paul, Col may represent an earlier and milder stage of the same imprisonment described in Phil; or there were two different imprisonments. Of course, if Col and Eph are pseudonymous, the whole setting of imprisonment may be fictional, with the historical imprisonment of Phlm used metaphorically for Paul's suffering.

[35]Yet R. P. Martin, *Colossians* (NCBC) 22–32, argues strongly for Ephesus. In the late 2d century the Marcionite prologue to Col placed Paul's imprisonment at Ephesus; in the early 4th century Eusebius supported Rome, mentioning Aristarchus (Col 4:10) who went with Paul to Rome (Acts 27:2). The description of the imprisonment there (Acts 28:31) wherein Paul was allowed to preach openly and without hindrance befits the unapprehensive approach to imprisonment in Col.

from the genuinely Pauline Phlm, we have very little internal evidence for the place of origin or date of Col. From external evidence, seemingly Ignatius (writing *ca.* 110) knew Eph, and so that letter is not normally dated later than 100. Since the writer of Eph probably drew on Col (rather than vice versa), a date for Col no later than the 80s seems indicated. A number of the characters mentioned in Col (and Phlm) are associated in the NT with Rome (p. 508 above).[36] However, if the genuinely Pauline Phlm was written from Ephesus (as favored in Chapter 21 above), the dependence of Col on Phlm and the whole Lycus valley setting of Col, geographically close to Ephesus, make that city the most likely place of origin for a pseudonymous Col.

If one posits a considerable number of deuteroPauline letters, the existence of a Pauline school of disciples at Ephesus, who after Paul's death continued his heritage in the 80s, is not implausible.[37] Yet how could a writer of that school address Col to the Lycus River valley Christians who possessed the letter sent to Philemon twenty-five years previously?[38] Presumably it would have mattered to them if they knew that Col, despite surface appearances, was not actually written by Paul who had died long before. If therefore the writer desired to gloss over the pseudonymous character of the letter, he might have presented Col as stemming from long ago, namely, at the same time as Phlm, but only recently recovered. In the course of addressing the area around Colossae, now in ruins from an earthquake[39]—an area to a house-church of which Paul once wrote Phlm—the writer in the Pauline school of the 80s would be wrapping himself in the apostle's mantle by borrowing from Phlm the dramatis personae who constituted Paul's connection to the Lycus valley. A syncretistic false teaching now threatened the next generation of Christians there, and the writer's intention would have been to remind them of what Pauline missionaries had told them about Christ and to develop that christology to refute the new error.

No assurance is possible; but together the arguments tilt toward the school

[36]A postscript would place the origin of Eph at Rome, and that might support a Roman origin for Col.

[37]The suggestion has been made that the school was a continuation of the group of disciples that Paul had gathered in the lecture hall of Tyrannus at Ephesus (AD 54–56; Acts 19:9). For a Johannine school of writers, see pp. 370, 389 above—plausibly also at Ephesus.

[38]Remember that Phlm was not a purely private letter, for the community that met in Philemon's house was also addressed (Phlm 2). Other scenarios are imaginable, e.g., Phlm was never actually sent but remained in the possession of the Ephesus school.

[39]A major earthquake devastated Laodicea in AD 60–61 and presumably the other two cities as well. Nothing in Col suggests a catastrophe in the recent past. Some think that Colossae was not rebuilt or was reduced to a village; numismatic evidence for the continuance there of a Roman city appears in the *next* century. The list of names in Col 4:7–17 may indicate a small Christian community, so that no large resettlement need be posited.

position mentioned in the last paragraph. What is assured is that Col belongs in the Pauline heritage. I am treating it in the deuteroPauline section of this *Introduction* because that is how most critical scholars now treat it.

Issues and Problems for Reflection

(1) The Col hymn professes that Christ Jesus is the image of the invisible God—God's Son in whom all things were created, in whom all the fullness of God was pleased to dwell, and through whom all things were reconciled to God. How within fifty years (at the latest) did Christians come to believe that about a Galilean preacher who was crucified as a criminal? Like the other NT hymns, Col 1:15–20 offers a challenge to understanding the development of NT christology (see BINTC). Given the fact that most scholars judge hymns in the Pauline letters to be prePauline or nonPauline in origin, one should note where "high" christological statements in those hymns are similar to statements in the prose of the undisputed letters, e.g., compare Col 1:16 and I Cor 8:6.

(2) Against the philosophy of the false teachers Paul describes a Christ who is preeminent, superior to every principality or power. This message was written to a 1st-century Christian community that had been brought into existence a relatively brief time before. What does such preeminence mean today when believing Christians represent a minority percentage of the world's population and there are few signs of Christ's superiority to what now pass for principalities and powers?

(3) The issue of who composed Col has importance, e.g., in knowing how far ecclesiology had advanced in Paul's lifetime. However, whether written in Paul's lifetime or afterward among a school of Pauline disciples, Col describes the church as the body of Christ and envisions the apostle as having suffered for the sake of Christ's body, the church. There are many Christians today, however, who profess a love of Christ but not for the church, even though the Nicene Creed, after three "We believe" clauses covering the Father, the Son, and the Spirit, has a fourth clause that reads, "We believe in one, holy, catholic, and apostolic church." How does Col speak to this dilemma?

(4) Compare the five household codes in the NT (n. 20 above) and the differences among them (both as to groups mentioned in one and not another, and the tone of the instructions). Are the differences plausibly explicable from the respective social situations of the 1st-century communities addressed? On p. 609 above questions were raised about how to interpret the force of these codes today.

(5) Moule (*Colossians* 47–48) uses Col 1:3–14 to reflect on the substance and shape of prayer according to the Pauline tradition. It is a very interesting exercise to compare the beginnings of Paul's letters to see what he prays for.

(6) Col 4:10 identifies Mark as "the cousin of Barnabas," and 4:14 describes Luke as "the beloved physician." These identifications are lacking in Phlm 24. Are we seeing here a developing hagiography? Other NT works report more about Mark and Luke (pp. 158–60, 267 above) that is worthwhile analyzing in response to this question.

Bibliography on Colossians

COMMENTARIES AND STUDIES IN SERIES (* = plus Phlm; ** = plus Eph; *** = plus Phlm, Eph; **** = plus Phlm, Eph, Phil): Abbott, T. K. (ICC, 1897**); Barth, M., and S. Blanke (AB, 1994); Bruce, F. F. (NICNT, 1984***); Burgess, J. (ProcC, 1978); Caird, G. B. (NClarBC, 1976****); Dunn, J.D.G. (NIGTC, 1996*); Houlden, J. L. (PC, 1970****); Hultgren, A. J. (ProcC, 1993); **Lohse, E.** (Hermeneia, 1971*); Martin, R. P. (NCBC, 2d ed. 1978*; IBC, 1992***); Moule, C.F.D. (CGTC, 1962*); Mussner, F. (NTSR, 1971); O'Brien, P. T. (WBC, 1982*); Patzia, A. G. (NIBC, 1990***); Reumann, J. (AugC, 1985); Rogers, P. V. (NTM, 1980); Wedderburn, A.J.M. (NTT, 1993); Yates, R. (EC, 1993).

Anderson, C. P., "Who Wrote 'The Epistle from Laodicea'?" JBL 85 (1966), 436–40.

Arnold, C. E., *The Colossian Syncretism* (Grand Rapids: Baker, 1996).

Baggott, L. J., *A New Approach to Colossians* (London: Mowbray, 1961).

Barbour, R. S., "Salvation and Cosmology: The Setting of the Epistle to the Colossians," SJT 20 (1967), 257–71.

Bornkamm, G., "The Heresy of Colossians," CAC 123–45.

Brown, R. E.,** "The Pauline Heritage in Colossians/Ephesians," BCALB 47–60.

Bruce, F. F., "St. Paul in Rome, 3. The Epistle to the Colossians," BJRL 48 (1966), 268–85.

Cannon, G. E., *The Use of Traditional Materials in Colossians* (Macon, GA: Mercer, 1983).

Collins, R. F., CLPDNW 171–208.

Cope, L.,* "On Rethinking the Philemon-Colossians Connection," BR 30 (1985), 45–50.

De Maris, R. E., *The Colossian Controversy* (JSNTSup 96; Sheffield: Academic, 1994).

Dunn, J.D.G., "The Colossian Philosophy: A Confident Jewish Apologia," *Biblica* 76 (1995), 153–81.

Evans, C. A., "The Colossian Mystics," *Biblica* 63 (1982), 188–205.

Francis, F. O., "The Christological Argument of Colossians," in *God's Christ and His People,* eds. W. A. Meeks and J. Jervell (N. A. Dahl Festschrift; Oslo: Universitetsforlaget, 1977), 192–208.

———, ed., CAC. (A collection of significant essays).

Harris, M. J.,* *Colossians and Philemon* (Grand Rapids: Eerdmans, 1991).

Hartman, L., "Humble and Confident. On the So-Called Philosophers in Colossians," *Studia Theologica* 49 (1995), 25–39.

Hooker, M. D., "Were There False Teachers in Colossae?" in *Christ and Spirit in the New Testament,* eds. B. Lindars and S. S. Smalley (C.F.D. Moule Festschrift; Cambridge Univ., 1973), 315–31.

Kiley, M., *Colossians as Pseudepigraphy* (The Biblical Seminar; Sheffield: JSOT, 1986).

Knox, J.,* "Philemon and the Authenticity of Colossians," JR 18 (1938), 144–60.

Lightfoot, J. B.,* *St. Paul's Epistles to the Colossians and to Philemon* (London: Macmillan, 1892). A classic.

Lyonnet, S., "Paul's Adversaries in Colossae," CAC 147–61.

Martin, R. P., *Colossians. The Church's Lord and the Christian's Liberty* (Grand Rapids: Zondervan, 1973).

Martin, T. W., *By Philosophy and Empty Deceit. Colossians as Response to a Cynic Critique* (JSNTSup 118; Sheffield: Academic, 1996).

O'Neill, J. C., "The Source of the Christology in Colossians," NTS 26 (1979–80), 87–100.

Pokorný, P., *Colossians. A Commentary* (Peabody, MA: Hendrickson, 1991).

Reicke, B., "The Historical Setting of Colossians," RevExp 70 (1993), 429–53.

Robertson, A. T., *Paul and the Intellectuals: The Epistle to the Colossians* (Garden City, NY: Doubleday, 1928).

Rowland, C., "Apocalyptic Visions and the Exaltation of Christ in the Letter to the Colossians," JSNT 19 (1983), 73–83.

Sanders, E. P., "Literary Dependence in Colossians," JBL 85 (1966), 28–45.

Saunders, E. W., "The Colossian Heresy and Qumran Theology," in *Studies in the History and Text of the New Testament,* eds. B. L. Daniels and M. J. Suggs (K. W. Clark Festschrift; Salt Lake City: Univ. of Utah, 1967), 133–45.

Schweizer, E., *The Letter to the Colossians* (Minneapolis: Augsburg, 1982).

CHAPTER 28

EPISTLE (LETTER) TO THE EPHESIANS

Among the Pauline writings only Rom can match Eph as a candidate for exercising the most influence on Christian thought and spirituality. Indeed Eph, which has been called the "crown of Paulinism" (C. H. Dodd), is more attractive to many because it spares them the complex argumentation of Rom. Especially appealing to an ecumenical age is the magnificent Eph view of the church universal and of unity among Christians. The writer has been called the supreme interpreter of the apostle (before the appearance of Martin Luther, some Protestants would add) and "Paul's best disciple."

Who is this writer? Already in the 16th century Erasmus, noting that the style of Eph with its ponderous sentences is quite different from that of Paul's main letters, thought that Eph could be by someone else. In 1792 E. Evanson queried Paul's authorship; and throughout the 19th century arguments against Paul as a writer were presented with increasing systematicization. Yet even in the 20th century there have been major defenses of Paul as the writer (E. Percy in German in 1946; M. Barth and A. van Roon in 1974). A fair estimate might be that *at the present moment about 80 percent of critical scholarship holds that Paul did not write Eph.* After the *General Analysis* treats the basic message of the letter as it comes to us (in which Paul is presented as the sender[1]), subsections will be devoted to: *Ecclesiology of Eph and "Early Catholicism," To whom and by whom, What genre, Background of the ideas, Issues for reflection,* and *Bibliography.*

General Analysis of the Message

Paul is a prisoner for the Lord (3:1; 4:1; 6:20), and Tychicus is being sent to tell the recipients about him (6:21–22). Otherwise there is no story in Eph, recounting Paul's past dealings with the audience or any details about them.

[1]My only presupposition is that "in Ephesus" was lacking in the original ms. of 1:1 (p. 626 below), and so the letter was addressed "To the saints who are also faithful in Christ Jesus."

part of the letter with a doxology, almost as if just thinking about Christ causes him to praise God (3:20–21).

The IMPERATIVE OR PARAENETIC SECTION OF THE BODY (4:1–6:20) explicates the implications of this great plan of God with thirty-six verbs in the imperative.[6] In 1:4 Paul said that God chose "us" in Christ before the foundation of the world to be holy and without blemish in the divine presence. In 4:1 he leads into directives for living a life worthy of such a calling. First, Paul spells out seven manifestations of oneness in the Christian life (4:4–6).[7] He continues by pointing out how the ascended Christ[8] poured forth a diversity of gifts to equip Christians for building up the body of Christ: apostles, prophets, evangelists, pastors, and teachers (4:7–12). When such gifts were discussed in I Cor 12, they were dividing Christians; now without having to correct people, Paul can proclaim that they help "the saints" attain to the unity of faith, to the measure of the stature of the fullness (*plērōma*) of Christ, and thus to grow up into Christ the head of the body (4:13–16).[9]

Since Gentiles and Jews have been made one, Christian Gentiles are no longer in dark ignorance and cannot live in the uncleanness and lusts of their former life (4:17–24). In 2:15 Paul spoke of Christ's work in creating a new human being from Jew and Gentile, and now he instructs this new human being not to live according to the old pattern of life. The rules for a new life reflect the demands of the Ten Commandments about how not to treat others (4:25–5:5). Paul sees two contrasting ways of "walking," corresponding to light and darkness, to the devil and the Holy Spirit, to truth and falsehood. This dualism produces children of light and sons of disobedience (5:6–20), the wise and the unwise. The Christians who have been addressed in 1:1 as saints are to have no part in the unfruitful works of darkness. The "Awake, O sleeper . . ." of 5:14 probably comes from a hymn.[10] Rather than carousing, Christians are to sing and make melody to the Lord.

Eph 5:21–6:9 specifies the way of Christian life in terms of a household code for *wives*/husbands, *children*/fathers, *slaves*/masters. The overall pat-

[6]D. E. Garland and R. A. Culpepper treat Eph 4:1–24 and 4:25–5:20 in RevExp 76 (1979), 517–27, 529–39.

[7]Also noteworthy as signs of unity are some ten instances of verbs and nouns beginning with *syn*, "together with," e.g., 2:6: raised up together with and seated together; 2:21: joined/held together with; 3:6: heirs together with.

[8]On the descent-ascent of Christ, see G. B. Caird, StEv II (1964), 535–45. Sometimes the pattern has been compared to Johannine christology.

[9]Unlike the pressing admonition about the false philosophy and angel worship in Col 2:8–23, the reference in Eph 4:14 to the danger of being tossed about by every wind of doctrine and by human cunning is both brief and general. It could be applicable in any time or place without anything specific in mind.

[10]Does the "arise from the dead" mean that the resurrection takes place at baptism? (See also 2:5–6 and the discussion of the realized eschatology of Col on pp. 612–13 above.) Eph does not speak of a future resurrection of Christians or of the parousia.

tern of the subjection/obedience of the first party, and the obligation of the second party (to whom subjection is due) to exemplify characteristics of Christ are the same as in the household code of Col 3:18–4:1; but the Eph code is a third longer than that of Col, and there are interesting differences. Eph (5:21) begins with an instruction to be subject to one another out of reverence for Christ; and, of course, that affects husbands to wives, as well as wives to husbands. Thus the opening of this code modifies more radically the established order than did the code in Col. The lyric language of 5:25–27 (sometimes thought to come from a baptismal hymn) brings Christ and the church into the relationship of husband and wife, so that respectively the subjection and the love are given a uniquely Christian stamp. The obligation of the husband to love is treated more extensively than the obligation of the wife to be subject, and both are rooted in God's initial plan for union in marriage (5:31 = Gen 2:24).[11] The children/fathers instruction is also fortified with an OT motif. The Eph change in the slave/master relationship is largely in the master section: Not only should the master be impartial in treating the slaves as in Col; he should forbear threatening—with the reminder that Christ is the master of the master. The radical thrust of the gospel is putting pressure on those who have authority and power.

Employing the figurative language of armor and weapons, a final exhortation concerns the ongoing battle with the principalities and powers (Eph 6:10–20).[12] We have heard that the exalted Christ has been seated above all such powers (1:20–21) and that the mysterious plan of God for all has been made known to them through the church (3:9–10). Yet now we discover that such realized eschatology has not entirely replaced future eschatology, for the divine struggle with the powers and the rulers of the present darkness continues. Paul asks for prayers for himself that in this struggle he may be allowed to proclaim the mystery of the gospel. The magnificent final self-description as "an ambassador in chains" (6:20) capsulizes the motif of triumphing with God's help; no human hindrance can prevent Paul from pursuing the vocation he announced at the beginning: "an apostle of Christ Jesus by the will of God" (1:1).

In the CONCLUDING FORMULA (6:21–24) minimal greetings refer to one companion, Tychicus, who is being sent to the addressees as in Col 4:7–8.

[11]J. P. Sampley, *"And the Two Shall Become One Flesh": A Study of Traditions in Ephesians 5:21–33* (SNTSMS 16; Cambridge Univ., 1971). Here Eph agrees with I Cor 6:9 by rooting the Christian attitude toward marriage in the creation story, even as did Jesus (Mark 10:7–8; p. 141 above).

[12]R. A. Wild, CBQ 46 (1984), 284–98.

Ecclesiology of Ephesians and Early Catholicism

Worthy of special comment is Eph's exaltation of the church that goes beyond the already high estimation in Col. Even though Col had a universal concept of "church," half of its four uses of *ekklēsia* were to local church (4:15,16); there is no such local reference in the nine uses in Eph. These are all in the singular and designate the universal church. As in Col 1:18,24, the church is Christ's body and he is the head (Eph 1:22; 5:23). Yet in Eph the church has a cosmic role. According to the most common interpretation of 1:21–23 Christ has been made head over all things (including angelic powers) "for the church," and through the church (3:10) the wisdom of God is made manifest to those powers. Glory is given to God in the church (3:20). Christ loved the church and gave himself over for her (5:25)—that is different from the idea that Christ died for sinners (Rom 5:6,8) or for all (II Cor 5:14–15). Christ's goal was to sanctify the church, cleansing her by the washing of water with the word, rendering her without spot or blemish. He continues to nourish and cherish her (Eph 5:23–32).[13] In Chapter 27 above, *Issue* 3, I commented that many Christians today might have problems with the Col picture of Paul offering his sufferings for the sake of the church. How much more might they have a problem with the Eph picture where the church is the goal of Christ's ministry and death!

This is a convenient moment to mention briefly the issue of "Early Catholicism," which the ecclesiology of Eph is thought to exemplify. The term designates the initial stages of high ecclesiology, sacramentalism, hierarchy, ordination, and dogma—in short the beginning of the distinctive features of *Catholic* Christianity. At the beginning of the 20th century A. von Harnack suggested that there was no early Catholicism in the NT; rather, such theology and church organization were a development that began in the 2d century under the influence of the Greek spirit, distorting the pristine evangelical character of Christianity (to which the Reformation returned). In a challenge to that position E. Käsemann has been prominent in contending that there is "Early Catholicism" in the NT itself, but that these developments were not necessarily normative for Christianity.[14] He resorted to the principle of "the canon within the canon." Just as Paul distinguished between

[13]See Sampley, "*And.*" On aspects of Eph ecclesiology, see S. Hanson, *The Unity of the Church in the New Testament: Colossians and Ephesians* (Uppsala Univ., 1946); B. M. Metzger, *Theology Today* 6 (1949–50), 49–63; C. F. Mooney, *Scripture* 15 (1963), 33–43; J. Gnilka, TD 20 (1972), 35–39; J. L. Houlden, StEv VI (1973), 267–73; F.-J. Steinmetz, TD 35 (1988), 227–32.

[14]See Chapter 2 above, n. 40; Harnack, *What* 190ff; Käsemann, "Ministry and Community in the New Testament," in KENTT (Germ. orig. 1949), 63–134; "Paul and Early Catholicism," in *New Testament Questions of Today* (Philadelphia: Fortress, 1967; Germ. orig., 1963), 236–51; Küng, *Structures* 151–69; L. Sabourin, *Theology Digest* 35 (1988), 239–43; R. E. Brown, NJBC 66.92–97.

the letter and the Spirit (II Cor 3), so the Christian cannot make an infallible authority out of the canonical NT but must distinguish the real Spirit within the NT. In relation to Paul, for Käsemann (a Lutheran) one cannot appeal to the deuteroPauline writings as the authoritative interpreters of the gospel of Paul; one is closer to that in Gal and Rom with their spirit of justification by faith.

There is an arbitrariness, however, in this type of judgment, for it asserts the right to reject those voices in the NT with which one does not agree. Other Christians and even churches may be less explicit in their judgment; but in fact, even if it is only through a lectionary, all tend to give more weight to some parts of the NT than to others. A church that stresses the ecclesiology of Eph, for instance, most likely does so because its own high ecclesiology resembles it. In any real solution one must recognize that there are important differences among the NT books on issues such as ecclesiology, sacramentalism, and church structure. A church (or a Christian) may make a theological decision to give preference to one view over another. Yet an awareness of what is said in the NT on the other side of an issue can modify some of the exaggerated or objectionable features of one's own position. Repeating the NT passages that support one's views may give reassurance, but listening to the scriptural voices on the opposing side enables the NT to act as a conscience.

To Whom and By Whom?

(1) To WHOM? The directional address is dubious textually; for the italicized phrase in 1:1b, "To the saints who are *in Ephesus* and/also (the) faithful in Christ Jesus," is lacking in important mss.[15] Other factors also call into question whether the letter was directed to the Ephesian Christians. Somewhere in most of his letters Paul mentions pertinent personal circumstances or previous activities, and toward the end he usually includes greetings from and to named people who are meaningful to the community addressed. These are absent from Eph with the exception of a reference to Paul's chains and to Tychicus (6:20–21). Paul had spent some three years at Ephesus (AD 54–57; Acts 20:31); and so it is almost inconceivable that in a friendly letter to Christians there he would not have included some greetings and reminis-

[15]In the Chester Beatty Papyrus II (P^{46}; *ca.* 200), the original hand of the important 4th-century Codices Sinaiticus and Vaticanus, and the text used by Origen and probably by Marcion (who called this letter "To the Laodiceans") and Tertullian. Some argue that Laodicean title was original but changed to Ephesus because of the bad reputation of Laodicea (Rev 3:15–16). For all the possibilities, see E. Best in *Text and Interpretation,* eds. E. Best and R. M. Wilson (M. Black Festschrift; Cambridge Univ., 1979), 29–41; and PAP 273–79.

cences. Moreover, in Eph 1:15 the writer says, "I have *heard* of your faith in the Lord Jesus." In 3:2 he assumes that the recipients have "heard" of his stewardship of God's grace, and in 3:7–13 he explains his ministry to them. How could Paul speak so indirectly of his relations to the Ephesian Christians? Eph 2:14 seems to treat as a fait accompli the breaking down of the wall of enmity between the community of Israel and the Gentiles; it is not patent that this had been accomplished in Ephesus or in the other communities of the Pauline mission during Paul's lifetime. Indeed, since Eph never mentions Jews and 2:11 speaks to "you, Gentiles in the flesh," one has the impression that Eph is addressed to a community that is entirely Gentile. That is scarcely true of the situation envisaged in Acts 19:10 in the mid 50s, when the Ephesian mission had converted "Jews and Gentiles alike." Thus, of the thirteen letters in the NT that carry the name of Paul, Eph, the least situational, may have been the only one not directed to a destination more specific than to Christians (probably chiefly in Asia Minor) who regarded Paul as a great apostle.

That Eph could be directed to any of or all the saints in Christ Jesus has led a number of scholars (beginning with Archbishop Ussher in the 17th century) to envision it as a circular letter meant to be read in many different cities, with a space left blank for the name of the individual site to be filled in each time. (Thus, the mss. that have "in Ephesus" would preserve the copy read at Ephesus; Marcion's ms. was of the one read at Laodicea.) However, evidence for the use of such letters in early Christianity is insufficient, particularly for the blank-space idea. A more common approach (to be discussed below) is that another genre of literature has been adapted to the letter form.

(2) BY WHOM? *The relationship to Col.* If Eph is not really a letter to the Ephesian Christians but some type of more general work, who wrote it?[16] In the preceding chapter, we discussed with a fair amount of detail the issue of whether Paul wrote Col and found that the evidence favored, but not conclusively, a writer other than Paul. In striking ways Eph resembles Col in overall structure and verbal parallels. That may be calculated in various ways, e.g., between one third and one half of the 155 verses in Eph are parallel to Col both in order and content. One quarter of the words of Eph are found in Col, and one third of the words of Col are found in Eph.[17] Table 7 as presented

[16]See in Cross, *Studies* 9–35, the debate over the Pauline writing of Eph (for, J. N. Sanders; against, D. E. Nineham).

[17]See J. Coutts, NTS 4 (1957–58), 201–7; J. B. Polhill, RevExp 70 (1975), 439–50. Particularly close are Eph 1:1–2 to Col 1:1–2; Eph 1:22–23 to Col 1:17–19; Eph 2:13–18 to Col 1:20–22; Eph 4:16 to Col 2:19; Eph 5:19–20 to Col 3:16; Eph 5:22–6:9 to Col 3:18–4:1 (with considerable verbal agreement); and Eph 6:21–22 to Col 4:7–8.

TABLE 7. COMPARING EPHESIANS AND COLOSSIANS

Topic	*Eph*	*Col*
(1) Redemption, forgiveness	1:7	1:14,20
(2) The all-inclusive Christ	1:10	1:20
(3) Intercession for the readers	1:15–17	1:3–4,9
(4) Riches of a glorious inheritance	1:18	1:27 (hope of glory)
(5) Christ's dominion	1:21–22	1:16–18
(6) You he made alive	2:5	2:13
(7) Aliens brought near	2:12–13	1:21–22
(8) Abolishing the commandments	2:15	2:14
(9) Paul the prisoner	3:1	1:24
(10) Divine mystery made known to Paul	3:2–3	1:25–26
(11) Paul, minister of universal gospel	3:7	1:23,25
(12) Paul to make known the mystery to all	3:8–9	1:27
(13) Lead a life worthy of your calling	4:1	1:10
(14) With all lowliness, meekness, patience forbearing one another	4:2	3:12–13
(15) Christ unites members of church	4:15–16	2:19
(16) Put off old nature and put on new nature	4:22–32	3:5–10,12
(17) No immorality among you	5:3–6	3:5–9
(18) Walk wisely and make the most of the time	5:15	4:5
(19) Sing songs, hymns, and spiritual songs, giving thanks to God	5:19–20	3:16–17
(20) Tables of household duties for husbands, wives, children, parents, slaves, and masters	5:21–6:9	3:18–4:1
(21) Paul the prisoner exhorts persistence in prayer	6:18–20	4:2–3
(22) Tychicus sent to inform church about Paul and to encourage them	6:21–22	4:7–8

here shows parallel topics.[18] Inevitably the vocabulary, style, and theology arguments that were invoked against the Pauline writing of Col (pp. 610–13 above) have been invoked against the Pauline writing of Eph. The vocabulary argument that Eph has some eighty words not found in the undisputed Pauline letters[19] loses much of its force when we know that about the same number may be found in Gal which matches Eph roughly in length and in the number of diverse words it uses. Other data are more noteworthy: A florid style is like that of Col but even more expansive and hyperbolic (e.g., almost fifty uses of "all"), producing sentences of remarkable length like Eph 1:3–14 and 4:11–16.[20] There are piled up adjectives and genitives, and

[18]Adapted from Puskas, *Letters* 130–31, with the kind permission of the author and of the Liturgical Press. The "topics" are derived from Eph and follow its order. A more elaborate table of parallels is offered by Moffatt, *Introd. NT* 375–81, who prints out the wording of the passages.

[19]Of note: *Satanas* is used seven times in the undisputed Pauline letters, never *diabolos,* which is used twice in Eph.

[20]C. J. Robbins, JBL 105 (1986), 677–87, points out that the lengthy sentence is characteristic of the periodic structure described by the Greek rhetoricians.

redundant style and terms quite uncharacteristic of the Pauline usage in the undisputed letters. Also there are differences between Col and Eph that complicate a judgment about the writer. Eph is longer and has bodies of material lacking in Col, e.g., much of the hymn in Eph 1:3–14 and the paraenesis in 4:1–14. On the other hand, the attack on the false philosophy in Col 2 and the long set of greetings in Col 4 are missing in Eph. Shared motifs like "body," "head," "fullness," "mystery," and "reconciliation" often have a somewhat different tone in Eph.[21] In discussing the message we have seen other differences, e.g., in the household codes and ecclesiology.

Although some scholars continue to accept Paul as the writer of Eph,[22] the thrust of the evidence has pushed 70 to 80 percent of critical scholarship to reject that view, including a significant number who think that Paul wrote Col. Within that percentage *probably most would posit a writer of Eph different from the person who composed Col.*[23] Other aspects of Eph must now be examined to determine more about that writer.

(3) BY WHOM? *The relationship to the other Pauline letters.* On a much lesser scale than the similarity between Eph and Col, parallels between Eph and the other Pauline letters have been recognized. A careful list of parallels to the seven undisputed letters (with dubious evidence for II Thess) is given in G. Johnston, IDB 2.110–11; the most impressive are to Rom, I-II Cor, and Gal.[24] If Paul wrote Eph, he could have drawn on his previous writings (if they were available to him in prison); yet would he have been likely to reuse them in this fashion? We have seen that in a sense Rom is the first commentary on Gal, but Paul's use of themes from Gal in Rom represents the refinement of his own ideas by an innovative thinker facing a new situation. Most scholars would interpret the reuse of Pauline letters in Eph as a more secondary procedure.

[21]While in Col the mystery revealed in Christ is God's plan of salvation for the Gentiles, in Eph the mystery is the union of Jews and Gentiles in the same body of Christ (3:3–6)—indeed, the union of all things in heaven and on earth in him (1:9–10).

[22]A few scholars have argued that Paul wrote Eph and that someone else digested its ideas into Col. If Paul wrote both letters, Col might have been written at the end of the "first" Roman imprisonment (AD 61–63) and Eph just a bit later from the same situation, or else (on the evidence of the Pastorals that Paul left Rome and returned again) during the "second" Roman imprisonment (*ca.* 64–66). Yet since Tychicus, who carried the letter to Colossae (Col 4:7–8), seems to have carried Eph as well (Eph 6:21–22), some have theorized that Paul wrote Phlm, Col, and Eph at the same time and sent them with Tychicus: Phlm to Philemon and his house-church as a recommendation for Onesimus; Col to the community at Colossae; Eph to be read more generally to various churches in the same area (Johnson, *Writings* 354).

[23]That means more than simply a different penman taking dictation from the writer of Col, for greater freedom of expression is posited. E. Best, NTS 43 (1997), 72–96, argues that the relationship of Eph to Col does not stem from written copying but from discussions between two Pauline disciples.

[24]If there are parallels between Eph and the Pastoral Letters (Eph 2:3–7 and Titus 3:3–7), the dependence may be on the part of the latter. Parallels to Luke-Acts and Rev are debatable; and the more impressive ones to I Pet (n. 31 below) may represent dependence on a common tradition.

An adventurous explanation was proposed by Goodspeed and supported in part by Knox. It expands the idea that the slave Onesimus was released by Philemon and came back to Ephesus to become the bishop there several decades after Paul's death (see Chapter 21 above, *Subsequent career*). Interest in Paul had been catalyzed by the appearance of Acts; and that inspired Onesimus to gather in Ephesus copies of the letters, and to compose from them Eph as a summary of Paul's ideas, placing it at the head of the collection.[25] The special closeness to Col is explicable because, next to Phlm, that was the letter with which Onesimus was most involved, having accompanied Tychicus, who carried it to Colossae.

Although Goodspeed's theory is attractive, it is almost totally a guess and has little following. Other guesses identifying the writer as a known disciple of Paul include *Timothy* because he is thought to be the scribe who wrote Col, *Tychicus* because he is mentioned in both Col and Eph (Mitton), and *Luke* because of a proposed connection of Eph with Acts.[26] It is noteworthy that such proposals often involve a Pauline disciple working with collected Pauline letters at Ephesus. The theory of a pseudonymous Col posits the existence of a Pauline school at Ephesus, a member of which in the 80s composed Col, using background material from Phlm. That school might very well have been the context for gathering Paul's letters.[27] *A plausible theory, then, would be that on the basis of the undisputed Pauline letters and especially of Col* (*which had been composed in the school earlier*) *someone in the Ephesian school of Paul's disciples produced Eph as an encouraging portrayal of aspects of Pauline thought.* If "in Ephesus" was missing from the original, it may have been added in a copy by a scribe who knew that the composition of the letter was connected with that city.[28] A control for dating a pseudonymous Eph to the 90s is generally thought to be supplied by reminiscence of Eph 5:25,29 in the letter written by Ignatius *ca.* 110 to *Polycarp* (5:1), bishop of Smyrna, thirty-five miles north of Ephesus. Probably, too, by the 90s there was at least an incipient collection of Paul's letters on which the writer of Eph could have drawn.

[25]In fact, however, Eph is not placed first in any known ancient listing or collection of Paul's letters.

[26]See the list of parallels in Puskas, *Letters* 133–34. Some are rather tenuous. See also E. Käsemann in SLA 288–97. Acts 20:17–38 directs to the elders of Ephesus Paul's last words to the churches he founded.

[27]Claims that the thought of Eph has resemblances to that of John (e.g., Allan), traditionally associated with Ephesus, may also favor Ephesus as the place of composition. Although Eph is a "captivity letter," the question of which of Paul's three imprisonments was the setting is not really important if one thinks that the letter is deuteroPauline and the references to imprisonment have been borrowed from Col.

[28]Or else it represented an early guess by a copyist as to a possible destination.

What Genre?

In the preceding section I spoke with deliberate vagueness under (1) of "another genre of literature adapted to the letter form" and under (3) of an "encouraging portrayal of aspects of Pauline thought." The resemblances to a letter are marginal; but the ancient Greek letter form went beyond letters in the strict sense (p. 410 above), so that Eph could almost function as a speech or address given to the audience of Pauline churches. It may be a writing that straddles Deissmann's dividing line between "Epistles" and "Letters." Many scholars have made an effort to be precise, with the assumption that the minimal elements of letter format (1:1–2 and 6:21–22) borrowed from Col are only incidental to the message. Theological tractate, manifesto, meditation, and homily are some of the proposed descriptions. Soards (*Apostle* 153) may be close to the most common view when he speaks of synthesizing and developing Pauline themes to produce "a grand Pauline theology in the form of a standard Pauline communication . . . for a new time and place." There are, in fact, passages in Eph that do summarize characteristic Pauline thought, e.g., 2:8–10;[29] yet Eph is scarcely a comprehensive summary, for only a few aspects, such as unity, triumphal ecclesiology, and exalted christology, are stressed.

Those more interested in formal analysis have concentrated on the congratulatory tone of Eph and spoken of epideictic rhetoric (p. 412 above), specifically a letter using praise as a basis for an appeal (often to a more authoritative audience). Paul, however, is a superior figure, a saintly apostle idealized as "*the* prisoner" for Christ in 3:1; 4:1. What he writes is not so much praise of the recipients as enthusiastic evaluation of what has been achieved in Christ for all Christians and indeed for the whole universe.[30] Rather than appealing, he encourages growth in the Christian life—thus general exhortations not prompted by any specific problems.

A strong context of communal prayer has been detected in Eph. In that vein, another thesis finds baptismal language in 1:13–14; 4:5,30; 5:8,26 (see Kirby, *Ephesians*) and would see Eph as a fuller teaching to those who had recently been baptized, whence the encouraging tone. The closeness of Eph to I Pet, often thought to be a baptismal homily, has contributed to this thesis.[31] (Even without a specific orientation to baptism, however, the writer,

[29]A. T. Lincoln, "Ephesians 2:8–10: A Summary of Paul's Gospel," CBQ 45 (1983), 617–30.

[30]H. L. Hendrix, *Union Seminary Quarterly Review* 42 (1988), 3–15, compares Eph to honorary decrees inscribed to celebrate benefactors; these would offer parallels to the ponderous grammatical constructions and the hyperbole.

[31]Compare Eph 1:3 to I Pet 1:3; Eph 1:20–21 to I Pet 3:22; Eph 2:19–22 to I Pet 2:5–6,9; Eph 3:4–5 to I Pet 1:10–12. See J. Coutts NTS 3 (1956–57), 115–27. Puskas, *Letters* 139–40, thinks of

consciously or unconsciously, may have used theological language familiar to him and his addressees from a common Christian tradition already being taught at baptism.) The fact that the first half of Eph (the "doctrinal" section; see Summary Page) starts and ends with a doxology and a prayer has suggested to some a liturgical background. Kirby, *Ephesians,* would find in chaps. 1–3 the pattern of a Jewish blessing, perhaps for use at the eucharist, and in various parts of Eph echoes of a Pentecost covenant-renewal ceremony.

Conclusion: Without being too specific about the precise literary form, we may make the following observations. *Paul's undisputed letters in the 50s* show a man wrestling with the issue of the return of Christ and the general fate of Christians, as well as struggling with Jewish Christians who insisted on circumcision for Gentiles and the works of the Law. For those who believe, he invoked a Jesus put to death for their trespasses and raised for their justification. Most of Israel did not accept Jesus' claims; nevertheless Paul proclaimed that eventually they would. Although he had success among the Gentiles, he reminded them that they were only a wild olive branch grafted on the tree of Israel. Believers are united in Christ's (risen) body, having been baptized into him; and they should live in anticipation of Christ's return amid trumpet blasts. *In Eph* those struggles seem past,[32] and Paul's mission is triumphing. He who once described himself as the least of all the apostles (I Cor 15:9) is now described as the least of all the saints (Eph 3:8). His career is seen as an integral part of the mysterious plan of God for the whole of creation in Christ (3:1–12). To the Paul of Eph has been given an understanding, not only of the redemption accomplished by the crucifixion/resurrection, but also of the full plan of God where everything in heaven and earth is subject to an exalted Christ and united in him. This is visible in the church that is now seen as the chef d'oeuvre of Christ's accomplishment, since Jews and Gentiles, without losing their own identity, have been made one in the church.[33] The Paul of Eph does not need to em-

---

Eph as a baptismal homily adapted for general circulation among the churches of western Asia by being put in letter format by a writer from the community where it was proclaimed. Some would see the relationship to I Pet as an argument for the origin of Eph in Rome.

[32]There is only one reference to the Law in Eph (2:14–15): Christ "has broken down the dividing wall of hostility in his flesh, having abolished the law of commandments with its ordinances." On this, see C. J. Roetzel, ZNW 74 (1983), 81–89.

[33]Some scholars think that Eph was written as a universalist corrective, to reprove both Jewish Christian exclusion of Gentiles, and Gentile Christian exclusivism that would scrap the salvation-history heritage from Israel or dissociate Christianity from a Judaism now regarded by the Romans as dangerous because of the Jewish Revolt of 66–70. The text of Eph, however, has a joyful air of achieved unity that reinforces the addressees by reminding them of this marvel accomplished by God through Christ—it does not reprove or warn them. The paraenetic section (Eph 4:1–6:20) is so general that no specific threat, e.g., gnostic libertinism, need be posited.

phasize the second coming because so much has already been accomplished in Christ.

Can this outlook be verified in the last years of Paul's life?[34] We do not know what happened to Paul by way of theological change in the 60s just before he died, but in many aspects the outlook of Eph is certainly different from the outlook of the last undisputed letters. More likely, then, we should think of Eph as the continuation of the Pauline heritage amid his disciples who came to see how the unified church of Jews and Gentiles (now existing in places in Asia Minor?) fitted into God's plan and brought to culmination the gospel proclaimed by Paul. One of the disciples had written Col a decade previously (the 80s) to correct a dangerous teaching in the Lycus valley. But that danger had now passed (perhaps through the influence of Col); and another writer, elated by experiencing a unified church, wanted to share with all the saints the developments of Paul's christology and ecclesiology that made such a magnificent result possible. Many of the ideas of Col were taken over and mixed with ideas from letters written by Paul himself, in order to give the fullest expression to the Pauline vision of how Christ and the church fit into God's plan.

For some an Eph not written by Paul himself loses much of its authority. Yet a thesis in which it stems from a school of Paul's disciples, besides rooting the work solidly in the Pauline heritage, glorifies the apostle by the quality of his disciples. During his lifetime he attracted a number of truly distinguished co-workers in preaching the gospel: Timothy, Titus, Silvanus, Luke, Aquila, Priscilla, etc. (Chapter 17 above, n. 3). In the last third of the 1st century they and unrecorded others carried on his work and applied his insights to new problems, just as the apostles carried on and developed the work of Jesus. In considering the role of the deuteroPauline letters one may think of the historical prophet Isaiah who was not diminished because for two centuries after his death his image inspired prophets to write in his tradition and to add their work to his as an integral part of the Isaian prophecy.

Background of the Ideas

If we accept that "in Ephesus" was a later addition, there is little in the letter to tell us the background of the recipients, and no clear indication that the thoughts expressed in Eph were meant to correct their wrong ideas or bad influences on them. Practically, then, our discussion will center on the background of *the writer's ideas.* Some of his emphases reflect Col's re-

[34]The blandness of Eph has forced adherents of Pauline authorship to attribute the work to the old age of the apostle when all passion was spent.

sponse to a false philosophy, e.g., Eph's exalted christology and the subjection of the principalities, the powers, and the devil. But what about other ideas, e.g., the emphasis on the church and on cosmic unity; the dualism between the children of light and the works of darkness (5:8–10), and the ascension of Christ above the heavens (4:8–10)?

The usual range of Greek philosophies is proposed. Those who saw gnostic influence in Col (on the false philosophy or on the writer) tend to see gnostic influence here, in terms either of the writer's employing gnostic language and thought to counter heresy, or of developing a Christian gnosticism as the best way to explain Christ's role in the world. They claim that the Jesus of Eph has become a gnostic redeemer who, instead of breaking down the wall that separated the heavenly realm from the earthly, has broken down the dividing wall between Israel and the Gentiles (2:14–16) and has now returned to the heavenly realm bringing out from this world those who were prisoners (4:9–10). Incorporation into Christ's body has been compared to the gnostic theme of incorporation into the cosmic body of the heavenly man. Much of the evidence for the gnostic ideas, however, stems from later than the 1st century, and some of the analogies are far-fetched (e.g., the derivation of the idea of the wall[35]). Also there are emphases in Eph that would be rejected by many of the later gnostics, e.g., that God created the world and planned to redeem it through Christ's blood (Eph 3:9; 1:7–10), and that marriage between a man and a woman is something sacred and intended by God (Eph 5:21–33). At most, one might allow the possible influence on Eph of elements that would eventually be woven together into gnostic systems.

Other scholars propose a Jewish background for some of the writer's ideas. Eph is much more semitized than the undisputed Pauline letters. For instance, in both hymnic style and theological content parallels have been detected in the DSS (Qumran) literature.[36] The theme of mystery (*mystērion*) that occurs six times in Eph is close to the picture of mysteries in the Qumran literature.[37] There too we find a dualistic picture of the world dominated by the spirits of light and darkness, even as Eph 6:12 speaks of "the world rulers of this darkness." The Qumran literature describes the sons of light who walk in the light, distinct from the sons of darkness who walk in the darkness,

[35]If one has to guess, given the temple imagery in 2:21, the dividing wall mentioned five verses earlier may more plausibly recall the wall that kept the Gentiles out of the inner section of the Jerusalem Temple court, reserved for Jews.

[36]K. G. Kuhn, PAQ 115–31; F. Mussner, PAQ 159–78. One should be careful to distinguish between the unprovable claim that the writer of Eph was directly influenced by the Qumran literature or Qumran Essenes and the demonstrable fact that the Qumran literature shows us ideas prevalent among 1st-century Jews. Murphy-O'Connor, "Who," once suggested that Eph was written under Paul's direction by a scribe (amanuensis) who was a converted Essene.

[37]See Chapter 27 above, n. 19. C. C. Caragounis, *The Ephesian Mystērion* (CBNTS 8; Uppsala: Gleerup, 1977), traces it to the use of *mystērion* in Daniel, and thus another Jewish background.

even as Eph 2:2 knows of the sons of disobedience. Codes for behavior comparable to the household code of Eph are also found in the Qumran community rules. Elsewhere in Judaism the theme of cosmic unity in a body has a certain parallel in Philo's thought, where the world is a body with the Logos as its head. In an overall picture, then, the outlook of Eph can be explained by the writer's drawing on the Scriptures, developments of Jewish thought in the Hellenistic world, and Christian beliefs, especially as vocalized within the Pauline tradition. Therefore, neither Pagan mystery religions nor gnosticism need be posited as a major shaping factor.

Issues and Problems for Reflection

(1) Eph 2:19–20 describes Christians as "fellow citizens with the saints and household members of God who are built upon the foundation of apostles and prophets, with Christ Jesus himself as the cornerstone." In I Cor 3:10–11 Paul says, "I laid a foundation . . . No other foundation can anyone lay than the one that has been laid, which is Jesus Christ." The difference about the foundation in these two statements has constituted an argument for positing that Eph was written by a Pauline disciple rather than by Paul. Passages such as Matt 16:18; Rev 21:14; Matt 21:42; Acts 4:11; I Pet 2:4–8 show that both interpretations of the foundation image were known outside the Pauline circle. Do the two interpretations lead to different pictures of the church?

(2) All foundational images have been criticized as too static. Whether Christ is a cornerstone or a foundation, that imagery portrays him chiefly as supportive of the church but not active in it. The imagery in John 15 of Jesus as the vine pumping life into the branches is more effective in conveying the idea that Jesus is a dynamic presence. Yet Eph 2:21–22 follows the foundation/cornerstone pictorialization immediately with imagery of growth (a plant) and being built together (a building) into a dwelling place of God. What aspects of the church emerge from this combination?

(3) I Cor 12:28 lists God's appointments in the church thus: "First apostles; second prophets; third teachers, then miracles, then healing gifts, helping, administrating, various kinds of tongues." Eph 4:11 has Christ giving apostles, prophets, evangelists, pastors (shepherds), and teachers. Is the shift from God to Christ significant? Have functions or ministries become complicated in the interim between I Cor and Eph, or were evangelists and pastors already present under the vague Corinthian description of administrating? How do evangelists differ from apostles (see Acts 21:8; II Tim 4:5)? I Pet 5:1–4 has Peter, an apostle, in a pastoring role (also John 21:15–17).

(4) Eph 4:4–6 lists seven factors ("one body . . .") that bind Christians

together. How many of those are still shared by Christians even in a divided Christianity? Is the failure to mention "one eucharist" significant, e.g., was the eucharist a disunifying factor (see I Cor 11:17–22)? It has been noted also that "one church" is *not* mentioned. However, is there any evidence in either the undisputed Pauline letters or in Eph that Pauline thought would have tolerated disunited churches?

(5) Eph 5:21–32 attests to a high spiritual estimation of marriage, comparing it to the relationship between Christ and his body which is the church, a relationship that is part of the divine mystery. "Christ loved the church and gave himself over for her in order to sanctify her, having cleansed her by the bath of water in the word, that he might present to himself the church in splendor, without spot or wrinkle . . . holy and without blemish." With adaptation this imagery should be applicable to the Christian husband and wife. Is this very high view of marriage reconcilable with I Cor 7:8 which stresses that the unmarried should remain unmarried (like Paul)? The latter was governed by a strong apocalyptic viewpoint wherein the things of this world are passing away, whereas Eph gives voice to a realized eschatology wherein the community consists of married families. There are elements of both attitudes in the teaching of Jesus (Matt 19:5–9,12); and Christians have sought to preserve both by placing a premium on celibacy for the sake of the kingdom and by exalting matrimony as a sacrament or a state of life uniquely blessed by God.

(6) In Col 1:13,16; 2:10,15 and Eph 1:21; 2:2; 3:10; 6:12 we hear of forces called rulers/principalities (sg. *archē,* 6 times); prince (*archōn,* 1), powers (*dynamis,* 1), authorities (*exousia,* 8), thrones (*thronos,* 1), dominions/lordships (*kyriotēs,* 2).[38] A special combination appears in Eph 2:2: "the prince [*archōn*] of the power [*exousia*] of the air." These forces are related to whatever is in heaven, on earth, and under the earth in Phil 2:10; and to the angels, principalities, and powers of Rom 8:38; and to every principality, authority, and power of I Cor 15:24. Usually evil or, at least, capable of being understood as rivals to Christ, they are superhuman (angelic or diabolic [Eph 6:11]) and have a type of control over human destiny, perhaps because they are somehow attached to planets or stars (see the *stoicheia* on pp. 605–6 above). How is the Pauline vision of Christ's superiority over them related to the Synoptic Gospel picture of Jesus expelling demons as a manifestation of the coming of the kingdom? A modern demythologizing interpretation

[38]See G.H.C. Macgregor in *New Testament Sidelights,* ed. H. K. McArthur (A. C. Purdy Festschrift; Hartford [CT] Seminary, 1960), 88–104; H. Schlier, *Principalities and Powers in the New Testament* (New York: Herder and Herder, 1961); A. T. Hanson, *Studies Paul's Technique,* 1–12; W. Wink, *Naming the Powers: The Language of Power in the New Testament* (Philadelphia: Fortress, 1984); C. E. Arnold, JSNT 30 (1987), 71–87, and *Ephesians: Power and Magic: the Concept of Power in Ephesians in the Light of Its Historical Setting* (SNTSMS 63; Cambridge Univ., 1989).

would see them as powerful earthly agents that seek to dominate people's lives (government, military, etc.), but does such a reduction to human tyranny retain what the Pauline writers meant to convey? Eph 6:12 explicitly distinguishes between a struggle against principalities, powers, and world rulers (pl. of *kosmokratōr*) of this present darkness and a struggle against flesh and blood.

Bibliography on Ephesians

COMMENTARIES AND STUDIES IN SERIES: Allan, J. A. (TBC, 1959); Barth, M. (2 vols.; AB, 1974); Beare, F. W. (IB [vol. 10], 1953); Best, E. (NTG, 1993); Foulkes, F. (TNTC, 1963); Kitchen, M. (NTR, 1994); **Lincoln, A. T.** (WBC, 1990; NTT, 1993); Mitton, C. L. (NCBC, 1976); Sampley, J. P. (ProcC, 1993); Swain, L. (NTM, 1980); Taylor, W. F. (AugC, 1985); Zerwick, M. (NTSR, 1969). See also the *Bibliography* of Chapter 27 for works marked with more than one asterisk, treating both Col and Eph.

Allan, J. A., "The 'In Christ' Formulations in Ephesians," NTS 5 (1958–59), 54–62.
Barth, M., "Traditions in Ephesians," NTS 30 (1984), 3–25.
Brown, R. E., "The Pauline Heritage in Colossians/Ephesians," BCALB 47–60.
Bruce, F. F., "St. Paul in Rome, 3 and 4. The Epistle to the Ephesians," SJT 48 (1966), 268–85; 49 (1967), 303–22.
Cadbury, H. J., "The Dilemma of Ephesians," NTS 5 (1958–59), 91–102.
Cross, F. L., *Studies in Ephesians* (London: Mowbray, 1956).
Dahl, N. A., "Cosmic Dimension and Religious Knowledge [Eph 3:18]," in *Jesus und Paulus,* eds. E. E. Ellis and E. Grässer (W. G. Kümmel Festschrift: Göttingen: Vandenhoeck & Ruprecht, 1975), 57–75.
Goodspeed, E. J., *The Meaning of Ephesians* (Univ. of Chicago, 1933).
———, *The Key to Ephesians* (Univ. of Chicago, 1956).
Kirby, J. C., *Ephesians, Baptism, and Pentecost* (Montreal: McGill Univ. 1968).
Koester, H., ed., *Ephesos—Metropolis of Asia* (Valley Forge, PA: Trinity, 1995).
Lincoln, A. T., "The Use of the OT in Ephesians," JSNT 14 (1982), 16–57.
Martin, R. P., "An Epistle in Search of a Life-Setting," ExpTim 79 (1968), 296–302.
Mitton, C. L., *The Epistle to the Ephesians* (Oxford: Clarendon, 1951).
Murphy-O'Connor, J., "Who Wrote Ephesians?" TBT 1 (1965), 1201–9.
Robinson, J. A(rmitage), *St. Paul's Epistle to the Ephesians* (2d ed.; London: Clarke, 1922). A classic.
Schnackenburg, R., *The Epistle to the Ephesians* (Edinburgh: Clark, 1991).
van Roon, A., *The Authenticity of Ephesians* (NovTSup 39; Leiden: Brill, 1974).
Westcott, B. F., *Saint Paul's Epistle to the Ephesians* (London: Macmillan, 1906).

CHAPTER 29

PASTORAL LETTER: TO TITUS

After some observations on *the "Pastoral" Letters in general,* discussing the title and the similarities among the group, I shall use this Chapter and the next two (30, 31) to treat them in the order Titus, I Tim, II Tim. As we shall see, there is a major debate about whether Paul wrote them, but I prefer to leave that issue to p. 662 below and to discuss them at face value first. In the treatment of Titus, after *Background* and *General Analysis,* subsections will deal with *Presbyter/bishops, Issues for reflection,* and *Bibliography.*

The Pastoral Letters in General: Title, Interrelationship

The Title. Many refer to the three as "Epistles" (p. 410 above). Yet they have the letter format, with a beginning that identifies the sender and the intended recipient, and (I Tim excepted) a conclusion extending greetings and a blessing. As for "Pastoral," that designation has been applied to them since the early 18th century as a recognition of their central concern—no longer the missionary expansion that dominated the first years of Christianity, but the care of evangelized communities after the missionaries had moved on either geographically or through death.[1] This is a care that we recognize as "pastoral." That term is appropriate in another way because a prominent theme in Titus and I Tim is church structure or order, i.e., the appointment of officials to administer the Christian community; and often we designate such figures "pastors." If the NT symbolism for the missionary is the fisher(man), the symbol for the one who guides and feeds those won over by the missionary is the shepherd (or *pastor* in Latin). I shall repeat the designation "Pastoral Letter" in the title of the Chapter treating each of these works because, more than any other letters attributed to Paul, these are profitably considered together and in relation to each other.

Interrelation from the Viewpoint of Order: Overall they are very homogeneous in style and atmosphere. A logical deduction is that either the same person wrote them or, if X wrote one and Y wrote the others, Y has taken great pains to mimic X. Nevertheless, important scholars have objected that

[1]II Tim 4:6–8 eloquently portrays Paul as about to die.

Summary of Basic Information about Titus

DATE: If by Paul, *ca.* AD 65. If pseudonymous (80 to 90 percent of critical scholarship), toward the end of the 1st century, or (less probably) early 2d century.

TO: Titus in Crete (newly founded churches?) from a Paul depicted as recently departed from there and now in coastal Asia Minor (Ephesus?) or western Greece (Macedonia?), on his way to Nicopolis.

AUTHENTICITY: Probably written by a disciple of Paul or a sympathetic commentator on the Pauline heritage several decades after the apostle's death.

UNITY AND INTEGRITY: Not seriously disputed.

FORMAL DIVISION:
- A. Opening Formula: 1:1–4
- B. Thanksgiving: None
- C. Body: 1:5–3:11
- D. Concluding Formula: 3:12–15.

DIVISION ACCORDING TO CONTENTS:
- 1:1–4: Address/greetings to Titus
- 1:5–9: Church structure and the appointment of presbyter/bishops
- 1:10–16: False teaching that threatens the community
- 2:1–3:11: Community behavior and belief:
  - 2:1–10: Household code
  - 2:11–3:11: What Christ has done and its implications
- 3:12–15: Concluding greetings and blessing.

treating the three as a group has blinded interpreters to their individual differences. In particular there is an increasing insistence that at least II Tim deserves separate consideration.[2]

As for genre, some would compare Titus and I Tim to the *Didache* (*ca.* AD 100–120), an early church manual that also has warnings against false teachers/prophets. The church manual genre is well attested later as well (*Didascalia Apostolorum, Apostolic Constitutions*); but R. F. Collins, CLPDNW 110–11, is right in questioning the comparison because the Pastorals do not give detailed directives on how the church order is to function. II Tim does not deal with church order, and Titus does so only in a sketchy manner. More technically Puskas (*Letters* 183) would argue that Titus and I Tim represent deliberative, paraenetic rhetoric, while II Tim exemplifies demonstrative, epideictic rhetoric—see pp. 411–12 above. Fiore, *Function,* stresses the various hortatory techniques in the Pastorals and the parallel of literary form to the Socratic and pseudo-Socratic letters. We shall see that II Tim has the atmosphere of a farewell address; moreover it has certain

[2]As we shall see in treating II Tim, Murphy-O'Connor would find over thirty points on which Titus and I Tim agree against II Tim; even when they use the same terms, it is often with a different nuance. He and other scholars would maintain that two writers were involved, with the writer of II Tim closer to authentic Pauline style.

parallels to the Captivity Letters, i.e., Phil, Phlm, Col, and Eph written from imprisonment.

A major issue is the order in which they were composed. That cannot be learned from the present canonical order (I-II Tim, Titus) which is simply an arrangement by descending length. If the letters are pseudepigraphical, we must be cautious about making judgments based on the contents, for some of the details might not be historical. According to what is related, the church situation envisioned in Titus is less established and detailed than that envisioned in I Tim; and since the letters claim to be addressed to different geographical destinations (Crete and Ephesus respectively), perhaps the churches in the eastern Mediterranean were not all at the same stage of development. Yet similar church development does not necessarily tell us which letter was written first. The death of Paul is envisioned as approaching in II Tim; and so logically, if he wrote all three, he probably wrote that last. However, II Tim is not concerned with the same structural issues as Titus and I Tim; and so it is not inconceivable that II Tim was written first (perhaps by Paul) and that after his death an unknown writer composed Titus and I Tim, imitating the style of II Tim in order to deal with issues of church structure that had now become acute. In short, any order of composition is possible. Yet since our custom has been to begin by taking the letters at face value, there is a certain appropriateness in the order Titus (less developed church structure), I Tim (more developed church structure), II Tim (Paul dying). Quinn, *Titus* 3, points out that this order, attested in the Muratorian Fragment (late 2d century) and Ambrosiaster (4th century), is probably the oldest.

The Background (of Titus)

Although the letter does not depend for its meaning on a knowledge of Titus' career, in the NT Titus (never mentioned in Acts) is described as having been converted by Paul[3] and brought to the Jerusalem meeting in AD 49 (Gal 2:1–3) to demonstrate how genuine a Christian an uncircumcised Gentile could be. In the crisis between Paul and the church of Corinth, where Paul had been publicly embarrassed during his "painful visit," Titus carried the letter written "with many tears" from Ephesus to Corinth. He was successful in effecting a diplomatic reconciliation, so that he brought to Paul in Macedonia good news from Corinth (*ca.* 56–57: II Cor 2:1; 7:6–16; pp. 541–43 above, #8–10). He was later sent to Corinth to gather the collection that Paul would bring to Jerusalem in 58 (II Cor 8:6,16,23; 12:17–18; #11).

[3]Titus 1:4: "My true son in the common faith."

The present letter assumes that Paul has been in Crete with Titus and has left him there to correct anything that is still defective, specifically to appoint presbyters in every Christian community (Titus 1:5). It is not stated where Paul is when he writes the letter, although the Asia Minor coast (Ephesus) and Greece (Macedonia or Achaia) are localizations that would fit his plan to spend the winter in Nicopolis, most probably the city in western Greece (3:12). Four people are mentioned in Titus 3:12–13, two of whom (Artemas, Zenas) are otherwise unknown. *Tychicus* from Asia Minor, who is with Paul, was said in Acts 20:4–5 to have accompanied Paul as he left Corinth on his way to Jerusalem, passing through Macedonia and Troas, from which he sailed past Ephesus. He is also mentioned as the conveyer of both Col (4:7–9) and Eph (6:21–22), letters from a captivity setting, perhaps in Ephesus (pp. 616, 630 above). *Apollos,* who in his travels will pass through Crete, was last heard of at Ephesus when Paul sent I Cor (16:12). These details might tip the scales slightly in favor of the Ephesus region as the real or imagined place from which Paul is writing to Titus; and if the composition of the Pastorals implies a sequence, it would have been after Paul left Ephesus and went to Macedonia that he wrote I Tim (1:3).

Nothing in the career of Paul narrated in Acts or the other Pauline letters (outside the Pastorals) fits the details recounted in the preceding paragraph. From those sources Paul's only visit to Crete was during the voyage that carried him as a prisoner to Rome *ca.* 61; the ship stopped at Fair Havens and followed the coast of Crete, only to be driven off by a storm (Acts 27:7–14). Rom 15:19 tells us that Paul had been in Illyricum by AD 58, but after that visit he wintered in Corinth (p. 543 above, #12). Most scholars who accept Paul as the writer of Titus or at least the accuracy of the details given in Titus posit a "second career" for the apostle in the mid-60s during which he was released following his two-year captivity in Rome narrated in Acts 28:30 (AD 61–63) and went back east, namely to Crete, Ephesus, and Nicopolis. II Tim is brought into this theory to posit a terminus of Paul's second career in another Roman captivity and execution there in 65–67.[4]

General Analysis of the Message

Below after a short comment about the Opening Formula, the message in the Body of Titus will be organized under three headings: church structure,

[4]Sometimes the affirmation that Paul wore chains seven times (*I Clement* 5:6) is invoked as evidence for this; yet J. D. Quinn, JBL 97 (1978), 574–76, contends that it stems simply from a count of the seven available NT works that mentioned imprisonment (Acts, II Cor, Eph, Phil, Col, Phlm, and II Tim). For the "second career" of Paul, see L. P. Pherigo, JBL 70 (1951), 277–84; O.F.A. Meinardus, BA 41 (1978), 61–63, and *Paul's Last Journey* 112–47; J. D. Quinn, *Studia Biblica 1978* (JSNTSup 3; Sheffield: Academic, 1980), 289–99.

false teaching, and community relations and belief. I shall follow the same procedure in Chapter 30 below on I Tim, pointing out how that letter complements the picture given in Titus. Only when we have considered both letters will I examine where the overall picture fits best into 1st- and 2d-century Christian thought and practice, and the related issue of whether these are writings appropriate to Paul's lifetime.

OPENING FORMULA (1:1–4). This is both long and formal; indeed only Rom, written to a community that Paul had never visited, is noticeably longer. Is it plausible that Paul needed to introduce himself thus to a disciple who had known him for years? Many scholars answer negatively, using this inconsistency to challenge writing by Paul and even proposing that we are given here an introduction to the three Pastorals planned as a pseudepigraphical corpus. Others would explain the formality on the grounds that, although addressed to Titus, the letter was meant to function as public support for Titus in accomplishing a difficult task as a delegate of Paul,[5] and so to be read aloud in the churches. Since a major concern is to preserve the faith of Christians in Crete, at the beginning Paul is shown as insisting that one of the duties of an apostle is to be concerned with the faith of God's elect.

BODY (1:5–9): *First theme: Church structure or order.* This is a main issue in the Pastorals (or at least in Titus and especially I Tim),[6] as was recognized in one of the oldest references to them. The Muratorian Fragment (late 2d century) says that although they were written from personal feeling and affection, they are held in honor in the church catholic in the matter of ecclesiastical order. Such order is a concern in Titus because of the danger presented by false teachers. The letter tells us that during his stay in Crete Paul had not established a fixed structure, and so he is now entrusting that task to Titus who had remained after Paul's departure. I Tim envisages a community organized under presbyter/bishops and deacons, while Titus mentions only the appointment of presbyter/bishops. The qualifications demanded of these figures were to guarantee that they would provide a leadership faithful to Paul's teaching and thus protect the faithful from innovations, as we shall see in a subsection below.

BODY (1:10–16): *Second theme: false teaching.* Titus attacks a pressing danger. However, the description of the teachers is phrased polemically;[7]

[5]Commentators have at times wrongly described Titus as the bishop of Crete (and Timothy as the bishop of Ephesus). There is insufficient evidence, however, that the structure of one bishop for a locale had developed when the Pastorals were written. Moreover, Titus and Timothy are presented in the letters as missionary companions and legates of Paul, rather than as permanent residential supervisors.

[6]The tone of the emphasis is important: The letters do not try to legitimize the kind of church structure they describe; they take it for granted but seek to insure its installation and effectiveness.

[7]R. J. Karris, JBL 92 (1973), 549–64.

and only with difficulty can one discern between precise information and vague generalization. Thus, it is hard to diagnose the teaching from claims that the opponents are insubordinate, idle talkers who ought to be silenced, deceivers who upset households, teachers working for monetary gain,[8] with tainted minds and consciences—people denying God by their deeds, who are vile, disobedient, and unfit for any good deed. The quotation in Titus 1:12 from Epimenides of Cnossus (6th century BC) vilifying the Cretans as liars and lazy gluttons suggests that the false teachers are native to Crete; and yet the description of the false teachers at Ephesus in I Tim 1:3–11 is not dissimilar.

Christians of Jewish ancestry ("those from the circumcision") come under fire in Titus 1:10, and the implication that they follow humanly crafted rules declaring things impure (1:15) might favor the thesis they were using their strict traditions to interpret the Mosaic Law (see Mark 7:8). Yet the meaning of Jewish myths/fables in 1:14 is not clear. Are these developments in Jewish apocrypha with their stress on calendric details and on the roles of angels? Or are Jewish gnostic speculations about human origins in mind? (The thesis of a gnostic error was held already in 1835 by F. C. Baur, and J. B. Lightfoot spoke of a "Judaism crossed with gnosticism.") The statement that the teachers profess to know God (1:16) might point in the latter direction. Do the elements pointing in both directions suggest that the author was facing a syncretism that combined Jewish and gnostic elements?[9] The vagueness of what is described warns us how uncertain is any judgment that would date Titus to the mid-2d century because it attacks fully developed gnosticism. Indeed, the description that touches so many bases and still remains vague might have been meant to make this letter (and I Tim as well) applicable to any foreseeable false teachers who would come along.

BODY (2:1–3:11): *Third theme: Community relations and belief.* This takes up about two thirds of Titus. The first section (2:1–10) is a household code of which we have seen examples in Col 3:18–4:1 and Eph 5:21–6:9 (pp. 608, 623–24 above).[10] Those were neatly divided into advice for three pairs with the subjected component mentioned first: *wives*/husbands, *children*/fathers, *slaves*/masters. The pattern here is less regular: older men/older

[8]Does this hint that they are paid for teaching (as are presbyters in I Tim 5:17)? Or by their teaching do they attract a following from whom they then request money? Or is this simply a general supposition, similar to that shared today by many people in reference to media preachers?

[9]The picture is not greatly clarified by the condemnation in 3:9 of foolish inquisitiveness, genealogies, dissensions, and controversies over the Law. Are these disputes within the community the product of a consistent false teaching?

[10]Verner, *Household,* argues effectively that the concept of the church as the household of God is a key notion in the Pastorals: The household is the basic unit in the church, and the church is a social structure modeled on the household.

women, younger women/younger men/ slaves. Moreover, the issue is not the relationship of the older men to the older women, but the general edifying comportment of both and their training of younger counterparts.[11] Yet in 2:4–5 where women are told to love and be submissive to their husbands, and in 2:9 where slaves are told to be submissive to their masters, Titus comes close to the household codes of Col and Eph. The demand for sober, dignified behavior, similar to that placed on the presbyters in 1:7–9, is traced to sound doctrine and is meant to embellish the teaching of God our Savior (2:10), so that Christian belief and manner of life are to be uniform. (By relating their behavior to Christian belief and doctrine the Cretan Christians could differentiate their deportment from similar behavior that could be inculcated by Greek philosophers[12] simply as a more rational way of life.)

In 2:11–3:11, with a proselytizing interest the author gives pastoral instructions based on what Christ has done. Before conversion Christians were foolish and disobedient, slaves to passion (3:3); but the "great God and Savior of us Jesus Christ"[13] gave himself to redeem and purify a people of his own zealous for good deeds (2:13–14)—indeed, for the salvation of all (2:11; see also 3:4–7, which may be a hymn). In his undisputed letters Paul held himself up as a model to be imitated (Phil 3:17). He repeats that in the Pastorals (I Tim 1:16; II Tim 1:13),[14] and now he wants the Cretan Christians to be models (Titus 2:7) to attract others to the faith. Part of this modeling of good deeds will consist in being submissive to rulers and authorities (3:1)[15] and being courteous to all, including outsiders (3:2). Nothing is more harmful to such a public image than foolish inner-Christian dissensions and quarrels (3:9–10).

CONCLUDING FORMULA (3:12–15). The information supplied here has already been discussed at the end of the *Background* subsection, for it feeds into the thesis of a "second career" of Paul beyond that narrated in Acts and raises acutely the issue of historicity to be discussed on p. 669 below. The final greetings envision a wider audience than Titus.

[11]Note that older women are to teach younger women—cf. I Tim 2:12 which forbids a woman to teach or have authority over men.

[12]See S. C. Mott, "Greek Ethics and Christian Conversion: the Philonic Background of Titus ii 10–14 and iii 3–7," NovT 20 (1978), 248–60.

[13]I judge that most probably this is a text that calls Jesus God (BINTC 181–82); see also M. J. Harris in *Pauline Studies,* eds. D. Hagner and M. J. Harris (Exeter: Paternoster, 1980), 262–77.

[14]Indirectly or directly in the Pastorals, uniquely chosen by God as a herald, Paul is a model of many virtues that would help the communities, e.g., of perseverance in suffering, of enduring hope, of faithful teaching, and of correcting error.

[15]Some would include this instruction in the household code. It continues the theme of an orderly society (wives submissive to husbands, slaves to masters), but certainly goes beyond the relationships within a household.

Presbyter/bishops in the Pastorals

Although scholars are not in total agreement about what is envisaged, here are likelihoods:[16]

(1) In each community there were to be appointed presbyters. Normally, as the designation *presbyteroi* (a comparative adjectival noun from "old," *presbys,* whence "elders") indicates, these would be older, experienced men[17] of the community. In antiquity sixty was often the recognized age when one became an old man or old woman (see I Tim 5:9); yet the age of the "elders" was surely not so exactly calculated. Moreover a younger man particularly noted for good judgment might be considered "old" in wisdom. Christian presbyters were to have two major overall functions. First, seemingly as a group, they were to give the whole community direction,[18] e.g., by guiding policy decisions and supervising finances. The relation of a presbyter to an individual house-church is unclear; but the presbyters presided over the whole community and therefore perhaps over a group of house-churches. Second, they were to exercise pastoral or shepherding care for individual Christians in matters of belief and moral practice. The Jewish synagogue had groups of elders who performed the first, more general task;[19] and the Christian presbyteral structure was influenced by that model.

(2) In the Pastorals "overseer, bishop" (*episkopos*[20]) is another title for the

[16]By anticipation I include the evidence of I Tim with that of Titus, with the assumption that I Tim 3:1–7 and 5:17–22 described the same structure. The following are a sample of the many treatments: E. Schweizer, *Church Order in the New Testament* (SBT 32; London: SCM, 1961); R. Schnackenburg, *The Church in the New Testament* (New York: Herder and Herder, 1965); R. E. Brown, *Priest and Bishop: Biblical Reflections* (New York: Paulist, 1970); "*Episkopē* and *Episkopos:* The New Testament Evidence," TS 41 (1980), 322–38; B. Holmberg, *Paul and Power: The Structure of Authority in the Primitive Church* (CBNTS 11; Lund: Gleerup, 1978); P. Perkins, *Ministering in the Pauline Churches* (New York: Paulist, 1982); B. Witherington III, *Women in the Earliest Churches* (SNTSMS 59; Cambridge Univ., 1988); D. L. Bartlett, *Ministry in the New Testament* (Minneapolis: Fortress, 1993), esp. 150–84; R. A. Campbell, *The Elders* (Edinburgh: Clark, 1994). See specifically J. P. Meier, "*Presbyteros* in the Pastoral Epistles," CBQ 35 (1973), 323–45.

[17]Although in the NT we have evidence for women apostles, women prophets, women deacons, and a formal group of "widows," it is not indicated that there were women presbyters. *Presbyterai,* a feminine comparative noun from "old," appears in I Tim 5:2; but the comparison with younger women suggests that there Paul is speaking of older women as an age bracket rather than of women presbyters holding a recognized office.

[18]I Tim 5:17 contends that the presbyters who "preside" well are worthy of double honor. Without supplying titles, the first (I Thess 5:12) and the last (Rom 12:8) of the undisputed Pauline letters use the same Greek verb in reference to "presiding" over others (caution: English translations vary). Thus the basic idea of church order was older than the Pastorals, even though in them the structure now has greater articulation and perhaps greater regularity.

[19]While this is true, we should acknowledge that there is not much evidence for the title of elder associated with the Jewish synagogue; see A. E. Harvey, "Elders," JTS 25 (1974), 318–32.

[20]Literally one who sees or looks (*skopein*) over (*epi*); compare English "periscope" by which one looks around (*peri*). Reflecting the Latin *videre,* "to see," or *intendere,* "to look," plus *super,* "over," other possible renditions are "supervisor" and "superintendent," although the latter has a

presbyteros (whence "presbyter/bishop"), particularly in the second function of pastoral care of individuals.[21] Because in Titus and I Tim *presbyteros* is used in the plural and *episkopos* only in the singular, some have thought that the structure involved one presbyter from among the others who served as bishop or overseer in relation to the whole community. Most probably that is a wrong interpretation: The singular *episkopos* in Titus 1:7, following "anyone" of the presbyters in 1:5–6, is generic, describing what every presbyter/bishop should be (similarly I Tim 3:1–2). Thus, we may speak of presbyter/bishops in the communities envisioned by Titus and I Tim with the reasonable confidence that there was an overseeing group rather than a solitary overseer/bishop—the latter being a development attested only later. Yet it is clear from I Tim (5:17: perhaps a church structure more developed than that of Titus, with greater specification of duties) that not every presbyter exercised the same kind of pastoral overseeing, for only some preached and taught. In I Tim there are directions about community worship (2:8–10); and so silence about presbyter/bishops presiding at the liturgy is probably not accidental—presumably this was not one of their functions. Moreover, there is no comparison in the Pastorals of the role of the presbyter/bishops (and the deacons in I Tim) to the pattern of Christ (and the apostles) or to that of the sacred order of priests (and levites) in the OT. Thus one can scarcely speak of hierarchy.[22] Nor is any explicit theology developed about the structure, although undoubtedly in the writer's mind it contributed to making the church of the living God a pillar and bulwark of truth (I Tim 3:15).

(3) Before appointment, the qualifications of potential presbyter/bishops were to be examined carefully. We saw that I Cor 12:28 describes administrative capabilities as a charism or gift of the Spirit, even as Rom 12:6–8 counts "presiding over others" among charisms. In the Pastorals there is no indication that *ipso facto* a person who had (or claimed to have) the charism of administration or presiding would be recognized as a presbyter/bishop.

---

secular usage that it may be wise to avoid. Also because of the ambiguity of "oversight," the task of these men is better described as "supervision" or "overseeing."

[21]Johnson, *Writings* 401, makes the claim that the community structure envisioned at Ephesus resembles the structure of the diaspora Jewish synagogues. However, it is not clear that the synagogue officials exercised the type of pastoral care over individuals exercised by the Christian bishops. A Jewish parallel for that is found, rather, in officials of the Dead Sea Scrolls community called "supervisors" or "examiners" (Hebrew *mĕbaqqēr* or *pāqîd,* the literal equivalent of *episkopos*) who were described as shepherds and were responsible for the individual behavior of those under their care. Others would seek a parallel in the Greek pattern of an *episkopos* as a supervising functionary within special societies, including religious groups, or as a financial manager.

[22]Unfortunately in modern misusage "hierarchy" is applied to almost any structure (particularly in the church) where some are over others, as if the term were "higher-archy." Rather it should refer only to ordering or structure thought to be sacred (*hieros*) inasmuch as it resembles the order in the heavenly realm or an order established by God. Campbell, *Elders,* would argue that the designation "elders" in the NT did not refer to an office in any strict sense but constituted an honor.

Presumably if a person met the qualifications and was appointed presbyter/bishop, that appointment would have been regarded as taking place under the guidance of the Spirit, but that is never said;[23] and so the Pastorals' structure is often contrasted with charismatic leadership.

To probe that contrast, let me list from Titus 1:6–9 (and, to save repetition, from I Tim 3:1–7[24]) the qualities and qualifications expected of the presbyter/bishop. Four categories may be distinguished: (a) Negative descriptions of disqualifying behavior or attitudes: not arrogant; not quick-tempered, not violent*, *not quarrelsome,* not a heavy drinker*, not greedy for gain, *not loving money.* (b) Positive descriptions of desired virtues and abilities: faultless, *above reproach,* hospitable*, *gentle,* loving good, devout, just, showing good sense*, self-controlled, *sober, dignified.* (c) Life-situation to be expected of a public figure who would be setting a standard for the community: he has been married only once*;[25] his children are believers; they are not loose-living or insubordinate; *he is not a recent convert.* (d) Skills related to the work to be done: *he has a good reputation with outsiders; he manages well his own household; he is an adept teacher;* he holds fast the trustworthy word which accords with the teaching of sound doctrine.

The qualifying virtues described in (a) and (b) are sometimes called institutional: They would result in the selection of presbyter/bishops whom a congregation could like, admire, and live with. The qualifications do not have a dynamic thrust and would not be inclined to produce leaders who change the world. It has sometimes been noted humorously that Paul himself might have difficulty meeting the qualifications; for, if we judge from Gal, he could be quick-tempered and undignified in his language. But then Paul was an apostle and a missionary, not a residential bishop. He was a figure

[23]There are about six references to the (Holy) Spirit in the Pastorals but none of them in clear relation to presbyteral structure. For instance, the Pastorals' gifts of the Spirit are of a different order from those envisioned in I Cor 12, e.g., II Tim 1:7: "For God did not give us a spirit of timidity, but a spirit of power, of love, and of self-discipline." Yet Paul speaks to Timothy (II Tim 1:14): "Guard this beautiful entrustment by the Holy Spirit dwelling within us"; and I Tim 3:1 regards the work of the bishop as beautiful and to be aspired to. I Tim 4:14 speaks of the role of Timothy (which involves community care) as a "gift" (*charisma*), given through prophecy with the laying on of hands of the presbytery.

[24]Qualifications shared by Titus and I Tim are marked by an asterisk; qualifications mentioned only by I Tim are italicized.

[25]Even though it is expected in the Pastorals that the presbyter/bishop be married, as we can detect from remarks about household and children, this particular qualification, "husband of one wife," is not a directive that the presbyter/bishop must have a wife (as often used in antiCatholic polemic), but that he cannot have had more than one wife, i.e., cannot have remarried after divorce or the death of a spouse (or, a fortiori, be polygamous where that was permitted by society). That is shown by the parallel demand of the widow in I Tim 5:9, "wife of one husband"—a widow no longer has a husband and so it refers to her having been married only once (see Chapter 30 below, n. 12). The remarrying of widowers or widows, while tolerated, was not regarded as an ideal, probably on the basis that husband and wife constituted one flesh (I Cor 6:16; 7:8).

whose restless dynamism might have grated on people if he had attempted to stay and supervise a church for a decade.

The demands in (c) distance the Pastorals from a charismatic approach to ministry.[26] A person with remarkable leadership abilities (which could be considered a charism given him by the Spirit) would not be eligible to be a presbyter/bishop if his children were not Christian—a situation that might have occurred frequently to those converted in midlife. Why this ineligibility? Because as leader of the community his family life had to set an ideal example for the community.

(4) In 1:5 Titus is told to appoint presbyters in Crete, but we are not told how a continuity of presbyters will be preserved once he departs. Presbyters already exist in Ephesus, and no clear indication is given in I Tim as to how that came about. No matter how the appointment or selection came about,[27] was there a designating action that in the language of the later church might have been considered an ordination? Some appeal to I Tim 4:14, "Do not neglect your gift [*charisma*] that you have in you, given to you through prophecy with the presbytery's laying on of hands," and understand it as making Timothy a presbyter; but we have no other evidence for Timothy in this role. Another understanding of the verse would have the laying on of hands oriented toward Timothy's general mission, just as II Tim, which never mentions presbyters, traces Timothy's spiritual gift to Paul's laying on of hands (1:6–7). More helpful could be I Tim 5:22 where, in a passage immediately following the discussion of the behavior of elders, Timothy is urged not to be hasty in the laying on of hands or participating in others' sins. That could describe an action in the designation of elders, but some interpret it as a reference to absolving sinners. On the general bases of later church history and of Jewish practices in reference to rabbis, one may strongly suspect that, at the time the Pastorals were written, presbyters were installed by the laying on of hands. Yet, once again, we may doubt that there was as yet uniformity in the Christian churches.

[26]Nevertheless, most likely structure and charism coexisted temporally (but perhaps in different places) in the geographic spread of the early church, e.g., in the 50s I Thess 5:12–13 supposes structure, while I Cor 12 supposes a variety of charisms.

[27]Described procedures in the early church are not uniform. In Acts 14:23 Paul appoints presbyters in every church and moves on, but we are never told how they were replaced. Acts 20:28 speaks of the Holy Spirit having made the presbyters of Ephesus overseers (*episkopoi*). In *Didache* 15:1–2 people are told to choose for themselves bishops (and deacons). After claiming that the apostles appointed their first converts to be bishops and deacons (42:4), *I Clement* 44:2 has them leaving instructions that after death other approved men (*andres*) should succeed to their ministry (*leitourgia*).

Issues and Problems for Reflection

(1) Whether or not Paul wrote the Pastoral Letters will be left to the next Chapter on I Tim. A factor that enters the discussion is whether the style and vocabulary is Pauline. To get an idea of the problem, we can use the first chapter of Titus as an example. Features therein that are found in the undisputed Pauline writings include: the reference to God's elect or chosen (1:1; only Paul in the NT); the divine plan about salvation in Christ which has existed from all eternity or before creation (1:2–3); Paul's having been entrusted with manifesting this through preaching (1:3); and the grace and peace greeting (1:4). Features not found in the other Pauline Letters (outside the Pastorals) include: Paul as the servant *of God* (1:1); "knowledge of the truth" (1:1, although Paul uses both nouns separately); "God our Savior" (1:3); officials known as presbyters (cf. "bishops" in Phil 1:1); many of the qualifications in 1:7–8 (not arrogant, not quick-tempered, not violent, not a heavy drinker, not greedy for gain, hospitable, loving good, showing good sense, devout [*hosios*], self-controlled); the phrase "sound doctrine" (1:9); and some of the description of the opponents in 1:10 (and 1:16: insubordinate, idle talkers, deceivers, tainted, vile). Evaluating such evidence is always a dubious point because Paul might have given considerable freedom to a scribe.[28] Here, however, most scholars postulate a writer other than Paul.

(2) In the Pastorals there is emphasis on sound doctrine (Titus 1:9; 2:1; I Tim 1:10; II Tim 4:3) and knowledge of truth (Titus 1:1; I Tim 2:4; II Tim 2:25; 3:7), as well as being sound in faith (Titus 1:13; 2:2), retaining sound words (I Tim 6:3; II Tim 1:13), and being nourished on "the word of the faith" (I Tim 4:6—an unPauline expression). Clearly a certain content and phraseology had become part of Christian belief. Although some have contended that for the earliest Christians faith meant only trust in Jesus or belief that he was sent by God, from certain NT passages we can see that christological content quickly entered the picture, namely, a belief in who Jesus was/is. For example, see Rom 1:3–4 for a prePauline christology that may date back to the early 40s. However, by the last third of the 1st century (at least) Christians had moved to insisting on greater precision in expressing christology because there could be different understandings of the early formulations. In Matt 16:16; 26:63 it is not enough to state that Jesus is the Christ (Messiah), but that he is so in such a way that he is truly the Son of God. Thus doctrine becomes part of faith. The Pastorals reflect what will become increasingly characteristic of Christianity in the 2d through the 4th

[28]Yet since I Tim was almost certainly written by the same person who wrote Titus, the scribe would have had to be someone who traveled with Paul over a period of time.

centuries: an ever-sharpening insistence on orthodoxy (correct faith content), combined with orthopraxy (correct behavior).

(3) On pp. 609–10 above a question was raised about the modern application of instructions given in the household codes. That issue is exacerbated by elements of prejudice evident in the Titus code (2:1–10). The dangers of slander and excessive wine are mentioned only in reference to the older *women.* The duties of slaves are recounted, including a warning against pilfering; but nothing is said to the masters in a relationship where society was less likely to curb the oppressive potentialities of the masters than to punish slaves. One may argue that the omission occurred because relatively few Christians in Crete were masters, but that does not resolve the problem produced by such a code in later times when it might give the impression that Christianity favored those who had higher social or economic status. Other NT passages should be read as a corrective.

(4) There is a hymnic description of salvation and baptism in 3:4–7 that is called "a sure (faithful) saying" (3:8)[29] and that may involve earlier tradition. Many of the ideas therein (e.g., freely by grace, renewal, bath) are Pauline or deuteroPauline (Rom 3:24; 12:2; Eph 5:26), but rebirth (*palingenesia*) is not used elsewhere by Paul. Some would derive the image from Stoicism or the mystery religions; but the idea that the acceptance of Christ is so important that it can be deemed a new birth (from God) has particular significance against a background of Judaism, where birth from a Jewish parent (mother) made one a member of God's chosen people. See Matt 19:28 for the word, and John 3:3–8 and I Pet 1:3,23 for the idea. Chapter 22 above, *Issue* 4, discusses baptism in Pauline practice.

Bibliography on the Pastoral Letters in General and on Titus

COMMENTARIES AND STUDIES ON THE (THREE) PASTORAL LETTERS IN SERIES: Barrett, C. K. (NClarBC, 1963); Davies, M. (EC, 1996; NTG, 1996); **Dibelius, M., and H. Conzelmann** (Hermeneia, 1972); Donelson, L. R. (WBComp, 1996); Fee, G. D. (NIBC, 1988); Fuller, R. H. (ProcC, 1978); Guthrie, D. (TNTC, 1957); Hanson, A. T. (NCBC, 1982); Houlden, J. L. (PC, 1976); Hultgren, A. J. (AugC, 1984); Johnson, L. T. (NTIC, 1996); Karris, R. J. (NTM, 1979); **Kelly, J.N.D.** (HNTC, 1960); Knight, G. W. (NIGTC, 1992); Lock, W. (ICC, 1924); Oden, T. (IBC, 1989); **Quinn, J. D.** (*Titus;* AB, 1990); Taylor, F. T., Jr. (ProcC, 1993); Young, F. M. (NTT, 1994).

[29]G. W. Knight, *The Faithful Sayings in the Pastoral Epistles* (Grand Rapids: Baker, 1979); R. A. Campbell, JSNT 54 (1994), 73–86. There are five of these sayings in the Pastorals (including I Tim 1:15; 3:1a; 4:9; II Tim 2:11), and some would see them as catechetical maxims derived from Paul, or confessional statements constructed from Pauline soteriological themes. The formula does not occur in the undisputed Paulines, but see "faithful is God" of I Cor 10:13.

Barrett, C. K., "Pauline Controversies in the Post-Pauline Period," NTS 20 (1973–74), 229–45.

———, "Titus," in *Neotestamentica et Semitica* (M. Black Festschrift; Edinburgh: Clark, 1969), 1–14.

Bratcher, R. G., *A Translator's Guide to Paul's Letters to Timothy and Titus* (New York: United Bible Societies, 1983).

Brown, L. A., "Asceticism and Ideology: The Language of Power in the Pastoral Epistles," *Semeia* 57 (1992), 77–94.

Brown, R. E., "The Pauline Heritage in the Pastorals: Church Structure," BCALB 31–46.

Collins, R. F., "The Image of Paul in the Pastorals," *Laval théologique et philosophique* 31 (1975), 147–73.

———, "The Pastoral Epistles," CLPDNW 88–130.

Colson, F. H., "Myths and Genealogies—A Note on the Polemic of the Pastoral Epistles," JTS 19 (1917–18), 265–71.

Donelson, L. R., *Pseudepigraphy and Ethical Argument in the Pastoral Epistles* (Tübingen: Mohr-Siebeck, 1986).

Elliott, J. K., *The Greek Text of the Epistles to Timothy and Titus* (Salt Lake City: Univ. of Utah, 1968).

Ellis, E. E., "The Authorship of the Pastoral Epistles," *Paul and His Recent Interpreters* (Grand Rapids: Eerdmans, 1961), 49–57.

Fiore, B., *The Function of Personal Example in the Socratic and Pastoral Epistles* (AnBib 105; Rome: PBI, 1986).

Grayston, K., and G. Herdan, "The Pastorals in the Light of Statistical Linguistics," NTS 6 (1959–60), 1–15.

Hanson, A. T., *Studies in the Pastoral Epistles* (London: SPCK, 1968).

———, "The Use of the Old Testament in the Pastoral Epistles," IBS 3 (1981), 203–19.

———, "The Domestication of Paul," BJRL 63 (1981), 402–18.

Harrison, P. N., *The Problem of the Pastoral Epistles* (Oxford Univ., 1921).

———, *Paulines and Pastorals* (London: Villiers, 1964).

Lemaire, A., "Pastoral Epistles: Redaction and Theology," BTB 2 (1972), 25–42.

Malherbe, A. J., "Medical Imagery in the Pastorals," in *Texts and Testaments,* ed. W. E. March (San Antonio: Trinity Univ., 1980), 19–35.

Metzger, B. M., "A Reconsideration of Certain Arguments against the Pauline Authorship of the Pastoral Epistles," ExpTim 70 (1958–59), 91–94.

Morton, A. Q., S. Michaelson, and J. D. Thompson, *A Critical Concordance to the Pastoral Epistles* (Wooster, OH: Biblical Research, 1982).

Moule, C.F.D., "The Problem of the Pastoral Epistles: A Reappraisal," BJRL 47 (1965), 430–52.

Rogers, P. V., "The Pastoral Epistles as Deutero-Pauline," ITQ 45 (1978), 248–60.

Soards, M. L., "Reframing and Reevaluating the Argument of the Pastoral Epistles toward a Contemporary New Testament Theology," in *Perspectives on Contemporary New Testament Questions,* ed. E. V. McKnight (T. C. Smith Festschrift; Lewiston, NY: Mellen, 1992), 49–62.

Towner, P. H., "The Present Age in the Eschatology of the Pastoral Epistles," NTS 32 (1986), 427–48.

Verner, D. C., *The Household of God: The Social World of the Pastoral Epistles* (SBLDS 71; Chico, CA: Scholars, 1983).

Wild, R. A., "The Image of Paul in the Pastoral Letters," TBT 23 (1985), 239–45.

Wilson, S. G., *Luke and the Pastoral Epistles* (London: SPCK, 1979).

Ziesler, J. A., "Which Is the Best Commentary? X. The Pastoral Epistles," ExpTim 99 (1987–88), 264–67.

CHAPTER 30

PASTORAL LETTER: THE FIRST TO TIMOTHY

There are two letters to this disciple of Paul in the NT canon, but neither shows an awareness of the existence of the other (contrast II Pet 3:1). "First" does not tell us that the one so designated was written first, but only that it is longer than the other that has consequently been called "second." The subject matter of I Tim resembles that of Titus; but again nothing in either missive shows awareness of the other, nor do we know which of the three Pastorals was written first.

After a discussion of the *Background,* the *General Analysis* will be divided according to the pattern used for Titus (pp. 641–44 above). Subsections will be devoted to: *Who wrote Titus and I Tim,* the *Implications of pseudepigraphy for the Pastorals,* and *Issues for reflection.*

The Background

Some biographical details about Timothy, drawn from Acts and the rest of the Pauline corpus, can be useful since they may have shaped the writer's image of the recipient. Timothy lived at Lystra in SE Asia Minor and presumably was converted as a result of Paul's evangelizing there *ca.* AD 46. When the apostle passed through once more *ca.* 50, Timothy joined him as a traveling missionary and remained at his service as a faithful helper through Paul's subsequent career. According to Acts 16:1–3, although Timothy's father was a Gentile, his mother was a Jewish Christian; and so Paul had him circumcised lest Jews be scandalized.[1] During the "Second Missionary Journey" of 50–52, Timothy accompanied Paul through Phrygia and Galatia and over to Europe (Philippi, Thessalonica, and Beroea). He was sent back to strengthen the Thessalonians, and rejoined Paul in Corinth

[1]Many would challenge the accuracy of Acts here because in Gal 2:3 Paul states that he refused to have Titus circumcised. Yet Titus, if born of two Gentile parents, was a Gentile, whereas Timothy, as the son of a Jewish mother, may have been considered a Jew. Despite scholars' assumptions, in Paul's writings there is no clear indication that he thought Jews should not be circumcised. II Tim 1:5 gives the name of Timothy's mother as Eunice, and that of his grandmother (also a Jewish Christian) as Lois.

Summary of Basic Information

DATE: If by Paul, *ca.* AD 65. If pseudonymous (80 to 90 percent of critical scholarship), toward the end of the 1st century, or (less probably) early 2d century.

TO: Timothy in Ephesus (with the possibility that Ephesus may represent churches already in existence for quite a while) from a Paul depicted as recently departed from there and now in Macedonia.

AUTHENTICITY: Probably written by a disciple of Paul or a sympathetic commentator on the Pauline heritage several decades after the apostle's death.

UNITY AND INTEGRITY: Not seriously disputed.

FORMAL DIVISION:

A. Opening Formula: 1:1–2
B. Thanksgiving: None
C. Body: 1:3–6:19
D. Concluding Formula: 6:20–21.

DIVISION ACCORDING TO CONTENTS:

1:1–2: Address/greetings to Timothy
1:3–11: Warning against false teachers
1:12–20: Paul's own career and charge to Timothy
2:1–15: Ordering of public worship (especially for men and women)
3:1–16: Instructions for bishop and deacons
4:1–5: Correction of false teaching
4:6–5:2: Encouragement for Timothy to teach
5:3–6:2: Instructions for widows, presbyters, and slaves
6:3–10: Warning against false teachers and love of money
6:11–21a: Charge to Timothy
6:21b: Concluding blessing.

bringing good news (I Thess 3:6; Acts 18:5), so that his name was joined to Paul's in sending I Thess (1:1). He aided Paul in the evangelizing of Corinth (II Cor 1:19); but we lose track of him for the years when according to Acts 18:18–19:1 Paul went back to Caesarea, Jerusalem, and Syrian Antioch, only to start out again ("Third Missionary Journey") through Galatia and Phrygia for Ephesus. During Paul's stay in Ephesus in 54–57 Timothy was with him at least part of the time.[2] In late 56 or early 57, probably to collect money to be taken to Jerusalem, Paul sent him from Ephesus into Macedonia (Acts 19:22; I Cor 4:17; 16:10) with the understanding that eventually he would go to Corinth. Seemingly Timothy reached there just after I Cor was delivered. It was not well received, and so Timothy hastened back to Paul in Ephesus to report on this. Probably Timothy was with Paul when the apostle finally left Ephesus in the summer of 57; for when Titus brought good news

[2]His name is joined to Paul's in Phil 1:1 and Phlm 1, and those letters may have been sent from Ephesus.

of the resolution of the Corinthian situation, Paul and Timothy sent II Cor (1:1) from Macedonia. Timothy spent the winter of 57–58 with Paul in Corinth, during the time Rom (16:21) was sent. Acts 20:4–5 has him with the apostle at the beginning of the journey from Corinth to Jerusalem before Pentecost of 58; he went on ahead and awaited Paul in Troas. That is the last mention of Timothy in Acts. During the period of the composition of the undisputed Paulines (*ca.* 51–58?), Timothy's name was listed as co-author on I Thess, Phil, Phlm, and I Cor. Because it is also joined to Paul's in Col 1:1 and respectable scholars judge that letter to have been written by Paul from Rome, Timothy is often thought to have been with Paul in the Roman imprisonment of 61–63; but that is far from certain.

Through the years Paul wrote warm evaluations of Timothy. In I Thess 3:2 Timothy is portrayed as Paul's "brother" and God's servant in the gospel of Christ. Paul wrote to the Philippians (2:19–23): "I have no one like him"; he is son to Paul in the service of the Gospel, and he does not look after his own interests but Christ's. In I Cor 4:17; 16:10–11, Timothy is described as Paul's beloved and faithful child, not to be despised for he does the work of the Lord.

How does the biographical information in I Tim fit into this picture? In its attitude toward Timothy I Tim (along with II Tim) is very close to the undisputed Pauline letters: Timothy is a beloved son to Paul and a servant to God; he is to be an example even as he learned from Paul; he is not to be despised. Beyond this I Tim describes Timothy as a youth (4:12; 5:1) who had a gift, given to him "through prophecy with the laying on hands of the presbyters" (4:14); he has also been subject to frequent illness (5:23). At the time of writing he was at Ephesus, left there by Paul who had gone into Macedonia (1:3), hoping to return to Ephesus soon (3:14–15; 4:13). This information does not fit into the career of Paul and Timothy that I have just recounted, derived from Acts and the undisputed Pauline letters. For instance, when Paul left Ephesus for Macedonia in 57, Timothy did not remain behind. Accordingly, as with the letter to Titus (p. 641 above), scholars have posited a "second career" of Paul after his captivity in Rome ended in 63. They contend that Paul went back to Ephesus (despite Acts 20:25,38, where he told the elders of Ephesus *ca.* 58 that they would never see him again), and that then sometime in the mid-60s he left Timothy there and went on to Macedonia.[3]

[3]Some object that by that time Timothy would have been a Christian for almost twenty years and probably older than thirty-five, and thus scarcely in his youth! Yet Paul, who may have been in his early thirties at the time of the stoning of Stephen, is described in that scene in Acts (7:58) as a young man. Paul, in his undisputed letters speaks of Timothy as his child, but such a figurative expression yields little precision.

General Analysis of the Message

The "Division According to Contents" in the Summary above shows a complicated sequence in I Tim, with a good deal of to-and-fro. At times Paul tells Timothy what to do (1:3–20; 4:6ff.); at other times he speaks directly to community problems (e.g., in chap. 2). Topics begun in an early section are taken up again later (false teaching, church structure). Quinn would argue that instructions for Timothy are arranged in two segments, one (1:3–3:13) situated before and one (4:6–6:21a) situated after a core of prophetic texts, hymnic and oracular (3:14–4:5) that are proposed and interpreted for Timothy by Paul.[4] More simply, I shall follow the organization of contents adopted in the treatment of Titus, even though they are not treated in the same order in I Tim. Thus, after a short comment about the Opening Formula, the message will be studied under three headings: church structure, false teaching, and community relations and belief. Scattered pericopes dealing with these will be brought together.

Opening Formula (1:1–2). This is shorter than that of Titus. Instead of the unusual "servant of God" found there, the apostle identifies himself as commissioned by God our Savior and Christ Jesus our hope, thus building a basis on which he can issue church instructions. The address to Timothy and the greeting are virtually the same as those to Titus.

Body (3:1–13; 5:3–22a). *Theme of church structure or order.* This topic was treated first in Titus and involved only the appointment of presbyter/bishops in Crete. The situation is more complicated in I Tim, for the treatment of the structure at Ephesus is spread over two strangely unconnected segments, the first describing the bishop (overseer) and deacons, the second describing widows and presbyters. Quinn, *Titus* 16, treats these as instructions for two different church orders, the first directed to Gentile house-congregations at Ephesus, the second (especially in the matter of presbyters) addressed to the Jewish house-churches. That is unwarranted, and we need posit no more than one basic church structure among the Pauline congregations at Ephesus,[5] even if that structure was more complicated than the one envisioned in Crete (Titus). Christianity at Ephesus dated back at least to the 50s, whereas Christianity in Crete may not have been planted till several decades later. The fact that I Tim 5:19–20 proposes a process at Ephesus for bringing accusations against a presbyter suggests an institution that has been in existence for some time. Most qualifications stipulated in Titus 1:5–9 for the combined presbyter/bishops who are the teachers of the community are

[4]For another structural analysis, see P. G. Bush, NTS 36 (1990), 152–56.

[5]If the Gospel according to John was written in the Ephesus area, there would have been other, nonPauline Christian congregations with different attitudes toward structure.

stipulated in I Tim 3:1–7 for the bishop(s).[6] In all likelihood those bishops were presbyters; but since 5:17 indicates that only certain presbyters were involved in preaching and teaching, probably not all presbyters were bishops.[7] The claim that anyone aspires to the role of a bishop aspires to a noble function (3:1) shows how highly the position was esteemed.[8] The warning for those who are bishops not to become conceited (3:6) would make special sense in such a situation.

Alongside the presbyter/bishops at Ephesus there are deacons (3:8–13) who are to have similar qualifications: respectable, not given to too much wine, not pursuing dishonest gain, married only once, managing their children and household well. Why some men are presbyter/bishops and others are deacons is not clear. It is specified in 3:10 that the deacons are to be tested before being allowed to serve, and so they may represent a younger group.[9] Yet there may have been social or economic distinctions about which we have no information and can only guess, e.g., deacons might not have been wealthy enough to have a large house at which the Christian community could meet—if possessing such a space was expected of presbyter/bishops as part of the demand that they be hospitable. The root verb *diakonein* suggests service; and deacons may have rendered service more menial than that provided by the presbyter/bishops. The promise that those deacons who serve well will gain an excellent standing suggests the possibility of moving on to be presbyter/bishops (which could explain why the qualifications are the same). Probably there are also women deacons[10] (3:11) for whom qualifications are listed: respectable, temperate, trustworthy. Presumably they rendered the same kinds of service supplied by the men deacons, but some have *speculated* that at certain times women deacons performed duties for women that men deacons performed for men. Unfortunately we know nothing precise about that service since not a word is said in I Tim as to what the

[6]The word occurs only in 3:2 as a generic singular (p. 646 above).

[7]Thus there may already be a movement toward specification that will ultimately lead to one presbyter being assigned authority over all: the type of episcopate urged by Ignatius of Antioch.

[8]This is designated "a faithful saying." But a variant reading of 3:1 has "a human saying," presumably meaning that ambition in aspiring to be a bishop reflects human values in need of qualification: J. L. North, NovT 37 (1995), 50–67.

[9]In 5:1 directions are given for the relations between *presbyteroi* (comparative form from "old") and *neōteroi* (comparative form from "young"), and some would argue that just as presbyters (elders) were bishops, "youngers" were deacons. However, since 5:2 deals with the relationship between older women (*presbyterai*) and younger women (*neōterai*), 5:1 is probably talking about the relationship between older men and younger men—an age designation, not a reference to office.

[10]Discussed by J. H. Stiefel, NTS 41 (1995), 442–57. After a treatment of male deacons in 3:8–10, the next verse begins "Women also." Grammar strongly favors the interpretation that this means "women (who are deacons)" rather than "women (wives of deacons)." The wife of the deacon is mentioned as a distinct role in 3:12. Moreover, it is clear that the term *diakonos* could refer to men and women (e.g., Phoebe in Rom 16:1—see there for avoiding the unbiblical term "deaconess").

deacons are to do for the Christian community. In Acts 6:1–6 *diakonein* is used for waiting on tables, and from that has developed the idea that the deacons waited on tables and distributed food. Yet historically it is a misinterpretation to regard as deacons Stephen and the Hellenist leaders chosen in that Acts scene;[11] at most one may wonder whether Luke was interpreting them in the light of deacons he knew in the churches of the 80s. Since Stephen and Philip preached, that could mean that the later deacons preached and taught.

Widows (5:3–16) constituted another group at Ephesus. They had fixed community status, but it is not clear that they should be described as holding an office or constituting an order. Paul would make a clear distinction between women who are widows only because their husbands are dead, and those who have a special church role for whom he lists qualifications. The special ("true") widows must be sixty years old, have been married only once (and thus committed to remaining single[12]), not have children or grandchildren to be cared for, have brought up their children well, and be well known for good deeds. It is envisioned that these are women without personal wealth (5:5,16), and so the church provides for them from the common goods (Acts 6:1). Elements of their role in the church included praying night and day,[13] extending hospitality even in menial tasks (washing "the feet of the saints"), helping those in need. (We have no idea how this widows' role differed from that of the men and women deacons.)

What is peculiar in Paul's description is the clearly hostile tone toward widows who should not be enrolled among the special group of widows. These ineligible widows ought to be taking care of their children or grandchildren. He fears that the younger among them might even be "merry widows," indulging in pleasure and sensual desires that could overcome their dedication to Christ, visiting about and gossiping, looking for another husband, and thus breaking their lifetime pledge to their first husband. In the long run, then, Paul judges it better that young widows remarry and have children rather than give scandal. "Some have already turned away after Sa-

[11]"To wait on tables" is figurative language for being responsible for the community's funds and their distribution. If we were to use the anachronistic language of later decades to describe the seven Hellenist leaders who were responsible for the community's direction, common finances, and public preaching, they would have the role of bishops.

[12]Some have tried to understand the expression simply in terms of a woman having been faithful to her husband, no matter how often she married; but inscriptions of this period used an equivalent adjectival expression ("having one husband") as a laudatory description of a widow who had restricted herself to one marriage.

[13]The description in Luke 2:36–37 of the pious Jewish widow Anna who never left the Temple and worshiped night and day, fasting and praying, may be related to the ideal of the Christian widow in the communities known to Luke.

tan" (5:15). J. M. Bassler[14] has suggested that some of the women thus declared ineligible (perhaps not only widows, but divorced or unmarried women) may have been insisting on greater freedom of expression. They would also have been the target of the more general corrections in I Tim 2:11–15 that want women to be submissive and, since they are easily deceived, forbidden to teach men. We shall return to that issue after we look at the false teaching.

BODY (1:3–20; 3:14–4:10; 6:3–5): *Theme of false (and true) teaching.* False teaching is described in several places in I Tim, and we cannot be sure that the same danger is always in mind. As in the letter to Titus, there is much polemic in the description,[15] making it difficult to know what precisely was the basic error. Paul (1:13–16) mentions that he himself was converted from being a blasphemer and persecutor by the merciful grace of Christ—implicit encouragement that others now opposed to sound doctrine can be converted, for Christ came into the world to save sinners. Timothy, despite his youth, has had prophecies made about him, has followed sound doctrine, and is capable of being a good minister of Christ (1:18–19; 4:6) in counteracting the false teachers. Alongside an indication of the Jewish background of the opponents who would be teachers of the Law (1:7), there is an unclear reference to their devotion to myths and genealogies (1:4; 4:7; cf. Titus 1:14; 3:9; II Tim 4:4). The condemnation of sins against the Ten Commandments (implicit in 1:8–10) measures the teachers by a general standard of orthopraxy. But some of the criticized issues are more specific: The opponents forbid people to marry and order them to abstain from certain foods (4:3). (More obscurely, moreover, as teachers [or perhaps religious gurus] they are very interested in making money: 6:5,10.) This leaves us with the same query raised in treating Titus: Does the teaching reflect a background in Jewish apocrypha, or Jewish gnosticism ("falsely called knowledge" [*gnōsis*]: 6:20), or a combination of the two? Soards, arguing that Paul's insistence on traditional values means that he is struggling against an arrogant individualism, contends that the probable object was Cynic philosophy.[16] Individual Cynic philosophers spoke with sarcasm and skepticism about God or the gods and about traditional religious beliefs and praised those who

[14]JBL 103 (1984), 23–41.

[15]E.g., I Tim 6:3–5: Anyone who teaches something other than sound and pious doctrine is conceited, knowing nothing, morbid about controversies and quarrels over words, thus producing envy, strife, blasphemies, wicked suspicions, and wrangling among the depraved and using religion for gain.

[16]"Reframing" 54–65; see also Fiore, *Function.* It is difficult to know whether we should bring II Tim into the diagnosis of the error attacked in Titus and I Tim. II Tim 2:17–18 denounces men who contend that the resurrection is already past, and Soards cites Cynic rejection of an afterlife.

did not marry and raise a family; they were accused of being mercenary. In part, a decision about the tone of the false teaching[17] depends on our analysis of those in the community whom those teachers most affected, to which we now turn.

BODY (2:1–15; 4:11–5:2; 5:22B–6:2; 6:6–19): *Theme of community relations and belief.* This is harder to delineate in I Tim than it was in Titus because part of it is woven into the condemnation of false teaching, e.g., 1:8–11. As in Titus 2:1–10 there is a *household code* but in a scattered form. Thus, in I Tim 5:1–2 there are instructions about the interrelations of the older and the younger members of the community, male and female; in 2:8–15 there are instructions for men and women on how to behave during worship; in 6:1–2 slaves are told to show no less respect to Christian than to nonChristian masters (once again with no corresponding admonition to masters); in 2:1–2 prayer is inculcated on behalf of those in authority.

The instructions for men and women in worship are disproportionately corrective of women. A stress on modesty and decency in dress leads into a demand that women be quiet and submissive while they learn (2:9–12). "I do not permit a woman to teach or to have authority over men" may refer primarily to a worship context[18] but probably extends farther, as the reference to Eve suggests. Normally these verses are read as a general attitude toward women; and in today's context they will be heard as extremist in limiting women's roles, especially when combined with a reproving attitude toward young widows in 5:11–15.[19] Yet there has been support recently for another way of interpreting this passage against the background of the letter's attack on false teaching.[20] That these were *wealthy* women is suggested by the warning against gold, pearls, and costly attire (2:9); and this may be connected to the castigation of self-indulgent widows having the leisure to

[17]Some would be far more skeptical about attempts to discern the thought of the opponents criticized in I Tim. Johnson (*Writings* 397): "When the elements of slander (e.g., the accusation of cupidity) are removed, however, they simply represent once more the sort of elitist esoteric groups we so often encounter in the religiosity of the Hellenistic world."

[18]Given that a church structure with authoritative groups of presbyters (elders) echoes the synagogue pattern of presbyters, many observe that the prohibition against women teaching in the assembly or having authority over men resembles synagogue practice.

[19]Often the negative attitude toward women in the Pastorals is contrasted with a more favorable attitude toward an ecclesiastical role for women in the undisputed Pauline letters (e.g., toward Prisca, Phoebe, and Junia in Rom 16:1,3,7; I Cor 16:19, and the equalizing statement in Gal 3:28). That comparison, however, should also take into account I Cor 14:35, "It is shameful for a woman to speak in church" (see also Col 3:18).

[20]On women in I Tim 2:9–15, consult A.D.B. Spencer, JETS 17 (1974), 215–221; R. and C. Kroeger, *Reformed Journal* #10 (Oct. 1980), 14–18; G. W. Knight, NTS 30 (1984), 143–57; A. Padgett, *Interpretation* 41 (1987), 19–31; C. S. Keener, *Paul, Women & Wives* (Peabody, MA: Hendrickson, 1992); S. Motyer, VE 24 (1994), 91–102; H. S. Baldwin et al., *Women in the Church: A Fresh Analysis of 1 Timothy 2:11–15* (Grand Rapids: Baker, 1995); also the debate between D. J. Moo and D. B. Payne, *Trinity Journal* NS 1 (1980), 62–83; 2 (1981), 169–222.

flit about from house to house (5:6,13); see also the attacks on wealth in 6:9,17. If the false teachers were making such women the target of their message, that would explain the charge that the teachers were seeking monetary gain (6:5).[21] Thus, not women in general but women who became the spokespersons of the error to which they had been enticed would have been the object of the prohibition of teaching and holding authority (2:12).[22] In visiting from house to house the women may have been spreading the error. The women who do this false teaching are compared to Eve who deceived Adam (2:13–14); and the salvation of women through bearing children (2:15,[23] echoed in the urging of young widows to remarry and bear children in 5:14) may have been an invocation of the authority of Gen 3:16, in order to contradict the teachers who forbade marriage (I Tim 4:3). Such a scenario is not impossible in the context of the late 1st and early 2d centuries. Attention has been called to apocryphal *Acts* composed in the 2d century that exemplify a teaching rejecting eating meat, drinking wine, and participating in sexual intercourse. The *Acts* also envision a permanent Christian widowhood that offers independence from marriage and family life and occasionally display gnostic tendencies. Some would see women having a role in the composition of such *Acts*[24] and think that the criticism of "godless and silly myths" in I Tim 4:7 was directed against this kind of tradition.

Beyond the household code one may notice a particular distrust of wealth in 6:5–10,17–19, including the famous "The love of money is the root of all evils" (6:10). A notable number of *hymnic passages* supports the writer's

[21]Also II Tim 3:2,6–7 describes false teachers as lovers of money who make their way into households and capture weak women.

[22]That this is not directed universally against women receives some support from Titus 2:3, where older women are told to teach. If a limited directive is accepted, however, one should still recognize that the expressions of the Pastorals (especially, for instance, II Tim 3:6–7) can be offensive and need to be qualified by an emphasis on the social situations of the time that affected the writer's outlook.

[23]This might sound like salvation through works, but it is modified by a demand for faith, love, and holiness. In the total Pauline picture it should be balanced by Paul's praise of celibacy in I Cor 7:25–38.

[24]S. L. Davies, *The Revolt of the Widows. The Social World of the Apocryphal Acts* (Carbondale, IL: Southern Illinois Univ., 1980), argues that the apocryphal *Acts of John, Peter, Paul, Andrew, Thomas,* and *Xanthippe* were written by Christian women (who were celibate) for other Christian women. He points to relationships between wonder-working Christian preachers and the portrayal of women in these *Acts.* Widows in such literature might include a woman who had left her husband or never married. D. R. Macdonald, *The Legend and the Apostle* (Philadelphia: Westminster, 1983), maintains that elements of genuine Pauline radicalism were continued in the *Acts of Paul and Thecla* (AD 160–190), as stories about women teaching in the Pauline tradition were passed on and developed by celibate women storytellers. (See n. 33 below and R. A. Wild, *Chicago Studies* 24 [1985], 273–89.) For Macdonald the Pastorals were written by literate men aligned with the developing episcopacy and were directed against women who were prophets and storytellers; they represent a polemic attempt to domesticate apocalyptic radicalism by appealing to the example of Paul. This theory fits into a dubious trend to see the Pastorals as an attempt to correct the apostle's heritage; see pp. 663, 668 below.

moral instructions, the most famous of which is 3:16, where in six short poetic lines the mystery of religion/godliness (*eusebeia*) is praised in terms of what has happened to Christ.[25] Hymnic elements have also been recognized in 6:7–8 and the benediction of 6:15–16. The latter has a resounding liturgical ring in its lines: "The blessed and only Sovereign; the King of kings, and Lord of lords; the one who alone is immortal, dwelling in unapproachable light, whom no one has ever seen or can see." This blessing would have been seen as giving to Christ titles that might elsewhere be claimed by the emperor. Jesus has become part of a monotheistic creedal statement of the "truth" in 2:4–5, "There is one God; there is one mediator between God and human beings, Christ Jesus himself human."

In the CONCLUDING FORMULA (6:20–21) one does not find the greetings that terminate most Pauline letters, including Titus and II Tim, but only a passionate plea to Timothy. Just as some interpret the long Opening Formula of Titus as an introduction to the Three Pastorals, so some regard the abrupt ending of I Tim as a preparation for the already planned II Tim. Such a collective planning for the group will be challenged below (pp. 668–69).

Who Wrote Titus and I Timothy?

We have enough evidence now to consider this issue; and since II Tim is partially a different problem, let us leave that till the next Chapter. Paul is the apparent writer, even to the extent of supplying details about his personal travels. Yet for reasons to be listed below, that has been challenged for the last 200 years. A suggested alternative is a close Pauline disciple carrying out the implicit designs of the master,[26] in other words the same solution suggested for other deuteroPauline writings. (Such a solution may or may not accept the historicity of the biographical details that appear in the Pastorals.) Yet some scholars would place a greater distance between Paul and the writer of the Pastorals. Some would see them as written not by a disciple of Paul but by a sympathetic commentator on the Pauline heritage (including some information about Titus and Timothy that he wove into a fictional sequence) who wanted to strengthen local church organization against incipi-

[25]See R. H. Gundry in *Apostolic History and the Gospel,* ed. W. Gasque and R. P. Martin (F. F. Bruce Festschrift; Grand Rapids: Eerdmans, 1970), 203–22; also E. Schweizer, "Two Early Christian Creeds Compared," in *Current Issues in New Testament Interpretation,* eds. W. Klassen and G. F. Snyder (O. Piper Festschrift; New York: Harper, 1962), 166–77, compared with I Cor 15:3–5.

[26]Although he is critical of this solution, Johnson, *Writings* 387, supplies a good description of what might have happened: An adaptation of the Pauline message for a new generation, emphasizing structure and order, while resisting ascetical and egalitarian excess; an acceptance of a diminished eschatological expectation; growth in church structure; increased accommodation to the world after the apostle's death; hailing Paul as a hero whose authentic genius becomes part of the "deposit" of faith for future generations.

ent gnosticism. More radically, others would see them as a nonPauline attempt to correct the apostle's heritage: At a time when the memory of Paul was being invoked dangerously by Marcion and by apocryphal *Acts,* the Pastorals would have been written to domesticate that memory and bring the apostle into the mainstream.[27] Indeed, forgery has been suggested, as part of a design to deceive the readers. Part of the issue is whether the contents of the Pastorals can feasibly be assigned to Paul's lifetime (i.e., to a "second career" in the period 63–66 after that recounted in Acts). Those who describe the Pastorals as pseudepigraphical assign them to the 80s–90s, the early 2d century, or the last third of that century. Let us look at different factors (not all of the same worth) that have entered into scholars' decisions. In describing them, I shall point out that they are rarely unambiguous. If that produces a confusing result, the effect is realistic; for resolving with great assurance the issue of who wrote the Pastorals and when does not respect the evidence. Beyond the question of Pauline authorship, a somewhat detailed discussion of these factors is justified because many of them concern essential aspects of the continuity between Paul's life and the ongoing churches that were shaped by his mission.

(1) The Pastorals' use of particles, conjunctions, and adverbs differs notably from Paul's undisputed usage. Also roughly one quarter of the vocabulary of the Pastorals does not appear in the other Pauline letters,[28] but that cumulative statistic does not do justice to the fact that the vocabulary of *II* Tim is much less foreign to the Pauline heritage. By comparison with the undisputed Pauline letters, the collective vocabulary of the Pastorals is less Septuagintal and closer to that of the ethical directions of the popular Greek philosophers, and the style is less Hebraic and more colorless and monotonous (longer sentences, less varied use of particles, etc.). More specifically, for instance, epithets from Hellenistic piety are ascribed exuberantly to both God and Christ in a distinctive way: "our great God and Savior" (Titus 2:13); "the blessed and only Sovereign, the King of kings and Lord of lords" (I Tim 6:15).[29] The value of the vocabulary and style argument has been queried because of Paul's possible use of scribes to whom he might have given liberty that would affect statistical comparison (but see Chapter 29

[27]It is not accurate, however, to contend that the Pastorals were meant to rehabilitate the memory or image of Paul or defend his vilified name; his authority is simply assumed.

[28]Noteworthy vocabulary of Titus and I Tim is found in Luke-Acts. See p. 666 below. The statistical linguistic analysis applied by K. Grayston and G. Herdan, "Pastorals," was challenged by T. A. Robinson, NTS 30 (1984), 282–87.

[29]Much has been written on the "unique" christology of the Pastorals with their emphasis on salvation in the *epiphaneia* ("manifestation, appearance") of Christ Jesus, an appearance in the flesh and in the second coming. (As to vocabulary, the term occurs five times in the Pastorals but never in the undisputed Paulines, which use *parousia.*) The discussion goes beyond the scope of this *Introduction,* but it is well summarized by CLPDNW 111–18.

above, n. 28). The subject matter in the Pastorals, especially that pertinent to church structure, is different from that of the other Pauline letters—a factor that could explain some vocabulary difference. Moreover Pauline vocabulary and style are strangely mixed with the nonPauline. Nevertheless, the statistics create a doubt about Pauline writing, especially when combined with other arguments.[30]

(2) In general, a similar report would be generated by a comparison of the theology and ethics of the Pastorals with that of the undisputed Paulines. Familiar Pauline terms (law, faith, righteousness) appear but with a slightly different nuance. Overall the same differences can be found in the other Pauline letters but not in so concentrated a manner. In the Pastorals there is an unusual amount of polemic, often stereotypical.

(3) As explained in the *Background* section of the Chapters on Titus and I Tim, the data about Paul's ministry and whereabouts cannot be fitted into what we know of Paul's life before the Roman imprisonment of 61–63. If the material is historical and Paul actually wrote these letters, they demand our positing a "second career" in the mid-60s. *Terminus a quo:* Titus and I Tim could not have been written, therefore, before 64–66.

(4) Some who would place the Pastorals late in the 2d century point to the fact that they are missing from Marcion's canon (*ca.* 150); yet Tertullian (*Adversus Marcion* 5.21) contends that Marcion knew and rejected them.[31] They are also missing from the Beatty Papyrus II (P^{46}; *ca.* 200[32]); but that papyrus codex contains only Pauline letters addressed to communities (Chapter 15 above, n. 2) and makes no claim to be a complete collection. The Rylands Papyrus, P^{32}, from about the same period, contained Titus. Some have claimed that the Pastorals were written to correct the apocryphal *Acts of Paul and Thecla* (late 2d century), which puts great stress on remaining a virgin and has a woman teaching men (n. 24 above); yet in the opposite direction we may be seeing in the Pastorals material that later ap-

[30]In a very careful treatment Johnson, *Writings* 386, judges that neither appeal to the outlook of an aging apostle nor mention of a second generation seems adequately to account for the differences in the Pastorals. Yet he raises the issue of whether Paul could have spoken and written to his more educated Hellenistic associates, Timothy and Titus, in a manner different from that which he used for his communities.

[31]See p. 14 above on Marcion. Titus and I Tim emphasize the authority of presbyters to teach, and Marcion ran afoul of the presbyters of the Roman church. II Tim 3:15–16 speaks of the OT Scriptures as inspired by God and useful for teaching—a view that Marcion would not approve. Some have argued that the Pastorals were written to refute Marcion (and thus composed after the middle of the 2d century), but then one might have expected a clearer and more consistent correction of Marcion's rejection of the OT. Puskas, *Letters* 178, 180 argues that there may be a reference to Marcion's *Antitheses* in I Tim 6:20; but he thinks the contact may have come with the early Marcion before he went to Rome (*ca.* AD 140), thus allowing a date for the Pastorals in the early 2d century.

[32]Or earlier (Y. K. Kim, *Biblica* 69 [1988], 248–57).

pears full-blown in the *Thecla Acts*.[33] Although this *Acts* shares in part the characters and places mentioned in II Tim, its description of Paul's journey does not correspond closely to the Pauline travels reflected in the Pastorals; and if the details of the Pastorals are not historical, the most one can say is that they and the *Thecla Acts* exhibit a similar tendency to expand the career of Paul. Toward the end of the 2d century the Muratorian Fragment is already accepting the Pastorals as authoritative. Polycarp, *Philippians* 4:1, is close to I Tim 6:10 and 6:7 and to the widow motif of 5:3–6; and most judge that Polycarp's letter (AD 120–130) has been influenced by the Pastorals and not vice versa. *Terminus ante quem:* Thus the external evidence slightly favors the Pastorals having been writen before AD 125.

(5) The false teaching that is criticized is often judged to be a Judaizing gnosticism that developed later than Paul's lifetime. Although this identification has been supported by prestigious scholars (M. Dibelius, H. Conzelmann), we have seen that the exact nature of what is being criticized in the Pastorals is hard to discern. There is insufficient evidence in the Pastorals to suggest that one of the great gnostic systems of the 2d century was the target of criticism.

(6) Also in relation to dating, it is argued that the church structure envisioned in the Pastorals goes beyond Paul's lifetime. True, none of the undisputed Pauline letters mentions presbyters; but church structure is not the subject of those writings, and so the silence could be accidental. Moreover, there is an equivalence between those called presbyters and the bishop (overseer) or bishops; and Phil 1:1 mentions the latter. (The claim that the *episkopoi* of Phil and those of the Pastorals are very different is without substantiation, since Phil supplies us no information on those figures.) Accordingly we cannot be certain when the presbyteral structure that was widespread in the last third of the 1st century (Acts 14:23; I Pet 5:1–4; Jas 5:14) became common. Although the oncoming death of Paul is mentioned only in II Tim (not Titus or I Tim), the concern with leaving behind an established church structure would be understandable as Paul's consciousness of mortally passing from the scene grew stronger. This concern would also be understand-

[33]Characters mentioned negatively in II Tim include Demas (4:10), Phygelus and Hermogenes (1:15), Hymenaeus and Philetus (who falsely teach that the resurrection of believers has already taken place: 2:17–18), and Alexander the coppersmith (4:14). By confused conflation Demas and Hermogenes the coppersmith surface in the *Thecla Acts* as deceptive companions of Paul who turn against him, try to have him killed, and offer to teach that the resurrection has already taken place. Salutations are sent to the household of Onesiphorus in II Tim 4:19, after he has been mentioned favorably in 1:16–18, with the possible implication that he is deceased ("May the Lord grant him to find mercy on the Day of the Lord"); he appears with his household as friends of Paul in the *Acts*. Comparatively the *Acts* seems to be an expansion of the material in II Tim.

able soon after Paul's death as the newly orphaned churches sought reassurance.

(7) According to Titus the principal structure to be inaugurated in Crete by Titus' appointment is that of presbyter/bishops; I Tim supposes the existence in Ephesus of presbyter/bishops (with some specialization of the presbyters) and deacons. The bipartite structure is not far from that of *Didache* 15:1 (*ca.* AD 100?) which urges that people appoint for themselves bishops and deacons to take the place of wandering apostles and prophets, and that of *I Clement* 42:4,5; 44:4–5; 54:2 (*ca.* AD 96), which refers to presbyter/bishops and deacons. It is distinct from the tripartite structure urged by Ignatius in most letters (*ca.* 110), namely, one bishop, presbyters, and deacons. Therefore, if one were to posit a linear progression (which is surely too simple a picture), the Pastorals would be placed in time before the writings of Ignatius.[34]

(8) As many have noted, in atmosphere and vocabulary the Pastorals are very close to Luke-Acts,[35] to the point that some have thought that the same person wrote them, or that one was written in partial dependence on the other. The reference in II Tim 3:11 to Paul's sufferings and what happened to him "at Antioch, at Iconium, and at Lystra" echoes the journey of Paul recounted only in Acts 13:14–14:20. The idea of presbyters in every town (Titus 1:5) is found in Acts 14:23. Presbyters who were bishops/overseers (Titus, I Tim) are attested in Acts 20:17,28. Aged widows who refuse remarriage and spend night and day in prayer are attested in I Tim 5:5,9 and Luke 2:36–37. A farewell address of Paul in the light of his coming departure is found in both II Tim 3:10–4:8 and Acts 20:18–35; the II Tim farewell is addressed through Timothy to the church at Ephesus and the Acts farewell is directed to the presbyter/bishops of Ephesus. The most plausible dating of Luke-Acts is the 80s.

(9) I Tim implies the existence of a certain type of false teaching at Ephesus. If we accept that information as historical, we must take into account that the letter to the angel of the church at Ephesus in Rev 2:1–7 (probably written in the 90s) and Ignatius' *Ephesians* (*ca.* 110) do not describe a similar heresy. Was it stamped out by I Tim which was written to Ephesus earlier than those two letters, whence the praise in Rev 2:2 for having put false apostles to the test, and in *Ephesians* 8:1 for not having been deceived? Or

[34]Puskas, *Letters* 180, would place the Pastorals outside Ignatius' sphere by contending that they were addressed to areas not yet influenced by the monepiscopal (one-bishop) system. To accept that theory one must regard as nonhistorical the references to Ephesus in I Tim 1:3; II Tim 1:18; 4:12, for in Ignatius' time monepiscopacy was established there.

[35]See J. D. Quinn in Talbert, *Perspectives on Luke-Acts* 62–75. Knight, *Pastorals,* thinks Paul may have used Luke as a secretary in writing the Pastorals.

did the heresy develop after those two letters, so that I Tim was written after them?

(10) More than the undisputed Pauline letters, the Pastorals contain a large amount of biographical material, especially recent missionary activities not otherwise attested: where Paul hopes to spend the winter, what happened to him at his first judicial hearing (in Judea or in Rome), and the names and occasionally the whereabouts of some fifteen friends and enemies of Paul who are mentioned nowhere else in the NT. Did someone other than Paul invent such details and scatter them over three letters? Modifying his proposals in several writings, P. N. Harrison has suggested that genuine Pauline notes were incorporated into the Pastorals (Titus 3:12–15; parts of II Tim, esp. chap. 4). Yet these notes do not make a truly sequential narrative; and today the thesis has relatively little following.[36] Drawing on the example of pseudepigraphical writings attributed to Plato, Donelson (*Pseudepigraphy*) contends that personalia intended to impress the reader and to lend an appearance of genuineness are typical of ancient pseudepigraphy. One should not forget, however, that many of these details play a role in the hortatory thrust of the Pastorals; they bring out aspects of the life of Paul that should be imitated. Also the personalia are not without significance for dating, especially if we include those in II Tim. Such details would require knowledge of other Pauline letters and Acts (see p. 678 below), and would those works have been easily available before AD 100?

(11) If the Pastorals are the creations of a pseudepigrapher, why did he choose as his pattern letters addressed to individuals (of which there is only one undisputed Pauline instance: Phlm) instead of the much more common pattern of letters addressed to communities? Why did he not shape letters of Paul to Crete and to Ephesus instead of Titus and I Tim? If the Pastorals were written in the 2d century and the biographical details reported in them are fictional, why has their fate (acceptance into the biblical canon) differed so sharply from other fictional compositions by or about Paul, e.g., *III Corinthians, Letter to the Laodiceans, Acts of Paul and Thecla,* which were not accepted?

(12) Those who do not believe in inspiration and those who do but without a literalist understanding of the divine communication do not find the notion of pseudepigraphy an obstacle in itself when it is understood in terms of disciples continuing the Pauline tradition and assuming the mantle of the apostle to speak loyally in his name to new problems facing a later generation. It is hard to see, however, how a proposal that the writer of the Pastorals

[36]See D. Cook, JTS NS 35 (1984), 120–31. Linguistically and stylistically these passages, he contends, were written by the same hand as the rest of the respective letters.

was intentionally deceptive and consciously desired to counteract Paul's genuine heritage can be fitted into any notion of inspiration, even a sophisticated one.[37]

In varying ways the factors just listed have contributed to a situation where *about 80 to 90 percent of modern scholars would agree that the Pastorals were written after Paul's lifetime,*[38] *and of those the majority would accept the period between 80 and 100 as the most plausible context for their composition.* The majority would also interpret them as having some continuity with Paul's own ministry and thought, but not so close a continuity as manifested in Col and Eph and even II Thess.

Implications of Pseudepigraphy for the Pastoral Letters

If one accepts pseudepigraphical authorship, virtually every issue pertinent to the letters has to be rethought.[39] No one can pretend to give definitive answers to the questions that now arise, but readers should know the issues.

Authority of the Pastorals? The authority of the historical Paul as an interpreter of Jesus Christ is based on God's call and the revelation given to him, as well as his response to God's grace by self-sacrificing fidelity to the apostolic mission. Disciples of Paul who accompanied him and shared his apostolic mission acquired a shared authority. Yet for the disciples of the disciples inevitably the bloodline of authority begins to run thin. If the writer of the Pastorals is a disciple several times removed from the historical Paul, do his instructions have the same force as those of the historical Paul? The answer to that question may well reflect one's acceptance of inspiration and biblical authority—if the Spirit has given all these writings to Christ's church, then as Scripture the Pastorals have no less a divine guarantee than the undisputed Pauline letters.

Composition as a Group? Did the pseudepigraphical writer compose the letters separately as a problem arose in real places, e.g., Crete, Ephesus, and

[37]A particular problem arises when inspiration is identified with revelation. L. M. Maloney (STS 361) objects to attributing authority to the Pastorals, and in particular their oppressive attitude toward women. Following E. Schüssler Fiorenza, she takes the position that no text that is destructive of the personal worth of women can be the revealed word of God. More classically one could hold that the Pastorals are inspired, i.e., given by God to the church, without maintaining that all the attitudes affirmed in the Pastorals are revealed. For instance, the revealed message may be that the exercise of church authority is affected by the social situation in which it is framed, and that accordingly in any system of authority oppressive attitudes of some sort are inevitable. Our recognition of oppressive attitudes in the past (e.g., in the Pastorals) should warn us that future generations will recognize oppression in the present, even among those who would never think of themselves as oppressive.

[38]CLPDNW 109, quotes H. von Campenhausen: "It is not the individual arguments against the genuineness, important as they are, which are decisive, but their complete and comprehensive convergence against which there are no significant counter-arguments."

[39]S. E. Porter, *Bulletin for Biblical Research* 5 (1995), 105–23.

Rome (where Paul died)? That would be the easiest solution; for if one posits a master design from the start, why would the writer have planned two letters to Timothy when he could have incorporated Paul's approaching death in the first letter? Also questionable is positing that the writer started with a master design for Paul's travels that we can detect from treating the letters as a group, namely, a Paul who is supposed to have left Crete (Titus) for Ephesus from which, in turn, he departed for Macedonia (I Tim) to winter at Nicopolis in Dalmatia (Illyricum), only to be taken again in captivity to Rome (II Tim).

Historicity of the Travels? More radically one has to ask whether there is any historicity at all in the "second career" of Paul. Of course, even if he wrote several decades later, the writer might have known details about Paul's last years not preserved elsewhere; and there is also Harrison's theory of the incorporation of some older Pauline fragments in the Pastorals. Nevertheless, most who posit pseudepigraphy think of a fictional embellishment on the grounds that imaginative settings are often part of the genre. By creating a plausibly realistic background from the type of apostolic ministry Paul once exercised, the writer would be appealing to Paul as the apostle par excellence.

Historicity of the Geographical Addresses? We have to ask whether the surface directions of the Pastorals (to Titus in Crete, to Timothy at Ephesus in I Tim, to Timothy probably in Asia Minor in II Tim) are authentic. Geographically, were Crete and Ephesus really addressed (even if decades after Paul's death)? Would the recipients not have known these could not be from Paul? Or were the letters directed more widely so that sites from the Pauline tradition were mentioned to illustrate types of Christian churches—Crete to exemplify churches now being newly formed, and Ephesus to illustrate churches long in existence?[40]

Historicity of the Personal Addressees? In one theory of pseudepigraphy Paul has become the model apostle, prophet, and teacher, giving instruction to church situations beyond his time—a voice that speaks even to dangers yet to come. What about the two disciples to whom this Paul addresses himself? Were Titus and Timothy still on the scene when the Pastorals were written, so that in some way, even if from beyond the grave, these letters buttressed their attempts to continue the Pauline heritage? Or were they dead and were these letters written to regions where they had worked in order to bless, support, and develop structures established by those disciples of Paul? Or were the names simply chosen from Pauline history and used paradigmat-

[40]I do not see sufficient evidence for Quinn's suggestion that Crete represented Jewish Christian churches, and I Tim was addressed in part to those churches and in part to Gentile churches.

ically to address in general church leaders and churches decades later? Those who favor the last-mentioned solution in effect see the Pastorals as doubly pseudonymous: historically not written by Paul, and not addressed to Timothy and Titus.

Historicity of Places of Composition? While Titus does not specify the place from which it was written, either Ephesus or Macedonia is likely; I Tim indicates Macedonia; II Tim indicates Rome. Are these truly indicative of where the Pastorals took their origins, or again have places from Paul's life been chosen to embellish the message? The church of Rome wrote to the church of Corinth with advice and correction *ca.* AD 96, holding up the example of Peter and Paul who contended unto death, and citing elements of Paul's life beyond the career described in Acts (*I Clement* 5:2–7). The similarities to the Pastorals are clear, and so at least the Roman origin posited in II Tim might be historical for the Pastorals—not Rome when Paul was dying but Rome where he had died and was now venerated as an apostle par excellence. One's view on that question will depend to some extent on the discussion in the next Chapter, where we consider the possibility that Titus and I Tim might have been written in imitation of a II Tim that was closer to Paul.

Issues and Problems for Reflection

(1) Numerous issues and problems have been raised in the preceding two subsections, and they are fundamental for understanding the Pastorals. But underlying all the various decisions there is a fundamental question for the meaning of the Pastorals today: Are the instructions of the Pastorals about church structure/order a legitimate continuation of the Pauline tradition? That question can be asked even if one rejects the idea that the Pastorals are a deliberate forgery designed to impose nonPauline ideas, since even a loyal and well-meaning disciple can unconsciously distort a master's heritage.[41] Sometimes because of scholars' roots in churches that lack an episcopate and sometimes because of their own dislike of such a fixed structure, they have argued that the stress on structure in the Pastorals is a perversion of Paul's appreciation of charisms—a parade example of the corrupting influence of "Early Catholicism" (p. 625 above). Others have noted that in I Cor 12 and 14 Paul indicated that charisms could cause problems and that passages like I Thess 5:12 ("those over you in the Lord"), Phil 1:1 ("bishops and deacons"), and Rom 12:8 (understood as referring to presiders or lead-

[41]However, one must still ask whether such a distortion would be possible if one views the Pastorals as inspired Scripture.

ers) show that Paul was not opposed to authoritative structures. They would argue that a more articulated structure like that of the Pastorals was a necessity if the churches were to avoid disastrous divisions once the authoritative apostle had been removed from the scene through death. Even though sociological factors inevitably shape the growth of authoritative structures if a society is to survive, in the classical theology of churches that accept ancient tradition, the development of the structure of presbyter/bishops and of deacons was directed by God as normative. Indeed, even the postNT development of a tripartite structure of one bishop, presbyters, and deacons is taken by many churches as both normative and irreversible. Obviously the stance taken on the issue has ecumenical import.

(2) If one regards the developing structure in the Pastorals as loyal to strains in Paul (or further as authoritative, normative, and even irreversible), does that mean it is irreformable? This structure developed in a particular type of society (male-dominated) in particular circumstances (acute danger of false teaching). To what extent did those particularities influence the development, creating possibilities of distortion? Does a directive like "I do not permit a woman to teach or to have authority over a man" (I Tim 2:12) constitute permanent guidance for a church directed by male presbyter/bishops, or is it simply the product of a time when most women did not have the same education as men? Holding on to a received faith is contrasted to the coming of false teaching (1:19; 4:1). Do such alternatives allow for beneficial new ideas to challenge unreflective repetition? Are they not one-sided in favoring the status quo? If the Pastorals have developed a more stable structure than that dependent on charisms, has I Cor 12 lost all relevance for such a structured church? Does it portray simply a past stage of early church life? Or in order to be faithful to the whole NT, must not a church structured by appointed officials also have room for those raised up in a nonsystematic way through the gift of the Spirit? To what extent must those thus gifted by the Spirit show obedience and respect to officials who are part of a structure that was called into being by the same Spirit? These are enduring issues in the Christian churches.

(The general *Bibliography* for the Pastoral Letters is found at the end of the preceding Chapter on Titus.)

CHAPTER 31

PASTORAL LETTER: THE SECOND TO TIMOTHY

Readers are reminded that nothing in this letter conveys an awareness of previous Pastoral Letters having been written to Timothy or Titus, and that therefore we have no direct indication that II Tim was written after Titus or I Tim. Although stylistically it is very similar to them, it is not concerned with church structure, which for them is a central issue.[1]

After discussion of *Possibilities about the Pastorals* and the *General Analysis,* subdivisions will be devoted to: the *Inspiration of Scripture as described in 3:15–16, Issues for reflection,* and *Bibliography.*

II Timothy and Possibilities about the Pastorals

Paul's life situation pictured in Titus and I Tim, as we saw, could not be fitted into his "original career" known from Acts and the undisputed Pauline letters. Consequently in each case scholars posit a "second career" (actual or fictional) for Paul after his being released from the Roman captivity of 61–63. That career would have included a ministry alongside Titus in Crete, a return to Ephesus (where he left Timothy in charge), and then a departure to Macedonia. Most contend that what II Tim tells us about Paul and Timothy is also unable to be fitted into the "original career"; and so they look on it as an ending to the "second career" in which (actually or fictionally) *ca.* 65 Paul was once more imprisoned in Rome (II Tim 1:16–17; 2:9)[2] and wrote II Tim just before he died in 66–67.

A serious minority, however, argues that II Tim can be fitted into Paul's career described in Acts. Specifically II Tim is deemed reconcilable with the assumption that after the two years of relatively easy detention in Rome (the last reference in Acts 28:30–31), Paul was subjected to harsher jailing that led to his death there *ca.* 64 or shortly afterwards. II Tim would have been written in a context just before that death without any "second career" lead-

[1]In all that follows the article of Murphy-O'Connor, "2 Timothy," is very important.

[2]The first clear reference to a second imprisonment in Rome occurs early in the 4th century in Eusebius, EH 2.22.2.

Summary of Basic Information

DATE: Written either *first* or *last* of the Pastorals. If by Paul, perhaps through a secretary, *ca.* 64 or shortly after (if written *first*) or 66–67 (if *last*). If pseudonymous (80 to 90 percent of critical scholarship), in the late 60s shortly after Paul's death (if written *first*) or decades later, most likely toward the end of the 1st century (if *last*).

To: Timothy (in Troas? in Ephesus?) from a Paul depicted as imprisoned and dying in Rome.

AUTHENTICITY: Probably written by a disciple of Paul or a sympathetic commentator on the Pauline heritage (either soon after Paul's death with historical memories, or decades later with largely fictional biographical content). Yet it has a better chance of being authentically Pauline than do the other Pastorals.

UNITY AND INTEGRITY: Not seriously disputed.

FORMAL DIVISION:

A. Opening Formula: 1:1–2
B. Thanksgiving: 1:3–5
C. Body: 1:6–4:18
D. Concluding Formula: 4:19–22.

DIVISION ACCORDING TO CONTENTS:

1:1–5: Address/greetings to Timothy; recollection of his family background
1:6–18: Encouragement to Timothy from Paul in prison, feeling himself abandoned
2:1–13: Instruction on faithful preaching of the gospel, ending in a poetic saying
2:14–3:9: Examples of true teaching vs. false teaching
3:10–4:8: Final encouragement to Timothy based on the example of a Paul about to die
4:9–18: Practical charges to come and be wary; Paul's situation
4:19–22: Concluding greetings and benediction.

ing to a second imprisonment *ca.* 65. How do the data of II Tim fit into that minority hypothesis? We are not told where Timothy was; but when he would come to Paul he was to be accompanied by Mark and to bring a cloak and books that the apostle left at Troas (4:11,13). From the surface evidence, therefore, one might assume that Timothy was at Troas;[3] and that is not implausible on the basis of other NT evidence. Acts 20:5–13 reported that in 58 on his way to Jerusalem and eventual imprisonment in Caesarea and Rome, Paul met Timothy at Troas and spent seven days there.[4] If II Tim were

[3]Most assume that Timothy is at Ephesus because that is where I Tim left him. Yet, II Tim may have been written before I Tim and thus have antedated the (fictional) career created for Paul there. Moreover, in II Tim 4:12 Paul says, "I sent Tychicus to Ephesus"—an odd phrasing if Timothy, the recipient of the letter, is imagined to be at Ephesus where he should not have needed to be informed of this.

[4]That II Tim was looking back to Paul's journey to Jerusalem in 58 receives support from the references to leaving Erastus at Corinth and Trophimus at Miletus (4:20), for this journey proceeded from Corinth in Greece through Troas to Miletus (the only other NT reference to the last site: Acts 20:2–3,6,15). Yet how can that information be reconciled with Acts 21:29 where Trophimus has

written from Rome *ca.* 64 in his continued imprisonment, Paul's career would not have brought him back to Troas after 58 to retrieve things he might have left there (perhaps because he had hoped to pick them up when he traveled from Jerusalem via Rome to Spain: Rom 15:24–25). Troas was a place that historically Paul had wanted to evangelize. When he left Ephesus in the summer of 57, he had begun successfully to preach the gospel at Troas, but was forced by his anxiety over Corinth to move on quickly to Macedonia (II Cor 2:12–13). Timothy may have picked up the task, whence Paul's addressing the letter to him there. II Tim 4:16 has Paul tell Timothy that in his first defense (at Rome?) no one took his part and all deserted him. It may be that his one and only Roman imprisonment had now turned harsh (perhaps because that defense was not successful), and it was important that Paul tell Timothy what was happening at Rome[5] in order to summon his closest confidant to one last meeting before Paul's approaching death (4:6–8). Paul's foreboding would have been verified in Rome in 64 (or even later) when Nero began to execute Christians.

By way of overall judgment, there is no convincing objection to this minority proposal, and so we must read II Tim without any presuppositions about how it is related to the other Pastorals.[6] Indeed, there are four serious possibilities:

(1) All three Pastorals are genuinely by Paul, written in the order Titus, I-II Tim during a "second career" *ca.* 65–67, culminating in a second Roman imprisonment.

(2) II Tim is genuinely by Paul, written *ca.* 64 or shortly afterwards at the end of his one, prolonged Roman imprisonment that led to his death. Titus and II Tim are pseudonymous, written later, most likely toward the end of the 1st century, partly in imitation of II Tim. A "second career" was created.

---

come with Paul to Jerusalem in this journey? Did Paul send him back to Miletus? Or has the writer made a mistake?

[5]In the hypothesis of a "second career" Paul was with Timothy for a period at Ephesus in 64–65 (thus before II Tim was written); is it likely that he would never have told Timothy in person about how he had been deserted at Rome? If II Tim was the first Pastoral to have been written and it did shortly precede Paul's death, the whole "second career" in the mid-60s demanded by Titus and I Tim is not historical.

[6]Johnson, *Writings* 382, contends that if II Tim were to be read with the other captivity letters (Phlm, Col, Eph) rather than with Titus and I Tim, its strangeness would be greatly diminished. The vocabulary and theology difference of II Tim from the undisputed Paulines is much less than that of Titus and I Tim. Although the application of the title "Savior" to Christ (II Tim 1:10, found also in Titus 2:13; 3:6; Eph 5:23) is very Hellenistic, it is also genuine Pauline usage (Phil 3:20). The theology of II Tim 1:9 is also Pauline: God saved us not in virtue of our works but in virtue of the divine purpose and the grace that God gave us in Christ Jesus ages ago.

(3) All three Pastorals are pseudonymous, but II Tim was written not long after Paul's death as a farewell testament by someone who knew Paul's last days, so that the biographical details therein would be largely historical, even if dramatized with some license. Titus and I Tim were written pseudonymously later, most likely toward the end of the 1st century, partly in imitation of II Tim. A "second career" was created.

(4) All three Pastorals are pseudonymous, written in the order Titus, I-II Tim most likely toward the end of 1st century. A "second career" was shaped (probably fictionally) for Paul with a second Roman imprisonment, so that he might speak final words about issues now troubling areas once evangelized by the apostle.

Although the majority of scholars favors a variant of (4), in my judgment (3) best meets some of the problems listed in Chapter 30 above in discussing the authorship of Titus and I Tim, and the implications of pseudepigraphy.

Perhaps a caution would be useful before we begin the *General Analysis.* The complicated debate about sequence, authorship, and date should not be allowed to obscure the power of this letter read simply as it is presented: an eloquently passionate appeal of the greatest Christian apostle that his work continue beyond his death through generations of disciples. Paul has committed his life to God in Christ, and amidst his sufferings he knows that God will protect what has been thus entrusted (II Tim 1:12). He may be chained; but the gospel he has proclaimed, which is the word of God, cannot be chained (2:9). Some scholars have complained that the Paul of II Tim has become a boaster; rather he is portrayed as offering the only argument left him in prison and at the brink of death—the example of a life lived in a way that could encourage those whom he addresses. If Paul has contributed enormously to making the love of Christ (in both senses) real to Christians, in no small way II Tim has contributed to making Paul loved.

General Analysis of the Message

The OPENING FORMULA (1:1–2) resembles that of I Tim but designates Paul an apostle by "the will" of God, rather than by "the command" of God. In that II Tim more closely approaches the normal pattern of the undisputed letters (I Cor 1:1; II Cor 1:1). Similarly closer to authentic Pauline practice is the presence of a THANKSGIVING (1:3–5), a feature lacking in I Tim. Its concentration on Timothy illustrates the very personal character that distinguishes II Tim from the other Pastorals. The information about Timothy's Jewish mother and grandmother, which we have no reason to doubt, is reported without the slightest hint that belief in Christ constituted a conflict with Judaism. (Indeed, in 3:14–15 Timothy will be urged to continue in what he has learned from his childhood, specifically the Jewish Scriptures.) This appreciative attitude is reminiscent of the atmosphere of Rom 9:1–5 and may support the Roman context claimed by II Tim 1:17.[7]

The BODY (1:6–4:18) of II Tim is about 20 percent shorter than that of I Tim, and the contents are less scattered. It takes Timothy's personality and situation into account and reflects Paul's loneliness and suffering in prison as death approaches. In some ways, then, II Tim constitutes the third of Paul's final testaments in the NT, the first being the Letter to the Romans (perhaps the last preserved genuine Pauline writing) sent from Corinth in the winter of 57–58 with a consciousness that he would face difficult times at Jerusalem but with hope that he would be able to come to Rome and go on to Spain; and the second being the Miletus sermon delivered to the presbyter/bishops of Ephesus (Acts 20:17–36) as Paul went to Jerusalem in the summer of 58 conscious he would never see them again. In neither of those, however, is death so specifically envisaged as in II Tim 4:7–8, in words that, if even if Paul did not pen them, are worthy of his eloquence: "I have fought the good fight; I have finished the race; I have kept the faith; henceforth there is laid up for me the crown of righteousness."

There are various examples of the literary genre of last-testamentary discourses or farewell speeches in the Bible.[8] Let me list characteristics of this genre, at the same time indicating the II Tim passages in which they are found. The speaker, announcing with a tone of sorrow the imminence of his departure (4:6–8), utters words of reassurance that the dear one(s) left behind should not be afraid or insecure (2:1–2,14–15; 4:1–2).[9] Often the speaker recalls his own situation and past life (1:11–13,15–18; 3:10–17), urges unity among those he is leaving behind (2:14,23–25), foresees dangers from enemies (2:16–17; 3:1–9,12–13; 4:3–4), and encourages fidelity, promising reward for it (2:11–13; 3:14; 4:8). He expresses love for those (children)

[7]The Jewish liturgical language that appears in Paul's self-description in II Tim 4:6, "I am already being poured out (like a libation on the altar)," resembles terminology of similar derivation in Rom 3:25 (Christ as an expiatory sacrifice); 12:1 (presenting one's body as a living sacrifice); and 15:16 (Paul's ministering in the priestly service of the gospel of God so that the offering of the Gentiles might be acceptable).

[8]BGJ 2.598–601; Chapter 11 above, n. 46. Yet these discourses are not letters; and citing Greco-Roman parallels, Johnson (*Writings* 391–92) would argue that II Tim is closer to the literary genre of the personal paraenetic letter written to exhort someone to pursue something and to abstain from something else, often by holding up examples to emulate and polemicizing against adversaries. Probably elements of several different genres are found in II Tim.

[9]We have to be wary of historicizing some of the sentiment that may represent the normal self-expression of the genre. For instance, we cannot conclude that Timothy was very insecure. Nor should the instruction to Timothy to do the work of an evangelist in 4:5 be construed as evidence that Timothy had the church office called "evangelist" (Acts 21:8; Eph 4:11).

he is leaving behind (1:4–5; 2:1 "my son"). In the farewell atmosphere of II Tim, a Messiah who was crucified as a criminal has as his herald Paul who is in prison as a criminal. Yet by Paul's words that scandal is turned into a defiant cry of victory, and an encouragement to Timothy and all those who suffer for the gospel. Two passages catch the tone of the message. "You have followed my teaching, way of life, endurance, faith, patience, love, steadfastness, persecutions and sufferings . . . yet from all these the Lord rescued me" (3:10–11). "Proclaim the word, be persistent in season and out of season, convince, reprimand, exhort in all patience and teaching" (4:2).

The problem of false teaching, which II Tim shares with Titus and I Tim, is part of the farewell discourse's foreseen danger. In one instance the false teaching described in II Tim is quite specific: Hymenaeus and Philetus[10] are teaching that the resurrection is past already (2:17–18). That may lie close to what is combated by Paul (*ca.* 56–57) in I Cor 15:12.[11] In other ways the II Tim description of the falsity is more ambiguous, for the accumulated abuse of those who will come in the last times (II Tim 3:1–9) could fit almost anyone. The catalogue of vices in 3:2–5 is fairly standard[12] (but closer to the one in Rom 1:29–31 than to the one in I Tim 1:9–10), and the disparagement of women in 3:6–7 is similarly generalized. This could be the stock language of apocalyptic danger.[13] If Titus and I Tim were written later, the writer of those letters may have taken his cue from this section of II Tim, making the description more specific in the light of actual dangers then being encountered.[14] The creative transmission of tradition from the apostolic generation to the next generation of teachers is envisioned in 1:13–14; 2:1–2; and that would have encouraged a third and fourth generation of Pauline disciples to continue the tradition of the master: "What you have heard from me . . . entrust to faithful people who will be fit to teach others also."

The Body Ending in 4:9–18, with its directions to Timothy and its account of Paul's situation, leads into the greetings of the CONCLUDING FORMULA (4:19–22). It is impossible to be sure how many of the characters and inci-

[10]We know nothing of *Philetus;* but *Hymenaeus,* whom Paul criticizes here as upsetting the faith, is the one whom (seemingly more seriously) in I Tim 1:20 Paul delivers to Satan that he might learn not to blaspheme—a sequence that favors the precedence of II Tim.

[11]See R. A. Horsley, NovT 20 (1978), 203–31, for this interpretation of the Corinthian error. Further, II Tim's reference, "What you have heard from me through many witnesses" (2:2), resembles the emphasis in I Cor 15:11 where, after naming other witnesses, Paul writes, "Whether, then, it was I or they, thus we preach and thus you believed." The allusion to the crown of righteousness laid up for Paul (II Tim 4:8) is similar to the imagery of running for the prize in the athletic games (I Cor 9:24–27).

[12]See N. J. McEleney, "The Vice Lists of the Pastoral Epistles," CBQ 36 (1974), 203–19.

[13]E.g., the resistance of the Egyptian magicians Jannes and Jambres to Moses is cited in 3:8, while the rebellion of Korah against Moses is cited in Jude 11.

[14]Another possible example of specification: II Tim 2:22 hints that Timothy is young; his youth is specified in I Tim 4:12.

dents mentioned in this sequence are genuine reminiscences of Paul's (first or second) captivity in Rome, or imaginative decoration by a pseudepigrapher put together from reminiscences found in the other Pauline letters and Acts.[15] The latter position has implication for dating, since we may wonder whether those works would have been easily available to a pseudepigrapher before AD 100.

Inspired Scripture (3:15–16)

This passage contains the famous words: "All/every Scripture [is] inspired by God and useful for teaching, for reproof, for correction, and for training in righteousness." Grammatically the distributive "every" is the more likely translation, i.e., "every passage of Scripture" with a reference back to the "sacred writings" known to Timothy from his childhood (3:15). There is no doubt that "Scripture" designates all or most of the books we call the OT; only by later church teaching can it be applied to the NT, which in its full form (as now accepted in Western Christianity) did not come into general acceptance for another two hundred or more years. No verb "is" appears in the Greek; and so this could be a qualified statement, viz., "Every Scripture that is inspired by God is also useful . . ." No matter how one translates the verse, the primary emphasis indicated by the context is less on the inspiration of all Scripture passages than on the utility of inspired Scripture for continuing what Timothy has learned from his childhood in order to teach and correct and thus to counteract evil impostors. The goal is that a leading person in the community "who belongs to God may be proficient, equipped for every good work" (3:17). Implicitly this is an indication that the Pauline writer posits a strong connection between the Scriptures of Israel and his own view of Jesus Christ.

The word for "inspired" in relation to Scripture in 3:16 is "breathed [into]

[15]*Demas,* who has deserted and gone off to Thessalonica, was with Paul when he wrote Phlm 24 (from Ephesus *ca.* 55?) and Col 4:14 (from where? genuinely Pauline?). *Crescens,* who has gone to Galatia or Gaul, is otherwise unknown; but if Gaul is the correct reading, the Pauline mission has spread to Western Europe! *Titus* has gone to Dalmatia, but before or after the time in Crete implied in Titus 1:5? *Alexander,* the coppersmith, has done Paul much harm. A Jew with that name was dragged into the Ephesus riot *ca.* 56 (Acts 19:33), most likely to dissociate the Jewish community from Paul the troublemaker. An Alexander was put under a ban in I Tim 1:20 to be handed over to Satan. If we are to think of him, does the derogatory comment in II Tim 4:14–15 refer to a situation before that envisioned in I Tim? When Rom (16:3) was written in 58, *Prisca* (Priscilla) and *Aquila* were in Rome; now they are back in Asia Minor near or with Timothy. Of *Pudens, Linus,* and *Claudia* we hear nothing in the other Pauline letters or Acts, although Irenaeus (AH 3.3.3.) lists Linus as a bishop (i.e., prominent presbyter) of the church of Rome after Peter's death. At an early period a Christian in Rome named Pudens gave a piece of land subsequently connected with a titled church. On the role of some of the II Tim characters in *The Acts of Paul and Thecla,* see Chapter 30 above, n. 33.

by God," a term found not in the Greek Bible, but in preChristian Pagan literature and the *Sibylline Oracles.* A somewhat similar description is found in II Pet 1:20–21 in reference to the prophecies of Scripture: "Not ever is prophecy brought forth by human will; rather people who were carried along by the Holy Spirit spoke from God."[16] The Qumran literature refers to what "the prophets revealed through God's holy spirit" (1QS 8.16). Josephus and Philo, Jewish writers contemporary with the NT, also speak of a movement from God in the production of the "sacred Scriptures."[17] The texts in II Tim and II Pet are very important in the development of a Christian belief in the inspiration of the Scriptures (OT and NT); yet one should recognize that there is nothing specific about how the divine movement takes place, beyond a symbolic description like "breathed into."

Issues and Problems for Reflection

(1) Christians have various views about inspiration, focused on the person of the writer or on the written product, or on both (Chapter 2 above, B). For instance the classical Roman Catholic description since the encyclical *Providentissimus Deus* of Pope Leo XIII (1893) is that by supernatural power God moved and impelled the human authors and assisted them when writing so that the things that God ordered (and only those) they rightly understood, willed faithfully to write down, and finally expressed in apt words with infallible truth. Another view concentrates on the truth and inerrancy of the Bible rather than on the process. Drawing on II Tim 3:15–16, one might reflect on the extent to which the various approaches have gone beyond the Scriptural information and why.

(2) A famous apocalyptic apprehension is voiced in II Tim 4:3–4: "A time is coming when people will not endure wholesome teaching, but with itching ears will accumulate to themselves teachers to suit the desires of their heart, and will turn their ears away from the truth and turn to myths." Almost every generation of Christians, especially in the more traditional churches, has invoked this description as fulfilled in its own time. Nevertheless, that fear has too often made ecclesiastical institutions constantly defensive against new ideas. In such an atmosphere there will come a moment when

[16]Mark 12:36 has Jesus saying that David spoke a psalm verse "in the Holy Spirit" (affirmed also by Peter in Acts 1:16), while Acts 28:25 has the Holy Spirit speaking through Isaiah the prophet.

[17]With sophistication Philo, *De vita Mosis* 2.35.188–91, distinguishes three possibilities: (a) The prophet interprets divine utterances spoken to him by God personally; (b) The utterance occurs in a question-and-answer dialogue between the prophet and God; (3) The prophetic spokesperson speaks as a divine oracle, a *porte-parole* possessed by God. Although Philo thought the last was the prophet par excellence, many today would favor the first as a better description of prophecy. But prophetic literature is only part of the Scriptures.

no ideas constitute a greater danger than new ideas, and when deaf ears are more prevalent than itching ears.

Bibliography on II Timothy

(See also the *Bibliography* for the Pastoral Letters in general in Chapter 29 above.)

Cook, D., "2 Timothy IV.6–8 and the Epistle to the Philippians," JTS 33 (1982), 168–71.

Johnson, L. T., "II Timothy and the Polemic Against False Teachers: A Re-examination," JRS 6/7 (1978–79), 1–26.

Malherbe, A. J., " 'In Season and Out of Season': 2 Timothy 4:2," JBL 103 (1982), 23–41.

Murphy-O'Connor, J., "2 Timothy Contrasted with 1 Timothy and Titus," RB 98 (1991), 403–18.

Prior, M. P., *Paul the Letter-Writer and the Second Letter to Timothy* (JSNTSup 23; Sheffield: JSOT, 1989).

Skeat, T. C., "Especially the Parchments: A Note on 2 Timothy 4:13," JTS NS 30 (1979), 173–77.

PART IV

THE OTHER NEW TESTAMENT WRITINGS

Hebrews

I Peter

James

Jude

II Peter

Revelation (The Apocalypse)

CHAPTER 32

LETTER (EPISTLE) TO THE HEBREWS

By all standards this is one of the most impressive works in the NT. Consciously rhetorical, carefully constructed, ably written in quality Greek, and passionately appreciative of Christ, Heb offers an exceptional number of unforgettable insights that have shaped subsequent Christianity.

Yet in other ways Heb is a conundrum. Our treatment of the Pauline letters usually began with a subsection entitled *Background,* based on information in the respective letter about the author, locale, circumstances, and addressees. Heb tells us virtually nothing specific about any of these issues, and almost all our information pertinent to background must come from an analysis of the argumentation advanced by the author. Therefore we shall begin with the *General Analysis* of the argumentation. Let me caution that the "Division According to Contents" in the accompanying Summary Page (used in the *Analysis*) is simply a convenient way of highlighting some of the main ideas. It makes no pretense of being the structure intended by the author of Heb—for that readers must consult the first subsection following the *Analysis,* which treats *Literary genre and structure* and pays particular attention to the structure detected by A. Vanhoye (accepted by many today). Subsequent subsections will be concerned with *Thought milieu, By whom/where/when, Addressees, Issues for reflection,* and *Bibliography.*

General Analysis of the Message

In the eschatological context of the last days,[1] the INTRODUCTION (1:1–3) immediately affirms the superiority of Christ over all that has gone before in Israel. The main contrast is between two divine revelations: one by the prophets and the other by a preexistent Son through whom God created the world and who has now spoken to us. The description, in language that may be drawn from a hymn,[2] shows that the writer is interpreting Christ against the back-

[1]See also the phraseology of 9:26: "Now once for all he has appeared at the end of the ages." Eschatology is a key theme in Heb: C. K. Barrett in *The Background of the New Testament and Its Eschatology,* eds. W. D. Davies and D. Daube (C. H. Dodd Festschrift; Cambridge Univ., 1956), 363–93; C. E. Carlston, JBL 78 (1959), 296–302; S. D. Toussaint, *Grace Theological Journal* 3 (1982), 67–80.

[2]J. Frankowski, BZ NS 27 (1983), 183–94.

Summary of Basic Information

DATE: 60s or more likely 80s.

FROM: Not specified; greetings extended from "those from Italy."

TO: Addressees not identified but, based on content, to Christians who are attracted by the values of the Jewish cult; surmises would place them at Jerusalem or Rome, with the latter more likely.

AUTHENTICITY: Author not identified; later church attribution to Paul now abandoned.

UNITY AND INTEGRITY: Not seriously disputed.

FORMAL DIVISION: (see p. 690 below for Vanhoye's proposal).

DIVISION ACCORDING TO CONTENTS:

1:1–3:	Introduction
1:4–4:13:	Superiority of Jesus as God's Son
	1:4–2:18: Over the angels
	3:1–4:13: Over Moses
4:14–7:28:	Superiority of Jesus' priesthood
8:1–10:18:	Superiority of Jesus' sacrifice and his ministry in the heavenly tabernacle inaugurating a new covenant
10:19–12:29:	Faith and endurance: availing oneself of Jesus's priestly work
	10:19–39: Exhortation to profit from the sacrifice of Jesus
	11:1–40: OT Examples of faith
	12:1–13: The example of Jesus' suffering and the Lord's discipline
	12:14–29: Warning against disobedience through OT examples
13:1–19:	Injunctions about practice
13:20–25:	Conclusion: blessing and greetings.

ground of the OT portrayal of divine Wisdom. Just as Wisdom is the effusion of God's glory, the spotless mirror of God's power who can do all things (Wisdom 7:25–27), God's Son is the reflection of God's glory and the imprint of God's being, upholding the universe by his word of power (Heb 1:3). Going beyond the Wisdom pattern, however, the Son is a real person who made purification for sins; and that accomplishment is intimately related to the Son taking his seat at the right of the Majesty.

SUPERIORITY OF JESUS AS GOD'S SON (1:4–4:13). This extraordinarily "high" christology is now worked out in the Son's superiority over the angels and over Moses. *Superiority over the angels (1:4–2:18)*[3] is worked out through a chain or catena of seven OT quotations in 1:5–14 that match the designations of the Son in the introductory description of 1:1–3.[4] The super-

[3]Let me alert readers that I am following here a sequence of themes, rather than a formal division (to be explained in the first subsection below); and in a carefully planned work like Heb the latter is important. For instance, since 1:4 is a subordinate clause, formal structure would require that it be placed with 1:1–3 even though it introduces a new theme.

[4]J. P. Meier, *Biblica* 66 (1985), 504–33; also K. J. Thomas, NTS 11 (1964–65), 303–25; J. W. Thompson, CBQ 38 (1976), 352–63. Notice that the OT citations do not simply gloss the argument but are a constitutive part of it.

angelic status of Christ as Son is sublime exaltation indeed, if we remember that in the Jewish heritage angels were "sons of God," that in DSS two angels who were respectively the spirits of truth and of falsehood dominated all humanity, and that angels were the mediators of the Law. Particularly significant is Heb 1:8–9 in which, employing the words of Ps 45:7–8, the writer has God address to Jesus words never addressed to an angel: "Your throne, O God, is forever and ever . . . therefore (O) God, your God has anointed you with the oil of gladness"—one of the important NT texts where Jesus is called God (BINTC 185–87). In NT times there was a danger among some of placing angels above Christ, but we need to be cautious about assuming that such an error circulated among the intended audience of Heb. To assert the exalted status of Jesus, superiority over the angels may have seemed to the writer an obvious illustration.

As frequently in Heb, the descriptive (doctrinal) section leads into a moral exhortation (2:1–4): If the message of the Law declared by angels was valid, how can we escape if we neglect the great salvation declared by the Lord Jesus and "attested to us by those who heard"? (The quoted clause seems to place the writer of Heb not with the apostolic witnesses but with the next generation.) One finds introduced in 2:5–18 an outlook that colors the christology of Heb, viz., combining lowliness and exaltation. Using Ps 8:5–7 the author points out that God's Son who was for a while made lower than the angels now has everything subject to him. To a community that is despondent because of hardship the author holds up in Christ God's plan for humanity: not exaltation without suffering but exaltation through suffering. If the exaltation of God's Son was soteriological, he was not concerned with saving angels. Rather Christ tasted death for every human being; and God has brought many to glory through Jesus, the pioneer of their salvation made perfect through suffering (2:10). This theme of the wandering people of God being led by Jesus the forerunner to the heavenly sanctuary and place of rest will recur again in 4:11,14 and 6:20.[5] In his role as pioneer the Son partook of the flesh and blood of the children of God, and was made like his brothers and sisters in every respect, so that he might become a merciful and faithful high priest to make expiation for the sins of the people. Because he himself has suffered and been tempted, he is able to help those who are tempted (2:14–18). This portrayal, which will be developed in greater detail in chaps. 4–5, represents one of the great NT testimonies to the incarnation.

Superiority over Moses (3:1–4:13) is exemplified in 3:1–6 by the greater glory of the builder over the house building, of the son over the servant in a household (cf. John 8:35). "The apostle and high priest of our confession" is

[5]Some would find here an echo of gnosticism (see the subsection below, *Thought Milieu*).

another example of the magnificent titles given to Jesus. In 3:7–4:13 the writer once more turns to exhortations based on Scripture, but now centered on the exodus of Israel. The Christians addressed are in danger of growing weary because of discouragement. Those among the Israelites who were disobedient failed to achieve the goal of entering God's rest in the Holy Land. Similarly this is a testing for those who believe in Jesus, as Heb 4:12 makes explicit in one of the most famous passages in the NT, describing the word of God as sharper than any two-edged sword piercing even between soul and spirit, able to discern reflections and thoughts of the heart.

SUPERIORITY OF JESUS' PRIESTHOOD (4:14–7:28). The opening verse states the dominant theme: "We have a great high priest who has passed through the heavens, Jesus the Son of God." Although Heb and John share the notion of an incarnation, we do not find in John a description of the reality of Jesus' humanity comparable to that offered by this section of Heb. A high priest who is able to sympathize with our weaknesses, Jesus was tested in every way as we are, yet without sin (4:15). Like the Israelite high priest Christ has not exalted himself but was appointed by God, a point illustrated by royal coronation psalms (5:1–6). Describing Jesus' suffering in the days of his flesh when he brought prayers and supplications to the One who had the power to save him from death (5:7–9), the writer affirms that Jesus learned obedience despite his being Son. (These verses show familiarity with the tradition of Jesus' passion whereby he prayed to God about his impending death.[6]) When he was made perfect, he became the source of eternal salvation to all who obey him (cf. Phil 2:8–9).

In 5:11–14 the writer turns again to exhortation, reprimanding the immaturity of the recipients who can still take only milk, not solid food. The description of six points of elementary teaching in 6:1–2[7] is a bit embarrassing for Christians today—would that many knew even those! That apostasy from Christ is a concern of the writer becomes clearer in 6:4–8 (also 10:26–31), as he warns that there is no repentance after being enlightened[8] (i.e., baptized: John 9; Justin, *Apology* 1.61.12; 65.1). Yet he gives rhetorical assurance that he has no doubts about the future of his addressees, whose loving work will

[6]BDM 1.227–34 and 2.1107–8 point out similarities between Heb and the Mark/Matt form of Jesus' bipartite prayer in Gethsemane and on the cross where he prays to be delivered from death amidst the weakness of his flesh. According to both Heb and Mark/Matt, Jesus' prayer was answered in that he conquered death and became the source of salvation. (Heb may have developed its account through dependence on an early Christian hymn, while in the prayer on the cross Mark uses Ps 22.) In 13:12 Heb shows awareness of the tradition found also in John 19:17 that Jesus died outside the walls of Jerusalem.

[7]Some find here a traditional Christian catechism; the "laying on of hands" probably refers to the receiving of the Holy Spirit (Acts 8:17; 19:6).

[8]Surveying attempts to wrestle with the severity of this, D. A. de Silva, JBL 115 (1996), 91–116, thinks that believers have accepted the patronage of God through Jesus and Heb is taking aim at apostasy that violates such patronage.

not be overlooked by God (6:9–12). God is faithful to promises, and that serves as a guarantee for the effectiveness of Jesus' intercession in the inner heavenly shrine as a high priest according to the order of Melchizedek (6:13–20). The whole of chap. 7 is devoted to the superiority of this priesthood possessed by Jesus over the levitical priesthood (and could be treated with chaps. 8–10 of Heb as well as with the chaps. that precede). Through the DSS (11Q *Melchizedek*) we have learned more about the mysticism that surrounded Melchizedek as a heavenly figure.[9] Actually, however, to understand the argument in Heb little more is needed than the OT and the rules of contemporary exegesis, e.g., the failure to mention Melchizedek's ancestry permits one to argue as if he had no father or mother. Several points constitute the superiority of Melchizedek: He blessed Abraham; his priesthood was accompanied by the Lord's oath; and above all a priest according to the order of Melchizedek is eternal (Ps 110:4). There is no longer a need for numerous (levitical) priests who are replaced after death because Jesus who has the Melchizedek priesthood continues forever, making intercession (7:23–25).[10] When he offered himself, this holy, blameless, undefiled high priest, separated from sinners and exalted above the heavens, effected a sacrifice that is once for all (7:26–27).

SUPERIORITY OF JESUS' SACRIFICIAL MINISTRY AND OF THE HEAVENLY TABERNACLE, INAUGURATING A NEW COVENANT (8:1–10:18). The idea that Jesus is a high priest before God leads to the notion of a heavenly tabernacle. Exod 25:9,40; 26:30, etc., describes how God showed Moses the heavenly model according to which the earthly tabernacle was built. In Heb 8:2–7 this antecedent may be influenced by a Platonic scheme of reality in which the heavenly tabernacle set up by God is true, while the earthly tabernacle is a copy or shadow. The levitical priests who serve this shadow sanctuary have a ministry inferior to that of Christ, even as the first covenant is inferior to the second covenant mediated by Christ. Heb 8:8–13 (see also 8:6), picking up the language of new covenant from Jer 31:31–34, makes it clear that the first covenant made with Moses is now old, obsolete, and passing away.

In chap. 9 the writer presents a prolonged comparison between Jesus' death and the ritual of the Day of Atonement (Yom Kippur) carried out in the transportable sacred edifice of Israel's desert wanderings, the Tabernacle or Tent

[9]Kobelski, *Melchizedek;* also FESBNT 221–43; M. de Jonge and A. S. van der Woude, NTS 12 (1965–66), 301–26; J. W. Thompson, NovT 19 (1977), 209–23.

[10]W. Horbury, JSNT 19 (1983), 43–71, compares the approach to priesthood in Heb with that of various Jewish writings. As background for seeing Jesus as priest, some appeal to the DSS and the expectation therein of a priestly Messiah, but that expectation is of a priest from the order of Aaron distinct from a Davidic Messiah. Heb is emphatic that Jesus is not a levitical (= Aaronic) priest and applies to Jesus psalms pertinent to the Davidic Messiah. The writer is probably not appealing to an established Jewish expectation but using biblical imagery to clothe a conviction about Jesus. *Testament of Levi* 8:14, "From Judah a king will arise and establish a new priesthood," is probably a Christian interpolation or editing.

with its divisions, curtains, and altars. Although the developed comparison may stem from the author, the fact that both he (9:5) and Paul (Rom 3:25) appeal to the image of the *hilastērion,* the place of expiation where the blood of the sacrifices was sprinkled to wipe out sins,[11] suggests a wider awareness that Jesus' death could be compared to levitical sacrifices. What is unique to Heb is the parallel drawn between the high priest going once a year into the Holy of Holies with the blood of goats and bulls and Jesus going once for all into the heavenly sanctuary with his own blood,[12] thus ratifying the new covenant. There he now appears in the presence of God "on our behalf" (9:24); and having been offered once to bear the sins of many, he will appear a second time to save those who are eagerly waiting for him (9:28).[13]

The superiority of the sacrifice of Jesus made with his own blood is reiterated with emphasis in 10:1–18, e.g., "for all time a single sacrifice for sins" (10:12). The basic thesis is that God prefers obedience to a multiplicity of sacrifices. The obedience of Jesus' sacrifice is phrased in 10:5–9 through a passage from Ps 40:7–9: "A body you prepared for me . . . Behold I have come to do your will as it is written of me at the head of the book." This sacrifice has made perfect forever those who are being given a share in Jesus' own consecration; their sins are forgiven, and so there is no longer a need for offerings for sin.

FAITH AND ENDURANCE: AVAILING ONESELF OF JESUS' PRIESTLY WORK (10:19–12:29). Through the way opened by Jesus, those whom the writer calls "brothers" should enter the Holy Place by Jesus' blood with faith, hope, and love, meeting together as a community (10:19–25). If they sin deliberately, there is no longer a sacrifice for sins, but horrible punishment: "It is a fearful thing to fall into the hands of the living God" (10:26–31).[14] Yet there is no reason for discouragement. In times past after they were first converted and baptized ("enlightened"), they joyfully accepted abuse, affliction, and persecution. Now again they need endurance and faith so as to save their souls

[11]It is also called a "propitiatory" or "mercy seat." Some object to this designation because it suggests that an angry God is being propitiated or appeased. For the debate see J. A. Fitzmyer, NJBC 82.73–74; L. Morris, NTS 2 (1955–56), 33–43.

[12]"Through the greater and more perfect tabernacle not made by hands, i.e., not of this creation . . . he entered once and for all into the Holy Place" (9:11–12). Some understand the tabernacle to be the body of Christ, but more likely it is the heavenly regions through which Jesus passed to the highest heavens. The fact that he carries his blood to heaven means that his sacrifice was not completed on the cross, for an essential part of such a sacrifice was bringing the blood to the place of expiation to sprinkle it there.

[13]The ascent into heaven from the cross with his blood to be followed by the parousia does not seem to leave room for a resurrection and appearances. That impression is refuted not only by 13:20, but also by the analogy of other NT works. Luke 23:43 has Jesus going to Paradise on the day of his death; yet Luke 24 describes resurrection appearances.

[14]This is probably an adaptation of the unforgivable sin against the Holy Spirit encountered elsewhere in the NT (see Chapter 7 above, n. 11). Although there were various interpretations of it, apostasy evidently was a frequent candidate.

(10:32–39). In 11:1–40 the writer, having begun by giving a famous description of faith ("The assurance [or reality] of things hoped for, the conviction [or evidence] of things not seen"), launches into a long list of OT figures who had that kind of faith or faithfulness.[15] At the end (11:39–40), faithful to his contrast between the old and the new, he points out that all these people of faith did not receive what had been promised, for "God had foreseen something better for us, so that without us they should not be made perfect."

As a transition (12:1–2) the writer urges his readers, "surrounded by so great a cloud of witnesses," to keep their eyes fixed on Jesus, "the pioneer and perfecter of faith." In 12:3–13 he points out that they would not really be God's children without the discipline of suffering that God applies. Jesus endured great hostility whereas the readers have not yet endured to the point of shedding their blood. Heb 12:14–29 dramatizes penalties for disobedience from the OT; it ends with the warning that God is a consuming fire, echoing Deut 4:24.

FINAL EXHORTATION (13:1–19).[16] Containing Heb's only detailed concrete ethical injunctions, this is the area in which Heb comes closest to Pauline style. After some imperatives on issues of community life characteristic in NT works, Heb 13:7 appeals to the faith of past leaders in the history of the community who preached the gospel.[17] One can appeal to the past because "Jesus is the same yesterday, today, and forever" (13:8)—another unforgettable example of the eloquence of writer. But the writer also appeals for obedience to the present leaders who watch over the readers' souls (13:17).

CONCLUSION (13:20–25). The exhortation closes with a blessing invoked through "the God of peace who brought again from the dead our Lord Jesus, the great shepherd of the sheep" (13:20). Amidst the greetings, the references to Timothy who has been released and those from Italy are some of the very few clues in Heb as to the place of origin and destination.

Literary Genre, Structure

In 1906 W. Wrede, a distinguished German scholar, published a work the title of which can be translated "The Literary Riddle of the Epistle to the He-

[15]P. M. Eisenbaum, *The Jewish Heroes of Christian History; Hebrews 11 in Literary Context* (SBLDS 156; Atlanta: Scholars, 1997). For a similar list praising famous men, see Sirach 44–50 and Wisdom 10, works written in the Hellenistic period. Plutarch, a contemporary of the author of Heb, offers parallel accounts of figures as icons of Greco-Roman history.

[16]F. V. Filson, *"Yesterday": A Study of Hebrews in the Light of Chapter 13* (SBT 4; Naperville, IL: Allenson, 1967).

[17]Does the reference to "the outcome of their conduct" mean that they died a martyr's death? We shall see below the plausibility that Heb was addressed to Roman Christians, and some have seen in the past leaders a reference to Peter and Paul.

brews." H. E. Dana comments, Heb "begins like a treatise, proceeds like a sermon, and closes like an epistle."[18] Yet there are problems with the application of each of those genres to Heb. Despite its careful exposition of the superiority of Christ, Heb is not simply a theological *treatise.* The writer has expounded his doctrine for the apologetic purpose of preventing the addressees from abandoning faith in Christ in favor of the idealized values of the Israelite cult. In regard to Heb as a *sermon,* Heb calls itself a "word of exhortation" (13:22), and there are clauses such as "we are speaking" (2:5; 5:11; 6:9). Using the categories of Aristotelian rhetoric (p. 412 above), Attridge (*Hebrews* 14) states, "It is clearly an epideictic oration, celebrating the significance of Christ." But there is also an element of deliberative rhetoric, for Heb calls for action in terms of faithfulness and perseverance. Today some distinguish a homily (which is tied closely to the text of Scripture) from a sermon (which is more topical)—the argumentation in Heb draws heavily on Scripture. As for being a *letter,* only the instructions in chap. 13 and, in particular, the *Conclusion* in 13:20–25, give Heb a resemblance to the letter form known from Paul's writings.[19] Perhaps we should settle for the relatively simple description of Heb as a written sermon or homily with an epistolary ending.

The structural analysis of Heb by A. Vanhoye has had wide influence.[20] Working with features like catchwords, inclusions (i.e., the end of a section matching the beginning), alternations of genre, Vanhoye detects an elaborate concentric composition, consisting of an Introduction (1:1–4) and Conclusion (13:20–21), surrounding five chiastically arranged sections[21] (each of which has several subsections):

I. 1:5–2:18: The name superior to the angels (Eschatology)
II. 3:1–5:10: Jesus faithful and compassionate (Ecclesiology)
III. 5:11–10:39: The central exposition (Sacrifice)
IV. 11:1–12:13: Faith and endurance (Ecclesiological paraenesis)
V. 12:14–13:19: The peaceful fruit of justice (Eschatology).

Certainly many of the features Vanhoye points out are present in Heb; it is a work artistically planned with careful structure. Attridge's analysis of the

[18]Cited by R. E. Glaze, Jr., *No Easy Salvation* (Zachary, LA: Insight, 1966), 9.

[19]A few scholars have argued that chap. 13 or 13:22–25 was added precisely for that purpose, but see R.V.G. Tasker, ExpTim 47 (1935–36), 136–38.

[20]His earlier writing is summarized in *Structure and Message of the Epistle to the Hebrews* (Rome: PBI, 1989); briefly Attridge, *Hebrews* 15–16; and for variants: J. Swetnam, *Biblica* 53 (1972), 368–85; 55 (1974), 333–48; G. H. Guthrie, *The Structure of Hebrews: A Text-Linguistic Analysis* (NovTSup 73; Leiden: Brill, 1994). Further: D. A. Block, *Grace Theological Journal* 7 (1986), 163–77; J. Swetnam, *Melita Theologica* 45 (1994), 127–41.

[21]In the chiasms the theme of I matches that of V (Eschatology); the theme of II matches that of IV (Ecclesiology). A popular alternative divides Heb into three sections with the transitions (4:14–16; 10:19–25) marked by exhortations building confidence.

structure (*Hebrews* 19) is heavily influenced by Vanhoye's; he regards it as a definite advance over simple catalogues of contents and thematic structures, which, he complains, often focus on christological affirmations that skew the text by making it primarily a dogmatic work. Yet concentration on content need not have that result, and too formal an approach may be in danger of divorcing Heb from the clear apologetic goal that it seeks to achieve by stressing the superiority of Christ.[22] Is it a contradiction to encourage that attention be paid both to a formal approach that respects the complexity of the work and to a more thematic study? Because this NT *Introduction* is intended to give a basic familiarity with the contents of each NT book, I chose to follow a thematic approach in the *General Analysis* above; but readers are encouraged to pursue further investigation by availing themselves of insights from the formal approach.

Thought Milieu

Beyond the issue of structure is the question of the writer's intellectual milieu and background. We may begin with parallels to PHILO. The writer of Heb manifests allegorical skill in his appeals to Scripture,[23] a skill similar to that exhibited by Philo (see Sowers, *Hermeneutics*) and by the *Epistle of Barnabas*. Heb's description of the penetrating power of God's word (4:12) resembles Philonic language (*Quis rerum divinarum heres* 26; #130–31). As with Philo, sometimes the thought categories he employs have parallels in contemporary philosophy, particularly Middle Platonism (p. 88 above).[24] This does not mean the writer of Heb was a formal or well-trained philosopher. He is less thorough in terms of philosophy and Platonism than is Philo; but he had at least a popular acquaintance with ideas of his time. In both writers cultic images are used to symbolize other elements. For Heb 8:5 and 9:23–24 the Israelite sacrifices and liturgy in the earthly sanctuary are copies or shadows of the corresponding realities in the heavenly sanctuary, even as the Law is a shadow of the good

[22]Some analyses of Heb have overdone the apologetic thrust, but I shall point out below that one should not overlook the double goal of preventing apostasy and of correcting a misunderstanding of the gospel that underappreciates what Christ has done.

[23]He uses the LXX. His occasional differences from the LXX form known to us exemplifies a lack of uniformity among 1st-century AD Greek versions. Most likely it does not show that the author cited the Hebrew Scriptures, pace G. E. Howard, NovT 10 (1968), 208–16; Buchanan, *Hebrews* xxvii–xxviii; see K. J. Thomas, NTS 11 (1964–65), 303–25; J. C. McCullough, NTS 26 (1979–80), 363–79.

[24]See Thompson, *Beginnings;* R. Williamson, SJT 16 (1963), 415–24; L. D. Hurst, SBLSP 1984, 41–74. Montefiore, *Hebrews* 6–8, links Heb to Alexandrian Judaism but lists important differences from Philo. S. G. Sowers, *The Hermeneutics of Philo and Hebrews* (Richmond: Knox, 1965); R. Williamson, *Philo and the Epistle to the Hebrews* (Leiden: Brill, 1970); L.K.K. Dey, *The Intermediary World and Patterns of Perfection in Philo and Hebrews* (SBLDS 25; Missoula, MT: Scholars, 1975).

things to come (10:1). Yet Heb's contrast between the earthly and the heavenly in relation to cult does not stem simply from the nature of the factors involved. In part it stems from the eschatological change introduced by Christ,[25] and eschatology is not one of Philo's (or Plato's) emphases. Thus the relation to Philo is at most indirect: some of the same thought milieu but no direct familiarity.

Much more dubious is the attempt to find a GNOSTIC background in the imagery of Heb. Both Bultmann and Käsemann had detected this in the picture of Jesus the pioneer or forerunner leading the wandering people of God to their heavenly rest (although Käsemann later acknowledged that the thrust to find gnostic elements was overdone). In gnostic thought the souls or sparks of the divine from another world[26] that are lost in this material world are led by the revelation of the gnostic redeemer from this world to the world of light. Also there are examples of dualism in Heb, e.g., the earth below and the heavenly country (11:15–16); two ages (2:5; 6:5; 9:26). There are serious objections to the gnostic proposal, however. Although we know Middle Platonism existed in the thought ambiance of the late–1st century world in which Heb was written, we are not certain how developed or widespread gnosticism was. Dualism was not confined to gnosticism. The portrait of a pioneer leading the people of God has a sufficient backdrop in the Moses/Joshua role of leading Israel to the Promised Land, which is mentioned prominently in Heb. Also, the way in which Jesus played a role as a pioneer was through his suffering (2:9–10)—a very ungnostic idea.

After the discovery of the DSS at QUMRAN there was considerable enthusiasm for thinking that Heb might be associated with Christian Jews of that background, indeed, might be addressed to Essene priests.[27] The DSS sectarians were fiercely opposed to apostasy, and so those who had become Christians might have had a guilt complex impelling them to return. The Qumran community also had a strong priestly and liturgical cast and was very close-knit; those who had left to follow Christ might have had a deep nostalgia for what they had left behind. It is generally thought that the Qumranians did not participate in the cult of the Jerusalem Temple, whence perhaps Heb's failure to call upon that Temple for its examples. The DSS employ the new covenant motif even as does Heb. Most scholars, however, are skeptical about Qumran influence on Heb. The Qumran *Temple Scroll* has God direct the building of the Temple, and so there should have been in Heb no reluctance to appeal sym-

[25]See G. W. MacRae, *Semeia* 12 (1978), 179–99.

[26]Some would find in Heb 2:11 (the sanctifier and the sanctified have all one origin) the gnostic idea of the heavenly preexistence of souls, but 11:15–16 holds up to people a journey to a heavenly homeland where they have never been before.

[27]For divergent views, see Y. Yadin, *Aspects of the Dead Sea Scrolls* (Scripta Hierosolymitana 4 [1958]), 36–55; F. F. Bruce, NTS 9 (1962–63), 217–32; F. C. Fensham, *Neotestamentica* 5 (1971), 9–21.

bolically to an ideal Temple. The writer's idea of Jesus as a priest according to the order of Melchizedek is almost the opposite of the Qumran expectation of a priestly Messiah descended from Aaron. As recipients, Christians from a Qumran ambience are no more plausible a target of Heb than Christians influenced by another form of Judaism. Attridge (*Hebrews* 29–30) contends correctly, "There is no single strand of Judaism that provides a clear and simple matrix within which to understand the thought of our author or his text."

Another hypothesis appeals to Acts 6:1–6 (and the sequel constituted by Stephen's speech in Acts 7) which distinguishes between two species of Jewish Christians (both of whom made Gentile converts): the HELLENISTS who in the person of Stephen took a radically deprecatory stance toward the Jerusalem Temple (7:47–50), and the Hebrews, who in the person of Peter and John went regularly to the Temple (3:1). Could the writer of Heb have been a Hellenist preacher trying to win over Hebrew Christians[28] to his persuasion? Many think of John as a Gospel of Hellenist theology, and Heb is close to John in its attitude toward replacing the Israelite cult. Although (pp. 697–98 below) the title "To the Hebrews" stems far more likely from an analysis of the contents, could it have had more literal roots? Albeit attractive, this hypothesis too remains unprovable.

If the contents do not identify the background of Heb with a clearly defined vein of thought or ideological group, do other questions pertinent to Heb help?

By Whom, From Where, and When?

BY WHOM? Some refer to Heb as pseudonymous; but "anonymous" is more accurate since no claim is made within the work about its writer. Yet by the end of the 2d century some were attributing Heb to Paul. Reflecting Alexandrian tradition, Beatty Papyrus II (P^{46}), our earliest preserved text of the Pauline letters (containing ten addressed to communities), places Heb after Rom.[29] Acceptance as a work of Paul came slower in the Western church. Both in Alexandria and Rome, however, in official late-4th and early-5th century canonical lists, Heb was counted within the fourteen Pauline letters, sometimes placed before the personal letters (I-II Tim, Titus, Phlm), more often at the end of the collection. Gradually the name of Paul was introduced into the title of the work, appearing both in the Vulgate (and English translations drawn from it)

[28]See W. Manson, *Hebrews;* R. W. Thurston, EvQ 51 (1979), 22–39. The majority of scholars thinks of Roman Christians as the addressees. If Rome was evangelized from Jerusalem (p. 562 above), the tone of its Christianity might well have been close to that of the Hebrews who dominated Jerusalem Christianity once the Hellenists were driven out by persecution (Acts 8:4–5; 11:19).

[29]We shall see below that there are close connections between Heb and Rom, but is that in part because Heb was sent to Rome or from Rome?

and the KJV. Factors that contributed to the attribution to Paul include: (a) The appearance of the name of "brother Timothy" in 13:23—otherwise Timothy's name is found only in Acts and ten letters of the Pauline corpus, and he is called "brother" by Paul in I Thess 3:2; Phlm 1; and II Cor 1:1 (and Col 1:1). Yet Timothy must have been close to many other Christians as well. (b) The benediction and greetings in 13:20–24 (and to a lesser extent, the ethical imperatives of chaps. 12–13) resemble a Pauline letter ending. (c) Hab 2:3–4, cited in Heb 10:37–38, is used by Paul in Gal 3:11; Rom 1:17. Yet the writer of Heb does not relate the passage to justification by faith rather than by works, which is the Pauline interpretation. (d) Elements in the phrasing and theology of Heb have parallels in works bearing Paul's name.[30]

Nevertheless, the evidence against Paul's writing Heb is overwhelming. The elaborate, studied Greek style is very different from Paul's, as Clement and Origen already recognized. Common Pauline expressions ("Christ Jesus," some ninety times) never appear in Heb. More important, the outlook is not Paul's. Whereas the resurrection is a major factor in Paul's theology, in Heb it is mentioned only once (13:20, in a subordinate clause); and conversely the major Heb theme of Christ as high priest does not appear in Paul. Paul denied that he received his gospel from other human beings; God revealed the Son to him (Gal 1:11–12). How could he have written that the message was declared first by the Lord "and attested to us by those who heard" (Heb 2:3)?

Among those who do not accept Pauline authorship,[31] the two most common suggestions for authorship involve a known companion of Paul or a figure totally unknown, with the latter as the most common choice. The most learned figure of the patristic era, Origen, was content to leave anonymous the actual writer (whom he thought a possible secretary of Paul), remarking that only God knew who wrote Heb. Others made guesses about the writer or (if they assumed he was Paul) about the secretary he employed. Tertullian attributed Heb to Barnabas; and, in fact, the early–2d century *Epistle of Barnabas* has an Alexandrian style of allegory similar to that of Heb. However, that "epistle" is also anonymous, and the attribution of it to Barnabas is no more solid than the attribution of Heb to Paul. Other ancient attributions of Heb were to Luke and

[30]E.g., self-humbling of Christ to the point of death (Heb 2:14–18; Phil 2:7–8); greater glory than Moses (Heb 3:2–3; II Cor 3:7–8); his obedience (Heb 5:8; Phil 2:8; Rom 5:19); *hilastērion,* "expiation" (Heb 9:5; Rom 3:25); the offering or sacrifice of Christ (Heb 9:28; I Cor 5:7); Abraham as an example of faith (Heb 11:8; Gal 3:6–9); running the race as an idiom (Heb 12:1; I Cor 9:24); addressing the recipients as "saints" (Heb 13:24; Rom 1:7 and passim). Differences exist in all these parallels.

[31]In the early centuries Heb was thought to lose authority if Paul did not write it. Now the realization that we do not know who wrote many of the NT books has removed this objection to anonymity.

Clement of Rome. Luther attributed it to Apollos,[32] described in Acts 18:24 with attributes that could fit the writer (a Jew, a native of Alexandria, eloquent, well versed in the Scriptures); and that suggestion has attracted a considerable following. Priscilla and Aquila had contact with Apollos (Acts 18:26), and each of them has been proposed as writer. Silas and Philip have also been suggested.[33]

We have to be satisfied with the irony that the most sophisticated rhetorician and elegant theologian of the NT is an unknown. To employ his own description of Melchizedek (7:3), the writer of Heb remains without father or mother or genealogy. The quality of his Greek and his control of the Scriptures in Greek suggest that he was a Jewish Christian with a good Hellenistic education and some knowledge of Greek philosophical categories. His allegorical style of hermeneutics has parallels in Philo and in Alexandrian interpretation; but that interpretation was taught elsewhere, and so the claim that the writer of Heb came from Alexandria is unproved. Those from whom he learned about Christ (2:3) may have had a theological outlook similar to that of the Hellenist movement and its freer attitude toward the Jewish cultic heritage.

FROM WHERE? The dubious thesis that Heb was written from Alexandria would be of little service in any case, for we know nothing of the origins of the Christian church in Alexandria. The argumentation in Heb based on the Jewish liturgy and priesthood has made Jerusalem or Palestine a more prominent candidate. (Yet Heb's presentation of the liturgy reflects "book-knowledge" of the LXX more than attendance at the Jerusalem Temple, which is never mentioned.) As we saw above, parallels have been found between the attitude of Stephen, the Hellenist leader at Jerusalem, and that of the writer of Heb; both depend heavily on the Scriptures and distrust a divine house made with hands.[34] Actually, however, according to Acts 8:4; 11:19, the Hellenists functioned mostly outside Jerusalem and even outside Palestine. The greetings extended to the readers from "those who come from Italy" (Heb 13:24) reminds some of the presence of Roman Jews at Jerusalem on Pentecost (Acts 2:10); and indeed, if the letter was addressed to Roman Christians, Acts 28:21 suggests frequent correspondence between Judea and Rome. Nevertheless, theo-

[32]In Luther's Sept. 1522 German NT translation Heb was one of the four works not printed in the traditional NT order, but moved to the end. For Luther they were not among the "true and certain main books" because in former times they were seen in a different light (i.e., not of apostolic origin).

[33]The prize for dubious ingenuity goes to the suggestion that Mary, the mother of Jesus, is responsible for the content of the letter: J. M. Ford, TBT 82 (1976), 673–94. Earlier in CBQ 28 (1966), 402–16, she thought that Heb was written by a Paulinist reacting to Apollos' activity *in Corinth.*

[34]To be precise, however, Stephen was opposed to a Temple made with hands but favorable to the earlier tabernacle. Heb sees the replacement of the earthly tabernacle.

ries about the place whence Heb was sent are almost as much a guess as theories about the writer.

WHEN? This question is partially related to the answer to the previous questions. At the lower end of the spectrum, the writer of Heb does not belong to the first generation of Christians since apparently he is dependent on those who heard the Lord (2:3); and his readers/hearers have been believers for a while (5:12; 10:32). At the upper end, a limit is set by *I Clement* 36:1–5 (probably written in the late 90s, but not later than 120) which echoes Heb 1:3–5,7,13.[35] Thus the most frequent range suggested for the writing of Heb is AD 60 to 90, with scholars divided as to whether it should be dated before the destruction of the Jerusalem Temple (hence to the 60s) or after (hence to the 80s). If Paul, Apollos, Aquila, or Priscilla wrote the work, a date no later than the 60s would be suggested since most of them would have been dead by the 80s. The release of Timothy (from captivity: 13:23), a seemingly historical factor, is not an obstacle to a later date; for Timothy was younger than Paul (see p. 655 above) and could well have lived into the 80s.

The main supporting factor for dating in the 60s is the silence of Heb about the destruction of the Jerusalem Temple (AD 70). A reference to that destruction could have reinforced the writer's thesis that Jesus replaced the Jewish liturgy, priesthood, and holy place. However, nowhere in the letter does the writer show any interest in the Temple (and it may not have been the major holy place for him since in the OT God did not command that it be built); thus we have no way to know how its destruction would have fitted into his argumentation. The references to the cult in the present tense (Heb 8:3; 9:7; 13:11) do not prove that sacrifices are continuing in the Temple;[36] for Josephus' *Ant*, written twenty years after the destruction of the Temple, also uses the present tense.

A supporting factor for a writing date in the 80s is the strong emphasis on the replacement of the Jewish feasts, sacrifices, priesthood, and earthly place of worship—indeed the first or old covenant is being replaced by the new (8:7–8,13). The earlier Christian picture had been one of radically renewing the institutions of Israel; but after 70 and the destruction of the Temple the perception changed, as can be witnessed in John (pp. 334, 344). Christ was now seen to have replaced what went before. Similarly it was in the last third of the century that the custom of using "God" for Jesus became more prominent. However, although theologically Heb seems more at home in the 80s, one must rec-

[35]More than twenty passages in *I Clement* are thought to echo Heb, e.g., a list of OT examples of faith in *I Clement* 10–12 and 17, comparable to Heb 11.

[36]The most difficult passage, however, is 10:1–2, where rhetorically the writer argues that the sacrifices offered year after year cannot make people perfect: "Otherwise would not the sacrifices have ceased to be offered?"

ognize that an argument for dating that draws on comparative theology is very weak, since "advanced" theological insights did not all come at the same time in every place. Nothing conclusive can be decided about dating, but in my judgment the discussion about the addressees into which we now enter favors the 80s.

To Which Addressees?

Let us begin with the letter's title. Most scholars agree that the title "To the Hebrews" was *not* supplied by the author. Yet it appears in Beatty Papyrus II (P^{46}), the oldest ms. we possess, and was already in use *ca.* 200 in Egypt and North Africa. (No other rival title has ever appeared as a destination.) Almost certainly it represents a conjecture attached to the work because of an analysis of the contents that deal so largely with Israelite cult.

What can be determined about the addressees and their locale from the contents of Heb? Three stages are reflected in the letter,[37] the first two of which are in the past. (a) At the beginning, in the author's estimate, they were properly enlightened (and baptized into Christ; see p. 686 above). The community received the Christian message from evangelists whose work was accompanied by the working of miracles. The activity of the Holy Spirit was part of that experience (2:3–4; 6:4–5). Whether through Jewish upbringing or through Christian evangelization the addressees valued the religious wealth of Judaism. The argumentation supposes that the community of Christians who read/heard Heb would understand allusive reasoning based on the Jewish Scriptures[38] and had both a good knowledge of and favorable attitude toward the cultic liturgy of Israel. (b) Then (how soon?) they were afflicted by some type of persecution, hostility, and/or harassment (10:32–34). They were deprived of property, and some were put in prison. Imprisonment suggests the involvement of local officials against the Christians.

(c) By the time Heb is written the crisis of active persecution seems to have passed, but there is ongoing tension and despondency, and future danger. Abuse from outsiders is still an issue (13:13), but more seriously members of the group are becoming "dull" and "sluggish" (5:11; 6:12) and have wrong ideas. An exaggerated nostalgia for the Jewish roots of the Christian proclamation seems to be part of the picture. Specifically, the author thinks that some put too much value on the Israelite cultic heritage, not appreciating the enormous change brought about God through Christ whereby what belongs to the

[37]Necessarily we depend on the author's wording, but we should be aware of the possibility of rhetorical exaggeration in some of the descriptions.

[38]Heb has even been said to be materially a midrash (loose commentary) on Pss 95; 110; and Jer 31:31–34, phrased in rhetorical Greek prose.

old covenant is passing away. Furthermore, it seems that there were even some in danger of abandoning altogether the riches brought to them by faith in Christ. Apparently those affected by this outlook had already ceased meeting together in prayer with other Christians (10:25). The arguments advanced in Heb about the superiority of Christ[39] (especially over Moses) and the replacement of the Jewish sacrifices and high priesthood, along with the exhortations that accompany these arguments, are meant both to inculcate a proper understanding of the gospel and to discourage any backsliding. The author warns sternly about the difficulty of receiving forgiveness for a deliberate sin committed after receiving knowledge of the (Christian) truth. He uses the example of endurance during past persecution to encourage steadfastness now, amidst present hostility which may well increase.

What emerges from an analysis of the letter about the history of the addressees is very general; and so the Christian community of almost every city in the ancient world has, at one time or another, been suggested as the destination of Heb. The greatest attention, however, has been on Jerusalem and Rome. The suggestion about the *Jerusalem area* is related to the assumption that the addressees were Jewish Christians who were constantly tempted to return to their ancestral religion by the attraction of the Temple liturgy and sacrifices which they could see continuing in Jerusalem. In this theory a Christian in Italy, who was writing to these Jewish Christians living in Palestine or Jerusalem to urge them not to abandon Christ, included greetings from "those from Italy" (13:24). By way of evaluation, the idea that some of the addressees were Christians of Jewish ancestry is not implausible. Yet Gentile Christians often shared the mentality of the strain of Jewish Christians who converted them (p. 301 above); and so it is quite possible that a mixed community of Christians was addressed, rather than simply Jewish Christians. The idea that the proximity of the Temple constituted the magnet drawing the addressees to the Israelite cult fails to take into account that there is no reference to the Temple in Heb, and that a book-knowledge of the LXX Scriptures could supply Heb's picture of the cult. Indeed, the failure to mention the Temple militates against Jerusalem/Palestine as the place addressed. Moreover, how would the persuasive thrust of Heb fit what we know of Jerusalem Christians? Our evidence suggests that, after the Hellenists were driven out *ca.* AD 36, Jewish Christians in Jerusalem did worship in the Temple (Acts 21:23–24,26); and so, if Heb was written to them before 70, why would they need a directive not to return to what they had given up? If Heb was written after 70, how could Christians return to a sacrificial cult that no longer functioned?

[39]In the oratory of Heb, comparison is a major feature; some twenty-seven comparatives have been counted. *Synkrisis* or "comparison" was a technical term in Greek rhetoric, but one can also find this pattern in rabbinic reasoning.

Some difficulties are avoided by the subthesis that Heb was addressed to a special Jerusalem group, e.g., to converted priests (Acts 6:7) who presumably would not have been allowed to offer sacrifice after professing Jesus, or to the Jewish Christians who fled from Jerusalem in the 60s rather than join the revolt against Rome and could no longer go daily to the Temple. Yet even with those groups could a second-generation Christian, not of apostolic rank, writing in the 60s, have hoped that his corrective or dissuasive would be influential in a city where James, the brother of the Lord and faithful adherent of the Jewish cult, had such eminence? Why would the author compose in elegant *Greek* a dissuasive to Jewish Christian priests who would have known Hebrew as part of the liturgy, or to Jewish Christians of Judea for whom Hebrew or Aramaic would have been a native language?[40]

The theory that Heb was addressed to the Christian community in the *Rome area*[41] is more recent (seemingly first proposed about 1750). What factors favor it? Acts 18:2 implies that Jewish Christians were among Jews expelled from Rome under Claudius (*ca.* AD 49?); and so no matter whence Heb was sent to Rome, there could have been Christians from Italy[42] to send back greetings. The reference to past sufferings and imprisonment of the community addressed (10:32–34) could make excellent sense if Heb was written to Rome in the 80s, for the Roman Christians had been fiercely persecuted by Nero in 64–68 when both Peter and Paul died there. Heb's challenge to the present generation of addressees, "You have not yet resisted to the point of shedding blood" (12:4), may suggest a date before the 90s when under the Emperor Domitian investigations of exclusive Oriental cults endangered Christians (pp. 805–9 below).

The parallels between themes in Paul's letter to the Romans *ca.* 58 and Heb could be explained if Heb were written to the same community a decade or two later. Of all Paul's letters Rom is the most sensitive to the values of Judaism; it

[40]What light is cast on the recipients by Heb 13:23: "Our brother Timothy has been released and with him I shall see you if he comes soon"? The NT does not portray Timothy in prison; he is never mentioned as coming to Jerusalem (see p. 655 above), and we are not certain that people there would have known much about him. Christians at Rome, however, would have known Timothy. In Rom 16:21 Timothy is the first person whose greetings Paul shares with the Roman Christians. II Tim, apparently sent from imprisonment in Rome, invites Timothy to come to Paul there (1:17; 4:9).

[41]In Italy there were Christians at Puteoli (Pozzuoli) on the Bay of Naples, at Pompeii and Herculaneum, and probably at Ostia; yet only Rome could have been the principal addressee, for Heb implies a place with a considerable Jewish Christian heritage, where Timothy was known, where the gospel was preached by eyewitnesses (2:3), and where seemingly leaders died for the faith (n. 17 above).

[42]In "Those *from Italy* send you greetings," grammatically the italicized phrase may describe residence (living in Italy) or extraction (Italians). The scribe of Codex Alexandrinus understood it in the former sense, for he added to 13:25 "Written from Rome." But if the phrase is understood in the latter sense, Heb could have been sent from almost any place (Italians greeting Italians). If it was sent from Jerusalem/Palestine, Acts 2:10 reports Roman Jews there at Pentecost; and according to Acts 10:1 the Italian cohort was stationed at Caesarea *ca.* 40 (historically accurate?).

also uses a considerable amount of Jewish liturgical language (p. 563 above). Heb could have been written to correct exaggerations in those attitudes. Paul urged the Romans (12:10) to be leaders (*prohēgoumenoi*) of one another in honor. Heb 13:7 refers to the leaders (*hēgoumenoi*) of the addressees who in the past set an example by "the outcome of their conduct" (their death? martyrdom?) and faith (those who died under Nero?), and 13:17 refers to leaders at the time of writing (80s?) who are accountable for the care of souls. *I Clement* 21:6, written from Rome *ca.* 96–120, speaks of honoring "our leaders." There are also parallels between Heb and I Peter, written from Rome; but we shall reserve those to the next Chapter where the thought-background of I Peter will be discussed.

A major argument for a Roman destination is that knowledge of Heb was attested at Rome earlier than at any other place. As we saw in discussing dating, a passage from Heb is cited in *I Clement* written in Rome and thus within a relatively short time after the writing of Heb being written. In mid-2d century Justin, writing at Rome, shows knowledge of Heb. One cannot explain this easily by claiming that Heb was known in Rome because it had been sent *from* that city, for writers of the Roman church have views different from those in Heb.[43] More probable is the view that Heb, designed as a corrective work, was received by the Roman church but not enthusiastically appropriated there. Indeed, such an explanation is almost necessitated by Rome's attitude toward the canonical status of Heb. Even though Alexandrian and Eastern knowledge of Heb is first attested nearly a century after Roman knowledge,[44] the letter was accepted as canonical in the East rather quickly and attributed to Paul. Apparently Rome did not accept such an attribution, for throughout the 2d century. Roman writers fail to list Heb as Scripture or among the letters of Paul.[45] One may theorize that the Roman community which first received Heb knew that it did not come from Paul but from a second-generation Christian teacher. Although he was worthy of respect, he did not have the authority of an apostle (an attitude understandable in a church priding itself in having two apostolic "pillars," Peter and Paul [*I Clement* 5:2–7]). Trinitarian controversies helped to change the picture, for Heb (especially 1:3) was invaluable in the orthodox defense of the full divinity of Christ against the Arians. Then the opinion that

[43]*I Clement* differs markedly from Heb by having a positive estimation of levitical cult; *Hermas* is less rigorous than Heb on the question of forgiveness after baptism.

[44]Only at the end of the 2d century does Heb surface clearly in the East with the Alexandrian Pantaenus, and in North Africa with Tertullian.

[45]Heb is not mentioned among biblical books by *Hermas,* the OT commentaries of Hippolytus (+ 235), Canon Muratori, and the Roman presbyter Gaius (Caius). The latter's silence lends support to joining Heb and John as examples of a more radical (Hellenist) Christianity. (See Chapter 11 above, n. 96, on Gaius' resistance to the acceptance of John in the Roman church.) As late as 380, Ambrosiaster, a bellwether of Roman feeling, commented on thirteen letters of Paul but not on Heb.

Paul wrote Heb won the day in the larger church (*ca.* 400), and Rome was willing to accept it as the fourteenth letter of the apostle.

I have gone into the subject of addressees at greater length because it is more important than when and from where Heb was written. If Heb was written to Rome, addressing a generation later than that which received Rom and just before the generation reflected in *I Clement,* we have an insight into the ongoing struggles of a Christian community that proved to be one of the most important in the history of Christianity.[46]

Issues and Problems for Reflection

(1) The (high) priesthood of Jesus Christ is a major theme of Heb.[47] To some extent this development is a surprise since the historical Jesus was emphatically a layman, critical to some degree of Temple procedure and treated with hostility by the Temple priesthood. The solution of Heb that his was a priesthood according to the order of Melchizedek may be original, but the idea of Jesus' priesthood is found in other NT works, chiefly in relation to his death. In particular, John 10:36 and 17:19 use in reference to Jesus "consecrate, make holy," the verb employed by Exod 28:41 for Moses' consecration of priests. Many think that the description of the seamless tunic stripped from Jesus before he died was influenced by the tunic of the Jewish high priest (Josephus, *Ant.* 3.7.4;#161).[48] Does the idea of Jesus' priesthood stem from picturing his death as a self-offered expiatory sacrifice? Rom 3:25 describes Christ in this way (see also I John 2:2).

(2) After reflecting on the texts in the preceding paragraph, one may ask how the appropriation of Israelite liturgical language (Tabernacle, Temple, priesthood, sacrifices, feasts) for Jesus affects the use of that language for later Christians. The attitude has not always been consistent. Even some literalist groups do not mind speaking of the church or the Christian community as a temple; the language of tabernacle or temple is used for the Christian meeting house by groups that proclaim themselves Bible Christians. Many have no objection to the description of Holy Thursday/Easter as a Christian Passover. Yet they may reject vigorously the terminology of sacrifice and priest in Christian

[46]A continuation of the picture of Roman Christianity may be found in BMAR 159–83.

[47]B. Demarest, *A History of the Interpretation of Hebrews 7,1–10 from the Reformation to the Present* (Tübingen: Mohr-Siebeck, 1976); A. Vanhoye, *Old Testament Priests and the New Priest According to the New Testament* (Petersham, MA: St. Bede's, 1986); J. M. Scholer, *Proleptic Priests: Priesthood in the Epistle to the Hebrews* (JSNTSup 49; Sheffield: JSOT, 1991).

[48]Just as in Heb Jesus replaces much of the Israelite cult, in John the Word comes to "tent among us," replacing the Tabernacle or Tent (1:14); Jesus' risen body replaces the Temple sanctuary (2:21); and themes in his speeches replace themes of major feasts (7:2,37–39; 10:22,36); he is condemned to death as a sacrificial lamb at the hour lambs are being sacrificed in the Temple (1:29; 19:14,36).

cult, despite the fact that already *ca.* 100 *Didache* 14 finds Mal 1:11 ("pure sacrifice") fulfilled in the eucharist. In loyalty to the once-for-all outlook of Heb, churches that *do* use sacrificial terminology often stress that the eucharist is no new sacrifice but the liturgical making-present of the sacrifice of Christ. Although already *ca.* 100 *I Clement* 40:5; 42:1,4 juxtaposed the Jewish high priest, priest, and levite to Christ, the bishop, and the deacon, the first clear use of "priest" for the principal Christian eucharistic minister (the bishop) comes at the end of the 2d century.[49] By the 4th century all eucharistic ministers were considered to be Christian priests, sharing in Christ's priesthood according to the order of Melchizedek. It is worth reflecting on what values the use of Israelite cultic language preserves, and the problems it raises. (See pp. 722–23 below for the priesthood of believers.)

(3) A somewhat different issue is raised by comparing Heb with other NT thought on the eucharist. Except for a possible reference in 9:20, Heb does not mention the eucharist; but it seems most unlikely that the author would not have known of it. Is the silence accidental? In other NT thought, Luke 22:19; I Cor 11:24–25, "Do this in remembrance of me," and I Cor 11:26, "As often as you eat this bread and drink this cup, you proclaim the death of the Lord until he comes" imply an ongoing eucharistic ritual re-presenting the sacrifical death of Jesus. How would the author of Heb with his idea of a once-for-all offering of Christ (7:27) have reacted to that view? A few radical scholars have argued that Heb was written in part to reject an ongoing eucharistic cult. Scholars also debate whether for Heb the one sacrificial offering of Jesus on the cross continues in heaven, the sphere of the eternal. In that case may we do justice to the thought of Heb by suggesting that the eucharist should be seen as an earthly participation in that continued sacrifice?

(4) Even though continuity is not totally rejected, more specifically than any other NT work, Heb speaks of the obsolescence of the *diathēkē,* "covenant," that God made with Moses, e.g., 8:13.[50] That covenant is becoming obsolete, growing old, ready to vanish away (also 10:9: He takes away the first in order to establish the second). In the opposite direction some today would completely do away with the terminology "Old" and "New" in reference to either covenant or testament, substituting "First" and "Second," or "Israelite" and

[49]H.-M. Legrand, *Worship* 53 (1979), 413–38.

[50]The Greek word may also be translated "testament," e.g., it may mean "covenant" in 9:15 and "testament" [RSV: "will"] in 9:16,17. Because Jesus' death is a self-sacrifice, he is both the sacrifice that seals the covenant and the testator who makes a will or last testament. Although Jer 31:31–34; 32:40 (Ezek 37:26) speaks of a new eternal covenant, that image is not emphasized in subsequent Jewish literature until the DSS. S. Lehne, *The New Covenant in Hebrews* (JSNTSup 44; Sheffield: JSOT, 1990); J. Dunnill, *Covenant and Sacrifice in the Letter to the Hebrews* (SNTSMS 75; Cambridge Univ., 1992).

"Christian."[51] Does that shift render justice to the various insights about newness in the NT (especially with its references to "new covenant") that do not have the connotation of replacing the obsolescent? On a deeper level many Christian theologians deny that the covenant of God with Israel (through Abraham? through Moses?) has become obsolescent or been replaced. In its declaration *Nostra Aetate,* Vatican Council II warned "the Jews should not be presented as rejected . . . by God, as if such views followed from the Holy Scriptures." Leaving aside all connotations of rejection, however, how should Christians react to the covenant between God and Moses? Can they say that it is still valid and yet, in loyalty to Paul and Heb, not be bound by its demands?[52]

(5) At the time Heb was written, the Tabernacle had not existed in Israel for a thousand years. Why does the author of Heb draw his analogies from the Tabernacle or Tent (e.g., chap. 9) rather than from the Temple? Was his choice dictated by the fact that God was portrayed as instructing Moses how to build the Tabernacle (Exod 25–26) whereas God was not reported in the OT as dictating how to build the Solomonic Temple (II Chron 2–3) or the Second Temple after the Exile (Ezra 3)?[53] Moreover, the Temple had been subjected to considerable prophetic correction, and that had not been true of the desert Tabernacle. Also, even though God had dictated how to build the earthly Tabernacle, it no longer existed; that fact may have served the author as a model for reasoning how the levitical sacrifices and priesthood might cease to exist even though God had dictated their performance. Finally, the Tabernacle was the sacred cultic place for Israel in its desert wanderings, and Heb is addressed to Christians depicted as a wandering people on its way to heavenly rest. Jesus could be portrayed as entering the heavenly sanctuary of which the earthly Tabernacle was only a copy and preparing the way for people to follow.

Bibliography on Hebrews

COMMENTARIES AND STUDIES IN SERIES: **Attridge, H. W.** (Hermeneia, 1989); Bruce, F. F. (NICNT, 1964); Buchanan, G. W. (AB, 1972); Casey, J. (NTM, 1980); Davies, J. H. (CCNEB, 1967); **Ellingworth, P.** (EC, 1991; NIGTC, 1993); Ellingworth, P., and E. A. Nida (TH, 1983); Fuller, R. H. (ProcC, rev. ed., 1995); Guthrie, D. (TNTC, 1983); Hagner, D. A. (NIBC, 1990); Hewitt, T. (TNTC, 1960); **Lane, W. L.** (2 vols.; WBC, 1991); Lindars, B. (NTT, 1991); Moffatt, J. (ICC, 1924);

[51]The problem with the latter substitution is that Christians of the NT regarded themselves as the Israel of God. Also see p. xxxiv above.

[52]See N. Lohfink, *The Covenant Never Revoked* (New York: Paulist, 1991).

[53]In chaps. 40–42 Ezekiel received a vision on how the new, eschatological Temple should be built; but most regard the description as utopian in the sense that it was never built. In the DSS *Temple Scroll* God speaks in the first person describing how the Temple should be built. On the Tabernacle see C. R. Koester, *The Dwelling of God* (CBQMS 22; Washington, DC: CBA, 1989).

Montefiore, H. W. (HNTC, 1964); Smith, R. H. (AugC, 1984); Trotter, A. H. (GNTE, 1996); Wilson, R. M. (NCBC, 1987).[54]

SURVEYS OF RESEARCH: Hagen, K., *Hebrews Commenting from Erasmus to Bèze 1516–1598* (Tübingen: Mohr-Siebeck, 1981); McCullough, J. C., IBS 2 (1980), 141–65; 3 (1981), 28–45; Koester, C. R., CRBS 2 (1994), 123–45.

BMAR 139–58.

Cody, A., *Heavenly Sanctuary and Liturgy in the Epistle to the Hebrews* (St. Meinrad, IN: Grail, 1960).

D'Angelo, M. R., *Moses in the Letter to the Hebrews* (SBLDS 42; Missoula, MT: Scholars, 1979).

deSilva, D. A., *Despising Shame. Honor Discourse and Community Maintenance in the Epistle to the Hebrews* (SBLDS 152; Atlanta: Scholars, 1996). Social relationships.

Evans, L. H., *Hebrews* (Waco, TX: Word, 1985).

Hagner, D. A., *Hebrews* (San Francisco: Harper, 1983).

Héring, J., *The Epistle to the Hebrews* (London: Epworth, 1970).

Horton, F. L., *The Melchizedek Tradition: A Critical Examination of the Sources to the Fifth Century A.D. and in the Epistle to the Hebrews* (SNTSMS 30; Cambridge Univ., 1976).

Hughes, G. H., *Hebrews and Hermeneutics* (SNTSMS 36; Cambridge Univ., 1979).

Hughes, P. E., *A Commentary on the Epistle to the Hebrews* (Grand Rapids: Eerdmans, 1977).

Hurst, L. D., *The Epistle to the Hebrews: Its Background of Thought* (SNTSMS 65; Cambridge Univ., 1990).

Isaacs, M. E., *Sacred Space: An Approach to the Theology of the Epistle to the Hebrews* (JSNTSup 73; Sheffield: JSOT, 1992).

Käsemann, E., *The Wandering People of God* (Minneapolis: Augsburg, 1984; German orig. 1957).

Kistemaker, S. J., *Exposition of the Epistle to the Hebrews* (Grand Rapids: Baker, 1984).

———, *The Psalm Citations in the Epistle to the Hebrews* (Amsterdam: Soest, 1961).

Kobelski, P. J., *Melchizedek and Melchireša'* (CBQMS 10; Washington, DC: CBA, 1981).

Manson, W., *The Epistle to the Hebrews* (London: Hodder & Stoughton, 1951).

Peterson, D., *Hebrews and Perfection* (SNTSMS 47; Cambridge Univ., 1982).

Pursiful, D. J., *The Cultic Motif in the Spirituality of the Book of Hebrews* (Lewiston, NY: Mellen, 1993).

Thompson, J. W., *The Beginnings of Christian Philosophy: The Epistle to the Hebrews* (CBQMS 13; Washington, DC: 1982).

Westcott, B. F., *The Epistle to the Hebrews* (3d ed.; London: Macmillan, 1909). A classic.

[54]I am particularly indebted to the contributions of Prof. C. R. Koester, who is preparing a new commentary on Heb in the AB series.

CHAPTER 33

FIRST LETTER OF PETER[1]

We now turn to what, since Eusebius in the early 4th century, have been known as the (seven) Catholic or General Epistles, a designation that (at least in Eastern Christianity) was deemed appropriate for works addressed to the church universal, namely Jas, I-II Pet, I-II-III John, and Jude.[2] Under their present titles, coming in canonical sequence after the Pauline corpus (including Heb), they have the air of presenting the witness to Jesus of those who had seen him in his earthly career, namely, two members of his family (James and Jude) and two of the most important of the Twelve (Peter and John).[3] At times these writings confirm prominent elements in Paul's message (I Pet); at times they represent a very different atmosphere (I-II-III John; Jude); at times they come close to indirect confrontation with Paul (Jas; II Pet). Almost every feature about these Catholic Epistles/Letters is debated in scholarship: the genre (truly letters?[4]), their addressees (some specific, some not), and the actual writer.[5]

Following my usual procedure with disputed writings, I shall first treat these epistles as they now come to us. In each Chapter that means presenting

[1]In the rather arbitrary canonical order (next note) Jas follows Heb. To help the flow of thought in this *Introduction* I have chosen to treat I Pet here after Heb for three reasons. First, we saw that Heb may well have been sent to Rome in the 80s, and I Pet may have been sent from Rome in the 80s. Second, Heb, which follows the Pauline letters, was long (even if wrongly) attributed to Paul and has some similarities to Pauline thought and background, and I Pet has many similarities to Pauline thought. Third, James has no connection with Rome and is hostile to a (Pauline?) stress on faith rather than works. It claims as author James, while the Letter of Jude claims as author "Jude the brother of James." II Pet draws on Jude. Therefore treating the writings in the order followed here (Pauline letters, Heb, I Pet, Jas, Jude, II Pet) has a logical flow. The Johannine Epistles were already treated above in Chapters 12, 13, and 14, following the Johannine Gospel.

[2]EH 2.23.25: "the seven [epistles] called Catholic." In Western Christian usage "Catholic" had the connotation of "canonical." The canonical order was probably dictated by the listing of the "pillars" of the Jerusalem church in Gal 2:9: "James and Cephas [= Peter] and John," with Jude appended.

[3]In some Eastern church lists quite logically these epistles stand between Acts and the Pauline corpus.

[4]I John has no marks of the letter format; I Pet and Jas have elements of the format, but the content is closer to a homily (I Pet), marked with oratorical aspects of a debate/diatribe (Jas).

[5]I-II-III John offer no personal name. Although the other four do, scholars generally agree that II Pet is pseudonymous, and debate about Jas and Jude, with the majority favoring pseudonymity. Although disputed, I Pet has the best chance of stemming directly or indirectly from the claimed writer.

Summary of Basic Information

DATE: If written by Peter, 60–63; more likely 70–90.

TO: An area in northern Asia Minor (perhaps evangelized by missionaries from Jerusalem).

AUTHENTICITY: Possibly by Peter using a secretary; more likely by a disciple carrying on the heritage of Peter at Rome.

UNITY: Although the vast majority now opts for unity, some would see two documents joined: one (1:3–4:11) where "persecution" was only a possibility, and one (4:12–5:11) where the community was actually undergoing it.

INTEGRITY: Those who detect the presence of a confessional fragment and/or hymns usually think they were included by the writer.

FORMAL DIVISION:

A. Opening Formula: 1:1–2
B. Body: 1:3–5:11
 1:3–2:10: Affirmation of Christian identity and dignity
 2:11–3:12: Appropriate behavior for bearing good witness in a Pagan world
 3:13–5:11: Christian behavior in the face of hostility
C. Concluding Formula: 5:12–14.

a *Background* of the figure whose name appears in the title. Even if that person did not write the respective work, the claim to his authorization suggests that the emphasis in the writing is related to his image. Thus we begin with the writing attributed to Peter, the most important 1st-century follower of Jesus, even if one outranked by Paul in terms of written NT impact. I Pet is one of the most attractive and pastorally rich writings in the NT, and it deserves careful attention.

After the *Background* and the *General Analysis* of I Pet, subsections will treat: the *Suffering described; I Pet 3:19; 4:6 and the descent of Christ into hell; Relation to the Pauline tradition; From and to whom, where, and when; Issues for reflection;* and *Bibliography.*

The Background

Simon,[6] who very quickly came to be called Cephas (Aramaic: *Kēpā'*, "rock") or Peter (Greek: *Petros* from *petra,* "rock"),[7] is always named first in the lists of the Twelve and was clearly the most important of that group

[6]Or Symeon—reflecting a Greek form of the name closer to the Semitic original; see below on II Pet 1:1.

[7]Despite occasional challenges, "Cephas" and "Peter" refer to the same man: D. C. Allison, JBL 111 (1992), 489–95. In ten Pauline uses of the name, "Cephas" is used eight times and "Peter" twice. There is a large bibliography on Peter in the NT of which I name only books: O. Cullmann,

during Jesus' lifetime. The unanimous Gospel tradition is that he denied Jesus and failed in loyalty during the arrest (BDM 1.614–21). Nevertheless, after the appearance of the risen Jesus to Simon Peter (Luke 24:34; I Cor 15:5; John 21), he was restored to preeminence and exercised a leadership role among the followers of Jesus in Jerusalem in the first few years (Acts 2–5; p. 291 above). The portrayal of him as the most active missionary among the Twelve, venturing to accept new groups into the Christian community (Acts 8:14–25; 9:32–11:18), gets backing from Gal 2:8; for Paul considers Peter's apostolate as one against which to measure himself. According to both Acts 15 and Gal 2:1–10 Peter was a major figure at the Jerusalem meeting of AD 49 that decided on the acceptance of the Gentiles. Subsequently he functioned in the church of Antioch (where there was a controversy with Paul) and by the year 55 there was a group of Christians at Corinth that regarded him as their patron (I Cor 1:12; 3:22). He was martyred (John 21:19) in Rome sometime between 64 and 68 during Nero's persecution. *I Clement* 5, written from Rome, treats Peter and Paul as the most righteous pillars of the church who were persecuted unto death.

Peter's image remained extremely important after his death, as we can recognize in Gospel passages that most likely were committed to writing after 70. In John 21 he is portrayed as the leading fisherman (missionary) among the Twelve, bringing to Jesus a huge catch of fish, and then as the shepherd (pastor) commissioned to feed Jesus' sheep. In Luke 22:32 he is the one told by Jesus, "Strengthen your brothers." In Matt 16:18 Peter who has responded in faith to the Messiah, the Son of God, is the one on whom Jesus will build the church and to whom he will give the keys of the kingdom of heaven. It is against such background that we must understand this letter written in Peter's name.

Two other figures are mentioned in I Pet 5:12–13 as present with Peter in Babylon (Rome): Silvanus, "whom I regard as a faithful brother, through whom I have written to you"; and Mark, "my son." As for the first, Acts 15:22,32 mentions Silas, a Jewish Christian prophet of the Jerusalem church who risked his life for the sake of the Lord (15:26). Along with Judas Barsabbas he bore the instructions of the Jerusalem meeting of AD 49 (at which Peter and Paul were present) to Antioch. According to 15:36–18:5, as a substitute for Mark who went with Barnabas to Cyprus, Paul chose Silas to be a missionary companion during the "Second Missionary Journey," at least as

---

Peter: Disciple, Apostle, Martyr (2d ed.; Grand Rapids: Eerdmans, 1968); O. Karrer, *Peter and the Church: An Examination of Cullmann's Thesis* (Quaestiones Disputatae 8; New York: Herder, 1963); R. E. Brown et al., PNT; T. V. Smith, *Petrine Controversies in Early Christianity* (WUNT 2/15; Tübingen: Mohr-Siebeck, 1985); P. Perkins, *Peter: Apostle for the Whole Church* (Columbia, SC: Univ. of S. Carolina, 1994).

far as Corinth, where Silas is mentioned for the last time in Acts. He is the same as Silvanus[8] whom Paul identifies as a co-writer in I Thess 1:1, a letter written from Corinth during that Journey.[9] Silvanus's preaching at Corinth at that time is recalled in II Cor 1:19. How Silas/Silvanus came to Rome we do not know, but presumably Peter would have known him as "a faithful brother" from Jerusalem days.

As for Mark, readers are asked to review the discussion (pp. 158–59 above) of whether John-called-Mark and Mark were the same person. To summarize, it is possible that a Jewish Christian named Mark, whom Peter knew in Jerusalem (Acts 12:12) and who had been a companion of Paul (early on and then again later), came to Rome in the 60s in Paul's last days and that there he became helpful to Peter.

General Analysis of the Message

OPENING FORMULA (1:1–2). I Pet uses the same type of Jewish letter greetings that Paul employed, although I Pet modifies the standard "grace and peace" by adding "be multiplied to you" from the OT letter format exemplified in Dan 3:98 (4:1). The fact that the writer does not use the name Simon (cf. II Pet 1:1) but "Peter" suggests that the witness borne in the letter (e.g., 5:1) appeals not so much to the eyewitness memory of Jesus' ministry but to the testimony of one who has served as a great apostle and is now looked on as "a pillar" of the church (Gal 2:9, even if Paul dislikes the phrase). The address is "To the exiles of the diaspora," a term used in the OT for Jews living outside Palestine, the true home of the chosen people. However, it is reasonably clear from the contents of the letter that the recipients are Gentile Christians who are now the "chosen" people (1:1–2; 2:4,9) in the diaspora—in the sense of being scattered among Pagans and perhaps also in the sense of being away from their heavenly home. The specific geographical designation suggests the crescent-shaped route of the carrier of the letter in northern Asia Minor:[10] He will land at one of the Black Sea ports (e.g., Sinope) of *Pontus,* move southward through the eastern tip of *Galatia* into *Cappadocia,*[11] then westward to the province of *Asia,* and finally northward on a road leading up from Ephesus to a Black Sea port at the *Bithynia* end of the province of Bithynia-Pontus. Noteworthy in I Pet's formula is the

[8]A Latinized form of Silas and a Roman cognomen or family name.

[9]A similar reference is found in II Thess 1:1, but that work may be pseudepigraphical and simply copying from I Thess 1:1.

[10]On the geography see C. J. Hemer, ExpTim 89 (1977–78), 239–43.

[11]After AD 72 eastern Pontus, Galatia, and Cappadocia had been woven into one province.

triadic mention of God the Father, the Spirit, and Jesus Christ (cf. II Cor 13:14).

FIRST SECTION OF THE BODY (1:3–2:10): *Affirmation of Christian identity and dignity.* I Pet lacks a Thanksgiving so characteristic of the Pauline letters. In its place the Body of the letter opens with a remarkably affirmative section stressing the dignity of the Christian believers. The description strongly echoes the imagery of the exodus from Egypt and the experience at Sinai. Like the Hebrews at the first Passover who were to gird up their loins, the addressees are to gird up their minds (1:13). Those who came into the desert yearned to return to the fleshpots of Egypt, but the Christian addressees are not to be conformed to the desires of their former ignorance. The demand of God at Sinai, "Be holy because I am holy" is repeated (Lev 11:44; I Pet 1:16); and there are echoes of the golden calf, the paschal lamb, and God's ransom of Israel (Deut 7:8) in the reminder that the addressees were ransomed not with silver and gold but with the precious blood of Christ as an unblemished lamb. A reference to the beginning of Christian life is found in 1:3 and 1:23: "You have been born anew, not from perishable seed but imperishable."

Since 3:18–22 is specific, "Baptism which corresponds to this now saves you," many scholars think that the writer was drawing his imagery from baptismal parlance wherein entering the Christian people of God was understood through the analogy of Israel's beginnings as God's people. Some are very specific in having I Pet use the language of a baptismal hymn or hymns that can be reconstructed.[12] Others think of a baptismal liturgy used in Rome, with baptism being conferred between 1:21 and 1:22. Because of the Passover symbolism, a special Easter vigil baptismal liturgy has been proposed.[13] Another thesis suggests a baptismal homily covering the whole of 1:3–4:11.[14] For our purposes there is no real need to be so precise. One covers the basic thrust of the section if one thinks of the writer evoking language and traditional Scripture passages heard at baptism by the addressees who had been evangelized by missionaries with a very deep attachment to the traditions of Israel. (Below I shall suggest that this area of Asia Minor had been evangelized from the Jerusalem of Peter and James.)

The climax of this section comes in 2:4–10, centered around two sets of three OT texts: The set in 2:6–8 is centered on Christ as the stone selected

[12]Proposals include 1:3–5; 1:18–21; 2:21–25; 3:18–22; 5:5b–9, with parallels to the hymn in Titus 3:4–7. Elements of a baptismal creed or confession have been detected in I Pet 3:18,19,21d,22; 4:5. See K. Shimada, AJBI 5 (1979), 154–76.

[13]Cross, *I Peter.* To the contrary, Moule, "Nature"; T.C.G. Thornton, JTS 12 NS (1961), 14–26.

[14]In this the influence of Ps 34 has been proposed (I Pet 2:3 = Ps 34:9; I Pet 3:10–12 = Ps 34:13–17).

by God but rejected by some human beings;[15] and the set in 2:9–10 is centered on the Christian community, once no people but now the people of God. The important v. 9 interprets Exod 19:6 (LXX), "You shall be to me a kingdom, a body of priests, and a holy nation," i.e., the privileges of Israel that are now the privileges of Christians.

SECOND SECTION OF THE BODY (2:11–3:12): *Appropriate behavior for bearing good witness in a Pagan world.* Given the dignity of the Christian people, there is a standard of conduct that can set an example for the surrounding Pagans in order to counteract their low estimate of Christians. This leads to the final of the five NT household codes (2:13–3:7) that we began discussing in Chapter 27 above.[16] There is no attention given here to changing the existing social and domestic order (even if it is unjust), but only how to behave in the present situation in a way that exemplifies the patience and self-giving of Christ. (See the queries raised on pp. 609, 650 above.) The I Pet code deals with Christians being subject to the emperor and governors, slaves being subject to their masters, and the reciprocal relationship of wives (being subject) and husbands (being considerate). Thus structurally it is less balanced than the triad of reciprocal relationships in Col 3:18–4:1 and Eph 5:21–6:9 and lacks their discussion of children/fathers. In one way the I Pet code is not close at all to the older men/older women and younger women/younger men emphasis in Titus 2:1–10, but in another way the two household codes share the goal of edifying comportment that would attract others to the faith. I Pet shares the motifs of prayer/respect for those in authority and of modest dress for women with the household code(s) now scattered in I Tim (2:1–2); 2:8–15; 5:1–2; 6:1–2. Like Titus and I Tim and unlike Col and Eph the I Pet code talks only about the duty of slaves toward their masters and not vice versa. We shall see in n. 21 below that in terms of institutional ministry I Pet may again be closer to the Pastorals than to Col and Eph.

As for details, being subject to the king (emperor) and governors who punish evildoers will show that the Christians are not evildoers despite what people say. Slaves are to be patient when they are beaten unjustly, even as the sinless Christ left an example patiently accepting insults and suffering. (The passage in 2:21–25 shows how intimately the portrait of the Suffering Servant in Isa 53 had been woven into the Christian description of Christ's

[15]See T. D. Lea, *Southwestern Journal of Theology* 22 (1980), 96–102.

[16]More technically some are also community codes dealing with behavior at liturgy and in relation to public authority. D. L. Balch, *Let Wives Be Submissive: The Domestic Code in I Peter* (SBLMS 26; Chico, CA: Scholars, 1981); also J. W. Thompson, ResQ 9 (1966), 66–78. Although the code in this instance has to match the morals expected by the surrounding society so that non-Christians will see the Christians as laudable, the writer would see such virtuous behavior as flowing from having been born anew (1:22–23). Some who take the baptismal-liturgy approach to I Pet would see in the slaves, wives, and husbands groups coming to be baptized.

passion.) The exhortation to the slaves ends on the note that their wounds have been healed and that Christ is the shepherd and guardian of their souls.

This portion of I Pet concludes in 3:8–12 by addressing "all of you" with five brief imperatives on how to treat one another so that they can live as a truly Christian community, and the promise of a blessing from the Lord, quoted from Ps 34:13–17. Perhaps once more I Pet is echoing standard baptismal oratory, for Jas 1:26 reflects Ps 34:14 (see n. 14 above).

THIRD SECTION OF THE BODY (3:13–5:11): *Christian behavior in the face of harassment.* A subsection below will treat the issue of whether the suffering in I Pet stems from persecution or alienation.[17] The latter seems more plausible, and I shall work with that hypothesis. Christians are suffering, being reviled and abused by their fellow Gentiles who cannot understand the strange turn that the gospel has produced in the converts' lives, making them asocial. But Christians have the example of Christ, the righteous who suffered for the unrighteous. His death was not the end, for he was made alive in the spirit, and then went to proclaim his victory over the evil angels who were imprisoned in a pit after they had sinned with women and brought about the flood (3:18–19; see subsection below). From that flood Noah and others, eight in all, were saved,[18] just as Christians have been saved through the cleansing waters of baptism (3:20–21).

The Christians are alienated because they cannot live the way their Pagan neighbors do. We have seen lists of vices in the Pauline letters (pp. 566, 677 above), but in 4:3–4 the list seems to be shaped by a malevolent picture of Pagan feasts in which Christian Gentiles no longer participated. I Pet 4:5–6 promises that a judgment by the God of the living *and the dead* will deal with the injustice that those who accepted the gospel preaching about Christ are encountering. If some of them have died despised by others ("judged in the flesh according to human standards"), they will survive ("live in the spirit according to God"). This judgment of all things is coming soon because the end of all things is at hand (4:7). As for the present, amidst the hostility of their neighbors they can survive if they love, support, and serve one another (4:8–11).[19]

Since Christ showed that suffering was the path to glory, Christians should

[17]D. Hill, NovT 18 (1976), 181–89, makes the interesting point that the concentration on suffering in I Pet is not unrelated to the references to baptism. Becoming a Christian makes one see the role of suffering in the light of Christ's passion. See also R. Hall, ResQ 19 (1976), 137–47.

[18]J. P. Lewis, *A Study of the Interpretation of Noah and the Flood in Jewish Literature* (Leiden: Brill, 1968).

[19]The writer speaks of charisms: whoever speaks; whoever serves (*diakonei*). Does the latter refer to deacons (also n. 21 below), and does the writer consider them marked by a charism? Yet we are about to see (5:1–3) that the writer urges the presbyters/elders not to tend the flock by constraint. That does not sound as if they have presented themselves as having an administrative charism (I Cor 12:28); probably they were chosen by others.

not be surprised if "a fiery ordeal" and greater sufferings come (4:12–19). Judgment will begin with the Christian community, "the household of God" (v. 17). Therefore Peter who was a witness to the sufferings of Christ as well as a partaker in the glory to be revealed encourages the presbyters of the community to take care of the flock (5:1–4).[20] The implied church structure is well established. They seem to be receiving wages, for I Pet insists that they should be shepherds eagerly and not for shameful gain. The model for them is Christ the chief shepherd.[21]

Closing the Body of the letter are a set of admonitions (5:5–9), piled one upon the other. Corresponding to the care exercised by the presbyters must be the obedience shown by those under their authority. The need for watchfulness is stressed. The imagery, echoing Ps 22:14, is memorable: "Your adversary the devil is prowling around like a roaring lion looking [for someone] to devour." Consolingly, the doxology (5:10–11) offers the pledge that in this struggle Christ will confirm, strengthen, and establish the Christians after they have suffered a little.

CONCLUDING FORMULA (5:12–14). Peter now intervenes with personal greetings, perhaps added in his own hand. They are formulated somewhat differently from the greetings that characterize Paul's letters. It is not clear whether writing "briefly through Silvanus" means that Silvanus is the bearer (cf. Acts 15:23: "writing through their hand") or the secretary (amanuensis). Some think that "briefly" tilts the odds toward the latter. I have discussed Silvanus and Mark in the *Background* above. The church of Rome[22] joins her greeting to Peter's.

[20]He could speak as an apostle, but to those in authority he has a better chance at persuasion if he speaks as "a fellow presbyter." The emphasis in "witness" is probably not primarily on eyewitness but on testifier: Because Peter had experienced both the suffering and glory of Christ, he could bear witness. The "glory" may refer to the resurrection, but II Pet 1:16–18 understood the "glory" as a reference to the transfiguration.

[21]On church order in I Pet 5:1–5, see J. H. Elliott, CBQ 32 (1970), 367–91. For Christ the shepherd as a model for shepherding the church, see John 10:11 + 21:15–19. The shepherding language in I Pet is very much like that addressed in Acts 20:28 to the presbyters/overseers (bishops) of Ephesus; and the admonitions resemble in tone those in Titus 1:5–8. Are the "youngers" (a comparative like "elders," i.e., presbyters) who are urged to be subject to the elders/presbyters in I Pet 5:5 deacons, so that like the Pastorals, I Pet presumes a two-tier ministry of presbyter/bishops and deacons? See Chapter 30 above, n. 9.

[22]"She who is at Babylon"; that designation serves as imagery in post-AD 70 Jewish literature for a Rome that had destroyed the second Jerusalem Temple even as Babylon had destroyed the first. For the use of a female figure to symbolize a church, cf. II John 1,13. *I Clement,* written several decades later, is from the church of Rome to the church of Corinth and, according to respectable tradition, written by Clement who may have been the delegated spokesman for the presbyters at Rome. Yet he never names (himself as) the writer of the letter; and though he admires Peter (*I Clement* 5), Clement does not have Peter speak for the Roman church. I Peter names Peter as the writer and has him speak for the church at Rome.

The Suffering Described: Imperial Persecution or Alienation?

The several passages dealing with suffering in I Pet have attracted attention, entering the discussion of the dating and purpose of the letter. For instance, if one thinks that Peter wrote the letter (by himself or through a secretary), one might interpret the indications that the readers are experiencing or have experienced trials of some kind (1:6) and are being treated by the Gentiles as evildoers (2:12) as references to the struggles at Rome between Jews who believed in Christ and Jews who did not—struggles that caused the Emperor Claudius to expel Jews from Rome *ca.* AD 49 (p. 433 above). The trial by fire that is about to come on the addressees (4:12) and the anticipated, same sufferings about to come on Christians throughout the world (5:9) might reflect persecution[23] in Rome in *Nero's time* after the fire of 64, about to begin or already starting, and the Christian fear that it might spread through the Empire. If one thinks the work is pseudonymous and written about 90, the references could be to imperial harassment in *Domitian's time:* some interrogations/trials already, but fear of greater intensity and even of active persecution (pp. 805–9 below).[24] But if imperial persecution was the issue, whether by Nero or by Domitian, would I Pet command, "Honor the king [emperor]" (2:17; also 2:13)?

A more recent tendency has been to refer I Pet's suffering/trial language not to imperial persecution but to local hostility wherein nonChristians spoke badly of Christians, treating them as evildoers (2:12), defaming their conduct (3:16), vilifying them (4:4), and insulting them because of their belief in Christ (4:14). Christians would have constituted a new cult, exclusive and, to outside eyes, secretive and subversive—suspect of immorality or even of atheism because they did not participate in the public cult and thus insulted the gods. On the one hand, "trial by fire" (4:12) might seem overly hyperbolic for such treatment;[25] on the other hand, this explanation accounts very well for the atmosphere of alienation that pervades the letter. The strong stress on the dignity of Christians and their status would be meant to encourage a group being ostracized by their countrymen, a group that can be ad-

[23]In fact, however, the word for persecution never occurs in I Pet; the writer speaks of testing/trial and suffering. Reicke's theory that I Pet was written as an admonition against Christian involvement in anti-imperial Zealot-style subversive activity has had little following. See C. F. Sleeper, NovT 10 (1968), 270–86.

[24]The minority of scholars who place the writing of I Pet after 100 can find in 4:16 ("being made to suffer as a Christian" and not being ashamed but glorifying God "because of the name") a reference to the persecution Pliny the Younger conducted in Pontus-Bithynia *ca.* 110 in the emperor *Trajan's time* with its test of recognizing Christians by their unwillingness to curse Christ.

[25]Yet it may simply be a figurative image for eschatological suffering. *Didache* 16:5 predicts that in the last days there will be "a fiery ordeal"; and II Pet 3:12 says that on the day of the Lord the elements will melt with fire.

dressed as homeless and sojourners (2:11; also 1:1,17). They are like Israel in the exodus on the road to the Promised Land; they should not look back to their former status as did the Israelites (1:14), but press on to their imperishable inheritance (1:4). Although they may have been accepted by their neighbors before, they were then "no people" in God's eyes and had not received God's mercy (2:10 echoing Hos 1:9; 1:6); now they are a chosen race, a royal priesthood, a holy nation, God's own people (I Pet 2:9). Well does J. H. Elliott entitle his convincing analysis of I Pet "A Home for the Homeless."

I Pet 3:19; 4:6 and the Descent of Christ into Hell

Two texts in I Pet are of import for this issue:

3:18–20: (Christ was put to death in the flesh and made alive in the Spirit) "in which having gone he made proclamation to the spirits in prison. Formerly they had been disobedient when God's patience waited in the days of Noah."[26]

4:6: "For this reason the gospel was preached also to the dead, in order that, having been judged in the flesh by human estimation [literally, 'according to men'], they might live in the Spirit in God's eyes ['according to God']."

A number of vague NT texts indicate that Christ, presumably after his death, descended beneath the earth (Rom 10:7; Eph 4:9), that he took up from below dead saints (Matt 27:52; Eph 4:8), and that he triumphed over the evil angelic powers (Phil 2:10; Col 2:15). Among the 2d-century apocrypha the *Ascension of Isaiah* 9:16; 10:14; 11:23 has Christ despoil the angel of death before rising from the dead and ascending into heaven, after which the angels and Satan worshiped him. The *Odes of Solomon* 17:9; 42:15 have Christ open the doors that were closed and those who were dead run toward him. Melito of Sardis (*On the Pasch* 102) has Christ say: "I am the one who trampled hell, bound the strong one, and snatched people away and up to heaven on high." Later the *Gospel of Nicodemus* has a whole narrative of Christ's descent into hell to deliver the OT saints—the source of the legends of the harrowing of hell. From the 4th century through the 6th an article was making its way into the Apostles' Creed: "He descended into hell." The clause is a curiosity in the sense that the church has never decided the exact purpose of that journey. Indeed, some modern churches have deleted the clause as meaningless for contemporary faith. That is an overreaction, for

[26]This is often thought to be part of a baptismal hymn or confession comparable to the hymn in I Tim 3:16: "Manifested in the flesh, made alive in the spirit, seen by angels." The last clause there is interesting given the second interpretation of I Pet 3:18–20 explained above.

certainly it is a way of expressing figuratively that Christ's death affected those who had gone before. But in what way? Do the two I Pet texts refer to the same preaching? And what is the relationship between the I Pet texts and the creedal clause? These are the questions we now seek to answer. That during the *triduum mortis* (three days [or parts thereof], from Friday night to Sunday morning, that his body was in the tomb[27]), Christ went down to the place of the dead is open to two major interpretations that have been intertwined with the interpretation of the I Pet texts.

(1) *For salvific purposes.* This is the oldest interpretation, dating at least to early in the 2d century. In *Gospel of Peter* 10:41, as Christ is being brought forth from the tomb by two immense angels followed by the cross, a voice from heaven asks, "Have you made proclamation to the fallen-asleep?" The cross makes obeisance in answering, "Yes." The context suggests that the preaching would be beneficial, as clearly affirmed by Justin, *Dialogue* 72, written *ca.* 160. Clement of Alexandria (*ca.* 200) offers the first attested interpretation of I Pet 3:19 in this way, a view attractive to Origen who held that hell was not eternal. A modification of the approach to avoid that implication about hell holds that Christ went to limbo in order to announce to the deceased *saints* that heaven was now open for them and/or to offer sinners a second chance if they accepted the proclamation.[28]

(2) *For condemnatory purposes.* If one interprets 3:19 in the light of 4:6, the proclamation to the spirits in prison is the same as evangelizing the dead and has to have had a salvific intent. However, W. J. Dalton[29] has made a strong case that the two verses do not refer to the same event. I Pet 4:6 does not have Christ do the preaching; rather it refers to the preaching about Christ which is the proclamation of the gospel. Christians who accepted the gospel and have since died are alive in God's eyes (as in I Thess 4:13–18). I Pet 3:19, on the other hand, does have (the risen) Christ do the preaching but to the spirits in prison, without any mention of the dead. In Semitic anthropology "spirits" (as distinct from "shades") would be an unusual way to

[27]Despite the parabolic Matt 12:40, the Gospel narratives do not spell out that Jesus' body was in the grave three days, but only that it was placed in the tomb on Friday before sunset and was no longer there Sunday morning. From God's viewpoint there would be no dimension of time from the death to the resurrection. Consequently in that respect what was happening to Jesus between death and resurrection is a pseudo-problem: According to Christian faith he was with God, even as Christians believe that those who die in God's love are with God between their death and their resurrection.

[28]A further modification, proposed hesitantly by Augustine, replaced Origen's interpretation in the West: The salvific proclamation of Christ to the disobedient contemporaries of Noah was not after their death but during their OT lifetime. This reflects a view, attested elsewhere in the NT, that Christ was active in the OT period, as a type of preexistence (BINTC 133–34).

[29]*Christ's Proclamation to the Spirits: A Study of 1 Peter 3:18–4:6* (2d ed.; AnBib 23: Rome: PBI, 1989). See also B. Reicke, *The Disobedient Spirits and Christian Baptism. A Study of 1 Pet. iii 19* (Copenhagen: Munksgaard, 1946).

refer to the dead; more likely it would refer to the angels. The reference to disobedience in the days of Noah suggests that these are the angels or sons of God who did evil by having relations with earthly women according to Gen 6:1–4, a wickedness that led God to send the great flood from which Noah was saved (6:5ff.). In preNT Jewish mythology the story of these wicked angels is greatly elaborated, e.g., God had the spirits rounded up and imprisoned in a great pit under the earth until the day when they would be judged (*I Enoch* 10:11–12; *Jubilees* 5:6). I Pet 3:19 has the risen Christ go down there to proclaim his victory and crush the Satanic forces. The imagery is similar to that of John 16:11 where the return of Jesus to God marks the condemnation of the Prince of this world, and that of Rev 12:5–13 where when the Messiah is born (through resurrection) and taken up to heaven, the devil and his angels are cast down. In my judgment this is the most plausible explanation of 3:19.

Relation to the Pauline Tradition

H. Koester (*Introd. NT* 2.xi) treats I Pet (and II Pet) in connection with the legacy of Paul and the transformation of Pauline theology into ecclesiastical doctrine. That is a somewhat extreme example of the detection of Pauline influence on I Pet, and it has been disputed or greatly qualified by others who think of a Petrine school of writers with a trajectory of its own. We need to consider the similarity between I Pet and the Pauline tradition under several headings since the diagnosis of the relationship is important for the reconstruction of early Christianity.

Similarity of format. As we have seen, the Opening Formula and the Concluding Formula of I Pet resemble those found in Paul's letters, but with some significant differences. Since most NT letters are associated with Paul, there is not enough other comparative material to tell whether the Pauline letter format is unique to Paul. Some similar elements in I Pet may represent common Christian letter format and may not be derived from direct knowledge of the Pauline letters.

Similarity of phraseology and thought. These words and phrases in I Pet are an example: in Christ (3:16; 5:10,14), freedom (2:16), charism with examples (4:10–11), the sufferings of Christ (*pathēmata:* 1:11; 4:13; 5:1), righteousness (*dikaiosynē:* 2:24; 3:14).[30] How widespread was such terminology? In some instances the phrase may be distinctively Pauline, e.g., "in Christ" occurs 164 times and "charism" occurs fifteen times in the Pauline

[30]Kelly, *I Peter* 11, lists parallels that I Pet has to Rom, Eph, and the Pastorals. K. Shimada, AJBI 19 (1995), 87–137, argues that direct literary dependence of I Pet on Paul cannot be proved.

writings, and nowhere else in the NT except I Pet. In other instances we are dealing with terms attested elsewhere in the NT, e.g., freedom brought by Christ is found in Mark, Luke, and John; Christ's sufferings, in Heb 2:9–10. In particular several of the proposed parallels between I Pet and Eph (p. 631: used by some to date I Pet quite late) are attested elsewhere with variations, e.g., Christ as the cornerstone (I Pet 2:7; Eph 2:20—see Matt 21:42) and the household code (p. 710 above).

Significant differences from Paul. Although I Pet speaks of righteousness or justification, it does not specify "by faith," which is the Pauline theme. There are no references in I Pet to a tension between faith and works, the church as Christ's body, Christ's preexistence before creation, etc.

Finally, some general similarities in the theological message, e.g., the salvific death and resurrection of Christ and the efficacy of baptism (I Pet 3:18–22), need not reflect direct knowledge of Paul's letters. Paul says specifically that he and Cephas (and others) had a common preaching (I Cor 15:11 in reference to 15:5–7). The cultic parallels between I Pet and Rom (priestly ministry of preaching and spiritual offerings in Rom 15:16 compared to I Pet 2:5) may be traceable to an appreciation of Jewish cult among Roman Christians—the very situation Heb would have been written to correct.[31] Both Silvanus and Mark had been with Paul; they could have been possible channels of Pauline influence on the writer, if the references to them in 5:12–13 are historical. I Pet was written from Rome, a city where at least some of the church would have been influenced by Paul's letter to the Romans and where Paul and Peter may actually have crossed paths in the 60s. Thus one need not posit that the writer had read much of the Pauline corpus. We can think of I Pet as a largely independent work, no closer to Paul's thought or farther from it than historically Peter would have been from Paul toward the end of their lives. The two men represented different strains of Christian missionary activity, and I Pet and II Pet can be considered a Petrine corpus distinct from the much larger Pauline corpus. In the latter (thirteen letters), as we have seen, there are seven genuine writings by Paul himself and six other writings that many judge (with varying degrees of likelihood) to be pseudonymous, e.g., II Thess quite possibly by Paul, but Eph most probably not. In the Petrine corpus (two letters[32]) there is I Pet, probably pseudonymous as we shall see, but difficult to judge; and II Pet, much more

[31]In BMAR 128–58 I have related both I Pet and Heb to the Roman church in the postPauline period AD 65–95, one written from Rome, the other to Rome (by someone who knew the Roman situation). Some themes they share include Christians as "exiles" (I Pet 1:1; 2:11; and Heb 11:13: *parepidēmoi*); sprinkling with the blood of Christ (I Pet 1:2; Heb 12:24); Christ as shepherd (I Pet 2:25; 5:4; and Heb 13:20).

[32]The noncanonical corpus is larger: *Gospel of Peter, Acts of Peter, Letter of Peter to Philip,* and *Apocalypse of Peter.*

clearly a postPetrine composition by an admirer who may have been a disciple.

From and To Whom, Where, and When?

We shall try to answer a number of questions on the basis of data mentioned in I Pet. It may be worthwhile remembering however, that if I Pet should be a totally fictional pseudepigraphon with no relation whatsoever to Peter, then all the data (e.g., geographical and personal names) might be fictional as well; and many of the questions would be completely unanswerable.

FROM WHOM? Of all the Catholic Epistles I Pet has the best chance of being written by the figure to whom it is attributed. A major argument advanced for composition by Peter is the knowledge of Jesus' words shown in the work. Since there is no explicit quotation, one must decide whether possible echoes are more likely attributable to the memory of an earwitness (favoring composition by Peter) or to knowledge of preached tradition and/or the written Gospels (making composition by Peter most unlikely).[33]

What arguments militate against authenticity? Let me list and comment on them, with the more persuasive coming *last.* (1) The excellent quality of the Greek, exhibiting a rich vocabulary, and the citation of the LXX form of the OT make it unlikely that I Pet was composed by a Galilean fisherman.[34] However, since I Pet 5:12 may indicate that Silvanus (Silas) was an amanuensis (secretary), if he were given considerable freedom and knew Greek well, he could have phrased Peter's thoughts. (2) The dependence of I Pet on the Pauline writings does not match the historical relations between Peter and Paul, which were hostile. Actually neither the dependence (see subsection above) nor the hostility should be exaggerated. Some relationship to Paul could be explained by the locale (both of them were in Rome in the 60s) or by common co-workers (Silvanus and Mark). As for addressees, the contention that I Pet was sent to Pauline territory is dubious, as we shall see below. (3) References to a "fiery ordeal" (4:12) and the experience of suffering required of the brotherhood throughout the world (5:9) suggest a universal imperial persecution, and there was none in Peter's lifetime. However,

[33]Echoes include: I Pet 1:4 and Matt 6:20; I Pet 1:17 and Luke 11:2; I Pet 2:19–20 and Luke 6:32–33; I Pet 3:9 and Matt 5:39; I Pet 3:14 and Matt 5:10; I Pet 4:14 and Matt 5:11. E. Best, NTS 16 (1969–70), 95–113, argues that the resemblances are to a few blocks of material in Matt and Luke and suggest an oral rather than written dependence; they do not support Peter as the author of I Pet. See, however, R. H. Gundry, NTS 13 (1966–67), 336–50; *Biblica* 55 (1974), 211–32.

[34]The response that people in business in Galilee, especially on a trade route such as that around Capernaum, learned Greek is irrelevant. They may have picked up enough Greek for commerce but scarcely the ability to write literary Greek.

since there was no universal persecution of Christians until the 2d century, this interpretation of the suffering would require a dating too late to be plausible. The passage may mean no more than harassment and the common Christian demand to take up the cross.

(4) The church organization implied in 5:1 with established presbyters, seemingly appointed and salaried, fits the last one third of the century better than Peter's lifetime (n. 21 above). That may be true; but the reference to varied charisms in 4:10–11 suggests a transitional period, earlier, for instance, than that envisioned by I Tim, which was addressed to Ephesus in the Province of Asia (cf. I Pet 1:1). Goppelt uses this observation to argue for an 80–85 dating. (5) The writer calls himself "Peter" rather than Simon or Simon Peter. This seems to be the mark of a disciple stressing the authority implicit in the symbolic designation. (6) There are indications in the circumstances to be discussed in the following paragraphs that also make more plausible a date not too long after Peter's martyrdom and the fall of Jerusalem. Accordingly a greater number of scholars posit pseudepigraphical composition, not by a purely fictional claimant but by a representative of those at Rome (a school of disciples?) who regarded themselves as the heirs of Peter.[35] In ABD 5.278 J. H. Elliott writes, "Speaking in the name of their martyred leader, this Petrine branch of the family of God in 'Babylon' assured fellow members of the household dispersed through Asia Minor of the bonds of suffering, faith, and hope which united the worldwide Christian brotherhood."

FROM WHERE? The farewell greeting in 5:13 includes "she who is at Babylon." A few scholars have tried to refer this to a geographical Babylon in Egypt or Mesopotamia (partially at times with Reformation interest to avoid attributing authority to the church of Rome). Today, almost universally,[36] it is agreed that this letter was written from Rome. The excavations on Vatican Hill, showing a firm ancient tradition of honoring the site where Peter was buried,[37] confirm the information in *I Clement* 5, written *ca.* AD 96–120 from Rome, about Peter having contended unto death. Thus a letter from that city bearing Peter's name would have been perfectly appropriate.

TO WHOM AND WHERE? I Pet 1:1 is addressed "To the exiles of the dias-

[35]M. L. Soards, "1 Peter, 2 Peter, and Jude as Evidence for a Petrine School," ANRW II.25.5 (1988), 3828–49. Achtemeier, *1 Peter* 43, opts for I Pet as a pseudonymous letter drawing on traditions associated with Simon Peter.

[36]In his first edition, Beare, *First Peter,* regarded the Babylon information as fictional and argued that I Pet was written in the region to which it was addressed (a view that he later abandoned). That localization was to explain the echoes of the mystery religions of Asia Minor that Beare detected in I Pet—a view that should also be abandoned.

[37]The question of whether Peter's bones have been found is much more disputable. See D. W. O'Connor, *Peter in Rome* (New York: Columbia Univ., 1969); G. F. Snyder, BA 32 (1969), 1–24.

pora in Pontus, Galatia, Cappadocia, Asia, and Bithynia." That Gentiles were the main focus is suggested by 2:10: "Once you were no people, but now you are God's people." Any Christians could be exiles of the diaspora in the sense of being away from their true home with Christ in heaven, but the expectation that the addressees would understand the heavy dose of exodus imagery in I Pet suggests Gentile Christians who had been catechized with a strong appreciation of Judaism. In 2:9 the Christians have taken on all the privileges of Israel.

Are the five places mentioned, all in Asia Minor, adjacent Roman provinces or more restricted regions or districts within those provinces reflecting ancient national origins? If the former, the whole western half of Asia Minor is meant and Paul had been in Galatia and at Ephesus in Asia. If the latter (which is more plausible[38]), northern Asia Minor is meant; and Paul had probably not been in most of that area, e.g., Acts 16:7 says that the Spirit of Jesus did not allow Paul into Bithynia, and Acts does not mention his going into Pontus, Cappadocia, or northern Asia. We have no evidence that Peter had been to that locale either, but there is another possibility that would explain a letter bearing his name addressed to it. Three of the five names (Cappadocia, Pontus, and Asia) are mentioned in Acts 2:9 in a list of devout Jews in Jerusalem who heard Peter preach on Pentecost and asked to be baptized. That list of people (which includes Rome) may well be programmatic of what Luke knows to have been the spread of Jerusalem Christianity, a Christianity that did not insist on circumcision or the Sabbath but, more than Paul's mission, remained insistent on the Jewish heritage. In treating Gal, we saw that those who came to Galatia (a fourth area mentioned in I Pet) and preached there a gospel other than Paul's probably claimed to represent the Jerusalem authorities, so that in 2:9 Paul refutes them by insisting that James, and Cephas, and John extended the right hand of fellowship to him. Peter was a representative of Jerusalem Christianity, and part of his popularity at Rome may have stemmed from the fact that the Roman church was also the product of the Jerusalem mission. That background could explain very well why Peter or a disciple using his name wrote from Rome to the churches of Asia Minor: They and Rome shared the same history, and Peter was an authority for both of them.

Yet, one may ask, instead of having the letter come from Rome, would it not have been more logical for the Jerusalem church (and perhaps, James)

[38]Bithynia and (western) Pontus, names separated by I Pet, had constituted one province for over a century. And if one would argue that eastern Pontus is meant, that had been joined to the province of Cappadocia by AD 63–64, and then Cappadocia to the province of Galatia by 72. Could the northern part of that composite province be intended in the (geographical?) word order of I Pet 1:1 (p. 708 above)?

to have addressed pastoral advice to areas evangelized by its missionaries? Several observations may be helpful. Although both Peter and James had a certain communality as representatives of Jerusalem Christianity (Gal 1:18–19; 2:11–12; I Cor 9:5: "brothers of the Lord" and Cephas), Peter is portrayed as a mobile missionary with responsibility for an opening to the Gentiles (Acts 9:32–11:18; 12:17), while James remained in Jerusalem as the leader of the Jewish Christian community. Therefore, Peter's may have been the appropriate image for addressing churches found in purely Gentile areas.[39] Moreover, according to Christian tradition, the Jewish Revolt produced a major disruption in the Jerusalem church, for the Christians of that city refused to take a part in the war and went across the Jordan to Pella. Thus the Roman conquest of Jerusalem in AD 70 may have ushered in a period when the Christians in Rome took over the evangelistic enterprise formerly operated from the Jewish capital.[40] In *I Clement* (*ca.* 96–120) the Roman church addressed admonitions to the church at Corinth, and Ignatius wrote to the Roman church *ca.* 110, "You have taught others" (*Romans* 3:1).

WHEN? At the upper end of the possible chronological scale I Pet is cited by or known to several early–2d century witnesses, e.g., II Pet 3:1, Polycarp's *Philippians,* and Papias (EH 3.39.17),[41] and thus a date after 100 is unlikely. At the lower end of the scale, we need to posit a date after Peter reached Rome. Since there is no reference to Peter in the letter Paul wrote to Rome in 58, presumably I Pet could not have been written before the early 60s. If Peter wrote the letter, the possible range would be 60–65. If the letter is pseudonymous, written by a disciple, the range would be 70–100. One might doubt that the respect for the emperor inculcated in 2:13,17 would have been likely during the time of Nero's persecution which began after the fire of 64 (he was assassinated in 68) or in the final years of Domitian's reign (81–96), after the revolt of 89, when he let loose his hostility toward those of suspicious outlook (p. 807 below). Thus the two ranges can be reduced

[39]As we shall see in the next Chapter, Jas, directed to the twelve tribes in the diaspora, may well have been written from Jerusalem or Palestine to mixed Jewish/Gentile Christians for whom the name of James would carry authority. There are certain similarities between I Pet and Jas besides the diaspora phraseology of the Opening Formula: theme of trials (I Pet 1:6; Jas 1:2); begotten/brought forth by the word (I Pet 1:23; Jas 1:18); example of the grass withering (I Pet 1:24; Jas 1:10); putting away all evil (I Pet 2:1; Jas 1:21); passions that wage war (I Pet 2:11; Jas 4:1); covering a multitude of sins (I Pet 4:8; Jas 5:20); "God opposes the proud but gives grace to the humble" and so be humble (I Pet 5:5–6; Jas 4:6–7); resist the devil (I Pet 5:8–9; Jas 4:7).

[40]Acts symbolically moves the story from Jerusalem to Rome with the latter serving as the site where it is announced: "Let it be known to you that this salvation of God has been sent to the Gentiles; they will listen" (28:28). That symbolism may represent a historical development.

[41]An even earlier witness to I Pet might be *I Clement:* same opening greeting asking that grace and peace be multiplied; same assurance that love covers a multitude of sins in I Pet 4:8 and *I Clement* 49:5; same quote about God resisting the proud in I Pet 5:5 and *I Clement* 30:2. Kelly, *1 Peter* 12, lists other parallels.

to 60–63 and 70–90. Pastoral care for Asia Minor exercised from Rome would be more intelligible after 70. Similarly the use of "Babylon" as a name for Rome makes better sense after 70, when the Romans had destroyed the second Temple (n. 22 above); all the other attestations of this symbolic use of the name occur in the post-70 period. The best parallels to the church structure portrayed in I Pet 5:1–4 are found in works written after 70 (n. 21 above). All this tilts the scales in favor of 70–90,[42] which now seems to be the majority scholarly view.

Issues and Problems for Reflection

(1) As for canonicity, I Pet and I John were the first of the seven Catholic Epistles to gain wide acceptance as canonical. We saw above early–2d century witnesses to I Pet. Eusebius (EH 3.3.1) mentions I Pet first in discussing the writings of the apostles and affirms that it was used by the elders of ancient times (unlike II Pet). Strangely I Pet is not mentioned in the Muratorian Fragment, but that absence may stem from the poorly preserved character of that list. P^{72}, a papyrus of the 3d century, contained I Pet, II Pet, and Jude. Along with I John and James, I Pet was accepted by the Syriac-speaking church in the 5th century.

(2) In the history of ecclesiology I Pet 2:9 has played an important role. It describes the baptized Christian community as a royal priesthood.[43] The sacrifices they offer are spiritual sacrifices (2:5), namely their virtuous life.[44] In Reformation struggles it was employed against the Roman Catholic maintenance of an ordained priesthood on the grounds that a priesthood distinct from the priesthood of the Christian community is not justified by the NT. Several observations need to be made. *First,* there is no indication that the term "priest" was used for any Christian official in NT times. Priestly terminology seems to have been introduced in the 2d century in relation to the use of sacrificial language for the eucharist (see p. 573 above). *Second,* the description of the people of God as a royal priesthood is OT terminology (Exod 19:6): Israel had both this ideal and a specially consecrated priesthood with powers and duties different from those who were not priests.

[42]Achtemeier, *1 Peter* 30, favors the earlier years of the 80–100 range. I Pet has a household code; if Col is deuteroPauline, then the other four household codes belong to the last third of the 1st century.

[43]Sometimes this is called the priesthood of all believers, but that may too individualistic. It is not clear that the writer would call an individual Christian a priest. Also it is not clear whether the writer had a theology of the priesthood of Christ to which to relate the community priesthood.

[44]D. Hill, JSNT 16 (1982), 45–63, however, points to a connection between liturgical expression and Christian living, so that the spiritual sacrifices would include prayers and even eucharistic liturgy.

Therefore the notion that a priesthood of the baptized community excludes the existence of specially ordained priests is not justifiable biblically. (See above pp. 701–2 as to whether the unique priesthood and sacrifice of Christ excludes specially ordained priests.) Worthy of reflection, however, is how churches that have the concept of a specially ordained priesthood can strive to maintain a proper insistence on the universal Christian priesthood. *Third,* I Pet 2:9 is comparable to Rev 1:6 where in liturgical language Jesus Christ is praised for having "made us a kingdom, priests to his God"; and Rev 5:10 where the seer says of those in heaven who have been ransomed for God by Christ, "You have made them a kingdom and priests to our God." Thus there is an eschatological tone to the communal priesthood.[45]

(3) The addressees of I Pet are alienated from their surrounding society because of their Christian beliefs and practices. In today's first world, particularly in the United States, to blend into the surrounding society is almost an ideal, with the result that Christians who do not are looked on as sectarian. If we leave aside the particular ancient context of Gentiles recently become Christian in Roman-controlled Asia Minor, is there truth for all times to be retained from I Pet's descriptions of the Christians as aliens? To what extent does Christian identity demand distinctiveness from a nonChristian society?

(4) Whatever nuance one gives to his purpose, Christ's going to make proclamation to the spirits in prison who had been disobedient in the days of Noah (I Pet 3:19—see subsection above) means that his victory was applied to those who lived and acted in OT times. That description has imaginative elements, but it represents a Christian instinct that Christ's victory affected not only those who followed temporally but also those who preceded—a temporal universality as part of the theology that all are saved through Christ. (See also Matt 27:52.) How do Christians reconcile such dependence on Christ with a belief that people who have not known Christ are judged by God according to the way they lived in light of their own knowledge and conscience?

(5) I Pet 2:9 speaks to the Gentiles as God's chosen people having all the prestigious privileges of Israel in the OT. Where does that type of theology leave the Jews who did not believe in Jesus? Would the writer say that they were no longer a royal priesthood, a holy nation, God's own people? Or does he simply not think of them because they are not an issue in the area he addresses?

[45]See Elliott, *Elect,* on the priesthood concept in I Pet; also R. E. Brown, *The Critical Meaning of the Bible* (New York: Paulist, 1981), 96–106, on priesthoods in the NT. For comparison to Philo's concept, T. Seland, JSNT 57 (1995), 87–119.

Bibliography on I Peter

COMMENTARIES AND STUDIES IN SERIES (* = also on II Peter; ** = also on II Peter and Jude): **Achtemeier, P. J.** (Hermeneia, 1996); Best, E. (NCBC, 1971); Bigg, C. (ICC, 2d ed., 1902**); Craddock, F. B. (WBComp, 1995**); Cranfield, C.E.B. (TBC, 1960**); Danker, F. W. (ProcC, rev. ed., 1995); Davids, P. H. (NICNT, 1990); Elliott, J. H. (AugC, 1982**); Grudem, W. A. (TNTC, 1988); Hillyer, N. (NIBC, 1992**); Kelly, J.N.D. (HNTC, 1969**); Krodel, G. A. (ProcC, 1977); Leaney, A.R.C. (CCNEB, 1967**); Martin, R. P. (NTT, 1994**); Michaels, J. R. (WBC, 1988); Perkins, P. (IBC, 1995**); Senior, D. P. (NTM, 1980*); Stibbs, A. M., and A. F. Walls (TNTC, 1959). See also the *Bibliography* of Chapter 34 below for works marked **.

BIBLIOGRAPHIES AND SURVEYS: Martin, R. P., VE 1 (1962), 29–42; Elliott, J. H., JBL 95 (1976), 243–54; Sylva, D., BTB 10 (1980), 155–63; JETS 25 (1982), 75–89; Casurella, A., *Bibliography of Literature on First Peter* (Leiden: Brill, 1996).

Beare, F. W., *The First Epistle of Peter* (3d ed.; Oxford Univ., 1970).

Combrink, H.J.B., "The Structure of 1 Peter," *Neotestamentica* 9 (1975), 34–63.

Cranfield, C.E.B., *The First Epistle of Peter* (London: SCM, 1950).

Cross, F. L., *1 Peter: A Paschal Liturgy* (London: Mowbray, 1954).

Elliott, J. H., *The Elect and the Holy. An Exegetical Examination of 1 Peter* (NovTSup 12; Leiden: Brill, 1966).

———, *A Home for the Homeless. A Social-Scientific Criticism of 1 Peter* (new ed.; Minneapolis: A/F, 1990).

———, "Disgraced Yet Graced: The Gospel According to 1 Peter in the Key of Honor and Shame," BTB 25 (1995), 166–78.

Furnish, V. P., "Elect Sojourners in Christ: An Approach to the Theology of I Peter," *Perkins Journal* 28 (1975), 1–11.

Goppelt, L., *A Commentary on I Peter* (Grand Rapids: Eerdmans, 1993; German orig., 1978).

Jonsen, A. R., "The Moral Teaching of the First Epistle of St. Peter," *Sciences Ecclésiastiques* 16 (1964), 93–105.

McCaughey, J. D., "On Re-Reading 1 Peter," *Australian Biblical Review* 31 (1983), 33–44.

Moule, C.F.D., "The Nature and Purpose of I Peter," NTS 3 (1956–57), 1–11.

Munro, W., *Authority in Paul and Peter* (SNTSMS 45; Cambridge Univ., 1983).

Neyrey, J. H., "First Peter and Converts," TBT 22 (1984), 13–18.

Selwyn, E. G., *The First Epistle of Peter* (2d ed.; London: Macmillan, 1947).

Senior, D. P., "The First Letter of Peter," TBT 22 (1984), 5–12.

Talbert, C. H., *Perspectives on First Peter* (Macon, GA: National Ass. of Baptist Profs. of Religion, 1986).

Thurén, L., *The Motivation of the Paraenesis: Discovering Argumentation and Theology in 1 Peter* (JSNTSup 117; Sheffield: JSOT, 1995).

van Unnik, W. C., "The Teaching of Good Works in I Peter," NTS 1 (1954–55), 92–110.

CHAPTER 34

EPISTLE (LETTER) OF JAMES

Among the "Catholic Epistles" we now come to a work called by Luther an epistle of straw ("right strawy epistle"), but which has come into its own in our time as the most socially conscious writing in the NT. After the *Background* and *General Analysis,* subsections will treat: *James and Paul (2:24), James and Matthew, Anointing of the sick (5:14–16), Literary genre, By and to whom, where, and when?, Canonicity, Issues for reflection,* and *Bibliography.*

The Background

Leaving to a subsection below the historical issue of who wrote the epistle, here we are interested in identifying the figure presented as the author: "James, a servant of God and of the Lord Jesus Christ." In the NT there are several men named "James" (Greek *Jakōbos,* derived from the Hebrew for "Jacob," the patriarch from whom descend the twelve tribes). At least two of them, both members of the Twelve, may be dismissed as extremely unlikely candidates for authorship: the brother of John and son of Zebedee, James ("the Great") who died in the early 40s; and James (son?) of Alphaeus of whom we know nothing.[1] A totally unknown James, not mentioned elsewhere in the NT, has been suggested (to explain why the work failed to get wide acceptance); in later tradition, it is thought, he would have been confused with James the brother of the Lord.

A short cut around the last suggestion brings us to the only truly plausible candidate: *James listed first among the "brothers" of Jesus* in Mark 6:3; Matt 13:55,[2] not a member of the Twelve but an apostle in a broader sense

[1]The mistake of identifying him with James the brother of the Lord has been frequently repeated in hagiography (and it is this wrongly conflated James who is usually denoted by the designation James "the Less"). Acts 1:13–14 is lucidly clear in distinguishing between the Twelve and the brothers of the Lord; also I Cor 15:5,7.

[2]Since these brothers are associated with Mary (Mark 3:31–32; John 2:12), if one had only the NT one would assume that they were the children of Mary and Joseph, born after Jesus—a view held in antiquity by Tertullian and by most Protestants today. Yet already in the early 2d century, they were identified as the children of Joseph by a previous marriage (*Protevangelium of James* 9:2). This interpretation is maintained in much of Eastern Christianity, and Bauckham (*Jude Relatives* 31) says that it "has a better claim to serious consideration than is often nowadays allowed." The

Summary of Basic Information

DATE: If pseudonymous, after the death of James *ca.* 62, in the range 70–110; most likely in the 80s or 90s.

TO: A homily employing diatribe, shaped in a letter format to "the twelve tribes in the dispersion," i.e., probably Christians outside Palestine quite conservative in their appreciation of Judaism.

AUTHENTICITY: Claimed author is James (the brother of the Lord); but most think it was written by someone (a disciple?) who admired the image of James as the Christian authority most loyal to Judaism.

UNITY AND INTEGRITY: Not seriously disputed today.

DIVISION ACCORDING TO CONTENTS (TOPICS):

1:1:	Greetings (Opening Formula)
1:2–18:	The role of trials and temptations
1:19–27:	Words and deeds
2:1–9:	Partiality toward the rich
2:10–13:	Keeping the whole Law
2:14–26:	Faith and works
3:1–12:	Power of the tongue
3:13–18:	Wisdom from above
4:1–10:	Desires as the cause of division
4:11–12:	Judging one another as judging the Law
4:13–17:	Further arrogant behavior
5:1–6:	Warning to the rich
5:7–11:	Patience till the coming of the Lord
5:12–20:	Admonitions on behavior within the community.

of the term (I Cor 15:7; Gal 1:19). There is no evidence that he followed Jesus during the public ministry (Mark 3:21,31–32; 6:1–4); rather he stayed behind in Nazareth with the other relatives. Yet the risen Jesus appeared to him (I Cor 15:7; *Gospel of the Hebrews* 7), and seemingly from then on he was a prominent figure (Gal 1:19). That is reflected in the Coptic *Gospel of Thomas* 12, where Jesus tells the disciples that after his departure they should go to James the Just, "for whose sake heaven and earth have come to exist." Once the Jerusalem church was structured, James (accompanied by the elders) was portrayed as the presiding leader and spokesman.[3] He was executed by stoning in the early 60s at the instigation of the high priest

claim that he was a cousin of Jesus was introduced in the 4th century by Jerome and became common in the Western church. See, however, J. P. Meier, CBQ 54 (1992), 1–28. In Roman Catholicism the thesis that Mary remained a virgin after Jesus' birth is generally evaluated as infallibly taught by the ordinary magisterium.

[3]Gal 2:9; Acts 12:17; 15:13–22; 21:18. See K. Carroll, BJRL 44 (1961–62), 49–67. The implications that Peter's departure from Jerusalem (Acts 12:17) had for leadership in the church are discussed on p. 302 above.

Ananus II who, when the Roman prefect was absent, convened a Sanhedrin and accused James ("the brother of Jesus who was called the Messiah") of having transgressed the Law (Josephus, *Ant.* 20.9.1; #200).[4] Several apocrypha bear the name of James (*Protevangelium of James; Apocryphon of James;* and two *Apocalypses*), but none betrays knowledge of the letter we are discussing.

For our letter the most important element of background is the imagery of James as a conservative Jewish Christian very loyal to observing the Law. He was not an extreme legalist, for both Acts 15 and Gal 2 agree that he sided with Paul in declaring that the Gentiles did not have to be circumcised when they came to believe in Christ. Yet the speech that appears on his lips in Acts 15:13–21 offers the most traditional reason for that acceptance of Gentiles by applying to them elements of Lev 17–18 applicable to strangers living within Israel.[5] Paul interpreted the decision at Jerusalem to mean freedom from the Law for Gentile converts, but at Antioch "certain men came from James" and challenged the mingling at table of Jewish Christians and Gentile Christians who did not observe the food laws. According to Acts 21:18–25, when Paul arrived at Jerusalem *ca.* 58, James told him how many Jews had been converted in Jerusalem and instructed him to be purified and go to the Temple. In later tradition (the *Pseudo-Clementine* writings) James was looked on as the bishop of bishops by Jewish Christians who despised Paul.[6] He was given the sobriquet "the Just," which Eusebius (EH 2.23.4–7) explained in terms of his having lived as a Nazirite (an ascetic especially dedicated to God) and his praying so often in the Temple that his knees became as calloused as those of a camel. It is not surprising then that, whether or not written by James, the NT letter that bears his name echoes in many ways traditional Jewish belief and piety.

[4]There is no reason to doubt the authenticity of Josephus' reference to James' death; J. P. Meier, *Bible Review* 7 (1991), 20–25. Legends developed about his death, e.g., in the 3d century Clement of Alexandria reported that he was thrown off the pinnacle of the Temple (EH 2.1.5; cf. Hegesippus in EH 2.23.15–16).

[5]Although Acts 15:22–23 reports that the apostles, elders, and the whole Jerusalem church sent a letter to Antioch, Syria, and Cilicia insisting on James' demands, Acts 21:25 has James and the elders ("we") send the letter.

[6]Besides the subapostolic church writings associated with Clement, a presbyter of the church of Rome (*I* and *II Clement* in Appendix II below), a body of pseudonymous literature tells a fictitious story about how Clement was converted to Christ, traveled with Peter, and ultimately found lost family members—the *Pseudo-Clementines.* Composed originally in Greek *ca.* the 4th century (?) from earlier material that is sometimes called a basic document (*ca.* 150–200?), the main components are entitled *Homilies* and *Recognitions* (the latter preserved only in Syriac and Latin). James is a hero in this literature, which is strongly attached to Judaism and is antiPauline. The *Pseudo-Clementines* played a major role in F. C. Baur's early-19th-century analysis of Christian origins which depicted the Jewish Christianity represented by James as the antithesis to Pauline Christianity—a depiction that goes considerably beyond the NT evidence.

General Analysis of the Message

OPENING FORMULA OR GREETINGS (1:1). Jas spends little time on christological reflection; some have even thought of it as a Jewish writing only slightly adapted for Christian use. Nevertheless, the coupling of "God" and "the Lord Jesus Christ" in the first line shows the traditional Christian faith of the writer. Interpreted against an OT background, "To the twelve tribes in the diaspora" should mean that the addressees were Jews dispersed outside the Holy Land. Yet Christians considered themselves the renewed or new Israel; and I Pet, addressed to Gentile Christians, is written (1:1) "To the exiles of the diaspora." Many scholars would argue, therefore, that Jas was or could be addressed to Gentile Christians. Nevertheless, in Jas there is no correction of vices that in the eyes of Jews were characteristically Gentile (idolatry,[7] sexual impurity); the "twelve tribes" is more Jewish than the I Pet address; the addressees meet in a "synagogue" (2:2); and the leading Jewish Christian authority is pictured as the author. We might be well advised, then, to think of the addressees as Christians strongly identified by the Jewish heritage.

Abraham, Moses, and various OT prophets were called "servant of God"; and all believers in Jesus could be thus entitled (Rev 1:1). Thus in Jas 1:1 the leader of the Jerusalem church and the brother of the Lord is designating himself modestly, even as Jesus commanded (Matt 23:8–12).

TRIALS, TEMPTATION, WORDS, DEEDS (1:2–27). The "grace and peace" greeting of Paul's letters (also I Pet 1:1) is lacking in Jas, as is the Thanksgiving element in the letter format. Indeed, after 1:1 Jas bears little semblance to a regular letter, as the writer launches immediately into a series of exhortations. The attitude and subject matter strongly echo the late Wisdom books of the OT,[8] adapted to an eschatological outlook and combined with the emphases in the teaching attributed to Jesus in Q, e.g., material in the Sermon on the Mount (Matt 5–7) and scattered in Luke 6 and elsewhere (Table 2 in Chapter 6 above). On the other hand, the format resembles that of the Greco-Roman diatribe. The issue of Literary Genre will be treated in a subsection below, as well as the debate about the sequence of thought in Jas. Here in the *General Analysis* our concern is to do justice to the main topics, following a division according to content. Most of what Jas is saying is clear

[7]Contrast I Pet 1:18; 2:10. Jas 2:19 simply assumes monotheism.

[8]Sirach and Wisdom more than Proverbs. The Wisdom books are an excellent witness to the practical morality expected of Jews in their personal, family, and business lives. As an example of Wisdom style, note the metaphors taken from the world around us (rather than from revelation) in the first chapter of Jas: the waves of the sea (1:6), the sun burning the grass (1:11), the person looking in the mirror (1:23).

even on first reading; and so we shall be concentrating on why the topics were chosen and what the treatment tells us about the situation of the writer and the addressees.

Jesus had warned his followers that they would undergo testing and trials during which they would need faith in God's ability to meet their needs (Matt 5:11; 24:9–13). The presence of a similar passage at the beginning of I Pet (1:6–7) may mean that encouragement in the face of trials was a standard part of baptismal instructions,[9] and thus not indicative that the addressees were especially persecuted or harassed. On the other hand, the alternating address (Jas 1:9–11) to those of low estate and of wealth, contrasting their fate, is striking. Here Jas is close to the Lucan form (6:20,24) of the beatitude for the poor with the accompanying woe for the rich. Several other passages in Jas (2:1–9; 5:1–6) attack the rich, so that the poor/rich issue most likely reflects a social situation known to the writer in his own church[10] from which he extrapolates for others. (The name of James raises the image of the Jerusalem church with its emphasis on sharing goods: Acts 2:44–45; 4:34–37; 5:1–11; 6:1; Gal 2:10.) In dealing with responsibility for evil, following in the tradition of Sirach 15:11–13, Jas 1:13 is firm, "God tempts no one." Rather, in language worthy of DSS dualism between light and darkness, God is the Father of lights (Jas 1:17).[11] God brings forth Christians by the word of truth and wills that they be like the firstfruits which in the Israelite liturgy belong to God (Jas 1:18).[12] But for that to happen, Christians cannot simply be hearers of the word (of the gospel); they must manifest its working in their lives—a practical moral theme to which Jas will return in 2:14–26. From the beginning, however, it is worth noting that the good works flow from the power of the gospel word that has been implanted. There is nothing

[9]The beatitude in Jas 1:12 promises the crown of life to the person who endures temptation. In Rev 2:10 Jesus promises the crown of life to those who remain faithful. I Pet 5:4 promises the unfading crown of glory when the great Shepherd comes. In II Tim 4:8 Paul is confident that there is in store for him a crown of righteousness to be given by the righteous Judge on the last day.

[10]Some would think simply of the *'anāwîm* of the late OT period who are poor *in spirit,* i.e., those who accept being (and even choose to be) economically poor because they reject this world's values. The descriptions in Jas, however, suggest the economically poor, defrauded of wages and preyed on, without being clear about the extent to which this poverty was benevolently chosen or accepted. Jas rails against the arrogantly materialistic rich whose wealth was indiscriminately acquired. See R. Crotty, *Colloquium* 27 (1995), 11–21.

[11]See also *Testament of Abraham* (recension B) 7:5; also I John 1:5: "God is light."

[12]"Bring forth" is the action of a woman giving birth from her womb; for the male image of divine begetting, see John 1:12–13. The Mosaic Law was described as the word of truth in Ps 119:43, while Eph 1:13 calls the gospel of salvation the word of truth. The risen Christ himself is the firstfruits from the dead (I Cor 15:20), and the 144,000 redeemed by him are the firstfruits presented to God and the Lamb (Rev 14:4). L. E. Elliott-Binns, NTS 3 (1956–57), 148–61, traces the ideas in Jas 1:13–18 to Gen rather than to Hellenistic influence.

theoretical about the religion advocated in Jas 1:27: a religion manifested in taking care of needy widows and orphans and keeping oneself undefiled by the world.

RICH AND POOR, AND THE WHOLE LAW (2:1–13). Although Wisdom Literature abounds in similes and metaphors introduced simply as illustrations, it is hard to think that the picture painted here in Jas is purely theoretical. One gets the impression that Jas and the addressees live in Christian communities that come together into what is still being called a synagogue (literal rendering of 2:2, often translated as "assembly"), and that there rich members tend to be received with favor and special distinctions. The inevitable institutionalization of a community called into being by the preached gospel has taken place, and Jas (2:5) is correctively calling on what they were taught in the past about the poor inheriting the kingdom. Particularly eye-catching is the claim that the rich Christians[13] are oppressing "you" and dragging "you" into court. (In 5:6 Jas accuses the rich of having condemned and put to death the just.) Was the writer facing an actual situation similar to that criticized by Paul in I Cor 6:1–8 where Christians were resorting to secular courts to settle their disputes, or is this simply a generalized echo of OT language (Amos 8:4; Wisdom 2:10)? As previously for Jesus (Matt 22:39–40, from Lev 19:18), so now for Jas 2:8–10, love of neighbor sums up the Law and the commandments; and to offend on this point makes one guilty of breaking the Law as a whole.[14] The stunning expression "law of liberty" in Jas 2:12 (repeated from 1:25) challenges a dichotomy between law and freedom.

FAITH AND WORKS (2:14–26). The writer begins in the style of the Greco-Roman diatribe with an imaginative example of his own creation, illustrating the disastrous results of indifference to good works.[15] He then (2:21–25) offers biblical examples of the importance of works from the accounts of Abraham in Gen 15:6 and 22:16–17, and of Rahab in Joshua 2.[16] Scholarly

[13]Jas 2:7 accuses them of blaspheming the noble name that has been called on them (at baptism?). Those "on whom the Lord's name is called" is an OT description of God's chosen people (Deut 28:10; Amos 9:12).

[14]Jas never mentions "works of the Law" or circumcision as Paul does, nor does he refer to ritual laws. C. H. Felder, *Journal of Religious Thought* 39 (1982–83), 51–69 argues that "law" in this section means the moral law of the OT and of the Jesus tradition, as contrasted with discriminatory partiality. See also L. T. Johnson, "Leviticus 19 in James," JBL 101 (1982), 391–401. Although the atmosphere is strongly Jewish, M. O. Boyle, NTS 31 (1985), 611–17, points to evidence in stoicism for the idea that breaking even one precept makes one a transgressor of the law.

[15]On the style of 2:14–26, J.D.N. van der Westhuizen, *Neotestamentica* 25 (1991), 89–107. Jas 2:18 portrays (disparagingly) someone treating faith and works almost as if they were two different charisms so that one person has faith and another does works. Jas would allow only one gift: a faith that manifests itself in one's life.

[16]Jas' use of Abraham is closer to standard Jewish thought than is Paul's use; cf. Sirach 44:19–21; I Macc 2:52; *Jubilees* 19:9. (See R. N. Longenecker, JETS 20 [1977], 203–12; M. L. Soards, IBS 9 (1987), 18–26). The faithful deeds of Rahab are praised in Heb 11:31; *I Clement* 12.

discussion of this passage has been dominated by the contrast between Jas' insistence on the insufficiency of faith without works and Paul's rejection of the salvific value of works (of the Mosaic Law). Leaving all that until the first subsection below, here I would point out simply that Jas is working out in practice Jesus' warning that not everyone who says, "Lord, Lord," will enter the kingdom of heaven (Matt 7:21). In any period outsiders would certainly judge Christians by the commonsense standard of 2:26 that faith without works is dead; for them it would be a case of "putting one's money where one's mouth is."

FAULTS THAT DIVIDE A CHRISTIAN COMMUNITY (3:1–5:6). In a series of paragraphs Jas treats one example after another of sins and shortcomings that are particularly threatening to the harmony required by the commandment to love one another. Like an OT wisdom teacher, the writer in 3:1–12 clusters examples (bit in horse's mouth, rudder on a ship, fire, poison, bitter water), eloquently describing the damage that can be done by the loose tongue, particularly on the part of teachers.[17] His irony in 3:9 is redolent of Ps 62:5; Sirach 5:15(13): The tongue is used both to bless God and to destroy human beings created in God's image! Just as faith has to be manifested in works, so also wisdom (3:13–18—Jas seems still to be thinking of teachers). If Jesus said, "By their fruits you shall know them," (Matt 7:16), the wisdom from above is recognizable by its fruits (pure, peaceable, moderate, etc.) We are not far here from the beatitudes as we shall see when we compare Jas and the Sermon on the Mount, or from Paul's fruit(s) of the Spirit in Gal 5:22.

This emphasis on how the wise should live leads into a condemnation of the various envies and desires that divide people and make them so unhappy (4:1–10)[18]—desires that are the opposite of the spirit of the beatitudes. The quotation from Prov 3:34 in Jas 4:6 ("God resists the proud but gives grace to the humble") sums up the thought. (The same passage is quoted in I Pet 5:5, and both Jas and I Pet use "God" rather than the "Lord" of the LXX; apparently a common Christian usage of certain OT passages had developed, perhaps in "catechetical" training.) Judging one's brother or sister is con-

[17]Jas 3:1 prepares the way for this discussion of wisdom by warning "Let not many become teachers." If teaching were totally a charism from the Spirit (see I Cor 12:28, and the rejection in I John 2:27), would there have been choice about being a teacher? Thus community life envisaged in Jas seems to have had an office of teacher even as it has presbyters (Jas 5:14).

[18]Does the initial criticism of wars indicate that Jas was written after the troubled 60s when the Jewish Revolt against Rome forced Christians to decide whether they should participate? Or is Jas still thinking of teachers who stir up Christian divisions? In 4:4 Jas attacks "You adulteresses." Most commentators understand this as a symbolic reference to God's people who are unfaithful, against the background of the prophets railing against Israel as God's unfaithful spouse (Jer 3:9; Ezek 16; Hos 3:1). Yet the plural in Jas is troubling, and copyists who read "adulterers and adulteresses" seemingly thought of sinful individuals. L. T. Johnson, NovT 25 (1983), 327–47, points to the theme of envy in Jewish Hellenistic moral literature.

demned in Jas 4:11–12 as arrogance over against the Law of God the supreme lawgiver and judge. The attack on arrogance continues in 4:13–17, where readers are reminded that they are not masters of their own life. (Compare the uncertainty about tomorrow to Prov 27:1.) The theme of the rich, already treated twice (1:9–11; 2:1–9) returns as a blistering attack in 5:1–6, reminiscent of the curses against them in the prophets (Amos 8:4–8)[19] and the preaching of Jesus.[20] The appeal to be patient until the coming of the Lord in Jas 5:7–11 is related to the expectation that the poor will get little justice in this world at the hands of the rich. A refutation of the notion that Jas is not Christian in outlook may be found in the emphasis on the parousia in this section.[21]

PARTICULAR ADMONITIONS ABOUT BEHAVIOR IN THE COMMUNITY (5:12–20). Oaths, prayer, and correction of the wayward are the final subjects treated, still seemingly in the context of the forthcoming final judgment. The emphatically negative attitude toward taking oaths in 5:12 (see Sirach 23:9–11) again brings Jas very close to Matt's Sermon on the Mount (5:33–37). A special subsection below will be devoted to Jas 5:14–16, which illustrates not only liturgical prayer for the sick (powerful like that of Elijah) but a special anointing with oil by the presbyters, healing both sin and sickness. Implied here is a community life with assigned functionaries. Given the strongly admonitory atmosphere of much of Jas, one might think of the writer as stern and even unforgiving. The last lines (5:19–20) come then as a surprise: He is very concerned with bringing back (and implicitly forgiving) those who have deviated. (Here Jas could be contrasted to Heb 10:26–31.) If for I Pet 4:8 charity covers a multitude of sins, for Jas the activity of seeking out the lost does that.

Jas 2:24 and Paul on Faith and Works

In Gal 2:16 Paul affirmed: "A person is not justified by works of the Law but through faith in/of Jesus Christ." Slightly later he stated in Rom 3:28, "A person is justified by faith, apart from the works of the Law." By contrast Jas 2:24 claims, "A person is justified by works and not by faith alone."[22] The

[19]Defrauding laborers of their wages (Jas 5:4) is condemned in the OT (Lev 19:13; Deut 24:14–15). Jas is also reflecting the complaints against the mistreatment of the righteous in the Wisdom Literature, e.g., Wisdom 2:18–20.

[20]Particularly in Luke: 6:24; 12:15–21,33–34; 14:33; 16:19–25; 18:22–25.

[21]The eschatology of Jas differentiates it from the general run of Hellenistic teaching, and brings it closer to the atmosphere of the kind of Jewish wisdom visible in DSS. T. C. Penner, *The Epistle of James and Eschatology* (JSNTSup 121; Sheffield: JSOT, 1995).

[22]The contrast was sharpened by Luther who inserted an "alone" in the Romans passage: "by faith alone." The reformer answered the "blockheads" who objected that this word was not present

wording is remarkably close, and in the context both writers appeal to the example of Abraham in Gen 15:6.[23] Thus, it is very difficult to think that the similarity is accidental; one of the views is a reaction to the other. The faith/works issue is a major emphasis for Paul in Gal and Rom, whereas it is more incidental in Jas.[24] Few would contend that Paul shaped his position in reaction to Jas, and so it would seem that the writer of Jas is correcting a Pauline formula. Or to be more precise, he is correcting a misunderstanding of a Pauline formula. Paul was arguing that observance of ritual works prescribed by the Mosaic Law, particularly circumcision, would not justify the Gentiles;[25] faith in what God had done in Christ was required—a faith that involved a commitment of life. The writer of Jas is thinking of people who are already Christian and intellectually believe in Jesus (even as the devil can believe: 2:19) but have not translated that belief into life practice; and he is insisting that their works (not ritual works prescribed by the Law but behavior that reflects love) must correspond to their faith—something with which Paul would agree, as can be seen from the "imperative" sections of his letters insisting on behavior.[26] If the writer of Jas had read Rom, he should have been able to see that Paul and he were not dealing with the same issue: Paul was *not* proclaiming justification through a faith that did not involve living as Christ would have his followers live. For that reason it seems more logical to think that, when Jas was being written, a Pauline formula had been repeated out of context and given a misinterpretation that needed to be corrected.

Paul probably repeated the faith/works formula often in his preaching, and so we cannot tell where and when the writer of Jas encountered the misuse of it. (Of course, the writer of Jas may not have known that it was Paul's formula that was being misrepresented or misunderstood.) It is tempting to think that it was the (misunderstood) repetition of the precise formula

---

in the Greek of Rom: "It belongs there if the translation is to be clear and vigorous" (*Luther's Works* 35.188). For the general topic of faith and works in James and Paul, see J. Jeremias, ExpTim 66 (1954–55), 368–71; J. T. Burtchaell, *Interpretation* 17 (1963), 39–47; W. Nicol, *Neotestamentica* 9 (1975), 7–24; J. G. Lodge, *Biblica* 62 (1981), 195–213; W. Dyrness, *Themelios* 6 (#3, 1981), 11–16.

[23]Jas 2:21–23 combines this with the example of Abraham's obedience in Gen 22:9–18, especially vv. 16–17. For the style of argumentation, see I. Jacobs, NTS 22 (1975–76), 457–64; Soards, n. 16 above.

[24]It is a misinterpretation to make the dispute with Pauline ideas a dominant motif in Jas; it is a small issue in a much wider exhortation.

[25]There are many passages in the Pauline heritage, however, where "work(s)" is used positively to mean good works in general, e.g., I Thess 5:13; Rom 13:3; Eph 2:10.

[26]Also Gal 5:6: "faith working through love"; I Cor 13:2: "If I have a faith that can move mountains and do not have love, I am nothing"; Rom 2:13: "It is not the hearers of the Law who are righteous before God but the doers of the Law"; and the insistence on obedience in Rom 6:17; 16:19,26; II Cor 10:6; Phlm 21. Yet one can be fairly sure that Paul would never have phrased his positive imperative about behavior in the "works, not faith alone" language of Jas 2:24.

from Gal 2:16 or from Rom 3:28 that Jas was correcting. When we discussed Rom, I suggested that Paul wrote the letter to the Roman Christians in part to correct misrepresentations of his position that were in circulation there, perhaps coming from Jerusalem, the mother church of the mission that had brought Christianity to Rome. Word of what Paul had written in Gal (including his critique of the pillars of the Jerusalem church) could have been brought (back) to Jerusalem by the preachers in Galatia whom Paul was attacking. If Jas were written in the late 50s in Jerusalem, it might have contained a reaction to what was being reported (with bias) about Paul's thought expressed in Gal. Presumably Jas would have been transmitted to communities in danger of being corrupted by such Pauline ideas. If one posits a later composition of Jas, the reaction might have been shaped by reports of what Paul had written in Rom—see pp. 563–64 above for the possibility that Paul sent a letter to the Roman Christians in part because they had some influence with the Jerusalem authorities. All this involves guessing, but we shall return to the issue in later subsections.

Jas and Matt on the Jesus Tradition

The closeness in content between Jas and sections of Matt that present Jesus' teaching is remarkable, as may be seen from a list of the parallels to Matt's Sermon on the Mount.[27]

Jas 1:2: Consider it all joy when you encounter various trials.
  Matt 5:11–12: Blessed are you when they revile and persecute you . . . Rejoice and be glad.
Jas 1:4: That you may be perfect, and complete, lacking in nothing.
  Matt 5:48: Be perfect therefore as your heavenly Father is perfect.
Jas 1:5: Ask from God who gives to all generously and without reproach.
  Matt 7:7: Ask and it will be given to you.
Jas 1:19–20: Be slow to anger, for human anger does not accomplish God's righteousness.
  Matt 5:22: All who are angry with their brother[/sister] shall be liable to judgment.
Jas 1:22: Be doers of the word and not only hearers, deluding yourselves.
  Matt 7:24: Everyone who hears these words and does them.

[27]Outside the Sermon, these are possible parallels: Jas 1:6 = Matt 21:21 (faith, doubt, sea); Jas 2:8 = Matt 22:39 (love neighbor as oneself); Jas 3:1 = Matt 23:8 (against teachers); Jas 3:2ff. = Matt 12:36–37 (against careless speech); Jas 5:7 = Matt 24:13 (persevering until the end); Jas 5:9 = Matt 24:33 (Judge/Son of Man at gates). See M. H. Shepherd, JBL 75 (1956), 40–51.

Jas 2:5: Has not God chosen the poor of this world to be . . . heirs of the kingdom?

Matt 5:3: Blessed the poor in spirit, for theirs is the kingdom of heaven.[28]

Jas 2:10: Whoever keeps the whole Law but fails in one point becomes guilty of all.

Matt 5:19: Whoever breaks one of the least of these commandments and teaches people thus will be called least in the kingdom.

Jas 2:13: Judgment is without mercy to one not exercising mercy.

Matt 5:7: Blessed are the merciful because they shall receive mercy.

Jas 3:12: Can a fig tree bear olives, or a vine figs?

Matt 7:16: Do people pick grapes from thorn bushes, or figs from thistles?

Jas 3:18: The harvest of righteousness is sown in peace by those who make peace.

Matt 5:9: Blessed are the peacemakers because they shall be called sons of God.

Jas 4:4: Friendship with the world is enmity toward God.

Matt 6:24: You cannot serve God and mammon.

Jas 4:10: Humble yourself before the Lord and he will lift you up.

Matt 5:5: Blessed are the meek because they will inherit the earth.

Jas 5:2–3: Your wealth has rotted and your clothes have become moth-eaten; your gold and your silver are rusted . . . You have laid up treasure [= punishment] for the last days.

Matt 6:19–20: Do not treasure up for yourselves treasures on earth where moth and decay destroy, and thieves break in and steal; treasure up for yourselves treasures in heaven.

Jas 5:9: Do not complain against one another that you may not be judged.

Matt 7:1: Do not judge that you may not be judged; for with the judgment that you judge, you will be judged.

Jas 5:10: Take as an example of suffering and patience the prophets.

Matt 5:12: Thus they persecuted the prophets who were before you.

Jas 5:12: Do not swear either by heaven or by earth or with any other oath, but let your "yes" be "yes" and your "no" be "no."

Matt 5:34–37: Do not swear at all, neither by heaven . . . nor by earth . . . Let your word be "Yes, yes," "No, no."

Notice that despite the closeness of theme, neither the wording of the parallels nor the order in which they appear is the same. Accordingly most schol-

[28]This is one of several instances where Jas is closer to the Lucan parallel (6:20, which here, in turn, is closer to the original Q form): "Blessed are you who are poor, for yours is the kingdom of God." P. H. Davids, in *Gospel Perspectives: The Jesus Tradition outside the Gospels,* ed. D. Wenham (Sheffield: JSOT, 1985), 63–84; D. B. Deppe, *The Sayings of Jesus in the Epistle of James* (Chelsea, MI: Bookcrafters, 1989); P. J. Hartin, *James and the Q Sayings of Jesus* (JSNTSup 47; Sheffield: JSOT, 1991).

ars think that the writer of Jas knew not Matt but a Jesus tradition of the type that Matthew knew, similar to Q (n. 28 above).

Anointing the Sick (5:14–16)

The passage is introduced in 5:13 by suggesting prayer as a response for suffering and praising God in song as a response to feeling cheerful. Our key concern is the response suggested for one who is sick:

> "[14]Let that person call the presbyters/elders of the church; and, having anointed [him/her] with oil in the name of the Lord, let them pray over him/her. [15]And the prayer of faith will save the one who is ill; and the Lord will raise him/her up; and if that person has committed sins, he/she will be forgiven. [16]Therefore confess sins to one another, and pray for one another that you might be healed."

In subsequent church usage the healing of the sick through anointing by a priest was evaluated as a sacrament; and inevitably Jas 5:14–15 featured in debates between the Reformers and Rome over the number of sacraments. Session XIV of the Council of Trent (DBS 1716–19) defined that extreme unction[29] was a sacrament instituted by Christ and promulgated by James, and that the presbyters of the church whom James urges to be called in are not just senior community members but priests ordained by the bishop. A number of points about that statement need to be clarified to facilitate dialogue:[30]

(1) Trent made its statement in light of the 16th-century debate and the established understandings of that period. Trent was defining that extreme unction met the criterion of "sacrament" that had developed in the Middle Ages. It did not define that the anointing of the sick was understood as a sacrament in the 1st century; and indeed we have no evidence that the term sacrament was used that early. Similarly it was defining that this sacred action should be administered by those who in the 16th-century church (and long before) constituted clergy, namely, ordained priests, and not simply senior members of the lay community. Trent did not define (although those present at the Council may have assumed) that when Jas was written there were clearly established roles of bishops, priests, and rites of ordination. (See pp. 646–48, 702 above for those issues.) An ecumenically sensitive probe of 1st-century practice both by Roman Catholics who accept the au-

[29]This became the designation when in the Middle Ages the Western church confined anointing to the gravely or terminally ill.

[30]On healing in Jas, see K. Condon, *Scripture* 11 (1959), 33–42; J. Wilkinson, SJT 24 (1971), 326–45; D. J. Harrington, *Emmanuel* 101 (1995), 412–17. Also J. Empereur, *Prophetic Anointing* (Wilmington: Glazier, 1982); P. F. Palmer, "Who Can Anoint the Sick?" *Worship* 48 (1974), 81–92.

thority of the Council and by other Christians might phrase the sacramental issue thus: At that time was prayer over the sick and anointing for healing and forgiveness by acknowledged authorities (called presbyters) looked on as a specially holy action continuing the work of Jesus?

(2) Presbyters are to be called in to help the sick. There was a tradition that both Peter and Paul did healings (Acts 3:6; 5:15; 14:8–10; 28:8). In the 50s in the church at Corinth there were those who were acknowledged to have a charism of the Spirit for healing (I Cor 12:9,28,30). We saw that in the development of church structure, particularly in the last third of the 1st century, those who were designated or selected as presbyters in the community took on some of the roles that formerly or elsewhere were filled by those who were acknowledged to have a charismatic gift (see pp. 646, 670 above). Thus it is quite understandable that the role of prayerful healing could be assigned to presbyters.

(3) Anointing with oil in the name of the Lord is first in the sequence of what the presbyters are expected to do. Olive oil was used medicinally in antiquity. Lev 14:10–32 gives anointing with oil a place in confirming the cleansing from leprosy; Isa 1:6 speaks of wounds being softened or eased with oil; Jer 8:22 presupposes the healing power of the balm of Gilead. (Besides having medicinal value, oil was thought to have magical value, especially in exorcisms.) In NT times Mark 6:13 recounts an aspect of the work of the Twelve whom Jesus sends out in 6:7: "They anointed with oil many who were sick and healed them." Would Mark have us think that this was part of what Jesus sent them to do? Matt 10:1 indicates that healing diseases and infirmities was commanded. Throughout Jas there are echoes of the Jesus tradition, and so the practice described in Jas 5:14–15 may have been seen as a continuation of something Jesus had once commanded.[31] Is that implied in having the anointing "in the name of the Lord"?[32]

(4) The prayer of faith over the sick by the presbyters will save (heal?) the sick person, and the Lord will raise the person up; and if the person has committed sins, they will be forgiven (5:15). (The description is phrased as a sequence, but one composite action is probably envisioned.) Visiting those who are ill and praying for sick friends was encouraged in the OT, e.g., Ps

[31]Jesus himself is never reported to have used oil to heal or drive out demons. That he could have been thought to command what he did not himself practice is not a difficulty if we remember his command to his disciples to baptize in Matt 28:19, even though that Gospel never recounts that Jesus himself baptized.

[32]More likely "the Lord" is Jesus, rather than God; exorcism and healing in the name of Jesus is well attested (Matt 7:22; Luke 10:17; Mark 16:17; Acts 3:6; 4:30; 16:18). Laws, *James* 228–29, makes a good case that "in the name" does not refer to an exorcist's invocation, but a healing done by someone acting under the command of Jesus and in an exercise of his power. That is precisely the view that led the later church to regard this anointing of the sick as instituted by Christ.

35:13–14; Sirach 7:35. Praying to God for the healing of sickness often had a special tone because sin was seen as the root and cause of sickness. For instance, the friends who visited Job wanted to pray for and with Job by getting him to acknowledge his sin, and then God would cure him. Such belief is attested in the 2d century BC in Sirach 38:9–15: "My child, when you are sick, delay not to pray to God, who will heal you. Flee wickedness, let your hands be just; cleanse your heart from all sin . . . The person who sins against the Maker will be defiant toward the doctor." The DSS *Prayer of Nabonidus* describes the king afflicted by a malignancy, praying to God Most High, and being forgiven his sins by an exorcist (García Martinez ed. 289).[33] A continuation of a connection between sin and sickness may be implied in I Cor 11:29–30 where profanation of the eucharist is related to the situation wherein many are ill, weak, and dying. In the Gospels Jesus portrays himself as a physician (Matt 9:12; Luke 4:23); and for those whom he cured, being "saved" sometimes covers both being healed of their illness and being forgiven their sins.[34] Against that background Jas 5:15 makes good sense: The prayer of faith will save the sick in a double way—raise them up from the sick bed and forgive their sins.

(5) The relation of 5:16 ("Therefore confess sins to one another, and pray for one another that you might be healed") to what precedes is very disputed. From Reformation times, in opposition to Trent's doctrine of extreme unction administered by ordained priests, some have regarded v. 16 as an interpretative specification of vv. 14–15: the presbyters were simply elderly members of the community, and the prayer (and the anointing) were simply the activity of community members—no authorities or the early equivalent of "clergy," if an anachronistic term is permitted. Others like Dibelius (*James* 255), recognizing that v. 16 is envisioning an activity different from that authorized in vv. 14–15, insist that the two are irreconcilable: V. 16 is an interpolation.[35] Still others, rejecting the desperate solution of an interpolation, have thought of v. 16 as complementary: There was a special sacred action by the presbyters designed to heal, but there was *also* community confession, prayer, and healing. (*Didache* 4:14 instructs: "You shall confess your offenses in church, and not come forward to your prayer with a bad conscience.") The last mentioned interpretation seems to have the greatest following and does justice to an early attitude where the emergence of desig-

[33]This attitude continued in later Judaism: in the Babylonian Talmud, *Nedarim* 41a, R. Alexandri states that no sick person is cured of a disease until that person's sins are forgiven. See also *Baba Bathra* 116a, "Whoever has a sick person in the house should go to a sage who prays mercy for that person."

[34]Mark 5:34; 10:52; notice the connection in Mark 2:5–12.

[35]Theologians have sought to find another sacrament here: penance or sacramental confession.

nated authorities had not yet rendered otiose community-shared sacred actions.

Literary Genre[36]

In 1:1 Jas has an Opening Formula; but it lacks news about the sender, greetings extended, and all semblance of a Concluding Formula.[37] The contents imply certain features of church life, e.g., synagogue meetings where both rich and poor are present, and a structure wherein certain people are designated as teachers and presbyters. Yet nothing specific identifies the addressees. Thus one may say that Jas is closer to an Epistle than to a Letter in Deissmann's division (p. 410 above), although, as we saw, that division does not allow for a sufficient variety of letters. Some interpreters claim that Jas was not intended for a specific group of Christians, but was simply an eclectic collection of moral instructions applicable to all. That analysis, however, does not do justice to the background and emphasis of those instructions. For instance, as pointed out above, the address "To the twelve tribes of the diaspora," when combined with the contents, suggests a certain "brand" of Christian quite loyal to the heritage of Israel and not as "liberal" as the Jewish/Gentile Christians represented by the adherents of Paul who had dispensed with many of the attachments to the Law—in other words the type of Christianity represented in his lifetime by the historical James, the brother of the Lord. Many object that if this were the case, Jas should have had passages stressing the food laws or the Jewish feasts, etc. Yet that objection assumes that Jas was written to adherents who would need correction on those points. Rather the silence of Jas on such issues and the tone of encouragement suggest that the addressees were of the same mind-set as the writer, needing no admonition on doctrinal matters but only on points where they have been affected by the baneful influence of secular society (unjust partiality, preferring the rich) and of distorted Pauline thought (faith, not works). This would make sense if Jas was sent out from Jerusalem or Palestine, directed specifically to those in churches originally converted or influenced by missionaries from the Jerusalem church. We shall return to this possibility in the next subsection.

What genres and styles can be detected in Jas? This collection of moral

[36]See H. S. Songer, RevExp 66 (1969), 379–89.

[37]F. O. Francis, ZNW 61 (1970), 110–26, contends that lack of a formal close is not uncommon in Hellenistic epistolary style. He would find two introductory thematic statements in 1:2–11 and 1:12–25, with the body of the document treating them in reverse order. L. Thurén, NovT 37 (1995), 262–84, offers a rhetorical analysis dividing Jas into 1:1–18; 1:19–27; 2:1–5:6; 5:7–20.

observations and instructions, often in a gnomic and proverbial style, presented with a strong hortatory tone resembles in content and style a whole body of OT Wisdom Literature,[38] as pointed out above in the *General Analysis.* After the OT period a Jewish vein of wisdom was continued both in Greek (e.g., *The Sentences of Pseudo-Phocyclides*[39] probably written by a very Hellenized Jew after 100 BC) and in Hebrew (e.g., *Pirke Aboth,* collecting material from before AD 200). Gentile Greco-Roman philosophical literature (Epictetus, Plutarch, Seneca) also offered tractates of ethical teaching;[40] and in certain of its conglomerations of maxims Jas agrees with convictions and sentiments found there (but see n. 21 above). As for Christian influence Jesus was remembered as sometimes playing the role of a man of wisdom, as may be seen in the Q collection of teaching preserved in Matt and Luke. Above we saw how close Jas is to Matt precisely in this area. Besides loyalty to the *didache,* or teaching of Jesus, Jas exhibits a strong eschatological outlook typical of early Christian expectation of the parousia (5:7–9). There was moral wisdom/teaching in the writings of Paul as well (frequently in the imperative section of the letters), but in Jas this constitutes the whole epistle. If, by developing christology almost to the point of doctrine, the NT differs considerably from the writings and thoughts of Israel and, a fortiori from Greco-Roman literature, Jas reminds us of an uncompromising insistence on morality that is very much in continuity with Israel and would be approved by many Gentiles as well.

As with some of the Jewish writings in the Hellenistic period, Jas does not hesitate to use genres known in the Greco-Roman world to convey its teaching.[41] Aspects of the diatribe (p. 89 above) are prominent in Jas. For example, a thesis is established by a series of examples in 2:14–26; the "you . . . I/we" conversation between the writer and the hearers/readers runs through much of the letter; also there is a constant series of imperatives; direct address to theoretical opponents, e.g., 4:13; 5:1; and rebuttal of objections, e.g., 1:13; 2:18. Yet elements of diatribal argumentation are found in many different forms of literature, and one can scarcely equate Jas with some of the more formal Greco-Roman school diatribes. Jas is also paraenetic both in style and content, e.g., the appeals to remembered exhortations known already and to models to be imitated.[42] Yet in its transmission of traditional moral exhortations in the form of maxims paraenesis is almost a

[38]On the issue of wisdom in Jas, see B. R. Halson, StEv 4 (1968), 308–14; J. A. Kirk, NTS 16 (1969–70), 24–38. Note that there is no personification of wisdom in Jas.

[39]P. W. van der Horst, OTP 2.565–82.

[40]See Malherbe, *Moral.*

[41]D. F. Watson, NTS 39 (1993), 94–121; NovT 35 (1993), 48–64.

[42]L. G. Perdue, ZNW 72 (1981), 241–46; *Semeia* 50 (1990), 14–27; J. G. Gammie, *Semeia* 50 (1990), 41–77; R. W. Wall, *Restoration Quarterly* 32 (1990), 11–22.

secondary genre since it appears within works that are dominantly of another genre and reflect different social settings. Jas has also been identified as a protreptic (encouraging) discourse, an exhortation to follow one way of life as superior to another, for it upholds the superiority of the Judeo-Christian moral life reflecting the Law. This genre does more justice to Jas as a deliberate rhetorical writing and not simply a random collection of maxims. If one reflects on how all that is combined with the Letter Opening, one will probably emerge with a mixed classification for Jas.

By and To Whom, Where, and When?

BY WHOM? Was the work really written by James of Jerusalem before his death in AD 62? Let us sample arguments invoked to support an affirmative answer. Would not a later attempt at pseudonymity have used the honorific title "brother of the Lord" rather than "a servant of God" (1:1), or have made specific references to Jesus and supplied some fictional biographical data? Also the Jewish atmosphere of the letter fits composition by the leader of the Jerusalem church. Yet such arguments do not refute the possibility of a disciple or knowledgeable admirer of James, using a modest title that the historical James applied to himself and writing in such a way as to continue his thought. James of Jerusalem was one of the most important people in NT Christianity, and a pseudepigrapher might have seen no need to introduce him to the addressees (especially if they were in churches evangelized from Jerusalem). The Greek employed in Jas is fluent, even eloquent, and shows polished style;[43] there is little chance that it has been translated from Hebrew/Aramaic and that the writer's mother tongue was Semitic. The Scripture employed is the LXX, not the Hebrew Bible. Therefore it is unlikely that a villager from Nazareth wrote it personally. One might appeal to the use of a scribe; but as we shall see, other factors favor the thesis that the letter was written after James' lifetime by one who respected that figure's authority. Speculations as to the exact identity of the writer then become useless.

WHEN? By way of external evidence, the *Pseudo-Clementine* literature (the earliest source of which stems from *ca.* 150–220) honors James as the bishop of bishops and posits a much more advanced hostility between James and Paul than is apparent in Jas.[44] Jas seems to have been known by the

[43]Greek hexameter can be found in 1:17; an Attic imperative in 1:19; etc.

[44]This literature (n. 6 above) shows knowledge of the canonical Gospels. R. E. Van Voorst, *The Ascent of James: History and Theology of a Jewish-Christian Community* (SBLDS 112; Atlanta: Scholars, 1989), esp. 79–80. Also F. S. Jones, *An Ancient Jewish Christian Source . . . Recognitions 1.27–71* (Atlanta: Scholars, 1995).

author of the *Shepherd of Hermas,*[45] which was probably written in Rome about 140. Thus Jas would have been written sometime before that date. By way of internal evidence, as we saw by comparing Jas with Matt's Sermon on the Mount, the writer knows, but in different phrasing, the type of Jesus teaching found in Q and the Gospels. Therefore, dependence on the written Gospels is not probable. The writer also knows the Pauline tradition about faith and works preserved in Gal and Rom, written in the 50s, but seemingly through inaccurate popularization. These relationships to the Jesus and Paul traditions might have been possible before 62, but a more likely date would be the last third of the 1st century. Church structure of the type implied in 3:1 where there is an office (not simply a charism) of teacher and in 5:14–15 where presbyters have a specific, indeed a quasiliturgical role also suggests a late 1st-century date. A date much later than that is not plausible. By the first half of 2d century the likelihood would increase that the writer of Jas would have known the written Gospels and Epistles.

FROM WHERE? TO WHOM AND WHERE? There is scant evidence for settling these questions. A special sensitivity for the poor, knowledge of the Jesus tradition, reference to the early and late rain typical of Palestinian climate (5:7)[46] have suggested Jerusalem or Palestine as the place of origin. According to Hegesippus (EH 3.19–20), the descendants of Jesus' family (called the Desposyni), especially the grandsons of Jude, "his brother after the flesh," ruled the churches in Palestine until the time of Trajan (98–117). Although James was venerated more widely, certainly Christians in the Palestinian churches would have had a special veneration for James, the original leader of the Jerusalem community. The oldest source of the proJames *Pseudo-Clementines* is thought to have been composed at Pella, about 60 miles NE of Jerusalem, across the Jordan, where Jerusalem Christians are said to have gone before the destruction of the city in 70.

The moral exhortation in Jas is clearly directed to a community or communities (not to individuals or a single household) as a voice against a dominant culture (1:27; Johnson, *James* 80–88). Yet Jas is not sectarian in the sense of only being against outsiders; it is chiefly concerned with correcting Christian insiders who should know better. The use of Greek, of the LXX, and the reference to the diaspora (1:1) suggest an audience beyond Palestine. The strong Jewish tone has made many think of a Jewish Christian writer and audience. Yet Gentile Christians usually took on the coloration of the

[45]Double-mindedness (Jas 1:8; cf. *Mandates* 9.1); the idea of God-given Spirit dwelling in the addressees (Jas 4:5; cf. *Mandates* 5.1.2); bridling the tongue, the whole body, and the evil desire (Jas 1:26; 3:2; cf. *Mandates* 12.1.1). See Laws, *James* 22–23; Johnson, *James* 75–79. Possibly *I Clement,* also a Roman church document, used Jas; that would mean Jas was written before 120.

[46]Of course, this could be simply an OT echo (e.g., Deut 11:14).

Jewish missionaries who converted them, and so there was also a vein of Jewish/Gentile Christianity that was very loyal to Judaism. If Jas was sent out from Jerusalem (or from the remnants of the Christian community in Palestine after AD 70) "To the twelve tribes in the diaspora," it could have been meant for those Jewish/Gentile Christian communities originally evangelized from Jerusalem—communities marked by James' fidelity to Judaism. One of those communities might have been Rome; for Jas was known in Rome by the early 2d century. When received there, it could have served to correct exaggerations of the viewpoint toward works expressed by Paul in Rom. Was it cited at Rome (*Hermas,* and possibly *I Clement*) because it corresponded to the still dominant proJewish outlook there (pp. 561–62 above)? By the mid-2d century, however, the figure of James was being lionized by Jewish Christians who were regarded as heretical (*Pseudo-Clementines*); and so enthusiasm for works bearing his name may have waned—whence the failure to list Jas in canonical enumeration of late-2d century Rome. There is too much guesswork in this proposal, but it militates against the idea that Jas was a very general composition without defined goal and pastoral intent.

Canonicity of Jas[47]

Jas is not mentioned in the Muratorian Fragment, thought to represent the Scriptures of Rome at the end of the 2d century. The Old Latin translation of Jas found in the Codex Corbeiensis (9th-century preservation) and placed with the extracanonical writings raises the possibility that Jas was translated into Latin in the 3d century (and perhaps later than other Catholic Epistles). Thus the evidence suggests that in the West *ca.* 200 Jas was not considered canonical, even though it had been known quite early in Rome as we saw in discussing the *Shepherd of Hermas.* In the early 3d century in the Greek-speaking East, Origen acknowledged the letter, albeit as one of the disputed books, citing it twenty-four times and attributing it to James the apostle, the brother of the Lord.[48] In the early 4th century Eusebius (EH 2.23.24–25; 3.25.3) was still listing it among the disputed books of the NT; yet by the late 4th century Athanasius gave evidence of the acceptance of Jas in the Greek-speaking churches of the East. Jerome's not totally enthusiastic inclusion of it in the Vulgate and Augustine's authority meant acceptance in the

[47]J. A. Brooks, *Southwestern Journal of Theology* 12 (1969), 41–55.

[48]Probably Origen knew of it, not from his native Alexandria but from his stay in Palestine. Eusebius (EH 6.14.1) claims that "Jude and the remaining Catholic Epistles" had been commented on earlier by Clement of Alexandria, but none of Clement's preserved writings show knowledge of Jas.

West. At this same time, however, it was not accepted in the Syriac-speaking church. Finally at the beginning of the 5th century Jas appeared in the official Syriac translation, the Peshitta, even though some of the contemporary leaders of that church show no awareness of it.

We are uncertain why Jas was so slow in finding acceptance. Did some who knew it fail to recognize that the "James" of 1:1 was the church leader of Jerusalem? Did others challenge the attribution in 1:1 as fictional? Or did its circulation primarily in Christian circles loyal to the Law make it suspect in the larger church? Did its lack of christology make it unacceptable as a General (Catholic) Epistle?

The ancient disagreements about Jas contributed to new doubts in the Reformation period. Erasmus accepted it but questioned its attribution to the Lord's brother, as did Cardinal Cajetan. In the (September) 1522 edition of his translation into German, Luther attempted to put Jas with Heb, Jude, and Rev at the end of the NT as of lesser quality than "the true and certain, main books of the New Testament." Major factors in the Reformation opposition to Jas, besides disputes in antiquity, were the support it gave to extreme unction as a sacrament and its affirmation, "Faith apart from works is useless" (2:20), which conflicted with Luther's exaltation of faith. Even though Luther found many good sayings in it, Jas was a strawlike epistle when compared to the true gold of the gospel. As late as the 1540s in his "table Talk" he was wishing that Jas be thrown out of discussion at the University of Wittenberg, for it did not amount to much. Luther's reorganization of the canon was subsequently abandoned, and thanks to Melanchthon the apparent contradiction between Jas and Paul was harmonized. Yet in subsequent centuries, particularly within Protestantism, Jas was often looked on as an inferior NT witness, especially when compared to Paul's letters. It was sometimes dismissed as the late product of Ebionite or extreme Jewish Christianity.

By the second half of the 20th century, however, with a heightening of the Christian sense of social morality, Paul's reticence about changing social structures (e.g., his tolerating slavery) came under increased criticism, whereas Jas entered into favor. The maxim, "What profit, my brothers and sisters, if someone say that he or she has faith and does not have works," exemplified by supplying clothes for those who are poorly clothed, food for those who are hungry every day (Jas 2:14–16), was seen as a significant corrective for socially insensitive Christianity. The lack of christological affirmation in Jas remains a problem ("Jesus Christ" only twice: 1:1; 2:1); but to a generation raised on liberation theology, social concern was more important. (More perceptively one might comment that Jas shows a profound understanding of how to translate christology into meaningfulness for

Christian living, even as did Jesus himself; for though introduced in the Synoptic Gospels as the Son of God, Jesus did not preach that identity explicitly but explained the good news of the kingdom to the poor, the hungry, and the persecuted.) Many, therefore, resonating with Jas 1:27 whereby real religion is to visit orphans and widows in their need, would disagree sharply with the claim that Jas is an epistle of straw. This change of outlook is an enduring warning about depreciating one or the other NT work as inferior. What one generation despises, another generation may esteem as the heart of the gospel.

Issues and Problems for Reflection

(1) The issue of structure is not without importance, e.g., how much of what follows 3:1 refers primarily to teachers? Are they still in mind throughout chap. 4? Dibelius (*James* 5) describes Jas as paraenesis, i.e., a gathering of ethical materials from many sources with little or no continuity, except perhaps by "stitch-words" or "chain-words" that connected a number of subunits. More refined study, however, stresses that paraenesis can have form and development; and the majority of recent commentators would not see Jas as without structure, even though they may not agree on the details of that structure. Some argue that the structure was externally controlled, e.g., a midrash or homiletic interpretation of Ps 12(11); or the length of installments used in preaching.[49] The most likely of these hypotheses would find the selection of topics dictated by patterns already established in baptismal homilies or catechetical instruction about expected morals, as illustrated by the many parallels with I Pet. Cargal (*Restoring*) surveys the proposals and then seeks to apply the semiotic theory of Greimas. His units are not easily reconciled with topics and rhetorical indications, e.g., he considers 1:22–2:13 a section, despite the new address in 2:1. Still others would detect a theological organization of the material in Jas, e.g., around the principle of a twofold inclination (*yēṣer* or *yetzer*) in every human being, toward good and toward evil (see Jas 1:8; 4:8; and Marcus, "Evil"). Readers may compare the structure in several commentaries on Jas to see whether and how different divisions affect meaning.

(2) We can see a growth in OT reflections on the issue of people's responsibility for the evil that they do. The affirmation that God hardened Pharaoh's heart so that he did not do what God commanded through Moses (Exod 4:21; 7:3–4; etc.; also II Sam 24:1; Isa 6:9–10) is a formula that does not

[49]Respectively, M. Gertner, *Journal of Semitic Studies* 7 (1962), 267–93, esp. 267–78; P.B.R. Forbes, EvQ 44 (1972), 147–53.

adequately distinguish between God's foreknowledge and God's causality. Theological progression is found in the perception whereby a figure other than God moves people toward evil: at first, an angelic figure who in himself is not evil (the Satan of Job 1:6–12; Zech 3:1–2) and then an evil angelic tempter or devil (I Thess 2:18; Matt 4:1–11). Nevertheless, modern society blames much on heredity, which is a substitute for blaming God, and among religious people there can be an exaggeration of "the devil made me do it" motif. Jas 1:13–16 constitutes a challenge on both scores by its emphasis on personal accountability for the response to temptation or testing. The complete rejection of the existence of an intelligent principle of evil, however, although also encountered today, runs against much NT evidence and traditional Christian teaching.

(3) At the height of the civil rights crisis in the United States, in respect to certain churches it was often claimed that one could read Jas 2:1–7 and substitute "white" and "black" for "rich" and "poor" and have a sermon of immediate relevance. With the integration of churches, however, one should not think that the challenge offered by Jas has lost its relevance. Let us imagine a very socially conscious Christian parish that one cannot charge with indifference to the poor. Still can the administrator of the parish escape from giving special attention to the generous rich? The possibility of further gifts of money will soon disappear if public acknowledgment is not made of large donors (whether in the bulletin, by a plaque, or through an annual listing of gifts). Is it possible to live in this world and not show partiality? Even as does Jesus in the Gospels, is Jas issuing a challenge that will never be fulfilled completely till the kingdom comes?

(4) A subsection was devoted to Jas 5:14–16 and to divided Christian thought about whether the anointing of the sick is a sacrament. Leaving aside for the moment a particular priestly anointing of the sick, one cannot deny that Jas has picked up and continued a major concern for healing that stems from Jesus. Paul knows of charismatic healers, and some today would still insist on their presence in the church. Most Christians do not think they have been given a special charisma for healing. What responsibility have they toward continuing the early Christian emphasis on healing or care of the sick, especially in a culture that more and more entrusts healing to the medical profession and health organizations?

Bibliography on James

COMMENTARIES AND STUDIES IN SERIES (* = also on Jude;** = also on Jude and I and/or II Pet): Adamson, J. B. (NICNT, 1976); Blackman, E. C. (TBC, 1957); Chester, A. (NTT, 1994); Davids, P. H. (NIGTC, 1982; NIBC, 1984); Dibelius, M.

(Hermeneia, 1975); Gench, F. T. (ProcC, rev. ed., 1995); **Johnson, L. T.** (AB, 1995); Kugelman, R. (NTM, 1980*); **Laws, S.** (HNTC, 1980); Martin, R. A. (AugC, 1982); Martin, R. P. (WBC, 1988); Perkins, P. (IBC, 1995); Reicke, B. (AB, 1964**); Ropes, J. H. (ICC, 1916); Ross, A. (NICNT, 1954); Sidebottom, E. M. (NCBC, 1967**); Sloyan, G. S. (ProcC, 1977); Tasker, R.V.G. (TNTC, 1956); Townsend, M. J. (EC, 1994); Williams, R. R. (CCNEB, 1965).

Adamson, J. B., *James: The Man and His Message* (Grand Rapids: Eerdmans, 1989).

Baker, W. R., *Personal Speech-Ethics in the Epistle of James* (WUNT 2.68; Tübingen: Mohr-Siebeck, 1995).

Cabaniss, A., "A Note on Jacob's Homily," EvQ 47 (1975), 219–22.

Cargal, T. B., *Restoring the Diaspora: Discursive Structure and Purpose in the Epistle of James* (SBLDS 144; Atlanta: Scholars, 1993). A semiotic approach.

Geyser, A. S., "The Letter of James and the Social Condition of His Addressees," *Neotestamentica* 9 (1975), 25–33.

Hort, F.J.A., *The Epistle of St James* (London: Macmillan, 1909). An incomplete commentary (to 4:7) by a famous 19th-century scholar.

Marcus, J., "The Evil Inclination in the Epistle of James," CBQ 44 (1982), 606–21.

Martin, R. P., "The Life-Setting of the Epistle of James in the Light of Jewish History," *Biblical and Near Eastern Studies,* ed. G. A. Tuttle (W. S. LaSor Festschrift; Grand Rapids: Eerdmans, 1978), 97–103.

Mayor, J. B., *The Epistle of St James* (3d ed.; London: Macmillan, 1913).

Mitton, C. L., *The Epistle of James* (Grand Rapids: Eerdmans, 1966).

Moffatt, J., *The General Epistles* (London: Hodder & Stoughton, 1928).

Reese, J. M., "The Exegete as Sage: Hearing the Message of James," BTB 12 (1982), 82–85.

RevExp 66 (#4, 1969) was devoted to Jas.

CHAPTER 35

LETTER (EPISTLE) OF JUDE

Origen found Jude "packed with sound words of heavenly grace." Yet today, except for the memorable phrasing in Jude 3 "to contend for the faith once for all delivered to the saints," most people find this very brief work too negative, too dated, and too apocalyptic to be of much use. In addition, Jude has a remarkable number of textual difficulties, reflecting liberties taken in transmission, perhaps because the work was not treated as authoritative. There is no use denying the difficulties; indeed, it may be helpful to read the introductory subsection on the *Literary Genre of Apocalyptic* in Chapter 37 below before studying Jude. Nevertheless, Jude does give us a look into how a church authority responded to dangers, real or foreseen, as Christians began to divide from within.

After the *Background* and *General Analysis,* subdivisions will be devoted to these special issues: *Jude's use of noncanonical literature, Literary genre, By and to whom, from where, and when?, Canonicity,* and *Bibliography.*

The Background

Below in a subsection we shall discuss whether this was in fact written by Jude. Here we are asking which figure was intended when the writer described himself as "Jude, the servant of Jesus Christ and the brother of James." The same Greek name *Ioudas*[1] is rendered in the English NT both as Judas and Jude—the second rendering in order to avoid confusion with Iscariot, the one who gave Jesus over. If we leave the Iscariot aside, there is a Jude (son?) of James near the end of the list of the Twelve "whom Jesus named apostles" in Luke 6:16.[2] We know nothing about him, and there is no reason to think he was our writer for whom the "the apostles of our Lord Jesus Christ" were a separate group (Jude 17). Acts 15:22,27–33 has a

[1]Derived from the Hebrew for Judah, one of the twelve sons of Jacob/Israel.

[2]Also Acts 1:13. Presumably he is the "Judas/Jude not the Iscariot" portrayed in Jesus' company at the Last Supper in John 14:22. This Judas/Jude does not appear in the Marcan list of the Twelve (which in 3:18 has Thaddaeus) or in the Matthean (10:3: Thaddaeus or Lebbaeus). See Chapter 7 above, n. 7, for the hybrid "Jude Thaddaeus."

Summary of Basic Information

DATE: Virtually impossible to tell. A few scholars place it in the 50s; many in 90–100.

FROM/TO: Probably *from* the Palestine area where the brothers of Jesus were major figures *to* Christians influenced by the Jerusalem/Palestinian church(es). Some scholars think Jude was written in Alexandria.

AUTHENTICITY: Very difficult to decide. If pseudepigraphical, by one for whom the brothers of Jesus were authoritative teachers.

UNITY AND INTEGRITY: Not seriously disputed.

FORMAL DIVISION:

A. Opening Formula: 1–2

B. Body: 3–23:

- 3–4: Occasion: Contend for the faith because of certain ungodly intruders
- 5–10: Three examples of the punishment of disobedience and their application
- 11–13: Three more examples and a polemic description of the ungodly intruders
- 14–19: Prophecies of Enoch and of the apostles about the coming of these ungodly people
- 20–23: Reiterated appeal for faith; different kinds of judgment to be exercised

C. Concluding Doxology: 24–25.

prophet Judas/Jude (called Barsabbas) sent with Silas to Antioch, carrying the decision of James and the others from the Jerusalem meeting of AD 49. A few scholars would argue that metaphorically he was the "brother" (= Christian friend and fellow-worker) of James as the author of Jude designates himself.

However, the most common and plausible suggestion of why the writer identified himself through a relationship to James is that *the intended Jude was one of the four named brothers of Jesus* (third in Mark 6:3: "James and Joses and *Judas* and Simon," and fourth in Matt 13:55) and thus literally the brother of James. With such family status, this Jude would have had the kind of authority implied by the author's stated intention to write a more general work "about our common salvation" (Jude 3)—a project conceived before the problem arose that caused him to send this short missive correcting the presence of intruders. He can recall what the apostles foretold (v. 17); and so, although not an apostle, he is presenting himself as a master with some standing in the tradition. The writer may have known Hebrew, if Bauckham is correct in his contention that Jude's use of Scripture implies the Hebrew text form rather than the LXX.[3] In the self-designation of v. 1, Jude would be identifying himself modestly as a servant in relation to Jesus (see Jas 1:1), but more specifically as brother of James the famous leader of the Jerusalem church, probably because the letter was sent from Jerusalem/Palestine. In that area Jude would have had authority if we can judge from the tradition about his career. Seemingly the brothers of the Lord became missionary apostles (in the Pauline sense: I Cor 9:5); but their main mission may have been within Palestine, where Julius Africanus (EH 1.7.14) reports that the family of Jesus congregated. Hegesippus (EH 3.19–20) tells us that the grandsons of Jude, Jesus' "brother after the flesh," were leaders of churches in the Palestine area until the time of Trajan (98–117).[4] Bauckham's detailed study of the tradition (*Jude Relatives* 45–133) makes a good case that members of the family were dominant forces among Christians both in Galilee and Jerusalem.[5] Let us assume, then, in what follows that this is a letter sent in the name of Jude, brother of Jesus and of James. (On the parentage of the brothers, see Chapter 34 above, n. 2.)

General Analysis of the Message

OPENING FORMULA (vv. 1–2). Technical questions as to literary genre and the identity of the addressees will be treated later. Here we note that for Jude (as for Paul: Rom 1:6; I Cor 1:24) Christians are those "called"; moreover, they have taken over a traditional designation of Israel as "the darling (beloved)" of God (Deut 32:15; 33:5,26).

THE BODY (vv. 3–23) is framed by references to faith in vv. 3 and 20. In the Body Opening *the occasion is expounded in vv. 3–4.* The writer speaks to the "beloved" addressees of "our common salvation"—apparently one already being shared as in the deuteroPauline Eph 2:8, whereas in the earlier Pauline writing salvation was yet to be granted in the eschatological future (I Thess 5:8–9; I Cor 3:15; Rom 5:9–10). Jude thinks of faith as a traditional body of teaching (probably both doctrinal and moral) "once for all delivered to the saints" in times past, and he regards himself as having the right to expound it. His plans to do so on a general level have been interrupted by

[3]*Jude Relatives* 136–37. The attempt to locate the composition of Jude in Alexandria, e.g., J. J. Gunther, NTS 30 (1984), 549–62, has had limited following. One would expect the LXX to be the Scripture used there.

[4]In the list of the Jewish bishops of Jerusalem (EH 4.5.3–4; 4.22.4) Symeon/Simon (James' brother or cousin?) succeeds James. Recorded at the end of the list are Joseph/Joses and Jude (the names given in Mark/Matt to Jesus' brothers). This would be in the time of Emperor Hadrian (*ca.* 130) if the list is sequential.

[5]Judas/Jude became popular in some circles (especially gnostic) in Syria, but confusedly. Jude the brother of Jesus was amalgamated with Thomas (Didymus) whose name meant "twin," and emerged as Judas Thomas, the twin brother of Jesus.

the appearance of "certain ungodly people [*anthrōpoi*]" who turn the grace of God into licentiousness and deny the Lord Jesus Christ (v. 4).[6] The polemic description of outsiders "slipping in" to cause havoc appears already in Gal 2:4, and becomes common in the last third of the 1st century (Acts 20:29; II Tim 3:6; II John 10). Yet we must remember that we are hearing these figures described hostilely, and they may have considered themselves evangelizing missionaries. Some would see the intruders as teachers because of the reference to "shepherding themselves" in v. 12, but from the condemnation in v. 4 we can construct little of their teaching.

Three Examples of the Punishment of Disobedience and Their Application (5–10). As we shall see, some exegetes doubt that Jude was addressed to a real situation; for them it was a general epistle meant to be applied wherever the occasion demanded. If one thinks of a real situation, the writer seems to assume that the addressees know what is erroneous in the teaching he attacks; and so he concentrates on how God will refute it. (Is it conceivable that he has heard of strange teachings but not with enough specificity to list them?[7]) He offers in vv. 5–7 three examples from Israelite tradition in which God punished disobedience. (When he politely assumes that his readers are familiar with these examples, is he envisioning Jewish Christians who have been brought up with this background, or Gentile Christians who have had to be taught this?) Even though a generation had been brought out of Egypt by the Lord,[8] in the desert many showed their lack of faith and were destroyed by death before Israel entered the Promised Land (Num 14). Angels of God left their privileged place in heaven to lust after women (Gen 6:1–4), and God locked them beneath the earth in darkness till judgment day (*I Enoch* 10:4–6; chaps. 12–13).[9] Sodom and Gomorrah practiced immorality and were punished by fire (Gen 19:1–28). These three examples are fol-

[6]There are different possible readings: "deny the only Master [= God] and our Lord J. C." or "deny our only Master and our Lord Jesus Christ" (as II Pet 2:1 understood it). Denying God could indicate that these were atheists or polytheists (but there is nothing else in the letter to support this) or that they were gnostics rejecting the OT creator God. Denying Jesus Christ could mean an objectionable christology or a lifestyle unbefitting a Christian. Some maintain that these teachers are challenging "Jude's" authority over the hearers/readers, but there is nothing in the letter of the "listen to what I said rather than to them."

[7]II John 10 wants anyone excluded who does not bring the teaching the writer holds, and II Tim 4:3 warns that people will gather around them teachers who will say what itching ears want to hear. Such a general admonition about teaching does not exclude the possible presence of specific troubles facing the community addressed.

[8]Mss. differ on whether to read "Jesus," "the Lord," or "God" in v. 5. The Lord may mean Jesus, e.g., I Cor 10:4 describes Christ as the rock encountered in the desert wanderings. On this verse see: M. Black in *Apophoreta* (Festschrift E. Haenchen; Beihefte ZNW 30; Berlin: Töpelmann, 1964), 39–45; C. D. Osburn, *Biblica* 62 (1981), 107–15; A.F.J. Klijn, *New Testament Age,* ed. W. C. Weinrich (Festschrift B. Reicke; Macon, GA: Mercer, 1984), 237–44; J. Fossum, NTS 33 (1987), 226–43.

[9]Some would see a classical reference to Hesiod's account (*Theogony* 713–35) of the Titans bound in chains and consigned to the darkness of Tartarus, but that is more plausible for II Pet 2:4

lowed in vv. 8–10 by applicable commentary (v. 8: "In similar manner these . . .")—an interpretative pattern strongly defended by Ellis and Bauckham as a key to the structure of Jude. Although the application resumes the overall condemnation of v. 4 by issuing three accusations against the ungodly intruders, it is not clear how exactly the accusations match the three examples of vv. 5,6,7 (perhaps in reverse order?). These people defile their flesh (like the Sodomites), reject lordship (God or Christ?) and revile the glorious ones (angels?)—probably we need not search for specific erroneous doctrines that gave rise to such generalized polemic.[10] In vv. 9–10 the derisive presumptuousness of the adversaries is contrasted with the modesty of the supreme archangel Michael who did not blaspheme when the devil tried to claim Moses' dead body, but only rebuked him—a story derived from the Moses legend that had developed beyond the account of Moses' death in Deut 34.[11] Clement of Alexandria is one of several early witnesses who tell us that Jude derived this account from the *Assumption of Moses,* an apocryphon that has been lost to us.[12]

Three More Examples and a Polemic Description of the Ungodly Intruders (11–13).[13] In a "woe" against the adversaries, the writer bunches three examples of those who in rabbinic tradition (*'Aboth R. Nathan* 41.14) "have no share in the world to come": Cain (whose evil had been expanded in later tradition beyond murder, e.g., I John 3:12), Balaam (who for a bribe taught Midianites how to lead Israel into idolatry—Num 31:8; Deut 23:5; Josh 24:9–10, as expanded in later tradition[14]), and Korah (who mutinied against Moses and Aaron: Num 16). The writer then (vv. 12–13) lets loose a torrent of colorful invective against the ungodly "these" of whom he spoke previously, indicative of their evil, the insubstantiality of their claims, and their ultimate punishment. Once more this polemic tells us nothing very exact about the adversaries. The most interesting image is that of corrupting the love feasts (v. 12), since it reminds us of the early Christian *agapē* meals, linked with the eucharist and often unfortunately the subject of dispute

---

(which does refer to Tartarus) than for Jude. *Hearers* familiar with Greek mythology may have been reminded of Hesiod; but methodologically, since the Jewish background of the account is explicit, need we assume that the *writer* knew and drew on the classical Greek story?

[10]Those who search for specific ideas sometimes propose that the libertines were disparaging the angels for having given the Law to Moses.

[11]S. E. Loewenstamm, "The Death of Moses," *Studies on the Testament of Abraham,* ed. G.W.E. Nickelsburg (Missoula, MT: Scholars, 1976), 185–217.

[12]The *Testament of Moses* (seemingly 1st century AD) has been incompletely preserved. Was the *Assumption* a separate work or the lost ending of the *Testament*? See Appendix II.

[13]On these verses: G. H. Boobyer, NTS 5 (1958), 45–47; J. P. Oleson, NTS 25 (1979), 492–503; C. D. Osburn, CBQ 47 (1985), 296–303; W. Whallon, NTS 34 (1988), 156–59.

[14]There is a more positive picture of Balaam in Num 22–24, where he refused bribes offered by King Balak and would not prophesy against God's will; but the negative picture won out, as we see from Philo, Josephus, and rabbinic comments.

(I Cor 11:17–34). One gets the impression that the intruders had made their way into the very heart of the group(s) addressed.

Prophecies of Enoch and of the Apostles about the Coming of these Ungodly People (*14–19*). It is part of the style of warnings like that of Jude to recall that the coming of the impious was foretold for the last times (I Tim 4:1; II Tim 3:1ff.); and indeed Jesus himself is recalled as giving such an apocalyptic notice about false messiahs and false prophets in the last times (Mark 13:22). Jude 14–15 begins with a prophecy against the ungodly delivered by Enoch, the mysterious figure who walked with God and was taken up to heaven without dying; but once more the writer reaches beyond the reference in Gen (5:23–24) to Jewish tradition, this time as preserved for us in *I Enoch* 1:9.[15] Some would find an antecedent for the polemic description of the ungodly by Jude 16 in the *Testament* (*Assumption*) *of Moses* 7:7,9; 5:5, but the parallelism is far from clear. The writer then turns to a prophecy of the apostles, "In the last times there will be scoffers, walking according to their own ungodly desires." No such passage is preserved in the NT; and so the writer seemingly is drawing on a wider Christian tradition, just as he drew on an Israelite tradition wider than the OT.

Reiterated Appeal for Faith; Different Kinds of Judgment To Be Exercised (*20–23*). Despite the proportionately greater space given to polemic, one could argue that these verses represent both the purpose and true climax of the letter. In v. 3 the writer wanted "to write to you, beloved, encouraging you to contend for the faith." By way of inclusion he spells out how to contend in v. 20: "Beloved, build yourselves up in your most holy faith." This is to be done by praying in the Holy Spirit and keeping themselves in God's love—good advice at any time but now made more urgent, for while waiting for the mercy to be shown them at the judgment by the Lord Jesus Christ, those addressed have to deal with the scoffers who do not have the Spirit (v. 19).[16] Given the amount of polemic thus far, one is surprised to find nuance in the treatment to be meted out: Those who doubt or hesitate are to be shown mercy; others are to be saved and snatched from the fire; and still others to be shown mercy with extreme caution, hating their corruption.[17] Evidently Jesus' own cautions about community judgments have not been without effect (Matt 18:15–22).

[15]The Jude citation is closer in certain places to the Aramaic fragment of *I Enoch* preserved at Qumran than to either the Ethiopic or fragmentary Greek text. See C. D. Osburn, NTS 23 (1976–77), 334–41.

[16]Webb, "Eschatology," points out that Jude is concerned not only with future judgment but also with present judgment exercised in and through the community to separate out the intruders.

[17]Greek copies of Jude differ textually about what should happen and whether the writer distinguishes three groups or two. See S. Kubo, in *New Testament Text Criticism*, eds. E. J. Epp and G. D. Fee (Oxford: Clarendon, 1981), 239–53; J. M. Ross, ExpTim 100 (1989), 297–98.

CONCLUDING DOXOLOGY (vv. 24–25). No personal messages to the addressees conclude Jude. Rather, Jude concludes with a solemn doxology, probably drawn from the liturgy but adapted to the endangered state of the addressees. Jude blesses the one and only (*monos* = monotheism) God who can keep them safe without failing and bring them exulting to judgment without stumbling (cf. I Thess 5:23; I Cor 1:8). The Christian modification of this Jewish monotheistic praise is that it is through Jesus Christ our Lord—not far from one Lord and one God of Eph 4:5–6 (see Jas 1:1).

Jude's Use of Noncanonical Literature

This use has been a problem: Throughout the centuries theologians have contended that if the author was inspired, he should have been able to recognize what was inspired and what was not. (Sometimes the argument went the other way: Because the author of Jude was inspired, the books he cited, like *I Enoch,* must have been inspired.) Today most deem this a pseudoproblem which presupposes a simplistic understanding of inspiration and canonicity. Divine inspiration was acknowledged when a book was declared canonical by Israel or the Christian church.[18] Although there was common agreement among the Jews of the 1st century AD that "the Law and the Prophets" were inspired and canonical, there was not unanimity about "the other Writings."

Yet the lack of a fixed canon, an answer given by many scholars to the problem of Jude's citations, may not be to the point. Seemingly Jews and early Christians used books as sacred and with authority (and thus virtually treated them as inspired) without asking whether they were on the same level as the Law and the Prophets. We cannot confine Jude's dependence on the noncanonical to the citation of *I Enoch* in vv. 14–15 and that of the *Assumption of Moses* in v. 9. In addition, the punishment of the angels in v. 6 is derived from *I Enoch;* and the polemic in v. 16 may draw on the *Assumption of Moses.*[19] In the Cain and Balaam examples of v. 11, Jude is dependent on tradition about the biblical characters that has been developed far beyond the biblical account. Also in vv. 17–18 he cites words of the apostles not found in books that Christians would ultimately judge to be biblical. In other words, the writer accepts and feels free to cite a wide collection of Israelite

[18]Some Christians think that the inner movement of the Spirit enables them to recognize what is inspired; but the disagreements produced by such private inspiration make most turn to an external criterion.

[19]Some scholars would see parallels between the *Testaments of the Patriarchs* and Jude 6–7 on the angels and Sodom (*T. Naphthali* 3:4–5; *T. Benjamin* 9:1). However, there are Christian elements in the *Testaments,* and it is difficult to know which way possible influence would go.

and Christian traditions, and is not confined to a collection of written books ever deemed canonical by any group that we know. Thus canonicity may never have entered the writer's mind.

Literary Genre

Recently the study of Jude has been revived by new approaches to the letter. For instance, Neyrey has concentrated on the use of social science models and perspectives to complement other methods. The welfare of the group, not of individuals, would be paramount in antiquity. Neyrey reminds us of the patron-client pattern wherein God and Jesus would be regarded as heavenly benefactors and the writers as their agents. Attacks on what the writers judge beneficial for the group would be treated indignantly as attacks on God.

Considerable attention has also been paid to literary issues and rhetorical structure according to Greco-Roman standards (e.g., Charles, *Literary* 20–29). Of the forms of rhetoric (pp. 411–12 above), one can detect deliberative rhetoric in Jude's exhortations, dissuasives, and warnings. Yet there are also elements of epideictic rhetoric in the pungent emotions expressed and evoked, and of judicial rhetoric in the accusations and woes. At the same time the use of parallelism and threefold (triadic) illustrations in Jude's argumentation echoes the OT.

If one seeks to apply Deissmann's Epistle/Letter distinction (p. 410), which is Jude? It has slightly more Christian letter format than Jas. Rather than the flat "greetings" of Jas 1:1, "the mercy and peace and love" of Jude 2 is not far from the opening "grace, mercy, peace" of I and II Tim and II John. Jas ended without any sign of concluding greeting; Jude 24–25 has a majestic doxology that may be compared to the praise ending Rom (16:25–27).

The address "To the Twelve Tribes in the Dispersion" in Jas 1:1 may be more precise than Jude's "To those who are called, beloved in God the Father and kept safe for Jesus Christ" (v. 1), which could be applied to any Christians. Yet, internally the contents of Jude seem to be more specific about the situation of those addressed. That leads us into a very difficult issue: How much of the polemic in Jude is to be taken literally, and how much is traditional language? That we must be cautious is indicated by the fact that some of the description of the opponents in Jude 16 may be drawn from the *Assumption of Moses;* and in turn a great deal of the polemic in II Pet is simply taken over from Jude, as we shall see in the next Chapter. All three writers were scarcely facing the same situation, and so there was a convention of reusing polemic descriptions. Does that mean that Jude is addressed to all churches, describing no particular heresy but alerting all to a general problem, as a number of scholars now claim? Perhaps one need not go that far. There is no claim made in Jude to be addressing one community, as there was in many of the Pauline letters. Nevertheless, the situation described in Jude 3–4 may be factual: namely, an initial intention to address a general exhortation to Christians for whom Jude would have authority (thus presumably those who would have a connection with the mother church[es] in Jerusalem/Palestine with which Jude's name was associated), interrupted by the urgent recognition that false teaching had been introduced in some of those communities. Certainly the polemic description of the unworthiness of those responsible could be traditional (e.g., "certain ungodly people," in vv. 4, also 10–13,16–19) without dismissing the historicity of their presence. What about the dangerous teaching? One could construct from the description a situation wherein Jewish/Gentile churches taught to respect the Jewish heritage and its moral demands (as one would expect of areas where the names of Jude and James of Jerusalem were primary authorities) were being undermined by Christians strongly influenced by the Gentile world who claimed that the gospel had freed believers from moral obligations. In order to condemn such libertine ideas, Jude would be resorting to evil examples from Israelite tradition about attempts to seduce Israel or its outstanding figures. If this minimum reconstruction be allowed, given the presence of letter-format elements, there is reason to judge that Jude has the specificity to be described as a Letter, rather than as an Epistle.

By and To Whom, From Where, and When?

To be honest we have little information to answer such questions, perhaps less than for any other NT work.

BY WHOM? Did the brother of Jesus and James really write this short letter (even through a scribe), or was a disciple, or even one more remote, using Jude's name? Some would defend authenticity by arguing that Jude was not important enough for someone to have invoked his name in a pseudonymous composition, but that contention overlooks the importance of the relatives of Jesus and the descendants of Jude in the Jerusalem/Palestine churches. No one is able to establish positively that Jude wrote the letter; but we can ask whether there is an aspect of the letter that excludes authenticity. For example, was it written from a place other than Palestine where Jude lived, or in a style that he is not likely to have possessed, or at a time later than his life?

FROM WHERE? Authenticity would favor the place of origin as Palestine, since James was the leader of the Jerusalem church and the descendants of

Jude remained important in Palestine.[20] Jude does not cite the OT verbatim, but the allusions seem to depend on a knowledge of the Hebrew Scriptures rather than on a use of the LXX (quite unlike the procedure in most of the NT, including Jas); and that gives an edge to Palestine over the Greek-speaking Christian centers. Numerous Aramaic copies of *I Enoch,* an apocryphon cited in Jude, have been found at Qumran; and although ultimately *I Enoch* circulated more widely and in other languages, there is evidence to suggest that the writer of Jude knew the Aramaic form (n. 15 above).

What does the *style of argumentation* tell us about the place of origin? The writer has a good command of Greek vocabulary and is more than adequate in the use of conjunctions, participial phrases, and alliterations. Accordingly, some would contend that Greek was his mother tongue. Other scholars argue that a native speaker of Hebrew or Aramaic could have learned this Greek style by being taught rhetoric and immersing himself in Jewish Hellenistic literature. Bauckham would find in the arrangement of examples from the Jewish tradition in Jude exegetical techniques reminiscent of the way texts are joined in some of the DSS commentaries. If one doubts that a Galilean villager, like Jude the "brother" of Jesus, could have written the letter himself, there is always the possibility of his having employed a scribe more educated in Greek. Thus, the argument from style does not exclude authenticity and origin in Palestine, even if it somewhat favors pseudonymity.

WHEN? The range of feasible proposals runs from AD 50 to 120. The argument for a 2d-century dating because Jude was addressed to gnostics has little value as we shall see in the next paragraph. Nor is the argument pertinent that, because in vv. 3 and 20 it presents faith as a body of teaching, Jude represents "Early Catholicism." Not only is that phenomenon not datable, but also Jude lacks features that scholars classify as Early Catholic, e.g., neglect of the parousia (contrast vv. 14,21,24) and insistence on authoritative church structure. Indeed one cannot date Jude too late because it was used extensively by the author of II Peter, itself probably to be dated no later than 125–150. At the other end of the spectrum some have tried to date Jude after Jas, assuming that they were both written to the same audience and that since Jas does not mention false doctrine, Jude must have been written later

[20]Some would argue for Syria, where Jude the brother of Jesus became popular, especially in gnostic literature. However, he was often known there as Judas Thomas or Didymus (n. 5 above), not simply as Jude "the brother of James" (Jude 1). The suggestion that in Syria, in order to counteract the gnostic appeal to Judas Thomas, a pseudepigrapher chose "Jude" is implausible: To gain authority he would have added the description "brother of Jesus." Soards ("1 Peter") would associate Jude with I Pet and II Pet as the work of a Petrine school; but that would be more likely if Jude drew on II Pet, rather than II Pet on Jude. In the latter case Jude was known to the Petrine school (in Rome, presumably).

when suddenly "ungodly people" arrived. That is too much to base on the fact that Jude identifies himself as the brother of James. The reference to the words spoken beforehand by the apostles of our Lord Jesus Christ (v. 17) sounds as if the apostles (the Twelve?) belong to a past generation,[21] but that would be true any time in *the last third of the 1st century.* In that period also one can find instances of the use of "faith" to describe a body of beliefs and practices, as in Jude 3.[22] If Jude himself wrote the work, his being listed as third or fourth among the brothers of Jesus suggests that he was one of the youngest; and so he could have been alive as late as AD 90–100, which may be the most plausible date for the letter. Thus dating may slightly favor pseudonymity, but certainly does not prove it.

TO WHOM? Once again this is an exercise of more or less intelligent guessing. Some have sought to identify the intended audience of Jude from the error attacked. If it is libertinism, could it stem from a misunderstanding of Paul's proclamation of freedom from the obligations of the Mosaic Law (thus Rowston, "Most")? This might indicate an audience in the Pauline sphere of influence. Yet there is no implicit citation of Paul as there was in Jas 2:24; and the polemic against possible libertine features in Jude 4,7,8,16,18,19 is too general and stereotypic to enable us to be specific about the source. The charge in v. 8 that the ungodly intruders revile the glorious ones has fed much speculation about their identity, but that is surely a case of explaining the obscure by the more obscure. An implication that the "ungodly people" were gnostics has been found in the assurance given to the addressees that "you once and for all were given knowledge of all things" (v. 5), and the claim that the ungodly intruders blaspheme "what they do not know" (v. 10). The indictment that the opponents were denying God in v. 4 and the insistence on the one and only God in v. 25 are interpreted as attacks on the gnostic rejection of the creator God, but both the interpretation and reading of v. 4 are dubious (n. 6 above). The reference to Cain in v. 11 has been associated with a 2d-century group of gnostics called Cainites who regarded the OT God as responsible for evil (see Jude 8: they reject lordship [of God?]). It should be obvious how unwarrantedly speculative these claims are, even were the polemic of Jude to be taken literally. They stem from dubious assumptions about widespread gnosticism in 1st-century Christianity, so that almost every reference to knowing things masks a gnostic claim.[23]

[21]The contention that Jude is simply referring to past predictions not to past apostles is not overly persuasive.

[22]True, that approach to faith could be found earlier (Gal 1:23), but "once for all delivered to the saints" does not give the impression of a recent event.

[23]For rejecting a gnostic analysis of the opponents, see Eybers, "Aspects."

Realistically, the attack on the ungodly people in Jude does not help us to identify or locate the addressees.

From the self-identification of the writer as the brother of James it has been surmised that Jude was meant for the audience addressed by Jas. Yet Jude lacks "To the twelve tribes in the diaspora" of Jas 1:1, as well as any reference, explicit or implicit, to a letter by James. It is not implausible that both Jas and Jude were written to regions where the "brothers of Jesus" would be highly respected, but that could be a wide area involving different churches. Consonant with that picture is the supposition that the addressees knew a wide range of Jewish tradition, so that they would have found convincing the examples cited in Jude. More than that we cannot say.

Canonicity of Jude

Already by the early 2d century Jude was important enough to be copied by the author of II Pet. *Ca.* 200 in the West (Muratorian Fragment, Tertullian) Jude was being acknowledged as Scripture. In the East about the same time, according to EH 6.14.1, Clement of Alexandria commented on it; and certainly Origen respected it although he was aware that others rejected it. Two papyri, P^{72} and P^{78}, attest to the use of Jude in the 3d–4th centuries. Yet Jude's utilization of an apocryphal book like *I Enoch* raised problems, and in the early 4th century Eusebius still listed it among the disputed books. Finally by 400, with the contributions of Athanasius and Jerome to the formation of the canon, Jude was accepted in the Greek-speaking East and the West. Acceptance in the Syriac-speaking churches came in the 6th century.

In his 1522 NT Luther placed Jude along with Jas, Heb, Rev at the end as of lesser quality; and both Cardinal Cajetan and the Protestant Oecolampadius saw problems with it. However, there was no continued debate about it in subsequent centuries comparable to that about Jas because it was not that theologically important. Although considerable bibliography has been devoted to it, Jude has not had a great role in shaping the thought of the churches.

* * *

Usually we have concluded our discussion of a NT book with "Issues and Problems for Reflection." Jude, however, is a very short work; and today most would not appreciate or find germane its argumentation from Israelite tradition about the angels who sinned with women, Michael's battle over the body of Moses, Sodom, Balaam, and Korah. We owe Jude reverence as a book of Sacred Scripture, but its applicability to ordinary life remains a formidable difficulty. It is interesting to note that in the three-year liturgical lectionary in use in the Roman Catholic and other prominent churches, a lectionary that covers a very large portion of Scripture, Jude is never read on any of the 156 Sundays, and on only one weekday (where vv. 17,20–25, scarcely the heart of the letter, form the pericope).

Bibliography on Jude

COMMENTARIES AND STUDIES IN SERIES: Asterisks mark commentaries on Jude in the *Bibliographies* of Chapters 33 (I Pet), 34 (Jas), and 36 (II Pet).

Bauckham, R. J., *Jude and the Relatives of Jesus in the Early Church* (Edinburgh: Clark, 1990). Chap. 3, pp. 134–78, summarizes research on Jude.

Charles, J. D., *Literary Strategy in the Epistle of Jude* (Scranton Univ., 1993). Reuses previous articles in various journals; long bibliographies.

Dunnett, W. M., "The Hermeneutics of Jude and 2 Peter: The Use of Ancient Jewish Traditions," JETS 31 (1988), 287–92.

Ellis, E. E., "Prophecy and Hermeneutic in Jude," in *Prophecy and Hermeneutic in Early Christianity,* ed. E. E. Ellis (WUNT 18; Tübingen: Mohr-Siebeck, 1978), 221–36.

Eybers, I. H., "Aspects of the Background of the Letter of Jude," *Neotestamentica* 9 (1975), 113–23.

Hiebert, D. E., "Selected Studies from Jude," BSac 142 (1985), 142–51, 238–49, 355–66.

Joubert, S. J., "Language, Ideology, and the Social Context of the Letter of Jude," *Neotestamentica* 24 (1990), 335–49.

———, "Persuasion in the Letter of Jude," JSNT 58 (1995), 75–87.

King, M. A., "Jude and 1 and 2 Peter: Notes on the Bodmer Manuscript," BSac 121 (1964), 54–57.

Rowston, D. J., "The Most Neglected Book in the New Testament," NTS 21 (1974–75), 554–63.

Thekkekara, M., "Contend for the Faith: The Letter of Jude," *Biblebhashyam* 15 (1989), 182–98.

Watson, D. F., *Invention, Arrangement, and Style: Rhetorical Criticism of Jude and 2 Peter* (SBLDS 104; Atlanta: Scholars, 1988), 29–79.

Webb, R. L., "The Eschatology of the Epistle of Jude and Its Rhetorical and Social Functions," BulBR 6 (1996), 139–51.

Wisse, F., "The Epistle of Jude in the History of Heresiology," *Essays on the Nag Hammadi Texts* (Festschrift A. Böhlig; Leiden: Brill, 1972), 133–43.

Wolthuis, T. R., "Jude and Jewish Traditions," CTJ 22 (1987), 21–41.

———, "Jude and Rhetoricism," CTJ 24 (1989), 126–34.

CHAPTER 36

SECOND EPISTLE (LETTER) OF PETER

In all likelihood this pseudonymous work was chronologically the last NT book to be written; and, as we shall see, despite a somewhat bland first impression it has been in our times the subject of acrimonious debate. After the *Background* and *General Analysis,* subdivisions will be devoted to: *By and to whom, from where, and when?, Canonicity and Early Catholicism, Issues for reflection,* and *Bibliography.*

The Background

Given our practice of beginning by treating the work as it now stands, what background about Peter is supposed beyond that already presented for I Pet (Chapter 33 above)? The writer invokes the historical career of Symeon Peter (1:1) by using for this "apostle of Jesus Christ" a Greek form of his personal name close to the Hebrew original (not "*Simōn*" but "*Symeōn*" from *Šimĕʿōn*—elsewhere for Peter only in Acts 15:14) and by highlighting his eyewitness presence at the transfiguration (2:16–18). He wraps himself in the mantle of the author of I Pet in "Now this, beloved, is the second letter I write to you" (3:1). He knows of what "our beloved brother Paul wrote to you according to the wisdom given him, speaking of these things as he does in all his letters" (3:15–16). Indeed, a bit patronizingly Symeon Peter hints at his own superior teaching position as an interpreter of the Scriptures, since in Paul's letters "There are some things hard to understand that the ignorant and unstable distort to their own destruction, as they do the other writings (Scriptures)." Without naming his source, he quotes large sections from the letter of Jude, the brother of James (modifying what might be objectionable therein), thus drawing on a tradition venerated by those Christians for whom "the brothers of the Lord" were authorities. Gone are the struggles when Paul made snide remarks about James and Cephas (Peter) as "so-called pillars" of the Jerusalem church and opposed Cephas face to face (Gal 2:9,11). We are much closer to the outlook of *I Clement* 5:2–5, written from Rome between 96 and 120, which speaks of both Peter and Paul as pillars of the church. If in the 2d century the Jewish Christians of the *Pseudo-Clementine* literature were exalting James over against Paul who did harm, and if Mar-

Summary of Basic Information

DATE: After Pauline letters; after I Pet and Jude; most likely AD 130, give or take a decade.

TO/FROM: Probably to a general audience of eastern Mediterranean (Asia Minor?) Christians who would have known Pauline writings and I Pet. Perhaps from Rome, but Alexandria and Asia Minor have been suggested.

AUTHENTICITY: Pseudonymous, by someone desiring to present a final message with advice from Peter.

UNITY AND INTEGRITY: No major dispute.

FORMAL DIVISION:
A. Opening Formula: 1:1–2
B. Body: 1:3–3:16
  1:3–21: Exhortation to progress in virtue
  2:1–22: Condemnation of false teachers (polemic from Jude)
  3:1–16: Delay of the second coming
C. Concluding Exhortation and Doxology: 3:17–18.

cion was exalting Paul as the only apostle and rejecting the Jewish heritage, the Simeon Peter who gives instructions in II Pet is a bridge figure seeking to hold together the various heritages. In that sense this is a very "Catholic Epistle."

General Analysis of the Message

The OPENING FORMULA (1:1–2) is II Pet's only substantial gesture toward a letter format. It gives a general description of the addressees as "those who have received a faith of the same value as ours." This is not meant to assure Gentile converts that they have the same faith as Jewish Christians (as in Acts 11:17), but to affirm that through "the divine righteousness of our God and Savior Jesus Christ"[1] all Christians have the same faith as the original companions of Jesus, for whom Symeon Peter is the spokesman par excellence (1:16). In other words, as in Eph 4:5, there is only one Christian faith. Many call attention to "faith" here as a deposit of beliefs in place of the Pauline sense of trust, even though Paul could write of "faith" in a more objective sense (e.g., Gal 1:23). The "grace and peace be multiplied" greeting is copied from I Pet 1:2.[2] The "knowledge [*epignōsis*] of Jesus our Lord"

[1]"Righteousness" (*dikaiosynē*) has a double connotation here, both of divine *power* making those affected righteous and of *justice* since it does so without distinction (pp. 576–77 above). This is one of the clearer passages where the NT calls Jesus "God": BINTC 184.

[2]Other passages where II Pet echoes I Pet would include: *2:5* and I Pet 3:20b: Noah and those with him saved from the flood; *2:14* and I Pet 4:3: sin without stopping; *2:18* and I Pet 4:2: fleshly

(II Pet 1:2) is a theme that will be repeated later in II Pet, for it is the antidote to false teaching.

THE BODY (1:3–3:16). *II Pet 1:3–21, an Exhortation*[3] *to Progress in Virtue,* uses terms heaped on one another in luxuriant abundance (e.g., 1:5–7: faith, virtue, knowledge, self-control, perseverance, godliness, affection for each other, love). In a memorable phrase the writer wants his addressees "to become sharers of the divine nature" (1:4), a more abstract, Greek way of phrasing I Pet 5:1 "sharer in the glory that is to be revealed" (or of I John 1:3: *koinōnia* with the Father and the Son).[4] Christians who do not make progress become blind and forget that they were cleansed from their sins (II Pet 1:9)—a theology of baptism as an enlightenment (cf. Heb 6:4) and a washing.

Speaking as Peter facing death, the writer in 1:12–15 wants to leave the addressees this reminder so that after his departure they will be able to recall that he spoke of such things. He has the authority to do so because the truths about Christ that he (and the other apostles: "we") proclaimed were not "cleverly devised myths" but eyewitness testimony to God's own revelation from heaven at the time of the transfiguration acknowledging Jesus as the beloved divine Son (1:16–19). The reference to the transfiguration is probably II Pet's exegesis of I Pet 5:1 where Peter describes himself as "a sharer in the glory that is to be revealed." We must still ask, however, why II Pet sees the transfiguration so useful as a source of assurance, instead of, for instance, appealing to the famous appearance of the risen Christ to Peter (I Cor 15:5; Luke 24:34)? Does the transfiguration serve in 1:16 as an affirmation of the promised "parousia of our Lord Jesus Christ" (which is being denied by scoffers [3:3–4]) because it was closer to the kind of theophany expected in the last days than was a resurrection appearance? Is there an appeal to the transfiguration because the writer wants to establish a certain priority of Peter over Paul (3:15–16), who could claim to have seen the risen Christ but not the transfigured Christ of the ministry? Is the authority of the transfiguration safer than that of a resurrection appearance because the writer wants to reject the myths of gnostic visionaries who very frequently used the risen Christ as the source of speeches establishing their doctrine?

Prophecy also enters into the II Pet picture. According to 1:14 Jesus an-

---

desires; *3:1:* the reference to a previous letter; *3:2* and I Pet 1:10–12: the OT prophets and the Christian apostles or preachers; *3:14* and I Pet 1:19: "spotless and blemish-free." See G. H. Boobyer in *New Testament Essays,* ed. A.J.B. Higgins (Memorial T. W. Manson; Manchester Univ., 1959), 34–53.

[3]F. W. Danker, CBQ 40 (1978), 64–82, points to a type of Roman emperor style where the imperial benefactor addresses civic assemblies in the realm.

[4]This is the common view; but A. Wolters, CTJ 25 (1990), 28–44, argues that there is no Greek element in II Pet 1:4, for it refers to covenantal partnership.

nounced beforehand Peter's (forthcoming) death—a tradition that one finds also in John 21:18–19. Also in II Pet 1:19, after the "we" who were on the holy mountain for the transfiguration, "we have the prophetic word made more sure" probably means OT prophecies[5] of God's appearance, intervening in the last days. This brings us to the most famous passage in II Pet (1:20–21): "All prophecy of Scripture is not a matter of one's own interpretation; for not ever is prophecy brought forth by human will; rather people who were carried along by the Holy Spirit spoke from God."[6] Who is the "one" of "one's own"? Some understand it to be the prophet (who is not given to formulate prophecy on his/her own); others understand it of the recipient of prophecy. In the latter explication the passage seems to challenge the right of private interpretation of Scripture, and has been attacked as an aspect of II Pet's "Early Catholicism" (subsection below). Also, although the passage speaks specifically of (OT) prophecy, it has been employed to defend the divine inspiration of all Scripture. Such issues should not make us forget that the writer's primary intent was to support the veracity of the expected parousia of Christ.

The Polemic Condemnation of the False Teachers (*2:1–22*) feeds into that goal by comparing the opponents to the false prophets who troubled Israel.[7] That the writer has in mind a specific false assertion about the parousia will become apparent in 3:3–4, but to prepare the way he uses polemic that could fit almost any erroneous teachers. Indeed, although he never informs his readers, he has taken over this polemic en masse from Jude,[8] using in whole or in part nineteen of Jude's twenty-five verses. Several features of difference are noteworthy. The "noncanonical" examples of Jude (argument over the body of Moses; and the *I Enoch* prophecy) are not used, seemingly because the writer of II Pet had a more fixed sense of what constituted Scripture. From the Jude 5–7 triad of those punished by God, namely, the people in the desert, the angels, and Sodom and Gomorrah, II Pet 2:4–8 has kept the second and third but substituted the flood for the first, probably under the influence of the usage of the flood in I Pet 3:20. There is a more Hellenized version of the punishment of the angels: in everlasting chains and darkness

[5]However, J. H. Neyrey, CBQ 42 (1980), 504–19, treating 1:16–21, thinks that the II Pet writer is defending his interpretation of the transfiguration as a prophecy of the parousia.

[6]See J. T. Curran, TS 4 (1943), 347–68; D. E. Hiebert, "Selected 2 Pet," 158–68.

[7]H.C.C. Cavallin, NovT 21 (1979), 263–70; D. E. Hiebert, "Selected 2 Pet," 255–65. For the implication of predicted ruin in 2:1, see A. D. Chang, BSac 142 (1985), 52–63.

[8]Cf. *II Pet 2:1–2* and Jude 4 on the secret coming of false teachers/ungodly people, their heresies, licentiousness, and denying the Master; *2:4,6* and Jude 6–7 on the examples of the rebellious angels and Sodom and Gomorrah; *2:10–16* and Jude 8–13 on deriding lordship, being like animals, assorted condemnations, and the Balaam example.

for Jude 6, but in Tartarus for II Pet 2:4.[9] Unlike Jude, II Pet (2:5–9) is interested in those who were exempted from divine punishment—Noah from the flood, Lot from Sodom and Gomorrah—as proof that God knows how to rescue the godly from the trial. Also II Pet omits the reference to unnatural lust that was present in the Jude 7 allusion to Sodom and Gomorrah.

When II Pet 2:10–16 also echoes Jude 8–13, there are again differences, e.g., Balaam's ass (2:16) becomes a part of that biblical reference. In 2:17–22 II Pet stresses several times a particular aspect of the wickedness of the false prophets not prominent in Jude. They escaped from the pollutions of the world through a knowledge of Christ, and now they have become entangled again, so that the final state is worse than the first.[10] It would have been better for them not to have known the way of righteousness than to have turned back after knowing it. As illustration, 2:22 cites a biblical proverb about a dog returning to his vomit from Prov 26:11, and another about a pig that had been washed clean wallowing in the mire. The latter, not from the OT, was known in Semitic wisdom (Syriac *Ahikar* 8:18) and Greek tradition (Heraclitus, Democritus, Sextus Empiricus).

Delay of the Second Coming (*3:1–16*). The polemic continues, adapting elements from Jude 16–17. Up to now the charges have been so general (even as they were in Jude), that we could not tell much of what might be being said by actual false prophets/teachers if there were any; but in 3:4 II Pet becomes specific, seemingly quoting the scoffing that is his target. False teachers are denying the promise of the parousia on the grounds that the leaders ("fathers") of the first Christian generation have died and "all things have continued as they were from the beginning of creation."[11] To refute this, the writer uses several strategems. First (3:1), he invokes prestige by wrapping himself in the mantle of Peter who in a previous letter (I Pet) had exhibited correct understanding. Second (3:2), he makes clear that the object of that understanding, which supports the parousia, consists of predictions by the prophets and the apostles.[12] As Symeon Peter, he can be authoritative on

[9]See B. A. Pearson, *Greek, Roman and Byzantine Studies* 10 (1969), 71–80. Fornberg (*Early* 53) suggests the influence of the Eleusinian mysteries.

[10]See D. A. Dunham, BSac 140 (1983), 40–54.

[11]This may be ordinary skepticism about religious prognostication of the future; but by way of more formal parallel, the Epicureans argued against God's providence on the grounds that no divine judgment of the world had taken place. C. H. Talbert, VC 20 (1966), 137–45, adapting Käsemann's thesis, argues that II Pet was not directed against early Christian disturbance over the delay of the parousia but against gnostics who advocated a realized eschatology and an entirely present salvation that permitted libertine practice.

[12]Jude 14–17 had cited the prophecy of Enoch and the prediction of the apostles (in whose number Jude was not included).

both prophecy and apostleship: In 1:19 he claimed, "We have the prophetic word made more sure," and in 1:1 he identified himself as "an apostle of Jesus Christ"—indeed he has spoken as "we" for the other apostolic eyewitnesses (1:16–18). In 3:14–16 he adds the witness of "our dear brother Paul" who told them in his letters to try to be found blameless in God's sight at the forthcoming judgment, even if the ignorant and unstable twist his words. Third (3:5–7), the writer offers proof that all things have not continued as they were from the beginning of creation. The God who manifested power in creation flooded the world; and that same God will judge the created heaven and earth with fire, destroying the ungodly, thus punishing the false teachers and ensuring the parousia.[13] Fourth (3:8–10), he dismisses the "delay" of the parousia in terms of the inscrutability of divine "time" which is not our time: In the eyes of the Lord a thousand years are a day (Ps 90:4). If there is a delay, it is because the Lord is forbearing and wants to allow time for repentance (3:9)—a view that explains why II Pet has called attention to Noah and Lot who were spared in times of divine punishment. Eventually, however (as Jesus predicted in Mark 13:32,36), the day of the Lord will come unexpectedly, like a thief; and the earth and all its works will be found out.[14] Therefore (3:11–16) facing such ultimate dissolution, the addressees should live lives of holiness and godliness in order to be found without spot or blemish.

CONCLUDING EXHORTATION AND DOXOLOGY (3:17–18). This is an effective summation of what has gone before. In the literary format of this dying speech, Symeon Peter issues a final warning to be on guard against the deceit of the lawless who will cause the addressees to lose their stability. Then he comes back to his initial wish (1:5–8) that they make progress, not only in grace but also in the knowledge of "our Lord and Savior Jesus Christ." The doxology gives glory not only now but until the day of eternity, a day that Symeon Peter has given assurance is surely coming (3:7).

By and To Whom, Where, and When?

BY WHOM? In discussing I Pet, we saw that serious scholars supported Simon Peter as the writer (through a scribe), even if the odds somewhat favored pseudonymity. A comparison of I Pet and II Pet shows that the same writer did not compose both works, as noted already by Jerome in the 4th

[13]S. Meier, BZ NS 32 (1988), 255–57.

[14]The end of 3:10 is difficult: Is "found out" the correct reading? Is it a negative idea (as might be implied by preceding clauses that have the heavens pass away and the elements burned up)? See F. W. Danker, ZNW 53 (1962), 82–86; A. Wolters, *Westminster Theological Journal* 49 (1987), 405–13; D. Wenham, NTS 33 (1989), 477–79.

century. For instance, there are OT quotations in I Pet but not in II Pet; some 60 percent of the vocabulary of II Pet is not found in I Pet;[15] the style of II Pet is more solemn, even pompous and labored; and the mind-set about issues like the second coming is quite different. That, plus factors to be discussed under dating below, makes it clear that II Pet is pseudonymous, written presumably by someone in the Petrine tradition.[16] Indeed, the pseudonymity of II Pet is more certain than that of any other NT work.

WHEN? At one end of the spectrum, II Pet was certainly in existence by AD 200, since the text is preserved in the 3d–century Bodmer P[72] and it was known by Origen. At the other end, a number of "afters" point to a date no earlier than *ca.* 100, e.g.: *after* the apostolic generation was dead and expectations of the second coming during their lifetime had been disappointed (II Pet 3:4—thus after 80); *after* I Pet (II Pet 3:1[17]) which may have been composed in the 80s; *after* Jude which may have been composed *ca.* 90; *after* there was a collection of Pauline letters (II Pet 3:15–16) which probably did not take place much before 100; *after* those letters were seemingly being reckoned as Scripture (3:16: "as they do the other writings [Scriptures]")—a development attested for Christian writings in the early 2d century; *after* there was a well-known tradition of a prediction by Jesus of Peter's death (1:14)—the prediction in John is in a section (21:18–19) probably not added to the Gospel until after 100, even if it contained earlier tradition. There are other features that indicate lateness, e.g., harmonizing of Peter and Paul as consonant authorities with implicit superiority given to Peter; a sensitivity to exclude the noncanonical references in material taken over from Jude. Yet within the dating spectrum of AD 100–200, nothing cited in this paragraph requires a date after the first half of the 2d century. Thus a date of 130, give or take a decade, would best fit the evidence.

FROM WHERE? II Pet was written from a place where Peter was an authority even after his death (which is appealed to in 1:14–15) and where I Pet, a collection of Pauline letters, and Jude would have been known.[18] If the Ro-

[15]In particular, while I Pet uses *apokalypsis* for future coming/appearance of Jesus, II Pet uses *parousia.*

[16]The 2d century saw a whole body of pseudepigraphical Petrine literature that was not accepted as canonical (Chapter 33 above, n. 32).

[17]Does "*Now* this, beloved, is the second letter I write to you" indicate that the writer wants to suggest that I Pet had been written not too long before?

[18]None of these contributing items would be changed by pseudonymity because one has to ask why the writer chose the auspices under which he wrote. Arguing from a knowledge of II Pet in the *Apocalypse of Peter,* which is *possibly* of Alexandrian provenance and *possibly* to be dated *ca.* 135, Kelly opts for Alexandrian provenance of II Pet. Were collected Pauline letters known so early in Alexandria? As typical of his interests, Neyrey in his *2 Peter* (128–32) devotes his attention to the social location of the author: a male, not an aristocrat, writing in a city of Asia Minor (also Fornberg) where he had access to a wide variety of Christian documents. But in which city of that description would Peter's last testament have been a plausible composition?

man community was founded from Jerusalem, eventually it may have come to know Jude, a letter written under the auspices of the brother of James, the leader of the Jerusalem church. Paul wrote to Rome and eventually died there. I Pet was written from Rome, and that city where Peter died a martyr's death would have been a most appropriate site for composing II Pet as a type of farewell address by the great apostle. The images of Peter and Paul were harmonized at Rome as *I Clement* 5 testifies. Rome is then at least a plausible candidate for the composition of II Pet within a Petrine "school."

TO WHERE? I Pet (1:1) was addressed to areas in Asia Minor, areas perhaps evangelized by Jerusalem but to which, after the destruction of Jerusalem, Rome could now speak in the name of Peter, who had spent a good deal of his life in the Jerusalem church before coming to Rome. II Pet 1:1 is addressed "to those who have received a faith of the same value as ours," which could mean all Christians. Yet 3:1 supposes the same audience as I Pet. Also there is an assumption in II Pet 3:15–16 that the audience had been addressed by Paul and knows all (many of) his letters. Thus not all Christians but those in the eastern Mediterranean (probably Asia Minor) were probably in view.[19] The Hellenization of II Peter (e.g., Tartarus in 2:4) would also fit that area. The very general instructions and polemic of II Pet do not allow us to diagnose the theological problems of the addressees (other than disappointment about the failure of Jesus to return); rather they make II Pet an epistle applicable to many situations and times.[20]

EPISTLE OR LETTER? In discussing Jude a whole subsection was devoted to *Literary Genre,* including whether it was an Epistle or Letter in Deissmann's terminology (p. 410 above). That does not seem necessary here. The opening two verses do follow a letter format but with an address applicable to all Christians. The doxology at the end is much less ample than that of Jude and not really indicative of a letter. The exhortation and instruction that constitute a good part of the work are not precise, and the polemic against the false teachers is taken over en masse from Jude. Thus specific communities that one could name and their problems do not seem to be envisaged. The writer is presenting a homily that constitutes Peter's last will and testament to Christians who would be influenced by his reputation—a homily fitted into minimum letter format. Even granted the diversity of Hellenistic letters, "Epistle" covers II Pet better than "Letter."

[19]The debate among older commentators as to whether the addressees were Jewish or Gentile Christians is particularly pointless here since they would have had their roots in missionary activity of various strains in which memories of Peter, Paul, and probably James of Jerusalem were influential.

[20]Not necessarily those addressed in Jude, from which II Pet borrowed.

Canonicity and Early Catholicism

Of the twenty-seven NT books II Pet had the least support in antiquity. In the Western church (unlike Jude) II Pet was either unknown or ignored until *ca.* 350, and even after that Jerome reported that many rejected it because it differed in style from I Pet. In the Eastern church Origen acknowledged disputes about it. Bodmer P[72] (3d century) shows that II Pet was being copied in Egypt; yet in the early 4th century Eusebius did not treat it as canonical, and most of the great church writers of Antioch ignored it. Nevertheless, during the 4th century II Pet was making its appearance in some Eastern and Western church lists (Athanasius, III Carthage); and by the early 6th century even the Syriac-speaking church was accepting it. Despite that checkered history Luther did not relegate II Pet to the back of his 1522 NT (as he did Jas, Jude, Heb, and Rev), probably because he did not have great difficulty with its teaching. In modern times, however, particularly among more radical Protestant scholars II Pet has been attacked; and the occasional voice has been raised for removing it from the canon because of a dislike of its "Early Catholicism."

Käsemann is the leading exponent of the presence of "Early Catholic" features in II Pet. In his attempt to correct gnostics who rejected the parousia, the writer of the epistle stressed that faith was a body of beliefs. The prophetic Scriptures were not a matter of one's own interpretation but had to be interpreted by authoritative teachers like Peter. A chain of apostolic authority from the eyewitnesses of Jesus' ministry was now assumed. Käsemann also complains that the Pauline ideas of faith as trust and of justification are absent and that Hellenistic philosophic terminology ("partakers of the divine nature") has been substituted for the existential language of the early books. In the eyes of Käsemann (a Lutheran) all this would eventually produce the kind of Christianity exemplified by Roman Catholicism and represented a wrong direction. Passionately he demands ("Apologia" 195):

> What are we to say about a Church, which is so concerned to defend herself against heretics, that she no longer distinguishes between Spirit and letter; that she identifies the Gospel with her own tradition and, further, with a particular religious world-view; that she regulates exegesis according to her system of teaching authority and makes faith into a mere assent to the dogmas of orthodoxy?

A logical implication would be that the church made a mistake in canonizing II Pet, and indeed radical voices have been raised for deletion.

Disagreement with this approach has been expressed on two scores. First, a challenge has been mounted against the right of interpreters to decide that what favors their theology and their church inclination is the true message of the NT and that what does not is a distortion. To what extent is the objection to Early Catholicism a reflection of Protestant disagreement with aspects of Roman Catholicism and Eastern Orthodoxy? Would it not be healthier to recognize that the individual church traditions capitalized on *selected* ideas in the NT, and that dialogue among the churches will be facilitated when each tradition calls itself to account for what it has neglected? If Christian groups can eliminate from the canon what they do not agree with, how has Scripture the ability to make them rethink? Second, Fornberg and others have questioned whether Käsemann's analysis of the thought of II Pet as Early Catholicism is correct. Did the author of II Pet really stand so simply for the approaches indicated in Käsemann's paragraph quoted above? In the Early Catholic thesis are we not reading the writer's reaction to a particular set of problems in the light of much later Reformation issues? Also many of the ideas at issue (faith as believed truths, importance of apostolic authority, authoritative interpretations, danger of untraditional private teachers) are found widely in the NT, including the undisputed Pauline letters. II Pet can provide an opportunity to discuss the validity of those ideas, but the dialectic isolation of them may not facilitate a valid exegesis of the writer's intent.

Issues and Problems for Reflection

(1) "Faith" as a deposit of beliefs (II Pet 1:1) is often contrasted pejoratively with the Pauline sense of faith as trust in what God has done in Christ. Granted that one must respond to God's grace with faith as trust and commitment, is it likely that Christianity could have continued without formulating its beliefs? Confessions like "Jesus is Messiah, Lord, etc." were necessary not only so that those asked to commit themselves could know what God's graciousness consisted in but also eventually because others denied this identity. Today some Christian churches refuse to formulate a creed beyond the Scriptures, but that should not disguise the fact that there is an incipient body of beliefs in the Scriptures themselves. Thus faith as trust and faith as a body of beliefs can be seen as complementary.

(2) Although a certain adaptation to the language of Greek philosophy that contrasts this world to the eternal is noticeable in several later NT works like Acts and the Pauline Pastorals, nowhere is it more apparent than in II Peter, e.g, an ideal of godliness (*eusebeia* in 1:3,6,7; 3:11), and of being sharers in divine nature escaping the corrupt world (1:4). Granted that this was not the original language of Jesus' message, is it a corruption of that

message, as some opponents of "Early Catholicism" would contend, or is it an inevitable thrust of the proclamation of a gospel of incarnation? In the latter direction cannot one argue that when preachers have refused to phrase the gospel in the language and cultures of other people, they have weakened their mission and limited the understanding of what God has done in Christ? Such rephrasing need not mean the rejection of previous expressions and formulations or the loss of past insights.

(3) II Pet 3:7,12–13 constitutes the NT evidence that heaven and earth will be destroyed by fire at the end of time,[21] to be replaced by a new heaven and a new earth. (Actually Christians who take that literally often dispense with any earthly replacement and think of a nonmaterial heaven as the replacement.) The apocalyptic idea of a new heaven and earth echoes Isa 65:17; 66:22; fire is a traditional element in divine punishment (Matt 3:10; 5:22; 13:40,50; 18:8–9). Besides reflecting the biblical idiom, the writer may be making himself intelligible also to those whose primary background included the Stoic doctrine of an immense conflagration that would consume the finite and be followed by regeneration in a never-ending cycle. Theologically, the belief that II Pet is an inspired writing could insure the truth of the parousia (Christ's ultimately bringing about God's kingdom) which is a major point in this epistle; but did the author have any divine revelation about what would occur at the end of time? Must Christians believe in the destruction of the world as we know it by fire? See R. L. Overstreet, BSac 137 (1980), 354–71.

(4) In many ways II Pet resembles II Tim. Each is a last testament of a famous apostle; and each appeals to the witness of the apostle, respectively Peter and Paul. Each is concerned about the intrusion of false teachers upon whom opprobrium is heaped. For guidance each assumes a deposit of faith. It is a worthwhile exercise to pick out other theological parallels as an example of how in different sections of the church at the end of the NT period similar attitudes and answers were developing.

Bibliography on II Peter

COMMENTARIES AND STUDIES IN SERIES (* = also on Jude): **Bauckham, R. J.** (WBC, 1983*); Danker, F. W. (ProcC, 2d ed., 1995*); Green, M. (TNTC, 2d ed., 1987*); Knight, J. (NTG, 1995*); Krodel, G. A. (ProcC, rev. ed., 1995); Neyrey, J. H. (AB, 1993*). Also works marked with a single asterisk in the *Bibliography* of Chapter 33 on I Pet, and with a double asterisk in the *Bibliography* of Chapter 34 on Jas.

[21]See C. P. Thiede, JSNT 26 (1986), 79–96 on the conflagration.

Surveys of Research: Snyder, J., JETS 22 (1979), 265–67; Hupper, W. G., JETS 23 (1980), 65–66; Bauckham, R. J., JETS 25 (1982), 91–93; ANRW II.25.2 (1988), 3713–52.

Abbott, E. A., "The Second Epistle of St. Peter," *Expositor* 2/3 (1882), 49–63, 139–53, 204–19. A major early study.

Cooper, W. H., "The Objective Nature of Prophecy According to II Peter," *Lutheran Church Quarterly* 13 (1940), 190–95.

Crehan, J., "New Light on 2 Peter from the Bodmer Papyrus," StEv 7 (1982), 145–49.

Deshardins, M., "The Portrayal of the Dissidents in 2 Peter and Jude," JSNT 30 (1987), 89–102.

Ernst, C., "The Date of II Peter and the Deposit of Faith," *Clergy Review* 47 (1962), 686–89.

Farmer, W. R., "Some Critical Reflections on Second Peter," *Second Century* 5 (1985), 30–46.

Fornberg, T., *An Early Church in a Pluralistic Society: A Study of 2 Peter* (CBNTS 9; Lund: Gleerup, 1977).

Green, M., *2 Peter Reconsidered* (London: Tyndale, 1961).

Grispino, J. A., and A. Dilanni, "The Date of II Peter and the Deposit of Faith," *Clergy Review* 46 (1961), 601–10.

Harvey, A. E., "The Testament of Simeon Peter," in *A Tribute to Geza Vermes,* eds. P. R. Davies and R. T. White (Sheffield: JSOT, 1990), 339–54.

Hiebert, D. E., "Selected Studies from 2 Peter," BSac 141 (1984), 43–54, 158–68, 255–65, 330–40.

James, M. R., *2 Peter and Jude* (Cambridge Univ., 1912).

Käsemann, E., "An Apologia for Primitive Christian Eschatology," KENTT 169–95.

Klinger, J., "The Second Epistle of Peter: An Essay in Understanding," *St. Vladimir's Theological Quarterly* 17/1–2 (1973), 152–69.

McNamara, M., "The Unity of Second Peter. A Reconsideration," *Scripture* 12 (1960), 13–19. A rare voice arguing that it consists of two or three letters.

Mayor, J. B., *The Second Epistle of St. Peter and the Epistle of St. Jude* (New York: Macmillan: 1907).

Picirilli, R. E., "Allusions to 2 Peter in the Apostolic Fathers," JSNT 33 (1988), 57–83.

Robson, E. I., *Studies in the Second Epistle of St. Peter* (Cambridge Univ., 1915).

Watson, D. F., *Invention*, 81–146, on II Pet.

Witherington, B., III, "A Petrine Source in 2 Peter," SBLSP 1985, 187–92.

CHAPTER 37

THE BOOK OF REVELATION (THE APOCALYPSE)

We now come to the book that stands at the end of the canonical NT even though it was not the last NT book to be composed—II Pet has that distinction. Either of the two names that appear in the title of this Chapter may be used for the book (please note, however, that one should not call the book Revelation*s*), and both literally mean "unveiling." Yet "Apocalypse" (from the Greek title of the book: *Apokalypsis*) has the advantage of catching the esoteric character of the genre of this work, so that it is not simply thought of as revelation in the ordinary religious sense of a divine communication of information. That remark leads us into the leading difficulty about the book.

Rev is widely popular for the wrong reasons, for a great number of people read it as a guide to how the world will end, assuming that the author was given by Christ detailed knowledge of the future that he communicated in coded symbols. For example, preachers have identified the Beast from the Earth whose number is 666 as Hitler, Stalin, the Pope, and Saddam Hussein, and have related events in Rev to the Communist Revolution, the atom bomb, the creation of the State of Israel, the Gulf War, etc. The 19th and the 20th centuries have seen many interpreters of prophecy who used calculations from Rev to predict the exact date of the end of the world. Up to the moment all have been wrong! Some of the more militant exponents of Rev have aggravated law-enforcement authorities to the point of armed intervention (the Branch Davidians in Waco, TX). On the other hand, many believing Christians do not think that the author knew the future in any sense beyond an absolute conviction that God would triumph by saving those who remained loyal and by defeating the forces of evil. That evaluation can be defended through a study of the *Literary genre of apocalyptic,* with which we shall begin. After that will come the *General Analysis,* a bit longer than usual, because Rev is difficult to understand: "This book, more than any other New Testament writing, demands commentary" (Harrington, *Revelation* xiii). Then subsections will be devoted to: *Structure,* the *Role of liturgy, Millenarianism* (20:4–5), *Authorship, Date and life-situation (persecution under Domitian?), Issues for reflection,* and *Bibliography.*

Summary of Basic Information

DATE: Probably between AD 92 and 96 at the end of the Emperor Domitian's reign.

TO: Churches in the western sector of Asia Minor.

AUTHENTICITY: Written by a Jewish Christian prophet named John who was neither John son of Zebedee nor the writer of the Johannine Gospel or of the Epistles.

UNITY: Only a few scholars contend that two apocalypses (from the same hand or school) have been joined—an attempt to explain the repetitions and seemingly different time perspectives.

INTEGRITY: The writer may have included visions and passages that were already part of Christian apocalyptic tradition, but overall the work is entirely his own.

DIVISION ACCORDING TO CONTENTS:

A. Prologue: 1:1–3

B. Letters to the Seven Churches: 1:4–3:22
   Opening Formula with attached praise, promise, and divine response (1:4–8)
   Inaugural Vision (1:9–20)
   Seven Letters (2:1–3:22)

C. Part I of the Revelatory Experience: 4:1–11:19
   Visions of the Heavenly Court: The One Enthroned and the Lamb (4:1–5:14)
   Seven Seals (6:1–8:1)
   Seven Trumpets (8:2–11:19)

D. Part II of the Revelatory Experience: 12:1–22:5
   Visions of the Dragon, the Beasts, and the Lamb (12:1–14:20)
   Seven Plagues and Seven Bowls (15:1–16:21)
   Judgment of Babylon, the Great Harlot (17:1–19:10)
   Victory of Christ and the End of History (19:11–22:5)

E. Epilogue (with Concluding Blessing): 22:6–21.

The Literary Genre of Apocalyptic

"Apocalypticism" usually refers to the ideology of works of this genre or of the groups that accepted them. Some prefer to use the noun "apocalypse" as the designation for the genre; but to avoid confusion with the NT book being discussed, let us use the nominal adjective "apocalyptic" in that role.[1] The fact that this designation is derived from the title of the NT book tells us that in some ways Rev is a model for the genre—a genre difficult to

[1]I give here only some sample books from the abundant literature: H. H. Rowley, *The Relevance of Apocalyptic* (3d ed.; London: Lutterworth, 1963); D. S. Russell, *The Method and Message of Jewish Apocalyptic* (Philadelphia: Fortress, 1964); K. Koch, *The Rediscovery of Apocalyptic* (SBT NS 22; Naperville, IL: Allenson, 1972); P. D. Hanson, *The Dawn of Apocalyptic* (Philadelphia: Fortress, 1978); ed., *Visionaries and Their Apocalypses* (Philadelphia: Fortress, 1983); *Old Testament Apocalyptic* (Nashville: Abingdon, 1987); C. Rowland, *The Open Heaven: A Study of Apocalyptic in Judaism and Christianity* (New York: Crossroad, 1982); D. Hellholm, ed., *Apocalypticism in the Mediterranean World and the Near East* (Tübingen: Mohr-Siebeck, 1983); J. J. Collins, *The Apocalyptic Imagination* (New York: Crossroad, 1987); S. L. Cook, *Prophecy and Apocalypticism* (Minneapolis: A/F, 1995). Also *Journal for Theology and the Church* 6 (1969); CBQ 39 (#3; 1977); *Semeia* 14 (1979); 36 (1986); CRBS 2 (1994), 147–79.

define, in part because we do not find truly comparable examples of it in our contemporary literature. There are, of course, modern books by people who have fertile imaginations or who claim visions about the future, specifically about Satan being let loose, and the end of the world; but most of these are imitations or innovative applications of Dan and Rev.

As we turn to aspects of apocalyptic, qualifiers like "frequently," "often," and "sometimes" are required because very little of what follows is true of all apocalypses. Characteristic of biblical apocalypses is a narrative framework in which a revelatory vision is accorded to a human being, most often through the intervention of an otherworldly being,[2] e.g., by an angel who takes him to a heavenly vantage point to show him the vision and/or to explain it to him. Sometimes to get there the visionary has to travel a distance to the ends of the earth or make a vertical journey through various heavens. The secrets revealed involve a cosmic transformation that will result in a transition from this world to a world or era to come and a divine judgment on all. (NT Christian apocalyptic differs from Jewish apocalyptic of the same period in that the new era has already begun because of the coming of Christ.) The vision of the supernatural world or of the future helps to interpret present circumstances on earth, which are almost always tragic. As we shall see, apocalyptic had its roots in prophecy; and prophets too had a supernatural experience wherein they were brought into the heavenly court that meets in God's presence and introduced to the mysterious plan of God (Amos 3:7; I Kings 22:19–23; Isa 6). In apocalyptic, however, the visions of the otherworldly have become far more luxuriant, most often accompanied by vivid symbols (ideal temple, liturgical settings, cosmic phenomena, menagerie of fantastic beasts, statues) and mysterious numbers.[3] The prophetic message too involves present circumstances on earth (international and national politics, religious practice, social concern), but the situation and solution are different from those in apocalyptic. When the circumstances to which the writing prophet addresses himself are prosperous and comfortable, he may condemn the situation as spiritually and morally barren and warn of impending disaster within the confines of history (invasions, captivity, fall of the monarchy, destruction of the Temple); when the circumstances

[2]J. J. Collins, ABD 1.279. Apocalypses are "intended to interpret present, earthly circumstances in light of the supernatural world and of the future, and to influence both the understanding and behavior of the audience by means of divine authority" (A. Yarbro Collins, *Semeia* 36 [1986], 7). Although the Bible mentions women prophets, in biblical apocalyptic the visionaries are all men.

[3]Below we shall distinguish different periods of Israelite history in which apocalypses were written; the later ones take much of their symbolism from the earlier apocalyptic books. It has been estimated that about 65 percent of the verses of Rev have OT allusions; yet it is very difficult to find a single explicit quotation of the OT. S. Moyise, *The Old Testament in the Book of Revelation* (JSNTSup 115; Sheffield: Academic, 1995).

are desperate because of captivity or oppression, the prophet may offer hope in terms of return to the homeland or the destruction of the oppressor and a restoration of the monarchy. Apocalypses are most often addressed to those living in times of suffering and persecution—so desperate that they are seen as the embodiment of supreme evil. If history is laid out in a pattern of divinely determined periods (enumerated in various ways), the author is living in the last of them.[4] Hope of a historical solution has disappeared in favor of direct divine intervention that will bring all to an end. Very often in a strongly dualistic approach, the apocalyptist envisions what is happening on earth as part of a titanic struggle in the other world between God or God's angels and Satan and his angels. In some apocalypses pseudonymity is a key factor. The writer takes the name of a famous figure from antiquity, e.g., Daniel, a legendary wise man; Enoch, who was taken up to heaven; or Ezra, the great lawgiver. Such a figure lends authority to an apocalypse, for he can predict exactly all that will happen between his time and the present time when the author is writing (because, in fact, all that has already happened).[5] Indeed, when we know the subsequent history, a way to date such works is to pinpoint the period when the accuracy of the portrayal of history stops and inaccuracy or vagueness begins.

To illustrate the history of Jewish and Christian apocalyptic and its variety, let me mention some representative examples of the genre. Our oldest illustration of biblical apocalyptic, and one indicative of its beginnings, may be dated to the Babylonian exile. That catastrophe, following the capture of Jerusalem, destruction of the Temple, and fall of the monarchy, began to call into question the possibility of salvation within history. Although the Book of Ezekiel is dominantly prophetic in the sense that the prophet expected deliverance in history, the extravagant imagery of his visions (Ezek 1–3; 37) and his idealistic anticipation of the New Israel virtually go beyond history (40–48) and overlap into apocalyptic style and anticipation. Indeed, Ezek supplied a major part of apocalyptic language and images that would be used in the future: the four living creatures (looking like a man, lion, ox, eagle), an enthroned figure above the firmament described in terms of gems and precious metals, eating scrolls, the harlot, the wicked prosperous city-

[4]L. Hartman, NTS 22 (1975–76), 1–14, gathers evidence to show that the apocalyptists were not concerned with assigning a date for the end time, but with impressing on the audience the urgency of the situation.

[5]Rev does not lay out past history in a pattern of symbolically represented periods as do *I Enoch* and Dan; it does not instruct people to seal up or hide its message as do Dan and *II Baruch.* There is no reason to think that Rev is pseudonymous; the use of John as a pseudonym would make sense only if the author were claiming apostolic authority, but he is not. The genuine identification of the visionary as a man named John may be accounted for by the fact that Rev is partly prophecy, as we shall see.

kingdom blasphemous in its arrogance (Tyre in chaps. 27–28), Gog of Magog, measuring the Temple, etc. A combination of prophetic historical message with apocalyptic elements and imagery (the Day of the Lord, hordes of destructive locusts) is found in the Book of Joel, of uncertain date but probably postexilic. From the same general period comes Zech 4:1–6:8, with its visions (interpreted by an angel) of lampstands, scrolls, four different colored horses; and from sometime later come deutero Zechariah and trito Zechariah (Zech 9–14), with an allegory of the shepherds and pictures of judgment and an ideal Jerusalem. See also Isa 24–27.[6]

Another important period for the appearance of apocalyptic writing was the 3d and 2d centuries BC when the Greek dynasties in Egypt (Ptolemies) and Syria (Seleucids), descended from Alexander the Great's conquest, became more authoritarian in their rule of Judea. In particular the persecution of the Jewish religion in favor of the worship of the Greek gods under the Seleucid king, Antiochus IV Epiphanes (176–164 BC) sharpened a sense of diabolic evil that only God could overcome. The idea of an afterlife had now developed clearly among some Jews, and that opened the possibility of eternal happiness replacing an existence marked by suffering and torture. In this period we move from prophetic books with apocalyptic traits to full-fledged apocalypses. The initial section of *I Enoch* (chaps. 1–36) was composed in the 3d century BC, and to the treasury of apocalyptic symbolism it contributed pictures of the final judgment and of wicked angels who fall and are locked up till the last days. A later section of the book (chaps. 91–105) lays out predetermined history in a pattern of weeks. Dan, the greatest OT biblical apocalypse, was written *ca.* 165 BC. The vision of four monstrous beasts followed by the heavenly coronation of a son of man (chap. 7) and the vision of the seventy weeks of years (chap. 9) had a strong impact on later apocalypses. The rise of the DSS community was related to the troubles in the mid-2d century BC; and there were strong apocalyptic elements in DSS thought, as witnessed in QM, a plan for the war of the last times between the sons of light and the sons of darkness. Still another major period of the production of Jewish apocalypses was in the decades after AD 70 and the Roman destruction of the Jerusalem Temple—the ancient Babylonian devastation relived 650 years later. *IV Ezra* and (slightly later) *II Baruch* were composed in that era when Rome was the embodiment of evil.[7]

We do not know whether the author of Rev knew Jesus' long apocalyptic

[6]W. R. Millar, *Isaiah 24–27 and the Origin of Apocalyptic* (Harvard Semitic Monograph 11; Missoula, MT: Scholars, 1976). Also J. Fekkes, III, *Isaiah and Prophetic Traditions in the Book of Revelation* (JSNTSup 93; Sheffield: JSOT, 1994).

[7]For seventeen apocalypses amid the Jewish pseudepigrapha, see R. J. Bauckham, JSNT 26 (1986), 97–111.

discourse (Mark 13 and par.), but he knew traditional apocalyptic elements that circulated among 1st-century Christians. For instance, in the Pauline tradition there is a strong apocalyptic sense of Christ bringing about the endtimes, as well as anticipations of the resurrection of the dead and the antichrist figure (I Cor 15; II Thess 2).[8] Rev, however, is the most apocalyptic book in the NT. Nero's vicious persecution of Christians in Rome and seemingly harassment under Domitian (see subsection below), set in the broader context of deification of the emperor, gave a diabolic tinge to a struggle between Caesar and Christ; and the destruction of the Jewish Temple was seen as the beginning of divine judgment on all those who opposed Christ. Rev reuses many of the elements from Ezek, Zech, the Isaian Apocalypse, and Dan; but it does so with remarkable creativity. Moreover, other features, like the letters to the churches, the joining of Christ the Lamb to the heavenly court, and the marriage of the Lamb, attest to originality. Christian apocalypticism continued after the NT period both in circles remembered as orthodox (*Shepherd of Hermas; Apocalypse of Peter*) and among the gnostics (*Apocryphon of John; Apocalypse of Paul*).[9] To this day catastrophic times continue to revive the apocalyptic spirit among some Christians (and some Jews), as they come to believe that the times are so bad that God must soon intervene.

Although, as just seen, one can trace a lineage from prophetic writing to apocalyptic writing,[10] some of the major preChristian Jewish apocalypses were written when prophecy no longer flourished—a period when Wisdom Literature was more abundant and Israel had come into contact with Greco-Roman civilization. That situation casts light on two aspects of apocalyptic. First, some have claimed that apocalyptic replaced prophecy. That is not accurate: There are works with mixed elements of the two genres, and that is certainly true of Rev. Although the seer of Rev entitles his work *apokalypsis,* he speaks of it six times as a prophecy, specifically at the beginning and end (1:3; 22:19). Indeed the letters to the churches (1:4–3:22) have elements of prophetic warning and consolation.[11] As Roloff (*Revelation* 8) ob-

[8]For a comparison of the eschatology of Rev 20 and Paul, see S.H.T. Page, JETS 23 (1980), 31–43. There is also a strong apocalyptic tone in Jude (taken over by II Pet), but it is difficult to date that work in relation to Rev. For the larger picture, see P. S. Minear, *New Testament Apocalyptic* (Nashville: Abingdon, 1981); also *Apocalyptic and the New Testament,* eds. J. Marcus and M. L. Soards (J. L. Martyn Festschrift; JSNTSup 24; Sheffield: JSOT, 1989).

[9]In the article cited in n. 7 above, Bauckham, 111–14, argues that one cannot stop with OT pseudepigrapha, for up to AD 200 Christian and Jewish apocalyptic remained close together.

[10]On apocalyptic and prophecy: B. Vawter, CBQ 22 (1960), 33–46; G. E. Ladd, JBL 76 (1957), 192–200; D. S. Russell, *Prophecy and the Apocalyptic Dream* (Peabody, MA: Hendrickson, 1994).

[11]See D. Hill, NTS 18 (1971–72), 401–18; M. E. Boring, SBLSP (1974), 2.43–62; F. D. Mazzaferri, *The Genre of the Book of Revelation from a Source-critical Perspective* (BZNW 54; Berlin: de

serves, the self-proclamation of Jesus Christ is heard in those letters; and it was one of the tasks of Christian prophets to announce to the communities the will of the exalted Christ. Second, there are certain similarities between strains in apocalyptic and Wisdom Literature. Few would go as far as G. von Rad in deriving apocalyptic from the wisdom tradition, but a deterministic view of history (laid out in numerical patterns) and a display of erudition sometimes mark both traditions. In *I Enoch* 28–32; 41; 69, for instance, one finds detailed descriptions of various kinds of trees, an interest in astronomical secrets, and an appreciation of knowledge in general. Wisdom Literature existed in other countries, and some portions of the Hebrew Wisdom Literature drew on foreign sources. Similarly, not only ancient Semitic creation myths but the Greco-Roman myths about the gods have left their mark on apocalyptic imagery, especially in the descriptions of the beasts and the warfare between good and evil. The worship of the goddess Roma, queen of heaven, may have been combined with the OT female Zion figure in shaping the imagery of the mother of the Messiah in Rev 12.

Finally we should be aware that the figurative language of apocalyptic raises hermeneutical issues. Many times one can detect a historical referent in the description, e.g., that one of the grotesque beasts of Dan or Rev refers to a specific world power (the Seleucid Syrian kingdom, Rome). Yet sometimes the symbols are polyvalent, e.g., the woman in Rev 12 may symbolize Israel giving birth to the Messiah as well as the church and her children in the wilderness under Satanic attack after the Messiah has been taken up to heaven. (She could also be the same as the bride of the Lamb, the New Jerusalem, who comes down from heaven in 21:2, but there is less agreement on that.) Beyond the question of the writer's intent the symbolism of apocalyptic compels imaginative participation on the part of the hearers/readers. It finds its full meaning when it elicits emotions and feelings that cannot be conceptualized. Therefore, the identification of the 1st-century referents in a purely descriptive way does not do justice to the persuasive power of Rev (E. Schüssler Fiorenza, *Revelation* [ProcC 31]). Apocalypticists of a later period are wrong in thinking that various items in biblical apocalyptic represent exact foreknowledge of events that would take place 1,000–2,000 years

Gruyter, 1989). These features have convinced a minority of scholars that Rev should be classified as prophecy rather than apocalypse. For arguments that Rev is better classified as (at least predominantly) an apocalypse, see J. J. Collins, CBQ 39 (1977), 329–43; D. Hellholm, *Semeia* 36 (1986), 13–64; D. E. Aune, *ibid.* 65–96. In defending the idea of both prophecy and apocalyptic, E. Schüssler Fiorenza, *Book* 133–56, 175–76, would argue that the writer patterned his letters on the authoritative Pauline letter form, so that the whole work is a prophetic-apostolic letter written in a concentric chiastic pattern. Our evidence is insufficient that the Pauline letter form was that unique, that widely known, and that definitive at this early period.

later; but those involved in such movements understand the power of this literature better than do dispassionate exegetical inquiries content with historical identifications.

General Analysis of the Message

A. Prologue (1:1–3). The book is announced as the "revelation of Jesus Christ," i.e., the revelation given by Christ about the divine meaning of the author's own times and about how God's people will soon be delivered. This revelation is delivered by an angel to a seer named John[12] who, as we shall discover in v. 9, is on the small island of Patmos in the Aegean Sea, some sixty-five miles southwest of Ephesus. The island location may have affected some of the imagery in the book, e.g., the beast that rises from the sea. The blessing in v. 3, the first of seven in Rev, indicates that this prophetic message is meant to be read aloud and heard, probably at liturgies in the churches addressed.

B. Letters to the Seven Churches (1:4–3:22). This begins with an *Opening Formula (1:4–5a)*, as if the seven letters to come are part of one large letter.[13] The basic elements attested in NT Opening Formulas (Paul, I Pet; p. 413 above) are present here; but the Opening's triadic patterns are phrased in the symbolic style that pervades this book. In a description that proceeds from reflection on Exod 3:14, God is the one who is and was and is to come. Similarly three phrases describe Jesus in terms of his passion and death (faithful witness), his resurrection (firstborn from the dead), and his exaltation (ruler of earthly kings). The "seven spirits" of Rev 1:4 is obscure; see also the seven spirits of God (3:1; 4:5; 5:6). Perhaps the image refers to the Holy Spirit, for that figure should be included in the normal triadic grace with Father and Son (II Cor 13:13[14]; I Pet 1:2; II Thess 2:13–14).[14]

Baptismal language may be echoed in the *doxology of Christ in 1:5b–6* since what has been accomplished by his blood and the resultant dignity of Christians in terms of kingdom and priesthood, echoing Exod 19:6, are

[12]In Rev angels intervene at every turn; that John is preeminently a seer is exemplified by the emphasis on all that "he *saw*," a verb that occurs some fifty-five times in the book.

[13]Or given the concluding blessing in 22:21, it might seem that the whole work was a letter; but most of what intervenes is closer to revelatory narrative. The presence of a letter in an apocalyptic work is not unparalleled; see *II Baruch* 78–87.

[14]The seven gifts of the spirit of God in the LXX of Isa 11:2–3 could account for describing the Holy Spirit in this way. Others, however, would argue for a reference to the seven angels who serve before the heavenly throne (Tobit 12:15; *I Enoch* 90:21; Rev 8:2). Still others think of the guardian angels of the seven churches.

themes found in I Pet 1:2,19; 2:9.[15] It reminds the addressees of their identity; and *Rev 1:7 is an OT echo* (Dan 7:13; Zech 12:10), assuring them that Christ will come in judgment on all enemies. To the seer who ends his praise and promise with a prayerful "Amen," *in 1:8 the Lord God affirms* the triadic designation of 1:4 (who is, was, and is to come), prefacing that with "I am the Alpha and Omega," and concluding it with "the Almighty." The first and the last letters of the Greek alphabet signal God's existence at the beginning and the end; the designation *Pantokratōr,* "Almighty," is a favorite in Rev (nine times; elsewhere only II Cor 6:18) and was to become standard in the Byzantine church for depicting the majestic, all-powerful, enthroned Christ.

Inaugural Vision (1:9–20). John, speaking of the tribulation and endurance of the addressees, explains that he has been at Patmos "because of the word of God." Most interpret that to mean imprisonment or exile, a background that would explain the atmosphere of persecution in Rev. (In fact, Patmos was one of the small isles used for exile, and there was a type of banishment that could be imposed by a Roman provincial governor.) Moved in the Spirit "on the Lord's Day," he hears and "sees" a voice (even as prophets saw words: Isa 2:1; Amos 1:1; etc.). The Sunday context may account for the plausible echoes of Christian liturgy in the heavenly visions of the seer (see subsection below). That he can see a voice and that a constant "like" governs the seer's descriptions warn us that we have moved beyond a realm confined to the external senses into one of spiritual experience and symbolism. The vision of Christ is resplendent with rich symbolism, much of it derived from Dan. Christ is not only identified with "one like a son of man" (Dan 7:13), but also described with attributes belonging to the Ancient of Days (Dan 7:9 = God). The setting amidst the seven golden lampstands (Rev 1:12) prepares for the seven churches but also is evocative of the Jerusalem Temple (I Chron 28:15, from Exod 25:37) where God had been seen in a vision by Isaiah (Isa 6). The seven stars in the right hand were regal and imperial symbolism—a preparation for later visions in Rev that will pit Christ against Caesar. The imagery of this initial vision will be mined for descriptions of Christ in the letters to follow.

Letters to the Seven Churches (2:1–3:22). These are very important for understanding the whole book. They give us more information about a group

[15]In Rev 1:6 and 5:10 Christ or the Lamb has made the saintly believers a kingdom and priests to his God and Father—thus seemingly an already acquired privilege. In 20:4–6 the souls of the those who had been beheaded for their testimony to Jesus and who had not worshiped the beast will be priests of God and Christ and reign with him a thousand years—thus seemingly a future privilege. This is related to the priesthood issue in I Pet (pp. 722–23 above); also A. J. Bandstra, CTJ 27 (1992), 10–25.

of churches in western Asia Minor than most of the other NT books do about their addressees. When we come to the great visions of chaps. 4ff., we need to keep reminding ourselves that these are reported in order to convey a message to the Christians of those cities. Part of the misuse of Rev is based on the misunderstanding that the message is primarily addressed to Christians of our time if they can decode the author's symbols. Rather the meaning of the symbolism must be judged from the viewpoint of the 1st-century addressees—a meaning that needs adaptation if we are to see the book as significant for the present era.

The accompanying Table 8 shows the arrangement of the letters,[16] remarkably parallel in some ways, yet strikingly diverse in others. For instance, in terms of the judgment passed by the Son of Man who dictates the letters, nothing bad is said of Smyrna and Philadelphia; nothing good is said of Sardis and Laodicea. Before turning to details in the letters, let me make a general assessment of the message. Three sorts of problems confront the seven churches: false teaching (Ephesus, Pergamum, Thyatira); persecution (Smyrna, Philadelphia); and complacency (Sardis, Laodicea). Most modern readers who know something about Rev think of persecution as the only issue addressed and consequently reinterpret the book in the light of threatening situations today. The struggle against complacency may be much more applicable to modern Christianity. The false teaching is very conditioned by the 1st century in one way (eating meat offered to idols), and yet the underlying issue of Christians conforming in an unprincipled way to the surrounding society remains a very current problem.

The longest letter is to Thyatira which ironically is the least known city; the shortest is to Smyrna, a very famous city. There are abundant OT references in most of the letters, but relatively few in those to Sardis and Laodicea. The cities, all found in the western section of Asia Minor, are listed in an order that suggests a circular route for the letter carrier, beginning from Ephesus, going north through Smyrna to Pergamum, then southeast, and finally (after Laodicea) presumably west, working his way back to Ephesus. (Despite the plausibility of that proposal, it should be noted that no circular post road has been found.) The titles or descriptions of Christ that begin the letters echo in varying degrees descriptions in chap. 1.

Details in the rest of the letters (consisting of the status of the church,

[16]D. E. Aune, NTS 36 (1990), 182–204, in discussing various proposals about the literary genre of the letters, points out parallels to imperial edicts with four parts: *praescriptio* (opening declaration), *narratio* (reported information about the addressees), *dispositio* (commands as to what should be done), and *sanctio* (sanction to bring about observance). Into this mold the prophetic proclamations of the seer have been poured. This suggestion should warn us against the tendency to see the letters of Rev simply as an imitation of Pauline style (n. 11 above). T.M.S. Long, *Neotestamentica* 28 (1994), 395–411, debates the use of reader-response interpretation by using 2:1–7 as an example.

admonitions or encouragement, and a promise) reflect the geographic and commercial situation of the respective city, for evidently the seer knew the area well.[17] By way of example, in 2:7 the promise to Ephesus, "I will give to eat from the tree of life which is in the paradise of God" may echo the fact that the great temple to Artemis, one of the seven wonders of the ancient world, was built on a primitive tree shrine and the enclosure of the temple was a place of asylum.[18] The crown or garland of life in 2:10 may be evoked by Smyrna's position with its beautiful buildings rising to the crown of Mt. Pagus. Pergamum as the site of the throne of Satan may refer to the status of the city as the principal center of the imperial cult in Asia Minor; for a temple to the spirit of Rome existed there as early as 195 BC, and in gratitude to Augustus a temple to the godhead of Caesar had been built there in 29 BC.[19] (Indeed, there were imperial temples in all the cities addressed, except Thyatira.) The warning to Sardis about coming like a thief at an unexpected hour (3:3) may reflect the history of that city, which was captured twice by surprise; and the reference to a new name for the faithful among the Philadelphians (3:12) may echo the several times the city's name was changed (Neocaesarea, Flavia). Useless lukewarm water to be spit out of Jesus' mouth is used to image the Laodicean church (3:16), a contrast with the hot spring baths at nearby Hierapolis and the cold drinking water of Colossae.

Some churches are strong; some are weak; but whether commending or reprimanding, the writer frequently uses designations that are not clear to us. We do not know the views of the Nicolaitans at Ephesus and Pergamum (2:6,15). Are they Christians of libertine moral practice? Are they gnostics? It is not clear whether at Pergamum those who hold the teachings of Balaam (2:14) are the same in whole or part as the Nicolaitans; their attitudes seem to be responsible for seductively promoting idolatry and fornication, perhaps by claiming that all things are permitted. Whether the "Jezebel" at Thyatira

[17]The classic treatment is W. M. Ramsay, *The Letters to the Seven Churches of Asia* (London: Hodder & Stoughton, 1904; updated ed. by M. W. Wilson; Peabody, MA: Hendrickson, 1994). More recently see O.F.A. Meinardus, *St. John of Patmos and the Seven Churches of the Apocalypse* (New Rochelle: Caratzas, 1979); Yamauchi, *Archaeology* (1980); C. J. Hemer, *The Letters to the Seven Churches of Asia in Their Local Setting* (JSNTSup 11; Sheffield: JSOT, 1986). Meinardus also deals with the subsequent history of the churches. In the 2d century, a decade and a half after Rev was written, Ignatius wrote to Christians at Ephesus, Philadelphia, and Smyrna; and to Polycarp, the bishop of Smyrna; see C. Trevett, JSNT 37 (1989), 117–35. Somewhat later is the account of Polycarp's martyrdom at Smyrna.

[18]Artemis was Diana of the Ephesians; for Paul's trouble with the man who made her silver shrines, see Acts 19:23–40(41). This tree imagery also echoes Gen 2:9; 3:22 and possibly the cross as a tree; the writer has selected OT imagery in light of the local situation.

[19]Or the "throne" could refer to the great altar of Zeus on the hill 800 feet above the city (now magnificently preserved in a Berlin museum), while "Satan" may be related to the serpent emblem of the Aesculapius cult that flourished there.

TABLE 8. LETTERS TO THE ANGELS OF THE CHURCHES (REV 2–3)

Items in each Letter	**Ephesus** (2:1–7)	**Smyrna** (2:8–11)	**Pergamum** (2:12–17)
Titles or description of the speaker (Christ):	The One holding the seven stars in right hand and walking among the seven golden lampstands	The First and the Last who died and came to life	The One having the two-edged sword
Status of the church: GOOD THINGS acknowledged by speaker: .... Status of the church: BAD THINGS speaker has against them	I know your deeds, labor, endurance; not tolerant for wicked; you tested would-be apostles, finding them false; you endure patiently for my name's sake; not weary .... Have abandoned first love	I know your tribulation; rich despite poverty; blasphemed by those calling themselves Jews who are only a synagogue of Satan .... NOTHING BAD SAID	I know you dwell where Satan's throne is; you hold fast my name; did not deny faith in me; Antipas my faithful witness was killed among you where Satan lives .... Some hold teachings of Balaam who seduced Israel to idol food and immorality; some hold teaching of Nicolaitans
Admonitions; encouragements:	Remember whence you have fallen; repent and do the former works; if not, I will come to remove your lampstand from its place; you hate the works of the Nicolaitans which I hate	Do not fear what you are about to suffer; the devil will throw some in prison to test you, and you will have tribulation ten days; be faithful unto death, and I will give you the crown of life	Repent; if not, I will come soon and war against them with the sword of my mouth
Promise to whoever has ears to hear what the Spirit says to the churches:	To the victor I will give to eat from the tree of life which is in the paradise (-garden) of God	The victor will not be harmed by the second death	To the victor I will give the hidden manna and a white stone inscribed with a new name that no one knows except the recipient

TABLE 8. Continued

Thyatira (2:18–29)	**Sardis** (3:1–6)	**Philadelphia** (3:7–13)	**Laodicea** (3:14–21)
The Son of God, having eyes like a blazing fire and feet like burnished bronze	The One having the seven spirits of God and the seven stars	The Holy and True One having the key of David; opens—none can shut; shuts—none can open	The Amen, faithful and true Witness; the *Archē* (ruler or beginning) of God's creation
I know your deeds, love, faith, service, endurance; your latter deeds exceed former .... You tolerate the woman Jezebel a "prophetess" whose teaching seduces to immorality and idol food; I gave her time but she refuses to repent	NOTHING GOOD SAID .... I know your deeds; you have the name of being alive but are dead	I know your deeds; I have opened before you a door that can't be shut; you have little power but have kept my word and not denied my name .... NOTHING BAD SAID	NOTHING GOOD SAID .... I know your deeds; you are neither cold nor hot, but lukewarm; am about to spit you out of my mouth. You claim to be rich, affluent, not needy; you do not know that you are wretched, pitiable, poor, blind and naked
I will throw her into sickbed, and into great affliction those who commit adultery with her, unless they repent their works; I will put her children to death. All the churches will know I am the searcher of minds and hearts; I will give to each of you according to your works. But I lay no burden on the rest of you who do not hold this teaching, who have not known the deep things of Satan; but hold fast what you have till I come	Awake; strengthen what remains and is about to die; I have not found your works complete before my God. Remember and keep what you received and heard; repent; if you are not awake, I shall come as a thief at an hour you know not. But you have a few names who have not soiled their garments; they shall walk with me in white for they are worthy	I will make synagogue of Satan (not really Jews; they lie) come and bow before your feet. Because you kept my word of endurance, I will keep you from the hour of trial about to come on the whole world, to test those dwelling on earth. I come soon; keep what you have so that no one can take your crown	I advise you to buy from me gold refined by fire in order to be rich, and white garments to be clothed in lest your naked shame be shown, and eyesalve in order to see. Those whom I love I reprove and chastise, so be zealous and repent. Behold I stand at the door and knock; if anyone hears my voice and opens the door, I will enter and we will eat together
To the victor who keeps my works to the end I will give power over the nations to rule them with a rod of iron as when earthen vessels are broken, even as I have received it from my Father; I will also give the morning star	Thus the victor will be clad in white garments; and I shall not erase his/her name from the book of life but confess it before my Father and before His angels	I will make the victor a pillar in the temple of my God, never to leave it; I will write on him/her the name of my God and of His city (the new Jerusalem descending from heaven, from my God), and my own new name	To the victor I will grant to sit with me on my throne, as I was victorious and sat with my Father on His throne

(2:20–21) is a Pagan figure (a sibyl) or a woman in the Christian community we do not know. The designation of those at Smyrna and Philadelphia who "call themselves Jews" but are in fact a synagogue of Satan (2:9; 3:9) may reflect a usage where believers in Christ, instead of using the self-designation "Israel," speak of themselves as the true Jews. The overarching message that spans the seven letters and matches the theme of the rest of the book is to stand firm and make no concession to what the author designates as evil. The optimistic promises to the victor in each letter fit the goal of encouragement that is characteristic of apocalyptic.

C. Part I of the Revelatory Experience: (4:1–11:19). As we shall see in the subsection on *Structure* below, it is very difficult to diagnose the author's overall organizational plan in the body of Rev, once we get beyond the letters to the churches. Yet many scholars detect two large subdivisions, one beginning with the open door in heaven seen in 4:1, the other, after the opened heavens in 11:19, beginning with the great sign seen there in 12:1. It will be helpful to review the outline at the beginning of this Chapter to see the parallelism between the two. This first Part opens with chaps. 4 and 5 depicting the heavenly court centered on God and the Lamb; in that vision a scroll with seven seals is mentioned. Beginning in 6:1 the Lamb opens the seals, the seventh of which (8:1) introduces the visionary to seven angels with seven trumpets which begin to be blown in 8:6.

Visions of the Heavenly Court: The One Enthroned and the Lamb (4:1–5:14).[20] We have just acknowledged that the seer knows the local situation in Asia Minor; simultaneously he sees what is happening in heaven as part of his understanding that "what must take place after this" interweaves earth and heaven. Drawn from Ezek 1:26–28, precious gems, not anthropomorphic features, are used to describe the Lord God seated on the heavenly throne; and the lightning and the four living creatures echo the vision of the cherubim in Ezek 1:4–13; 10:18–22. The twenty-four elders/presbyters, however, seem to have a different background. The number twenty-four, used nowhere else in apocalyptic literature, may consist of two groups of twelve, representing the old and new Israel.[21] The hymn of worship to the enthroned God by the living creatures and the elders/presbyters reproduces the threefold "Holy" of the seraphim in Isa 6:3 and centers on the creation.

A matching vision in Rev 5 centers on the Lamb,[22] introduced by that personalized animal's ability to open the scroll with the seven seals which is

[20]For analogies in Jewish apocalyptic, see L. W. Hurtado, JSNT 25 (1985), 105–24.

[21]Others think all twenty-four are OT saints (sometimes including John the Baptist); still others see them as the angelic court.

[22]This title is used for Jesus some twenty-nine times in Rev; the background is either the Servant of the Lord who went to his death as a lamb to the slaughter (Isa 53:7), or the paschal lamb, or both.

written on both sides. The Lamb, which stands as though slain, is identified as the Lion of the tribe of Judah, the Root of David, who has conquered. (Clearly here paradoxical symbolism outstrips descriptive logic.) The hymn sung to Jesus the victorious Davidic Messiah has a refrain about being "worthy" similar to that in the hymn to God in the preceding chapter. Thus God and the Lamb are being put on virtually the same plane, with one being hailed as the creator and the other as the redeemer.

Seven Seals (6:1–8:1). The first four seals opened by the Lamb (6:1–8) are the four different colored horses, respectively white, red, black, and pale (green?), ridden by the famous four horsemen of the Apocalypse, representing respectively conquest, bloody strife, famine, and pestilence. The colored-horse imagery is derived from Zech 1:8–11; 6:1–7; and the description of the horsemen and the selection of the disasters, which are part of the eschatological judgment of God, may have been shaped by contemporary circumstances, e.g., the Parthian attacks upon the Romans.[23] The fifth seal (6:9–11) depicts souls of the martyrs (killed in the Neronian persecution in the 60s?) under the heavenly altar, which is the counterpart of the Jerusalem Temple altar of holocausts (see 11:1). They cry out for God's punitive justice on the shedders of blood, but the judgment is delayed a little longer until the predetermined number of martyrs be completed. The sixth seal (6:12–17) describes cosmic disturbances that are part of God's punishment. They are not to be taken literally (as they are by some who keep seeking to identify them in occurrences of our time), for they are the traditional imagery repeated again and again in apocalyptic.[24] Even the great ones of the earth will not escape the wrath of the Lamb.

Before he describes the seventh seal (8:1ff.), the seer narrates in chap. 7 an intervening vision wherein angels, holding back the four winds (cf. *I Enoch* 76), are told not to wreak harm until the servants of God have been sealed on their foreheads to indicate that they belong to God. It is not clear why the vision makes a distinction between the symbolic number of 144,000 Christians (12,000 from each tribe[25]) and the innumerable multitude from every nation tribe, people, and tongue whose white garments have been washed in the blood of the Lamb. The former group, the unblemished who are firstfruits by martyrdom or by continence [see Rev 14:1–5], is somehow

[23]Although sometimes in apocalyptic four animals have been used to describe past stages in world history, that is not the case here. The Parthian horsemen used bows (Rev 6:2).

[24]Earthquake in Amos 8:8; Joel 2:10; the sun and moon darkened in Amos 8:9; Joel 2:10; falling like figs in Nahum 3:12. These images are also found in the apocalypse attributed to Jesus in Mark 13:8,24,25.

[25]With Levi replacing Dan, the tribe which was considered unfaithful and idolatrous (Judg 18; I Kings 12:28–30) and which had Satan as a prince guardian (*Test. of Twelve Patriarchs: Dan* 5:6). Attested later is the tradition that the antimessiah or antichrist would come from the tribe of Dan.

more select; but scarcely Jewish Christian distinguished from Gentile Christians, or OT saints distinguished from followers of Christ. An interesting suggestion is that the two descriptions offer different perspectives of the church: The church is the heir and continuation of Israel (144,000 from the twelve tribes) and yet reaches out to the whole world (multitude from every nation, etc.). Or since the 144,000 are on earth waiting to be sealed, and the multitude are in heaven standing before the Lamb, the descriptions could be describing a church that is both earthly and heavenly, both militant and triumphant. (See Boring, *Revelation,* 129–31.) The peace brought by being in the presence of God is beautifully described in 7:16–17: no more hunger or thirst, no more burning or scorching heat, as the shepherding Lamb leads them to springs of living water.

Seven Trumpets (8:2–11:19). The opening of the seventh seal in 8:1 is climactic since logically the scroll can now be read and the judgment of the world should be revealed; but as in a Chinese-box puzzle, another seven (seven angels with seven trumpets) is now unveiled. The half-hour silence that begins the vision creates a contrast with the trumpet blasts to follow. In 8:3–5 the context becomes more highly liturgical and dramatic as incense[26] is mixed with the prayers of the saints, and there is accompanying thunder, lightning, and earthquake. The seven trumpets are divided as were the seven seals with an initial group of four (hail, sea turned to blood, star called "Wormwood," darkening of the heavenly bodies); but now the background is the plagues of the exodus.[27] As those plagues prepared for the liberation of God's people from Egypt, so these plagues prepare for the deliverance of God's people (those sealed; see 7:3) in the final days. That only one third is affected indicates that this is not the whole of God's judgment (cf. Ezek 5:2). These are eschatological symbols, and precise identifications with catastrophes that occur in our time are useless.

In Rev 4:8 the four living creatures sang a triple "Holy" to honor the Lord God seated on the throne; by contrast in 8:13 an eagle cries out with a triple woe, anticipating the last three trumpet blasts of judgment. The vision of the fifth trumpet (9:1–11) concerns locusts that look like battle horses emerging from the bottomless pit; it combines the eighth Egyptian plague (Exod 10:1–20) with Joel 1–2, and (along with the next woe) may also be colored by the Parthian invasions of the Empire from the East. The demonic is now being let loose, as indicated by the name of the king of the locusts: "Destruction" in both Hebrew and Greek (9:11). This is the first of the three woes.

[26]Is there any likelihood that incense had already become part of the Christian cult on earth, or is this simply the imagery of the Jerusalem Temple?

[27]Perhaps contemporary events added to the symbolism, e.g., the eruption of Vesuvius in AD 79 as a backdrop for the great mountain burning with fire in Rev 8:8.

The sixth trumpet (9:13–21) has angels release an immense number of cavalry from beyond the Euphrates who had been waiting for the appointed time. Despite these horrendous and diabolic punishments, the rest of humankind refuses to believe. As after the sixth seal, so after the sixth trumpet the sequence is interrupted to recount intermediary visions preparatory for the seventh in the series, a trumpet that will not be sounded till 11:15. In 4:1 the seer was taken up to heaven through an open door; but in 10:1–2 he is back on Patmos as the mighty angel comes down from heaven with the little scroll. This angel is described in the trappings of God, of the transfigured Jesus (Matt 17:2), and of Rev's initial vision of the Son of Man (1:12–16). Accompanying the angel's appearance are the seven thunders (10:4), which intriguingly the seer is forbidden to write down. (Is that because their contents are too horrible, or is it simply mystification?) This immense angel who spans land and sea warns that when the seventh trumpet is sounded, the mysterious plan of God promised by the prophets (Amos 3:7) will be fulfilled. The instruction given the seer to eat the little scroll, which is sweet in the mouth but bitter in the stomach, echoes Ezekiel's prophetic inauguration (2:8–3:3). Different from the larger scroll in 5:1,[28] it involves the pleasant news of the victory of the faithful and the bitter news of the painful disaster coming on the world that the seer has to prophesy.

The apocalyptic imagery of the visionary experience recounted in chap. 11 may also reflect contemporary history. From background supplied by the arrangement of the Jerusalem Temple, a distinction is made between the temple sanctuary area (*naos*) belonging to God and the court outside the sanctuary. The measurement of the sanctuary of God and those who worship there (11:1–2) is a sign of protection. That area may represent the heavenly or spiritual temple and/or the Christian community protected amidst destruction. By contrast the outer court that is given over to the Gentiles to trample may represent the earthly Temple of Jerusalem destroyed by the Romans in AD 70 (see Luke 21:24) and/or a Judaism no longer protected by God. Does the same time period throw any light on the two prophetic witnesses, two olive trees, and two lampstands (11:3–4) who will preach with miraculous power until they are killed by the beast from the pit in the great city where the Lord was killed? The 1,260 days (also 12:6) of their prophesying is equivalent to the forty-two months of the Gentiles' trampling the Temple court and the three-and-a-half times or years of 12:14; Luke 4:25; Jas 5:17. (These various ways of calculating half-seven are related to Dan 7:25; 9:27; 12:7 as the time when the evil Antiochus Epiphanes was let loose to perse-

[28]Various suggestions have been made about the two scrolls, e.g., larger = OT and smaller = NT; or larger = Part I of Rev and smaller = Part II.

cute the Jewish believers.) Is the seer speaking of purely eschatological figures, or were there two historical martyrs during the Roman destruction of Jerusalem that contributed to the picture? The OT accounts of Zerubbabel and Joshua the high priest (Zech 4:1–14), and of Moses and Elijah supply some of the imagery, but that does not exclude references to contemporary figures.[29] Jerusalem is meant; but the agents seem to be Gentiles not Jews, for they refuse to bury the bodies in a tomb (Rev 11:9). Since 14:8; 16:19; etc. use "the great city" for Rome, is there a double meaning, and is the martyrdom of Peter and Paul in Rome in the 60s in mind? In any case the two figures are made victorious by being taken up into heaven, and an earthquake wreaks havoc on the city. That is the second of the three woes (11:14).[30]

The seventh trumpet is finally sounded in 11:15–19, signaling that the kingdom of the world has become the kingdom of our Lord and his Christ, to which proclamation there is a hymn of the twenty-four elders/presbyters. This might make us think that the end of the world had come. But there is much more to follow, for the opening of God's temple in heaven to show the ark of the covenant (11:19)[31] introduces Part II, even as the open heavenly door in 4:1 introduced Part I.

D. Part II of the Revelatory Experience: 12:1–22:5. Just as Part I began with two chapters of inaugural visions, Part II begins with three chapters of inaugural visions. They introduce characters, the dragon and the two beasts, who will figure prominently in the rest of the book. Indeed these chapters have been looked on as the heart of Rev.

Visions of the Dragon, the Beasts, and the Lamb (12:1–14:20). Certainly some of the imagery of Gen 3:15–16 and the struggle between the serpent and the woman and her offspring are part of the background for chap. 12 (see 12:9). The woman clothed with the sun, having the moon under her feet and on her head the crown of twelve stars, represents Israel, echoing the dream of Joseph in Gen 37:9 where these symbols represent his father (Jacob/Israel), his mother, and his brothers (the sons of Jacob who were looked on as ancestors of the twelve tribes).[32] There is also the mythic sea-serpent imagery, which is found in biblical poetry as Leviathan or Rahab (Isa 27:1;

[29]R. J. Bauckham, JBL 95 (1976), 447–58 argues for the adaptation of Jewish expectations about Enoch and Elijah; A. Greve, NTA 22 (1978), #209, argues for contemporary figures: James the brother of John and James the brother of the Lord (martyred in the early 40s and 60s respectively).

[30]The third is to come quickly but Rev never spells out when it does come. Woes without a numerical specification are pronounced in Rev 12:12; 18:10,16,19.

[31]According to II Macc 2:4–8 the ark was hidden by Jeremiah in a secret place until the scattered people of God would be gathered again and the glory of the Lord seen in the cloud.

[32]In the description of the woman in 12:1, A. Yarbro Collins (*Combat* 71–76) sees an echo of the attributes of the high goddesses in the ancient world. In subsequent theology, especially the Middle Ages, the woman clothed with sun was identified with Mary the mother of Jesus.

51:9; Pss 74:14; 89:11; Job 26:12–13; etc.) and even outside Israel. Boring, *Revelation* 151, points to a myth centered on an island near Patmos, namely, Delos, the birthplace of Apollo, son of the God Zeus and slayer of the dragon of Delphi. This victory of light and life over darkness and death was appropriated by the Roman emperors as propaganda for the Golden Age that they were introducing, and both Augustus and Nero presented themselves as Apollo. Is Rev using the imagery of the myth to reverse the propaganda: Instead of slaying the dragon, the emperor is the tool of the dragon?

The metaphorical birth-giving of the people of God is an OT theme (Isa 26:17; 66:7–8), and Zion brings forth an individual child in *IV Ezra* 9:43–46; 10:40–49. In Rev the woman brings forth her child the Messiah (Ps 2:9) in pain; this is an instance of Jewish expectations of the birth pangs of the Messiah, meaning the wretchedness of the world situation that becomes a signal for the coming of God-sent deliverance (Micah 4:9–10). The dragon (the ancient serpent, Satan) tries to devour the child, who escapes by being taken up to God. This leads to a war in heaven; and the dragon is cast down to earth[33] where, in anger with the woman, he makes war on her offspring (12:6,13,17). There is no reference here to Jesus' physical birth or Jesus as an infant (and then a jump to his ascension to God), but to Jesus' "birth" as the Messiah through his death. The birth symbolism for death is found in John 16:20–22: On the night before he dies, Jesus says that the disciples' sorrow is like that of a woman about to give birth to a child; but that sorrow will be forgotten for joy once the child is born, i.e., through Jesus' return from the dead.[34] As for Satanic opposition, John 12:31; 14:30; 16:11 depict Jesus' passion and death as a struggle with the Prince of this World who is cast out even as Jesus returns to his Father. The subsequent struggle portrayed in Rev between the dragon and the woman (now the church[35]) and her children in the wilderness[36] lasts 1,260 days and three-times-and-a-half, i.e., the time of persecution that will lead into the endtime; but she is pro-

[33]The story in 12:7–12 of the victory by Michael and his angels in a great battle and the rejoicing in heaven may be an insert from another source. An earlier dispute between Michael and Satan over the body of Moses is mentioned in Jude 9.

[34]Acts 2:24 speaks of God raising up Jesus, having loosed the "pangs" of death; Col 1:18; Rev 1:5 refer to Jesus as the firstborn from the dead; and Rom 1:4; Acts 13:33 regard the resurrection of Jesus as the begetting of God's Son.

[35]The coming of the Messiah through the sufferings of Israel is run together with the sufferings of the church that will lead to the second coming of the Messiah, for the church must remain in the wilderness after the Messiah is taken up to God, until he returns again. It is debated whether this woman is also the bride of the Lamb (Rev 19:7) and the New Jerusalem (21:2,9). The plasticity of apocalyptic symbols could allow a figure who is both mother and bride, and both on earth and coming down from heaven.

[36]Is this a reference to the flight of Christians from Jerusalem *ca.* 66 across the Jordan to Pella at the time of the Jewish Revolt against Rome? Thus S. G. Sowers, TZ 26 (1990), 305–20.

tected by God (with eagle's wings; cf. Exod 19:4). Taking his stand on the sands of the sea (Rev 12:18[17]), the dragon employs in his campaign on earth two great beasts, one from the sea, the other from the land.[37]

The first beast rises from the sea (13:1–10) with ten horns and seven heads. Dan 7 had illustrated the use of four chimerical beasts to represent world empires, with the ten horns on the fourth beast representing rulers. Accordingly the beast in Rev combines elements of Dan's four as a way of symbolizing that the Roman Empire (which came to the cities addressed in Rev from the West across the sea) is as evil as all the others combined. The seven heads are explained in 17:9–11 as the seven hills (of Rome) and also as the seven kings, five of whom have fallen, the sixth is, and the seventh is yet to come for a little while; then that passage adds an eighth that goes to perdition. Domitian is probably to be counted as the eighth,[38] the last one known to the author if he wrote during Domitian's reign. The claim that one of the heads seemed to have a mortal wound but was healed may represent a legend of Nero redivivus (i.e., come back to life).[39] In the imagery of Rev, as well as waging war against the holy ones (13:7), the Empire had caused people to worship the devil (13:4), and thus to be excluded from the book of life (13:8).

The second beast, the one from the earth (13:11–18), is an evil parody of Christ. It has two horns like a lamb but it speaks like a dragon; later it is associated with a false prophet (16:13; 19:20; 20:10); it works signs and wonders, like those of Elijah; it has people marked on the right hand or the forehead, even as the servants of God are sealed on their forehead (7:3; 14:1). This beast portrayed as rising from the earth, i.e., from the land mass of Asia Minor, is emperor worship[40] (and the Pagan priesthood promoting

[37]This same imagery of the two beasts is found in *I Enoch* 60:7–8; *IV Ezra* 6:49–52; *II Baruch* 29:3–4.

[38]Various ways of understanding the counting have been proposed, depending on whether one starts with Julius Caesar or Augustus, and on which emperors are counted (see Table 1 above for chronology). If one counts from Augustus, the first five who had fallen would include Nero; if one omits the three transitional emperors of the year 69 (is that justifiable?), the sixth "who is" would be Vespasian, and the seventh who is to come but remain briefly would be Titus, Domitian's predecessor, who reigned only three years. If Rev was written during Domitian's reign, it is being backdated to Vespasian's time (when the Jerusalem Temple was destroyed). Backdating is not unusual in apocalypses, for, as explained on p. 776 above, there is then accurate "advance" knowledge up to the present.

[39]Juvenal, *Satires* 4.38 and Pliny the Younger, *Panegyric* 53.3–4, both writing just after Domitian's reign, regarded that emperor as a second Nero.

[40]S. J. Scherrer, JBL 103 (1984), 599–610, argues that signs and wonders were part of the panoply of emperor worship. See also L. J. Kreitzer, BA 53 (1990), 210–17; J. N. Kraybill, *Imperial Cult and Commerce in John's Apocalypse* (Sheffield: Academic, 1996). Provincial cults approved by the Roman Senate existed in Pergamum for Augustus, and in Smyrna for Tiberius and Livia; S. Friesen, BAR 19 (#3; 1993), 24–37, contends that the large temple of the Sebastoi at Ephesus was dedicated to Vespasian, Titus, and Domitian.

it), which began very early there. The wound of the beast by the sword (13:14) may be Nero's suicide; the survival, Domitian's reign. The description in 13:18 ends with perhaps the most famous image in Rev: The number of the beast, a human number that calls for understanding, is 666. By gematria (where letters also serve as numerals, as in Latin) the Hebrew consonants transliterating the Greek form of the name Nero Caesar total to 666.[41]

The Lamb and the symbolically numbered 144,000 (14:1–5) are a consoling picture, meant to reassure Christians that they will survive the assaults of the dragon and the two beasts. (The image of the harp music enters many popular and even humorous pictures of heaven.) The language of chastity certainly means that they have not yielded to idolatry, but may also be an allusion to sexual continence (I Cor 7:7–8).

Three angels (14:6–13) proclaim solemn admonitions: an eternal gospel directed to the whole world, stressing the need to glorify God because the hour of judgment has come; a woe to Babylon (Rome); and a severe warning that those who have worshiped the beast and bear its mark will undergo hell fire. A voice from heaven blesses those who die in the Lord. Then (14:14–20) the Son of Man with a sickle in his hand and more angels execute a bloody judgment, throwing the vintage of the earth into the winepress of God's fury.

Seven Plagues and Seven Bowls (15:1–16:21). Comparable to the seven seals and trumpets of Part I of Rev, we now hear of seven plagues and seven bowls containing them that portend the final judgment. But before they are poured out, we are shown in chap. 15 a scene in the heavenly court where the Song of Moses is sung, echoing the victory of the Hebrews crossing the Reed (Red) Sea (cf. Exod 15:1–18). Amid clouds of incense the heavenly temple/tabernacle supplies the angels with the contents of the bowls. Once more the plagues preceding the exodus of the Hebrews from Egypt (Exod 7–10) serve as background, although this time their effect is no longer limited to one third of the world as it was with the seals. The frogs that issue from the mouth of the false prophet are three demonic spirits who perform signs like the magicians of Egypt. A famous image is supplied by Rev 16:16: Armageddon as the place of the final battle with the forces of evil.[42] The seventh bowl (16:17–21) marks the climax of God's action; its contents smash Rome into parts as a voice proclaims, "It is done."

Judgment of Babylon, the Great Harlot (17:1–19:10). This fall of Rome is now described in vivid detail, following the OT convention of portraying

[41]An ancient variant is 616 (noted in the footnotes of many Bibles), which would be the numerical value of the Hebrew letters transliterating the Latin form of the name Nero Caesar.

[42]A Greek transliteration of Hebrew *har Mĕgiddô,* the Mount of Megiddo, i.e., the pass through the plain of Esdraelon in Israel where armies from the North and the South often clashed.

cities marked by idolatry or godlessness (Tyre, Babylon, Nineveh) as harlots, bedecked by wealth from commerce, and those who accept their authority as fornicators who will lament over the city's fall (Isa 23; 47; Nahum 3; Jer 50–51; Ezek 16; 23; 26–27[43]). In Rev 17:7 the angel explains the mysterious meaning of the harlot and the beast from the sea which she rides, but we have to speculate about the symbolism of the numbers (see above under 13:1). The doom of Babylon/Rome, drunk with the blood of the martyrs (particularly under Nero), is dramatically proclaimed in chap. 18 by angels in a great lament. Just as ancient Babylon was symbolically to be cast into the Euphrates (Jer 51:63–64), so Babylon/Rome is to be thrown into the sea (Rev 18:21).[44] Counterpoised to the lament on earth is a chorus of joy in heaven (19:1–10). In that rejoicing we hear of the marriage of the Lamb and his bride (19:7–9) that anticipates the final vision of the book. The theme of the marriage of God and the people of God stems from the OT (Hos 2:1–25[23]; Isa 54:4–8; Ezek 16—sometimes in contexts of unfaithfulness). Now it has been shifted to Christ and the believers (John 3:29; II Cor 11:2; Eph 5:23–32).

Victory of Christ and the End of History (19:11–22:5).[45] Reusing elements from previous visions, the seer describes Christ as a great warrior leading the armies of heaven, as the King of kings, and the Lord of lords (19:16; I Tim 6:15). The carrion birds are called together to eat the defeated armies[46] that followed the two beasts, both of whom are thrown into the lake of fire symbolizing eternal damnation. Chap. 20 describes the millennial reign of Christ, which has given rise to numerous theological disputes in the history of Christianity (subsection below). Only the Satanic dragon remains from the triad of beasts, and now he is shut up in a pit for a thousand years while Christ and the Christian martyr saints reign on earth. The saints who died once will live forever as priests of God and of Christ, for over them the second death (final destruction) has no power (20:6). After the thousand

[43]J.-P. Ruiz, *Ezekiel in the Apocalypse [16:17–19:10]* (Frankfurt: Lang, 1989).

[44]E. Corsini (*Revelation*) contends that Rev does not refer to the future (second coming, etc.) but to the first coming of Christ and the aftermath of his crucifixion and resurrection. He would see the harlot as Jerusalem (which put Jesus to death), for that city was destroyed by the Roman beast.

[45]On this section, see M. Rissi, *The Future of the World* (SBT NS 23; London: SCM, 1972); W. J. Dumbrell, *The End of the Beginning: Revelation 21–22 and the Old Testament* (Exeter: Paternoster, 1985).

[46]Some find the picture of the Word of God with his robes dipped in blood and the banquet to eat the flesh of enemies (19:13,17,18) too vengeful for the moral standards of the gospel. But as A. Yarbro Collins has pointed out, Rev functions in part as a catharsis, to help those who feel themselves powerless before ruling authorities to get a sense that they are powerful since God is on their side and will make them triumph. Thus a strong depiction of the victory is necessary to accomplish the goal of overcoming marginalization and frustration.

years Satan is let loose to gather Gog and Magog, all the nations of the earth;[47] but fire will come down from heaven and consume them, while the dragon will now be thrown into the lake of fire where the beasts had been cast. As both death and hell yield up the deceased, the dead are judged before the throne of God according to what is written in the book of life; and the second death takes place (20:11–15).

To replace the devastation of the first heaven and first earth, there is a new heaven and a new earth, and a New Jerusalem that comes down from heaven (21:1–22:5), like a bride adorned for her husband (see 19:9). The dwelling of God with human beings is described lyrically, offering hope for all who live in the present vale of tears: no more tears, death, or pain, or night; a city as beautiful as a precious jewel built on foundation walls bearing the names of the Twelve Apostles of the Lamb; a city perfectly cubic in shape, immense enough to contain all the saints. In that city there is no temple or sun or moon, for the Lord God and the Lamb are present there as its light; and nothing unclean is found within its perimeters. As in Paradise of old, a river of the water of life flows through the city watering the tree of life; and the saints shall live there forever.

E. EPILOGUE (WITH CONCLUDING BLESSING) 22:6–21. John the seer and the words of prophecy are highlighted, just as they were in the Prologue (1:1–3). He is told not to seal up the words, for the time is near. As in the inaugural vision before the Seven Letters (1:9–20), the Lord God, speaking as the Alpha and the Omega, lends authority to the words of warning and of invitation heard by the seer. The audience is admonished not to add or subtract from the prophetic words of the book.[48] In response to the affirmation of Jesus that he is coming soon, John the seer utters an impassioned "Amen. Come, Lord Jesus," an echo of one of the oldest prayers used by Christians (I Cor 16:22).

Having begun in letter format, Rev ends in the same way (22:21) with a very simple Concluding Blessing on "all the saints," i.e., those who have not yielded to Satan or the beasts.

[47]Gog of Magog (i.e., of the land of Gog) leads the forces against Israel in Ezek 38–39; the name is probably derived from Gyges, the 7th-century BC king of Lydia. That one person in Ezek has become two in Rev illustrates the plasticity of images in apocalyptic.

[48]Because eventually Rev was placed last in the canon, some have taken this admonition (21:18–19) to refer to the NT: no more Scripture and nothing authoritative beyond the NT. That is not what was meant. This is simply another example of traditional care for preserving an apocalypse, e.g., *II Baruch* 87:1 and *IV Ezra* 14:46–47 (where Ezra is cautioned to keep the seventy apocalyptic books from the public). Moreover, a book like II Pet was written after Rev and became part of the NT.

Structure of the Book

One commentator has observed that almost every interpreter brings to the study of the structure of Rev a set of presuppositions that find expression in the ultimate outline suggested for the book, with the result that there are almost as many outlines as there are interpreters.[49] Scholars discern structure in two ways: on the basis of either external factors or internal contents. External factors suppose a judgment about what has most shaped the book, e.g., Christian liturgy, Greek drama, imperial games, or set apocalyptic patterns visible in other apocalypses, Jewish and Christian. Obviously there are elements that Rev shares with these external factors, but it is questionable whether any one of them so dominated the author's mind that he structured his book on it. As for the set pattern discernible in other apocalypses, as I pointed out above (pp. 776, 778) the combination of prophecy and apocalyptic in Rev has some unique features. Although it might seem secure to allow the internal contents to speak for themselves, that is not so easy in apocalyptic. Apocalypses introduce readers into the mysterious plans of God, revealing part of what is concealed from normal vision. Thus, inevitably in their own procedures there is an atmosphere of the mysterious and of concealment. Almost by design the authors proceed in a way that defies human logic. For instance, it seems illogical that having explained six of the seven seals and trumpets, the seer of Rev goes off on a tangent before explaining the seventh, and in the case of the seals that the seventh begins another seven. Also it is not unusual that a formula, having been repeated several times, will suddenly be varied, without any intent to change meaning or give a different direction.[50] Thus in this literary genre structure is often quite difficult to diagnose from the contents.

By way of example, A. Yarbro Collins (*Combat* 19) concentrates on an organizational principle of seven, and between the Prologue and Epilogue finds six interlocking sets of seven: letter messages (1:9–3:22), seals (4:1–8:5), trumpets (8:2–11:19), unnumbered visions (12:1–15:4), bowls (15:1–16:21), unnumbered visions (19:11–21:8). As we have mentioned, consistency is not always characteristic of patterns in apocalyptic; yet if seven is the organizing pattern, one is tempted to ask why there are six sevens and

[49]A careful discussion of theories is found in C. R. Smith, NovT 36 (1994), 373–93. J. Lambrecht is correct in *L'Apocalypse* 77–104 when he says that three sections of Rev are agreed on: the Prologue (1:1–3); the Letters to the Seven Churches (1:4–3:22); and the Epilogue and blessing (22:6–21). Therefore most disputes are about the structure of 4:1–22:5.

[50]There are good biblical antecedents for such variation, e.g., of seven references to punishment in Amos 1–2, all are phrased as "I will send fire," except the fifth (1:14) which suddenly shifts to "I will kindle fire."

not seven,[51] why some sevens are numbered and some are not, why she has to count two passages as interspersed appendixes (17:1–19:10 and 21:9–22:5) because they do not fit into the seven pattern, and why the unnumbered visions might not also be considered appendixes.[52]

There seems to be a certain amount of repetition in Rev because several times the impression is given that the end has come (11:15–19; 16:17–21), only to have more visions. That may simply be part of the literary form, as a way of expressing the inexpressible. Part II in relation to Part I (pp. 786, 790 above) seems repetitive. Scholars have explained this in various ways: (a) Some contend that the two parts treat the same material from different points of view,[53] e.g., Part I deals with God's judgment on the entire world, while Part II treats that material from the point of view of the church with stress on God's control of the demonic. A variant is that Part I deals with the church and the Jewish world; Part II, with the church and the Gentiles. Yet the themes are hard to divide so evenly. (b) Others think of temporal sequence with Part I referring to things that have already happened and Part II of things yet to come.[54] True, there are some references to past events in Rev, e.g., in 11:2 the court outside the sanctuary (= the earthly Temple of Jerusalem?) "has been given" to the nations to be trampled; but the author does not symbolically lay out past history in detail as do other apocalypses. (c) Still another approach would detect a spiraling movement from glory in heaven to tribulation on earth and back. The heavenly chaps. would be (in whole or part) 4–5; 7:9–17; 11:15–19; 15; 19; 21:1–22:5; the intervening earthly chaps. would be 6:1–7:8; 8:1–11:14; 12–14; 16–18; 20. That approach, besides emphasizing the heaven-earth dimension of Rev, blocks the book from being misinterpreted as vision of sequential future history.

With such a variance of opinions I have thought it wise above not to advocate any particular structure. The division I have given is simply a way of listing contents and makes no pretense of being the author's intended plan. A knowledge of contents is an essential help to readers if they then wish through further reading to investigate in greater depth the issue of structure.

[51]There is another way of counting a seven-part structure, with Prologue and the Epilogue as the first and the seventh, separated by five sections.

[52]Smith (n. 49 above) offers several other quite different outlines based on contents and favors one based on seeing the phrase "in the Spirit" (1:10–11; 4:1–2; 17:1–3; 21:9–10) as beginning sections. See also E. Schüssler Fiorenza, *Book* 159–80.

[53]The idea that there is a recapitulation goes back as far as Victorinus of Pettau (*ca.* 300). C. H. Giblin, CBQ 56 (1994), 81–95, sees three recapitulating stages, progressively enunciating God's holy war on behalf of God's harassed people.

[54]A variant is the approach of the French scholar M.-É. Boismard (JB) who would find two apocalypses, one written in the time of Nero, and one written in the time of Domitian, combined in a very complicated pattern in Rev.

The Role of Liturgy[55]

The visions of the seer of Rev include simultaneously what is happening in heaven and on earth. The vision of heaven is set in a liturgical context. The one like a Son of Man who speaks to John and utters a message for the angels of the seven churches stands in the midst of seven gold lampstands (1:12–13). The worship of God and the Lamb dominates what is happening in heaven. In chap. 4, with an appearance like that of precious gems, God is seated on a throne accompanied by twenty-four elders/presbyters on their thrones.[56] A menorah of seven torches burns before the throne. Like the seraphim in Isa 6, the four living creatures who are cherubim chant a trisagion (the hymn with the threefold "Holy"); and all join in a "Worthy are you" hymn praising the creator God.[57] In chap. 5, as the Lamb stands in this setting and receives a scroll, a new "Worthy are you" hymn is sung praising Jesus for having ransomed people from every background, until every creature in heaven and on earth and under the earth joins in with a beatitude to One on the throne and the Lamb. Other hymns are scattered throughout the book, along with harp music (14:2). In 11:19 we are told of God's temple in heaven that is opened to show the ark of the covenant; and from that temple amidst the smoke of God's glory come forth angels carrying bowls (presumably full of burning coals) to be poured on the earth (15:5–8). Rev ends (22:20) by echoing the traditional Christian prayer, "Amen, come, Lord Jesus."

Much of the liturgical imagery is patterned on the Jerusalem Temple,[58] the place of God's glory on earth with its altar, hymns, lampstands, and incense. The several references to Christians as priests to God, seemingly both now and in the eschatological future (n. 15 above), also come from that ambiance. On a general scale, A. Farrer thinks of Rev drawing on images that were used at various Jewish feasts. Another suggestion is that the seer envi-

[55]M. H. Shepherd, *The Paschal Liturgy and the Apocalypse* (Richmond: Knox, 1960); also: O. A. Piper, *Church History* 20 (1951), 10–22; L. Mowry, JBL 71 (1952), 75–84. In terms of the divine worship of Jesus, R. J. Bauckham, NTS 27 (1980–81), 322–41, compares Rev and the *Ascension of Isaiah* and argues that this worship was typical of Christian apocalyptic.

[56]Probably in a semicircle with God's throne in the middle and twelve on each side.

[57]Among the many hymns in the NT (pp. 232, 489 above), those in Rev are the most specifically identified as such. They are of a choral type and not spontaneous or individual utterances. J. J. O'Rourke, CBQ 30 (1968), 399–409, argues for the use of preexistent hymnic material in the composition. W. C. van Unnik, *Mélanges Bibliques en hommage au Béde Rigaux,* eds. A. Descamps and A. de Halleux (Gembloux: Duculot, 1970), 445–61, points to wide use of "worthy" in the Hellenistic world, particularly in relation to divine secrets and holy books.

[58]Jewish liturgical background is not peculiar to Rev. The author of Heb, thinking of the Tabernacle, describes Christ the priest ascending to heaven and opening the veil of the celestial Holy of Holies to enter with his blood and thus to complete what was begun on the cross.

sions the celebration of an ideal Feast of Tabernacles in the heavenly Jerusalem, based on Zech 14:1–21.[59]

A major question is whether *Christian* liturgy also shaped the author's imagery. The frequency of white garments (3:5,18; 4:4; etc.) has suggested to some scholars a background wherein the newly baptized put on white garments. More specifically, because of the strong emphasis on the Lamb, M. H. Shepherd would propose a paschal liturgy at which people were baptized. Since the seer receives his vision on the Lord's day (1:10), the weekly Christian reunion for worship is a possibility. That could be the context in which Rev would have been read aloud and heard (1:3; 22:18).[60] Some would find a reference to the eucharistic meal in "the marriage supper of the Lamb" (19:9). Most evidence for early Christian worship/feasts stems from documents (Ignatius, Justin, Hippolytus) that are dated from a period after that of Rev. We can list parallels to Rev as a possible witness to the liturgical atmosphere that influenced the seer, but it is also possible that Rev influenced those later witnesses. *Ca.* AD 110 Ignatius (*Magnesians* 6.1; also *Trallians* 3.1) describes the bishop having the first seat among the elders/presbyters like God and the assembly of the apostles. Did that shape John's vision of the heavenly assembly with God on the throne and the twenty-four elders/presbyters around God? *Ca.* AD 96–120 *I Clement* 34.6–7 describes the singing of the trisagion by the heavenly myriads (as do the seraphim in Rev 4:8), and then urges Christians, being assembled with one accord, to cry out with one voice to God. In considering the frequency of hymns in Rev, we should remember the common view that Rev was written in western Asia Minor in the late 90s. In his investigation of Christians in a nearby region of Asia Minor ten or fifteen years later, Pliny the Younger (*Epistles* 10.96.7) reported that they sang hymns to Christ as to a god. *Ca.* AD 150, drawing on a liturgy that must have been in place for some time, Justin (*Apology* 1.67) describes a weekly meeting on the Lord's Day when the Gospels and the writings of the prophets were read. Did that practice influence John's vision of the scroll being unsealed during the heavenly liturgy? According to Justin's *Dialogue* 41 the purpose of the eucharistic remembrance among Christians was to give thanks to God for having created the world and for having delivered us from evil—the themes of the "Worthy" hymns in Rev 4 and 5.[61] From all this what can be said is that by the 2d century Christians believed not only that

[59]J. A. Draper, JSNT 19 (1983), 133–47; H. Ulfgard, *Feast and Future. Revelation 7:9–17 and the Feast of Tabernacles* (CBNTS 22; Stockholm: Almqvist, 1989).

[60]See D. L. Barr, *Interpretation* 40 (1986), 243–56.

[61]This outlook is still found today in the Preface of the eucharistic canon, which begins by acclaiming the worthiness of God to be praised and ends with a threefold "Holy."

the earthly liturgy was meant to have a simultaneity with the heavenly worship so that one participated in the other, but also that they should follow the same pattern. Given the enormous distortion of Rev today as a detailed prediction of the future, the use of the book in the liturgical readings of the church year may be a healthy context for getting close to at least one aspect of the original milieu.[62]

Millenarianism (The Thousand-Year Reign: 20:4–6)

In its prevision Rev states that at the end those who had been beheaded for their testimony to Jesus and for the word of God and who had not worshiped the beast came to life and reigned with Christ a thousand years, while the rest of the dead did not come to life until the thousand years were ended. The origins of such a belief may be found in a certain tension between prophetic and apocalyptic expectations. If one reviews the history of Messianism (e.g., NJBC 77:152–63), an anticipation that survived the Babylonian exile was that one day God would restore the kingdom of David under a model anointed king, the Messiah; indeed, earlier Scripture was reread with this understanding (e.g., Amos 9:11). Even though idealized and pictured as definitive, this would be an earthly, historical kingdom, and most often its relation to the endtime was not specified. On the other hand, in a pessimistic view of history, some apocalyptic literature pictured God's direct final intervention without any mention of the restoration of the Davidic kingdom (Isa 24–27; Dan; *Assumption of Moses; Apocalypse of Abraham*).

One way of combining the two expectations was to posit two divine interventions: (1) a restoration of an earthly kingdom[63] or period of blissful prosperity to be followed by (2) God's endtime victory and judgment. Where there was a strong influence of Greco-Roman thought, the classical expectation of a Golden Age may have shaped the Jewish depiction of the messianic kingdom. Various numbers were used to symbolize the duration of the expected period. In a section described as an "Apocalypse of Weeks" (3d–2d century BC), *I Enoch* 91:12–17 proposes that after seven of the ten weeks of years are past, the eighth is to be a period of righteousness; the ninth is the

[62]See U. Vanni, NTS 37 (1991), 348–72. For promotion of this idea, see D. Dumm, *Worship* 63 (1989), 482–89; J.-P. Ruiz, *ibid.* 68 (1994), 482–504. The latter cites Vatican Council II, *Sacrosanctum Concilium* (on the Liturgy) 1.8: "In the earthly liturgy, by way of foretaste, we share in that heavenly liturgy which is celebrated in the holy city of Jerusalem." C. Rowland, *Priests and People* 8 (1994), 428–31, an expert in apocalyptic, narrates his attempt to preach on Rev in the context of Anglican evensong.

[63]A. S. Geyser, NTS 28 (1982), 388–99, argues that the author of Rev was expecting the Messiah to restore the twelve-tribe Jewish kingdom and was representative of the expectation of the Judean church.

period marked for destruction; and in the tenth the angels are judged, leading to eternity. In *IV Ezra* 7:28 (late 1st century AD), after God brings an evil age to an end, the Messiah reigns for 400 years with the righteous on earth. Then comes the resurrection of the dead and the judgment. A similar tradition of the souls of the righteous being raised at the time of the Messiah's appearance is found in *II Baruch* 29–30 (early 2d century AD).

In Christian apocalyptic I Cor 15:23–28 offers this sequence: first the resurrection of Christ; then of those belonging to Christ who reigns until he has put all his enemies under his feet; then the end when Christ delivers the kingdom to God destroying every rule, authority, and power. In the late-1st century AD *Ascension of Isaiah* 4.14–17, after Beliar has ruled as an antichrist for 1,332 days, the Lord will come with his angels and saints and throw Beliar into Gehenna; then there will be a period of rest for those who are in this world, and after that they will be taken up into heaven.

The variation of the numbers in these expectations should warn us that none of the writers had an exact knowledge about future time spans and (for the most part) probably never intended to convey exactness. Indeed, according to the analysis above of the expectation of a first divine intervention to establish a kingdom or ideal time in this world and of a second divine intervention to replace the temporal world by the eternal, we can see the two interventions simply as symbolic ways of predicting divine victory over evil forces that are an obstacle to God's kingdom or rule over the whole world. The writer of Rev, then, would have used the thousand-year reign of Jesus on earth, not to describe a historical kingdom, but as a way of saying that eschatological expectations will be fulfilled.

Nevertheless, throughout Christian history some have taken the thousand years of Rev quite literally and speculated about it. (It is worth reminding ourselves that only one passage in Rev consisting of two verses mentions the millennium; there has been an enormous, indeed an extravagant growth, from small beginnings.) That belief was widely held in the 2d and 3d centuries among those considered orthodox (Papias, Justin, Tertullian, Hippolytus, Lactantius) and heterodox (Cerinthus and Montanus). However, the danger that the expectations of the abundance and happiness were becoming too sensual and worldly gradually led to a rejection of millenarianism (chiliasm). Origen allegorized the millennium to represent the spiritual kingdom of God on earth; Augustine understood the first resurrection to refer to conversion and the death to sin, and the second resurrection to refer to the resurrection of the body at the end of time. Church writers of the 4th century tell us that Apollinaris (Apollinarius) of Laodicea was a chiliast (his writings on the subject have been lost), and the Ecumenical Council of Ephesus (431) condemned his fanciful theories.

Especially in the subsequent Western church, from time to time millennial expectations have been revived in various forms. The Cistercian Joachim of Flora (1130–1202), after a thousand years of Christianity, proclaimed a new era of the Spirit, represented by monasticism, to come about 1260, which would move beyond the era of the Father (OT) and of the Son (NT). Although millenarianism was rejected by the Augsburg Confession, some "left-wing" groups spawned by the Reformation embraced it, e.g., the Zwickau prophets, T. Münzer, and John of Leiden. The coming of persecuted Protestants to North America was often accompanied by hopes of establishing a religiously perfect kingdom in the New World. In the United States during the 19th century millennialist groups proliferated, usually with one foot in Dan and the other in Rev, and sometimes reinforced by private revelations. These are exemplified in the followers of William Miller and Ellen G. White (Seventh-Day Adventists), Joseph Smith (Mormons), and Charles T. Russell (Jehovah's Witnesses). In some evangelical groups sharp divisions arose between Premillennialists and Postmillennialists: the former with the view that the golden age will come only after the evil present era is destroyed by the second coming; the latter, exhibiting optimistic liberalism, with the view that the present age will be gradually transformed into the millennium by natural progress in society and religious reform. A form of the premillennial movement featured dispensationalism, identifying periods of time in world history (e.g., as exemplified in the Scofield Reference Bible). Usually the thesis was that we are living in the sixth dispensation, and the seventh is about to come. The larger, established churches remain convinced that, although the final stage in the divine plan will be accomplished through Jesus Christ, the thousand years are symbolic and no one knows when or how the end of the world will come. Acts 1:7 sets the tone: "It is not for you to know times and seasons that have been set by the Father's own authority." As late as 1944 the Roman Catholic Church condemned even a mitigated form of millenarianism (DBS 3839).[64]

Authorship

The seer of Rev four times calls himself John. Justin Martyr (*Dialogue* 81.4) identifies him as John, one of the apostles of Christ. That he was an apostle is highly implausible since he has a vision of the New Jerusalem

[64]For a bibliography on millennial writing, see J. R. Stone, *A Guide to the End of the World* (New York: Garland, 1993); for a survey and exegesis, see J. W. Mealy, *After the Thousand Years: Resurrection and Judgment in Revelation 20* (JSNTSup 70; Sheffield: JSOT, 1992). An evaluation is supplied by S. Harding, "Imagining the Last Days," in *Accounting for Fundamentalism*, eds. M. E. Marty and R. S. Appleby (Vol. 4 in a 5-volume project; Univ. of Chicago, 1994), 57–78.

descending from heaven with the names of the twelve apostles of the Lamb on its foundation walls (21:14), thus implicitly a group distinct from himself. Already in the 3d century a careful study of language, style, and thought correctly convinced Dionysius of Alexandria that Rev was not written by the man responsible for John's Gospel[65] and I-II-III John, whom he assumed to be John the apostle. Consequently Dionysius attributed Rev to John the Elder/Presbyter—a distinction reflecting the reference to two Johns, John one of the Twelve and John the presbyter, by Papias (*ca.* 125; p. 398 above). However, since "John" was a common name among NT Christians, the conclusion that does the most justice to the evidence is that the seer of Rev was an otherwise unknown John.

What can be learned about the author from Rev itself? The Greek of the work, which is the poorest in the NT to the point of being ungrammatical, probably reflects one whose native language was Aramaic or Hebrew.[66] The impact produced by the fall of Jerusalem is important in shaping his vision, and so the thesis of some scholars that he was a Jewish Christian apocalyptic prophet who left Palestine at the time of the Jewish Revolt in the late 60s and went to Asia Minor (probably to Ephesus from which he was exiled to Patmos) has plausibility. Like an OT prophet he can speak authoritatively to the Asia Minor Christians,[67] and regard himself as the voice of the Spirit (see the refrain "the Spirit says to the churches" at the end of each of the seven letters). His apocalypse/prophecy is not simply a rereading of the OT but an eschatological message from God in comment on the present situation.[68]

The issue of Rev's relationship to the Johannine tradition is complicated. Certainly it should not be considered a Johannine writing in the sense in which that designation is applied to John and I-II-III John. Yet there are interesting parallels to elements in the Johannine literature, especially the

[65]The Greek of the Gospel of John is simple but grammatical. The Greek of Rev is sometimes irregular. Many key Gospel terms are absent from Rev, e.g., "truth," "eternal life," "remain in," "darkness," and "believe."

[66]G. Mussies, *The Morphology of Koine Greek as Used in the Apocalypse of St. John* (NovTSup 27; Leiden: Brill, 1971). S. Thompson, *The Apocalypse and Semitic Syntax* (SNTSMS 52; Cambridge Univ., 1986), would argue that Rev represents a Jewish-Greek dialect. S. E. Porter, NTS 35 (1989), 582–603, suggests simply that the author has limited linguistic Greek competence, with the result that his writing falls within the vulgar range of 1st-century Greek. More provocative (and less likely) suggestions are that the author deliberately used poor Greek to show his contempt for Greco-Roman civilization or combined the profane language of this world with the inexpressible, sacred language of the heavenly court.

[67]He knows the churches and seems to be known to them, and so he may have visited them all. Clearly there are many prophets (11:18; 22:9); but behind the letters to the churches there is an assumption of the writer's authority that suggests more than an itinerant, wandering prophet. Aune, "Social," makes an interesting point that, despite his authority, he seeks to establish a sympathetic rapport with his addressees: "Your brother and companion in the tribulation" (1:9).

[68]E. Schüssler Fiorenza, *Book* 133–56, esp. 135–37.

Gospel, that suggest a relationship,[69] e.g.: Christ as the Lamb (but different vocabulary); Christ as the source of living water (John 7:37–39; Rev 22:1); Christ as light (John 8:12; Rev 21:23–24); looking on Christ as one pierced (John 19:37; Rev 1:7); the Word (of God) as a name or title for Jesus (John 1:1,14; Rev 19:13); the importance of "the beginning" (John 1:1; 8:25; Rev 3:14; 21:6); "I am" statements of Jesus (John passim; Rev 1:8,17–18; 2:23; etc.); the image of the spouse of Christ for the people of God (John 3:29; Rev 21:2,9; 22:17); reference to the mother of Jesus and the mother of the Messiah as "woman" (John 2:4; 19:26; Rev 12:1,4,13; etc.); a stress on witness/testifying (both passim); an end to the role of the Jerusalem Temple (John 2:19–21; 4:21; Rev 21:22); a hostile attitude toward "Jews" (John passim; Rev 2:9; 3:9); a major conflict with the devil/Satan (John 6:70; 8:44; 13:2,27; Rev 2:9,13,24; etc.). There are also parallels to the Epistles: the theme of God as light (I John 1:5; Rev 21:23; 22:5); the coming of the antichrist(s) (I John 2:18,22; Rev 13:11); false prophets (I John 4:1; Rev 2:20; 16:13; 19:20; 20:10); a female figure and her children represent a/the church (II John 1,13; Rev 12:17); and there are evil children as well, of the devil or of an evil woman (I John 3:10; Rev 2:20,23).

Nevertheless, such similarities are far less than those between the Gospel and Epistles of John. Moreover, there are many significant differences between Rev and the Johannine works.[70] Consequently, in the view of the majority of scholars one does not have justification for speaking of the author of Rev as a member of the Johannine School of writers who wrote the body of the Gospel, the Epistles, and redacted the Gospel. To do justice to all the factors, however, one should probably posit some contact between the seer and the Johannine tradition or writings. A good case can be made that the early stage of the Johannine tradition was shaped in Palestine or a closely adjacent area, and that some or all of the Johannine community later moved to the Ephesus area. A similar career has been posited for the prophet/seer of Rev. Early and late periods of possible contact can find support from theological observations. For instance, there was a future eschatology (which is dominant in Rev) in an early stage of the Gospel tradition (even if it has small voice in the developed Gospel) and in the Epistles which, al-

[69]Thus Swete, *Apocalypse* cxxvi–cxxx, from his detailed comparison of Rev and the Gospel as to vocabulary, grammar, and style. See also du Rand, *Johannine* 244–48. The tendency to dissociate Rev sharply from the Johannine orbit is illustrated by E. Schüssler Fiorenza, *Book* 85–113, who argues that the seer seems to be more familiar with Pauline than with Johannine School traditions.

[70]Beyond different vocabulary and style, there are significantly different outlooks. For example, the dominant eschatology in the Gospel is realized, so that there is little concentration on the future coming of Christ. The Gospel refers to the Scripture and cites it formally; Rev has no citations of Scripture. However, for modern support of the thesis that John the apostle wrote both John and Rev, and that the similarities far outweigh the differences, see Smalley, *Thunder.*

though written later than the Gospel, appeal back to the beginnings of the tradition. Thus the 50s or 60s in Palestine and/or the 80s or 90s in Ephesus are plausible times and places of contact.

Date and Life-Situation: Persecution under Domitian?

Within Rev there are certain indications that can help us to date the book. In the letters to the churches there is no indication of the presence of a supremely authoritative bishop as when some of the same churches are addressed by Ignatius *ca.* 110. If the worship arrangement of twenty-four elders around the One seated on the throne in Rev 4:4 suggests the presence of presbyters (elders), the seer may be closer to a period reflected in Titus and I Tim (90s) and *Didache* 15:1 (slightly later?) where presbyters/bishops and deacons are being/have been installed, but have not yet replaced apostles and prophets. Some addressees tested and some tolerated false prophets (Rev 2:2,20); the latter may reflect an outlook close to that of *Didache* 11:7 where prophets cannot be tested.[71]

Symbolic elements in Rev have more often been regarded as the key to the dating of Rev.[72] For instance, the reference to five deceased kings (seen as Julius through Claudius, Nero's predecessor) in 17:9–10 has made many posit composition in whole or in part in Nero's time (AD 54–68).[73] Yet it is more historical to date Augustus as the first emperor, and 17:11 seems to imply that an eighth king might be ruling. Nero is referred to (the number 666 in 13:18), but perhaps as dead (the mortally wounded head). Moreover, too many elements in Rev seem irreconcilable with Nero's lifetime. Many think that Rev implies the destruction of the earthly Temple by the Gentiles (the symbolism of the outside court in 11:2; and the use of Babylon symbolism for Rome), emperor worship, and persecution in Asia Minor; but Nero ruled before the destruction of the Jerusalem Temple, rejected having a temple to his divinity, and conducted no recorded persecution outside Rome.

Accordingly, for a long time the scholarly majority has held that Rev was written during the reign of Domitian (81–96)[74] who ruled after the destruc-

[71]Caution about all such speculation is dictated by the reminder of Aune, "Social," that Rev is not interested in the polity of the churches addressed but in a supralocal world of apostles, prophets, and saints. Thus silence could be accidental.

[72]It should be noted, however, that a scholarly minority insists that Rev employs pure symbolism without any reference to calendric history, and thus is useless for dating. Close to that are interpretations that would have Rev simply attacking contemporary culture with no reference to Roman persecution (R. H. Smith, CurTM 22 (1995), 356–61). More nuanced is A. Yarbro Collins, *Forum* 8 (1992), 297–312: attacking not only Roman panoply but also the then current world-view.

[73]A. A. Bell, Jr., NTS 25 (1978–79), 93–102.

[74]Already *ca.* 170 Irenaeus (AH 5.30.3) dated the visions of Rev "toward the end of Domitian's reign."

tion of the Jerusalem Temple and signed himself as Lord and God, and could be considered Nero come back again. In n. 38 above we saw how the calculation of kings could apply to Domitian. As part of this thesis it was assumed almost as a given fact that an Empire-wide persecution of Christians was conducted by Domitian in his last years. Now, however, one sees frequently, again almost as a given fact, the rebuttal claim that there was no persecution under Domitian (81–96).[75] Between these two views is there an intermediate possibility? Let us review the evidence,[76] since the position taken on Domitian may affect the dating of other NT works, e.g., I Pet, and perhaps Jude.

Domitian's father Vespasian (69–79) and his brother Titus (79–81) had been emperor before him, and during their reigns his ambitions were frustrated for he exercised little real power. In his own reign he was a reasonably good administrator but less judicious and popular than his family predecessors. Autocratic to an extreme, Domitian paraded his authority, wearing the marks of his triumphs even in the Senate, and made his control so absolute that his consultation of the Senate was perfunctory. He styled himself "Lord and God."[77] The enduring effect of his reign was to move Roman governance closer to an absolute monarchy. Although he never revoked the ancient privileges of the Jews, he was more rigorous than his predecessors in enforcing the poll tax on the Jews (*fiscus judaicus*). A revolution by Saturninus, the governor of Germany, in 89 exacerbated Domitian's tendency to seek vengeance; and he became insistent in seeking out treason. The historian Suetonius (*Domitian* 8.10) describes his last years as a reign of terror; that may be exaggerated, but the names of at least twenty opponents executed by Domitian are preserved. Not only political enemies but those of a different outlook (philosophy) were a target, as part of his campaign for the purity of the official religion. In 95 he both executed his cousin, the consul Flavius Clemens, and banished Clemens' wife Flavia Domitilla (Domitian's niece) for treason and for atheism.[78] Plots to overthrow Domitian multiplied; and in September 96, before his forty-fifth birthday, he was assassinated in a

[75]See E. T. Merrill, *Essays in Early Christian History* (London: Macmillan, 1924), 148–73; L. L. Wellborn, BR 29 (1984), 35–54; F. G. Downing, JSNT 34 (1988), 105–23. L. L. Thompson, *Revelation*, is a determined attempt to exonerate Domitian. A. Yarbro Collins, BR 26 (1981), 33–45, challenges the persecution but still dates Rev to Domitian's reign.

[76]For Domitian's relation to Jews and Christians: E. M. Smallwood, *Classical Philology* 51 (1956), 1–13; P. Keresztes, VC 27 (1973), 1–28; L. L. Thompson, *Historia* 31 (1982), 329–42.

[77]Suetonius, *Domitian* 8.13; Martial, *Epigrams* 10.72. In fact, however, there has been no evidence of that designation on any coin, inscription, or manuscript. Coins show him enthroned as "father of the gods." Encouragement to worship the emperor seems to have come from the peoples of the East rather than from the emperor himself.

[78]Suetonius (*Domitian* 8.15) reports the execution of Clemens on the grounds of very tenuous suspicions; Cassius Dio (*Roman History* 67.14.2) reports the atheism charge.

conspiracy involving his own wife Domitia and one or both of the praetorian prefects.

How did Domitian's suspicions and severity affect Christians? In the early 300s Eusebius (EH 3.18.4) reports a persecution and martyrdoms in the fifteenth year of Domitian (AD 96). What is the evidence for that? (1) Cassius Dio (*ca.* AD 225) says that the atheism for which Clemens and Domitilla were respectively executed and banished was "a charge on which many others who drifted into Jewish ways were condemned." At other times charges of atheism were laid against Christians, and some would have regarded them as members of a Jewish sect. The Eusebius passage refers to the banishment of Flavia Domitilla, a niece of Flavius Clemens because of her testimony to Christ. That there was a Christian woman named Domitilla is suggested by the catacomb containing Christian burials that bears her name; but she may have been confused with the Flavia Domitilla, the wife of Clemens (mentioned above), who was attracted to Judaism—an attraction attested among wives of the nobility. A similar confusion is witnessed in the identification of Clement, the prominent presbyter of the Roman church who wrote *I Clement,* with the consul Flavius Clemens, the victim of Domitian.[79] The similarity of names (Domitilla, Clement) raises the possibility that members of the household of Flavius Clemens—servants who took the masters' names—may have been attracted to Christianity, sparked by the interest of the patrons in Judaism.

(2) Melito of Sardis (AD 170–180) addressed a petition to the emperor of his time claiming that, of the preceding emperors, only Nero and Domitian, "persuaded by certain malignant persons, desired to bring our doctrine into ill repute." Since Nero certainly persecuted Christians, this may be a tactful way of reporting a persecution by Domitian. *Ca.* 197 Tertullian (*Apologeticum* 5.4) writes that Domitian, who was similar to Nero in cruelty, attempted to do what Nero had done (assault the Christian sect with the imperial sword) but because of humane reasons soon stopped what he had begun and even restored those whom he had banished. The modifying conclusion of Tertullian's description seems strange if he was inventing the whole report.

(3) *I Clement* 1:1 (AD 96–120) explains the writer's delay in addressing his letter to Corinth in terms of "sudden and repeated *happenings and experiences* that have befallen us." Many scholars have translated the two nouns as "misfortunes and calamities" and interpreted them as a reference to persecution under Domitian, usable to date *I Clement* to *ca.* 96 when Domitian died. That is an overinterpretation of 1:1. However, the appeal of the writer

[79]This confusion may be implicit in the legends about Clement in the *Pseudo-Clementine Literature,* the roots of which date back to AD 150–200. See Chapter 34 above, n. 6.

in chap. 5 to noble examples "of our own generation" centers on the persecution that brought about the death of the most righteous pillars Peter and Paul. That passage suggests a date not too much later than the 60s when the two apostles died. The statement in 7:1 that part of his reason for writing about such things is that "we are in the same arena, and the same struggle is before us" suggests that something comparable to the Neronian persecution is being experienced or anticipated.

(4) A connection between Nero and Domitian as hostile figures to Christians is suggested by the most probable interpretation of Rev 13:3, where one of the heads seemed to have been mortally wounded (Nero was stabbed to death) but was healed so that the blasphemies were renewed (n. 39 above) and war was waged against the holy ones. Since Rev was written in Asia Minor, the hostile picture indicates persecution there.

(5) Writing in Asia Minor (Pontus-Bithynia) in 110, Pliny the Younger (*Epistles* 10.96.6) tells of those charged with professing Christ who said they had ceased to be Christians twenty years ago, thus *ca.* 90. That date hints at persecution there in the latter years of Domitian.

(6) Hegesippus (*ca.* 160–180) is part of the ancient authority cited in EH 3.19–20 to the effect that, as a result of Domitian's orders that the descendants of David should be put to death, the grandsons of Jude, the brother of Jesus according to the flesh (p. 750 above), were interrogated but dismissed as being of no consequence. Eventually Domitian by an injunction caused the persecution against the church to cease.

The evidence does not warrant our attributing to Domitian a persecution in Rome of a ferocity nearly approaching Nero's. It does warrant the likelihood that in his distrust of possibly dangerous deviations Domitian showed hostility to Gentiles who abandoned the state religion for the Oriental cults that advocated the exclusive worship of one aniconic God (Judaism and probably Christianity). During his reign some "cultists" were executed, especially when their religious stance might be connected to political opposition. Under Nero antiChristian activities do not seem to have extended outside Rome; but under Domitian investigations were more widespread, e.g., to Asia Minor and Palestine. Whether or not by Domitian's personal orders, local authorities may have undertaken their own investigations, especially in areas where Christians had annoyed their Pagan neighbors who judged them antisocial and irreligious. The Christians' refusal to join in the public cult and perhaps to honor the divinized Domitian, when reported by those hostile to them, would have resulted in tribunals and sentences and martyrdom.[80]

[80]In AD 110 Pliny followed a pattern that seems to have been well established (*Epistles* 10.96–97): He did not seek out Christians; but once they were denounced, they were prosecuted.

The instances may have been very limited, but the memory of what Nero had done in Rome thirty years before would have colored Christian apprehension of what might be coming. (Notice that in Rev 2:10; 3:10 the persecution is going to come.) The exile of the prophet John to Patmos, the killing of Antipas at Pergamum (2:13), local ostracizing, disparity of wealth, and social discrimination producing alienation[81] would have been added together to shape the overall picture of oppressive Roman rule in Rev. Finally, subsequent Christian tradition, influenced by later full-scale Roman persecution, would have simplified and made the two emperors equally guilty of persecution. This analysis of Domitian's reign that combines a basis in fact for some persecution or harassment of Christians with reactive Christian exaggeration seems more responsible to the evidence than either denying harassment of Christians under Domitian or supposing major persecution.

Issues and Problems for Reflection

(1) In antiquity there were problems about the canonicity of Rev, in part in relation to whether or not John (the apostle) was thought to be the author. The book was widely accepted in the Western churches. (The rejection by Gaius who also rejected the Gospel according to John was not significant.) In Asia Minor toward the end of the 2d century, opposition to Montanist beliefs about a new outpouring of the Spirit caused the Alogoi to reject Rev (as well as John). Elsewhere in the East, once Dionysius of Alexandria (*ca.* 250) showed that Rev was not written by John the apostle, the work was often rejected, especially in reaction to the use of Rev as a support for sensual chiliasm. Nevertheless, Rev was accepted in the 4th century by Athanasius, and eventually the Greek-speaking church came to accept it. However, it continued to be rejected in Syria and by the Syriac-speaking church. In Reformation times, Luther assigned Rev to a secondary status; Zwingli denied that it was Scripture; and it was the only NT book on which Calvin did not write a commentary. Today there is no major problem of a denial of canonical status. However, Rev is overused in the wrong way (e.g., as exact predictions of the future); and reaction to such overuse sometimes prevents others from seeing its genuine value. It may well be important, then, to propose for discussion a strong clarifying statement—one that will scandalize some Christians, but is acceptable to the majority of Christians (and implies no rejection of inspiration or revelation). God has not revealed to human

[81]We saw in treating I Pet (p. 713 above) that there were factors in the way that Christians were treated that isolated them, but one must also recognize that the attitude of the author of Rev would encourage alienation. He wants Christians to have nothing to do with Roman power, wealth, and pomp.

beings details about how the world began or how the world will end, and failing to recognize that, one is likely to misread both the first book and the last book in the Bible. *The author of Rev did not know how or when the world will end, and neither does anyone else.*

(2) How can Rev be presented in a way that is both factual and meaningful? The first step may be to insist that the book be read through as a whole. That avoids the tendency to pick out a few symbolic references and to speculate about them. The second step is to insist that it was addressed to the seven churches and its details and historical context pertain to the 1st century rather than to the 20th or 21st century. (Vawter's pamphlet listed below can be helpful on a very elementary level.) That will dispense with the fanciful decoding of Rev (and Dan) in the light of today's headlines. Yet such factual knowledge by itself could result in a history lesson about Roman political administration in the late 1st century—scarcely a salvific message. As a further step, therefore, other aspects of Rev and of apocalyptic in general need emphasis.

To a contemporary culture that idolizes science and calculable knowledge, apocalyptic is an enduring witness to a reality that defies all our measurements; it testifies to another world that escapes all scientific gauges and finds expression in symbols and visions. That world is not created by imagination, but images serve as an entrée. Artists ranging from Pieter Brueghel through William Blake to Salvador Dali have understood that. On a psychological level Jung sought an entry into that world through symbols. On a religious level mystics have offered insight. Liturgy properly understood brings ordinary believers into contact with this heavenly reality. To a world that accepts only what it can see, hear, and feel, Rev is the final scriptural gateway to what the eye has not seen and the ear not heard. Because its visions are filled with theological symbols, not with photographic reproductions, Rev does not give an exact knowledge of that other world, a world that cannot be translated into human concepts. Rather, it attests forcefully that at every moment of human history, even the most desperate moment that causes people to lose hope, God is present. The Lamb standing as though slain is the ultimate guarantee of God's victorious care and deliverance, especially for the downtrodden and oppressed.[82]

(3) The question of the NT attitude toward what we call the secular government has often been an issue in seeking guidance for the attitude to be

[82]The commentary and articles by C. Rowland are particularly helpful in seeing the value of Rev's presentation of God's truth. See also E. Schüssler Fiorenza and A. Boesak, *Comfort and Protest: Reflections on the Apocalypse of John of Patmos* (Philadelphia: Westminster, 1987); W. Ewing, *The Power of the Lamb: Revelation's Theology of Liberation for You* (Cambridge, MA: Cowley, 1994).

expected of Christians today. (In such a search it is important to realize that a separation between the secular and the religious is inexact for NT times when, for instance, emperor worship was a way of inculcating pious respect for rulers' authority.) Actually there is no consistent NT instruction about "secular" governance; what promotes God's cause is what receives approval. Because most Christian works were written at a time when there was no persecution, respect and prayers for governing authorities were inculcated (Rom 13:1–7; I Pet 2:13–17; I Tim 2:1–4), in part as a sign that Christian peculiarities did not constitute a threat to civil order. According to Luke 20:20–26 and Matt 22:15–22 (cf. 17:24–27), Jesus declined a challenge to refuse to pay taxes to Caesar; and Acts 22:25–29 shows no embarrassment in portraying Paul as invoking his Roman citizenship in order to obtain just treatment from the authorities. In Rev, however, Rome is a harlot drunk with the blood of the martyrs and a Satanic tool. In discussing Domitian's reign we saw that probably there was no massive persecution of Christians in the 90s, and so some would contend that the seer is overreacting. Yet one could contend that he was more perceptive than other Christians in seeing what would inevitably happen to Christians, given the claims of the Empire. Notice that despite the horrendous picture of Rome in Rev, the readers are not urged to take up arms in revolt and no participatory role is assigned them in the eschatological battle. They are to endure persecution and remain faithful.[83]

Bibliography on Revelation

COMMENTARIES AND STUDIES IN SERIES: Bauckham, R. J. (NTT, 1993); Beasley-Murray, G. R. (NCBC, 1974); Boring, M. E. (IBC, 1989); **Caird, G. B.** (HNTC, 1966); **Charles, R. H.** (2 vols.; ICC, 1920); Corsini, E. (GNS, 1983); Court, J. (NTG, 1994); Ford, J. M. (AB, 1975); Giblin, C. H. (GNS, 1991); Harrington, W. J. (SP, 1993); Krodel, G. A. (AugC, 1989); Laws, S. (GNS, 1988); Michaels, J. R. (GNTE, 1992); Morris, L. (2d ed.; TNTC, 1987); Mounce, R. H. (NICNT, 1977); Rowland, C. (EC, 1993); Schüssler Fiorenza, E. (ProcC, 1991); Sweet, J.P.M. (PC, 1979); Wall, R. W. (NIBC, 1991); Yarbro Collins, A. (NTM, 1979).

L'Apocalypse johannique et l'Apocalyptique dans le Nouveau Testament, ed. J. Lambrecht (BETL 53; Leuven Univ., 1980). Contains important articles in English.

Aune, D. E., "The Social Matrix of the Apocalypse of John," BR 26 (1981), 16–32.

Bauckham, R. J., *The Climax of Prophecy: Studies in the Book of Revelation* (Edinburgh: Clark, 1992).

Blevins, J. L., *Revelation* (Atlanta: Knox, 1984).

[83]On the politics of Rev: A Yarbro Collins, JBL 96 (1977), 241–56; J. C. Garrett, Jr., *Journal of Church and State* 18 (1976), 433–42; 19 (1977), 5–20.

Bruce, F. F., "The Spirit in the Apocalypse," in *Christ and Spirit in the New Testament,* eds. B. Lindars and S. S. Smalley (Cambridge Univ., 1973), 333–44.
Buchanan, G. W., *The Book of Revelation* (Lewiston: Mellen, 1993).
Court, J., *Myth and History in the Book of Revelation* (Atlanta: Knox, 1979).
Ellul, J., *Apocalypse: The Book of Revelation* (New York: Seabury, 1977).
Farrer, A., *The Revelation of St. John the Divine* (Oxford: Clarendon, 1964).
Feuillet, A., *The Apocalypse* (New York: Alba, 1965). Represents two-source approach. Also his *Johannine Studies* (New York: Alba, 1964), 181–292.
Fuller, R. C., *Naming the Antichrist* (New York: Oxford, 1995).
Guthrie, D., *The Relevance of John's Apocalypse* (Grand Rapids: Eerdmans, 1987).
Hanson, A. T., *The Wrath of the Lamb* (London: SPCK, 1957).
Hughes, P. E., *The Book of Revelation: A Commentary* (Grand Rapids: Eerdmans, 1990).
Interpretation 40 (#3; 1986). Entire issue dedicated to Rev.
Kealy, S. P., *The Apocalypse of John* (Wilmington: Glazier, 1987).
Kiddle, M., *The Revelation of St John* (London: Hodder & Stoughton, 1940).
Koester, C. R., "On the Verge of the Millennium: A History of the Interpretation of Revelation," *Word & World* 15 (1995), 128–36. Whole issue devoted to Rev.
Ladd, G. E., *A Commentary on the Revelation of John* (Grand Rapids: Eerdmans, 1972).
Laws, S., *In the Light of the Lamb: Imagery, Parody, and Theology in the Apocalypse of John* (Wilmington: Glazier, 1988).
Malina, B. J., *On the Genre and Message of Revelation* (Peabody, MA: Hendrickson, 1995).
Metzger, B. M., *Breaking the Code* (Nashville: Abingdon, 1993).
Minear, P. S., *I Saw a New Earth* (Washington: Corpus, 1968).
Morris, L., *The Revelation of St John* (London: Tyndale, 1969).
Murphy, F. J., "The Book of Revelation," CRBS 2 (1994), 181–225. Excellent bibliography.
O'Leary, S. D., *Arguing the Apocalypse: A Theory of Millennial Rhetoric* (New York: Oxford, 1994).
Perkins, P., *The Book of Revelation* (Collegeville, MN: Liturgical, 1983).
Pippin, T., *Death and Desire: The Rhetoric of Gender in the Apocalypse* (Louisville: W/K, 1992).
Prévost, J.-P., *How to Read the Apocalypse* (New York: Crossroad, 1993). Good teaching tool, with pictures and charts.
Roloff, J., *The Revelation of John* (Minneapolis: A/F, 1993).
Schüssler Fiorenza, E., *Invitation to the Book of Revelation* (Garden City, NY: Doubleday, 1981). Revised as a ProcC in 1991 (see above).
———, *The Book of Revelation: Justice and Judgment* (Philadelphia: Fortress, 1985). Her collected essays; referred to above as *Book.*
Smalley, S. S., *Thunder and Love: John's Revelation and John's Community* (Milton Keynes: Word, 1994).
Swete, H. B., *The Apocalypse of St. John* (3d ed.; London, Macmillan, 1909).
Talbert, C. H., *The Apocalypse* (Louisville: W/K, 1994).

Thompson, L. L., *The Book of Revelation: Apocalypse and Empire* (New York: Oxford, 1990).

(Vawter, B.), *Revelation: A Divine Message of Hope* (Pamphlet 51; New Haven: Knights of Columbus, 1956). This pamphlet, which does not bear the author's name, is a very good, simple introduction for those puzzled by the book.

Vorster, W. S., "'Genre' and the Revelation of John," *Neotestamentica* 22 (1988), 103–23.

Wainwright, A. W., *Mysterious Apocalypse* (Nashville: Abingdon, 1993).

Yarbro Collins, A., *The Combat Myth in the Book of Revelation* (Missoula: Scholars, 1976).

———, *Crisis and Catharsis: The Power of the Apocalypse* (Philadelphia: Westminster, 1984).

———, "Reading the Book of Revelation in the Twentieth Century," *Interpretation* 40 (1986), 229–42.

APPENDIXES

I The Historical Jesus

II Jewish and Christian Writings Related to the New Testament

APPENDIX I

THE HISTORICAL JESUS

A brief survey of scholarship on the historical Jesus is germane to this *Introduction.* The NT is a small library of books written within a hundred years of Jesus' death by those who believed he was the Messiah. Thus without him there would be no NT. Also developments in the study of the historical Jesus have marked major changes in the direction of NT scholarship, so that this survey can familiarize readers with what has happened in research. Finally, a great deal of publicity has surrounded studies of this question in the last few years; and without explanation, beginners may acquire a distorted view of directions and importance.

Two Hundred Years (1780–1980) of the Modern Quest

For some 1,800 years Christianity largely took for granted that the Gospel portrayal of Jesus with all its christological evaluations was a literally factual account of Jesus' lifetime.[1] The "Enlightenment" or the 18th-century movement that exalted human reason and empirical scientific investigation inevitably led to a new approach to the Bible. The same historical principles used to study other ancient works first began to be applied to the NT by R. Simon, a Catholic priest (1690), and by the Protestant scholar, J. D. Michaelis (1750).[2] H. S. Reimarus, whose work was published posthumously in 1778, was the first to develop a picture of Jesus distinct from the Christ described in the Gospels. The former was a Jewish revolutionary who attempted unsuccessfully to establish a messianic kingdom on earth, while the latter was the fictional projection of those who stole his body and pretended he had risen from the dead. Unfortunately, then, from the beginning, the application of systematic historical research to Jesus was mixed with a rationalism (touted as scientific but actually very lacking in objectivity[3]) that a priori

[1]That does not mean that this period was lacking in insights about the differences among the Gospels that make the 18th- to 20th-century quests more intelligible; see H. K. McArthur, *The Quest Through the Centuries* (Philadelphia: Fortress, 1966).

[2]For a very useful survey of NT studies in the modern period, see J. S. Kselman and R. D. Witherup, NJBC 70.

[3]No Jesus research is purely objective, but the better balanced investigations admit to their presuppositions and the corresponding limitations.

denied the possibility of the supernatural. Often the search for the historical Jesus has been conducted with an overtone of freeing Jesus from the theological impositions of the later church, but in fact many of the searchers have imposed their own skepticism and antitheological biases on the picture they claim to have "found." In 1835 D. F. Strauss, a student of F. C. Baur (p. 30 above), published a *Life of Jesus* based on the principle that the Gospels had transformed and embellished by faith the picture of Jesus so that what resulted was mythical. The change was so profound that he judged it almost impossible to write a historical account of Jesus' life. From that stance but moving in different directions B. Bauer (1877) argued that Jesus and Paul never existed, and E. Renan (1863) portrayed a purely human Jesus. In such investigation the Fourth Gospel was soon dismissed as a theological creation and thus a totally unreliable historical source, while Mark (along with Q) was attentively studied as a key to the human Jesus. However, in 1901 W. Wrede (p. 153 above) argued that Mark was also the product of theology in which Jesus was presented as divine, and so not a reliable historical source. Behind the different exemplars of what has been called the "first quest" of the historical Jesus was the implication that modern theology ought to change according to what scholars now discerned about Jesus.

In *The Quest for the Historical Jesus* (*. . . From Reimarus to Wrede;* Ger 1906; Eng 1910), A. Schweitzer passed judgment on more than a hundred years of such "historical Jesus" research. He contended that most of the investigation described above told us more about the investigators than about Jesus, for they were describing their own mirror-image reflection. Following the lead of J. Weiss, Schweitzer argued that the previous quest had overlooked Jesus' apocalyptic outlook in which he saw himself as the Messiah who by his death would bring about the end of the world. For Schweitzer, therefore, Jesus was a noble failure. In *The So-Called Historical Jesus and the Historic Biblical Christ* (Ger 1892; Eng 1964) M. Kähler presented another skeptical reaction to the "Jesus research" by arguing that it was impossible to separate out the historical Jesus from the Christ of faith, since the NT writings all focus on the latter. The Christ of faith is the one who has been proclaimed by Christians and the only one to be concerned with. R. Bultmann moved in the same direction. In BHST (Ger 1921), he used form criticism not only to classify what was said about Jesus in the Synoptic Gospels but also to judge its historicity; and he attributed the highest percentage of the Jesus tradition to the creativity of the early Christians. Thus the quest for the historical Jesus was a virtual impossibility. Bultmann's pessimism about what can be known of Jesus historically corresponded to his theological principle (influenced by a Lutheran background) that one should not seek a historical basis for faith. Thus, if we may simplify, contrary to the "quest"

Bultmann would not change theology according to "discoveries" about the historical Jesus which were irrelevant to belief. Paradoxically Bultmann did not wish to dispense with the exalted Gospel picture of Jesus, for the proclamation of that Gospel picture offers a challenge today for people to believe that is existentially similar to the challenge that Jesus offered to people in his lifetime. Those who respond by belief, God delivers from the hopeless incapacity of their own human abilities.

The reaction to Bultmann, largely led by his own students, constituted the "new" (or second) quest of the historical Jesus. In 1953 E. Käsemann gave a lecture published as "The Problem of the Historical Jesus" (KENTT 15–47) in which he pointed out the danger of the gap Bultmann had opened up: If there is no traceable connection between the glorified Lord of the Gospels and the historical Jesus, Christianity becomes a myth. For Käsemann faith, rather than being indifferent, requires an identity between the earthly Jesus and the exalted Lord. Recognizing that the Gospel sources are not coldly factual biography, he sought to develop criteria for determining what is historical in the Gospel tradition. Other "Post-Bultmannians" sought to determine historical features beneath the Gospel presentation;[4] the result included various portrayals of Jesus of religious significance, e.g., one who regarded himself as God's eschatological representative, exemplifying God's love and values by his actions, teachings, or authority and offering the possibility of an encounter with God. Bultmann's influence remains in that an existential touch dominates in all such portrayals—a Jesus to whom one can relate but not one who offers explicit christological formulation, for that is the product of subsequent Christian reflection.

After 1980: The Jesus Seminar and Related Scholars

The rest of this Appendix will deal with the last quarter of the 20th century, for the date 1980 is approximate.[5] One may speak of two tendencies, although the more conservative one is generally treated as the study of christology rather than as historical Jesus research. (Pursuit of that topic belongs more to a book on NT theology than to a NT *Introduction;* for that reason this Appendix devotes only one paragraph to it.) A willingness to attribute explicit christology to the lifetime of Jesus got new life in late–20th

[4]E.g., G. Bornkamm, *Jesus of Nazareth* (New York: Harper & Row, 1960); E. Fuchs, *Studies of the Historical Jesus* (SBT 42; London: SCM, 1964); H. Conzelmann, *Jesus* (Philadelphia: Fortress, 1973). For surveys: J. M. Robinson, *A New Quest of the Historical Jesus* (SBT 25; London: SCM, 1959); R. E. Brown and P. J. Cahill, *Biblical Tendencies Today: An Introduction to the Post-Bultmannians* (Washington, DC: Corpus, 1969).

[5]In choosing whom to discuss I found very helpful Witherington, *Jesus Quest.* This period has been described as the "Third Quest"; see M. E. Boring, *Interpretation* 50 (1996), 341–54.

century scholarship, as once more it became respectable to hold that Jesus actually thought he had a unique relationship to God and reflected that outlook in his speech and attitudes. "Son of Man" is a title that many scholars think he used of himself. "Messiah" remains a title that others may have used of him during his lifetime, whether or not he accepted the designation.[6] The Qumran discoveries show that titles like Son of God and Lord were known in Semitic-speaking circles of Palestine during Jesus' time. Moreover, the scholarly practice of assigning the introduction of certain christological titles to specific postJesus stages in the geographical and temporal spread of Christianity is now seen to be too simple. Therefore, a continuity between Jesus' lifetime and the Gospel portraits may be more inclusive than hitherto thought. Readers are encouraged to explore the trend to emphasize this continuity, for it has major following among highly reputable scholars.[7]

THE JESUS SEMINAR. A more radical tendency in studying Jesus has received greater attention, sometimes because its proponents have advertised their results in the media. This Seminar was founded in 1985 by R. Funk with J. D. Crossan as co-chair; it has consisted of some fifty to seventy-five scholars who meet regularly, write papers, and vote on decisions about what the historical Jesus did and said.[8] The color-coded voting was designed to catch attention: red = he undoubtedly said this or something very much like it; pink = probably he said something like this; gray = the ideas are his even though he did not say this; black = he did not say it.

Although partly drawing on criteria developed by the Post-Bultmannians, the Seminar stands out in several ways. *First,* it has operated to a remarkable degree on a priori principles, some of them reflecting antisupernatural bias.

[6]Since the "Messiah" issue will appear in the discussion to follow, some fictions need to be laid to rest. One encounters the affirmation that there were many would-be messiahs in Palestine at this time. In fact there is no evidence that any Jew claimed or was said to be the Messiah before Jesus of Nazareth (or until a century after his death). Thus one must offer an explanation for the unanimity attested in the NT that Jesus was the Christ (Messiah). As Witherington, *Jesus Quest,* points out, very important scholars posit an affirmation or confession of messiahship during Jesus' lifetime: M. de Jonge, *Jesus, the Servant Messiah* (New Haven: Yale, 1991); J.D.G. Dunn, in *The Messiah,* ed. J. H. Charlesworth (Minneapolis: A/F, 1992), 365–81; P. Stuhlmacher, *Jesus of Nazareth—Christ of Faith* (Peabody, MA: Hendrickson, 1993); N. T. Wright, *Who Was Jesus?* (Grand Rapids: Eerdmans, 1992), and his other books on Jesus.

[7]BINTC offers detailed argumentation and bibliography for the affirmations in this paragraph and (214–17) an evaluation of books on christology. For surveys, see Cowdell and Hultgren in the *Bibliography* below.

[8]For typical essays, see H. Shanks (moderator), *The Search for Jesus* (Washington, DC: Biblical Archaeology Society, 1994). The number of participants has varied (e.g., 200), depending on how one counts all who ever took part and/or those who simply received mailings. The membership is self-selective (and most often of a particular mind-set); for when the seminar was inaugurated, many scholars refused to take part. As of 1995 its membership contained no active members of the NT faculties at Harvard, Yale, Union (NYC), Princeton (Seminary), Duke, Emory, Vanderbilt, the University of Chicago; or of the major European faculties.

For instance, the bodily resurrection had no real chance of being accepted as having taken place. The session dealing with the authenticity of Jesus' predictions of his passion and death was dominated by the initial refusal of most of the participants to allow the possibility that Jesus could have spoken of his impending death by virtue of "super-ordinary" powers; accordingly they voted black on eleven Synoptic passion predictions. Again, almost as a principle, the eschatological character of Jesus' ministry has been dismissed, with an obvious negative result in judging the authenticity of Gospel statements that echo such an outlook.

Second, the results have been exceptionally skeptical. Of the sayings attributed to Jesus in the four Gospels, some 50 percent were voted black and 30 percent gray, leaving less than 20 percent that have a chance of being authentic (red or pink). A red vote was accorded to no statement of Jesus in John and to only one saying peculiar to Mark!

Third, from the beginning the seminar has sought popular media coverage to an extraordinary degree—one reviewer has compared it to the style of P. T. Barnum. Claiming that scholarly views appearing in books and scientific journals do not reach the general public, the leading figures in the Jesus Seminar have turned to newspaper interviews and TV talk shows, attracting attention even in Sunday supplements and periodicals like *GQ*. Part of the piquancy is attributable to a proclaimed intention to liberate Jesus from the tyranny of the "religious establishment," represented in church or doctrinal tradition and Christian worship. Thus after almost every seminar session bombshell announcements are released to catch the public's eye, e.g., that Jesus did not utter the Lord's Prayer or any of the beloved words that appear in John. An impression has been created that these scandalous sound bites represent where scholars now stand.

In fact, however, although spokesmen for the Jesus Seminar like to pretend that the chief disparagement of their stances comes from "fundamentalists," scholarly evaluations and reviews of the productions of the Jesus Seminar[9] have often been bluntly critical, e.g., those by NT professors like A. Culpepper (Baylor), R. B. Hays (Duke), L. T. Johnson (Emory), L. E. Keck (Yale), J. P. Meier (Catholic University), and C. T. Talbert (Wake Forest/ Baylor). One finds therein such devastating judgments as: methodologically misguided; no significant advance in the study of the historical Jesus; only a small ripple in NT scholarship; results representing the Jesus the researchers wanted to find; the pursuit of a specific confessional agenda; and dangerous

[9]Many of the reviews have concentrated on R. W. Funk et al., *The Five Gospels* (New York: Macmillan, 1993). The fifth gospel is the Coptic *Gospel of Thomas,* the first edition of which the seminar participants posit to have existed in the 50s, and along with Q, to have antedated Mark.

in giving a false impression. We cannot here enter the discussions in detail,[10] but I shall make pertinent evaluative observations as I conclude this Appendix.

Various participants in the Jesus seminar have written their own books,[11] but here we shall discuss separately only J. D. Crossan and M. J. Borg. The Seminar has dealt largely with the sayings of Jesus; these writers have fleshed out pictures of Jesus in the direction of some of the implications of the Seminar.

J. D. CROSSAN[12] bases his presentation of Jesus on sources that he would date before 60: e.g., the reconstructed Q and apocryphal gospels (*Gospel of Thomas, Secret Gospel of Mark,* an early form of the *Gospel of Peter*). He draws on social analyses of Roman rule in Palestine in Jesus' lifetime that posit much political unrest and assume as applicable to Nazareth a power pattern attested in larger cities. Jesus is seen as a combination of an itinerant Cynic preacher and illiterate Galilean peasant, who was strongly egalitarian.[13] The historicity of Jesus' infancy narrative is dismissed by Crossan on the analogy of a 12th-century AD account of Moses' life (*Sepher ha-Zikronot*—see BBM 600). There are no demons, and so Jesus performed no exorcisms in the strict sense even though he delivered individuals from duress that they regarded as possession. There were elements of magic[14] as

[10]One of the most common objections to the Seminar is its arbitrariness in dismissing the historicity of well-attested aspects of the Gospel portrait of Jesus, e.g., his exorcisms (contrast G. H. Twelvetree, *Jesus the Exorcist* [WUNT 2.54; Tübingen: Mohr-Siebeck, 1993]) or his eschatological outlook (even though some of the evidence for the sayings about the coming Son of Man meets the criteria for judging what is authentic).

[11]Some are not formally scholars, e.g., Episcopal Bishop John Spong, whose works stripping Jesus of christology Johnson, *Real Jesus,* treats under the heading of "Amateur Night." In BBM 702–4 I comment on Spong's *Born of a Woman* (San Francisco: Harper, 1992), including the observation, "I do not think that a single NT author would recognize Spong's Jesus as the figure being proclaimed or written about." G. O'Collins (*Tablet* 248 [1994], 529–30), in a withering review of Spong's *Resurrection: Myth or Reality?* (San Francisco: HarperCollins, 1994), points out extraordinary inaccuracies and ends: "My advice for his next book . . . is to let some real experts check the text before publication." While not members of the Jesus Seminar, A. N. Wilson (*Jesus* [London: Norton, 1992]) and S. Mitchell (*The Gospel According to Jesus* [New York: HarperCollins, 1991]) are popularizers of a similar Jesus whom they consider to have been wrongly divinized.

[12]*The Historical Jesus: The Life of a Mediterranean Jewish Peasant* (San Francisco: Harper, 1991); *Jesus, A Revolutionary Biography* (San Francisco: Harper, 1994).

[13](See also B. Mack's attempt to work back behind Mark to a Jesus as a Cynic preacher; p. 88 above). Crossan describes Jesus and his followers as hippies; and for L. E. Keck (*Christian Century* [Aug. 24–31, 1994] 785), Crossan imagines Jesus as the center of a Galilean Camelot. All Crossan's points are debatable. He himself admits (*Jesus* 121–22) that we cannot know whether or how much Jesus knew about Cynicism; the *only* preserved evidence about Jesus' literacy (Luke 4:16), even if uncertain, would have Jesus read; he was not a peasant in the sense of one of the rural poor who eke out their living from the land; to support egalitarianism Crossan must deny that Jesus chose the Twelve—a dismissal that implies what Paul presents as tradition (I Cor 15:3–5) was his creation.

[14]The magic element is related to the thesis of M. Smith, *Jesus.* For a strong defense of a proper distinction between miracles (such as those attributed to Jesus) and magic, see Meier, *Marginal* 2.538–52.

Jesus operated outside the normal religious lines, but there were no supernatural miracles. Most of the passion account was created from reflection on the OT; there was no Jewish trial of Jesus; he was executed by the Romans; and his body was probably eaten by the dogs; there was no bodily resurrection. Inevitably Crossan has been accused of flights of imagination that compromise his claims to a historical approach.[15]

M. J. Borg is in many ways in harmony with the Jesus Seminar, e.g., the "preEaster" Jesus was not a Messiah or a divine savior, nor was he eschatologically concerned with the end of the world—such views would make Jesus irrelevant for our times.[16] Reflecting his own faith pilgrimage, Borg is attempting to find a meaningful Jesus; and his eloquence about Jesus' own spirituality has attracted some who would otherwise find the Seminar's claims offensive. Borg offers a compassionate[17] sage who taught a subversive wisdom (indeed one who regarded himself as a spokesman of divine wisdom), and a prophetic social critic who by the inclusivity of his appeal rejected a politics of holiness that involved separation. Key to his picture is that Jesus was a charismatic, spirit-led holy man—one who had frequent mystical experiences of God or the Spirit and became a channel of that Spirit to others. Thus he was similar to Ḥoni the rainmaker of the 1st century BC and the Galilean Ḥanina of the 1st century AD.[18] Aspects of Borg's presentation might find wide acceptance, but many would maintain that sufficient justice is not done to essential Gospel evidence by Borg's portrayal of a Jesus who had no definitive revelation and did not present himself as having a distinctive role in the final (i.e., eschatological) action by God that had now begun. The question has been raised whether once again, as with the discovery of the liberal Jesus in the last century, the quest is not producing the Jesus the quester wished to find.

[15]B. F. Meyer, CBQ 55 (1993), 576: "As historical-Jesus research, it is unsalvageable. Not that a long historical struggle has turned out to have been in vain, for there are no signs of any such struggle having taken place."

[16]*Jesus, A New Vision* (San Francisco: Harper, 1987); *Meeting Jesus Again for the First Time* (San Francisco: Harper/Collins, 1994). Borg rejects as incomplete many common Christian reactions to Jesus: e.g., the picture of Jesus as a divine savior leads to believing things *about* Jesus; Jesus as a moralistic teacher leads to Christian life as being good. Borg would put primary emphasis on Jesus as shaping a relationship with God that involves transformation.

[17]So compassionate that Borg's Jesus seems to make no absolute demands of moral purity; the more severe Jesus, e.g., in his demands about marriage, does not emerge.

[18]All this can be challenged. Jesus is not particularly remembered as a mystic or as communicating the Spirit to others during his ministry. The parallel to Ḥoni and Ḥanina reflects the thesis of G. Vermes, *Jesus the Jew* (Philadelphia: Fortress, 1973); but the charismatic miracle-worker picture of such figures is historically dubious and reflects dependence on later rabbinic literature, which in this case aggrandized them—see Meier, *Marginal* 581–88. In the earliest tradition Ḥoni was a man of persuasive prayer that brought God's extraordinary help. Jesus is not remembered as working his miracles by praying for God's help.

After 1980: Miscellaneous Views

We turn now to a miscellany of scholars whose approaches are partially or very different from those of the Jesus Seminar (which some of them criticize sharply).

E. P. SANDERS,[19] rather than appealing to a Greco-Roman pattern like the Cynic preacher, stresses the Jewishness of Jesus, who was an eschatological prophet (not a social reformer) heralding a new age for which Israel would need restoration. Comparatively he does not construct his picture of Jesus on a collection of sayings but shows more confidence in the basic Gospel pattern of the facts and deeds of Jesus' life.[20] He acknowledges the tradition that Jesus worked miracles (which should not be confused with magic), but Sanders would attribute them to natural rather than supernatural causes. He doubts the historicity of the polemics between Jesus and the Pharisees, for Jesus' positions on the Law lay within a tolerable variance. The historically offensive element was Jesus' offering sinners a place in the kingdom without requiring repentance. The critique of Sanders by other scholars, besides challenging such a repentance-free attitude, has contended that there was more conflict between Jesus and his Jewish contemporaries than Sanders allows.[21] There has also been a complaint that Sanders does not pay sufficient attention to "sayings" of Jesus in the parables and the Sermon on the Mount.

SCHOLARS PORTRAYING JESUS AS A SOCIO-POLITICAL ACTIVIST: Although his portrayal of the social aspects of Palestine has appealed to some of the Jesus Seminar participants, *G. Theissen*[22] differs from the Seminar strongly in stressing the antiquity of the material in the canonical Gospels. He describes Galilee and Judea as ripe for revolt *during Jesus' public ministry* and fits into that context a picture of Jesus and his followers as radical (pacifist) wandering charismatics who had abandoned or renounced family and

[19]*Jesus and Judaism* (Philadelphia: Fortress, 1985); *The Historical Figure of Jesus* (London: Penguin, 1993).

[20]Jesus was born about 4 BC, lived in Nazareth, underwent baptism by JBap, called disciples (including a group of Twelve), preached God's kingdom (which had both a present and future aspect), went to Jerusalem, was involved in a controversy over the Temple, was interrogated by Jewish authorities and executed by the Romans. At times his disciples, who claimed to have seen him after his death, came into conflict with Jews who did not believe in him.

[21]M. Casey, *From Jewish Prophet to Gentile God* (Louisville: W/K, 1991) sees Jesus as a prophetic preacher of repentance who had real conflicts with the Pharisees and foresaw that his death as a martyr would be accepted by God. B. D. Chilton, *Tyndale Bulletin* 39 (1988), 3–18, argues that there were cultic differences between Jesus and the Pharisees.

[22]His most formal treatment of Jesus is a type of novel, *The Shadow of the Galilean* (Philadelphia: Fortress, 1987); but it reflects earlier social studies, especially *Sociology of Early Palestinian Christianity* (Philadelphia: Fortress, 1978). See also his *Gospels Context.*

home.[23] More radically *R. A. Horsley* (rejecting the image both of a Cynic preacher and a wandering charismatic) would imagine Jesus to have been a social revolutionary against the violent and greedy power elite. Historically Jesus was not a messianic type; rather his contemporaries saw a resemblance to the reforming social-political prophets of old, e.g., Jeremiah.[24] In Horsley's view the religious parties or "sects" mentioned by Josephus (Sadducees, Pharisees, Essenes) had little influence on the population of Galilee, which was highly peasant in makeup. Jesus tried to reorganize village life in Palestine into a kingdom of this world, expecting God to overthrow the various Roman and Jewish political rulers of Palestine.[25] Those whom he "healed," he sent back to their villages to join in the cause. Obviously there is only a tenuous connection between such a Jesus (and his historical followers) and the NT Christian groups who had a high christology and a primarily religious thrust.

SCHOLARS INTERPRETING JESUS IN TERMS OF DIVINE WISDOM (SOPHIA): These are hard to classify. OT Wisdom Books (Proverbs, Sirach, Wisdom of Solomon) portray a personified female wisdom figure who was either the first of God's creation (Prov 8:22) or emerged from God's mouth (Sirach 24:3) or was an emanation of God's glory (Wisdom 7:25), and who took part in creation. Scholars of many backgrounds would recognize that an adaptation of this figure played an important role in the NT understanding of Jesus' divine origins.[26] But how much of this adaptation goes back to Jesus himself? (It is important to recognize that this is not simply an issue of whether Jesus was a sage or one who spoke as a wise man.) To some extent this has been tied in with feminist approaches to the NT. *E. Schüssler Fior-*

[23]Although Theissen makes valuable social observations in his many writings, this political analysis is highly disputable and may reflect a retrojection of the restless, revolutionary situation of later decades (BDM 1.676–705). Moreover, both Jesus and his named followers who had a craft and possessions did not come from the extreme poor (Theissen has modified his stance on this somewhat); and one may ask whether their leaving aside possessions (which is presented eschatologically in the Gospels) can be related so directly to the social, political situation.

[24]*Jesus and the Spiral of Violence* (San Francisco: Harper, 1987); *Sociology and the Jesus Movement* (New York: Crossroad, 1989). Although Horsley's helpful contribution has been to insist on a distinction among would-be kings, prophets, bandits, and Zealots (BDM 1.682–93), many insist that Jesus would have been seen as more than a prophet, thus possibly as a Messiah. (Does any OT prophet speak with the authority attributed to Jesus in the Gospels?) For a critique of Horsley's attempt to apply his outlook to the narratives of Jesus' birth (*The Liberation of Christmas* [New York: Crossroad, 1989]), see BBM 625–26.

[25]There is not much Gospel evidence of Jesus' addressing himself primarily to villagers as distinct from town or city dwellers or of his confronting the political power elite, even though his words criticized values that both peasants and elite would have embraced. Those who disagree with Horsley often insist that he has exaggerated the social class dimension of Jesus' ministry, neglecting the eschatological and spiritual aspects.

[26]See E. A. Johnson, ETL 61 (1985), 261–94 for a good survey.

enza,[27] who like some in the Jesus Seminar looks on the *Gospel of Thomas* as an important early source and speculates about the Q community, contends that Jesus regarded God as *Sophia* and himself as Sophia's child and prophet. A major proof for this is the Lucan form (7:35) of the Q saying "Wisdom [understood as God] is justified by all her children [by Jesus]."[28] There are also passages where Jesus uses female images of himself, e.g., Luke 13:34, but they scarcely establish God as Sophia. Despite Schüssler Fiorenza's contention, it is hard to know whether Jesus, who consciously spoke in a wisdom language (e.g., in parables), translated his relationship to God into the Sophia mold. Schüssler Fiorenza would hold that this ancient level was followed by a later level in which Jesus himself was identified as Sophia, even if the terminology was shifted to male titles like "Lord." That is the very level, however, that other scholars would regard as the earliest,[29] for many would judge that Jesus saw himself as uniquely related to God in a relationship that went back to his origins. Some of the prePauline hymns, such as Phil 2:6–11 which may be very early, and passages in John (BINTC 205–10), reflect the influence of the wisdom imagery on such a relationship.

J. P. MEIER has attempted the most ambitious modern reconstruction of the historical Jesus.[30] In principle willing to consider all sources, he examines and rejects the apocryphal gospels as unhelpful; and while he posits Q, he does not reconstruct a Q community or primitive gnostic or feminist groups more genuine than the Christians who produced the NT. Meticulous about methodology, he applies some of the same criteria as the Jesus Seminar but with clarity about their limitations; and he avoids a priori exclusions of the eschatological, supernatural, and the miraculous.[31] He treats both the sayings and works of Jesus. Against the tendency to characterize Jesus as a Cynic, a wandering charismatic, etc., Meier stresses the difficulty of any classification of Jesus, who was a "marginal Jew," differing from others in very many aspects of his life and teaching. Meier sees a Jesus heavily influ-

[27]*Jesus: Miriam's Child and Sophia's Prophet* (New York: Continuum, 1994), which develops motifs of her *In Memory.* From her analysis of Jesus as leading an egalitarian renewal movement in tension with the dominant patriarchal ethos of his time—plainly an analysis phrased in modern terminology—it is difficult at times to move back to Jesus' historical mind-set, for surely he would not have thought in those terms.

[28]Even if we leave aside the possibility that the form in Matt 11:19, which does not mention Wisdom's children and has no "all," may be older, this is not a lucid text (see Meier, *Marginal* 2.152–53). The contention that there was a Q community that honored God as Sophia goes considerably beyond the evidence. The much stronger grounds for Jesus praying to God as *'Abbā'*, "Father," do not favor such a nonpatriarchal view of God.

[29]See B. Witherington III, *Jesus the Sage: The Pilgrimage of Wisdom* (Minneapolis: A/F, 1994).

[30]*A Marginal Jew.* The first two published vols. total 1,600 pages; the third will cover the parables, the last days of Jesus' life, and his death.

[31]In *Marginal* 2.686–98 Meier favors the historicity of three blind-man healings (Mark 8:22–26; 10:46–52; John 9:1–7); thus he does not exclude John from historical research about Jesus.

enced by JBap, whose eschatological message of necessary repentance he accepted. "A miracle-working eschatological prophet wearing the mantle of Elijah," Jesus did not proclaim a social program but the kingdom of God in the sense of God's coming to transform people and rule in the last times. This rule was already making itself present in Jesus' ministry of healing and exorcism; indeed Meier regards as early church creations sayings that place the future coming of the kingdom within an imminent time period after Jesus' death. From Meier's massive work a more traditional Jesus emerges—one having considerable in common with the Jesus Christ described in Paul and the Gospels. NJBC 78:22 anticipates Meier's third volume dealing with Jesus' teaching and traces his authority to a claim to know directly and intuitively the will of God in any given situation. Patently that has strong christological implications.

Evaluative Observations

(1) Some speak as if modern methods give a great deal of assurance about the "historical Jesus," no matter how limited that picture. That is simply not true on at least two scores. *First,* portrayals of the historical Jesus are drawn by scholars who are very divided in their judgments about the Gospels.[32] Even if, as most think, Matt and Luke drew on Mark, was John independent of Mark, so that we have two separate witnesses? Is there anything historical in John's presentation of Jesus? If, as most think, Matt and Luke drew on a Q collection of Jesus' sayings, was that source more ancient than Mark? Does the projected Q reflect a community who knew or believed nothing of Jesus beyond what is in Q? Can we reconstruct a preMarcan source? Do noncanonical materials (none of which in their present form antedate the 2d century) tell us anything historical about Jesus? *Second,* scholars are also divided about the real value of the criteria for discerning the historical Jesus. Those criteria are designed to eliminate anything for which there could be another derivation, e.g., what could have come from contemporary Judaism or Christian preaching. Yet a rigorous application of such criteria would leave us with a monstrosity: a Jesus who never said, thought, or did anything that other Jews said, thought, or did, and a Jesus who had no connection or relationship to what his followers said, thought, or did in reference to him after he died.

(2) What is meant by "the historical Jesus"? That designation refers to what after nearly 2,000 years we can recover of the life of Jesus of Nazareth

[32]For example, see Appendix IX in BDM 2.1492–1524, where M. L. Soards studies 35 different reconstructions of the preMarcan passion narrative and illustrates vividly the lack of scholarly agreement.

by the application of modern criteria to records written by those who believed that he was God's unique agent for the salvation of all (Messiah, Lord, Son of Man, Son of God, God). Necessarily the results are very limited; and it is a major mistake to think that the "historical (or reconstructed) Jesus," a totally modern portrayal, is the same as the total Jesus, i.e., Jesus as he actually was in his lifetime. Indeed, by generous estimate, were scholars agreed on a portrait of the "historical Jesus," it would not cover one hundredth of the actual Jesus. It is equally a mistake to equate "the historical (reconstructed) Jesus" with the real Jesus—a Jesus who really means something to people, one on whom they can base their lives. See pp. 105–6 above.

(3) The preceding observation warns us against the foolishness of making the "historical Jesus" portrayed by a scholar or a seminar of scholars the norm of Christianity, so that constantly the tradition of the Christian churches would have to be altered by the latest portrayal. On the other hand, the Bultmannian reaction to the quest, which almost makes faith independent of (inevitably uncertain) historical research, need not be the only solution. Indeed, one can argue that churches and believers should not be indifferent to careful historical scholarship about the Bible. Rather, leavening and rephrasing traditional ideas under the impact of careful scholarship is better than either overthrowing the ideas or ignoring scholarship. Following the principle of *fides quaerens intellectum* (faith seeking intellectually respectable expression), Christian belief has nothing to fear from solid, careful scholarly research. Such a position requires openness on both sides. On the part of church authorities, there should be a recognition that past phrasings of faith are time-conditioned and are susceptible to being rephrased.[33] Through critical biblical study, what was once assumed to be a necessary aspect of belief (e.g., creation in six days with rest on the seventh) may prove to be only a dramatic way of phrasing what remains essential (namely, that no matter how things came into existence, it was through God's planning and power). For their part scholars would do well to avoid a rhetoric whereby their discoveries are presented as certain, making the discoverers the infallible arbiters of Christian faith. Biblical books are documents written by those who believed in the God of Abraham and the Father of Jesus Christ; good sense suggests that communities sharing that faith have an authority in dealing with those books.

(4) The historical Jesus "uncovered" (but actually reconstructed) in the Jesus Seminar and by some of the authors discussed above could scarcely be the object of Christian church proclamation. If Jesus was a wise Cynic

[33]The Roman Catholic Church, which is often regarded as the most dogmatic in its presentation of Christian belief, recognized this in *Mysterium Ecclesiae* issued by the Roman Congregation for the Doctrine of the Faith in 1973.

preacher and teacher and nothing more, why should there be a religion based on him, given the prominence of other ancient teachers (Aristotle, Plato, Seneca, etc.)? If Jesus was chiefly a deluded apocalyptic preacher who wrongly thought the end of the world would come soon, why continue to proclaim him as the savior of the world? If Jesus' resurrection from the dead is simply a way of expressing the conviction that he is with God, why is he to be worshiped, given the many other saintly people who are surely with God? Those who advance such views of Jesus often claim they are trying to reshape Christian belief and proclamation. More bluntly, however, their views of Jesus would make traditional Christian belief illusory and traditional proclamation irresponsible.

(5) Apocryphal gospels are a major tool in the more radical "historical Jesus" research with the supposition that in whole or part they antedate the canonical Gospels and are a more reliable guide to what Jesus was like. For instance, the collection of Jesus' sayings found in the Coptic *Gospel of Thomas* is claimed to represent a collection already in existence in 50s or 60s and (alongside Q) to constitute evidence for Jesus as a Cynic preacher. While reputable scholars do argue that some of the material in *GTh* may represent early tradition, many others argue that all or most of *GTh* is dependent on the canonical Gospels and thus casts no light on the historical Jesus.[34] Crossan would make all the canonical Gospels dependent for the basic narrative of Jesus' passion and death on sections of the *Gospel of Peter* which, in his judgment, contain a very early account showing that the passion story was not based on memories of what happened but on imaginative inventions suggested by OT passages. In fact, however, most scholars who have reviewed Crossan's work disagree strongly, contending that directly or indirectly *GPet* depends on the canonical Gospels, and thus offers no independent information about the historical passion and death of Jesus.[35] Despite frequent claims in the media, it is far from established that we have any extensive sources of historical knowledge about Jesus beyond the NT.

Bibliography on the Historical Jesus

The topic is tangential to the main purpose of this *Introduction* which is concerned with the *books* of the NT; and so here only a very limited list is offered, indicating possibilities for further study. Some of the works on NT Theology and the Surveys of NT Research mentioned in the *Bibliography* of Chapter 1 above have sections on the historical Jesus.

[34]The situation is well summed up by G. J. Riley, CRBS 2 (1994), 232: "The single most controversial issue facing scholars is whether or not the GTh is a genuine witness to an independent stream of tradition reaching back to Jesus."

[35]See BDM 2.1317–49; A. Kirk, NTS 40 (1994), 572–95; C. A. Evans, BulBR 6 (1996), 159–65.

Bockmuehl, M., *This Jesus: Martyr, Lord, Messiah* (Edinburgh: Clark, 1994).
Chilton, B. D., and C. A. Evans, eds., *Studying the Historical Jesus* (Leiden: Brill, 1994).
Cowdell, S., *Is Jesus Unique? A Study of Recent Christology* (New York: Paulist, 1996).
Davies, S. L., *Jesus the Healer* (New York: Continuum, 1995).
Evans, C. A., *Life of Jesus Research: An Annotated Bibliography* (Leiden: Brill, 1996).
———, *Jesus and His Contemporaries* (Leiden: Brill, 1995).
———, and S. E. Porter, eds., *The Historical Jesus* (Sheffield: Academic, 1995).
Gnilka, J., *Jesus of Nazareth* (Peabody, MA: Hendrickson, 1997).
Hengel, M., *Studies in Early Christology* (Edinburgh: Clark, 1995).
Hultgren, A. J., *The Rise of Normative Christianity* (Minneapolis: A/F, 1994).
Johnson, L. T., *The Real Jesus* (San Francisco: Harper, 1995).
Meier, J. P., *A Marginal Jew* (3 vols.; New York: Doubleday, 1991–).
———, "Why Search for the Historical Jesus?" BRev 9 (#3; 1993), 30–32, 57.
———, "Dividing Lines in Jesus Research Today," *Interpretation* 50 (1996), 355–72. Several other articles in this issue are relevant to this Appendix.
Neill, S., and N. T. Wright, *The Interpretation of the New Testament: 1861–1986* (2d ed.; New York: Oxford, 1988).
Scott, B. B., "From Reimarus to Crossan: Stages in a Quest," CRBS 2 (1994), 253–80.
Senior, D. P., "The Never Ending Quest for Jesus," TBT 34 (1996), 141–47.
Strimple, R. B., *The Modern Search for the Real Jesus* (Philippsburg, NJ: P & R, 1995).
Wilkins, M. J., and J. P. Moreland, eds., *Jesus under Fire: Modern Scholarship Reinvents the Historical Jesus* (Grand Rapids: Zondervan, 1995).
Witherington, B., III, *The Jesus Quest: The Third Search for the Jew of Nazareth* (Downers Grove, IL: InterVarsity, 1995).
Wright, N. T., *Jesus and the Victory of God* (Minneapolis: A/F, 1996).
———, *The Original Jesus* (Grand Rapids: Eerdmans, 1996).

APPENDIX II

JEWISH AND CHRISTIAN WRITINGS PERTINENT TO THE NEW TESTAMENT

As Jewish background for the NT, besides the OT (including the Deuterocanonical Books), there are a series of extracanonical writings from the 3d century BC into the 2d century AD, including the DSS, the Apocrypha, and the works of Josephus.[1] There are also Christian writings from the period AD 90–200, some of them considered apocryphal, some called "Apostolic Fathers," and (on opposite sides) gnostic[2] and early patristic writings. References have been made to these in this *Introduction,* and the goal here is to supply in the briefest manner some useful information on the most important. Greater detail can be found in NJBC 67 and 80:34–82.

Jewish Writings[3]

THE DEAD SEA SCROLLS. The title "Qumran Literature" covers some ten scrolls and thousands of fragments found, beginning in 1947, in caves near Qumran on the NW shore of the Dead Sea. Written or copied between the late 3d century BC and the early 1st century AD, the approximately 800 mss. represented consist of OT books, including many of the Deuterocanonical Books (often in a variety of textual traditions); Apocrypha (often in the long-lost original languages); and compositions of the particular community of Jews who lived at the Qumran settlement. Most scholars identify this community as Essenes (first subsection in Chapter 5 above), and think that they moved to Qumran during the Maccabean era (*ca.* 150 BC), only to be destroyed by the Romans *ca.* AD 68. A figure called "the Righteous Teacher," probably of a priestly family of the purest Zadokite lineage, is thought to be

[1]Philo should also be included, but has been treated on pp. 91, 95 above.

[2]Marcion should also be included, but has been treated on p. 14 above.

[3]Although most (or all) of the NT and some of the Christian writings to be discussed in the next subsection were composed by those who were born Jews, the present heading is meant to cover works written by Jews who were not Christian.

either the community founder or its most important figure. The most important community compositions are **QS,**[4] the community rule of life (150–125 BC); **QSa,** a short addendum to the rule looking toward the last days; **QSb,** another addendum consisting of blessings; **QH,** a collection of hymns or psalms, many perhaps composed by the Righteous Teacher; **QM** (1st century AD), an imaginative description of the final war to be waged between the forces of good and evil; **QpHab,** the "p" indicating a *pesher* or line-by-line commentary on an OT book (e.g., Habakkuk), applying it to Qumran life-circumstances; **QapGen** (25 BC–AD 25), an elaboration of Gen in Aramaic; **3Q15** (late 1st century AD, and perhaps not stemming from the Qumranians), a copper scroll or plaque in Hebrew close to that of the Mishna, describing where Temple treasures were buried; **11QMelch** (50–25 BC), fragments of an eschatological midrash found in Cave 11 dealing with Melchizedek as a heavenly figure; **11QTemple** (1st century AD), a very long scroll of God's revelations to Moses about how the Temple should be built. Despite claims to the contrary, there is no clear evidence of Christian influence or component in the Qumran DSS.

I (ETHIOPIC) ENOCH. Apocalyptic writing about what was seen by Enoch (whom God took from the earth in Gen 5:24) circulated in Aramaic from 300 BC onward. There are fragments of some dozen Enoch mss. among the DSS; in addition the disparate collection we know as *I Enoch* is preserved partially (33 percent) in Greek, and completely in Ethiopic. Divided into five books, it contains imaginative expansions of the fall of the angels in Gen 6:1–4; apocalyptic descriptions and dream visions (comparable to Dan); astronomical speculations; apocalyptic divisions of world eras; and in chaps. 37–71 elaborate visionary discourses or parables that describe a preexistent Son of Man. This parable section has not been discovered in the DSS fragments, and so some would claim that it was a Christian composition. Later works are *II* (*Slavonic*) *Enoch* and *III* (*Hebrew*) *Enoch.*

JUBILEES. This 2d-century BC rewriting of Gen 1–Exod 14 is related to other apocryphal Moses material. Fragments of some dozen Hebrew mss. of *Jub* have been found in the Dead Sea area; about one quarter of *Jub* is preserved in Lat; but the whole book has been preserved only in Ethiopic. It attributes evil to the fallen angels. The most notable characteristic is calendric interest, dividing the history of the world into 49 periods (jubilees) of 49 years each. The calculation of the year reflects a solar calendar of 364 days (12 months of 30 days and 4 intercalary days), in which the same dates fall on the same day of the week every year—a calendar followed also by

[4]Readers will often see a document with a prefaced numeral designating the number of the Qumran cave in which it was found, thus, 1QS, which means the ms. of QS found in Cave 1.

the Qumran community which protested against the Maccabean use of a lunar calendar in Temple observance.

(LETTER OF) ARISTEAS TO PHILOCRATES. Reflecting the large Jewish community in Alexandria, this small 2d-century BC book (not a letter) narrates the (*legendary*) origin of the translation of the Pentateuch from Hebrew into Greek. Under King Ptolemy II Philadelphus (285–246 BC) the royal librarian, who desired a copy of the Jewish Law for the famous library at Alexandria, arranged that seventy-two elders (six from each tribe) be sent by the high priest in Jerusalem. They produced the LXX (Septuagint, from the Latin for the rounded number seventy), although in fact that name is applied to the Greek translations and compositions of the *whole* OT made over four centuries, beginning probably before 300 BC (NJBC 68.63).

LIVES OF THE PROPHETS. There are numerous Greek mss., many of them with Christian additions. The best Greek ms., a 6th-century AD codex in the Vatican Library, treats twenty-three Jewish prophets without *obvious* Christian interpolations. The work was probably written in Palestine before AD 70. Whether the original was in Greek drawing on Semitic sources, or in Hebrew or Aramaic and then translated into Greek is uncertain. The stated goal is to supply the name of the prophet, where he was from, where and how he died, and where he was buried; but the amount of information varies greatly, with the life of Joel the shortest, and that of Daniel relatively long. As background for the Gospels, the *Lives* attest a biographical interest in the prophetic figure, disproportionately concentrated on the death (at times narrating a martyr's death not attested in the OT), as well as an attempt to supply a known place of burial.

TESTAMENT (OR ASSUMPTION) OF MOSES. Antiquity knew of both a *Testament of Moses* and an *Assumption of Moses*. An untitled Latin work that has survived, although entitled *Assumption* by its first editor, is Moses' final speech or testament (cf. Deut 31–34) to Joshua about the future history of Israel, coming to a conclusion with the Roman intervention after Herod the Great's death. It was probably composed in Aramaic or Hebrew and revised before AD 30. Jude seems to refer to the lost *Assumption*.

IV MACCABEES. This philosophical discourse or "diatribe" on the supremacy of Jewish religious reason over human passions and sufferings is illustrated by OT examples, especially the martyrs of II Macc 6–7. Composed in Greek in the diaspora (Antioch? Alexandria?) probably *ca.* 40 AD, it embodies a theology of vicarious suffering in martyrdom that inspired Christian commemoration of martyrs.

IV EZRA OR THE APOCALYPSE OF EZRA.[5] A work known as 2 Esdras (or

[5]M. E. Stone (Hermeneia; Minneapolis: A/F, 1990) offers a major commentary.

IV Esdras in the Latin Vulgate) contains sixteen chapters, of which chaps. 1–2 and 15–16 are Christian compositions. Chaps. 3–14 constitute *IV Ezra,* a Jewish work of *ca.* AD 90–120, originally written in Hebrew or Aramaic but now preserved most completely in Latin. It consists of seven dialogues/visions involving Shealtiel who was taken captive at the time of the Babylonian destruction of Jerusalem (I Chron 3:17; Ezra 3:2), confusingly identified as Ezra (who lived a century later). The parallel between that period and the aftermath of the Roman destruction of Jerusalem in AD 70 sparked a florescence of Jewish apocalyptic literature contemporary with the later part of the NT, exemplified by works bearing the name of Ezra and Baruch.

II BARUCH, OR THE SYRIAC APOCALYPSE OF BARUCH. Preserved in a Syriac translation from the (original?) Greek, this Jewish work from AD 95–120 is dependent on *IV Ezra* or a source common to both. Baruch, the secretary of Jeremiah who lived at the time of the Babylonian destruction of Jerusalem, served as an appropriate if fictional subject to issue prophetic/apocalyptic warnings and encouragement. There is also *III Baruch or the Greek Apocalypse of Baruch,* probably composed in Egypt AD 70–150; it probes the mysteries of the heavenly realms.

PSALMS OF SOLOMON. Preserved in medieval Greek mss. and Syriac, these eighteen psalms were originally composed in Hebrew in Palestine (Jerusalem) 65–40 BC. Because they interpret the Roman invasion by Pompey as punishment of the corruption of the Sadducee high priests, they have been attributed to the Pharisees (although other antiSadducee groups, like the Qumran Essenes, are a possibility). Descriptions in Pss 17–18 of the anticipated Davidic Messiah who will conquer the Gentiles and establish a kingdom for the tribes of Israel are important background for the NT.

FLAVIUS JOSEPHUS. Born in Palestine of a priestly clan in AD 37, Josephus ben Matthias died after 94, probably in Rome. Although he was a commander of Jewish forces in Galilee during the revolt against Rome (66–70), he surrendered to Vespasian, who set him free when he predicted that the Roman general would become emperor. From 69 on he was a client of Vespasian's "Flavian" imperial family (whence "Flavius"), so that Titus brought him to Rome and installed him in the imperial palace. There in the 70s he wrote *The Jewish War* (originally in Aramaic, but translated into Greek) as propaganda to show the futility of revolting against the Romans. *Ca.* 94 he finished the *Jewish Antiquities* (*Ant.*) in 20 vols., a massive history of the Jews from patriarchal to Roman times. (His minor works were *Life,* his autobiography, and *Against Apion,* a defense against Pagan slanders.) Josephus offers invaluable but not impartial information about the postbiblical period, and sometimes a comparison of the *War* and the *Ant.* shows his biases. The famous *Testimonium Flavianum* (*Ant.* 18.3.3; # 63–64) is Josephus' witness to Jesus; shorn of later Christian additions it tells of Jesus' astonishing deeds and teaching and that Pilate condemned him to death upon the indictment of "the first-ranking men among us."[6]

TESTAMENTS OF THE TWELVE PATRIARCHS. (For this literary form, see p. 352 above.) If Jacob blesses his twelve sons in Gen 49, this work (preserved in late Greek mss. but composed before AD 200) contains the testament of each of those twelve to his own sons. Its witness to messianic expectations is important. There are Christian passages, and scholars are divided: Were they additions to a Jewish original written just before 100 BC, or was the basic work a Jewish Christian composition drawing on earlier sources? Defending the latter position is the important commentary by H. W. Hollander and M. de Jonge (Leiden: Brill, 1985). De Jonge's valuable translation is found in Sparks, *Apocryphal OT.*

SIBYLLINE ORACLES. From 500 BC poetic oracular statements or prophecies by sibyls (Cumae, Delphi, etc.) were valued and preserved, but eventually the collections perished. Jews and Christians imitated these Pagan oracles, and this Greek work in fourteen books represents a combination of two collections, ranging from *ca.* 150 BC to AD 650. It is not always possible to distinguish Jewish from Christian oracles.

Christian (and Gnostic) Writings

GOSPEL OF THE HEBREWS. This Jewish Christian gospel, independent of Matt and apparently known to Papias (*ca.* 125), survives only in a few patristic quotations. They treat of the descent of the preexistent Christ into Mary, the coming of the Holy Spirit on Jesus at his baptism, and the resurrection appearance of Jesus to James (his brother) at a eucharistic meal. It should not be confused with the *Gospel of the Nazaraeans* that has variants of Matt, or the *Gospel of the Ebionites* that has variants based on Matt and Luke.

SECRET GOSPEL OF MARK (*SGM*). Passages from this work appear in an 18th-century copy of an otherwise unknown letter of Clement of Alexandria (*ca.* 175–200) that M. Smith reported finding in 1958 in a Palestinian monastery. According to Clement, Mark wrote an account of the "Acts of the Lord" (canonical Mark) in Rome; then after Peter's martyrdom Mark brought his notes to Alexandria and expanded the earlier work into "a more spiritual gospel" for the use of those being brought to perfection—a guide to the mysteries that would lead into the inner sanctuary of the truth hidden by the seven veils. Mark left this second edition to the Alexandrian church, in the archives of which it was kept and read only to those being initiated

[6]See BDM 1.373–76; J. P. Meier, CBQ 52 (1990), 76–103.

into the great mysteries. Unfortunately Carpocrates (a 2d-century heretic) got a copy which, Clement claimed, he was misinterpreting for his "blasphemous and carnal doctrine." The most important passage in *SGM* concerns Jesus raising a young man from the tomb who then loved Jesus and came to him at night with a linen cloth over his naked body. Some scholars (H. Koester, Crossan) would argue that this is closer to the larger original "Marcan" composition, and that canonical Mark is a secondary abbreviation because some passages in *SGM* were considered scandalous. Most think of *SGM* as a conflated pastiche from the canonical Gospels used to support esoteric initiations (as Clement suggests). See Chapter 6 above, n. 20.

GOSPEL OF PETER (*GPet*). This Greek work was known in the 2d century and hesitantly rejected as unsound by Bishop Serapion of Antioch. The only sizable portion, preserved in a codex from *ca.* 800, treats a segment of the passion from the final trial of Jesus to the resurrection. There are elements in it that are clearly not historical: Herod and the Jews put Jesus to death; Pilate has to ask Herod's permission for the body; the cross that was put into Jesus' tomb comes forth and speaks. Crossan, however, contends that large portions of *GPet* are older than the canonical passion accounts, which drew on it. Most scholars regard *GPet* as an imaginative expansion of the canonical Gospels, whether known by reading or hearing. See Chapter 6 above, n. 4 and n. 21.

PROTEVANGELIUM OF JAMES. This work, preserved in many Greek mss. beginning in the 3d century, was in circulation by mid-2d century. Dealing with Mary's family, her upbringing and marriage to Joseph, as well as the birth of Jesus, it claims to have been written by James (presumably because as "brother of the Lord" he would have known the family history). Its incorrect knowledge of Judaism shows that it is not a historical account, even though it may contain some reliable items of earlier tradition. The *Protevangelium* gives the names of Mary's parents as Joachim and Anne, has Mary presented at the Temple at an early age, describes the "brothers" of Jesus as children of Joseph by a previous marriage, and suggests that Mary gave birth to Jesus painlessly and without any rupture of the hymen. It has had great influence on religious art and the development of mariology.[7]

INFANCY GOSPEL OF THOMAS. The original Greek survives only in very late mss., although there are Latin and Syriac texts from the 5th century. It consists of a number of legendary episodes showing the miraculous powers of the boy Jesus from age five through twelve. (The best known is how he

[7]This and the next-listed apocryphon are translated with notes in R. F. Hock, *The Infancy Gospels of James and Thomas* (Santa Rosa, CA: Polebridge, 1995).

made clay birds fly.) Christologically it is meant to show that the boy Jesus had the same powers (and the same opposition) as the adult Jesus.

ODES OF SOLOMON. It is uncertain whether the original composition (by a Jewish Christian in the early 2d century AD, probably in Syria) was in Hebrew or Aramaic or Greek; but the most complete presentation of the forty-two *Odes* is in Syriac. Although some think of them as gnostic, they have parallels to Jewish apocalyptic and the DSS, as well as to certain aspects of the Fourth Gospel. The *Odes,* expressing joy at the appearance of the Messiah, may have had baptismal use.

I CLEMENT.[8] A letter-treatise from the church of Rome to the church of Corinth in order to support some Corinthian presbyters who had been deposed. Dionysus of Corinth (*ca.* 170) attributed it to Clement, an important figure of the Roman church (corresponding secretary and/or leading presbyter?).[9] Most date it *ca.* 96 (partially in dependence on the thesis of persecution under the Emperor Domitian: pp. 805–9 above), although 96–120 would be a more certain time range. The letter stresses authority and has the (twofold) church structure of bishops and deacons stem from the apostles (p. 648 above). A homily on repentance and leading a holy life known as II CLEMENT[10] (mid-2d century?), not written by the same author, may stem from the aftermath of the Corinth-Rome interchange in *I Clement.*

DIDACHE.[11] More fully known as *The Teaching (Didachē) of the Lord through the Twelve Apostles to the Nations,* this is an instructional handbook on ethics and liturgical practices (baptism, eucharist). Whether it is a unified composition is uncertain. The closeness to Matt has made Syria at the beginning of the 2d century the most plausible situation for its earliest sections. Its eucharistic teaching has parallels to Johannine language; the picture of church organization (bishops and deacons replacing prophets and teachers: p. 646 above) seems to imply a preIgnatius situation.

LETTERS OF IGNATIUS OF ANTIOCH.[12] The bishop of Antioch was arrested,

[8]This and the next five paragraphs select from early church writings called "The Apostolic Fathers," because they were thought in general to be written in the subapostolic period, i.e., after the passing of the apostles. Some of them were written before the final works of the NT. The Greek text plus a (not-too-satisfactory) Eng translation is found in Loeb Classical library, by K. Lake (2 vols.; New York: Putnam's, 1912); also a paperback Eng ed. by J. N. Sparks (New York: Nelson, 1978).

[9]The structure of one bishop presiding over the presbyters does not seem to have been established in the Roman church much before mid-2d century AD, but anachronistically Clement would be later identified as bishop. See BMAR 159–83. For the *Pseudo-Clementine* literature, see Chapter 34 above, n. 6.

[10]K. P. Donfried, *The Setting of Second Clement* (NovTSup 38; Leiden: Brill, 1974).

[11]B. S. Walters, *The Unknown Teaching of the Twelve Apostles* (San Jose, CA: Bibliographies, 1991); C. N. Jefford, ed., *The Didache in Context* (NovTSup 77; Leiden: Brill, 1994); J. A. Draper, *The Didache in Modern Research* (Leiden: Brill, 1996).

[12]W. R. Schoedel (Hermeneia; Philadelphia: Fortress, 1985) offers detailed commentary.

condemned, brought to Rome as a criminal and executed there *ca.* 110. During the journey he was visited by Christian representatives; and he wrote seven letters to the *Ephesians, Magnesians, Trallians, Romans, Philadelphians, Smyrneans,* and to *Polycarp* (the bishop of Smyrna). Except for *Romans,* the letters attest to and support the threefold structure of one bishop, presbyters, and deacons, because the authority of the bishop can be a bulwark against division and heresy. In *Smyrneans* 8.2 he uses the expression "the catholic church" (*hē katholikē ekklēsia*).

LETTER OF POLYCARP (to the Philippians). This cover letter for a collection of Ignatius' letters may be composite, with chaps. 13–14 written shortly after Ignatius' visit and while he was still alive (13.1–2), but chaps. 1–12 after his martyrdom (9.1). In any case a date between 110 and 135 is likely. Polycarp is advising the Philippian church about the treatment of a presbyter who had misused funds. He seems to show knowledge of various Pauline writings and is especially close to the Pastorals. In a chain of 2d-century church writers Polycarp (who himself was martyred in Smyrna in 155–160—the *Martyrdom of Polycarp*) was acquainted at the earlier end with Ignatius and at the later end with Irenaeus (the bishop of Lyons who wrote the 5-volume *Adversus Haereses* against the gnostics in 180–190 and may have been martyred *ca.* 202).

SHEPHERD OF HERMAS.[13] Some in the early church elevated this vibrant call to conversion of heart, composed in Rome before AD 150, to the level of canonical Scripture; for instance, it was part of the 4th-century Codex Sinaiticus of the NT. Sold in the past from one master to another, Hermas seems to have been a manumitted slave who was a prophet (probably not a presbyter). From an angel-shepherd he received revelations and dictation that are written down in three sections of the document: five Visions; twelve Mandates (or commandments); and ten Similitudes or parables. The apocalyptic Visions are hard to diagnose. The instructions on virtue in the Mandates suppose a spiritual anthropology in which good and bad spirits are active (cf. the DSS and the *Didache*) and have to be discerned. The Similitudes (the longest section of the book) strongly stress the care of the poor. *Hermas* testifies to the survival of a strong Jewish bent in Roman Christianity.

THE EPISTLE OF BARNABAS.[14] This treatise was written in Greek by an unknown author (probably a Gentile), employing the allegorical style of OT interpretation in vogue at Alexandria. It too was contained in Codex Sinaiti-

[13]For an excellent brief treatment of this complicated document, C. Osiek, BRev 10 (#5; 1994), 48–54.

[14]There are many unresolved problems about this work; see J. C. Paget, *The Epistle of Barnabas* (WUNT 2.64; Tübingen: Mohr-Siebeck, 1994).

cus. The ethical instruction of *Barnabas* involves the "two ways," i.e., the way of light and the way of darkness (a theme strongly emphasized in DSS dualism). Although the author is heavily influenced by Jewish thought, he criticizes Jewish ritual. Many find in 16:3–4 a reference to Hadrian's plan to build a temple to Zeus on the site of the destroyed Jerusalem Temple, and that suggests a date before 135.

WRITINGS OF JUSTIN MARTYR. A Gentile from Palestine (modern Nablus), he spent time in Ephesus, and was martyred in Rome *ca.* 165. He had tried Greek philosophies before he became a Christian. In 156 he addressed an *Apology* to the Emperor Antoninus Pius defending Christianity against slanders, and later wrote the *Dialogue with the Jew Trypho.* "Trypho" may be a figure constructed out of Jewish spokesmen or attitudes of the time, but the work gives us an idea (albeit biased) of Jewish objections to Christianity and the refutations developed against them.

DIATESSARON OF TATIAN. Born in the East in the Euphrates area, Tatian came to Rome, was converted to Christianity, and became a pupil of Justin. He wrote against Greek culture and then returned to Mesopotamia in 172. The tradition is that he was a heretic (advocating over-asceticism, exemplified by an opposition to marital relations associated with Encratism). He is remembered for composing the *Diatessaron* (a harmony from the four Gospels and some noncanonical material); but we do not know whether he wrote it in Rome or back in the East, and whether in Greek or (more probably) in Syriac. It had enormous influence and served in place of the canonical Gospels for centuries in the Syriac-speaking church. The original was lost; and so the *Diatessaron* has had to be reconstructed from later harmonies and particularly from St. Ephrem's commentary on it.[15]

GOSPEL OF THOMAS (*GTh*).[16] At Nag Hammadi in Egypt, some 300 miles south of Cairo near the site of a 4th-century monastery, there were discovered in 1945 thirteen Coptic codices containing some forty-six different tractates, almost forty of which were not known previously. They are translations of earlier Greek documents; and many are gnostic (of various types), but the line between Christian ascetic and gnostic is not always definable. *GTh,* a collection of 114 sayings of the living (risen) Jesus, is the most important treatise for NT purposes. (Although called a gospel, such a sayings collection without a biographical framework offers a parallel to the hypothetical Q source of Matt and Luke.) Seventy-nine have some parallel in the Synoptic tradition, and there has been considerable debate as to whether the

[15]This is available in an edition by C. McCarthy (New York: Oxford, 1994). For a survey of research: W. L. Petersen, *Tatian's Diatessaron* (VC Supplement 23; Leiden: Brill, 1994).

[16]For recent research, G. J. Riley, CRBS 2 (1994), 227–52.

GTh form of some of them is more original. In the Jesus Seminar all or most of *GTh* is treated as a composition of the 50s antedating the canonical Gospels; but the majority of scholars thinks that, although *GTh* may have preserved some original sayings of Jesus, as a whole the work is a composition of the 2d century and reflects at times incipient gnosticism. In themselves the sayings are often obscure without the interpretive key supplied by the gnostic myth of the fall from heavenly origin to this world of ignorance, and the possibility of return through knowledge. See Chapter 8 above, *Issue* 6; and Chapter 9, n. 48.

GOSPEL OF TRUTH. The original of this eloquent Nag Hammadi homiletic reflection on Jesus was composed in Greek in the 2d century AD and may have been written by the famous gnostic teacher Valentinus. The gnostic myth of the fall of Sophia from the divine realm to this world seems to underlie its picture of Jesus as the manifestation of the unknowable Father God. It reflects paraphrases of the canonical Gospels.

Bibliography: General Works

Jewish Writings:

Evans, C. A., *Noncanonical Writings and New Testament Interpretation* (Peabody, MA: Hendrickson, 1992). Very brief information on all noncanonical works, Jewish and Christian.

DEAD SEA SCROLLS: Bibliography at end of Chapter 5 above; also NJBC 67.79–117.

APOCRYPHA (OT): Most complete collection is OTP.
The Apocryphal Old Testament, ed. H.F.D. Sparks (Oxford: Clarendon, 1994).
Apocrypha and Pseudepigrapha of the Old Testament, ed. R. H. Charles (2 vols.; Oxford: Clarendon, 1913).

JOSEPHUS: Bibliography at end of Chapter 4 above.

Christian (and Gnostic) Writings:

APOCRYPHA (NT): Most complete collection is HSNTA.
The Apocryphal New Testament, ed. J. K. Elliott (Oxford: Clarendon, 1993).
The Apocryphal Jesus, ed. J. K. Elliott (New York: Oxford, 1996). Select texts from the apocryphal gospels.

EARLY CHURCH WRITERS: For more detail and bibliography, see NJBC 80.34–82.
Wagner, W. H., *After the Apostles. Christianity in the Second Century* (Minneapolis: A/F, 1994).

GNOSTICS: A bibliography on gnosticism appears at the end of Chapter 5 above.

INDEXES

I Bibliographical Index of Authors
II Index of Subjects

INDEX I.
BIBLIOGRAPHICAL INDEX OF AUTHORS

References to the works of other authors are found both in the footnotes and in the bibliographies at the end of chapters. Let me emphasize that those bibliographies are *not* lists of recommended books—in my judgment some of the listed items are idiosyncratic and even wrong in their direction. But this *Introduction* is meant for the use of readers and teachers with various interests and views different from mine; deliberately, therefore, the bibliographies include a wide range of entries. Footnotes contain entries pertinent to particular subjects or sections of a chapter (and often cite works far more important than those listed in the bibliographies).

This index, which covers both bibliographies and footnotes, does not register discussions of authors' views; rather it lists the page on which readers can find the data about a book or article. Throughout the *Introduction* references to books are made by giving the author's last name and one or two significant words from the title, and such abbreviated titles of bibliography books are included in this index to facilitate searching for the full data. (For "Commentaries and Studies in Series," the abbreviated title is the biblical book treated in the chapter.) Other works (articles in bibliographies; footnote references) are indicated simply by the numbers of the pages on which they appear.

Family names beginning in *de, di, du* and in *van, von* are listed under *d* and *v* respectively; ä, ö, ü are treated as if ae, oe, and ue.

Aageson, J. W. *Written* 442
Abbott, E. A. 772
Johannine 379
Abbott, T. K. *Colossians* 618
Abrahamsen, V. 485
Achtemeier, P. J. 140, 150, 151, 155, 471
1 Peter 724
Mark (ABD & ProcC) 168
Romans 583
Adam, A.K.M. *Postmodern* 25
Adamson, J. B. *James* 746
James Man 747
Ahern, B. A. 612
Aland, B. *NT Text Criticism* 53
Aland, K. "Problem" 588
Aland, K. and B. *Text NT* 53
Albright, W. F. *Matthew* 222
Alexander, L. 227
Alexander, N. *1–3 John* 393
Allan, J. A. *Ephesians* 637
"In Christ" 637
Allison, D. C. 706
Matthew 222
New 176
Allison, R. W. 524
Ambrozic, A. M. *Hidden* 168
Anderson, B. W. *Books* (TBOB) 15
Anderson, C. P. 618
Anderson, G. 91
Anderson, H. *Mark* 168

Anderson, H. G. 576
Anderson, J. C. (Survey) 223
Mark 168
Matthew's Narrative 223
Anderson, P. N. *Christology* 379
Arnold, C. E. 636
Colossian 618
Arzt, P. 415
Ashton, J. *Interpretation & Understanding* 379
Attridge, H. W. 121
Hebrews 703
Aune, D. E. 779, 782
"Problem" 123
"Social" 811
Aus, R. *2 Thess* 598
Avi-Yonah, M. *Encyclopedia* 72

Baasland, E. 481
Bacon, B. W. 398
Gospel 379
Studies 223
Badenas, R. 570
Báez-Camargo, G. *Archaeological* 72
Baggott, L. J. *Colossians* 618
Bailey, J. A. 365, 598
Bailey, K. E. 245
Baird, W. 545
NT Research 19
Baker, W. R. *Personal* 747
Balch, D. L. 710
NT Social 71
Social History 223
Balchin, J. F. 603
Baldwin, H. S. 660
Ball, D. M. 347
Balz, H. *Exeget. Dictionary* 18
Bandstra, A. J. 781
Banks, R. 522
Paul's 442
Barbour, R. S. 618
Barclay, J.M.G. 425, 469
"Conflict" 465
Obeying 481
Barr, A. *Diagram Synoptic* 123
Barr, D. L. 799
Barraclough, R. 95
Barré, M. 537
Barrett, C. K. 337, 353, 538, 556, 557, 651, 683
Acts 331
1 Corinthians 538
2 Corinthians 557
Essays 379
Essays on Paul 569
Freedom 481
John 379
Luke Historian 276
NT Background 93
Pastorals 650
Paul 442
Romans 583
Bartchy, S. S. 519
Barth, G. 188
Barth, K. *Christ & Romans* 583
Philippians 500
Barth, M. *Colossians* 618
Ephesians 637
"Traditions" 637
Bartlet, V. 400
Bartlett, D. L. 645
Romans 583
Barton, S. C. 131
Bassler, J. M. 597, 659
Pauline Theol. 1 444
Bates, W. H. 548
Batey, R. A. 69
Bauckham, R. J. 772, 777, 790, 798
Climax 811
Jude Relatives 760
Palestinian 70
Revelation 811
2 Peter 771
Bauer, B. 818
Bauer, D. R. 174, 175
Treasures 223
Baumert, N. 524
Beale, G. K. *Right* 38
Beall, T. S. *Josephus* 93
Beardslee, W. A. *Literary* 25
Beare, F. W. *Ephesians* 637
First Peter 724
Philippians 500
Beasley-Murray, G. R. 144
John & Gospel 379
Revelation 811
2 Corinthians 557
Beasley-Murray, P. 603
Beavis, M. A. 132
Bechtler, S. R. 570
Beck, N. A. 137
Becker, J. *Paul* 442

Beker, J. C. *Heirs* 588
NT Introd. 16
Paul books 442
Bell, A. A., Jr. 805
Bell, I. H. *Cults* 94
Belleville, L. L. 471, 538, 544
Bellinzoni, A. J. *Two-Source* 123
Benko, S. *Pagan Rome* 94
Benoit, P. *Jesus* 612
Bernard, J. H. *John* 379
Best, E. 156, 612, 626, 629, 718
Ephesians 637
1 Peter 724
Mark 168
Romans 583
2 Corinthians 557
Temptation 168
Thessalonians 465
Betz, H. D. 481, 551
Essays & Sermon 178
Galatians 481
Matthew 222
2 Corinthians 557
Betz, O. 81, 155
Beutler, J. 348
Bickerman, E. J. *Chronology* 72
Maccabees 78
Bieringer, R. *Corinthian* 539
Studies 557
Bigg, C. *1 Peter* 724
Bilezikian, G. C. *Liberated* 168
Birdsall, J. N. 53
Bittner, W. 364
Black, C. C. 24, 144, 150, 158, 161, 393
Exploring (under Culpepper) 380
Black, M. 191, 751
Romans 583
Blackman, E. C. *James* 746
Marcion 14
Blanke, S. *Colossians* 618
Blenkinsopp, J. *Corinthian* 539
Blevins, J. L. *Messianic* 153
Revelation 811
Bligh, J. *Galatians* 481
Block, D. A. 690
Blomberg, C. L. 133, 244
Matthew 223
Bloomquist, L. G. *Function* 500
Blount, B. K. *Cultural* 46
Boccaccini, G. *Middle Judaism* 70
Bock, D. L. *Luke* 276
Bockmuehl, M. *This Jesus* 830
Boers, H. 465
Justification 481
Boesak, A. 810
Bogart, J. *Orthodox* 393
Boismard, M.-É. 327, 368, 389
Boobyer, G. H. 752, 763
Borg, M. J. 823
Borgen, P. 65, 324, 364
Bread & Logos 346
Paul 481
Philo writings 95
Boring, M. E. 131, 778, 819
Continuing 124
Hellenistic 93
Matthew 222
Revelation 811
Sayings 124
Bornkamm, G. 398, 557, 618, 819
Paul 442
Tradition 223
Boswell, J. 529
Botha, P.J.J. 161
Boucher, M. I. 132
Bovon, F. *Luke Theologian* 276
Boyle, M. O. 730
Braaten, C. E. *Reclaiming* 46
Bratcher, R. G. xxxvi
Timothy 651
Braun, W. 248
Brawley, R. L. 272
Briggs, R. C. (Survey) 393
Brinsmead, B. H. *Galatians* 481
Broadhead, E. K. *Prophet* 168
Brocke, M. 180
Bromiley, G. W. (abridg. Kittel) 18
Broneer, O. 521, 539
Brooke, A. E. *1–3 John* 393
Brooks, J. A. 743
Brown, A. R. *Cross* 539
Brown, C. 133
Brown, J. P. 149
Brown, L. A. 651
Brown, R. E. 80, 86, 112, 180, 301, 328, 353, 372, 377, 391, 607, 618, 625, 637, 645, 651, 723, 819
BBM, BCALB, BDM, BEJ xxv
BGJ, BINTC, BMAR, BNTE, BROQ xxvi
Community 379
"Further" 583
MNT, NJBC xxix, 16

Brown, R. E. (*continued*)
Once 331
PNT xxx
Brown, R. M. 27
Brown, S. 370
Apostasy 276
Origins 16
Browning, W.R.F. *Luke* 276
Bruce, F. F. 19, 465, 603, 618, 637, 692, 812
Acts 331
Colossians 618
Commentary Acts 332
Epistles John 393
1 Corinthians 538
Galatians 481
Hebrews 703
NT History 70
Paul 442
Philippians 500
Survey 393
Thessalonians 465
Bryan, C. A. *Preface* 168
Buchanan, G. W. 371
Hebrews 703
Revelation 812
Buck, C. H. Jr. 553
Paul 445
Buckel, J. *Free* 482
Bujard, W. 610
Bultmann, R. 89, 568
BHST xxvi
1–3 John 393
John 379
Second Corinthians 558
Theology 18
Burge, G. M. *Anointed* 353
John 379
Burgess, J. *Colossians* 618
Burkert, W. *Greek Religion* 94
Burkett, D. 339
Burkill, T. A. 150
Burnett, F. W. 198
Burney, C. F. 333, 370
Burridge, R. A. *What* 123
Burtchaell, J. T. 733
Philemon's Problem 510
Burton, E. D. *Galatians* 481
Bush, P. G. 656
Bussby, F. 117
Butler, B. C. *Originality* 123
Byrne, B. 368, 519
Reckoning 584
Romans 583
Byrskog, S. *Jesus* 223

Cabaniss, A. 747
Cadbury, H. J. 227, 269, 637
Acts 332
Making & Style 276
Cahill, P. J. 819
Caird, G. B. 623
Colossians 618
Luke 276
NT Theology 18
Philippians 500
Revelation 811
Callan, T. 227
Calloud, J. 24
Campbell, D. A. 478, 567
Campbell, R. A. 538, 650
Elders 645
Campbell, T. H. 423
Cannon, G. E. *Use* 618
Caragounis, C. C. 634
Cargal, T. B. *Restoring* 747
Carlston, C. E. 188, 191, 683
Carrington, P. *Mark* 168
Carroll, J. T. *Response* 276
Carroll, K. 726
Carson, D. A. 333, 364
John 379
Showing 539
Survey 379
Triumphalism 558
Carter, W. 178, 195
Matthew 223
Cartlidge, D. R. *Documents* 93
Casey, J. *Hebrews* 703
Casey, M. 824
Cassidy, R. J. 191
Jesus 276
John's Gospel 379
Political 276
Society 332
Casurella, A. *Bibliography* 724
Catchpole, D. R. 186
Quest 124
Cavallin, H.C.C. 764
Cerfaux, L. *Christ* 442
Christian & Church 442
Chafin, K. L. *1 Corinthians* 538

Chang, A. D. 764
Chapman, J. 400
Charles, J. D. *Literary* 760
Charles, R. H. *Apocrypha* 840
Revelation 811
Charlesworth, J. H. 368, 820
John DSS 80
OTP xxx
Chenderlin, F. 538
Chester, A. *James* 746
Childs, B. S. *Introd. OT* 24
New 16
Chilton, B. D. 378, 824
Studying 830
Chow, J. K. *Patronage* 539
Church, F. F. "Rhetorical" 510
Clark, G. 522
Clark, K. W. 211
Clarke, A. D. *Secular* 539
Cody, A. *Heavenly* 704
Coetzee, J. C. "Holy" 393
Cohen, S.J.D. 81
From 70
Josephus 72
Cole, D. P. 433
Cole, R. A. *Galatians* 481
Mark 168
Coleman, P. 529
Coleridge, M. 228
Collange, J.-F. *Philippians* 500
Collins, J. J. 774, 775, 779
Collins, R. F. 178, 465, 651
Birth & Studies 465
CLPDNW 589
Introd. NT 16
Proclaiming 442
TTC xxxii
Colson, F. H. "Myths" 651
Combrink, H.J.B. 724
Comfort, P. W. *Early* 53
Condon, K. 736
Conzelmann, H. *Acts* 331
1 Corinthians 538
Gentiles 70
Interpreting 17
Jesus 819
Outline 18
Pastorals 650
Theology 276
Cook, D. 667, 680
Cook, J. G. *Structure* 168
Cook, M. J. 150, 211
Cook, S. L. 774
Cooper, E. J. 393
Cooper, W. H. 772
Cope, L. 504, 618
Coppens, J. 607
Corsini, E. *Revelation* 811
Cosgrove, C. H. *Cross* 482
Court, J. *Myth* 812
Revelation 811
Cousar, C. B. *Galatians* 481
Coutts, J. 627, 631
Cowdell, S. *Is Jesus* 830
Craddock, F. B. *1 Peter* 724
Luke 276
Philippians 500
Craffert, P. F. 427
Crafton, J. A. *Agency* 558
Cranfield, C.E.B. *First Epistle* 724
1 Peter (TBC) 724
Mark 168
Romans 583
Romans Shorter 584
Creed, J. M. *Luke* 276
Crehan, J. 772
Cribbs, F. L. 365
1 Peter 724
Studies 637
Cross, F. L. *Studies* 637
Cross, F. M., Jr. *Ancient* 94
Crossan, J. D. 112, 132, 822
Sayings 93
Crotty, R. 729
Crouch, J. E. 608
Crump, D. M. 236
Culliton, J. T. 612
Cullmann, O. 377, 706
Joh. Circle 380
Salvation 18
Culpepper, R. A. 368, 623
Anatomy & Exploring & School 380
1–3 John 393
Luke 276
Cunningham, P. A. *Jewish* 442
Curran, J. T. 764

Dahl, M. E. 535
Dahl, N. A. 471, 516, 576, 637
Studies in Paul 442
Daines, B. 612
Dalton, W. J. 498, 715

D'Angelo, M. R. *Moses* 704
Danker, F. W. 763, 766
1 Peter 724
2 Peter 771
Luke & Jesus 276
2 Corinthians 557
Danove, P. L. 148
Darr, J. A. *Character* 276
Daube, D. 191, 510, 518
Davids, P. H. 735
1 Peter 724
James 746
Davidsen, O. *Narrative* 168
Davies, J. H. *Hebrews* 703
Davies, M. 530
Matthew 222
Pastorals 650
Rhetoric 380
Davies, S. L. 661
Jesus 830
Davies, W. D. 178, 683
Invitation 17
Matthew (with Allison) 222
Paul 442
Dawes, G. R. 520
Dawsey, J. M. *Lukan* 277
Deardorff, J. W. *Problems* 123
de Boer, M. C. 299, 387, 388, 439, 525, 539
From Jesus 380
Joh. Perspectives 380
Deissmann, A. *Light* 93
de Jonge, M. 372, 687, 820, 835
EJ xxvii
Delobel, J. *NT Text Criticism* 53
Demarest, B. 701
De Maris, R. E. 525
Colossian 618
Deming, W. *Paul* 519
Denaux, A. 89, 364
Deppe, D. B. 735
Derrett, J.D.M. 510
Deshardins, M. 772
de Silva, D. A. 686
Deutsch, C. *Lady* 223
Dewey, J. 28, 150, 152
Dexinger, F. 75
Dey, L.K.K. 691
Dibelius, M. 22, 607
James 746–747
Pastorals 650
Paul 442
Studies 332
DiCicco, M. M. 547
Dillon, R. J. 227, 260
Dodd, B. 478
Dodd, C. H. 105, 132, 389
1–3 John 393
Historical & Interpretation 380
Meaning Paul 442
Romans 584
Doig, K. F. *NT Chronology* 72
Donahue, J. R. 132, 145, 153, 156, 161, 199
Donelson, L. R. *Pastorals* 650
Pseudepigraphy 651
Donfried, K. P. 89, 199, 324, 400, 575, 837
"Chronology" 445
"Cults" 465
Theology 442
Thessalonians 465
TRD xxxii
Doty, W. G. *Letters* 420
Doughty, D. J. 488
Dowd, S. E. 143
Downing, F. G. 121, 806
Cynics 94
Drake, A. E. 604
Drane, J. W. *Paul* 443
Draper, J. A. 799, 837
Drury, J. *Tradition* 277
Duke, P. D. 336
Duling, D. C. 27
NT Introd. 17
Dumbrell, W. J. 794
Dumm, D. 80
Duncan, G. S. 500
Dunderberg, I. 116
Dungan, D. L. *Documents* 93
Interrelations 123
Sayings 443
Dunham, D. A. 765
Dunn, J.D.G. 150, 283, 443, 472, 612, 618, 820
Christology 493
Colossians 618
1 Corinthians 538
Galatians (BNTC & NTT) 481
Jesus, Paul 482
Romans 583

Dunnett, W. M. 760
Dunnill, J. *Covenant* 702
Dupont, J. *Salvation* 332
Sources 331
du Rand, J. A. *Johannine* (survey) 379
Dutile, G. 557
Dyrness, W. 733

Easton, B. S. 363
Early 332
Ebeling, G. *Truth* 482
Edwards, J. R. 131
Romans 583
Edwards, O. C., Jr. *Luke's* 277
Edwards, R. A. *Concordance* & *Theology* (Q) 124
Edwards, R. B. *1–3 John* 393
Egelkraut, H. L. 244
Ehrman, B. D. *Orthodox* & *Text NT* 54
Eisenbaum, P. M. *Jewish* 689
Elder, L. B. 519
Ellington, J. *2 Corinthians* 557
Ellingworth, P. *1 Corinthians* 538
Hebrews 703
Elliott, J. H. 27, 510, 711, 719, 724
Elect & *Home* 724
1 Peter 724
Elliott, J. K. *Apocryphal* 840
Greek 651
Language 168
Manuscripts 54
Elliott, N. *Rhetoric* 584
Elliott-Binns, L. E. 729
Ellis, E. E. 161, 436, 452, 539, 651, 760
Eschatology 277
Luke 276
Paul Interpreters 442
Pauline Theology 443
Paul's Use 443
"Pseudonymity" 589
World 380
Ellis, P. F. *Genius* 337
Matthew 223
Ellul, J. *Apocalypse* 812
Empereur, J. 736
Engberg-Pedersen, T. *Paul* 443
Epp, E. J. 327
NTIMI 16
Studies 54
Ernst, C. 772
Esler, P. F. *Community* 277
First 70
Evans, C. A. 142, 618, 829
Jesus books 830
Joh. Writings (under Porter) 381
Luke 276
Luke Scripture 277
Nag Hammadi 95
Noncanonical 840
Paul 443
Pauline (under Porter) 444
Studying (under Chilton) 830
Word 337
Evans, C. F. *Luke* 276
Evans, L. H. *Hebrews* 704
Ewing, W. *Power* 810
Eybers, I. H. "Aspects" 760

Falk, H. *Jesus* 80
Fallon, F. T. *2 Corinthians* 557
Farmer, W. R. 123, 148, 772
CHI xxvii
Formation 18
Gospel & *Synoptic* 123
Farrer, A. 124
Revelation 812
Farris, S. *Hymns* 232
Fee, G. D. *1 Corinthians* 538
God's Presence 443
NT Exegesis 46
Pastorals 650
Philippians 500
Studies 54
Fekkes, J., III 777
Felder, C. H. 27, 608, 730
Feldman, L. H. *Jew Gentile* 70
Josephus writings 72
Fensham, F. C. 692
Ferguson, E. 4
Backgrounds 70
Feuillet, A. 392
Apocalypse 812
Joh. Studies 812
Filson, F. V. 393, 689
Fine, S. 75
Finegan, J. *Archaeology* 72
Chronology 72
Myth 94

Fiore, B. *Function* 651
Fisher, F. L. *1 Corinthians* 538
Fitzgerald, J. T. 544
Fitzmyer, J. A. 77, 83, 141, 144, 189, 207, 420, 423, 433, 492, 544, 551, 582, 688
According Paul 443
Biblical Commission 46
Bibliography 16
FESBNT, FTAG xxvii
Luke 276
Luke Theologian 277
Paul 443
Responses—DSS writings 94
Romans 993
Scripture 46
Spiritual 584
Wandering 83
Fleddermann, H. T. *Mark* 124
Flender, H. *St. Luke* 277
Foakes Jackson, F. J. *Beginnings* 332
Foerster, W. *Gnosis* 95
Forbes, C. 545
Forbes, P.B.R. 745
Ford, J. M. 272, 695
Revelation 811
Forestell, J. T. *Word* 380
Fornberg, T. *Early* 772
Texts 69
Fortna, R. T. 348
Fourth Gospel 380
Gospel Signs 380
Fossum, J. 603, 751
Foulkes, F. *Ephesians* 637
Fowl, S. E. 440, 473
Fowler, R. M. 136
Let 169
Frame, J. *Thessalonians* 465
France, R. T. *Bibliographic* 16
GP xxvii
Matthew 222
Francis, F. O. 392, 606, 607, 618, 739
CAC xxvi
Pauline 442
Franklin, E. *Christ & Luke* 277
Frankowski, J. 683
Franzmann, M. *Jesus* 95
Freed, E. D. 351, 371
Apostle 443
NT Introd. 17
Frend, W.H.C. *Archaeology* 72
Freyne, S. 69
Galilee & World 70
Fridrichsen, A. 133
Friedrichsen, T. A. 115
Friesen, S. 792
Fuchs, E. 819
Fuller, R. C. *Naming* 812
Fuller, R. H. *Critical Introd.* 17
Hebrews 703
Miracles 133
NT Study 19
Pastorals 650
Fung, R.Y.K. *Galatians* 481
Funk, R. W. 186, 400, 420, 821
Parallels 94
Furnish, V. P. 439, 443, 500, 724
"Corinth" 539
2 Corinthians 557
Theology 443
Fusco, V. 255

Gärtner, B. *Areopagus* 311
Gager, J. G. *Kingdom* 70
Gamble, H. Y. 12
Books 10
NT Canon 18
Textual 584
Gammie, J. G. 740
García Martínez, F. *People;* DSS writings 94
Gardner, P. D. 520
Gardner-Smith, P. 363
Garland, D. E. 191, 197, 500, 623
Garrett, J. C., Jr. 811
Garrett, S. R. 242
Gasque, W. *History* 331
Gaston, L. 432
Paul 482
Gaventa, B. R. 332, 471, 517
Geddert, T. J. 144
Geldenhuys, N. *Luke* 276
Gench, F. T. *James* 747
Georgi, D. 553
Opponents 558
Gerhardsson, B. 116, 144, 177, 181
Gertner, M. 745
Getty, M. A. 510
Philippians 500
Geyser, A. S. 747, 800

Giblin, C. H. 248, 337, 598, 797
Revelation 811
Threat 598
Gibson, J. B. 177
Gill, D.W.J. 522
Greco-Roman 70
Gillespie, T. W. 523
Gilliard, F. 463
Gillman, J. 465
Glasson, T. F. *Moses* 380
Glaze, R. E., Jr. 690
Glover, R. 317
Gnilka, J. 625
Jesus 830
Philippians 500
Godsey, J. R. 559
Gooch, P. D. 520
Goodenough, E. R. 510
Philo 95
Goodman, M. 198
Goodspeed, E. J. 589
Key & Meaning 637
Goosen, G. *Studying Gospels* 123
Goppelt, L. *I Peter* 724
Theology NT 18
Gordon, T. D. 482
Goulder, M. D. 301, 324, 606
Luke 277
Midrash 223
Type 332
Gowler, D. B. 238
Grabbe, L. L. *Judaism* 70
Grant, F. C. *Hellenistic & Roman Religion* 94
Grassi, J. A. 358, 368
Grayston, K. *1–3 John* 393
"Pastorals" 651
Green, J. B. *Hearing* 46
Luke & Luke-Acts 276
Green, M. *2 Peter* 771
2 Peter Reconsidered 772
Greenlee, J. H. *Introduction* 54
Greenwood, D. C. *Structuralism* 24
Greve, A. 790
Grispino, J. A. 772
Grosheide, F. W. *1 Corinthians* 538
Grudem, W. A. *1 Peter* 724
Guelich, R. A. *Mark* 168
Sermon 178
Guerra, A. J. 569
Romans 584
Guilding, A. 346
Gundry, R. H. 207, 612, 622, 718
Mark 169
Matthew 223
Gunther, J. J. 750
St. Paul's (Opponents) 500
Guthrie, D. 586
"Development" 589
Galatians 481
Hebrews 703
NT Introd. 17
Pastorals 650
Relevance 812
Guthrie, G. H. 690

Haas, C. *1–3 John* 393
Haenchen, E. *Acts* 332
John 379
Hafemann, S. J. 544
Hagen, K. *Hebrews* 704
Hagner, D. A. 372
Hebrews 703 (NIBC), 704
Matthew 222
Hahneman, G. M. *Muratorian* 18
Hall, D. R. 405
Seven 19
Hall, R. 711
Hall, R. G. 471
Halson, B. R. 740
Hamerton-Kelly, R. G. 91
Gospel 169
Hammond, N.G.L. *Oxford Classical* 70
Hansen, G. W. *Abraham* 482
Hanson, A. T. 636, 651
Pastorals 650
Studies Pastorals 651
Studies Paul 443
Wrath 812
Hanson, P. D. 774
Hanson, R.P.C. *Acts* 331
II Corinthians 558
Hanson, S. 625
Harding, S. 802
Hare, D.R.A. *Mark* 168
Matthew 222
Harnack, A. (von) *Luke* 277
NT Studies 332
What 44
Harner, P. B. 180
Relation 380

Harrill, J. A. 519
Harrington, D. J. 223, 612, 736
Matthew 222
NT Bibliography 16
Paul 443
Harrington, W. J. *Revelation* 811
Harris, E. 337
Harris, M. J. 644
Colossians 618
2 Corinthians 558
Harrison, P. N. 510
Paulines & Problem 651
Harrisville, R. A. 478
Bible 19
1 Corinthians 538
Romans 583
Hartin, P. J. 735
Hartman, L. 144, 776
"Humble" 619
Harvey, A. E. 645, 772
Hastings, A. *Prophet* 277
Hatton, H. *1 Corinthians* 538
Hauser, A. J. 26
Havener, I. *Q* 124
Haverly, T. P. 152
Hawkin, D. J. *Johannine* 380
Hawthorne, G. F. *Dictionary* 443
Philippians 500
Hay, D. M. *1 and 2 Corinthians* 539
Pauline Theol. 2,3 444
Haynes, S. R. *To Each* 46
Hays, R. B. 482, 529, 567
Echoes 443
Faith 482
Hedrick, C. W. 130, 132
Nag Hammadi 95
Heil, J. P. *Mark* 169
Romans 584
Held, H. J. 181
Hellholm, D. 774, 779
Hemer, C. J. 708, 783
Acts 332
Henaut, B. W. 116
Hendrickx, H. 132, 133
Hendriksen, W. *Romans* 584
Hendrix, H. L. 458, 631
Hengel, M. *Acts* 332
"Hymns" 490
Jews & Judaism 71
Pre-Christian Paul 443
Question 380
Studies 169
Studies Christology 830
Hennecke, E. HSNTA xxviii
Herdan, G. 663
Héring, J. *First Cor* 539
Second Cor 558
Hebrews 704
Hester, J. D. 471
Hewitt, T. *Hebrews* 703
Hiebert, D. E. "Selected Jude" 760
"Selected 2 Pet" 772
Hill, D. 711, 722, 778
Matthew 222
Hill, R. C. 346
Hillyer, N. *1 Peter* 724
Hobart, W. K. 269
Hobbs, H. H. *Epistles John* 393
Hock, R. F. 836
Social 425
Hodgson, R. *Nag Hammadi* 95
Hoffman, R. J. 14
Hoffmann, D. L. 92
Holladay, C. R. 84, 500
Fragments 93
Holland, G. S. *Tradition* 598
Hollander, H. W. 835
Holmberg, B. 27, 645
Holmes, M. W. *Text NT* 54
Holwerda, D. E. 353
Hong, I.-G. *Law* 482
Hooker, M. D. 478, 493, 522, 619
Mark 168
PAP xxx
Hoppe, L. J. *Synagogues* 72
Horbury, W. 374, 687
Horsley, R. A. 527, 677, 825
Hort, E. *Bible* 16
Hort, F.J.A. *James* 747
Horton, F. L. *Melchizedek* 704
Horvath, T. 405
Hoskyns, E. *Fourth Gospel* 380
Houlden, J. L. 180, 625
Colossians 618
1–3 John 393
Pastorals 650
Philippians 500
Howard, G. E. 210, 493, 570, 691
Paul 482
Howard, W. F. 389
Fourth Gospel 379
Howell, D. B. *Matthew* 223

Hubbard, B. J. 203
Hughes, F. W. *Early* 598
Hughes, G. H. *Hebrews* 704
Hughes, P. E. *Hebrews* 704
Revelation 812
2 Corinthians 557
Hull, J.H.E. 283
Hultgren, A. J. 478
Colossians 618
Pastorals 650
Paul's Gospel 583
Rise 830
Humphrey, H. M. *Bibliography* 168
Risen 169
Hunter, A. M. *Interpreting* 19
Mark 168
Hupper, W. G. 772
Hurd, J. C. *Bibliography* 16
"Good News" & *Origin* 539
"Pauline" 445
Hurst, L. D. 493, 691
Hebrews 704
Hurtado, L. W. 151, 786
Mark 168

Isaacs, M. E. *Sacred* 704

Jacobs, I. 733
Jacobson, A. D. *First* & "Literary" 124
James, M. R. *2 Peter* 772
Jefford, C. N. 837
Jenson, R. W. *Reclaiming* 46
Jeremias, J. 132, 180, 733
Jerusalem 72
Jervell, J. GCHP xxvii
Luke & *Unknown* 277
Jervis, L. A. 524
Purpose 584
Jewett, R. 464, 465, 482, 500, 559
Chronology 445
Paul 443
Thessalonian 465
Johanson, B. C. *To All* 465
Johnson, E. A. 825
Johnson, E. E. *Pauline Theol. 3* 444
Johnson, L. T. 222, 265, 271, 680, 730, 731
Acts 331
James 747
Luke 276
Pastorals 650
Real Jesus 830
Writings 17
Johnson, M. 184
Johnson, S. E. *Griesbach* 123
Mark 168
Paul 443
Johnson, T. F. *1–3 John* 393
John 379
Johnston, G. 353, 629
Jonas, H. *Gnostic* 95
Jones, D. L. 86
Jones, F. S. 741
Jones, P. R. 392
Jongeling, B. *Bibliography* 94
Jonsen, A. R. 724
Joubert, S. J. 760
Judge, E. A. 412
Juel, D. H. *Luke-Acts* 277
Mark 168
Master 169
Messiah 145
Thessalonians 465
Just, A. A., Jr. 261

Kähler, M. 818
Käsemann, E. 44, 576, 603, 625, 630, 819
"Apologia" 772
KENTT xxviii
Perspectives 443
Romans 584
Testament 380
Wandering 704
Karrer, O. 707
Karris, R. J. 241, 573, 642
Invitation Acts 332
Invitation Luke 277
Luke: Artist 277
Pastorals 650
What 276
Kaye, B. N. 465
Kaylor, R. D. *Paul's* 584
Kazmierski, C. R. 156
Kealy, S. P. *Apocalypse* 812
Mark 168
Keck, L. E. 150, 553, 822
Paul 443
SLA 277
Kee, D. 554
Kee, H. C. 27, 129, 133
Community 169
Understanding 17

Keener, C. S. 660
Kelber, W. H. 116, 145
Mark's Story 169
Kelly, J.N.D. *Pastorals* 650
1 Peter 724
Kennedy, G. A. *NT Interpretation* 26
Kenny, A. 588
Kent, H.A.A. *Heart Opened* 558
Keresztes, P. 806
Kermode, F. 153
Kertelge, K. *Romans* 583
Kiddle, M. *Revelation* 812
Kiley, M. *Colossians* 619
Kilgallen, J. J. 295
First Corinthians 539
Luke 277
Kilpatrick, G. D. *Origins Matt* 233
Principles 54
Kim, Chan-Hie, *Form* 420
Kim, Y. K. 664
Kimelman, R. 374
King, M. A. 760
Kingsbury, J. D. 185, 223
Christology 169
Conflict Luke 277
Conflict Mark 169
Matthew books 222, 223
Kinman, B. R. 253
Kinukawa, H. *Women* 169
Kirby, J. C. *Ephesians* 637
Kirk, A. 112, 740, 829
Kissinger, W. S. 178
Kistemaker, S. J. *Heb & Psalm* 704
Kitchen, M. *Ephesians* 637
Kittel, G. TDNT 18
Klassen, W. 418
Klijn, A.F.J. 500, 751
Klinger, J. 772
Kloppenborg, J. S. *Formation* 124
other Q writings 124–125
Knight, G. W. 650, 660
Pastorals 650
Knight, J. *2 Peter* 771
Knox, J. 14, 550, 619
Chapters 445
Philemon 510
Knox, W. *Acts* 332
Kobelski, P. J. *Melchizedek* 704
Koch, K. 22, 774
Kodell, J. 277
Koenig, J. *Philippians* 500
Koester, C. R. 531, 704, 812
Dwelling 703
Symbolism 335
Koester, H. 100, 112, 216, 460, 465, 489, 598
Ephesos 637
"History" 169
Introd. (NT) 17
Kopas, J. 241
Kopp, C. *Holy Places* 73
Kraabel, A. T. 299
Kraft, R. A. *Early Judaism* 71
Kraybill, J. N. 792
Kreitzer, L. J. 792
2 Corinthians 557
Krentz, E. 16, 35, 490, 598
Galatians 481
Krodel, G. A. *Acts* 331
1 Peter 724
2 Peter 771
Revelation 811
2 Thessalonians 598
Kroeger, R. and C. 660
Kruse, C. *2 Corinthians* 557
Kselman, J. S. 817
Kubo, S. 753
Kümmel, W. G. *Introduction* 17
NT Investigation 19
Theology NT 18
Küng, H. *Structures* 44
Kürzinger, J. 209
Kugelman, R. *James* 747
Kuhn, K. G. 634
Kurz, W. S. 551
"Kenotic" 500
Luke-Acts 277
Kysar, R. *1–3 John* 393
Fourth Evangelist 379
John (AugC, ABD) 379
Maverick & Story 380

Ladd, G. E. 614, 778
Revelation 812
Theology 18
Lake, K. *Beginnings* 332
Lambrecht, J. 132, 149, 185, 463, 557, 568
L'Apocalypse 811
Pauline Studies 443
Lamouille, A. 327

Lampe, G.W.H. 539
Lane, E. N. 491
Lane, W. L. *Hebrews* 703
Mark 168
Langevin, P.-E. *Bibliographia* 16
Lategan, B. C. 470
La Verdiere, E. A. 270
Law, R. *Tests* 394
Laws, S. *James* 747
Light 812
Revelation 811
Layton, B. *Gnostic* 95
Lea, T. D. 589, 710
Leaney, A.R.C. *1 Peter* 724
Jewish 71
Luke 276
Lee, D. A. 358
Symbolic 335
Lee, E. K. *Religious* 380
Lee, M. V. 485
Leenhardt, F. J. *Romans* 584
Legrand, H.-M. 702
Lehne, S. 702
Lemaire, A. 651
Lentz, J. C., Jr. *Luke's Paul* 332
Leon, H. J. *Jews* 561
Léon-Dufour, X. *Dictionary* 18
Levinsohn, S. H. *Acts* 332
Lewis, J. P. 545, 711
English Bible xxxvi
Lewis, L. A. 510
Lieberman, S. *Hellenism* 71
Liefeld, W. L. *Acts* 331
Lienhard, J. T. *Bible* 18
Lietaert Peerbolte, L. J. 597
Lieu, J. M. 372
Epistles 400
1–3 John 393
Lightfoot, J. B. *Colossians* 619
Galatians 482
Notes I Thess 466
Notes II Thess 598
Philippians 500
Lightfoot, R. H. *Mark* 169
St. John 380
Lincoln, A. T. 631, 637
Ephesians 637
Theology 443
Lindars, B. 130, 364, 377
Behind 380
Hebrews 703
John 379
Lindemann, A. *Interpreting* 17
Linnemann, E. 125
Litfin, D. 516
Loader, W. *Christology* 380
1–3 John 393
Lock, W. *Pastorals* 650
Lodge, J. G. 733
Loewenstamm, S. E. 752
Logan, A.H.B. *Gnostic & NT Gnosis* 95
Lohfink, N. 31, 703
Lohmeyer, E. 180
Lohse, E. *Colossians* 618
Long, A. A. *Hellenistic* 94
Long, T.M.S. 782
Longenecker, R. N. 466, 730
Galatians 481
Longstaff, T.R.W. *Synoptic* 123
Louw, J. P. 380
Lüdemann, G. *Early* 332
Opposition 443
Paul 445
Lührmann, D. 125, 466
Galatians 492
Itinerary 46
Lull, D. J. *Galatia* 482
Luter, A. B. 485
Luz, U. *Matthew* 222
other Matt books 223
Lyonnet, S. 619
Lyons, G. *Pauline* 443

Macdonald, D. R. 661
No Male 482
MacDonald, J.I.H. 575
Macgregor, G.H.C. 636
John 379
Structure (under Morton) 277
Mack, B. L. *Lost* 125
Myth 169
Who 17
Mackay, B. S. 498
MacMullen, R. 491
MacRae, G. W. 372, 692
NTIMI 16
Studies 95
Maddox, R. *Purpose* 277
Madros, P. *Pride* 558

Magness, J. L. 148
Malatesta, E. *Epistles John* 392
Interiority 394
St. John 379
Malbon, E. S. 152, 156
Narrative 169
New 46
Malherbe, A. J. 95, 405, 461, 466, 495, 651, 680
Ancient & Moral 420
Paul 466
Paul Philosophies 95
Malina, B. J. *Calling* 223
Genre Rev 812
Social writings 27
Windows 71
Maloney, L. M. 668
Mandell, S. 191
Mann, C. S. *Mark* 168
Matthew 222
Manson, T. W. "St. Paul" 598
Manson, W. *Hebrews* 704
Marcus, J. 128, 132, 153, 162, 470, 573, 747
Apocalyptic 778
Way 169
Marrow, S. B. *John* 380
Paul 443
Marsh, J. *John* 379
Marshall, I. H. 500, 579
Acts 331
1–3 John 393
Luke (NIGTC) 276
Luke: Historian 277
NT Interpretation 47
Philippians 500
Theology (under Donfried) 442
Thessalonians 465
Marshall, P. *Enmity* 539
Martin, B. L. *Christ* 443
Martin, C. J. 608
Martin, D. B. 526
Martin, R. A. 318
James 747
Studies 443
Martin, R. P. 491, 603, 637, 724, 747
Colossians 618
Colossians Lord 619
1 Peter 724
James 747
Mark 168
NT Books 16
NT Foundations 17
Philippians 500
2 Corinthians 557
Spirit 539
Martin, T. W. 471, 606, 619
Martin, V. 374
Martyn, J. L. 467, 473, 545
Galatians (AB) 481
"Galatians" TBOB 482
Gospel John & History 380
"Law-Observant" 482
SLA (under Keck) 277
Marxsen, W. *Introd. NT* 17
Mark 169
NT Foundations 18
Mason, S. *Josephus NT* 72
Josephus Pharisees 93
Massaux, E. 216
Mastin, B. A. *John* 379
Matera, F. J. 272
Galatians 481
NT Ethics 18
What 168
Matlock, R. B. *Unveiling* 443
Matson, D. L. 310
Matsunaga, K. 377
Matthews, V. H. "Atlases" 78
Mattill, A. J., Jr. 332
Bibliography 331
"Johannine" 380
Luke 277
May, D. M. 27
Mayor, J. B. *James* 747
Second 772
Mazzaferri, F. D. 778
McArthur, H. K. 817
McCarthy, C. 839
McCaughey, J. D. 724
McCullough, J. C. 691, 704
McDonald, L. M. *Formation* 19
NT Introd. 16
McEleney, N. J. 137, 677
McGaughy, L. C. 199
McGown, W. 603
McIver, R. K. 218
McKeever, M. C. *Luke-Acts* 276
McKenzie, S. L. *To Each* 46
McKim, D. K. *Guide* 46
McKnight, E. V. 22, 37
Meaning & New 46
McLaren, J. S. *Power* 71

McNamara, M. 772
Meade, D. O. *Pseudonymity* 589
Meagher, J. C. *Clumsy* 169
Mealand, D. L. 588
Mealy, J. W. 802
Mearns, C. L. 466
Meeks, W. A. 372, 521, 612
CAC xxvi
First 444
GCHP xxvii
Prophet-King 380
Writings 443
Meier, J. P. 216, 522, 538, 645, 684, 726, 727, 826, 830, 835
Law History 224
Marginal 830
Matthew (ABD) 222
Matthew (Glazier) 224
Vision 224
Meier, S. 766
Meinardus, O.F.A. 641, 783
Paul books 444
Mendels, D. *Rise* 71
Mendelson, A. *Philo* 95
Menken, M.J.J. 379, 598
2 Thessalonians 598
Menninger, R. E. *Israel* 224
Menoud, P. H. 547
Menzies, A. *Second Cor* 558
Menzies, R. P. 283
Merrill, E. T. 806
Metzger, B. M. 589, 625, 651
Breaking 812
Canon 19
Index Christ 16
Index Paul 442
Manuscripts 54
New 17
Text & Versions 54
Textual Commentary 54
Meurer, S. *Apocrypha* xxxv
Meyer, B. F. 823
Reality 47
Meyer, M. W. 86, 112
Meyer, P. D. 125
Meyers, E. M. Bibliography 72
Encyclopedia 73
Michaelis, J. D. 817
Michaels, J. R. *John* 379
1 Peter 724
Revelation 811
Millar, W. R. 777
Miller, J. E. 530
Miller, R. J. *Complete Gospels* 101
Mills, W. E.:
BBR: xxv, 168, 223, 276, 331, 379, 538, 583
Bibliography: Acts 331
Index Paul 442
Minear, P. S. 361, 368, 778
I Saw 812
Obedience 584
Minn, H. R. *Thorn* 547
Minor, M. *Literary-Critical* 25
Mitchell, M. M. *Paul* 539
Mitchell, S. 475, 822
Mitton, C. L. *Ephesians* (NCBC) 637
Epistle Eph 637
James 747
Moessner, D. P. 244
Moffatt, J. *First Cor* 539
General Epistles 747
Hebrews 703
Introd. NT 17
Moir, I. *Manuscripts* 54
Moloney, F. J. 339, 377, 378
Moloney, L. M. 668
Momigliano, A. *Pagans* 71
Monloubou, L. 25
Montefiore, H. W. *Hebrews* 704
Moo, D. J. 660
Romans 583
Moody, D. *1–3 John* 393
Mooney, C. F. 625
Moore, G. F. *Judaism* 71
Moore, M. S. 622
Moore, S. D. 25
Mark (under Anderson) 168
Morgan, R. 19
Romans 583
Morgan-Gillman, F. 459
Morland, K. A. 471
Morris, L. 346, 688
1 Corinthians 538
John 379
Luke 276
Revelation 811, 812
Thessalonians 465
Morton, A. Q. *Concord. Pastorals* 651
Critical 539
Making 169
Paul 588
Structure 277

Moses, A.D.A. 190
Mott, S. C. 644
Motyer, S. 660
Moule, C.F.D. 651
Birth NT 17
Colossians 618
Mark 168
"Nature" 724
Mounce, R. H. *Matthew* 222
Revelation 811
Mowry, L. 798
Moxnes, H. 271
Theology 584
Moyer, J. C. (under Matthews) 73
Moyise, S. 775
Müller, J. J. *Philippians* 500
Mullins, T. Y. 547
Letter Format articles 420
"Thanksgivings" 510
Munck, J. 398, 458, 482, 569
Acts 331
Paul 444
Munro, W. *Authority* 724
Murphy, F. J. 812
Religious 93
Murphy-O'Connor, J. 428, 433, 447, 493, 516, 519, 520, 522, 525, 527, 538, 539, 550, 551, 552, 603
Becoming 444
1 Corinthians 538
2 Corinthians 557
Holy Land 73
PAQ xxx
Paul Life 444
Paul the Letter-Writer 420
"Pauline Missions" 445
St. Paul's Corinth 539
"2 Timothy" 680
"Who" 637
Mussies, G. 803
Mussner, F. 634
Colossians 618
Myers, C. *Binding* & *Who* 169

Nanos, M. D. 561
Nardoni, E. 139, 531
Navone, J. *Themes* 277
Neale, D. A. 241
Neil, W. *Acts* 331
Neill, S. *Interp. NT* 830
Neirycnk, F. 111, 112, 115, 116, 121, 125, 149, 150, 364
FGN xxvii
Gospel Mark 168
Gospel Matt 223
Minor Agreements 123
Q-Synopsis 125
Nelson, P. K. 257
Nepper-Christensen, P. 211
Neufeld, D. *Reconceiving* 394
Neumann, K. J. 588
Neusner, J. 82, 300, 579
Christianity 71
Judaism 93
Social World 71
Neville, D. J. *Arguments* 123
New, D. S. *OT Quotations* 123
Newman, B. M. *John* 379
Newport, K.G.C. 197
Neyrey, J. H. 223, 270, 472, 724, 764
Ideology 381
Paul 444
2 Peter 771
Social 278
Nicholson, G. C. *Death* 380
Nickelsburg, G.W.E. 71
Nickle, K. F. 553
Nicol, W. 733
Sēmeia 381
Nida, E. A. *Hebrews* 703
John 379
Nineham, D. E. 627
Mark 168
Nolland, J. 174, 175
Luke 276
Norden, E. *Agnostos* 490
North, J. L. 657
Nygren, A. *Agape* 533
Romans 584

O'Brien, P. T. 621
Colossians 618
Gospel 444
Introductory 420
Philippians 500
O'Collins, G. 822
Luke 278
O'Connor, D. W. 719
O'Connor, M. 24

O'Day, G. R. *John* 379
Revelation 336
Oden, T. *Pastorals* 650
O'Fearghail, F. *Luke-Acts* 278
Ogg, G. *Chronology* 445
O'Grady, J. F. *Four* 123
Olbricht, T. H. 26, 466
O'Leary, S. D. *Arguing* 812
Oleson, J. P. 752
Olsson, B. *Structure* 381
Omanson, R. L. *2 Corinthians* 557
O'Neill, J. C. 473, 619
Puzzle 394
Theology 332
Oostendorp, D. W. *Another* 558
Orchard, B. 161
Matthew & Order 124
O'Rourke, J. J. 798
Orr, W. F. *1 Corinthians* 538
Osburn, C. D. 751, 752, 753
Osiek, C. 838
Galatians 481
O'Toole, R. F. 315
Unity 278
Otto, R. E. 487
Overman, J. A. 69
Matthew (NITC) 222
Matthew's Gospel 224
Overstreet, R. L. 771

Padgett, A. 660
Page, S.H.T. 778
Pagels, E. H. *Gnostic Gospels* 95
Johannine 381
Paget, J. C. 198, 838
Painter, J. 391
Quest & Reading John 381
Palmer, P. F. 736
Pamment, M. 368, 371
Pancaro, S. *Law* 381
Parkin, V. 150
Parsons, M. C. 225, 281
Paschal, R. W. 377
Patte, D. *Matthew* 224
Paul's Faith 444
Structural 24
Patterson, S. J. 120
Patzia, A. G. 589
Colossians 618
Making NT 17
Payne, D. B. 660
Pearson, B. A. 527, 765
Penna, R. *Paul* 444
Penner, T. C. 732
Percy, E. 610
Perdue, L. G. 740
Perkins, P. 89, 645
Dialogue & Gnosticism 96
James 747
1–3 John 393
John 381
Mark 168
Peter 707
1 Peter 724
Reading NT 17
Revelation 812
Perriman, A. 612
Perrin, N. 23, 132, 155
NT Introd. 17
"Towards" 169
Pervo, R. I. 225
Luke's Paul & Profit 332
Peterlin, D. *Paul's* 501
Petersen, N. R. 25, 132, 575
Perspectives 169
Rediscovering 510
Petersen, W. L. 839
Peterson, D. *Hebrews* 704
Pettem, M. 263
Petuchowski, J. J. 180
Pherigo, P. 641
Phipps, W. E. 519
Picirilli, R. E. 772
Pickering, S. 216
Pilch, J. J. Social writings 27
Pilgaard, A. 84
Pilgrim, W. E. 265
Pinnock, C. H. 466
Piper, O. A. 394, 798
Piper, R. A. Writings on Q 125
Pippin, T. *Death* 812
Plevnik, J. 466
Plummer, A. *1 Corinthians* 538
Luke 276
Plymale, S. F. 236
Pogoloff, S. M. *Logos* 539
Pokorný, P. *Colossians* 619
Polhill, J. B. 400, 627
Pollard, T. E. 498, 603
Joh. Christology 381

Polzin, R. M. 24
Portefaix, L. *Sisters* 501
Porter, S. E. 26, 668, 803, 830
Approaches 47
Joh. Writings 381
NT Introd. 16
Pauline Writings 444
Powell, J. E. *Evolution* 224
Powell, M. A. 25, 197
God 224
Treasures (under Bauer) 223
What 276
Pregeant, R. *Engaging* 47
Preiss, T. 510
Prévost, J.-P. *Apocalypse* 812
Price, J. L. *Interpreting NT* 17
Prior, M. P. *Paul* 680
Pryor, J. W. *John* 381
Przybylski, B. *Righteousness* 224
Pummer, R. 296
Pursiful, D. J. *Cultic* 704
Purvis, J. D. 371
Puskas, C. B. *Introd. NT* 17
Letters 420

Quarles, C. L. 579
Quast, K. *Reading* 539
Quesnell, Q. *Mind* 169
Quinn, J. D. 268, 410, 586, 641, 666
Titus 650

Radice, R. D. *Philo* 95
Räisänen, H. 137, 153, 482
NT Theology 19
Paul 444
Rahner, H. 86
Rahtjen, B. D. 498
Rajak, T. *Josephus* 72
Ramsaran, R. A. 527
Ramsay, W. M. 783
Galatians 482
Luke 269
St. Paul 444
Rappaport, U. *Josephus* 72
Rapske, B. 315
Ravens, D.A.S. *Luke* 278
Reed, J. T. 415, 498
Reese, J. M. 747
Thessalonians 465
Reicke, B. 619, 715
James 747
Luke 278
NT Era 71
Reid, B. E. 241, 243
Reiling, J. *Luke* 276
Reim, G. 381
Reimarus, H. S. 817
Reimer, J. R. *Women* 332
Reinhartz, A. *Word* 381
Renan, E. 818
Rengstorf, K. H. *Concordance* 72
Rensberger, D. *Joh. Faith* 381
Reumann, J. 501, 576
Colossians 618
Rhoads, D. M. *Israel* 71
Mark 169
Rice, G. E. 274
Richard, E. 293, 335, 465
Jesus 18
New 278
Thessalonians 465
Richards, E. R. *Secretary* 420
Richards, W. L. *Classification* 393
Richardson, A. *Introd. Theology* 18
John 379
Miracle 133
Word Book 18
Richardson, N. *Panorama* 278
Riches, J. 71
Century 19
Matthew 222
Ricoeur, P. *Essays* 47
Ridderbos, H. N. *Paul* 444
To Galatia 482
Riesenfeld, H. 510
Riley, G. J. 829, 839
Resurrection 372
Riley, H. *Making* 124
Ringe, S. H. 237
Acts 331
Rissi, M. *Future* 794
Robbins, C. J. 628
Robbins, V. K. 123, 147, 227, 322
Jesus & New 169
Roberts, C. 216
Robertson, A. *1 Corinthians* 538
Robertson, A. T. *Paul* 619
Robinson, J. A(rmitage) *Ephesians* 637

Robinson, J.A.T. 163, 612
Priority 381
Wrestling 584
Robinson, J. M. 603, 819
Nag Hammadi 95
Problem 169
Q writings 125
Robinson, M. A. 49
Robinson, T. A. 663
Robinson, W. C., Jr. *Way* 278
Robson, E. I. *Studies* 772
Roetzel, C. J. 578, 632
Letters 444
World 95
Rogers, P. V. *Colossians* 618
"Pastoral" 651
Rohrbaugh, R. I. 162
Roloff, J. *Revelation* 812
Ropes, J. H. 478
James 747
Rose, H. R. *Religion* 95
Rosenblatt, M.-E. 298
Paul 332
Rosner, B. S. *Paul* 517
Ross, A. *1–3 John* 393
James 747
Ross, J. M. 753
Rowland, C. 619, 774, 800, 810
Revelation 811
Rowley, H. H. 774
Rowston, D. J. "Most" 760
Ruckstuhl, E. 363
Rudolph, K. *Gnosis* 96
Ruef, J. *1 Corinthians* 538
Ruiz, J.-P. 794, 800
Russell, D. S. 774, 778
Russell, R. 598
Russell, W. 482
Ryan, R. 241
Ryken, L. *Literary Criticism* 47

Sabourin, L. 442, 625
Safrai, S. *Jewish People* 71
Saldarini, A. J. 197
Matthew's 224
Pharisees 93
Salom, A. P. 389
Sampley, J. P. *"And"* 624
Ephesians 637
Pauline 442
Sanday, W. *Romans* 583
Sanders, E. P. 824
Jewish Christian 93
Jewish Law & Judaism 93
"Literary" 619
Paul books 444
Sanders, J. A. 277, 443
Canon & Torah 24
Sanders, J. N. 627
John 379
Sanders, J. T. 272, 420, 523, 622
Hymns 490
Schismatics 71
Sandmel, S. *Genius* 444
Philo 95
Saunders, E. W. "Colossian" 619
Savage, T. B. *Power* 558
Saw, I. 524
Schaberg, J. 203
Scharlemann, M. H. 295
Schelkle, K.-H. *Theology NT* 18
Scherrer, S. J. 792
Schiffman, L. H. 374
Schlatter, A. *Romans* 584
Schlier, H. 636
Schlueter, C. J. 463
Schmid, J. *Mark* 170
Schmidt, D. 598
Schmithals, W. 302, 466, 501
Gnosticism 539
Paul 444
Schnackenburg, R. 178, 645
Ephesians 637
Joh. Epistles 394
John 381
Schneider, G. *Galatians* 481
Schneiders, S. M. 45
Revelatory 47
Schnelle, U. *Anti-Docetic* 381
Schoedel, W. R. 837
Schoeps, H. J. *Paul* 444
Scholer, D. M. 388
Nag Hammadi & Studies 96
Scholer, J. M. 701
Scholes, R. 151
Schottroff, L. *Let* 47
Schreiner, T. R. *Interpreting & Law* 444
Schubert, P. *Form* 420
Schuchard, B. G. 351
Schürer, E. *History* 71

Schüssler Fiorenza, E. 539, 810, 826
Aspects 94
Book 812
In Memory 27
Invitation 812
Revelation 811
Searching (STS) 27
Schütz, J. *Paul* 444
Schwartz, D. R. *Studies* 71
Schwartz, S. *Josephus* 72
Schweitzer, A. *Paul* 445
Quest 818
Schweizer, E. 363, 612, 645, 662
Colossians 619
Luke 278
Mark 170
Matthew 224
Theological Introd. 17
Scobie, C.H.H. 296, 371
Scott, B. B. 830
Scott, M. *Sophia* 346
Scroggs, R. 131, 529
Christology 381
Scullion, J. J. 580
Seccombe, D. P. 265
Seeley, D. 25, 142, 492
Segal, A. F. *Paul* 445
Rebecca 71
Segovia, F. 354, 393
Farewell & Love 381
Seifrid, M. A. 576
Seitz, C. R. xxxiv
Seland, T. 723
Sellew, P. 150, 152
Selwyn, E. G. *1 Peter* 724
Senior, D. P. 145, 161, 200, 724, 830
1 Peter 724
Passion John 381
What 223
Shanks, H. 820
Shaw, R. H. 596
Shedd, R. 335
Sheeley, S. M. *Narrative* 278
Shepherd, M. H. 734, 798
Shepherd, T. 131
Shepherd, W. H., Jr. 278
Sherk, R. K. 475
Sherwin-White, A. N. *Roman* 71
Shimada, K. 709, 716
Shiner, W. 156
Shuler, P. L. *Genre* 123
Sidebottom, E. M. *James* 747
Silva, M. *Philippians* 500
Sim, D. C. 215
Skeat, T. C. 216, 680
Sleeper, C. F. 713
Slingerland, D. 433
Sloan, R. B., Jr. 237
Sloyan, G. S. *1–3 John* 393
James 747
John & What 379
Smalley, S. S. 361, 379
1–3 John 393
John 381
Thunder 812
Smallwood, E. M. 806
Jews 71
Smit, J. 471
Smit Sibinga, J. 216
Smith, A. *Comfort* 466
Smith, C. R. 796
Smith, D. M. *Anatomy (NT)* 17
Composition 381
1–3 John 393
Joh. Christianity 381
John 379
John among Gospels 364
Smith, M. 112, 835
Jesus 86
Smith, R. H. 805
Hebrews 704
Matthew 222
Smith, T. V. 707
Snodgrass, K. 274
Snyder, G. F. 519, 719
First Corinthians 516
Snyder, J. 772
Soards, M. L. 35, 318, 471, 510, 529, 719, 730, 827
Apocalyptic 778
Apostle 445
"Reframing" 651
Soares-Prabhu, G. M. 207
Songer, H. S. 394, 739
Souter, A. *Text* 19
Sowers, S. G. 691, 791
Sparks, H.F.D. 271
Apocryphal 840
Spencer, A.D.B. 660
Spicq, C. *Lexicon NT* 18

Spivey, R. A. *Anatomy (NT)* 17
Spong, J. 822
Squires, J. T. *Plan* 278
Stagg, F. 394
Staley, J. L. 337
Print's & Reading 381
Stambaugh, J. E. *NT Social* 71
Stanley, D. M. 466
Stanton, G. N. 13
Gospel 224
Gospels & Gospel Truth? 124
"Matthew" 123
TIMT 223
Stauffer, E. *NT Theology* 18
Stein, D. *Parables* 132
Stein, R. H. 115
Synoptic 124
Steinmetz, F.-J. 625
Stemberger, G. 82
Jewish 94
Stendahl, K. 439, 568
Final 584
Paul among Jews 445
School 207
Stenger, W. *Introd. NT* 47
Stephenson, A.M.G. 548
Stepp, P. L. 568
Sterling, G. E. 129
Stern, E. *Encyclopedia* 73
Stern, M. *Jewish People* 71
Stewart-Sykes, A. 548
Stibbe, M.W.G. *John* 379
other John books 382
Stibbs, A. M. *1 Peter* 724
Stiefel, J. H. 657
Stirewalt, M. L., Jr. 421, 564
Stock, A. *Method Mark* 170
Method Matthew 224
Stöger, A. *Luke* 276
Philemon 510
Stoldt, H.-H. *History* 124
Stone, J. R. 802
Stone, M. E. *Fourth Ezra* 833
Jewish Writings 94
Stott, J.R.W. *1–3 John* 393
Men 17
Romans 584
Stowers, S. K. *Diatribe & Rereading* 584
Strachan, R. H. *Second Cor* 558
Strack, H. L. *Introd. Talmud* 82
Strauss, D. F. 818
Strauss, M. L. 275
Strecker, G. 178, 211
1–3 John 393
Minor 124
Streeter, B. H. 394
Strimple, R. B. *Modern* 830
Stuhlmacher, P. *Jesus* 820
Romans 584
Styler, G. M. 124
Suggs, M. J. 184, 445
Sullivan, F. A. 531
Sumney, J. L. 598
Identifying 558
Sundberg, A. C., Jr. 4
Swain, L. *Ephesians* 637
Swartley, W. M. *Israel's* 123
Sweet, J.P.M. 583
Revelation 811
Swellengrebel, J. L. *Luke* 276
Swete, H. B. *Apocalypse* 812
Swetnam, J. 690
Sylva, D. (survey) 724
Syreeni, K. 178

Talbert, C. H. 271, 276, 571, 765
Apocalypse 812
Literary Patterns 278
Luke-Acts & Reading Luke 278
Reading Corinthians 540
Reading John 382
Perspectives 278
Perspectives I Pet 724
What 123
Tambasco, A. *Days* 445
Tannehill, R. C. 25, 165
Narrative 278
Tasker, R.V.G. 690
2 Corinthians 557
James 747
Taylor, F. T., Jr. *Pastorals* 650
Taylor, G. *Paul* (under Buck) 445
Taylor, J. "Making" 332
Taylor, K. A. "Living Bible" xxxvi
Taylor, M. J. *Companion* 445
Taylor, N. H. 144
"Composition" 558
Paul 445

Taylor, V. *Formation* 124
Mark 170
Taylor, W. F. *Ephesians* 637
Tcherikover, V. *Hellenistic* 71
Teeple, H. *Literary* 382
Telford, W. R. 142, 168
Mark 168
TIM xxxi
Tellbe, M. 488
Tennant, F. R. 580
Tenney, M. 337
Terian, A. 95
Thackeray, H.St.J. *Josephus* 72
Theissen, G. 27, 824
Gospels Context 124
Psychological 445
Social 540
Thekkekara, M. 760
Thiede, C. P. 771
Earliest & *Eyewitness* 164
Thielman, F. 578
From Plight 482
Philippians 500
Thiselton, A. C. *New* 47
Thomas, K. J. 684, 691
Thomas, W. D. 501
Thompson, C. L. 522
Thompson, G.H.P. *Luke* 276
Thompson, J. W. 684, 687, 710
Beginnings 704
Thompson, L. L. 806
Revelation 813
Thompson, M. M. *Humanity* 382
Thompson, M. R. *Magdala* 241
Thompson, S. 803
Thompson, W. G. 192, 270
Paul 445
Thomson, I. H. *Chiasmus* 421
Thornton, T.C.G. 709
Thrall, M. E. 551, 554, 558
1 Corinthians 538
2 Corinthians 557
Throckmorton, B. H. 149
Thüsing, W. *1–3 John* 393
Thurén, L. 739
Motivation 724
Thurston, R. W. 693
Tiede, D. L. 84
Luke 276
Prophecy 278
Timmins, N. G. 364
Tinsley, E. J. *Luke* 276
Tolbert, M. A. 132
Sowing 170
Tolmie, D. F. 352
Tombs, D. *Approaches* 47
Tompkins, J. P. *Reader* 47
Toussaint, S. D. 683
Towner, P. H. 652
Townsend, J. T. 273
Townsend, M. J. *James* 747
Trevett, C. 216, 783
Trible, P. 26, 27
Trilling, W. *Conversation* 445
Trobisch, D. *Paul's* 12
Trocmé, E. *Formation* 170
Trompf, G. 522
Trotter, A. H. *Hebrews* 704
Trudinger, P. 388, 594
Tuckett, C. M. 112, 120, 153
Luke 276
Luke's Literary 278
Q writings 125
Revival 124
Turner, H.E.W. 158
Turner, N. "Q" 125
Twelvetree, G. H. 822
Tyson, J. B. 155, 482
Images & *Luke-Acts* 272

Ulfgard, H. 799
Urbach, E. E. *Sages* 94

Vaage, L. E. *Galilean* 125
Vaganay, L. *Textual* 54
Van Belle, G. *Joh. Bibl.* 379
Signs 382
van der Horst, P. W. 740
VanderKam, J. C. *DSS Today* 94
van der Loos, H. 133
Vander Stichele, C. 524
van der Westhuizen, J.D.N. 730
van der Woude, A. S. 687
Vanhoye, A. 690, 701
van Iersel, B.M.F. *Reading* 170
van Minnen, P. 423
Vanni, U. 800
van Roon, A. *Authenticity* 637
Van Segbroeck, F. FGN xxvii
Luke Bibl. 276
van Tilborg, S. *Reading* 368

van Unnik, W. C. 276, 332, 398, 544, 724, 798
Tarsus 445
Van Voorst, R. E. 741
Readings 47
Vassiliadis, P. 125
Vaughan, W. J. 481
Vawter, B. 377, 603, 778, 813
Vellanickal, M. *Sonship* 382
Verbrugge, V. D. 525
Verheyden, J. 144
Vermes, G. 823
DSS English & Complete DSS 94
Verner, D. C. *Household* 652
Via, D. O. 24
Ethics 170
Vielhauer, P. 324, 526
Vincent, M. R. *Philippians* 500
von Wahlde, U. C. 382, 391, 400
Earliest 382
Vorster, J. N. 584
Vorster, W. S. 144, 394, 813
Votaw, C. W. *Gospels* 123

Wachtel, K. 216
Waetjen, H. C. *Reordering* 170
Wagner, G.:
EBNT xxvii, 168, 223, 276, 331, 379, 393, 481, 583
Wagner, W. H. *After* 840
Wainwright, A. W. *Mysterious* 813
Wainwright, E. M. *Toward* 224
Wainwright, G. 464
Walasky, P. W. 278
Walker, W. O. 522
"Acts" 332
Wall, R. W. 740
Revelation 811
Waller, E. 186
Walsh, P. G. 87
Walter, E. *First Corinthians* 540
Walters, B. S. 837
Walters, J. C. 561
Walther, J. A. *1 Corinthians* 538
Wanamaker, C. A. 466, 493
Thessalonians 465
Wansbrough, H. 116
Wansink, C. S. 494
Ward, R. B. 519
Watson, D. F. 26, 400, 405, 740
Invention 760
Watson, F. 550
Paul 445
Watson, N. *1 Corinthians* 538
2 Corinthians 557
Watty, W. W. 142
Wead, D. W. *Literary* 382
Weatherly, J. A. 272
Weaver, D. J. 182
Webb, R. L. "Eschatology" 760
Webb, W. J. 551
Wedderburn, A.J.M. 284, 442, 584, 612
Colossians 618
NT Gnosis (under Logan) 94
Romans 584
Theology (with Lincoln) 443
Weeden, T. J. 155
Mark 170
Weima, J.A.D. 421
Bibliography 465
Neglected 421
Wellborn, L. L. 540, 806
Wenham, D. 133, 440, 766
GP xxvii
Wenham, J. *Redating* 124
Westcott, B. F. 576
Ephesians 637
Epistles 394
Hebrews 704
History Canon 19
John 382
Whallon, W. 752
Whitacre, R. A. *Joh. Polemic* 382
White, J. L. 421, 510, 519
Body & Light 421
White, L. M. *Social World* 72
Whitely, D.E.H. 538
Theology 445
Wiefel, W. 561
Wiens, D. 295
Wikenhauser, A. *NT Introd.* 17
Wilcox, M. *Semitisms* 332
Wild, R. A. 624, 652, 661
Wilder, A. N. *Rhetoric* 26
Wiles, M. E. *Spiritual* 382
Wilkins, M. J. *Jesus* 830
Wilkinson, J. 736
Jerusalem 73
Willett, M. E. 346
Williams, D. J. *Acts* 331
Thessalonians 465

Williams, J. F. *Other* 170
Williams, R. R. *Acts* 331
1–3 John 393
James 747
Williams, S. K. 478, 482
Williamson, L. *Mark* 168
Williamson, R. 691
Willimon, W. H. *Acts* 331
Willis, W. L. 520
Wilson, A. N. 822
Wilson, M. W. 783
Wilson, R. M. 91, 482, 527
Gnosis 96
Hebrews 704
Wilson, S. G. 268, 278
Gentiles & Luke/Law 278
Luke Pastorals 652
PAP xxx
Related 72
Wilson, W. G. 389
Wilson, W. T. 571
Wimbush, V. L. 519
Wind, A. 382
Windisch, H. 353
Winger, M. 470, 480
Wink, W. 636
Winter, B. W. *Literary Setting* 93
TBAFC 331
Winter, S.B.C. 510
Wire, A. C. 524
Wisse, F. 760
Witherington, B., III 388, 645, 772, 817, 826
Conflict 540
Jesus Quest 830
John's Wisdom 382
Paul's Narrative 445
Philippians 500
Witherup, R. D. 298, 299, 817
Conversion 285
Cross 200
Wolfson, H. A. *Philo* 95
Woll, D. B. *Joh. Conflict* 382
Wolters, A. 763, 766
Wolthuis, T. R. 760
Worden, R. D. 125
Worgul, G. S. 612
Wortham, R. A. 463
Wrede, W. *Messianic* 153
Wright, A. G. 254
Wright, D. F. 112, 529
Wright, N. T. 491, 603, 820
Interp. NT (under Neill) 830
Jesus books 830
NT People 17
Wuellner, W. 26

Yadin, Y. 692
Yamauchi, E. 606
Archaeology 73
Gnosticism 96
Yarbro Collins, A. 144, 775, 805, 806, 811, 813
Beginning 170
Combat & Crisis 813
Revelation 811
Yates, R. 482, 606
Colossians 618
Yonge, C. D. *Philo* 95
Yorke, G.L.O.R. 612
Young, F. M. *Meaning* 558
Pastorals 650

Zehnle, R. F. 290
Zeitlin, S. *Rise* 72
Zerwick, M. *Ephesians* 637
Ziesler, J. A. 576, 652
Galatians 481
Pauline 445
Romans 584
Zwiep, A. W. 274

INDEX II.
SUBJECT INDEX

A few authors are listed here, not for bibliographical purposes (see preceding index), but because there is a discussion of their views.

Abraham and descendants (seed) 175, 470, 472–473, 479, 567, 570, 733
Acts, apocryphal 661, 663, 664–665, 667, 678
Acts of the Apostles 8, 14, 42, 279–332
  authorship 322–327
  differences from Paul's theology 273, 323–326
  historicity (accuracy) 284, 292, 297, 298, 300, 301, 306, 308, 316, 318–327, 422–423, 426, 427, 431, 432, 436, 452, 458, 464, 557
  longer text 49, 280, 327
  organization, plan 280, 281, 296, 303, 309
  (and) Paul's Pastorals 294, 305, 313, 666
    (*see also* Paul, "second career")
  sermons (speeches) 284–286, 290, 295–296, 300, 304, 311, 313, 314, 318–319, 453
  sources 316–319
  title "Acts" 279
  "We" (Paul's companion) 225, 267–269, 310, 313, 315, 317, 321, 322–327, 433, 456, 487
  (*see also* Luke, Gospel: authorship, summaries; Paul)
Adam 236, 492, 524, 567–568, 580–582, 661
Aelia Capitolina xli, 63
Agapē (*see* Love)
Agapē meal 522, 752–753
Akiba (Aqiba), Rabbi xli, 63, 82
Alexandria xxix, xxxv, xxxix, 9, 12, 13, 49–51, 65, 91, 101, 311, 434, 527, 693–695, 833, 835
Angels (spirits) 148, 203, 229, 257, 281–282, 302, 339, 343, 359, 636, 643, 715–716, 751, 752, 775, 776, 780, 787, 791, 793, 832, 838
  and Christ 200, 257, 604, 606, 617, 684–685, 714
  (*see also* Demon; Powers)
Anointing the sick 732, 736–739, 746
Antichrist (antiGod, false Christs) 385–387, 395, 397, 403, 590, 595, 597–598, 778, 787, 804
  man of lawlessness 590–591, 593, 594–597
AntiJudaism 39, 166–167, 196, 202, 206, 222, 327, 463, 473, 723, 786, 804
  "the Jews" in John 339, 341, 357–358, 370, 374–375, 390, 804
  (*see also* Pharisees, NT critique)
Antioch (Syrian), church at 11, 36, 62, 162, 195, 212–215, 269, 284, 286, 301–303, 305, 308–309, 324, 428, 430, 456, 727, 837
Antiochus IV Epiphanes 56, 57, 303, 597, 777, 789
Apocalypse (*see* Revelation, Book)
Apocalyptic 121, 199, 328, 506, 587, 594, 677, 771, 810, 818, 829, 832, 834, 838
  genre, development 8, 774–780
  in Paul 324, 440, 453, 461–463, 480, 506, 509, 514, 519, 525, 571, 583, 596, 607, 636, 679, 778
  signs 144, 590–591, 594, 595–596
  (*see also* Eschatology; Mark, apocalypse)
Apocrypha 587, 600, 606, 754, 829, 831
  (*see* Deuterocanonical Books)

Apollos 70, 311, 434, 515–517, 525, 527, 535, 536, 641, 695, 696
Apostle(s): 130, 227, 279, 317, 523, 531, 574, 749, 750, 753, 758, 805
  as NT authors 10, 109, 208–211, 216, 268
  as preachers 108, 284–285, 289–290
  false 541, 545, 547, 549, 550, 554–556
  teaching of 289, 765–766, 769–770
  women as 359, 574, 675
  (*see also* Twelve)
Aqiba (*see* Akiba)
Aquila and/or Priscilla (Prisca) 311, 433, 452, 513–515, 520, 562, 564, 575, 660, 678, 695, 696
Aretalogy 102–103
  (*See also Theios anēr*)
Aristeas, Letter of 56, 529, 833
Armageddon 793
Ascension, exaltation (of Jesus) 262, 280, 281, 493, 623
Ascension of Isaiah 714, 798, 801
Assumption of Moses (*see Moses, Assumption*)
Audience (reader) interpretation 21, 36–38, 84–85, 103, 238–239
Augustine (St.) 113, 439, 559, 580, 715, 743, 801
Augustus, Emperor xxxviii, 58–59, 67, 69, 85, 86, 233, 253, 423, 483, 513, 519, 791, 792, 805
Author/writer distinction 41, 411, 413, 585–586, 610

Babylon, name for Rome 712, 719, 722, 793, 794
Baptism (Christian) 46, 92, 108, 141, 203, 281, 285–286, 300–301, 329, 341–342, 348, 351, 367, 377, 388, 490, 521, 525, 532, 536, 537, 568, 612–613, 622–624, 631–632, 650, 686, 688, 709, 711, 714, 729, 763, 780, 799, 837
  (*see also* John the Baptist)
Bar Cochba (*see* Simon bar Cochba)
Barnabas 85, 139, 279, 291, 298, 301, 303–306, 308–309, 317, 428, 431–432, 476, 521, 618, 707, 694
Barnabas, Epistle of 50, 588, 691, 694, 838–839
Baruch, II xli, 8, 414, 580, 776, 777, 780, 792, 795, 834
Baur, F. C. 30, 35, 320, 441, 467, 556, 586, 613, 643, 727, 818
Beatitude(s) 164, 171, 178–179, 205, 233, 239, 246, 729
Beatty, C. (*see* Papyrus)
Beloved Disciple 338, 352, 357–359, 361, 368–371, 373–375, 384, 398, 399
Bible translations (*see* Translations)
Birkat ha-mînîm 82, 214, 374
Bishops (*see* Presbyters)
Body of Christ 108, 354, 441, 454, 518, 521, 526, 612, 617, 622, 623, 631, 688, 716
Body of Letter (*see* Letters)
Bultmann, R. 22–23, 89, 440, 568, 818–819, 828
  theory about John 333, 342, 363, 366, 370, 372, 377, 384, 392
  (*see also* Post-Bultmannians)

Cabirus, Cabiri 87, 458, 460
Caligula, Emperor xxxix, 60, 86, 144, 430, 597
Canon, canonicity viii, 4, 10–15, 51–52, 693, 722, 743–745, 754–755, 759, 764, 767, 769–770, 795, 809, 838
  center of (canon within) 43–44, 625–626, 770
  OT canon xxxiv–xxxv
Canonical criticism 24, 42–44
Catholic (*see* Early Catholicism; Roman Catholic)
Catholic Epistles (in general) 7, 383, 410–411, 413, 419, 705, 722, 743, 744, 762
Celibacy (*see* Marriage)
Census (of Quirinius) xxxviii, 60, 233, 321
Cephas (*see* Peter)
Charism 516, 523–524, 531–533, 571, 646–648, 670, 671, 711, 716, 737
Chiliasm (*see* Millenarianism)
Christian (the name) 286, 301
Christology (christological titles) 103, 108, 120, 128, 140, 153, 156–157, 164–165, 175, 183, 184, 218, 229, 234–235, 262, 264, 284–286, 294, 339, 347, 350, 360, 388, 397, 401, 405, 490, 492, 684–685, 691, 754, 780, 781, 787, 799, 819–820, 822, 826, 837
  Pauline 439–440, 491–493, 499, 565, 596–597, 602–604, 611–612, 617, 649, 663
  preexistence (incarnational) christology 337–338, 347, 364, 371, 374, 391, 492–493, 683, 686, 717, 826, 835
  (*see also* Son of God; Son of Man)

Chronologies xxxviii–xli, 312, 362, 428–429, 445
Church 6, 189, 191–193, 215–216, 218, 329, 567, 612, 617, 622, 625–626, 635, 788, 791, 804, 805
governance, structure 7, 295–296, 302, 305, 313, 330, 361, 368, 376, 398, 404, 437, 441, 464, 499, 523–524, 571, 623, 624, 626, 635, 638–639, 642, 645–648, 656–659, 665–666, 670–671, 711–712, 719, 731
(*see also* Presbyters)
unity 349, 356, 620, 622, 623, 632–633, 635–636
use of the name 189, 193, 287, 402
(*see Koinōnia*)
Circumcision 299–301, 305–310, 330–331, 438, 469–473, 479, 566, 653
Claudius, Emperor, xxxix, 60, 430, 433, 513, 562, 571, 575, 576, 699, 713, 805
Clement, First Letter viii, xli, 12, 51, 62, 221, 398, 418, 436, 439, 494, 495, 516, 544, 588, 608, 648, 666, 670, 696, 700–702, 712, 719, 721, 727, 742, 743, 761, 768, 799, 807–808, 837
Second Letter 51, 100, 416, 588, 837
(*see also* Pseudo-Clementine Literature)
Codices (Greek) of the NT 50–51
Collection, Paul's for Jerusalem 287, 315, 434, 435, 477, 496, 525, 543, 546, 549, 553–554, 563, 574, 654
Colossae 504, 599–601, 605, 616, 783
Colossians, Letter to 6, 441, 453, 502, 504, 507–508, 587, 599–619
by Paul (?) 159, 453, 585, 599, 600, 610–615
from where 507, 615–617
relation to Phlm 601, 602, 609, 614–616
Corinth 66, 511–513, 837
Paul's adversaries at 526–528, 553–556
(*see also* Apostles, false)
Paul's dealing with 311–312, 433, 513–515, 541–543, 559–560
Corinthians:
First Letter to 429, 434, 511–540
unity 512, 515, 517, 535
lost letters to 10, 434, 515, 518, 541, 543, 544, 548
Second Letter to 312, 429, 434, 541–558
unity 541, 548–551
Co-senders (*see* Letters/Epistles, co-author)
Covenant (renewal, new) 3–4, 77, 284, 338, 632, 687–688, 692, 696, 702–703
(*see also* Testament)
Creed (Apostles', Nicene) 464, 617, 714, 770
Cynics 85, 88–89, 120, 122, 425, 461, 487, 519, 520, 605, 659–660, 822, 824–826, 828, 829

Deacon(s) 294, 499, 574, 642, 657–658, 671, 711–712, 837
women 452, 559, 574, 657
Dead Sea Scrolls (DSS, Qumran) 75–77, 80, 81, 141, 164, 232, 248, 288, 320, 372–373, 385, 387, 389, 479, 551, 568, 582, 606, 611, 634–635, 646, 679, 685, 687, 692–693, 702, 703, 729, 738, 753, 757, 777, 820, 831–833, 837, 838, 839
list of 832
Death, NT attitudes toward 349, 461–462, 486–487, 499, 552
Deconstruction 25
Deissmann, A. 410
(*see also* Letters, NT)
Deliberative or demonstrative (*see* Rhetoric)
Demon (bad angels, Beelzebul, Beliar, devil, Satan) 129, 131, 140, 157, 177, 185, 236–237, 242, 246, 255, 257, 292, 347, 351, 365, 375, 385, 386, 388, 551, 590–591, 595, 628, 636, 659, 712, 746, 776, 777, 783, 788, 791, 794–795, 822
Deuterocanonical (Books) xxxv, 64, 425, 831
DeuteroPauline writings ix, 6, 12, 419, 437, 441, 453–455, 586–588, 592–596, 632–633, 662–668, 674–675
Diatribe 9, 89, 90, 519, 564, 566, 705, 726, 728, 730, 740, 833
Diatessaron of Tatian 13, 14, 839
Didache viii, xli, 100, 216, 218, 303, 587, 608, 639, 648, 666, 702, 713, 738, 805, 837, 838
Dikaiosynē (*see* Justification)
Divorce (*see* Marriage)
Domitian, Emperor xli, 62–63, 86, 595, 597, 699, 713, 721, 778, 792–793, 797
persecution under? 803–809, 811, 837

"Early Catholicism" 44, 625–626, 670, 757, 764, 769–771
Ebionites (*Gospel of the*) 214, 835

Education in NT times 68–70
Egerton (*see* Papyrus)
Emperor worship 86, 458, 492, 513, 597, 783, 792–793, 806
Enoch 587, 753, 776, 790, 832
I Enoch 44, 716, 751, 753, 754, 759, 764, 776, 777, 779, 780, 787, 792, 800, 832
Ephesus 11, 62, 312–313, 434, 448, 656, 666, 782, 783, 803
John and 334, 368, 390, 392, 616, 630, 656, 804
Paul and 312, 433–435, 477, 485, 489, 495–496, 515, 541–543, 601, 615, 616, 630, 641, 654–656, 666
Ephesians, Epistle to 6, 441, 454, 587, 620–637
author 620, 627–630
compared to Col 614, 616, 623–625, 627–629, 633
destination of 620, 626–627
Epicurean(s) 84, 89, 311, 425, 461, 564, 765
Epideictic (*see* Rhetoric)
Epistles (*see* Letters)
Eschatology 120, 128, 192, 194, 195, 218–219, 240, 245, 247, 248, 251, 254–256, 275, 281, 283–284, 342, 367, 385, 386, 389, 417, 440, 514, 552, 565, 572, 580, 612–613, 623, 624, 633, 636, 683, 690, 692, 732, 787, 788, 804, 822, 827
(*see also* Apocalyptic)
Essenes (Jewish "sect") 76–81, 91, 605, 831, 834
(*see also* Dead Sea Scrolls)
Ethics 74, 178–179, 191, 220, 265, 289, 376, 390, 391, 397, 401, 425, 469, 480, 517, 578, 689, 740, 745
interim 509–510, 519–520, 530
(*see also* Household codes)
Euaggelion ("gospel") terminology 99–101, 104
Eucharist 6, 42, 46, 68, 108, 136, 137, 256, 261, 269, 289, 303, 313, 324, 330, 345–346, 351, 361, 367, 377, 378, 388, 514, 521–523, 537, 538, 632, 636, 702, 722, 837
meaning of 288–289
Europe, evangelization of 310, 433, 456, 484, 500
(*see also* Rome, church at)
Ezra, IV xli, 8, 580, 777, 791, 792, 795, 801, 833–834

Faith 340–344, 346–349, 358–360, 390, 533, 688–689, 730–731, 744, 748, 753 (and passim)
alone (*sola fides*) 43, 567, 732–733
content of (body of beliefs) 387, 649–650, 750, 757–758, 762, 769–770, 771
of Christ 469, 477–478
(*see also* Justification)
False teachers/ing 304, 385, 386, 395, 397, 399, 404, 594, 596, 601–608, 611, 613, 616, 617, 642–643, 659–660, 661, 666–667, 677, 751–753, 764–766
(*see also* Apostles, false)
Farewell (*see* Testament)
Feasts (*see* Liturgy)
Form criticism 22–23

Galatians, Letter to 65, 429, 434, 467–482
area addressed 433, 468, 471, 475–476
dating 468, 476–477
(and) Rom 562, 563
Gamaliel (I) 233, 292–293, 321, 425
Gloria in excelsis (*see* Hymns, Lucan)
Gnosis, gnosticism, gnostics 13, 14, 85, 92–93, 215, 216, 297, 372, 376, 391, 488, 492, 527, 556, 572, 595, 604, 606–607, 634, 635, 643, 659, 661, 663, 665, 685, 692, 751, 757, 758, 763, 765, 769, 778, 783, 826, 831, 837, 840
"God" applied to Jesus (*see* Jesus, as God)
God-fearer 270, 299, 514
Goodspeed, E. J. (Pauline theory) 508–509, 630
Gospel(s):
eyewitness (literal) accounts? 21, 109–110, 210–211, 817
formation (three stages) viii, 107–111
four 12–13
harmonization 48, 110–111, 115, 195, 236, 359
meaning and genre 7, 22, 99–107
writing of 7–8, 12–14, 109–110
(*see also* Prefaced Gospel titles; Synoptic Gospel; and individual Gospels)
Greco-Roman (or Pagan):
religious world 65, 83–93, 102–103, 152, 305, 311, 425, 448, 458, 460, 485,

491, 513, 566, 605, 606, 751–752, 779, 783, 786, 791, 800
social world 63–70, 447–448
(*see also* Poor; Slave[s])
Griesbach hypothesis 113–116, 122, 164–165, 275

Habakkuk (faith passage) 479–480, 565–566
Hadrian, Emperor xli, 63–64, 750, 839
Hanukkah (Dedication) feast 57, 75
Hebrews, Gospel of the 209, 726, 835
Hebrews, Letter to 9, 91, 683–704, 717, 744, 798
addressees 11, 684, 693, 695, 697–701
author 419, 453, 684, 690, 693–695
date 684, 696–697
title 9, 693, 697
Hellenists 213, 293–297, 300, 301, 317, 320, 321, 658, 693, 695, 698, 700
Hermas, Shepherd of xli, 50, 377, 700, 742, 743, 778, 838
Hermeneutics (in general) 4, 20–47
Hermetic literature/thought 85, 371, 492, 604
Herod the Great xxxviii, 58–60, 176, 253, 575
Historical criticism 21, 35–40
Historical Jesus (*see* Jesus, quest of)
Homosexuality 528–530, 566
House-church 68, 156, 271, 397, 399, 403, 504, 505, 508, 516, 526, 563, 564, 574, 605, 616, 645, 656
physical setup 522
Household codes (behavior) 425, 453, 602, 608–610, 617, 623–624, 643–644, 650, 660–661, 710
applicability today 609–610
Hymns (in the NT) 489–493, 683, 686, 709, 714, 786–787, 790, 798, 799
Lucan Canticles (Gloria, Magnificat) 67, 232–234, 239, 266, 274, 288, 489
Pauline 237, 440, 453, 491–493, 523, 533–534, 571, 572, 600–604, 617, 622–624, 629, 644, 650, 661–662
Prologue of John 232, 337–338, 360, 383–384, 389, 392, 489, 492, 603

Ignatius of Antioch viii, xli, 15, 63, 108, 215, 216, 274, 391, 398, 403, 413, 418, 495, 509, 616, 630, 666, 731, 783, 799, 805, 837–838
Inclusion 336–337, 349, 351, 360
Infancy narratives (*see* Jesus, infancy)
Inspiration of Scripture 29–32, 41, 236, 530, 667–668, 670, 678–679, 754, 764, 771
Roman Catholic position 30–32

James, Epistle of 9, 214, 705, 721, 725–747, 755
and Matt 728, 732, 734–736
James of Jerusalem, brother of Jesus 6, 61, 80, 166, 293, 295, 298, 302, 524, 534, 699, 721, 725–727, 741, 750, 790, 835
(and) Paul 42, 43, 213, 304, 307–309, 314, 428, 431–432, 435, 439, 453, 469, 472, 474, 556, 727, 730–734, 739, 744, 761
James, Protevangelium of viii, xli, 101, 725, 727, 836
James son of Zebedee, brother of John xxxix, 61, 302, 320, 368, 725, 790
Jamnia (Yavneh) xl, 81–82, 191, 211, 214, 215
Jerusalem church
community life 286–289, 293–296, 302, 320, 721
evangelizing mission 284, 296–297, 301, 456, 562, 709, 720–721, 739
meeting at (about Gentiles, *ca.* AD 49) 287, 295, 305–309, 428, 431, 475–477, 553, 707, 727, 749
(*see* Collection, Paul's; Poor)
Jesus (of Nazareth)
as God 141, 337, 360, 388, 492, 581, 596–597, 644, 685, 696, 762
brothers (family) of 131, 135, 211, 241–242, 302, 725–726, 742, 749–750, 836
(*see also* James; Jude; Mary)
education, trade of 67–69, 107, 135, 187, 822, 825
expectation of the end 182–183, 190, 198–199, 255, 281, 361, 686
free from sin 556–557
infancy (narrative) of 45, 59, 100, 110, 114, 165, 171, 173–176, 205–206, 218, 227, 228–235, 270
language spoken by 69, 108
life/political context 59–60, 84, 107, 824–825
quest of historical viii, 104–107, 121–122, 817–830
"Jesus Seminar" 105, 820–824, 826, 828, 840
limitations of 106, 827–829
(*see also* Schweitzer, A.)

Jesus (of Nazareth) (*continued*)
temptation/testing of 128, 177, 236–237, 255
virginal conception of 39, 175, 217, 219, 229
(*see also* Christology; Law; Messiah; Miracles; Name of; Parables; Passion; Priest; Resurrection; Transfiguration)
Jewish, Jew(s):
relation to Christians 52, 62, 66, 82, 459
(*see also* AntiJudaism; Pharisees, NT critique)
religious world in NT times 65, 75–83
revolt vs. Rome 61, 144, 214, 272, 632, 731, 791, 803, 834
sects 75–82, 825, 834
(*see also* Essenes; Pharisees; Sadducees)
terminology "Jews" xxxiii, 75, 463
Johannine community 93, 373–376, 383, 390–392, 403–405
Johannine School (witnesses, writers) 370, 384, 389, 391, 398–399, 402, 404, 616, 803–805
John, Epistles of 9, 373–376, 383–405, 414–415, 705, 803
author 383, 389, 395, 396, 413, 803–804
dates 389–390, 396, 402
John, Gospel of 7, 13, 81, 88, 93, 100, 333–382, 635, 693, 700, 701, 818, 821, 837
author 334, 369, 803–804
date 334
locale 334, 337, 373–375, 804, 826
redactor 336, 342, 354, 360, 366–368, 377
relation to Synoptics 105, 150, 177, 344, 345, 350, 351, 356–360, 362–365, 369, 377
sources 334, 360, 363–365
stylistic features 333–337
(*see also* Beloved Disciple; Hymns, Prologue; Lamb of God; Luke, relation to John; Spirit, Paraclete)
John, apostle, son of Zebedee 362, 368, 369, 383, 398, 439, 802–804, 809
John the Baptist 80, 105, 128, 135, 139, 143, 177, 183–184, 221, 229–233, 235–236, 240, 250, 266, 285, 312, 338, 342, 373, 786, 827
John the Presbyter/Elder 368, 369, 398
John the prophet/seer (author of Rev) 10, 774, 776, 780, 795, 802–803, 809
Josephus, writings of xli, 62, 79, 561, 679, 752, 831, 834–835
Jubilees, Book of 716, 832–833
Judas Iscariot 145, 199–200, 255–256, 292, 347, 351–352, 357, 419, 748
death of 114, 201, 282
Jude (Judas), brother of Jesus 413, 586, 742, 748–750, 756–757, 808
Jude, Letter of 705, 743, 744, 748–760, 764–765, 778
Justification (righteousness) 141, 171, 324, 440, 441, 456, 536, 559, 565–567, 570, 576–577, 579, 581, 626, 694, 717, 732–734, 762
Justin (Martyr) 158, 271, 686, 715, 799, 801, 802, 839

Kerygma 108
Kingdom and kingship 128, 130–132, 140, 157, 177, 186, 192, 218, 248, 251, 275, 281, 285, 328, 335, 461, 525, 602, 612, 827
Knox, J. (Pauline theories) 508–509, 550, 600, 630
Koine Greek 70, 287
Koinōnia (community) 81, 214, 287–288, 291, 293, 294, 301, 306, 308, 309, 329–330, 384, 397, 432, 521–523, 553, 563, 763

Lamb (of God) 336, 338, 701, 709, 778, 786–788, 793–795, 798, 799, 804, 810
Laodicea 599–601, 616, 783
Letter to 10, 508, 600, 626, 627, 667
Last Testament (*see* Testament)
Law (Mosaic or Jewish):
Jesus and 137, 179, 188, 215, 234, 263, 272, 289, 308, 469, 824
Paul and 43, 179, 212–213, 314, 427, 432, 449, 469–470, 472–473, 480, 518, 521, 566, 570, 572–573, 578–581, 611, 632, 643, 733, 758
Letters/Epistles (NT) 5–7, 9, 12, 395, 401, 409–421, 705
Body 397, 401–403, 415–417
co-author (co-sender, scribe, secretary) 411, 413, 471, 473–474, 507, 565, 575, 585, 594, 595, 601, 611, 615, 630, 649, 663, 708, 712, 757, 766

Concluding Formula 397, 403, 418–419
"Epistle" vs. "Letter" (Deissmann) 392, 410–411, 631, 638, 739, 755, 768
format, genre 5–7, 9, 410–419, 459, 462, 502, 631–632, 689–691, 705, 739–741, 755–756, 762, 768, 780, 782
how composed 411, 419
of recommendation 403, 545, 555, 564, 575
Opening Formula 396, 401, 413–415
ordering (arrangement) of ix–x, 383, 409–410, 419, 640, 705
Thanksgiving 415, 450, 462–463, 471
(*see also* Rhetoric, types of)
Literal sense of Scripture 21, 35–40
Liturgy (cult, feasts, ritual, worship) 75, 108, 152, 261, 303, 328, 330, 344, 346, 347, 349, 378, 415, 521–522, 537, 563, 567, 573, 611, 622, 631, 646, 660, 662, 676, 688, 691, 695, 697, 700, 701, 709, 710, 717, 729, 754, 780, 781, 798–800
Lives of the Prophets 102, 833
Lord's Prayer 52, 109, 164, 179–180, 205, 216–218, 246, 288, 821
Love 245, 352, 354, 375, 377, 385–387, 393, 395, 397, 449–450, 523, 531, 533–534, 567, 572, 577
Luke, disciple of Paul 7, 267–269, 317, 326, 587, 618, 630, 694
Luke, Gospel of 7, 225–278
authorship 226, 267–269, 322–327
community (locale) 11, 226, 269–271
date 273–274
geography in 226, 237, 238, 242, 244, 251, 263, 269
orderliness, historicity 39, 227, 233, 236, 239, 256, 258, 264, 267, 319, 321
plan of 226, 228, 259–260
purpose, 271–272, 322
relation to Acts 225, 228, 258, 259, 261–263, 280–282, 290, 296, 305, 314, 315, 317
relation to John 225, 238, 244, 245, 250, 258, 261, 275, 357, 360, 362, 365, 378
relation to Mark 113–115, 191, 225, 242–244, 251, 255, 257, 258, 260, 263–266, 365
sources 111–122, 255, 262–268, 316–318
summaries, Luke-Acts use of 237, 286, 291, 295, 319
(*see also* Hymns, Lucan)
Luther, M. 14, 44, 274, 439, 467, 559, 563, 567, 568, 576, 608, 620, 695, 725, 732–733, 744, 759, 769, 802, 809
LXX (*see* Septuagint)

Maccabees, IV 833
Magic, magician, magi, magus 45, 86, 104, 129, 134, 137, 176, 188, 205, 234, 304, 822, 824
(*see also* Simon Magus)
Magnificat (*see* Hymns, Lucan)
Mandaeans 92, 363, 372
Man of lawlessness (*see* Antichrist)
Marana tha 5, 180, 288, 526, 795, 798
Marcion(ite) 4, 12, 14, 15, 100, 399, 439, 467, 474, 481, 570, 595, 600, 615, 626, 627, 663, 761–762, 831
Mark (John Mark) 7, 127, 158–161, 303, 304, 309, 317, 369, 431, 508, 618, 707–708, 718, 835
Mark, Gospel of 7, 13, 126–170, 818, 821, 835–836
apocalypse (chap. 13) 144–145, 163, 173, 590, 753, 777–778, 787
author 158–161
basic message 157
dating 163–164
endings (appendix) of 53, 127, 148–149, 245, 261
intercalation (sandwich) 131, 134, 135, 142, 145, 180, 196
locale (from, to) 127, 161–163
Galilee vs. Jerusalem 162
sources 111–114, 149–152, 154–156
view of disciples 155, 156, 165, 187
(*see also* Messianic Secret)
Mark, Secret Gospel of xli, 101, 112, 149, 154, 161, 164, 822, 835–836
Marriage 252, 510, 518–519, 530, 537, 608–609, 624, 636, 647, 710
divorce 140–141, 179, 194, 250, 289, 519, 530
Mary Magdalene 147, 241, 350, 358–359
Mary, mother of Jesus 33, 34, 115, 116, 131, 135, 165, 175, 185, 219, 229–232, 234, 241–242, 266, 282–283, 340, 358, 369, 398, 695, 725–726, 790, 835
(*see also* Jesus, brothers of)
Matthew, the apostle 208–209
Matthew, Gospel of 7, 171–224, 730, 732, 734–736, 837

Matthew, Gospel of (*continued*)
author (Jew or Gentile?) 172, 196, 211–212
community (locale) 11, 175, 179, 182, 212–216
dating 216–217
discourses (sermons) in 109, 117, 173, 178–180, 182–183, 185–187, 191–193, 198–199
original language of 112–113, 117, 209–211
sources of 111–122, 203–208
structure 172–174, 202
(*see also* Beatitudes; Lord's Prayer; Sermon on the Mount)
Messiah (Davidic), Messianism 100, 104, 108, 288, 343, 347, 791, 800, 820, 834, 837
Jesus as 175, 229, 275, 286, 329, 338, 343, 349, 360, 374, 427, 687, 791, 818, 820, 823, 825
Messianic Secret 129, 153, 156
Midrash 82, 697, 745
Millenarianism (millennial reign, chiliasm) 12, 44, 794, 800–802, 809
Miracles of Jesus 133–134, 136, 155, 171, 180–181, 186, 188, 205, 237, 240, 242, 247, 266, 557, 822, 823, 827
signs/works 339–340, 360, 363
Mishna 26, 68, 79–80, 81–83, 146, 345, 832
Moses, Assumption (Testament) of 752, 753, 754, 755, 800, 833
Moses and Christ 9, 176, 178, 179, 184, 197, 290, 338, 346, 371, 374, 545, 685–686, 692, 698
(*see also* Law, Jesus and)
Muratorian Fragment 4, 267, 436, 576, 600, 640, 642, 665, 700, 722, 759
Mystery (*mystērion*) 86, 133, 453, 517, 583, 601, 602, 607, 622, 629, 632, 634
Mystery religions 86–87, 371, 425, 568, 572, 605, 607, 635, 636, 650, 719, 765

Nag Hammadi 92, 101, 363, 372, 839, 840
"Name" of Jesus 286, 290, 291, 329, 356, 402, 490, 737
Narrative Criticism 25–26, 45, 238
Nazaraeans, Gospel of the 199, 209, 212, 835
Nero, Emperor xl, 61, 86, 162, 163, 270, 302, 436, 561, 571, 597, 674, 699, 700, 707, 713, 721, 778, 787, 791, 792–794, 797, 805–809
redivivus (= Domitian) 593–594, 792, 808
New Testament, composition of 3–19
order of ix, 419, 705
Nicene creed (*see* Creeds)

Odes of Solomon 363, 489, 587, 714, 837
"Old" Testament (use of term) xxxiv, 10, 43
Onesimus 452, 504–509, 614
collector of Paul's letters (?) 509, 630
Opening Formula (*see* Letters)
Orality (oral teaching) 28, 112, 115–116, 206
Original sin 580–582
"Our Father" (*see* Lord's Prayer)

Pagan (use of term) 65, 74
Papacy 221–222
Papias 6, 13, 109, 112, 116, 158–161, 209–211, 216, 376, 398, 721, 801, 803, 835
Papyrus, papyri 50, 412, 414, 722, 759
Beatty 12, 50, 410, 575, 626, 664, 693
Bodmer 50, 759, 767, 769
Egerton 143
Magdalen 316
Oxyrhynchus 418, 489
Rylands 50, 664
Parables of Jesus 111, 120, 131–133, 143, 156, 185–187, 196, 199, 220, 241, 245–249, 266, 335, 348, 354, 365, 824, 826
Paraclete (*see* Spirit)
Paraenetic (*see* Rhetoric)
Parousia (second coming, judgment) 6, 139, 148, 203, 339, 371, 386, 389, 395, 462–464, 590, 591, 594–598, 613, 623, 633, 663, 688, 753, 757, 763–767, 771, 781, 791, 829
Passion of Jesus 145–148, 166–167, 199–203, 257–260, 356–358, 463, 534, 823, 836
predictions of 138, 140, 142, 189, 191, 195, 199, 243, 252, 821
Pastoral letters of Paul 410, 435, 436, 441–442, 454–455, 543, 587, 594, 638–680, 830
author 649, 662–668, 672–675
(and) Luke 268, 663, 666
order of 638, 640, 653, 662, 668–669, 672–675
(*see also* Timothy; Titus)
Patmos 780, 781, 789, 791, 803
Paul (Saul):
as apostle 298, 303, 323–324, 413, 427, 450, 462, 470, 472, 473, 505, 517,

520, 535, 536, 547, 556, 565, 571, 613–614, 624, 642, 647, 668, 675
(and) church 453, 464, 499, 612, 617, 622, 625–626, 635, 638, 642, 656–659
conversion of 296, 298, 313–315, 424, 430, 448–450, 471, 659
dating 312, 314–315, 426, 428–430, 433
death/last years of xl, 6, 302, 436, 495, 499, 633, 638, 640, 641, 665–666, 672–675, 689, 699
disciples of 413, 452–453, 481, 614, 616, 630, 633, 678
(*see also* Timothy; Titus)
early years, origins 323, 423–426, 570
education 59–60, 84, 425–426, 448, 566
eloquence/rhetoric 411–412, 425, 451–452, 454, 514, 516–517, 521, 545, 564, 568, 569, 628, 631
imprisonment(s) of 273, 314–315, 428, 434–436, 455, 486–487, 493–496, 502, 507–508, 601, 614, 615, 622, 630, 640, 641, 655, 664, 672–675, 699
Judaizing opponents 469–474, 488–489, 554, 769
labor (trade, work) 312, 425, 447, 458, 486, 513, 514, 592
life (portrayals) of 84, 422–437, 446–448, 545–546, 563–564
(and) Peter 42, 213, 238, 304–309, 427, 430, 431–432, 439, 453, 467, 469, 526, 537, 555–556, 707, 717, 718, 720, 761, 763, 766, 767, 771
(and) Roman officials 310, 312, 314–315, 459, 469, 484, 485, 487
"second career" 641, 644, 655, 663–665, 667, 669, 672–675, 678
(and) sexual issues 460, 517–519, 528–530, 536–537
(and) social issues 480, 500, 505–507, 509
(*see also* Household codes)
(and) synagogues/Jews 273, 304–305, 326, 425–426, 431, 438, 448, 453, 458, 463
"thorn in the flesh" (ailment) 468, 475, 476, 547
(*see also* Apocalyptic, in Paul; Deutero-Pauline writings; Women, in Paul)
Pauline journey(s) 262, 304–305, 309–314, 321, 325, 430–435, 475–476, 525, 573–574, 595, 601, 640, 653–654, 666, 669, 673–674, 707–708
to Spain 435, 436, 494, 564, 574, 674
Pauline letter writing 5–7, 12–13, 585–586
school of 586, 600, 616, 621, 630, 633, 804
(*see also* Letters/Epistles)
Peter (Cephas, Simon) 116, 160, 165, 187–189, 191, 193, 204, 214, 218, 243, 258, 261, 264, 290–292, 299–302, 317, 321, 338, 352, 356, 359, 361, 368–369, 376, 398, 404, 428, 515, 521, 524, 527, 534, 535, 537, 555–558, 678, 706–708, 761–762
confession of Jesus 138, 189–190, 221, 274–275, 346–347, 349
death of xl, 6, 302, 436, 495, 689, 707, 719
(and) James 302–303, 307, 472, 537
(*see also* Paul, and Peter; Rome, Peter at)
Peter, Gospel of viii, xli, 10, 11, 101, 112, 149, 154, 206, 216, 715, 822, 829, 836
Peter, Letters of:
First 66, 313, 453, 705–724, 745, 766–767
and Pauline writings 631–632, 716–717
Second 453, 588, 596, 705, 717, 755, 761–772, 795
School of writers 717, 719, 757, 767–768
Pharisees (Jewish "sect") 77–80, 163, 198, 834
NT critique 78–79, 82, 122, 184–185, 188–189, 196–198, 202, 215, 222, 238, 246, 248, 250, 291, 293, 348, 471, 605, 824
misuse of hypocrite 79, 215, 246, 251
Philemon, Letter to 68, 429, 434, 493, 494, 501–510, 609, 614–616
Philippi 66, 310, 325, 457, 458, 483–485, 543, 838
Philippians, Letter to 325, 429, 434, 483–501, 610–611
from where 484, 493–496, 507–508
hymn 491–493, 498
unity 484, 498–500
Philo 60, 65, 77, 80, 91, 219, 283, 372, 527, 529, 551, 604, 635, 644, 679, 691–692, 695, 752, 831
Phoebe 559, 564, 574, 575, 657, 660
Platonism 88, 533, 604, 605, 687, 691–692, 829
Plērōma ("fullness") 92, 604, 606, 622, 623
Pliny (the Younger) 62–63, 86, 489, 502, 713, 792, 799, 808
Polycarp xli, 12, 100, 389, 399, 414, 416, 418, 484, 496, 595, 608, 630, 665, 721, 783, 838

Poor (and wealthy) 67, 213, 233, 239, 246–247, 250, 252, 254, 265, 270–271, 287, 387, 522, 553, 729, 742, 746
(*see also* Collection, Paul's)
Post-Bultmannians 819, 820
Powers (Principalities) 602, 604, 606, 608, 617, 622, 624, 625, 634, 636–637
(*see also* Angels)
Predestination 582, 745–746
Preexistence (*see* Christology)
Prefaced Gospel/NT titles (prologues) 4, 100, 109, 158, 208, 494, 507, 585, 615
Presbyter(s) (presbyter/bishop[s]) 7, 63, 81, 305, 313, 375, 395–399, 413, 464, 499, 524, 641–648, 656–658, 660, 665–666, 671, 711–712, 718, 736–738, 742, 786, 790, 798, 805, 837, 838
how selected 648
one bishop (monepiscopacy) 63, 274, 396, 403, 642, 646, 657, 671, 678, 799, 805, 837, 838
types of 398–399
words "presbyter," "bishop" 645–646
Priest(s):
Christian 573–575, 646, 701–702, 722, 736, 780–781, 798
Jesus as 573, 686–688, 693, 694, 701, 722
Principalities (*see* Powers)
Prisca/Priscilla (*see* Aquila)
Prologues (*see* Prefaced Gospel/NT titles)
Protevangelium (*see James*)
Psalm numbering/versification xxxii
Psalms of Solomon 51, 489, 587, 834
Pseudepigraphy (pseudonymity) 502, 585–589, 592–596, 610–615, 627–630, 632, 640, 642, 649, 662–671, 674–675, 678, 705, 718–719, 721, 766–767, 776
Pseudo-Clementine literature 214, 727, 741, 742, 743, 761, 807

Q (Gospel source) 7, 13, 40, 89, 116–122, 149, 179, 184, 204, 205, 214, 235, 236, 239, 265, 316, 728, 736, 740, 742, 818, 821, 822, 826, 827, 829, 839
community? 40, 120, 826
table of material 118–119
Qumran (*see* Dead Sea Scrolls)

Rapture, the 464
Recommendation (*see* Letter of)
Redaction Criticism 23–24, 116, 152, 171
Resurrection (and appearances):
of Jesus 110, 147–149, 202–203, 260–262, 281, 298, 367, 524–525, 534–535, 688, 694, 763, 791, 821, 823, 829, 835
of the dead 524–525, 534, 535, 552, 623, 711, 778, 795
resuscitations by Jesus, Peter 134, 240, 299, 313, 349
Revelation:
close of 536
divine 32–35, 41, 449, 471, 480, 536
natural 566
Revelation, Book of (Apocalypse) 8–9, 453, 489, 587, 595, 723, 744, 773–813
relation to John's Gospel 803–805
title 773
(*see also* Apocalyptic; John the prophet)
Revolt (*see* Jewish, revolt vs. Rome)
Rhetoric(al criticism), types of 26–27, 45, 91, 411–412, 471–472, 505, 516, 517, 547, 564, 581, 604, 631, 634, 676, 690, 698, 739–741, 745, 755
Righteousness (*see* Justification)
Roman:
political history xxxviii–xli, 57–63
roads 64, 447, 457, 483–485, 495
(*see also* Greco-Roman)
Roman Catholic (councils, documents, liturgy, teaching) xi, xxxv, 19, 31–34, 43–44, 52–53, 107, 111, 131, 141, 148, 189, 197, 218, 220, 221, 274, 328, 376, 377, 385, 390, 441, 529, 578, 579, 600, 625, 679, 703, 722, 726, 736, 738, 760, 769–770, 800, 802, 828
Romans, Letter to 313, 429, 434–436, 559–584, 615, 699–700
goal of 562–564
(*see also* Justification; Law, Paul and; Original sin)
Rome
church at 11, 62, 161–162, 221, 302, 311, 315–316, 456, 508, 560–562, 573, 693, 699–701, 717, 743, 838
Jews at (expulsion of) 433, 523, 561, 562, 572, 575, 699
Paul's imprisonment 273, 302, 436, 494–495, 508, 615, 641, 655, 664, 670, 673, 699
Peter at 159, 161, 221, 302, 670, 678, 699, 707, 719, 761, 768, 835

writings from/to 270, 699, 712, 717, 837, 838
Rylands (*see* Papyrus)

Sacraments 41, 44, 46, 107, 367, 377–378, 521, 626, 636, 736–739
(*see also* Baptism; Eucharist)
Sadducees (Jewish "sect") 76–80, 211, 254, 290, 314, 435, 605, 834
Samaritans xxxviii, 56, 57, 62, 78, 244, 245, 251, 296–297, 321, 342–344, 371, 374
Sanhedrin, makeup of 146
Satan (*see* Demon)
Schools of NT writers (*see* Johannine school; Pauline letter writing; Peter, Letters of, School)
Schweitzer, A. 182, 818
Scribe(s) (*see* Letters/Epistles, co-author)
Secret Gospel of Mark (*see Mark, Secret Gospel*)
Seneca 90, 410, 513, 740, 829
Sensus plenior of Scripture 42
Septuagint (LXX, Greek Scriptures) xxix, xxxv, 36, 56, 91, 99, 208, 219, 234, 268, 425, 479, 530, 691, 695, 698, 710, 718, 741, 742, 750, 757, 833
Sermon on the Mount 377, 728, 732, 734–735, 742, 824
Shepherd of Hermas (*see Hermas*)
Sibylline Oracles 529, 674, 835
Simon bar Cochba xli, 61, 63, 82
Simon Magus 85, 86, 205, 242, 297, 304
Sin (*see* Original Sin; Spirit, sin against)
666 (symbolic number) 773, 793, 805
Slave(s), slavery 67–68, 425, 426, 480, 503–507, 510, 608–609, 710
Social/sociological criticism (background, concerns) 27, 30, 38, 238, 287, 425, 480, 485, 500, 503, 514, 522, 744–745, 755, 767
Socrates, Socratic 88, 102, 152, 639
Solomon (*see Odes of; Psalms of*)
Son of God 9, 37, 84, 100, 108, 128, 129, 146, 156–157, 184, 187, 189, 190, 199, 218, 219, 221, 229, 235, 298, 339, 342, 349, 360, 390, 439, 449, 490, 565, 649, 686, 707, 745, 785, 820, 828
Son of Man 126, 130, 156, 184, 199, 203, 218, 243, 286, 296, 339, 348, 371, 781, 789, 793, 798, 820, 832
Sophia (*see* Wisdom)
Sophists 90–91, 120, 156
Source Criticism 21–22, 35, 40
(*see also* Sources under individual NT writings)
Spirit (Holy) 31, 110, 129, 131, 165, 175, 185, 190, 218, 229, 236, 246, 262, 272, 280, 283, 286, 291, 295, 297, 300–301, 312, 330, 331, 347, 358, 360, 376, 386–391, 404, 532, 545, 554, 565, 569, 582, 647, 686, 697, 753, 764, 780, 797, 803, 823, 835
Paraclete 352–355, 378, 385, 389, 391
sin against 131, 185, 246, 388, 688
Spiritual sense of Scripture 41–42
Stephen xxxviii, 11, 279, 293–296, 319, 320, 426–428, 658, 693, 695
(*see also* Hellenists)
Stoic(s), Stoicism 84, 85, 90, 311, 425, 520, 531, 552, 566, 605, 650, 771
(*see also* Diatribe)
Structuralism (Semiotics) 24–25, 152
Synagogue:
departure of Christians from 66, 82, 108, 197, 214–216, 270, 354, 374, 404–405
origin/existence 64, 75
Synoptic (Gospel) interrelationship 111–116
(*see also* individual Gospels)

Tabernacle 139, 687–688, 695, 701, 703
Talmud 83, 599, 738
(*see also* Mishna)
Tanak xxxiv
Targum(s) 36, 82, 208
Teachers (*see* False teachers)
Temple of Jerusalem 75, 267, 294, 295–297, 299, 347, 370, 435, 546, 563, 573, 634, 692–693, 698, 703, 781, 787, 798, 832
destruction of xl, 61, 182, 253–255, 273, 350, 427, 696, 721, 722, 777, 778, 789, 792, 834
Jesus and 109, 143, 144, 163, 196, 198, 200, 203, 217, 234–235, 253–254, 336, 340–341, 343, 349, 405
Testament:
last (farewell discourse) 313, 352, 453, 563, 639, 676–677, 768, 771, 833
term for Scripture xxxix, 3–4
(*see also* Covenant)

Testament of Moses (*see Moses, Assumption*)
Testaments of the Twelve Patriarchs 352, 687, 754, 787, 835
Testimonia 566, 570, 573
Testimonium Flavianum 834–835
Text of Greek NT: 48–54
  critical editions 52
  ms. families 49, 51
  Textus receptus 49, 52
Textual Criticism 21, 48, 54, 748
Thanksgiving of Letter (*see* Letters)
Theios anēr ("divine man") 84, 103, 155, 554
Thessalonica 310–311, 456–459, 595
Thessalonians:
  First Letter to 311, 324, 433, 441, 456–466, 592–593, 708
  Second Letter to 441, 453, 588, 590–598
    authorship 587, 591, 592–596
Thomas, Gospel of 101, 112, 117, 120, 121, 143, 220–221, 248–249, 360, 372, 726, 821, 822, 826, 829, 839–840
Thomas, Infancy Gospel of 234, 836–837
Tiberius, Emperor 60, 792
Timothy (disciple of Paul) 326, 413, 456, 458–460, 462, 493–496, 517, 541, 587, 601, 614–615, 630, 653–655, 673–676, 694, 696, 699
  circumcision of 309–310, 653
  First Letter to 638–640, 645–648, 653–671
  Second Letter to 638–640, 672–680
Titles of NT works (*see* Prefaced Gospel/NT titles)
Titus 307, 326, 413, 543, 546, 587, 640–641, 653
  Letter to 639–652
    authorship 662–668
Titus, Emperor xli, 61–62, 561, 792, 834
Tongues, speaking in 514, 531–532, 545
Tosepta 83
Trajan, Emperor xli, 62–63, 713, 750
Transfiguration of Jesus 139, 190, 243, 534, 712, 761, 763
Translations of the NT xxxv–xxxvii, 52–53
Truth, Gospel of 249, 840
Twelve, the 6, 15, 24, 134, 182, 195, 228, 239, 244, 279, 282–283, 292, 294, 298, 302, 303, 321, 323, 347, 398, 574, 706, 707, 725, 737, 795, 803, 822, 824
  appearances of risen Jesus to (Eleven) 149, 203, 261–262, 281, 358–361, 524, 534
  list of 130, 182, 208, 239, 282, 748
  (*see also* Apostles)
Typical sense of Scripture 41–42

Vespasian, Emperor xl, 61, 792, 834
Vulgate (Latin translation) 52

"Way," the 81, 287, 314, 315
"We" (Paul's companion) (*see* Acts)
Western Non-Interpolation (Luke-Acts) 49, 226, 256, 262, 274
Widow(s) 658–659
Wisdom (personified; Sophia) 92, 184, 218, 246, 333, 338, 346, 374, 491, 492, 603–604, 684, 740, 825–826, 840
Wisdom Literature (OT) 491, 608, 728, 730, 740, 778–779, 825
Women, role of: 92, 645, 775
  as apostles 359, 574, 675
  in the Gospels 147, 154–155, 175, 241, 260
  in Paul 310, 452, 454, 481, 484–485, 500, 523–524, 645, 657–661, 668, 671
Word (*logos* of God) 91–92, 337–338, 353, 371, 383–384, 389, 490, 492, 686, 794, 804
Worship (*see* Liturgy)